# The Encyclopedia of Taxation and Tax Policy

JOSEPH J. CORDES
ROBERT D. EBEL
and
JANE G. GRAVELLE
Editors

# The Encyclopedia of
# Taxation and Tax Policy

THE URBAN INSTITUTE PRESS
Washington, D.C.

Published in cooperation with the National Tax Association

**THE URBAN INSTITUTE PRESS**
2100 M Street, N.W.
Washington, D.C. 20037

Library of Congress Cataloging in Publication Data

The Encyclopedia of Taxation and Tax Policy/Joseph J. Cordes, Robert D. Ebel, and Jane G. Gravelle, editors.

Includes index and bibliographical references.

1. Taxation—Encyclopedias.   I. Cordes, Joseph J.   II. Ebel, Robert D.   III. Gravelle, Jane G.

HJ2305.E53                              1999                         98-40996
336.2′003—dc21

ISBN 0-87766-682-2 (cloth, alk. paper)

Printed in the United States of America

**THE URBAN INSTITUTE** is a nonprofit policy research and educational organization established in Washington, D.C., in 1968. Its staff investigates the social and economic problems confronting the nation and public and private means to alleviate them. The Institute disseminates significant findings of its research through the publications program of its Press. The goals of the Institute are to sharpen thinking about societal problems and efforts to solve them, improve government decisions and performance, and increase citizen awareness of important policy choices.

Through work that ranges from broad conceptual studies to administrative and technical assistance, Institute researchers contribute to the stock of knowledge available to guide decision-making in the public interest.

# Contents

# Preface

Topics of taxation and tax policy have suddenly come alive. Discussions of tax policy—how it "works" and what it is, or ought to be, about—are as old as the ancient practice of commandeering grain and livestock for a sovereign's use. But there is a new and urgent emphasis arising from several factors, a long time in the making, that have both culminated and converged in the past decade.

First, far-reaching developments have forced the revisiting of basic questions of the economic, social, and political role of governments, and thus the structure and level of the public's finances. These developments include a trend (not only in this country but even in traditionally centralist nations such as those of the Middle East) of transferring fiscal power from central to subnational governments, the fiscal crisis (many would argue the failure) of the welfare state in developed economies, and the collapse of command economies in both the developing world and the "transition countries" of the former socialist countries of Europe and East Asia. So while Justice Oliver Wendell Holmes's observation that taxes are the price we pay for a civilized society still holds, it is also true that the role, size, and financing of government are under more scrutiny than perhaps ever before.

Second, the globalization of the marketplace in an era of record public-sector presence is affecting that marketplace. Measured in terms of trade as a share of product, this country has been heavily global before—in the early 1900s, for instance—but it is only in the post-1970s era that worldwide market competition and the focus on competitiveness have become topics for national and subnational tax policy attention. With this change have come not only the questioning of the size of the public sector but also arguments for both major and minor changes in tax rules—from the overhaul of the U.S. tax system (for example, the income vs. consumption and flat tax debates) to a proliferation of federal, state, and local tax incentive programs (from certain tax shelters to enterprise zones).

A third factor is the explosion of electronic technology, a dramatic and emerging story. Developments in the ways we communicate electronically are changing not only the way governments administer taxes (the number of state income tax returns has risen from 200,000 to more than 1,200,000 since 1992) but also the way tax bases can be measured and how they grow and decline. For example, the advent of the remote electronic seller as a competitor to the Main Street retailer is putting unprece-dented pressures on the long-term revenue integrity and the economic neutrality of conventional tax bases. State and local transactions taxes are the best example of this problem.

These changes in the economic and technical environment have been accompanied by dramatic advances in the body of knowledge about economics. In the past 20 years the frontiers of public finance theory have been expanded and the literature on financing the public sector and how taxes work and affect behavior has burgeoned. How one frames public-sector decisionmaking has changed (for example, public choice theory, cost-benefit analysis, optimal taxation), and so have the tools (from sophisticated spreadsheet models to the development and maturity of mathematical and statistical microsimulation techniques). And there are entirely new fields. The examination of state and local finances has long been part of the study of public finance, but much of what is now studied as part of fiscal decentralization and intergovernmental relations has been developed since the early 1960s, using models developed since the 1970s for assignment of powers, intergovernmental grants, and local public goods.

Why does it all matter? From the scholastic writings of St. Thomas Aquinas (c. 1225–1274), who tried to resolve the issue of what was a "just price," to those of the 19th century classical economists—Smith, Malthus, Ricardo, and Marshall, who called their discipline "political economy"—a core question has been how to make institutions, public as well as private, responsive to people's needs so that society as a whole is better off.

In sum, the issues of taxation and tax policy combine the best human motives—paying for needed services that people acting privately have no incentive to offer—and what some would call the worst social organization—using the power of governments to commandeer part of individuals' income for collective pursuits. These motives and misgivings are why, throughout history and increasingly today, those of us involved in taxation and tax policy worry about and debate broad questions ranging from "proper" criteria for distributing the tax payment responsibility, to the structure of fiscal relationships among governments, to the practices of evading taxpaying responsibilities. Equally important are the detail questions—for example, inventory accounting, trust fund finance, apportionment of multistate and multinational business income, and the provisions that fit under the rubric of "tax shelters."

But whether the topics are as broad as the principles of just taxation or as narrow as the mechanisms of a tax credit in support of low-income housing, what pulls it all together and makes it important is the fact that a system of taxation is more than a compendium of dry tax law and arcane economic data. It is an expression of community relationships among individuals and between the people and their governments.

\*\*\*

Research on this book began four years ago at the instigation of the members of the National Tax Association (NTA), a unique organization that represents a cross section of tax practitioners and administrators, policymakers, business executives, and academics. They identified a major gap in the economic policy knowledge base: Despite the availability of a robust scholarly literature (such as the *National Tax Journal*), many excellent textbooks, and a growing amount of information over the Internet, there is no single source that has been subjected to rigorous peer review (this leaves out much of what is available on the Internet) and that is at the same time learned and readable on the key issues that matter in public finance.

To create this source, they proposed to draw on the best tax scholars and practitioners to put together the first *Encyclopedia on Taxation and Tax Policy*. The goal of the *Encyclopedia* is to provide a reference book—a complete guide—to public-sector tax and tax-related issues, in a manner that makes the complex understandable. The format was chosen to offer the generalist a quick and reliable introduction to a topic (accompanied by references for further reading) and also to give the tax specialist the benefit of the best thinking of other experts.

Thus, this volume will serve as a one-stop source on a definition, a concept, or an overview of a topic. For those who do not study or "practice" public finance or who are new to a topic, the *Encyclopedia* will provide an essential and thorough introduction to that topic.

It also will offer a road map of where to go when related issues arise. This will be *the* place to "look it up." That is a huge advantage. In many circumstances the *Encyclopedia* essay will provide all, or nearly all, one needs to know.

For the more serious student, even a cover-to-cover reading can make good sense. Although one will not remember or even fully understand every essay, the volume in its entirety will provide a complete overview of the discipline.

And for the specialist—whether tax executive, state tax director, research analyst, policymaker, or academic—this *Encyclopedia* becomes an indispensable resource on topics outside one's own area of specialization.

The essays in the *Encyclopedia* cover the range of tax issues. Included (with a range of examples for each) are (1) broad essays on fundamental economic concepts and behavior (tax incidence, effects of taxes on labor supply, savings, portfolio choice); (2) essays on more specialized economic and tax concepts (capital export neutrality, cost of capital, tax illusion); (3) essays on each type of tax levied in the United States (income, property), along with essays on taxes levied in other countries or under consideration (the national value-added tax, the flat tax) and essays on nontax revenues; (4) essays on important features of current taxes (deductions for charitable contributions, taxation of multinational corporations, circuit breakers); (5) essays on tax measurement and accounting (revenue estimating and forecasting, basis, depreciation, deferral); (6) essays on tax administration and related topics (tax evasion, property tax assessment); (7) essays on techniques and tools of tax analysis (generational accounting, general equilibrium models, progressivity measures); (8) essays on institutions (the nature and role of congressional committees, federal and state tax offices, public interest groups); and (9) essays on related public finance issues (budgets and budget processes).

\*\*\*

Selecting the authors for each of the essays in this book was easy: The membership of the National Tax Association comprises the nation's top experts in public-sector economics. Thanks in large part to NTA members, who combine a historical understanding of public financing with an up-to-date "hands-on" perspective, the best authors were identified and the list of essay topics grew, reflecting the range of expertise and interests of the membership.

\*\*\*

It was a pleasure to work with all the contributors to the *Encyclopedia*, who not only met their several deadlines but also willingly rewrote their essays as new evidence, laws, and regulations evolved during the review and preparation process. We also received invaluable help and support from the members of the NTA's Board of Directors, especially Helen Ladd, Gerald Bair, Sandy Navin, Emil Sunley, William Fox, Wayne Eggert, and Eugene Steuerle. Our special thanks also to Frederick Stocker, who was the NTA's executive director when this important project was initiated.

The process of getting the book in publishable form was a demanding one, and it could not have been accomplished without the superb help of Ann Cordes, who provided important organizational support in the early stages of the project, and Tom Holbrook, who assisted in the final preparation of the manuscript. At NTA, Joan Casey and Jennifer

Gravelle were key to getting the manuscript ready for publication and advising on presentation. We also wish to thank the referees who critically reviewed the entire manuscript. Margaret Carroll did a first-rate job of copyediting the entire work. And we acknowledge the highly professional review and handling that Felicity Skidmore, Blair Potter, Scott Forrey, and Helena Mickle of the Urban Institute Press brought to the publication.

The Editors

Joseph J. Cordes
Robert D. Ebel
Jane G. Gravelle

# Foreword

"Nothing is certain but death and taxes," as the old saying goes. Taxes have the additional characteristic of providing invaluable insights into how citizens relate to one another and to their government. Who pays taxes, how much, on what basis, and for what services are central questions of fairness in a society.

The editors of *The Encyclopedia of Taxation and Tax Policy* are acutely aware of the role taxes play in society. Taxes "combine the best human motives—paying for needed services that people acting privately have no incentive to offer—and what some would call the worst social organization—using the power of governments to commandeer part of individuals' income for collective pursuits," they note in their preface. Therefore, they have structured the book to cover broad tax issues, such as ability to pay, tax evasion, and fairness in taxation, as well as narrower ones, such as the inverse elasticity rule, seigniorage, and capital import neutrality. Moreover, the entries' concise definitions, knowledgeable and clearly written essays, and references to other sources of information are intended to appeal not only to specialists seeking out the thinking of other experts, but to general readers as well.

The *Encyclopedia* was a formidable undertaking. It was begun with the encouragement of members of the National Tax Association, who identified the need for an authoritative, comprehensive, readable guide to key issues of public finance. Nearly five years in the making, the book draws on the expertise of more than 150 contributors from all areas of tax scholarship and practice.

"Making the complex understandable" was the editors' goal in compiling the *Encyclopedia*, and this they have achieved. Some entries correct widely held misconceptions among the public and the popular press. For example, the mortgage interest deduction is by no means the principal tax benefit of owning a home (untaxed imputed rent is), and computing the average size of the marriage penalty is extremely difficult (because the partners' behavior after splitting up, and thus the taxes they would pay, cannot be determined in advance). The entry defining sumptuary taxes (a type of excise tax designed to discourage the consumption of specific commodities or services) notes that they are more familiarly known as sin taxes. Another engaging entry points out that some farm owners seeking to offset high nonfarm income may be "farming the tax code" rather than the land.

The *Encyclopedia* occupies a unique place as the first reference work in the Institute's distinguished list of books on federal and state taxation and tax policy. Since much of the usefulness of a reference book lies in its currency, the Institute and the editors have committed themselves to updating and revising the *Encyclopedia* periodically. I expect this ongoing effort will continue to meet the need for a first-rate reference work in public finance, a need as certain as taxes.

William Gorham
President
The Urban Institute

# A

## Ability to pay

Richard A. Musgrave

Harvard University and University of California at Santa Cruz

*One of two widely held principles of fair taxation.*

Dating back to Adam Smith, this principle calls for people to contribute to the cost of government in line with their ability to pay. Accomplishing this requires that tax burdens be assigned so that individuals with a higher ability to contribute will pay more. Thus, tax liabilities are to be distributed so as to equalize burdens across taxpayers whose capacities differ. The principle is appealing, and a further discussion of its merits and of how equal burdens are to be defined is given elsewhere. Here, some major problems of implementing ability-to-pay taxation are noted.

To begin with, an index has to be chosen to measure taxable capacity or ability to pay. Two centuries ago, this was seen in terms of property and wealth, which then came to be replaced by income as the best indicator. More recently, there has been increasing support for the use of consumption as the most desirable base.

Because ability to pay relates to the taxpaying capacity of individuals, ability-to-pay taxation calls for taxation to be in direct and personal form. This condition is met by the personal income tax, but not by indirect consumption taxes such as the sales or value-added tax. This objection, however, would not apply to an expenditure tax, assessed on the taxpayer's total consumption. Therefore, it would permit the use of exemptions and progressive rates as under the income tax.

*Cross references:* consumption taxation; fairness in taxation; tax equity analysis.

## Adjusted current earnings

Mark Booth

Congressional Budget Office

*A broad measure of a corporation's income used to calculate federal income tax liability from the alternative minimum tax.*

In the Tax Reform Act of 1986, Congress designed the alternative minimum tax (AMT) system for corporations, creating a broader measure of the federal income tax base that included an adjustment based on adjusted current earnings (ACE). Congress defined ACE to conform closely with earnings and profits as described in the Internal Revenue Code. From 1987 through 1989, Congress temporarily placed in effect a broadly similar adjustment based on book income, after which the adjustment based on ACE became effective. Congress instituted the AMT system with the adjustments for ACE or book income to ensure that corporate taxpayers with significant economic income could not substantially reduce or eliminate their income tax through the use of tax-preferred exclusions, deductions, and credits.

In 1991, ACE contributed about half of the broader tax base under the AMT system compared with the regular tax system, although this proportion may be overstated because it does not include base broadening from reduced use of credits and net operating losses (Gerardi et al. 1994). Some of this substantial contribution, however, was likely a result of the lingering effects of the transition from the adjustment based on book income to the adjustment based on ACE. Tax law changes enacted in the Omnibus Budget Reconciliation Act of 1993 should gradually reduce the importance of ACE beyond 1993. Tax law changes in the Taxpayer Relief Act of 1997, however, will conform the AMT tax base more closely to the regular tax before the ACE adjustment is considered, making the ACE adjustment more important.

### Computing ACE

Corporations calculate ACE after the specific AMT adjustments to the regular income tax base for certain excluded income and allowed deductions. Corporations first make these specific adjustments—most importantly to depreciation of capital assets—to compute an interim measure of their

AMT base, called preadjustment alternative minimum taxable income (AMTI). To compute ACE, they then make three further modifications, the "adjustment based on ACE": (1) to include income, such as tax-exempt income, that is required in calculating earnings and profits but not required in calculating preadjustment AMTI; (2) to exclude deductions, such as the dividends-received deduction, that are allowed in calculating preadjustment AMTI, but not in calculating earnings and profits; (3) to include other income or exclude other deductions as specified separately, such as for depreciation, that are unrelated to earnings and profits.

After computing ACE, corporations calculate their (postadjustment) AMTI by adding an amount equal to 75 percent of the difference between ACE and the preadjustment AMTI to the preadjustment AMTI. In effect, the income included and deductions disallowed by the adjustment for ACE are taxed at only 75 percent of the 20 percent tax rate applied to the full AMT base. In contrast, the specific adjustments made to calculate the preadjustment AMTI are, in effect, taxed at the full 20 percent rate.

### Specific components

Analysts estimate depreciation to be the most important adjustment based on ACE, at least until the tax law changed in 1993. (We cannot know with certainty the magnitude of the various adjustments because corporations do not report them separately on their income tax returns.) In general, for an asset placed in service after 1989, but before 1994, ACE requires that depreciation be calculated using the straight-line method over the asset's useful lifetime. For equipment investment, this depreciation method compares unfavorably with that allowed for purposes of calculating preadjustment AMTI, which allows firms to accelerate depreciation at a rate not to exceed one and one-half times the straight-line rate (the 150% declining balance method). For assets placed in service from 1981 through 1989, ACE requires that the remaining basis be depreciated under the straight-line method, rather than allowing some acceleration as under the depreciation system used to calculate preadjustment AMTI. (These calculations are further complicated, in some cases, by the required use of the depreciation lifetime used for book purposes.)

The Omnibus Budget Reconciliation Act of 1993 repealed the separate depreciation calculation for ACE, effective for property placed in service after December 31, 1993. Many people had criticized the depreciation adjustment for ACE because it further complicated corporate tax accounting. The adjustment for ACE should now become much less significant over time as corporations replace old property with new property that does not require

any adjustment. However, the Taxpayer Relief Act of 1997 conformed AMTI depreciation recovery periods to regular depreciation periods, making ACE relatively more important in the AMT base but making it less likely that firms will fall under the AMT.

The other specific adjustments based on ACE that are unrelated to earnings and profits will remain in effect. These include adjustments for depletion allowances, intangible drilling costs, construction period carrying charges, long-term contracts, installment sales, asset bases following ownership changes, and inventories that use the last in, first out (LIFO) accounting method. The adjustments based on earnings and profits, such as for tax-exempt income and the dividends-received deduction, also remain in effect.

### Other aspects

A corporation's adjustment based on ACE may be negative in certain years—reducing preadjustment AMTI—if past positive adjustments were a result of timing effects. For example, to the extent that some of a corporation's depreciation for purposes of ACE is delayed but not permanently disallowed, the adjustment for ACE could become negative at the later time when the depreciation is allowed. This timing effect does not occur from permanent adjustments for ACE, such as those resulting from tax-exempt income or the dividends-received deduction. In any given year, the adjustment based on ACE may reduce preadjustment AMTI only to the extent that the adjustments in previous years had increased preadjustment AMTI (net of previous reductions).

The transition in 1990 from the adjustment based on book income to the adjustment based on ACE caused a temporary surge in AMT payments that estimators did not expect when the Tax Reform Act of 1986 was enacted. Corporate liabilities from the AMT, measured as the incremental amount resulting from the AMT, rose from $3.5 billion in 1989 to $8.1 billion in 1990 and $5.3 billion in 1991. Analysts had expected that the major differences between ACE and book income would roughly offset in the aggregate. In particular, analysts expected that the longer depreciation lives required by ACE and its greater inclusion rate (75% rather than 50% for book income) would roughly offset other factors, such as the rule that the adjustment for book income could not be negative. Analysts have now revised their earlier assumptions about the differing depreciation lives. In addition, business-cycle movements, in particular the recession that began in 1990, may have contributed to the increase in AMT liabilities in 1990 and 1991 compared with 1989.

## Additional readings

Bonafide, Robert T. "A View from the Trenches." *National Tax Journal* 40 (September 1987): 465–67.

Gerardi, G. Geraldine, Hudson Milner, and Gerald Silverstein. "The Effects of the Corporate Alternative Minimum Tax: Additional Results from Panel Data for 1987–1991." In *National Tax Association—Tax Institute of America, Proceedings of the Eighty-Sixth Annual Conference, 1993.*

Lyon, Andrew B. *Cracking the Code: Making Sense of the Corporate Alternative Minimum Tax*. Washington, D.C.: The Brookings Institution, 1997.

*Cross references:* alternative minimum tax, corporate; basis; earnings and profits.

# Adjusted gross income

Susan C. Nelson
Department of the Treasury

*A measure of an individual taxpayer's net income used in calculating personal income taxes.*

---

Adjusted gross income (AGI) is defined by section 62 of the Internal Revenue Code as gross income from all sources not specifically excluded, minus certain deductions. Because AGI is a creature of the tax code, its components have changed over the years with tax law changes.

AGI can be understood in part by comparison with other measures of income. Compared with a measure of comprehensive income, AGI is primarily a measure of money income, but one that does not include many forms of money income that would be part of comprehensive income. From the perspective of the economy as a whole, AGI is similar to personal income in the National Income and Product Accounts (NIPA) but differs from it primarily in the same ways it differs from comprehensive income. In terms of the income tax system, AGI is the broadest measure of income but, compared with taxable income (the income measure to which tax rates are actually applied), it does not reflect personal differences that affect individuals' ability to pay taxes.

## Components of AGI

The major sources of income in AGI in 1994 included wages and salaries; taxable interest and dividends; business income from partnerships, Subchapter S corporations, sole proprietorships, and farms; capital gains; taxable pension and Individual Retirement Account (IRA) distributions; unemployment compensation; and some Social Security benefits. The deductions taken in reaching AGI included trade and business expenses, expenses attributable to rents and royalties, and certain losses from the sale or exchange of property. The Form 1040, on which individuals calculate their income tax, refers to other deductions allowable in reaching AGI as "Adjustments to income" or as "Statutory adjustments." For 1994, these adjustments included primarily alimony payments, moving expenses, certain savings for retirement (such as contributions to Keogh plans for the self-employed and to IRAs for employees and their spouses), one-half of the self-employment tax, and a health insurance deduction for the self-employed.

## Recent changes in the definition of AGI

Tax law amendments had changed this definition of AGI somewhat in the previous 15 years, generally expanding it. The most significant revisions came in the Tax Reform Act of 1986 (TRA86). Among these were the full inclusion of long-term capital gains (previously, 40% was included in the AGI, and before 1979, 50% had been included). TRA86 also imposed limits on "passive losses" that would be allowed in calculating AGI. It changed moving expenses and unreimbursed employee business expenses from income "adjustments" to itemized deductions. (Starting in 1994, moving expenses were again allowed as an adjustment to income instead of as an itemized deduction.) It eliminated the adjustment to income for a married couple with a second earner and the exemption for the first $400 of dividends received. Working to narrow the definition of AGI, it allowed self-employed individuals a deduction for up to 25 percent of their health insurance premiums.

Other legislation has made more modest changes in the definition of AGI. Legislation in 1991 added the adjustment to income for one-half of an individual's self-employment tax. In 1984, half of Social Security benefits were for the first time included in the AGI for taxpayers with other income of $25,000 ($32,000 for married couples), and in 1994 the share was increased to 85 percent for individuals with other income of $34,000 ($44,000 if married). Similarly, in 1979 unemployment compensation was initially added to AGI for persons with other income of $20,000 ($25,000 for couples), and in 1987 for all taxpayers regardless of other income. The Economic Recovery Tax Act of 1981 (ERTA) and TRA86 both substantially revised the depreciation schedules, with ERTA liberalizing the deductions and TRA86 tightening them. Consequently, a given amount of business profits (as measured for the company's books and records) would contribute less to AGI in the early 1980s than it would after 1986. Recent tax revisions have added deductions for self-employed individuals' health insurance and education deductions, as well as restoring some of the deduction for IRAs that had been curtailed in 1986.

## Comparison with comprehensive income, personal income, and taxable income

AGI can be compared conceptually and quantitatively to other frequently used measures of income.

Comprehensive income, or the Haig-Simons definition of income as consumption plus changes in net worth, is a broader concept of income than AGI. Haig-Simons is a comprehensive measure of income ("economic income") defined as the increase in an individual's power to consume (sum of consumption plus net wealth).

AGI excludes most forms of nonmoney income as well as some types of money income. Components of comprehensive income not in AGI include imputed rent on owner-occupied housing, unrealized capital gains, and in-kind fringe benefits of employees. Including any of these in income for tax purposes would entail substantial valuation problems. Sources of money income that are missing from AGI include welfare payments, interest on state and local government bonds, employer-provided contributions for health and pension plans, and income on savings through life insurance. These forms of income are excluded more for policy than for administrability reasons.

Personal income in the NIPA is also broader, on balance, than AGI (it amounted to $6.2 trillion in 1992, compared with $4.2 trillion of AGI), but AGI includes $0.8 trillion in sources of income that are missing from personal income. The largest of these is personal contributions to Social Security and related programs ($293 billion), followed by taxable private pensions ($160 billion) and net capital gains ($130 billion). Personal income includes the following major items that are not in AGI: transfer payments ($771 billion), employer-provided fringe benefits ($402 billion), investment income of life insurance or private pension funds ($228 billion), and differences in accounting treatment between NIPA and tax regulations ($54 billion). In addition, there is a $630 billion discrepancy, or gap, between AGI as reported to the Internal Revenue Service and AGI as the NIPA would calculate it. Much of the gap represents noncompliance with the tax code (Park 1994).

For tax purposes, AGI represents a broad measure of net income; however, in most respects it does not reflect differences in personal circumstances that the public wants to take into account before levying taxes. Such differences include family size,

marital circumstances, or particularly large expenditures for purposes that the public either wants to encourage (such as charitable contributions or home ownership) or views as appropriate adjustments to a measure of ability to pay (such as state and local income taxes, extraordinary medical expenses, or extraordinary casualty losses). More specifically, in 1994 AGI ($3.96 trillion) exceeded taxable income ($2.6 trillion) by the amount of personal exemptions ($563 billion) plus the amount of either itemized deductions ($493 billion) or the standard deduction ($397 billion) (Internal Revenue Service 1997: 38, 48).

## Additional readings

Internal Revenue Service. *Statistics of Income Bulletin* (various years). Washington, D.C.

Park, Thae S. "Relationship between Personal Income and Adjusted Gross Income, 1991–1992." *Survey of Current Business* (August 1994): 51–53.

Pechman, Joseph A. *Federal Tax Policy.* Washington, D.C.: The Brookings Institution, 1987.

*Cross references:* charitable deductions; family, tax treatment of; health expenditures, tax treatment; income tax, federal; individual retirement accounts; interest deductibility; itemized deductions; Social Security benefits, federal taxation.

# Airport and Airway Trust Fund

Joseph J. Cordes
Mindy M. Nichols
George Washington University

*A trust fund established in 1970, financed by aviation excise taxes and dedicated to funding public investments in the air transport system.*

The Airport and Airway Trust Fund was established on July 1, 1970, by the Airport and Airway Revenue Act of 1970. The 1970 act created new aviation user taxes that were to be deposited into the trust fund. These taxes, and interest earned on the deposits, were to be used to meet specified airport and airway obligations in the United States. Authorized expenditures from the trust fund include monies spent on such things as qualified airport planning and construction, safety measures, and related departmental administrative expenses.

The original act that created the trust fund was amended in 1973, 1976, and 1979 to authorize spending for additional items of aviation-related ex-

## TABLE 1

### Aviation Tax Revenues Dedicated to Trust Fund

| Tax | Current Tax Rate | Percentage of Trust Fund Receipts |
|---|---|---|
| Airline Ticket Tax | 10% | 87.5 |
| Airline Cargo Tax | 6.25% | 5.2 |
| General Aviation Fuel Tax | $0.14 per gallon on gasoline; $0.175 per gallon on other fuels | 4.0 |
| International Departure Tax | $6 per person | 3.3 |

*Source:* U.S. House of Representatives Committee on Ways and Means, 1991.

penditure. These included increased funding for safety and security equipment costs, snow-removal and noise-suppression equipment, construction of physical barriers and landscaping to reduce the effects of airport noise on areas adjacent to public airports, and airport terminal development (i.e., public, nonrevenue-producing areas including baggage facilities and passenger-moving equipment), and specified amounts for maintenance of airway facilities. The Omnibus Budget Reconciliation Act of 1990 increased the aviation taxes that finance the trust fund by 25 percent.

In recent years, approximately 75 percent of the funding for the Federal Aviation Administration (FAA) has come from the trust fund. More specifically, the trust fund has financed 100 percent of FAA spending for airport improvement, facilities and equipment, and research, engineering, and development, and about half of FAA spending on operations; the other half has come from the Treasury's general fund.

Table 1 summarizes the various aviation taxes whose revenues are dedicated to the trust fund. The most important and visible of these is the Air Passenger Ticket Tax, which accounts for almost 90 cents of every tax dollar flowing into the trust fund. In recent years, these aviation taxes have raised about $5 billion annually, and the FAA has estimated that receipts would have been about $6 billion in fiscal 1996 had the taxes not lapsed. Since 1990, the trust fund has funded about $40 billion in spending on construction and safety improvements at airports, and on technological upgrades to the air traffic control system.

In recent years, several policy issues have been raised about the Airport and Airway Trust Fund. All users of U.S. airways and airports have expressed concern—also raised by beneficiaries of other federal trust funds—that in the 1990s Congress has been reluctant to authorize the full spending of trust fund revenues because trust fund surpluses have contributed to reducing the federal budget deficit.

There have also been debates about whether the current mix and form of taxes that finance the trust fund allocate the costs of funding public aviation infrastructure fairly among the different users. General and business aviation users of airports believe that the taxes they pay into the trust fund represent a fair share of the benefits they receive from public investments in aviation infrastructure, but commercial users believe that general and business aviation users are effectively subsidized by the trust fund, because it is largely financed by the tax on passengers of commercial airlines.

The nation's seven largest airlines have called on Congress to replace the current airline ticket tax, which is assessed on an ad valorem basis on the price of airline tickets, with a new set of user fees equal to $2 per airplane seat ($1 per seat for commuter planes); $4.50 per passenger; and $.005 per passenger per nonstop/origin and destination mile. This proposal has been opposed by "low-cost" carriers who contend that taxes based on a percentage of ticket prices will be lower for low-cost airlines than the proposed set of user fees.

The airline ticket tax also attracted public attention at the end of 1995, when aviation user taxes failed to be reenacted as part of the budget impasse between the president and Congress. From January of 1996 to the present, the ticket tax has lapsed, been temporarily restored, and then lapsed again. Many tax analysts have assumed that the airline ticket tax was effectively shifted forward to passengers in the form of higher ticket prices. If so, one would expect airline ticket prices to fall and rise in response to these changes in the tax. Although this did happen in some cases, the response of airline ticket prices to the off again, on again nature of the ticket tax has been more complex. For example, when the tax temporarily lapsed, many airline passengers did not see reductions in ticket prices.

One explanation for this behavior is that airlines were concerned that the tax would be imposed retroactively, even though it had lapsed, and thus continued to "collect" it. But this does not fully explain why some airlines lowered their ticket prices and others did not when the tax lapsed temporarily. Another possibility is that the response of airlines reflected different degrees of competition in regional markets, combined with strategic pricing behavior—such as price leadership—exhibited by airlines functioning in imperfectly competitive market environments.

The Taxpayer Relief Act of 1997 has restored the ticket tax in a new form: an excise tax of 7.5 percent (9% for FY 1998 and 8% for FY 1999) along with a $2.25 per passenger fee, indexed for inflation in 2003 ($1 for FY 1998 and $2 for FY 1999). The tax applies to commercial purchases of air mileage awards as well. The aviation fuel and air cargo taxes have been extended permanently. The international departure tax has been increased to $12, and a $12 tax has been imposed on international arrivals.

### Additional readings

U.S. General Accounting Office. *Airport and Airway Trust Fund: Effects of the Trust Fund Taxes' Lapsing on FAA's Budget*. Washington, D.C., 1996.

U.S. House of Representatives, Committee on Ways and Means. *Overview of the Federal Tax System*. Washington, D.C., 1991.

*Cross references:* benefit principle; excise taxes; fairness in taxation; user charges, federal.

# Alcoholic beverage taxes, federal

Thomas F. Pogue
University of Iowa

*Taxes are of decreasing importance as sources of revenue and in their impact on individuals' consumption decisions.*

In fiscal year 1996, alcoholic beverage taxes accounted for less than 1 percent of federal revenues, down from more than 5 percent in 1950. Moreover, they absorb a small and diminishing share of consumers' budgets—less than 0.2 percent of Americans' total consumption spending in 1994.

The taxes are fixed dollar amounts per unit of beverage—in 1996, $13.50 per proof-gallon of distilled spirits; $18 per 31-gallon barrel of beer; $1.07 per gallon of table wine. At these rates, the alcohol in distilled spirits is taxed most heavily, at $.21 per ounce; alcohol in beer and wine is taxed at $.10 and $.07 per ounce, respectively.

Alcoholic beverage tax rates have been adjusted only infrequently. From 1951 to 1997, the tax on distilled spirits was increased twice (1985 and 1991), and the taxes on beer and table wine were increased once (1991). In the periods between increases, inflation greatly eroded the real value of the taxes, defined as the purchasing power that consumers lose because of the taxes. From 1951 through 1990, inflation, as measured by the Consumer Price Index, reduced the real tax on distilled spirits by 76 percent and the real taxes on beer and wine by 80 percent. The 1991 increase in the tax on wine, from $.17 to $1.07 per gallon, was more than sufficient to restore the real tax to its 1951 value; and in 1995 the real tax on wine was still 7 percent higher than in 1951. However, the 1991 tax increases for distilled spirits and beer were not enough to offset inflation. By 1995, the real taxes on distilled spirits and beer had

fallen to 22 percent and 34 percent, respectively, of their 1951 levels. To maintain the 1951 levels, the tax on distilled spirits would have to have been $62 in 1995 instead of $13.50, and the tax on beer $53 instead of $18.

Congress could have prevented such erosion by indexing the taxes so that they automatically increase enough to offset inflation; or it could have stated the taxes as a percentage of selling price. But it has chosen to do neither.

Taxes on alcoholic beverages are commonly regarded as less fair than broad-based income and consumption taxes because they depend on individuals' purchases of those beverages, which are not closely related to either their ability to pay taxes or the benefits they receive from the government. The taxes are not horizontally equitable because persons with the same income purchase different amounts of the beverages and therefore bear different tax burdens (see Horizontal equity). Indeed, about 30 percent of all families escape the taxes because they do not buy alcoholic beverages. The taxes are also regressive, absorbing a larger percentage of the income of low-income persons than of middle- or high-income persons (see Progressivity, measures of). The significance of this regressivity is diminished, however, by the fact that about one-half of the poorest one-fifth of families do not purchase alcoholic beverages. Further, alcohol taxes are less regressive when related to lifetime income rather than income for any single year.

In addition to generating revenue, the taxes make alcoholic beverages more expensive, causing consumers to shift some of their purchases to other products. Studies have shown that alcohol abusers, as well as individuals who drink moderately, reduce their consumption of alcohol when beverage prices rise in response to either taxes or other factors. Drinking by young and underage persons appears to be especially sensitive to alcohol prices. See Leung and Phelps (1993) for a review of these studies.

The potential for reducing abusive consumption is the main rationale for taxing alcoholic beverages more heavily than most other products. Individuals who drink excessively not only harm themselves as they impair their health and decrease their productivity and income; they also impose *external* costs on others, including loss of life and property due to alcohol-related accidents, as well as a share of the medical and other costs of alcoholism. The prices on which alcohol abusers base their consumption decisions do not include external costs. Abusers therefore underestimate the costs that their alcohol consumption imposes on society at large. And they consume more than they would be willing to pay for if they had to pay prices that reflect external costs. The result is an inefficiently high level of production and consumption of alcoholic beverages.

Alcoholic beverage taxes counter the effects of this underpricing. Higher taxes lead to higher alcohol prices, which in turn lead to decreases in abusive consumption and external costs. The taxes can, in principle, be set high enough to push market prices to levels that fully reflect external costs. However, combined federal, state, and local taxes are currently well below this level. Pogue and Sgontz (1989) placed external costs at more than $.60 per ounce of alcohol consumed, stated in 1995 dollars. More recent estimates by Miller and Blincoe (1994) are even higher, about $1.40 per ounce of alcohol consumed just for the external cost of alcohol-related crashes. The latter estimate is equivalent to about $4.60 per six-pack of beer and $14.30 per fifth of 80-proof distilled spirits. Even if these estimates are off by half, they imply that external costs are large relative to the taxes on alcoholic beverages. Further, federal taxes are much weaker deterrents to abusive consumption today than they have been in the past because of the aforenoted decrease in the real value of the taxes on beer and distilled spirits.

A growing number of studies advocate increasing alcoholic beverage taxes to reduce abusive consumption and the related external costs. Cook and Moore (1994) argue that higher taxes would be especially effective in reducing alcohol use by youths. To maintain their effectiveness, the taxes should, of course, be indexed so that their real values do not fall with inflation. To avoid tax competition among states, taxes aimed at reducing external costs should be levied by the federal government. And because external costs depend on the amount of alcohol consumed, equal taxes should apply to beverages with equal alcohol content, which is not the case now.

Taxes on beer and distilled spirits could be increased from their 1995 levels by as much as 194 and 359 percent, respectively, without exceeding their highest post-Prohibition real values, reached in 1951. Although smaller increases would not restore the taxes to these peak values, they would nevertheless generate a significant amount of revenue. For example, the Congressional Budget Office (U.S. Congress 1995: 398) estimates that increasing all taxes on alcoholic beverages to the equivalent of $.25 per ounce of alcohol would increase revenue by more than $4 billion annually over the 1996–2000 fiscal years. And, unlike an increase in the income tax, increases in alcoholic beverage taxes would generate revenue without reducing incentives to supply labor and save.

Proposals to increase taxes on alcohol, whether to reduce external costs, increase revenue, or both, commonly meet with several objections. First, as noted above, the taxes are widely perceived as unfair because they are based on purchases of alcoholic beverages rather than ability to pay. Second, they penalize the many individuals who do not consume excessively in order to limit abusive consump-

tion by a few. There is thus a tradeoff of costs: External costs are decreased, but only by imposing higher costs (higher tax burdens) on moderate drinkers. The tax rate that minimizes the sum of these two categories of cost is termed the *optimal* tax. Studies that have estimated the optimal tax conclude that it is considerably larger than current taxes. The need for this cost tradeoff would, of course, be eliminated if it were possible to tax only abusive consumption, but that is not feasible. Third, because higher federal taxes would reduce alcohol consumption, state and local governments would also have to increase their tax rates on alcoholic beverages or suffer revenue losses. Finally, although higher taxes may reduce external costs, they may not be the least costly and disruptive means of doing so. Opponents of alcoholic beverage taxes advocate other measures—educating the public, especially youths, about the dangers of alcohol abuse; treating abusers; controlling access by minors; increasing penalties for driving while under the influence of alcohol. Alcoholic beverage taxes are seen as appropriate for financing these measures but not for financing general government.

In sum, increasing and maintaining the real values of federal alcoholic beverage taxes would entail several difficult tradeoffs. It would reduce abuse and external costs but penalize those who consume moderately. It would generate revenue, without curtailing work and saving incentives. But the resulting distribution of tax burdens would be less fair than if the revenues were obtained from personal or corporate income taxes. Because individuals evaluate these tradeoffs differently, there is no consensus on the question of whether federal alcoholic beverage taxes should be increased or allowed to erode with inflation, as they have during the past four decades. [See U.S. Congress, Congressional Budget Office (1990), for additional bibliographic references and details on alcoholic beverage taxes.]

### Additional readings

Cook, Philip J., and Michael J. Moore. "This Tax's for You: The Case for Higher Beer Taxes." *National Tax Journal* 47 (3) (September 1994): 559–73.

Joint Committee of the States to Study Alcoholic Beverage Laws. *Impact on Alcoholic Beverage Control of Taxation and Mark-up.* Cleveland, 1953.

Leung, Siu Fai, and Charles E. Phelps. "The Demand for Alcoholic Beverages." In *Economic Research on the Prevention of Alcohol-Related Problems*, edited by Gregory Bloss and Michael Hilton. Rockville, MD: National Institutes of Health Publication No. 93-3513, 1993.

Manning, Willard G., Emmett B. Keeler, Joseph P. Newhouse, Elizabeth M. Sloss, and Jeffrey Wasserman. "The Taxes of Sin: Do Smokers and Drinkers Pay Their Way?"

*Journal of the American Medical Association* 261 (11) (March 1989): 1604–9.

Miller, Ted R., and Lawrence J. Blincoe. "Incidence and Cost of Alcohol-Involved Crashes in the U.S." *Accident Analysis and Prevention* 25 (5) 1994: 583ff.

Pogue, Thomas F., and Larry G. Sgontz. "Taxing to Control Social Costs: The Case of Alcohol." *American Economic Review* 79 (1) (March 1989): 235–43.

U.S. Congress, Congressional Budget Office. *Federal Taxation of Tobacco, Alcoholic Beverages, and Motor Fuels.* Washington, D.C.: U.S. Government Printing Office, 1990.

U.S. Congress, Congressional Budget Office. *Reducing the Deficit: Spending and Revenue Options.* Washington, D.C.: U.S. Government Printing Office, February 1995.

*Cross references:* consumption taxation; excise taxes.

# Allocation rules, multinational corporations

Barbara Rollinson
Department of the Treasury

Carol Doran Klein
Arthur Andersen, LLP

*Rules that determine how multinational corporations must divide expenses between domestic source and foreign source income for tax purposes.*

## Overview

Multinational corporations often incur expenses in one country that support operations in another country. In order to determine how much tax is owed to any one country, it is necessary to determine how to treat these expenses. Some of them may be readily traceable to income earned in a single country; however, some expenses may support income that is earned in more than one place. For example, a corporation with operations in the United States and Canada may undertake research and development (R&D) in the United States that leads to a new product that is produced and sold in both the United States and Canada. As another example, a U.S. corporation may decide to expand its operations in the United States and in the rest of the world and finance this worldwide expansion by borrowing (and thus incurring interest expense) in the United States. In both of these cases, expenses incurred in the United States support the production of both U.S. and foreign source income and, therefore, both U.S. and foreign source income should bear a portion of the expenses.

In the absence of specific rules about how to treat these expenses, companies would have an incentive to claim them in countries in which they faced the highest marginal income tax rates. Therefore, higher tax countries have an incentive to prevent taxpayers from assigning all of these expenses to their high tax income. Like so many tax issues affecting multinational corporations, countries recognize that unless they make an effort to resolve differential tax treatment of these types of expenses, double deduction or no deduction anywhere may result. Bilateral income tax treaties usually provide that when a corporation organized in one country has branch operations in another country, each country recognizes that there are situations in which expenses incurred in one country benefit operations in the other and thus should be allowed as a deduction in the other country. In addition, tax treaties usually contain provisions for resolving cases of double taxation, including that caused by differential treatment by the tax authorities in each country that leads to no deduction of an item of expense in either country.

## U.S. rules

The Internal Revenue Code provides expense allocation rules for situations in which a foreign branch, or other types of foreign operations, are involved. In general, the goal is to match the expenses with the income generated by these expenses. If the income is deemed to arise within (or without) the United States, then the expense will also be allocated against income from sources within (or without) the United States. If the income is deemed to arise partly from within and partly from without, then the expense will be apportioned between income from sources within and without the United States.

This overall goal of matching income and expense is achieved in different ways for different types of expenses. In the case of expenses that are readily traceable to an item of income earned in a specific country, the expenses are matched with and offset against that item of income. When the expenses are linked to more than one item of income, a ratable part of these expenses is allocated to and reduces each of the types of income. The treatment of this latter type of expense is the subject of extensive rules in the U.S. Internal Revenue Code and its Regulations. In keeping with the general rule of matching income and expense, most of these expenses may be allocated in proportion to the income they generate. For example, general and administrative expenses usually may be allocated based on the gross income. For two types of expenses, interest and R&D, the goal is the same but, because of the nature of the expenses and their potential importance, the approach is somewhat more refined.

## Interest expense

Interest expense is allocated based on the theory that money is fungible. In other words, if a company incurs debt to finance an expansion at one of its plants, the debt can be considered as supporting the maintenance of cash on hand during the expansion or other existing assets. Thus, a dollar of borrowing can be viewed as supporting all of the company's assets. To implement this theory, generally, a company must classify each of its assets based on the type of income the asset produces and then allocate the interest expense based on the value of the assets. (The minor exceptions to this general rule are for interest expense associated with special transactions, such as certain types of nonrecourse debt and integrated financial transactions.)

A multinational corporation that has assets and incurs interest expense in U.S. and foreign subsidiaries must determine which assets and what interest expense get divided in this way. Before the Tax Reform Act of 1986, each separately incorporated entity allocated its own interest expense based on its own assets. This practice allowed companies to isolate their debt in subsidiaries that held no assets and would be classified as non-U.S. assets. Since the Tax Reform Act of 1986, however, the U.S. Internal Revenue Code has generally required a group of affiliated U.S. corporations to allocate interest expense as if all the members were a single corporation. Thus, the assets of any U.S. company that is at least 80 percent owned by a common parent, and any interest expense incurred by those same companies, are allocated using affiliated group apportionment ratios. For this purpose, foreign corporations are not included in the affiliated group. This so-called "water's edge" fungibility means that if a U.S. company owns 100 percent of a Canadian company, the value of its stock in the Canadian company will be included in the U.S. company's assets, but the underlying assets held by the Canadian company and the interest expense the Canadian company incurs will not be included. Some have argued that water's edge fungibility should be replaced with "worldwide" fungibility. Under worldwide fungibility, assets and interest expense of both U.S. and foreign subsidiaries that are part of a worldwide group would be taken into account. A practical difficulty with implementing worldwide fungibility under the current scheme of asset-based allocation is that U.S. multinationals would be forced to require their foreign subsidiaries to classify their assets for U.S. tax purposes.

## Research and development

Fashioning a general rule to determine how to allocate R&D "properly" has proved to be a more difficult undertaking. R&D expenses incurred in a given year are currently deductible, yet they frequently generate future income. In addition, R&D may not relate to all of the taxpayer's income because it may support only certain product categories. However, requiring companies to provide special analyses showing how R&D should be allocated would be an expensive and imprecise undertaking. Thus special regulations provide general rules for allocating R&D. R&D is divided up based on the standard industry classification to which it relates. Because R&D is assumed to be most valuable in the country in which it is undertaken, a certain percentage of this R&D is allocated exclusively to the country in which most of it is undertaken, and the remainder is allocated in proportion to domestic and foreign sales of the corporation in those same standard industry classifications.

Determining the appropriate percentage for the exclusion apportionment fraction has proved quite controversial. For a number of years, Congress passed special legislation that set temporary amounts for this percentage. The current exclusive apportionment percentage of 50 percent found in the regulations is supported by a 1995 Treasury study that reiterates the diversity of "proper" percentages depending on the type of R&D and the company's business structure.

The regulations also offer the option of dividing R&D expenses based on the relative amounts of gross income within and without the United States. If this method is selected, 25 percent of the R&D expenses are allocated exclusively to the location in which most of the R&D is undertaken. In addition, this option is limited by a "floor," which provides that the allocations to foreign source income must be at least 50 percent of those that would have been allocated to foreign source income under the sales method. The reason for this backstop is that comparing gross income is something of a mismatch since the definition of foreign gross income includes, for example, dividends from a foreign corporation; thus, foreign gross income may be much closer to a net concept than domestic gross income.

## Impact of U.S. allocation rules on multinational corporations

U.S. corporations are taxed on their worldwide income and allowed a foreign tax credit for foreign taxes paid up to the amount of tax that would have been paid in the United States. U.S. allocation rules, which have the result of classifying some expenses incurred in the United States as foreign source, do not literally affect the deductibility of an item of expense for U.S. tax purposes. Instead, these rules affect the calculation of a U.S. corporation's foreign tax credit limitation. An increase (decrease) in expenses classified as foreign decreases (increases) a corporation's foreign tax credit limitation. For corporations whose foreign operations are largely in low-tax locations or that earn types of income that are lightly taxed abroad, the allocation rules have little practical impact because these corporations are still able to credit all foreign taxes paid. Conversely, for corporations operating predominantly in locations with tax rates higher than those found in the United States, these rules operate to restrict the foreign tax credits actually allowed by the corporation.

## Additional readings

Department of the Treasury. *The Impact of the Section 861-8 Regulation on U.S. Research and Development*, June 1983.

Department of the Treasury. *The Relationship between U.S. Research and Development and Foreign Income*, May 1995.

Hufbauer, Gary Clyde. *U.S. Taxation of International Income*. Washington, D.C.: Institute for International Economics, 1992.

Organization for Economic Cooperation and Development. *Model Double Taxation Convention on Income and Capital*. Paris: OECD, 1995.

*U.S. Internal Revenue Code.* Sections 861, 862, and 864 and the Regulations under each of these sections.

*Cross references:* foreign tax credit; multinational corporations, taxation.

# Alternative minimum tax, corporate

Andrew B. Lyon
University of Maryland

*A complex tax (either federal or state) designed to increase the income tax on businesses that the legislature believes pay too little relative to "standard" rules of taxation.*

## Overview

Minimum taxes are intended to increase tax payments from taxpayers who, under the rules of the regular tax system, are believed to pay too little tax relative to a more standard measure of their income. The U.S. federal income tax has both a personal and a corporate alternative minimum tax (AMT). Standard rules of business income taxation call for the recognition of income as it accrues, that is, at its receipt or when all events have occurred that fix the right to receive the income, whichever comes first. Deductions are permitted only when definite liabilities have been incurred. These standard rules are strongly influenced by (but differ somewhat from) both financial accounting practices and economic principles of income measurement. (Note that both standard rules and regular tax rules depart from economic measures of income by not allowing a deduction for the opportunity cost of equity-financed capital. The standard rules, as embodied in the AMT, additionally depart from economic principles by making little or no attempt to adjust measured income for the effects of inflation. The regular tax system gives some consideration for inflation through accelerated depreciation for equipment and valuation rules for inventory.)

Rules of the regular tax system make many departures from the standard rules, in a manner that generally results in a lower measure of income. The motives for these departures—or tax preferences—may include an aim for simplicity, an incentive for certain activities, political influence, or better accounting for other economic factors such as inflation.

Corporate and individual minimum taxes were first put into the U.S. tax code in 1969. Initially, the minimum tax functioned much like an excise tax on specified tax preferences in excess of some fixed amount. As part of the Tax Reform Act of 1986, the corporate minimum tax was significantly modified to cover a much broader range of preferences and is now called the alternative minimum tax. It is an *alternative* tax because the rules for this minimum tax constitute a complete, alternative set of rules to the regular tax system. It is a *minimum* tax because a corporation must pay the larger of its AMT or its regular tax liabilities.

## AMT calculation

The AMT has its own rules for the measurement of income and deductions, and it has separate tax rates. While closely following the rules of the regular system, the AMT has a broader definition of income and a less generous set of deductions. Further, most business tax credits, such as the credit for research and experimentation, cannot be used to reduce tax payments under the AMT.

Given the larger measure of taxable net income under the AMT, practically all corporations would pay AMT were it not for the fact that the tax rate under the AMT is lower than the maximum tax rate under the regular tax system. The tax rate under the AMT is 20 percent, while the average tax rate under the regular tax system is about 34 percent for firms with more than $100,000 of income. Because the regular tax rate is 70 percent higher than the AMT rate, a firm's income must be at least 70 percent greater under the AMT before it must make payments under this system. It might at first appear that such a significant percentage change in net income would require that the AMT use tremendously different measures of includable income or allowable deductions relative to the regular tax system. But for the typical manufacturing firm, gross receipts and deductions are 10 to 20 times larger than its net income. A 5 to 10 percent change in includable receipts or allowable deductions is sufficient to create an AMT liability.

The starting point for the determination of income for AMT purposes is the corporation's regular taxable income. Regular taxable income is modified by a series of additional computations, termed *adjustments* and *preferences*. Adjustments can either increase or decrease taxable income, whereas preferences are calculated on a property-by-property basis and only enter to the extent that they are positive. Adjustments include a portion of accelerated depreciation on buildings and equipment, amortization of pollution control facilities, mining exploration and development expenses, income reported under the completed contract method of accounting, and installment sales income.

Preferences include percentage depletion, intangible drilling costs, bad debt deductions of financial institutions, and interest on certain bonds that would otherwise be tax-exempt. Between 1987 and 1989, an additional preference was one-half the amount by which a corporation's book income (with certain modifications) exceeded its taxable income for AMT purposes. This preference was enacted as an explicitly temporary measure and was replaced in 1990 with an alternative measure of income, adjusted current earnings. Since 1990, 75 percent of the difference between adjusted current earnings and the firm's taxable income for AMT purposes is included in income.

AMT income may effectively be reduced by up to 90 percent through net operating losses and foreign tax credits, both of which are recalculated using AMT principles. The 20 percent tax rate is applied to this measure of income, yielding tentative minimum tax, and this amount is compared to the firm's regular tax liability before all credits except the foreign tax credit. If the tentative minimum tax is larger, the firm pays the excess as AMT, in addition to its regular tax liability. If the firm's regular tax liability exceeds its tentative minimum tax, it may further reduce its regular tax by allowable business credits, but generally not below its tentative minimum tax. For firms with large amounts of business credits, such as the credit for research and experimentation, the AMT may serve to increase the

firm's tax liability by delaying the use of these credits even if the firm pays no AMT.

A major element of the increase in tax liability under the AMT involves differences in the timing of deductions. Because firms may switch between the AMT and the regular tax, a system of credits for taxes paid under the AMT and adjustments to the basis of depreciated property is needed to prevent the AMT from collecting taxes in excess of the value of the timing preference. The tax credit for AMT payments can only be used to offset future regular tax liability. Further, it may not be used to reduce regular tax payments below the tentative minimum tax (the same floor that limits the use of most business tax credits). A firm that pays AMT and eventually claims all of its AMT credits will have the same total tax liability over this period as it would have had in the absence of the AMT. Because the AMT credits are taken *after* the firm's AMT payments, however, the AMT has resulted in an acceleration of tax payments. The cost to the firm of this acceleration is the forgone earnings on these funds. If a firm must wait a long time before claiming its AMT credits, this cost may be a sizable fraction of the AMT payment. Calculations indicate that firms undertaking investment in equipment while temporarily subject to the AMT generally face a higher cost of capital than firms on the regular tax (Lyon 1990). Interestingly, firms that are presently on the regular tax and are anticipating a short period of AMT liability in the future may face increased investment incentives as a result of the tax.

## AMT revenues

Between 1987 and 1992, AMT revenues were between $2.7 billion and $8.6 billion (1992 dollars), or between 3 and 9 percent of the regular tax revenues collected in those years. AMT credits claimed over this period were about one-fifth of the AMT paid (U.S. General Accounting Office 1995).

In each year between 1987 and 1992, firms paying AMT represented only 1 to 2 percent of all corporations. AMT incidence was much more likely, however, for larger firms. Approximately 20 to 30 percent of firms with assets in excess of $250 million paid AMT each year between 1987 and 1992. The General Accounting Office (GAO) has estimated that, among a sample of corporations with assets in excess of $50 million, 49 percent paid AMT in at least one year between 1987 and 1991. Firms paying AMT in at least one year accounted for nearly two-thirds of the corporate assets in the GAO sample.

A 1993 legislative modification to the calculation of the AMT is expected to reduce the future incidence of the AMT to some degree. A much more significant change was enacted in 1997, which substantially narrowed the differences between regular and AMT depreciation by equating recovery periods.

## Why an AMT?

The existence of the minimum tax appears to be an inconsistency in the formulation of tax law. One part of the tax system gives special deductions, exclusions, and incentives, and another part of the tax system takes them away (Graetz and Sunley 1988). Why, then, a minimum tax?

Some analysts believe the minimum tax is an appropriate "second-best" method to reduce the magnitude of deviations from economic measures of income if political constraints prevent their direct elimination. Corporations for which income measured under the minimum tax differs greatly from income measured under the regular tax are likely to pay minimum tax. Taxable income under the minimum tax, however, is not the same as economic income. Further, because a firm undertaking a tax-preferred activity can still avoid the minimum tax if the firm additionally undertakes other activities without such preferences, tax-preferred activities will still attract investment. If one desires, for reasons of efficiency, to limit the amount of the economy's resources devoted to a given tax-preferred activity, the minimum tax will not be as effective as a direct reduction in the tax preference for that activity.

Others argue that the minimum tax does just what it is supposed to do. It allows tax policy to meet two social objectives: providing tax incentives to encourage particular activities and ensuring, for reasons of fairness, that corporations with positive incomes pay at least some tax. Of course, ultimately corporate taxes are borne by people, and the fact that a given corporation pays a low rate of tax may not have implications for equity among individuals. If the fairness concern is that individuals who earn income from certain corporate activities pay too little tax on this income, this directly conflicts with the assumed objective of encouraging the activity through a tax preference.

## Additional readings

Graetz, Michael J., and Emil M. Sunley. "Minimum Taxes and Comprehensive Tax Reform." In *Uneasy Compromise: Problems of a Hybrid Income-Consumption Tax*, edited by Henry J. Aaron, Harvey Galper, and Joseph Pechman. Washington, D.C.: The Brookings Institution, 1988.

Lyon, Andrew B. "Investment Incentives under the Alternative Minimum Tax." *National Tax Journal* 43 (December 1990): 451–65.

Lyon, Andrew B. *Cracking the Code: Making Sense of the Corporate Alternative Minimum Tax*. Washington, D.C.: The Brookings Institution, 1997.

U.S. General Accounting Office. *Experience with the Corporate Alternative Minimum Tax*. GAO/GGD-95-88, 1995.

*Cross references:* adjusted current earnings; alternative minimum tax, personal; capital cost recovery; cost of capital; income tax, corporate, federal; taxable income, corporate.

# Alternative minimum tax, personal

David Weiner
Congressional Budget Office

*An additional tax paid by some individuals that can result from the use of certain tax preferences. (See also Alternative minimum tax, corporate.)*

The personal alternative minimum tax (AMT) requires individuals to calculate their income tax a second way, differently from the regular income tax. Separate tax rates and definitions of taxable income apply in each of these tax systems. The AMT limits the use of certain tax preferences, or exceptions to a comprehensive measure of income. A taxpayer's final liability is the greater of the tax liabilities calculated under the regular tax system and the AMT system. The AMT is defined as the amount by which the tax calculated under the broader AMT base, the tentative minimum tax, exceeds regular tax liability. The tax base under the AMT is broader than that under the regular tax, and the top marginal tax rates are lower than under the regular tax. Relatively few taxpayers pay AMT, and the amount collected from the AMT has been small relative to that collected from the regular income tax (table 1).

**TABLE 1**

**AMT Statistics for Selected Years**

|  | Tax Year | | |
| --- | --- | --- | --- |
|  | 1983 | 1988 | 1994 |
| Returns with Income Tax | 78,016 | 87,135 | 87,619 |
| Returns with AMT | 265 | 114 | 369 |
| Total Income Tax Liability | $274.2 | $412.9 | $559.1 |
| AMT Liability | $2.5 | $1.0 | $2.2 |

*Notes:* Numbers of returns are in thousands. Dollar amounts are in billions.
*Source:* Statistics of Income, Internal Revenue Service (Washington, D.C.: U.S. Government Printing Office, various years).

## History of the AMT

The AMT has its origins in the "add-on" minimum tax, which was first introduced into the tax system in 1969. Unlike the dual tax systems of the AMT, the minimum tax was a separate tax in which a flat 10 percent rate was applied to certain tax preferences in excess of an exempted amount of $30,000. A taxpayer's total liability was the sum of the regular tax and the minimum tax. The minimum tax was introduced in order to collect some taxes from wealthy individuals who paid little or no tax because they took advantage of tax preferences to reduce their taxable income. The minimum tax was strengthened in 1976 when the exemption amount was changed to the greater of $10,000 or half the taxes paid under the regular tax. The rate was also increased to 15 percent.

The AMT was introduced into the tax system by the Revenue Act of 1978, coexisting with the minimum tax. The preferences for certain itemized deductions and excluded capital gains were moved from the minimum tax to the AMT. By using the AMT rather than the minimum tax, taxpayers would only pay additional tax on capital gains income if their AMT exceeded their regular tax liability. Congress anticipated that "capital formation will be facilitated and every individual will pay at least a reasonable amount of tax with respect to large capital gains." The AMT exempted the first $20,000 from tax and had a graduated rate schedule of 10, 20, and 25 percent.

In 1982, Congress repealed the minimum tax and expanded the AMT. Most preference items under the minimum tax were moved to the AMT. The exemption was increased to $30,000 for a single taxpayer and $40,000 for taxpayers filing jointly. A flat rate of 20 percent was applied to alternative minimum taxable income after the exemption was deducted.

The next major revision to the AMT occurred with the Tax Reform Act of 1986. Additional preference items were added to expand the AMT base. One of the largest preference items—the excluded portion of long-term capital gains—was eliminated from the regular tax (and thus as a preference under the AMT). The AMT rate was raised to 21 percent, and the AMT exemption was phased out for high-income taxpayers. For each dollar that the alternative minimum taxable income exceeded a specified threshold, the exemption amount was reduced by 25 cents. For taxpayers with large amounts of income, the exemption was completely eliminated. Finally, AMT generated in the current year could in some circumstances be taken as a credit against regular tax liability in future years.

In 1990, Congress raised the top marginal income tax rate to 31 percent and the AMT rate to 24 percent. The top marginal income tax rate was in-

creased again in 1993, and a graduated rate schedule of 26 and 28 percent was introduced to the AMT. The exemption amounts were increased to $45,000 for married individuals and $33,750 for unmarried individuals.

Harvey and Tempalski (1997) claim that the AMT will grow rapidly because regular tax exemptions are indexed and AMT exemptions are not; they predict 9 million taxpayers will be affected within 10 years.

The 1997 tax reduction added two important credits: the child credit and education credits, which will cause some additional taxpayers to be subject to the AMT.

## Tax preferences

Tax preferences are exceptions to a comprehensive measure of income under an ideal income tax. The items considered tax preferences for purposes of the AMT have changed over time. These preferences are items that can be excluded from regular taxable income or deductions allowed under the regular tax that would not be allowed under a comprehensive income tax. Not all tax preferences are included in the AMT, and the list has changed over time. The preferences described below are among those included under the tax law in effect in 1993.

The use of exemptions and deductions is limited under the AMT. While the AMT has its own exemption level, it does not allow deductions for personal exemptions or the standard deductions allowed under the regular tax. Some itemized deductions, including miscellaneous itemized deductions and deductions for taxes paid, are completely disallowed. Others are more limited. For example, medical deductions are allowed only to the extent that they exceed 10 percent of adjusted gross income, compared with 7.5 percent under the regular tax. Deductions for investment interest and home mortgage interest are subject to separate rules under the AMT, which can reduce the size of the deduction compared with the regular tax. The itemized deductions allowed under the minimum tax are not, however, subject to the itemized deduction limitation that applies to higher-income individuals under the regular tax.

Many of the other preferences under the AMT are associated with the timing of income and deductions for investors in noncorporate businesses. Deductions for depreciation of equipment, oil depletion allowances, allowances for intangible drilling costs, or mining exploration and development costs are allowed at a slower rate under the AMT than under the regular tax. The difference between deductions allowed under the regular tax and the AMT is included in the alternative minimum taxable income. Other examples of timing preferences include deductions associated with a financial institution's bad debt, deductions for newspaper circulation expenses, deductions for research and experimentation expenses, and the use of the "percentage-of-completion" or the "installment" methods of accounting. It is these timing preferences that generate credits that can be taken against future regular tax liability.

## Justification for the AMT

The minimum tax and the AMT were originally designed to ensure that wealthy individuals pay some income tax. These individuals would not be able to avoid paying income taxes through the use of certain tax preferences or tax shelters. Aside from a general sense of fairness, it has been argued that overall confidence and compliance with the tax system could be undermined if nonwealthy taxpayers feel that wealthy taxpayers pay little or no income tax.

While the minimum tax provided a disincentive for the use of any specified tax preferences, the AMT only discourages the use of an "excessive" amount of tax preferences. That is, individuals with tax preferences are affected by the AMT only to the extent that their tentative minimum tax is greater than their regular tax. For example, most taxpayers with itemized deductions take a deduction for state and local income taxes. While this is a preference item under the AMT, most taxpayers are unaffected because this deduction by itself is not enough to generate a tentative minimum tax greater than the regular tax.

The AMT has been associated with efforts to expand the tax base to a more comprehensive measure of income. The most recent significant change to the AMT took place with the Tax Reform Act of 1986, which expanded the income tax base under both the regular tax and the AMT. While the AMT tax base is broader than that under the regular tax, the list of preference items is much smaller than comprehensive lists of tax preferences such as those in the tax expenditure budget.

The AMT does limit the advantage of certain tax preferences for some taxpayers, but it is not without cost. While relatively few taxpayers pay the AMT, many taxpayers must calculate their tax under both the AMT and the regular tax to determine if they owe any AMT liability. The AMT, with its separate schedule of itemized deductions, exemptions, depreciation schedules, and rates, adds significantly to the complexity of tax calculations.

## Additional readings

Harvey, Robert P., and Jerry Tempalski. "The Individual AMT: Why It Matters." *National Tax Journal* 50 (September 1997): 453–74.

Moran, Beverly I. "Stargazing: The Alternative Minimum Tax for Individuals and Future Tax Reform." *Oregon Law Review 69* (1990): 223–68.

U.S. Congress, Joint Committee on Taxation. *General Explanation of the Revenue Provisions of the Tax Equity and Fiscal Responsibility Act of 1982.* 97th Cong., JCS-38-82.

U.S. Congress, Joint Committee on Taxation. *General Explanation of the Tax Reform Act of 1986.* 99th Cong., JCS-10-87.

*Cross reference:* income tax, federal.

# Apportionment
## Robert P. Strauss
Carnegie-Mellon University

*Involves the division of a business's multijurisdictional taxable economic activities among taxing jurisdictions.*

---

Apportionment of a tax base can be contrasted to *allocation* of a tax base and *harmonization* of jurisdictions' taxes. *Allocation* involves the attribution of certain types of business receipts of a multistate business, usually investment income (dividends, interest, and royalty income), to *one* taxing jurisdiction. *Harmonization* denotes the extent to which taxing jurisdictions recognize, for their own tax purposes, taxes imposed by other jurisdictions on the same taxpayer. State corporate income taxes typically do not allow the deduction of other states' corporate income taxes in determining businesswide taxable income.

The current state business tax apportionment laws reflect the historical evolution of the realities of U.S. businesses. When markets were local or regional in character, geographic attribution of the profits due to the sale of tangible and intangible personal property was unnecessary. Indeed, business taxation in colonial times typically involved the imposition of a local real property tax and the collection of various fees related to the privilege of doing business in the area. As the corporate form became more popular during the Industrial Revolution as a means of raising capital and insulating investors from some business risks, the states devised various incorporation fees, often based on the extent of capitalization. These fees were variously called franchise or capital stock taxes, and they persist to this day, although the limitations on the amount per firm that can be collected lighten their burden and typically eliminate them from serious state tax planning considerations. It should be noted that a series of U.S. Supreme Court cases in the 19th century generally supported a state's right to impose a tax for the privilege of doing business and also supported as permissible measurement of the privilege to include net income.

Before the voluntary development in 1957 among the states of a model business tax statute with extensive apportionment rules, the Uniform Division for Income Tax Purposes Tax Act, business taxpayers typically reported state income on the basis of accounting records of their establishments in the state. Such separate accounting of an establishment's revenues, expenses, and profits and losses, however, has largely been replaced by the proportionate attribution of business income to states in which the business has sufficient activity, on the basis of such state-specific factors as payroll, property, and sales. The first two factors may be viewed as supporting attribution on the basis of the origin of the activity of a multijurisdictional business, while the last (sales) factor may be viewed as supporting attribution on the basis of access to markets in which one does business, or the destination of the activity of a business.

The general purpose of apportionment is to avoid, reduce, or eliminate the risk of multiple taxation of multistate business activity. The extent to which any state may tax an interstate business is regulated by the Commerce, Due Process, and Equal Protection clauses of the U.S. Constitution and attending case law and, in the case of state corporate income taxes, by a specific federal statute that defines when a multistate business may be initially subjected to a state corporate income tax.

Public Law (PL) 86-272 provides specific guidelines for the determination of a business's taxability under a state corporate income tax for businesses engaged in the interstate sale of tangible personal property. Under PL 86-272, taxability or *nexus* in a state is not established if a business merely solicits orders for the sale of tangible personal property into the state in question. Solicitation by nonemployees of the business—for example, contract sales representatives—the displaying of goods in a state by business employees, and the shipment of the business's goods by business employees in a business-owned vehicle into a state are protected activities under PL 86-272 and presumptively do not constitute nexus. Maintenance of an office (owned or rented), ownership of other real property, ownership of inventory, solicitation of orders by employees with the authority to accept them, purchasing, or frequent installation by business employees in the state, on the other hand, are not protected activities and are sufficient to constitute nexus (taxability) in the state in question.

State taxation of other aspects of interstate business is not protected by federal statute but has been limited by a series of Supreme Court decisions.

The Uniform Division Act distinguishes between income to be apportioned among taxing states and income, primarily from investments, to be entirely allocated to the state of a corporation's commercial domicile. Under the act, income taxable in State A is determined by averaging the payroll, property, and sales (on a destination basis) fractions of such activities attributable to State A as compared with all states in which the business is taxable, and multiplying this percentage by the businesswide taxable income:

$$Taxable\ Income_A = \frac{1}{3}\left(\frac{Payroll_A}{Payroll} + \frac{Property_A}{Property}\right.$$
$$\left. = \frac{Sales_A}{Sales}\right) \cdot Taxable\ Income$$

A variety of complications arise and are dealt with in the act to implement this equation. For example, real property is measured at cost (as contrasted with market), while rental property is included in the property factor by capitalizing it, usually at 12.5 percent; compensation of executives is sited to the commercial domicile of the corporation, and specific rules are suggested to deal with employees who work in multiple jurisdictions. Difficult issues arise in the treatment of the location of factors in states without an income tax, and the treatment of sales to tax-exempt organizations and governments. Administrative considerations, technological change, and the nature of particular service industries (especially telecommunications, banking, and transportation) have led to the development of industry-specific apportionment rules. The Multistate Tax Commission (MTC), a voluntary organization of states, continues to refine and detail this basic formula, which member states subsequently adopt through amendments to their business tax statutes and through adoption of MTC regulations.

The apportionment equation presumes that the business's income is known; however, in the case of multitiered corporations, the nature of the filing unit, as defined by state tax law, interacts with the apportionment formula in affecting the state-by-state business tax liability. The states vary considerably as to whether they permit or require a corporation to file on a consolidated, combined, unitary, or separate basis. A consolidated corporate filing unit for federal income tax purposes includes all domestic subsidiaries owned 80 percent or more by the parent corporation (typically a holding company). Were this consolidated entity subjected to state corporate income taxation, the denominators in the equation would reflect the property, payroll, and sales of the consolidated corporation, and the income would reflect the income of the aggregation of these subsidiaries. However, since PL 86-272 limits application of a state corporate income tax to only those parts of a corporation with substantial contact, business would typically resist such an inclusive definition of the filing unit for a state's corporate income tax. Combined reporting involves the aggregation of only those subsidiaries that are taxable in a state; in some states, the aggregation prohibits the offsetting of positive income in some subsidiaries with negative income in others. Issues arise as to whether the aggregation is *before* or *after* apportionment to each specific state.

Application of a state unitary filing requirement entails identifying and aggregating those parts of a multistate corporation that have various economic links with each other (operational interdependence, functional integration, centralized management and span of control, purchasing policy, etc.), and one of which has sufficient contact in the state under PL 86-272 to permit state taxation. States have applied unitary filing requirements to the worldwide activities of domestic- and foreign-headquartered corporations. California has been the most innovative and aggressive in the application of the unitary principle of business taxation, and was upheld in two important Supreme Court cases dealing with the unitary taxation of a domestically headquartered company and an internationally headquartered company, respectively, *Container Corporation of America* v. *California Franchise Tax Board* in 1983, and *Barclays Bank* v. *California Franchise Tax Board* in 1994.

While the equation above is the most common apportionment rule embodied in state corporate income tax statutes, the U.S. Supreme Court has been quite permissive in finding that variants of it do not represent an undue burden on interstate commerce. A number of states have tried to emphasize the sales factor more heavily than the other factors in the equation to raise further revenues from out-of-state firms, and have provided optional formulas (one, two, or three factors in the equation) to tax local firms more favorably. As of 1997, Iowa, Missouri, Nebraska, and Texas require or permit the use of a one-factor sales or gross receipts formula.

### Additional readings

Commerce Clearing House. *All State Tax Guide*. Chicago, 1995.

Gordon, Roger. "A Critical Look at Formula Apportionment." In *Final Report of the Minnesota Tax Study Commission*, edited by Robert D. Ebel and Therese J. McGuire. Boston: Butterworths, 1986.

Hellerstein, Jerome R., and Walter Hellerstein. *State Taxation. 1. Corporate Income and Franchise Taxes*. 2d ed. Boston: Warren, Gorham, and Lamont, 1993.

Martinez-Vazquez, Jorge, and Martin Grace. "Corporate Taxation: The General Franchise Tax." In *Taxation and Economic Development: A Blueprint for Ohio Tax Re-*

*form*, edited by Roy Bahl. Columbus, Ohio: Battelle Press, 1995.

*Cross references:* income tax, corporate, state and local; Multistate Tax Commission.

# Automatic stabilizers

Robert M. Coen
Northwestern University

*Built-in features of the fiscal system that tend to reduce fluctuations in economic activity.*

Just as shock absorbers on an automobile smooth out road bumps without action on the part of the driver, automatic stabilizers cushion the economy to external shocks without explicit action on the part of government authorities. The principal examples of automatic stabilizers are the income tax and unemployment benefits. A negative macroeconomic shock, such as a decline in foreign demand for a nation's exports, causes output and employment in export industries to contract. As workers in the export sector experience declines in their incomes, they will be inclined to reduce consumption spending, thereby spreading the initial shock to other parts of the economy and magnifying its effect. Automatic stabilizers limit these repercussions by sustaining disposable income when pretax, pretransfer income declines. For example, if wages are subject to a marginal tax rate of 20 percent, a worker whose wage income declines by $1,000 will suffer only an $800 loss in disposable income, because tax liability falls by $200. An unemployed worker whose wage income falls to zero will nonetheless have positive disposable income equal to unemployment benefits received. Under a positive macroeconomic shock, automatic stabilizers act to restrain the growth of disposable income and spending when pretax income rises.

Automatic stabilizers can reduce economic fluctuations, but they cannot eliminate them because they do not fully replace lost income. Furthermore, they cannot reverse a cumulative decline in output or restrain a cumulative increase. Discretionary fiscal actions may also be needed to increase stability, just as the driver of a car may increase the smoothness of the ride by reducing speed or steering to avoid potholes. However, discretionary stabilization policy requires that authorities forecast the need for policy changes and then implement the changes. Because of lags in data collection, forecasting errors, and lengthy legislative processes, discretionary actions may be ineffective or even destabilizing. By contrast, an income tax collected via withholding at the source operates as a stabilizer automatically and immediately whenever income changes. Unemployment benefits are not quite as automatic, since unemployed workers must file claims to receive them.

Intermediate between passive reliance on automatic stabilizers and active use of discretionary policies are stabilization policy rules, sometimes referred to as feedback rules or formula flexibility. An example would be a rule stipulating that tax rates are to be reduced during recessions and increased during booms. Such a rule eliminates the implementation lags that beset discretionary policies, but not recognition lags, because information still needs to be collected and analyzed to determine the state of the economy. Automatic stabilizers have the distinct advantage of eliminating both recognition and implementation lags.

## Effectiveness of automatic stabilizers

The power of automatic stabilizers depends principally on the extent to which taxes change when income changes—that is, on the marginal tax rate. (Transfers such as unemployment benefits may be thought of as negative taxes, such that the larger the fraction of lost earnings replaced by unemployment benefits, the higher the marginal tax rate.) The marginal tax rate can be expressed as the product of the average tax rate, $t$, and the revenue elasticity of the tax system, $E$. While $t$ might be set to finance a desired ratio of public expenditures to output, $E$ depends on the design of the fiscal system. For example, a progressive income tax has an $E > 1$ and provides greater built-in stability than a flat-rate income tax, for which $E = 1$. Any fiscal system for which $E$ is positive provides some degree of built-in stability.

Musgrave and Miller (1948) proposed an index of built-in stability that measures the percentage of national output (gross domestic product, or GDP) change prevented by the cushioning effect of the fiscal system. In a static, Keynesian macroeconomic model, the index takes the form $\alpha = \beta Et / (1 - \beta + \beta Et)$, where $\beta$ is the marginal propensity to spend out of disposable income, $0 < \beta < 1$. If $E$ is zero, there is no built-in stability and $\alpha$ is zero. For reasonable values of $E = 1.1$, $t = 0.3$, and $\beta = 0.6$, the tax system would reduce by 33 percent the decline in GDP resulting from a decline in exogenous demand, relative to a situation in which $E$ is zero. Kiefer (1980) surveys estimates of $\alpha$ for the federal income tax and the fiscal system as a whole.

Greater stability of the U.S. economy after 1945 may be attributed in part to a higher ratio of federal receipts to GDP, since for a given value of $E$, $\alpha$ increases as $t$ increases. On the other hand, built-in stability is reduced by tax reforms that are intended to reduce excess tax burdens by cutting marginal tax rates and indexing personal exemptions and tax brackets to inflation, while leaving $t$ unchanged. Also, shifts in tax sources away from those with high $E$s (personal and corporate income taxes) to those with smaller $E$s (sales, excise, payroll, property, and estate taxes) tend to reduce built-in stability.

The Musgrave-Miller index has several deficiencies. Automatic stabilizers tend to create budget deficits during recessions that must be financed by borrowing or monetary expansion. Increased government borrowing may raise interest rates and thereby reduce investment spending, negating part of the cushioning effect of the stabilizers. The index does not distinguish between real and nominal changes in income or between demand and supply shocks, and it does not consider effectiveness in moderating fluctuations in the price level as well as output. In a dynamic economy with lagged responses of spending to income or production to demand, a sensible goal for stabilization policy may not be to reduce the effect of a shock on the level of GDP, but rather to minimize the variance of GDP around its full-employment level. The variance depends in complex ways on the lags, as well as on the nature of recurring stochastic shocks to the economy, and full-employment GDP may itself be affected by automatic stabilizers. Depending on the economic structure, an income tax may be either stabilizing or destabilizing (Johansen 1974). Nonetheless, the major insights provided by the index remain valid in a variety of settings.

Rational-expectation macroeconomic models have shown that activist stabilization policies are likely to be ineffective, but they support the role of automatic stabilizers that serve to decentralize changes in taxes on the basis of information that becomes known to central authorities only with lags (McCallum and Whitaker 1979). If strict Ricardian equivalence holds, then an income tax cannot act as a built-in stabilizer. A reduction in current taxes leads to an expectation of higher future taxes, leaving the present value of taxes, which determines current spending, unchanged. However, if consumers cannot fully differentiate between idiosyncratic income shocks and those that are common to all workers, there will be imperfect capitalization of future taxes, and the reduction in consumption due to a common income shock may be smaller the higher the marginal income tax rate (Christiano 1984).

## Implications for budget analysis and policy

If at the onset of a recession the government's budget is balanced, it will go into deficit during the recession, as automatic stabilizers do their job. A policy rule or constitutional amendment that requires an annually balanced budget would therefore undermine automatic stabilizers. To adhere to such a policy, tax sources with very small *E*s would have to be adopted, or discretionary changes in tax rates and expenditure programs would have to be enacted to offset the fiscal impacts of automatic stabilizers, but these are likely to be destabilizing, requiring that tax rates be increased in recessions. An alternative budget policy that allows automatic stabilizers to operate would set the average tax rate to achieve a balanced budget *when the economy is operating at high employment,* permitting deficits to be run in recessions and surpluses in booms (Friedman 1948). Because state and local governments are usually required to maintain balanced budgets, their fiscal systems cannot contribute much to built-in stability.

Because of automatic stabilizers, the conventionally measured budget deficit is often an inaccurate gauge of discretionary fiscal policy. A rise in the official deficit does not necessarily indicate active pursuit of expansionary fiscal programs; it may simply reflect the operation of built-in stabilizers. To assess discretionary fiscal policy, the impact of the state of the economy on budget receipts and expenditures must be removed, resulting in a cyclically adjusted measure referred to as the high-employment, standardized-employment, or structural deficit (Brown 1956; Council of Economic Advisers 1962: 78–82). Estimates of the structural deficit by the Congressional Budget Office (U.S. Congress 1995: 77–82, 91) indicate that in recent years, a one percentage point increase in unemployment adds about $40 billion to the conventional deficit after one year and $60 billion after two years, reflecting the functioning of automatic stabilizers.

## Additional readings

Brown, E. Cary. "Fiscal Policy in the Thirties: A Reappraisal." *American Economic Review* 46 (December 1956): 857–79.

Christiano, Lawrence J. "A Reexamination of the Theory of Automatic Stabilizers." In *Monetary and Fiscal Policies and Their Applications*, edited by Karl Brunner and Allen Meltzer. Amsterdam: North-Holland, 1984.

Council of Economic Advisers. *Annual Report*. Washington, D.C.: U.S. Government Printing Office, 1962.

Friedman, Milton. "A Monetary and Fiscal Framework for Economic Stability." *American Economic Review* 38 (June 1948): 245–64.

Johansen, Leif. "Some Aspects of Automatic Stabilizers." In *Public Finance and Stabilization Policy*, edited by Warren L. Smith and John M. Culbertson. Amsterdam: North-Holland, 1974.

Kiefer, Donald W. "The Automatic Stabilization Effects of the Federal Tax Structure." In *The Business Cycle and Public Policy, 1929–80*. U.S. Congress, Joint Economic Committee. Washington, D.C.: U.S. Government Printing Office, 1980.

McCallum, Bennet T., and John K. Whitaker. "The Effectiveness of Fiscal Feedback Rules and Automatic Stabilizers under Rational Expectations." *Journal of Monetary Economics* 5 (1979): 171–86.

Musgrave, Richard A., and M. H. Miller. "Built-In Flexibility." *American Economic Review* 38 (March 1948): 122–28.

U.S. Congress. Congressional Budget Office. *The Economic and Budget Outlook: Fiscal Years 1996–2000*. Washington, D.C.: U.S. Government Printing Office, 1995.

*Cross references:* rainy day funds; revenue elasticity (tax elasticity).

# Average effective tax rate

Richard Sansing
Yale University

*The ratio of a taxpayer's nominal tax liability to income.*

---

The average effective tax rate is a widely used, albeit theoretically dubious, measure of tax burdens, particularly corporate tax burdens. Corporate effective tax rates have also been used in studies examining the relationship between tax burdens and firm size, as part of the debate over whether large firms face higher political costs. The appropriate way to measure both the ratio's numerator and denominator continues to be debated, even though the usefulness of the average effective tax rate for decisionmaking purposes has not been established.

Many attribute the increases in nominal corporate tax burdens in the Tax Reform Act of 1986 (TRA86) to the low average corporate effective tax rates calculated and publicized by lobbying groups such as Citizens for Tax Justice. Subsequent research documents an increase in corporate effective tax rates in the years following the enactment of TRA86.

Financial accountants define the corporate average effective tax rate as: *income tax expense for financial reporting purposes divided by pretax accounting income*. Income tax expense is pretax accounting income less "permanent differences" between pretax financial accounting income and taxable income, multiplied by the statutory tax rate. Interest income from state and municipal bonds that is exempt from tax is an example of a permanent difference. A firm facing a 40 percent tax rate with $100 of pretax financial accounting income that includes $10 of tax-exempt interest income would report an income tax expense of $36 = [($ 100 − $10) × 0.4], and would have an effective tax rate of 36 percent.

Others define the effective tax rate differently, including only the current portion of the income tax expense in the numerator. This approach excludes the deferred income tax expense, which is the product of the statutory tax rate and the difference between accounting income and taxable income due to timing differences in the definitions of accounting and taxable income—for example, differences in the calculation of depreciation. Continuing the above example, suppose a corporation with a pretax financial accounting income of $100 and $10 of tax-exempt interest income reports a depreciation expense of $85 for tax purposes but only $65 for book purposes. The firm's income tax expense of $36 consists of a current income tax liability of $28 = [$100 − $10 − ($85 − $65)] × 0.4 and a deferred tax liability of $8. With only the current portion of the federal income tax expense in the numerator, the average effective tax rate is 28 percent instead of 36 percent.

The exclusion of deferred taxes from the numerator is a matter of considerable controversy because it compares a cash basis numerator to an accrual basis denominator. Some argue that deferred income tax expense should be included in the numerator to provide a consistent comparison, while others argue for the inclusion of the present value of deferred taxes to reflect the fact that these taxes may not actually be paid for many years. Finally, even the current portion of the income tax expense may not equal the actual income taxes paid; the two may differ because the subsidiaries included in consolidated financial statements may differ from those included in the consolidated tax return.

Although most of the debate over corporate effective tax rates has focused on the numerator, the appropriate denominator is also open to question. Fullerton (1984) defines the denominator as "correctly measured corporate income." However, financial accounting income is not, and does not purport to be, equivalent to economic income. Economic income is not well-defined if markets are either imperfect or incomplete. In practice, the accounting principle of conservatism tends to understate income. For example, asset appreciation is not recognized until a sale occurs, and most research and development expenditures are expensed when incurred. The effective tax rate measure will fail to reflect such tax-preferred investments, because it reflects the difference between taxable income and financial accounting income, not the difference between taxable income and economic income.

The average effective tax rate omits the implicit taxes on tax-favored investments. Demand for tax-favored investments forces investors to bear an im-plicit tax in the form of a lower pretax rate of return than they could obtain from an investment with a less favorable tax treatment. Recent empirical work provides evidence consistent with the implicit tax hypothesis in the corporate sector. Adding implicit taxes to both the numerator and denominator of the effective tax rate definition provides a more accurate measure of a firm's tax burden. In addition, the effective tax rate only reflects a taxpayer's nominal tax burden; it reveals nothing about which individuals bear the real economic burden of the tax.

Another problem in interpreting an effective tax rate is that it depends on the change in firm size. Suppose assets are depreciated faster for tax purposes than book purposes. If the corporation just replaces assets as they wear out, this difference will not cause the effective tax rate to differ from the statutory tax rate; higher depreciation on new assets will offset lower depreciation on old assets. The firm must be growing for the book-tax difference to cause the effective tax rate to decrease. If the firm is shrinking, the book-tax difference will cause the effective tax rate to exceed the statutory tax rate. Even though the proper inference regarding the difference between the effective tax rate and the statutory tax rate depends on the rate of firm growth, previous effective tax rate studies have not reported changes in firm size.

Differences regarding the definition of pretax financial accounting income and taxable income imply that the numerator and denominator may have different signs. A firm with a current tax liability of $10 and a pretax financial accounting loss of $100 has an effective tax rate of −10 percent, as does a firm with pretax financial accounting income of $100 receiving a $10 refund (due to a carryback of a current tax loss). That firms in two very different situations have the same effective tax rates casts doubt on the meaning of the measure.

Other issues related to the measurement of effective tax rates include whether to compare domestic taxes to domestic income or worldwide taxes to worldwide income, and whether to include non-income taxes and/or shareholder-level taxes in the numerator.

The debate over effective tax rates reflects the absence of a theoretical foundation regarding their use. This stems from a more basic problem: the decision context in which the effective tax rate measure is to be used is rarely, if ever, specified. Since the various measures cannot be compared under a fineness criterion, one measure can only be judged superior to another if it leads to a better decision on the part of the user of the information, which requires the specification of a user and a decision context. Arguments over which measure is better in the absence of a specific decision context cannot be resolved.

## Additional readings

Beaver, William. *Financial Reporting: An Accounting Revolution.* 2d ed. Englewood Cliffs, N.J.: Prentice Hall, 1989.

Beaver, William, and Joel Demski. "The Nature of Income Measurement." *The Accounting Review* 54 (1979): 38–46.

Birnbaum, Jeffrey, and Alan Murray. *Showdown at Gucci Gulch.* New York: Random House, 1987.

Citizens for Tax Justice. *Corporate Taxpayers and Corporate Freeloaders,* edited by Robert S. McIntyre. Arlington, Va.: Tax Analysts, 1985.

Clowery, Grant, Ed Outslay, and James Wheeler. "The Debate on Computing Corporate Effective Tax Rates—An Accounting View." *Tax Notes* 30 (March 10, 1986): 991–97.

Dworin, Lowell. "On Estimating Corporate Tax Liabilities from Financial Statements." *Tax Notes* 29 (December 2, 1985): 965–71.

Egger, John. "Citizens for Tax Justice's Latest Misrepresentation of Corporate Tax Burdens." *Tax Notes* 29 (December 2, 1985): 956–63.

Fullerton, Don. "Which Effective Tax Rate?" *National Tax Journal* 37 (1984): 23–42.

Fullerton, Don. "The Use of Effective Tax Rates in Tax Policy." *National Tax Journal* 39 (1986): 285–93.

Gupta, Sanjay, and Kaye Newberry. "Corporate Average Effective Tax Rates after the Tax Reform Act of 1986." *Tax Notes* 55 (May 4, 1992): 689–702.

Porcano, Thomas. "Corporate Tax Rates: Progressive, Proportional, or Regressive." *Journal of the American Taxation Association* 7 (Spring 1986): 17–31.

Scholes, Myron, and Mark Wolfson. *Taxes and Business Strategy.* Englewood Cliffs, N.J.: Prentice Hall, 1992.

Shevlin, Terry, and Sue Porter. "The Corporate Tax Comeback in 1987: Some Further Evidence." *Journal of the American Taxation Association* 14 (Spring 1992): 58–79.

Spooner, G. "Effective Tax Rates from Financial Statements." *National Tax Journal* 39 (1986): 293–306.

Wilkie, Patrick. "Empirical Evidence of Implicit Taxes in the Corporate Sector." *Journal of the American Taxation Association* 14 (Spring 1992): 97–116.

Wilkie, Patrick, and Steve Limberg. "The Relationship between Firm Size and Effective Tax Rate: A Reconciliation of Zimmerman [1983] and Porcano [1986]." *Journal of the American Taxation Association* 11 (Spring 1990): 76–91.

Zimmerman, Jerold. "Taxes and Firm Size." *Journal of Accounting and Economics* 5 (August 1983): 119–49.

*Cross references:* capital cost recovery; deferral of tax; marginal effective tax rate; taxable income, corporate.

# B

## Banks, state taxation

Bill Fox
University of Tennessee

*Due to their institutional (e.g., regulatory) history, financial institutions, such as banks, have been treated differently from nonfinancial institutions for state tax purposes. As banking changes, however, state tax policy may also change.*

The structure of state bank taxes across the United States has been driven by judicially imposed restrictions on the ability of states to tax national banks and by congressional legislation (see Symons 1984). These limitations on state taxation arose because, in times past, nationally chartered banks were regarded as instrumentalities of the U.S. government. The banks issued currency, served as fiscal agents, and acted as depositories of public monies. State-chartered banks could be taxed with any structure, but given the restrictions on the taxation of national banks, states limited their taxation of state-chartered banks to what was permissible for national banks. The major reason was so that state banks would not be placed at a competitive disadvantage. Moreover, state banks could avoid the higher taxes by applying for and receiving a national charter.

In *McCulloch* v. *Maryland,* Congress was seen by the U.S. Supreme Court as having the power to permit any form of state taxation of national banks that it deemed appropriate. Congress has acted on several occasions to authorize states to impose taxes on national banks. The most recent legislation became effective in 1976 and represents two significant steps in federal tax policy for national banks. First, states are permitted to impose any type of tax on banks without the necessity of obtaining further congressional approval, as long as the tax does not discriminate against national banks. Second, whether a tax discriminates against national banks is measured by comparing the tax on national banks with the tax on state banks, rather than with that on nonbanking corporations. Thus, the only limitation in existing legislation is that a state must tax national banks in the same manner as it taxes banks chartered in the state.

### Current bank tax structure

A combination of shifting federal legislation, historical developments that led states to initially impose dissimilar tax structures, and unique characteristics of the banking industry has resulted in differences between many states' tax structures for banks and other corporations. Bank taxes are usually structured using some combination of corporate income, franchise, and share taxes. Base definitions for the corporate income tax are often a variant of the federal corporate income base definition, but the specific characteristics differ by state. The base for share taxes is the value of banking shares, deposits, or some other indicator of intangible personal property. The importance of share taxes comes from the history of federal legislation. Share taxes were the only permissible form for taxing national banks until 1926, when Congress first permitted states to adopt an income-based franchise tax. Franchise taxes are levied with either a corporate income tax or a share tax base. Thus, state taxes have either income or intangible property as the tax base, and the franchise tax is a legal distinction, rather than a conceptually different tax base. However, the legal distinction is important, because court rulings indicate that the income from federal securities can only be taxed using a nondiscriminatory franchise or other nonproperty tax. Thus, states imposing a corporate income tax on banks cannot tax the interest from federal securities. Twenty-four states use their franchise tax to tax the interest from federal securities.

Currently, 15 states impose a corporate income tax on banks, 40 have a franchise tax, and 7 use share taxes. These state totals include 15 states that levy more than one form of taxation. Moreover, a number of states impose franchise taxes using both an income and a share base. Banks are taxed with the Single Business Tax in Michigan. Louisiana, Nevada, and Wyoming have no statewide tax on banking.

Tax rates on income (using either an income- or a franchise-based tax) range from 12.54 percent in Massachusetts to 0 percent in 12 states. Rates on intangible assets (using either a share tax or a franchise tax) are more difficult to compare because of the widely different bases. The business and occupations tax in Washington (which is actually levied on receipts) has the highest rate at 1.5 percent, and 31 states are lowest with a 0 percent tax rate. Data on tax revenues from the banking industry are available for some states. For example, New York collects 30 percent as much from banks as from nonbank corporations, Massachusetts collects 25 percent as much, and Delaware 20 percent as much. On the other hand, Vermont collects only 5 percent as much from banks as from nonbank corporations.

Income for multistate corporations is normally apportioned across states using either separate accounting or formulary apportionment. A common means for formulary apportionment of nonbanking corporations is a three-factor formula that apportions to a state the share of a corporation's income that corresponds to the arithmetic average of the firm's percent of sales, payrolls, and property located in the state. Historically, state tax structures have given less consideration to apportionment of bank income than to income earned in other industries because banks were presumed to earn their income in a single state. A recent survey of the states found that only 32 permit apportionment, and of those, only 18 permit banks to use the three-factor formula (see Kincaid and McCray 1988). Some states, such as Massachusetts, allow no apportionment and require that all domiciled banks' income be taxed in the state, regardless of where it is earned. Other states may permit interstate banks to apportion, but may not have developed explicit rules for apportioning bank income.

## Changing environment and tax structure

The environment in which banks operate has changed radically in recent years. Development of interstate banking, branchless banking, and loan securitization are three sources of this transformation. First, state-level expansions of interstate banking powers have permitted accelerated interstate banking. At least 46 states and the District of Columbia have passed legislation permitting some form of interstate banking.

Federal legislation has been an important element in the changing bank environment, as a number of federal actions, including the Garn-St. Germain Act and the International Banking Act of 1978, have expedited interstate banking.

Second, branchless banking has been facilitated by technological advances in the collection, storage, and transmission of information. For example, computer technology has allowed "electronic banking" to be operationally and economically feasible through automated teller machines, electronic funds transfer systems, and many other means.

Third, securitization of loan activity, which has developed rapidly during the past decade, is perhaps the single most important way financial institutions are able to engage in cross-state activity. Securitization is not a new phenomenon, dating back at least to activities of the Federal National Mortgage Association (Fannie Mae) in the 1930s, but it has accelerated as a result of standardization of mortgage contracts and, more recently, development of computer technology that has permitted securitization of nonmortgage loans.

Changes under way in the banking industry have invalidated the assumption of firms that operate within a single state. In response, several states, including Indiana, Minnesota, New York, Tennessee, and West Virginia, have reformed their bank tax structures. The reform process is just beginning, and it is too early to determine the general thrust of how states will tax financial institutions, since considerable differences have resulted across the states thus far.

The reforms have been targeted to three major issues. First, states have attempted to define financial institutions for tax purposes. Historically, states have often defined banks based on a regulatory definition, such as whether the firm takes deposits and makes loans. Those states modifying their definition of financial institutions tend to define them as firms that are in substantial competition with banks (West Virginia) or moneyed capital (California), or are doing the business of a financial institution (Tennessee).

Second, efforts have been made to rationalize the geographic distribution of taxation on a financial institution's income. The motivation has been a desire to tax income generated by financial institutions with multistate presence. Formulary apportionment has been used in all states making changes. A driving force in the formula's structure in each state has been a decision regarding whether financial institutions should be taxed on a destination or origination basis. Minnesota and Tennessee have developed formulas patterned on destination principles, and New York has followed origination principles. Indiana has adopted a dual tax structure that uses origination-based rules for domiciled financial institutions (with a credit for taxes paid in other states) and destination rules for nondomiciled financial institutions.

Important considerations in revised formulas have been the number of factors, the specific factors to be used, and how the situs of the factors are to be established. The number of factors has varied from the one-factor receipts-based formula used in Tennessee to three-factor formulas adopted in states such as New York. Much consideration of the specific factors has centered on the property factor. New York substituted deposits for the property factor, California uses intangible property rather than real property, and Minnesota uses both real and intangible property in the property factor. Origination-based formulas tend to establish situs where the financial institution is located, destination-based formulas where the market is located.

Third, nexus has been redefined because branchless banking and loan securitization activities of financial institutions can only be taxed with a broader definition of nexus than that which has traditionally been used. Minnesota and Tennessee have defined nexus to exist for financial institutions that have either a physical presence in the state or regularly solicit for business in the state. Both states have de minimus rules that exclude financial institutions with limited connections to the state from taxation.

## Additional readings

Fox, William F. "Taxation of Insurance Companies." In *Final Report of the Minnesota Tax Study Commission*, edited by Robert D. Ebel and Therese J. McGuire. Boston: Butterworths, 1986.

Kincaid, John, and Sandra B. McCray. "State Taxation and the Rise of Interstate Banking: A Survey of States." *Intergovernmental Perspectives* 14 (Fall 1988): 18–22.

Symons, Edward L., Jr. "State Taxation of Banks: Federal Limitations." *The Banking Journal* 99 (9) (October 1984): 817–41.

Tannenwald, Robert, and Ranjana G. Madhusdhan. "State Taxation of Bank Income with Unlimited Interstate Branching." In *Proceedings of the Annual Conference on Taxation*. National Tax Association, 1995.

*Cross references:* apportionment; income tax, corporate, state and local.

# Basis

Joseph J. Cordes
George Washington University

*The amount a taxpayer uses to determine the cost of acquiring an asset, which is used to determine the asset's capital gain or loss.*

The basis of an asset is a key element in computing a taxpayer's capital gain or loss upon the sale of that asset. In the simplest case, when shares of corporate stock were all acquired at the same time, the basis would be the purchase price of the stock plus any brokerage fee. For example, if 100 shares of corporate stock were purchased at $20 per share (including brokerage fees) and later sold for $30 per share (net of broker commissions), the capital gain would be the difference between the $2,000 purchase price of the stock, which is its basis, and the $3,000 received from the sale.

Determining the basis of physical assets, such as real estate property, is more complicated because one must take into account any improvements made by the owner, as well as any depreciation claimed on the asset. Thus, a landlord who buys a house as a rental-income property would increase the basis by the amount of any improvements made on the house, and decrease the basis by the amount of any depreciation deductions claimed. For example, if the property were initially purchased for $50,000, and the landlord subsequently made $5,000 worth of improvements and claimed a total of $20,000 in depreciation, the *adjusted basis* of the property would be $35,000 = ($50,000 + $5,000 − $20,000).

In both cases, the basis is adjusted to properly measure the change in the taxpayer's wealth attributable to the asset. If the cost of improvements were not added to the initial purchase price, the capital gain (loss) triggered by the sale would overstate (understate) the taxpayer's true gain (loss) because the sales price of the asset would presumably include the value of the improvements made. Similarly, failure to subtract depreciation deductions from the basis would cause the capital gain (loss) registered upon sale to understate (overstate) the owner's gain (loss) by the amount of tax deductions for depreciation that the owner had already been able to claim over the asset's life.

Some administrative complications in determining the basis are encountered by increasing numbers of taxpayers who acquire shares of stock in a company, or in a mutual fund, over a period of time, as occurs, for example, when dividends are automatically reinvested. When the time comes to sell the shares in the company or fund, what basis should be used to determine the taxpayer's capital gain or loss? If the shareholders have kept good records as to when different shares of stock were acquired, they can give written instructions that the sale is to consist of stock purchased at specific dates. In this case, the basis is determined by the purchase price of shares acquired on those dates. If the taxpayers cannot identify when particular shares of stock were purchased, they must normally use a first in, first out rule under which the basis is determined by using the price per share paid for the earliest purchase. Taxpayers with shares in a mutual fund can, however, use the average cost of shares acquired as their basis.

When assets are transferred between parties rather than sold, numerous rules apply to determine the basis. One such rule that affects individual taxpayers is the provision for determining basis when, for example, a parent makes a gift of an asset to a child. In this case, the basis of the asset is *carried over* from its original owner to the recipient of the gift. Assets transferred by inheritance qualify for a *stepped-up* basis. In this case, the heir's basis is the fair market value of the inherited asset at the time of the original owner's death. In effect, the stepped-up basis at death wipes out any taxes that would have been owed on capital gains.

One recurring issue in defining the basis of capital assets has to do with the proper treatment of inflation. Because the tax basis is stated in dollars of the year it was purchased, while the sale price is stated in the inflated dollars of more recent years, simply subtracting the basis from the asset's sales price will overstate the taxpayer's real capital gain when the asset is sold. The most direct way of addressing this problem is to index the basis to take inflation into account. Several administrative proposals have been made to adjust the basis for inflation, but none has been implemented to date.

**Additional readings**

U.S. Congress. Congressional Budget Office. *Indexing Capital Gains*. Washington, D.C.: U.S. Government Printing Office, 1990.

*Federal Tax Handbook*. Paramus, N.J.: Prentice Hall, 1990.

*Cross references:* capital gains taxation; corporate reorganizations; depreciation recapture; inflation indexation of income taxes.

# Basis adjustment

Joseph J. Cordes
George Washington University

*A reduction in the basis, used to determine tax deductions for depreciation of physical assets.*

Depreciation deductions for physical assets are determined by applying a schedule to the acquisition cost, or depreciable basis, of the asset. A basis adjustment reduces the amount of the asset that can be depreciated by the amount of any tax credits that the taxpayer receives in connection with purchase of the asset. For example, if a piece of equipment costs $1,000, and the firm is eligible to receive an investment tax credit equal to 10 percent of the cost of the investment, the after-tax cost of making the investment to the taxpayer would be $900. In such cases, it can be argued that the amount of capital cost recovery should be based on the taxpayer's out-of-pocket outlay of $900 rather than the purchase price of $1,000. A way of achieving this result would be to adjust—reduce—the depreciable basis of the asset by the amount of the credit claimed.

A basis adjustment was required for the original investment tax credit adopted in 1962 but was dropped in 1964. A half basis adjustment was enacted in 1982 and remained in force until 1986, when the investment credit was abolished.

One reason for adjusting the depreciable basis when an asset qualifies for an investment tax credit

is that it reduces the advantage that the credit gives to assets of shorter durabilities. Since the present value of depreciation deductions is larger for short-lived assets, adjusting the basis has the effect of reducing the economic value of the investment credit relatively more for short-lived than for long-lived assets. This partially offsets the fact that the investment credit reduces the user cost of shorter-lived assets relatively more than it does the user cost of longer-lived assets.

**Additional reading**

Gravelle, Jane G. *The Economic Effects of Taxing Capital Income*. Cambridge, Mass.: MIT Press, 1994.

*Cross references:* cost of capital; investment tax credits.

# Benefit principle

Joseph J. Cordes
George Washington University

*Along with the ability-to-pay principle, one of the two major approaches for considering the fairness of taxation.*

The benefit principle, which dates to the 17th century, holds that people should pay taxes according to the benefits they receive from government programs. This requires that public expenditures be financed by taxes that place a heavier burden on taxpayers who derive greater benefits from those expenditures. The merits of the benefit principle are discussed further under the heading "Fairness in taxation." This entry briefly summarizes the main advantages and limitations of using the benefit principle to judge the fairness of particular taxes.

The most attractive feature of the benefit principle is that it puts the government-taxpayer relationship and the relationship between consumers and producers in the marketplace on equal footing. Under this view, governments provide goods and services that are of value to taxpayers, and taxes, although compulsory, become analogous to prices that people should pay for these services. Just as it is fair for consumers to "pay for what they get" in the marketplace, so too it is fair for them to pay taxes according to how much they benefit from government spending.

More recently, taxing according to benefits received has also been seen as a way of confronting taxpayers with the true cost of government goods and services. It is hoped that this will lead taxpayers to make better-informed decisions about the size and scope of government. Taxpayers are more likely to demand more government services if they believe that these services are "free" than if they must pay the costs in the form of benefit taxes or user charges.

There are, however, some factors that limit the applicability of the benefit principle in gauging the fairness of financing government. One is that it is very hard to accurately measure the benefits that people receive from a wide range of goods and services. For example, how would one measure the individual benefits from the peace of mind that people get from having their borders defended, or from government programs that improve the environment? In some cases, these problems can be overcome by using tax bases that bear some relation to benefits received. For example, federal and state gasoline taxes enjoy wide support as benefit-based taxes because people believe that how much one benefits from federal and state highways bears some relationship to the amount of gasoline that one buys. Similarly, many economists believe that government goods and services are reflected in residential property values such that property taxes are often seen as a local benefit tax.

At the same time, taxes are compulsory, not voluntary, and the benefit principle does not account for a taxpayer's ability to pay. In several cases, application of the benefit principle and application of the ability-to-pay principle can cause the same tax to be viewed differently. For example, gasoline taxes are often seen as regressive taxes because consumers generally pay a lower share of their income in such taxes as their income rises. But, from the standpoint of the benefit principle, gasoline taxes are seen as providing a rough kind of tax fairness by distributing the burden of paying for public roads according to how much people drive.

### Additional reading

Musgrave, Richard A. *The Theory of Public Finance*, ch. 4. New York: McGraw-Hill, 1959.

*Cross references:* ability to pay; Airport and Airway Trust Fund; fairness in taxation; fuel taxes, federal; property tax, real property, residential; tax price; Tiebout model; user charges, federal.

# Border tax adjustments

Charles Vehorn
International Monetary Fund

*International tax arrangements on goods traded between countries to avoid double taxation or nontaxation.*

### Introduction

The tax treatment of goods shipped from one country to another would create serious economic dis-

tortions if some goods were taxed in both countries while others escaped taxation in both countries. Border tax adjustments make economic distortions in the prices of traded goods less likely to occur. These adjustments can follow either the destination principle or the origin principle (both principles are discussed more fully in subsequent entries). The destination principle, which is the most common international practice, provides for taxation only by the importing country. This country sets the tax rate, levies the tax, and retains the revenue for itself. Any tax paid by the exporter on inputs is refunded by the exporting country. The origin principle provides for taxation only by the exporting country. Any production that originates in the country, whether consumed at home or exported abroad, is taxable, whereas imports are exempt.

### Type of taxes involved

Border tax adjustments are made for indirect taxes such as the sales tax—at either the retail level or intermediate level—the value-added tax (VAT), a cascading turnover tax, excise taxes, or state monopolies. Although some would argue that border tax adjustments should be made for direct taxes as well, General Agreement on Tariffs and Trade rules apply the origin principle to such taxes (income taxes, payroll taxes, Social Security charges, and property taxes) and make them ineligible for adjustments. Thus, this entry focuses only on indirect taxes.

The mechanism of adjustment varies depending on the type of tax. Messere (1994) has described the method of adjustment for selected consumption taxes (see table 1). For example, under a VAT an exporter normally would receive a refund for taxes paid on inputs by claiming a credit (as documented by the purchase invoice and verified at the border) on the VAT return. In VAT terminology, exported goods are zero-rated (see Value-added tax, national, for further discussion). The importer, on the other hand, pays the domestic rate of VAT on all imports, at the time of either importation or subsequent domestic sales. Trade between two countries following the destination principle ensures that exports and imports will be subject to the VAT only once, by the importing country. Cases of double taxation or nontaxation are avoided.

Complications arise if a country attempts to make border tax adjustments for "taxes occultes" (hidden taxes). Taxes occultes can be defined as consumption taxes on (1) auxiliary materials used in the transportation or production of goods (e.g., energy, fuel, lubricants, packing, stationery); (2) durable capital equipment (e.g., machinery, buildings, vehicles); and (3) services (e.g., transportation, advertising) (OECD 1968). These hidden taxes were far more troublesome in cascading tax systems of the 1960s and earlier than in more current systems

**TABLE 1**

**Border Tax Adjustment Mechanism under Different Types of General Consumption Taxes**

EXPORTS

| | Type of Tax | Method of Adjustment | Amount of Refund |
|---|---|---|---|
| A | Manufacture and wholesale sales tax | Exporter does not usually pay tax, but sometimes tax already paid is refunded | Usually none, but if tax is paid then actual amount is refunded |
| B | Retail sales tax (RST) | Exporter does not pay tax | None |
| C | Value-added tax (VAT) | Exporter does not normally pay tax, but any tax paid on inputs is refunded* | Actual amount of tax paid is refunded* |
| D | Cascading tax | Tax already paid by exporter is refunded | Estimated tax paid on similar domestic products sold in the home market |

IMPORTS

| | Type of Tax | Method of Adjustment | Amount Charged |
|---|---|---|---|
| A | Manufacture and wholesale sales tax | Domestic rate of tax charged, sometimes at time of importation and sometimes on subsequent domestic sales | Same as tax charged on similar domestic products |
| B | Retail sales tax (RST) | As in A, but more often charged later on subsequent domestic sales | Same as tax charged on similar domestic products |
| C | Value-added tax (VAT) | As in A* | Same as tax charged on similar domestic products* |
| D | Cascading tax | Tax paid at time of importation | Estimated tax paid on similar domestic products sold in the home market |

*This is according to the transparent VAT system originally preferred by the EC Commission under which exporters pay VAT on their inputs and get it refunded when goods are exported; importers pay VAT at the time of importation. Some countries with a VAT have adopted the RST model. Currently, all EC countries use the model under the deferred payment method applying to intracommunity trade.
*Source:* Ken Messere, "The International Consumption Tax Ruler." *Bulletin for International Fiscal Documentation* 48 (December 1996): 665–80.

using the VAT. Excise taxes on gasoline also represented a source of taxes occultes. Since these taxes were hidden, it became virtually impossible to make a precise border tax adjustment, so most adjustments were based on averaging, and disputes concerning over- or undercompensation emerged. As more countries moved to the VAT, the concerns about adjustments for hidden taxes lessened (Messere 1979).

If trading partners were to do nothing when goods crossed their borders, the tax consequences would vary depending on the type of tax in each country. If, for example, the exporting country imposed a retail sales tax and the importing country a manufacturer sales tax, then a consumer good could escape taxation by both countries. If, on the other hand, an exporting country imposed a manufacturer sales tax and the importing country a retail sales tax, then double taxation could occur (Messere 1994).

### Arguments for and against

Most of the arguments either for or against border tax adjustments depend on assumptions about tax shifting. If the tax is fully shifted forward (i.e., fully reflected in the price to consumers), neutrality is maintained between a domestic good and a similar imported good, and international trade is not affected by refunding taxes paid to exporters. If the

tax is partially shifted forward, imports may be inhibited and exports enhanced (OECD 1968).

The two main arguments in favor of border tax adjustments following the destination principle could be characterized as the "benefits to consumers argument" and the "competition argument." If consumers bear the tax burden and receive the benefit from government spending, consumption taxes should be collected in the country where consumers reside rather than where producers reside. The second argument points out that, in the absence of rebates and equalizing import taxes, firms in countries with high consumption tax rates cannot compete with firms in countries with low consumption tax rates, unless taxes are adjusted at the border.

One argument against border tax adjustments notes that it may not be appropriate to seek neutrality on the revenue side of a government's budget while ignoring neutrality on the expenditure side. Differences in certain government expenditures (such as infrastructure) may reduce business costs disproportionately, giving certain firms in one country an advantage over similar firms in other countries. Some have generalized this argument by stating that trade between countries can be affected by various nonfiscal factors (minimum wage laws, social welfare programs, natural resources). So why single out adjustments for distortions from taxation without making adjustments for other distorting factors? The response to this argument is that the tax factor is inherently different from these other factors. If the government did nothing with respect to border tax adjustments, it would in fact be applying the origin principle.

## Current policy issues

### European Community

The European Community (EC), in moving toward a single market, must focus on the tax implications of intracommunity trade. As a first step, all members had to substitute a VAT for turnover taxes and follow the destination principle. In 1987, the EC Commission proposed a VAT clearinghouse system to facilitate removal of border controls. Under this proposed system, the destination principle would be maintained. However, exporters would collect VAT from importers and importers would claim credit for the VAT they paid to exporting countries. The exporting country would then be required to report the amount of tax collected on exports to a clearinghouse, which would calculate net flows to ensure that the country of destination received the correct amount of revenue (Kopits 1992). One important drawback to the clearinghouse system is that it can only be successful to the extent that each member country correctly reports the tax collected by exporters and the tax credit claimed by importers, while at the same time ensuring that any fraud is quickly detected.

Instead of the clearinghouse, however, the EC adopted a transitional regime that began on January 1, 1993. This system was to be in effect for at least four years and extended automatically thereafter until a definitive system had been developed. Under the transitional regime, exports to VAT payers in another country continue to be zero-rated. The importer is formally liable for the VAT on the imports, but is also allowed to take a credit for these purchases against the VAT collected on sales. The transitional regime relies heavily on information-sharing, maintains the destination principle, avoids use of an administratively complicated clearinghouse mechanism, and protects the importer from any prefinancing costs of the VAT (Hill and Rushton 1993).

### Former Soviet Union countries

The problem faced by countries in the former Soviet Union (FSU) is identical to that faced by EC countries. How should trade between FSU countries be treated under the VAT? Almost all FSU countries initially followed the VAT model adopted by the Russian Federation in 1991. In that original VAT law, imports were not taxed, regardless of whether the goods were from FSU countries or countries other than the FSU. Exports to countries outside the FSU were zero-rated. Exports to FSU countries were apparently subject to VAT, but with certain restrictions

that allowed a credit for imports, so a modified origin principle prevailed. At the end of 1992 the Russian Federation changed its VAT law, appearing to reflect the destination principle. Exports were zero-rated and all imports were subject to the VAT. However, another provision in the law allowed trade between FSU countries to be regulated by international agreements, including an agreement between most FSU countries that exports, rather than imports, would be subject to VAT (Sunley and Summers 1995). A few FSU countries have enacted new tax laws stipulating use of the destination principle for all trade, including interrepublic trade.

## Additional readings

Hill, Roderick, and Michael Rushton. "Harmonizing Provincial Sales Taxes with the GST: The Problem of Interprovincial Trade." *International VAT Monitor* (October 1993): 21–32.

Kopits, George. "Overview." In *Tax Harmonization in the European Community: Policy Issues and Analysis*, edited by George Kopits. Washington, D.C.: International Monetary Fund, 1992.

Messere, Ken. "A Defense of Present Border Tax Adjustment Practices." *National Tax Journal* 32 (December 1979): 481–92.

Messere, Ken. "The International Consumption Tax Rules." *Bulletin for International Fiscal Documentation* 48 (December 1994): 665–80.

Organization for Economic Cooperation and Development. *Border Tax Adjustments and Tax Structures in OECD Member Countries*. Paris: OECD, 1968.

Sunley, Emil M., and Victoria P. Summers. "An Analysis of Value-Added Taxes in Russia and Other Countries of the Former Soviet Union." *Tax Notes International* 10 (June 19, 1995): 2049–72.

*Cross references:* consumption taxation; destination principle; origin principle; value-added tax, national.

# Budget-balance requirement

Ronald Snell
National Conference of State Legislatures

*Most states have legislation mandating that expenditures not exceed revenues.*

Requirements that states balance their budgets are often said to be a major difference between state and federal budgeting. State officials certainly take seriously an obligation to balance the budget, and in the debate over a federal balanced budget in the early and mid-1990s, much of the discussion centered around those states with balanced budgets. This entry is concerned with the nature, definition, and enforcement of state balanced-budget requirements.

## Nature of state balanced-budget requirements

All states except Vermont have a legal requirement to balance their budget. Some are constitutional, some are statutory, and some have been derived by judicial decision from constitutional provisions about state indebtedness that do not, on their face, call for a balanced budget. The General Accounting Office has commented that "some balanced budget requirements are based on interpretations of state constitutions and statutes rather than on an explicit statement that the state must have a balanced budget."

The requirements vary in stringency from state to state. In some states, the requirement is that the introduced budget be balanced, or that the enacted budget be balanced. In others, policymakers are required to ensure that expenditures in a fiscal year stay within the cash available for that fiscal year. Yet other states may carry unavoidable deficits into the next fiscal year for resolution.

There are three general kinds of state balanced-budget requirements:

1. The governor's proposed budget must be balanced (43 states and Puerto Rico).
2. The budget the legislature passes must be balanced (39 states and Puerto Rico).
3. The budget must be balanced at the end of a fiscal year or biennium, such that no deficit be carried forward (37 states and Puerto Rico).

Such provisions can be either constitutional or statutory, but are more rigorous if they are constitutional since they are not subject to legislative amendment. Some states have two or all three of the possible balanced-budget requirements, and a few have only a statutory requirement that the governor submit a balanced budget. Weighing such considerations, 36 states have rigorous balanced-budget requirements, four have weak requirements, and the other 10 fall in between those categories.

## What has to be balanced?

State balanced-budget requirements in practice refer to operating budgets, not capital budgets. Operating budgets include annual expenditures—such items as salaries and wages, aid to local governments, health and welfare benefits, and other expenditures that are repeated from year to year. State capital expenditures, mainly for land, highways, and buildings, are largely financed by debt. Court decisions and referendums on borrowing have led to the exclusion of expenditures funded by long-term debt from calculations of whether a budget is balanced.

In practice, the following kinds of state revenues and expenditures also have little impact on state balanced budgets:

—Almost all federal reimbursements or grants to a state are committed to specific purposes, and the governor and legislature have little discretion over the use of most federal funds.
—Transportation trust fund money raised from state motor fuel taxes is usually earmarked for highways and other transportation purposes.
—Some tax collections may be diverted to local governments or other specified purposes without appropriations.
—Some states allow agencies or programs to collect and spend fees, charges, or tuition without annual or biennial appropriations.

In each of these cases, it is practically impossible for revenues and expenditures to get out of balance, since expenditures are controlled by available funds.

Thus it is not surprising that "balancing the budget" tends to focus on the general fund, even though general-fund expenditures compose only 50 to 60 percent of total state spending.

## Enforcement of balanced-budget requirements

State requirements to balance the budget do not impose legal penalties for failure to do so. There are, however, two sorts of enforcement mechanisms. Prohibitions against carrying deficits into the next fiscal year and restrictions on the issuance of state debt help to enforce balanced-budget provisions by making it difficult to finance a deficit. In many states, governors or joint legislative-executive commissions can revise budgets after they are enacted to bring them into balance.

Unlike the federal government, states are not able to issue debt routinely. Issues of general obligation debt require at least the approval of the legislature and, in many states, voter approval. The issue of revenue bonds requires legislation to create an agency to issue the bonds and the creation of a revenue stream to repay the debt. These practices place the issuance of debt fully into public view. However, it is extremely rare for a state government to borrow long-term funds to cover operating expenses. Louisiana did in 1988 and Connecticut did in 1991. There do not appear to be any other examples of this practice from recent years.

A legislature and a governor can jointly revise a budget at any time. But most legislatures are not in session throughout the year, and some legislatures meet for only a few months every other year. Requiring legislative consent for every change in a budget would impose delays or the costs of special sessions. Therefore, many state constitutions allow governors or special commissions to revise budgets after they have been enacted to bring expenditures into line with revenues.

Thirty-six states allow governors some degree of authority to reduce spending when it is necessary to maintain a balanced budget, even if enacted budgets call for specific amounts of expenditure. Some states prohibit executive budget revisions, and many restrict the amounts and nature of such reductions. Some states have, in addition, joint legislative and executive boards or commissions that are constitutionally permitted to make budget revisions—for example, to deal with unforeseen revenue shortfalls, emergencies, or unanticipated federal funds.

### Practice

State balanced-budget rules are not as rigid as those recommended for the federal government in the early 1990s, which would have forbidden total expenditures above total revenues in any year, as well as new borrowing. By this standard, states routinely run deficits because they borrow to finance capital expenditures. But this does not violate state balanced-budget requirements. Nor does rolling deficits in operating funds forward from one fiscal year to the next, if a state constitution permits the practice.

Fiscal stress, however, can induce governors and legislators to adopt expedients so they can observe the letter, if not the spirit, of balanced-budget requirements. Among these are selling state assets, postponing payments to vendors, reducing payments to pension funds, borrowing from one state fund to finance expenditures from another, and using "creative" accounting. Such expedients reflect the stress that can arise between legal demands for a balanced budget and political demands for the continuation of state programs without tax increases. The fact that such expedients tend to be limited to times of fiscal stress is in itself a measure of how seriously state elected officials take their responsibility to produce balanced budgets.

### Additional readings

Advisory Commission on Intergovernmental Relations. *Fiscal Discipline in the Federal System: National Reform and the Experience of the States.* Washington, D.C., 1987.

Briffault, Richard. *Balancing Acts: The Reality behind State Balanced Budget Requirements.* New York: Twentieth Century Fund Press, 1996.

Snell, Ronald K. *State Balanced Budget Requirements: Provisions and Practice.* Denver, Colo.: National Conference of State Legislatures, 1996.

*Cross references:* budgeting, state; budget policy, state and local; budget processes, state.

## Budgeting, state
Ronald Snell
National Conference of State Legislatures

*There is a similarity of state practices regarding the budgeting framework and administrative process.*

The state budget process is central to the administration of state government. In addition to allocating resources, budgets set policy, review and evaluate policy, and lay the foundation for future planning and program review. This discussion is concerned with the elements of state budget processes that are found in most states.

State practices are fairly similar. Important structural differences include the nature of a state's requirement to balance the budget; an annual or biennial budget cycle; the governor's authority to revise the enacted budget; and whether earmarked or federal funds are subject to the appropriations process. The most important political difference among states is the balance between legislative and executive authority in composing the budget. Governor's line-item vetoes are one element in the legislative/executive balance, but tradition and partisanship are equally decisive.

### The framework of budgeting—the fiscal period

Budgets are for a specific period of time: a fiscal year or a biennium. Although 20 states enact budgets on a biennial schedule, only North Dakota, Oregon, and Wyoming enact true biennial budgets. Elsewhere, biennial states enact separate budgets for two fiscal years at once. The relative advantages of annual and biennial budgets have been debated at length, and states occasionally change from one to the other. Nebraska shifted to biennial budgeting in 1987, Connecticut did so in 1991, and Arizona is now in the process of moving to a biennial budget. No state has moved in the other direction in the past decade. The current state and federal interest in biennial budgeting is motivated by the hopes of saving time and political energy, and of having more opportunity for program evaluation and review. The overall experience of states, however, is that neither budget cycle has overwhelming advantages or disadvantages.

Fiscal years begin on July 1 for all but four states. July 1 is the date on which the federal fiscal year began until the federal government changed to October 1 in 1974. Alabama and Michigan adopted the federal practice. New York begins its fiscal year April 1 and Texas on September 1. The advantage of a fiscal year that begins in or after the middle of a calendar year lies in the legislative calendar. State legislatures that are not in session year-round convene in January or February, and a July beginning for the new fiscal year allows time to enact a budget.

## The framework of budgeting— balanced-budget requirements

State balanced-budget requirements give revenue forecasting even more importance for states than it has for the federal government, which can routinely borrow to maintain programmed expenditures. States are less able to do so. State long-term, general-obligation borrowing requires at least legislative approval and may take a vote of the people. Constitutional and statutory restraints on state borrowing put teeth into balanced-budget provisions.

Balanced-budget provisions themselves do not require all states to make sure a year's expenditures are less than the year's resources. Thirty-eight states are constitutionally prohibited from carrying over a deficit from one fiscal year (or biennium) to the next—the most rigorous antideficit provision. In other states, the requirement is that a governor submit a balanced budget, or that the budget enacted by the legislature be in balance.

Most states, in most years, balance their operating budgets. Capital expenditures are not necessarily included in determining whether a budget is balanced and some other obligations may be omitted. Recessions or unforeseen fiscal problems can force state governments to take extreme measures to comply with the letter of the law, such as shifting resources among state accounts ("internal borrowing"), counting the sales of assets or the proceeds of borrowing as revenues, deferring vendor payments or contributions to retirement funds, or sophistry in accounting. Such measures are sometimes attacked as evidence of bad faith on the part of governors and legislators. However, the real issue is the tension between demands for a balanced budget and demands that spending for state programs be sustained.

## The budgeting process—the executive budget

All states follow the model of executive budgeting. Executive budget offices and staff draft a proposed budget to submit to the legislature. As a rule, executive budget proposals are comprehensive—they include all sources of funding and expenditures, with the possible exceptions of state authorities and enterprises that generate their own revenue. The governor's budget also includes proposals for the budgets of other elected state officials—many states elect officials such as the treasurer, the attorney general, the auditor, and the superintendent of public schools, who may have substantial budgets to administer.

In most states, the proposed executive budget dominates the legislative budgeting process. In some states it is adopted with relatively few changes, and in most it establishes the agenda of budget discussion and negotiation. In most states, the executive budget is the only comprehensive planning document the state produces. Strong legislative budget processes dominate in a few states—Arizona, Colorado, and Texas, for example—and in those the executive budget may be largely disregarded.

## The budgeting process—executive and legislative coordination

Whether the executive or legislative branch dominates the budget process, there is generally far more cooperation between the legislative and executive branches than is typical for Congress and the president. The agenda-setting role of the executive budget in many states is one reason. Another is the executive line-item veto in the 41 states where it exists. A final reason is the political expectation that a state will enact a balanced budget before the beginning of its fiscal year, an expectation that is almost always met. Late budgets and vetoes are most likely when a state is experiencing serious fiscal difficulties. Otherwise, executive and legislative negotiations are intended to resolve budget disagreements, and avoid vetoes and late budgets. Governors used line-item vetoes in only 5 of the 41 states that permitted them in 1993 (Snell 1995).

## Postenactment budget revisions

Although budgets become effective only after legislative enactment and executive approval, many states allow budget revisions to be made without involving the entire legislature. Most legislatures are not in session throughout the year, and some legislatures meet for only a few months every other year. Requiring legislative consent for every change in a budget would impose delays or the costs of special sessions. Therefore, 36 states allow governors some degree of authority to reduce spending when it is necessary to maintain a balanced budget, even if enacted budgets call for specific amounts of expenditure.

Some states prohibit executive budget revisions. Many states restrict the amounts and nature of such revisions. Some states have, in addition, joint legislative and executive boards or commissions that are constitutionally permitted to make budget revisions—for example, to deal with unforeseen revenue shortfalls, emergencies, or unanticipated federal funds. Thus, state constitutions do not necessarily require as strict a separation of legislative and executive authority as the federal constitution does for the federal government.

Governors and legislatures may make significant midyear changes in a budget, as needed. Additional appropriations or appropriations for new purposes are called *supplemental* appropriations. Legislatures that convene at the beginning of a calendar year usually find a list of proposed supplementals awaiting their consideration, with its length and amount depending on the problems that have arisen to that point in the fiscal year and on the revenue available for use.

## Administration of the budget

Budget administration is the responsibility of the executive branch, although the legislative and judicial branches protect their independence by maintaining control of their budgets. Other elected executive branch officials administer their budgets, and they and the judiciary occasionally clash with governors when governors see a need for government-wide budget cuts (legislators are less likely to disagree with governors on this point, for political reasons).

Budget administration is usually centralized in a budget or accounting office, which releases funds to agencies on a schedule (the allotment process). Such offices are usually responsible for monitoring revenues and expenditures, and issuing monthly reports at least for internal use, but increasingly for public information. Such central budget offices may include or coordinate their work with state purchasing offices and personnel departments. The current trend is to decentralize purchasing and personnel management to agencies as much as possible. Financial auditing may be the responsibility of an executive official. Performance auditing and program review, however, are often the responsibility of a legislative agency (44 legislatures have one) and are closely tied to legislative budget oversight.

## Additional readings

Axelrod, Donald. *Budgeting for Modern Government*. 2d ed. New York: St. Martin's Press, 1995.

Clynch, Edward J., and Thomas P. Lauth, editors. *Governors, Legislatures, and Budgets: Diversity across the American States*. New York: Greenwood Press, 1991.

Eckl, Corina L. *Legislative Authority over the Enacted Budget*. Denver: National Conference of State Legislatures, 1992.

Grooters, Jen. *Legislative Budget Procedures in the 50 States*. Denver: National Conference of State Legislatures, 1998.

National Association of State Budget Officers. *Budget Processes in the States*. Washington, D.C., 1995.

National Conference of State Legislatures. *State Strategies to Manage Budget Shortfalls*. Denver, 1996.

Rosenthal, Alan. *Governors and Legislatures: Contending Powers*. Washington, D.C.: Congressional Quarterly Press, 1990.

Snell, Ronald K. *Fundamentals of Sound State Budgeting Practices*. Denver: National Conference of State Legislatures, 1995.

*Cross references:* budget-balance requirement; budget policy, state and local; budget processes, state.

# Budget policy, state and local

Jeffrey I. Chapman
University of Southern California

*The environment of state and local budget policy delineated by changing size and composition, unsettled issues, and cries for reform.*

## Importance of state and local budgets

The importance of the state and local sector has greatly increased since 1960. During the 34-year period from 1960 to 1994, for example, the share of spending by state and local governments in total government spending rose from just over 40 percent to 49 percent, and the share of general revenue collected by state and local governments rose from just over 33 percent to almost 51 percent of revenue collected by all levels of government.

## Changing composition of state and local expenditures

There have been some significant changes in the composition of state and local expenditures over the past several decades. Table 1 illustrates dramatic changes in three categories of state expenditures: Public welfare and corrections expenditures have more than doubled, while expenditures on highways have fallen by about two-thirds. As table 2 shows, for local governments there have been fewer dra-

## TABLE 1

### State Direct Expenditures: Percentage Distribution (Fiscal Years)

|                     | 1960 | 1970 | 1980 | 1990 | 1994 |
|---------------------|------|------|------|------|------|
| Higher Education    | 16   | 22   | 20   | 18   | 17   |
| Public Welfare      | 12   | 19   | 24   | 27   | 32   |
| Health and Hospitals| 11   | 10   | 11   | 10   | 10   |
| Corrections         | 2    | 2    | 3    | 5    | 5    |
| Highways            | 34   | 22   | 13   | 11   | 11   |
| Interest            | 3    | 3    | 5    | 6    | 5    |
| Other               | 22   | 22   | 24   | 23   | 21   |

*Source: Government Finances*, selected years; www.census.gov.

matic expenditure changes, with only highway expenditures falling by about 50 percent. Conversely, what is notable is that so many expenditure categories have not changed over the 30 years.

Tables 3 and 4 show that the composition of state and local revenues has remained quite stable. Table 3 shows only a few categories of revenue sources that have changed much since 1960. In particular, the total amount of taxes, as a percentage of total revenues, has decreased because the decline in sales taxes and other taxes has offset the increase in income taxes. Charges have nearly doubled to offset this tax decline. This has probably resulted in increased efficiency if the charges have been accurately set. However, it has also probably increased regressivity.

## TABLE 2

### Local Direct Expenditures: Percentage Distribution (Fiscal Years)

|                     | 1960 | 1970 | 1980 | 1990 | 1994 |
|---------------------|------|------|------|------|------|
| Local Education     | 44   | 44   | 41   | 40   | 40   |
| Public Welfare      | 6    | 8    | 6    | 5    | 5    |
| Health and Hospitals| 6    | 6    | 7    | 8    | 9    |
| Police and Fire     | 8    | 7    | 8    | 8    | 8    |
| Highways            | 10   | 6    | 6    | 5    | 5    |
| Interest on Debt    | 3    | 4    | 4    | 5    | 5    |
| Other               | 23   | 25   | 28   | 29   | 28   |

*Source: Government Finances*, selected years; www.census.gov.

## TABLE 3

### State Revenue Sources: Percentage Distribution (Percent of General Fund)

|                     | 1960 | 1970 | 1980 | 1990 | 1994 |
|---------------------|------|------|------|------|------|
| Intergovernmental   | 21   | 24   | 23   | 22   | 24   |
| Total Taxes         | 55   | 53   | 48   | 47   | 44   |
| Property            | 2    | 1    | 1    | 1    | 1    |
| Personal Income     | 7    | 10   | 13   | 15   | 14   |
| Sales               | 32   | 30   | 23   | 23   | 22   |
| Other               | 14   | 11   | 11   | 8    | 7    |
| Charges and Misc.   | 8    | 10   | 12   | 15   | 14   |
| Other               | 3    | 5    | 8    | 1    | 1    |
| Insurance Contracts | 13   | 11   | 15   | 15   | 17   |

*Source: Government Finances*, selected years; www.census.gov.

## TABLE 4

### Local Direct Revenue Sources: Percentage Distribution (Fiscal Years)

|                     | 1960 | 1970 | 1980 | 1990 | 1994 |
|---------------------|------|------|------|------|------|
| Intergovernmental   | 27   | 34   | 39   | 33   | 34   |
| Total Taxes         | 49   | 43   | 33   | 35   | 35   |
| Property            | 43   | 36   | 25   | 26   | 26   |
| Personal Income     | 1    | 2    | 2    | 2    | 2    |
| Sales               | 4    | 4    | 5    | 5    | 5    |
| Other               | 2    | 1    | 1    | 2    | 2    |
| Charges and Misc.   | 13   | 14   | 18   | 20   | 20   |
| Utility             | 10   | 7    | 9    | 9    | 9    |
| Other               | 2    | 2    | 2    | 3    | 3    |

*Source: Government Finances*, selected years; www.census.gov.

Table 4 shows roughly similar results for local governments. Total taxes have declined as a percentage of total revenues; however, in this case the decline has occurred because of the fall in property taxes. Again, this decline has been offset by the increase in charges and miscellaneous. It should be noted that local governments receive about 9 percent of their total revenues from utilities, whereas the state receives about 1 percent.

## Budget issues today

Any analysis of state and local budgeting must address several policy issues, among them: (1) a lack of any theory of budgeting; (2) budget and fiscal stress, including tax and expenditure limits; (3) budgetary structures; (4) operating versus capital budgets; and (5) increasing interaction between state and local budgets.

### Lack of budgetary theory

Currently, there is no unified budgeting theory for state and local government. However, there are some potential candidates for a beginning discussion. For example, the models of principal-agent relationships (Eisenhardt 1989), which are concerned with controlling both measurable and nonmeasurable outputs, might be a useful starting point. Alternatively, controlling the levels of taxes and expenditures might be addressed through a Tiebout analysis (Dowding et al. 1994). Finally, since the budget itself is a political document, some elements of game theory might be appropriate in its analysis.

### Budgets, tax and expenditure limits, and fiscal stress

The focus of state and local tax and expenditure limits is on the budget. Since it is the document that reflects the outcome of the public decisionmaking process, it becomes the document controlled by these constraints. To the extent that budgets are politically constrained, fiscal stress is likely. The budget will not realize forecasted revenues and will not be able to allocate resources to all claimants.

### Budgetary structures

Much discussion concerning budgets revolves around the types of approaches that can be used to facilitate the budget as either a control, management, or planning device (Lynch 1994). A line-item budget, in which the budget is concerned with inputs such as number of employees and their salaries, the amount of capital, and the amount of materials and supplies, is principally a control device. The budget can be performance-based, in which performance measures are developed by the jurisdiction and then adequate funding is established to ensure meeting those benchmarks. For example, the desired number of minutes for an ambulance to arrive at an emergency scene is determined and then financed. Decisions are made at the performance level, and these budgets are used for management decisions. The third type of budget is planning oriented. In this type, the mission of a particular agency is defined and then budget decisions are made to support this mission. A subcomponent of this type of budget is the modified zero-based budget that asks each agency manager to predict what would happen if specified increments or decrements of the budget were to occur. Although zero-based budgeting was not absolutely successful at the national level, some state and local jurisdictions have successfully used a modified form. Another subcomponent of this type of budget is the entrepreneurial budget, in which decisions are decentralized to make each manager accountable for results (Cothran 1993). It should be noted that underlying all of these budgets is the simple line-item form, which must always be followed, regardless of any other sophisticated methodology. This makes the other budget formats more expensive than the line-item form.

### Operating versus capital budgets

The operating budget of a jurisdiction is designed to control, manage, or plan the jurisdiction's current activities. The capital budget is designed as a plan for obtaining and financing long-term capital assets, usually accumulated through the issuance of debt. Although most state and local jurisdictions have moved to a separation of operating and capital budgets, there still may be confusion over the appropriate use of each. This is especially true when the operating budget contains payments for such debt-like instruments as certificates of participation, which are not technically debt. Further confusion occurs when earmarked fund accounting appears in the operating budget, yet the funds are used to fi-

nance long-run capital projects. Although there are formal accounting rules designed to force the reporting of these transactions correctly and consistently (Government Finance Officers Association 1994), many jurisdictions do not follow the full Governmental Accounting Financial Reporting standards.

### Intergovernmental budget relationships

Over time, the relationships between state and local budgets have become more complex. Local governments are now closely tied to state budgets and state controls. On the expenditure side, this tie relates to state-mandated services financed by the local government, while on the revenue side, it relates to state subventions and tax-sharing with the local governments. For some states, when their revenues fall, they may take some of these revenues back from the local governments. This "shift-and-shaft" federalism can cause fiscal stress at the local level while the state solves its budgetary problems. A side effect of this activity is the disengagement of the state and local budget cycles, since the mandates and revenue shifts are sometimes decided after the local budget is adopted.

## Budget reforms

Recommending budget reforms has always been a popular subject (for examples, see Schick 1990 or the California Citizens Budget Commission 1995). In particular, two sets of reforms seem to be consistent among all recommendations.

One is that the budget should become a useful source of information for public decisionmaking. The other is that budgets should be comprehensive, using standardized data formats, written in plain English, accompanied by a narrative summarizing the actions taken, and understandable by both elected officials and the citizens.

The budget should also be an honest reflection of decisions undertaken. An explicit discussion of tax expenditures, the use of special funds, and a statement of fiscal condition should be an integral part of the budget document. In addition, a presentation of current expenditures, the baseline trend—including cost-of-living allowances and caseload increases—and budget expenditures should be presented, so that actual changes can be determined.

State and local governments do not have the luxury of the continuous deficit finance that the national government has utilized over the past several decades. These governments can be exceedingly stretched between constituent demands for fewer taxes and more service entitlements. Because of this, the issues that face state and local budgets tend to carry more emotional weight than those at the national level, and consequently it is far more difficult to reach consensus.

## Additional readings

California Citizens Budget Commission. *Reforming California's Budget Process* (preliminary report). Los Angeles: Center for Governmental Studies, 1995.

Cothran, Dan A. "Entrepreneurial Budgeting: An Emerging Reform?" *Public Administration Review* 53 (5) (September/October 1993): 445–54.

Dowding, Keith, Peter John, and Stephen Biggs. "Tiebout: A Survey of the Empirical Literature." *Urban Studies* 31 (4/5) (1994): 767–97.

Eisenhardt, Kathleen M. "Agency Theory: An Assessment and Review." *Academy of Management and Review* 14 (1) (1989): 57–74.

Government Finance Officers Association. *Governmental Accounting, Auditing and Financial Reporting*. Chicago, 1994.

Lynch, Thomas. *Public Budgeting in America*. 4th ed. Englewood Cliffs, N.J.: Prentice Hall, 1994.

Schick, Alan. *The Capacity to Budget*. Washington, D.C.: The Urban Institute, 1990.

*Cross references:* budget-balance requirement; budgeting, state; budget processes, state.

# Budget process, federal

## Al Davis
House Budget Committee

*Annual procedures whereby the president submits a budget for congressional review and disposition.*

The U.S. government has an annual budget cycle. The cycle normally begins with the president's budget submission early in the calendar year. The president's budget translates many of his political priorities into a plan of action. Then Congress responds. At a minimum, Congress must pass annual appropriations bills, or one or more "continuing resolutions," which may substitute for appropriations bills. In many years, Congress does more. It passes legislation that changes the permanent laws affecting revenues and spending, such as Medicare. The congressional budget process is used to coordinate budget-related congressional action.

## Time horizon

In the 1970s, presidential and congressional budgets typically covered one year. During the 1980s, the budget time horizon grew longer. Five-year congressional budgets became the norm and are now required by law. Even longer projections have sometimes been made. For example, the budget resolution approved in 1996 covered a seven-year period. The new congressional majority wanted to balance the budget and it took seven years to show that the plan could achieve balance, relying as it did on savings to grow from cutting the rate of growth of spending.

A longer budget horizon promotes better planning and discourages gimmicks that create only one-time savings or one-time revenue gains. A longer horizon also discourages spending initiatives or tax cuts that are small for many years but balloon in later years. However, over a longer time period, technical estimating limitations become more severe. Moreover, the policies assumed in a very long-range budget may not be sustainable, because the current Congress cannot tie the hands of future Congresses. This fact is particularly salient in the case of appropriations, because they are made annually and do not become part of permanent law.

## Economic assumptions

Underlying any federal government budget is a set of economic assumptions. For example, a president may decide that his program will be "good for the economy" and he may assume in his budget that economic growth will be higher, or inflation or unemployment lower, than in recent years. His assumptions may be more optimistic than the consensus of private economic forecasters. Congress is likewise free to decide on its own economic assumptions for the congressional budget resolution.

The levels of revenues, entitlement spending, and deficits in the budget are quite sensitive to the underlying economic assumptions. Optimistic assumptions can bring budgets closer to balance and minimize the size of spending cuts or revenue increases needed to bring the budget into balance. Presidential budgeting during the late 1980s was criticized for using "rosy scenario" economic assumptions to make it look as if the president's program would achieve a balanced budget.

The power of economic assumptions can be illustrated: In early 1997, the Congressional Budget Office (CBO) estimated that if interest rates became one percentage point lower than the CBO had projected through the year 2002, with no change in inflation, the budget deficit would be lower by $48 billion in 2002. In 1997, the congressional budget resolution assumed a deficit reduction of $34 billion in the year 2002 to come mainly from a reduction in interest rates, which, in turn, was to come from law changes to reduce budget deficits. Lower interest rates reduce the cost of federal debt service. As a result, the congressional budget did not have to recommend law changes that by themselves would balance the budget. Once policies were recommended to move the budget close to balance, the assumption was that a dividend from lower debt service costs would bring the budget the rest of the way into balance.

So-called technical assumptions, such as those about patterns of medical service use, are also very important in making budget projections. Typically, the congressional budget process relies on the CBO to make these assumptions.

Economic and technical assumptions can change over time. These changes can greatly alter perceptions about budgetary problems and influence the federal government's response. For example, in September 1993, despite the enactment of major deficit reduction earlier in the year, the CBO projected a year 2002 deficit of $320 billion. In January 1997, less than four years later, that office's comparable projection for the year 2002 was only $188 billion, even though very little deficit-reduction legislation had become law during 1994, 1995, and 1996. The deficit reestimate was mainly a result of better-than-forecast economic performance from 1994 through 1996 and revisions in noneconomic assumptions. Later in 1997, Congress used a somewhat more optimistic deficit projection based, in part, on the assumption that deficit-reduction legislation would itself reduce interest rates and help balance the budget. The dramatic improvement in the deficit outlook between late 1993 and 1997 made it possible for Congress to cut taxes while projecting a balanced budget.

When the federal budget was far out of balance, the major limiting factors on congressional budget action were the difficulty in reaching agreement and lawmakers' level of tolerance for painful cuts in spending or painful increases in taxes. If the federal budget comes to balance, the budget agenda may become much more sensitive to relatively small changes in budgetary projections. For example, if a $20 billion deficit is projected at some time in the future, Congress might want to eliminate the deficit. If a $20 billion surplus is projected, Congress might want to cut taxes or increase spending. Such swings in policy could occur, even though they would be driven by statistically tiny errors in budgetary projections, given that total spending and revenues will soon exceed $1,750 billion.

## President's budget—level of detail and specifics

The president's budget is not just a set of highlights and suggestions, or a presentation of the president's political preferences—although it is surely that. The president's budget is normally presented in great "line-item" detail. Large documents are printed and backed up with detailed supporting materials from the government agencies. Because of the president's prominence as a nationwide elected official, his ability to marshall the resources of the executive branch, and, in comparison, Congress's representation of so many varied points of view, the president's budget is often the point of departure for subsequent congressional decisions.

## Congressional budget

The present congressional budget process was implemented in the Congressional Budget Act of 1974. That legislation was partly a congressional response to concerns over President Nixon's unilateral and aggressive withholding of authority to spend. The new budget act created a new, less one-sided mechanism. The legislation was also a response to the criticism that Congress lacked a mechanism for coordinating the response of its numerous committees to the president's budget, or for coordinating an alternative budget. The drafters of that legislation did not wish to take away more power than necessary from the then-standing committees of Congress. When they created the new budget committees, they did not eliminate other committees, nor did they intend that the budget committees become creators of "line-item" authorization law changes or appropriations bills. The mission of the budget committees and the budget resolution is to provide guidelines and targets for the money-related actions of other committees. The budget resolution allows Congress to speak with one voice to its various committees.

The original budget act included a variety of procedural rules, and since its passage the Senate has added its own special procedural rules, which are too extensive to discuss in this entry. The act also established the CBO, which produces studies related to the budget and estimates the budget effects of proposed legislation, except for changes in revenues, which are generally estimated by the Joint Committee on Taxation. The CBO is independent of the executive branch and is separate from the much smaller staffs of the House and Senate budget committees.

The congressional budget takes the form of a resolution that is voted on by the House and the Senate, first separately and then in response to a conference committee recommendation. The final budget resolution is not submitted to the president for his approval or veto. The congressional document is normally quite different in character from the president's budget.

## Content of a budget resolution

The report accompanying the budget resolution includes a statement of underlying economic assumptions. These are recommended by the budget committees and need not be identical to the president's, or the same as the advisory assumptions normally suggested by the CBO.

The congressional budget resolution presents total spending, total revenues, the recommended change in revenues, the budget deficit (or surplus), and the implied level of federal debt that is subject to statutory limit. (If that level of debt is higher than the amount authorized by current law, Congress must later vote to raise the "debt ceiling," even though it has already voted on a budget that will create higher debt. This must-pass debt legislation often becomes a vehicle for legislative riders, one of which was the original Gramm-Rudman-Hollings law discussed further on.) In the budget resolution, spending is broken down among 20 budget "functions" covering such categories as defense, international affairs, agriculture, transportation, Medicare, other health services, and net interest. The "functions" include many government programs and do not track one-for-one with congressional committee jurisdictions.

Officially, the amounts in the budget resolution no longer include the Social Security trust funds, which are expected to run surpluses for many years. Nevertheless, committee report language typically provides projections for the budget including Social Security, and the budget has been discussed in terms of the total, including Social Security. For example, when the 1997 budget resolution was presented as a plan for balancing the budget, that balance was achieved only with Social Security Trust Fund surpluses included. The official numbers in the budget resolution continued to show deficits, because they did not include Social Security surpluses.

The report on a budget resolution also includes committee "allocations" (i.e., ceilings) and a revenue floor, and it may include "reconciliation instructions." Allocations and the floor on revenues are enforced through points of order in the House and Senate. Most often, it takes 60 votes in the 100-member Senate to waive a point of order against considering legislation that would cause spending to exceed a budget allocation or revenues to be cut below the floor. In the House, the "rule" controlling amendments and debate may waive points of order, and the rule is subject to a majority vote.

One allocation is made to the Appropriations Committee. Appropriations are made each year for fixed dollar amounts. This one allocation covers a great deal of spending. For example, for fiscal year 1997, spending determined by appropriations was about $550 billion, one-third of total spending including Social Security. For a "budget year" (e.g.,

for calendar year 1997, the "budget year" was the coming fiscal year, 1998), this allocation is enforceable by a point of order. In the more than 20 years since the process began, total appropriations have been held quite closely to the allocation in the budget resolution.

Because there is only one budget resolution allocation for all appropriations, program-by-program assumptions that the budget committees may have used may not be very influential. On the other hand, if a major issue, such as a division of funds between defense and nondefense, were to be articulated and fully debated, the assumption might greatly influence the subsequent appropriations process.

The rest of the budget comprises revenues and "mandatory" spending. Mandatory spending includes "entitlements," which are created by laws that entitle certain classes of people to benefits. The largest entitlements are Social Security ($365 billion in 1997) and Medicare ($213 billion). Mandatory spending also includes obligatory spending, such as interest on the federal debt ($244 billion in 1997) and payments arising from court decisions. Typically, neither tax law nor underlying authorizations specify numerical amounts; rather, they set the terms and conditions under which individuals pay taxes and receive benefits such as Social Security. Unlike spending subject to appropriations, revenues and mandatory spending will be whatever results from the underlying law. For this reason, revenues and mandatory spending are more difficult to predict, and they are more difficult to control than spending subject to appropriations.

While detailed appropriations are the responsibility of a single committee in the House and Senate, responsibility for revenues and mandatory spending is spread among many committees. The report on a budget resolution creates allocations for each of the authorizing committees. These allocations cover the total amount of mandatory spending contemplated in the budget resolution. Because the authorizing committees have different program responsibilities, the program implications of these multiple allocations may be clearer than for the single allocation provided for annual appropriations. For example, if the Committee on Ways and Means has a spending allocation that is significantly below the current law level, Congress most probably knows whether Medicare reductions are likely and, if so, the broad outlines of the probable changes.

Although there are points of order against considering legislation that would cause spending to exceed an allocation, or revenues to fall below the floor, points of order are powerless to reduce spending that would occur under existing law, or to raise revenues. For this reason, management of mandatory spending, unlike appropriations, also takes place through "reconciliation instructions" to the various authorizing committees. These instructions do not have to be included in a budget resolution, but they frequently have been included since budget deficits became a concern. Reconciliation instructions are numerical targets stretching over several years. Recently, the time span has been five years or more.

After 1981 and through 1993, the instructions have been to reduce mandatory spending and/or raise revenues. In 1995, however, the new congressional majority began to include an instruction for a major tax cut. A tax cut was ultimately enacted in 1997.

Historically, Congress has usually come quite close to meeting the reconciliation targets, although in one year a reconciliation effort was abandoned, and once, during the mid-1980s, reconciliation action was not completed until early in the next session of Congress. In 1995, reconciliation was not completed because the president vetoed the implementing legislation. In 1996, Congress completed action on only one of three reconciliation bills that were planned in the budget resolution.

## Level of detail and specifics

The level of detail reported in budget resolutions is much less than in the president's budget. This is not to say that the numbers in a budget resolution are arbitrary. To win a majority of votes for budget resolutions, the budget committees, the congressional leadership, committee chairs, and others must reach understandings about the assumptions behind the numbers in a budget resolution. Budget committee reports may or may not be specific about these understandings.

Reconciliation amounts are usually net numbers, and committees have frequently included both pluses and minuses in their reconciliation recommendations. For example, the tax-writing committees might have been reconciled to raise $50 billion in added revenue over several years. Such an instruction would not normally preclude tax cuts when they are paid for with other changes. For example, a committee might include $60 billion of added revenues and $10 billion of tax cuts to arrive at the net increase of $50 billion. A committee might even pay for tax cuts with spending reductions rather than tax increases.

## Misunderstandings about the congressional budget process

The congressional budget process is sometimes misunderstood. As explained above, the congressional budget resolution frequently lacks the kind of detail that some observers may wish to have. There may not be an up-or-down vote on a budget resolution that reflects the president's budget submission.

There is no one up-or-down vote that sends an entire congressional budget to the president for his signature (or veto). The budget resolution is not sent to the president.

A vote on a House-Senate conference agreement on the budget resolution is not the end of budget-related votes. After this vote, there are votes on separate appropriations bills (House, Senate, and conference agreements), which can number up to 13. There may be votes on interim appropriations measures called "continuing resolutions." There are often votes on a reconciliation bill.

## Gramm-Rudman-Hollings fixed deficit targets

In 1985, budget law took a new turn when the Gramm-Rudman-Hollings (GRH) law was enacted. This law pushed budget statutes beyond the point of establishing institutions and procedures. It required that budget deficits be brought down to specified amounts. The budget was to be balanced in 1991. If Congress did not enact legislation sufficient to do so, automatic spending cuts would be triggered. This automatic mechanism did not include tax increases. The manner in which spending would be cut was specified by formula, and some programs were exempted—for example, Social Security.

In 1990, the 1985 GRH law was replaced. The original ambitious deficit targets had proved politically unattainable. Before 1990, Congress had delayed and revised the targets. In 1990, Congress passed major deficit-reduction legislation and changed the law to emphasize prevention of future legislation that would increase budget deficits. The pursuit of further deficit reduction then became, once again, a matter of judgment, rather than law.

## Pay-as-you-go and caps

The 1990 law established a two-part control mechanism. Spending subject to appropriation was made subject to a separate series of annual caps. If this spending exceeded the cap in any year, there would be an automatic cut in programs subject to appropriation.

The second part of the mechanism was called "pay-as-you-go." Pay-as-you-go covered the rest of the budget: mandatory spending and revenues. In simplified terms, if the cumulative effect of mandatory spending and revenue legislation is to raise the budget deficit in any one year, then "sequestration" is triggered. Mandatory spending programs like Medicaid and farm price supports are cut across-the-board, except that Medicare can be cut by no more than 4 percent, and numerous programs, such as Social Security and unemployment compensation, are exempt. There is no automatic increase in revenues.

In 1993, as part of another deficit-reduction bill, the caps and pay-as-you-go mechanisms were extended. In 1997, the mechanisms were again extended as part of another deficit-reduction bill.

## Constitutional amendment to balance the budget

In 1995, the major budget process issue became a proposed constitutional amendment to require a balanced budget. In the Senate, in both 1995 and 1996, that amendment fell a few votes short of the necessary two-thirds needed to send it to the states for possible ratification. However, in 1997, the constitutional amendment seemed less urgent to supporters, because of the passage of legislation that reduced program spending enough to balance the budget.

## Line-item veto

In 1996, Congress passed a law to give the president the power to react to enacted legislation by canceling funding for items drawing upon appropriations, to cancel new items of mandatory spending, or to cancel "limited tax benefits," if the president found that such cancellations would reduce budget deficits. That power became effective in 1997 and expires after the year 2004. After cancellations by a president, the burden is on Congress to enact legislation overturning the cancellations. The law provides for expedited congressional procedures to make it less difficult than normal for Congress to work its will in this matter. In 1997, the president canceled a number of items that were included in appropriations bills, one item of added direct spending from a budget reconciliation bill, and two "limited tax benefits" from a tax bill. Court review of the constitutionality of several of these actions has begun.

## Budget surpluses

In September 1997, the CBO projected that a small budget surplus would emerge in the year 2002, counting Social Security. The projection assumed that future Congresses would adhere to the caps on spending subject to appropriations and assumed no economic recession in the year or two preceding 2002. In fact, the budget surplus occurred somewhat earlier. For fiscal 1998 (the 12 months ending September 30), the budget recorded a $70 billion surplus (the figure includes excess payroll taxes being collected for Social Security). Although these surpluses are projected to vanish when the baby boomers retire and the costs of Social Security and Medicare escalate more rapidly, Congress and the president have begun to debate the unfamiliar issue of whether to run budget surpluses—i.e., to move closer toward balance in the non–Social Security budget—or whether to cut taxes and raise spending.

## Additional readings

Council of Economic Advisors. *Annual Report of the Council of Economic Advisors and Economic Report of the President*. Washington, D.C.: U.S. Government Printing Office, annual.

Office of Management and Budget. *Budget of the United States Government*. Washington, D.C.: U.S. Government Printing Office, annual.

*Cross references:* revenue estimation, federal; revenue forecasting, federal; Social Security Trust Fund.

# Budget processes, state
Bruce A. Wallin
Northeastern University

*Annual procedures whereby state governors submit budgets for legislative review and disposition.*

While state governments in the United States are often noted for their diverse approaches to politics and policies, their budget processes are to a great extent very similar (Hutchison and James 1988).

In almost every state, proposed budgets are put together in the executive branch. Most state fiscal years run from July 1 to June 30, and governors begin the process in July or August by having their budget offices send out instructions for budget requests to the various departments and agencies. These instructions usually give each spending unit a rough idea of what they might expect in continued, expanded, or (rarely) reduced resources. By the fall, agency requests are received by the budget office and reviewed, often with an eye toward cutting expenditures seen as unnecessary. Hearings on the budget requests may be conducted within the executive branch and might include representatives of the governor, budget officials, and department heads, who may wish to appeal the decisions of the budget office. The governor then prepares a final budget proposal, which includes projected revenues and appropriations, and a budget message (Rosenthal 1990).

Governors customarily submit proposed budgets to their state legislatures in late January or early February. Most commonly, the budget is referred to one committee in each house, usually called the "appropriations" committee. This is very different from (and far more efficient than) budgeting at the federal level, where each house has a budget committee, 13 authorization committees, and an appropriations committee, divided into many subcommittees. After committee hearings, debates, markup sessions (where bills are gone over and changed line by line), and votes, the budget bill is sent to the floor of the whole chamber, where it may be amended and is ultimately voted on.

Budget bills usually originate in the lower house, mirroring the practice for revenue bills at the federal level, and following the philosophy that all revenue actions should be initiated in the chamber closest to the people in terms of number of constituents per representative and frequency of elections. A similar process then occurs in the Senate, with committee work preceding debate and final action on the Senate floor. In most cases, a budget that passes a state senate will differ in some manner from the budget that passes the house, and a conference committee will be appointed by legislative leaders to work out a compromise. That compromise must then be approved by both houses of the state legislature.

The budget bill is then sent to the governor. Governors may sign the bill, veto the entire bill (which almost never occurs), or in most states sign it with a line-item veto, allowing the governor to strike portions of the bill that he or she dislikes. Any vetoes then return to the state legislature for override attempts, usually requiring two-thirds of the state legislature. Some evidence suggests that while the item veto is thought of only as a tool of fiscal restraint, it is frequently used to alter policy (Gosling 1986). Item vetoes are rarely overridden.

Important variations in state budget processes do exist. In 21 states, the budget is a biennial one, passed every two years instead of annually. The argument for biennial budgeting is that it is more efficient, allowing the legislature to spend time on other important policy issues, time that would otherwise be consumed by the budget process. Evidence on the effect of biennial budgeting on state policy is unclear, to a great extent because there is no agreement on how to identify "good policy." In another variation, 15 states have joint budget committees, with representatives of both houses of the state legislature receiving the budget from the governor.

In a few states, including California, Rhode Island, and Nebraska, a super-majority of legislators is needed to pass a budget. The goal of super-majority approval is fiscal discipline, the argument being that it will be more difficult to get, say, two-thirds of a state legislature to agree to a budget with unnecessary spending.

Finally, variations exist in the veto powers of governors. Governors in 43 states have the power of line-item veto, meaning that they can veto portions of a budget passed by the legislature. But in 26 states, governors may also veto language in an appropriations bill, giving them more power (Council of State Governments 1996). In addition, provisions for override vary by state. Giving the governor the most power is an override that calls for two-thirds of *elected* legislators to override; less restrictive is the provision for override by two-thirds *present* at the time of the vote.

The roles of the main participants in the state budget process are fairly typical in all states. The governor may be viewed as budget balancer for two reasons. First, the governor is the one individual in the process who represents the entire state, and a balanced budget is a common denominator for most citizens, at least in principle. Second, submitting a budget in balance gives the governor power over the legislature in determining the ultimate shape of the budget. Facing a proposed budget in balance, a legislature desirous of tax cuts would have to find expenditure reductions to finance them, while a legislature that sought to increase spending over a governor's request would have to find the added revenues to finance it. It is usually easier to accept the broad parameters of the governor's budget.

State legislators can generally be characterized as spenders or tax-cutters, as they seek to please their constituents by bringing benefits back to their districts, or use the budget to reward special interests who may have provided the rationales for budget items, and perhaps gained access by means of campaign contributions. Department or agency heads are also generally spenders, since in the public sector size of budget is a measure of success, a substitute for profit in the private sector. Most individuals who head agencies also believe in their mission and are therefore likely to want to spend more, and have a clientele of their own to serve.

The governor has much more power in the state budgeting process than the president does in federal budgeting. First, governors usually submit a budget in balance, which as already noted makes it more difficult for the legislature to change. Second, governors have an informational advantage over state legislators, and the imbalance of staff resources at the state level tilts much more strongly toward the executive than it does at the federal level. Third, in many states the job of state legislator is a part-time one, or at least allows legislators to pursue other professional activities, giving the governor the advantages of time and focus. Fourth, the line-item veto gives a governor more power than the president has traditionally had, and is generally stronger than the version recently enacted by Congress, which allows a simple majority of members to specify a law as not subject to presidential line-item veto.

State budgeting for the most part continues to be "traditional" or "line-item" budgeting, with incrementalism the prevailing decision system employed. As a consequence, most of the emphasis of state budgeting is placed on analyzing the change in inputs from the previous year's budget (Rosenthal 1990: 136). While producing stability and making it easier to compromise, incrementalism does result in some programs outliving their usefulness, or at least growing beyond need. Comprehensive reform measures have for the most part been unsuccessful, including zero-based budgeting and planning, programming, budgeting systems (National Conference of State Legislatures 1995). Zero-based budgeting sought to have programs analyzed from top to bottom, with varying output levels estimated for various levels of resources. Planning, programming, budgeting systems sought to move from line-item budgeting to the presentation of budgets in program packages, with multiyear planning and performance measures. Both reforms failed as a result of calculation problems, as well as political and organizational resistance. Successful reforms have included better revenue estimating, often involving joint legislative-executive committees, and multiyear forecasting of both revenues and expenditures. Performance budgeting has increasingly found its way into state budgeting, especially on the executive side.

Budgeting at the state level is greatly affected by legal, political, economic, and demographic variables. Legally, all states except Vermont are either statutorily or constitutionally required to balance their budgets. Most states also have limits on how much they can borrow, usually expressed as a percentage of appropriations. Twenty-one states face constitutional or statutory tax and/or expenditure limitations (TELS), most a product of the tax revolt kicked off by California's Proposition 13 in 1978 (Advisory Commission on Intergovernmental Relations 1991). Taxes are often limited to a percentage of the tax base, or expenditure growth may be tied to inflation plus population growth. These TELS usually require a super-majority override by the legislature, or public override by referendum. Political variables include tax competition—the fear that taxpayers will flee a state if its tax burden is much higher than that of a neighboring state.

Many exogenous variables have an important impact on state budgeting. Most important is the economy. A drop in economic performance reduces revenues while simultaneously causing increased expenditures for welfare and unemployment programs. Important demographic variables include the number of school-age children, as education spending is one of the two largest expenditure commitments of states; the number of youth in the 16–24 high-crime cohort, which has a great impact on the fastest-rising state expenditure, corrections; and the number of elderly, which affects state budgets most directly through increased Medicaid expenditures funneled to nursing homes. Finally, federal policies also have an impact on state budgets, through increases or decreases in federal aid, or through the imposition of federal mandates, especially those that are unfunded. While Congress recently passed a law limiting the use of unfunded mandates, it was not made retroactive.

In sum, because of balanced-budget requirements, limits on revenue increases for fear of taxpayer flight, and built-in expenditure pressures based on inflation and increasing populations served, state budgeting is revenue-constrained. Surges in revenue will allow states to embark on additional spending or to pursue tax cuts. But in the absence of such revenue windfalls, state budgeting is for the most part highly routinized, with incremental decisions made by actors constrained by their environment.

### Additional readings

Advisory Commission on Intergovernmental Relations. *Significant Features of Fiscal Federalism 1991*. Vol. 1. Washington, D.C., February 1991.

Council of State Governments. *Book of the States*. Lexington, Ky., 1996.

Gosling, James J. "Wisconsin Item-Veto Lessons." *Public Administration Review* 46 (July–August 1986).

Hutchison, Tony, and Kathy James. *Legislative Budget Procedures in the 50 States: A Guide to Appropriations and Budget Processes*. Denver: National Conference of State Legislatures, September 1988.

National Conference of State Legislatures. *Fundamentals of Sound State Budgeting Practices*. Denver, May 1995.

Rosenthal, Alan. *Governors and Legislatures: Contending Powers*. Washington, D.C.: Congressional Quarterly Press, 1990.

*Cross references:* budget-balance requirement; budgeting, state; budget policy, state and local.

# Business location, taxation and

William T. Bogart
Case Western Reserve University

*The relationship between government fiscal and regulatory policy and firm site choice and investment decisions.*

The effect of government policy on a firm's site selection and investment decisions is a familiar question to government officials and academics alike. Although this entry focuses on a business's decision to locate in various regions or states in the United

States, the concepts are applicable to international location problems as well. There has long been a consensus among academics that government fiscal policy plays almost no role in interregional location decisions and at best a supporting role in intraregional or intrametropolitan location decisions. This consensus has been challenged in recent years, but there is still no broad support in the academic literature for the proliferation of state and local government programs designed to affect firm location decisions. Because taxes raise revenue to finance government services, and since government regulations can have effects similar to taxes, the broad sweep of government activity is considered here, rather than the more narrow focus of taxes.

## Theory of business location

In order to understand the relationship between taxation and business location, it is necessary to consider the general theory of business location. Economic theory typically assumes that firms make decisions in an attempt to maximize profits (revenues minus costs). Both revenues and costs can vary with the firm's location. One component of costs is the expense of the local public sector. Local taxes add to the cost of doing business, while local government services can reduce the cost of doing business, either directly (e.g., infrastructure) or indirectly (e.g., good schools are a source of skilled workers). The level of local taxes can also affect the relative advantage of the nonprofit corporate form.

Two conditions must be met for government policy to have an effect on a firm's location decision. The first is that some aspect of government policy must vary over space. If every government levies the same taxes, provides the same public services, and administers the same regulations, then a firm's location decision will be made entirely on the basis of factors other than government policy. The second condition is that the increase in profits resulting from government policy in one location relative to the other exceeds any loss in profits resulting from the location choice. For example, if a company stands to save $2 million in taxes by moving from one place to another at a cost of $4 million in lost profits, it will not make the move. Economists investigating the variation in taxes relative to other factors have typically found that the other factors (e.g., labor costs, access to markets) dominate the firm's decision at the intermetropolitan or interregional level. However, once a firm has decided to locate in a particular metropolitan area, intergovernmental differences can play a significant role. One ongoing controversy is the incidence of taxes levied on businesses. If the taxes are completely shifted, then nominal differences in taxes at various locations are irrelevant for a firm's decisions.

## How taxes affect business location

There are two ways that taxes and government spending affect business location decisions. The first is directly through increasing (in the case of taxes) or decreasing (in the case of public services) the cost of doing business. The second is indirectly through the effects of government policy on output markets or factor markets.

The level and mix of state and local government taxes varies greatly in the United States. This would seem to be prima facie evidence for taxes as an important factor in business location decisions. There are two ameliorating factors that should be noted, though. First, state and local taxes are deductible from income for the purposes of computing federal taxes owed. This reduces the variability among states, as high state taxes are partially compensated for in part by lower federal taxes. Second, the taxes may be capitalized into asset values, especially land, so that the economic incidence of the tax is not on the firm facing the nominal incidence of the taxes.

Since states differ in the emphasis of their tax systems on various factors of production, the relative attractiveness of a location will depend on the type of firm—for example, labor-intensive versus capital-intensive. Two important topics for analysis are therefore the relative mobility of production factors and the possibility of substituting among production factors. Wasylenko and McGuire (1985) demonstrate that location determinants vary by industry, and the effect of taxes will therefore also vary by industry.

It is also important to identify the appropriate tax rate to be used in the analysis: marginal or average. For a firm considering an incremental expansion, the marginal effective tax rate is the most relevant. For a firm considering a relocation, the average effective tax rate is the most important.

In addition to its direct effect on a firm's profits, government policy also has indirect effects. For example, if the public school system is excellent, a firm might face a labor market with a large supply of qualified workers. Regulatory policy, in the form of zoning laws and building codes, for example, at the local level, workers compensation schemes and unemployment insurance at the state level, and environmental policy at the federal level, can also affect a company's cost of doing business. Because federal laws apply everywhere in the country, it might at first seem surprising to find them making a difference among locations. Recently, though, there has been concern that Superfund and related legislation and regulation have created a disadvantage for "brownfield" locations (industrial sites) relative to "greenfield" locations (undeveloped or agricultural sites). Because brownfields are typically located in the older parts of metropolitan areas, especially central cities, the environmental legislation has added another reason for companies to avoid locating in central cities in favor of surrounding areas. Central cities typically have higher taxes than their suburbs, making it difficult to precisely identify the reason for a given location decision. The nature of the environmental liability and the incentive to pursue "deep pockets" also reduce the efficacy of central cities' programs designed to make themselves more attractive relative to the suburbs.

## Evidence

Two methods are used to identify the effect of government policy on firm location. The first is to survey businesses on the importance of government policy in their location decisions, the second to statistically test the relationship between measurable aspects of government policy and business location decisions. Both of these methods have drawbacks. The survey method suffers from a sample selection bias in two respects. The first, and most serious, is that only businesses that have both chosen to locate in a particular area and survived until the survey date will be included. The second is the typical survey problem of nonresponse. The other main problem facing the survey method is the difficulty in identifying the marginal effect of a particular government policy, holding all other relevant variables equal.

The statistical methods also have some problems. One is sample selection bias, because the places where development incentives are used do not represent a random sample. A second statistical problem in evaluating the effectiveness of economic development programs is that they are usually small relative to the local economy, making their impact more difficult to identify. The third problem, related to the other two, is distinguishing the independent effect of the program in question from unobservable local characteristics. Papke (1993) summarizes the statistical problems and demonstrates the state of the art in addressing them.

There had been a long-standing consensus among academics using both methodologies that government policy had either no effect or only a small effect on firms' location decisions. This general finding had four basic explanations: (1) that taxes did not vary much across locations, (2) that the variation in taxes was exceeded by the variation in other factors, such as labor costs or access to markets, (3) that the taxes could be shifted, and were therefore irrelevant for the firm's location decision, and (4) that high taxes were accompanied by high levels of desirable public services.

The consensus that government policy has little effect has been challenged in recent years. The most comprehensive survey of the empirical literature is found in Bartik (1991). Newman and Sullivan (1988) provide an excellent introduction to the econometric literature. Table 1 summarizes the econometric evidence. There are two principal conclusions. One is that taxes are a more important determinant of intrametropolitan business location decisions than of intermetropolitan business location decisions. The second is that econometric analysis that controls for specific community characteristics is more likely to find that taxes are important.

A related question is whether government policies designed to promote business location are self-financing—that is, whether the additional tax revenues provided by the business exceed the cost of providing the incentive. Most econometric studies do not directly address this question. However, to the extent that incentives do not affect business location decisions, they clearly are not self-financing. This raises the question of why governments would provide the incentives at all. Using survey evidence from Ohio, Morse and Farmer (1986) demonstrated that an economic incentives program can be self-financing even if it affects the location decision of only a small fraction of firms. Courant (1994) provides a thoughtful critique of the economic literature, suggesting that research needs to focus on the contribution of tax incentives to the quality of life in an area.

## Government policy in the 1980s and 1990s

Despite the long-held academic consensus on the ineffectiveness of state and local government economic development programs, such programs have proliferated in the 1980s and 1990s. Bartik (1994) summarizes existing state and local government programs, distinguishing among so-called "first-wave" (attraction of branch plants), "second-wave" (providing free government services to new and small businesses), and "third-wave" (providing government services through quasi-market organizations) development policies. Eisinger (1993) argues that states are moving toward "third-wave" policies in order to achieve maximum visible effect with minimal commitment of resources.

There are two possible reasons that these programs have continued to spread despite lukewarm academic endorsement. One is that the government officials anticipated the recent academic findings in support of these policies. The other is that government officials find themselves in a "prisoners' dilemma" with respect to offering incentives, whereby they are offering incentives rather than relying on their own merits because of the threat of other governments luring businesses away. Wassmer (1993) documents this process in the Detroit metropolitan area. Since the prisoners' dilemma results from an inability to make credible commitments, a way of resolving this problem is to have higher-level governments forbid lower-level governments from of-

## TABLE 1

### Summary of Econometric Studies of Tax Effects on Business Location

| Type of Study | Percentage of Studies with at Least One Statistically Significant Negative Tax Effect | Mean Elasticity of Business Activity with Respect to Taxes [Range] | Median Elasticity |
|---|---|---|---|
| Inter-Area Studies | 70% (57 studies) | −0.25 (s.e. = 0.05) [−1.40 to 0.76] (48 studies) | −0.15 |
| Inter-Area Studies with Controls for "Fixed Effects" | 92% (12 studies) | −0.44 (s.e. = 0.11) [−1.02 to 0.00] (11 studies) | −0.35 |
| Inter-Area Studies with Public Service Controls | 80% (30 studies) | −0.33 (s.e. = 0.09) [−1.40 to 0.76] (25 studies) | −0.27 |
| Intra-Area Studies | 57% (14 studies) | −1.48 (s.e. = 0.54) [−4.43 to 0.62] (9 studies) | −1.59 |
| Intra-Area Studies Using Specific Community Data | 70% (10 studies) | −1.91 (s.e. = 0.60) [−4.43 to 0.62] (7 studies) | −1.95 |

*Source:* Adapted from table 2.3 in T. Bartik, *Who Benefits from State and Local Economic Development Policies?* Kalamazoo, Mich.: Upjohn Institute for Employment Research, 1991.

fering incentives. This has not proven politically tractable at either the state or federal level. The inability to make credible commitments not to offer incentives has also undermined attempts at voluntary cooperation among local governments.

## Additional readings

Bartik, Timothy. *Who Benefits from State and Local Economic Development Policies?* Kalamazoo, Mich.: Upjohn Institute for Employment Research, 1991.

Bartik, Timothy. "What Should the Federal Government Be Doing about Urban Economic Development?" Staff Working Paper 94-25. Kalamazoo, Mich.: Upjohn Institute for Employment Research, 1994.

Eisinger, Peter K. "State Economic Development in the 1990s." Working Paper 18. Madison, Wis.: The Robert M. LaFollette Institute of Public Affairs, 1993.

Mark, Stephen, Therese J. McGuire, and Leslie E. Papke. "The Effect of Taxes on Economic Development." In *Taxing Simply, Taxing Fairly*, Final Report of the District of Columbia Tax Revision Commission. Washington, D.C.: District of Columbia Tax Revision Commission at www.dctrc.org, 1998.

Morse, George, and Michael Farmer. "Location and Investment Effects of a Tax Abatement Program." *National Tax Journal* 39 (1993): 229–36.

Newman, Robert J., and Dennis Sullivan. "Econometric Analysis of Business Tax Impacts on Industrial Location: What Do We Know, and How Do We Know It?" *Journal of Urban Economics* 23 (1988): 215–34.

Papke, Leslie. "What Do We Know about Enterprise Zones?" In *Tax Policy and the Economy*, edited by James Poterba. Cambridge, Mass.: MIT Press, 1993.

Wassmer, Robert. "The Use and Abuse of Economic Development Incentives in a Metropolitan Area." *Proceedings of the Eighty-Sixth Annual Conference, National Tax Association* (1993):146–57.

Wasylenko, Michael, and Therese McGuire. "Jobs and Taxes: The Effect of Business Climate on States' Employment Growth Rates." *National Tax Journal* 38 (1985): 497–511.

*Cross references:* commuter taxes; enterprise zones.

# C

# Capital cost recovery

James Mackie
Department of the Treasury

*Income tax features intended to allow businesses to recover the costs associated with the depreciation in value of tangible assets that are used to produce income.*

Income tax regulations generally do not allow a deduction for the cost of a new asset when purchased. Instead, they spread out the deduction over a period roughly consistent with the asset's useful economic lifetime. The amount allowed as an annual deduction reflects (however roughly) the reduction in the value of the capital asset each year. It is called depreciation, or capital cost recovery.

## Depreciation and measurement of economic income

### Depreciation defined

Let's begin with an income tax based on the idealized concept of economic income. Economic income is a measure of the change in a household's real economic well-being that has occurred over some accounting period, typically taken to be a year. It is defined as the household's change in wealth, measured before consumption purchases. Changes, up or down, in the (market) value of its capital assets, including buildings and machines, are part of a household's overall change in wealth and are included in economic income. When assets fall in value from year to year, they are said to depreciate, and this depreciation must be allowed as a deduction when measuring and taxing economic income.

### Depreciation versus current cash outlays or expenses

A distinguishing feature of capital is its durability. A capital asset has value beyond the end of the year in which it is purchased. Consequently, it is inappropriate to deduct the full cost of a new capital asset in the year in which it is purchased because that cost does not represent a change in wealth. In fact, the initial purchase of a capital asset, such as a machine, has no effect on economic income. When a businessman purchases a machine, he simply exchanges one asset, money, for another asset of equal worth, the machine. Rather than the initial purchase price, it is the change in the value of the machine over the year that affects economic income. Because the machine is durable, any fall in value typically will be much less than the full price paid for the machine. The decline in value is likely to continue for many years after the machine is purchased and should reduce income in each of these years.

While the machine's value may rise over the course of a year, there are many reasons to expect that typically a machine's value will fall over time. For one thing, it might physically wear out as it is used to produce output. Alternatively, new and superior types of machines might become available, thereby reducing the market value of this now obsolete machine. However motivated, the fall in the value of the machine—its depreciation—should be allowed as a deduction in computing the businessman's taxable income. Of course, if the machine rises in value, this appreciation should also be taxable.

## Inflation, real changes in asset values, and depreciation

Inflation can lead to changes in asset values that do not reflect changes in economic well-being, and so needs to be accounted for in measuring economic income. For example, suppose that over the course of a year the general price level doubles. Then, if a businessman's assets also double in value, he is no better off, in terms of the real (inflation-adjusted) purchasing power of his assets, than he was at the beginning of the year. Only if the value of his assets more than doubles will he be better off. Consequently, purely nominal growth in asset values should not trigger tax liability; the tax system should adjust—index—for inflation.

In indexing for inflation, one measures values at a consistent price level—for example, in end-of-year prices. If the general price level doubles, then measuring the real change in asset values requires first doubling all beginning-of-year asset values. This implies that depreciation allowances that are appropriate without inflation need to be increased proportionately with the increase in the general price level. Otherwise, depreciation allowances will decline in real value over time, causing overtaxation. The following example illustrates this point.

Suppose that at the beginning of the year, the businessman has an asset worth $100. The asset wears out at a rate of 10 percent per year, and its relative price does not change. If there is no inflation, then at the end of the year the asset is worth $90, so $10 is the proper depreciation allowance.

In contrast, suppose there is 50 percent general price inflation. Then at the end of the year, the asset is worth $135 [$90 × (1 + the inflation rate)]. But the $35 nominal increase in value is due only to inflation in the general level of prices; it does not represent real purchasing power.

Far from rising in value, measured in constant (year-end) prices the asset has declined in value, or depreciated, from $150 [$100 × (1 + the inflation rate)] to $135, or by $15. To account for the 50 percent inflation rate, the depreciation deduction allowed under the tax law must increase from $10 (no inflation) to $15. If the depreciation system were not indexed for inflation, the taxpayer would owe tax on $5 of purely nominal income and so would be overtaxed relative to the standard set by economic income. Proper income measurement requires a 50 percent increase in the depreciation allowance, exactly equal to the increase in the price level.

In the next year, without inflation in either year, the depreciation allowance would be $9 (10% of $90). With a 50 percent inflation rate in both year 1 and year 2, however, the proper depreciation allowance would be $20.25, reflecting the change in the value of the asset, measured in end-of-year-2 prices. Hence, to index the second year's no-inflation depreciation allowance of $9 requires multiplying by a factor of 2.25, which equals (1 + the inflation rate in year 1) × (1 + the inflation rate in year 2) and represents the total increase in the general price level over the two-year period since the asset's original purchase.

## Depreciation in practice

Deviations from the standard provided by measuring and taxing economic income are common in real-world tax systems. These deviations can often be interpreted as attempts to meet other criteria or to compromise between competing objectives.

### Administrative concerns and depreciation as changes in market value

Simplicity and ease of administration are important features of the tax system. Unfortunately, they conflict with a desire to measure and tax economic income. The measurement of depreciation as changes in market values is often one casualty of the conflict between accurate income measurement on the one hand, and simplicity and administrability on the other. Typically, income tax systems provide for depreciation allowances without reference to actual or estimated changes in the market value of the assets. For example, tax systems often allow a constant fraction of an asset's initial purchase price as a depreciation deduction (so-called straight-line depreciation). Although these schedular depreciation deductions are unlikely to match real economic depreciation, schedular deductions are simpler than would be a system based on actual or estimated changes in market values.

### Administrative concerns and indexation for inflation

Another common casualty of the conflict between income measurement and simplicity/administrability is indexation of depreciation allowances (as well as many other components of the tax system) for inflation. Practical proposals to index depreciation for inflation are often criticized as unworkably complex, administratively burdensome, and subject to taxpayer abuse and manipulation. Taxpayer abuse is especially problematic if depreciation is indexed, while other features of the tax code, such as interest income and expense, are not, thereby creating arbitrage opportunities.

### Accelerated depreciation as an investment incentive

Another conflict comes between the desire to tax income, perhaps because of a belief that it represents an equitable tax base, and the desire to encourage efficient amounts of saving and investing. Since saving/investing is done out of after-tax income, and then the return earned on the amounts saved and invested is also taxed, an income tax overtaxes future consumption relative to current consumption. Although not strictly accurate, it is common to refer to this problem as one of overtaxing, hence discouraging saving and investment.

One way to reduce the effective tax burden on investment income is to offer so-called accelerated depreciation allowances. Depreciation allowances that are pushed forward in time, relative to those that "ought" to be allowed (e.g., based on changes in the economic value of assets over time), are referred to as accelerated depreciation allowances. The extreme example of accelerated depreciation is immediate "expensing" of capital outlays, under which the full cost of an investment is deducted in the year it is purchased. Accelerated depreciation can be rationalized as a compromise between the goals of measuring and taxing economic income on the one hand, and providing an "adequate" incentive to save and invest on the other.

Accelerated depreciation allowances are more valuable to taxpayers because they receive the cash flow from depreciation earlier in the investment's life. Because of the time value of money, an earlier deduction is worth more to the taxpayer than one or a series of deductions occurring later in time. The earlier deduction is said to have a larger present value. One of the important components in the cost of capital is the present value of the cash flow from depreciation. By increasing this present value, accelerated depreciation reduces the cost of capital and the associated effective tax rate and so provides an investment incentive.

The benefit from accelerated depreciation can also be understood by analogy to an interest-free loan. In the early years of an asset's life, accelerated depreciation gives the taxpayer larger depreciation allowances than those implied by, say, economic income accounting. During each of these early years, the government in effect loans the taxpayer an amount equal to the difference between the tax reduction based on accelerated depreciation and that implied by economic depreciation. But in later years, this pattern reverses as allowed depreciation deductions eventually fall below economic depreciation. During the latter years, the taxpayer repays the loan, but without interest. Accelerated depreciation thus provides the taxpayer with an interest-free source of investment funds.

### Depreciation in relation to tax neutrality

While accelerated depreciation might help reduce distortions in the consume/save choice, it can create distortions in the allocation of investment funds across projects. Accelerated depreciation is almost certain to give some assets lower effective tax rates than others and so violate the tax neutrality standard.

Neutrality, the uniform taxation of all investments, is a commonly accepted tax policy goal. It is rooted in a concept of economic efficiency that defines an allocation of investment as efficient if it is impossible to increase output by shifting funds from one investment project to another. Efficiency thus requires that all investments have the same pretax returns, which means they must also have the same effective tax rate. A tax based strictly on economic income meets the neutrality criterion—it imposes an effective tax rate equal to the statutory tax rate on all investments.

Starting from a system that measures and taxes economic income, a shift to accelerated depreciation is almost certain to violate tax neutrality. For one thing, accelerated depreciation is likely to offer a tax reduction only for so-called depreciable assets (e.g., machinery, buildings). Other assets (e.g., inventories and land) typically are not depreciated and so will not receive a tax reduction. For another, if past practice is any indication, only some depreciable assets will qualify for accelerated depreciation, and even among those that do qualify, the degree of acceleration probably will vary from asset to asset. Assets that do not qualify for accelerated depreciation, or that qualify only for limited acceleration, will have a higher effective tax cost than do assets that fully qualify, thereby violating the neutrality standard.

### Accelerated depreciation in lieu of indexing depreciation for inflation

As discussed, inflation can overtax investment income when depreciation is not indexed. This overtaxation can be reduced by offering accelerated depreciation allowances. Thus, accelerated depreciation can be justified as a simple way to index implicitly for inflation. The indexation provided by accelerated depreciation is rather crude, however, as it is unlikely to be set properly for every asset at any one inflation rate, nor to be adjusted continuously to follow changes in the inflation rate over time.

### Additional readings

Feldstein, Martin. "The Welfare Cost of Capital Income Taxation." *Journal of Political Economy* (April 1978).

Gravelle, Jane G. "The Capital Cost Recovery System and the Corporate Income Tax." Report No. 79-230. Washington, D.C.: Congressional Research Service, 1979.

Hulten, Charles R., and Frank C. Wykoff. "The Measurement of Economic Depreciation." In *Depreciation, Inflation and the Taxation of Income from Capital*, edited by C.R. Hulten. Washington, D.C.: The Urban Institute Press, 1981.

Rosen, Harvey S. "The Personal Income Tax." In *Public Finance*, 3rd ed., ch. 16. Boston: Richard D. Irwin, 1992.

U.S. Department of the Treasury. "What Is to Be the Tax Base?" and "A Model Comprehensive Income Tax." In *Blueprints for Basic Tax Reform*, ch. 2 and 3. Washington, D.C.: U.S. Government Printing Office, 1977.

*Cross references:* cost of capital; income tax, corporate, federal; income tax, federal; marginal effective tax rate; taxable income, corporate.

# Capital export neutrality

Peggy B. Musgrave
University of California, Santa Cruz

*A term introduced and developed in the 1960s to describe a situation in which the overall burden of taxation on capital owned by resident entities of a given country is the same whether that capital is invested abroad or at home.*

In tax terms, the same proportionate tax wedge exists between the before- and after-tax rates of return wherever the capital is invested. Thus the tax system neither encourages nor discourages capital export, and the investor's choice of investing in the domestic economy or in foreign economies will not be influenced by tax considerations. Capital export neutrality is thus to be distinguished from capital import neutrality, which requires equal tax treatment for all capital invested within a given country, regardless of the nationality of its ownership (see "Capital import neutrality" entry).

The economic significance of capital export neutrality is the international efficiency in resource allocation that it promotes. In the absence of tax inducements or barriers to international capital flows, capital will tend to be invested where returns are the highest, rather than where there are tax advantages to be had. Since maximization of world output and income requires that investment be located where it is the most productive, capital export neutrality is consistent with the world production efficiency criterion (Rosen 1991: 362–63).

Capital export neutrality requires that investments made at home and abroad be taxed at the same effective rate of tax, allowing for differences in tax-based definition as well as in statutory rates. This is not readily achieved because the total tax burden on foreign investment income may involve taxation in both the host country (where the income is earned) and the home country (where the investing corporation is "resident"). If the residence (capital-exporting) country confers a tax exemption for investment income earned abroad, only the source (capital-importing) country's tax applies. Unless the rates of tax in the two countries are equal, capital export neutrality will not prevail, with the tax differentials resulting in either a tax penalty or a tax incentive for investing abroad. On the other hand, imposition of the residence tax on top of the source tax results in a strong tax impediment to investment abroad. The residence country may neutralize this penalty by permitting a full credit for the foreign tax against its own tax liability, with a refund if the former exceeds the latter. Thus, given the source country's primary entitlement to tax, the country of residence has the capability of achieving capital export neutrality by taxing global income accompanied by the neutralizing mechanism of the foreign tax credit.

Following this principle, the United States, along with several other industrialized countries, applies its federal corporation tax to the global (domestic and foreign) income of resident corporations with a credit for foreign tax so as to secure capital export neutrality. Since application of residence taxation with a tax credit for taxes paid to outside jurisdictions presents administrative and compliance problems within a closely interdependent market, the member states of the United States apply source taxation only. Consequent nonneutralities resulting from rate differentials for capital flows among them thus remain, though at lower rates. This problem also applies to the highly integrated European Common Market, which is seeking some degree of capital export neutrality through source taxation imposed at rates within maximum and minimum limits.

While global, residence-based taxation with a foreign tax credit offers an important means to capital export neutrality, it may fall short of a complete solution:

1. In theory, the concept should be extended to require equalization of net fiscal burdens, allowing for those government expenditure benefits that reduce the costs of production and raise the rate of return to capital. Since it is generally assumed that such expenditure benefits are not closely related to the level of corporate income tax, the concept of capital export neutrality is usually applied to taxes in isolation.

2. Because the tax burden on capital income involves both corporate and individual income taxes, both should be allowed for in a fully neutral treatment. But to do so becomes highly complex if corporate and individual income taxes are subject to varying degrees of integration from country to country (Sato and Bird 1975). However, since most decisions to invest abroad are made at the corporate level, it has been customary to examine the conditions for capital export neutrality as they apply to the corporate income tax alone.

3. The requirement that effective rates be equalized for investments made at home and abroad rests on the usual assumptions that the burden of the corporate tax falls on corporate profits. If shifting occurs, the conditions for capital export neutrality have to be adjusted accordingly (P. Musgrave 1969: 111–115).

4. Capital export neutrality obtained through global residence taxation calls for foreign profits of domestic corporations to be taxed concurrently, whether earned in a foreign incorporated subsidiary or in a foreign branch. To avoid taxing foreign incorporated subsidiaries directly, the United States defers its tax on profits of the foreign incorporated subsidiary until distributed as dividends, a practice that is inconsistent with capital export neutrality.

### Additional readings

Musgrave, Peggy B. *United States Taxation of Foreign Investment Income: Issues and Arguments*. Cambridge,

Mass.: International Tax Program, Harvard Law School, 1969.

Musgrave, Richard A. "Criteria for Foreign Tax Credit." In *Taxation and Operations Abroad*. Princeton: Tax Institute Symposium, 1960.

Richman (Musgrave), Peggy B. *Taxation of Foreign Investment Income: An Economic Analysis*. Baltimore: Johns Hopkins Press, 1963.

Rosen, Harvey S. *Public Finance*. 3rd ed. Boston: Irwin, 1991.

Sato, Mitsuo, and Richard M. Bird. "International Aspects of the Taxation of Corporations and Shareholders." Washington, D.C.: International Monetary Fund, *Staff Papers*, July 22, 1975.

*Cross references:* capital import neutrality; national neutrality.

# Capital gains taxation

Gerald Auten
Department of the Treasury

*Treatment of the changes in value of capital assets such as corporate stock, real estate, or a business interest.*

Under a pure net accretion (Haig-Simons) approach to income taxes, real capital gains would be taxed each year as they accrued and real capital losses would be deducted. Capital gains are generally taxed only when "realized" by sale or exchange, however, because it would be difficult to estimate the value of many assets, it would be viewed as unfair to tax income that had not been realized, and it could force the liquidation of assets to pay the tax on accruals. Taxation upon realization, however, leads to other problems, which require policy compromises.

## Current law

Since 1987, realized capital gains have been fully included in adjusted gross income. Beginning with assets sold on or after May 7, 1997, long-term capital gains on assets held at least 18 months will be taxed under a separate rate schedule. Long-term gains in the 15 percent tax bracket will be taxed at a 10 percent rate, and those in higher tax brackets will be taxed at 20 percent. Gains on assets held from 12 to 18 months will be taxed at ordinary tax rates but will be eligible for an alternative rate of 28 percent (as under prior law). Beginning in 2001, capital gains in the 15 percent bracket on assets held at least

five years will be taxed at 8 percent. Capital gains in the 28 percent and higher brackets on assets purchased in 2001 or later and held for at least five years will be taxed at 18 percent. Depreciation on real estate is "recaptured" subject to a maximum rate of 25 percent.

Capital losses can be used to offset capital gains, and a maximum $3,000 of capital losses can be used to offset other taxable income. Unused capital losses can be carried forward to future years. The limit on the capital loss deduction is necessary to prevent taxpayers from recognizing capital losses but not capital gains.

The Taxpayer Relief Act of 1997 also substantially changed the taxation of capital gains on principal residences. The one-time exclusion of up to $125,000 of capital gains on residences for taxpayers age 55 and over, and the rollover of capital gains from one residence to another, were replaced with an exclusion of up to $500,000 ($250,000 for nonjoint returns). The new exclusion can be claimed whenever the taxpayer meets the eligibility requirement of owning and occupying the residence for at least two of the previous five years and using the exclusion only once in a two-year period. Prior law had been criticized as being complex, distorting certain housing decisions, and generating little tax revenue.

When appreciated assets are transferred by bequest, the basis is stepped up to the value of the assets on the date of death. Thus, the accrued gains on assets held at death are not taxed under the income tax, although they may be subject to the estate tax.

A 50 percent exclusion for capital gains from the sale of certain small business stocks purchased at the time of issue and held for at least five years was introduced in 1993. Eligible businesses must have less than $50 million in assets (including the proceeds of the stock issue) and meet certain other requirements. The 1997 act allowed a rollover provision for such gains and provided for a maximum rate of 14 percent.

## History of capital gains taxation in the United States

From 1913 to 1921, capital gains were taxed at ordinary rates, initially up to a top rate of 7 percent. Because of concern that the higher income tax rates introduced during World War I reduced capital gains tax revenues, from 1922 to 1934 taxpayers were allowed an alternative tax rate of 12.5 percent on capital gains on assets held at least two years. From 1934 to 1941, taxpayers could exclude percentages of gains that varied with the holding period. For example, in 1934 and 1935, 20, 40, 60, and 70 percent of gains were excluded on assets held 1, 2, 5, and 10 years, respectively. Beginning in 1942, taxpayers could exclude 50 percent of capital gains on assets held at least six months or elect a 25 percent alternative tax rate if their ordinary tax rate exceeded 50 percent. Capital gains tax rates were increased significantly in the 1969 and 1976 Tax Reform Acts. The 1969 act imposed a 10 percent minimum tax, excluded gains, and limited the alternative tax to $50,000 of gains. The 1976 act further increased capital gains tax rates by increasing the minimum tax rate to 15 percent. In 1977 and 1978, the maximum tax rate on capital gains reached 39.875 percent with the minimum tax and 49.875 percent including an interaction with the maximum tax. In 1978, Congress reduced capital gains tax rates by eliminating the minimum tax on excluded gains and increasing the exclusion to 60 percent, thereby reducing the maximum rate to 28 percent. The 1981 tax rate reductions further reduced capital gains rates to a maximum of 20 percent.

The Tax Reform Act of 1986 repealed the exclusion of long-term gains, raising the maximum rate to 28 percent (33 percent for taxpayers subject to certain phaseouts). When the top ordinary tax rates were increased by the 1990 and 1993 budget acts, an alternative tax rate of 28 percent was provided. Effective tax rates exceeded 28 percent for many high-income taxpayers, however, because of interactions with other tax provisions. The new lower rates for 18-month and five-year assets were adopted in 1997. Nominal and effective tax rates for the period 1984–1995 are shown in table 1.

## Economic issues in capital gains taxation

### Inflation

Taxing nominal gains raises the effective tax rate on real capital gains and can lead to imposition of a tax in cases of real economic losses. Several studies have shown that a large percentage of reported capital gains reflect the effects of inflation, with the capital gains of lower- and middle-income taxpayers commonly representing nominal gains but real economic losses. The indexing of the cost or basis of an asset has frequently been proposed to correct for inflation.

### Deferral

From the standpoint of economic accretion, the deferral of capital gains taxes until realization reduces the present value of the tax, thereby reducing the effective tax rate below the statutory tax rate. (The combination of deferral and inflation can produce effective tax rates much higher or lower than the statutory tax rates.)

### Lock-in effects

Because capital gains are taxed only when realized, high capital gains tax rates discourage the realization of capital gains and encourage the realization of capital losses. Investors induced to hold appreciated assets because of capital gains tax when they would otherwise sell are said to be "locked in." Lock-in effects impose efficiency losses when investors are induced to hold suboptimal portfolios with inappropriate risk or diversification, or forgo investment opportunities that may offer higher expected pretax returns. Investors with appreciated property may also incur unnecessary transaction costs to avoid capital gains taxes if they obtain cash from their investment by using it as security for a loan, or reduce their risk by selling short an equivalent asset (short against the box). The financial incentive to be locked in is greater for long-held, highly

## TABLE 1

### Realized Capital Gains and Taxes Paid on Capital Gains, 1984–95

| Year | Total Positive Realized Capital Gains ($ billion) | Taxes Paid on Capital Gains ($ billion) | Effective Tax Rate on Capital Gains (%) | Gains as Percent of Gross Domestic Product (%) | Maximum Tax Rate on Long-Term Gains (%) |
|------|------|------|------|------|------|
| 1984 | 140.5 | 21.5 | 15.3 | 3.7 | 20.0 |
| 1985 | 172.0 | 26.5 | 15.4 | 4.3 | 20.0 |
| 1986 | 327.7 | 52.9 | 16.1 | 7.7 | 20.0 |
| 1987 | 148.4 | 33.7 | 22.7 | 3.3 | 28.0 |
| 1988 | 162.6 | 38.9 | 23.9 | 3.3 | 28.0 |
| 1989 | 154.0 | 35.3 | 22.9 | 2.9 | 28.0 |
| 1990 | 123.8 | 27.8 | 22.5 | 2.2 | 28.0 |
| 1991 | 111.6 | 24.9 | 22.3 | 2.0 | 28.9 |
| 1992 | 126.7 | 29.0 | 22.9 | 2.1 | 28.9 |
| 1993 | 152.3 | 36.1 | 23.7 | 2.4 | 29.2 |
| 1994 | 152.7 | 36.2 | 23.7 | 2.2 | 29.2 |
| 1995 | 180.1 | 44.3 | 24.6 | 2.5 | 29.2 |

*Notes:* Realized gains include positive amounts of both short- and long-term capital gains. The maximum rate includes the effects of the 3 percent phaseout of itemized deductions for high-income taxpayers (computed for 1994 as $29.188 = 28 + 0.03 \cdot 39.6$). Taxpayers in the income range over which personal exemptions are phased out or subject to certain other phaseout provisions could pay higher effective tax rates. In 1988 through 1990, taxpayers in the so-called "bubble" tax bracket paid a 33 percent tax rate on capital gains.
*Source:* U.S. Treasury Department, Office of Tax Analysis.

appreciated assets and is increased by the step-up in basis at death.

### Behavioral responses and revenues

Behavioral responses associated with capital gains tax rates are complex. In the absence of tax law changes, transitory fluctuations in income and tax rates may induce taxpayers to accelerate or defer realizations of gains. Similarly, taxpayers time realizations to take advantage of differential tax rates on short- and long-term gains. Statutory changes in tax rates are likely to result in short-run and long-run responses. Taxpayers may initially react to a cut in the capital gains tax rate by unlocking significant amounts of accumulated capital gains (such as the 49% increase in long-term gains after the 1978 capital gains tax reduction). The long-run response, which is generally thought to be smaller, would include higher realizations from more rapid turnover, from sales of more long-held assets, and from sales of assets that would otherwise be held for life or given to charity. Responses to increased tax rates are not necessarily symmetric as there is little inducement for a large short-run response, and taxpayers may gradually reduce realizations as they adjust portfolios and learn avoidance methods in response to the higher tax rates (such as seemed to occur after rate increases in the 1970s and after the 1986 Tax Reform Act).

Empirical studies have provided widely ranging estimates of the responsiveness of capital gains because of the apparent sensitivity to the implicit assumptions inherent in the data and methodologies used. Using a cross-section sample of 1973 tax returns in a study that may have influenced the 1978 capital gains tax cut, Feldstein et al. (1980) estimated an elasticity of realizations of corporate stock gains for wealthy taxpayers with respect to tax rates of about $-3.8$ and concluded that reducing rates from 1970s levels would increase tax revenues. Auten and Clotfelter (1982) used panel data to separate the response into short-run and long-run components; they estimated short-run elasticities generally larger than $-1.0$ and long-run elasticities generally averaging about $-0.5$ (0.8 at a 20% tax rate), implying that rate reductions might lead to increased revenues in the short run but lower revenues in the long run. A recent micro-data study by Burman and Randolph (1994) found a large transitory response ($-6.4$) and a small permanent response ($-0.2$) based on the variation in state capital gains tax rates. Time series studies generally find elasticities between $-0.5$ and $-0.9$, implying that the realizations responses offset a large part but not all of the effects of tax rate changes.

The question of whether the short- and long-run responses to lower capital gains rates are large enough to offset the lower rate has been debated for over 70 years and is likely to remain controversial.

### Savings and investment effects

Capital gains tax rates may affect the savings rate through the after-tax rate of return, but this effect is generally believed to be small. Capital gains tax rates may affect the quantity of investment through the cost of capital, and the allocation of investment through effects on the relative returns to risk-taking. Preferential tax rates for capital gains may increase the proportion of higher-risk investment such as in startup or venture capital businesses.

By reducing the expected variance of after-tax returns, a flat-rate income tax with full deduction of losses would increase risky investment. However, the current income tax system may discourage risky investment because of progressive tax rates and limits on the deduction of losses.

### Income conversion

Preferential tax rates for capital gains induce taxpayers to attempt to convert ordinary income into capital gains taxed at a lower rate. Executive compensation may be shifted from salaries to stock options. Many tax shelters before the 1986 act were based on investments that permitted operating losses created by the deduction of expenses at ordinary tax rates and the deferred taxation of capital gains at a preferential rate.

### Distribution of tax burden

The income distribution effects of lowering or raising capital gains tax rates has been an important issue affecting debates about capital gains rate changes. Capital gains are more highly concentrated among high-income households than other forms of income, and therefore it is argued that capital gains rate cuts would be regressive.

### Equity and efficiency

Tax equity implies that capital gains income should be taxed at the same rates as other income. However, if the responsiveness to tax rates is greater for capital gains than for other forms of income, the excess burden of the income tax would be reduced by providing a lower rate for capital gains than for other income.

## Additional readings

Auten, Gerald, and Charles Clotfelter. "Permanent vs. Transitory Effects and the Realization of Capital Gains." *Quarterly Journal of Economics* 97 (November 1982): 613–32.

Auten, Gerald, and Joseph Cordes. "Cutting Capital Gains Taxes." *Journal of Economic Perspectives* 5 (Spring 1991): 181–92.

Burman, Leonard, and William Randolph. "Measuring Permanent Reponses to Capital-Gains Tax Changes in Panel Data." *American Economic Review* 84 (4) (September 1994): 794–809.

Congressional Budget Office. *How Capital Gains Tax Rates Affect Revenues: The Historical Evidence.* Washington, D.C., March 1988.

Congressional Budget Office. *Perspectives on the Ownership of Capital Assets and the Realization of Capital Gains.* Washington, D.C., 1997.

Feldstein, Martin, Joel Slemrod, and Shlomo Yitzhaki. "The Effects of Taxation on the Selling of Corporate Stock and the Realization of Capital Gains." *Quarterly Journal of Economics* 94 (June 1980): 777–91.

Gravelle, Jane G. *The Economic Effects of Taxing Capital Income.* Ch. 6. Cambridge, Mass., and London: MIT Press, 1994.

U.S. Congress, Joint Committee on Taxation. *Proposals and Issues Relating to the Taxation of Capital Gains and Losses (JCS–10–90),* March 23, 1990.

U.S. Treasury Department, Office of Tax Analysis. *Report to Congress on the Capital Gains Tax Reductions of 1978.* Washington, D.C.: U.S. Government Printing Office, 1985.

Zodrow, George. "Economic Analyses of Capital Gains Taxation: Realizations, Revenues, Efficiency and Equity." *Tax Law Review* 48 (3) (1993): 419–527.

*Cross references:* elasticity, demand and supply; income tax, corporate, federal; income tax, federal; portfolio choice.

# Capital import neutrality

Peggy B. Musgrave
University of California, Santa Cruz

*A situation in which the same effective tax rate applies to all capital income earned within a given country, regardless of the investor's country of residence.*

Capital import neutrality, to take an example, would mean that capital income earned on investments in France would be taxed at the same rate regardless of whether the investments were made by U.S., German, or French residents (R. Musgrave 1960; P. Musgrave 1969: 119–20). Capital import neutrality is met when an international tax system is based on the source principle. Thus, in the example given above, only France, the country of source, would be entitled to tax capital income arising in France. Countries of residence would in effect provide tax exemption for foreign-source income. This contrasts with "capital export neutrality," in which capital income accruing to investors residing in a given country is taxed at the same rate wherever that income is earned, whether at home or abroad. This is accomplished by having the country of residence permit foreign tax to be credited against its own tax (see "Capital export neutrality" entry).

Unfortunately, it is difficult to meet both standards at the same time. Only if effective tax rates were the same in all countries could capital import and export neutrality be met simultaneously. But tax rates differ, the two criteria are in conflict, and tax policy with respect to foreign investment has to choose between the two.

Opinions differ as to which of these two neutrality concepts should be given priority. The case for capital export neutrality rests on the proposition that, in order to secure worldwide efficiency in capital allocation, the choice of location should not be affected by tax considerations. This is accomplished under a system of residency taxation combined with foreign tax credit. In contrast, source taxation and capital import neutrality attract capital to low-tax countries and thus distort international capital allocation. That distortion will be larger the greater the tax differentials, including, in particular, the presence of tax havens. Even though U.S. investors in France would pay the same tax rate as U.K. investors in France, they would each have to pay different taxes depending on whether they invest at home or abroad. Only if all tax rates were the same would this not be the case.

Proponents of capital import neutrality hold that firms, when competing in foreign markets, should not be handicapped (as they would be under capital export neutrality) because their residence lies in a higher-tax country (Vogel 1988). This competitive disadvantage is debatable (Shoup 1974: 36–38), but the question is whether it should be viewed as causing inefficient allocation. Different rates of corporate tax among countries reflect differences in domestic tax policy that may give rise to differing rates of capital formation. Once taken, be it wise or unwise, that policy choice should bear equally on the level of both domestic and foreign investment. There would seem to be no reason to counteract the overall effect by favoring foreign versus domestic investment. It should also be noted that capital import neutrality may be met at the expense of horizontal equity in taxation, which requires that all those entities residing in a given country be subject to the same tax treatment by that country.

While economists mostly support the superior efficiency case for export neutrality, this occurs at a cost. A source-based system is much simpler to administer and comply with than a residence-based system, particularly if combined with the foreign tax credit. The choice of economic efficiency is thus bought at the cost of additional administrative complexity. This may well be why many countries apply a "territorial" or source-based tax system, a system that leaves capital flows open to tax rate differentials. However, this is a defect that may be remedied by rate equalization, although this is at the cost of some loss of independence in tax policy. In concluding, it is noted that the case for capital import neutrality in taxation may be strengthened if allowance is made for the offsetting effects of public expenditure benefits, in which case source taxation and capital import neutrality may cause less interference with capital export neutrality (Gandenberger 1983).

### Additional readings

Gandenberger, Otto. "Kapitalexportneutralitat versus Kapitalimportneutralitat." *Aufsatze zur Wirtschaftspolitik*. Forschungsinstitut für Wirtschaftspolitik an der Universitat Mainz, 1983.

Musgrave, Peggy B. *United States Taxation of Foreign Investment Income: Issues and Arguments*. Cambridge, Mass.: International Tax Program, Harvard Law School, 1969.

Musgrave, Richard A. "Criteria for Foreign Tax Credit." In *Taxation and Operations Abroad*. Tax Institute Symposium, 1960.

Shoup, Carl S. "Taxation of Multinational Corporations." In *The Impact of Multinational Corporations on Development and International Relations*. Technical Papers: Taxation. New York: United Nations, 1974.

Vogel, Klaus. "The Search for Compatible Tax Systems." In *Tax Policy in the Twenty-First Century*. New York: John Wiley, 1988.

*Cross references:* capital export neutrality; national neutrality.

# Charitable deductions

William C. Randolph
Department of the Treasury

*Preferential tax treatment of expenditures or gifts to organizations that the law qualifies as having a socially beneficial characteristic and for which the donor is not motivated by direct benefit when making the contribution.*

Since 1917, individual federal taxpayers have been allowed to deduct gifts to charitable and certain other nonprofit organizations. Such organizations (hereafter called "charitable") were already exempt from the income tax. A charitable deduction extended the benefits of exemption to individual taxpayers, so that income donated to charitable organizations was exempted from all levels of income taxation.

The deduction was intended to subsidize the activities of private organizations that provide viable alternatives to direct government programs. The 1917 law increased tax rates, and the deduction was introduced to alleviate congressional concern that the higher tax rates would discourage private charity (Wallace and Fisher 1977). To control the revenue loss, total charitable deductions were limited to 15 percent of taxable income. Corporations were first allowed a deduction in 1935.

Under the current federal income tax, individuals who itemize deductions can deduct contributions to certain organizations operated for religious, charitable, scientific, literary, or educational purposes. The list also includes domestic government entities, fraternal societies, organizations that prevent cruelty to children or animals, and several other types of socially beneficial organizations. Organizations must be operated in a nonprofit form and are subject to other restrictions.

Types of deductible contributions include cash, financial assets, and other noncash property such as real estate, clothing, and art work. In general, the law limits gifts of cash or other non–capital gains assets to no more than 50 percent of the (slightly modified) adjusted gross income. Contributions of capital gains property are generally limited to 30 percent of adjusted gross income. Both individuals and corporations can carry forward contributions that exceed the limits and use them as deductions in later years. Samansky (1993) provides a comprehensive discussion of current law.

A donation of appreciated capital gains property can be deducted at its full current market value. The capital gains portion is, in effect, deducted twice. It is implicitly deducted once against itself because the capital gains will never be taxed. It is also explicitly part of the itemized deduction, so that other income is shielded from taxation.

In 1991, individual deductions totaled $60.6 billion and corporate deductions totaled $4.8 billion. For fiscal 1995, the Joint Committee on Taxation estimates the tax expenditure at $17.3 billion for deductions by individuals and $1.2 billion for deductions by corporations.

The deduction subsidizes giving by lowering the price that people must pay privately to support charitable organizations. A charitable contribution of one dollar that is deducted from taxable income lowers the donor's tax bill and thus decreases the resources available for the donor's other consumption, the price, by less than a dollar. For example, if a donor's marginal tax rate is 30 percent, a deductible one-dollar cash gift to charity will reduce the donor's taxes by 30 cents, so the price of the gift to the donor will only be 70 cents.

This price reduction affects giving in two ways, which economists refer to as income and substitution effects. The income effect results because the reduced price effectively makes more income available for all consumption. If people normally give more as income rises, the income effect of the price reduction will induce people to increase giving. The substitution effect arises because the reduced price makes giving cheaper relative to other commodities, which will induce people to give more. Empirical studies indicate that both the income and substitution effects cause people to increase charitable giving (Clotfelter 1985).

Many policy justifications have been offered for the charitable deduction. Some argue that an ideal income tax should not treat gifts to charity as part of an individual's income (Andrews 1972). Under this view, an income tax should reallocate resources that would have been used for private consumption and use them for public consumption. Because charitable giving is not used for the giver's private consumption, it would not be fair to include it in the tax base.

Some argue that private charitable activity is superior to direct government activity (Belknap 1977). For example, private social and religious organizations provide some services that substitute for government programs, such as providing food or shelter for the poor. The tax deduction and tax exemption subsidize those organizations while avoiding the direct participation of government, which might be more intrusive and also risk violating the constitutional principle of separation of church and state. A similar argument can be made for encouraging donations to private educational institutions. Not only might the tax deduction be less intrusive than direct government spending, but private institutions sometimes approach education differently from public institutions. Competing approaches can encourage pluralism and increase innovation.

Another justification for the deduction and the exemption is that private charitable organizations may provide social goods more efficiently than the government. Because taxes are mandatory and the burden of taxation and governance is spread among many people, individuals can have little incentive to increase government efficiency. In the private nonprofit sector, however, competition among organizations for donations creates an incentive for the organizations to operate efficiently.

Popular policy justifications can often be reduced to descriptions of the many socially desirable activities of charitable organizations. To an extent, this justification is simply an individual expression of taste for more of a good thing. It is natural for such people to argue for a subsidy that encourages others, whose tastes may differ, to give more.

Even if tastes did not differ, however, some charitable activities would be supplied inadequately if there were no subsidy. This is because the activities may create additional social benefits, external to those experienced by a donor. A person who donates money to help the poor, for example, receives private satisfaction from the act of generosity, but other people, aside from the poor, also benefit from a reduction in poverty. The donor does not account for this external benefit, however, but decides how much to give by comparing the private cost of a contribution with the private satisfaction received. Consideration of the additional external benefits would warrant a larger donation. All potential donors could be made better off as a group if they were either compelled through taxes or encouraged by subsidy to give more.

Examples of subsidized activities with external benefits abound. Education and religion can improve moral conduct, decrease crime, and increase civic responsibility. Education can decrease poverty. Education and scientific research increase general knowledge and speed the rate of technological progress, which can improve the standard of living. In each case, benefits extend to people beyond those who provide voluntary financial support or benefit directly from the activities.

Economic efficiency of the tax subsidy provided by the charitable deduction can be evaluated by comparing costs with benefits. The cost of a deductible charitable contribution is shared with other taxpayers. The after-tax cost is borne privately by the donor, but the amount by which the deduction reduces taxes is an additional social cost shared with other taxpayers. Cost-sharing occurs, whether it means that taxes must be increased or government spending decreased to make up for the tax revenue forgone as a result of the deduction.

The amount of external benefit provided by the subsidy increases with the satisfaction that other potential donors experience if the subsidy increases giving, measured by the extent by which the amount of charity would have been inadequate without a subsidy, and the degree to which the subsidy actually does increase giving. External benefits can be difficult to measure and probably vary greatly among subsidized activities. For example, people probably benefit by different amounts from poverty reduction and scientific innovation. Further, many subsidized organizations provide a mix of public services that have external social benefits with social goods that could be provided adequately to organization members through the use of membership fees. A subsidized increase in such services would provide no external benefits. Finally, even if a charitable activity has external benefits, the tax subsidy only increases the external benefits to the extent that it increases giving.

Substantial empirical research suggests that the subsidy does increase giving (Clotfelter 1985), although the estimated size of the effect is not very robust in more recent evidence (Steinberg 1990). Some published evidence suggests that the subsidy increases certain types of charitable giving more than others. For example, Schiff (1990) found that giving to support elementary education is more sensitive to the subsidy than giving to health and medical charities. This evidence suggests that the most efficient policy might subsidize different types of charity at different rates. Randolph (1995) suggests that studies have generally overstated the degree to which the subsidy increases giving, which weakens, somewhat, its economic policy justification.

Economists often argue that a deduction is not the best device for providing a subsidy. An efficient subsidy would vary with the amount of external benefits, whereas the tax subsidy rate provided by a charitable deduction varies only with the giver's tax rate. A deduction thus provides larger subsidies to charitable organizations favored by higher-income taxpayers, because they face higher marginal tax rates. The deduction also currently provides no subsidy for gifts by people who do not itemize deductions. Some argue that a tax credit would be a fairer and more efficient form of subsidy because the subsidy rate would not depend as much on the giver's level of income (Hochman and Rodgers 1977).

### Additional readings

Andrews, William D. "Personal Deductions and the Ideal Income Tax." *Harvard Law Review* 86 (December 1972): 309–85.

Belknap, Chauncey. "The Federal Income Tax Exemption of Charitable Organizations: Its History and Underlying Policy." In *Research Papers Sponsored by the Commission on Private Philanthropy and Public Needs*. Vol. IV. U.S. Department of the Treasury (1977): 2025–43.

Clotfelter, Charles T. *Federal Tax Policy and Charitable Giving*. Chicago: University of Chicago Press (for National Bureau of Economic Research), 1985.

Hochman, Harold M., and James D. Rodgers. "The Optimal Tax Treatment of Charitable Contributions." *National Tax Journal* 30 (1) (March 1977): 1–18.

Randolph, William C. "Dynamic Income, Progressive Taxes, and the Timing of Charitable Contributions." *Journal of Political Economy* 103 (4) (August 1995): 709–38.

Samansky, Allan J. *Charitable Contributions and Federal Taxes*. Charlottesville, Va.: The Michie Company, 1993.

Schiff, Jerald. *Charitable Giving and Government Policy: An Economic Analysis*. New York: Greenwood Press, 1990.

Steinberg, Richard. "Taxes and Giving: New Findings." *Voluntas* 1 (2) (November 1990): 61–79.

Wallace, John A., and Robert W. Fisher. "The Charitable Deduction under Section 170 of the Internal Revenue Code." In *Research Papers Sponsored by the Commission on Private Philanthropy and Public Needs*. Vol. IV. U.S. Department of the Treasury (1977): 2131–61.

*Cross references:* adjusted gross income; itemized deductions; Joint Committee on Taxation, U.S. Congress; nonprofit organizations, federal tax treatment.

# Child care expenses: the child care credit

Amy E. Dunbar
University of Iowa

*A nonrefundable credit based on employment-related expenses of household-type services for the care of children.*

The Internal Revenue Code provides tax benefits in the form of a credit or exclusion for child care expenses incurred by taxpayers deemed to be gainfully employed. The credit was enacted in the Tax Reform Act of 1976 by repealing Section 214, which allowed an itemized deduction for child care expenses, and replacing it with Section 44A (redesignated as Section 21 by the Tax Reform Act of 1984). The Section 129 dependent care exclusion for assistance from employers was enacted by the Economic Recovery Tax Act of 1981 and subjected to a $5,000 cap by the Tax Reform Act of 1986.

Both the credit and the exclusion are subject to earned income ceilings that limit the qualified child care expenses in any taxable year to an amount not in excess of the earned income of the employee or, if the employee is married, the lower of the employee's earned income or the earned income of his or her spouse. Thus, these benefits generally are not available to one-earner couples. (Spouses who are full-time students or incapable of caring for themselves are deemed to earn $200 per month for one dependent or spouse being cared for, or $400 per month for more than one.)

From 1976 to 1981, a credit of 20 percent of qualified child care expenses was allowed, with a maximum credit of $400 for each of the taxpayer's first two dependents. The 20 percent credit was the same for all taxpayers. In an effort to make the credit more progressive, Congress enacted a sliding scale credit in 1982, which is 30 percent of qualified expenses for taxpayers with incomes of $10,000 or less. The credit is reduced by 1 percent for each $2,000 or fraction thereof of income above $10,000. For taxpayers with adjusted gross income (AGI) above $28,000, the credit rate is 20 percent. The maximum credit for a taxable year ranges from $720 for a taxpayer whose AGI is $10,000 or less to $480 for a taxpayer whose AGI exceeds $28,000. When there is more than one dependent, the maximum credit ranges from $1,449 to $960. Effective in 1989, the Family Support Act of 1988 reduced dollar-for-dollar the amount of expenses eligible for the credit by the amount of expenses excludable from income under Section 129.

## Focus of research

This entry focuses on the child care credit, examining its impact on the progressivity of the federal individual income tax from 1979 through 1988. (See Altshuler and Schwartz 1996, who use a life-cycle approach to examine the progressivity of the credit, and Gentry and Hagy 1996, who examine the distributional effect of both the credit and the exclusion.)

The child care tax benefit progressivity issue has been addressed by Congress several times. The 1976 conversion of a deduction to a credit and the 1982 change to a sliding scale credit were intended to increase the credit's progressivity. Congress again addressed the perceived regressivity of the credit in the Revenue Reconciliation Act of 1989 debates, but no changes to the credit were enacted at that time.

Table 1 reports the total child care credit and total credits claimed during the 1979–1988 period on all returns filed as reported by Publication 1304, *Individual Income Tax Returns*. The child care credit represents a large portion of the total credits claimed, increasing substantially over the sample period. ("Total credits" as reported in Publication 1304 do not include the earned income credit that was refunded or offset against taxes other than income taxes. For example, in 1988, individual taxpayers paid approximately $413 billion in income tax after credits and received $12 billion in credits (including $5 billion of earned income credit), of which $4 billion was child care credit.) This research extends Dunbar and Nordhauser's (1991) progressivity research on the child care credit by (1) using the

Kakwani index in addition to the Suits index, (2) considering the impact of the income distribution on these indices, and (3) adding two years, 1987 and 1988, to the sample period. A comparison of the Suits and Kakwani tax indices is provided in Formby et al. (1984) (see also Progressivity, measures of). This research extends the Suits and Kakwani tax indices for credit purposes.

The Suits credit index (S) relates cumulative credits with cumulative income. The value of S ranges from −1 to 1, with the −1 to 0 range representing a regressive credit and the 0 to 1 range representing a progressive credit. The Kakwani credit index (K) considers two relationships: cumulative credits with cumulative tax returns and cumulative income with cumulative tax returns. The value of K ranges from −1 to 2, with the −1 to 0 range representing a regressive credit and the 0 to 2 range representing a progressive credit.

Because the S is based upon an integration that is performed with respect to income, while K is based upon an integration with respect to tax returns, Formby et al. (1984: 303) noted that the two indices may provide conflicting implications when time-series or cross-sectional comparisons are made. (See Suits 1977 for the approximation procedure used to compute the integrals used in the Suits tax index. The Kakwani tax index is derived in Kakwani 1976.) They state, however, that "there is no apparent conceptual reason to prefer one of the measures over the other. For this reason, both K and S warrant consideration when progressivity is measured."

## Index computation

Three alternative measures of "income" are used to provide some assurance that the conclusion will not be dependent on the income measure: taxable income (TI), AGI, and expanded AGI (EXPAGI). EXPAGI modifies AGI by

1. adding the untaxed portions of capital gains, dividends, interest, and unemployment compensation;
2. adding back adjustments to income for deductible IRA and Keogh retirement plan contributions and the deduction for the working married couple; and

## TABLE 1

**Total Credits Claimed on All Returns and Credits Claimed on Sample Returns (thousands of dollars)**

| | 1979 | 1980 | 1981 | 1982 | 1983 | 1984 | 1985 | 1986 | 1987 | 1988 |
|---|---|---|---|---|---|---|---|---|---|---|
| Child Care Credit | 793,143 | 956,439 | 1,147,907 | 1,501,453 | 2,051,462 | 2,648,834 | 3,127,702 | 3,397,090 | 3,438,314 | 3,812,849 |
| Total Credits | 6,780,186 | 7,215,839 | 7,905,294 | 7,854,493 | 8,190,737 | 9,263,308 | 10,248,044 | 7,020,731 | 6,329,438 | 7,047,140 |

*Source:* Internal Revenue Service.

3. adding back amounts subtracted from AGI for net partnership losses, net S corporation losses, net estate or trust losses, and net rental losses.

Taxpayers were ranked by the three measures of income and placed in deciles. The cumulative credit and cumulative income tax after all credits (ITAC), and income tax before the child care credit but after all other credits (ITBC), were determined for each decile. The credit indices were determined based on the proportion of the specific credit relative to income reported by taxpayers in each decile. Likewise, the ITAC and ITBC indices were determined based on the proportion of tax relative to income reported by taxpayers in each decile. If the credit index is positive (negative), the credit is progressive (regressive). To determine the impact of the credit on the income tax and to confirm the sign of the credit indices, the ITAC and ITBC indices were compared. If the ITAC index was greater (lesser) than the ITBC index, the credit increased (reduced) the progressivity of the income tax.

## Sample data

The data for 10 years, 1979–1988, were obtained from the Ernst & Young/University of Michigan Tax Research Data Base, specifically the Individual Tax Model Files (model data). The model data are drawn from a stratified sample of returns. Each return has an integer-weighting factor that allows a researcher to simulate the population of the returns filed in each year. The sum of the integer weights corresponds to the population of returns filed in each year. Each year's sample represented on average 97 percent of the returns filed in each year after the elimination of returns from other years that were filed in the sample year and returns that reported additional special taxes. (For example, distributions from a pension plan may be subject to a special tax. The distribution, however, is not included in income on the tax return. Thus, the return could reflect taxes but no taxable income. Because this research determines progressivity by comparisons of various income measures with tax liability, returns that reflected additional taxes were eliminated.)

## Results

S and K values were positive across years for all income measures, with the exception of the Ks for 1979–1981 for the AGI income measure and the 1979 index for the EXPAGI income measure. S using the TI measure ranged from 0.2337 in 1981 to 0.4372 in 1988; K ranged from 0.1444 in 1979 to 0.3010 in 1988. S using the AGI measure ranged from 0.0244 in 1979 to 0.2854 in 1986; K ranged from −0.0278 in 1979 to 0.1916 in 1986. S using the EXPAGI measure ranged from 0.0565 in 1979 to 0.2899 in 1986;

K ranged from −0.0074 in 1979 to 0.1898 in 1986. Regardless of the income measure used, S and K ITAC indices were higher than ITBC indices in every year, confirming that the child care credit contributed to the progressivity of the income tax during 1979–1988.

Table 2 reports the cumulative distributions of AGI, ITAC, ITBC, and credit by decile for 1981 and 1983. This table confirms Dunbar and Nordhauser's (1991) conclusion that the child care credit became more progressive after the 1981 law change that increased the credit rate for low-income taxpayers. S increased from 0.0444 in 1981 to 0.1683 in 1983; K increased from −0.0023 to 0.0956. The increase in S and K can be attributed in part to the 1982 law change that increased the credit. In addition, these indices become more progressive because the distribution of AGI becomes more unequal.

To determine the impact of the change in AGI distribution on the credit index, K can be recomputed holding the income distribution constant across 1981 and 1983. Recall that K considers two relationships: credit-returns and income-returns. If we hold the second relationship constant at 0.2689 (distribution of AGI in table 2) in 1981 and 1983, K would equal 0.0892 in 1983 instead of 0.0956. Thus, after controlling for the distribution of income, the credit index still increases.

## Conclusion

The child care credit contributes to the overall progressivity of the federal income tax. The tax law change in 1982 increased the progressivity of the child care credit, although the lower deciles continue to reflect regressivity. Many taxpayers are in the lower deciles because they are one-earner families. If such taxpayers are married, they are generally precluded from claiming the credit. If Congress wishes to increase the progressivity of the credit, the credit could be increased further for low-income taxpayers or the credit for high-income taxpayers could be phased out.

## Additional readings

Altshuler, Rosanne, and Amy Ellen Schwartz. "On the Progressivity of the Child Care Tax Credit: Snapshot versus Time-Exposure Incidence." *National Tax Journal* 49 (1996): 55–71.

Dunbar, Amy, and Susan Nordhauser. "Is the Child Care Credit Progressive?" *National Tax Journal* 44 (1991): 519–28.

Formby, John P., Terry G. Seaks, and W. James Smith. "Difficulties in the Measurement of Tax Progressivity: The Case of North America." *Public Finance* 39 (1984): 297–313.

## TABLE 2

**Distribution of Adjusted Gross Income (AGI), Income Tax After Credits (ITAC), Income Tax Before Child Care Credit (ITBC), and Child Care Credit: Cumulative Percentages by Sample Decile for Two Years Surrounding Tax Law Change**

| | | 1981 | | | | | 1983 | | |
|---|---|---|---|---|---|---|---|---|---|
| Decile | AGI | ITAC | ITBC | Child Care | Decile | AGI | ITAC | ITBC | Child Care |
| 1 | 0.69% | 0.01% | 0.01% | 0.00% | 1 | 0.67% | 0.01% | 0.01% | 0.00% |
| 2 | 2.72% | 0.21% | 0.21% | 0.03% | 2 | 2.66% | 0.24% | 0.24% | 0.12% |
| 3 | 6.14% | 1.19% | 1.19% | 1.65% | 3 | 6.02% | 1.20% | 1.21% | 2.13% |
| 4 | 11.00% | 3.37% | 3.38% | 6.76% | 4 | 10.79% | 3.32% | 3.37% | 10.08% |
| 5 | 17.48% | 7.28% | 7.32% | 15.22% | 5 | 17.17% | 6.98% | 7.09% | 22.20% |
| 6 | 25.91% | 13.26% | 13.31% | 25.64% | 6 | 25.46% | 12.77% | 12.93% | 34.20% |
| 7 | 36.70% | 21.96% | 22.02% | 37.03% | 7 | 36.14% | 21.22% | 21.43% | 48.44% |
| 8 | 50.34% | 34.16% | 34.24% | 54.47% | 8 | 49.70% | 33.14% | 33.37% | 64.43% |
| 9 | 67.93% | 51.90% | 52.00% | 76.95% | 9 | 67.10% | 50.17% | 50.41% | 81.90% |
| 10 | 100.00% | 100.00% | 100.00% | 100.00% | 10 | 100.00% | 100.00% | 100.00% | 100.00% |
| Suits Index | | 0.2199 | 0.2189 | 0.0444 | | | 0.2253 | 0.2224 | 0.1683 |
| Kakwani Index | | 0.1711 | 0.1704 | −0.0023 | | | 0.1733 | 0.1713 | 0.0956 |
| Distribution of AGI | | | | 0.2689 | | | | | 0.2657 |
| Distribution of Credit | | | | 0.2678 | | | | | 0.3135 |

Gentry, William M., and Allison P. Hagy. "The Distributional Effects of the Tax Treatment of Child Care Expenses." In *Empirical Foundations of Household Taxation*, edited by Martin Feldstein and James M. Poterba. National Bureau of Economic Research, 99-128. Chicago: University of Chicago Press, 1996.

Kakwani, Nanok C. "Measurement of Tax Progressivity: An International Comparison." *Economic Journal* 87 (1976): 71–80.

Suits, Daniel B. "Measurement of Tax Progressivity." *American Economic Review* 67 (1977): 747–52.

*Cross references:* family, tax treatment of; income tax, federal.

# Circuit breaker

John E. Anderson
University of Nebraska

*A mechanism that provides a state income tax credit for selected taxpayers with high local property tax burdens.*

A circuit breaker is a targeted means of providing property tax relief. The term *circuit breaker* is adapted from the common home electrical device that trips when an electrical circuit is overloaded. In similar fashion, a property tax circuit breaker is designed to trip, providing relief, when a taxpayer is overloaded with property tax burden.

The credit mechanism is defined by specifying two parameters. First, we must define what is meant by being overburdened with property taxes. Circuit breakers do that by specifying a threshold proportion of income taken by the property tax beyond which the taxpayer is presumed to be overburdened. Second, the size of the tax credit must be specified as some share of the property tax in excess of the threshold proportion of income. Note that the circuit breaker mechanism presumes an ability to pay that is reflected by the taxpayer's income. When the property tax is high relative to income, the taxpayer is overburdened and is deserving of relief.

The general form of a circuit breaker credit mechanism can be described as a credit ($C$) for which a taxpayer qualifies when property tax liability ($P$) exceeds some threshold proportion ($b$) of income ($Y$). The credit is specified as a fraction ($a$) of the property tax in excess of the proportion of income $bY$.

$$C = a[P - bY], \text{ if } P > aY,$$
$$C = 0 \text{ otherwise.}$$

For example, a state can specify the circuit breaker as providing a 50 percent credit for property taxes paid in excess of 5 percent of income. In that case $a = 0.50$ and $b = 0.05$. If a taxpayer's property tax bill exceeds 5 percent of income, the taxpayer qualifies for the credit. If the property tax bill is less than 5 percent of income, the taxpayer does not qualify and receives no credit. The credit is then 50 percent of the property tax liability in excess of 5 percent of income: $C = 0.5[P - 0.5Y]$. Table 1 lists the credit amount for several hypothetical taxpayers with income $Y$ and property tax liability $P$.

A taxpayer with an income of $20,000 first qualifies for the credit when property taxes exceed $1,000 (5% of income). Hence, a taxpayer with an

**TABLE 1**

**Circuit Breaker Examples**

| Income<br>Y | Property Tax<br>P | Credit<br>C | Net Property Tax<br>after Credit<br>P − C |
|---|---|---|---|
| 20,000 | 1,000 | 0 | 1,000 |
| 20,000 | 1,500 | 250 | 1,250 |
| 20,000 | 2,000 | 500 | 1,500 |
| 40,000 | 2,000 | 0 | 2,000 |
| 40,000 | 3,800 | 900 | 2,900 |

income of $20,000 and property tax liability of $1,500 would qualify for a credit of $250 (50% of the difference between $1,500 and $1,000). The credit then reduces the effective property tax from $1,500 to $1,250. If the property tax were to rise to $2,000, the credit would increase to $500, reducing the net property tax liability to $1,500.

Similarly, a taxpayer with an income of $40,000 first qualifies for the credit when property tax liability exceeds $2,000 (5% of $40,000). A taxpayer with this income and a property tax bill of $3,800 would qualify for a credit of $900 (50% of the difference between $3,800 and $2,000), reducing the property tax bill to $2,900.

Both homeowners and renters can be included in a circuit breaker program. In the case of renters, a share of the rent paid to the landlord is assumed to be allocated to paying the property tax. That share of the rent is counted as property tax payment to local governments. The circuit breaker then applies as in the case of a homeowner.

The state can specify a maximum credit to be earned. For example, the credit ceiling could be $1,000. Regardless of the taxpayer's property tax liability in relation to income, a credit of no more than $1,000 would be provided. The state can also specify several different sets of parameters $a$ and $b$ in the general formula above. For example, the credit could be more generous for the elderly, with $a = 1.0$ and $b = 0.03$. In that case, an elderly taxpayer would qualify for the credit when the property tax liability first exceeds 3 percent of income, and the credit would be a full 100 percent of the property tax in excess of 3 percent of income.

A primary advantage of this form of property tax relief is that state resources are targeted specifically to those taxpayers most in need of it. If the state has $100 million it can spend on providing local property tax relief, that sum will be more effectively used when it is targeted to specific taxpayers than if it is spread across all property owners. Alternative mechanisms of providing property tax relief, such as a homestead exemption, spread the relief across all homesteads. The state's resources are not targeted to those most in need. Of course, defining an overburdened taxpayer is a problem. While a person whose property tax bill exceeds 5 percent of income

may indeed be overburdened with local property tax, that person may simply have chosen to spend an extremely large share of income on housing. While housing expenditures generally fall as a share of income as income rises, there are certainly exceptions. Circuit breaker mechanisms define need in terms of property tax relative to income. In order to eliminate relief to very high income taxpayers or to those with exceptionally large housing expenditures, a phaseout mechanism for high-income taxpayers or a cap on the credit can be applied.

A fully refundable credit makes the state's income tax more progressive, regardless of the tax rate structure. With a fully refundable property tax credit, a taxpayer without income tax liability can file a return, claim the credit for property taxes, and receive a check from the state. Some states have a single flat income tax rate, yet have progressive income tax systems because of their reliance on a circuit breaker mechanism. For convenience of property tax payment, the credit is sometimes frontloaded. That is, the state credit is received before the property tax bill is due the local government.

Because the circuit breaker mechanism provides *state* income tax relief for *local* property taxes paid, the state government is making an indirect commitment to fund local government activity. The precise workings of a given state's circuit breaker mechanism should therefore be considered in tandem with that state's method of distributing state resources to local governments. Revenue-sharing formulas, aid distribution formulas, grants, and equalization mechanisms are all methods that states use to facilitate local government provision of public goods and services.

Thirty-one states in the United States have adopted circuit breakers since the mid-1960s. The parameters of the circuit breakers vary widely from state to state. In some cases the circuit breaker provides a small amount of aggregate property tax relief to a narrowly targeted group of taxpayers. In other cases, hundreds of millions of dollars of property tax relief are provided to large numbers of taxpayers. Homeowners, renters, the elderly, and the disabled are all provided property tax relief in varying degrees by the circuit breaker mechanism. Details on each state's circuit breaker mechanism are provided in ACIR (1994). For a thorough review of the role of circuit breakers in providing property tax relief, see Gold (1979).

Two states, Michigan and Wisconsin, use the circuit breaker mechanism to provide property tax relief for agricultural property owners. While most states provide preferential treatment for agricultural property through use value assessment or a classified property tax system, these two states have chosen to employ a circuit breaker mechanism on the state income tax. Farmers whose property taxes are high relative to their income receive a credit on the state income tax for some portion of the property tax they pay to local governments.

Incentive effects of circuit breakers are a potential concern. If, on the margin, a taxpayer pays only 50 percent of the property tax, the price of local public goods, such as education, is significantly reduced. The taxpayer may then be more likely to vote for additional local public goods, increasing demand for those goods and putting upward pressure on property tax rates. While in theory this potential effect is worth consideration, in practice the demand for local public goods is known to be quite inelastic (unresponsive to price). Besides, only a fraction of the taxpayers receive the benefit of the circuit breaker credit. The others face the full price of local public goods, not subsidized by the credit. Thus, the effect of the circuit breaker is not likely to raise property tax rates.

Capitalization of the circuit breaker tax relief is also worth consideration. To the extent that the circuit breaker reduces the property tax, we would expect the market value of property to reflect the reduced tax liability. Tax relief can be expected to be at least partially capitalized into higher property values.

### Additional readings

Advisory Commission on Intergovernmental Relations (ACIR). *Significant Features of Fiscal Federalism*. Vol. 1. Washington, D.C.: 1994.

Gold, Steven D. *Property Tax Relief*. Lexington, Mass.: D.C. Heath, Lexington Books, 1979.

Sjoquist, David L. "Taxation of Real Property." In *Taxation and Economic Development: A Blueprint for Ohio Tax Reform*, edited by Roy Bahl. Columbus, Ohio: Battelle Press, 1995.

*Cross references:* homestead exemption and credit programs; property tax, real property, residential.

# Commuter taxes

Robert W. Wassmer
California State University, Sacramento

*The history of state and local use of employment-based taxation designed to charge for public services that accrue to persons who work, but do not reside, in a jurisdiction.*

The term *commuter taxes* usually refers to an income or payroll tax that is paid by individuals to the jurisdictions where they work but do not reside. This can occur if residence is in one state and employment in another. The burden of this interstate situation has been nearly eliminated by most states allowing a credit, or income exemption, for income taxes paid to other states. Commuter taxes are considered here to be an intrastate issue that arises where local jurisdictions can levy local income taxes. A tax of this type is most likely to occur within a metropolitan area and be placed on a suburban resident who commutes to central city employment.

This entry presents the history of commuter taxes in the United States, statistics on their use, the motivation behind their adoption, and an economic evaluation of their desirability and impact.

### History

The first local tax on labor income was adopted by Philadelphia in 1938 in response to increased expenditure needs and declining property values brought on by the Great Depression. Toledo next adopted a payroll tax in 1946. Adoptions followed in St. Louis (1948) and in other cities in Ohio and Pennsylvania. In the 1960s and 1970s, cities adopted local income taxes for the additional reasons of providing property tax relief and collecting revenue from central city workers who were increasingly living in surrounding suburbs. In 1962, Detroit adopted a local tax whose base was federal adjusted gross income, and residents were taxed at only half the rate of nonresidents. New York City adopted a similar tax in 1966 and was the first and only city to apply a progressive rate structure.

### Statistics

Commuter taxes were in use in 12 states in 1991: Alabama, California, Delaware, Indiana, Kentucky, Michigan, Missouri, New Jersey, New York, Ohio, Oregon, and Pennsylvania. Indiana, Kentucky, and Oregon were the only states to use the tax at the county level. The local income tax rate on nonresidents is lower than on residents in the states of Indiana, Kentucky, Michigan, New York, Ohio, and Pennsylvania. California, New Jersey, and Oregon are the only states where the employer, as opposed to the employee, is legally responsible for paying a local tax assessed on total payroll.

In 1991, commuter taxes were levied by a total of 3,643 local jurisdictions in the United States. Seventy-eight percent of these jurisdictions were in Pennsylvania; 14 percent were in Ohio. The range of commuter tax rates in 1991 varied from 0.45 percent in New York City to 4.31 percent in Philadelphia. Most commuter tax rates in the United States are near 1 percent. In 1948, only 0.4 percent of all local general revenue came from the individual income tax. This percentage peaked at 2.4 percent in 1987 and 1988. By 1990, it had fallen to 1.9 percent.

These figures mask the fact that cities using a local tax rely heavily on its revenue. In the 1990–91 fiscal year, Philadelphia derived 47 percent of its own-source revenue from local payroll taxes.

## Motivation

Local jurisdictions have been motivated to impose an income tax on nonresidents based on three general arguments. The first is that a local income tax, of any sort, provides needed revenue diversification. Diversification was sought in the 1970s after many states imposed local limits on property taxation. Local income taxes allowed cities and counties to meet these property tax limits, and also yielded a lower rate of taxation on the alternate base of local sales. This is important because the burden (or hurt) imposed by any tax more than doubles when the rate of taxation doubles. Diversification through the adoption of a local income tax, like portfolio diversification, also provides greater total revenue stability.

A second justification for commuter taxes is that when people commute from an area of residence to another area of employment, the benefits of locally provided services can spill over jurisdictional boundaries. City services that benefit both residents and commuters (such as streets, sanitation, public safety, and cultural amenities) may be under-provided if only residents are asked to pay for them. Ladd and Yinger (1989) found that, for large U.S. cities, a 10 percent difference in employment per capita (i.e., more commuters) results on average in a 2.9 percent greater city expenditure on all general services, and a 3.9 percent increase in police and fire expenditure.

Considering the concept of benefit taxation, it is also appropriate to ask commuters to pay taxes to their jurisdiction of employment in proportion to the benefits they derive from the services provided by it. If commuters derive fewer benefits than residents, it is also appropriate to set the nonresidential income tax rate lower than the resident rate. Counterarguments to this motivation for commuter taxes include cries of "taxation without representation," and claims that if local business taxes are shifted forward and/or backward, commuters already pay for city services in the form of higher prices for goods and services purchased within the city and/or lower wages.

The third, and probably least noble, motivation given for the imposition of a commuter tax is that it allows a jurisdiction to export taxes to nonresidents for the sole purpose of lower local residential or business tax rates, or greater local expenditure. Because both actions benefit local elected officials in the short term, there is a strong political motivation to pursue such exporting. Alternatively, the exportation of a city commuter tax may be justified on the equity basis of "ability to pay." The argument given is that through little direct fault of its own, a central city often contains the poorest population and the harshest atmosphere in which to provide local services in a metropolitan area. Normal levels of local government service in a central city would hence require highly regressive taxes. Central city tax exporting reduces the need for this form of taxation and has been argued to be socially optimal. The taxation of commuters at a level greater than benefits received from local services also discourages affluent residents, who are employed in the central city, from moving to the suburbs.

## Evaluation

Local commuter income taxes can be evaluated based on the criteria of public perception, simplicity, equity, and efficiency. In the annual public opinion survey conducted by the Advisory Commission on Intergovernmental Relations in 1987 (ACIR 1987), people were asked which form of revenue should be used by their local government to meet additional costs. Property taxation and income taxation finished equally behind the choices in preferred order of user charges, sales taxation, and no new taxes. Even though local income taxation is federally deductible, the public may still dislike its further use because of the heavy reliance on income taxation by both states and the federal government.

The local income tax deserves praise for its simplicity. The existence of state and federal income taxes solves many administrative problems. Simplicity also lies in the broad base and low rates that characterize most local income tax systems in the United States. Equivalent tax rates on a comprehensive tax base also verify that the local income tax meets the standard measure of horizontal equity. The near elimination of double taxation through usually allowing only one type of jurisdiction in a state to levy local income taxes, and basing local income taxation on either place of residence or employment, also enhances the local income tax's fairness.

Except for cases in which the pretax outcome is deemed undesirable, a tax is considered more efficient the less it does to alter market outcomes. To understand how economic outcomes are altered in the presence of a commuter tax, it is necessary to determine who pays the tax. A fundamental finding of public finance is that a tax statute has very little to do with who really pays the tax. An employee, even though legally responsible for payment, could demand higher wages in the presence of a commuter tax and hence shift his or her tax payment partially (or completely) back onto the employer. Conversely, an employer asked to make local payroll taxes could shift them forward onto employees by paying lower wages.

The more employment is concentrated in a metropolitan area's central city that levies a commuter tax, the greater the likelihood for the tax to be paid by commuters in the form of lower after-tax wages. This is caused by the difficulty that workers in a metropolitan area face in trying to escape the commuter tax by finding work in the suburbs. The more likely commuter taxes are to be paid by business in a central city where the tax is levied, the greater the employment opportunities available in suburban cities that do not levy the tax. In this case, central city business pays the commuter tax in the forms of a lower profit, or a lower return on immobile inputs (such as land). This situation puts central city business at a disadvantage and in the long run it could cause relocation to the suburbs.

With respect to this issue, Ladd and Yinger (1989) assume that local payroll taxes are fully paid by employees. After examining 78 of the largest U.S. cities in 1982, they concluded that the export potential of a commuter income tax is approximately 2.5 times that of the local property tax, and six times greater than a local sales tax. Because many of these large cities continue to face fiscal problems, and in the early 1980s only 15 used a commuter income tax, Ladd and Yinger strongly recommend its greater use. They do not consider that if employers pay part of the commuter tax, then its imposition may drive business to the suburbs and possibly make the long-term fiscal crisis of central cities even worse. As evidence, Grieson (1980) found that the 1976 increase in the Philadelphia income tax rate from 3.31 to 4.31 percent caused a long-term decline of 10 percent in the city's 1975 employment level. Stull and Stull (1991) have also found that an additional percentage point added to a city's local income tax in the Philadelphia metropolitan area would cause the average home value in the city where the increase occurred to fall by approximately 4 percent.

So far, there is little empirical evidence to support the contention of commuter exploitation of central cities. After accounting for the benefits that San Francisco bestowed upon suburban commuters, and the revenue that commuters provided the city through the forward and backward shifting of existing business taxes other than a commuter tax, Smith (1972) concluded that nonresident workers pay more than their fair share in central city taxes. Greene et al. (1974) looked at the net benefit flow from Washington, D.C., to its suburbs and also found that, if the dollar cost of service is counted, suburban residents are paying at least their fair share. Alternatively, if a welfare measure based on what suburban residents would actually be willing to pay for central city services was used, suburbia would gain a net flow of benefits. Even under this finding, Greene et al. note that commuters are already paying their fair share of indirect taxes to the central city and a com-

muter tax would not charge the appropriate suburban residents for the net flow of benefits they receive. After looking over these studies and others, Bradford and Oates (1974) concluded that suburban exploitation appears to be of "minor quantitative importance"; nevertheless, they do recommend further study. A well-done recent study on the desirability of instituting a commuter tax in Washington, D.C., was recently completed by Strauss (1997). He concluded that a tax between 0.5 and 1 percent on commuter wages could be appropriately justified in that city.

## Additional readings

Advisory Commission on Intergovernmental Relations. *Changing Public Attitudes on Government and Taxes.* Washington, D.C., 1987.

Advisory Commission on Intergovernmental Relations. *Local Revenue Diversification: Local Income Taxes.* SR-10. Washington, D.C., August 1988.

Advisory Commission on Intergovernmental Relations. *Significant Features of Fiscal Federalism.* 2 vols. M-180. Washington, D.C., February 1992.

Aronson, J. Richard, and John L. Hilley. *Financing State and Local Governments.* 4th ed. Washington, D.C.: The Brookings Institution, 1986.

Bradford, David F., and Wallace E. Oates. "Suburban Exploitation of Central Cities and Government Structure." In *Redistribution through Public Choice*, edited by Harold M. Hochman and George E. Peterson. Washington, D.C.: The Urban Institute, 1974.

Break, George F. *Financing Government in a Federal System.* Washington, D.C.: The Brookings Institution, 1980.

Fisher, Ronald C. *State and Local Public Finance.* 2d ed. Chicago: Irwin, 1996.

Greene, Kenneth V., William B. Neenan, and Claudia D. Scott. *Fiscal Interactions in a Metropolitan Area.* Lexington, Mass.: Lexington Books, 1974.

Grieson, Ronald E. " Theoretical Analysis and Empirical Measurements of the Effects of the Philadelphia Income Tax." *Journal of Urban Economics* 8 (1980): 123–37.

Ladd, Helen F., and John Yinger. *America's Ailing Cities: Fiscal Health and the Design of Urban Policy.* Updated edition. Baltimore: Johns Hopkins Press, 1989.

Smith, R. Stafford. *Local Income Taxes: Economic Effects and Equity.* Berkeley: Institute of Governmental Studies, 1972.

Strauss, Robert P. "The District of Columbia's Individual Income Tax: Structure, Characteristics, and Policy Alternatives." In *Taxing Simply, Taxing Fairly*. Washington, D.C.: Tax Revision Commission at www.dctrc.org, 1998.

Stull, William J., and Judith C. Stull. "Capitalization of Local Income Taxes." *Journal of Urban Economics* 29 (1991): 182–90.

# Consumption taxation

Gilbert E. Metcalf
Tufts University

*Taxation based on consumption, as opposed to some other measure of ability to pay, most notably income.*

## Forms of consumption taxes

To understand the different ways in which consumption taxes can be implemented, it is useful to begin with the Haig-Simons definition of income: income ($Y$) equals consumption ($C$) plus changes in wealth ($W$) ($Y = C + \Delta W$). First, note that the key difference between income and consumption taxation is the inclusion or exclusion of $\Delta W$ in the tax base. Changes in wealth—or savings—are not taxed by consumption taxes but are taxed by income taxes. Second, note that this relationship suggests that consumption can be taxed directly (e.g., via a sales or excise tax) or indirectly by imposing an income tax with deductions for increases to savings (and inclusion of withdrawals from savings in the tax base). A national sales tax on all goods and services would be one way to implement a consumption tax, while an income tax with IRA treatment of all savings would be a way to implement the consumption tax indirectly. The expenditure tax proposed by Kaldor (1955) is an example of this indirect approach. Recently, it has been revived as a component of the Nunn-Domenici USA Tax Plan.

Value-added taxes (VATs) provide a third method of implementing consumption taxes. Value added in production is the difference between the sale price of produced goods and services and the cost of goods and services used in production. A VAT can be viewed as a national sales tax where the tax is collected in increments at each stage of production, from the producers rather than from the retail seller. A key feature of a consumption-style VAT is that investments by the firm are deducted (expensed) rather than depreciated. The effective tax rate on investment equals zero if a firm can expense its investment. While taxes are paid on the returns to that investment (i.e., on the value of goods and services generated by the investment), those taxes can be viewed as the government's share of the return to the investment because of its equity stake in the investment following the tax deduction resulting from expensing.

As described above, all financial transactions are ignored when calculating value added. All cash proceeds into the firm (stock sales, proceeds from borrowing) are ignored, as is all cash out (dividends, interest, debt repayment). This approach is often characterized as the $R$ (for real transactions) base approach, a terminology credited to Meade (Institute for Fiscal Studies 1973). Alternatively, one can include all financial transactions ($R + F$ base). Thus, all cash proceeds are included as taxable income, and all cash outflows are deducted. So long as the same tax rate applies to all transactions, these two approaches generate the same tax consequences to a firm. The present discounted value of taxes paid on proceeds from borrowing, for example, should just equal the present discounted value of taxes saved by deducting principal and interest on that debt. The $R + F$ approach is better suited for use in taxing financial services where value added is difficult to disentangle from financial activities (borrowing and lending).

As an accounting identity, value added is allocated to workers (wages) and capital owners (dividends and retained earnings). However, as noted above, investment expensing means that the taxes on value added allocated to capital owners are offset by the reduction in taxes due to expensing. In other words, the only capital owners who will incur the burden of a consumption tax are those who own capital before a consumption tax is implemented (ignoring transitional rules). This gives rise to the distinction between "old" and "new" capital and is an important issue in tax reforms.

It is often claimed that a consumption tax is a combination of a wage tax plus this lump sum tax on old capital. There are (at least) two important observations to make about this claim. First, if a future observer sees that individuals file tax returns paying taxes on their wage income only, that observer will not be able to say if this is a "wage" or a "consumption" tax. To distinguish between the two forms of taxation, the observer would need to know what happened to old capital at the time of the reform. If a wage tax has been enacted along with a levy on existing capital, then the observer would be looking at a consumption tax. In other words, the distinction between a wage tax and a consumption tax based on treatment of old capital may mislead an observer. We would enact what looks like a consumption tax, but what really is a wage tax, by forgiving the tax on old capital and vice versa.

Second, the claim would suggest that in the absence of old capital, wage and consumption taxes are equivalent. But consider an entrepreneur who thinks up a great idea after the new law has been enacted and sells it for $1 million. (Or perhaps he finds oil on a previously worthless piece of property and sells it for $1 million.) All consumption financed by this $1 million would escape taxation under a wage tax. A personal cash flow tax would tax all cash coming to an individual, with a deduction for any savings (into qualified accounts); in this case, the consumption financed by proceeds from the sale of the idea would be taxed. In certain cases, the U.S. Treasury staff's blueprints (U.S. Treasury Department 1977) allow for a tax prepayment option in which additions to savings are not deducted, nor are the principal and return from that savings taxable (when withdrawn for consumption). While tax prepayment is a useful—perhaps essential—option for certain assets (houses, jewelry, etc.), it could not be used for taxing returns such as our entrepreneur receives. In this context, the tax prepayment approach would be identical to a wage tax.

Variations on these approaches to taxing consumption abound; generally, the focus on how one implements a consumption tax follows from administrative and distributional concerns arising from windfall gains and losses in the transition from some existing tax system to the consumption tax system. One popular variant is the Hall-Rabushka Flat Tax, which is a two-part tax. The business tax is essentially a VAT with a deduction allowed for compensation to workers. The second tax is a personal tax on compensation at the same tax rate. Described this way, the shifting of the labor tax component from the business tax to a personal tax has no economic effect. The motivation for shifting the labor tax component is to allow a generous personal exemption to effect greater tax progressivity. A slight variant on the Hall-Rabushka Flat Tax is Bradford's (1987) X Tax. It differs in having a progressive rate structure on the personal tax, the top rate of which equals the business tax rate.

An important unresolved question is whether bequests and gifts should be included in the base of a consumption tax when the tax is explicitly levied on consumption. Clearly, the receipt of gifts should not trigger a consumption tax liability. One might argue that the gift of a bequest (or other monetary gift) should be treated as consumption (and hence taxed) because the bequest generates consumption benefits for the donor. An altruistic motive (e.g., Blinder 1974) might justify the consumption benefits of the gift. However, the donor of a gift derives utility from his or her ability to increase the bequest recipient's utility. Because the purchasing power of the gift is reduced by the consumption tax, the donor now receives less utility from a given bequest. In effect, the donor has been taxed on the gift, and explicit inclusion of the bequest in the consumption tax would constitute double taxation. Under a strategic bequest motive (e.g., Bernheim et al. 1985), the gift can be viewed as a payment for services from the recipient. Because these services (visits, home care, affection) are likely to be untaxed, the consumption tax should properly tax bequests. The Meade Commission's approach to taxing bequests was to propose a separate wealth tax to "encourage dispersion in the ownership of wealth" (Institute for Fiscal Studies 1973: 518).

## Historical antecedents

The intellectual arguments for consumption taxation can be traced back to Thomas Hobbes. Writing some 350 years ago, he argued that ". . . the Equality of Imposition consisteth rather in the Equality of that which is consumed, than of the riches of the persons that consume the same" (Hobbes 1651: 387). His argument was based on the logic that the state provides protection for the enjoyment of life and that taxes are the price of that protection. Because consumption is the material manifestation of the enjoyment of life, so should consumption be the base of taxation. Or as Hobbes put it, "For what reason is there, that he which laboureth much, and sparing the fruits of his labour, consumeth little, should be more charged, than he that living idly getteth little, and spendeth all he gets: seeing the one hath no more protection from the Commonwealth than the other?"

More recently, Kaldor (1955) argued for an expenditure tax as a surtax to coexist with the current income tax in the United Kingdom. More recently still, the Meade Commission (Institute for Fiscal Studies 1973) in the United Kingdom and the U.S. Treasury Department (1977) have made forceful cases for consumption taxation. Despite these proposals, no country has shifted its tax system wholly to a consumption base. However, there has been a shift in the mix from income toward consumption taxation in a number of ways in the last 20 years. First, the European Community (EC) passed two directives in 1967, in which it mandated all EC members to implement VATs. As a result, the mix of consumption and income taxes has shifted to the point where consumption taxes (VATs, excise taxes, etc.) constitute between 15 and 25 percent of tax revenues for the EC countries (see Metcalf 1995). Second, there has been a tremendous growth in defined contribution pension programs and other tax-deferred savings programs in the United States and other industrialized countries. Current estimates are that roughly 50 percent of personal savings in the United States receive consumption tax treatment (Gale 1995).

## Rationale for consumption taxation

There are three major reasons that many economists have advocated a shift from income to consumption taxation: simplicity, efficiency, and fairness. The essential argument for simplicity is that income is difficult, if not impossible, to measure accurately, while the measurement of consumption is relatively straightforward. Most of the complexity in the current income tax system arises from the need to measure income. Two oft-cited examples are depreciation and capital gains. A consumption tax of any of these forms would eliminate these problems. Capital expenditures are expensed (deducted) under a consumption tax and capital gains are ignored. On the other hand, efforts to achieve distributional goals can add complexity to a consumption tax. For example, every VAT in place in Europe and other industrialized countries has exemptions and multiple rates, which add considerable complexity to the tax code. Transitional concerns are also likely to add complexity. For example, most serious consumption tax plans in the United States have gone to great lengths to preserve basis in existing assets and to prevent the taxation of withdrawals from savings accumulated before tax reform.

The major case for efficiency is that a consumption tax eliminates the intertemporal consumption distortion by ending the tax on savings. Moreover, reducing the effective tax on capital will encourage economic growth through greater rates of investment. With respect to the effect of consumption taxation on savings, the intertemporal distortion depends importantly on the rate of return subject to taxation. As Bradford (1995) has shown, a consumption tax only exempts the risk-free return from taxation. Given that the risk-free return is a small component of the total return on savings, the efficiency gains from a consumption tax vis-à-vis an income tax may be modest. Moreover, while a consumption tax may reduce intertemporal distortions, there still remains a distortion between the consumption of purchased goods and nonpurchased goods—most notably leisure. In addition, when comparing income and consumption taxes, a higher tax rate would be required to raise the same amount of revenue with the consumption tax versus the income tax, given the nontaxation of savings.

Finally, some economists have argued for a shift to consumption taxation based on fairness. Hobbes employed a benefits principle to justify consumption taxation. More recently, Kaldor (1955) argued that the difficulties associated with taxing income are so great that a shift to an expenditure tax would in fact raise more revenue from the very wealthy than income tax does—a view at sharp variance with conventional wisdom.

The common perception is that a consumption tax would be highly regressive compared with an income tax. This follows from the fact that the savings rate relative to income rises with income. Whether a consumption tax need be more regressive than an income tax depends on (1) the degree of progressivity of the income tax being replaced, (2) the structure of the consumption tax being contemplated, and (3) the way in which progressivity is measured. Ignoring the first point here, there are several comments to be made. First, progressive elements can be built into a consumption tax: progressive rate structure and personal exemptions, to name two. Second, conventional measures of pro-

gressivity in the tax code use annual income to measure economic well-being. This approach biases measures of tax progressivity in a downward direction. If people are making consumption decisions on the basis of lifetime income, then consumption income ratios will be very high for "low" income individuals and very low for "high" income individuals who might have the same lifetime income. Not all economists are convinced by the lifetime income analysis, however. A revenue-neutral tax shift from income to consumption taxation would undoubtedly result in high-income taxpayers receiving a tax cut. This fact creates substantial political difficulties for the enactment of a consumption tax. It should be noted, however, that much of the objection here is really an objection to the ending of the double taxation of capital income that occurs under the current income tax system. The same problem would arise in a shift to an integrated income tax system.

## Conclusion

In practice, consumption is inherently easier to measure than income, and the dynamic efficiency gains from encouraging savings and investment could be large. However, that argument is weakened by the difficulties associated with transiting from the current income tax system to a proposed consumption tax system. In addition, concerns about the fairness of moving from an income to a consumption tax base loom large in the tax reform debate.

To date, the transitional difficulties have stood as a major obstacle to wholesale change. However, there has been piecemeal change, and the current U.S. tax system is a hybrid of an income tax and consumption tax system that has gradually shifted from a predominant reliance on income as the tax base toward a greater reliance on consumption as the tax base. In so doing, we have come (perhaps unconsciously) to the result proposed by Kaldor 40 years ago: "However inadequate the system of income taxation may be in relation to the objectives which it seeks to attain, it is inconceivable that, within any foreseeable period, it should be wholly abandoned in favor of an alternative system based on personal expenditure. The most that can be hoped for therefore is to introduce a spending tax that can be operated side by side with the income tax, and that would take some of the weight off the income tax without imposing an excessive administrative burden" (Kaldor 1955: 224).

## Additional readings

Bernheim, B. Douglas, Andrei Shleifer, and Lawrence H. Summers. "The Strategic Bequest Motive." *Journal of Political Economy* 93 (1985): 1045–76.

Blinder, Alan. *Toward an Economic Theory of Income Distribution*. Cambridge, Mass.: MIT Press, 1974.

Bradford, David. "On the Incidence of Consumption Taxes." In *The Consumption Tax: A Better Alternative?* edited by Charles Walker and Mark Bloomfield. Cambridge, Mass.: Ballinger, 1987.

Bradford, David. "Consumption Taxes: Some Fundamental Transition Issues." In *Frontiers of Tax Reform*, edited by Michael J. Boskin. Stanford: Hoover Institution Press, 1995.

Gale, William. "Reinventing the Federal Tax System." *The Brookings Review* (Fall 1995).

Hobbes, T. *Leviathan*. New York: Penguin Books, 1651 (Penguin edition published in 1968).

Institute for Fiscal Studies. *The Structure and Reform of Direct Taxation: Report of a Committee Chaired bv Professor James E. Meade.* London: George Allen and Unwin, 1973.

Kaldor, Nicolas. *An Expenditure Tax*. London: George Allen and Unwin, 1955.

Metcalf, Gilbert. "Value Added Taxation: A Tax Whose Time Has Come?" *Journal of Economic Perspectives* 9 (1995): 121–40.

U.S. Treasury Department. *Blueprints for Basic Tax Reform*. Washington, D.C.: U.S. Government Printing Office, 1977.

*Cross references:* expensing; fairness in taxation; flat tax; progressivity, measures of; retail sales tax; value-added tax, national; value-added tax, state.

# Corporate reorganizations

David Reishus
The Economics Resource Group, Inc.

*Tax treatment of corporate mergers, acquisitions, and reorganizations.*

Corporate transactions—mergers, acquisitions, reorganizations, and the like—constitute one of the most complex areas in tax policy and practice. There are myriad legal methods and corresponding tax rules under which ownership transfers of corporate assets can occur. The unifying economic principle of these various transactions is the transfer of ownership or change in identity of a corporate business activity. The numerous alternatives by which these transfers can occur make appropriate and consistent taxation difficult, if not impossible. The difficulties are not solely legal or administrative, but confront fundamental issues in corporate tax policy: What is the appropriate treatment of corporate distributions; when is income recognized; and how broad is the corporate tax base?

## Tax treatment of corporate transactions

The taxation of transfers of ownership in corporate businesses generally follows one of two paradigms. The first is that of a sale of assets. In a sale, the seller is taxed on realized gain or loss and the buyer obtains a basis in the assets equal to the purchase price. The second paradigm is that of a merger or reorganization of corporate enterprises in which the tax attributes of the corporate entities continue in some form, and thus no recognition of gain is triggered. The word "reorganization has a precise definition in U.S. tax law which generally results in a tax-free transaction at both the shareholder and corporate level" (Bittker and Eustice 1994: Ch. 12). Reorganization and merger are used in a broad sense to denote changes in corporate identity and ownership.

The oversimplified taxonomy, summarized in figure 1, highlights the alternative tax outcomes at both shareholder and corporate levels available under U.S. tax law. The two basic paradigms recur in most other countries. The problems of categorization, neutrality, and integrity of the tax system persist with the more integrated corporate tax systems in place in a number of European countries. Bittker and Eustice (1994) provide a thorough introduction to relevant U.S. tax law.

At the shareholder level, a transaction is treated as either a sale or a tax-free reorganization. In the latter, shareholders exchange stock in one corporation for stock or securities in another. As a result, control of the assets of the first corporation come under control of another corporation's shareholders. Properly structured, the exchange of stock will not trigger tax to any party. The transferring shareholders have the same bases in the second company's stock as they previously held in the first.

A transfer of stock for cash or other types of property will be treated as a sale. Capital gain (or loss) will be recognized and taxed to the extent the sale price exceeds (is less than) a selling shareholder's basis in the stock. The buyer obtains a basis in the stock equal to the purchase price. Indeed, purchasing all of the stock in a corporation for cash is the simplest mechanism for transferring ownership of corporate assets. An important alternative transaction involves the sale of all the assets in a corporation followed by a distribution of the proceeds to shareholders. At the shareholder level, such a distribution is generally treated as a sale of stock by the shareholder, with tax paid on any capital gain realized.

At the corporate level, the two paradigms also apply. At one extreme, the tax attributes of a corporation, along with its assets, remain essentially intact following a tax-free reorganization. The tax attributes of the corporation—asset bases, accounting methods, net operating loss carryforwards, for-

**FIGURE 1**

**Simplified Taxonomy of Corporate- and Shareholder-Level Tax Outcomes by Method of Acquisition**

| | Shareholder Level | |
| --- | --- | --- |
| | *Taxable*<br>Seller: Shareholder tax on gain (or loss) on shares.<br>Buyer: Basis in shares equal to purchase price. | *Nontaxable*<br>Seller: No current tax carryover basis in shares.<br>Buyer: No current tax. |
| *Corporate Level* | | |
| *Taxable*<br>Target: Corporate tax on gain (or loss) plus applicable recapture; corporate tax attributes extinguish.<br>Acquirer: No current tax; step-up (or down) basis in assets to purchase price, plus good will if required. | *Cash acquisition of corporate assets with distribution of cash to selling shareholders.* | *Exchange of stock for securities satisfying statutory reorganization requirements; election for taxable corporate-level treatment.* |
| *Nontaxable*<br>Target: No current corporate tax.<br>Acquirer: Carryover basis in assets; use of tax attributes of target with limitations. | *Cash acquisition of shares.* | *Exchange of stock for securities satisfying statutory reorganization requirements.* |

*Source:* Author.

eign tax credit carryforwards—continue. The use of the acquired attributes by the new corporation, however, may be restricted for policy reasons. The assets of the corporation are not treated as having been sold, and no recognition of gain occurs.

At the other extreme, the corporation sells its assets. This sale triggers gain or loss, along with any applicable recapture, and thus generates corporate tax liability to the selling corporation. The buyer obtains a new basis in the assets. Goodwill, defined as the excess of the purchase price over the value attributable to tangible assets, may be created. The new owner depreciates assets and amortizes goodwill, based on these new values. To the extent that the proceeds from a sale of substantially all of the assets of a corporation are distributed to its shareholders, this distribution is treated as a sale to the shareholders, as discussed above. The selling corporation's tax attributes may be extinguished if a distribution of proceeds to shareholders occurs.

Shareholder and corporate tax treatment are coordinated in a fashion. Sales that occur at one level only, such as a sale of shares by shareholders or a sale of assets by a corporation without a liquidating distribution to shareholders, are taxed at one level only. A stock-for-stock exchange qualifying as a tax-free reorganization generally results in no tax at either the shareholder level or the corporate level, although an election permits treatment as a sale at the corporate level. Finally, a sale of assets with a liquidating distribution results in sales treatment at both the corporate and shareholder levels.

## The elusive search for neutrality

Application of the two alternative paradigms to economically similar transactions highlights problems of consistency and neutrality. Neutrality in this context means neither encouraging nor discouraging transfer of corporate enterprises. The alternative legal mechanisms for effecting economically similar outcomes and the interplay with other aspects of the corporate tax system make such a goal elusive. For example, the tax consequences at both the corporate and shareholder levels can be dramatically different depending on whether the selling shareholder receives cash or stock, even if the stock is widely traded, highly liquid, and easily used as collateral.

Nonlinearities in the corporate tax system may inherently provide an incentive to merge. For example, if tax losses do not fully offset profits in an economic sense, two separate corporations, one with losses and one with gains, may pay more tax than if they merged and combined their tax attributes. In an attempt to limit mergers as a means of trading in losses or other tax attributes, complex rules have been developed to limit their use postmerger. The shuffling of corporate identities in mergers highlights the problem of the level at which corporate profits are taxed. Are profits of the whole corporate sector, each corporation, or historical lines of business the appropriate target of the corporate tax? Like tax rules for affiliated groups and the dividend-received deduction, merger tax rules display aspects of all levels.

To the extent that a corporate transaction does not meet the requirements for tax-free treatment, a sale occurs and tax liability is triggered. The tax due on a corporation's sale serves as a disincentive to its acquisition, just as taxation on realization of capital gains tends to "lock in" gains and discourage sales of appreciated property. A corporation selling assets immediately recognizes gain (or loss). The buyer obtains a step-up (or step-down) in the bases of the assets that—depending on the details of the transaction and depreciation schedules, recapture rules, goodwill amortization, ordinary income and capital gains tax rates, and other factors—may compensate over time for the immediate tax consequences to the seller. The balance in current U.S. tax law usually tips so that the immediate adverse tax consequences to the selling corporation exceed the ultimate benefits to the buyer, thus discouraging corporate asset sales.

The use of debt, particularly in leveraged buyouts, has also been identified as a tax incentive for corporate mergers (Bulow et al. 1990). To the extent that interest deductibility encourages the use of debt, this incentive is widespread and not limited to corporate mergers. While the use of debt in corporate mergers has been a focus of concern, there is little agreement on whether interest deductibility provides the incentive to merge or not.

The treatment of cash in acquisitions poses problems for the integrity of the classical two-tier corporate tax regime. In general, cash earned by corporations that is distributed to shareholders is treated as a dividend and taxable in full as ordinary income to individual shareholders. To the extent that the double taxation of dividends traps assets in corporate form, acquisitions of corporate assets may be encouraged relative to new investments (King 1989a). Moreover, in a cash acquisition, selling shareholders only pay tax (at capital gains rates) to the extent that the proceeds exceed basis in their stock. Thus, cash that leaves the corporate sector via an acquisition may bear less tax than that paid out as dividends. As such, the tax system further encourages cash acquisitions as a means of moving equity beyond the reach of the corporate income tax (Joint Committee on Taxation 1989). The amount of cash leaving the corporate sector via acquisition is large; in 1985, during the mid-1980s merger boom, $70 billion left via cash acquisitions, exceeding the level of cash dividends in that year (Bagwell and Shoven 1989). Solutions to this problem are complex and may generate nonneutralities and perceived inequities of their own (Warren 1993). Corporate tax integration, as implemented in a number of countries, reduces the tax wedge between dividends and distributions via cash acquisitions but does not eliminate the need to identify dividend and sale treatment for a transaction.

## Do taxes affect corporate mergers?

Several studies have measured the impact of specific tax provisions on the incentive for mergers. The ability to accelerate the use of net operating loss carryforwards and the potential benefits from asset step-ups have little impact on the aggregate level of corporate acquisition activity, even though in specific instances they, and other minor rules, are important. Auerbach and Reishus (1988) find these tax provisions have little effect on the probability of merger. Hayn (1989) finds modest impact of these provisions on the premiums obtained in an acquisition.

Hayn (1989) and others find that the form a merger takes, whether a taxable cash acquisition or a tax-free reorganization, is strongly influenced by tax factors. The type of tax benefits available at the corporate level affects whether cash or stock is used and thus the corresponding tax treatment. In general, qualifying as a tax-free reorganization for those desiring that status increases the likelihood of merger completion. Buyers may use cash for nontax reasons, such as in limiting exposure to the seller's legal liability or in responding to a tender offer. When cash is used, the immediate tax charge may discourage acquisitions.

Leveraged buyouts, acquisitions involving large increases in debt, have been the object of specific study. Kaplan (1989) and Schipper and Smith (1991) both found large savings in taxes after these transactions, most of which was a result of increased interest deductions. Thus, to the extent the acquisition is necessary to obtain such a highly leveraged corporate structure, interest deductibility encourages leveraged buyouts.

The role of trapped equity stemming from the double taxation of dividends in inducing acquisition activity is less certain. The pure trapped equity model suggests that any tax advantage to acquisitions relative to new investments works solely through stock market pricing. Time-series analyses by King (1989b) and Modén (1993) provide modest support for this influence on aggregate acquisition activity. To the extent that cash acquisitions are tax-favored relative to dividends, cash acquisitions (but not stock acquisitions) may be further encouraged.

In summary, current evidence suggests that tax factors have only a modest impact, with exceptions in particular cases, on the aggregate level of corporate mergers and the choice of merger partners. Taxation does influence the form of a merger, whether cash or stock, and thus its tax status, which may indirectly influence economic outcomes. Interest deductibility may encourage leveraged buyout mergers, to the extent that the acquisition is necessary to achieve the high leverage. The influence on an unintegrated or partially integrated corporate tax system on corporate acquisitions may be profound but is empirically highly uncertain and contentious.

## Additional readings

Auerbach, Alan J., and David Reishus. "The Effect of Taxation on the Merger Decision." In *Corporate Takeovers: Causes and Consequences*, edited by Alan J. Auerbach. Chicago: University of Chicago Press, 1988.

Bagwell, Laurie Simon, and John B. Shoven. "Cash Distributions to Shareholders." *The Journal of Economic Perspectives* 3 (3) (Summer 1989): 129–40.

Bittker, Boris I., and James S. Eustice. *Federal Income Taxation of Corporation and Shareholders*. 6th ed. Boston: Warren, Gorham, and Lamont, 1994.

Bulow, Jeremy I., Lawrence H. Summers, and Victoria P. Summers. "Distinguishing Debt from Equity in the Junk Bond Era." In *Debt, Taxes, and Corporate Restructuring*, edited by John B. Shoven and Joel Waldfogel. Washington, D.C.: The Brookings Institution, 1990.

Hayn, Carla. "Tax Attributes as Determinants of Shareholder Gains in Corporate Acquisitions." *Journal of Financial Economics* 23 (June 1989): 121–53.

Joint Committee on Taxation. *Federal Income Tax Aspects of Corporate Financial Structures*. Report prepared by the staff of the Joint Committee on Taxation. January 18, 1989.

Kaplan, Steven. "Management Buyouts: Evidence on Taxes as a Source of Value." *The Journal of Finance* 44 (3) (July 1989): 611–32.

King, Mervyn. "Economic Growth and the Life-Cycle of Firms." *European Economic Review* 33 (1989a): 325–34.

King, Mervyn. "Take-over Activity in the United Kingdom." In *Mergers and Merger Policy*, edited by James Fairburn and John Kay. Oxford: Oxford University Press, 1989b.

Modén, Karl-Markus. *Tax Incentives of Corporate Mergers*. Stockholm: The Industrial Institute for Economic and Social Research, 1993.

Schipper, Katherine, and Abbie Smith. "Effects of Management Buyouts on Corporate Interest and Depreciation Tax Deductions." *The Journal of Law and Economics* 34 (2) (pt. 1) (October 1991): 295–341.

Warren, Alvin C., reporter. *Reporter's Study of Corporate Tax Integration*. American Law Institute, Federal Income Tax Project. March 31, 1993.

*Cross references:* income tax, corporate, federal; integration, corporate tax.

# Cost of capital

Jane G. Gravelle
Congressional Research Service, Library of Congress

*The amount that must be paid for the use of capital, either real or financial, usually measured as an annual percentage rate.*

## Defining the cost of capital

The term "cost of capital" is often used differently by economists, financial commentators, and businessmen, although it refers in general to the amount that must be paid for the use of capital, either real or financial. The financial press sometimes seems to equate the cost of capital with the interest rate. Businessmen may mean the required return the firm must earn (the hurdle rate) to undertake a given investment project.

Following Jorgenson's (1963) work, which crystallized the concept, economists generally use the term to mean the implicit rent that is paid in a given period for the use of capital goods (e.g., machinery). This measure is also called the "user cost of capital" or the "rental price of capital." As used by economists, the cost of capital is the price of capital, just as the wage rate is the price of labor. Cost-of-capital measures are derived from a discounted cash flow method, where the present value of the stream of expected earnings sums to the cost of the asset.

To illuminate the differences between uses of the "cost of capital" term, consider how the measure is altered by the introduction of depreciation, risk, inflation, and taxes.

First however, there are circumstances under which all uses of the cost of capital would be the same—when there is a uniform level of risk and thus a single type of financial asset (e.g., only bonds), and there is no depreciation, no taxes, and no inflation. In this case, the cost of capital is the rate of interest, denoted $i$. If the interest rate is 6 percent, the cost of capital is 6 percent, or 6 cents per dollar of capital.

### Introducing depreciation

Suppose the capital in question is a machine, whose value falls by a certain percent each period as the machine gets older and experiences wear, tear, and obsolescence. If the firm were renting this machine from a lessor, its rent would include not only interest on the use of capital but also an amount to compensate the lessor for the deterioration in value of the machine. Suppose the machine loses 10 percent of its value each year. In that case, the cost of capital for the machine is the sum of the interest paid ($i$) and the depreciation rate ($d$), or $i + d$. If the interest rate is 6 percent and the depreciation rate is 10 percent, the cost of capital is 16 percent, or 16 cents per dollar of capital.

The user cost of capital, inclusive of depreciation, therefore varies across different types of assets. It is larger for machinery, which depreciates more quickly, than for structures.

### Introducing risk—debt versus equity finance

The cost of capital will not be represented properly by using the interest rate if there are different forms of financial investments. Equity investments generally earn higher rates of return than debt investments, presumably owing to the greater riskiness of equity investments. Typically, the cost-of-capital measure is adjusted to incorporate that risk by providing a weighted average of debt and equity. For example, if a firm borrows $f$ percent of its capital, pays an interest rate of "$i$," and has a required equity return of $E$, then the cost of capital will be: $fi + (1 - f)E + d$.

### Introducing inflation

The interest rate, or the equity return, in the cost-of-capital formula should be the real rather than the nominal return. The nominal interest rate during an inflationary period is composed of two parts: the real return and the inflation premium necessary to retain the real value of the asset. For example, if the interest rate is 6 percent and the inflation rate is 4 percent, the real interest rate is only 2 percent. When a firm repays the nominal principal in cheaper dollars, that repayment plus the inflation premium is just enough to maintain the real value of the principal.

### Introducing taxes

Hall and Jorgenson (1967) incorporated taxes into the cost of capital; economists have since further refined this measure. If there were no inflation, and if taxable income were measured correctly, the cost of capital to a firm would be the interest rate, if debt-financed. The firm pays no tax on interest because although the profits of its investments are taxed, they are fully offset by the deductibility of the interest. However, the firm must pay a tax on the equity return to stockholders or other equity owners; thus, if $E$ represents the rate of profit after the tax required by equity interests, the cost of capital for equity finance is $E/(1 - u)$, where $u$ is the firm's tax rate. With depreciation, and a mixture of debt and equity finance, the cost of capital is: $fi + (1 - f)E/(1 - u) + d$.

When inflation is present, but tax depreciation is measured correctly (i.e., reflects true economic decline but is restated in nominal dollars each period), the cost of the debt-financed investment, net of depreciation, is $i(1 - u) - p/(1 - u)$, where $i$ is the nominal interest rate and $p$ is the inflation rate. Note that this value is smaller than the real interest rate $(i - p)$ with no tax. This is because the firm can deduct nominal interest. Thus, the firm's after-tax real cost of borrowing is $i(1 - u) - p$, smaller than the $(i - p)/(1 - u)$ cost if the inflation premium were not deductible. This real cost is grossed up by the tax rate if economic income is otherwise correctly measured.

In general, tax depreciation is measured according to tax accounting rules that neither adjust for inflation nor reflect the true pattern of economic depreciation. In this case, the cost of capital is $(R + d)(1 - uz - k)/(1 - u)$, where $z$ is the present value of tax depreciation deductions per unit of investment, $k$ is any investment credit allowed, and $R$ is the weighted after-tax discount rate of the firm $f[i(1 - u) - p] + [1 - f]E$. $E$ is assumed to be the real rate of profit. The value of $z$ may be larger than economic depreciation $[d/(R + d)]$ because tax depreciation is accelerated, but this effect is offset by the fact that depreciation deductions are not normally indexed for inflation (and thus would be discounted at the nominal discount rate, $R + p$, making the value of $z$ smaller.

For many applications, there is an additional, crucial measure: the pretax rate of return, or the net cost of capital. This measure is taken by calculating the cost of capital and then subtracting the depreciation rate. The measure that is left is the pretax rate of return, subsequently denoted as $r$.

## Applications of the cost-of-capital measure

The cost-of-capital measure is used in several ways: in summarizing the often complex features of the tax code into a single measure of effective tax rate, in assessing the effects of tax changes on the allocation and size of the capital stock, and in measuring the efficiency consequences of tax policy.

### Effective tax rates

The cost-of-capital measure can be used to construct effective marginal tax rates. One measure is the *firm level* effective tax rate, which shows the effects of features such as investment credits and tax depreciation. This measure of effective tax rate is derived by subtracting the firm's after-tax rate of return from the pretax rate of return, and dividing by the pretax rate of return, or $(r - R)/r$. It thus shows what fraction of the internal pretax rate of return, $r$, is paid in taxes. If economic income is equal to taxable income (in a present-value sense), the effective tax rate will be the firm's statutory marginal tax rate.

Effective tax rates typically vary across assets. To aggregate these measures, the pretax returns on different assets should be weighted by the contribution of the asset to the total capital stock to obtain an overall pretax return, and hence an overall effective tax rate.

Another measure of effective tax rate is the *total* effective tax rate. To measure this tax burden, one must measure the real after-tax rate of return to investors. This return would be a weighted average of the after-tax real interest rate, or $i(1 - t) - p$, where $t$ is the tax rate of the bondholder. The equity rate in the corporate sector will be $E(1 - v)$, where $v$ is the real effective personal-level tax burden (arising from dividend and capital gains taxation).

There is some disagreement as to how to weight and measure different tax rates. For example, $v$, in a traditional model, represents the sum of the effective personal-level taxes on corporate stock: taxes on dividends and effective real tax burdens on capital gains. Some proponents of the "new view" of dividends distinguish between equity investment obtained through new stock issues and investment of retained earnings, arguing that the dividend tax is not an effective burden on this latter (and dominant) source of equity finance. Another issue is whether the ratio of debt-to-equity finance at the margin is the same as the ratio on average, and how risk might be treated in measuring tax rates.

### Effects of tax changes on the cost of capital and investment

The cost-of-capital measure is important, given its role as a measure of the price of capital inputs, in estimating the effects of tax policy changes on the size and allocation of the capital stock. One issue is the extent to which changes in tax liability alter interest rates or equity returns. To hold rates of return (either the firm's after-tax rate, or the individual investor's after-tax rate of return) constant will lead to a different result than if, say, the capital stock is held constant. Thus, assessment of the effects of tax changes on the cost of capital and on investment will depend not only on how investment responds to changes in price but also on whether the estimate takes into account feedbacks from the economy as a whole.

It is important to distinguish between the gross cost of capital (inclusive of depreciation) and pretax return (which is sometimes referred to as the net cost of capital). The percentage change in the price of capital appropriate for assessing changes in investment demand should be measured as a fraction of the gross (depreciation-inclusive) cost; this effect will be smaller than the percentage change in pretax return for assets that depreciate.

Another application of the cost-of-capital measure is in calculations of the efficiency effects of a tax change. In general, a tax system results in the most efficient allocation of capital if the pretax returns are equal across all assets. The cost-of-capital concept is necessary to derive the pretax return; this measure, in turn, provides input for assessing whether a tax change leads to more or less economic efficiency.

### Magnitude of the cost of capital

Most estimates of the firm's discount rate ($R$) range in the neighborhood of 4 to 6 percent for a corporate firm. The cost of capital after all taxes (i.e., after personal taxes) would be slightly lower. Overall effective tax rates in the U.S. economy as of 1994 have been estimated at around 30 percent (including owner-occupied housing), suggesting an overall pretax rate of return of around 7 percent. All of these rates of return are net of any inflation premium. The depreciation rate averages about 15 percent for equipment, 2 to 3 percent for structures, and about 3 percent overall, including land and inventories that do not depreciate. Gravelle (1994) contains data on effective tax rates and the magnitude of the measures used to compute the cost of capital.

### Additional readings

Gravelle, Jane G. *The Economic Effects of Taxing Capital Income.* Cambridge, Mass.: MIT Press, 1994.

Hall, Robert E., and Dale W. Jorgenson. "Tax Policy and Investment Behavior." *American Economic Review* 58 (June 1967): 391–414.

Jorgenson, Dale W. "Capital Theory and Investment Behavior." *American Economic Review* 54 (May 1963): 247–59.

*Cross references:* capital cost recovery; deferral of tax; marginal effective tax rate.

# D

# Deferral of tax

Emil M. Sunley
International Monetary Fund

*A tax strategy or plan whereby income may be deferred or postponed for some period of time.*

---

The concept of tax deferral relates to the timing of tax payments. Taxpayers prefer to pay taxes tomorrow, next year, five years from now, or in the hereafter, rather than today. This is because a dollar today is worth more than a dollar in the future. Tax deferral is sometimes suggested to be unimportant because it involves "only postponing" a tax payment that will eventually have to be made. But as Surrey (1971) points out, deferral of taxes is analogous to the government making interest-free, nonrecourse loans without collateral. Moreover, taxes deferred are taxes partly forgiven, and taxes deferred forever are taxes forgiven.

Just as taxpayers prefer to pay taxes later, the government prefers to receive tax payments now instead of in the future. If the government receives a dollar of taxes today, it can be invested to earn interest, or it can be used to reduce the amount of borrowing the government otherwise would have to do, thus saving interest payments on the avoided debt.

Many tax incentives or preferences take the form of tax deferrals. Examples from the U.S. income tax include accelerated depreciation, the deferral of income from controlled foreign corporations, the deferral of interest on U.S. savings bonds, and the deferral of capital gains on home sales. Taxing capital gains when realized involves deferral of taxation, as the gains may have accrued over a number of years. Sophisticated tax planning often involves a mastery of tax rules in order to minimize taxes by deferring them to the future.

## The value of tax deferral

According to Andrews (1991), the value of tax deferral can be measured in four ways: interest on the deferred tax, present value of the deferred tax, increase in the after-tax rate of return, and the effective tax rate on the investment.

Possibly the simplest way to measure the value of deferring taxes is to compute the *interest earned* by investing the funds that would not be available if the taxpayer had to pay the taxes currently. Suppose a taxpayer defers paying $1,000 of tax and invests the funds, earning a 10 percent after-tax return. If he defers the tax one year, he earns $100. If he defers the tax two years, he earns $210 ($100 each year plus an additional $10 by investing the $100 earned the first year for one year). If he defers 10 years, he earns $1,594 ($100 a year compounded at 10%).

A second way of measuring the value of deferring tax is to compute the *present discounted* value of the deferred tax. The taxpayer's discount rate is crucial to understanding this way of measuring the value of deferral. The discount rate is essentially the after-tax rate of return that the taxpayer can earn on invested funds. If a taxpayer can defer paying $1,000 of tax for one year and her discount rate is 10 percent (i.e., she can earn a 10% after-tax return), then she needs to set aside $909.09 today to have $1,000 a year from now when the tax must be paid ($1,000 = $909.09 × 1.1). Thus, the present discounted value of paying $1,000 in tax a year from now is $909.09, assuming the taxpayer's discount rate is 10 percent. Thus, deferring tax one year is equivalent to paying only 90.9 percent of the tax liability. If $1,000 of taxes can be deferred 10 years, the present value is only $385.54, again assuming a 10 percent discount rate. Thus, deferring the tax 10 years is equivalent to paying only 38.6 percent of the tax liability.

These first two methods—interest earned and present discounted value—are closely related. The first approach looks at how much will be available in, say, 10 years if taxes are deferred, while the second approach looks at how much would have to be set aside today to pay the taxes in the future. To see this, recall that if $1,000 of taxes can be deferred for 10 years, the taxpayer can earn $1,594 over the 10-year period. At the end of 10 years he will have $2,594 available—the initial $1,000 plus the $1,594 of after-tax earnings. The present discounted value of $2,594 10 years from now and discounted at 10 percent is $1,000 ($1,000 = $2,594 × .3855). Or put another way, if a taxpayer has a tax liability of $2,594 10 years hence, he needs to set aside $1,000 today, assuming he can earn 10 percent after taxes on these funds.

The third method of measuring the value of deferral looks at *after-tax rate of return*. If a taxpayer in the 28 percent tax bracket puts his money in a savings account paying 10 percent, he has to pay tax each year on the earnings and thus his after-tax rate of return is 7.2 percent. Suppose the tax rules allow a taxpayer to defer paying tax for five years. If the

**TABLE 1**

**Effective Tax Rates for Different Tax Deferral Periods and Discount Rates**
**(Nominal tax rate = 28%)**

| Discount Rate (percent) | Period of Deferral (Years) | | | |
|---|---|---|---|---|
| | 0 | 5 | 10 | 25 |
| 5 | 28.0 | 26.1 | 23.9 | 18.4 |
| 10 | 28.0 | 24.4 | 20.6 | 12.8 |
| 20 | 28.0 | 21.6 | 15.8 | 7.8 |

Source: Author's calculations.

taxpayer invests $1,000 in the savings account, his account will grow to $1,610.51 at the end of five years. He will then have to pay taxes of $170.94 (28 percent on the $610.51 of interest earnings), leaving $1,439.57 after tax. His after-tax rate of return is 7.56 percent, because $1,000 invested at 7.56 percent per year compounded will grow to $1,439.57 in five years. Thus, deferring tax for five years in this example increases the after-tax rate of return from 7.2 to 7.56 percent.

A final method of measuring deferral is the *effective tax rate*. This method is closely related to the after-tax rate of return because the effective tax rate on an investment is defined as the percentage reduction in the rate of return resulting from taxes (i.e., the difference between the before-tax and after-tax rates of return divided by the before-tax rate of return expressed as a percentage). In the savings account example, the before-tax rate of return was 10 percent and the after-tax rate of return 7.56 percent when the taxpayer was allowed to defer taxes for five years. Thus taxes reduced the rate of return by 24.4 percent (from 10 to 7.56%). When the interest income was taxed currently, the after-tax rate of return was 7.2 percent, giving an effective tax rate of 28 percent, which is just equal to the nominal tax rate.

For a taxpayer in any given tax bracket, deferral is worth more the longer the period of deferral and the higher the rate of return that can be earned on invested funds (and thus the higher the taxpayer's discount rate). Table 1 measures the value of deferral by computing the effective tax rate for a taxpayer in the 28 percent tax bracket, assuming various periods of deferral and various before-tax rates of return. Lower effective tax rates indicate that deferral is more valuable. As shown in table 1, if the before-tax rate of return is 10 percent, the effective tax rate is 28 percent if there is no deferral, 24.4 percent if deferral is for 5 years, 20.6 percent if deferral is for 10 years, and 12.8 percent if deferral is for 25 years. Similarly, if the period of deferral is 10 years, the effective tax rate is 23.9 percent if the before-tax rate of return is 5 percent, but it falls to 15.8 percent if the before-tax rate of return is 20 percent. Deferral is also worth more the higher the taxpayer's mar-

ginal tax rate because the amount of taxes that can be deferred on a given amount of income varies directly with the taxpayer's marginal tax rate.

Tax deferral is often combined with other incentives or preferences. For example, employer contributions to a pension plan are excluded from the employee's income in the years the contribution is made, and the income earned on the funds in the pension plan is not taxable when earned. Instead, the taxes on both the employer contribution and the earnings are deferred until the employee receives a pension or other distribution from the plan. There may be an additional benefit from this treatment because many taxpayers are in lower tax brackets after retirement.

## Examples of U.S. tax deferral preferences

Capital gains are taxed only when realized. This is clearly a practical solution because of the difficulty of valuing assets each year. But this practical solution provides a significant tax benefit. A person who invests in a savings account is taxed each year on the interest earnings whether or not the funds are withdrawn from the account. In contrast, a person who invests in non-dividend-paying stock only pays tax on any gain (or recognizes a loss) when the stock is sold. This tax deferral reduces the effective tax rate on appreciating assets. In addition to deferral, the gain may never be taxed because under U.S. law, if appreciated stock passes at death to an heir, the unrealized capital gains at the time of death are not taxed.

The most important investment incentive in the United States and many other countries is accelerated depreciation. The tax law allows the cost of depreciable assets to be recovered more rapidly than the actual decline in the value of the assets— that is, economic depreciation. Accelerated depreciation is a deferral preference because the total amount of depreciation allowed over the life of the asset is unaffected. By being able to claim depreciation deductions earlier, the taxpayer can defer taxes to a later year. Because it is difficult to measure the actual decline in the value of assets, it is difficult to know just how much tax deferral is permitted under various depreciation rules. Companies, however, generally take slower depreciation for book or financial purposes, which may indicate that companies believe the depreciation allowed for tax purposes to be accelerated relative to the actual decline in the value of the assets. In fact, the tax savings resulting from the difference between book and tax depreciation becomes the deferred tax item on the liability side of the company's balance sheet.

Before the Tax Reform Act of 1986, accelerated depreciation on real estate and machinery and equipment was one of the key elements of tax shelters. These tax-favored investments produced artificial losses that sheltered other income from taxation.

Immediate write-off or expensing (sometimes called instantaneous depreciation) is an extreme form of accelerated depreciation. Although only allowed in the United States for a limited amount of depreciable assets (under section 179 of the Internal Revenue Code), for research and experimentation expenditures, and for certain exploration and development costs of oil and mineral properties, it would be a normal rule under a cash-flow tax. As Brown (1948) showed, expensing results in the after-tax rate of return on the investment being the same as the before-tax rate of return, implying a zero effective tax rate on the investment.

The income of foreign corporations controlled by U.S. shareholders is generally not subject to U.S. taxation. The income becomes taxable only when the shareholders receive dividends or other distributions. This permits U.S. companies to defer tax on their foreign income until it is distributed.

A final example is the deferral of tax on U.S. savings bonds interest. Interest on these bonds is only taxable when the bonds are redeemed, unless the investor elects to pay tax currently—and few do. These bonds can be quite attractive investments for individuals who expect to hold them until retirement, when they will be in a lower tax bracket.

## Additional readings

Andrews, William D. *Basic Federal Income Taxation*, pp. 256–64. Boston: Little, Brown and Company, 1991.

Brown, E. Cary. "Business-Income Taxation and Investment Incentives." In *Income, Employment, and Public Policy: Essays in Honor of Alvin H. Hansen*. New York: W. W. Norton & Co., 1948.

Surrey, Stanley S. "The Tax Reform Act of 1969—Tax Deferral and Tax Shelters." *Boston College Industrial and Commercial Law Review* 12 (February 1971): 307–18.

*Cross references:* capital cost recovery; capital gains taxation; cost of capital; expensing; marginal effective tax rate; multinational corporations, taxation.

# Depletion, cost and percentage

Jane G. Gravelle
Congressional Research Service, Library of Congress

*Deductions to reflect the using up of mineral deposits.*

Depletion deductions are allowed to recover investment costs in a mineral reserve, which becomes de-

pleted as minerals are extracted. These investment costs include the costs of acquiring mineral properties (purchase of lease bonuses) and exploration costs. There are two depletion methods—cost and percentage. Cost depletion allows recovery of costs at the same estimated rate as the mineral is extracted; it is an appropriate method for recovering costs (although its value is reduced by inflation). Percentage depletion allows an arbitrary deduction of a percentage of gross sales and, in some cases, may be many times the original cost. Percentage depletion is limited to independent producers of oil and gas and then allowed only for limited quantities (up to 1,000 barrels of oil a day or the gas equivalent); it is allowed at a 15 percent rate. Marginal (stripper) wells receive special benefits. Percentage depletion is allowed at a variety of different rates for other minerals. Despite the limits on percentage depletion for oil and gas, the subsidy value of percentage depletion is largest for these fuels: $0.6 billion, compared with $0.3 billion for other fuels (primarily coal) and $2 billion for nonfuel minerals.

Percentage depletion originated with oil and gas and was a substitute for discovery value depletion, enacted in 1918 and allowing recovery of market value rather than cost. For many years, percentage depletion for oil and gas was one of the most hotly debated tax subsidies. In later years, percentage depletion was justified on the grounds of maintaining a domestic oil and gas capacity for national defense in the face of low-cost foreign production. The provision was repealed for major producers when prices rose dramatically in the 1970s. The provisions for other minerals, which were enacted after those for oil and gas, and justified in part to provide parity, were retained.

The oil and gas production industry retains important tax subsidies, but they are in the form of the ability to expense or rapidly recover a large fraction of the cost of finding mineral deposits.

## Additional reading

U.S. Congress, Senate, Committee on the Budget. *Tax Expenditures*. Washington, D.C., December 1996.

*Cross references:* capital cost recovery; expensing; inflation indexation of income taxes.

# Depository institutions, federal taxation

Edith Brashares
Department of the Treasury

*Special tax provisions that deviate from those of the general corporate income tax are provided to certain institutions that derive income from lending.*

While most providers of financial services are taxed under the general corporate income tax rules (see Corporate income tax, federal), some are subject to special tax provisions. In particular, a distinction is made between depository institutions that derive most of their income from lending activities in which funds are taken from depositors and lent to borrowers, and "nondepository" institutions that do not take deposits, but instead borrow to finance or securitize loans. Nondepository institutions are neither given special tax treatment nor as regulated as depository institutions. In general, bank holding companies are considered nondepository institutions and can engage in nonbanking activities.

Unlike the other depository institutions, credit unions are exempt from federal income tax. (Internal Revenue Code section 501(c)1 exempts federally chartered credit unions, while 501(c)14 exempts state-chartered credit unions from paying federal income taxes.) Credit unions are not-for-profit, have a mutual organization structure in that the owners and depositors are one and the same, and distribute earnings back to members. Membership is limited to those sharing a "common bond," such as the same profession. Repeal of this tax exemption, for at least some credit unions, was proposed in 1971, 1973, 1978, 1985, and 1992 (see American Bankers Association 1989 for further discussion).

The remaining depository institutions, thrifts and banks, are subject to federal income tax. Thrifts include domestic building and loan associations, savings and loan associations, mutual savings banks, and cooperative nonprofit mutual banks. While most consumers today would consider thrifts and banks as interchangeable, there are differences that have historic roots. In general, thrifts had a primary objective of taking deposits from individuals and using the funds to provide home mortgages, while banks used deposits from both individuals and businesses to finance commercial and industrial, as well as consumer, loans. These operating differences were reflected in distinctions in tax treatment, though the tax differences have narrowed as thrift and bank activities have become similar.

Special tax treatment of depository institutions has generally reflected the fact that their primary income derives from taking deposits and lending. Depository institutions are subject to special rules with respect to bad debts, gains and losses on debt obligations, and insolvent institutions' priorities for payments. Because depository institutions can deduct interest expense to purchase and carry bonds, unlike other taxpayers, who are more restricted, banks and thrifts are subject to special rules with respect to tax-exempt bonds. Other special provisions include interest exclusion on some obligations, net operating loss, alternative minimum tax treatment, and provisions that apply to thrifts (see Rook 1989 for more details).

## Bad debts

Taxpayers, other than certain depository institutions, are required to use the specific charge-off method to account for bad debts. Essentially, a deduction for a bad debt is allowed when a loan becomes partially or totally worthless. Large banks and thrifts with assets of $500 million or more are required to use the specific charge-off method. Treasury regulations allow banks and thrifts to treat debts as worthless for tax purposes when they are charged off for regulatory purposes (conclusive presumption). This generally allows the losses to be recognized sooner.

Small banks and thrifts can use the reserve method for accounting for bad debts, but are limited to using the experience and fill-up methods for determining reserve deductions. For growing institutions, the reserve method generally accelerates future loss deductions and is equivalent to an interest-free loan from the government equal to the tax rate times the reserve amount. Under the experience method, the reserve is based on the six-year moving average of charge-offs less recoveries (net charge-offs) during the year as a percentage of the amount of loans outstanding at the end of the year. The deduction for bad debts is then the amount by which this percentage times the amount of loans at the end of the year exceeds outstanding reserves adjusted for net charge-offs. The fill-up method allows a deduction for the difference between base year reserves (1987) and current reserves (determined after the reduction for current year losses). This method was very popular before the base year was fixed in 1986, particularly for thrifts.

The Tax Reform Act of 1986 repealed the bad debt reserve method by large banks as well as nondepository institutions. In addition, as a result of the Tax Reform Act of 1969, small banks were no longer eligible to use the percentage of eligible loan reserve method for determining reserves after 1988. Under this method, a bank's allowable reserve equaled a specific percentage of its eligible loans.

The bad debt reserve deduction was the change in allowable reserves plus net charge-offs. (See Neubig and Sullivan 1987 for a discussion of the effects of the 1986 act on banks.)

Depository institutions that no longer qualify for reserve treatment are required to recapture (include in income) all or part of bad debt reserves. Recapture is intended to prevent the duplication of deductions—first as a reserve addition and then when the loan is charged off.

Currently, when a small bank or thrift becomes large, reserve recapture is done using either the four-year spread or the cutoff method. Under the four-year spread approach, 10 percent of reserves are recaptured into income in the first year, 20 percent in the second, 30 percent in the third, and 40 percent in the fourth. However, if the institution has a large net operating loss deduction that is expiring, it can choose instead to recapture more in the first year, two-ninths of the residual in the second, three-ninths in the third, and four-ninths in the fourth year. Under the cutoff approach, the reserve associated with a stock of loans outstanding at the time of recapture cannot be added to. The amount of the reserve is then adjusted for net charge-offs, while the amount of the associated stock of loans is adjusted for charge-offs and loan collections. If adjusted reserves exceed adjusted loans, then the difference is recaptured and the reserve balance is decreased by this amount. If adjusted reserves are less than or equal to the adjusted loans, then none of the reserve is recaptured. The cutoff method can effectively delay when the recapture occurs. These two recapture methods were also allowed in 1986 when the reserve method was repealed for large banks.

When reserve recapture was necessary for thrifts in 1996, the recapture regime was different, reflecting the regulatory problems with recapturing pre-1988 reserves and the additional special assessment paid by thrifts to capitalize the deposit insurance fund. In general, the amount of post-1987 reserves recaptured was included ratably over six years. Large thrifts recaptured the excess of total reserves over pre-1988 reserves (excluding supplemental reserves). Small thrifts also excluded post-1987 experience-based reserves from recapture because they could continue to use experience-based reserves. Post-1987 experience reserves would be recaptured later under rules applicable to banks if a thrift became a large depository institution. (This approach forgives tax on pre-1988 reserves of former thrifts so that small thrifts would be treated on a par with larger thrifts. However, small banks that become large banks would still be liable for recapture of their post-1987 experience-based reserves.) For the first two years following the tax law change, though, thrifts satisfying a residential loan requirement could suspend recapture. The loan require-

ment was that the principal amount of residential loans made by the taxpayer during the year had to meet or exceed the average of the principal amount of residential loans made by the taxpayer during the six most recent taxable years beginning before January 1, 1996. (See Brashares and Koch 1997 for details on the 1996 tax law changes and prior tax treatment of thrifts.)

Before the tax changes in 1996, whereby thrifts were treated the same as banks, thrifts received preferential bad debt treatment in exchange for satisfying certain criteria. Thrifts had to have a thrift charter and satisfy the qualified thrift asset test. In general, thrifts could choose the most advantageous approach each year for determining additions to reserves for residential loans (qualifying): (1) percentage of taxable income, (2) experience, or (3) fill-up. While reserves were adjusted each year for the amount of net charge-offs, the reserve addition under the percentage of taxable income method was the amount by which 8 percent of taxable income (determined without regard to the bad debt deduction) exceeded the addition to reserves for nonresidential (nonqualifying) loans. However, the deduction could not exceed the amount needed to increase reserves to 6 percent of qualifying loans. (In addition, total reserves plus surplus could not exceed 12 percent of deposits.) Unlike the experience method, the amount of the deduction was unrelated to bad debt experience and could result in reserve growth without relation to loan losses. Before 1986, the percentage allowed was higher and essentially enabled thrifts to pay little tax by having large additions to reserves. (When thrifts were first taxed [1952], the rate was 100%. The rate was lowered to 60% in 1969, 40% in 1976, and 8% in 1986.)

## Gains and losses as ordinary income

For both banks and thrifts, gains and losses realized on the sale or exchange of a debt obligation are treated as ordinary, instead of a capital gain or loss, if the debt obligation was acquired after July 11, 1969. This restriction limited tax avoidance when capital gains received significant preferential treatment (see Capital gains taxation). An obligation obtained before this time has the gain or loss allocated ratably between long-term capital gain or loss from before July 12, 1969, and the ordinary income or loss after July 11, 1969. The capital gain portion is limited to the net gain recognized on all sales or exchanges of debt obligations for the year.

## Insolvent depository institutions

Given the overriding concern with insuring depositors against losses from the insolvency of the institution, it is not surprising that insolvent institutions receive special treatment with respect to tax payment. Taxes cannot be collected, except employment taxes, when the collection would diminish an institution's assets necessary for payment of its depositors.

## Interest expense and exclusion

To discourage interest rate arbitrage using tax-exempt bonds (see Tax-exempt bonds), the interest expense deduction is effectively denied for purchasing and carrying most tax-exempt bonds acquired after August 7, 1986. The disallowed interest expense is the average adjusted tax bases of tax-exempt obligations acquired after August 7, 1986, over the average adjusted tax bases of all assets times the total interest expense. Tax-exempt bonds acquired before August 8, 1986, but after 1982 limit interest disallowance to 20 percent. Before 1983, there was no disallowance. The 20 percent disallowance continues to apply to certain small-issue bonds, particularly those where the issuer anticipates issuing no more than $10 million of obligations in a year.

Before repeal in 1996, depository and other financial institutions were encouraged to make loans to employee stock ownership plans (ESOPs) by excluding 50 percent of the interest on certain securities acquisition loans made after July 18, 1984 (see Employee stock ownership plans). The 1989 tax law changes added restrictions, such as the ESOP being obliged to own 50 percent or more of the stock after the acquisition.

## Net operating losses

Like other taxpayers, a bank can carry a net operating loss back 3 years or forward 15 years (see Net operating losses). However, the loss attributable to a bank's bad debt deduction could be carried back 10 years or forward 5 years if the bank used the specific charge-off method, and the net operating loss was for a taxable year beginning after 1986 and before 1994. For losses attributable to tax years beginning after 1975 and before 1987, unlike other taxpayers, all banks were entitled to a 10-year carryback and a 5-year carryforward period. The longer carryback was granted to offset the effect of phasing down the percentage of eligible loans reserve method. Similarly, for losses in tax years between 1981 and 1986, thrifts were entitled to a 10-year carryback and a 5-year carryforward before 1987.

## Alternative minimum tax

Unlike the other corporate alternative minimum tax provisions, the preference for bad debt reserves affected only depository institutions (see Alternative minimum tax, corporate). The preference, repealed in 1996, was for the excess of the bad debt deduction over the experience reserve deduction and primarily affected thrifts.

## Special thrift provisions

While most corporations are not entitled to deduct dividends that they pay, thrifts can deduct "dividends" that are more accurately described as interest paid to depositors. The key requirement is that the depositor can withdraw the paid or credited dividend amount on demand. Similarly, banks and other nonmutual corporations that receive dividends from mutual savings banks or savings and loans associations must treat the dividends as interest and not eligible for the dividends-received deduction.

As with other taxpayers, the tax treatment of distributions to shareholders that are not redemptions or liquidations comes first from earnings and profits in the taxable year. The next sources, by rank, are somewhat unique to thrifts. These sources are earnings and profits accumulated in tax years beginning after December 31, 1952 (when thrifts became taxable), pre-1988 reserve for losses on qualifying loans to the extent that additions to this reserve exceed those that would have been allowed under the experience method, and supplemental reserves for losses on loans. For redemption and liquidation distributions, the first source is pre-1988 reserves for qualifying loans followed by supplemental reserves, earnings and profits for the taxable year, and earnings and profits accumulated in taxable years beginning after December 31, 1952.

Federal Savings and Loan Insurance Company (FSLIC) payments reimbursing losses as part of 1988 and 1989 transactions are exempt from tax. Tax law in 1993 clarified that FSLIC assistance was compensation for losses and disallowed a loss deduction. Net operating losses as a result of these loss deductions were limited.

## Additional readings

American Bankers Association. *The Credit Union Industry: Trends, Structure, and Competitiveness.* Prepared under the Direction of the Secura Group. Washington, D.C.: American Bankers Association, November 10, 1989.

Brashares, Edith, and Cathleen Koch. "Changing the Tax Treatment of Thrifts: The Importance of the Rules of the Game." Mimeograph. Paper presented at the American Economic Association Annual Meetings, New Orleans, January 1997.

Neubig, Thomas S., and Martin A. Sullivan. "The Effect of the Tax Reform Act of 1986 on Commercial Banks." In Office of Tax Analysis, Department of the Treasury, *Compendium of Tax Research 1987.* Ch. 10. Washington, D.C.: U.S. Government Printing Office, pp. 279–305.

Rook, Lance W. *Federal Income Taxation of Banks and Financial Institutions.* 6th ed. Boston: Warren, Gorham, and Lamont, 1989.

*Cross references:* banks, state taxation; income tax, corporate, federal; tax-exempt bonds.

# Depreciation recapture

Joseph J. Cordes
George Washington University

Larry Ozanne
Congressional Budget Office

Leonard E. Burman
The Urban Institute

*A provision in tax law that is intended to limit the ability of taxpayers to convert otherwise fully taxable income into tax-preferred capital gains.*

---

Accelerated depreciation can become a means of converting ordinary income into preferentially taxed capital gains. For an example of accelerated depreciation, suppose that an apartment building is built for $100,000 by a taxpayer in the 28 percent tax bracket, that the preferential tax rate on capital gains is 20 percent, and that $50,000 in depreciation deductions are allowed before the building is sold for $80,000. The taxpayer's adjusted basis—cost less depreciation deductions—is $50,000. However, the true economic depreciation is actually only $20,000 ($100,000 − $80,000). The $30,000 capital gain (sales price less adjusted basis) in this example is entirely a result of accelerated depreciation deductions. Without depreciation recapture, the capital gains tax would be $6,000 (20 percent of $30,000). This is really a tax on the rental income previously earned from the building that was deferred because of accelerated depreciation. Thus, accelerated depreciation creates deferred income of $30,000, which is then taxed as a capital gain, thereby giving the investor the opportunity to convert that income into a form that is taxed at 20 percent instead of 28 percent.

When capital gains are taxed at preferential rates, opportunities for converting ordinary income into capital gains in the manner described above can be reduced by requiring that depreciation deductions be recaptured.

Recapture means that the portion of a gain that corresponds to past depreciation deductions is taxed at ordinary income tax rates. In the example just given, none of the measured capital gain would be taxed preferentially because the depreciation deductions of $50,000 exceed the measured capital gain of $30,000. Only an increase in value over the original purchase price (adjusted for out-of-pocket costs) would qualify for the lower capital gains rate. For example, if the building in the above example were sold for $110,000, the initial measured gain would be $60,000, of which $50,000 would be recaptured and taxed at ordinary rates and $10,000 would be taxed at the lower capital gains rate.

Although the concept of requiring that accelerated depreciation be recaptured is simple in principle, the regulations governing recapture are among the more complex elements of tax law. Nonetheless, tax experts recognize the necessity of recapture to avoid creating incentives for tax shelters and the accompanying incentives for investors to engage in tax arbitrage, such as those that existed in the early 1980s. These incentives are strongest, and hence the need for a strong and workable recapture provision is greatest, when the tax code allows highly accelerated depreciation while simultaneously taxing capital gains at preferential rates. Tax changes that were enacted in 1986 reduced the effective need for recapture rules considerably by aligning tax depreciation more closely with the economic depreciation of assets and by taxing capital gains at the same rate as other income. Subsequent changes in tax law that reintroduced a preferential tax rate for capital gains for some investors have increased the role of recapture provisions. Currently, all depreciation on equipment is recaptured at ordinary rates, while depreciation on structures is taxed at ordinary rates, capped at 25 percent, with the top rate on long-term capital gains set at 20 percent and the top rate on ordinary income at 3.6 percent.

*Cross references:* basis; capital cost recovery; capital gains taxation; tax arbitrage; tax shelters.

# Destination principle

George Carlson
Arthur Andersen, LLP

*In designing general business (e.g., value-added) and transaction (e.g., sales) taxes, a choice is made between taxing goods where they are produced ("origin") or where they are purchased or consumed ("destination"). In an open economy, the choice may strongly affect tax productivity, equity, and efficiency.*

---

Under the destination principle of taxation, goods and services are taxed where they are purchased or consumed, rather than where they are produced or originate. Destination-basis treatment can be contrasted with the origin principle, under which goods and services are taxed where they are produced. Consider the case of a sales or value-added tax levied by Jurisdiction B. With respect to goods and services that are produced in Jurisdiction A (the origin) but sold in Jurisdiction B (the destination), the destination principle is implemented if Jurisdiction B applies what are popularly known as "border tax adjustments" to imports and exports. Specifically, Jurisdiction B should apply the tax to goods imported from Jurisdiction A and rebate or "forgive" the tax on exports. (Domestically produced and consumed goods and services are, of course, taxed by Jurisdiction B as well.) The effect of these so-called destination principle border tax adjustments is to ensure that all goods sold in Jurisdiction B (the destination jurisdiction) are taxed, regardless of where they are produced or originate. Similarly, goods or services produced in Jurisdiction B but exported and sold elsewhere are not taxed by Jurisdiction B under the destination principle.

International tax and trading rules, established by the General Agreement on Tariffs and Trade, provide that destination principle border tax adjustments can be applied to taxes on products, such as excise, sales, or value-added taxes (also known as indirect taxes), but not to direct taxes, such as income and social insurance taxes. Thus, indirect taxes can be imposed at the border on imports, but no explicit adjustments can be made for direct taxes with respect to either imports or exports. In countries with federal systems of government, such as the United States and Canada, subnational governmental entities may also be able to levy taxes. If so, the movement of goods and services among these subnational units of government requires a choice between the destination and origin principles. In the United States, for example, states tend to follow a destination principle method of taxation.

The primary effect of the destination principle is to tax consumption, rather than production. All goods and services sold in the destination jurisdiction are taxed, provided they are not specifically exempted from the tax base. Many jurisdictions, for example, choose to exempt food and medicine and other "necessities" from taxation for reasons of fairness and equity. But provided a good or service is generally subject to taxation, the destination principle demands that the tax be levied no matter where the good or service was produced. Only the destination of the sale of the good or service is relevant in determining tax liability. Because the destination of a service (e.g., financial advice) can be less certain than that of a good (e.g., an automobile), it may be more difficult to apply the destination principle to some services than to goods.

A completely general tax applied uniformly to either the consumption or production of all goods will not affect the allocation of resources in an economy. In an open economy, this implies that the choice of either origin or destination principle border tax adjustments is irrelevant to resource allocation. In particular, assuming a comprehensive tax applying to all products, the choice of either the destination principle or the origin principle will not affect the distribution of resources, or the direction or extent of trade between two countries. There is a monetary difference between the two principles in that a general tax imposed under the origin principle will initially worsen the country's trade balance, causing an offsetting devaluation in its currency, whereas a general tax imposed under the destination principle will have no trade balance repercussions. This is another way of saying that currency depreciation and destination principle border tax adjustments produce the same results. Finally, there is a fiscal difference in that taxes on imports are collected by the destination jurisdiction.

# Dividends, double taxation of

Joseph J. Cordes
George Washington University

*Taxation that comes about in the U.S. tax system because corporate profits are taxed once by the corporate income tax and then again when these profits are distributed to shareholders.*

Income that is earned by corporations in the United States is currently subject to two levels of tax. Corporate profits are subject to the corporate income tax. When these profits are distributed to the shareholders who own the corporations, these distributions are also included in the shareholders' taxable income.

The consequence of this system is that the return on equity investments in corporate activities is taxed twice. For example, if the statutory corporate tax rate is 34 percent and the personal tax rate is 33 percent, one dollar of corporate earnings is first reduced by 34 cents in corporate profits taxes, which leaves the corporation with 66 cents that can either be kept as retained earnings or paid out in dividends. If the 66 cents is paid out in dividends, this amount would be included in a shareholders' taxable income and would be subject to the personal tax of 33 percent, leaving the shareholder with 44 cents. This situation may be contrasted with a dollar that is earned by, for example, a business that is not incorporated. In that case one dollar of earnings would be subject only to the personal income tax, and the owners of the unincorporated business would get to keep 66 cents.

Double taxation of corporate earnings has long been considered a nettlesome problem of the U.S. tax system, and it is believed to affect business behavior in several ways. One that has received particular attention is the corporation's decision as to how much of its after-tax earnings to retain and how much to pay out to shareholders in dividends. Another is the corporation's decision about how to finance its investments.

## Retained earnings versus dividend payout

One way corporations can reduce the sting of the double tax is to retain earnings rather than pay them out in dividends. If the retained earnings are invested wisely by the corporation, each dollar of retained earnings should increase the value of the firm, which raises its share price. Such price appreciation translates into a capital gain for shareholders; and although capital gains are ultimately subject to tax, they are taxed more lightly than dividends, mainly because of tax deferral. Although retained earnings are neither good nor bad in and of themselves, economists believe that the decision to retain earnings or pay them out should be based on nontax considerations.

## Equity versus debt finance

Double taxation also makes equity finance "more costly" to the corporation than debt finance. This is because corporations are allowed to deduct interest payments on corporate taxes as a business expense but are not allowed to take a tax deduction for the costs of equity finance. As a consequence, the returns from corporate investments that are ultimately paid out to bondholders are subject to only one level of tax. In effect, this means that one dollar of investment that is financed by debt needs to earn a lower overall rate of return in order to pay bondholders their required return after tax, because this dollar is subject only to the personal income tax, than does one dollar of investment that is financed by equity, which is subject to both the corporate and personal income taxes.

## Policy implications

Double taxation of corporate equity has given rise to calls for integrating the corporate and personal income taxes. This is discussed in more detail in the entry Integration, corporate tax. The tax system also has features that are designed to attenuate the effects of double taxation, including the tax treatment given to Subchapter S corporations.

*Cross references:* dividends-received deduction; income tax, corporate, federal; income tax, federal; integration, corporate tax; Subchapter S corporation.

# Dividends-received deduction

George A. Plesko
Massachusetts Institute of Technology

*A deduction that corporations may take in some cases for dividends received from other corporations.*

The dividends-received deduction (DRD) has been present in some form since the establishment of the corporate income tax in 1909. The rationale for the DRD is to eliminate the possibility of taxing corporate income more than twice—the traditional U.S. approach to corporate income. In the absence of a DRD, intercorporate dividends would be taxed at least three times: first as income to a corporation, then as income to the corporation receiving the distribution, and then again when the income is distributed to the individual shareholders. To the extent that there is additional intercorporate ownership, this income could be subject to even more layers of corporate taxation.

The DRD is generally governed by sections 243–246 of the Internal Revenue Code, which define the types of eligible dividends and the holding period requirements (currently 45 days). Allowable deductions vary depending on the type of stock (preferred versus common) and the type of company paying the dividend (public utility, small business, or foreign). Initially, the DRD was equal to 100 percent of all dividends received, but the deduction level has changed, or been restricted, several times since its inception, frequently since 1986. From 1913 to 1917, the DRD was eliminated, but it was reinstated at 100 percent in 1918. The DRD remained at 100 percent until 1937, when it was reduced to 90 percent and later further reduced to 85 percent. In 1965, a two-tier DRD was established, with the allowable exclusion based upon the amount of ownership. If the companies were members of an affiliated group (80% or more ownership), the DRD was 100 percent. Dividends from nonaffiliated companies were classified as "portfolio dividends" and subject to an 85 percent deduction. The Tax Reform Act of 1986 reduced the DRD to 80 percent for portfolio dividends. As part of the Omnibus Budget Reconciliation Act of 1987, the DRD for portfolio dividends received or accrued after December 31, 1987, was reduced to 70 percent in the case of ownership of less than 20 percent of the corporation. This ownership-dependent three-tiered level of DRD continues today.

Although interest payments are more tax-favored for the paying corporation than dividends, the existence of the DRD has created opportunities for corporations to issue dividend-paying stock that closely resembles debt. Jassy (1986) has shown how the DRD creates arbitrage opportunities for firms with net operating losses.

## Additional readings

Jassy, Everett L. "Issuances of Floating Rate Preferred Stock by Special Purpose Subsidiaries of Loss Corporations." *Tax Lawyer* 39 (3) (1986): 519–62.

Lind, Stephen A., Stephen Schwarz, Daniel J. Lathrope, and J.D. Rosenberg. *Fundamentals of Corporate Taxation*. Mineola, N.Y.: Foundation Press, 1987.

Schaffer, D.C. "The Income Tax on Intercorporate Dividends." *Tax Lawyer* 33 (1) (Fall 1979): 161–82.

*Cross references:* dividends, double taxation of; income tax, corporate, federal; integration, corporate tax.

# E

## Earmarking of taxes

Frederick Stocker
Professor Emeritus
Ohio State University

*In contrast to the practice of combining all revenues in a general fund and allocating them to expenditures through a budgeting process, earmarking reserves revenues from certain sources for particular expenses.*

Earmarking refers to the practice of dedicating a specific stream of tax revenue to a specific expenditure purpose. The most common contemporary example is the dedication of highway revenues (gas taxes, motor vehicle registration fees) to the construction and maintenance of streets and highways.

Earmarking is important in state and local fiscal systems. In 1988, 23 percent of state tax revenue came from earmarked sources, a share that remained more or less stable for a decade but was far below the 51 percent share for 1954. The earmarked share exceeded 50 percent in three states and was less than 10 percent in six (National Conference of State Legislatures 1990).

State taxes most often earmarked are excise taxes on motor fuel, tobacco, alcoholic beverages, and insurance. Among broad-based taxes, the most significant are state general sales taxes and corporate income taxes, although typically only a small portion of revenue from these sources is earmarked. By state program area, earmarking is most extensive in connection with highways and local government assistance.

Earmarking provisions are sometimes contained in state constitutions, sometimes in the statutes. The former are obviously more restrictive and more durable.

At the federal level, examples of earmarking are found in the Old Age, Survivors, Disability, and Health Insurance programs, where payroll taxes are set aside in trust funds. The Highway Trust Fund and the Airport and Airway Trust Fund are other major examples.

Generally, public finance and public administration experts disapprove of earmarking on the grounds that it rigidifies the public budget, depriving elected officials of the freedom to allocate funds among competing expenditure programs in accordance with currently perceived needs. It causes some parts of the budget to be overfunded relative to what elected representatives would otherwise have appropriated, and other parts to be underfunded. Also, earmarking is criticized for removing part of the public budget from the same legislative scrutiny and oversight given to general fund expenditures.

It is for these same reasons that proponents of certain government programs often favor earmarking as a guarantee that their function will receive continued funding, regardless of shifting legislative priorities. Common also is the practice of earmarking revenues for a popular cause (e.g., education) to help pass an otherwise unpopular general tax increase.

### Many faces of earmarking

Earmarking is not a single, clearly defined phenomenon; rather, it covers many different fiscal practices and institutional arrangements. At one extreme, earmarking can be thought of as essentially what happens in private market exchange, where proceeds from the sale of privately produced goods are "earmarked" to finance production costs. To recognize this is to see that in the public sector a common form of earmarking occurs in such enterprises as water and sewer systems, transit systems, and the like, where user revenues are dedicated to production of an essentially private good.

Similarly, special districts (transit districts, airport districts) illustrate a form of earmarking in that their revenues, most commonly user charges but sometimes including general tax levies, are set aside for support of the special purpose(s) of the district.

Although rarely referred to as "earmarking," clearly all revenue received by school districts is dedicated to education purposes.

Special levies of units of general government (a state, county, or city) can also be said to be earmarked to their designated purpose. An example is a county property tax levy for children's services. Earmarking is a central feature of "tax increment financing," whereby taxes paid by a business are used to pay the costs that the government incurs in providing it with facilities and services (e.g., job training).

All bond issues involve earmarking, most clearly in the case of revenue bonds (where debt service is met from a specified revenue stream) but also with general obligation debt, where a portion of general tax revenues is pledged to meet interest and principal. This is perhaps the least controversial form of earmarking.

While these examples indicate the pervasive nature of earmarking, most debate has focused on earmarking revenues for services that demonstrate a high degree of publicness and for which the quid pro quo is far from clear. We find a continuum ranging from situations in which benefit taxes are feasible and acceptable (the gas tax applied to highway expenditures), through taxes where there is a less clear but still plausible connection with the designated purpose (setting aside hunting and fishing license revenues for outdoor recreation programs and facilities), to those where there is no logical connection at all (earmarking lottery profits for education or for social services to the elderly).

## The benefits basis of earmarking

Earmarking finds its strongest equity rationale in the benefits connection, where it represents an extension into the tax-financed sector of the quid-pro-quo concept that is the accepted basis for private market transactions. Dedication of highway user tax revenues for highway purposes represents the benefit principle at its best (notwithstanding the tenuous relationship between taxes paid and benefits received by different categories of highway users). The equity rationale for earmarking general taxes finds its limit in the fact that there are very few services or facilities for which there is a corresponding "earmarkable" tax.

## Earmarking and the allocation of resources

The conventional indictment of earmarking is that it *presumptively* distorts budget allocations in a less efficient direction, by constraining decisions of the legislature. This indictment, however, is not always pertinent, because earmarking often does not apply to *marginal* dollars. If revenues from the earmarked source are less than the legislature would have appropriated in any case, earmarking does not increase the total funding, except perhaps temporarily. Its role is purely cosmetic. The classic example is the earmarking of lottery profits for education.

While earmarking may not increase total funds for the targeted function, it may nevertheless weaken opposition to particular revenue measures that otherwise would fail. Earmarking of profits from (taxes on) gambling is clearly an aid to legalization of such activities. The time-honored practice of selling a new tax by earmarking the money for education is a familiar if transparent strategem for softening taxpayer resistance. To the extent that this ruse succeeds, the earmarked function presumably shares in the additional funds to at least the same extent that it would in any revenue gain from non-earmarked sources.

From the standpoint of economic efficiency, such uses of earmarking are criticized as "little more than fraud," leading to a counterefficient tendency toward overtaxing and overspending (Oakland 1985). This criticism presumes (1) that earmarking does in fact increase political support for the tax increase and (2) that increased revenues produce an inefficient overexpansion in the public budget rather than a correction of some (yet to be explained) tendency toward underfinancing of the public sector.

Earmarking has been defended as a strategy for "unbundling" items in the public budget. If public expenditures were financed through a system of direct voting by citizens on a series of tax/expenditure issues, it would be possible to avoid the "package deal" that characterizes government general fund budgets (Buchanan 1963). Voters would be given wider scope for public choice, and the resulting budget allocations would, arguably, be more reflective of citizen preferences. This thesis argues the advisability of presenting voters a number of discrete programs or projects, each accompanied by a tax, rather than an omnibus package.

In recent years, this view seems to be gaining acceptance, perhaps reflecting growing skepticism by the public that their elected representatives are capable of spending tax money wisely, where it does the most good. General tax levies have had less success in the legislatures and at the polls than those earmarked for specifically designated purposes. If this trend continues, earmarking will become more prevalent in state/local fiscal systems.

Underlying the earmarking question is the perennial conflict between rules and discretion in public-sector decisionmaking. Constitutional and, to a lesser extent, statutory earmarking provides a rule constraint on legislative action or direct democracy. The absence of such constraints leaves revenue allocation to discretionary choice. Conflicting preferences in this matter are likely to continue.

## Additional readings

Borg, Mary O., and Paul M. Mason. "The Budgetary Incidence of a Lottery to Support Education." *National Tax Journal* 41 (March 1998): 75–85.

Buchanan, James M. "The Economics of Earmarked Taxes." *Journal of Political Economy* 71 (October 1963): 457–69.

Ebel, Robert D. "Earmarking of Taxes." In *A Fiscal Agenda for Nevada*, edited by Robert D. Ebel. Reno: University of Nevada Press, 1990.

National Conference of State Legislatures. *Earmarking of State Taxes*. Denver, 1990.

Oakland, William H. "Earmarking and Decentralization." In National Tax Association, *Proceedings of the Seventy-Seventh Annual Conference*. Columbus, Ohio (1985): 274–77.

*Cross references:* benefit principle; budget processes, state; user charges, federal.

# Earned income credit

Jonathan Barry Forman
University of Oklahoma College of Law

*A refundable income tax credit for low-income working taxpayers (U.S. Code, Title 26, Section 32).*

The earned income credit was originally enacted in 1975, and over the years it has grown to be one of the principal antipoverty programs in the federal budget. The credit was expanded significantly by the Omnibus Budget Reconciliation Act of 1993, and in 1998 some 18 million taxpayers were expected to claim more than $27 billion of earned income tax credits, with an average credit per taxpayer of almost $1,480 per year (U.S. Congress 1996: 809). In 1998, some families will be entitled to claim an earned income tax credit of up to $3,756 per year.

Unlike other tax credits for individuals (e.g., the dependent care credit), the earned income tax credit is refundable. That is, if the earned income tax credit exceeds the taxpayer's tax liability, the Internal Revenue Service will refund the difference. In 1998, for example, of the roughly $27 billion of earned income tax credits expected to be claimed, some $23 billion will be attributable to the portion of the credit that exceeds taxpayers' tax liabilities.

Literally, the statute provides that a taxpayer's earned income tax credit will equal a specified percentage of the taxpayer's earned income up to a maximum dollar amount (U.S. Code, Title 26, Section 32). The maximum credit amount is available to taxpayers over a certain income range and is phased out as a taxpayer's income increases beyond a specified phaseout floor. The Internal Revenue Service publishes tables each year to help taxpayers and their employers determine the proper amount of credit.

Three separate schedules apply, depending upon how many qualifying children the taxpayer has. For 1998, a taxpayer with one child was entitled to an earned income tax credit equal to 34 percent of up to $6,680 of earned income. Those earning between $6,680 and $12,260 could claim the maximum credit of $2,271 (roughly 34% × $6,680). Finally, those earning more than $12,260 would see that $2,271 credit amount reduced by 15.98 percent of the amount of earned income (or adjusted gross income, if higher) above $12,260, resulting in no credit for taxpayers earning $26,473 or more.

Similarly, taxpayers with two or more children could claim a credit of 40 percent of up to $9,390 of earned income for a maximum credit of $3,756 in 1998, but those earning more than $12,260 would see their credit phase down to zero dollars at $30,095 of income. Finally, taxpayers without children could claim a credit of up to 7.65 percent of up to $4,460 of earnings for a maximum credit of $341 in 1998, but those earning more than $5,570 saw their credit phase down to zero dollars at $10,030 of income.

These maximum earned income credit amounts will expand even beyond 1998, as the applicable earned income and phaseout amounts are indexed for inflation.

To be a "qualifying child" within the meaning of the earned income credit, an individual must satisfy a relationship test, a residency test, and an age test. The relationship test is satisfied if the child is the taxpayer's son, stepson, daughter, or stepdaughter; a descendant of the taxpayer's son or daughter; or the taxpayer's foster or adopted child. The residency test is satisfied if the child has lived with the taxpayer at least one-half of the taxable year. The age test is satisfied if the child is (1) under age 19, (2) a full-time student under age 24, or (3) permanently and totally disabled. Also, to be eligible for the credit, childless taxpayers must be over age 25 and under age 65.

The earned income credit is available to both employees and independent contractors, as the term "earned income" is defined to include wages, salaries, tips, and other employee compensation, and the net earnings from self-employment. To claim the credit, a taxpayer must file Internal Revenue Service Form 1040 or Form 1040A. Since 1991, taxpayers with children must also fill out Schedule EIC to claim the credit.

Taxpayers with children may elect to receive advance payment of a portion of their earned income credit in their paychecks throughout the year. To receive the credit in advance, a taxpayer must fill out Internal Revenue Service Form W-5, the Earned Income Credit Advance Payment Certificate, and give it to his employer. The employer then includes a portion of the employee's advance earned income credit amount along with wages, and the remainder of the credit is refunded only after the taxpayer files an income tax return. The Internal Revenue Service publishes tables to help employers determine the proper amount of advance payment. For example, an employee earning between $128 and $235 a week in 1998 gets a $26 per week paycheck increase by electing to receive advance payment of the credit.

## History of the credit

The earned income credit grew out of the welfare reform efforts of the early 1970s (Forman 1988: 45–58). The credit was originally added to the Internal

Revenue Code by the Tax Reduction Act of 1975. Over the years, the credit has been expanded, and it is now one of the principal antipoverty programs in the federal budget.

As originally adopted in 1975, the earned income tax credit was intended to offset the Social Security taxes of low-income workers with children and to provide those taxpayers with an increased incentive to work. An eligible taxpayer could claim a refundable credit equal to 10 percent of the taxpayer's earned income for the taxable year, which did not exceed $4,000 (a maximum credit of $400). That $400 maximum credit was reduced one dollar for each 10 dollars of income in excess of $4,000. Thus, the credit was completely phased out at an income level of $8,000. As enacted, the original earned income tax credit was available to taxpayers only for calendar year 1975.

Subsequent revenue acts extended the credit, and it was made a permanent part of the Internal Revenue Code by the Revenue Act of 1978. The Deficit Reduction Act of 1984 increased the maximum amount of the earned income tax credit and renumbered it to its current location in the Internal Revenue Code (U.S. Code, Title 26, Section 32). The credit was expanded significantly by the Tax Reform Act of 1986, and it has been indexed for inflation since 1987. The Omnibus Budget Reconciliation Act of 1990 also expanded the credit and added a supplemental credit amount for families with two or more children.

The Omnibus Budget Reconciliation Act of 1993 expanded the credit even further and made a small credit available to certain childless workers (up to $341 in 1998). By the year 2000, more than 19 million families are expected to claim almost $30 billion of earned income credits, with an average credit per family of almost $1,565 (U.S. Congress 1996: 809).

## Analysis

The earned income tax credit is an income transfer program that provides significant financial assistance to low-income workers, especially those with children. Unlike increasing the minimum wage, the expansion of the earned income credit over the past two decades has provided benefits targeted to help the working poor. Also, unlike most other welfare programs or a negative income tax, the earned income tax credit provides significant work incentives to low-income workers (Forman 1988: 67–77). Indeed, as currently structured, the earned income tax credit is one of the federal government's largest and most effective antipoverty programs.

Unfortunately, the earned income tax credit is not without its problems. For example, a recent study estimated that between 80 and 86 percent of eligible taxpayers actually received the credit in 1990

(Scholz 1994). While this is a relatively high participation rate when compared with other transfer programs such as food stamps and Aid to Families with Dependent Children, it still means that approximately 2 million families eligible for the credit in 1990 failed to obtain it. Moreover, remarkably few taxpayers elect to receive their credits by means of the advance payment mechanism. In 1989, for example, only about 40,000 families received advance payments, less than 0.5 percent of those eligible (U.S. General Accounting Office 1992).

Compliance with the earned income tax credit is also a problem. For example, Internal Revenue Service audit data indicate that 42 percent of recipients claimed too large a credit in 1988 and that about 32 percent of recipients were not entitled to any credit at all that year (Stathis 1993). Compliance with the advance payment rules is also problematic: An estimated 49 percent of the individuals who filed income tax returns in 1989 and who had definitely received the advance payment failed to report that receipt on their return, and an estimated 45 percent of those who had received advance payment of the credit failed to even file returns (U.S. General Accounting Office 1992).

Finally, the earned income tax credit has also been implicated in some perverse disincentives for work and marriage. While the credit unequivocally increases the incentive to work in the phase in range of the credit (up to $9,390 of earnings for workers with two children in 1998), the combination of income and Social Security taxes and the phaseout of the credit may discourage work by an even greater number of relatively low-income workers falling in the applicable phaseout ranges (e.g., from $12,260 to $30,095 of earnings for workers with two or more children in 1998). Lowering the phaseout rate could reduce this work disincentive, but it would also stretch out the phaseout range, which in turn would subject more taxpayers to the lowered phaseout rate.

Worse still is the earned income tax credit's impact on marriage. For example, consider a two-earner family with two children. If each earns $10,000 and they file a joint return, the family will get an $1,811 refund. If they divorce and each takes a child and files as head of household, they may each claim a $2,271 earned income tax credit. This is a $2,731 a year incentive for divorce (Feenberg and Rosen 1994).

President Clinton has touted the expansion of the earned income tax credit by the Omnibus Budget Reconciliation Act of 1993 as part of a grander scheme to reform the welfare system and to "make work pay" for low-income Americans. Given the concerns about participation, compliance, and the perverse disincentives for work and marriage, it seems likely that Congress will reconsider the credit's operation in coming years. One option would be to replace the current earned income tax credit with an exemption from Social Security taxes for the first $10,000 of wages, and to supplement the exemption with a refundable family allowance tax credit based upon the number of children in the family (Yin, Scholz, Forman, and Mazur 1994). This approach would reduce marginal tax rates and their disincentive effects on low-income workers. Moreover, a Social Security tax exemption would reach 100 percent of low-income workers, and it would be less complicated than first collecting Social Security taxes and then using the earned income tax credit to refund them.

## Additional readings

Feenberg, Daniel R., and Harvey S. Rosen. "Recent Developments in the Marriage Tax." National Bureau of Economic Research Working Paper No. 4705. Cambridge, Mass.: April 1994.

Forman, Jonathan Barry. "Improving the Earned Income Credit: Transition to a Wage Subsidy Credit for the Working Poor." *Florida State University Law Review* 16 (1) (1988): 41–101.

Scholz, John Karl. "The Earned Income Tax Credit: Participation, Compliance, and Antipoverty Effectiveness." *National Tax Journal* 47 (1) (March 1994): 63–85.

Stathis, Jennie S. "Statement of Jennie S. Stathis, Director of Tax Policy and Administration Issues, General Government Division, General Accounting Office, before the Subcommittee on Select Revenue Measures and Human Resources." U.S. House of Representatives, Committee on Ways and Means, GAO/T-GGD-93-20. Washington, D.C., March 30, 1993.

U.S. Code, Title 26, Section 32.

U.S. Congress, House of Representatives, Committee on Ways and Means. *The Green Book: Background Material and Data on Programs within the Jurisdiction of the Committee on Ways and Means*. Washington, D.C.: U.S. Government Printing Office, November 1996.

U.S. General Accounting Office. "Earned Income Tax Credit: Advance Payment Option Is Not Widely Known or Understood by the Public." GAO/GGD-92-26. Washington, D.C., February 1992.

Yin, George K., John Karl Scholz, Jonathan Barry Forman, and Mark J. Mazur. "Improving the Delivery of Benefits to the Working Poor: Proposals to Reform the Earned Income Tax Credit Program." University of Florida Law School. *American Journal of Tax Policy* 11 (2) (1994): 225–98.

*Cross references:* budget process, federal; fairness in taxation; labor supply, taxes and; progressivity, measures of; tax equity analysis.

# Earnings and profits
## Mark B. Booth
Congressional Budget Office

*A tax accounting concept to distinguish between corporate distributions to shareholders, as either ordinary income or capital.*

When a corporation distributes cash or other property to a shareholder, it must, for tax purposes, classify the distribution as either a dividend or a return of capital. To classify distributions, corporations must compute a measure from the Internal Revenue Code called "earnings and profits" (E&P), which represents either a flow of annual income, called "current E&P," or a cumulative amount of income, called "accumulated E&P," measured as accruing from the beginning of the federal income tax in 1913. The classification has important federal tax consequences for shareholders. Individuals, for example, generally pay tax at ordinary income tax rates on dividends, pay no tax on a return of capital that is less than their invested basis, and pay tax at a limited rate on capital gains. E&P has several other applications in the federal tax code unrelated to classifying dividends, such as determining a part of the base of the alternative minimum tax for corporations (see Adjusted current earnings entry), but those applications are much more limited in scope and are not discussed in detail here.

The tax code limits dividends to that being paid out of a corporation's current or accumulated E&P. No limit applies, for example, if a corporation has a positive balance of accumulated E&P or a positive amount of current E&P in the year of distribution (both as measured before deducting distributions), and its annual distributions do not exceed either measure: those annual distributions are considered dividends for tax purposes. The limit to the amount of distributions that must be considered dividends is called the "E&P limitation," and it has changed little since 1936. In determining the classification of a distribution, a corporation first compares the value of the distribution to its current E&P. If none or only a portion of the distribution is considered a dividend under that test, the corporation then compares the distribution to accumulated E&P to determine if a greater portion qualifies as a dividend. If only a portion of a corporation's total distributions are dividends, certain rules are applied to allocate the distribution types and amounts to specific shareholders based on factors including the chronological order of distribution and the E&P limit exceeded.

## The computation

A corporation generally computes its current E&P the way it computes its taxable income; however, it may not use the tax-preferred treatment of certain income and expenses that the tax code does allow for when calculating taxable income. It also must make certain other adjustments to its taxable income. These changes make current E&P correspond much more closely to the concept of economic income than taxable income. Accumulated E&P is computed by adding up all the annual amounts of current E&P, be they positive or negative (loss).

Accelerated depreciation generates the most significant difference between current E&P and taxable income. When calculating current E&P, a corporation must depreciate its assets using a straight-line method. In addition, tax-exempt interest income, such as from municipal bonds or life insurance contracts, must be included in E&P. Also, when calculating current E&P, corporations may not account for income using the preferential completed contract or installment sales methods of accounting, and those in the extractive industries may not use the preferential treatment of costs termed "percentage depletion." Additional differences include the treatment of charitable contributions and capital losses. Federal income taxes and distributions themselves are also deducted to determine current E&P.

The E&P limitation conceptually defines dividends as being paid out of a corporation's economic income earned either during the year of distribution or over the entire period since 1913. If a distribution exceeds the E&P limitation, the excess is considered a return of capital that the shareholder contributed to the corporation. The shareholder is not subject to tax, up to the amount of the shareholder's invested basis in the corporation. If the distribution also exceeds the basis of the shareholder's investment, then the excess is taxed as a capital gain to the shareholder.

## Criticisms of E&P and the limitation

The measure of E&P is criticized as being too complex and costly for corporations to compute. Corporate reorganizations particularly add to the complexity.

The E&P limitation is also very imprecise when applied to specific distributions. Corporations—especially large, publicly traded ones—often experience rapid turnover of their shareholders, and the annual and cumulative measures of E&P do not track the transactions between corporations and specific shareholders well. For example, a shareholder may purchase stock in a corporation that recorded large losses in E&P in the first year of ownership, but at least a portion of any distribution that year would still be a taxable dividend if the corporation had remaining accumulated E&P; so too would a distribution in subsequent years, regardless of accumulated E&P, if the corporation then recorded even small current gains.

## Possible reforms

Requiring corporations to allocate specific distributions to the earnings and investments of specific shareholders would impose an administrative burden that is generally considered to be prohibitively expensive. Short of that reform, it is not clear that incremental changes to the E&P limitation would significantly improve its precision.

To reduce the complexity of the federal tax code, several groups and individual analysts over the years have endorsed the complete elimination of the measure of E&P and the E&P limitation. One alternative would be to tax all (nonliquidating) distributions as dividends, but that treatment would treat true returns of capital as taxable income to shareholders. Another alternative would be to rely on state law defining dividend distributions, but that treatment might be difficult to enforce and could encourage tax avoidance strategies because federal income tax rates are much higher than those of the states.

If policymakers eliminated or reformed the use of E&P, other applications of E&P in the tax code would also need to be addressed, including the alternative minimum tax and foreign tax credit.

## Additional readings

American Bar Association, Section on Taxation, Earnings and Profits Work Group. "Elimination of 'Earnings and Profits' from the Internal Revenue Code." *Tax Lawyer* (Winter 1986): 285–330.

Blum, Walter J. "The Earnings and Profits Limitation on Dividend Income: A Reappraisal." *Taxes* (February 1975): 68–87.

U.S. Department of the Treasury. "Integration of the Individual and Corporate Tax Systems." Washington, D.C.: U.S. Government Printing Office, January 1992.

Westin, Richard A. *Tax Lexicon.* Arlington, Va.: Tax Analysts, 1989.

*Cross references:* adjusted current earnings; alternative minimum tax, corporate.

# Education financing, state and local

David N. Figlio
University of Oregon

*The primacy of the state and local role in the financing of primary and secondary education.*

The financing of primary and secondary schooling in the United States is almost exclusively the responsibility of state and local governments. This reliance on state and local revenue can be traced to the 10th Amendment to the U.S. Constitution, which reserves for the states all functions (such as education provision) not expressly granted to the federal government. As such, education became a state responsibility, and each state consequently has established a system of free public schools.

Until the early 20th century, local schools were financed almost exclusively with the property tax. Early in this century, states began to increase their role in directly financing local public education. This state support, commonly known as "state aid," was first used as a tool to help enforce state mandates on the length of the school year or minimum teacher qualifications, for instance. Early state aid took the form of flat grants, in which state support was distributed on a per capita, per student, or per teacher basis. However, even as the state share of school financing increased, the local property tax remained by far the dominant vehicle for school funding. In 1920, more than 83 percent of school revenues came from the local property tax.

During the early 20th century, the property tax came under increased criticism as a means of funding schools. Disparities in the taxable property of residents led to wide differences in the quantity and quality of educational programs provided across districts. Early writers, such as Morrison (1930), Mort (1933), and Strayer and Haig (1923), argued that the unequal distribution of educational opportunity further exacerbated the already substantial problems associated with an unequal distribution of wealth. These authors' central argument was that states should intervene to guarantee that each district provide at least a minimum amount of educational service while maintaining reasonably comparable tax burdens.

The impetus for school finance reform increased, coming to a head in the early 1970s. Authors such as Coons, Clune, and Sugarman (1970) echoed the sentiment that the school finance systems in place at the time violated the rights of some children, who had no control over where they lived, to quality education. However, the U.S. Supreme Court, ruling in *San Antonio Independent School District* v. *Rodriguez,* rejected the argument that equal educational opportunity is constitutionally guaranteed. Following this ruling, school finance reforms have been pursued on a state-by-state basis. Thirteen states have now carried out school finance reform via litigation, and others have changed state aid formulas through legislation.

Today state and local sources are (on average) equally important in school finance. In the 1991–92 school year, 44.3 percent of school revenues came from local sources and 46.4 percent came from state sources. The federal role in financing primary and secondary education has grown as well, but is still less than 7 percent of total revenues. The split of state and local sources, however, is by no means similar across states. In 1991–92, state spending as a share of total revenues was as high as 90.3 percent in Hawaii, 73.8 percent in New Mexico, and 71.6 percent in Washington, and as low as 8.5 percent of total revenues in New Hampshire and 28.9 percent in Michigan. Likewise, the way in which state revenues are distributed to local school systems varies substantially from state to state, as is described further on. States are still dramatically changing their school finance systems, either through legislation (Michigan and Kentucky) or through court rulings (Wyoming and New Hampshire).

## Rationale for school finance reform

As already mentioned, a dominant rationale for the school finance reforms that have occurred over the past three decades centers around equity in the provision and finance of education. There are several main issues regarding equity. One major concern with the school finance system that existed before the 1970s involves equality of educational opportunity. There exists a widely held belief that school spending translates into student achievement and future labor market success, although this argument is still being actively debated (see further on). There exist considerable differences across communities in their abilities to pay for public schooling, largely determined by marked differences in tax bases, and this could lead to wealthier districts spending substantially more on education than poorer districts and reaping the benefits associated with this increased spending.

Data from before the school finance reform movement appear to support this perception. In the early 1970s, disparities in school spending were dramatic: Nationally, the 95th percentile school district spent 6.6 times as much per pupil as did the fifth percentile district in the 1971–72 school year, and the 95th percentile district raised almost 13 times the own-source revenues per pupil as did the fifth percentile district. And even within states these differences were large: In California, these two ratios were 5.5 and 5.8, respectively, while in Texas they were 9.1 and 11.7. Moreover, per pupil spending on education and per pupil own-source revenues collected are (not surprisingly) very highly correlated with community wealth. For instance, in 1971–72, the correlation coefficients between median family income and per pupil spending or own-source revenues were close to 0.6.

With such vast differences in spending, which were intimately tied to wealth, there was a genuine concern that children in lower-means districts were systematically being given lower prospects for future success. Indeed, these spending differences probably *understated* the true degree of differences in education provision, as low-spending, low-income districts likely had a larger percentage of high-need students who are costlier to educate (Downes 1995).

The reliance on the property tax as the primary source of local education finance leads to possible inequities in school funding within districts. Only a fraction of the households within any school district have school-age children, but all pay property taxes at the same rate, regardless of usage of the education system. Moreover, the property taxes are likely to be the most burdensome on the elderly, who live on fixed incomes and for whom the house is likely the principal source of wealth (but for whom the demand for quality public education is probably lowest). The argument that property-tax-based school finance subsidizes households with school-age children at the expense of those without school-age children (particularly elderly households) and those who choose to send their children to private school was therefore another equity motivation for school finance reform. For these and other reasons, states have moved from primarily local-revenue-based school finance systems to those in which state aid is a prominent feature.

## State aid to local school districts

Every state has a different system of financing schools, but several common general formulas are used to distribute state aid. There are four basic types of formulas: flat grants, foundation grants, power equalization programs, and full state funding. Readers interested in a more thorough treatment should consult Monk (1990) or Salmon et al. (1989).

*Flat grants* provide a specified number of units of state support for each unit of quantifiable need. "Need" in flat grants typically takes the form of average daily attendance or school district enrollment and is independent of the receiving school district's fiscal capacity. Still, flat grants based on pupil counts do work to equalize school spending, as they at least help to deal with one dimension of fiscal capacity—the need, as measured by the number of pupils. Indeed, as the size of a population-based flat

grant increases, the state approaches equalization of tax burdens and educational spending. The extreme case of a flat grant is full state funding (present in Hawaii), in which the state's grant fully covers the costs of providing public schools.

In addition to being based on pupil counts, flat grants may be categorical, in that the aid is targeted to a particular purpose, rather than being general aid. Examples of categorical aid include subsidization of student transportation; directed funds for particular groups, such as disabled students or students from disadvantaged backgrounds; or support for particular curricular areas, such as vocational or foreign language education. Most federal aid to schools is categorical in nature.

Flat grants may also take the form of *matching grants*, in which the grant is linked to a particular investment by the receiving district. Many matching grant formulas are inversely tied to district wealth, which helps to equalize the financial burden of providing educational services. Interestingly, many early programs of state aid took the form of matching grants that worked *against* equalization, as grants tended to be linked to teacher counts, and wealthier districts were more likely to have higher teacher counts per pupil.

Unlike flat grants, *foundation* programs attempt to establish an inverse relationship between state aid and fiscal capacity. The basic formula for a foundation aid program has two components. First, the state sets a "foundation" level—the level of spending intended to guarantee a minimum acceptable level of education provision. This foundation may simply be a function of enrollment or attendance, or may take into account cost differences from district to district. From this foundation, the state subtracts some common tax rate times the total value of the school district's tax base. This subtracted portion of the formula is the share of the foundation level of school provision that the state expects the school districts to cover. In addition, foundation grants allow for optional local tax levies so that school districts desiring to spend above the foundation level may do so. As with flat grants, foundation grants are imperfect. Critics of foundation grants often argue that foundation levels may be set too low; that the foundation program is too inflexible, as the foundation level must be frequently reset to keep up with inflation or changes in costs; and that foundation grants may not achieve equalization because the optional tax levies can enable wealthier districts to outspend poorer districts.

A third class of state aid programs intended to further equalize school district spending is called *power equalization*. In one form of power equalization, percentage equalization, the state matches local education spending at a rate that varies inversely with the school district's fiscal capacity. Percentage equalization plans differ from the programs mentioned above in that they encourage local tax effort beyond the foundation rate. However, virtually all state percentage equalization plans cap the level of matching that states will provide to districts. Moreover, like the plans mentioned above, in practice, percentage equalization does not attain wealth neutrality; that is, per pupil expenditures are still related to district wealth.

District power equalization programs attempt to eliminate district wealth as a determinant of school district spending. In a district power equalization formula, a district's state aid is the difference between its state-determined revenue entitlement tied to its tax rate and the level of revenue generated by the local school tax. The aim of these programs is to guarantee that each school district selecting a particular level of tax effort will have the same spending level, regardless of district wealth. These programs generally incorporate so-called "recapture" provisions, in which school districts remit to the state any tax collections above the revenue entitlement. This negative state aid component of these programs (also occasionally found in foundation aid programs) tends to make district power equalization programs politically difficult to implement. In addition, while district power equalization programs are the most wealth-neutral of the state aid formulas described here, there may still be substantial differences in per pupil spending across districts because districts may choose different levels of tax effort.

In general, political considerations preclude a state from adopting one of the above programs in pure form. In order to attain legislative passage, states sometimes incorporate "hold harmless" clauses, in which a district may choose between the funds due to it under the current formula or those that would accrue under an existing formula, whichever is greater. Other compromises may include provisions for guaranteeing a district a minimum amount of state funding even if not entitled under the existing formula. Salmon et al. (1989) provide a useful classification of the basic form of each state's support programs.

## Does money matter?

A central issue surrounding school finance reform involves the question of whether expenditures matter in contributing to student outcomes, such as academic achievement or labor market success. If money does not matter, then the discussion of school spending equalization ceases to be as important an issue if the rationale of equalization is equality of educational opportunity. Hanushek (1986) summarizes the existing "education production function" literature by stating that "there is no systematic relationship between school expenditures and student performance." However, this result has been called

into question by recent authors such as Ferguson (1991), Figlio (1997), and Husted and Kenny (1996). There is a similar lack of consensus regarding the effects of school spending on labor market outcomes. While Card and Krueger (1992) find a positive relationship between school quality and future wages, their conclusion is questioned by Betts (1995) and Heckman et al. (1995). The primary conclusion that should probably be drawn from the existing literature relating school spending to outcomes is that the effect of spending is not yet completely understood.

## Additional readings

Betts, Julian. "Does School Quality Matter? Evidence from the National Longitudinal Survey of Youth." *Review of Economics and Statistics* (February 1995): 231–47.

Card, David, and Alan Krueger. "Does School Quality Matter? Returns to Education and the Characteristics of Public Schools in the United States." *Journal of Political Economy* 100 (February 1992): 1–40.

Coons, John E., William H. Clune, and Stephen D. Sugarman. *Private Wealth and Public Education.* Cambridge, Mass.: Harvard University Press, 1970.

Downes, Thomas. "Compensating for Cost Disparities with Equalization Aid: Can It Be Done? Should It Be Done?" Working paper, Tufts University, 1995.

Ferguson, Ronald. "Paying for Public Education: New Evidence on How and Why Money Matters." *Harvard Journal of Education* 28 (1991): 465.

Figlio, David N. "Did the 'Tax Revolt' Reduce School Performance?" *Journal of Public Economics* 65 (September 1997): 245–69.

Hanushek, Eric A. "The Economics of Schooling." *Journal of Economic Literature* 24 (September 1986): 1141–77.

Heckman, James, Anne Layne-Farrar, and Petra Todd. "Does Measured School Quality Really Matter? An Examination of the Earnings-Quality Relationship." NBER Working Paper No. 5274. Cambridge, Mass., September 1990.

Monk, David H. *Educational Finance: An Economic Approach.* New York: McGraw-Hill, 1990.

Morrison, H.C. *School Revenue.* Chicago: University of Chicago Press, 1930.

Mort, P.R. *State Support for Public Education.* Washington, D.C.: American Council on Education, 1933.

Murray, Sheila E. "Two Assays on the Distribution of Education Resources and Outcomes." In *Proceedings of the Annual Conference on Taxation, 1996.* Washington, D.C.: National Tax Association, 1997.

Salmon, Richard, Christina Dawson, Stephen Lawton, and Thomas Johns. *Public School Finance Programs of the United States and Canada.* Blacksburg, Va.: American Education Finance Association, 1989.

Strayer, G.D., and Robert Murray Haig. *Financing of Education in the State of New York.* New York: MacMillan, 1923.

*Cross references:* tax and revenue capacity; tax limitations; Tiebout model.

# Education tax credits, higher education, federal

Dennis Zimmerman
Congressional Research Service, Library of Congress

*Tax credits created in 1997 for postsecondary education.*

The Taxpayer Relief Act of 1997 created two tax credits for postsecondary education expenses. One, the Hope Scholarship Credit, can be claimed for each student in the family (including the taxpayer, the spouse, or their dependents) for two taxable years for expenses incurred attending a qualified education program. Each student's credit is equal to 100 percent of the first $1,000 of qualified tuition and fees and 50 percent of the next $1,000. Tuition and fees financed with scholarships, veterans' education assistance, and other income not included in gross income for tax purposes do not qualify (with the exception of gifts and inheritances).

The other, the Lifetime Learning Credit, provides a 20 percent credit for the first $5,000 of qualified tuition and fees (the first $10,000 after 2002) that taxpayers pay for themselves, their spouse, or their dependents. The credit is available for any number of years and for any level of postsecondary education.

Both credits are phased out for single taxpayers with a modified adjusted gross income over $40,000 ($80,000 for joint-return taxpayers). Neither credit is refundable, and the sum of these and other credits is limited to the excess of the taxpayer's regular income tax liability over the minimum tax.

## Rationales for the credits

Federal subsidy of higher education has three potential economic justifications: a capital market failure; external benefits; and nonneutral federal income tax treatment of physical versus human capital. Subsidies that correct these problems are said to provide taxpayers with "social benefits."

### Capital market failure

Many students find themselves unable to finance their postsecondary education from earnings and personal or family savings. Student mobility and a lack of property to pledge as loan collateral require that commercial lenders charge high interest rates on loans for postsecondary education to reflect their high risk of default. As a result, students often find themselves unable to afford postsecondary loans from the financial sector. By definition, this financial constraint bears more heavily on lower-income groups than on higher-income groups and leads to inequality of opportunity. It is also inefficient because these students, on average, might be expected to earn a rate of return on postsecondary education loans that is higher than the rate of return earned on the alternative loans made by the financial sector.

This "failure" of the capital market is attributable to the legal restriction against pledging an individual's future labor supply as loan collateral— that is, against indentured servitude. Since allowing indentured servitude is something modern society rejects, the federal government pursues an alternative strategy to correct this market failure—it provides a guarantee to absorb most of the financial sector's default risk associated with postsecondary loans to students. This financial support is provided through the Federal Family Education Loan Program and the Direct Loan Program. These programs guaranteed approximately $34 billion of loans for postsecondary education in fiscal year 1997. Outlays in 1997 for the default costs of guaranteed loans made in prior years totaled almost $3 billion. This guarantee is an entitlement, and it equalizes the financing cost for some portion of most students' education investment. When it is combined with Pell grant programs for lower-income students, it appears that at least some portion of the capital market failure has been corrected and equality of opportunity has been improved.

### External benefits

Some benefits from postsecondary education may accrue not to the individual being educated, but rather to the members of society at large. These external benefits are not valued by individuals, causing them to invest less than is optimal for society (even assuming no capital market imperfections). External benefits are variously described as taking the form of better citizenship and increased productivity generated by knowledge.

Public subsidies to postsecondary education that are at least partially motivated by these external benefits, as opposed to the capital market failure addressed by the federal student loan and Pell Grant programs, are considerable. The state-local sector is by far the major contributor here, spending $50 billion on public (and some private) higher education systems in 1993–94 that provided relatively uniform subsidies to all student participants. The federal government provided $2.7 billion of interest subsidies through the student loan program in 1997 over and above the value of the guarantee being provided, several billion in work-study grants, and a variety of other assistance programs. Thus, federal and state-local subsidies to higher education that can be said to be designed to increase external benefits total tens of billions of dollars per year.

### Nonneutral taxation of human capital

A third potential justification sometimes advanced for providing subsidies to human capital investment is the possibility that investment in human capital is more heavily taxed than is investment in physical capital. Some believe this to be true because individuals are not allowed to recover education expenses such as tuition costs over their lifetime. But forgone earnings, scholarships, and government grants represent a larger share of an individual's human capital investment than do most students' direct outlays such as tuition, and these investments are effectively deducted when incurred because they are never included in income in the first place.

The effective marginal tax rate on physical capital investment is estimated to be about 33 percent. Using reasonable assumptions about marginal tax rates for an individual as a student and as a recipient of his education investment returns, the timing of these returns over a 40-year period, and the share of investment expensed, the tax on human capital investment is 25 percent, actually lower than the tax on physical capital.

### Summary

The return from investment in human capital receives more favorable treatment from the federal income tax than does the return from investment in physical capital. Thus, nonneutral income taxation cannot be used to justify subsidy of postsecondary education. The existence of a capital market failure and the presence of external benefits from higher education investments do provide justifications for public subsidy of higher education. However, the federal student loan program and Pell grants have partially corrected the capital market failure, and $50 to $60 billion of annual state-local and federal subsidies have probably gone a long way toward compensating for the existence of external benefits. At a minimum, additional subsidies such as the tax credit should be carefully targeted to those students still suffering from lack of access to capital or otherwise underinvesting in their own education.

### Effect of tax credit

Potential students induced to enroll in higher education by these credits cause investment in education to increase. But the overall effectiveness of the tax credit depends upon whether the cost of the marginal investment dollar of those already investing in higher education is reduced. For those whose tuition and fees exceed qualified tuition and fees, the credit applies to the last dollar of tuition and fees and the student's price is reduced by 50 percent with the Hope credit and by 20 percent with the Lifetime Learning Credit. The portion of the credit (and the federal revenue loss) that appears either as an increase in the quantity of education or as higher tuition depends upon the structure of the demand and supply schedules for higher education.

It is clear from the structure of these tax credits that tuition and fee payments will exceed qualified tuition and fees for a large number of students who are eligible for these credits. These students experience an income effect and a subsidy to participation but no marginal price effect. Moreover, because the subsidy is channeled through the tax system, students and families with lower income and little or no tax liability receive little or no benefit, even though these students are likely to have a larger participation response. The middle- and upper-middle-class students who receive tax benefits are likely to be relatively unresponsive to price changes, particularly with respect to participation. Thus, many of these families enjoy a windfall gain and the federal taxpayer gets no offsetting social benefits in the form of an increased quantity of investment.

### Additional readings

Gravelle, Jane, and Dennis Zimmerman. *Tax Subsidies for Higher Education: An Analysis of the Administration's Proposal.* Congressional Research Service Report 97-581 E, May 30, 1997.

Kane, Thomas J. "Beyond Tax Relief: Long-Term Challenges in Financing Higher Education." *National Tax Journal* (June 1997): 335–49.

McPherson, Michael, and Morton Owen Schapiro. *Keeping College Affordable.* Washington, D.C.: The Brookings Institution, 1991.

*Cross references:* child care expenses: the child care credit; education financing, state and local; income tax, federal.

# Elasticity, demand and supply

David N. Hyman
North Carolina State University

*Two measures of the sensitivity of buyers and sellers to price changes that play an important role in evaluating the effects of taxes.*

---

*Demand elasticity* measures the responsiveness of quantities demanded of an item relative to changes in its price. *Supply elasticity* gauges the responsiveness of quantities supplied of an item relative to changes in its price. Demand elasticity is usually called price elasticity of demand to distinguish it from measures of the sensitivity of amounts bought to changes in economic variables other than the item's price. Similarly, supply elasticity is commonly referred to as price elasticity of supply.

Price elasticity of demand is calculated by dividing the percentage change in the quantity demanded of an item by the percentage change in the price that caused it, other things being equal. The following formula can be used to calculate price elasticity of demand for small changes in price:

$$\text{Price Elasticity of Demand} = \frac{dQ/Q}{dP/P}$$

Where $Q$ is the initial quantity demanded, $dQ$ is the change in quantity demanded caused by the change in price $dP$, and $P$ is the initial price of the item.

Because the demand for a good is likely to fall as its price rises, the price elasticity of demand will be a negative number indicating the percentage change in the quantity demanded of an item resulting from a 1 percent change in its price. Price elasticity of demand is equal to the inverse of the negative slope of a demand curve ($dQ/dP$) multiplied by the ratio of the initial price of the item to its quantity demanded.

The absolute value of the price elasticity of demand can range from zero to infinity. When this value is between 0 and 1, demand is said to be inelastic; when it is greater than 1, demand is said to be elastic. The demand for an item is said to be of unitary elasticity if the absolute value of its price elasticity of demand is exactly equal to 1.

Knowledge of the price elasticity of demand is useful to businesses in forecasting changes in revenue from the sale of goods and services due to changes in market prices. Revenue is the price multiplied by the quantity of an item purchased in a market. If demand is inelastic, a price increase will result in an increase in revenue because the effects of a given percentage increase in price on revenue will not be offset by a larger percentage decline in quantity demanded. When demand is elastic, an increase in price will cause revenue to decline because the positive effect of the higher price on revenue will be swamped by the negative effect of a larger percentage decline in quantity demanded. The same logic can be used to forecast the effects of price declines on total revenue and expenditures on an item.

Supply elasticity is calculated in the same way as price elasticity of demand by dividing the percentage change in the quantity supplied by the percentage change in the price that caused that change in quantity. Because supply curves generally exhibit a positive slope, price elasticity of supply is a positive number. Supply is said to be inelastic when the price elasticity of supply is between 0 and 1. Supply is said to be elastic when its price elasticity exceeds 1.

Estimates of price elasticities of demand and supply are useful in forecasting the loss in efficiency in the use of privately owned resources in response to taxes. The excess burden of a tax is the cost of distortions in choices that result from that tax and is measured as the loss in net benefits from wasteful resource use over and above the dollar amount of tax paid. The excess burden of a tax depends on the willingness of buyers and sellers to adjust their behavior in response to tax-induced price changes. Taxes on goods or services traded in markets (including productive resources such as labor, capital, and land) inevitably affect the demand and supply of these items and therefore their market prices. The price changes, the responsiveness of buyers and sellers to tax-induced price increases, and therefore the excess burden of a tax depend on the price elasticities of demand and supply of the taxed items.

Other things being equal, the more elastic the demand for a taxed good or service, the greater the buyers' response to a tax-induced price increase and the greater the excess burden of a tax placed on its sale. Similarly, the excess burden of a tax will also vary with the price elasticity of supply of the taxed item. Other things being equal, the higher the price elasticity of supply of a good or service, the greater the excess burden of a tax on its sale.

To minimize the excess burden of taxes, it would be best to tax goods and services whose demand or supply is highly inelastic. For example, because the overall supply of land in a nation is usually considered to be perfectly inelastic, a tax on land results in no excess burden. Similarly, the excess burden of a tax on goods with few good substitutes (such as certain drugs or basic foodstuffs) would also be very low because there would be little change in the quantities of these items demanded in response to any tax-induced price increases.

The price elasticity of demand and supply of a taxed good or service will also influence the incidence of the tax between buyers and sellers of taxed goods and services. When demand is highly inelastic, buyers will not respond to a tax-induced price increase by substantially reducing quantity demanded. A tax increases the cost of selling each unit of a product and therefore usually decreases the willingness of sellers to supply given quantities. If price elasticity of demand for a taxed item were zero, the sellers could raise the price they charge by the tax per unit and not cause a decrease in quantity demanded.

If demand for an item is not of zero elasticity, an attempt by sellers to raise the price of their product by the full amount of the tax will cause a surplus of the product on the market because buyers will want to buy less at a price that includes the full tax. In this case, the new market equilibrium price will be somewhere between the initial price and the sum of that price and the tax per unit, with the tax being shared by the buyers and sellers. Buyers would pay a higher price than before, and sellers would receive a lower net price after paying the tax per unit. In general, other things being equal, the more inelastic the demand for a taxed item, the greater the share of the tax paid by buyers in terms of a price increase.

The incidence of a tax between buyers and sellers is also affected by the price elasticity of supply. If sellers are to succeed in shifting a portion of a tax on a good or service they offer for sale in markets, they must make the good scarcer in the market. The price elasticity of supply indicates the willingness and ability of sellers to reduce quantities supplied in response to a tax. For example, the price elasticity of supply of labor of prime-aged males in the workforce has been estimated to be zero. This implies that a tax on labor services (as results from an income or payroll tax) will not cause these workers to reduce their number of hours of work. Because workers do not respond to the tax by working fewer hours, labor is not made scarcer, and its price (wages or salaries) cannot rise in the marketplace. Under these circumstances, the entire tax on labor income must be borne by workers who will not shift any of the cost of the tax to the buyers (the employers) in the market. In general, the more inelastic the supply of a taxed good or service, the greater the incidence of that tax on the sellers in the market.

In the long run, supply is generally more elastic than it is in the short run. An industry of constant costs is one whose long-run supply curve is a flat line that is infinitely elastic at all points. In such industries, the minimum possible average cost of producing a product is constant and does not vary in the long run with the number of firms in the industry. Many industries in the United States have perfectly elastic supply curves in the long run. Firms in these industries will incur losses as a result of a tax on the sale of their product. Firms that fail will leave the industry, and as this occurs market supply will decrease and market price will rise. Price will continue to rise until it equals the minimum possible

average cost of production plus the tax, so that the net price received by sellers just equals their minimum possible cost. In cases where supply is perfectly elastic in the long run, a tax will be shifted forward fully to buyers.

*Cross references:* excess burden; incidence of taxes; inverse elasticity rule; labor supply, taxes and.

# Employee stock ownership plan
## Gerald Mayer
Congressional Research Service, Library of Congress

*An employee benefit plan that is required to invest primarily in the stock of the sponsoring employer.*

The employee stock ownership plan (ESOP) is a defined contribution plan. Unlike a defined benefit plan, where an employer agrees to pay employees a given amount of retirement benefits, under a defined contribution plan, an employer agrees to make contributions to accounts set up for each employee. An ESOP qualifies under the tax code as either a stock-bonus plan or a combination stock-bonus plan/pension plan (also called a money-purchase pension plan). An ESOP may be combined with other kinds of employee benefit plans, such as a profit-sharing plan or a 401(k) plan.

Unlike other pension plans, ESOPs must invest most of their funds in the stock of the sponsoring employer. ESOPs are also unique among employee benefit plans in their ability to borrow money to buy stock. An ESOP that has borrowed money to buy stock is a leveraged ESOP; an ESOP that acquires stock through direct employer contributions of cash or stock is a nonleveraged ESOP.

Although employers are not required to provide a pension plan for their employees, private employers that do provide such plans must meet the legal requirements of the Employee Retirement Income Security Act of 1974 (ERISA). Like other defined contribution plans, ESOPs qualify for certain tax benefits. In particular, employer contributions to an ESOP may be deducted by the employer as a business expense. (For tax years beginning after December 31, 1997, this provision does not apply to contributions made by an S corporation to repay an ESOP loan.) Employees are not taxed on employer contributions to the ESOP or on the earnings on invested funds until they are distributed.

ESOPs also qualify for special tax benefits. Contributions to a leveraged ESOP are subject to less restrictive limits than contributions to other qualified employee benefit plans. For loans made before the enactment of the Small Business Job Protection Act of 1996, which became law on August 20, 1996, qualified lenders may exclude more than 50 percent of the interest earned on an ESOP loan from their gross income if the ESOP owns more than 50 percent of the company's stock. An employer may deduct dividends paid on stock held by an ESOP if the dividends are paid to plan participants or if the dividends are used to repay a loan that was used to buy the stock. A stockholder in a closely held company may defer recognition of the gain from the sale of stock to an ESOP if, after the sale, the ESOP owns at least 30 percent of the company's stock and the seller reinvests the proceeds from the stock's sale in a U.S. company. For tax years beginning after December 31, 1997, the last two provisions do not apply to stock in an S corporation.

To qualify for the above tax benefits, an ESOP must meet the minimum requirements established in the Internal Revenue Code. Many of these requirements are general ones that apply to all qualified employee benefit plans. Other requirements apply specifically to ESOPs. In particular, ESOP participants must be allowed voting rights on stock allocated to their accounts. In the case of publicly traded stock, full voting rights must be passed through to participants. For stock in closely held companies, voting rights must be passed through on all major corporate issues. For lenders to qualify for the 50 percent interest exclusion on ESOP loans, full voting rights must be passed through to participants on stock acquired with the loan. Closely held companies must give employees the right to sell distributions of stock to the employer (a put option), at a share price determined by an independent appraiser. An ESOP must allow participants who are approaching retirement to diversify the investment of funds in their accounts.

ESOPs have multiple objectives. The creation of ESOPs is intended to broaden stock ownership. As a kind of defined contribution plan, ESOPs are designed to provide employees with a source of retirement income. ESOPs are also intended to provide employers with a tax-favored means of financing. In contrast to conventional debt financing, both the interest and the principal on an ESOP loan are tax-deductible. The 50 percent interest exclusion may allow lenders to charge below-market interest rates on ESOP loans.

The effectiveness of ESOPs in broadening stock ownership depends largely on the effect of pension plans on private saving. Evidence suggests that private pension plans tend to have a positive effect on the net rate of private saving. Therefore, ESOPs probably have some effect on the distribution of stock ownership. Because ESOPs are required to invest primarily in the stock of the sponsoring employer, the effectiveness of ESOPs in providing employees with retirement income depends, to a large extent, on the profitability of the sponsoring employer. Some evidence suggests that, when combined with employee participation in decision-making, ESOPs may improve worker productivity. Congress has questioned the effectiveness of ESOPs as a tax-favored source of finance and has repealed the 50 percent interest exclusion for ESOP loans.

### Additional readings

Blasi, Joseph R. *Employee Ownership: Revolution or Ripoff?* Cambridge, Mass.: Ballinger, 1988.

Blinder, Alan S., ed. *Paying for Productivity: A Look at the Evidence.* Washington, D.C.: The Brookings Institution, 1990.

Conte, Michael A., and Helen H. Lawrence. "Trends in ESOPs." In *Trends in Pensions 1992*, edited by John A. Turner and Daniel J. Beller. Washington, D.C.: U.S. Government Printing Office, 1992, pp. 135–48.

Mayer, Gerald. *Employee Stock Ownership Plans: Background and Policy Issues.* Library of Congress, Congressional Research Service Report 94-421 E, May 2, 1994.

U.S. General Accounting Office. *Employee Stock Ownership Plans: Benefits and Costs of ESOP Tax Incentives for Broadening Stock Ownership.* PEMD-87-8. Washington, D.C., December 29, 1986.

U.S. General Accounting Office. *Employee Stock Ownership Plans: Little Evidence of Effects on Corporate Performance.* PEMD-88-1. Washington, D.C., October 29, 1987.

Young, Karen M., ed. *The Expanding Role of ESOPs in Public Companies.* New York: Quorum Books, 1990.

*Cross references:* pensions, tax treatment; profit-sharing plans.

# Energy taxes

Geraldine Gerardi
Department of the Treasury

Eric Toder
The Urban Institute

*Excise taxes imposed on energy products or on final energy consumption.*

Over the past 25 years, there has been considerable discussion of new or additional taxes on energy. This interest was first sparked by the 1973–74 oil embargo and the subsequent concern over forging a national energy policy. Both the reasons for considering energy taxes and the specific tax bases considered have varied over the years, however, as perceptions of immediate national priorities have changed.

Taxes on energy have been considered for four major reasons: (1) to reduce adverse effects attributable to energy consumption, such as dependence on imported oil and global warming, (2) to capture windfall gains to domestic producers from decontrol and higher world oil prices, (3) to fund specific programs, and (4) to raise revenue to reduce large projected budget deficits.

Some of these concerns have been addressed in recent years. For example, in 1980 Congress enacted the Crude Oil Windfall Profits Tax to capture some of the gains to domestic producers as a result of the anticipated increase in oil prices following decontrol. The tax raised less revenue than expected when oil prices dropped in 1982, and it was repealed in 1988. Temporary taxes have also been imposed on crude oil and imported refined petroleum products to finance the cleanup of hazardous substances under the Superfund program and oil spills, and on motor fuels to finance the cleanup of leaking underground storage tanks. (Excise taxes on transportation fuels that are used to fund certain mass transit and highway construction and maintenance programs, aviation services and airport improvements, and the costs of water transportation have been in place for some time.) In 1993, the Clinton administration proposed a BTU tax, but Congress rejected it and enacted an increase in fuel taxes as part of a deficit-reduction package.

In addition to the energy taxes imposed and increased in recent years, environmental groups have discussed a tax on the carbon content of fossil fuels to address environmental concerns, in particular the effect of carbon emissions generated from the combustion of fossil fuels on potential global warming.

## Reasons for taxing energy

Tax experts normally favor taxes that are neutral and do not affect spending or investment patterns. Such a system is more equitable and conducive to economic efficiency, because relative prices will reflect true resource costs. Taxes on energy consumption are often justified, however, on the grounds that market prices do not reflect the full social costs of producing and consuming energy. Among the reasons advanced for energy taxes are several types of external effects.

### Dependence on imported oil

The United States remains heavily dependent on imported oil. Imports currently account for about one-half of U.S. oil consumption. Taxes that reduce energy consumption or increase domestic produc-

tion and encourage investment in conservation and alternative energy property will reduce U.S. dependence on oil and, it is argued, reduce the potential economic costs of any future oil supply interruption or sudden price rise. It is not clear, however, that energy taxes are the best alternative. Providing for government stockpiles or subsidizing private stockpiles is another option, and the United States has invested in a strategic oil reserve. The U.S. vulnerability to oil price shocks has also been lessened, relative to the 1970s when two such shocks occurred, by the reduced market power of the Organization of Petroleum Exporting Countries and increased worldwide competition in production.

### Conservation of nonrenewable resources

A second reason advanced for energy taxation is to reduce the depletion of nonrenewable resources. The fact that some resources are becoming scarcer or more expensive to extract does not provide a compelling reason to reduce energy extraction if capital markets are functioning properly. Federal income tax incentives that favor extraction, such as the expensing of intangible drilling costs, may encourage overproduction. Concern that resources are being used up too rapidly would suggest that these provisions be reviewed.

### Underpricing of energy: regulation and environmental costs

Although a rationale for energy taxes in the past was to offset regulatory policies that controlled energy prices, the phasing out of these regulations has eliminated this argument. A second argument is based on the presence of environmental costs—that is, energy is underpriced because its market price fails to take into account the damage to the environment from energy production and use. These environmental costs vary by type of fuel and use and the extent to which they are internalized to producers and consumers by existing environmental regulations. Recent proposals for a tax on the carbon content of fossil fuels reflect concerns about the effect of greenhouse gas emissions on global warming.

### Revenue raising

While not an economic justification for choosing energy taxes, such taxes might be high on the agenda of possible deficit-reducing measures, particularly because they are consumption taxes that may be attractive to those who favor greater reliance on taxes that do not discourage saving and capital formation. Objections to energy taxes have been raised on the grounds that they are regressive, burdening lower-income households relative to their annual income more than higher-income households. However, the measured regressivity of energy taxes is reduced when those taxes are distributed according to estimated lifetime income and when the indirect effects of the taxation of energy used to produce energy-intensive goods purchased by households are taken into account. Proponents of carbon taxes have argued that their revenues could be used to mitigate the regressivity of the tax or reduce other distortional taxes and ameliorate the decline in economic growth rates from the imposition of the carbon tax.

## Types of energy taxes

There are several types of energy taxes, and the choice of a particular tax would be influenced by the policy objective sought.

### Oil import fee

An oil import fee is the most direct way of reducing imports, because it will both discourage consumption and increase production (of domestic oil and of alternative fuels). An oil import fee should be imposed on both crude oil and refined petroleum products. Assuming that the tax does not cover other oil-intensive products (such as petrochemicals), there is an incentive to increase the importation of these products, with adverse effects for domestic producers. An oil import fee would differentially affect the prices of alternative consumer products and industries, increase state and local severance taxes, and increase the profits of domestic producers of oil and gas and, to some extent, producers of competing fuels, whose prices would also rise.

Taxing oil imports from all countries could create political problems for the United States. However, exempting imports from certain countries, such as Canada and Mexico, would reduce the tax base. Moreover, nonexempt countries could avoid the tax by channeling imports through exempt countries.

### Oil excise tax

Compared with an import fee, an oil excise tax would raise more revenue, but it would be a less efficient way of reducing imports, because it would not increase domestic production incentives. Its effects on consumer products and the incentive to import oil-intensive products would be similar to those of the oil import fee. It would not produce windfall benefits to oil producers or encourage domestic production, although it would benefit producers of alternative fuels and encourage their production.

### Broad energy taxes

Broad energy taxes are less targeted to reducing dependence on oil imports, because they encourage neither domestic production of oil nor production of other taxed fuels. If the objective is general conservation or environmental improvements, however, a broader-based tax would seem more appropriate. A tax justified on the grounds of depletion of nonrenewable resources should cover most, but not all, energy sources. A broad energy tax would be more evenhanded in its effects among industries and uses than an oil excise tax.

A broad energy tax could be imposed in several ways. The base could be the BTU content of the fuel or the value of the energy at some point in its production or sale. A tax on value (or *ad valorem* tax) could be imposed on producers or consumers; however, the relative impact of the taxes on final prices would vary depending on point of production. These broad-based taxes would include, in addition to oil, the other fossil fuels (natural gas and coal) and other types of energy such as hydroelectric, nuclear, and geothermal. Unless specifically excluded, such taxes would include renewable and/or nonpolluting energy sources, where the rationale for taxation (other than raising revenues and being more even across industries) is unclear.

Another type of energy tax is a carbon tax, which would be assessed only on fuels containing carbon (oil, coal, and natural gas). The main objective of a carbon tax is environmental, to reduce carbon emissions. A carbon tax would be based on the carbon content of the fuel (although such a tax would not be the same as a tax on carbon emissions, which depends on the efficiency with which the fuel is burned). A carbon tax would also have differential price effects among alternative fuels. The tax burden as a percentage of mine price (at the mine mouth or well head) would be substantially higher for coal than for oil or gas.

### Energy consumption taxes

Taxes on energy "consumption" are not well defined. Energy is not an end in itself, but a means of obtaining some other final product. For example, heat in one's home can be obtained by burning fossil fuel directly, by burning wood, by insulating or using machinery to store solar power, or by moving to a warmer climate. In practice, taxes on energy consumption end up being imposed on selected items of consumer expenditure and industrial purchases used for transportation, heating and cooling, and power generation. These might include motor fuels, electric power, oil and gas purchased directly, and oil, gas, and coal burned by factories. The tax is collected from intermediate sources or from the final consumer. A tax on the final consumer would be very complicated to collect. This tax would be designed to add the same percentage to the cost of all energy and would be more even among uses than more narrowly based taxes, but its objective is not clear.

### Motor fuel taxes

Motor fuel taxes are already imposed at both the federal and state levels. Traditionally, motor fuel revenues are allocated to trust funds. For example, the gasoline excise tax is allocated to the Highway Trust Fund; taxes on jet fuel are allocated to the Airport and Airways Trust Fund, and so forth. Between 1991 and 1997, a portion of the motor fuels excise tax was allocated to the general fund and used for deficit reduction. In 1993, taxes on gasoline and other fuels were increased as a deficit-reduction measure and the revenue from the tax increase was allocated to the general fund; in 1997, all funds were returned to the Highway Trust Fund, with a small portion dedicated to the mass transit account.

The most important of the motor fuel taxes is the gasoline tax, which is currently imposed at the federal level at 18.3 cents per gallon. Imposing taxes on gasoline that are not used for highway construction can be justified on the ground of pollution and congestion effects. Motor fuel taxes may not, however, be the best way to correct for these costs. For example, driving in rural areas does not produce the same external costs as driving in urban areas does.

Because motor fuels have a narrower base than oil excise taxes and energy taxes, the rates would have to be higher relative to sales prices to produce a given amount of revenue.

### Conclusion

Whether to adopt an energy tax, and what type to adopt, depends on the objectives. Present taxes are used primarily to fund specific programs and are sometimes motivated by user fee objectives. For many years, the most well-articulated argument for new types of energy taxes was to reduce dependence on oil imports. This objective would support an oil import tax or oil excise tax, even though these taxes would have many uneven effects and administrative complexities. Energy taxes aimed at revenue needs might be more broad-based, such as an ad valorem or a BTU tax, although in 1993 an increase in motor fuel taxes was ultimately adopted after Congress rejected a proposed BTU tax. Recently, environmental considerations are receiving more attention and have increased interest in a carbon tax to reduce the potential for global warming from greenhouse gas emissions.

### Additional readings

Bull, Nicholas, Kevin A. Hassett, and Gilbert E. Metcalf. "Who Pays Broad-Based Energy Taxes? Computing Lifetime and Regional Incidence." *The Energy Journal* 15 (1994): 145–64.

Gerardi, Geraldine, and Eric Toder. "The Economic Effects of Alternative Energy Taxes." *National Tax Journal* 37 (September 1984): 289–301.

Goulder, Lawrence H. "Environmental Taxation and the Double Dividend: A Reader's Guide." *International Tax and Public Finance* 2 (1995): 157–83.

Poterba, James. "Tax Policy to Combat Global Warming: On Designing a Carbon Tax." In *Global Warming: Economic Policy Responses*, edited by Rudiger Dornbusch and James Poterba. Cambridge, Mass.: MIT Press, 1991, pp. 71–97.

*Cross references:* excise taxes; fuel taxes, federal.

# Enterprise zones

Leslie E. Papke
Michigan State University

*Geographic areas targeted for economic development assistance.*

Enterprise zone programs are geographically targeted tax, expenditure, and regulatory inducements used by state and local governments since the early 1980s and by the federal government since 1993. While they differ in their specifics, all the programs provide development incentives, including tax preferences to capital and/or labor, in an attempt to induce private investment location or expansion to depressed areas and to enhance employment opportunities for the residents therein. Most enterprise zones are designated in urban areas, but occasionally rural areas are selected.

Typically, state and local zone programs provide larger tax credits for business investment than for employment incentives. Investment incentives include the exemption of business-related purchases from state sales and use taxes, investment tax credits, and corporate income or unemployment tax rebates. Labor subsidies include employer tax credits for all new hires or zone-resident new hires, employee income tax credits, and job-training tax credits. Some programs assist firms financially with investment funds or industrial development bonds.

Enterprise zones have been criticized as ineffective and inefficient in stimulating new economic activity. This criticism is part of a long-standing debate on the effects of intersite tax differentials on the location of capital investment. It is argued that if tax-induced investment only represents relocation from another state, then tax competition is a zero-sum game for the country as a whole. In addition, the preferential treatment of certain types of investment or employment within enterprise zones may induce decisions that would not be economically sound in the absence of the tax incentives.

Often, however, redistribution of economic activity within a state may be a desirable goal. If investment is relocated from local labor markets with low unemployment to local labor markets with higher unemployment, the incentives may generate efficiency gains for the economy as underutilized resources are tapped. Efficiency gains may also result if reductions in unemployment produce positive externalities, such as reductions in social unrest.

In addition to encouraging existing businesses to locate in particular geographic areas, the incentives may induce the creation of new businesses that would not otherwise have been started. Such new businesses could produce taxable profits and incomes that would reduce the revenue cost of the incentives.

A partial equilibrium model can predict the theoretical effects of enterprise zone incentives offered to firms in those zones. If the zones are small relative to the rest of the economy, the effect on zone wages and employment will depend on the supply elasticity of factors to the zone and on the demand elasticity for zone output. For plausible parameter values, a labor subsidy or an equal-cost subsidy to both zone capital and zone resident labor will raise zone wages. A capital subsidy alone may actually reduce zone wages. Employment effects are likely to be small if labor is inelastically supplied.

If the zones are relatively large and spillovers into the rest of the economy are considered, the effects are more difficult to predict. The net employment effects for the nation of a federal enterprise zone program depend on features of both zone and nonzone sectors of the economy: the relative sizes of the two sectors, the elasticity of factor substitution in the two sectors, the elasticity of zone and nonzone product substitution in consumption, and the aggregate supply elasticities of production factors. The greater the number of areas designated as enterprise zones, the smaller the effects on zone wages. If capital is relatively fixed in the aggregate, as many empirical studies suggest, the net effect will be to relocate productive facilities inside the zone.

An empirical evaluation of an enterprise zone program frequently measures the amount of investment undertaken after the designation, the increase in the number of firms in the zone, and the change in zone employment. Cost-effectiveness is measured by direct spending and forgone revenue per job created (or, if the goal of the program is zone-resident employment, cost per zone-resident job). These measures provide an accounting of the initial level of public investment required per zone job created. But they are not a full cost-benefit accounting of the program, because they do not account for second-round feedback effects (such as zone employee removal from welfare and income tax payments). In

addition, it is difficult to determine which jobs may be relocations.

The key methodological issue in the empirical evaluation is to separate the effects of zone designation from jobs and investments arising from other factors—for example, general upswings in the economy. In addition, the evaluation must account for the depressed economic characteristics that led to the initial zone designation. Survey or case study methodologies provide useful information on zone participation, but they cannot isolate zone effects.

Econometric analysis is better suited to analyzing the effects of zone programs. If zone sites are randomly selected, the effect of the program can be measured by comparing the performance of the experimental and control groups. Usually, however, enterprise zone designation is based on economic performance, so the data are nonexperimental. This sample selection problem can be addressed with a variety of econometric techniques.

Econometric analysis of a zone's success faces a practical difficulty in that conventional economic data are not available by zone. In most states, zones do not coincide with census tracts or taxing jurisdictions. As a result, zone areas cannot be pinpointed in standard data collections. Despite these difficulties, a number of studies have analyzed the federal program in Britain and the state and local enterprise zone initiatives in the United States.

In 1981, the United Kingdom began to designate areas as enterprise zones. The zones were small relative to U.S. zones, ranging in size from 100 to 900 acres, and consisting of vacant, unoccupied, or deteriorating industrial land within an economically declining community. In contrast to the state zones in the United States, British zone boundaries excluded both existing business and residential areas. The U.K. program focused almost exclusively on industrial development—community development was not a specific goal of the program. After a series of evaluations concluded that relocations were the source of activity in the zones, the British government is allowing the zones to expire.

In contrast to the United Kingdom, eligibility for state and local zone programs in the United States depends upon zone population characteristics. These include comparative unemployment rates, population levels and trends, poverty status, median incomes, and percentage of welfare recipients. At least 37 states have enacted enterprise zone programs as part of their economic development policies. They differ widely in purpose, coverage, and incentive provisions. For example, Michigan has only one zone, and Louisiana has more than 800.

The state of Indiana's enterprise zone program is considered by survey studies to be one of the most successful. In 1984, Indiana began to designate zones for a 10-year duration, subject to renewal. To qualify for consideration and possible designation, the area had to have an unemployment rate at least 1.5 times the average statewide unemployment rate, and a resident household poverty rate at least 25 percent above the U.S. poverty level. Its resident population had to be between 2,000 and 8,000 persons and its geographic area between 0.75 and 3 square miles, all with a continuous boundary.

The two largest tax incentives included in the Indiana enterprise zone program are: (1) a tax credit against local property tax liability equal to 100 percent of the property tax imposed on all inventories located in the zone; (2) a tax credit for employers hiring zone residents equal to 10 percent of wages, with a ceiling of $1,500 per qualified employee.

Indiana's employment tax credit, which targets the hiring of zone residents, is typical of other enterprise zone programs. Also like other programs, the value of the tax preferences is tilted heavily toward capital investment. But the inventory tax credit is an unusual mechanism for increasing investment because most states do not include inventories in a business's tangible personal property tax base and would instead typically provide incentives for investment in machinery or equipment rather than inventories.

Econometric analysis of Indiana zone and non-zone areas finds that zones have greater inventory growth and fewer unemployment claims than they would have in the absence of the zone designation. However, inventory investment appears to come at the cost of a drop in depreciable property. Moreover, despite the reduction in unemployment rates in the zones, a comparison of incomes from the 1990 Census suggests that zone residents are not appreciably better off with the Indiana zone program.

Cost-per-job estimates from zone programs are not that different from earlier U.S. experiences with job subsidies such as the JOBS program of the late 1960s and early 1970s and the Urban Development Action Grant Program in the late 1970s. However, costs per zone-resident job are considerably higher. For example, in Indiana, calculations indicate that the annual cost of an Indiana zone job in 1990 was $4,564, compared with $31,113 per zone-resident job. Note that, as in Indiana, local governments may bear the brunt of the cost of a state enterprise zone program if tax incentives are provided against local taxes without state reimbursement.

A new federal policy emphasizes increased geographic concentration of federal intervention. The Omnibus Budget Reconciliation Act of 1993 called for the creation of 95 enterprise communities (65 urban, 30 rural) and 9 empowerment zones (6 urban, 3 rural). The designations were to take place in 1994–95 and to last up to 10 years. Selected areas needed to demonstrate pervasive poverty, unemployment, and general distress, and applicants had to outline a plan of action that included local business and community interests.

Both enterprise communities and empowerment zones were to receive tax-exempt facility bonds, $3 million in Department of Heath and Human Services Social Service Block Grants, and priority for funds from many existing federal programs. Empowerment zones received additional benefits. The block grant amount was increased to $100 million and substantial employer tax benefits were added. Qualified employers receive a 20 percent employer tax credit for wages paid to qualified zone employees up to $15,000. Firms in empowerment zones may increase their Section 179 expensing by up to $20,000, to a total of $37,500 for qualified zone property.

The residence-based approach of the income tax credit differs significantly from another federal program designed to increase employment of the disadvantaged. The Targeted Jobs Tax Credit provides firms with a similar-sized subsidy for wages paid to targeted individuals—primarily welfare recipients and poor youth. Research has demonstrated that providing a subsidy based on individual characteristics may create a stigma that actually reduces the probability of being hired. Residence-based eligibility may eliminate this problem and encourage individuals who become employed to continue to live in the zone.

In 1997, the number of empowerment zones under federal law was expanded, and some revisions were made in the benefits. Special benefits were also enacted for the District of Columbia.

## Additional readings

Bartik, Timothy J. *Who Benefits from State and Local Economic Development Policies*. Kalamazoo, Mich.: W.E. Upjohn Institute for Employment Research, 1991.

Bishop, John, and Mark Montgomery. "Does the Targeted Jobs Tax Credit Create Jobs at Subsidized Firms?" *Industrial Relations* (Fall 1993): 289–306.

Brintnall, Michael, and R. Green. "Comparing State Enterprise Zone Programs: Variations in Structure and Coverage." *Economic Development Quarterly* 2 (1) (1988): 50–68.

Connecticut Department of Economic Development. *Enterprise Zones: The Connecticut Experiment*. Hartford, Conn., 1985.

Erickson, Rodney A., and S.W. Friedman. "Comparative Dimensions of State Enterprise Zone Policies." In *Enterprise Zones: New Directions in Economic Development*, edited by R.E. Green. Sage Focus Edition, 1991, pp. 136–54.

Gravelle, Jane G. "Enterprise Zones: The Design of Tax Incentives." CRS Report for Congress 92-476 S. Congressional Research Service, Library of Congress, June 3, 1992.

Papke, James A. *The Role of Market Based Public Policy in Economic Development and Urban Revitalization: A Retrospective Analysis and Appraisal of the Indiana Enterprise Zone Program—Year Three Report.* Center for Tax Policy Studies, Purdue University, 1990.

Papke, Leslie E. "What Do We Know about Enterprise Zones?" In *Tax Policy and the Economy* 7, edited by James M. Poterba. Cambridge, Mass.: MIT Press, 1993, pp. 37–72.

Papke, Leslie E. "Tax Policy and Urban Development: Evidence from the Indiana Enterprise Zone Program." *Journal of Public Economics* 54 (1) (1994): 37–49.

Roger Tym and Partners. *Monitoring Enterprise Zones: Year Three Report.* London: Department of the Environment, Her Majesty's Stationery Office, 1984.

Rubin, Barry M., and Craig M. Richards. "A Transatlantic Comparison of Enterprise Zone Impacts: The British and American Experience." *Economic Development Quarterly* 6 (4) (1992): 431–43.

Rubin, Barry M., and Margaret G. Wilder. "Urban Enterprise Zones: Employment Impacts and Fiscal Incentives." *Journal of the American Planning Association* 55 (4) (1989): 418–31.

Rubin, Marilyn, and R.B. Armstrong. "The New Jersey Urban Enterprise Zone Program: An Evaluation." Report prepared for the New Jersey Department of Commerce, Trenton, N.J., 1989.

Talbot, J. "Have Enterprise Zones Encouraged Enterprise? Some Empirical Evidence from Tynside." *Regional Studies* 22 (6) (1988): 507–14.

Thomas, C.J., and R.D.F. Bromley. "The Growth and Functioning of an Unplanned Retail Park: The Swansea Enterprise Zone." *Regional Studies* 21 (4) (1987): 287–300.

U.S. Department of Housing and Urban Development. "An Impact Evaluation of the Urban Development Action Grant Program." Office of Policy Development and Research, 1982.

U.S. General Accounting Office. *Enterprise Zones: Lessons from the Maryland Experience.* GAO/PEMD-89-2. 1988.

Wilder, M.G., and B.M. Rubin. "Targeted Redevelopment through Urban Enterprise Zones." *Journal of Urban Affairs* 10 (1) (1988): 1–17.

*Cross references:* budget policy, state and local; business location, taxation and; fiscal disparities; tax competition; tax-exempt bonds; zoning, property taxes, and exactions.

# Environmental taxes, federal

## Thomas A. Barthold
Joint Committee on Taxation, U.S. Congress

*Taxes levied on goods or services whose consumption or production is thought to affect the environment.*

---

Policymakers may implement environmental policy through the use of taxes or subsidies that affect market prices or rates of return, thereby altering the environmental consequences of private market outcomes.

Federal tax policy has long had environmental consequences, although it is only over the past 20 years that tax policy has been used as an environmental policy tool. Many existing tax provisions with environmental ramifications were not motivated by environmental concerns. For example, income tax provisions passed to assist the timber industry in the 1920s permitted expensing (rather than capitalization) of the costs of reforestation and planting. Combined with preferential capital gains treatment for harvested timber, these income tax provisions may have encouraged a more rapid harvest of domestic timberland. Similarly, Congress first enacted the federal motor fuels tax in 1932, but it is only recently that this tax began to be discussed as an environmental tax, aimed at addressing the externalities caused by automobile use.

Efforts at environmental tax policy began after the 1973 oil embargo, although at the time the focus of the policies was energy conservation rather than pollution reduction. In the Energy Tax Act of 1978, Congress enacted the gas guzzler excise tax, which varied with the Environmental Protection Agency's (EPA's) fuel economy rating of automobiles, and provided tax credits for residential energy conservation expenditures. While the gas guzzler excise tax remains in force today, Congress repealed the residential energy credits in 1986.

Since 1980, the use of tax policy to deal with environmental problems has accelerated, as policymakers have shown a much greater interest in so-called "market solutions" to environmental control than in direct regulation. Better-known examples include the excise taxes on petroleum and hazardous chemicals, enacted in 1980 to fund the EPA's hazardous waste site cleanup program (Superfund). In 1989, in the aftermath of the *Exxon Valdez* oil spill, Congress imposed an additional excise tax on petroleum and petroleum products to fund the Oil Spill Liability Trust Fund. In the same year, Congress imposed an excise tax on the manufacture of ozone-depleting chemicals. In 1992, Congress enacted income tax deductions for the purchase of "clean fuel" vehicles. At present, more than 50 federal tax code provisions may be classified as environmental.

Use of environmental taxes appears likely to continue. Congress has held hearings on a variety of environmental tax proposals. The EPA (1991) has discussed using taxes to deal with the problem of lead leaching into groundwater from landfills, the disposal of pesticide containers, and other environmental concerns. The most prominent recent example is President Clinton's proposal for a modified BTU (energy) tax.

Federal environmental tax policy generally falls into one of five categories: benefit taxes, taxes as insurance premiums, Pigouvian taxes (see below), liability taxes, or windfall profits taxes. First, Congress has assessed some taxes as user fees to fund specific direct-expenditure programs. This is sometimes called the benefit principle of taxation; those who benefit should pay the taxes, which approximate user charges. While the use of excise taxes imposed on highway motor fuels to fund expenditures from the Highway Trust Fund for the construction and repair of highways is the best-known example, the sport-fishing-equipment excise tax and the excise tax on motorboat fuels fund programs to ensure the survival of sport and other fish species.

Second, a tax may be assessed on an industry or group of consumers to fund an insurance pool against potential environmental risks arising from the taxed product. The tax is levied as an insurance premium in a mandated scheme of risk pooling. For example, the Oil Spill Liability Trust Fund tax imposes a tax of $.05 per barrel of domestic and imported oil. While the primary liability for damage from an oil spill remains with the owner of the oil, the tax funds a trust fund that may be drawn upon to meet unrecovered claims that may arise from an oil spill either upon the high seas or from ruptured domestic pipelines. The tax and trust fund represent a social insurance scheme with risks spread across all consumers of petroleum.

Third, the federal government has used the tax code to deliver Pigouvian subsidies or impose Pigouvian taxes, named after British economist Arthur C. Pigou, on polluters. The premise of such a tax (or subsidy) is that when an externality causes marginal social costs (or marginal social benefits) to diverge from private marginal costs (or private marginal benefits), the market outcome may not produce an efficient level of output. Pigou was the first to propose that a tax equal to the difference between marginal social cost and private marginal cost would lead the market to an efficient outcome. The tax internalizes the externality into private costs. Examples of Pigouvian subsidies are the (short-lived) residential energy credits, which were premised on the belief that private market prices did not reflect the full social benefit of energy conservation.

Examples of Pigouvian taxes are the gas guzzler excise tax and the excise tax on ozone-depleting chemicals.

Fourth, Congress has funded specific environmental programs by imposing environmental taxes on taxpayers deemed to be liable for past environmental damage, rather than on taxpayers perceived to benefit from the expenditure program. Such taxes cannot be interpreted as Pigouvian if they are not related to current externalities. Nor can such taxes be seen as insurance premiums if the primary expenditure purpose is to remedy past environmental damage. Examples of such "liability" taxes are the Superfund excise taxes on petroleum and chemicals and the Leaking Underground Storage Tank Tax imposed on fuels. These taxes fund trust funds, expenditures from which remedy past environmental damage.

The final category is that of windfall profits taxes. Regulatory control of supply may cause prices to rise beyond those that would prevail in a free market, creating high returns on the permitted sales. Alternatively, removal of previously existing price controls may cause prices to rise beyond those previously prevailing, creating high returns on existing sales. Economists refer to these increased profits as "inframarginal" or "windfall," meaning that they are profits on the level of the producers' economic activity that would have occurred without the change in regulatory policy. The most obvious example is the Crude Oil Windfall Profits Tax passed by Congress in 1980 in response to the deregulation of oil prices. This tax was repealed in 1988. Some have suggested that the tax on ozone-depleting chemicals is a windfall profits tax because production of and trade in these chemicals are governed by an international agreement.

Many taxes fall into more than one of these five categories. For example, motor fuels taxes may have both a benefit component and a Pigouvian component. In addition, environmental taxes often deviate from what economic theory would dictate. The taxes assessed as user fees only inexactly measure benefits; for example, not all motorboats are used for fishing. The taxes assessed as insurance premiums reflect imperfect pricing of risks; the Oil Spill Liability Trust Fund tax is imposed at the same rate regardless of whether the importer employs harder-to-rupture double-hulled or single-hulled tankers. The Pigouvian taxes imperfectly measure marginal social cost or benefit. The residential energy credits were inframarginal for all those taxpayers who were planning to invest in home insulation, even without the tax break.

Depending on their incidence, liability taxes may inexactly recoup damages from parties held responsible for past environmental damage. For example, the burden may fall on the current owners of enterprises rather than those who were the owners at the time the damage occurred. In practice, it may not be possible to identify the inframarginal units of production on which to impose a windfall profits tax.

The environmental taxes enacted probably deviate from theoretical precepts for several reasons. There are practical problems of design. It may be difficult to identify the tax base. Congress must also weigh the costs of administration and compliance against the benefits of a "perfect" environmental tax. In addition, other policy concerns such as economic development or defense needs may lead to compromises with environmental policy concerns.

The existing federal "environmental tax" provisions vary in their budgetary importance. The Office of Management and Budget (OMB) projected that federal motor fuels taxes would yield revenues in excess of $33 billion in 1998. The narrower scope of other tax provisions limits their budgetary effect. For example, OMB projects the excise tax on ozone-depleting chemicals to raise only $47 million in 1998. The Joint Committee on Taxation estimated the deduction for "clean fuel" vehicles to reduce revenues by less than $5.062 million in 1995. While small relative to the federal budget, such figures might be substantial relative to the affected industry. In addition, if the intent of a tax is Pigouvian, a small revenue yield might reflect that the tax has successfully altered behavior.

### Additional readings

Barthold, Thomas A., "Issues in the Design of Environmental Excise Taxes." *Journal of Economic Perspectives* 8 (Winter 1994): 133–51.

Cropper, Maureen L., and Wallace E. Oates. "Environmental Economics: A Survey." *Journal of Economic Literature* 30 (June 1992): 675–740.

Pigou, Arthur C. *The Economics of Welfare.* 4th ed. London: MacMillan & Co., Ltd., 1932.

U.S. Congress, House Committee on Ways and Means. *Hearings* Serial 101-98. March 6, 7, and 14, 1990.

U.S. Congress, Joint Committee on Taxation. *Present Law and Background Relating to Federal Environmental Tax Policy.* 1990.

U.S. Environmental Protection Agency. *Economic Incentives: Options for Environmental Protection.* March 1991.

*Cross references:* benefit principle; energy taxes; environmental taxes, state; excise taxes; fuel taxes, federal; Highway Trust Fund, federal.

# Environmental taxes, state

Robert A. Bohm
University of Tennessee at Knoxville

Michael P. Kelsay
Indiana University–Purdue University at Fort Wayne

*The states' tax and fee responses to activities judged environmentally harmful.*

In the most general terms, an environmental tax can be thought of as a user charge on the environment. Under this definition, any activity that has a negative environmental impact creates an obligation to pay the tax. At a minimum, revenue from the tax should be adequate to fund cleanup efforts. At best, the tax may provide incentives to reduce or eliminate the environmental problem altogether. Institutionally, environmental taxes are often called fees or charges, indicating that the revenue is designated for special purposes and is deposited in a restricted trust fund. When the word *tax* itself is used, common practice suggests that the revenue is deposited in the general fund. In this entry, these terms are used interchangeably to indicate a revenue instrument with an environmental base.

Environmental taxes take many forms at the state level. Some may be thought of as direct environmental taxes, the link with a recognizable environmental issue or problem being readily apparent. Into this group fall generation or emissions fees, disposal fees, and permit fees. A second group may be termed indirect environmental taxes. Here, the link to the environmental problem at hand may be rather remote. Into this group fall the so-called predisposal fees, and taxes on productive inputs and products that generate environmental costs when used. Indirect environmental taxes used by state governments are invariably thinly disguised product excise taxes.

Both direct and indirect environmental taxes may entail attempts to reflect differentially higher costs of treatment or higher risks associated with specific waste streams and activities with environmental impacts. For example, Tennessee levies a disposal charge on all solid waste disposed of in the state and a predisposal tax on the sale of automobile tires. Revenue from the disposal charge funds the bulk of the state's solid waste program. The tire predisposal tax is intended to reflect the higher costs inherent in the disposal of tires in landfills and the need for shredders. Alternatively, California charges higher rates for large-quantity generators of medical waste and differentiates its hazardous waste disposal fee based on the characteristics of the waste stream and the method of treatment.

State environmental taxes are levied over and above existing costs, charges, fees, or taxes in all but a few cases. Municipal solid waste services, for example, may be provided by local government and funded by user charges, through general revenues, or by private companies. State solid waste taxes or fees represent a surcharge added to the direct cost of this service. Environmentally based levies on products such as tires and motor fuels are likewise additional charges. The exception to this rule would be a case in which the state government itself is involved as primary provider of the service—solid waste services in Delaware and the District of Columbia, for example.

## State environmental taxes in 1995

Table 1 summarizes the major state environmental taxes in use in the 50 states and the District of Columbia, based on a survey completed in January 1995. In addition to a generic name for each type of tax, the table shows the number of states using the tax and the range of rate and base definitions. Permit fees, such as those used to fund state air quality programs and the National Pollution Discharge Elimination System, are not included in this summary.

Two generation fees are described in the table. The most frequently employed environmental tax, used in 44 states, is the hazardous waste generation fee. This is a two-part tax that, in most cases, combines an annual fee per facility and a volume fee per ton generated. The volume fee varies depending on on-site versus off-site method of treatment, storage, or disposal. Seven states impose a low-level radioactive waste generation fee. Typically, this tax is based on both waste volume and radioactivity level.

Missouri and Maine present two interesting examples of the hazardous waste generation fee. In Missouri, the tax consists of: (1) an annual registration fee of $1.00 per ton generated to a maximum

of $10,000.00; (2) an additional assessment of $25.00 per ton on all waste discharged, deposited, dumped, or placed on top of the soil for final action, and $2.00 per ton on all other waste transported off-site; and (3) 2.0 percent of gross charges and fees for disposal at hazardous waste landfill sites. The following fees are in place in Maine: large-quantity generators pay $40.00 per ton for waste generated and disposed of on-site in a licensed disposal facility; $100.00 per ton for waste stored from 90 to 180 days, and an additional $100.00 per ton for waste stored over 180 days; and $40.00 per ton or $30.00 per ton for waste transported off-site to a licensed facility for reuse, reclamation, or recycling. (These latter rates increase to $360.00 per ton and $270.00 per ton, respectively, if there is noncompliance with state waste-reduction goals.)

Forty-three states have enacted a hazardous waste disposal fee, and 36 have levied a solid waste disposal fee on municipal solid waste. Both of these taxes are in the form of surcharges, with widely varying rates between states. In addition, the rates can vary significantly within states. For example, in the case of the hazardous waste disposal fee in California, the rates range from $5.36 per ton for incinerated waste to $214.54 per ton for specific types of extremely hazardous waste.

In 38 states, the need for revenue to fund underground storage tank programs has led to the enactment of underground storage tank fees. Like the hazardous waste generator fee, this tax is often in two parts, an annual fee per tank and a rate per gallon stored. Two product excise taxes are commonly used for environmental purposes. The tire predisposal tax is in place in 28 states. With the exception of North Carolina's ad valorem approach and the District of Columbia's disposal calculation method, states levy this tax on a per tire basis, with the rate ranging from $0.25 to $2.00. A motor fuels tax, which provides funds for environmental programs related to fuel use, is in place in 14 states. In

## TABLE 1

### State Environmental Taxation in the United States 1995

| Tax | Number Using | Tax Rate and Base |
| --- | --- | --- |
| Hazardous Waste Generator Fee | 44 | From $300.00 to $200,000.00 annual fee per facility plus from $1.00 to $360.00 per ton generated |
| Hazardous Waste Disposal Fee | 43 | From $1.00 to $214.00 per ton |
| Underground Storage Tank Fee | 38 | From $10.00 to $30,000.00 annual fee per tank plus from $0.006 to $0.02 per gallon stored |
| Solid Waste Disposal Fee | 36 | From $0.10 to $42.00 per ton |
| Waste Tire Fee | 28 | From $0.25 to $2.00 per tire |
| Motor Fuels Fee | 14 | From $0.002 to $0.16 per gallon |
| Low-Level Radioactive Waste Generator Fee | 7 | From $3.00 to $13.00 per cubic foot |
| Coastal/Inland Spill Fee | 6 | From $0.20 to $0.80 per gallon of imported pollutant |
| Water Quality Fee | 4 | From $0.02 to $0.59 per gallon of solvent, oil, ammonia, or petroleum product |

some instances, funds from this tax are directed toward underground storage tank programs. Other uses include funding used oil collection programs. Two final taxes are the coastal/inland pollutant spill cleanup fee (six states) and the water-quality fee (four states). The cleanup tax is levied on a schedule of imported pollutants; the water-quality fee, used to fund water cleanup programs, is levied on selected water-polluting liquids.

## Environmental tax policy issues

To date, state environmental taxes have been levied on narrow bases with limited revenue goals. The jury remains out on the use of environmental taxes as more broadly based tax instruments. Likewise, little can be said about the incidence of these taxes. While a presumption of regressivity is common and probably correct, a firm conclusion cannot be documented.

Two factors have dominated the policy discussion surrounding the enactment of state environmental taxes. Paramount has been the need to provide revenue to fund expanding state environmental programs. The second factor has been a desire to provide incentives to reduce waste generation or encourage reuse and recycling. Economists have long argued for generation fees—that is, taxes directly on environmental emissions—as the best way to achieve the latter goal. Historically, these have been considered difficult to administer and politically impractical. However, as table 1 shows, states have begun to venture into this territory as better emissions monitoring becomes more commonplace and the pursuit of environmental quality rises on the political agenda.

Disposal fees and product excise taxes have long been the most popular forms of state environmental taxation. With easy-to-measure or familiar tax bases, they represent certain sources of revenue. Disposal fees paid directly by generators are equivalent to generation fees. In most cases, however, disposal of environmental waste is institutionally separate from generation, and the tax would have to be shifted to the generator to achieve the same incentive effect as an emissions fee. Still, disposal and product excise taxes do raise the cost of undesirable environmental practices, and these costs will be transmitted through the economy and alter behavior, albeit imperfectly. Furthermore, as has already happened in several states, these costs can be accentuated by means of differentially higher rates for particularly noxious waste or distasteful behavior.

## Additional readings

Anderson, Mikael. *Governance by Green Taxes.* New York: Manchester University Press, 1994.

Barthold, Thomas A. "Issues in the Design of Environmental Excise Taxes." *Journal of Economic Perspectives* (Winter 1994): 133–51.

Bohm, Robert A., and Michael P. Kelsay. "State and Local Government Initiatives to Tax Solid and Hazardous Waste." In *State Taxation of Business: Issues and Policy Options,* edited by Thomas Pogue. Westport, Conn.: Praeger, 1992.

Carlin, Alan. *The United States Experience with Economic Incentives to Control Environmental Pollution.* Washington, D.C.: U.S. Environmental Protection Agency, 1992.

Oates, Wallace. "Green Taxes: Can We Protect the Environment and Improve the Tax System at the Same Time?" *Southern Economic Journal* (April 1995): 915–22.

Organization for Economic Cooperation and Development. *Environment and Taxation: The Cases of the Netherlands, Sweden and the United States.* Paris: Organization for Economic Cooperation and Development, 1994.

Pigou, A.C. *The Economics of Welfare.* London: Macmillan and Company, 1938.

*Cross references:* environmental taxes, federal; severance tax, state.

# Estate and gift tax, federal

David Joulfaian
Department of the Treasury

*The federal tax treatment of wealth transferred in contemplation of, or at the time of, death.*

---

The estate and gift tax is the only wealth tax levied by the federal government. The estate tax was first enacted in 1916 and applied to the wealth of decedents with estates in excess of $50,000. It has undergone numerous changes, especially in 1976 and 1981, and it currently applies to taxable estates in excess of $600,000, with a maximum tax rate of 55 percent.

The gift tax was first enacted in 1924, repealed in 1926, and reenacted in 1932 in an attempt to reduce estate tax avoidance via the initiation of *inter vivos* gifts. In 1976, the gift tax was integrated with the estate tax under the Unified Transfer Tax, and a common tax rate schedule with a current maximum tax rate of 55 percent was established. Cumulative transfers, *inter vivos* gifts, and testamentary bequests below $600,000 were effectively exempt from taxation because the tax provides a unified tax credit of $192,800. Both estate and gift taxes are complemented by a generation-skipping transfer tax (GSTT) with a flat rate of 55 percent for cumulative transfers in excess of $1 million per donor.

## Purpose of the tax

The enactment of the estate and gift tax, and its evolving structure over the years, serve several legislative objectives. First and foremost, estate and gift taxes were enacted for their revenue yield. In 1996, these taxes yielded about $17 billion annually and accounted for about 1.2 percent of federal government receipts. The significance of this revenue source should not be understated, given that the estate tax is levied only on the wealthiest 1 percent of decedents' estates: the tax is paid by the estates of about 30,000 decedents from a decedent population of 2.2 million.

A second objective is that these taxes act as a backstop to the income tax, reducing the erosion of its base. Much of the capital income that escapes the income tax passes through the estate tax. Under the personal income tax, accrued capital gains are taxed only when realized, and interest income from state and local bonds, as well as proceeds from life insurance policies, among others, are tax-exempt. In contrast, all assets owned by decedents are likely to be included in their gross estates.

A third objective is a reduction in wealth concentration. By taxing the wealth holdings of the wealthiest estates, the estate and gift taxes are expected to reduce the size of bequests, reducing the wealth accumulated over generations. This is also accomplished by subjecting capital income that has escaped the personal income tax to estate taxation.

Another objective is taxation of each generation's wealth. Wealth transfers to grandchildren are taxed under the estate and gift taxes. However, because of the emphasis on taxing each generation, an additional tax—the GSTT—is also levied on these transfers. The rationale for the GSTT is that a tax should be levied on wealth transfers to children, coupled with another tax when they, in turn, transfer wealth to their children.

To minimize state objections to the enactment of death taxes by the federal government, the estate tax provides a tax credit for state death taxes, thereby keeping the state tax base intact. Effectively, the federal estate tax acts to minimize interstate competition for the wealthy, as the state death tax credit virtually offsets taxes levied by states on the wealthiest of estates.

## The tax base

The estate tax is levied on wealth held at death. This includes real estate, cash, stocks, bonds, businesses, pensions, and life insurance policies owned by the decedent, which form the gross estate. Estates may value these assets at their market value on the date of death or six months from that date. Similar property is also taxed under the gift tax when transferred during life. Cumulative lifetime gifts are added back to the taxable estate.

## Exclusions

The gift tax provides for an annual exclusion of $10,000 per donee. The estate tax provides for an exclusion of up to $750,000 for real property used on farms or in businesses. The exclusion is based on the difference between the market value of a property and the capitalized income from its use in business. Proceeds from life insurance policies on the life of the decedent but owned by others are also excluded from the estate. The GSTT provides an exemption of $1 million per donor.

## Deductions

1. *Marital Deduction.* All transfers of property between spouses, either through *inter vivos* gifts or bequests, are deductible from the estate and gift tax base.
2. *Charitable Bequest Deduction.* All sums of money donated to charitable organizations are deductible from the gross estate.
3. *Debts.* The gross estate is reduced by the amount of debts held at death. These debts include mortgages and outstanding medical expenses.
4. *Other Expenses.* These consist mostly of funeral expenses and expenses involving the settlement of the decedent's estate, such as attorney and executor commissions. They, too, are deductible from the estate tax base.

## Rate structure

The tax rate schedule ranges from 18 percent on the first $10,000 of taxable estate to 55 percent for the excess over $3 million of taxable estate. This rate schedule applies to the wealth at death plus the lifetime taxable gifts before credits have been applied. In 1997, taxable estates over $21 million faced a flat tax rate of 55 percent, with the benefit of the progressive rates phased out between $10 million and $21 million, creating a marginal tax rate of 60 percent. This will increase in steps to $24.1 million in 2006. Generation-skipping transfers are taxed at a flat rate of 55 percent, in addition to the estate and gift taxes.

## Tax credits

Several tax credits are available under the estate and gift tax. The largest of these is the unified credit. Through 1997, the value of the unified credit was fixed at $192,800—equivalent to an exemption of $600,000—for combined estate and gift taxes. Provisions enacted in 1997 increase the effective exemption to $1 million in steps by 2006 ($625,000 in 1998, $650,000 in 1999, $675,000 in 2000 and 2001, $700,000 in 2002 and 2003, $850,000 in 2004, $950,000 in 2005, and $1 million in 2006). The second largest credit is that for state death taxes. This credit is limited to a maximum of 16 percent of the federal taxable estate. State gift taxes do not benefit from a similar credit. The estate tax also provides for a credit for previously paid death taxes in order to minimize double taxation. In computing the heir's estate tax, the credit is set equal to the parent's estate tax on bequeathed wealth phased out over 10 years from the parent's date of death. The credit is not available for the estates of heirs dying more than 10 years after the parent's date of death.

## Tax deferral

Estates with closely held businesses and farmers may defer a fraction of the estate tax. This fraction is equal to the share of such assets in the estate, provided that it is in excess of 35 percent. The tax is deferred for a period of 15 years from the date of death, with the principal payable over the last 10 years. Interest payments are deductible against the estate tax, which requires filing tax returns over the deferral period. The benefit of this deferral is also available to estates that are subject to severe liquidity constraints, at the discretion of the Internal Revenue Service Commissioner.

## Income distribution

The possible effect on income and wealth distribution is an important consideration when levying estate and gift taxes. These taxes are levied on wealth and typically apply to the top wealth holders of the population. The revenue obtained from the estate and gift taxes, when redistributed, could have the net effect of reducing the concentration of wealth in the hands of a few people. More importantly, if the tax were designed such that it stimulates *inter vivos* gifts and bequests to a wider number of recipients, then it could be thought of as a tool to discourage concentrations of wealth.

There are some instances in which the estate and gift tax could cause greater inequality. If the estate tax, for instance, were to reduce savings, it would lead to lower levels of capital and lower the real rate of return to labor. By lowering labor income, this reduction may exacerbate existing inequalities between those who receive income from capital and those who receive income from labor. Another possible scenario occurs when wealth is transferred by donors who are more well off than the recipients. If such transfers are reduced by the estate and gift tax, then the level of inequality increases under the tax.

## Behavioral effects

Estate taxes have incentive effects for both donors and heirs. Higher estate taxes may reduce the work effort and savings of parents motivated to leave large bequests to their children. This substitution effect is the result of the tax raising the price of bequests. An offsetting effect is the income effect, whereby parents may have to increase their work efforts and savings to cover the higher taxes. It is not clear which effect dominates, and there is no empirical evidence to guide us.

Estate taxes also affect the heirs' work effort and savings. Recent evidence suggests that large inheritances may speed up the retirement decision. Even for those who remain in the labor force, one may also observe a reduction in labor supply. However, labor supply effects are generally small. Similarly, consumption is also observed to rise in the aftermath of inheritance. But, again, these effects are small.

## Additional readings

Bernheim, B. Douglas. "Does the Estate Tax Raise Revenue?" In *Tax Policy and the Economy* 1, edited by Lawrence H. Summers. Cambridge, Mass.: The MIT Press, 1987.

Cooper, George. "A Voluntary Tax? New Perspectives on Sophisticated Estate Tax Avoidance." Washington, D.C.: The Brookings Institution, 1979.

Davies, James B., and Peter Kuhn. "Intergenerational Transfers and the Distribution of Income and Wealth." In *Modeling the Accumulation and Distribution of Wealth*, edited by Denis Kessler and Andre Masson. New York: Oxford University Press, 1988.

Holtz-Eakin, Douglas, David Joulfaian, and Harvey Rosen. "The Carnegie Conjecture: Some Empirical Evidence." *Quarterly Journal of Economics* (1993): 413–36.

Joulfaian, David, and Mark O. Wilhelm. "Inheritance and Labor Supply." *Journal of Human Resources* (1994): 1205–34.

Kotlikoff, Lawrence, and Lawrence Summers, "The Role of Intergenerational Transfers in Aggregate Capital Accumulation." *Journal of Political Economy* (1981): 706–32.

Pechman, Joseph A. *Federal Tax Policy—Fourth Edition*. Washington, D.C.: The Brookings Institution, 1987.

Stiglitz, Joseph E. "Notes on Estate Taxes, Redistribution, and the Concept of Balanced Growth Path Incidence." *Journal of Political Economy* 8 (1978): 5137–50.

*Cross references:* fairness in taxation; family, tax treatment of; wealth taxation.

# Excess burden

Harry Watson
George Washington University

*Excess burden, also called efficiency cost or dead weight loss, occurs when a tax interferes with a taxpayer's economic decisions and efficient choice but generates no additional benefit to the tax collection agency.*

It might appear that taxation is simply a transfer of resources from taxpayers to the government and that, apart from the costs of complying with or administering a tax, the only burden of taxation is the financial inconvenience felt by taxpayers. Unfortunately, the burden borne by taxpayers is seldom limited to their direct tax payments—that is, their direct burden. With almost all taxes there is an additional—excess—burden that is not related to any explicit tax liability. Unlike direct burden, which is determined by tax statutes, excess burden is determined by the way in which a tax code alters the decisions made by taxpayers, so that it lacks the transparency of direct burden. As will be shown, this lack of transparency in no way lessens the potential adverse effects of the excess burden.

Excess burden arises when taxpayers are induced to make substitutions in order to ameliorate the impact of a tax. As most taxes alter relative prices or rates of return, such substitutions are a reasonable response on the part of taxpayers. For example, the introduction of an excise tax may induce consumers to substitute some untaxed goods for the now more expensive taxed good, and the introduction of a payroll tax may induce firms to substitute capital for labor. These substitutions suggest that taxpayers are making choices that, in the absence of taxation, would be considered inferior. It is these inferior choices that are the source of excess burden.

The cost of these substitutions for consumers is easily illustrated by the outcome of levying an excise tax on gasoline that is so high that no one buys any gasoline. As no revenue is collected, it is clear that there is no direct tax burden, but this does not mean that consumers do not suffer; most consumers would find relying exclusively on alternative forms of transportation to be quite burdensome. This cost to consumers is the excess burden of the tax, and most consumers would find it to be substantial. If the excise tax were then lowered enough so that some consumers were willing to buy gasoline, the excess burden would be reduced but not eliminated. Even with a lower excise tax, the pattern of automobile usage would differ from that observed in a no-tax world, in that consumers will have given up some of the benefits of using an automobile. This loss in benefits, which arises because the cost of driving relative to the cost of other forms of transportation has risen, represents the excess burden that remains with a lower excise tax.

Substitution effects are also costly for producers, as can be seen in the introduction of an income tax that discriminates between two different types of capital. Because the income tax reduces the resources available to the firm, the amounts of both types of capital used by the firm will decline. In addition, the differential tax treatment of capital will induce the firm to substitute capital with the lower after-tax cost for capital with the higher after-tax cost, resulting in a mix of capital that would not be found in a no-tax world. The tax-induced distortion in the mix of capital lowers the firm's productivity, and output will fall relative to the level of output that would have been produced had the income tax reduced the resources available to the firm but not discriminated between different types of capital. In this case, the tax-induced loss in productivity represents excess burden.

As these illustrations suggest, substitution effects, and the excess burden they create, arise when taxation alters relative prices or rates of return. Therefore, to determine whether a tax creates excess burden, it is only necessary to ask whether the tax alters any ratio of prices or rates of return. Using this criterion, all tax systems that are in use, including personal and corporate income taxes, commodity taxes, and wealth taxes, produce excess burden.

If a tax is not to create any excess burden, it must be designed so that taxpayers will find that making substitutions yields no benefits. Because the range of substitution possibilities is so great, this is tantamount to requiring that the tax base be unaffected by any taxpayer decisions, a situation that is referred to as lump-sum taxation. Thus, a tax for which liability is only a function of age or gender would be a lump-sum tax. While lump-sum taxes are attractive because they minimize excess burden, they can be quite regressive because their very nature precludes any link between a taxpayer's economic circumstances and tax liability.

Some insights into the factors that determine the magnitude of excess burden can be gained by considering a simple ad valorem excise tax. An approximation for the excess burden of this tax is given by

$$\left[\frac{\tau^2}{2}\right]\left[\frac{\epsilon\eta}{\epsilon + \eta}\right][PQ]$$

where $\tau$ is the ad valorem excise tax rate; $P$ and $Q$ are the market price and output levels, respectively; $\epsilon$ is the elasticity of demand; and $\eta$ is the elasticity of supply. As excess burden depends on the square of the tax rate, it will increase more than proportionately as the tax rate increases. The above expression implies that a 1 percent increase in the tax rate will produce a 2 percent increase in excess burden, which suggests that even small increases in tax rates can produce significant increases in excess burden. Increases in either elasticity, which reflect a greater willingness of consumers or producers to make substitutions, will also exacerbate excess burden. Conversely, if consumers or producers do not respond at all to the price changes, so that either $\epsilon$ or $\eta$ is zero, excess burden will be zero.

To appreciate the magnitude of excess burden, it is useful to divide the measure above by an approximation of the revenue this excise tax would raise, $\tau PQ$. In this case, the ratio of excess burden to revenue raised (the direct burden) is approximately

$$\left[\frac{\tau}{2}\right]\left[\frac{\epsilon\eta}{\epsilon + \eta}\right]$$

It is easy to find circumstances in which this ratio can be surprisingly large. For example, if the product is produced by a constant cost-competitive industry, so that $\eta$ is very large, and if $\epsilon$ is 2, then this ratio is just $\tau$. Thus, for a tax rate of 25 percent, excess burden is 25 percent of the tax revenue collected. Put differently, for this excise tax, each dollar collected by the government costs the private sector an additional $.25, a substantial charge for simply transferring resources from one sector of the economy to another.

Although most taxes are considerably more complicated than excise taxes, it is possible to derive excess burden expressions for these taxes that are quite similar to that for excise taxation. Given the relatively simple nature of these expressions, it may appear that calculating the excess burden of any tax would be a straightforward exercise. In theory, this conclusion is correct; expressions that provide exact measures of excess burden (which are somewhat more complicated than the approximate expression presented earlier) have been available for a number of years. In practice, the determination of excess burden is problematic because elasticity values, such as $\epsilon$ and $\eta$ in the case of an excise tax, are not easily obtained.

To appreciate the difficulties in implementing measures of excess burden, it is useful to consider the case of income taxation. An income tax may affect many relative prices, such as the price of current consumption relative to future consumption (savings) and the price of leisure relative to the price of other forms of consumption. As in the case of excise taxation, the degree to which taxpayers respond to these relative price changes—as reflected in the elasticity of savings with respect to changes in after-tax interest rates and the elasticity of labor supply with respect to after-tax labor income—plays a critical role in determining the magnitude of the excess burden. Unfortunately, a paucity of adequate data, combined with methodological disagreements, has produced a wide range of estimates for these elasticity values. Because excess burden is increasing in both these elasticities, using estimated values of these elasticities that are close to zero implies that the excess burden of income taxation is insignificant, whereas using estimated elasticity values that are large suggests that the excess burden of income taxation is a serious problem.

### Additional readings

Auerbach, Alan. "The Theory of Excess Burden and Optimal Taxation." In *Handbook of Public Economics*, edited by Alan Auerbach and Martin Feldstein. New York: North Holland, 1985.

Hyman, David. *Public Finance*, ch. 11. Orlando, Fla.: Dryden Press, 1999.

Rosen, Harvey. *Public Finance*, 4th edition, ch. 14. Burr Ridge, Ill.: Irwin, 1995.

# Excess profits tax

John Hakken
Coopers & Lybrand

*A high-rate tax levied either on business profits that exceed a normal or fair rate of return on invested capital or on the sales price of a commodity in excess of its normal price.*

Seeking to control the private gains from certain extraordinary government interventions in the economy, Congress has levied two different and quite distinct types of tax on "excess" profits. It enacted an "income-tax" type of excess profits tax on businesses as a temporary measure to control wartime profits during World War I, World War II, and the Korean War. Decades later, in 1980, when oil prices that had been regulated in response to the Arab oil embargo were decontrolled, it enacted an "excise-tax" type of excess profits tax on domestic oil production to limit the profits that oil companies would reap from higher oil prices. Nine years later, after the production of ozone-depleting chemicals was restricted by the Montreal Protocol, the Senate adopted another "excise-tax" type of excess profits tax on the domestic production of these chemicals to limit the profits that chemical producers could reap by curtailing their production and raising their prices. Instead, however, Congress eventually enacted an ordinary excise tax on these chemicals.

## The income-tax type

Each of the excess profits taxes that Congress enacted during wartime had a slightly different tax base, but all of the tax bases shared the same basic formula. Under that formula, a normal or fair amount of profit was determined for a consolidated group of businesses, and this amount was subtracted from the actual profits of the consolidated group, after certain conforming adjustments to actual profits had been made. The "normal" or "fair" amount of profit was generally calculated from some combination of: (1) actual profit during the prewar period, (2) the amount of invested capital during the prewar period, and (3) the change in the amount of invested capital since the prewar period. Whenever a business could show that its calculated normal profit had been distorted by some extenuating circumstance, adjustments, alternative calculations, or other remedies were generally available.

Congress enacted two different excess profits taxes during World War I. The War Act of 1917 levied an excess profits tax on both corporations and noncorporate businesses at graduated rates, from 20 to 60 percent. The normal return of each business was based on its average return on invested capital during the prewar period of 1911 through 1913, but it was restricted to between 7 and 9 percent. The normal profit for the tax year was then calculated by multiplying the business's average amount of invested capital during the tax year by its normal return on invested capital. The War Act of 1918 increased the top rate of the first excess profits tax to 65 percent and levied a second excess profits tax—called a war profits tax—only on corporations, at graduated rates up to 80 percent. Corporations had to pay either the excess profits tax or the war profits tax, whichever was larger. The normal profit during the tax year under the war profits tax was generally calculated by taking the actual average annual profit during the prewar period and adding 10 percent of the change in invested capital since the prewar period. Under both taxes, invested capital was valued on a historical basis and consisted of (1) paid-in cash, (2) business assets contributed by owners, and (3) retained earnings.

In light of the subsequent development of the excess profits tax, certain features of the World War I taxes are particularly noteworthy. The excess profits tax enacted in 1917, for example, is notable for being the only excess profits tax levied on noncorporate businesses. Apparently, the commingling of noncorporate business assets and personal assets, along with the unlimited liability of noncorporate business owners, blurred the concept of invested capital enough to make its application to noncorporate businesses impractical. During World War II and the Korean War, Congress relied on steeply graduated income tax rates and income surtaxes to

limit the profits of noncorporate businesses. A second notable feature of both World War I taxes is the way tax relief was granted. Because the tax rates were so high and the measurement of excess profits was so ad hoc, the Tax Commissioner was given broad discretion to grant businesses relief from the excess profits taxes whenever they appeared to be unduly burdensome. However, because the discretion was so broad and the basis for it so vague, the commissioner was flooded with relief requests. Therefore, subsequent excess profits taxes codified many relief provisions, stipulating the conditions for relief and enumerating the terms of that relief. The third notable feature is the difference in the way normal profits were computed under the two taxes. The excess profits tax enacted in 1917 required a business to historically reconstruct the entire amount of capital invested in it, so that a normal or fair rate of return could be applied to that amount (valued on a historical basis). The tax enacted in 1918 only required a business to adjust its prewar income for subsequent changes in invested capital, making the accounting for prewar investments unnecessary. Because the accounting was so much easier, subsequent excess profits taxes always offered businesses the option of computing normal profits by adjusting prewar income.

Between the two world wars, economists and lawyers thoroughly examined the theoretical underpinnings of the excess profits tax. Distinctions were drawn between excess profits taxes that compared current profits to prior profits during a base period, and excess profits taxes that compared current profits to profits that offered a hypothetical fair return on investment. Distinctions were also drawn between excess profits taxes that determined the excess profits of each business as a special case based on its profit history, and excess profits taxes that determined excess profits by universal rules, so that businesses with the same amount of income and the same amount of invested capital owed the same amount of excess profits tax regardless of their profit history.

In 1940, Congress levied an excess profits tax on corporations with graduated tax rates from 25 to 50 percent. After the United States entered World War II, and as its involvement grew, the tax on excess profits was raised three times, until the statutory rate reached a flat 95 percent during 1944 and 1945. Under the excess profits tax during World War II, corporations could compute their normal profit in one of two ways. Under the invested-capital method, the normal profit of a corporation equaled 8 percent of the first $5 million of invested capital, plus 6 percent of the next $5 million of invested capital, plus 5 percent of the remaining invested capital. The World War I definition of invested capital was expanded to include additional intangible assets and 50 percent of borrowed capital. (To make current profit conform to this concept of normal profit, 50% of the interest deduction was added back to income.) Under the earned-income method, normal profit equaled 95 percent of a corporation's "average" income during the 1936–1939 base period, plus 8 percent of any net addition to equity capital since the base period, minus 6 percent of any net reduction in equity capital since the base period. Excess profits were determined by deducting computed normal profits from actual profits after adjustments. Normal profits that could not be deducted during the current tax year could be carried forward or backward for two years. In addition, 10 percent of a corporation's excess profits tax payments were creditable against corporate income tax liabilities after the war.

In terms of the development of the excess profits tax, the ways in which the World War II tax attempted to adjust the calculation of excess profits for differences in investment risk are noteworthy. First, because a larger capital base allowed a corporation to reduce risk through diversification of its investments, the invested-capital method lowered the normal return on larger amounts of corporate capital. Second, because debt increased the risk to equity, the invested-capital method allowed a corporation to treat part of its borrowed capital as invested capital. Assuming that the corporation could borrow at an interest rate below the normal profit allowed on invested capital, the inclusion of borrowed capital effectively raised the normal profit rate allowed on leveraged corporate equity. Third, because corporations that were engaged in riskier business activities typically earned a higher average rate of return on their investment, the earned-income method did not place a ceiling on the normal rate of return. Fourth, because a corporation might not have earned a normal return during the base period as a result of risk, corporations were sometimes allowed to construct an "average" base period income from the typical incomes of similar businesses.

The excess profits tax that Congress levied during the Korean War was similar in most respects to the one levied during World War II. The tax rate, however, was only 30 percent, and the amount of excess profits tax could not exceed a ceiling of 20 percent of corporate income. Smaller corporations had a lower ceiling.

## The excise-tax type

The Crude Oil Windfall Profits Tax of 1980 imposed an excise tax on the domestic production of oil. The tax base for each barrel of domestic oil production was determined on a property basis and generally equaled the difference between the wellhead price of oil and the base price (adjusted for inflation), multiplied by one minus the state severance tax rate. In no case, however, could the annual tax base for

a property exceed 90 percent of the property's annual net oil income. For most domestic oil production (defined as tier 1 oil), the base price equaled the highest controlled price for oil produced from the property during May 1979 (which averaged $13 per barrel) less $0.21. For "stripper oil" production from low-volume wells (defined as tier 2 oil), the base price equaled $15.20 per barrel. This base price was then adjusted for differences in the quality and production location of the oil. For the production of newly discovered oil, heavy oil, and incremental oil from chemical injectants (defined as tier 3 oil), the base price equaled $16.55 per barrel. It, too, was adjusted for quality and location. The tax rates initially varied from 70 percent on the production of tier 1 oil down to 30 percent on the production of tier 3 oil. Independent oil producers were eligible for reduced tax rates on up to 1,000 barrels per day of tier 1 and tier 2 oil production. Subsequent amendments gradually lowered the tax rate on newly discovered oil to 15 percent and eliminated the tax on stripper oil from independent producers. As enacted, the windfall profits tax was scheduled to be phased out over 33 months beginning in 1988, once $227.3 billion in net revenue had been collected, but no later than 1991. When oil prices plunged in 1986, revenues from the windfall profits tax evaporated, prompting Congress to repeal the tax in 1988.

Despite the immense compliance burden involved in calculating the net income separately for each oil-producing property, oil producers used the net income limitation extensively to cut their tax liability under the windfall profits tax. The net income limitation proved most effective in cutting the tax on tier 1 oil because, for many properties, the tier 1 base price was only slightly above the average cost of producing a barrel of oil. Interestingly, the net income limitation was more effective in cutting the tax owed by oil producers when the price of oil was high rather than low because each additional dollar in price, which normally added a dollar to the tax base, added only $.90 to the tax base when the net income limitation was applied.

The excise tax on the production of ozone-depleting chemicals that the Senate (but ultimately not the full Congress) adopted in 1989 was closely related in concept to the windfall profits tax on the production of crude oil. The chemicals production tax would have imposed what amounted to a 100 percent tax on the manufacturer's sales price in excess of a base price based on 1987 sales. Moreover, the base price would have been adjusted for increases in production costs caused by inflation. Unlike the windfall profits tax on oil, the chemicals tax also would have imposed a minimum tax of $.60 per pound on both the production and importation of ozone-depleting chemicals to encourage the use of less harmful alternatives.

## Effects on economic efficiency

In theory, a tax on pure economic profit does not reduce economic efficiency because it does not change the allocation of economic resources. In other words, if an excess profits tax could be levied on pure economic profit, it would not change economic behavior. Anecdotal evidence strongly suggests, however, that past excess profits taxes did affect economic behavior. For example, the excess profits tax during World War II apparently encouraged manufacturers to advertise heavily to promote brand recognition that would benefit them after the war. With an effective excess profits tax rate of 85.5 percent, the after-tax cost of a dollar of advertising was only 14.5 cents. Likewise, the windfall profits tax on oil apparently encouraged some oil producers to adopt chemical recovery methods prematurely in order to get oil reclassified from tier 1 to tier 3, thereby reducing the tax by more than $5 per barrel on some production. Given the strong incentives from the high tax rates, the loss of economic efficiency under past excess profits taxes might have been substantial. In enacting such taxes, Congress had to balance the possible substantial loss of economic efficiency against the need to limit the redistributional consequences of government policies designed to redirect economic resources by regulating or deregulating industries or by engaging in war.

## Additional readings

Buehler, Alfred G. "The Taxation of Corporate Excess Profits in Peace and War Times." *Law and Contemporary Problems* 7 (Spring 1940): 291–300.

Chung, Edward. "Crude Oil Windfall Profit Tax, 1985." *Statistics of Income Bulletin* 6 (Fall 1986): 85–94.

Congressional Budget Office. *The Windfall Profits Tax: A Comparative Analysis of Two Bills*. Washington, D.C.: U.S. Government Printing Office, November 1979.

Keith, E. Gorden, and E. Cary Brown. "The Impact and Burden of Wartime Corporation Taxes. *Law and Contemporary Problems* 10 (Winter 1943): 121–32.

Peterson, C. Rudolf. "The Statutory Evolution of the Excess Profits Tax." *Law and Contemporary Problems* 10 (Winter 1943): 3–27.

Prentice-Hall. *Federal Excess Profits Tax*. New York: Prentice-Hall, 1954.

Shoup, Carl. "The Concept of Excess Profits under the Revenue Acts of 1940–42." *Law and Contemporary Problems* 10 (Winter 1943): 28–42.

Shoup, Carl. "The Taxation of Excess Profits." Parts I, II, and III. *Political Science Quarterly* 55 (December 1940): 535–55; 56 (March 1941): 84–106; 56 (June 1941): 226–49.

*Cross references:* energy taxes; environmental taxes, federal; income tax, corporate, federal.

# Excise taxes

## J. Fred Giertz
University of Illinois

*Taxes levied on the manufacture, sale, or consumption of a single good or service or on a relatively narrow range of goods or services.*

Excise taxes are an example of what have been traditionally called indirect taxes: taxes that are imposed on a transaction rather than directly on a person or corporation. Excise taxes are narrow-based consumption taxes, as compared with broad-based taxes such as a general sales tax or an expenditure tax. Excise taxes can be collected at various stages, including the point of production, the wholesale level, or the retail level.

Excise taxes are levied on either a unit or ad valorem basis. For unit (also known as specific) excises, the tax is denominated in terms of money per physical unit produced or sold. Examples include the U.S. government taxes of 18.41 cents per gallon of gasoline, $13.50 per gallon of distilled spirits, and $12 per departure and arrival international passenger airline ticket. Ad valorem excises are based on a percentage of the value of the product or service sold. The 10 percent federal tax (declining to 7.5% by the year 2000) on the cost of domestic airline passenger tickets and the 3 percent tax on the cost of telephone services are examples of ad valorem taxes.

## Rationale for excises

The use of excise taxes is explained or justified by a variety of rationales. They are sometimes employed because of ease of administration. In the past (and continuing today in some less-developed countries), excise taxes were applied only to products produced in sectors of the economy with well-developed markets. Broader-based taxes, such as the income and general sales taxes, are difficult to administer when most of the economic activity takes place outside a structured market setting.

Excise taxes are sometimes used as a means of implementing an ability-to-pay approach to taxation. So-called luxury taxes are an example of this approach. The United States currently levies an excise tax on expensive passenger vehicles. This tax is set at 10 percent of the value in excess of a floor amount of $30,000. The tax on high-value automobiles has also been explained as a means of making foreign imports (which comprise a large percentage of such vehicles) more expensive than domestic automobiles. By taxing items consumed disproportionately by higher-income individuals, excise taxes can achieve an element of progressivity. There are questions, however, concerning horizontal equity because not all people at the same income level have similar expenditure patterns for luxury items.

Excises are also levied on goods or services that are considered harmful or undesirable, in an attempt to discourage consumption. Taxes based on this rationale are labeled sumptuary excises. Examples include taxes on alcoholic beverages, tobacco products, and wagering. Because many of the goods and services taxed by sumptuary excises have relatively inelastic demands, these taxes may have only a limited impact on curtailing consumption. This presents an added benefit, however, for the government in that it provides a relatively stable source of tax revenue. Sumptuary taxes are often popular politically because many citizens do not engage in the taxed activities, whereas purchasers of the taxed items do so voluntarily. Such taxes may have negative consequences from the standpoint of vertical equity because sumptuary excises are often highly regressive.

Excises may also be imposed as a technique for dealing with negative externalities. This is related in some ways to the sumptuary excises. Taxes on "gas-guzzling" automobiles and gasoline can be explained as a kind of Pigouvian (corrective) tax to reduce the divergence of the private and social costs relating to pollution or congestion. Such taxes are usually an imperfect technique for internalizing externalities, because an efficient Pigouvian tax should be related to the marginal damage caused by an activity, which is not necessarily proportional to the level of consumption.

Finally, excise taxes may be employed as a means of implementing a benefits-received approach to taxation. Gasoline taxes are an example. Gasoline usage is closely related to highway travel, thereby providing a link between taxes paid and benefits received from roadways. This link is further strengthened by earmarking where the revenues collected from an excise tax are designated for use in providing government services related to the activity. Examples include the earmarking of motor fuel taxes for highways and taxes on airline tickets for air traffic control and facilities expansion.

## Economic impacts

The economic impacts of excise taxes are usually investigated using a partial equilibrium approach because excises apply to only one product or, at most, a narrow range of goods or services. An analysis of the incidence of an excise tax in a competitive industry is usually divided between its impacts in the short run and the long run. In the short run, an excise tax increases the price of the product, albeit by less than the full amount of the tax, and the price burden is shared by both the producers and the consumers. The exact effect depends on the elasticities of demand and supply for the product. The increase in price resulting from the tax will be greater as the elasticity of supply increases and the elasticity of demand falls. The impact on quantity will be greater as both the elasticity of demand and the elasticity of supply increase.

In regard to the sharing of the price burden, the more inelastic the demand, the larger the share of the tax borne by consumers. The more inelastic the supply, the larger the share borne by producers. In the limiting cases, the full price burden will be borne by consumers if demand is completely inelastic, whereas the full price burden will fall on producers if supply is completely inelastic.

In the long run, the price will increase by more than it does in the short run because of the exit of firms from the industry caused by losses created by the tax. In constant cost industries, the price will increase by the full amount of the tax; in increasing cost industries, by less than the amount of the tax; and in decreasing cost industries, by more than the amount of the tax. A constant cost industry is one in which industry costs are unaffected by the exit or entry of firms. An increasing cost industry is one in which the costs of all firms in the industry increase with the entry of new firms. In a decreasing cost industry, the costs of all firms fall with the entry of new firms.

In general, nothing can be said about the progressivity or regressivity of excise taxes because the answer depends on the consumption pattern by income class of each product that is taxed. As noted above, some excise taxes are highly regressive, such as those on tobacco and alcohol, while others, such as those targeting luxuries, may be progressive.

In regard to the welfare effects of excise taxes, excess burdens or deadweight losses generally result from the selective taxation of a small number of products. Such taxes distort consumer choices by driving a wedge between marginal cost and price. The more elastic the demand for a product, the greater will be the excess burden of an excise because such a tax will have a relatively large impact on the quantity consumed. In addition, the excess burden of an excise tax directly increases with the square of the tax rate—doubling the tax rate quadruples the welfare loss. This result argues for the use of a broad-based tax on a wide range of commodities rather than a high tax rate on a small number of goods.

It also follows from this that optimality can be achieved with a general set of selective excise taxes (given the amount of revenue to be collected) by setting excise tax rates for various products inversely to their elasticity of demand. While such a plan may be efficient in the sense that it minimizes excess burdens, it may have negative equity (distributional) consequences by taxing goods with inelastic demands (such as necessities) very heavily.

From the standpoint of efficiency, a general tax on all consumption at a uniform rate will generally dominate a partial system of taxation using excises. Such a tax does not distort consumer choices at the margin as excise taxes do. However, the general tax on consumption needs to be truly broad-based, with all goods (including leisure) part of the tax base. Such a broad base is extremely difficult to achieve.

## Use of excise taxes

Historically, excise taxes have played an important role in the tax systems of most governments. They have declined in relative importance, however, in the last hundred years because of the increased reliance on broad-based taxes such as income, general sales, and value-added taxes. Today, less-developed countries rely somewhat more heavily on excises than more highly developed countries.

In the United States, excise taxes are used by all levels of government, with states relying most heavily on this source. At the federal level in 1991, various excises (not including customs duties) amounted to $42 billion, or 6.5 percent of federal tax revenues. At the state level, excises accounted for $50 billion in tax revenues in 1991, or 16.2 percent of state tax revenues. Local governments collected $10 billion, or 4.5 percent of own-source tax revenues, from excises.

Federal government excises include taxes on various fuels, tires for highway use, truck trailers, "gas-guzzling" automobiles, luxury items (high-valued automobiles), air transportation, telecommunications services, wagering, alcohol, tobacco, and firearms. States generally apply excise taxes to a narrower range of items including motor fuels, alcohol, tobacco, and wagering.

Some local governments, especially municipalities, tax a similar range of activities, although usually at a lower rate than the state.

*Cross references:* ability to pay; benefit principle; earmarking of taxes; elasticity, demand and supply; energy taxes; excess burden; fuel taxes, federal; incidence of taxes; luxury taxes; optimal taxation; progressivity, measures of; tobacco taxes.

# Expensing

## Joseph J. Cordes
George Washington University

*System allowing a taxpayer to deduct—expense—the costs of acquiring a depreciable capital asset immediately as these costs are incurred, instead of taking a stream of depreciation deductions over the useful life of the asset.*

The financial effects of allowing investment costs to be expensed are illustrated in table 1 below. In this example, the asset is assumed to have a purchase price of $8,000 and to provide a stream of economic returns of $3,800 in the first year, $3,000 in the second year, and $2,000 in the third year. At the end of the third year, the asset is assumed to have exhausted its useful economic life, providing no further return and having no scrap or salvage value. Using standard techniques for evaluating investments, it can be shown that an investment with this profile of before-tax cash flows has an internal rate of return of 5.5 percent.

If the tax rate is assumed to be 50 percent and the investment is expensed for tax purposes, the government receives the stream of tax payments shown in column 2, and the investor realizes the stream of after-tax cash flows shown in column 3. In the year in which the asset is acquired, its full cost is deducted in computing taxable income, reducing the investor's tax liability by $4,000. In effect, the government provides the investor with a tax rebate equal to the tax rate multiplied by the cost of the asset. In subsequent years, no further deductions are taken, and the full amounts of the cash flows produced by the asset are taxed.

Using the techniques for evaluating pretax cash flows to evaluate the after-tax cash flows, it is easily shown that with expensing, the asset has an after-tax return of 5.5 percent, the same as the before-tax return. In this case, the marginal effective tax rate on the investment is zero.

This occurs because expensing reduces the after-tax returns and costs by the same proportion, determined by the tax rate. If the tax rate is 50 percent, the result under expensing is financially equivalent to one in which the government becomes a 50 percent partner in the investment. Through the tax system, the government shares 50 percent of the initial costs of the investment by allowing a deduction to be taken immediately, and then shares in 50 percent of the investment's proceeds. In other words, through the tax system, the investor keeps

## TABLE 1

| | Pretax Cash Flows (1) | Tax Liability With Expensing (1) × 50% (2) | After-Tax Cash Flow (1) minus (2) (3) |
|---|---|---|---|
| Initial Outlay | ($8,000) | ($4,000) | ($4,000) |
| Year 1 | $3,800 | $1,900 | $1,900 |
| Year 2 | $3,000 | $1,500 | $1,500 |
| Year 3 | $2,000 | $1,000 | $1,000 |
| Internal Rate of Return | 5.5% | N.A. | 5.5% |

*Notes:* Tax rate is assumed to be 50 percent.
Numbers in parentheses denote negative cash flows (outlays).

only 50 percent of the investment's returns, but also bears only 50 percent of the costs. As a result, per dollar invested, the investor earns the same return from the investment after taxes as before taxes.

Because expensing has the effect of exempting the normal or competitive return on capital assets from taxation, the capital-cost-recovery method is appropriate if the objective is to tax consumption instead of income. Thus, recent proposals for replacing the income tax with a consumption-based flat tax all have allowed outlays for new capital to be expensed. Similarly, a consumption value-added tax would allow outlays for new capital to be deducted in computing taxable value added.

If, however, the objective is to tax income instead of consumption, the appropriate method of capital cost recovery is to require the taxpayer to spread out deductions for the cost of the asset, based on the rate at which the asset depreciates in value over its useful lifetime—its economic depreciation. Under an income tax, allowing expensing of assets thus becomes a form of tax preference or tax expenditure, because it allows the competitive investment return of assets to go untaxed. In this case, opportunities for tax arbitrage can arise if taxpayers are allowed to expense the cost of assets, while at the same time allowing the interest expense of debt incurred to acquire these assets to be deducted.

*Cross references:* capital cost recovery; consumption taxation; flat tax; marginal effective tax rate; tax arbitrage; tax expenditures; value-added tax, national; value-added tax, state.

# Export source rule

## David Brumbaugh
Congressional Research Service, Library of Congress

*The U.S. Treasury regulation that in some cases results in an export tax benefit by permitting half of a firm's income from inventory exports to be attributed to foreign rather than U.S. sources.*

The export source rule produces a tax benefit because of the U.S. foreign tax credit—the basic U.S. mechanism for alleviating double taxation of foreign-source income in cases of overlapping U.S. and foreign tax jurisdictions. Firms that have sufficient foreign tax credits generated by other foreign-source income can use export tax credits to shield foreign-source export income from U.S. taxes. The result is a tax subsidy for exports—potentially larger for a firm than the more explicit foreign sales corporation tax benefit for exporters.

Under the U.S. system, taxpayers can credit foreign taxes they pay against U.S. taxes on a dollar-for-dollar basis. However, the tax code limits the total amount of foreign taxes that can be credited in a particular year; moreover, foreign taxes can offset only those U.S. taxes that apply to a firm's foreign—rather than domestic—source income. Foreign taxes that exceed U.S. taxes on foreign income are not creditable in the year they are paid and become "excess credits."

It is the foreign tax credit's limitation and excess credits that help create the source rule's tax benefit. If a firm has excess credits from existing foreign-source income, any additional income that can be attributed to foreign sources (that is "sourced" abroad) is either partly or fully shielded from U.S. taxes; the excess credits can be used to offset the U.S. taxes on the foreign-attributed income. In the context of exporting, if an exporting firm has foreign operations that have produced excess foreign tax credits, any export income that can be attributed to foreign sources is shielded by the credits and, in effect, exempted from U.S. tax. If an exporter is also able to source the income so that little or no foreign taxes apply to it, the export income attributed to foreign sources may also face few foreign taxes.

The tax code and associated regulations apply different source rules to different broad categories of exports. The rule for exports of inventory that is both produced and sold by an exporter engenders the largest potential benefit; rules for other property—for example, personal property—do not confer the same potential benefit. The benefit works as follows: Regulations issued under Internal Revenue Code Section 863 permit income from the production and sale of inventory to be sourced under a "50/50 split" rule. Fifty percent of the income is sourced where the property that was used to produce or sell the inventory is located; the remaining 50 percent is sourced under the so-called "title passage" rule—that is, where the property's title changes hands. Because the location of title passage is quite flexible, a firm can attribute half of its export income abroad under the 50/50 split rule. The half allocated on the basis of property is generally allocated to the United States; the half allocated under the title passage rule can be allocated abroad. A firm with excess credits that both produces and sells its exports can therefore exempt 50 percent of its export income from taxes.

The regulations and associated rulings do not permit firms to use the 50/50 split rule if an "independent factory price" exists—that is, a price established when a firm regularly exports and sells its output to unrelated distributors. Where such a price exists, regulations require that it be used to split income into production and selling components, with the production portion allocated to domestic sources and the selling portion allocated abroad. Allocation using the independent factory price eliminates most of the tax exemption available under the 50/50 split method. (For a more detailed explanation of how the source rule works, see U.S. Treasury 1993.)

The export source regulations were originally issued by the Treasury Department in 1922; they were drafted in response to a congressional mandate in the Revenue Act of 1921, which directed the Secretary of the Treasury to prescribe rules for determining the source of income where property is produced in one location and sold in another. The rules were thus not promulgated as an explicit means of stimulating exports.

More recently, however, policymakers have become aware of the rule's impact. Before the Tax Reform Act of 1986, the 50/50 split could apply to personal property as well as inventory. However, following the principle that income should be sourced where the economic activity that generated it occurs, the 1986 act required that income from exports of personal property be sourced in the United States rather than abroad. At the same time, Congress permitted the 50/50 split and its consequent exemption to continue in the case of inventory, citing concern that repeal would "create difficulties for U.S. businesses competing abroad" (Joint Committee on Taxation 1987). And beginning in 1987, the congressional Joint Committee on Taxation began listing what it termed "the inventory property sales source rule exception" in its annual compilation of tax expenditures. The source rule for inventory has thus become a consciously provided tax benefit for export production.

But if the provision's concern with competing abroad means that its purpose is to reduce the trade deficit, economic analysis indicates that it does not accomplish its goal. While the rule likely does increase U.S. exports on the one hand, exchange rate adjustments ensure that it increases imports by a like amount; the tax benefit is thus powerless to alter the trade balance. Indeed, under the current system of flexible exchange rates, any autonomous change in exports will trigger adjustments that neutralize any impact on the trade balance. Underlying the exchange rate adjustments is the more basic reason for a subsidy's inability to alter the trade balance: a trade deficit reflects an economy's aggregate decision to use more in the current period than it produces and to finance the difference by importing capital. It follows that the trade balance can change only if capital flows change; a trade deficit can decline only if capital imports also fall. Indeed, even if exchange rates were not flexible, this relationship implies that some alternative adjustment mechanism—for example, prices—would ultimately ensure a neutral effect on the trade balance.

This is not to say that the export source rule does not increase exports—only that any increase in exports is matched by an increase in imports. The source rule's tax exemption for export income does pose an incentive for firms to increase their exports; it reduces the pretax rate of return required to make export investment attractive and thus increases export investment and export supply. The extent to which exports actually expand depends on elasticities—of supply and demand for U.S. exports and, given the accompanying exchange rate adjustments, of supply and demand for U.S. imports. Based on Internal Revenue Service Statistics of Income data showing the extent to which the source rule benefit is used and on empirical estimates of elasticities, Rousslang (1994) estimated that if the rule had not been in effect in 1990, U.S. exports would have been $518 million lower—less than 0.2 percent of total U.S. merchandise exports in 1990. Thus, the impact of the export source rule on exports is probably quite small. Rousslang also estimated that the provision resulted in a tax revenue loss of between $726 million and $816 million.

Like other export subsidies, the source rule reduces the economic welfare of the subsidizing country—in this case, of course, the United States. The welfare loss has two sources: reduced economic efficiency and worsened terms of trade. The efficiency loss occurs because the subsidy induces the United States to trade more than it would if it simply exploited its comparative advantage in various products. In both exporting and importing more than it would without the rule, the United States is forgoing production of some import-competing goods in favor of export goods that it makes less efficiently. The resulting welfare loss is a "deadweight" loss that is not matched by a welfare gain elsewhere—overtrading on the part of the United States is necessarily matched by an inefficient level of trade on the part of its trading partners.

The second welfare loss is a transfer of economic welfare from the United States to its trading partners. The source rule expands exports because part of its subsidy is passed on by U.S. producers to foreign consumers in the form of lower prices—a transfer from U.S. taxpayers to foreign consumers.

## Additional readings

Rousslang, Donald J. "The Sales Source Rules for U.S. Exports: How Much Do They Cost?" *Tax Notes International* 8 (February 21, 1994): 527–35.

U.S. Congress, Joint Committee on Taxation. *General Explanation of the Tax Reform Act of 1986*. Washington, D.C.: U.S. Government Printing Office, 1987.

U.S. Department of the Treasury. *Report to the Congress on the Sales Source Rules*. Washington, D.C., 1993.

*Cross reference:* multinational corporations, taxation.

# F

# Fairness in taxation

Richard A. Musgrave

Harvard University and University of California at Santa Cruz

*A fundamental requirement of a good tax system.*

Few would deny that the tax burden should be distributed in a fair and equitable fashion, but views differ on what that implies. As Adam Smith saw it, "the subjects of every state ought to contribute towards the support of government, as nearly as possible, in proportion to their respective abilities; that is, in proportion to the revenue which they respectively enjoy under the protection of the state" (Smith 1776, vol. 2: 310). With this statement, Smith combined two principles of equitable taxation, more commonly viewed as distinct rules: (1) that contributions should be in line with benefits received, and (2) that the burden should be distributed in line with ability to pay. The two approaches differ in rationale and in their vision of fair taxation.

## Taxation as payment for benefits received

The benefit principle holds that people should pay for the public services they receive, just as they must pay for their private purchases in the market. If these payments are fair, so will be benefit taxation.

### Setting tax prices

In short, the benefit view calls for taxes to be seen as prices paid for public services, similar to what the consumer pays for private goods purchased in the market. The principle is the same for both sectors, but differences arise in application.

Consumers who purchase in the market pay a uniform price per unit of the same product but are free to adjust the amount bought. In this way, they equate price with the marginal utility they derive from their last unit. Because they must bid for goods in order to obtain them, they thereby provide signals to suppliers to furnish the desired amount. In this way, a competitive market secures an efficient assignment of resources, in line with what consumers prefer.

In the case of public goods, such as defense or weather forecasts, individual consumers are not free to vary their purchases. The same level of service is made available to all. But the marginal benefits derived by individual consumers will differ. In order to equate marginal benefit and price, their appropriate tax prices should differ accordingly. Moreover, as public goods are paid for by taxation and become available free of direct charge, consumers need not reveal their preferences by bidding in the market. Government, therefore, has no easy way to assess the correct tax price. A political process of budget voting is needed, to decide what services are to be provided and what tax prices are to be charged. If this democratic process is functioning well, its outcome will approximate a provision of public services that efficiently meets consumer demand. Its tax prices will also yield a burden distribution that is fair—that is, similar to that which would obtain had it been possible to charge market prices.

In short, benefit taxation fits into a natural order where, as suggested by John Locke (1689: 328) and Adam Smith (1776, vol. 1: 123), the invisible hand of the market—simulated in the provision for public goods by a political process—yields a result that is both efficient and just. But that claim of fairness requires the further premise that the distribution of income, out of which market purchases are made and benefit taxes are paid, must also be just (Wicksell 1896: 108). That condition is met in a view of distributive justice, such as that held by Adam Smith, that grants entitlement to earnings. Fair taxation in this setting means benefit taxation. Taxation has no redistributive role.

### Burden distribution

Such distributionally neutral taxation, however, does not call for a head tax, where each pays the same amount. High-income individuals under the benefit rule may be expected to place higher marginal values on a given provision of public goods, so that benefit taxes will rise with income. Whether they should rise at a slower, proportional, or faster rate depends on consumer demand. More specifically, the appropriate pattern will depend on what economists call the income and price elasticities of demand (Buchanan 1961: 227). Thus determined, the fair relation of tax to income will reflect consumer evaluations based on market-determined earnings, not (as in the ability-to-pay context) on what society considers to be a fair distribution of income. Herein benefit taxation basically differs from the ability-to-pay school of thought.

## Taxation in line with ability to pay

As distinct from the benefit rule, the ability-to-pay principle focuses on the tax side of the picture only. The taxpayer incurs a loss, and taxation should spread that loss in a fair and equitable fashion. This calls for taxpayers to contribute in line with their ability to pay.

### Choice of index

In order to implement ability-to-pay taxation, an index is needed by which to measure "ability." That index has traditionally been thought of in terms of income, with income seen to provide the best measure of economic capacity. It follows that those with equal income should pay the same, while those with higher incomes should pay more. The former, referred to as horizontal equity, follows readily from the rule that equals should be treated equally. But the latter, referred to as vertical equity, has remained controversial because it requires a determination of how much more higher-income taxpayers should pay.

### Equal sacrifice rules

As John Stuart Mill (1849: 155) put it, "equality ought to be the rule in taxation as it ought to be in all affairs of government. Whatever sacrifice it requires should be made to bear as nearly as possible with the same pressure upon all." Taxation in line with ability to pay thus became taxation so as to equate the sacrifice incurred.

Based on the premise that the utility of the last dollar of income falls as income rises, high-income person A should pay more so as to incur a sacrifice equal to that of low-income person B. The rule of "equal sacrifice" was subsequently given various interpretations, calling for equal absolute, equal proportional, or equal marginal sacrifice. These rules all let the amount of tax rise with income, more so the more rapidly marginal utility falls as income rises. Whereas the tax-to-income relationship under benefit taxation depended on consumer demand for public goods, it now hinges on the rate at which the marginal utility of income declines as income rises. With equal absolute sacrifice, taxation will be regressive, proportional, or progressive, depending on whether the elasticity of the marginal utility-of-income schedule falls short of, equals, or exceeds unity. Under the equal marginal rule, taxation is most progressive, with taxes collected by equalizing incomes from the top down until the necessary revenue is obtained.

### Least total sacrifice

There is no conclusive reason, as a matter of fairness, for preferring one over the other of these rules.

But economists, following Edgeworth (1897: 119), opted for the principle of equal marginal sacrifice, with Pigou (1928: 59) enshrining it as the "ultimate principle of taxation." By equating the marginal sacrifices incurred across taxpayers, the resulting burden distribution also serves to minimize aggregate sacrifice and thereby meets the economist's goal of maximizing society's aggregate welfare. In the process, the quest for fairness in taxation was thus joined with the utilitarian goal of maximizing aggregate welfare.

The premise of entitlement to earnings underlying the fairness view of benefit taxation no longer holds in this setting. With marginal income utility declining, equal marginal sacrifice calls for a high degree of progression. Indeed, as already concluded by Bentham (1802: 305), the logic of welfare maximization calls for income equalization—that is, for taxation to be extended beyond what is needed for the finance of public services and into a tax-transfer scheme to equalize incomes.

This case for highly progressive taxation was then qualified in two respects. First, as already stressed by Bentham, detrimental effects of taxation must be allowed for. Security of expectations and of property, as he argued, are given priority and are essential to accumulation. The reasoning from declining marginal utility of income to income equalization thus follows only on the unrealistic assumption that total income is fixed and remains unaffected by taxation. As economists now put it, taxation imposes a "deadweight loss" that must be taken into consideration. As taxes are imposed, the taxpayer will respond by engaging less in the taxed activity. This interferes with efficient resource use and imposes an additional burden, a deadweight loss that the taxpayer suffers but that does not add to Treasury revenues. That loss adds to the taxpayer's sacrifice and thus must be allowed for (see Optimal taxation entry). Because the deadweight loss rises rapidly with the marginal tax rate, the case for income equalization and progressive taxation has to be qualified considerably. A similar argument, focusing on the level of output, points to the "supply-side effects" of high marginal rates.

A further qualification was to discard a central assumption underlying the earlier utilitarian case for highly progressive taxation—that is, the premise of an observable and declining marginal utility-of-income function, similar for and comparable across all taxpayers. That concept was discarded some 50 years ago as unrealistic and replaced by the concept of a social welfare function. Based on the subjective view of individual members of society on how successive units of income should be valued, that function is to be arrived at via a democratic process. It thus expresses a consensus on how society views distributive justice and with it the fair distribution of the tax burden.

## *Impartiality*

The goal of least total sacrifice, as noted earlier, was embraced as matching the utilitarian goal of maximizing aggregate welfare. But why should welfare maximization be the fair and equitable goal? Bentham, the guru of utilitarianism (Bentham 1789: 3), laid down as his central proposition that individuals will seek to pursue their own happiness. From this he proceeded to the conclusion that therefore the interest of the community will be the sum of the interests of its members, so that government should seek to maximize that aggregate interest. But why should A, with superior endowment, agree, in pursuit of his or her own happiness, to a policy that requires him or her to pay higher taxes or make transfers to less-favored B, as would be needed to maximize aggregate welfare?

The goal of maximizing aggregate welfare, it appears, does not follow as a matter of self-interest. Its acceptance requires an ethical underpinning. Whereas in the context of benefit taxation that foundation was provided by entitlement to earnings, the underlying tenet now calls on individual members of society to view distributive justice from an impartial perspective. They should view the desirable state of distribution from behind a veil, without knowing what their own position therein will be (Rawls 1972: 136). They should value the interest of others as their own.

Judging from that position, individuals may favor a more or less equal distribution (and hence more or less progressivity in taxation), depending on their dislike of inequality. Or, as economists like to put it, their choice will depend on their willingness to gamble on doing better with inequality, as against playing it safe with a more equal distribution. Thus seen, self-interest again enters the picture, but only after the premise of impartiality has been accepted. A political process, as noted above, then serves to translate these individual preferences into a social welfare function; and, based on its weights, the tax burden is to be distributed so as to minimize the aggregate burden.

## Corrective taxation

So far, we have discussed general rules of fair taxation, such as the benefit and ability-to-pay principles. It remains to note that a fairness case may also be made for certain types of selective taxation that serve to correct unfair situations.

Even where entitlement to earnings is taken as the general rule, not all earnings may be seen to constitute deserved rewards. Thus, Henry George urged taxation of land rent, reflecting the Lockean stricture that such earnings are undeserved because natural resources are held in common, and no effort is involved in reaping the rent from them. Ever since

Aristotle and Thomas Aquinas called for taxation of usury interest, monopoly or excess profits have been viewed as undeserved, and hence appropriate sources of taxation. The fairness case here may be traced to the premise of a natural order in which only competitive earnings are seen as deserved. Indeed, that premise is needed if the invisible hand of the market is to be both efficient and just.

Of more recent concern, a fairness case may also be made for the taxation of activities such as smoking, activities that generate external costs and thereby burden others. Not only may most of these forms of selective taxation claim merit on grounds of fairness, they also are supported by the economist's quest for efficient taxation.

## Conclusion

As noted at the outset, the benefit and ability-to-pay rules offer differing views of fair and equitable taxation, reflecting their respective premises of distributive justice. Benefit taxation is fair in the context of an order that recognizes entitlement to earnings. People with higher incomes should pay more because they attach a higher monetary value to the public service. The ability-to-pay approach calls for a pattern of taxation that minimizes the aggregate loss and thus serves the goal of welfare maximization. People with higher incomes should pay more to meet that goal. Entitlement to earnings is disregarded, with the claim to fairness derived from an impartiality-based view of distributive justice. The expenditure side of the budget is not taken into account.

Although the two principles differ, they may also be combined. A person may accept entitlement to earnings as the general rule but accept distributional corrections for extreme inequality, especially at the lower end of the scale. This may well be the typical position, as suggested by actual patterns of effective rates of tax, with low or even negative rates at the bottom, followed by sharply rising rates toward the middle, and flattening out in the higher ranges.

But even where fairness is seen purely in ability-to-pay rather than benefit terms, there still remains the task of securing an efficient provision of public goods. Here, the efficiency role of benefit taxation—providing for linkage between tax and expenditure choices—is pivotal. A reconciliation between the two concerns is thus needed. In principle, although not readily matched in practice, this would be met by a two-part system, combining (1) a "distribution branch" of the budget, offering a tax transfer scheme so as to establish what is considered a fair state of distribution, with (2) a benefit tax-financed "allocation branch," which provides for an efficient level of public goods.

This entry deals with principles and norms of fair taxation; it is not a critique of tax practice. This requires no apology because norms have their impact, even in the "real world" of tax legislation. Their importance should not be underestimated, but they are only part of the picture. Tax politics and pressure groups also enter into it, and what appears on the books reflects the tension between these two sides of the picture.

## Additional readings

Bentham, Jeremy. *An Introduction to the Principles of Morals and Legislation*. Original 1789 work edited by L. Lafleur. New York: Hafner Press, 1948.

Bentham, Jeremy. "Principles of the Civil Code." In *The Works of Jeremy Bentham*. Vol. 1. Original 1802 work edited by J. Bowring. New York: Russell, 1962.

Edgeworth, F.Y. "The Pure Theory of Taxation." *Economic Journal 7*. Original 1897 work reproduced in *Classics in the Theory of Public Finance*, edited by R.A. Musgrave and A. Peacock. London: Macmillan, 1958.

Locke, John. *Two Treatises of Government*. Original 1689 work edited by P. Laslett. London: Cambridge University Press, 1960.

Mill, John Stuart. *Principles of Political Economy*. Books 4 and 5 (London: Longman's, 1921). Original 1848 work edited by D. Winch. London: Penguin Books.

Musgrave, Richard A. *The Theory of Public Finance*. New York: McGraw-Hill, 1959.

Musgrave, Richard A., and Peggy B. Musgrave. *Public Finance in Theory and Practice*. 5th ed. New York: McGraw-Hill, 1989.

Pigou, A.C. *A Study in Public Finance*. London: Macmillan, 1928.

Rawls, John. *A Theory of Justice*. Cambridge, Mass.: Harvard University Press, 1972.

Smith. Adam. *The Wealth of Nations*. Vols. 1 and 2. Original 1776 work edited by E. Cannan. New York: Putnam's, 1904.

Wicksell, Knut. "A New Principle of Just Taxation." Original 1896 work in *Finanztheoretische Untersuchungen*. Jena: Fischer. Reproduced in Richard A. Musgrave and Alan Peacock, 1958.

*Cross references:* ability to pay; benefit principle; environmental taxes, federal; environmental taxes, state; income tax, federal; tax equity analysis.

# Family, tax treatment of

Louis Kaplow

Harvard Law School and National Bureau of Economic Research

*One's income tax status is determined in part by one's family status (marital status and number of dependents).*

## Income tax treatment of married couples

Tax systems must allocate burdens among single individuals, married couples, and families with varying numbers of dependents. The U.S. federal income tax originally treated each taxpayer separately, as do many developed countries today, but it now treats married couples as a unit. This means, for example, that couples in which each spouse earns $25,000 pay the same tax as couples in which one spouse earns $50,000 and the other earns $0. With individual treatment, the latter couple would have a relatively higher tax burden because of the tax system's graduated rates: an individual with $50,000 of income pays more than twice the tax of a single individual with $25,000.

Aggregation of spouses' incomes is supported by those who believe that spouses typically share resources. In addition, enforcing separate taxation would be difficult. Couples could manipulate which spouse receives unearned income and incurs deductible expenses. Indeed, under the individual taxation regime, spouses in community property states were each taxed on half of earned income, and some states adopted community property laws, apparently so that their residents could receive this benefit.

But aggregation is blamed for discouraging the work effort of second earners (typically wives) whose labor supply is particularly responsive to effective wage rates and thus to taxes. Under individual taxation, a second earner would be taxed at a lower rate on initial earnings. The primary reason the income tax discourages second earners, however, is its failure to tax the imputed income of spouses who work in the home: if one earns $10,000 in the market, this will not be enough after taxes to pay $10,000 to hire someone to perform domestic work that one no longer has time to do. The child care credit is a partial remedy for some families, and a modest two-earner deduction previously existed. Larger earned income allowances and taxing the second (lower-earnings) worker's income at lower rates have been proposed.

In addition, the extent of actual sharing within the family has been questioned. If spouses largely retain control over their own earnings, it is argued that they should be taxed separately on those earnings. Unequal sharing, however, does not obviously favor a policy of heavier taxation of couples with unequal incomes. Part of any increased tax burden may be borne by the relatively poor spouse, whose poverty is greater the less equal the sharing.

Another feature of the current system is that it uses a separate rate schedule for married couples, which taxes them at higher rates than single individuals. That is, a married couple with $50,000 of income pays more than twice the tax of a single individual with $25,000 of income. Thus, prospective spouses with equal earnings face a marriage penalty. Despite this penalty, however, prospective spouses face a net subsidy if their earnings are sufficiently unequal. A single individual with income of $50,000 and another with income of $0 would pay less income tax if they married: the tax savings from income splitting (being taxed as if each spouse earned $25,000) exceeds the tax cost because of higher rates for married couples.

The primary rationale for applying a higher rate schedule to married couples is that economies of scale in living arrangements increase their ability to pay. Although scale economies increase well-being, they also imply that married couples benefit more per dollar of disposable income. This factor favors lighter taxation if higher taxes on those with higher incomes are justified on the grounds that marginal dollars are less valuable to the wealthy. Thus, it is ambiguous whether economies of scale favor higher or lower tax burdens on married couples. Also, many doubt that single individuals are unable to realize scale economies, by finding roommates if they wish. (Relatedly, the similarity between the economic situation of cohabiting adults and married couples is offered as an argument for taxing the latter as single individuals.)

## Income tax treatment of dependents

In addition to the different rates applied to married couples and single individuals, the income tax reflects family size by allowing an exemption, $2,650 in 1997, for each member, and a credit of $500 for each child under 17. These per-person allowances do not fall as family size increases, which would be analogous to the typical treatment in welfare programs. And the size of these allowances does not increase with income; rather, allowances are phased out at high income levels.

If the family really is the unit of taxation, it may seem more natural to treat dependents like spouses. For example, if a spouse reduces effective income by almost half, perhaps adding children should produce a similar result. France takes such an approach, while giving less weight to children than adults. The U.S. income tax makes a partial allowance of this sort by subjecting single individuals to a lower rate schedule if they have dependents.

Such an extension of the taxable unit from married couples to the entire family would significantly increase the tax benefits from having dependents for middle- and upper-income couples. The distributive rationale for this result is that, when children are present, adults need substantially more income before they reach any given living standard—say, before they are able to afford a summer home. In contrast, the constant exemption reflects a view of children as fixed costs, affecting parents' ability to pay no differently from leasing a sports car, which would have the same annual cost regardless of the purchaser's income.

More generous treatment of married couples and dependents is sometimes viewed as undesirable because it would favor the rich: A given exemption is worth more to those in higher tax brackets, and an increasing exemption would benefit them to an even greater extent. But determining proper taxation of married couples and families with dependents is distinct, in important respects, from deciding upon the degree of progressivity. After all, coherent redistribution is impossible unless one first decides to and from whom one is redistributing income and which units are properly characterized as rich and poor.

Most analysis of the proper treatment of families emphasizes the redistributive role of the income tax. If, instead, tax burdens depended in part on benefits received from the government, rather different principles would apply. For example, the receipt of many tax-funded benefits, like public education, increases with family size, suggesting that heavier burdens be placed on larger families—or at least reducing the force of arguments favoring more generous treatment.

## Social security and other transfer programs

Tax treatment of the family depends on more than the federal income tax, or the states' income taxes, which are much smaller in magnitude and usually treat families similarly. Social Security taxes, as well as Social Security benefit formulas and welfare programs, significantly affect the disposable income of different types of families. For all taxpayers but the rich, Social Security taxes are a sizable fraction of their tax burden, and these taxes do not adjust for family size in the same way as income taxes; nor do benefit rules respond in the same manner. To illustrate, a second earner entering the labor force bears the full effective burden of Social Security taxes but initially receives no increase in future retirement benefits. Similarly, the effect of the income tax on the poor cannot be determined without accounting for Social Security taxes and benefits and other transfer programs, including the earned income tax credit (EITC), which is formally part of the income tax. The marriage penalty from the EITC, for example, can be thousands of after-tax dollars for some lower-income couples. Also, it is more familiar to identify welfare payments than income tax exemptions as having a positive effect on fertility, although exemptions play a role and would have a more significant effect under some proposed alternatives.

## Gifts and bequests

Taxation of the family also concerns gifts and bequests. Indeed, a large portion of all giving, other than to public charities, is to family members, so tax issues concerning gifts have an important effect on the treatment of families. The income tax excludes gifts and bequests from donees' income and does not permit donors any deduction. (By contrast, spouses are implicitly each taxed on half of combined income; this is equivalent to assuming that resources are shared, giving a gift deduction to the higher-income spouse, and taxing the gift to the lower-income spouse.)

A comprehensive view of income might include gifts in donees' income, as they clearly increase ability to pay. Donors would still be denied a deduction on the theory that they have benefited by giving the gift at least as much as by direct consumption. (Also, as a quid pro quo may be present, some so-called gifts are really payments for services.)

A view that the tax system should maximize social welfare might be more favorable to gifts. Gifts do increase ability to pay, which is relevant for redistributive purposes. But gifts also have the desirable feature of the same economic resources providing a double benefit, to both donor and donee. Thus, economic welfare may be enhanced by subsidizing gifts.

The current system does not fully embrace either view. Existing income tax treatment of gifts is commonly rationalized on the grounds that taxing or subsidizing them would be difficult, particularly for myriad small gifts within the family. However, there is a gift and estate tax, separate from the income tax, levied on large gifts by the wealthy.

Gifts of property are also important in an income tax system because they result in future income from the property being taxed to the donee, often a child in a low tax bracket, rather than to the donor, who may be in the highest bracket. Rules concerning trusts and other assignments of income reduce this practice, but outright transfers of property, as well as some less-complete transfers, have long been permitted to shift the tax burden on future income to the donee. (Also, unrealized appreciation on property transferred as a gift is taxed to the donee; if given as a bequest, unrealized appreciation is never taxed.) Under the Tax Reform Act of 1986, however, unearned income of children under 14 is taxed to their parents, which eliminates much of the tax benefit from such transfers. This provision can be seen as embodying a view that—at least with respect to transfers of property—the entire (immediate) family is the unit of taxation, rather than just the married couple.

## Future research

Many rules affect the tax treatment of families, and no consensus exists about their proper form. Further illumination of these issues should be gained from analysis that unavoidably will become ever more complicated. Simple, intuitive appeals will be increasingly qualified or displaced by arguments that (1) give greater attention to the economics of the family, such as by analyzing decisions to marry, have children, and allocate resources among members (Becker 1991); (2) appeal directly to principles of distributive justice and economic welfare, as in the vast literature on optimal income taxation, rather than relying primarily on abstract ability-to-pay norms (Kaplow 1996); (3) integrate the effects of all major tax and transfer programs (Boskin and Puffert 1987); (4) adopt a lifetime perspective, often used in studies of tax incidence, because individuals spend parts of their lives in different family units; and (5) more closely examine other countries' tax systems, which vary greatly from that in the United States in their treatment of the family (Pechman and Engelhardt 1990).

## Additional readings

Becker, Gary S. *A Treatise on the Family*. Cambridge, Mass.: Harvard University Press, 1991.

Boskin, Michael J., and Douglas J. Puffert. "Social Security and the American Family." In *Tax Policy and the Economy*, vol. 1, edited by Lawrence H. Summers. Cambridge, Mass.: MIT Press, 1987.

Kaplow, Louis. "Optimal Distribution and the Family." *Scandinavian Journal of Economics* 98 (March 1996): 75–92.

Pechman, Joseph A., and Gary V. Engelhardt. "The Income Tax Treatment of the Family: An International Perspective." *National Tax Journal* 43 (March 1990): 1–22.

*Cross references:* ability to pay; child care expenses: the child care credit; earned income credit; estate and gift tax, federal; fairness in taxation; labor supply, taxes and; marriage penalty; optimal taxation; progressivity, measures of; Social Security benefits, federal taxation.

# Finance Committee, U.S. Senate

J.D. Foster, Ph.D.
Tax Foundation

*One of the three key fiscal committees of the U.S. Congress (along with the House Committee on Ways and Means and the Joint Committee on Taxation).*

The Senate Finance Committee may be the most powerful committee in the United States Senate because of the enormous range of vital issues over which it has jurisdiction. The committee has sole Senate committee jurisdiction over tax legislation, but its jurisdiction also includes the Social Security, Medicare, and Medicaid programs, and it is responsible for all legislation dealing with the national debt.

While the committee's most important work is the reporting of legislation to the full Senate, every year it also holds scores of hearings on issues falling within its jurisdiction. The purpose of those hearings is threefold: to establish a public record for legislative action; to allow citizens and interested parties to express their opinions and ideas directly to the committee; and to educate the members and committee staff. The committee also holds hearings on important executive branch nominees, including those for secretary of the Treasury, administrator of the Social Security Administration, and administrator of the Health Care Financing Administration.

As with all congressional committees, Senate Finance has a chairman drawn from the majority party and a ranking member drawn from the minority party. In general, the chairman and the ranking member are the most senior members (those who have served the longest on the committee) from their respective parties. The exception occurs when the senior member prefers to chair another committee of the Senate or when the senior member is part of his or her party's Senate leadership.

The committee chairman has tremendous power. The chairman chooses when the committee will hold hearings and the subject of those hearings. The chairman also determines whether and when legislation is to be considered. Thus, a chairman can move legislation swiftly, with the necessary members' support, or, acting alone, he or she can bury legislation indefinitely. Members can sidestep the committee by bringing legislation directly to the Senate floor and offering it as an amendment to other legislation. However, the prospects for success are always in doubt because of the lack of committee support and because of various floor rules, including germaneness requirements, that limit whether the amendment is in order for debate.

Members are appointed to the committee by their party caucuses according to each party's rules. The committee currently has 20 members; the ratio of majority to minority members tends to follow the ratio within the Senate as a whole. Typically, whenever the minority party has 45 or more members, the ratio in the committee is 12 to 8.

The committee maintains a relatively small staff, which is bifurcated into majority and minority staffs. The sizes of the staffs are limited by the available budget, which is divided 2 to 1 between the majority and minority staffs. Each staff has a director and a complement of tax, Social Security, and health care experts.

The committee has six subcommittees, covering Taxation and Internal Revenue Service Oversight; International Trade; Long-Term Growth, Debt, and Deficit Reduction; Social Security and Family Policy; Medicare, Long-Term Care, and Health Insurance; and Medicaid and Health Care for Low-Income Families. Each subcommittee has its own chairman and ranking member. These subcommittees hold hearings and initiate and report legislation to be considered by the committee as a whole. The primary purpose of the subcommittees is to allow members to develop expertise in legislative areas of particular interest to themselves and their constituents.

Frequently, the Senate majority and minority leaders have also been Finance Committee members, ensuring a close working relationship between Senate and committee leadership.

*Cross references:* Joint Committee on Taxation, U.S. Congress; Office of Tax Policy; Ways and Means Committee.

# Fiscal disparities

Helen F. Ladd
Duke University

*Differences across subnational governments in their abilities to meet the public expenditure need of their residents.*

Fiscal disparities refer to the variation across subnational jurisdictions in their ability to raise revenue to meet the public expenditure need of their residents. Fiscal disparities are a natural outcome of a federal system of government—that is, one in which certain fiscal responsibilities are assigned to the central or national level and others to lower levels of governments. In a unitary system of government, fiscal disparities would not arise.

In a federal system, fiscal disparities arise because the capacity to raise revenue to finance publicly provided services relative to the amount needed to provide a standard package of public services varies across jurisdictions. For example, a city with a large proportion of low-income residents will be disadvantaged relative to a city of wealthier residents, both because the residents' low income makes it difficult for the city to raise revenue for public services and because the concentration of poor people may require the jurisdiction to spend more per capita than other jurisdictions to provide a standard package of public services. The term *fiscal disparities* refers to these differences across subnational governmental units at any specific level of government. Thus, in the U.S. context, one can talk about the fiscal disparities across states at any point in time or among school districts, cities, or any other category of local government within a state or metropolitan area.

When fiscal disparities exist, one jurisdiction can provide a higher level of services at a given burden on its residents than another jurisdiction—or can provide a given level of services at a lower tax burden on its residents. Some observers view such disparities as an unfair consequence of a federal system of government—and one that higher levels of government should try to minimize through various forms of intergovernmental assistance. In addition, when there are fiscal disparities, some people may make inefficient decisions about where to live or work in their attempt to benefit from the fiscal advantages of the wealthier jurisdictions. Other observers discount the equity criticism on the grounds that if such disparities truly imposed burdens on the people living in the fiscally disadvantaged communities, those people would simply relocate to other jurisdictions with more favorable fiscal positions. Moreover, any attempt to offset the disparities could lead to inefficient levels of public services as taxpayer voters no longer faced the fiscal discipline of paying fully for all the services they chose to provide (see Fiscal equalization).

To determine the magnitude of fiscal disparities, one needs first to measure not only each jurisdiction's capacity to raise revenue but also the expenditure burdens placed on it. Failure to look at the spending side along with the revenue side could well give a misleading picture of a specific jurisdiction's fiscal condition and, consequently, of the disparities across jurisdictions. For example, based on the capacity side alone, a large city with an above-average capacity to raise revenue relative to the size of its population would appear to be in strong fiscal condition. However, once the large expenditure burdens placed on the city by its economically disadvantaged resident population and the large influx of daily commuters or shoppers are considered, the city's fiscal condition may not look so favorable.

Second, the measure of local fiscal condition should reflect the effects of factors that are outside the immediate control of local officials. In particular, one should not use actual revenues, tax rates, or spending levels as measures of expenditure need. This consideration is particularly important if the magnitude of a local government's adverse fiscal condition signals the need for more assistance from a higher level of government. Ideally, one would not want the local government to be able to manipulate the size of its claim on that assistance as it would be able to do if fiscal condition were measured using factors, such as tax levels or spending, over which local officials have some control.

Third, measuring fiscal condition, especially that of local governments, is complicated by the observation that expenditure responsibilities often differ among jurisdictions of the same type. This problem is particularly severe if one is comparing fiscal condition across large cities in different states. However, it can also arise within a state as, for example, when some cities have responsibility for kindergarten through 12th grade (K–12) education and others do not, or when some cities, such as San Francisco, have responsibility for county services as well as standard municipal services while others, such as Los Angeles, have responsibility for municipal services alone.

In addition to the use of simple measures such as per capita income, the literature focuses on two major approaches to measuring the revenue-raising component of fiscal condition. The first is the representative tax (or revenue) system as developed initially for states by the U.S. Advisory Commission on Intergovernmental Relations (ACIR). According to this approach, a jurisdiction's per capita capacity to raise taxes (or revenue, if capacity includes nontax revenue such as user charges and fees) is measured as the weighted average of its potential per capita tax bases where the weights are the average tax rates for each tax (for the whole country if the comparison is across states; within the state if the comparison is for local governments within a state). This approach answers the question of how much revenue a jurisdiction would raise if it were to tax all its potential tax bases at the average tax rate; however, it takes no account of the behavioral effects of tax rates on tax bases or of the implied burden on local residents. Its strengths are the ease with which it can be described and its links to tax bases and to how noneconomists think about capacity to raise revenue.

The second approach asks a somewhat different question. How much revenue per capita would the jurisdiction raise if it imposed a standard burden on local residents (where the standard burden is defined as the taxes borne by residents as a percentage of resident income), taking into account the ability of the jurisdiction to export tax burdens to nonresidents? This approach is conceptually more appealing to economists because of its closer link to the decisionmaking process they have modeled, but the need to estimate export ratios raises thorny implementation problems.

Similarly, there are two common approaches to measuring expenditure need. One is to adjust average per capita spending levels for workloads. Thus, for example, if one school district has more pupils relative to the population or more pupils with special needs than others, its expenditure need would be higher than that of other jurisdictions. An alternative approach is to use the statistical technique of regression analysis to develop cost indices that measure the costs in one jurisdiction relative to those in the average jurisdiction that arise because of the characteristics of that particular jurisdiction. Relevant characteristics for a city might include, for example, housing density, the poverty rate, and the amount of commercial property in the city. This approach is richer than the workload approach in that it can accommodate differences in the costs of service provision as well as the differences in workloads.

For many years, the ACIR measured the revenue-raising capacity of U.S. states. Recognizing the limitations of population as a measure of expenditure need, the ACIR in more recent years has introduced a measure of expenditure need based on a modified version of the workload approach. With the demise of the ACIR, additional work on fiscal disparities across states is likely to be limited. At the local level, a variety of recent studies have attempted to measure fiscal disparities for specific types of local governments within a state (Ladd 1994).

Two types of fiscal disparities have received significant attention: those across school districts within states and those within metropolitan areas. Starting with the *Serrano* v. *Priest* case in 1971, court cases in states throughout the country have focused public attention on disparities in the ability of local school districts to provide K–12 education for their students (see Education financing, state and local). Within metropolitan areas, the suburbanization of jobs and households has left many central cities with declining tax bases and increasing concentrations of poor households. These changes have led to a significant deterioration in the fiscal condition of central cities, both absolutely and relative to their suburbs.

### Additional readings

Ladd, Helen F. "Measuring Disparities in the Fiscal Condition of Local Governments." In *Fiscal Equalization for State and Local Government Finance*, edited by John E. Anderson. Westport, Conn.: Praeger, 1994: 21–54.

U.S. Advisory Commission on Intergovernmental Relations. *Measures of State and Local Fiscal Capacity and Tax Effort*. Report M-16. Washington, D.C., 1962.

*Cross references:* education financing, state and local; tax and revenue capacity; tax and revenue effort.

# Fiscal equalization

Helen F. Ladd
Duke University

*Policies to equalize the fiscal position of subnational governments.*

Fiscal equalization refers to attempts by a higher level of government within a federal system of government to reduce fiscal disparities among lower-level jurisdictions (see Fiscal disparities). For example, the national government might endeavor to offset fiscal disparities across states (in the United States) or provinces (in Canada), and states or provinces might try to reduce disparities across local governments such as counties, municipalities, or school districts. The higher level of government may achieve its ends through equalizing aid programs, through the redesign of fiscal institutions, or through tax-base sharing.

Fiscal equalization policies have been justified on both efficiency and equity grounds. The efficiency argument starts from the view that it is socially inefficient for mobile tax bases, such as business activity, to make location and investment decisions based on tax rate differentials that are not offset by corresponding differences in locally provided public services. By reducing those differences, an equalization program could potentially increase the efficiency of the location decisions of both firms and mobile households. However, to the extent that it props up inefficient governments, a program of fiscal equalization could potentially introduce new distortions. For example, assistance to poor communities or to communities with high costs of providing public services could inappropriately induce people to move to those communities (see Oakland 1994: 202). Whether or not it would do so depends on the cause of the disparities that the policy is intended to offset.

In general, the equity case for fiscal equalization tends to be stronger than the efficiency case. The most persuasive equity argument is categorical in that it applies to specific public services such as elementary and secondary education or public health. For example, the case for ensuring that all children have access at reasonable cost to an adequate level of education is quite compelling, given the importance of education to a child's future income and life chances. While many people would agree with this view for education, extending the logic to a range of other locally provided public services is more controversial and may vary across states or cultures.

A second equity rationale applies to differences in the revenue potential from natural resources across subnational jurisdictions. In principle, it may be desirable to use a policy of intergovernmental grants to spread the fiscal benefits of such natural resources to the state or the nation as a whole. However, as noted by Oakland (1994: 205), capitalization and other considerations may make it difficult to implement such a policy fairly.

Similarly, a case for fiscal equalization can be made when some jurisdictions include disproportionate numbers of dependent households or have other characteristics that raise the costs of providing a given package of public services. For example, a jurisdiction with a disproportionate share of low-income households is likely to have below-average capacity to raise revenue and above-average costs of providing a given level of public services to its residents. Consequently, to provide a given level of services to its residents, such a jurisdiction would require an above-average tax rate. This outcome would be undesirable for two reasons. First, by providing an incentive for middle- and upper-income households to leave the jurisdiction, the high tax rate would exacerbate the situation by increasing the concentration of poor households. Second, it would be unfair to the nonpoor households in those jurisdictions in that they would be bearing a burden that is more appropriately placed at a higher level of government (see Fiscal federalism).

A final, related, objective for an equalizing grant program is to make more equal the distribution of households' real incomes. While tax and transfer programs can best ensure that low-income households have adequate ability to purchase private goods and services, grants to communities with disproportionate numbers of low-income households may also be needed to ensure their access at reasonable cost to collectively determined goods and services, such as clean water and education. While the possibility that grants may be capitalized into housing prices may offset some of the benefits of such programs, it does not completely eliminate the argument for equalizing grants of this type. To the extent that factors such as disability, poverty, or discrimination restrict the mobility of low-income households, housing prices will not fully reflect differences in service quality or tax rates. In addition, even with full mobility, the impact of grants on hous-

ing prices is unclear because of complicated general equilibrium effects (Ladd and Yinger 1994).

The most widely used and discussed tool of fiscal equalization is intergovernmental aid. However, other tools are sometimes available. Consider, for example, the case of subnational governments in the United States. Because the powers of U.S. local governments are created by state constitutions and laws, state governments essentially define the rules under which local governments within each state operate. Consequently, states can achieve their equalization goals not simply by directing additional funds to needy jurisdictions but also by shifting responsibilities for certain expenditure functions (such as welfare or the judicial system, whose benefits extend beyond the boundaries of specific local governments) to a higher level of government or by empowering local governments to use additional taxes, such as payroll or wage taxes, to capture revenue from wealthier nonresidents. In addition, a state or a metropolitan area could introduce some form of tax-base sharing among local jurisdictions. The tax-base sharing program in the Minneapolis-St. Paul metropolitan area best illustrates that approach in the United States. Forty percent of the property tax base for new commercial and industrial property is put in a pool, taxed at a uniform rate, and redistributed to the local governments based on an equalizing formula (Luce 1998).

The main analytical issue with respect to equalizing aid programs is how to design formulas for distributing the aid. Not surprisingly, the appropriate design depends on the objective of the program. Consider, first, programs oriented toward particular categories of public services such as kindergarten through 12th grade (K–12) education. If the goal of the program is to ensure a minimum or threshold level of education services in all school districts, then aid should be in the form of a foundation grant. With such a program, each school district would receive enough aid so that, along with the revenue it would raise locally by imposing a minimum school tax rate, it could provide the minimum level of services. Assuming the goal were stated in terms of service levels rather than spending levels, the formula would have to take into account not only differences in the wealth of the school districts but also the fact that some districts have greater proportions of expensive-to-educate children. If, more generally, the goal were to ease the burden of providing a standard package of public services, the aid should vary inversely with a local jurisdiction's capacity to raise revenue and directly with its costs of providing that standard package. In this case, no additional incentive would be given for the local jurisdiction to attain the basic level of services. A third goal—that of ensuring equal service for a given level of sacrifice—could be achieved with a district power–equalizing grant. Finally, a goal of ensuring equal outcomes across districts would require that the state make all spending decisions and that local districts be prohibited from supplementing the state funds with locally raised revenues.

Views toward fiscal equalization have varied over time in the United States. In the 1970s, the federal government introduced a general revenue–sharing program designed to offset some of the fiscal disparities both across states and among local governments within states. That program, which ended in 1986, represented the most explicit attempt by the federal government to equalize the fiscal position of U.S. subnational governments. Other federal countries, such as Canada and Germany, have been much more aggressive in attempting to equalize the revenue-raising capacities of their subnational governments. At the state level, interest in policies to reduce within-state disparities varies across states. Partly in response to pressures from the courts, which have ruled that many state systems of education finance lead to unconstitutional disparities in educational opportunities, the states have most actively developed programs of equalizing aid for local school districts (see Education financing, state and local). For the many developing countries and former socialist countries moving to decentralize their governmental systems, the issue of fiscal equalization is now becoming increasingly relevant (see Shah 1994 and Bird, Ebel, and Wallich 1995).

## Additional readings

Anderson, John E., editor. *Fiscal Equalization for State and Local Government Finance*. Westport, Conn.: Praeger, 1994.

Bird, Richard M., Robert D. Ebel, and Christine I. Wallich, editors. *Decentralization of the Socialist State*. World Bank, 1995.

Ladd, Helen F., and John Yinger. "The Case for Equalizing Aid." *National Tax Journal* 47 (1) (1994): 211–24.

Luce, Thomas. "Regional Tax Base Sharing: The Twin Cities Experience." In Helen F. Ladd, *Local Government Tax and Land Use Policies in the United States: Understanding the Links*. Cheltenham, U.K.: Edward Elgar, 1998.

Oakland, William H. "Fiscal Equalization: An Empty Box." *National Tax Journal* 47 (1) (1994): 199–210.

Rafuse, Robert. *Representative Expenditures: Addressing the Neglected Dimension of Fiscal Capacity*. Washington, D.C.: Advisory Commission on Intergovernmental Relations, 1990.

Rye, C. Richard, and Bob Searle. "Expenditure Needs: Institutions and Data." In *Financing Decentralized Expenditures: An International Comparison of Grants*, edited by Ehtisham Ahmad. Cheltenham, U.K.: Edward Elgar, 1997.

Shah, Anwar. *The Reform of Intergovernmental Fiscal Relations in Developing and Emerging Market Economies*. World Bank, 1994.

*Cross references:* education financing, state and local; fiscal disparities; tax and revenue capacity; tax and revenue effort.

# Fiscal federalism

Richard M. Bird
University of Toronto

*The analysis of the problems that give rise to, and arise from, the existence of more than one level of government within the same geographical area.*

As originally developed by Musgrave (1959) and Oates (1972), the "theory of fiscal federalism" concerns the division of public-sector functions and finances in a logical way among multiple layers of government (King 1984). Much of the literature of fiscal federalism consists of relatively unrelated treatments of such issues as the "decentralization theorem" (Oates 1991), models for the assignment of powers (McLure 1993), discussions of intergovernmental spillovers and intergovernmental grants (Break 1980), fiscal mobility and migration (Wildasin 1991), and vertical fiscal imbalance and dependence (Hunter 1977). The theoretical discussion of local public goods that has taken place in the context of the Tiebout model (Wildasin 1986) is not part of "fiscal federalism" as defined here because it is concerned only with governmental relations at the same jurisdictional level. A more general, and relevant, theoretical framework to approach some of these problems might be the theory of overlapping clubs (Cornes and Sandler 1996), but as yet this has been little developed (Casella and Frey 1992).

Initially, stabilization and distribution were considered to be essentially "central" functions, with the only role for "subcentral" (state and local) governments arising in the allocative sphere. From this perspective, the main analytical task of fiscal federalism is to define the appropriate functions and finances of local governments as efficiently as possible—that is, in such a way as to maximize community welfare (often represented, for analytical convenience, by the Median Voter Theorem). In a territorial variant of the Benefit Principle, it was suggested at an early stage that each jurisdiction could be most efficiently mapped in terms of the spatial dimension of the services it provided. Thus, there would be "local public goods," "state public goods," and "national public goods," with the presumed beneficiaries of each financing their provision in an appropriate way (Olson 1969). In practice, the overlapping and multidimensional nature of most public-sector activities makes it difficult to apply this approach very rigorously, particularly because few lower-level governments have sufficient own-source revenues to finance the services logically assigned to them.

Given the greater interjurisdictional mobility of the base of the income tax relative to that of the consumption tax, and of the latter relative to that of the property tax (and the efficiency problems arising from tax exportation, when not precisely offset by benefit spillovers), most analysts suggest that the local public sector should be financed basically by user charges and "local" taxes, especially the property tax, and states by consumption taxes, with the income tax being left largely to the central (federal) government (Musgrave 1983). But this division of revenues means that state and local governments are likely to end up with greater expenditure responsibilities than can be financed from their own revenues. An important element of fiscal federalism from the beginning has thus been recognition of the probable need for intergovernmental grants to close the revenue gap. Considerable attention has been devoted to the appropriate design of such grants (Wilde 1971; Ahmed 1997), as well as to empirical analysis of their effects on local spending patterns (Gramlich 1977; Rubinfeld 1987).

The theory of fiscal federalism applies as well, or as badly, to local service units in a metropolitan area as to states in a federation. In principle, however, there are important analytical and policy differences, not only between local-metropolitan problems and federal-state problems but even between "tight" federations such as Germany and "loose" federations such as Canada—with the United States somewhere in between (Bird 1986). These differences arise in part from the differing nature and rigidity of the constraints imposed by political institutions. The question has attracted considerable attention in recent years, in part because of the emergence of nascent "federal" institutions in the European Union. However, fiscal federalism has little to say as yet about the dynamics of institutional change in emerging (or disintegrating) federations. Moreover, it offers little guidance in dealing with such important real-world intergovernmental finance problems as the appropriate size and scope of operation of local and intermediate-level governments in the newly emerging countries of the former Soviet bloc (Bird, Ebel, and Wallich 1995), where, for example, the potential impact on stabilization (Gramlich 1987) is a major concern.

In contrast, much good work has been done within this analytical framework on some of the problems arising from the common metropolitan area situation of divided political jurisdictions within an economically integrated region. A structure that puts people's places of work and residence in separate political jurisidictions, while making the latter primarily responsible for the most important local expenditure, education, has obvious implications for both efficiency and distribution (Wildasin 1986), as has been much explored in the literature on education finance. There is still much to be done, however, to satisfactorily explain local redistributive policies (Tresch 1981)—through, for example, education—and their impact on migration and other important economic variables (Wildasin 1991).

Much has been written about the virtues of decentralized government, from both a political and an economic perspective (Tullock 1994), but most of these supposed virtues can, in the conventional fiscal federalism framework, be achieved as well by regionally based central officials as by locally elected politicians. Perhaps some of the answers lie in the new "supply-side" theories of government (Breton 1996) that are beginning to be developed in the broad "public choice" framework (Mueller 1992), because there is considerable similarity between the assumptions underlying public choice theory and federalist theory (Ostrom 1971). As yet, however, little progress has been made with respect to articulating these arguments in either normative or positive terms in the conventional fiscal federalism analysis, other than as simple assertions.

Nonetheless, some important lessons have emerged from the fiscal federalism literature (Inman and Rubinfeld 1997). In particular, considerable progress has been made with respect to the appropriate assignment of tasks and finances in multilevel governments, especially with respect to the design and effects of intergovernmental grants (Wildasin 1997). While there is considerable variation in detail from state to state—let alone across countries—on the whole the observed assignment of functions to local and state governments accords broadly with the dictates of theory, with local governments being broadly responsible for "place-specific" services such as streets, water and sewerage works, refuse disposal, and fire and police services. In addition, in the United States, local governments are also generally responsible for providing primary and secondary education, although as a rule with substantial fiscal assistance from state governments; in other countries, education is often provided primarily by intermediate-level (state) governments and sometimes even by central governments. A common pattern everywhere is for one level of government to be involved in delivering a certain service while other levels are involved to varying degrees in financing and regulating it (Ter-Minassian 1997). Work on understanding the desirability and effects of alternative institutional structures of providing particular services is still in its infancy, though.

Local governments rely heavily on property taxes for revenue, while state governments rely on a mixture of sales and income taxes, and the federal government mainly on income (and payroll) taxes. The division of revenues differs in other countries: Although almost everywhere local governments get property taxes and central governments most income taxes, in some countries local income taxes—like national sales taxes—are much more important than in the United States (Owens and Panella 1991). Such taxes are invariably "piggybacked" on national taxes—that is, they take the form of surcharges. Only Switzerland comes close to matching the diversity of the state and local income and sales taxes found in the United States. Most other countries, whether formally federal or not, have much more territorially uniform fiscal systems. Although there is clearly vertical competition between levels of government for revenue, most attention has been paid in the literature to horizontal tax competition, perhaps because as a rule local governments have access only to those revenue sources that higher-level governments do not want for themselves.

Local governments almost invariably depend in part, and sometimes very heavily, upon transfers from upper-level governments to finance the services for which they are responsible. The appropriate level and design of such transfers has been an important concern in the fiscal federalism literature. Some argue, for example, that a system of unconditional fiscal equalization grants is an essential component of an efficient (and equitable) fiscal federal system (Boadway and Flatters 1982). Others assert that there is no place for such transfers (Oakland 1994). The theoretical literature suggests that the only clear efficiency case for intergovernmental payments is to compensate local governments for benefit spillovers to ensure that they provide the optimal amount of the public service in question. In practice, however, virtually no examples of the open-ended conditional matching grants called for by this theory are to be found in any country (Ahmed 1997). On the contrary, most countries (other than the United States) have some system of unconditional transfers intended to equalize some concept of fiscal capacity. Moreover, most conditional matching grants are limited in amount and probably best interpreted in a principal-agent framework (Ferris and Winkler 1991)—that is, as the equivalent of mandated functions being paid for, in large part, by transfers but with some local payment being called for. The latter is to ensure that local fiscal effort is maintained and also that, at the margin, local politicians remain electorally accountable for their actions to their constituents, as well as to the granting authority.

At the policy level, the Advisory Commission on Intergovernmental Relations (ACIR) (1990) carried out pioneering studies on fiscal disparities (sometimes referred to as "horizontal imbalance"), fiscal capacity, and fiscal effort. Curiously, this work has had its greatest policy impact in other federal countries such as Canada, where since 1967 a version of the ACIR's "representative tax system" concept has formed the basis of the federal-provincial equalization system—which itself was based in large part on a system developed in Australia in the 1930s (and since extended from revenue to expenditure equalization). Similar systems of federal-state transfers, often based on formulas and usually unconditional in nature, are characteristic of most federal countries (Shah 1994). Apart from the brief experience with a small "revenue-sharing" system in the 1970s (Juster 1977), the United States is unique among federal countries in that it has never had a system of federal-state equalization transfers—although there are, of course, many federal-state conditional transfers, as well as some experience with fiscal equalization at the state and local levels.

## Additional readings

Advisory Commission on Intergovernmental Relations. *1988 State Fiscal Capacity and Effort*. Information Report M-170. Washington, D.C., 1990.

Ahmad, Ehtisham, editor. *Financing Decentralized Expenditures: An International Comparison of Grants*. Cheltenham, U.K.: Edward Elgar, 1997.

Bird, Richard M. *Federal Finance in Comparative Perspective*. Toronto: Canadian Tax Foundation, 1986.

Bird, Richard M., Robert D. Ebel, and Christine I. Wallich, editors, *Decentralization of the Socialist State: Intergovernmental Finance in Transition Economies*. Washington, D.C.: World Bank, 1995.

Boadway, Robin, and Frank Flatters. "Efficiency and Equalization Payments in a Federal System of Government: A Synthesis and Extension of Recent Results." *Canadian Journal of Economics* 15 (1982).

Break, George F. *Financing Government in a Federal System*. Washington, D.C.: The Brookings Institution, 1980.

Breton, Albert. *Competitive Governments: An Economic Theory of Politics and Public Finance*. Cambridge, U.K.: Cambridge University Press, 1996.

Casella, Alessandra, and Bruno Frey. "Federalism and Clubs: Towards an Economic Theory of Overlapping Political Jurisdictions," *European Economic Review* 36 (1992): 639–46.

Cornes, Richard, and Todd Sandler. *The Theory of Externalities, Public Goods and Club Goods*. 2d ed. Cambridge, U.K.: Cambridge University Press, 1996.

Ferris, James M., and Donald R. Winkler. "Agency Theory and Intergovernmental Relationships." *Public Fi-

*nance with Several Levels of Government*, edited by Remy Prud'homme. The Hague/Koenigstein: Foundation Journal of Public Finance, 1991

Gramlich, Edward M. "Intergovernmental Grants: A Review of the Empirical Literature." In *The Political Economy of Fiscal Federalism*, edited by Wallace E. Oates. Lexington, Mass.: Lexington Press, 1977.

Gramlich, Edward M. "Subnational Fiscal Policy." *Perspectives on Local Public Finance and Public Policy* 3 (1987): 3–27.

Hunter, J.S.H. *Federalism and Fiscal Balance*. Canberra: Australian National University Press, 1977.

Inman, Robert P., and Daniel L. Rubinfeld. "The Political Economy of Fiscal Federalism." In *Perspectives on Public Choice: A Handbook*, edited by Dennis C. Mueller. Cambridge, U.K.: Cambridge University Press, 1997.

Juster, F. Thomas, editor. *The Economic and Political Impact of General Revenue Sharing*. Ann Arbor, Mich.: Survey Research Center, Institute for Social Research, University of Michigan, 1977.

King, David. *Fiscal Tiers: The Economics of Multi-Level Government*. London: George Allen and Unwin, 1984.

McLure, Charles E., Jr. *Vertical Fiscal Imbalance and the Assignment of Taxing Powers in Australia*. Stanford: Hoover Institution, 1993.

Mueller, Dennis C. *Public Choice II*. Cambridge, U.K.: Cambridge University Press, 1992.

Musgrave, Richard A. *The Theory of Public Finance*. New York: McGraw Hill, 1959.

Musgrave, Richard A. "Who Should Tax, Where, and What?" *Tax Assignment in Federal Countries*, edited by Charles E. McLure, Jr. Canberra: Australian National University Press, 1983.

Oakland, William. "Fiscal Equalization: An Empty Box?" *National Tax Journal* 44 (1994).

Oates, Wallace E. *Fiscal Federalism*. New York: Harcourt Brace Jovanovich, 1972.

Oates, Wallace E. "The Theory of Fiscal Federalism: Revenue and Expenditure Issues—A Survey of Recent Theoretical and Empirical Research." *Public Finance with Several Levels of Government*, edited by Remy Prud'homme. The Hague/Koeningstein: Foundation Journal of Public Finance, 1991.

Olson, Mancur. "The Principle of Fiscal Equivalence: The Division of Responsiblities among Different Levels of Government." *American Economic Review Papers and Proceedings* 59 (May 1969): 479–87.

Ostrom, Vincent. *The Political Theory of a Compound Republic*. Blacksburg, Va.: Public Choice Society, 1971.

Owens, Jeffrey, and Giorgio Panella, editors. *Local Government: An International Perspective*. Amsterdam: North-Holland, 1991.

Rubinfeld, Daniel. "The Economics of the Local Public Sector." In *Handbook of Public Economics*, vol. 2, edited by Alan J. Auerbach and Martin Feldstein. Amsterdam: North-Holland, 1987.

Shah, Anwar. *The Reform of Intergovernmental Fiscal Relations in Developing and Emerging Market Economies*. Policy and Research Series 23. Washington, D.C.: World Bank, 1994.

Ter-Minassian, Teresa, editor. *Fiscal Federalism in Theory and Practice*. Washington, D.C.: International Monetary Fund, 1997.

Tresch, Richard W. *Public Finance: A Normative Theory*. Plano, Texas: Business Publications, 1981.

Tullock, Gordon. *The New Federalist*. Vancouver: Fraser Institute, 1994.

Wildasin, David E. *Urban Public Finance*. London: Harwood Academic Publishers, 1986.

Wildasin, David E. "Income Redistribution in a Common Labor Market." *American Economic Review* 81 (1991): 757–74.

Wildasin, David E., editor. *Fiscal Aspects of Evolving Federations*. Cambridge, U.K.: Cambridge University Press, 1997.

Wilde, James E. 1971. "Grants-in-Aid: The Analytics of Design and Response." *National Tax Journal* 24 (1971): 143–55.

*Cross references:* benefit principle; education financing, state and local; fiscal disparities; fiscal equalization; median voter theorem; tax and revenue effort; tax exportation.

# Flat tax

William G. Gale
The Brookings Institution

*A proposal for fundamental tax reform that would replace the income tax system with a consumption tax, to be collected by levying a flat-rate tax on businesses and individuals.*

## Background

Consumption is income less savings. Thus, the only difference in principle between a consumption tax and an income tax is the treatment of the savings. An income tax taxes savings both when the money is earned and again when the savings earn interest. A consumption tax taxes saving only once: either when the funds are withdrawn and used for consumption or when the funds are first earned. Although this difference appears simple, consumption taxes come in many forms.

## The Hall-Rabushka flat tax

In the early 1980s, Robert Hall and Alvin Rabushka of the Hoover Institution developed a consumption tax system that achieves some of the administrative advantages of a value-added tax (VAT) relative to a sales tax, while also partially addressing concerns that consumption taxes impose a relatively heavier tax burden on lower-income taxpayers.

The Hall-Rabushka system is often called the "flat tax": It assesses a 19 percent tax on all businesses (corporate or otherwise)—identical to the VAT, except that wages, pension contributions, materials costs, and capital investments are deducted from the tax base. Individuals (or households) are assessed a 19 percent flat-rate tax on wages and pension benefits above an exemption of $25,500 for a family of four. No other income is taxable, and no other deductions are allowed.

The Hall-Rabushka proposal has served as the blueprint for several proposals to reform the federal tax system, including a proposal introduced by Representative Richard Armey (R-Texas) and Senator Richard Shelby (R-Alabama) and one offered by presidential candidate Steve Forbes (R) in the 1996 presidential primaries.

In comparison to the Hall-Rabushka proposal, the personal income tax in 1994 provided exemptions of $9,800 for a family of four, an earned income tax credit (EITC), and the choice of a $6,350 standard deduction or itemized deductions for mortgage interest, state and local income and property taxes, charity, and large health expenditures. Estimates indicate that in 1996, a family of four taking the standard deduction and the EITC, with all income from wages, would pay no federal income taxes on the first $23,700 of income, 15 percent on the next $31,000 or so, 28 percent on the next $53,000, and higher rates on additional income, reaching 39.6 percent on taxable income above $250,000.

Without the personal exemptions, the flat tax would be equivalent to a VAT, but with taxes on wages remitted by households rather than business. That is, the flat tax would be a consumption tax, even though it would look like a wage tax to households and a variant of a VAT to most businesses. Therefore, other than the exemptions, the economic effects of the flat tax should be essentially the same as those of a VAT or a sales tax.

The family exemptions make the flat tax progressive for low-income households. But at the high end of the income distribution, the tax is regressive, just like sales taxes and VATs.

The Hall-Rabushka proposal could be amended in several ways. Princeton economist David Bradford has proposed an X-tax similar to Hall-Rabushka but with graduated tax rates on household wage income to raise progressivity. (The business tax would be set equal to the highest tax rate on wage income.) The flat tax could also be modified to retain the EITC, allow a deduction for charitable contributions, and provide a tax credit (a one-to-one reduction in taxes paid under the flat tax) for payroll taxes paid. The credit would be a huge boon to lower- and middle-income households, because most now pay more in payroll taxes than in income taxes. These changes would, of course, require higher rates. But a tax system with these features might be able to retain the progressivity of the current tax system while also reaping most of the gains of the Hall-Rabushka proposal's broader base, generally lower rates, and simplified compliance. The question remains, though, of how large these gains would be.

## Evaluating the effects of adopting a flat tax

Analysts find it hard to predict with precision the effects of minor tax changes, and heated debate continues about the effects of the major 1980s tax reforms. Hence, efforts to evaluate the effects of uprooting the entire tax system must be appropriately qualified. (The economic effects of the flat tax are addressed by a number of contributions in Aaron and Gale 1996.)

A central issue in tax reform is always who wins and who loses. Under the flat tax, low-income households would lose because they now pay no income tax and are eligible for a refundable EITC of up to $3,370. Although the flat tax is more progressive than a VAT, it is more regressive than the current system. A flat tax would provide huge gains for high-income households, both because their marginal tax rate would fall and because they consume relatively less of their income than do low-income households. As a result, if a flat tax were to raise as much revenue as the current one, the tax burden for the middle class would have to rise. Consumption taxes are generally less regressive when viewed over longer periods of time because income changes from year to year, but they would raise tax burdens on lower- and middle-income households over any time frame. (For further discussion, see Gale et al. 1996 and Gentry and Hubbard 1997).

Perceptions of fairness may also be difficult to retain when, under the flat tax, some wealthy individuals and large corporations remit no taxes to the government while middle-class workers pay a combined marginal tax rate above 30 percent on the flat tax, state income tax, and payroll taxes.

As for simplicity, the flat tax would likely slash compliance costs for many businesses and households. But for many, the tax system is not that complicated.

And fundamental tax reform would not end the demands for special treatment that have so tangled the income tax. Ten years hence, we may find that what started as simplicity has once again become a confused jumble. Thus some simplification is likely with tax reform, but it is by no means a certain or lasting outcome. Moreover, many simplification gains could be made through changes in the income tax.

A third concern is how reform would affect different sectors of the economy. Removing the mortgage interest deduction and the deductibility of state and local property taxes may have profound effects on housing prices and home ownership, but the results would depend on how interest rates adjust, the sorts of grandfathering rules that are introduced, and other factors. How and when health insurance benefits and coverage rates would adjust to the elimination of tax-favored treatment of employer-provided health benefits is an open question.

Removing the deduction for charitable contributions would reduce overall giving and could affect its composition as well: Wealthy donors, for whom the write-off is now worth the most, tend to favor hospitals and universities; low-income donors, religious institutions.

Effects on businesses and investment would be complicated. The flat tax would eliminate corporate income taxes, put all businesses on an equal tax footing, reduce the statutory tax rate applied to business income, and make investment write-offs more generous. But it would also remove the deductibility of interest payments and of state and local taxes, and this could induce dramatic changes. For example, Hall and Rabushka estimate that General Motors' annual tax liability could rise to $2.7 billion from $110 million, while Intel's would fall by 75 percent. The effects of a consumption tax on international economic transactions and on the financial sector are potentially far-reaching and need to be examined carefully.

## Economic efficiency and growth

Ultimately, increased economic efficiency and growth must be one of the key selling points of a consumption tax. Without a significant gain in living standards, uprooting the entire tax system is probably not worth the risks, redistributions, and adjustment costs it would impose.

Efficiency gains might arise from five sources: the change of the tax base from income to consumption; a more comprehensive tax base, which eliminates the differential tax treatment of various assets and forms of income; lower tax rates, which raise the rate of return to working, saving, and investing and reduce incentives to avoid or evade taxes; reduced compliance costs; and the taxation of previously existing assets during the transition to a consumption tax (about which more later). All but the first and last are attainable under income tax reform.

Although estimates vary, a recent study suggests that a pure flat tax proposal with limited personal exemptions would raise economic output by between 2 and 4 percent over the first nine years and between 4 and 6 percent in the long run. But these results need to be interpreted carefully. First, many of the gains are also available through judicious reform of the income tax, in particular by making the taxation of capital income more uniform. Second, the estimates provided do not allow for child exemptions, as the Hall-Rabushka proposal and all of the recent flat tax proposals do. Allowing exemptions for children reduces the effects by about 2 percentage points (e.g., to 0–2% over 10 years). Third, the estimates apply to a pure, well-designed consumption tax. Compromises in the design, such as including mortgage interest deductions or allowing a transition, reduce the gains or turn them into losses. Allowing for transition relief alone is enough to reduce the impact on growth to zero in the long run. The estimates also show that, even for well-designed consumption taxes, efficiency losses are possible. (The estimates cited in this paragraph are taken from Auerbach 1997 and private communications with Kent Smetters. For additional analysis of the growth effects of tax reform, see Engen et al. 1997.)

A key element in raising growth and a major motivation for tax reform is increasing saving. Proponents typically point to two reasons why consumption taxes should spur saving. First, a revenue-neutral shift to a consumption tax would be expected to raise the after-tax rate of return on saving, while keeping total tax payments constant. Second, consumption taxes reallocate after-tax income toward high-saving households. Such reasoning is straightforward but incomplete. Saving is likely to rise only a little, if at all, for several reasons.

First, the current U.S. tax system is not a pure income tax; it is a hybrid between a consumption tax and an income tax. About half of private savings already receive consumption tax treatment. Funds placed in pensions, 401(k) plans, Keogh plans, and most individual retirement accounts (IRAs) are not taxed until they are withdrawn. The return on these investments, then, is the pretax rate of return. But the introduction of a consumption tax would reduce the pretax interest rate, so that the rate of return on these forms of saving would fall, which could reduce saving in these forms.

Second, pension coverage could fall. Under an income tax, pensions are a tax-preferred form of saving. But a consumption tax treats all saving equally, making it less likely that workers and employers would continue to accept the high regulatory and administrative costs of pensions. To the extent that workers did not resave all of their reduced pension contributions, saving would fall.

Third, under a pure consumption tax, all capital existing at the time of the transition is (implicitly) taxed again when the capital is consumed. But transition rules likely to be added to a consumption tax to avoid this double taxation would reduce or eliminate the long-term effect on saving and growth, as noted above.

## The transition: Can we get there from here?

Even if a consumption tax is the right system for an economy starting from scratch, it may not be the right way to *reform* an existing system.

The main transition issue is the taxation of "old capital"—capital assets accumulated earlier out of after-tax income whose principal would not have been taxed again under the income tax. Although some transitional treatment of old capital is typically thought to be likely, not having a transition—that is, implicitly taxing old capital again under a consumption tax—is arguably consistent with the three main goals of tax reform: efficiency, equity, and simplicity.

Certainly, not having a transition is simpler. The transition rules could be very complex, and the transition period could stretch out for years.

Not having a transition is also more efficient. Because future consumption can be financed only from future wages or existing assets, a consumption tax is a tax on future wages and existing assets. A consumption tax that exempts old assets is just a tax on future wages. And the same studies that show that a consumption tax (which taxes all old capital assets) is more efficient than an income tax also show that a wage tax is *less* efficient than an income tax—because not taxing existing capital requires higher tax rates on wages to raise the same revenue and hence distorts people's work decisions more. So exempting old capital removes any presumption that tax reform would result in a more efficient system.

Surely, the strongest argument for exempting old capital from taxes is fairness. The assets have already been taxed once; is it fair to tax them again? The answer may not be as obvious as it seems. First, a onetime implicit tax on existing capital is very progressive. The distribution of such capital is more skewed toward wealthy households than is the distribution of overall wealth, which in turn is more skewed than the distribution of income. Second, within any age group, wealthy households do most of the saving. Because these households would benefit most from eliminating the double taxation on future saving under a consumption tax, it is reasonable that they pay for some of the costs. Third, older households tend to have more assets than younger ones, and taxing existing capital places heavier burdens on older generations. But those older households have received transfers through Social Security and Medicare that far outreach what they

have put in. And the vast majority of income and wealth for most elderly households is in the form of future earnings (which have not yet been taxed), housing (which receives extraordinarily preferential treatment under the current tax), pension income (which already receives consumption tax treatment), Social Security benefits (which are not taxed under the flat tax), and Medicare benefits (which are not and would not be taxed). Relatively few elderly households finance much of their living expenses by other assets, and those that do tend to be very well off.

## Pros and cons of the flat tax

In principle, replacing the income tax with a consumption tax, such as the flat tax, offers the possibility of improving the efficiency, equity, and simplicity of the tax system. But these gains are uncertain and depend critically on the details of the reform. At least some of the gains could be made simply by modifying the existing system.

Idealized consumption taxes may always look better than actual income tax systems. Once in place, though, they would be subject to the same compromises and pressures as the income tax is. They could even lead to a system that is less efficient and less fair than the one we have.

## Additional readings

Aaron, Henry J., and William G. Gale, editors. *Economic Effects of Fundamental Tax Reform*. Washington, D.C.: Brookings Institution Press, 1996.

Altig, David, et al. "Simulating U.S. Tax Reform." National Bureau of Economic Research Working Paper 6248, October 1997.

Auerbach, Alan J. "Quantifying the Current U.S. Fiscal Imbalance." *National Tax Journal* 50 (September 1997): 387–98.

Engen, Eric, Jane Gravelle, and Kent Smetters. "Dynamic Tax Models: Why They Do the Things They Do." *National Tax Journal* 50 (September 1997): 657–82.

Gale, William G., Scott Houser, and John Karl Scholz. "Distributional Effects of Fundamental Tax Reform." In *Economic Effects of Fundamental Tax Reform*, edited by Henry J. Aaron and William G. Gale. Washington, D.C.: The Brookings Institution, 1996: 281–320.

Gentry, William, and R. Glenn Hubbard. "Distributional Effects of Adopting a National Retail Sales Tax." In *Tax Policy and the Economy*, vol. 11, edited by James M. Poterba. Cambridge, Mass.: MIT Press, 1997, pp. 1–47.

Hall, Robert, and Alvin E. Rabushka. *The Flat Tax*. Stanford: Hoover Institution Press, 1995.

*Cross references:* consumption taxation; tax reform, federal; value-added tax, national; value-added tax, state.

# Foreign corporations, federal taxation

Timothy J. Goodspeed
Hunter College—City University of New York

*Federal taxation of corporations owned by foreigners but incorporated and operated in the United States.*

Corporations owned by foreigners but incorporated and operated in the United States are generally subject to the same taxation rules applying to a corporation owned by U.S. citizens. In fact, tax treaties generally contain a nondiscrimination provision that requires equal treatment of U.S. and foreign companies.

Unless one looks at U.S. taxes paid by foreign-owned corporations, one might think that a reference to the federal corporate income tax and tax treaties would suffice for this entry. However, a look at available data indicates a puzzling surprise: Foreign-owned corporations operating in the United States pay surprisingly little U.S. tax compared with U.S.-owned companies operating in the United States. As reported by Grubert et al. (1993), the ratio of U.S. taxable income to assets was 0.58 for foreign-owned corporations and 2.14 for U.S.-owned corporations for 1987; the difference persists when sales are used in the denominator rather than assets and when the smaller categories of nonfinancial, manufacturing, and wholesale industries are examined.

The lack of U.S. tax revenue from foreign-owned companies relative to U.S.-owned companies has created a considerable amount of attention. The controversy has been centered on the amount of revenue that foreign-owned companies should be paying to the U.S. government as opposed to what they actually pay—that is, are foreign-owned firms able to avoid (or evade) paying tax to the U.S. government, or is the lack of revenue a natural consequence of differences between U.S.- and foreign-owned companies?

To get a handle on the approximate amount of revenue involved, one might begin by assuming that foreign- and U.S.-owned companies are alike. For reasons to be mentioned momentarily, foreign-owned companies are somewhat different from U.S.-owned companies, but suppose for the moment that they are the same. This is tantamount to assuming that the entire difference in tax revenues stems from tax avoidance or evasion on the part of foreign-owned companies. Because economic theory suggests that equivalent firms should have equal rates of return, one might suppose that the foreign rate of return of 0.58 should approximate the U.S. return of 2.14. Because *Statistics of Income Bulletin* (1990) data indicate that the total assets of the 45,000 foreign-owned companies operating in the United States in 1987 were $959 billion, one might expect taxable income of foreign-owned companies of about $20.5 billion and taxes paid of about $7 billion in 1987. Because foreign-owned companies actually paid $4.5 billion, one might suspect a 1987 shortfall of about $2.5 billion. However, the revenue shortfall has been suggested to be quite a bit larger than this. For instance, in his 1992 presidential campaign, Bill Clinton suggested that increased auditing by the Internal Revenue Service (IRS) of foreign corporations could raise $45 billion over a four-year period. The difference in the two figures may not be as great as first appears, because the Clinton estimates presumably referred to years after 1992, and the assets of foreign-controlled companies doubled between 1986 and 1990. Rather than try to determine an exact figure, one might consider the initial ballpark range to be $5 to $10 billion annually.

It is important to emphasize at this point that we have assumed that the entire revenue shortfall is a result of tax evasion. An important question is whether this assumption is justified or whether foreign-owned companies differ in certain fundamental ways from U.S.-owned companies.

What sorts of mechanisms might foreign-owned firms engage in to evade paying U.S. tax? The hypothesis put forward most often by members of Congress is "transfer pricing." (For a detailed description, see Transfer pricing.) In brief, suppose a parent company sells an input to its foreign subsidiary that the subsidiary uses to manufacture a product; the "transfer price" is the price charged by the parent in the sale of the input to its subsidiary. The potential for abuse results because both parent and subsidiary profits (and hence taxes) will be influenced by the price charged. The multinational may have an incentive to try to transfer its profits through judicious use of the transfer price so that high profits appear in the low-tax country and low profits in the high-tax country. In an attempt to eliminate such manipulative pricing practices, the U.S. government requires that the price be at "arm's length" of the price that would be charged by an unrelated party. The congressional claim is that foreign companies are evading U.S. taxes by not using arm's-length prices. The implication is that more IRS audits of foreign-owned companies could recover the lost revenue.

A somewhat different method to avoid U.S. tax is a technique known as "earnings stripping," under which loans are taken from related offshore companies. The large interest payments from these transactions are deducted in determining taxable income, consequently lowering taxable income and hence taxes paid. It should be noted that this would also result if foreign-owned companies took more legitimate loans from unrelated parties.

Both abusive transfer pricing and earnings stripping are methods by which foreign-owned companies may evade U.S. tax; if these are the cause of low foreign taxable income, there is a role for the IRS in cracking down on these activities. However, several natural business reasons may differentiate foreign and domestically owned companies and thus account for the difference in taxable income. These reasons include the fact that many foreign-controlled firms are recent acquisitions, exchange-rate issues, high startup costs of foreign-controlled firms, and a potentially lower cost of capital for foreign-controlled firms. After an acquisition, book assets are revalued; because many foreign-controlled firms are recent acquisitions, one would expect higher asset values and hence a lower rate of return for foreign relative to U.S.-owned companies. Exchange rates may be important because foreign-owned companies might tend to import proportionately more component parts. Thus, an unexpected fall in the dollar will increase costs and decrease profits in a higher proportion than to their U.S.-owned counterparts. Startup costs may be important because foreign-owned entities are likely to have large initial costs as they learn about the new foreign business environment; these large initial costs would presumably diminish over time. If foreign firms have a lower cost of capital than U.S.-owned firms, they may be willing to absorb a permanently lower return.

The results of Grubert et al. (1993) indicate that the revaluation of book assets after an acquisition, a maturation process of young foreign-controlled firms, and exchange-rate consequences for wholesale companies are important factors in explaining the difference in the rate of return of foreign versus domestically controlled companies. These natural business reasons account for about half of the difference in the rate of return of foreign versus domestically owned companies. Earnings stripping did not appear to have a significant effect. This leaves about half of the difference possibly attributable to transfer pricing but also suggests that the ballpark revenue figures calculated previously should be cut in half, to about $2.5 to $5 billion annually.

Some recent evidence suggests an even smaller estimate. Grubert (1997) updated the Grubert et al. (1993) studies using more recent data. He was able to explain up to 75 percent of the difference in returns of foreign versus domestically controlled companies. This suggests an even smaller revenue loss

of $1.25 to $2.5 billion annually. Collins et al. (1997) were unable to document transfer-price manipulation by foreign-controlled firms that have close to zero taxable income.

Another recent study (Pak and Zdanowicz 1994) suggests an astounding $30 billion annual loss in revenue as a result of tax evasion by foreigners. This study is interesting because it uses previously untapped data from the U.S. Customs Service, but it is not comparable to previously calculated figures. The $30 billion figure supposes that all illegal transactions are stopped, including money-laundering from drug activities. This is quite different from the transfer-pricing cases normally involving the IRS, which usually deal with legitimate business transactions. Moreover, product categories are sometimes too broad to allow an accurate assessment of price deviations. Nevertheless, it is a rich data set that can potentially be of great use.

Finally, one might note that a crackdown on transfer-pricing practices that is viewed as unfair by a particular country (e.g., Japan) may invite retaliatory action by that country. All of the revenue estimates thus far have ignored this possibility.

## Additional readings

Collins, Julie, Dean Kemsley, and Douglas Shackleford. "Transfer Pricing and the Persistent Zero Taxable Income of Foreign-Controlled U.S. Corporations." Unpublished manuscript, University of North Carolina, Chapel Hill, 1997.

Grubert, Harry. "Another Look at the Low Taxable Income of Foreign-Controlled U.S. Corporations." Unpublished manuscript, University of North Carolina, Chapel Hill, 1997.

Grubert, Harry, Timothy J. Goodspeed, and Deborah Swenson. 1993. "Explaining the Low Taxable Income of Foreign-Controlled Companies in the United States." In *Studies in International Taxation*, ch. 7, edited by Alberto Giovannini, R. Glenn Hubbard, and Joel Slemrod. Chicago: University of Chicago Press, 1993, pp. 237–70.

Pak, Simon J., and John S. Zdanowicz. "A Statistical Analysis of the U.S. Merchandise Trade Data Base and Its Uses in Transfer Pricing Compliance and Enforcement." Washington, D.C.: Bureau of National Affairs, Tax Management, Inc., May 11, 1994, pp. 50–57.

*Statistics of Income Bulletin*. Summer 1990.

*Cross references:* income tax, federal; multinational corporations, taxation.

# Foreign corporations, state taxation

Ben Miller
California Franchise Tax Board

*Taxation by the states of the income of foreign-country corporations.*

State taxation of the income of foreign country corporations is subject to constraints imposed by the Constitution of the United States, in limited areas by treaties entered into by the United States, and by state statutes. Such taxation could also be limited by federal statute, but at present there are no federal statutory limitations on state taxation of foreign corporation income.

A distinction needs to be drawn between the taxation of foreign corporations' income and consideration of those corporations' income and activities in a combined report under "unitary taxation." A foreign corporation that is engaged in a unitary business with domestic corporations may be included in a combined report that is used to determine the amount of income assigned to a state, regardless of whether or not the foreign corporation is itself doing business in the state [see *Barclays Bank PLC* v. *Franchise Tax Board*, 129 Led2d 244, 512 US 298 (1994), and *Container Corporation of America* v. *Franchise Tax Board*, 77 Led2d 545, 463 US 159 (1983)]. This is commonly referred to as worldwide combined reporting (WWCR). Under the jurisprudence of the U.S. Supreme Court, *consideration of income* in a combined report or for purposes of formulary apportionment does not constitute taxation of the foreign corporation. For purposes of this discussion, taxation of income will include consideration of income.

In most circumstances, states tax the income of foreign country corporations on the same basis as they tax the income of corporations organized within their own boundaries or in other states of the United States. (It should be noted that state statutes may be worded either to tax income directly or to impose a tax measured by income. Legal differences may arise from this semantic difference, but they have no application for the purposes of this discussion.) These methods vary between states. Some states, in assessing tax, consider only the results of a single entity, while others use combined or consolidated reporting. There are numerous variations in state practices with respect to combined and consolidated reporting.

For corporations doing business within and outside of state boundaries, almost all states determine the income assignable to activities within their boundaries on the basis of an apportionment formula, or formulary accounting. The apportionment formula compares various activities of the business within and without the state to determine the percentage of the business conducted within the state. Under formulary accounting, the entire income is considered, and geographic assignment is made on the basis of the application of the apportionment formula to the entire income. Some states, however, may use separate accounting to determine the income attributable to activities within their state, either because it constitutes allocable, or "nonbusiness," income under the Uniform Division of Income for Tax Purposes Act (UDITPA) or because they believe separate accounting fairly reflects the results of activities within their state. Some, but not all, states use formulary accounting to assign income arising from activities within the United States and separate accounting to determine what portion of the income being considered is earned within and outside of the United States. With respect to foreign (country) corporations, the use of separate accounting is more likely to determine income from activities within the United States and, perhaps also, within the individual state.

Under the Constitution, a state may not tax a foreign (country) corporation unless that corporation has sufficient activities within the state to establish a taxable "nexus." Traditionally, nexus has required an actual physical presence in a jurisdiction. A physical presence can arise if the corporation owns property that is present in the state or has employees located in the state. The physical contact must generally be both purposeful and regular. An agent may also create nexus. The determination of what kind of contact can create nexus is continually evolving. The current view is that a physical contact with the state is unnecessary and that "economic presence" suffices. Under this view, all that is required is that the corporation purposefully, and with some regularity, avail itself of the market presented by the state. Nexus for consideration of activities, and the results of those activities, that occur outside the boundaries of a state is provided by the "unitary business principle." This principle requires that the activities outside of the boundaries of the state bear some rational relationship to the activities conducted within the state. This rational relationship entails more than controlling ownership.

In general, tax conventions between the United States and other countries do not apply to taxes imposed by subnational jurisdictions. An exception to this rule developed in the mid-1970s with respect to nondiscrimination clauses. Tax conventions negotiated and approved since that time make the nondiscrimination clause applicable to subnational taxes. In 1975, an effort was made in the renegotiation of the tax convention with the United Kingdom to include a provision that would have prohibited the states from including the activities of foreign-incorporated entities in a worldwide combined report. The U.S. Senate refused to ratify the tax convention with this provision, and it was withdrawn. The revised tax convention was subsequently approved by the U.S. Senate and the United Kingdom, and a protocol—the Third Protocol—was agreed upon to recognize this change. No subsequent efforts to include such a provision in a tax convention have been accepted by the United States.

Friendship, commerce, and navigation (FCN) treaties contain both general nondiscrimination provisions and general provisions regarding income taxation, which are applicable to both national and subnational (state) jurisdictions. (It is understood that the position of the U.S. Department of State is that the more specific tax conventions are controlling over the general FCN treaties.) It appears that the language of the FCN treaties is broad enough to encompass the permitted use of the worldwide combined report method by states, but the issue is controversial. The California Supreme Court has interpreted the language of FCN treaties to allow for the use of worldwide combined reporting [see *Barclays Bank International, Ltd.*, v. *Franchise Tax Board*, 2 Cal.4th 708 (1992)]. This may be an issue that the U.S. Supreme Court will ultimately be called upon to consider.

The tax base to which state income tax statutes are applied varies greatly. Many states define the income base under consideration by reference to the Internal Revenue Code. For those states, the taxation of foreign (country) corporations will normally mirror that of the Internal Revenue Service. Income determined under the rules of the Internal Revenue Code and U.S. tax conventions will be the base for state tax purposes. Rules of "permanent establishment" and "effectively connected" income will be applicable. These rules may be applied in either a separate entity context or a combined report context, depending upon the state. In either event, the likelihood is that no consideration will be given to the activities and income of a foreign (country) corporation that occur or are assigned outside of the United States for federal tax purposes.

Other states provide their own definitions of income. In those cases, the determination of income is made under individual-state law and the state chooses whether it will conform to the Internal Revenue Code's definition of U.S. source income and expenses, effectively connected income, and other limitations on the taxation of foreign (country) corporations. Some states, even though conforming to or adapting the Internal Revenue Code's definition of income, may nonetheless consider all of the income of a foreign (country) corporation that is doing business within their boundaries and use an apportionment formula to determine how much of the overall income is taxable by the state. The state of New York is an example [see *Bass, Ratcliff & Gretton, Ltd.*, v. *State Tax Commission*, 266 US 271, 69 Led 282 (1924), and *Reuters, Ltd.*, v. *State Tax Commission*, 82 NY2d 112, 623 NI2d 1145 (1993)].

The U.S. Supreme Court in *Barclays Bank PLC* v. *Franchise Tax Board*, 129 Led2d 244, 512 US 298 (1994), upheld the right of the states to use worldwide combined reporting and consider the income of foreign-incorporated entities that are part of a unitary business, regardless of whether the foreign entities were directly engaged in business within the state. Since 1986, however, virtually all states have adopted either an elective or a mandatory "water's edge" reporting requirement in which they generally consider only the income of U.S.-incorporated entities and the U.S. income, as determined under the Internal Revenue Code, of foreign incorporated entities that have a presence in the United States.

## Additional reading

McLure, Charles E., Jr. *The State Corporation Income Tax*. Palo Alto, Calif.: Hoover Press, Stanford University, 1984.

*Cross references:* apportionment; foreign corporations, federal taxation; nexus.

# Foreign tax credit

Donald J. Rousslang
Department of the Treasury

*A credit that allows U.S. residents (individuals and companies) to subtract foreign income taxes paid from the U.S. income tax due on income earned abroad.*

The U.S. foreign tax credit is simple in concept. The United States employs a global tax system and, under the residence principle, taxes the income earned abroad by its residents. This foreign source income generally is also subject to tax in the foreign country under the source principle. To avoid double taxation of the foreign source income, a credit is given for foreign income taxes. That is, the taxpayer is allowed to subtract the foreign income tax from the tentative U.S. tax on the income (the U.S. tax before any allowance for foreign income taxes) and is required to remit only the difference (the residual tax) to the U.S. Treasury. The credit for foreign income taxes is limited to the tentative U.S. tax: The U.S. Treasury does not give a refund when the foreign income tax exceeds the tentative U.S. tax.

Foreign taxes other than income taxes (such as property taxes, excise taxes, payroll taxes, or value-added taxes) are deducted in deriving the taxable foreign source income, rather than being credited against the U.S. tax. All foreign income taxes can be credited against the tentative U.S. tax, including income taxes levied by local governments below the national level, such as by a province in Canada or by a canton in Switzerland. In contrast, income taxes imposed by U.S. states cannot be credited against the federal income tax; instead, they are deducted in deriving the income subject to the federal tax.

## The corporate foreign tax credit

The foreign tax credit is available to individuals with foreign source income, including wages earned abroad, but the great bulk of foreign tax credits goes to U.S. corporations with operations abroad. U.S. corporations earn foreign source income by operating branches abroad and by operating or investing in affiliates incorporated abroad. If the foreign source income is earned through a foreign branch, it is subject to U.S. tax in the same tax year in which it is earned. The tentative U.S. tax is simply the U.S. tax rate times the income of the branch. A credit is given for foreign income taxes and for any foreign withholding taxes that are levied when the branch remits the income to the U.S. parent. Losses incurred by a foreign branch can be deducted from the corporation's domestic source income to reduce the corporation's U.S. income tax. In succeeding years, however, if the branch becomes profitable, its income is treated as U.S. source income and no foreign tax credit can be claimed on it until the U.S. Treasury recovers the reduction in tax revenue caused by the branch's initial losses.

If the foreign source income is earned through a foreign affiliate that is a separate company incorporated abroad, the income generally is subject to U.S. tax only when it is remitted as dividends to the U.S. parent corporation. The U.S. tax on unremitted earnings is thus deferred until the earnings are repatriated. This is advantageous to the corporation because of the benefits associated with deferral of tax.

To be eligible for a credit for foreign taxes on the affiliate's income, the U.S. parent must own at least 10 percent of the affiliate. A foreign affiliate that is separately incorporated abroad and that is at least 10 percent owned by the U.S. parent is called a foreign subsidiary. A subsidiary distributes dividends to the U.S. parent from earnings and profits after foreign income taxes. To determine the tentative U.S. tax and the foreign tax credit for the dividends, it is necessary to construct the underlying foreign source income from which the dividends were derived. The formula for the tentative U.S. tax

$(T_A)$ on the underlying foreign source income is $T_A = t_{US}D/(1 - t_F)$, where $D$ is dividends, $t_{US}$ is the U.S. tax, and $t_F$ is the foreign income tax rate used for purposes of calculating the foreign tax credit (foreign income taxes paid divided by the subsidiary's earnings and profits as measured using the U.S. definition of taxable income). From the tentative U.S. tax, the U.S. corporation subtracts the sum of the foreign income taxes paid on the income underlying the dividends plus the foreign withholding taxes on the dividends. If the difference is positive, the U.S. corporation owes a residual U.S. tax. If the difference is negative, the U.S. corporation is said to have excess foreign tax credits.

In general, the U.S. parent corporation is allowed to sum the foreign source income and foreign taxes from all of its foreign operations, both branches and subsidiaries, when calculating the foreign tax credit and the residual U.S. tax. To be lumped together, however, the foreign source income must be within the same category of income (or income "basket"), as defined by the Internal Revenue Code. The main income baskets are for passive income (primarily interest, dividends, royalties, rents, or annuities received by the subsidiary), financial services income (income earned in banking, insurance, or finance), shipping income (income earned in international shipping), and general limitation income (primarily income earned abroad in the active conduct of a trade or business other than financial services, shipping, or income in the passive basket). Income in each of these baskets is subject to a separate foreign tax credit limitation. The maximum foreign tax credit that can be claimed in any basket (the foreign tax credit limitation) is the tentative U.S. tax. Any excess credits can be applied to offset the residual U.S. tax on foreign source income earned during the previous two years or the following five years, but if the credits cannot be used within that period, they are lost.

The separate income baskets help discourage U.S. corporations from moving offshore some types of highly mobile investments (such as international shipping, financial services, and portfolio loans) that can easily be located in low-tax countries. Subpart F of the Internal Revenue Code denies deferral for income from such investments, but U.S. corporations might still have a tax incentive to locate these activities abroad if they were allowed to combine the income and foreign taxes from these investments with those from other, less mobile, business activities that often generate excess foreign tax credits. The separate income baskets remove this incentive.

The foreign tax credit offsets most of the U.S. tentative tax on foreign source income. For example, in 1990 (the latest year for which tax data are available), total taxable foreign source income of U.S. corporations was about $89.7 billion. Foreign taxes on this income (income taxes and withholding taxes) amounted to about $27.4 billion, of which about $25 billion was creditable against the tentative U.S. tax. The residual U.S. tax on the income was about $4.7 billion.

## Credit versus deductions for foreign taxes

Taxpayers prefer receiving a credit for foreign taxes rather than a deduction, even if the foreign tax rate exceeds the U.S. rate and they are unable to credit all of the foreign taxes they pay. A simple example shows why. Denote foreign source income as $Y$, the U.S. tax rate as $t_{US}$, and the foreign tax rate as $t_F$. With a deduction for foreign income taxes, the U.S. tax is $t_{US}(1 - t_F)Y$, whereas with a credit the residual U.S. tax is $(t_{US} - t_F)Y$. From these formulas, we see that if foreign income taxes are deducted, the rate of U.S. tax on the income would equal $t_{US}(1 - t_F)$, which always exceeds the rate of residual U.S. tax after the foreign tax credit, $(t_{US} - t_F)$. If $t_F$ is greater than $t_{US}$, there is no residual U.S. tax after the credit, but a U.S. tax payment would be required if the foreign income taxes were deducted.

## The foreign tax credit and economic efficiency

According to conventional wisdom, for a capital-exporting country (a country that invests more abroad than it receives as inward foreign investment), a deduction for foreign taxes promotes national neutrality and maximizes the domestic income, whereas a foreign tax credit promotes capital export neutrality and maximizes the global income. Early statements of the conventional wisdom can be found in Richman (1963), Musgrave (1969), and Feldstein and Hartman (1979) (among others). More recently, Feldstein (1994) has challenged the view that national neutrality maximizes the domestic income: he concludes that it might well be in the national interest to tax foreign source income more lightly than domestic income, particularly when the foreign investment is highly leveraged through borrowing in foreign credit markets.

## Additional readings

Feldstein, Martin. "Tax Rules and the Effect of Foreign Direct Investment on U.S. National Income." In *Taxing Multinational Corporations*, edited by Martin S. Feldstein, James R. Hines, Jr., and R. Glenn Hubbard. Washington, D.C.: National Bureau of Economic Research, 1994.

Feldstein, Martin, and David Hartman. "The Optimal Taxation of Foreign Source Investment Income." *The Quarterly Journal of Economics* 93 (November 1979): 613–29.

Musgrave, Peggy B. *United States Taxation of Foreign Investment Income: Issues and Arguments*. Cambridge, Mass.: The Law School of Harvard University, 1969.

Richman (Musgrave), Peggy B. *Taxation of Foreign Investment Income: An Economic Analysis*. Baltimore: Johns Hopkins Press, 1963.

*Cross references:* capital export neutrality; deferral of tax; national neutrality.

# Franchise/privilege tax, state

Matthew N. Murray
University of Tennessee

*Defines and describes special levies on the privilege of doing business.*

A franchise is a right or privilege officially granted by the state, and a franchise tax is a special levy on this privilege. The privilege may reflect the right to start a business, to expand a business, or to sustain business activities over time. In some instances, the franchise provides unique privileges beyond simply the opportunity to conduct business. One example is the monopoly franchise that grants exclusive access to markets, as with public utilities. Another example is the corporate franchise that treats the business entity as a legal person subject to limited liability. Because business privileges are granted by the state and supported directly or indirectly by public-sector activities, the franchise tax represents an early form of benefit taxation.

Many taxes under many different guises have sought to tax business privileges generally and the corporate privilege specifically. Examples include occupation and license taxes; capital stock taxes; property taxes; special levies on utilities, financial institutions, and insurance companies; intangibles taxes; severance taxes; excess profits taxes; and the corporate income tax. More narrowly, the franchise tax itself typically takes the form of onetime or recurrent taxes on the corporate business enterprise. The tax is either a flat annual fee or is based on some measure of asset values.

## Historical evolution

The modern franchise tax has its roots in the 19th century as corporations evolved in the new American states and efforts were made to tax the *corporate* privilege. The states took the lead because they, not the federal government, chartered corporations. The base of the tax was usually some measure of capital stock or asset holdings, under the premise that unique privileges afforded through the franchise would be capitalized into the value of the enterprise. Initially, use of the franchise tax was confined to specific industries (such as financial institutions) and its application was through the property tax. For example, in 1805 Georgia implemented a capital stock tax on banks, although it was effectively a property tax extended to include personal property holdings. New York state's capital stock levy on insurance companies, introduced in 1828, was also structured as a property tax (Seligman 1897: 136–143).

As the corporate entity expanded its reach in the American economy, the taxation of businesses and corporations expanded as well (see Seligman 1897). Pennsylvania laid the groundwork for the broad state taxation of all corporations in the mid-19th century, and by 1891 the Pennsylvania tax on corporations had evolved into a tax on capital stock. By the turn of the century, franchise taxes on corporate capital stock were common across the states.

In the early years of its application, the franchise tax was the subject of considerable controversy and litigation. A number of important court decisions were handed down that heavily influenced the structure of today's franchise tax. For example, the courts concluded that the tax is not a property tax, because the tax base may bear little resemblance to actual property values. One implication is that states may circumvent the uniformity provisions that must typically be extended to taxpayers under the general property tax. The courts have also concluded that the franchise tax is a tax on privilege. In practice, this ruling has allowed states to tax the out-of-state capital of domiciled firms without violating the Interstate Commerce Clause of the U.S. Constitution.

### The modern franchise tax

The modern franchise tax is a somewhat ambiguous and ill-defined concept. If one relies simply on nomenclature, there were 26 states in 1997 that imposed a tax on corporations categorized under the rubric of "franchise tax" (Commerce Clearing House 1996). However, this classification scheme lends itself to confusion and misinterpretation. For example, the broad-based corporate franchise taxes in California, Florida, and New York are not included in this count, presumably because the base of these taxes is corporate income. For those 26 states with a "franchise tax," the tax may take the form of one-time or recurrent registration fees or, more commonly, taxes on some measure of capital stock. But this omits the comparable one-time origination/qualification fees and annual (or biennial) registration fees imposed by virtually every other state.

In those instances where the franchise tax falls on some measure of capital stock, the base will include some combination of shares of outstanding stock, surplus, undivided profits, and indebtedness, together intended to capture the extent of privileges granted through the franchise. One unique feature of the tax is that the base may include federal securities otherwise afforded preferential treatment under the tax code, because the courts have ruled that the tax is a privilege tax and not a property tax.

Apportionment practices vary substantially across the states. Some states choose to apportion domestic capital of in-state firms, paralleling treatment under the corporate income tax, whereas other states tax the entire domestic capital stock of in-state firms. Foreign firms are treated somewhat differently and can be taxed only on their in-state capital stock.

The rate structure of franchise taxes on corporate capital varies substantially across the states, with most states imposing taxes in the range of $1 to $3 per $1,000 of capital (see Commerce Clearing House 1997). Differential rates for foreign and domestic capital are not uncommon. (Pennsylvania has a franchise tax on foreign capital and a separate capital stock tax on domestic capital.) There are complications in some states, as with Georgia's 24-band rate structure and the practice in Illinois of separately taxing the capital stock of new enterprises, additional stock issuances, and the outstanding stock of incumbent firms.

In most states, franchise taxes (including one-time and recurrent levies) provide only a modest contribution to overall collections (Commerce Clearing House 1992). An exception is Delaware, where franchise taxes were 15.7 percent of collections in 1991. Louisiana follows in a distant second place, with franchise taxes representing 5.7 percent of collections in the same year. In 1991, 10 states derived less than 1 percent of total receipts from the franchise tax.

### Additional readings

Commerce Clearing House, Inc. *State Tax Handbook 1992*. Chicago, 1992.

Commerce Clearing House, Inc. *State Tax Handbook 1997*. Chicago, 1996.

Commerce Clearing House, Inc. *State Tax Guide*. Chicago, 1997.

Pogue, Thomas F., editor. *State Taxation of Business: Issues and Options*. Westport, Conn.: Praeger, 1992.

Seligman, Edwin R.A. *Essays in Taxation*. New York: The MacMillan Company, 1897.

# Fringe benefits

Robert Turner
Colgate University

*A variety of forms of compensation that are not taxed.*

For the purposes of tax policy, the most useful definition of fringe benefits is voluntary employer expenditures on noncash forms of compensation. If taxes were paid on comprehensive income, the form in which employees receive compensation would not affect their taxation. Indeed, the Internal Revenue Code (Section 61) defines gross income as including "all income from whatever source derived" and specifically notes that "compensation for services" is part of gross income. However, many fringe benefits are excluded from taxable income. These exclusions have implications for efficiency and equity and represent some of the largest tax expenditures in the U.S. tax system, totaling more than $100 billion.

## History

The U.S. income tax has always excluded some forms of compensation from the individual income tax base, while employers have always been allowed to deduct the cost of fringe benefits as well as wages from their taxable incomes. Employer contributions for accident and health insurance plans were nontaxable in the original income tax in 1913, although there was some ambiguity about the tax status of fringe benefits until the Internal Revenue Code of 1954. Similarly, term life insurance premiums became tax-exempt in 1920 and deferred compensation plans received favorable tax status in 1921.

By the early 1980s, several other fringe benefits had received statutory exclusions: up to $5,000 of death benefits, parsonage allowances, certain benefits provided to members of the Armed Services, meals and lodging for the convenience of the employer, group legal services, commuting through van pools, dependent care assistance, and employee educational assistance. The statutes governing van pooling and educational assistance expired in the mid-1980s. Many other miscellaneous fringe benefits had always been untaxed even without statutory provisions; the Tax Reform Act of 1984 formalized the exclusions of any miscellaneous fringe benefits that meet one of five criteria: a no-additional-cost service, a qualified employee discount, a working-condition fringe, a de minimis fringe, or a qualified tuition reduction. Special rules were written for parking, eating, and on-site athletic facilities.

Beginning in the 1970s, employers began providing fringe benefits in the form of cafeteria or flexible benefit plans whereby employees could choose from a menu of several compensation options, including cash and several fringe benefits. These fringe benefits were made nontaxable in 1978. A related approach is the flexible spending plan, or salary reduction arrangement, which allows employees to set aside pretax dollars to spend on certain expenses (mostly health and child care) not covered by existing benefit plans.

Most of the statutory fringe benefits receive tax preferences only if provided in a nondiscriminatory manner, dating back to 1942, when nondiscrimination rules governing pensions were instituted. Other important limits are the $50,000 limit on the amount of term life insurance that can be provided tax-free to employees, the various restrictions and funding rules for pension and stock plans initiated by the Employee Retirement Income Security Act of 1974, and nondiscrimination and plan qualification rules for health and life insurance plans.

Fringe benefits as a share of total compensation were quite low until the three decades after World War II, when there was a rapid expansion. This expansion was caused by an increase in the number of fringe benefits offered as well as increased employer contributions to the traditional benefit plans. Rapid growth of fringe benefits as a form of compensation stopped around 1980.

The tax advantage to employees of receiving fringe benefits depends on marginal tax rates. Because most fringe benefits are excluded from the federal, state, and Social Security tax bases, the tax price of fringe benefits (that is, the amount of after-tax wages that would be given up for a dollar's worth of fringe benefits) is considerably less than $1. Since 1980, the tax price has risen slightly as federal and state marginal tax rates have fallen. Because higher-income taxpayers generally have higher marginal tax rates, they receive a greater advantage.

## Efficiency effects

Not taxing fringe benefits gives rise to a consumption inefficiency because the goods that are provided as fringe benefits are made cheaper by the tax code. In this respect, health insurance has received the most attention. Many economists believe that the tax preference encourages more comprehensive health insurance to be provided and contributes to rising health care costs as consumers are shielded from the direct costs of their medical care.

The tax preferences given pensions and other deferred compensation plans may have an effect on national saving, although the effect is ambiguous because the tax preferences *ceteris paribus* lead to a larger government budget deficit. In addition, other forms of private saving may be affected by the amount of saving done in the form of pensions.

Tax preferences for fringe benefits may also have important effects in labor markets. The cost of labor is reduced differentially across firms and individuals, because the tax benefits increase with higher marginal tax rates. This effect may differ across workers, and some firms have cost advantages over others. Moreover, if employee preferences for fringes vary with skill levels, firms that use the skills of workers with a stronger preference for fringe benefits disproportionately may have lower costs than firms using other skill levels.

Because fringe benefits are tied to jobs, when compensation is paid in the form of fringes, labor mobility may be reduced, although this has some good as well as bad effects. Some kinds of fringe benefits, notably pensions, can also affect the timing of retirement as well as quitting behavior.

The labor market effects of not taxing fringe benefits depend greatly on whether employees sort themselves into firms based on their differing demands for the fringe benefits. Because the nondiscrimination rules that accompany the tax breaks given to fringe benefits mean that employers cannot tailor their fringe benefit offerings to each of their employees' wishes, heterogeneous preferences for fringe benefits should lead to a sorting equilibrium where some firms offer generous fringe benefit packages and others offer few or no fringes. Some firms are also more likely to replace the part of their workforce that do not want fringes with independent contractors, leasing arrangements, and part-time workers in order to satisfy the nondiscrimination rules. If workers are not perfect substitutes for each other, this leads to production inefficiencies. Sorting also exacerbates the adverse selection problem accompanying some fringe benefits such as health insurance, because less healthy workers will tend to congregate in firms offering more generous health insurance packages.

The importance of the distortions caused by the tax preferences given to fringe benefits depends on three things: the incidence of the tax preferences, the extent of job sorting that takes place, and the size of the effect tax preferences have on the amount of fringe benefits offered. Investigation of all of these issues is hampered by data problems.

Economic theory strongly suggests that the incidence of fringe benefit costs, and thus the incidence of tax preferences as well, is borne by the workers. Most of the arguments made in public debate about fringe benefits, however, are clearly based on the presumption that employers bear the costs (and receive the tax benefits). Statistical evidence has been inconclusive, although more and more studies are finding significant tradeoffs between wages and a variety of fringe benefits (consistent with employee incidence).

Empirical evidence regarding whether workers sort into jobs on the basis of fringe benefit offerings is meager. There seems to be support, though, for the hypothesis that some sorting occurs.

The relationship between tax incentives and the provision of fringe benefits has been the subject of many studies, although the data problems outlined earlier plague this research as well. There is some evidence that favorable tax treatment has led to an increase in the number of employees who receive various kinds of fringe benefits. There is also agreement that the tax advantage from paying compensation in the form of fringes rather than wages affects the share of fringes in total compensation. The magnitude of this effect, however, is uncertain. The results of some studies imply that full taxation of fringe benefits would cut by half or more the share of compensation paid in the form of fringes. Other studies find much smaller effects, with the fringe share of compensation falling by less than 15 percent if benefits were taxed fully.

## Should fringe benefits be taxed?

Tax preferences are usually justified on the grounds of economic efficiency, equity (horizontal and vertical), or administrative efficiency.

Tax preferences for fringe benefits may improve economic efficiency if private markets lead to an underprovision of the fringes as a result of market failures. Indeed, there has been definite congressional intent to encourage the private provision of many of the goods typically provided as fringe benefits. Economists, however, seem more concerned with the distortions caused by the tax preferences than with the market failures they might correct.

Horizontal equity has received much attention in the debate about taxation of fringe benefits. A common argument is that tax subsidies for fringes are horizontally inequitable because two workers with identical total compensation will pay different amounts of tax if one receives more compensation as wages and the other more fringe benefits. But the disparity may be more apparent than real if workers choose their mix of wages and fringes by sorting themselves among employers who provide different ranges of fringe benefits.

The impact on vertical equity also depends on the incidence of the tax preferences. If employers are able to appropriate the benefits, few would argue that vertical equity is improved. If employees receive the benefits, the issue is whether more benefits are received by well-off taxpayers or poorer taxpayers. Because the tax savings resulting from the tax preferences increase with marginal tax rates, this by itself suggests that taxing fringe benefits would improve vertical equity. Evidence also suggests that well-paid employees are more likely to receive a higher fringe share of compensation than low-paid workers, although there is some evidence that moderate-income workers receive a higher fraction of their compensation as health insurance than do high-income workers.

There is also some evidence that low-income workers respond more to tax incentives than do high-income workers, so it could be that taxing fringe benefits would lead low-income workers to receive far fewer fringes while high-income workers would still receive them. This might have important social consequences if fringe benefits provide goods that society values and that the government would provide if private markets did not.

One reason that fringe benefits have been excluded from the tax base is concern over the administrative complexity for the government, employers, and employees of including the value of fringe benefits as part of taxable income. Part of this complexity is simply the paperwork; another important element is uncertainty about the proper valuation of the benefits. While the employee's willingness to pay for the fringe benefit is theoretically the best measure of value, employer cost is administratively much easier (although it may be difficult for firms to allocate their total costs to individual workers properly).

## Proposals to tax fringe benefits

Three kinds of reforms of the tax treatment of fringe benefits have been proposed: limits on the amount of benefits that can be received tax-free, tax credits for some percentage of the value of the fringes as a replacement for the tax exclusion of fringes, and employer-based taxes. All of these options would reduce the tax benefits from receiving compensation in the form of fringes rather than wages.

Limits, or caps, on the amount of benefits that can be received tax-free would tend to improve efficiency and vertical equity by eliminating the tax benefits of fringes received by high-income taxpayers while retaining the tax benefits for those who do not receive as much of their compensation in the form of fringes. Because of the way that life insurance and pension benefits are valued, older workers would be especially hard hit by these limits. Also, because the costs of providing identical fringe benefits may differ substantially by region and industry, a single limit for all taxpayers may not be optimal. If limits are placed on specific benefits, other benefits would likely be substituted for them. To avoid this kind of response, a limit on the overall amount of compensation provided as tax-free benefits is an attractive option. Replacing the exclusion of fringe benefits with a tax credit could also improve efficiency and vertical equity. The credit would work better for fringes that are currently entirely excluded from the tax base than for fringes such as pensions, whose tax benefits are based on deferral of taxation.

Taxing employers instead of workers would be administratively less costly while still somewhat reducing the tax benefits of fringe benefits.

## Conclusion

Many economists and tax experts think that some form of taxation of fringe benefits would be desirable. They believe that both efficiency and equity would be improved. Potentially large amounts of revenue could be raised, which could be used to finance new government spending, lower other taxes, or reduce the government budget deficit. Public opposition is strong, however, and there is no indication that any reform will be enacted soon.

## Additional readings

Burman, Leonard, and Jack Rodgers. "Tax Preferences and Employment-Based Health Insurance" *National Tax Journal* 45 (September 1992): 331–46.

Kosters, Marvin H., and Eugene Steuerle. "The Effect of Fringe Benefit Tax Policies on Labor and Consumer Markets." *Proceedings of the Seventy-Fourth Annual Conference on Taxation*. Columbus, Ohio: National Tax Association, 1981, pp. 86–92.

Macaulay, Hugh Holleman, Jr. *Fringe Benefits and Their Federal Tax Treatment.* New York: Columbia University Press, 1959.

Munnell, Alicia H. "It's Time to Tax Employee Benefits." *New England Economic Review* (July/August 1989): 49–63.

Scott, Frank A., Mark C. Berger, and Dan A. Black. "Effects of the Tax Treatment of Fringe Benefits on Labor Market Segmentation." *Industrial and Labor Relations Review* 42 (January 1989): 216–29.

Turner, Robert W. "Fringe Benefits: Should We Milk This Sacred Cow?" *National Tax Journal* 42 (September 1989): 293–300.

U.S. Congress, Congressional Budget Office. *The Tax Treatment of Employment-Based Health Insurance*. March 1994.

U.S. Congress, General Accounting Office. *Effects of Changing the Tax Treatment of Fringe Benefits*. April 1992.

U.S. Congress, Joint Committee on Taxation. "Description of Certain Bills and Discussion of Issues Relating to Section 89 Nondiscrimination Rules Applicable to Certain Employee Benefit Plans." May 1989.

U.S. Department of Labor, Bureau of Labor Statistics. *Employee Benefits Survey: An MLR Reader*. Bulletin 2362. June 1990.

White, Richard A. "Employee Preferences for Nontaxable Compensation Offered in a Cafeteria Compensation Plan: An Empirical Study" *The Accounting Review* 58 (July 1983): 539–61.

Woodbury, Stephen J., and Wei-Juang Huang. *The Tax Treatment of Fringe Benefits*. Kalamazoo, Mich.: W.E. Upjohn Institute for Employment Research, 1991.

Zax, Jeffrey S. "Fringe Benefits, Income Tax Exemptions, and Implicit Subsidies." *Journal of Public Economics* 37 (November 1988): 171–83.

*Cross references:* employee stock ownership plan; health expenditures, tax treatment; horizontal equity; pensions, tax treatment; profit-sharing plans; vertical equity.

# Fuel taxes, federal

Kenneth D. Simonson
U.S. Small Business Administration

*Taxes levied by the federal government on gasoline, diesel fuel, and a variety of special fuels.*

The federal government imposes taxes on gasoline, diesel fuel, and a variety of special fuels. Although collections amount to only about 2 percent of total federal receipts, fuel taxes play a significant role in numerous policy debates.

Federal fuel taxes are divided at specified rates among general revenues and trust funds dedicated to highways, mass transit, aviation, environmental cleanup, and recreation. In addition, in every Congress, proposals are made to alter fuel taxes for such purposes as energy conservation, clean air, and funding intercity passenger rail. However, proposals to increase fuel taxes always draw substantial opposition, and fuel taxes account for a smaller share of federal receipts in 1998 than when they were first enacted in 1932.

## History

Beginning with Oregon in 1919, every state enacted gasoline taxes ranging from 2 to 7 cents per gallon. The first federal fuel tax on highway fuels was adopted in June 1932, at a 1-cent-per-gallon rate, as a one-year tax to reduce the deficit. The tax brought in 8 percent of federal receipts in fiscal 1933. Temporary extensions were enacted eight times from 1933 to 1956, at rates of 1 to 2 cents per gallon.

The Federal Aid Highway Act of 1956 established the Interstate Highway System and also created the Highway Trust Fund as a way to ensure the system's financing. All fuel tax receipts, along with revenues from tire, truck and bus, and highway-use taxes, were transferred to the trust fund. Fuel taxes

were raised to 3 cents per gallon in 1956 and to 4 cents in 1959.

In 1982, the fuel tax was raised to 9 cents per gallon, of which 1 cent was placed in a new mass transit account within the Highway Trust Fund. In 1984, the diesel tax, which is paid mainly by trucks, was raised to 15 cents in exchange for reducing the maximum tax on heavy trucks. An additional tax of 0.1 cents per gallon, dedicated to the new Leaking Underground Storage Tank (LUST) Trust Fund, was added in 1986.

Use of fuel taxes for general revenues resumed in 1990 with the enactment of a deficit-reduction package that included a five-year, 5-cent-per-gallon tax, split equally between the general fund and the Highway Trust Fund. In the next round of budget legislation, in 1993, the 1990 tax was extended to 1999 and redirected, starting in October 1995, to the Highway Trust Fund. At the same time, a new, permanent, 4.3-cent general-fund tax was imposed. In 1997, all general-fund revenues were returned to the Highway Trust Fund and the LUST tax of 0.1 cent, which had expired at the end of 1995, was reinstated.

As of mid-1998, the tax is imposed at a rate of 18.4 cents per gallon for gasoline (24.4 cents for diesel fuel). Of that, 0.1 cents goes to the LUST Trust Fund and 2.86 cents in the Highway Trust Fund goes to the mass transit account. Numerous exemptions or reduced rates have been enacted for certain fuels (for instance, three lower rates for ethanol blends) or users (for instance, farm, state and local government, and bus uses).

## Nonhighway taxes

Several other types of users pay fuel taxes. A fuel tax on noncommercial aviation fuel goes into the Airport and Airway Trust Fund. The tax on fuel used by vessels in commercial waterway transportation is placed in an Inland Waterways Trust Fund. Taxes on motorboat fuels go into the Aquatic Resources Trust Fund and the Land and Water Conservation Fund. Taxes on gasoline used in small power-tool and recreational engines go into a wetlands restoration program. Taxes on domestic and imported crude oil and imported petroleum products go into the Hazardous Substance Superfund. Imported cargo, including crude oil and refined products, is taxed for the Harbor Maintenance Trust Fund.

## Administration

The gasoline tax has always been collected at the producer or importer level. Collection of the diesel fuel tax has varied, however. Diesel fuel is chemically identical to heating oil, which is tax-exempt. To avoid taxing residential and commercial heating-oil users, the diesel tax has been imposed at the retail (truck stop) or wholesale-distributor level. Concerns about widespread evasion by vendors selling untaxed heating oil to taxable users led Congress, in 1993, to move the collection point for diesel fuel to the producer level and to require that untaxed fuel be dyed at the time it leaves the producer's terminal.

Historically, the Internal Revenue Service (IRS) did not devote much staffing to excise tax administration. Since the early 1990s, however, the IRS has worked jointly with state fuel tax administrators and the Department of Justice to crack down on fuel tax evasion. Nevertheless, federal and state rules for reporting and paying fuel taxes and for claiming exemptions or refunds still differ, making the taxes relatively complex for both the government and the taxpayers.

## Pros and cons

Fuel taxes provide a relatively stable and predictable level of funds, because highway fuel use changes little from year to year. Fuel taxes provide a simple, easily collected, although imprecise, measure of highway usage. These attributes make fuel taxes popular as one source of highway funding. Fuel taxes for other trust funds also serve in varying degrees as user fees that collect revenue from those who benefit from the expenditures that the taxes finance.

Advocates of fuel taxes for other purposes cite a variety of arguments. Some point to the fact that fuel taxes are broadly spread: Every consumer pays fuel taxes, explicitly when buying gasoline and implicitly as part of the cost of trucking goods. Some refer to the far higher rates of fuel tax in most industrialized countries as justification. Some say higher fuel taxes are warranted to pay for costs of importing and burning oil that are not reflected in the market price. These costs include defense outlays to ensure that the United States has secure sources of foreign oil, expenditures to fill and maintain the Strategic Petroleum Reserve, and costs of air pollution. A related argument for higher fuel taxes is to encourage development of renewable, domestic, or less-polluting fuel sources.

On the other side, some criticize fuel taxes for distorting market prices and causing producers and consumers to allocate personal and business spending inefficiently. Some oppose the gasoline tax because it is regressive; that is, lower-income families spend a higher percentage of income on the tax than do wealthier families. The tax also falls unevenly by location, occupation, and family size. Specifically, rural families, individuals who must use a vehicle in their jobs, and large families tend to spend more on gasoline than other families of the same income level, creating horizontal inequities. Some say that taxing only fuel is not an efficient or fair way to achieve environmental or national defense goals, which they feel should be addressed through taxes on all oil, all energy, general revenue sources, and/or through nontax means.

## Additional readings

Furchtgott-Roth, Diana. *The Measurement of Regressivity: The Case of the Motor Fuels Tax*. Discussion Paper 63. Washington, D.C.: American Petroleum Institute, December 1990.

Institute for Research on the Economics of Taxation. *The Impact, Shifting, and Incidence of an Increase in the Gasoline Excise Tax*. Washington, D.C., July 25, 1991.

Noto, Nonna A., and Louis Alan Talley. *Excise Tax Financing of Federal Trust Funds*. Report 93-6 E. Washington, D.C.: The Library of Congress, Congressional Research Service, January 5, 1993.

Poterba, James M. "Lifetime Incidence and the Distributional Burden of Excise Taxes." *American Economics Association Papers and Proceedings* 79 (May 1989): 325–30.

Talley, Louis Alan. *Federal Excise Taxes on Gasoline and the Highway Trust Fund: A Short History*. Report 97-853 E. Washington, D.C.: U.S, Library of Congress, Congressional Research Service, September 15, 1997.

U.S. Congress, Congressional Budget Office. *Federal Taxation of Tobacco, Alcoholic Beverages, and Motor Fuels*. August 1990.

*Cross references:* benefit principle; environmental taxes, federal; Highway Trust Fund, federal; user charges, federal.

# G

# Gaming taxation, state

Claude Louishomme
Donald Phares
University of Missouri—St. Louis

*State taxation of legalized gambling.*

## The context of gaming

Casino gaming has become a nationwide phenomenon in a relatively short time. In 1988, gaming existed in only two states: Nevada and New Jersey. By 1996, 22 states had Native American Indian casinos and 10 had non-Indian casinos. Expansion was driven by the gaming industry, changing attitudes toward gaming, and the search by states and localities for new revenues in an era of shrinking federal aid and growing citizen resistance to tax increases.

The enactment of the Indian Gaming Regulatory Act (IGRA) in 1988 marks a pivotal point in casino expansion. The IGRA was passed to bring economic development to the Indian nations. But the success of Indian casinos, such as Foxwoods in Connecticut, was not lost on the states. Several quickly moved to tap this source of new investment, jobs, and revenue. South Dakota was first, when it allowed limited stakes casinos in 1989. Colorado, Illinois, and Iowa followed in 1991. But Iowa and Illinois took a new approach with riverboat casinos, launched by Iowa in 1991 and beginning a trend. Riverboat casinos became operational in Mississippi in 1992, Louisiana in 1993, Missouri in 1994, and Indiana in 1995.

The expansion of locations where people can visit a casino marks a dramatic departure from the past. Nevada enjoyed a 45-year monopoly from 1931 until 1976, when a casino opened in Atlantic City. With the opening of casinos in seven states since 1989, the geography of the gaming industry has changed dramatically. The most recent successful drive occurred in Michigan when voters approved casinos for Detroit in 1997.

### Focus of this analysis

Ten states had non-Indian casinos operational in 1996; they are the focus here. Although each Indian tribe negotiates an agreement with a state, and an agreed-upon payment, Indian casinos are not taxed and are not required to report annual receipts, admissions, or other gaming statistics. Such data were compiled for this report, however, for the 10 states with non-Indian casinos.

### Gaming taxes and fees

States assess an assortment of taxes and fees on casino operations and patrons. In many instances, the locality in which a casino is located assesses additional taxes and fees. This analysis focuses primarily on statewide characteristics. These include the gaming tax rate and the tax on gaming revenues; other taxes and fees include device fees, application and annual license fees, and admission fees.

### Gaming tax rates

State gaming tax rates are assessed at either a fixed or a sliding rate, increasing with the amount taxed. Gaming tax rates are assessed on either the gross receipts (GR) or the adjusted gross receipts (AGR). The AGR is calculated by subtracting the winnings paid to patrons from gross receipts. States that tax at a fixed rate are Illinois (20% of AGR), Indiana (20% of AGR), Louisiana (18.5% of AGR), Missouri (20% of AGR), New Jersey (8% of GR), and South Dakota (8% of AGR).

States that tax on a sliding scale are Colorado, Iowa, Mississippi, and Nevada. In 1996, Colorado taxed the first $2 million of AGR at 2 percent, $2 to $4 million at 4 percent, $4 to $5 million at 14 percent, $5 to $10 million at 18 percent, and over $10 million at 20 percent. Colorado's rate structure clearly is geared toward smaller venues. Iowa taxes are set at 5 percent up to $1 million of AGR, 10 percent between $1 and $3 million, and 20 percent over $3 million. Mississippi's gaming tax has three rates and is applied to monthly gross revenues (MGR); casinos pay 4 percent on the first $50,000, 6 percent on the next $84,000, and 8 percent over $134,000. Nevada also bases its tax on MGR: 3 percent on the first $50,000, 4 percent on the next $84,000, and an additional 6.25 percent over $134,000.

### Other taxes and fees

In addition to the gaming tax that each of the 10 states with casinos assesses, they all subject these businesses to other taxes and fees such as device fees, annual licensing fees, and enforcement fees. States with gaming device fees are Colorado ($75 per slot and table), Mississippi (fees on slots and tables), Nevada (restricted and unrestricted slot flat fees, nonrestricted slot flat fees, nonrestricted game flat fees, annual slot tax, and fees on games), New

Jersey ($500 per year per slot machine), and South Dakota ($2,000 annual fee per device).

Three states have annual licensing fees: Iowa ($1,000), Louisiana ($100,000), and Mississippi ($5,000). In addition, Iowa and Missouri pass enforcement costs directly to the individual casinos. In Missouri, this is estimated to cost at least $600,000 per year per boat. New Jersey also has an additional 1.25 percent "alternative investment tax" on gross revenues.

### Admission fees

Four states with casinos charge an admission fee, four have no fee, and one (Louisiana) allows it as a local option. The four states with an admission fee are Illinois ($2), Indiana ($3), Iowa ($5,666 per week per boat), and Missouri ($2). States with no admission fees are Colorado, Mississippi, Nevada, and South Dakota. Louisiana allows local jurisdictions the option of charging a fee between $2.50 and $3.50.

As can be seen from this summary, states use a number of taxing instruments to derive revenues from casinos, but the casinos seem more than willing to incur these costs as a condition of doing business. The goal of the states in assessing these various taxes and fees is to generate revenue.

## Gaming revenues

### Gaming tax revenues

The main source of gaming revenues in 1996 was the gaming tax. This is applied to the house winnings, calculated either as GR or as AGR from all gaming. In 1996, gaming tax revenues totaled $1.86 billion. The four states with admission fees collected an additional $133 million. State gaming revenues totaled $1.99 billion in 1996.

In 1996, the 10 states with casino gaming collected a total of $1.8 billion in gaming tax revenues. Nevada led with $566 million. New Jersey was a distant second with $340 million. Illinois was third with $226 million. Then followed Louisiana with $216 million, Mississippi with $149 million, and Missouri with $114 million. The last four states each had gaming tax revenues of less than $100 million: Indiana ($75 million), Iowa ($70 million), Colorado ($59 million), and South Dakota ($45 million).

### Admission fee revenues

The four states with admission fees collected $132.4 million in admissions fees in 1996: Missouri $51 million, Illinois $50 million, Indiana $29 million, and Iowa $2.4 million.

Admission fee revenues constituted a significant portion of gaming tax revenues for three of the four states with these fees. In Missouri, for example, admission fee revenues represented 45 percent of gaming tax revenues and 31 percent of total state gaming revenues. In Illinois, admissions fees represented 22.3 percent of gaming tax revenues and 18.2 percent of total state gaming revenues. The comparable figures for Indiana were 38.9 percent and 28.0 percent. The figures for Iowa were 3.4 percent and 3.2 percent. The relatively low contribution of the Iowa admission fee is a function of how it is assessed. Whereas the other states assess per admission, Iowa assesses $5 annually per passenger.

### Total gaming tax revenues for 1996

Total state gaming revenue for 1996 was $1.99 billion. Not surprisingly, the two oldest gaming states, Nevada and New Jersey, were the largest revenue producers. Nevada led with 28.4 percent of the total, followed by Atlantic City at 17 percent. What is interesting is how quickly several new entrants into the gaming industry captured substantial shares of this expanding market. For example, Illinois generated 14 percent of the total and Louisiana 11 percent. Missouri (8.3%), Mississippi (7.5%), and Indiana (5.2%) also made impressive showings. Iowa, which was the state that started the riverboat casino movement in 1991, generated 3.6 percent. Not surprisingly, the states with limited stakes gaming, Colorado and South Dakota, generated only 2.9 percent and 2.2 percent, respectively.

## State general revenues and gaming revenues

Clearly, gaming has contributed significant amounts of revenue to state coffers. However, to get a clearer picture of the relative contribution of casino gaming to the fiscal health of state governments, we must look at revenues generated by this industry in terms of state revenue. We used data from the *1996 State Government Finances* and calculated "own-source" revenue by netting out intergovernmental, liquor store, and insurance trust revenues. Gaming revenues represent approximately 17 percent of own-source revenues in Nevada; next is South Dakota at 4 percent, Mississippi and Louisiana at 3 percent, Missouri and New Jersey at 2 percent, and all of the rest at 1 percent. Thus, while a total of almost $2 billion is raised, the fiscal impact is significant in only a few states. For all 10 states combined it is 2 percent.

## Uses of state gaming revenues

States use their gaming revenues in a variety of ways. Illinois and Missouri dedicate gaming proceeds to education. Indiana dedicates its revenues to infrastructure. Five states dedicate at least a portion of their revenues to specific areas. Nearly half of Colorado's gaming revenues go into general revenue. The rest is dedicated to tourism (0.2%), the State Historical Society (28%), the counties in which casinos are located (12%), and the casino cities (10%).

Tax receipts in Iowa are distributed in the following manner: 0.5 percent each to the city and county in which a casino is located, 0.3 percent to gambling treatment, and the balance to the general fund. In Louisiana, casinos are taxed at 18.5 percent of AGR. The gaming control board receives 0.5 percent, the state police gets 3 percent for enforcement, and the balance (15%) goes to the general fund. Mississippi divides its gaming receipts between a bond sinking fund (25%) and general revenue (75%). South Dakota dedicates 40 percent of it gaming revenues to tourism, 10 percent to Lawrence County, and 50 percent to a commission fund.

Gaming revenues in the two remaining states, Nevada and New Jersey, are not dedicated. Nevada revenues go into the general fund. In New Jersey, the governor and the state legislature decide how funds are to be allocated. For example, in 1996, the major programs funded by casino revenues in New Jersey were social services to the elderly such as pharmaceutical aid, energy assistance, a property tax reduction, residential care, and transportation assistance.

## Conclusion

Casino gaming has become readily available in many parts of the country. The phenomenon has swept the nation in less than a decade. Although the momentum for further expansion of the industry has slowed considerably, states that allow casino gaming have attached a number of taxes and fees to this industry and thus secured significant tax revenues, collectively some $2 billion in 1996. Gaming revenues are likely to continue to grow.

### Additional readings

Ebel, Robert D., editor. *A Fiscal Agenda for Nevada.* Reno: University of Nevada Press, 1990.

Gold, Steven D. "Casinos Are No Panacea for Ailing State Budgets." In *Casino Development: How Casinos Affect New England's Economy*. Proceedings of the Federal Reserve Bank of Boston Symposium, edited by Robert Tannenwald. Boston, Mass.: Federal Reserve Bank of Boston, 1995.

Goodman, Robert. *Legalized Gambling as a Strategy for Economic Development*. Northhampton, Mass.: United States Gambling Study, 1995.

Leven, Charles, Donald G. Phares, and Claude Louishomme. *The Economic Impact of Casino Gaming in Missouri*. St. Louis: Leven & Phares Associates, 1997.

Madhusudhan, Ranjana. "Betting on Casino Revenues; Lessons from State Experiences." *National Tax Journal* 49 (1996): 401–12.

U.S. Department of Commerce. Bureau of the Census. *State Government Finances*, various years.

*Cross references:* destination principle; earmarking of taxes; origin principle; retail sales tax; tax exportation.

# GATT

John H. Mutti
Grinnell College

*An acronym for the General Agreement on Tariffs and Trade.*

This organization was founded by a multilateral treaty negotiated in 1947 that established general rules to govern international trade. As a result of the eighth round of GATT negotiations concluded in 1993, the Uruguay Round, the GATT is now part of the World Trade Organization (WTO). The WTO is an umbrella organization that oversees multilateral trade rules, negotiating procedures, and dispute resolution mechanisms in several areas, including trade in goods, trade in services (the General Agreement on Trade in Services, or GATS), investment measures, and protection of intellectual property. A noteworthy achievement of the GATT is the substantial reduction in tariffs from the very high levels reached in the 1930s. Although the agreement deals primarily with trade relations, tariffs are not the only tax instruments or government fiscal policies treated by the GATT, and several GATT provisions and procedures are applicable to traditional public finance issues.

A fundamental principle of the GATT is that trade barriers be applied on a most-favored-nation (mfn) basis: The most favorable trade conditions offered to one country must be extended to all other signatories. The multilateral approach contrasts with the bilateral focus of international tax treaties. The mfn provision undoubtedly contributed to a more rapid reduction in trade barriers than would have occurred under strictly bilateral negotiations. The mfn provision also gives a country the opportunity to free-ride on the concessions of other countries without making its own reciprocal concessions. A country that fails to make meaningful offers, however, is unlikely to find that other signatories address items of greatest interest to it. Developing countries view this as a weakness of the GATT structure, and many countries who pursued inward-oriented development strategies felt no urgency in joining the GATT. For example, Mexico and Venezuela only acceded to the agreement in the 1980s. Because of many difficult issues raised by trade with nonmarket economies, China and Russia had not become members as of 1997.

An implicit goal of the GATT founders was to reduce tariffs while discouraging the use of other restrictive practices. Countries bind tariffs at existing rates and negotiate gradual reductions in them. If a government subsequently raises a bound tariff, other signatories may demand compensation through concessions on other goods, or retaliate by raising their own tariffs. With respect to other practices, such as quotas or discriminatory border treatment, the GATT attempts to prohibit or limit their use. More generally, it seeks to move to a system of transparent and predictable rules and away from the arbitrary and inconsistent application of discretionary standards. As tariff reductions have been achieved, these latter issues have become increasingly important.

Another important rationale behind GATT norms is the principle of national treatment. Once foreign goods enter a country and clear customs, they must be treated no worse than domestically produced goods. An explicit intent of this provision is to keep discriminatory domestic taxes and regulations from protecting domestic producers, because those measures otherwise could offset tariff concessions.

As GATT negotiations in the 1970s and 1980s came to include a wider set of domestic economic policies, the principle of national treatment played a central role. Exceptions to this principle initially allowed governments to determine appropriate domestic production subsidies, technical standards, and government procurement practices. While some limitations in these areas were established in the Tokyo Round concluded in 1979, the Uruguay Round concluded in 1993 went much further in clarifying acceptable practices in these areas. That round also addressed new concerns by expanding the basic framework for trade in goods to include trade in services, intellectual property protection, and trade-related investment measures.

An important distinction exists over the way a wider agenda was addressed in the Tokyo Round versus the Uruguay Round. In the Tokyo Round negotiations, the new items were treated in codes, and the provisions applied only between nations that signed the codes. Countries could pick and choose which items to sign, based on the expected benefits to them and the expected costs of accepting more limitations on their national policies. Most signatories were developed countries. In the Uruguay Round, new items were treated on an mfn basis, and countries who signed the agreement were to regard it as a single package of benefits and com-

mitments. Developing countries participated much more actively in this round of negotiations, which dealt with items such as agriculture and textiles that had previously escaped much GATT discipline.

An important GATT provision regarding taxes governs border tax adjustments that apply to products traded internationally. Production taxes on exports can be rebated, and production taxes faced by domestic producers can be imposed on imports. Because value-added taxes are regarded as taxes on products, they qualify for this border tax adjustment, whereas corporate income taxes do not. Although this distinction may rest on an incomplete analysis of the differential incidence of these taxes, it remains the basis for border tax adjustments, and rebating corporate income taxes constitutes a prohibited export subsidy.

A U.S. tax benefit for export income adopted in 1971 (Domestic International Sales Corporation [DISC] legislation) was subsequently found to be incompatible with GATT standards. This controversy provides a historical example of a further contentious aspect of GATT operations: the settlement of disputes. When a country brings a complaint against another contracting party, a panel of three to five impartial experts is appointed to evaluate whether the practice violates GATT standards. Previously, the panel report had to be accepted unanimously by the contracting parties. A country against whom the panel ruled could still block adoption of the panel report. For example, when U.S. practices under DISC were found to be incompatible with the GATT, panels also ruled that French and Belgian treatment of export income violated the GATT, but the latter two reports were not adopted. Even when reports are adopted, countries may be extremely slow to make their practices GATT-compatible. An important reform under the WTO is that a country can no longer unilaterally block a panel report, and a country that refuses to modify its practices may face retaliation on items covered by any WTO agreement.

A significant issue at the close of the 20th century is whether regional trade blocs or unilateral action by large countries will undermine the multilateral trading system promoted by GATT. Regional groups may have the positive effect of promoting greater concessions among members and may also create pressures to harmonize taxes and other aspects of fiscal policies. Small countries, however, are particularly vulnerable to a shift away from an mfn-based system.

### Additional readings

Jackson, John Howard. *The World Trading System*. Cambridge, Mass.: MIT Press, 1989.

Preeg, Ernest. *Traders and Diplomats*. Washington, D.C.: The Brookings Institution, 1970.

*Cross reference:* border tax adjustments.

# General-equilibrium models

Charles L. Ballard
Michigan State University

*Models that explicitly incorporate the interactions among markets, making them well-suited to studying the incidence and excess burden of taxes.*

Until the early 1960s, partial-equilibrium models (which look at a single market in isolation) were used in the vast bulk of research in the economics of taxation. A partial-equilibrium analysis usually begins by specifying a market supply curve and a market demand curve for the commodity in question. Taxes are then introduced, and this leads to changes in the equilibrium quantity and prices. These changes can be used to assess the incidence of taxes, as well as their efficiency effects.

In some cases, partial-equilibrium models pose few problems. This is especially true in the case of a tax on a relatively unimportant commodity, which would not be expected to have many effects on other markets. For example, a tax on hubcaps would probably have relatively minor general-equilibrium effects on other markets, such as those for steel, metalworkers, and automobiles. If the interactions with other markets are fairly small, it may be acceptable to ignore them by using a partial-equilibrium analysis. However, many of the most important tax policy questions of the last generation have dealt with taxes that have very substantial effects on other markets.

The shortcomings of partial-equilibrium models have been recognized for years. Authors such as Harry G. Brown (1939) and Richard Musgrave (1959) emphasized that taxes have effects on factor incomes, as well as on product prices. In 1955, Paul Wells presented a general-equilibrium analysis in diagrammatic form. However, these contributions lacked the precise mathematical basis necessary for quantitative answers to general-equilibrium questions.

**The Harberger model and its descendants**

An article by Arnold Harberger (1962) was a landmark for its rigorous, quantitative, general-equilibrium analysis of a tax policy question. Har-

berger's study focused on the corporation income tax in the United States, using a model with two sectors (corporate and noncorporate) and two factors of production (capital and labor). Although two-sector models of this type had not been used previously in public finance, they had a rich history in studies of international trade (Johnson 1971). In addition to building on the work of international-trade economists, another reason for using a two-sector model is that Harberger's methodology produces systems of equations that become extremely cumbersome when more than two sectors are studied. Unfortunately, the two-sector assumption forces Harberger to ignore much of the sectoral detail of the real economy.

The Harberger model assumes that the aggregate supplies of capital and labor are fixed. The model encompasses a time frame that is long enough to allow the capital stock to be reallocated from the corporate to the noncorporate sector. However, it does not allow us to study issues of long-run capital accumulation. In addition, Harberger's model is based on the techniques of differential calculus, so that the results are only strictly correct for small changes in tax rates.

Like any true general-equilibrium model, Harberger's model specifies the structure of consumer demand and the structure of production. The specifications yield a system of equations in variables such as the changes in the prices of corporate and noncorporate output, the changes in the prices of capital and labor, the changes in the amounts of capital and labor used in each sector, and the changes in sector output. Harberger solves the equations of the model using U.S. data for 1953–1959.

Harberger's most important conclusion was that capital bears approximately 100 percent of the burden of the corporate tax. The tax burden is borne both by the capital in the corporate sector *and* by capital in the noncorporate sector. This is because the total stock of capital is reallocated, until the net-of-tax returns are equalized in the two sectors. This can only occur if there is a decrease in the net-of-tax return to capital in the noncorporate sector. Clearly, this result could only have come from a general-equilibrium analysis.

Harberger finds the result regarding the incidence of the corporate tax to be quite robust. Different combinations of parameters generally give fairly similar results. After the appearance of Harberger's article, the model was extended and applied in a number of ways. Charles McLure (1969) extended the model to include more than one region, and Peter Mieszkowski (1972) emphasized the general-equilibrium effects of the property tax on capital prices. Michael Boskin (1975) estimated the annual welfare cost of the nontaxation of household activity to be at least $20 billion. These extensions and applications are summarized in McLure (1975).

## Computational general-equilibrium models

There was clearly a need for models that could easily incorporate large numbers of sectors. The models that arose to meet this need came in two rather different forms. The first was developed by Leif Johansen (1960) in a model for Norway. The Johansen approach is based on input-output analysis. Johansen-type models employ the techniques of matrix algebra to solve a system of linearized equations. This approach has achieved its greatest popularity in Australia, with the ORANI model and its descendants (Dixon et al. 1982). The Australian research effort has focused more on international trade and industrial policy issues than on taxation. However, tax policy issues have also been addressed (McDougall 1993).

By the late 1960s, Herbert Scarf (1973) had developed an algorithm that is guaranteed to calculate a general equilibrium for an economy with any number of producers and consumers. Scarf's model avoids the small-change assumption of the Harberger model, as well as the linearization assumption of Johansen-type models. Studies using the methods of Johansen or Scarf are called computational general equilibrium (CGE) analyses. Although Harberger-type models are still used, their popularity has gradually diminished, as CGE models have come into wider use.

The first major application of Scarf's methods in the area of taxation was by John Shoven and John Whalley (1972). In a reexamination of the corporate tax, Shoven (1976) found that a CGE model gave results similar to those of Harberger, for the two-sector model. However, when Shoven extended the CGE calculations to a 12-sector model, he found that the estimated efficiency cost of the corporation income tax was increased by about 40 percent. This indicates that the incorporation of more sectoral detail can have important effects on the results of a general-equilibrium simulation exercise. According to these CGE calculations, the ratio of excess burden to revenue for the corporation tax could be as great as 24 percent.

Even Shoven's calculations probably understate the efficiency cost of the corporate tax, because they (like Harberger's calculations) ignore the dynamic effects on capital accumulation. In the decade following Shoven's article, CGE modelers turned more of their attention to dynamic issues. Shoven, Whalley, and their colleagues eventually constructed a 19-sector model of the U.S. economy and tax system. This model calculates dynamic sequences of equilibria, using a repeated two-period structure. It allows researchers to study the effects of taxes on capital accumulation (Ballard et al. 1985). Among other

tax policy questions, Ballard, Fullerton, Shoven, and Whalley (BFSW) studied the integration of the corporate and personal income taxes. The model yielded the result that, in the long run, a significant portion of the corporation tax can be borne by labor. This is because the tax reduces the rate of capital accumulation. In the long run, this reduces the capital/labor ratio, and causes wages to be lower than they would otherwise have been.

One significant criticism of the general-equilibrium calculations of Harberger and of BFSW is that they assume that marginal capital tax rates and average capital tax rates are the same. The advantage of this approach is that it allows the researcher to "calibrate" the model precisely. Simulations performed with the model will precisely replicate the actual tax revenue observed in the economy. The problem is that this approach makes it very difficult to study separately the influences of different types of capital tax. In order to address this problem, many recent studies employ the cost-of-capital approach to the study of capital taxation. Working with a number of colleagues, Dale Jorgenson has developed a family of CGE models, some of which have more than 30 sectors (Jorgenson and Yun 1990). Marginal effective tax rates on capital are calculated for each sector, using the cost-of-capital approach. In addition, Jorgenson's models employ a flexible production structure that has proven especially useful for the investigation of energy taxes (Hudson and Jorgenson 1975).

Jorgenson and Yun (1990) find that tax reforms could lead to very substantial welfare gains. Some of the greatest potential gains come from indexation of the income tax base, and from incorporating the income of household assets into the tax base. According to Jorgenson and Yun, some tax reform proposals are associated with long-run gains of more than 10 percent of national wealth. This contrasts with welfare gains of 1 or 2 percent of wealth in the BFSW model. The difference may be explained in part by the difference in the dynamic specification. Jorgenson and Yun use a single, infinite-lived consumer. This specification leads to very large savings responses in the model. Consequently, the gains from dynamic tax policy changes may be overstated.

None of the studies mentioned so far allows us to consider the effects of tax policy changes on people of different ages. Alan Auerbach and Laurence Kotlikoff (1987) assess these effects using a general-equilibrium model. At any given time, the model includes 55 overlapping generations of life-cycle consumers. Over time, these consumers grow old and die, and new consumers are born. Auerbach and Kotlikoff use their model to study a wide variety of tax policy issues, including deficit finance, generational accounting, and Social Security. One of their most important insights has to do with the gains from moving toward a consumption tax. Under certain conditions, the long-run gains can be very large. However, a significant part of the long-run gain is merely a transfer from those who are old at the time of the policy change. The elderly are made worse off when we shift from an income tax to a consumption tax, because the consumption tax punishes dissaving, which is more likely to occur near the end of life.

Over the past two decades, there have been vast improvements in the speed of computers, and in the speed of the computational algorithms that are used for CGE models. As the computational techniques have become faster and more accessible, there has been an explosion in the number of studies using CGE models. Because of the flexibility of the approach, virtually any topic can be studied. Don Fullerton (1982) investigated revenue elasticities and the "Laffer Curve." He found that broad-based taxes in the United States are extremely unlikely to produce perverse revenue effects whereby increases in tax rates would lead to decreases in tax revenues. A study of environmental taxes (Ballard and Medema 1993) quantified the dramatic efficiency advantage of pollution taxes, relative to other sources of revenue. General-equilibrium modelers have also studied the interaction between taxes and the financial system (Slemrod 1983, and Galper et al. 1988). CGE models have also been used to consider the value-added tax (Ballard et al. 1987), marginal welfare costs for different capital taxes (Fullerton and Henderson 1989), and taxes and the housing market (Goulder 1989).

With the exception of the ORANI model in Australia, almost all of the studies mentioned above have dealt with aspects of the U.S. tax system, with rather little attention to international issues. However, studies such as those of Whalley (1980) and Laurence Goulder and Barry Eichengreen (1989) have focused on the interactions between the tax system and the international economy. Researchers have also applied CGE techniques to tax policy questions in a number of other countries, including Belgium (Dewatripont et al. 1991), Mexico (Serra-Puche 1984), the Philippines (Clarete and Whalley 1988), Sweden (Bergman and Lundgren 1990), and the United Kingdom (Piggott and Whalley 1985).

## Additional readings

Auerbach, Alan J., and Laurence J. Kotlikoff. *Dynamic Fiscal Policy*. Cambridge, U.K.: Cambridge University Press, 1987.

Ballard, Charles L., and Steven G. Medema. "The Marginal Efficiency Effects of Taxes and Subsidies in the Presence of Externalities: A Computational General Equilibrium Approach." *Journal of Public Economics* 52 (September 1993): 199–216.

Ballard, Charles L., John Karl Scholz, and John B. Shoven. "The Value-Added Tax: A General Equilibrium Look at Its Efficiency and Incidence." In *The Effects of Taxation on Capital Formation*, edited by Martin Feldstein. Chicago: University of Chicago Press, 1987.

Ballard, Charles L., Don Fullerton, John B. Shoven, and John Whalley. *A General Equilibrium Model for Tax Policy Evaluation*. Chicago: University of Chicago Press, 1985.

Bergman, Lars, and Stefan Lundgren. "General Equilibrium Approaches to Energy Policy Analysis in Sweden." In *General Equilibrium Modeling and Economic Policy Analysis*, edited by Lars Bergman, Dale Jorgenson, and Erno Zalai. Cambridge, Mass.: Basil Blackwell, Inc., 1990.

Boskin, Michael J. "Efficiency Aspects of the Differential Tax Treatment of Market and Household Economic Activity." *Journal of Public Economics* 4 (February 1975): 1–25.

Brown, Harry G. "The Incidence of a General Output or a General Sales Tax." *Journal of Political Economy* 47 (April 1939): 254–62.

Clarete, Ramon, and John Whalley. "Interactions between Trade Policies and Domestic Distortions in a Small Open Developing Country." *Journal of International Economics* 24 (May 1988): 345–58.

Dewatripont, C., Simon Erlich, Victor Ginsburgh, and Denise Van Regemorter. "The Effects on Unemployment of Reducing Social Security Contributions: A General Equilibrium Analysis for Belgium." In *Applied General Equilibrium Modeling*, edited by Henk Don, Theo van de Klundert, and Jarig van Sinderen. Dordrecht, Netherlands: Kluwer Academic Publishers, 1991.

Dixon, Peter B., Brian R. Parmenter, John Sutton, and D.P. Vincent. *ORANI: A Multisectoral Model of the Australian Economy*. Amsterdam: North-Holland Publishing Company, 1982.

Fullerton, Don. "On the Possibility of an Inverse Relationship between Tax Rates and Government Revenues." *Journal of Public Economics* 19 (October 1982): 3–22.

Fullerton, Don, and Yolanda K. Henderson. "The Marginal Excess Burden of Different Capital Tax Instruments." *Review of Economics and Statistics* 71 (August 1989): 435–42.

Galper, Harvey, Robert Lucke, and Eric Toder. "A General Equilibrium Analysis of Tax Reform." In *Uneasy Compromise: Problems of a Hybrid Income-Consumption Tax*, edited by Henry J. Aaron, Harvey Galper, and Joseph A. Pechman. Washington, D.C.: The Brookings Institution, 1988.

Goulder, Lawrence H. "Tax Policy, Housing Prices, and Housing Investment." *Regional Science and Urban Economics* 19 (May 1989): 281–304.

Goulder, Lawrence H., and Barry Eichengreen. "Savings Promotion, Investment Promotion, and International

Competitiveness." In *Trade Policies for International Competitiveness*, edited by Rob Feenstra. Chicago: University of Chicago Press, 1989.

Harberger, Arnold C. "The Incidence of the Corporation Income Tax." *Journal of Political Economy* 70 (June 1962): 215–40.

Hudson, Edward A., and Dale W. Jorgenson. "U.S. Energy Policy and Economic Growth 1975–2000." *Bell Journal of Economics and Management Science* 5 (Autumn 1974): 461–514.

Johansen, Leif. *A Multi-Sectoral Study of Economic Growth*. Amsterdam: North-Holland, 1960.

Johnson, Harry G. *The Two Sector Model of General Equilibrium*. Chicago: Aldine-Atherton Press, 1971.

Jorgenson, Dale W., and Kun-Young Yun. "Tax Reform and U.S. Economic Growth." *Journal of Political Economy* 98 (October 1990): S151–S193.

McDougall, R.A. "Short-Run Effects of a Carbon Tax." Centre of Policy Studies and Impact Project General Paper No. G-100, June 1993.

McLure, Charles E., Jr. "The Inter-Regional Incidence of General Regional Taxes." *Public Finance* 24 (3) (1969): 457–83.

McLure, Charles E., Jr. "General Equilibrium Incidence Analysis: The Harberger Model after Ten Years." *Journal of Public Economics* 4 (February 1975): 125–61.

Mieszkowski, Peter M. "The Property Tax: An Excise or a Profits Tax?" *Journal of Public Economics* 1 (April 1972): 73–96.

Musgrave, Richard A. *The Theory of Public Finance*. New York: McGraw-Hill, 1959.

Piggott, John R., and John Whalley. *U.K. Tax Policy and Applied General Equilibrium Analysis*. Cambridge, U.K.: Cambridge University Press, 1985.

Scarf, Herbert E. (with the collaboration of Terje Hansen). *The Computation of Economic Equilibria*. New Haven: Yale University Press, 1973.

Serra-Puche, Jaime. "A General Equilibrium Model for the Mexican Economy." In *Applied General Equilibrium Analysis*, edited by Herbert E. Scarf and John B. Shoven. Cambridge, U.K.: Cambridge University Press, 1984.

Shoven, John B. "The Incidence and Efficiency Effects of Taxes on Income from Capital." *Journal of Political Economy* 84 (December 1976): 1261–83.

Shoven, John B., and John Whalley. "A General Equilibrium Calculation of the Effects of Differential Taxation of Income from Capital in the U.S." *Journal of Public Economics* 1 (November 1972): 281–322.

Slemrod, Joel. "A General Equilibrium Model of Taxation with Endogenous Financial Behavior." In *Behavioral Simulation Methods in Tax Policy Analysis*, edited by Martin Feldstein. Chicago: University of Chicago Press, 1983.

Wells, Paul. "General Equilibrium Analysis of Excise Taxes." *American Economic Review* 45 (June 1955): 345–59.

Whalley, John. "Discriminating Features of Domestic Factor Tax Systems in a Goods Mobile–Factors Immobile Trade Model." *Journal of Political Economy* 88 (December 1980): 1177–1202.

*Cross references:* cost of capital; excess burden; incidence of taxes; income tax, corporate, federal; integration, corporate tax.

# Generational accounting

John Sturrock
Congressional Budget Office

*Generational accounting estimates how fiscal policy distributes resources among the average members of current and future generations.*

Because someone, sometime, must pay for all that government ever buys, current fiscal policy affects both current and future generations. If government does not pay for its purchases of goods and services with current taxes, it must raise future taxes to retire the ensuing debt or pay interest forever. If one generation pays less, another pays more. Sooner or later, someone pays.

## Fundamentals of generational accounting

To measure who pays how much, Alan Auerbach, Jagadeesh Gokhale, and Laurence Kotlikoff (1991) propose a system they call generational accounting. The system estimates the real (inflation-adjusted) net amount that the average member of any generation pays to all levels of government—federal, state, and local. A generation is defined by sex and year of birth. For example, current males comprise newborn boys, one-year-old boys, and so on; future females comprise girls born next year, the year after that, and so on.

Net amounts paid to government consist of net taxes—that is, taxes minus transfers. Transfers are government benefits (such as welfare, Medicare, or Social Security), which differ from government payments for purchases in that the recipients do not provide current goods or services. In effect, transfers constitute negative taxes. For example, if a person pays $10,000 in taxes in a given year and receives $4,000 in transfers, his or her net taxes equal $6,000. Generational accounting does not estimate who benefits from government purchases (payments to businesses and government workers to provide items such as defense, highways, or public education); the system calculates only who pays for purchases with their net taxes. To compare the net taxes of different generations on the same per capita basis, generational accounting expresses the results in terms of the net taxes each generation pays over its lifetime as a share of the income it earns over its lifetime.

### Theoretical assumptions

The calculations depend on two standard concepts—present value and the zero-sum constraint. Present value measures how much a future payment or receipt is worth today, depending on a discount (compound interest) rate. For instance, if the discount rate is 10 percent, a payment of $110 next year is worth $100 today; a payment of $121 two years from now is also worth $100 today. To find the present value of a stream of payments over many years, the analyst finds the present value of the payment in each year, then adds those present values together to find their sum.

The zero-sum constraint specifies that someone pays—future generations must pay with interest for government purchases not paid for by previous generations. That idea may be expressed as an equation:

$$PVF_t = NDG_t + PVG_t - PVC_t$$

where $PVF_t$ is the present value (in the base year $t$) of the net taxes of future generations, $NDG_t$ is the current net debt of government, $PVG_t$ is the present value of prospective government purchases, and $PVC_t$ is the present value of the net taxes of current (living) generations. The zero-sum constraint does not specify that government cannot borrow more or that it must ever retire any of its debt, only that it cannot borrow forever to pay interest.

### Empirical assumptions

The calculations of the elements of the zero-sum constraint depend on assumptions about the policy schedule for taxes and transfers. Taxes are broken into those that apply to payroll, labor income, capital income, home value, and other bases (mostly sales). Transfers are broken into Social Security, Medicare, Medicaid, food stamps, unemployment insurance, and other programs. The per capita schedule by age and sex for each tax or transfer is estimated from official survey data. For instance, the average 40-year-old woman pays about half as much in payroll taxes as the average 40-year-old man; the average 85-year-old man receives about three-quarters more in Medicare than the average 65-year-old man. Generational accounting assumes that such ratios remain fixed (although the calcula-

tions for Social Security include the scheduled changes in the normal retirement age).

The calculations for generational accounting also depend on demographic and economic projections. For a base population, the system uses the Social Security Administration's (SSA's) 75-year intermediate path. That population projection is extended through 2200 by assuming that the age- and sex-specific rates of fertility, mortality, and net immigration remain at their respective values in the last year of SSA's projection. After 2200, the age and sex of population is assumed to remain constant. Finally, the calculations depend on an assumed discount rate and on projected growth of effective labor productivity (output per work hour, adjusted for the age and sex of the worker). For example, a base calculation in 1997 set the real discount rate at 6 percent (about the historical real rate of return on equity) and assumed that productivity grew in the long run at 1.2 percent a year.

### The solution for the zero-sum constraint

Given such assumptions, the system finds the value of each element of the equation for the zero-sum constraint. The current value of government debt is estimated as the algebraic sum of past deficits. For the present value of prospective government purchases, the system starts with a stream of total purchases taken from an official long-term projection by the Office of Management and Budget or the Congressional Budget Office. Beyond the official horizon, per capita purchases by age are extended by assuming that they grow at the same rate as productivity. Those per capita amounts, together with the projected population by age, determine the extended stream of total prospective purchases. The entire stream is then discounted to find its present value.

The same general method applies to the present value of the net taxes of all current generations over their remaining lives. The system starts from an official projection of the total amount of each type of tax or transfer, finds the projected per capita amount by age and sex, extends the projection by assuming that the per capita amount by age and sex grows beyond the official projection at the same rate as productivity, discounts the resulting per capita stream for each current generation, and adds the resulting present values over the members of all current generations—current newborns through those age 90 or older.

Given the values of those three elements of the zero-sum constraint, its equation determines the present value of the net taxes of future generations. There is no way to say how future generations would share their overall burden. As an illustrative device, therefore, generational accounting assumes that future generations all pay net taxes at the same rate.

## TABLE 1

### Lifetime Net Tax Rates

| Year of Birth | Net Tax Rate (%) |
|---|---|
| 1900 | 24 |
| 1910 | 28 |
| 1920 | 30 |
| 1930 | 31 |
| 1940 | 33 |
| 1950 | 33 |
| 1960 | 33 |
| 1970 | 32 |
| 1980 | 31 |
| 1990 | 29 |
| 1995 | 29 |
| Future | 49 |

*Source:* Jagadeesh Gokhale, Benjamin R. Page, and John R. Sturrock, "Generational Accounts for the United States: An Update," Federal Reserve Bank of Cleveland, *Economic Review*, vol. 34, no. 4 (Winter 1997); to be reprinted in Alan J. Auerbach, Laurence J. Kotlikoff, and Willi Leibfritz, eds., *Generational Accounting around the World* (Chicago: University of Chicago Press, forthcoming).
*Note:* Future generations are those born after the base year, 1995.

To compare everyone on the same lifetime basis, generational accounting calculates the effective rate at which each generation pays net taxes over its entire life—its lifetime net tax rate. That calculation requires estimates of each generation's lifetime net taxes, past as well as prospective. Estimates of past net taxes use survey data (as far back as they go) to break each total tax or transfer into per capita amounts by age and sex. Given a generation's past and prospective net taxes, its net tax rate is the present value at birth of its lifetime net taxes as a percentage of the present value at birth of its lifetime labor income.

## Examples of the findings of generational accounting

As estimated in 1997, the lifetime net tax rates of successive U.S. generations had risen, then fallen over the century (table 1). The early rise largely paid for an increase in the share of output devoted to government purchases; the later decline coincided with longer lifetimes and higher per capita transfers for health care and Social Security. Most striking, the estimates revealed the extent to which policy had been biased against the future. To keep government purchases on their scheduled path, future generations would have had to pay lifetime net taxes at a rate that was 72 percent higher than that on current newborns—49 percent versus 29 percent. Of course, such an estimate predicted not what would happen, only what would have happened if the assumed policy schedule had remained fixed for current generations.

## Limitations and contributions of generational accounting

Like any empirical effort, generational accounting rests on uncertain or arguable premises. The estimates can vary under alternative forecasts of population and productivity or under different assumptions about who effectively pays a given tax or receives a given transfer. Generational accounting also assumes that prospective incomes are fixed, thereby ignoring the channel through which current deficits impose costs on young and future generations by reducing current national saving and hence prospective pretax income.

Finally, the results depend heavily on the assumed discount rate. For example, given the other base assumptions in 1997, the estimated lifetime net tax rate of future generations exceeded that of current newborns by 130 percent under a 9 percent discount rate and by 53 percent under a 3 percent discount rate. The higher rate approximates the real rate of return on private capital; the lower rate approximates the real rate of interest on long-term federal debt. The two rates differ largely because capital market participants assign different premiums to the risk of holding those assets. Prospective net taxes are also uncertain, but there is no market in them from which to infer the cost of their risk. Even if there were, people of different ages and with different lifetime incomes need not assign the same cost of risk to their prospective taxes and transfers and thus, need not discount them at the same rate.

Despite such limitations, generational accounting represents an important effort to show how fiscal policy affects various generations. Even when results are uncertain or approximate, they often reveal overall patterns and suggest issues for further analysis. The system offers valuable insights that should inform policymakers, explicitly representing future generations and framing issues on lifetime bases in terms of ultimate constraints.

Views expressed in this entry are those of the author and not necessarily those of the Congressional Budget Office.

## Additional readings

This entry is an abridged version of material from two sources:

Congressional Budget Office. *Who Pays and When? An Assessment of Generational Accounting* (1995).

Gokhale, Jagadeesh, Benjamin R. Page, and John R. Sturrock. "Generational Accounts for the United States: An Update." Federal Reserve Bank of Cleveland, *Economic Review* 33 (4) (fourth quarter 1997). Reprinted in *Generational Accounting around the World*, edited by Alan J. Auerbach, Laurence J. Kotlikoff, and Willi

Leibfritz. Chicago: University of Chicago Press, forthcoming.

Other references include:

Auerbach, Alan J., Jagadeesh Gokhale, and Laurence J. Kotlikoff. "Generational Accounts: A Meaningful Alternative to Deficit Accounting." In *Tax Policy and the Economy*, vol. 5, edited by David Bradford. Cambridge, Mass.: MIT Press, 1991, pp. 55–110.

Kotlikoff, Laurence J., *Generational Accounting: Knowing Who Pays, and When, for What We Spend*. New York: The Free Press, 1992.

*Cross references:* earmarking of taxes; Social Security benefits, federal taxation; Social Security Trust Fund.

# H

## Head tax

Joseph J. Cordes
George Washington University

*A tax levied in a fixed amount on individuals or households without regard to economic or other circumstances of the household.*

Head taxes are an example of a lump-sum tax. Because the amount of the tax is fixed, without regard to what the taxpayer does, it cannot affect the taxpayer's behavior (unless the taxpayer migrates from the jurisdiction that levies the head tax). Head taxes, or poll taxes as they are sometimes called, have mainly served as an intellectual benchmark against which to assess the incidence of other, more practical taxes. In 1990, however, the British government attempted to replace the residential property tax with an actual poll tax in the form of a flat rate community charge, levied on all adults in a jurisdiction. This tax proved to be enormously unpopular and played a significant role in the fall from power of then–prime minister Margaret Thatcher.

### Additional reading

Smith, Peter. "Lessons from the British Poll Tax Disaster." *National Tax Journal* 44 (4) (1991): 421–37.

## Health expenditures, tax treatment

Louise Sheiner
Federal Reserve Board of Governors

*Federal tax treatment of health expenditures made by individuals and by businesses on behalf of employees.*

The federal tax system provides favorable tax treatment to health expenditures in numerous ways, the most important being that employer-paid health insurance expenses are deductible for the employer and not included in employees' taxable wages; taxpayers with cafeteria plans may be able to deduct their share of premium payments and some out-of-pocket health expenses; and health expenditures exceeding 7.5 percent of adjusted gross income are deductible for taxpayers who itemize deductions.

This favorable tax treatment reduced income and payroll taxes by roughly $50 billion in 1997, making it one of the largest "tax expenditures" in the current income tax system (Joint Committee on Taxation 1996).

### Efficiency effects

The largest and most important of the tax expenditures for health is the exclusion of employer-paid health insurance premiums. As has long been recognized, the tax treatment of employer-paid health insurance provides an incentive for workers to be compensated in the form of health insurance rather than in cash wages. A $1 increase in employer-paid health expenditures costs only $(1 - t_i - t_p)/(1 + t_p)$, where $t_i$ is the income tax rate (federal plus net-of-federal state tax) and $t_p$ is the payroll tax rate. So, for an employee facing a 20 percent marginal income tax rate, an additional $1 in employer-paid health insurance costs only 67 cents.

Analyzing the effect of this tax subsidy is not straightforward. The current subsidy is not simply a subsidy for all health expenditures, but rather for health expenditures financed through employer-paid health insurance premiums. Monies spent by employers on health insurance premiums are excludable from taxable income, but employee health expenses for the employee's share of the insurance premium, for coinsurance and deductibles, and for noninsured health expenses are generally not deductible from taxable income. This tax structure can lead to distortions in three separate dimensions: how much health insurance to consume, how much health to insure, and whether to purchase insurance through an employer.

#### Effect on health expenses and health insurance

Feldstein and Friedman (1977) were among the first to analyze how this excludability of employer-paid health insurance premiums affects the structure of employer-paid health insurance. They found that the tax subsidy reduced coinsurance rates (increasing the share of health expenditures covered by insurance) by about 50 percent. Jack and Sheiner (1997) compared the efficiency consequences of a subsidy to health insurance with those of a broad subsidy to health care. On the one hand, limiting the subsidy to health insurance premiums leads consumers to purchase insurance that is more heavily weighted toward premiums—that is, with lower coinsurance and deductibles—thereby increasing health expenditures. On the other hand, providing a subsidy to out-of-pocket payments reduces the effectiveness of any *given* coinsurance and deductible at holding down health expenditures. However, for reasonable parameter estimates, Jack and Sheiner found that the first effect prevailed, and that a subsidy to health insurance alone leads to lower coinsurance rates and greater health expenditures than would a broader subsidy to all health expenditures. For example, in their model, the current subsidy reduces coinsurance rates by about 40 percent, whereas a tax system that also provided the same rate of subsidy to out-of-pocket health expenditures would reduce coinsurance rates by only about 25 percent. They calculated that these lower coinsurance rates increased health expenditures by 13 percent and 7 percent, respectively.

The Feldstein and Friedman and the Jack and Sheiner studies ignored two important elements of our current health system—that (1) employees typically are required to pay some fraction of their health insurance premiums in after-tax dollars; and (2) out-of-pocket health expenditures exceeding 7.5 percent of adjusted gross income are tax-deductible. Gruber and Poterba (1995) recalculated the tax subsidy to employer-paid insurance taking both of these factors into account. Their calculations suggest that the actual subsidy to employer-paid health insurance is only about 80 percent of the subsidy calculated above.

### The effect of the tax subsidy on pooling

The current tax system provides favorable tax treatment only to health insurance purchased through an employer. This subsidy encourages workers to purchase their insurance through their employer, rather than individually or through other associations. Two questions arise: Is employer-based health insurance a good thing, and, if so, would workers purchase insurance this way even without the tax preference? There are differing views as to whether an employer-based insurance system is advantageous (Burman and Rodgers 1992). On the one hand, if individuals choose where to work for reasons unrelated to health status, then employer-based insurance can avoid the adverse selection problems that plague the private insurance market. On the other hand, if the availability of health insurance influences job choice, then the link between health insurance and employment may distort the labor market. For example, workers with preexisting conditions or with a preference for a particular health insurance plan may be less likely to switch jobs, and workers may be less likely to work for small firms because these firms typically face higher health insurance costs.

It is questionable whether employment-based insurance could exist in the absence of some form of tax subsidy. If workers could get equally tax-advantaged health insurance through an individual market, then workers in good health might choose to drop employer insurance or to work in places that did not offer it, subjecting the employer-based insurance market to the same selection problems as those in the individual insurance market. Medical Savings Accounts (MSAs), which allow workers with high-deductible insurance plans to pay for health expenses with pretax dollars, may do the same thing. Employees who do not expect to incur large medical costs will be more likely to choose an MSA; employees with higher expected costs will then face higher health insurance premiums.

### Can the tax treatment of health expenditures explain the high rate of medical inflation?

While the tax treatment of health insurance clearly increases the level of health expenditures in this country, it is not known whether the tax system affects the growth rate of medical expenditures. The major factor underlying medical expenditure growth is the adoption of new technology, and most standard models with exogenous technology growth would imply that constant tax policy could not affect the growth rate of technology adoption. But, it is possible that tax policy affects the type of insurance coverage, and that insurance coverage affects take-up rates of technology (Pauly 1986). It is also possible that technology itself is endogenous, and that the level of health expenditures could affect the growth rate. None of these issues has been examined empirically.

### Additional readings

Burman, Leonard, and Jack Rodgers. "Tax Preferences and Employment-Based Health Insurance." *National Tax Journal* 45 (3) (1992).

Feldstein, Martin, and Bernard Friedman. "Tax Subsidies, the Rational Demand for Insurance and the Health Care Crisis." *Journal of Public Economics* 7 (April 1977): 155–78.

Gruber, Jonathan, and James Poterba. "Tax Subsidies to Employer-Provided Health Insurance." National Bureau of Economic Research Working Paper No. 5147, June 1995.

Jack, William, and Louise Sheiner. "Welfare-Improving Health Expenditure Subsidies." *American Economic Review* 87 (March 1997): 206–21.

Joint Committee on Taxation. "Estimates of Federal Tax Expenditures for Fiscal Years 1997–2001." JCS-11-96, November 26, 1996.

Pauly, Mark. "Taxation, Health Insurance, and Market Failure in the Medical Economy." *Journal of Economic Literature* 24 (June 1986): 629–75.

Cross references: fringe benefits; income tax, federal.

# Highway Trust Fund, federal

Kenneth D. Simonson
U.S. Small Business Administration

*Federal trust fund that finances highway construction and certain other federal spending on transportation.*

The federal Highway Trust Fund was created in 1956 to segregate revenues and outlays for highway construction from the rest of the federal budget. In large part, the fund continues as originally enacted, although there have been significant changes in both receipts and expenditures.

## History

Before 1956, the federal gasoline tax went into the general fund. Congress appropriated money for highway spending independently of the amount collected from any one tax.

The Federal-Aid Highway Act of 1956 set up the Highway Trust Fund to provide continuity in planning and spending on highways, with an assured source of funding. The trust fund was credited with receipts from taxes on motor fuels, tires, trucks, and buses. Expenditures from the fund were authorized for payments to states for construction of the Interstate Highway System and other federal-aid highways. The payments were made at specified matching rates, generally 90 percent federal funds for Interstate highways, 50 percent for primary routes. Construction of the Interstate system was expected to require 13 years, and taxes were authorized for 16 years, through June 30, 1972. The trust fund was also credited with interest on unspent receipts and was debited for refunds paid from the Treasury to nonhighway users of fuel and local transit systems. Later laws repeatedly extended the life of the fund and the taxes going into it.

The Surface Transportation Assistance Act of 1982 made the most sweeping changes in the trust fund since its inception. Congress acted on reports it had requested from the administration showing that projected revenues were insufficient to allow completion of the Interstate system and other spending, and that heavy trucks were not paying an amount proportionate to the pavement damage they caused. Accordingly, the act restructured highway taxes: It more than doubled fuel taxes (from 4 to 9 cents per gallon for gasoline and diesel) and ear-

marked 1 cent from each for a new Mass Transit Account. The truck tax, which had been imposed at a rate of 10 percent of the manufacturer's cost, was changed to a 12 percent retail excise tax, imposed at time of first retail sale or long-term lease. The tax on tread rubber, tires, and inner tubes became a tax on heavy tires only. A highway-use tax for heavy vehicles was hiked from $240 to a range of $100 to $1,900, depending on gross weight.

On the spending side, the act designated outlays for mass transit capital grants from the Mass Transit Account and created the so-called Interstate 4R program allowing expenditures for reconstruction, resurfacing, restoration, and rehabilitation, as well as the anticipated completion of the Interstate network.

Truck taxes were further modified in 1984 to cap the highway-use tax at $550. To make up the revenue, the diesel tax was increased to 15 cents per gallon. Additional extensions of taxes and spending, plus minor modifications to each, were enacted in 1987. Fuel taxes were increased again for both Highway Trust Fund and general fund purposes in 1990 and 1993.

The Intermodal Surface Transportation Efficiency Act of 1991 (ISTEA, popularly pronounced "ice-tea") significantly changed spending priorities. The act made what were intended to be final allocations for completing the Interstate system and created a new National Highway System, consisting of Interstates and other roads of "primary federal interest," to be supported by lower federal contributions, generally 80 percent. Although the chief focus of trust fund spending continued to be state-selected outlays on major highways, the act gave metropolitan planning organizations a voice in choosing projects. Highway construction was de-emphasized in favor of transit, bikeway, preservation, intermodal, and "intelligent vehicle/highway systems" projects. In short, what was formerly a purely highway construction funding mechanism was diversified into funding other modes and goals such as air quality improvement and technology support.

Legislation in 1997 returned the remaining 4.3 cents per gallon of general fund revenue to the trust fund, bringing trust fund rates to 18.3 cents for gasoline and 24.3 cents for diesel; 2.85 cents of those amounts are credited to the Mass Transit Account.

In fiscal 1997, the Highway Trust Fund was credited with $24 billion of taxes and $1 billion of interest. The Mass Transit Account received $4 billion of these amounts. Outlays totaled $22 billion from the Highway Account and $3 billion from the Mass Transit Account. ISTEA authorized expenditures through September 1997 and tax collections through September 1999. The Transportation Equity Act for the 21st Century (TEA-21) extends these rates through 2005.

## Policy issues

The United States is exceptional, if not unique, in the world in segregating fuel and other tax revenue for highway purposes. Support for the general principle of dedicating revenue collected from highway users is very widespread at the federal and state level. Nevertheless, several issues arise as to how the revenue should be apportioned and how broadly it should be spent.

One issue concerns the interdependence of trust fund and overall federal spending. Even though highway outlays come from an earmarked source, there are several constraints on this spending beyond having a positive balance in the trust fund. Total federal spending is dictated by the budget resolution adopted annually by Congress. The resolution caps "discretionary" spending, which includes transportation. Highway interests must compete with other transportation priorities, which in turn must win a share of the discretionary piece of the total budget.

The level of highway taxes is interrelated with both total federal receipts and highway spending. In most years, trust fund receipts closely match outlays. However, the bulk of receipts are derived from taxes on the number of gallons of fuel sold. Increasing fuel efficiency of both automobiles and trucks has meant that fuel tax receipts grow very slowly in the absence of tax rate increases, even though the number of vehicle miles of travel usually rises from year to year. At the same time, the costs of highway spending programs tend to rise in line with prices and wages generally, meaning that the number of highway projects financed by a given set of tax rates declines from year to year. Thus, highway spending proponents would like to see increasing highway tax rates. But highway taxes must go through the same legislative process as other taxes. In practice, this has meant that since 1990, highway taxes go up only as part of a large budget "reconciliation" bill that includes many tax and spending changes and that raises fuel taxes for mass transit and sometimes general fund, as well as highway, purposes.

A third issue concerns the mix of highway taxes. Legislation in 1982 attempted to charge automobiles, light trucks, and heavy trucks appropriate shares of the total tax burden. The 1982 allocation was based on methodology that was controversial at the time and became increasingly outdated as the proportions, miles traveled, and fuel economy of each type of vehicle changed. Yet a 1997 update by the Federal Highway Administration concluded that the mix of taxes in effect in 1996 did allocate tax burdens fairly equitably among vehicle types.

Furthermore, some critics argue that existing taxes fail to charge accurately for either pavement damage or congestion costs. They suggest that heavy trucks be charged a tax that varies with dis-

tance traveled and maximum weight per axle or overall, and that automobiles be charged for use of congested roads through tolls, possibly varying with time of day. Defenders of the current truck tax system say that a combination of fuel and tire taxes and a weight-based annual use tax approximates a tax on distance and vehicle weights without requiring the technology or extensive administrative burden required of true weight-distance taxes. Opponents of congestion pricing believe it is politically and, perhaps, technologically infeasible to collect tolls from all vehicles in crowded urban areas.

## Additional readings

Congressional Budget Office. *Innovative Financing of Highways: An Analysis of Proposals* (1998).

Small, Kenneth A., Clifford Winston, and Carol A. Evans. *Road Work: A New Highway Pricing and Investment Policy.* Washington, D.C.: The Brookings Institution, 1989.

Talley, Louis Alan. *Federal Excise Taxes on Gasoline and the Highway Trust Fund: A Short History.* Washington, D.C.: U.S. Library of Congress, Congressional Research Service Report 94-354 E, April 22, 1994.

U.S. Department of Transportation. *Federal Highway Administration. 1997 Federal Highway Cost Allocation Study.* August 1997.

U.S. General Accounting Office. *Highway User Fees: Updated Data Needed to Determine Whether All Users Pay Their Fair Share.* Report GAO/RCED-94-181, June 1994.

*Cross references:* benefit principle; earmarking of taxes; user charges, federal.

# Homeowner preferences, individual income tax

Jane G. Gravelle
Congressional Research Service, Library of Congress

*Income tax provisions that favor investment in owner-occupied housing.*

---

Housing is an important part of the capital stock, and owner-occupied housing receives favorable treatment. Two of the biggest tax expenditure items are the mortgage interest deduction (costing more than $40 billion per year in 1997) and the property tax deduction (costing about $16 billion).

Although these tax subsidies attract considerable attention, the fundamental benefit is that imputed rent is not included in income; if it were, business deductions for interest and property tax (along with depreciation and maintenence) would be appropriate. As a result of these tax preferences, the return on investment in owner-occupied housing is subject to negligible income taxes. Families are encouraged to own, rather than rent, housing and to consume too much housing.

There is disagreement as to the magnitude of the efficiency loss (which has been estimated to range from 0.1% to 1.0% of output). There are some arguments in favor of benefits for housing. They include the difficulty of taxing imputed rent and the possibility of spillovers for home ownership. Such spillovers have not been measured and are unlikely to be of a magnitude that would justify the significant tax benefits. Disallowing deductions would be a way of offsetting the benefit from exclusion of imputed rent, which is difficult to administer, but these options are imperfect. Disallowing mortgage interest deductions would not affect equity investments, for example. Disallowing property tax deductions might induce the states and localities to shift their sources of revenue.

The immense popularity of these provisions makes it unlikely that they would be altered.

### Additional readings

Berkovec, James, and Don Fullerton. "A General Equilibrium Model of Housing, Taxes, and Portfolio Choice." *Journal of Political Economy* 100 (April 1992): 390–429.

Gravelle, Jane G. *The Economic Effects of Taxing Capital Income.* Cambridge, Mass.: MIT Press, 1994.

*Cross references:* homestead exemption and credit programs; imputed income; income tax, federal; interest deductibility; itemized deductions; mortgage interest deduction.

# Homestead exemption and credit programs

Scott Mackey
National Conference of State Legislatures

*State and local programs that provide tax relief to owners of residential property.*

Homestead exemption and credit programs are the most widely used form of property tax relief. Forty-seven states have homestead exemptions or credits available to at least one class of qualified homeowner. Colorado, Missouri, and South Dakota are the exceptions. In the 47 states with programs, veterans and the disabled are the most common recip-

ients of tax relief. This entry focuses on homestead exemption and credit programs in the 36 states and the District of Columbia that have programs broadly available either to older Americans as a class or to all homeowners. The 11 additional states that provide relief only to veterans or the disabled are not discussed here.

### History

Most homestead exemption programs were created during the Great Depression to give poor homesteaders property tax relief that would help them avoid foreclosure. This helps explain why states with historically low property taxes, such as Oklahoma, still have very small exemptions on the books that in effect provide little tax relief. Homestead property tax exemptions are sometimes confused with state homestead exemptions, which prevent creditors from foreclosing on residences in bankruptcy proceedings. These are completely separate issues.

The early homestead exemptions programs were generally available to all homeowners. In 1957, New Jersey developed the first homestead exemption program targeted to older Americans. The 1960s and 1970s saw rapid growth in the number of states with targeted homestead exemption programs, with many of the new programs targeted to the elderly. However, since that time states have tended to make the programs available more broadly to all households, or to all low-income households (Gold 1979: 82–85).

### How the programs work

Homestead exemption programs reduce property taxes on residential property by exempting a certain amount of a home's value from taxation. Homestead exemption programs are usually mandated by state law, with local governments either absorbing the revenue loss or shifting the tax burden to other property. However, the 12 states shown in table 1 reimburse local governments for some or all of the property tax revenue lost as a result of homestead exemption programs.

Homestead credit programs are state-financed and may involve direct rebates to taxpayers or, like homestead exemptions, may reduce property tax bills directly. Arizona, Indiana, Mississippi, Minnesota, Nebraska, New Jersey, Ohio, Tennessee, Wisconsin, and the District of Columbia have homestead credit programs. These programs rebate a certain percentage of taxes due or provide a fixed credit to qualifying homeowners. New Jersey uses the latter method, providing a $250 rebate for elderly and disabled homeowners. Arizona provides all homeowners with a credit of 20 percent of the school tax bill up to $500. Table 2 ranks the gener-

**TABLE 1**

### State Reimbursement to Local Governments for Property Tax Revenue Loss Due to Homestead Exemption Programs

| State | Year | Reimbursement ($ millions) | Per Capita Reimbursement |
|---|---|---|---|
| Iowa | FY 93 | $98.0 | $34.83 |
| Louisiana | FY 93 | 90.0 | 20.95 |
| California | FY 94 | 342.9 | 10.99 |
| South Carolina | FY 93 | 40.0 | 10.98 |
| New Jersey | FY 93 | 58.1 | 7.37 |
| Indiana | FY 93 | 21.4 | 3.75 |
| North Dakota | FY 93 | 2.3 | 3.62 |
| Massachusetts | FY 93 | 19.1 | 3.18 |
| Wyoming | CY 93 | 1.1 | 2.34 |
| North Carolina | FY 93 | 8.0 | 1.15 |
| Oklahoma | CY 92 | 2.2 | 0.68 |
| Maine | FY 94 | 0.7 | 0.56 |

*Source:* National Conference of State Legislatures survey, summer 1994.

osity of state homestead credit programs in terms of per capita spending on homestead credit rebates.

The degree of property tax relief provided by homestead exemption programs varies tremendously from state to state. The tax reduction depends upon the dollar amount of the exemption provided and the assessment ratio used in determining the taxable value of the property. For example, in Louisiana, each homeowner receives a $7,500 homestead exemption, and California homeowners receive a $7,000 exemption. Louisiana's program is much more generous, however, because the state uses a 10 percent assessment ratio in determining the taxable value of the home. A $100,000 house in Louisiana has a taxable value of $10,000, so the $7,500 homestead exemption effectively exempts $75,000 in actual value from property taxes. In contrast, California's assessment ratio is 100 percent, so its homestead exemption is worth $7,000 in actual value.

In states without state-financed homestead exemption or credit programs, local governments can shift the tax burden from exempt property to non-

**TABLE 2**

### Homestead Credit Payments to Homeowners by State

| State | Year | Total Payments ($ millions) | Per Capita Payments |
|---|---|---|---|
| Indiana | FY 93 | $607.90 | $106.41 |
| Arizona | CY 93 | 120.00 | 30.49 |
| Mississippi | FY 94 | 68.00 | 25.73 |
| Wisconsin | FY 94 | 128.60 | 25.53 |
| Nebraska | FY 93 | 32.90 | 20.47 |
| Ohio | CY 92 | 52.50 | 4.76 |
| Tennessee | FY 93 | 8.70 | 1.71 |
| U.S. Total | | $1,018.60 | $29.06 |

*Source:* National Conference of State Legislatures survey, summer 1994. Data for Minnesota, New Jersey, and D.C. not available.

exempt property such as business property, vacation and second homes, and homes and other property owned by taxpayers who do not qualify for homestead exemptions. This is particularly true in states with generous homestead exemptions that are available to the general population, like those in Florida, Idaho, and Louisiana.

Florida estimated that some $78 billion out of a total taxable value of $690 billion, or 11 percent of all property, was exempt from taxation in 1993 as a result of its $25,000 homestead exemption (Florida Department of Revenue 1993: 9–10). For this reason, homestead exemption programs widely available to all homeowners may not provide the full amount of tax relief that they appear to provide. In the Florida example, the large amount of exempt property reduces the tax base and probably results in higher tax rates than would be necessary if all property were taxable. A hypothetical Florida couple with a $100,000 home receives a 25 percent reduction in the taxable value. However, if property tax mill levies were 11 percent higher to compensate for exempt property, the net tax reduction would be 17 percent, not 25 percent. Large homestead exemptions that are available to all homeowners shift the tax burden from homeowners to businesses.

Homestead credit programs avoid tax shifts because they are state financed. For this reason, these programs are popular with local officials. However, some states have found that homestead credit programs may increase local spending and taxes because local officials can increase tax rates without the full burden being borne by local taxpayers. Minnesota changed its Homestead and Agricultural Credit Program for this reason in 1991 (Baker and Hinze 1991).

## Participation issues

With homestead exemption programs, participation is automatic because the exemption is built directly into the property tax bill received by the homeowner. In some states, however, homestead credit programs require qualifying homeowners to claim their credit, often on a separate form submitted with income tax forms. Some elderly homeowners are not required to file an income tax form and therefore they may fail to claim their credit. State outreach programs are necessary to let qualifying homeowners know about the credit and how to apply for it; some states provide information about the credit with both income tax forms and property tax bills.

## Targeting homestead exemption and credit programs to the elderly

Tables 3 and 4 summarize the key features of homestead exemption and credit programs available

**TABLE 3**

**State Homestead Credit and Exemption Programs without Income Eligibility Guidelines: 1997**

| State | Value of Exemption for | |
| | Elderly Homeowners | All Homeowners |
| --- | --- | --- |
| Alaska | $150,000 | $10,000 (L) |
| Arizona (school)* | 20% of tax | 20% of tax |
| California* | $7,000 | $7,000 |
| District of Columbia | $30,000 | $30,000 |
| Florida | $25,000 | $25,000 |
| Hawaii | * | $40,000 |
| Idaho | * | * |
| Illinois | $16,500 | $16,500 |
| Indiana* | 4% of tax | 4% of tax |
| Iowa | $4,850 | $4,850 |
| Kansas (school) | $20,000 | $20,000 |
| Kentucky | $21,800 | — |
| Louisiana (all taxes except municipal) | $75,000 | $75,000 |
| Massachusetts | $2,000 | |
| Minnesota | * | * |
| Mississippi | Up to $240 tax and $60,000 | Up to $240 tax |
| New Mexico | $6,000 | $6,000 |
| Ohio* | 12.5% of tax | 12.5% of tax |
| Oklahoma* | $8,333 | $8,333 |
| South Carolina | $20,000 | — |
| Texas (school) | $15,000 | $5,000 |
| Texas (other local)* | $3,000 | $3,000 |
| Utah | 45% of value | 45% of value |
| West Virginia | $33,300 | — |
| Wisconsin (school) | $5,900 | $5,900 |

*Source:* National Conference of State Legislatures survey, December 1997.
(L) = Local option program
*Notes:
**Arizona**—Maximum tax rebate is $500.
**California**—The exemption can increase up to $150,000 if household income is less than $24,000.
**Hawaii**—Age 55 to 59: $60,000; age 60 to 64: $80,000; age 65 to 69: $100,000; age 70 and over: $120,000.
**Idaho**—Exemption is lesser of $50,000 or 50 percent of value for residential improvements.
**Indiana**—Local option to increase homestead credit to 8 percent of tax. See table 4 for additional exemption available to low-income elderly and disabled.
**Minnesota**—Minnesota's homestead exemption program is integrated with its property tax classification system.
**Ohio**—Additional exemptions for qualifying elderly and disabled homeowners are listed in table 4.
**Oklahoma**—An additional $1,000 assessed value exemption is available for households with incomes below $10,000.
**Texas**—Additional local option of up to 20 percent assessed value.

broadly to older Americans and to all households. States in table 3 offer homestead exemption programs without regard to the taxpayer's income, while states in table 4 target programs to low-income taxpayers. Both tables compare the treatment of elderly and nonelderly homeowners under state homestead exemption programs. Seventeen states offer the same benefits to elderly and nonelderly households, and 4 additional states offer benefits only to seniors. Seven states have programs

for the elderly and nonelderly alike, but offer more generous programs to seniors.

State decisions to target or not to target programs are based upon several factors. States that choose to provide benefits to all homeowners, without regard to income, are often using exemption and credit programs as part of a broader policy to shift taxes from the local to the state level or from residential property owners to businesses. Arizona's credit was adopted as part of a state tax increase to fund schools while providing property tax relief. Wisconsin's exemption was tied to passage of a state lottery, with funds earmarked for property tax relief.

### Targeting benefits to low-income households

Sixteen of the 24 states that provide more generous benefits to the elderly than to the general population require elderly homeowners to meet income criteria. Targeting programs in this manner allows states to provide tax relief to elderly homeowners on fixed incomes without providing relief to wealthy retirees. This reduces the revenue loss to local governments, or the state in the case of homestead credits or state-reimbursed homestead exemption programs.

New Jersey provides a $250 property tax reduction for elderly households with incomes below $10,000. North Dakota exempts homeowners age 65 and older with incomes below $13,500 from taxes on the first $44,000 of the value of their home. Elderly homeowners in Ohio with incomes below $16,500 receive a $14,285 homestead exemption in addition to the 12.5 percent property tax credit that is available to all homeowners regardless of age.

### Additional readings

Baker, Karen, and Steve Hinze. *Minnesota's Property Tax System: A Description of Changes Beginning in 1990*. St. Paul: Minnesota House of Representatives Research Department, 1991.

Florida Department of Revenue. *Ad Valorem Valuations and Tax Data*. Tallahassee, 1993.

Gold, Steven D. *Property Tax Relief*. Lexington, Mass.: D.C. Heath and Company, 1979.

Mackey, Scott. *State Tax Policy and Senior Citizens*. Denver: National Conference of State Legislatures, December 1994: 37–58. (This entry is excerpted and updated from Mackey 1994.)

*Cross references:* circuit breaker; property tax, real property, residential.

## TABLE 4

### State Homestead Credit and Exemption Programs with Income Eligibility Guidelines: 1997

| State | Dollar Value of Exemption for | | Income Cap |
|---|---|---|---|
| | Elderly Homeowners | All Homeowners | |
| Alabama (state) | Full | $40,000 | $12,000* |
| Alabama (local) | $50,000 | $20,000 | $12,000* |
| Delaware (nonschool) | $ 5,000 (L) | — | $ 3,000 |
| District of Columbia | Up to 50% of tax | — | |
| Georgia (local) | $10,000 | $ 5,000 | $10,000 |
| Georgia (school) | $25,000 | $ 5,000 | $10,000 |
| Indiana* | $ 9,000 | $ 6,000 | $15,000 |
| Montana | Up to $80,000 | Up to $80,000 | $16,034 |
| Nebraska* | 80% of AV | — | $23,000 |
| New Hampshire | $ 5,000 | — | $ 6,000* |
| New Jersey | $250 tax | — | $10,000 |
| New York | Up to 50% AV (L) | — | $16,500 |
| North Carolina | $13,000 | — | $11,000 |
| North Dakota | $44,000 | — | $13,500 |
| Ohio* | $14,285 | — | $16,500 |
| Tennessee | $15,000 | — | $10,000 |
| Utah* | 50% of tax up to $300 (L) | — | $18,400 |
| Virginia | Up to 100% AV (L) | — | $30,000 |
| Washington (local)* | $34,000 | — | $18,000 |

*Source:* National Conference of State Legislatures survey, December 1997.
(L) = Local option program
AV = Assessed value
*Notes:*
**Alabama**—Income cap applies to full exemption for elderly. Elderly with adjusted gross income less than $7,500 receive full exemption from local taxes.
**Indiana**—See table 3 for homestead credit program available for all homeowners.
**Nebraska**—Exemption varies with income and is capped at $40,000.
**New Hampshire**—Elderly homeowners receive a $5,000 exemption if income is below $6,000 and asset value is below $35,000.
**Ohio**—Elderly receive the $14,285 exemption plus the 12.5 percent homestead credit available to all homeowners (see table 3).
**Utah**—This is in addition to the program available to all homeowners.
**Washington** (local)—Exemption varies with income; amounts shown are the maximum benefit and the maximum qualifying income level.

# Horizontal equity

Joseph J. Cordes
George Washington University

*A principle used to judge the fairness of taxes, which holds that taxpayers who have the same income should pay the same amount in taxes.*

The principle of horizontal equity is a basic yardstick used to gauge whether tax burdens are fairly distributed. On the one hand, the idea that tax policy should strive for horizontal equity is uncontroversial (Musgrave 1990). It protects taxpayers against arbitrary discrimination, and also seems consistent with basic principles of equal worth. Some might also argue that horizontal equity comports with the principle of "equal protection under law" set forth in the United States Constitution.

On the other hand, some tax scholars maintain that the property of horizontal equity is not really an independent principle of tax fairness, but instead is subordinate to the concept of vertical equity, which holds that people with different incomes should pay different amounts of tax (Kaplow 1989). As a matter of logic, a tax system that assigned different tax burdens to people with different incomes should assign the same tax burden to people with the same income. Viewed in this way, equal treatment of equals in taxation is not an end in itself, but rather a means to ensuring that tax burdens are distributed in a way that is vertically equitable.

As Musgrave (1990) notes, however, horizontal equity can lay claim to being an independent standard of tax equity because it is consistent with a number of different underlying conceptions of tax fairness, although application of the vertical equity standard will differ. For example, the benefit principle of taxation holds that tax burdens should be assigned according to the benefits that taxpayers receive from government goods and services. If one assumes that the benefits taxpayers receive from government spending vary with their income level, a case can be made that taxation according to the benefit principle would require that taxpayers with the same income pay the same amount of tax. Under the benefit principle, vertical equity would require that taxpayers with different incomes pay different amounts of tax. But, depending on how benefits varied with income, vertical equity could require that benefit tax burdens be distributed regressively, proportionately, or progressively, depending on whether benefits from public goods and services rose less than proportionately, proportionately, or more than proportionately as income increased.

Under the ability-to-pay principle, people with the same incomes have the same ability to pay, and thus should pay the same amount in taxes. In contrast to the benefit principle, however, regressive taxes would not be deemed fair under the ability-to-pay principle, and there is a general presumption that vertical equity under the standard of ability to pay would require some degree of progression in tax burdens.

The point is that while different standards of tax fairness may give different answers about how people with different incomes should be taxed (e.g., regressively, proportionately, or progressively), in theory or in practice, they generally give a similar answer about how people with the same incomes should be taxed—namely, that tax burdens should be distributed in a manner that is horizontally equitable.

## Horizontal equity and consumption versus income taxation

Several conceptual issues should be kept in mind when applying the horizontal equity principle. One has to do with the measure of income that is used to group taxpayers as equals. The most commonly used yardstick is annual income, comprehensively measured. Many economists, however, believe that a taxpayer's lifetime income is a better measure. One's judgment about whether taxing income or consumption is consistent with horizontal equity depends on which definition of income one uses.

Consider, for example, the case of two people, Taxpayer A and Taxpayer B, who, for purposes of illustration, are assumed to live for only two periods of time. In the first period, both taxpayers work and earn $50,000; in the second, they retire and live from the proceeds of savings they collected in the first period. Assume that Taxpayer A saves $20,000 of income earned in the first period, and invests it at a return of 10 percent, while Taxpayer B saves only $10,000, also invested at 10 percent.

The question is do Taxpayers A and B have "equal incomes"? The answer depends on whether one measures income annually or over a taxpayer's lifetime. If annual income is used as the standard, then Taxpayers A and B would be seen to have the

same income in period one ($50,000), but Taxpayer A would have a higher income in period two because of investment income of $2,000 compared with only $1,000 of income for Taxpayer B. Applying the principles of horizontal and vertical equity would require that Taxpayers A and B pay the same tax in period one, and that Taxpayer A pay more taxes than Taxpayer B in period two.

Clearly, in this case, taxing income meets the standard of horizontal equity, but taxing consumption would not. The reason is that in period one, taxpayers A and B would pay taxes only on the amount of their income that is consumed, so that Taxpayer A would pay less in tax than would taxpayer B, even though they have the same amount of annual income.

If, however, one believes that lifetime income should be used to compare taxpayers, the answer changes. The reason is that from a lifetime perspective, Taxpayers A and B have the same lifetime income. They each earn $50,000 of income in period one, and this means that they have the same possibilities for consumption over their lifetimes. How they decide to allocate their consumption between present and future is a matter of personal preference. Taxpayer A would rather have more consumption in period two, and so saves more than does Taxpayer B. As a byproduct of these choices, the two taxpayers wind up with different amounts of *annual* income in period two, but this simply reflects the fact that Taxpayer A would rather consume less in period one and more in period two than would Taxpayer B. If lifetime income is the standard of comparison, it can be shown that taxing based on consumption achieves horizontal equity, while taxation of income imposes a heavier tax burden on people who have the same lifetime incomes as others, but who prefer to shift more of their lifetime consumption to later years through saving.

## Horizontal equity and implicit taxes

There are also situations in which horizontal "inequities" may be more apparent than real. Income received from tax-exempt bonds is a case in point. Suppose that Taxpayers A and B are identical in all respects save for the fact that Taxpayer A receives $7,000 in interest from tax-exempt bonds, while Taxpayer B receives $7,000 in fully taxable interest. Assume for purposes of illustration that the tax rate is 30 percent. It might seem that horizontal equity is violated because both taxpayers have the same measured income, even though Taxpayer B will pay $2,100 on his or her interest income, while Taxpayer A owes no tax on his or her tax-exempt interest.

But, as Bittker (1980) notes, the two taxpayers are not really in the same position. The reason is that tax-exempt bonds will pay a lower rate of interest because of their tax-free status. For example, if the interest rate on fully taxed bonds were 10 percent, and the tax rate 30 percent, the interest on tax-exempt bonds would be 7 percent. This means that in order to earn $7,000 in tax-exempt interest, Taxpayer A must have bought $100,000 of tax-exempt bonds, whereas Taxpayer B needed to buy only $70,000 worth of bonds to earn the same income. Many economists would say that Taxpayers A and B are really in the same position, because while Taxpayer B faces an explicit tax of 30 percent on interest earnings, Taxpayer A faces an implicit tax, levied in the form of the lower return received on the tax-favored investment.

## Cases in which horizontal equity does not apply

The standard of horizontal equity will have limited applicability when taxes are levied to account for the presence of external costs. For example, smokers and nonsmokers will face sharply different tobacco tax burdens, even when their incomes are the same. To the extent, however, that tobacco taxes are intended to force smokers to bear the external costs of smoking, the apparent violation of horizontal equity would not be seen as problematical.

## Application to tax policy

The concept of horizontal equity plays an important role in the evaluation of tax policy. For example, treating taxpayers with equal incomes equally was one of the central organizing principles of the landmark reform of the federal income tax that took place in the Tax Reform Act of 1986.

## Additional readings

Bittker, Boris. "Equity, Efficiency, and Income Tax Theory: Do Misallocations Drive Out Inequities?" In *The Economics of Taxation*, edited by Henry Aaron and Michael Boskin. Washington, D.C.: The Brookings Institution, 1980.

Kaplow, Louis. "Horizontal Equity: Measures in Search of a Principle." *National Tax Journal* 42 (2) (1989): 139–55.

Musgrave, Richard. "Horizontal Equity Once More." *National Tax Journal* 43 (2) (1990): 113–23.

*Cross references:* ability to pay; benefit principle; fairness in taxation; progressivity, measures of; tax reform, federal; tax reform, state; vertical equity.

# Implicit taxes

Harry Watson
George Washington University

*Costs, in the form of lower rates of return or higher prices, that may be borne by participants in untaxed or favorably taxed markets as a result of tax shifting.*

While taxpayers usually focus on the amount that they must remit to the government—their explicit tax burden—their true tax burden usually will not coincide with these payments. One reason for this discrepancy is that a tax in one market may be shifted to another market in the form of higher prices or lower rates of return. While these changes in prices or rates of return are not a direct result of explicit tax payments, they have the same economic consequences for taxpayers, and therefore can be viewed as implicit taxes.

Implicit taxes play an important role in incidence analysis—the question of who bears the economic, as opposed to statutory, burden of a tax. Measuring the incidence of a tax by looking only at explicit taxes paid will often produce a biased measure of burden in the presence of implicit taxes. The classic example of this bias is the belief that those who invest in state and municipal bonds in the United States face no tax burden; while they face no *explicit* tax burden, they do face a material *implicit* tax burden in the form of a lower no-tax rate of return. Because of the significant role played by implicit taxes in determining incidence, it is useful to understand the mechanism by which such taxes are created, the factors that influence their magnitude, and the form such taxes can take.

Implicit taxes are created when taxpayers attempt to ameliorate the impact of their explicit tax burden. In the case of income taxation, taxpayers may substitute tax-preferred investments for fully taxed ones. These tax-induced substitutions produce an increase in demand in markets that face a lower level of explicit taxation, which results in higher prices or lower rates of return in these markets. This process effectively shifts an explicit tax in one market to an implicit tax in another.

Consider, for example, the case of tax-exempt bonds. Suppose that initially the interest from all bonds is taxed fully at a rate of 30 percent, and that a decision is made to exempt the interest on bonds

issued by state and local governments from taxation. Assume that before the exemption is granted, all bonds offer a rate of 10 percent. When the exemption is granted, investors presumably would flock to buy tax-exempt municipal bonds, believing that these bonds would pay a tax-free return of 10 percent, compared with the after-tax rate of only 7 percent $[= 10\% - (10\% \times 0.30)]$ that they earn on fully taxed bonds. But this would boost the demand for tax-exempt bonds, which would allow the issuers of these bonds to command a higher bond price or, equivalently, offer a lower rate of return on them. Capital markets would adjust until the last dollar invested in either a fully taxed or a tax-exempt bond earned the same after-tax return. The result would be that investors in tax-exempt bonds would receive a return on their investment that was 30 percent less than the return they could earn by investing in fully taxed bonds. Thus, if they bought a fully taxed bond at, say, 10 percent, they would pay an explicit tax of 30 percent on their return. If they bought a tax-exempt bond, they would not have to write a check to the government, but they would also earn a return of only 7 percent, whereas in a world with no taxes, they would have been able to earn 10 percent. Thus, they would face an implicit tax of 30 percent.

The magnitude of implicit taxation depends in large part on how much latitude taxpayers have in lessening their explicit tax burden. This latitude depends critically on two factors: the form of the tax system and how responsive taxpayers are to economic incentives—that is, the elasticity of their response to changes in prices and rates of return.

Tax systems that are characterized by broad bases and uniform treatment of all items in these bases will leave taxpayers with limited opportunities to lessen explicit tax burdens, and therefore will generate few implicit taxes. For example, taxpayers who face a flat-rate income tax that provides uniform treatment for all forms of saving will find that no amount of portfolio juggling, apart from reducing the size of their portfolio, will alter their explicit tax liability. As portfolio adjustments provide few tax benefits, asset prices and rates of return will change little, and there will be no appreciable implicit taxation. Conversely, if the income tax provides numerous tax preferences, the range of opportunities for reducing explicit tax liability may lead to substantial alterations in taxpayer portfolios and, concomitantly, substantial changes in pretax rates of return. In this situation, the explicit tax on heavily taxed forms of saving will be shifted to those forms of saving that are treated preferentially.

For a given tax system, the magnitude of implicit taxes will reflect the elasticity of taxpayer response to changes in prices and rates of return. Generally, the more elastic the response, the greater is the magnitude of implicit taxation. Compare, for example, an excise tax levied on a lifesaving pharmaceutical with an excise tax levied on hardcover books. The absence of any substitutes for the lifesaving pharmaceutical means that taxpayers in need of such a product will not alter their demands for other goods or services—their response will be inelastic—and, as a result, other market prices will remain unaffected and no implicit taxes will be created. On the other hand, with an excise tax on hardcover books, one would expect taxpayers' responses to be quite elastic, resulting in a significant shift to paperbacks and a corresponding increase in their price. The magnitude of the price increase will be directly related to the ease of substituting a paperback for a hardcover book.

Unlike explicit tax burdens, implicit tax burdens may arise before any tax statutes are enacted. As long as taxpayers anticipate new tax codes or changes in existing ones, these anticipation effects will alter market behavior and market prices. Suppose that taxpayers believe that an investment tax credit, with a given structure, will be enacted but that the timing of enactment is uncertain. Because potential users of capital subject to the credit may delay investing with the expectation of receiving this credit, the market price of existing capital will fall, creating a capital loss—implicit tax—for owners of this capital. Thus, even though there has been no change in tax code provisions, and therefore no change in explicit tax liabilities arising from the credit, an implicit tax will have been levied on owners of existing capital.

Although most implicit taxes are produced by tax-induced changes in prices and rates of return, there are other ways in which such taxes can be created, a testament to their ubiquitous nature. Consider a market in which products can be distinguished on the basis of their quality (or by the level of services provided to consumers by producers). If an excise or sales tax is levied on these products, the producer of one of them can react by altering the price of the product or by altering its quality. In most cases, the imposition of the tax will lead to a higher tax-inclusive price for consumers, and the price increase represents the portion of the explicit tax paid by consumers. However, a producer may try to offset some of the decline in demand that results from the higher price by increasing product quality. This higher level of quality could reasonably be viewed as an implicit subsidy to consumers, a subsidy that lowers the true tax burden of consumers.

*Cross references:* fringe benefits; incidence of taxes; marginal effective tax rate; saving, taxes and.

# Imputed income

Jane G. Gravelle
Congressional Research Service, Library of Congress

*Income that is not received in monetary form and therefore is not typically subject to taxation. Imputed income, in economic theory, would include income from the flow from all durable goods, including assets held by consumers, and the value of leisure and unpaid work (such as food grown for home use).*

According to the reconciliation between adjusted gross income and personal income in the National Income and Product Accounts, in 1995 there was $240.2 billion of imputed income excluded from the tax base (this figure does not include employee fringe benefits). The largest item was $159.8 billion in the category of personal interest income, which includes the benefits of banking services provided free to customers in lieu of interest. The next largest item was $64.1 billion of imputed rental income on owner-occupied housing. There were also imputations for labor income, and for proprietor's income.

When the Treasury Department's Office of Tax Analysis prepares distributional tables, it uses an expanded income concept that includes imputed rent on owner-occupied housing.

*Cross references:* adjusted gross income; homeowner preferences, individual income tax.

# Incidence of taxes

George R. Zodrow
Rice University

*The analysis and measurement of who bears the final burden of a tax.*

One of the most fundamental questions addressed by public finance economists is that of who bears the final burden of a tax. The basic issue is that tax-induced changes in individual and firm behavior and the associated changes in commodity prices and factor returns are likely to imply that the final burden or "economic incidence" of a tax will be different from its "statutory incidence"—that is, a tax may be partially or fully "shifted" from one set of economic agents to another. Business taxes are a frequently cited example, as they may be either "shifted forward" as higher consumer prices or "shifted backward" as lower wages or land. The tax incidence literature provides many insights, and has played an important role in the development of tax policy (McLure and Zodrow 1994). Nevertheless, the incidence of many taxes—especially those on capital income, including corporate income taxes and local property taxes—is still a controversial topic. More generally, there is considerable disagreement about various theoretical issues, including the appropriate market structure for incidence analysis and the extent to which capital is mobile internationally; similarly, there is a lack of consensus on various empirical issues, including the parameter values that should be used in numerical simulations of the theoretical models.

Public finance economists have used three basic approaches to analyze tax incidence. The most common method analyzes the effects of taxes in a theoretical model of the economy; these models differ in many dimensions, including the number of markets analyzed, the extent to which factor supplies are assumed to be fixed, the method of capital accumulation, the nature of market competition, and the extent to which transitional issues are addressed. The second approach is closely related to the first, because it involves numerical simulations of tax effects in models that are basically complex variants of the analytical models described above. Finally, several analysts have studied incidence by estimating individual tax burdens directly using large micro-data sets. Each of these approaches, which have become increasingly sophisticated over time, is discussed below. Several excellent surveys of the incidence literature are available for further reference (Mieszkowski 1969; Break 1974; McLure 1975; Atkinson and Stiglitz 1980; Kotlikoff and Summers 1987; Atkinson 1994).

## Partial-equilibrium analysis

The simplest type of incidence analysis examines the impact of a tax in a "partial equilibrium" framework—that is, within the context of a single market, neglecting any tax-induced effects on other markets. Although relevant only when such effects can reasonably be assumed to be unimportant, partial-equilibrium models provide many insights. Most important, they demonstrate that incidence is determined primarily by the extent to which individuals or firms are able to change their behavior to avoid the tax; this flexibility is typically measured by price elasticities of demand and supply. For example, the

burden of an excise tax tends to be borne by consumers if demand is relatively inelastic—that is, if consumers are unable to substitute away from consumption of the taxed good; by comparison, the burden of an excise tax tends to be borne by producers if supply is fairly inelastic. In limiting cases, the tax is borne fully by a single group; for example, if demand is perfectly inelastic or supply is perfectly elastic (as is the case with constant returns to scale in production), consumers bear the entire burden of the excise tax. In addition, these same factors determine who bears the excess burden of a tax—the efficiency cost attributable to tax-induced distortions of individual and firm behavior. Finally, partial-equilibrium analysis can be used to demonstrate another basic tenet of incidence analysis—that the economic incidence of a tax in a competitive system depends solely on market conditions and is independent of its statutory incidence.

Nevertheless, partial-equilibrium analysis is clearly limited in that most taxes have important effects on markets other than the one in which they are assessed. Moreover, the focus in partial-equilibrium models on incidence in terms of producers and consumers is unsatisfactory, because one would like to go "behind the supply curve" and identify the factor owners who bear the producer portion of the tax burden, and go "behind the demand curve" to determine which types of consumers are adversely affected by tax-induced commodity price increases (McLure 1975).

## Static general-equilibrium analysis

These two problems are resolved in general-equilibrium models of tax incidence. Such models account explicitly for market interactions; for example, they consider the effects of tax-induced factor reallocations on all other markets in the economy. In addition, the effects of tax changes on individuals can be determined explicitly by specifying individual tastes and patterns of factor ownership.

The simplest general-equilibrium models are "static," in that total factor supplies are assumed to be fixed. Much of this research is based on the seminal article by Harberger (1962). (See also Musgrave 1953, 1959.) The Harberger model assumes perfectly competitive markets and zero initial taxes and has a single consumer, two production sectors, and two factors of production—capital and labor—that are perfectly mobile between the sectors, although fixed in total supply. The model is thus ideally suited to analyzing the intermediate-run effects of sector-specific taxes; it was initially used to examine the incidence of the corporate income tax, with the two production sectors representing corporate and noncorporate output.

The primary insight obtained from such models is that general-equilibrium effects in markets other than that in which a tax is introduced are often very important. For example, the imposition of a partial factor tax in the model drives the factor out of the taxed sector into the untaxed sector, tending to depress the overall return to the factor. (Note that the assumption of intersectoral mobility implies that the burden on any factor is shared among all factor owners rather than just the owners of the factor in the taxed sector.) Such models are theoretically characterized by a wide variety of incidence results; for example, the analysis of the corporate tax includes cases in which capital owners bear all (or even more than 100%) of the tax as well as cases in which capital owners benefit from the tax. Nevertheless, Harberger argued that for plausible parameter values, capital owners bear the full burden of the corporate income tax on equity income—a result that was generally confirmed in subsequent numerical simulation models (Shoven 1976).

The two-sector static general-equilibrium model has the significant advantage of being simple enough to be solved analytically for the factors that determine incidence as well as the parameters that establish their magnitudes; such analyses provide considerable insight into the market interactions that determine tax incidence. For example, the effect of the corporate income tax on the return to capital in the Harberger model can be decomposed into two components (Mieszkowski 1967). The first is a "substitution effect," which reflects reduced demand for capital in the taxed corporate sector and has an unambiguously negative effect on the return to capital. The second is an "output effect," which reflects reduced demand for corporate output because of its tax-induced increase in price; this has a negative (positive) effect on the return to capital if the taxed sector is capital (labor) intensive, as the reallocation of production from the taxed to the untaxed sector implies an excess supply of capital (labor), which must be eliminated by a reduction in its price. In general, commodity demand elasticities and the elasticities of substitution in production are the critical factors in determining the magnitudes of these effects.

The analytical static general-equilibrium model constructed by Harberger has been extended in numerous ways. One extension has been to allow consumers with different tastes. In this case, income redistribution affects consumer demands and thus relative consumer and factor prices and net incomes (Mieszkowski 1967). For example, a general tax on labor can be shifted in part to capital owners if the owners of labor consume the capital-intensive good to a disproportionate extent, so that a reduction in their incomes leads to reduced demand for capital. Second, the assumption of perfect factor mobility may be relaxed. In general, as suggested above, the burden of taxes in such cases falls on factors that are relatively immobile (McLure 1970, 1971). Third,

the assumption of perfect competition has been questioned, especially for analysis of the corporate tax. Although there is no widely accepted model of imperfect competition, most observers argue that more forward shifting of taxes to consumers is likely in this context (Katz and Rosen 1985). Fourth, because the Harberger model assumes that initial taxes are zero, excess burden effects cannot be analyzed because they are second-order effects and thus do not appear in a differential analysis. The extension to an existing tax structure allows explicit analysis of the burden of the efficiency costs of taxation (Ballentine and Eris 1975; Vandendorpe and Friedlaender 1976); such models are essential for the analysis of the incidence of tax reforms (Feldstein 1976; Zodrow 1981, 1992).

The primary problem associated with the analytical studies described above is that the number of markets and consumers must be severely limited to keep the models tractable. This problem has been attacked by utilizing the basic structure of the Harberger model in the construction of large-scale computable general-equilibrium models that analyze tax incidence in economies with many production sectors and types of consumers; for example, one such model includes 19 business sectors and 12 consumer groups (Ballard et al. 1985). These models have been used to analyze the incidence of differential taxation of industries and types of assets, and to determine the distribution of the tax burden of existing tax systems and potential reforms across various types of individuals. In addition, these numerical models have been extended to include considerations of risk and endogenous financial behavior (Slemrod 1983; Galper et al. 1988).

The basic static general-equilibrium model can also be used to analyze tax incidence in open economies, in which case one sector represents a small open economy and the second sector represents the rest of the world (or country in the case of a state or regional analysis). In the simplest cases, the main result is that, although capital still tends to bear the overall burden of a tax on capital in the small taxing jurisdiction, the outmigration of capital caused by the tax lowers returns to immobile factors in the jurisdiction by the sum of the tax and its excess burden (Brown 1924; Bradford 1978). The policy implication is that small open economies that face a perfectly elastic supply of a factor should not tax that factor (Slemrod 1988). More generally, increasing international mobility of capital suggests that open economy considerations should play an important role in tax incidence analyses, although the extent of international capital mobility is still a controversial issue (Harberger 1980; Feldstein and Bacchetta 1989).

Finally, the static general-equilibrium model has been used to argue that the property tax is primarily a tax on capital, because capital owners bear the average burden of property taxation in the nation, while tax differentials across jurisdictions cause higher commodity prices and lower factor returns in relatively high tax jurisdictions and the opposite effects in relatively low tax jurisdictions (Mieszkowksi 1972; Zodrow and Mieszkowski 1986). This view has been challenged, however, by those who argue that the property tax, when combined with the appropriate zoning restrictions or by perfect capitalization of fiscal differentials in land prices, is effectively a benefit tax for local public services (Hamilton 1975, 1976).

## Dynamic general-equilibrium analysis

The primary problem with the static analyses described above is that tax effects on total factor supplies are ignored; in particular, many observers have argued that this assumption is unreasonable when the incidence of a tax is borne by capital owners (although similar points could be made regarding the supply of labor and the stock of human capital). The following discussion outlines two basic approaches that have been used in analyzing tax incidence from a dynamic perspective—one based on the neoclassical growth model and the other based on the overlapping-generations life-cycle model.

Early approaches to dynamic tax incidence focused on adding taxes to the neoclassical growth model. In this case, capital income taxation reduces saving, which in turn lowers the equilibrium capital-labor ratio; as a result, labor productivity falls and wages decline, implying that the tax has been at least partially shifted from capital to labor. Indeed, in the special case in which capital owners save all their income and workers save none, the burden of a capital income tax is fully shifted to labor; more generally, the extent of shifting varies from about one-third to one-half (Krzyzaniak 1967; Feldstein 1974a). In addition, dynamic incidence analysis has demonstrated that the elasticity of supply of labor has no effect on the incidence of a labor income tax if saving rates, and thus long-run capital intensity, are unaffected by changes in labor supply (Feldstein 1974b).

More recent analyses of dynamic tax incidence have focused on tax effects within the context of overlapping-generations life-cycle models. These analyses have shown that dynamic tax incidence depends critically on how tax revenues are distributed across generations. (Similar issues arise in static models; however, most static analyses simply assume that tax revenues or government services accrue uniformly to all income groups.) For example, suppose that within the context of a two-period life-cycle model, capital income tax revenues are used to finance transfers to the elderly. In this case, saving declines because the elderly are drawing down their savings to finance consumption, and some (perhaps

all) of the burden of the tax is shifted from capital to labor (Diamond 1970). However, a markedly different result is obtained if revenues from the capital income tax finance transfers to the younger generation. In this case, the higher income level of the young, who are in the saving portion of their life cycle, implies increases in aggregate saving and capital intensity, such that wages increase and the return to capital falls.

Life-cycle dynamic models have also been used to examine the intergenerational incidence of tax reforms; the key factor in these analyses is the effect of alternative tax policies on the assets held by generations alive at the time of the reform's enactment. For example, under a switch from an income tax to a cash-flow consumption tax, double taxation of existing assets results in a huge welfare loss to the elderly, which in turn implies lower steady-state tax rates; by comparison, a switch to a wage tax confers a windfall gain to the elderly (who expected to be taxed on the income earned by such assets) and implies relatively high steady-state tax rates (Summers 1981a; Auerbach and Kotlikoff 1987).

Finally, both the static and dynamic analyses described above assume that capital reallocations are instantaneous and costless; however, in the presence of adjustment costs, tax incidence analysis must consider tax-induced changes in asset prices (Summers 1981b). Such asset price changes measure the windfall gains and losses attributable to the enactment of tax reforms and, if the adjustment period is long, may be a more important determinant of incidence than the long-run changes in factor prices stressed in most analyses. Moreover, the nature of such windfall gains and losses may be surprising. For example, the enactment of an investment incentive that applies only to a new investment is likely to result in a loss to the owners of existing capital assets; intuition dictates that equilibrium returns, which accrue to both new and old capital, will decline, because they are determined by the tax treatment of new investment, and these lower returns will be capitalized in the values of existing assets (Auerbach and Kotlikoff 1983).

## Empirical incidence analysis

Another approach to determining incidence uses micro-data sets to estimate individual tax burdens and thus estimate their distribution across individuals. These studies draw on the theoretical and empirical literatures to make assumptions about the incidence of various taxes, and typically include calculations for a variety of incidence assumptions. Such studies have generally found—depending on the incidence assumptions made, especially regarding the corporate income tax and property taxes—that the combined federal, state, and local tax structure in the United States is either modestly progressive or modestly regressive (Pechman and Okner 1974; Pechman 1985). The aggregation of all taxes, however, masks the progressivity of the federal income tax; one recent study estimates that effective individual income tax rates increase uniformly from −0.9 percent for the first income decile, to 16.5 percent for the top decile, to 20.8 percent for the top 1 percent of income earners (Pechman 1990).

Such studies have played an important role in tax reform debates; for example, their basic methodology was used by the U.S. Treasury in determining whether the various reform proposals considered before passage of the Tax Reform Act of 1986 satisfied the constraint of "distributional neutrality" (McLure and Zodrow 1987). Nevertheless, they have been criticized on a number of grounds. Although most critiques focus on the nature of the incidence assumptions used in the analyses, a separate issue is the use of annual income as a classifier. Many observers have argued that lifetime income is a better measure of ability to pay taxes, and that the distribution of tax burden should be measured by comparing lifetime income and taxes paid. Such calculations generally indicate that consumption taxes are less regressive and income taxes less progressive than do studies based on annual income (Davies et al. 1984; Poterba 1989; Fullerton and Rogers 1993). The lifetime approach to tax incidence analysis is, however, by no means universally accepted (Barthold 1993).

## Additional readings

Atkinson, Anthony B. "The Distribution of the Tax Burden." In *Modern Public Finance,* edited by John M. Quigley and Eugene Smolensky. Cambridge, Mass.: Harvard University Press, 1994.

Atkinson, Anthony B., and Joseph E. Stiglitz. *Lectures on Public Economics.* New York: McGraw-Hill, 1980.

Auerbach, Alan J., and Laurence J. Kotlikoff. "Investment versus Savings Incentives: The Size of the Bang for the Buck and the Potential for Self-Financing Business Tax Cuts." In *The Economic Consequences of Government Deficits,* edited by Lawrence H. Meyer. Boston: Kluwer-Nijhoff, 1983.

Auerbach, Alan J., and Laurence J. Kotlikoff. *Dynamic Fiscal Policy.* Cambridge, U.K.: Cambridge University Press, 1987.

Ballard, Charles A., Don Fullerton, John B. Shoven, and John Whalley. *A General Equilibrium Model for Tax Policy Evaluation.* Chicago: University of Chicago Press, 1985.

Ballentine, J. Gregory, and Ibrahim Eris. "On the General Equilibrium Analysis of Tax Incidence." *Journal of Political Economy* 83 (June 1975): 633–44.

Barthold, Thomas. "How Should We Measure Distribution?" *National Tax Journal* 35 (September 1993): 291–99.

Bradford, David F. "Factor Prices May Be Constant but Factor Returns Are Not." *Economics Letters I* (November 1978): 199–203.

Break, George F. "The Incidence and Economic Effects of Taxation." In *The Economics of Public Finance,* edited by Alan S. Blinder, Robert M. Solow, George F. Break, Peter O. Steiner, and Dick Netzer. Washington, D.C.: The Brookings Institution, 1974.

Brown, Harry G. *The Economics of Taxation.* New York: Holt, 1924.

Davies, James, France St-Hilaire, and John Whalley. "Some Calculations of Lifetime Tax Incidence." *American Economic Review* 74 (September 1984): 633–49.

Diamond, Peter A. "Incidence of an Interest Income Tax." *Journal of Economic Theory* 2 (September 1970): 211–24.

Feldstein, Martin S. "Incidence of a Capital Income Tax in a Growing Economy with Variable Savings Rates." *Review of Economic Studies* 41 (October 1974a): 505–13.

Feldstein, Martin S. "Tax Incidence in a Growing Economy with Variable Factor Supply." *Quarterly Journal of Economics* 88 (November 1974b): 551–73.

Feldstein, Martin S. "On the Theory of Tax Reform." *Journal of Public Economics* 6 (July–August 1976): 77–104.

Feldstein, Martin S., and Phillipe Bacchetta. "National Saving and International Investment." National Bureau of Economic Research Working Paper No. 3164, 1989.

Fullerton, Don, and Diane Lim Rogers. *Who Bears the Lifetime Tax Burden?* Washington, D.C.: The Brookings Institution, 1993.

Galper, Harvey, Robert Lucke, and Eric Toder. "A General Equilibrium Analysis of Tax Reform." In *Uneasy Compromise: Problems of a Hybrid Income-Consumption Tax,* edited by Henry J. Aaron, Harvey Galper, and Joseph A. Pechman. Washington, D.C.: The Brookings Institution, 1988.

Hamilton, Bruce W. "Zoning and Property Taxation in a System of Local Governments." *Urban Studies* 12 (June 1975): 205–11.

Hamilton, Bruce W. "Capitalization of Intrajurisdictional Differences in Local Tax Prices." *American Economic Review* 66 (December 1976): 743–53.

Harberger, Arnold C. "The Incidence of the Corporate Income Tax." *Journal of Political Economy* 70 (June 1962): 215–40.

Harberger, Arnold C. "Vignettes on the World Capital Market." *American Economic Review* 70 (May 1980): 331–37.

Katz, Michael L., and Harvey S. Rosen. "Tax Analysis in an Oligopoly Model." *Public Finance Quarterly* 13 (January 1985): 3–19.

Kotlikoff, Laurence J., and Lawrence H. Summers. "Tax Incidence." In *Handbook of Public Economics,* edited by

Alan J. Auerbach and Martin Feldstein. Amsterdam: North-Holland, 1987.

Krzyzaniak, Marian. "Long-Run Burden of a General Tax on Profits in a Neoclassical World." *Public Finance* (1967): 472–91.

McLure, Charles E., Jr. "Taxation, Substitution, and Industrial Location." *Journal of Political Economy* 78 (January–February 1970): 112–32.

McLure, Charles E., Jr. "The Theory of Tax Incidence with Imperfect Factor Mobility." *Finanzarchiv* 30 (1971): 27–48.

McLure, Charles E., Jr. "General Equilibrium Incidence Analysis: The Harberger Model after Ten Years." *Journal of Public Economics* 4 (February 1975): 125–61.

McLure, Charles E., and George R. Zodrow. "Treasury I and the Tax Reform Act of 1986: The Economics and Politics of Tax Reform." *Journal of Economic Perspectives* 1 (Summer 1987): 37–58.

McLure, Charles E., Jr., and George R. Zodrow. "The Study and Practice of Income Tax Policy." In *Modern Public Finance*, edited by John M. Quigley and Eugene Smolensky. Cambridge, Mass.: Harvard University Press, 1994.

Mieszkowski, Peter. "On the Theory of Tax Incidence." *Journal of Political Economy* 75 (June 1967): 250–62.

Mieszkowski, Peter. "Tax Incidence Analysis: The Effects of Taxes on the Distribution of Income." *Journal of Economic Literature* (December 1969): 1103–24.

Mieszkowski, Peter. "The Property Tax: An Excise Tax or a Profits Tax?" *Journal of Public Economics* 1 (April 1972):73–96.

Musgrave, Richard A. "General Equilibrium Aspects of Incidence Theory." *American Economic Review* 43 (May 1953): 504–17.

Musgrave, Richard A. *The Theory of Public Finance: A Study in Political Economy.* New York: McGraw-Hill, 1959.

Pechman, Joseph A. *Who Paid the Taxes, 1966–85?* Washington, D.C.: The Brookings Institution, 1985.

Pechman, Joseph A. "The Future of the Income Tax." *American Economic Review* 80 (March 1990): 1–20.

Pechman, Joseph A., and Benjamin A. Okner. *Who Bears the Tax Burden?* Washington, D.C.: The Brookings Institution, 1974.

Poterba, James M. "Lifetime Incidence and the Distributional Burden of Excise Taxes." *American Economic Review* 79 (May 1989): 325–30.

Shoven, John B. "The Incidence and Efficiency Effects of Taxes on Income from Capital." *Journal of Political Economy* 84 (December 1976): 1261–83.

Slemrod, Joel. "A General Equilibrium Model of Taxation with Endogenous Financial Behavior." In *Behavioral Simulation Methods in Tax Policy Analysis,* edited by

Martin S. Feldstein. Chicago: University of Chicago Press, 1983.

Slemrod, Joel. "Effect of Taxation with International Capital Mobility." In *Uneasy Compromise: Problems of a Hybrid Income-Consumption Tax,* edited by Henry J. Aaron, Harvey Galper, and Joseph A. Pechman. Washington, D.C.: The Brookings Institution, 1988.

Summers, Lawrence H. "Capital Taxation and Capital Accumulation in a Life Cycle Growth Model." *American Economic Review* 71 (September 1981a): 533–44.

Summers, Lawrence H. "Taxation and Corporate Investment: A q-Theory Approach." *Brookings Papers on Economic Activity.* Washington, D.C.: The Brookings Institution, 1981b, pp. 67–127.

Vandendorpe, Adolph L., and Ann F. Friedlaender. "Differential Incidence in the Presence of Initial Distorting Taxes." *Journal of Public Economics* 6 (October 1976): 205–29.

Zodrow, George R. "Implementing Tax Reform." *National Tax Journal* 34 (December 1981): 401–18.

Zodrow, George R. "Grandfather Rules and the Theory of Optimal Tax Reform." *Journal of Public Economics* 49 (November 1992): 163–90.

Zodrow, George R., and Peter Mieszkowski. "The New View of the Property Tax: A Reformulation." *Regional Science and Urban Economics* 16 (August 1986): 309–27.

*Cross references:* capital export neutrality; capital import neutrality; elasticity, demand and supply; general-equilibrium models; implicit taxes; life cycle model; lump-sum tax; tax equity analysis.

# Income tax, corporate, federal

Jane G. Gravelle
Congressional Research Service, Library of Congress

*A tax imposed on the profits of corporations, calculated by deducting costs—including interest payments—from gross receipts.*

## Brief history

The corporate income tax, enacted in 1909, actually predates the individual income tax, enacted in 1913. The corporate tax comes in a distant third (after the individual income and payroll taxes) as a source of federal tax revenue.

During its history, the statutory rate has fluctuated substantially, rising as high as 52 percent; currently the top rate is 35 percent. The tax is graduated, and closely held corporations may elect to be taxed as partnerships.

## Rationale for the corporate tax

A corporate tax has been justified by the special privileges the corporation receives (in terms of limited liability), the independent economic power of large corporations, the prevention of income-sheltering by high-tax-rate individuals (current tax rates make sheltering less important, however), and the tax's contribution to tax progressivity and revenue.

Many economists have been critical of the corporate tax, citing uncertainty as to the burden of the tax and its creation of a variety of distortions. They view limited liability as an efficient way to organize the raising of large amounts of capital and allocating risk, which should not be discouraged.

## Who bears the burden?

While the corporate tax is presumed to fall on shareholders in the short run, when the firm cannot change its capital stock, behavioral responses can alter the long-run burden. (Taxes on excess monopoly profits are not likely to be shifted, however.)

Who pays the corporate tax is relevant to issues of distribution and progressivity. Capital income is concentrated among higher-income individuals, and the tax contributes to progressivity if it falls on capital rather than labor.

Theoretical analysis indicates that corporate taxes are borne by all capital income. Harberger's (1962) landmark two-sector study shows how the reactions of investors to lower after-tax returns, following the imposition of the tax, serve to spread the tax. As the return falls in the taxed sector, investors shift their investments to the untaxed sector and its (initially) higher rates of return. This shift sets in motion a series of adjustments in prices, wages, rates of return, output, and factor allocations.

In equilibrium, the corporate sector becomes smaller, with higher relative prices, and with lower ratios of capital to labor, than it had before, while the noncorporate sector becomes larger, with lower relative prices and higher ratios of capital to labor than it had before. The pretax rate of return in the corporate sector rises, while the pretax return in the untaxed noncorporate sector falls, until it equals the after-tax return in the corporate sector. The effect on wages and labor shifts is indeterminate in direction. The magnitude and, for wages, the direction of these adjustments depend on how easily capital and labor can be substituted for production in each sector, how willing consumers are to substitute corporate and noncorporate products, and what the original allocations of capital and labor were. In some cases, capital can bear more than 100 percent of the tax and in some cases less than 100 percent, but overall there is a tendency for the tax to fall on capital.

This finding has held up through many modifications of the model, with the exception of models that allow the capital stock to change.

In a small, open economy, where capital is perfectly mobile and goods in international trade are perfect substitutes, the burden of capital income taxes imposed on capital used in a given country falls on that country's immovable factors (labor) because both worldwide prices and returns are fixed. Gravelle (1994a) shows that relaxing any of these assumptions will shift part of the tax burden away from labor, and back to capital; she finds that under reasonable assumptions, the burden still falls largely on capital.

Growth models of the tax introduce further complications in the form of a time dimension and uncertainty (see Fullerton and Rogers 1993). One must now distinguish between the burden on individuals living in the near-term and in the long-run equilibrium, and the incidence would then refer to lifetime incidence, rather than a cross section in a single year. If the savings response to a tax increase is negative, the burden of the corporate tax partially falls on labor in the long run, as the contraction in the total capital stock drives down the wage. At the same time, it is not clear that the corporate tax has caused the capital stock to fall, even on a theoretical basis (that answer depends in part on the disposition of the proceeds of the tax). Empirical evidence on the response of savings to changes in the rate of return is mixed (see Gravelle 1994b: Ch. 2 for a summary of this evidence).

At the same time, the relationships between sources of income and level of income (i.e., high-income individuals have more capital income) tend to be muted in a life cycle model, so that even if the corporate tax falls on capital (because savings do not respond to changes in the rate of return), the effect on progressivity may be lessened.

## Efficiency costs of the corporate tax

The corporate tax causes resources to be misallocated in the economy: too much capital relative to labor is used in the noncorporate sector and too little is used in the corporate sector, causing inefficient production. In addition, prices are distorted, causing too little corporate production. Most models of the corporate tax have produced welfare costs equivalent to a loss of about 0.5 percent of income, a not insignificant amount.

The following discussion elaborates on certain matters simplified by the original Harberger model.

## Fundamental changes in the structure of the model

Harberger's model explores a tax imposed on capital used to produce a particular type of good, while the corporate tax is imposed on firms because they are incorporated. The Harberger model does not allow taxed and nontaxed firms to produce the same product.

Several different methods of explaining the co-existence of corporate and noncorporate sectors in an industry have now been explored, generally relating to firm size. Gravelle and Kotlikoff (1989) suggest that large corporate firms benefit from scale advantages, while small firms benefit from entrepreneurial ability; hence, each form of production can coexist, given an imperfectly elastic supply of entrepreneurial skills. Other approaches (see Gravelle 1994b for a summary) allow corporate and noncorporate firms to produce differentiated products or allow different after-tax returns. Size might also play a role in these models (e.g., corporate products may be characterized by consistency and predictability, and corporate investments by liquidity and risk-sharing; noncorporate products and assets may be characterized by flexibility and the "personal touch").

While these models do not alter the estimates of burden, they increase the cost of distortions, because they allow for intra-industry substitution. There has been little empirical research, however, to establish the degree of substitutability of corporate and noncorporate capital directly, and such research is very difficult to perform.

## Marginal tax rates, personal-level taxes, and the treatment of dividends

At the personal level, taxes are imposed immediately on dividends, but retained earnings are not subject to tax until gains are realized (and never taxed if passed on at death). Capital gains have typically benefited from special rates or exclusions. Effective tax rates can also be affected by various special provisions (such as accelerated depreciation) and the failure to index for inflation. Current tax models generally employ more sophisticated measures of effective tax burdens that account for these factors.

This recognition of personal taxes, and of imprecisely measured income, does have several implications for the structure of corporate tax models. First, it means that the excess corporate tax (combined corporate and personal taxes on corporate income in excess of taxes on noncorporate income) varies from one individual to the next in a progressive tax system. Thus, some sort of portfolio effect should probably be included in any model of the corporate tax.

Second, the particular nature of the tax treatment of corporate source income at the personal level has given rise to extensive debate on the effects of taxes on dividends.

Because retained earnings are taxed more lightly than dividends, why do firms pay dividends? Firms wishing to distribute profits could effectively do so by repurchasing shares (causing share prices to go up). Several theories have been advanced to explain why firms pay dividends: they can be divided into the "traditional" and the "new" view of dividends (Zodrow 1991 provides a more extensive discussion of these views).

The new view presumes that dividends and capital gains are perfect substitutes and that firms cannot repurchase shares. Under the new view, dividend taxes in excess of capital gains taxes do not affect investment when that investment is financed out of retained earnings. By choosing reinvestment, the stockholder forgoes the excess dividend tax—a saving that offsets, in present value, future excess dividend taxes.

The new view also suggests that dividend taxes in excess of capital gains taxes are capitalized in the value of stock—hence the new view is sometimes referred to as the "trapped equity" view, or the "tax capitalization" view.

In the traditional view of dividends, they have some intrinsic value. Dividends may serve a signaling function: stockholders may not have full information about the profitability of a firm, and the payment of dividends might be used as a method to make clear that the firm is doing well. Agency cost may play a role: because of the separation of ownership and control in modern corporations and limited information, stockholders may wish to limit managerial discretion by requiring payment of regular dividends. Finally, shareholders may not view dividends and capital gains as perfect substitutes (because, for example, of differences in risk and transaction costs).

Empirical evidence has been mixed, but tends to favor the traditional view (see Gravelle 1994b: Ch. 4, for a summary of the empirical research). There are also some more straightforward empirical problems with the new view. Share repurchases (on the open market) can and do freely occur (at least in the United States), and firms sometimes issue new shares while paying dividends, a behavior inconsistent with the new view. At the same time, it is not entirely clear how the different traditional theories of tax should be incorporated into the tax burden.

The dividend tax debate is important for assessing the costs of distortions. Under the new view, the excess corporate tax is much smaller, and the efficiency gains reduced. If dividends and capital gains are imperfect substitutes, however, there is an additional element of distortion imposed by the current tax treatment along with the lock-in effect for corporate capital gains.

## The use of debt finance

Corporate firms could avoid the tax by using debt finance. Yet, U.S. corporations not only use equity capital, they use it in substantial amounts. What explains corporations' choice of taxed equity capital?

Clientele effects were initially used to explain debt/equity choices: with high individual tax rates, some individuals would face lower taxes on equity than on debt. However, this argument was inconsistent with the mixed portfolios held by individuals at different tax rates.

The increased risk of bankruptcy can explain why firms do not choose all debt finance, even though debt may be attractive because of the agency-cost issue discussed with reference to dividends—limiting managerial discretion through requiring periodic interest payments.

A final explanation is a portfolio explanation, in which debt is seen as an imperfect substitute for equity (because of differences, for example, in risk or in transactions costs).

None of these reasons alters the incidence effects of the corporate tax, but they do have implications for efficiency. Debt finance reduces the differential between taxes in the corporate and noncorporate sectors, but causes a distortion between debt and equity finance. There has been little empirical research on the magnitude of the substitutability of debt and equity, although the evidence that does exist suggests that it is small (see Gravelle 1994b for a discussion).

## Policy options

The excess corporate tax can be reduced in several ways. Dividend relief, common in other countries, could be provided by exclusion at the personal level, a deduction at the firm level, or a credit imputation method under which the firm withholds dividend taxes and the individual shareholder takes a credit for these taxes. The latter two methods preserve tax progressivity, and the last method can maintain some tax on otherwise tax-exempt entities (including foreign shareholders). Full partnership taxation could be achieved by providing a credit-imputation method for both dividends and retained earnings. Overall relief from double taxation could also be provided through elimination of individual-level taxes on dividends and capital gains.

In 1992, the U.S. Treasury Department undertook an extensive study of various methods, ultimately favoring dividend exclusion at the personal level. The firm-level deduction, which was actually proposed in 1984, did not allow the flexibility of imposing some tax on tax-exempt shareholders. The other methods were viewed as undesirable because of their complexity.

Treasury also explored a new and much more far-reaching approach—the Comprehensive Business Income Tax (CBIT). This proposal would tax all business income—from both debt and equity—at the firm level. Firms would not be able to deduct interest, but this interest would not be taxed to the recipient. This proposal would eliminate virtually all of the existing distortions, would not lose revenue (thus meeting both revenue and distributional objectives), and would be relatively simple to administer. CBIT does face some problems in transition and application to small businesses, and it might discourage foreign supplies of debt capital.

Even a partial reduction in the excess tax may be well worthwhile, because the excess burden of a tax rises with the square of the tax. The welfare gain per dollar of revenue may therefore be quite large, even with only a partial movement toward a neutral system.

## Additional readings

Fullerton, Don, and Diane Lim Rogers. *Who Bears the Lifetime Tax Burden?* Washington, D.C.: The Brookings Institution, 1993.

Gravelle, Jane G. "Corporate Tax Incidence in an Open Economy." *1993 Proceedings of the National Tax Association—Tax Institute of America*: 173–78. Columbus, Ohio, 1994a.

Gravelle, Jane G. *The Economic Effects of Taxing Capital Income.* Cambridge, Mass.: MIT Press, 1994b.

Gravelle, Jane G., and Laurence J. Kotlikoff. "The Incidence and Efficiency Costs of Corporate Taxation When Corporate and Noncorporate Firms Produce the Same Goods." *Journal of Political Economy* 97 (August 1989): 749–90.

Harberger, Arnold H. "The Incidence of the Corporation Income Tax." *Journal of Political Economy* 70 (June 1962): 215–40.

U.S. Department of the Treasury. *Report on Integration of the Individual and Corporate Tax Systems.* Washington, D.C.: U.S. Government Printing Office, January 1992.

Zodrow, George R. "On the 'Traditional' and 'New' Views of Dividend Taxation." *National Tax Journal* 45 (December 1991): 497–510.

*Cross references:* cost of capital; dividends, double taxation of; foreign corporations, federal taxation; incidence of taxes; income tax, federal; integration, corporate tax; inventory accounting; investment tax credits; marginal effective tax rate; multinational corporations, taxation; subchapter S corporation; taxable income, corporate; uniform capitalization rules.

# Income tax, corporate, state and local

Robert Strauss
Carnegie Mellon University

April Franco
University of Rochester

*A tax levied on the net income of general corporations subject to tax in 45 states and the District of Columbia.*

This tax is variously defined in state tax law as a direct tax on income, or as a franchise or privilege tax *measured* by net income. A number of states, most notably Massachusetts, New York, and Ohio, impose the larger of a net income tax or a tax on a corporation's net worth. The latter is viewed as a minimum tax imposed when net income is zero or negative. In addition to these state-level levies, there are a number of municipal corporate net income taxes; the most prominent is imposed by New York City at a rate of 8.85 percent (in addition to the state corporate net income tax rate of 9%). The states collected $21.6 billion of corporate net income taxes in 1992, or 13 percent of state general tax revenues. State corporate net income tax rates (as of 1997) vary among the states from as low as 1 percent, the lowest marginal corporate tax rate in Alaska and Arkansas, to as much as 10.5 percent, the highest marginal tax rate in North Dakota. Of the 45 state corporation income taxes, only 12 (Alaska, Arkansas, Hawaii, Iowa, Kentucky, Louisiana, Maine, Mississippi, New Mexico, Ohio, North Dakota, and Vermont) provide for a progressive rate structure; the others impose proportional tax rates. The top marginal tax rate in these 12 states' rates occurs on net incomes of between $50,000 and $250,000.

The general structure of the state corporate income tax base parallels that of the federal corporate income tax base, and all states either adopt or heavily refer to the Internal Revenue Code in the definition of receipts, deductions, and net income. Virtually all state corporate net income taxes define state-taxable corporate net income with reference to federal net income as shown on line 28 of federal corporate tax Form 1120; this initial measure of net income is then adjusted for federal constitutional and state policy purposes. Net income is reduced in all states by the amount of federal bond interest received by a corporation. Because state and local bond interest is exempt for federal tax purposes, all states increase federal corporate income by the amount of interest received on *other* states' bonds;

22 states add back interest earned on their own state and local bonds. Five states (Alabama, Iowa, Louisiana, Missouri, and North Dakota) allow a deduction for some or all federal corporate income taxes paid. The states vary considerably in their treatment of intercorporate dividends received. Some states allow the federal exclusion of dividends received by subsidiaries owned 80 percent or more by a parent taxable in their state, while others, notably California, tax all intercorporate dividends. Pennsylvania excludes from the measure of corporate income all dividends received. Currently, all states except California and New Jersey follow federal depreciation rules, but this conformity in depreciation deductions is relatively new. Many states, because of revenue uncertainties, chose not to allow the depreciation methods that Congress adopted in the Economic Recovery Tax Act of 1981 and then removed in the Tax Reform Act of 1986.

Application of state corporate net income taxes to corporations engaged in multistate business is governed by the federal Constitution through the Commerce, Equal Protection, and Due Process Clauses, U.S. Supreme Court decisions interpreting these constitutional protections, and Public Law 86-272 and its state constitutional and statutory counterparts. In 1959, the U.S. Supreme Court determined that state taxation of income earned in interstate commerce was not a violation of the Commerce Clause as long as the method of assessing the taxable income was in line with the local activities of the taxpayer in the state. The Supreme Court later provided a four-pronged test to establish the constitutionality of state taxes on interstate commerce. These tests involved whether the tax is: applied to an activity with substantial nexus, fairly apportioned, nondiscriminatory against interstate commerce, and fair relative to the services provided by the state to the taxpayer. The first of these tests is also part of Public Law 86-272. In the case of a property tax levied by a state in which the commerce involves a foreign country, two additional tests are used. If the tax is shown to subject foreign commerce to the risk of multiple taxation or to impair the federal government's ability to "speak with one voice," then the tax will be disallowed. Further, Public Law 86-272 determines whether or not a firm, engaged in the interstate sale of tangible personal property, may be subject to a state's corporate net income tax. Generally, an out-of-state business must have a permanent physical presence and employees in a state in order to be taxable under a state's corporate income tax.

Geographic attribution on a state-by-state basis of a multistate corporation's overall net income is accomplished through either the use of establishment-level books and records (*separate accounting*) or the proportionate attribution among states of overall income on the basis of the location of its payroll, property, and sales. In 1957, a model statute, the Uniform Division of Income for Tax Purposes Act, was developed by the states to define state-taxable net income and procedures recommended to determine in a practical manner the payroll, property, and sales of a multistate corporation. In addition, the model statute provides that investment income, defined as nonbusiness income, be entirely attributed or *allocated* to the commercial domicile of the corporation. Over the past 40 years, special apportionment rules have been developed for transportation, telecommunications, and financial institutions (see also Apportionment).

State taxation of the corporate form of business dates back to the early 19th century when corporate charters were initially granted through individual acts of state legislatures, and fees were collected for the privilege of incorporating and doing business in the state. It should be noted that the corporation generally succeeded earlier colonial business forms such as trading and joint-stock companies, because the corporate form offered limited liability as well as ease of investment to shareholders, and perpetuity to the business itself. Corporate registration fees were broadened in the middle of the 19th century in many states to levies on the measured capital stock (usually net worth) of the incorporated company. As incorporation became administered through state secretaries of state, and information was routinely collected on the officers and amount of capitalization of the newly formed corporation, these fees became general corporation taxes. Like the development of state personal income taxes, state adoption of the corporate income tax *preceded* federal enactment of the federal corporate income tax: Hawaii enacted the first corporate net income tax in 1901, eight years before Congress enacted the modern federal corporate income tax.

Unlike the corporate form in other industrialized countries, the U.S. corporation is a legal instrumentality of subnational governments. Until the turn of the 20th century, one corporation could not own shares of another. New Jersey was the first to permit, through state law, one corporation's ownership of another. Other states quickly followed as the business community pressured state legislatures for the authority to create such parent corporations or holding companies. Until the New Jersey statute was enacted, trusts were used to own corporations. Especially with the advent of the holding company, corporations enjoyed a number of distinct benefits: perpetual life, limited liability for shareholders or investors, and ready transferability or liquidity of investment interests. Additional benefits that corporations (and unincorporated businesses) enjoy include the definition, enforcement, and protection of private property rights and contracts, and various specific services provided by the state. Because of these benefits, and the legality of the corporation as

a separate entity, taxation of corporate net income has been justified under both the benefit and ability-to-pay theories of taxation.

Older industrial states, primarily in the East, which began imposing capital levies in the 19th century in conjunction with the corporate registration process, have tended to treat corporations that are part of a holding company as separate entities. States that began taxing corporations after the advent of the holding company form have generally looked to the overall corporation or the *unitary* business as the basis of taxation. California, which adopted its first corporate net income tax statute in 1929, has been the most aggressive in employing the unitary business tax concept.

There are three tests, resulting from a series of U.S. Supreme Court decisions, that are used in determining whether a business is unitary. They are the three-unities test, the dependency/contribution test, and the factors of profitability test. The first is a three-pronged test which holds that a business is unitary as long as any one of three tests is satisfied. They are tests of unity of ownership; unity of operation, which is linked to staff functions; and unity of use, which is linked to line functions. These tests are widely criticized for their ambiguity. The second test, dependency/contribution, establishes a business to be unitary when in-state operations depend upon, or contribute to, out-of-state operations. The final test, factors of probability, requires proof of functional integration, centralization of management, and economies of scale. It is important to notice that these tests are not discrete; there is substantial overlap because the same factors can be used as evidence in more than one test. The U.S. Supreme Court has offered no "bright line" test that would require a business to have a substantial flow of goods in order to be held to be unitary. In fact, it has declared that the prerequisite for that is a "flow of value, not a flow of goods."

Which of these tests is used in the state's determination of a unitary business depends primarily on the form of the business organization. Vertically integrated corporations will usually be treated as unitary, and horizontally integrated corporations will not. In the case of vertically integrated corporations, the tests of dependency/contribution and factors of profitability are used, while in the case of the horizontally integrated corporations, the three-unities test is used. In the case of vertically integrated corporations, the three-unities test does not "fit" well, and the California Supreme Court has indicated that it would apply less weight to this test. For a vertically integrated corporation, the need by one division for the raw materials or products provided by another division is viewed as proof for the dependency/contribution test. In the case of the factors of profitability test, proof is given by either centralized management or controlled interaction of the divisions. For a horizontally integrated corporation to be treated as unitary, there must be a sufficient degree of centralized management and central services. In 1982, the U.S. Supreme Court stated that the mere potential of contribution to income from functional integration, centralization of management, and economies of scale is not sufficient for a business to be held to be unitary; this contribution must actually occur. Further, the Supreme Court has noted no difference in applying the standards of central management and economies of scale to either vertically or horizontally integrated businesses.

The unitary business concept has effects in several areas of state corporate income tax. One area is in determining whether a business must use formula apportionment or separate accounting in determining taxable income. If a business is held to be unitary, then it must use formula apportionment. A second area is a test of whether an affiliated group of corporations must file on a combined report basis in a particular state. For instance, nearly one-quarter of the states require unitary businesses to file a combined report, and more than half have combined reporting.

While state application of the unitary business concept has been upheld by the U.S. Supreme Court, it continues to be the source of considerable friction between business taxpayers and state tax administrators. Business taxpayers often express the view that the ambiguity of the concept, especially when applied on a worldwide basis, encourages aggressive tax administration and materially increases the risk of multiple taxation. On the other hand, state tax administrators often express the view that multistate business taxpayers aggressively plan their state corporate income taxes, and utilize transfer pricing and other mechanisms to overstate income in nonincome tax states, and understate their income in states with corporate income taxes.

### Additional readings

Advisory Commission on Intergovernmental Relations. *Significant Features of Fiscal Federalism, vol. 1: Budget Processes and Tax Systems.* M-185, February 1993.

Commerce Clearing House. *All States Tax Guide.* Chicago, 1995.

Hellerstein, Jerome R., and Walter Hellerstein. *State Taxation. I. Corporate Income and Franchise Taxes.* 2d ed. Boston: Warren, Gorham, and Lamont, 1995.

McLure, Charles E. *The State Corporation Income Tax. Issues in Worldwide Unitary Combination.* Stanford: Hoover Institution Press, 1984.

*Cross references:* apportionment; income tax, corporate, federal; income tax, federal; multinational corporations, taxation; value-added tax, state.

# Income tax, federal

Emil M. Sunley
Janet Stotsky
International Monetary Fund

*A tax levied by the federal government on the incomes of individuals and businesses.*

At the federal level, the personal income tax is the most important revenue source, comprising 8.4 percent of gross domestic product in 1995, while the corporate income tax that year comprised 2.2 percent.

The income tax applies to every individual and entity having taxable income. Taxpayers are classified by the type of return they are required to file. Individuals file the individual tax return, and in 1994, 116 million of these forms were filed, making them the best-known and least-liked government forms. Corporations, trusts and estates, and partnerships file another form.

The base of the income tax falls far short of a comprehensive notion of income. The starting point is "gross income," defined broadly as "all income from whatever source derived." Taxable income is determined for both individuals and corporations by subtracting allowable exclusions, exemptions, and deductions from gross income.

## The personal income tax

For individuals, gross income includes wages and salaries, taxable interest, dividends, capital gains, rents, royalties, pension income including distributions from Individual Retirement Accounts (IRAs), business income from sole proprietorships, income from partnerships, income from estates and trusts, farm income, refunds of state and local income taxes (if they were previously deducted), alimony received, unemployment benefits, Social Security benefits over certain dollar limits, and other income. U.S. residents are generally taxed on worldwide income, although they may receive credit for taxes paid to foreign countries.

Gross income is a misnomer in two important ways. First, certain items are specifically excluded from gross income. These include gifts and bequests, death benefits, interest on tax-exempt state and local bonds, compensation for injuries or sickness, amounts received on accident and health plans, certain fringe benefits (the most important being pension contributions and health care benefits), and certain income transfers. Second, gross income is in some cases a net concept because certain expenses relating to earning income are netted out (e.g., from partnerships and Subchapter S corporations).

Taxpayers are allowed to deduct certain amounts, termed "adjustments," from gross income to arrive at adjusted gross income (AGI). The most important of these adjustments are one-half of self-employment taxes paid by the self-employed, qualified contributions to certain tax-deferred retirement accounts (IRAs and Keogh retirement plans), and alimony paid.

Taxable income is defined as AGI minus personal exemptions and either a standard deduction or allowable itemized deductions. Taxpayers could claim a personal exemption of $2,650 in 1997, an amount that is adjusted annually for inflation, for each taxpayer and dependent included on the tax return, although these exemptions are phased out for high-income taxpayers. Individuals can choose to itemize personal deductions or to claim the standard deduction—$4,150 for single individuals and $6,900 for married couples filing jointly in 1997. Itemized deductions consist of medical expenses over 7.5 percent of AGI; mortgage interest (with some restrictions); charitable contributions; state and local income and property taxes (but not sales or excise taxes or fees paid to state and local governments); casualty or theft losses over 10 percent of AGI; and unreimbursed employee business expenses, expenses incurred in earning investment income, and other miscellaneous expenses over 2 percent of AGI. Middle- and higher-income families and individuals are more likely to itemize their personal deductions because they tend to pay high state and local taxes and have larger home mortgage interest deductions. Overall, fewer than 29 percent of individual taxpayers itemize. In 1994, taxpayers reported taxable income of $2,598 billion.

The U.S. personal income tax has a rate schedule with five marginal tax rates—15, 28, 31, 36, and 39.6 percent. In 1997, the top marginal tax rate took the form of a 10-percent surcharge on the tax liability on taxable income over $271,050. In addition, various phaseout provisions for personal exemptions and itemized deductions can increase the effective marginal tax rate for many taxpayers. The combination of five brackets and phaseouts has resulted in a marginal tax rate schedule that does not vary smoothly with income. The interaction of the tax system with the earned income tax credit for low-income families and social security taxes, as well as with expenditure programs such as Social Security and Aid to Families with Dependent Children resulted in an even more complicated marginal tax rate schedule.

Individuals may file under four different rate schedules, applying to different forms of household composition. The most widely used schedules are for married couples filing jointly and for single individuals. The widths of the tax brackets are wider for the joint filers than for single filers. There is a rate schedule for married couples filing separately, but it is little used as it is seldom advantageous on tax grounds for married couples to file separately. The final rate schedule, which applies to heads of households, is generally used by unmarried individuals with a dependent child. It provides brackets that are wider than the rate schedule for single filers but narrower than the rate schedule for joint filers.

By permitting joint filing, the U.S. personal income tax imposes the same tax on married couples with the same income regardless of how the total income is split between the spouses, but imposes a different tax on a married couple and a single individual with the same income. One result of permitting joint filing is that the personal income tax results in both marriage penalties and marriage subsidies. If two individuals with about the same income marry, their tax burden under the joint rate schedule will be higher than it would be if they were both permitted to continue to file as single individuals. On the other hand, if two individuals with highly uneven incomes marry, the combined tax burden will be lower under joint filing. The introduction in recent years of higher marginal tax rates and the narrowing of tax brackets have increased the marriage penalty for couples with similar incomes.

Realized capital gains are included in full in taxable income, but long-term capital gains are subject to lower rates: no more than 28 percent for property held a year and 20 percent for property held 18 months. Eventually a rate of 18 percent will apply to gains held five years. (Taxpayers in the 15 percent bracket also receive lower rates.) Thus, for higher-income taxpayers, there is a significant difference between the tax rates on ordinary income and capital gains. Capital losses may be offset against capital gains and then against ordinary income, but no more than $3,000 per year in losses may be offset against ordinary income, with the remainder carried forward indefinitely. Taxpayers may exclude $250,000 of gain ($500,000 for a joint return) on the sale of a personal residence; this exclusion is available every two years.

Individuals who derive income from sole proprietorships may claim their income and expenses related to their business activities on a separate schedule, which is then integrated with the rest of the personal income tax.

After computing tax on taxable income, the individual taxpayer is allowed to claim certain tax credits. The most important of these are the earned income credit (a variable, vanishing credit targeted to low-income filers who work), the child credit, the education credit, the credit for child or dependent care, the credit for the elderly or disabled, the foreign tax credit, and the low-income housing tax credit. Of these, only the earned income credit is refundable (the excess of the credit over the tax liability is returned to the taxpayer). Many low-income households are not liable to tax (if their AGI is less than the total of their deductions and personal exemptions), but may still receive a tax credit refund through the earned income credit.

Individuals are also subject to the alternative minimum tax. This tax is computed by taking AGI, making adjustments and additions for tax preferences, and then subtracting certain itemized deductions and the personal exemption. The rate is 26 and 28 percent for individuals. Taxpayers pay the alternative minimum tax if it exceeds their regular tax.

The personal income tax is partly indexed to inflation. The personal exemption, the standard deduction, the maximum earned income and the phaseout base amounts of the earned income credit, and the bracket widths are all indexed to overall changes in the Consumer Price Index. Indexing of fixed dollar amounts was first enacted in 1981 for tax years after 1984, but frequent changes in the tax law since then have resulted in a number of discretionary changes in the indexed parameters. There is no indexing of depreciation, capital gains, or interest income and expense.

The main form of tax collection is based on withholding of employee earnings, instituted in 1943 with the dramatic expansion of the income tax to finance World War II. There is only very limited withholding of capital income. However, individuals with significant income outside the withholding system must estimate their tax liability and pay it in quarterly installments during the year. On their final tax return, taxpayers reconcile their final tax liability with amounts already paid.

### The corporation income tax

Taxable income for corporations and other entities required to file the corporation income tax return is defined as gross income less allowable deductions. Domestic corporations are, in general, taxed on worldwide income, although they may receive credit for tax paid to foreign countries. Most businesses use the accrual method of accounting, and businesses that have inventories are required to use the accrual method. Reserves typically are not allowed for tax purposes, although small banks can maintain tax-deductible reserves for bad debts and insurance companies can maintain reserves for future liabilities. Businesses may use either the last-in first-out (LIFO) or first-in first-out (FIFO) methods of inventory accounting. They depreciate machinery and equipment under accelerated methods and real estate using the straight-line method over lifetimes set to approximate the economic usefulness of the asset. They can also expense up to $18,500 of machinery and equipment each year (in 1998, rising over time to $25,000 by 2003). State and local taxes paid by a business are generally deductible business expenses for income tax purposes. Net operating losses can typically be carried back two years and forward 20 years, beginning in 1998.

The United States adheres to the classical system of a separate corporate tax with no tax relief for dividends paid by corporations or dividends received by individuals. Double taxation, however, is mitigated for Subchapter S corporations (small corporations taxed like partnerships), cooperatives, regulated investment companies, real estate investment trusts, and real estate mortgage investment conduits. In addition, domestic corporations are allowed a deduction of 70, 80, or 100 percent of dividends received from taxable domestic corporations, with the amount of the deduction dependent on the degree of ownership.

The formal tax rate schedule for corporations has progressive marginal rates of 15, 25, 34, and 35 percent, with the top rate applying to corporations with taxable income in excess of $10 million. The benefit of the lower tax rates, however, is phased out or recaptured over certain income ranges by imposing additional taxes of 3 or 5 percent. As a result, the marginal tax rate schedule for corporations can be said to have eight marginal rates of 15, 25, 34, 39, 34, 35, 38, and 35 percent, with the 39 and 38 percent rates being the marginal rates for taxable income in the income range over which the benefits of the lower marginal rates are phased out. The taxable income of certain personal service corporations is taxed at 35 percent.

Corporations can claim certain tax credits, including the foreign tax credit and the general business credit. The latter is an umbrella covering eight separate tax credits for investment, targeted jobs (for individuals in certain groups with high unemployment rates), alcohol used as fuel, research and development, and so forth.

Corporations pay tax on income from the sale of capital assets at the same rate as other income. Certain tax benefits, such as depreciation, are subject to recapture at ordinary income tax rates. Unlike individuals, corporations can only offset capital losses against capital gains. The remaining losses may be carried back three years and carried forward five years against capital gains.

Certain nonprofit organizations, including charitable, religious, educational, and medical organizations, trade associations, labor unions, and fraternal organizations, are exempt from corporate income taxes. These organizations are, however, subject to tax on business income derived from activities unrelated to their exempt purposes.

There is no indexing of business income for inflation. Depreciation allowances are based on historical cost. Accelerated depreciation is sometimes justified on the grounds that this compensates businesses for the use of historical cost basis in an inflationary environment. Though inventories are based on historical costs, businesses may choose whether to use LIFO or FIFO inventory accounting. LIFO offers some advantages in an inflationary environment. Financial assets are not indexed to inflation. There is no adjustment to the stock of debt based on changes in its value from inflation fluctuations. Nominal capital gains and nominal interest income are taxable, while nominal interest payments are deductible.

Corporations are also subject to an alternative minimum tax, which was designed to ensure that all corporations pay tax, even those benefiting from extensive tax preferences. The base of this tax is computed by recalculating taxable income, making adjustments, and adding back certain tax preference items. The rate of tax is 20 percent for corporations. In addition to the alternative minimum tax, corporations are subject to an environmental tax. The base for this tax is alternative minimum taxable income in excess of $2 million. The tax rate is 0.12 percent.

There is no withholding system for corporations. Instead, they are required to pay estimated taxes in quarterly installments, based on their estimated current earnings or, in some cases, previous earnings. On their final tax return, taxpayers reconcile their final tax liability with amounts already paid.

### Additional readings

Internal Revenue Service. *Statistics of Income–1992, Individual Income Tax Returns.* Washington, D.C., 1995: 31.

U.S. Office of Management and Budget. *Historical Tables: Budget of the United States Government, Fiscal Year 1997.* Washington, D.C., 1996: 32.

*Cross references:* adjusted gross income; alternative minimum tax, corporate; alternative minimum tax, personal; capital cost recovery; child care expenses: the child care credit; dividends, double taxation of; family, tax treatment of; income tax, corporate, federal; inventory accounting; itemized deductions; marriage penalty; nonprofit organizations, federal tax treatment; taxable income, corporate; withholding of taxes.

# Individual retirement accounts

Larry Ozanne
Congressional Budget Office

*Savings accounts with specific income tax incentives and penalties designed to encourage working people to save for retirement.*

Individual Retirement Accounts (IRAs) were first authorized in the Employee Retirement Income Security Act of 1974 (ERISA) as a means of encouraging working people to save for retirement. Recently, pre-retirement withdrawals from IRAs for higher-education costs and a first-time home purchase have been authorized. Unlike 401(k) and related salary reduction plans, IRAs are not run by employers. The enactment of IRAs extended to workers without pensions the same kind of tax advantages already granted to pension funds and the self-employed.

### History

Starting in 1975, individuals were allowed to set up separate accounts at financial institutions and deduct the value of their contributions from their current taxable income. Only employees without pensions were eligible to contribute, and their annual contributions were limited to 15 percent of pay or a maximum of $1,500. The investment returns of these accounts were also excluded from taxable income in the year earned, but withdrawals were to be included in taxable income in the year they occurred. To encourage use of the accounts for retirement saving, ERISA set a penalty of 10 percent additional tax on withdrawals by taxpayers before age 59½.

The Economic Recovery Tax Act of 1981 expanded IRA eligibility and increased maximum contributions. Starting in 1982, all persons with earnings could contribute to IRAs, whether or not they were in a pension plan, and the maximum contribution was increased to 100 percent of earnings or $2,000. In response, tax returns with IRA contributions jumped from 4 percent of all returns with wage and salary income in 1981 to 14 percent in 1982 and 18 percent in 1986.

Deductible IRA contributions were restricted by the Tax Reform Act of 1986. Starting in 1987, the act allowed deductible contributions only by an individual who was not covered by an employer pension plan, and who had adjusted gross income between $25,000 and $35,000 (or, for joint returns, $40,000 to $50,000). The restriction caused returns with IRA contributions to drop to 8 percent of all returns in 1987 and to decline slowly from there through the mid-1990s.

The Taxpayer Relief Act of 1997 substantially raised the income limits, which will eventually be $50,000 to $60,000 for single returns (the year 2005 and after) and $80,000 to $100,000 for joint returns (2007 and after). The act also allows individuals to elect back-loaded IRAs, called "Roth" IRAs, in which contributions are not deductible but withdrawals are not taxed—a treatment similar to that of a tax-exempt bond. These IRAs are phased out between $95,000 and $110,000 of income for singles, and $150,000 to $160,000 for joint returns. Virtually all taxpayers will thus be eligible for some type of fully tax-favored IRA. Regulations imposing penalties on premature withdrawals were also relaxed, so that the accounts may be used to save for higher-education expenses or the first purchase of a home.

## Effect on saving

IRAs have been popular among taxpayers. For example, during the years in which all taxpayers were eligible to contribute to IRAs, up to $40 billion of savings was deposited into IRA accounts annually. The large volume of IRA contributions, however, does not indicate that IRAs increased saving. IRAs increased personal saving only to the extent that people funded their contributions by reducing their consumption. Contributions funded by saving less in other accounts and by paying fewer taxes do not raise saving.

In principle, the incentive structure of IRAs could increase or decrease saving. The deferral of taxation on contributions and investment earnings until withdrawal increases the rate of return to saving. Because a higher return to saving has offsetting substitution and income effects, the net effect could be to increase or decrease saving. In addition, the limit on contributions means that persons able to contribute more than the limit without increasing their saving have only an income effect, which could reduce saving. Finally, features of the IRA and its marketing by financial institutions may have increased saving by making it easier for people to save. The heavy advertising of IRAs between 1982 and 1986 may have helped people focus on the importance of saving for retirement, and the deduction on contributions and the penalty on withdrawals may have helped people make and preserve their contributions. Backloaded IRAs are less likely to increase private savings because there is no up-front tax saving, and there is no future tax imposed on withdrawals.

Empirical studies have not been able to resolve the uncertainty about how IRAs affect saving, although many attempts have been made. The evidence for the full population is contradictory, but a limited consensus suggests that IRAs increased saving for nonelderly and less wealthy families.

The range of results is indicated by three pairs of analysts who have each measured saving for samples of families, estimated models of saving behavior, and used those models to predict how IRAs affected saving between 1982 and 1986. One pair, Venti and Wise (1986, 1990, 1991), estimate in three separate studies that if the contribution limit had been raised above $2,000, between 57 and 66 percent of additional IRA contributions would have come from reduced consumption. A second pair, Gale and Scholz (1995), estimate that the level would be at most 2 percent and that IRAs possibly increased consumption. The third pair, Joines and Manegold (1991), find that the expansion of eligibility in 1982 had no statistically significant effect on consumption for the full population.

Although Gale and Scholz and Joines and Manegold find no increase in saving for the full population, each pair finds an increase for a subpopulation. Gale and Scholz find that people under age 60, who could not withdraw from IRAs without paying the penalty, reduced their consumption by up to 35 cents per dollar contributed. Joines and Manegold find that people who had less than $25,000 of taxable financial assets in 1982 reduced their consumption by 63 cents per dollar contributed. Because Venti and Wise find large increases in saving for the full population, all three studies present evidence that IRAs increased saving for sizable subpopulations. Studies finding an increase in saving for subpopulations but not for the full population indicate either that the increases found for some subpopulations were small relative to saving for the full population or that other subpopulations reduced their saving.

More recently, Attanasio and DeLeire (1994) found little evidence of an IRA savings effect, using a methodology similar to Joines and Manegold.

## Additional readings

Attanasio, Orazio P., and Thomas C. DeLeire. "IRAs and Household Savings Revisited: Some New Evidence." National Bureau of Economic Research Working Paper 4900, October 1994.

Congressional Budget Office. *The Uncertain Effect of IRAs on Saving,* 1994.

Engen, Eric M., William G. Gale, and John Karl Scholz. "The Illusory Effects of Savings Incentives on Savings." *Journal of Economic Perspectives* 10 (Fall 1996): 113–38.

Gale, William G., and John Karl Scholz. "IRAs and Household Saving." *American Economic Review* 84 (December 1994): 1233–60.

Gravelle, Jane G. "Do Individual Retirement Accounts Increase Saving?" *Journal of Economic Perspectives* 5 (2) (Spring 1991): 133–48.

Hubbard, R. Glenn, and Jonathan S. Skinner. "Assessing the Effectiveness of Savings Incentives." *Journal of Economic Perspectives* 10 (Fall 1996): 73–90.

Joines, Douglas H., and James G. Manegold. "IRAs and Saving: Evidence from a Panel of Taxpayers." Mimeograph, Table 8. University of Southern California, September 1991.

Poterba, James, Steven Venti, and David A. Wise. "How Retirement Saving Programs Increase Saving." *Journal of Economic Perspectives* 10 (Fall 1996): 91–112.

Skinner, Jonathan. "Individual Retirement Accounts: A Review of the Evidence." *Tax Notes* (January 13, 1992): 201–12.

Venti, Steven F., and David A. Wise. "Tax Deferred Accounts, Constrained Choice and Estimation of Individual Saving," *Review of Economic Studies* 53 (1986): 593–94.

Venti, Steven F., and David A. Wise. "Have IRAs Increased U.S. Saving?: Evidence from Consumer Expenditure Surveys." *Quarterly Journal of Economics* 105 (3) (August 1990): 691.

Venti Steven F., and David A. Wise. "The Saving Effect of Tax-Deferred Retirement Accounts." In *National Saving and Economic Performance,* edited by B. Douglas Bernheim and John B. Shoven. Chicago: University of Chicago Press, 1991, p. 123.

*Cross references:* deferral of tax; income tax, federal; profit-sharing plans; saving, taxes and.

# Inflation indexation of income taxes

Vito Tanzi
International Monetary Fund

*Measures undertaken to prevent real income tax burdens from rising with general price inflation.*

### Indexation of income taxes

When the price level increases, the real burden imposed by income taxes may also increase. Indexing income taxes for inflation prevents this from happening by (1) adjusting tax rates, exemptions, and the standard deduction, and (2) adjusting how the base of the income tax itself is defined, to offset the effects of general increases in price level.

### Adjustments in tax rates, exemptions, and the standard deductions

Table 1 shows how inflation could affect the real tax burden of a taxpayer whose only source of income

was wages and salaries. The example assumes that in the absence of inflation, the taxpayer's income would be $40,000, and that the tax system would allow the taxpayer to claim a personal exemption of $4,000, and an additional standard deduction of $6,000. The example further assumes that taxable income between $0 and $30,000 is taxed at a rate of 10 percent, while each $1 of taxable income in excess of $30,000 is taxed at a rate of 20 percent.

Column (1) shows that if there were no inflation, the hypothetical taxpayer would face a tax liability of $3,000, which equals 7.5 percent of the taxpayer's total income.

Now assume that the price level increases by 10 percent, and that the taxpayer gets a cost-of-living increase of 10 percent from the employer. As can be seen from column (2), this would have the effect of increasing the taxpayer's income in "current dollars" from $40,000 to $44,000. If no adjustments were made in either the exemption or the standard deduction, the taxpayer's taxable income would increase from $30,000 to $34,000. If there were also no adjustments in tax rates, the "extra" $2,000 in income would also be taxed at the higher rate of 20 percent. Overall, the taxpayer would see tax liability increase from $3,000 to $3,800, which equals 8.6 percent of total income. Because the taxpayer is paying a larger percentage of income in tax than before, the real tax burden has increased.

There are two reasons why the real tax burden goes up in this example. One is that the exemption and the standard deduction are not increased to keep pace with inflation. In a world with no inflation, the combined effect of these two provisions was to exempt $10,000/$40,000, or 25 percent of the taxpayer's income, from tax. After inflation, if these amounts are not increased, they exempt only $10,000/$44,000, or just under 23 percent of income, from tax.

The other reason the real tax burden increases is that the taxpayer is moved into a higher tax bracket because of the cost-of-living increase. This phenomenon has been given the name of "bracket creep" to reflect the idea that unless tax rates are adjusted, inflation has the effect of pushing taxpayers into higher tax brackets.

Column (3) shows what would happen if personal exemptions, the standard deduction, and tax rates were adjusted for inflation. These adjustments would take the following forms: First, the amounts of the exemption and standard deduction would need to be increased by 10 percent. Second, the 10 percent tax bracket would need to be widened by increasing the upper limit by 10 percent, so that the higher tax rate would take effect at an income of $33,000 instead of $30,000.

If these adjustments were made, the taxpayer would face a postinflation tax liability of $33,000 instead of $34,000, and pay a tax on this income of

**TABLE 1**

**Effect of Inflation on Real Tax Burden**

| Items on Tax Return | No Inflation (1) | 10% Inflation, No Indexing (2) | 10% Inflation with Indexing (3) |
|---|---|---|---|
| Wages and Salaries | $40,000 | $44,000 | $44,000 |
| Personal Exemption | $4,000 | $4,000 | $4,400 |
| Standard Deduction | $6,000 | $6,000 | $6,600 |
| Taxable Income | $30,000 | $34,000 | $33,000 |
| Tax Liability | $3,000 | $3,800 | $3,300 |
| Tax Brackets | | | |
| $0–$30,000 | 10% | 10% | N.A. |
| Over $30,000 | 20% | 20% | N.A. |
| $0–$33,000 | N.A. | N.A. | 10% |
| Over $33,000 | N.A. | N.A. | 20% |
| Average Tax Rate | 7.5% | 8.6% | 7.5% |

N.A. = not applicable.

$3,300. The inflation-adjusted tax liability would equal 7.5 percent of the taxpayer's current dollar income of $44,000, which is the same real tax burden as before inflation.

Although this illustration is hypothetical, it is not fanciful. During the postwar period, increases in the price level pushed U.S. taxpayers into higher tax brackets, while at the same time eroding the value of personal exemptions and the standard deduction. These effects became especially pronounced in the 1970s and early 1980s as oil shocks accelerated the pace of general price increases.

From time to time, Congress and the president took measures to "cut taxes" by raising the amount of the personal exemption or by lowering personal income tax rates. These measures, however, only partially offset the increase in real tax burdens brought about by failing to index exemptions and the standard deduction, and by bracket creep.

The Economic Recovery Tax Act of 1981 marked a fundamental break with this pattern. The act provided, beginning in 1985, that exemptions, the standard deduction, and the width of tax brackets would be adjusted for inflation in a manner similar to that illustrated in the table. Since that time, these items have been adjusted by the Treasury Department each year, based on the Consumer Price Index. The result is that real tax burdens on wage and salary income no longer increase automatically with inflation.

## Inflation and the measurement of capital income

This illustration is only one way in which inflation can affect real income tax burdens. The amount of capital income, such as interest, capital gains, and profits reported on tax returns, also rises with inflation. Much of the increase in taxable income, however, may really be a return *of* capital, which in principle should not be taxed, rather than a return *on* capital, which should be included in the base of a comprehensive income tax.

Inflation poses more complicated issues for the proper measurement and taxation of capital income. These are best illustrated using the three most important examples: the measurement of income from capital gains, the depreciation deductions, and the measurement of interest income and expense.

### Capital gains

Consider first the case of income from capital gains. Suppose that if prices were stable, a real asset would have increased in value by 10 percent, from $100,000 to $110,000, over a given period. Thus, the capital gains, if realized through sale of the asset, would have been $10,000. Assume instead that over the same period the price level rises by 10 percent so that the nominal value of the asset grows at a rate of 20 percent, of which 10 percent represents inflation and 10 percent represents the real, or inflation-adjusted, return. In this latter case, the value of the asset at the time of sales is $120,000. Without an adjustment for inflation, the reported capital gain would be $20,000, which is more than twice the amount of the real or capital gain of $10,000. In extreme cases, failure to account for inflation may cause taxpayers to be taxed as if they had received a capital gain, when they had either no gain or even a capital loss. In the illustration above, if the real value of the asset appreciated at a rate of 0 percent instead of 10 percent when prices were stable, the taxpayer would have no capital gain. However, if prices rose by 10 percent its value would "increase" from $100,000 to $110,000, and without adjusting for inflation, the taxpayer would be taxed as if the capital gain had been $10,000, when in reality the gain was $0.

## *Depreciation*

The value of tax deductions for depreciation, which represent a return of capital rather than a return on capital, is also affected by inflation. Consider a piece of equipment that is initially purchased for $60,000 and that depreciates on a straight-line basis over three years. If prices were stable, and deductions for economic depreciation were allowed, the taxpayer would take a depreciation deduction of $20,000 each year for three years.

Suppose now that prices increase at a rate of 10 percent per year. In that case, allowing the taxpayer to take depreciation deductions based on the "historical" or non-inflation-adjusted basis of the depreciable asset would not allow the investor a full return *of* capital because the cost of replacing the services provided by the depreciating machine would rise each year by 10 percent.

## *Interest income and expense*

When prices are not stable, and inflation is anticipated, the monetary rate of interest will tend to be higher than the rate prevailing with price stability. If investors have perfect foresight about inflation, the monetary or nominal rate of interest can be assumed to approximate the sum of the real rate and the anticipated increase in the price level. Thus, if the anticipated rate of inflation were 10 percent and the real rate of interest were 5 percent, the nominal interest rate would approximate 15 percent.

In this case, in the absence of a tax on interest income, someone who lent $1,000 would receive $1,050 after one year. If prices were unstable, the lender would receive $1,150, but would not be any better off than if he or she had received $1,050 when prices were stable. This is because $100 out of the $150 of interest income just compensates the lender for the loss caused by inflation on the original financial capital of $1,000. Taxing the full $150 thus overstates the actual interest income received by the lender and paid by the borrower by the amount of $100.

## Indexing the tax base

The administrative measures that would need to be implemented in order to prevent inflation from mismeasuring capital income are more complex than those required to deal with bracket creep. In principle, capital gains can be indexed by increasing the taxable basis by the amount of inflation that has occurred since the asset was purchased. Thus, in the example above, the taxable basis of the asset at the time of sale would be multiplied by 110 percent, giving an inflation-adjusted basis of $110,000. The taxable capital gain would then be the difference between the sales price of the asset of $120,000 and the adjusted basis of $110,000, which would yield

the correct result of an inflation-adjusted capital gain of $10,000.

A similar adjustment could be made in the case of depreciable assets. In this case, the undepreciated basis of the asset would be increased each year to reflect the increase in the inflation rate, and this amount would then be divided by number of years remaining. Thus, in the above example, where prices rise at a rate of 10 percent per year, the undepreciated basis at the end of the first year would be $40,000 ($60,000 − $20,000). This amount would be multiplied by 1.10 to yield the inflation-adjusted basis of $44,000. Dividing by 2, the number of years remaining, would result in a year 2 (indexed) deduction of $22,000. Subtracting this amount from $44,000 would yield an undepreciated basis of $22,000, which when multiplied by 1.10 would yield a year 3 (indexed) depreciation deduction of $24,200.

In the case of interest income and expense, an appropriate remedy would be to subtract the inflationary component of interest payments in both interest income received by creditors and interest income paid by borrowers. Thus the borrower in the above example would be required to include $50 instead of $150 as taxable interest income, and the borrower would be allowed to deduct $50 instead of $150 as interest expense.

Both the capital gains exclusion and accelerated depreciation have been defended as crude ways of dealing with the effect that inflation has on the measurement of capital income. Economists agree, however, that these methods are very inexact ways of dealing with the problem, and that it would be preferable in principle to use more exact ways of indexing the tax base, such as those summarized above.

In the United States, proposals have been made from time to time to index capital gains and depreciation for inflation, following the procedures outlined above, and proposals were made to allow for partial indexing of interest payments in the Treasury Department's 1984 proposal for fundamental tax reform. Although the economic principles to be followed in indexing capital income are clear, implementing these principles in practice has proved to be administratively complex, which is one reason why these proposals have yet to be enacted.

Both the political impetus and the economic need for indexing the tax base for inflation are greatest when inflation rates are high. Thus, at the current low rates of inflation, it seems unlikely that significant efforts to index the tax base will be made.

One attractive feature of taxing individuals and business on the basis of consumption instead of income is that one does not need to worry about indexing capital income for inflation. This is because a consumption tax base would include neither capital gains nor interest payments in taxable income, and would not allow deductions to be taken for interest expense. Because the capital cost of assets would be deducted immediately, or expensed, the need to adjust capital cost recovery allowance to reflect the replacement cost of depreciating assets would also not be necessary.

## Additional readings

Congressional Budget Office. *Indexing Capital Gains*. Congress of the United States: Congressional Budget Office, 1990.

Halperin, Daniel, and C. Eugene Steuerle. "Indexing the Tax System for Inflation." In *Uneasy Compromise: Problems of a Hybrid Income-Consumption Tax*, edited by Henry Aaron and Harvey Galper. Washington, D.C.: The Brookings Institution, 1988, pp. 347–72.

Steuerle, C. Eugene. *The Tax Decade: How Taxes Came to Dominate the Public Agenda*. Washington, D.C.: The Urban Institute Press; distributed by University Press of America, 1992.

Tanzi, Vito. "Inflation and the Indexation of Personal Income Taxes in Theory and Practice." *Banca Nazionale Del Lavoro Quarterly Review* 118 (September 1976): 241–72.

U.S. Department of the Treasury, Office of the Secretary. *Tax Reform for Fairness, Simplicity and Economic Growth*. Vol. 2, ch. 9. Washington, D.C., 1984.

*Cross references:* capital cost recovery; capital gains taxation; consumption taxation; expensing; inflation tax; interest deductibility; personal exemption, federal; standard deduction, federal.

# Inflation tax

## G. Thomas Woodward
Congressional Research Service, Library of Congress

*A type of finance in which the government increases the supply of money and generates inflation to obtain real resources from the public.*

## Money creation and inflation

The inflation tax is based on the power of sovereign governments to regulate the money supply. Money—a symbol of purchasing power, such as a coin, note, or book entry—is a medium between selling and buying, used to avoid cumbersome barter. While a variety of entities can function as money, the right to furnish a basic medium of exchange is typically monopolized by the government.

To perform its transactions role, money need only symbolize wealth, not embody it. Thus, it is possible to profit from supplying money. Paper money, for example, is produced at a fraction of its value in the marketplace. Commodity monies, such as precious metals, may also produce a profit for the government if the metallic value of the coin is less than the coin's face value. Consequently, a government can obtain goods and services by creating and spending money into existence, reducing the reliance on explicit taxes.

The government can generate some revenue from money creation simply by satisfying the public's growing need for exchange media. But the need for money for transactions depends largely on the level of economic activity. And the physical capacity of the economy to produce typically places limits on how much additional money is needed. Money serves few purposes other than for exchange. Consequently, infusions of money in excess of what is demanded by economic growth result in efforts by the public to spend the excess on the limited goods and services that are available. This tends to bid up prices.

The revenue gained from money creation without inflation is called seigniorage. When the government goes beyond seigniorage and generates inflation to obtain resources, the additional revenue is said to result from an "inflation tax."

## Classification as a tax

The term "tax" stems from two characteristics of the process just described. First, through spending the newly created money, the government acquires command over resources. Second, through inflation, the public loses command over resources.

The first part of the process is simple. When the government spends money into existence, it acquires resources equal to the difference between the cost of producing the money and the money's purchasing power.

The second part occurs because the excessive creation of money generates inflation, and inflation reduces the purchasing power of the money already in the hands of the public. The real value of all previously issued government money decreases as the prices of goods and services rise. In a high money creation–inflation economy, the government may find that the inflation tax is virtually the only levy it can implement or enforce.

But heavy reliance on the inflation tax is usually short-lived; very large sums can be collected by the government only when the public ignores the rate at which it will be taxed. As with any tax, the revenue yielded depends on whether the public knows in advance what the tax rate will be, with more being collected if people do not expect the tax (or do not expect it to be so high) and fail to act to minimize their tax burden. In the case of inflation, they may reduce their tax obligation by using foreign currencies for transactions or by using cash management techniques that reduce the money balances they hold.

Because the inflation tax adjusts to the rate necessary to garner a given amount of revenue, it is effective in exploiting this difference between the expected and unexpected tax rate: if the public expects a given rate and reduces its money balances accordingly, the government increases the amount of money it creates to buy goods and services, and the inflation tax rises to an unexpectedly higher rate.

This automatic adjustment can create a dynamically unstable relationship that generates phenomenally high rates of inflation. If the revenue sought by the government is especially large, exceeding the maximum collectible by the tax when the public knows what the rate is, then the tax (and inflation rate) must always be higher than the public expects. And because rising inflation typically engenders expectations of more rising inflation, the inflation rate will have to accelerate to continue yielding the desired revenue. The result is a hyperinflation.

Using inflation to obtain revenues need not result in hyperinflation. It will only generate moderate inflation if the revenue aim of the government is modest. But out-of-control inflations are almost always caused by attempts to raise large amounts of revenue by the inflation tax.

**Problems with terminology**

A problem with the term "inflation tax" is that it suggests an equivalence between the inflation tax rate and the inflation rate. They are actually different. The tax rate is the amount of real resources obtained by the government divided by the real value of the money supply. This is less than the rate of increase in the overall price level. How much less depends on how quickly prices change in response to money creation and the pattern of government purchases with the newly created money.

Some analysts object to the use of the term inflation tax, regarding it as confusing. An alternative is to call all income from money-creation seigniorage. One advantage to this would be to avoid the confusion arising from inflation that does not derive from money creation. If, for example, the public learns to get by on less money for a given amount of economic activity, the current money supply will become too large and the price level will increase. The public experiences a loss in the value of its real money holdings, but no corresponding increase in government purchasing power occurs. Past seigniorage is transformed into inflation tax, *ex post*. This awkward result is avoided if no distinction

is made between seigniorage and the inflation tax to begin with.

**Additional readings**

Cagan, Phillip. "The Monetary Dynamics of Hyperinflation." In *Studies in the Quantity Theory of Money*, edited by Milton Friedman. Chicago: University of Chicago Press, 1956.

Keynes, John Maynard. *Treatise on Money*. New York: Harcourt Brace and Co., 1930.

Sargent, Thomas J., and Neil Wallace. "Rational Expectations and the Dynamics of Hyperinflation." *International Economic Review* (June 1973): 328–50.

*Cross references:* income tax, federal; inflation indexation of income taxes; seigniorage.

# Infrastructure financing
Holley H. Ulbrich
Clemson University

*Methods of financing public investments in physical capital, such as roads, schools, and public works.*

The term "infrastructure" carries many meanings, but it generally refers to physical capital—sometimes all capital, sometimes just public capital. The term infrastructure has even been extended to the intangible: Central European nations have been described as lacking the "social infrastructure" essential to democratic capitalism, such as a banking system, laws protecting property rights, and stock exchanges. In the narrow sense, however, infrastructure is generally understood to consist of public physical capital, such as roads, school buildings, water and sewer systems, and parks. Even with that narrower definition, the line between public and private infrastructure is fuzzy. One area may be served by a municipal water system, another by a private for-profit water supplier. Electricity is most often in the private sector, but the industry includes municipal retailers and federal wholesalers.

Public infrastructure as a share of total physical capital in the United States has declined from almost 50 percent in 1970 to about 40 percent in the 1990s (Economic Report of the President 1995: 105). The largest share of public infrastructure is in the state and local public sector—schools, roads and bridges, parks, jails, hospitals, and water and sewer systems.

## Why public capital?

In a market system, the market is the default provider of goods and services, and public provision must be justified by appeal to some form of market failure. For infrastructure, or physical capital, there are several such failures at work, all of which influence the method of financing.

1. Much public-sector physical capital has attributes of a public or at least quasi-public good. The marginal cost of an additional user of the services it provides is low to nonexistent. Up to some congestion level, the services of the physical capital are nonrival in consumption. Often the costs of enforcing exclusion of nonpayers exceed the benefits. These attributes characterize roads and parks in particular.

2. Public-sector capital usually has strong positive externalities, even those kinds that create capturable private benefits. Often those externalities accrue to adjacent landowners. The value of a house adjacent to an attractive park, for example, may increase, even if the current owner has no interest in the park. These benefits can be measured and captured more effectively through property taxes (tax-increment financing or special assessment) than through a private market pricing scheme.

3. Public infrastructure is generally used to provide services for which a disproportionate share of the cost is in the capital investment, with relatively low operating costs. (School buildings and education services are a notable exception.) This kind of cost structure makes it unlikely that the market will support more than one supplier in a given area, making the sole supplier a monopolist. Because monopolies usually produce less service at a higher price and are unresponsive to consumer demand, many countries choose to place such activities in the public sector. Municipal water and sewer systems are a good application of this rationale for public provision.

4. Arranging for private financing may be difficult for new or risky ventures, or when capital is built in anticipation of growth that may not occur. Government backing of such projects, either directly as owner or indirectly as guarantor, can lessen the lender's risk and make it easier to raise the needed funds. This role of government as financial guarantor goes far back into U.S. history. The Erie Canal was the most notable of many such 19th-century state-guaranteed infrastructure projects that proved hugely profitable.

## Financing infrastructure

While the federal government does not have a capital budget, state and local governments usually separate their capital spending from their operating budgets and borrow for part or all of their capital spending. In addition, states and especially local governments often operate their capital-intensive operations that sell services to citizens as separately accounted-for enterprise funds, so that there is no cross-subsidy in either direction between the enterprise activity and the general fund. For this reason, the focus here is on financing infrastructure in the state and local sector.

When the primary beneficiaries of most public capital are internal to the state, county, city, or special district, there is ample justification for the primary financing responsibility being at that level. In the 1960s and 1970s, however, a significant source of funding for state and local infrastructure was the federal government in the form of grants, especially for water and sewer projects and public housing. Today, that source of revenue has greatly diminished. Although federal aid for infrastructure could be defended as a form of fiscal equalization, it has not been a very efficient method. Fiscal equalization can be achieved by other methods that more effectively target poor states and poor individuals.

Financing of both infrastructure and operating costs has been marked by a shift away from dependence on general tax financing in favor of identifying beneficiaries and making them pay a reasonable share of the cost of the services they enjoy, in some cases with protection for the poor via subsidies. This trend is especially pronounced at the local level because of the property tax revolt. Many public services, such as fire and police protection, create general benefits in that they meet public "option demand"—paying for a service so that it will be there if needed, even if the payer never actually has to call for it. Other services primarily benefit users (park and recreation facilities) or adjacent landowners (road improvements). Both equity and efficiency considerations support the notion that beneficiaries of such services should pay to the extent feasible.

Public-sector capital is most often financed through capital markets. State and local governments enjoy the advantage of offering bonds whose interest is exempt from federal income taxes. Some bonds are general obligation bonds, backed by the full faith and credit of the issuing government; others are revenue bonds, with the revenue from the sale of services pledged to service the debt. Historically, general obligation bonds have been used for public infrastructure that does not generate a revenue stream, and revenue bonds have been used for infrastructure that does. School buildings, jails, police stations, and city halls do not directly generate revenue, but there is an identifiable revenue stream from college dormitories, stadiums, toll roads, water and sewer systems, and parking garages, which can be pledged to service the debt.

## Recent developments in infrastructure financing

The 1980s and 1990s have been marked by innovation and experimentation in financing infrastructure. The search for new ways to finance infrastructure was driven by high interest rates in the 1980s, declining federal grants, and pressures of growth on existing infrastructure. Currently popular techniques include public-private partnerships; state guarantees, intermediation, and debt subsidies; creation of new quasi-governmental bodies for the sole purpose of developing and financing infrastructure; and shifting of the cost to identified beneficiaries and away from taxpayers as a whole.

Public-private partnerships take many forms. Local governments may contract out a service, letting the contractor finance the infrastructure. Solid waste collection is often provided on this basis. In the 1980s, there was a brief flurry of sale-leaseback arrangements for public-sector capital, stimulated by tax loopholes that took advantage of tax-exempt municipal borrowing. That option has become less attractive because tax reforms have limited the use of such arrangements. There has also been some limited use of equity financing of public capital that generates a defined revenue steam, such as sewage treatment plants and landfills.

States have assumed some responsibility for helping local governments finance infrastructure, most often with help in borrowing rather than grants. Bond banks and revolving state loan funds are two widely used methods (Petersen et al. 1988). State guarantees can make it possible for local governments to borrow on more favorable terms. States can pool borrowing requests from many small communities, with or without a state guarantee, to get to a critical mass that reduces borrowing costs. Some states borrow on their own credit and use the proceeds to create credit banks that lend to local governments.

The last 15 years have seen increased use of special districts whose sole purpose is to fund (and in some cases, maintain or operate) particular kinds of infrastructure. Water and sewer districts have been commonplace for many years, but more recently, other kinds have appeared on the scene. Texas has pioneered the use of road districts. Montana uses neighborhood rural special-improvement districts. The Denver metropolitan area has a special toll road authority (National League of Cities 1987). Such special districts serve some combination of three purposes. They can provide residents with some of the benefits, including infrastructure, that one attains by being part of a municipality, without all the additional costs and restrictions. They can allow additional borrowing, and added tax levies to repay that borrowing, when general purpose local governments have exhausted their borrowing or tax-

ing capabilities. And special districts can ensure that the cost falls on those who are the primary beneficiaries. Special districts encompass a variety of entities ranging from those that are entirely tax-financed (typically roads, neighborhood parks, street lights, and beautification) to those entirely financed by user fees (water and sewer). What they have in common is a need to provide infrastructure to serve a defined area.

A final notable trend in infrastructure financing is the shift from general revenue financing to exactions from those who benefit, with increased diversity in how those beneficiaries are identified and how payments are extracted. Three of the more popular methods are impact fees, special assessments, and tax-increment financing. Impact fees on developers, special assessments for improvements, and tax-increment financing are increasingly commonplace ways to finance improvements that benefit a particular property, neighborhood, or defined area. New residents require not only the extension of water and sewer lines but also more police cars, fire substations, and public parks. Impact fees cover the additional capital costs imposed by developing vacant lots or adjacent tracts. Special assessments are more likely to pay for infrastructure improvements to serve already developed lots. Tax-increment financing seeks to capture the additional property tax revenue from the increase in property value that results from infrastructure improvements, and dedicates that revenue stream to paying the capital costs.

## Additional readings

*Economic Report of the President 1995*. Washington, D.C.: U.S. Government Printing Office, p. 105.

National League of Cities. *Financing Infrastructure: Innovations at the Local Level*. Washington, D.C.: 1987.

Ostrom, Elinor, Larry Schroeder, and Susan Wynne. *Institutional Incentives and Sustainable Development*. San Francisco: Westview Press, 1993.

Petersen, John E., Susan Robinson, Percy Aguila, Joni L. Leithe, and William Graham. *Credit Pooling to Finance Infrastructure: An Examination of State Bond Banks, State Revolving Funds, and Substate Credit Pools*. Government Finance Officers Association, September 1988.

World Bank. World Development Report: *Infrastructure for Development*. Washington, D.C.: World Bank, 1994.

*Cross references:* benefit principle; earmarking of taxes; fiscal federalism; tax-exempt bonds.

# Insurance industry, federal taxation

Jack Taylor
Congressional Research Service, Library of Congress

*Imposition of income taxes on insurance companies at corporate rates but with special accounting rules based on regulatory accounting methods, and limited taxation of beneficiaries, implying light federal taxation of the life, and possibly the property and casualty, insurance industries.*

Insurance involves the transfer of risk of financial loss from one person (the insured) to another (the insurer) for a fee (a premium). In the modern insurance industry, insurer companies pool the risks of many insureds to diversify their own potential liabilities, and pool the premiums received to earn a return while waiting to be used to pay claims. The industry thus offers two distinct but interrelated services, insurance and financial intermediation.

Insurance companies are subject to the federal corporate income tax on premium and investment income, but they are allowed to deduct additions to reserves for estimated future losses. Insurance policy owners and beneficiaries are not taxed on the investment income accumulated for them by the insurance companies, and they may also receive some distributions tax-free, especially in the case of life insurance. The net result of these special rules is to ensure that life insurance will be very lightly taxed and that other forms of insurance, notably property and casualty, will sometimes be undertaxed as well.

Because different forms of insurance are subject to different income tax rules, they will be discussed separately in later sections. They have in common, however, the continued use of reserve deductions to establish taxable income.

## Reserve accounting

The first modern income tax law in 1909 provided that the accounting rules used by insurance companies for regulatory and book purposes would also be used to calculate taxable income. (This was originally the case with most industries.) The purpose of the insurance accounting rules, however, was to ensure the solvency of the company and protect policyholders; they were therefore designed to prevent overstatement of income. It became obvious as time went by that deliberate overstatement of income was not the problem in tax accounting, and many of the regulatory rules have since been superseded.

The most important vestige of this regulatory accounting bias is the continued use of reserves to calculate taxable insurance income (although current tax law prescribes discount rates and other rules for reserves that are less conservative than the regulatory rules). Deductions from current income to cover future liabilities are not allowed in most tax accounting, which uses the stricter rule of allowing a deduction only when the liability is known with reasonable certainty as to both amount and time of payment. Because insurance companies are in the business of estimating such future liabilities, however, it has seemed reasonable to deduct additions to reserves as they are actuarially determined. Insurance company taxable income for any year, therefore, is net of that year's additions to reserves for policy obligations to be paid in future years.

## Property and casualty insurance

The tax rules basically separate insurance into "life" and everything else (with noncancelable health insurance included in "life" insurance). Nonlife companies are allowed a deduction for 80 percent of unearned premiums, plus additions to loss reserves discounted over the expected payment period for the policies reserved against. The discount rate is prescribed as the federal midterm rate (the average rate on outstanding federal government securities with maturities of three to nine years). (This is intended to represent a pretax rate of return on the companies' investments.) The payment period is established by reference to the industrywide payment pattern for each line of business (although a company can establish and use its own payment pattern from its own records).

The insured parties pay premiums to the companies that are tax-deductible for business insurance and nondeductible for personal insurance, and most benefits, when received, are tax-free unless they exceed the insured's basis in the lost property and create a capital gain. (Some liability insurance proceeds are taxable.)

A properly discounted reserve deduction for properly estimated losses would create no tax advantage; it would, in fact, be relatively tax-neutral. Current law, however, has several potential flaws that could undermine the assumed neutrality: (1) The prescribed discount rate may be lower than the earnings rate the company uses to set premiums and the actual earnings rate; if so, the initial deduction will be larger than required and some of the cost of the insurance will be paid for with tax-sheltered dollars (or, more likely, the benefit will go to reduce premiums and thus the cost of buying insurance as opposed to self-insuring). (2) Crediting reserves at the pretax discount rate does not allow recapture of excess deductions until claims are paid. (3) The payment pattern may be manipulable by the companies, allowing systematic overstatement of deductions. (4) Contested and uncertain liabilities may be deliberately included, again allowing overstatement of deductions.

To the extent that any of these biases exist, the nonlife insurance industry would enjoy a tax advantage.

There are special provisions reducing or eliminating taxes for smaller companies. Nonlife insurance companies with annual premiums of $350,000 or less are tax-exempt; those with premiums between $350,000 and $1.2 million may elect to be taxed on only their investment income, ignoring underwriting income.

## Life insurance

Life insurance is essentially insurance that depends on life expectancy or mortality rates, including non-cancelable accident and health insurance. A life insurance company in tax law is one in which more than half of its reserves are for life insurance. Qualifying as life insurance allows substantial tax advantages.

Life insurance policies often cover many years and are designed to accumulate large amounts of investment income ("inside buildup," in the jargon of the industry). Because this accumulating income represents the companies' obligation to pay benefits, it is deducted from the companies' taxable incomes as additions to policy reserves. The tax-free investment income, therefore, pays for a substantial part of the insurance coverage promised by the policies.

Although inside buildup is "credited" to the policies, it is not taxed to the policy owners either. It accumulates tax-free until it is paid out as death benefits, as policyholder dividends, or upon surrender of the policies. Death benefits are not taxed at all, and policyholder dividends and cash-surrender values are not taxed until they exceed the premiums paid for them.

In times past, companies used their own actuarial and interest rate assumptions in establishing reserves and funding policies, so policies could be significant tax shelters. Tightening of the law over the last decade or so has reduced the tax shelter opportunities; policies must now meet prescribed tests for actuarial and earnings assumptions to ensure that they are really insurance policies, and investing too much in a policy will now disqualify it for tax-free accumulation of inside buildup.

It remains true, however, that a substantial portion of the income generated by the industry is not taxed at either the corporate or the individual level.

Company taxation is further complicated by a peculiarity in the structure of the industry: A significant share of the business and assets of the industry derive from mutual companies, most very large, that are "owned" by their policyholders. Policyholder dividends are deductions for the companies, and stockholder dividends are not, so level taxation of the stock and mutual segments of the industry is a difficult problem.

The current solution is to disallow a portion of the mutual companies' policyholder dividends by use of a rather arbitrary formula (Section 809 of the Internal Revenue Code) that is supposed to equal the share of income paid to stockholders of stock companies. The formula does not work to anyone's satisfaction, and considerable argument has raged between the segments of the industry as to which is overtaxed.

"Small" life insurance companies also receive a special tax break. A company with less than $500 million in gross assets is allowed a deduction equal to 60 percent of the first $3 million of taxable income, reduced by 15 percent of the excess of taxable income over $3 million (thus phasing out the deduction at $15 million).

## Health insurance

Taxation of medical insurance involves some special problems, partly because of its close relationship to national health policy. Most medical insurance is purchased as an employee fringe benefit, deductible by the employer and tax-free to the employee. It ranges from typical indemnity insurance to prepayment for medical care from health maintenance organizations, increasingly with blurred lines between the types. And the entities offering the various types are covered under at least five tax regimes: (1) life insurance companies, (2) nonlife companies, (3) partially tax-exempt Blue Cross/Blue Shield organizations, (4) exempt HMOs and hospitals, and (5) for-profit, nonexempt hospitals or health providers taxable under the regular corporation income tax rules.

## Additional readings

Aaron, Henry J. *The Peculiar Problem of Taxing Life Insurance Companies*. Washington, D.C.: The Brookings Institution, 1983.

Graetz, Michael J., editor. *Life Insurance Company Taxation: The Mutual vs. Stock Differential*. Larchmont, N.Y.: Rosenfeld, Emanuel, Inc., 1986.

Harmon, William B., Jr. "Two Decades of Insurance Tax Reform." *Tax Notes* 57 (November 12, 1992): 901–14.

McLure, Charles E., Jr. "The Income Tax Treatment of Interest Earned on Savings in Life Insurance." In U.S. Congress, Joint Economic Committee, *The Economics of Federal Subsidy Programs, Part 3—Tax Subsidies*. Washington, D.C.: U.S. Government Printing Office, 1972.

Pike, Andrew D. "Reflections on the Meaning of Life: An Analysis of Section 7702 and the Taxation of Cash

Value Life Insurance." *Tax Law Review* 43 (Spring 1989): 491–587.

U.S. Congress. Joint Committee on Taxation. *Tax Reform Proposals: Taxation of Insurance Products and Companies.* Washington, D.C.: U.S. Government Printing Office, 1985.

*Cross references:* fringe benefits; income tax, corporate, federal; income tax, federal; insurance industry, federal taxation.

# Insurance industry, state taxation
## Thomas S. Neubig
Ernst & Young LLP

*State-level tax treatment of insurance companies.*

State taxation of insurance companies is important to the industry, to its competitors and customers, and to the states. In 1990, insurance companies paid more in state premium taxes ($7.4 billion) than in federal corporate income taxes ($5.7 billion). While federal income taxation has moved toward taxing all types of financial institutions more similarly, state taxation of insurance companies differs greatly from state taxation of banks and general business corporations.

State taxation of insurance companies may appear to be simple and straightforward with its reliance on premium taxation. In actual practice, premium taxation differs by state and by line of business, interacts with state income taxes and solvency assessments, includes favorable tax rules for domestic companies, and incorporates a unique system of retaliatory taxation.

## Premium taxation

All 50 states impose premium taxes on insurance companies for insuring risks or property in the state. Eight states allow special municipal taxation of insurance premiums. In 1991, premium taxes were 2.14 percent of insurance premiums (excluding annuities) and accounted for 2.5 percent of total state revenues.

Most states impose similar premium tax rates on both domestic and foreign insurers. Nine states, plus Puerto Rico, imposed higher premium tax rates on foreign versus domestic insurers in 1992.

Premium tax rates differ according to the type of insurance product. Fire insurance premiums are often taxed at higher rates, the extra tax being earmarked to local fire departments or state fire mar-

shals. Many states impose lower tax rates on health insurance and long-term care policies, and higher tax rates on workers' compensation policies. Twenty-three states do not levy a tax on Blue Cross/Blue Shield health plan premiums.

Premiums for annuities that are part of qualified pension plans are generally excluded from taxation, and nonqualified annuities are often excluded or subject to a lower premium tax rate. Fourteen states taxed some annuity considerations in 1992. In many states, premium taxes are "in lieu of" other taxes, such as state corporate income taxes. Premium taxes are relatively easy to administer, and they provide a stable source of revenue. Premium taxation dates back to the 19th century before the federal income tax. By contrast, the income tax rules for insurance companies at the federal level have evolved over the last 70 years and are still the subject of considerable debate.

A simple comparison of premiums to net income suggests that the typical 2 percent premium tax rate is equivalent to a high effective tax rate on net income, several times higher than states' general business tax rates on net income. Although tax-related price differentials may be small in percentage terms as a result of low state tax rates, premium taxes apply to a large tax base. Even small price differences for identical products can place competitors at a significant disadvantage, especially for financial service providers where margins are often low.

Because the insurance premium tax is a destination tax, allocated completely to the state of the insured risk, and all companies are generally subject to the same tax rate, companies can recover the tax cost through higher premiums without fear of losing market share. Premium taxes therefore are likely to be borne largely by resident households and local businesses.

With the growth of self-insurance and the emergence of direct competitors as the regulatory barriers between financial service providers erode, differences in state effective tax rates across providers and products can cause economic distortions and inefficiencies. Higher effective tax rates on insurance companies and their products increase the incentive to self-insure risks or to purchase comparable services from noninsurance companies.

## Income taxation

Eighteen states impose corporate income or franchise taxes on insurance companies. The income tax may apply only to domestic companies or to all companies. In most states, the income or franchise tax is creditable against the premium tax, or the premium tax is creditable against the income tax. Given the typical relationship between gross premiums and net income, most companies are effectively subject to just the premium tax.

## Retaliatory taxation

Retaliatory taxation is unique to the insurance industry. Retaliatory taxes are paid by a nondomicile (foreign) company selling premiums in a state with a lower tax burden than the insurer's state of domicile. For example, an Ohio-domiciled insurer selling insurance to Missouri residents would pay the Missouri rate of 2 percent, plus a retaliatory tax of 0.5 percent, equal to the excess of the 2.5 percent Ohio rate above the Missouri rate.

To determine the retaliatory tax rate, states increasingly include income taxes, fees, and in some cases guaranty fund assessments, in addition to premium taxes. Some also include other states' municipal taxes. Retaliatory taxes were enacted when most states had discriminatory tax rules against foreign insurers. The retaliatory tax system was designed to reduce tax barriers to interstate business activity of domestic insurers. Retaliatory taxation provides an incentive for states to keep their tax burdens on insurance companies in line with those of other states. If a state increases its tax rate or fees, its domestic insurers will pay higher retaliatory taxes to other states and the state will reduce its own retaliatory tax revenues.

## Domestic preferences

Domestic preferences for insurance companies typically take the form of excluding domestic companies from the premium tax with or without an alternative tax, different tax rates, or special credits or rate reductions targeted to domestic insurers.

The 1985 Supreme Court decision in *Metropolitan Life Insurance Co.* v. *Ward* found discriminatory state taxation to be unconstitutional. Since then, 17 states have removed domestic preferences; nevertheless, 18 states still had some form of differential taxation of domestic and foreign companies in 1992. In most cases, states have reduced premium tax rates on foreign insurers and made up the lost revenues by increasing premium tax rates on domestic insurers.

## Guaranty assessments

All 50 states have guaranty funds to pay claims of insolvent companies. Separate state guaranty funds are established for property and casualty companies, life insurance, annuities, and health policies. Guaranty fund assessments are levied as a percentage of premiums, when needed by a state to cover the costs of resolving an insurance company insolvency. Forty-three states provided a credit against the premium tax for at least some guaranty fund

assessments in 1992. The most common credit is for 100 percent of the eligible assessments taken pro rata over the next five years.

Guaranty fund assessments have increased sharply in the last few years. Assessments have averaged $850 million annually during the past five years, compared with less than $75 million annually before 1983.

## Other taxes and burdens

States impose other taxes and burdens on insurance companies. Insurance companies pay fees and licenses generally associated with the administrative costs of the state insurance regulatory agencies. In 1990, fees and assessments on insurance companies totaled $651 million, almost 50 percent more than the $439 million spent on state insurance department budgets.

Some states have considered extending their sales tax to services, including insurance services. A sales tax on gross insurance premiums would greatly overstate the value of insurance services, because insurance premiums generally include three elements: a pure insurance (transfer) element, a savings element, and a service (administrative, marketing, and entrepreneurial) element.

A sales tax on insurance services could further exacerbate the distortion between purchased insurance and self-insurance, and between savings through life insurance companies and other financial service providers. A sales tax could also have significant retaliatory tax implications for domestic insurers.

A more appropriate measure of insurance services might be the value added by the industry. A value-added tax base would be considerably smaller than gross premiums. The New Hampshire Business Enterprise Tax uses an additional approach to measuring insurance companies' value added, including employee compensation, interest paid on nonpolicyholder reserves, and shareholder dividends.

States also impose nontax burdens on companies. In many states, insurance companies are required to provide minimum benefit levels in their health insurance policies. New Jersey recently prevented insurance companies selling automobile insurance in the state from pulling out of that line of business without also withdrawing from all other lines of business. Florida imposed a temporary moratorium on insurance companies' canceling or not renewing personal property lines in the wake of the large losses from a hurricane. Insurance companies are required to pay assessments in some states for assigned risk pools, which sell insurance to the otherwise uninsured, or are required to participate in coverage of individuals in the state risk pool. The additional cost associated with assigned state risk pools creates an advantage for firms that can self-insure and avoid those costs.

## Additional readings

American Council of Life Insurance. *1992 Life Insurance Factbook*.

Grace, Martin, and Jorge Martinez-Vazquez. "The Taxation of the Insurance Industry." In *Taxation and Economic Development: A Blueprint for Ohio Tax Reform*, edited by Roy Bahl. Columbus, Ohio: Battelle Press, 1995.

Health Insurance Association of America. *Source Book of Health Insurance Data 1992*.

Insurance Information Institute. *1993 Property/Casualty Insurance Facts*.

Neubig, Thomas S., and Harold L. Adrion. "Value Added Taxes and Other Consumption Taxes: Issues for Insurance Companies." *Insurance Tax Review*, December 1993.

Neubig, Thomas S., and Michael Vlaisavljevich. "Economic Issues in State Taxation of Insurance Companies." In *State Taxation of Business: Issues and Options*, edited by Thomas F. Pogue. Westport, Conn.: Praeger, 1992.

*Cross references:* banks, state taxation; income tax, corporate, state and local; insurance industry, federal taxation.

# Intangible assets, income tax treatment

Jack Taylor
Congressional Research Service, Library of Congress

*In income tax accounting, those business assets that are not accounted for after valuing all physical and financial capital of the business.*

Purchasers of a business or professional practice may pay more than the market value of the firm's physical and financial assets because an ongoing business has name recognition, relationships with customers and suppliers, technical knowledge, established operations that have proven successful, rights represented by patents, copyrights, franchises, and licenses, and other such intangible factors that add to the income-earning potential of the firm. The more amorphous of these intangibles are sometimes called "goodwill" or "going-concern value." These intangible assets have proven to be a problem for income tax accounting because of uncertainties in measuring the income from them.

An asset that declines in value as it produces income requires an offsetting deduction from that income equal to the decline in value; income from machines that wear out as they produce must be netted against the machines' depreciation. Measuring income from them requires some measure of the rates at which they decline in value. An asset that does not decline in value presents no such problem; income from land, for example, requires no periodic deductions because land retains its value from purchase to resale (barring extraneous influences).

As with any asset, the capitalized value of an intangible is equal to the present value of its expected stream of future income. For intangible assets purchased as a part of a business, however, several difficulties arise. One problem is measuring the expected future income from the asset (i.e., valuing the asset). Another is determining the expected duration of the income stream (i.e., measuring the life of the asset). Even if both of these are established, a determination still needs to be made as to whether the income stream should be offset by any decline in the value of the asset (i.e., does the asset depreciate, as a machine would, or does it maintain its value from purchase to resale, as land would?).

These difficulties arise in the case of intangible assets whose value is determined by their relationship to a specific firm. Intangible assets that are usable in many firms, such as general-purpose computer software or purchased mailing lists, or that have market value apart from the firm, such as patents or copyrights, can be valued by reference to market prices and their lives determined by reference to general business practices, much as with tangible assets. But assets whose value depends on the continuation of a specific business are a different problem; at the very least, their market value is not the same apart from the business.

Intangible assets such as knowledge or a relationship with clients can have value and increase future income for two reasons. One is that some expense may be involved in creating the asset. The firm or professional practice may have to advertise, pay for training, join country clubs, buy lunches, or incur other expenses to acquire the asset in question. But even if no expense is involved, it still often takes time for the firm to form the relationships or acquire the knowledge needed to secure the future income. Purchasing an ongoing business that has already developed the necessary relationships or knowledge saves both the expenses and the opportunity costs that would otherwise be involved.

## The policy dispute

Policy arguments over whether or how intangibles should be depreciated for tax purposes have often been made by analogy to physical depreciable assets. Neutral taxation of depreciable physical capital generally requires that the amount allowed as a depreciation deduction vary with the expected life of the asset; so it was often assumed that similar treatment should apply to intangible assets.

However, there is an important difference in the tax treatment of the costs of creating and maintaining the two types of assets. The costs of creating physical assets are capitalized and deducted only as depreciation, the same treatment given the purchase price of a purchased asset. The costs of creating the types of intangible assets discussed here, however, are typically deducted as they are incurred (or are "opportunity costs" not subject to taxation). The same costs that serve to create the asset in the first place also serve to maintain its value in the hands of the purchasers; and by deducting the costs currently (or not reporting the opportunity costs), the taxpayer in effect writes off exactly the amount, other things being equal, that will maintain the value of the asset—that is, an amount equal to what the depreciation would be if it were depreciated. Thus the life of the asset is irrelevant; each asset is effectively a nondepreciable asset. This treatment actually gives these assets lower effective tax rates than capitalizing and depreciating them would (Gravelle and Taylor 1992). Neutral tax treatment requires that these assets be treated uniformly, not written off over estimated useful lives. In fact, a zero depreciation deduction for purchased intangibles is probably the most nearly neutral.

It should be obvious from this discussion that the correct distinction between types of assets is not physical and intangible, but capitalized and expensed, creation costs. Some intangible assets, such as over-the-counter software or motion picture films, are like physical assets in that their creation costs are fully capitalized, and neutral tax treatment requires that these assets be depreciated over their estimated useful lives.

It should also be obvious that none of these distinctions is totally clean in actual tax law. In the Internal Revenue Code, both intangible and physical capital assets are sometimes expensed. Patents, for example, may be produced by research and experimentation expenditures that are written off currently, and many of the repairs to machines and buildings that are actually capital in nature are deducted. The general principle remains in spite of the exceptions, however.

## The practical dispute

Valuing intangible assets, establishing their useful lives, and determining the proper deductions, if any, for their cost have been major questions in past U.S. federal tax policy. Taxpayers had an incentive to allocate greater portions of the purchase price of a business to depreciable physical assets or to intangible assets whose depreciation could be established and so reduce their future taxes. Disputes over the allocation of purchase prices became routine between taxpayers and the Internal Revenue Service (IRS) throughout the 1980s.

Taxpayers were able to use revenue projections to establish a value for such things as customer lists, "core deposits" of banks, or "insurance in force" for insurance companies and agencies. Reasoning that these customer relationships would decline over time as customers moved, died, or went to competitors, taxpayers also made statistical projections of the rate of decline to establish useful lives. Using the analogy with depreciable physical assets, they further reasoned that an annual allowance for depreciation based on the useful lives was required to properly measure income from the assets. Some lower courts accepted these arguments and some did not, although the IRS adamantly rejected them. The Supreme Court eventually decided (*Newark Morning Ledger*, 113 S.Ct. 1670 (1993)) that intangible assets could be depreciated if a value and a limited useful life could be established. This left a large backlog of cases in dispute between the IRS and taxpayers, however, and provided no general principles to help determine the proper useful life.

## Current tax treatment

Congress imposed a solution to the disputes, or at least to future disputes, in the Omnibus Budget Reconciliation Act of 1993 (PL 103-66). This act established a new category of amortizable asset called a "Section 197 intangible" (after the section of the Internal Revenue Code). The purchase price of these assets is to be written off by the straight-line method (equal deductions each year) over 15 years. These assets are defined as purchased (1) goodwill or going concern value, (2) information bases, know-how, relations with customers, suppliers, and workers, and similar items, (3) licenses, permits, and other government-granted rights, (4) covenants not to compete, and (5) franchises, trademarks, and trade names. Specifically excluded are self-created assets and financial assets, leases, patents and copyrights, computer software, films, sound recordings, books, sports franchises, and a few other categories. For the most part, the definitions correspond to the distinction between expensed and capitalized costs discussed earlier.

The 15-year write-off period is essentially arbitrary, chosen because it was approximately "revenue neutral," neither gaining nor losing revenue over the five-year period for which revenue estimates were made. The basis for the revenue estimate was that some intangibles were previously amortizable over periods shorter than 15 years and some would not have been amortizable at all. The average for revenue neutrality over the five years was calculated at

15 years. This, however, may hold the seeds for an additional tax policy problem, because in the long run far more amortization will be deductible than would have been the case under prior law and revenue losses will be much larger.

*Cross references:* capital cost recovery; cost of capital; depreciation recapture; uniform capitalization rules.

# Integration, corporate tax

## Glenn Hubbard
Columbia University

*Policies for reducing or removing the double tax on returns to corporate equity that can be imposed by the existence of a separate corporate and personal income tax.*

Current U.S. income tax laws treat corporations and their investors as separate entities. Under this so-called "classical" system of corporate taxation, two levels of tax are levied on earnings from investments in corporate equity. First, income earned by corporations is taxed at the corporate level. Second, when the corporation distributes dividends to shareholders, the income is taxed at the shareholder level as ordinary income. Undistributed earnings, which increase share values, are also double taxed, because they are taxed at capital gains rates when shares are sold.

In contrast, investors who conduct business activity in noncorporate form, such as a sole proprietorship or partnership (or in corporate form through a Subchapter S corporation), are taxed once on their earnings at their individual tax rate. Corporate earnings distributed as interest to suppliers of debt capital are generally deductible by the corporation, and thus not subject to tax at the corporate level.

Integration of the corporate and individual income taxes refers to any plan in which corporate income is taxed only once, rather than twice, both when earned and when distributed to shareholders as dividends.

## The need for integration

The classical corporate tax system distorts three economic and financial decisions—whether to (1) invest in noncorporate rather than corporate form; (2) finance investments with debt rather than with equity; and (3) retain rather than distribute earnings.

### Organizational form

Traditional arguments for integrating corporate and individual income taxes emphasize distortions of business organizational form. By taxing corporate equity income twice, the classical corporate tax system discourages equity-financed investments by corporate organizations. Also, it means that the corporate sector must earn a higher pretax rate of profit to prevent capital from flowing to the corporate sector. The tax distorts the allocation of resources by discouraging the use of the corporate form even when incorporation would provide nontax benefits—such as limited liability for the owners, centralized management, free transferability of interests, and continuity. Corporations may also be better able to exploit scale economies, while noncorporate organizations may be better able to encourage entrepreneurial skill. Distorting the choice between these business forms thus means diminishing the use of scale economies, as well. While the use of an S corporation can provide nontax benefits of the corporate form, while avoiding the problem of double taxation, there are a number of restrictions on their use that limit their applicability. Nonetheless, the use of S corporations has increased significantly.

### Corporate capital structure

Corporations have three alternatives for financing new investments: issuing new equity, using retained earnings, or issuing debt. The classical corporate tax system discriminates against equity financing of new corporate investment; because corporate profits are taxed twice, the cost of equity capital generally exceeds the cost of debt capital. Projects funded with new equity or retained earnings therefore require a higher pretax rate of return than projects financed with debt. The lower effective tax rate for debt-financed versus equity-financed corporate investment encourages the use of debt finance by corporations, holding nontax factors constant.

If debt issuance involved no nontax considerations, corporate borrowing would be an efficient type of "self-help" integration, because interest payments are deductible. But, while leverage has some nontax benefits, the most efficient financial arrangements will involve both debt and equity, with equity serving as a cushion against economywide fluctuations in profitability. Higher debt levels can also increase nontax costs of debt, including costs associated with financial distress.

Thus, a January 1992 Treasury Department report on integration concluded that tax-induced distortions in corporations' comparisons of nontax advantages and disadvantages of debt entail significant efficiency costs.

## *Corporate dividend distributions*

The current system of corporate income taxation may also distort a corporation's choice between distributing or retaining earnings and, if amounts are distributed, its choice of whether they are paid in the form of nondividend distribution, such as a share repurchase. Distributing earnings through dividends will be taxed relatively highly versus distributing earnings through capital gains generated by reinvested earnings or share repurchases.

Despite the tax disadvantage of paying dividends, corporations do so. Financial economists have offered two explanations as to why corporate dividends are paid despite the tax bias against dividend distributions. The first—known as the "traditional view"—argues that dividends offer nontax benefits to shareholders that offset their apparent tax disadvantage. For example, a high dividend payout may decrease managerial discretion over internal funds. Or dividends may provide signals to investors about a firm's prospects or relative financial strength.

The second explanation or "tax capitalization" view assumes that dividends offer no nontax benefits to shareholders relative to retained earnings. An additional assumption in this view is that corporations have no alternative to dividends (like share repurchases) for distributing funds to shareholders. As a result, investor-level taxes on dividends reduce the value of the firm as they are capitalized in share value, but would generally affect neither corporate dividend nor investment decisions. Under the assumptions of the tax capitalization view, corporate tax integration would not encourage corporations to increase dividend payouts, but would confer a windfall on holders of existing equity.

## Administrative means of achieving corporate tax integration

It would be relatively easy to design an integrated tax system if all shareholders were taxed at the same rate, shareholder and corporate tax rates were the same, all corporate income were taxed in the same manner, and the United States were a closed economy. The real world is not so simple, and evaluating alternative prototypes for integrating the corporate and individual tax systems requires making judgments on four issues, relating to the treatment of corporate-level tax preferences (e.g., accelerated depreciation or tax-exempt interest in municipal bonds); corporate income received by tax-exempt investors; corporate income received by foreign shareholders; and foreign taxes paid by U.S. corporations.

The Treasury Department's 1992 study of corporate tax integration was based on the following principles for judging different administrative prototypes for corporate tax integration: First, the benefit of corporate-level tax preferences should not be extended to shareholders. Second, corporate tax integration should not reduce taxes paid on corporate capital income by tax-exempt investors. Third, the benefits of integration should not be extended to foreign shareholders by statute, although benefits may be extended by treaty. Fourth, foreign taxes paid by U.S. corporations should not be treated identically by statute to taxes paid to the U.S. government, although extending the benefits of integration to foreign-source income could be accomplished through bilateral treaty negotiations.

## *Full integration*

One method of integration would treat the corporation as a conduit, taxing all corporate earnings, irrespective of whether they are distributed, once. One way to implement this would be a "shareholder allocation" prototype, in which shareholders would include their share of the corporation's income in their income subject to tax. Tax would be withheld at the corporate level, and shareholders could apply the credits for corporate taxes paid against their income tax liability. A disadvantage of this alternative is that corporate tax preferences would be passed along to shareholders, because such preferences would be included in the calculation of taxable income.

Avoiding such pass-throughs would be both inconsistent with the spirit of full integration and administratively complex. For this reason, and because of the general administrative complexity of this prototype, the Treasury report did not recommend its enactment.

## *Dividend relief*

Most proposals for integration have focused on eliminating the double taxation of those earnings that are distributed; in short, dividend relief. A number of options are possible. In an "imputation credit" system, tax is collected at the corporate level, but shareholders receive a credit to apply against investor-level taxes. In a "dividend deduction" system, corporations could deduct dividend payments just as they do interest payments in calculating taxable income. Or in a "dividend exclusion" system, shareholders would not be taxed on dividend income.

The imputation credit prototype might work this way: Corporations would determine their income for tax purposes, as they do now, and would pay corporate-level tax. Shareholders would include in their income the "grossed-up" amount of the dividend—that is, including both the dividend and the associated tax paid at the corporate level. They could apply toward individual tax payments a credit equal to the amount of corporate tax that would be associated with gross dividends. This system is similar to the taxation of wages and salaries for employees, in which an employee includes gross wages in taxable income and receives a credit equal to the amount of the tax withheld. In principle, an imputation system could be structured so as to conform to the Treasury's principles for integration, but doing so would be relatively complex. Nonetheless, the fact that most integrated tax systems use imputation credit prototypes suggests it will continue to be studied as a model for corporate tax integration in the United States.

A dividend-deduction system would treat dividends and interest payments symmetrically at the corporate level. Although this approach would be simple, it would violate the Treasury's recommendation that the benefits of integration not be extended to tax-exempt and foreign shareholders. Moreover, this proposal would be significantly more costly in terms of tax revenue than other alternatives.

The Treasury report recommended a dividend exclusion prototype for dividend relief as the most straightforward means of implementing the general policy recommendations requiring the least change from current law. Under this prototype, corporations would pay the corporate income tax, computing taxable income in the same way as under current law. However, dividends paid out of fully taxed corporate income would not be taxed again at the investor level.

If adopted, the Treasury proposal might work in the following manner: Fully taxed income would be tracked by corporations in an excludable dividend account (EDA) based on corporate taxes paid. For example, a corporate tax payment of $34 would permit $66 to be contributed to the EDA. That is, because the $34 of tax paid is equivalent to paying the statutory corporate tax rate on $100 of earnings, the corporation would be allowed to add $100 − $34, or $66, to its EDA, from which it could pay excludable dividends to its shareholders. Amounts of dividends distributed that are greater than the EDA balance, such as distributions from corporate tax preference income, would be taxable at the individual level.

Under the dividend exclusion prototype, tax-exempt investors would not pay tax on either "excludable" or "taxable" dividends, but would not be granted a refund of applicable corporate taxes. Essentially, those shareholders would bear the same tax burden on corporate equity income as they do now. Foreign shareholders would also be treated as they are under current law; a withholding tax of 30 percent on dividends paid by U.S. firms to foreign shareholders would remain (with lower rates available by treaty). With respect to foreign-source income earned by U.S. firms, corporations would be permitted to credit foreign taxes paid against U.S.

corporate tax (as under current law). However, the EDA would not be increased by U.S. corporate tax liabilities offset by foreign tax credits.

The Treasury report also considered, as a longer-run option, a broad extension of the dividend exclusion integration prototype to interest payments. This prototype—the Comprehensive Business Income Tax (CBIT)—would apply to all businesses, noncorporate and corporate, with the exception of very small firms. Under the CBIT prototype, neither deductions for payments to debt-holders nor those to equity-holders would be permitted, and a tax would be collected at the entity level (at a rate equal to the highest marginal individual tax rate). However, both interest and equity distributions would then be excludable from income by investors.

## Economic benefits of integration

The direction of the tax biases under an unintegrated system is clear. The size of the resulting inefficiency will be determined by how much households and firms respond to these tax considerations. These responses can be studied using computational general-equilibrium models.

Removing the double tax on corporate equity reduces the amount of revenue raised. For this reason, the Treasury report examined the gains in economic efficiency that would result from integration, assuming that other taxes are changed to offset the revenue effects of integration.

Based on simulations using several different general equilibrium models, the Treasury report concluded that the economic benefits from corporate tax integration appear to be significant. Gains would be culled from improved allocation of real resources, reductions in the likelihood of a firm's experiencing financial distress, and the shift toward allowing corporations to make capital structure and dividend decisions based on nontax benefits and costs.

The Treasury report offers estimates of how much the various prototypes would increase the amount of capital in the corporate sector. Depending on the prototype, model, and financing assumptions, this increase ranges from 2 to 8 percentage points. In addition the integration prototypes generally encourage corporations to use less debt. Estimated debt-to-asset ratios decrease by 1 to 7 percentage points. The integration prototypes encourage corporations to increase the portion of earnings distributed as dividends. Depending on the model, financing assumptions, and prototype, dividend payout ratios rise modestly by between 2 and 6 percentage points. By shifting resources into the corporate sector, reducing corporate borrowing, and encouraging dividends, the prototypes increase economic well-being by an amount that ranges from $2.5 to $26 billion per year.

### Additional reading

This article is based on Hubbard, R. Glenn. 1997. "Corporate Tax Integration: A View from the Treasury Department." *Journal of Economic Perspectives* 7(1): 115–32.

U.S. Department of the Treasury. *Integration of the Individual and Corporate Tax Systems: Taxing Business Income Once.* Washington, D.C.: U.S. Government Printing Office, 1992.

*Cross references:* dividends, double taxation of; general-equilibrium models; income tax, corporate, federal; income tax, federal.

# Interest deductibility

Michael J. McIntyre
Wayne State University

*The theory and practice underlying the deduction of interest expenses under an income tax.*

---

Most countries allow taxpayers to deduct interest payments under at least some circumstances and to prohibit or defer the deduction under other circumstances. Many individuals and most corporations claim an interest deduction, and the aggregate amounts are large. In 1986, the United States imposed significant limitations on the deductibility of interest. Nevertheless, it remains the most important deduction allowable under the U.S. income tax. According to the Statistics of Income figures published by the Internal Revenue Service, U.S. corporations deducted well over $600 billion in interest payments in 1994. Nearly 28 million individual taxpayers claimed the deduction in that year, for aggregate deductions of about $200 billion.

To regulate the deduction for interest payments, a country must provide a workable definition of interest that conforms, to the extent feasible, to economic realities. In general, interest may be defined as a rental payment for the use of someone else's money. A more ornate definition is needed, however, to specify what constitutes a genuine debt obligation. For example, the definition should make some attempt to distinguish debt from equity, so as to prevent closely held corporations from obtaining a deduction for disguised dividends. Detailed rules must also be provided to distinguish interest on a loan from repayment of the principal amount of the loan. Those rules tend to be particularly complex when the issuer of a debt instrument receives as loan proceeds less than the face amount of the debt instrument (so-called original issue discount bonds). Under such circumstances, the difference between the face amount of the loan and the amount received by the borrower constitutes economic interest.

The rules governing interest deductibility must also specify the timing of the deduction. In principle, a tax system that taxes only realized gains should not allow interest payments made to earn unrealized income to be deductible until that income is subject to tax. How to link a present interest payment with future income, however, is often a vexing question, as the discussion below suggests. Many countries have also faced serious political obstacles in adopting appropriate timing rules, at least in part because they had adopted overly generous interest deductibility rules before the importance of time-value-of-money issues was appreciated by their policymakers.

Tax theorists disagree sharply on the proper treatment of interest payments under a personal income tax and a corporate income tax. One prominent view is that the deductibility of interest payments on a loan ought to turn on the use made of the loan proceeds. To implement that principle, a tax system needs to adopt tracing rules that link specific interest payments to particular uses.

Tracing is easily accomplished whenever the lender requires the borrower to utilize the proceeds of a loan for a particular purchase. Such loans are typically called "purchase-money loans." The most common example is a mortgage that finances the purchase of a personal residence. Indeed, most real estate construction and acquisition loans are purchase-money loans. Purchase-money nonrecourse loans are a central feature of many tax shelter schemes.

Under other circumstances, tracing may be more difficult. For example, physical tracing is clearly impossible when a taxpayer has commingled borrowed and saved funds in a common account. To deal with the difficult cases, tax analysts have proposed various presumptive tracing techniques. These techniques are analogous to the inventory accounting rules used for linking the costs incurred to purchase goods of a certain type with the proceeds derived from the sale of such goods.

One such tracing technique is called "permissive stacking." Under permissive stacking, taxpayers are presumed to have used their borrowed money in accordance with the best available tax advice. Assume, for example, that G has $1,000 in her checking account, of which $500 came from a loan and the remaining $500 from savings. She writes two checks, one of $400 to pay a business expense and the other of $600 to pay for personal consumption. The permissive stacking rule assumes that she used borrowed money to pay the $400 business expense and is entitled to a deduction for 80 percent ($400/$500) of the interest payments on her loan.

An alternative to permissive stacking is "strict stacking." A strict stacking rule makes the assumption that taxpayers have spent their borrowed money for the use that provides the least favorable tax result. In the example above, G would be assumed to have paid for $500 of her personal consumption out of her $500 loan and to have paid the business expense of $400 from her savings. Thus, G would not be entitled to any interest deduction. Strict stacking is often a favored technique for limiting the scope of various tax-expenditure programs. For example, strict stacking has been recommended as a way to prevent borrowers from obtaining the benefits of tax incentives designed to encourage taxpayers to save.

The main competition to the tracing approach is the view that interest is inherently a current expense and ought to be deductible in all cases in an ideal income tax. Some proponents of this view would favor limitations on the deductibility of interest, however, in a less-than-ideal income tax system that gives preferences to certain categories of income. For example, they might not want home mortgage interest to be deductible unless the imputed income from home ownership is taxable. Similarly, they might favor deferring the deduction for interest used to purchase appreciating property if accrued gains are not taxable until they have been realized.

Proponents of tracing claim that their favored approach is consistent with the general treatment afforded to other deductions in an ideal income tax. They note that the deductibility of a rental payment for the use of property generally depends on the use made of that property. For example, an amount paid for an apartment is deductible if the apartment is used as a business office; the payment is not deductible if the apartment is used as a personal residence. Because interest is a form of rental payment—an amount paid for the use of someone else's money—the asserted analogy between interest and rent is strong.

Opponents of tracing contend that the fungibility of money makes tracing meaningless. For example, they note that in a tax system that made the deductibility of interest on a loan turn on the use made of the loan proceeds, a taxpayer holding $1,000 worth of stock and contemplating a $1,000 consumption expenditure would get a better tax result by selling the stock, using the proceeds to make the consumption expenditure, and then borrowing $1,000 to repurchase the stock. Proponents of tracing respond that the above example simply shows that a pure tracing system might impose some transactional costs on certain savers. To minimize those costs, they have proposed presumptive tracing ("permissive stacking") rules that would allow interest to be deductible when it is clear that the taxpayer would be able to claim the deduction through a mere rearrangement of his or her portfolio of assets.

Proponents of tracing contend that it is a fallacy to conclude that the fungibility of money supports the case for a universal deduction for interest. Their position is illustrated by the following example. F, a taxpayer, leases two identical automobiles at a monthly rental fee of $500 per car for his use and the use of his wife. F sometimes uses a car for business and sometimes for pleasure. His wife always uses a car for consumption purposes. For obvious reasons of convenience, F and his wife take whichever car is at the top of the driveway whenever they want to drive somewhere. The question arises as to how much of the automobile rental fees they should be allowed to deduct.

No one would seriously contend that the fungibility of F's cars justifies a deduction for the entire cost of renting them. F would not strengthen his claim for a full deduction, moreover, by demonstrating the administrative difficulties that he might encounter in distinguishing between the two cars. Because the cars are fungible, physical tracing of the rental fees to the business use of each car might not be necessary. The tax authorities might adopt a presumptive tracing rule for determining the portion of the rental fees attributable to business based on the ratio of business miles of use to total miles of use. The fungibility of rental cars, however, would not undermine the case for making the deductibility of rental fees turn on the use made of the rented property.

A second argument commonly made against tracing is that it would improperly advantage persons holding net assets over net borrowers. As an illustration of that argument, consider two taxpayers, both of whom have the same salary income. Mr. Ant, a thrifty person, holds a $1,000 money market certificate earning 10 percent interest; Mr. Grasshopper, who is a spendthrift, has accumulated no savings at all. Assume that Mr. Ant and Mr. Grasshopper each spend $1,000 on a personal vacation. Mr. Ant finances his vacation by cashing in his demand certificate. Mr. Grasshopper finances his by borrowing the $1,000 and paying $100 of interest. He and Mr. Ant spend all of their remaining net income on food and recreation. Both have enjoyed the benefit of a vacation worth $1,000, but Mr. Ant has $100 more than Mr. Grasshopper to spend on food and recreation. Unless permitted a deduction for his interest payment, Mr. Grasshopper will pay the same amount of tax as Mr. Ant, despite this difference in their power to buy food and recreational services.

Many tax systems include tax incentives and other special relief measures that ought to be evaluated in terms of spending goals. Whether interest on a loan should be deductible when the loan finances an activity favored by a tax incentive depends on the goals of that incentive, not on normative tax policy principles.

For example, the United States allows taxpayers to exclude the interest earned on state and local bonds from their income, presumably to subsidize the state and local governments that issue those bonds. Whether interest paid with respect to loans used to finance state and local bonds is deductible ought to depend on the utility of the deduction in advancing the goal of subsidizing state and local governments. Allowing the deduction will present taxpayers with arbitrage opportunities. Commentators do not agree as to whether those arbitrage opportunities are harmful or beneficial. If arbitrage is to be eliminated, however, the technique for doing so is strict stacking. Under strict stacking, a borrower holding state and local bonds will be considered to have purchased those bonds with borrowed money, up to the amount of the loan proceeds. Interest on the portion of the loan so linked with the purchase of the state and local bonds would be denied.

Most commentators agree that the deductibility of interest should be limited during periods of inflation. During such periods, a nominal interest payment typically includes not only genuine interest but also a payment to compensate the lender for the decline in the value of the principal amount of the loan. In substance, that latter portion is a prepayment of principal and should not be deductible. One way to prevent a deduction for the inflation component of nominal interest is to adopt a comprehensive indexing scheme. However, the perceived complexity of comprehensive indexing schemes has discouraged many governments from adopting them.

Some limitations on the interest deduction should be applied to taxpayers who are earning foreign income. Otherwise a country would be giving an improper incentive to invest abroad and would be ceding some of its jurisdiction to tax domestic income to foreign governments. Countries that exempt foreign income from taxation should prohibit taxpayers from deducting interest payments properly linked to the earning of foreign income.

Many countries, including the United States, impose their normal income tax on the worldwide income of resident taxpayers and then allow a foreign tax credit, subject to important limitations, for income taxes paid to foreign governments. The credit is typically limited to the amount of tax otherwise imposed on the taxpayer's foreign taxable income. Thus if a taxpayer's foreign taxable income is $100 and the tax rate is 35 percent, then the limitation on the credit would be $35. The foreign tax credit limitation cannot operate properly unless the credit country has appropriate rules for apportioning interest deductions between foreign and domestic sources.

The United States generally uses what is referred to as the asset method for linking interest payments with foreign and domestic income. Under that method, a taxpayer allocates its interest payments pro rata to its worldwide assets. Interest deductions are linked to foreign income to the extent that they have been allocated to assets that generate foreign income. Assume, for example, that a taxpayer has an asset having a value for tax purposes of $1 million that generates foreign income and also has an asset with a tax value of $4 million that generates domestic income. In computing the limitation on its foreign tax credit, the taxpayer is required under the asset method to attribute 80 percent of its interest deduction to domestic income and the remaining 20 percent to foreign income.

The tax reforms adopted in the landmark Tax Reform Act of 1986 generally make the deductibility of interest paid with respect to a loan depend upon the use made of the loan proceeds. Current U.S. law prohibits individuals from deducting consumer interest and limits the deduction for interest traceable to tax-shelter activities to the income (usually negligible) generated by those activities. Interest traceable to traditional investment assets is also limited to the income generated by those assets. As an incentive for home ownership and a response to political pressures, Congress continues to allow interest to be deductible when it is traceable to the purchase of the taxpayer's personal residence or to one other designated residence. Under some circumstances, individuals and corporations are required to capitalize interest payments made with respect to loans used to finance capital acquisitions. The U.S. limitations on the deductibility of corporate interest payments continue to be far more generous than would be appropriate under a tracing approach.

## Additional readings

Abreu, Alice G. "Distinguishing Interest from Damages: A Proposal for a New Perspective." *Buffalo Law Review* 40 (1992): 373–439.

Arnold, Brian J. "Is Interest a Capital Expense?" *Canadian Tax Journal* 40 (1992): 533–53.

Arnold, Brian J. "General Report: Deductibility of Interest and Other Financing Charges in Computing Income." *Cahiers de Droit Fiscal International* 79a. Deventer, Netherlands: Kluwer (1994): 489–541.

Auerbach, Alan J. "Should Interest Deductions Be Limited?" In *Uneasy Compromise: Problems of a Hybrid Income-Consumption Tax*, edited by Henry Aaron, Harvey Galper, and Joseph Pechman. Washington, D.C.: The Brookings Institution, 1988, pp. 195–221.

Block, Cheryl. "The Trouble with Interest: Reflections on Interest Deductions after the Tax Reform Act of 1986." *University of Florida Law Review* 40 (1988): 689–753.

Bossons, John. "Indexing for Inflation and the Interest Deduction." *Wayne Law Review* 30 (1984): 945–68; "Reply" 983–89.

Crane, Charlotte. "Matching and the Income Tax Base: The Special Case of Tax Exempt Income." *American Journal of Tax Policy* 5 (1986): 191–268.

Dixon, Darryl A. "A Consideration of the Theory of the Deductibility of Interest Payments from the Personal Income Tax Base." *National Tax Journal* 23 (1970): 168–76.

Dixon, Gordon D., and Brian Arnold. "Rubbing Salt into the Wound: The Denial of the Interest Deduction after the Loss of a Source of Income." *Canadian Tax Journal* 39 (1991): 1473–96.

Goode, Richard. *The Individual Income Tax*. Rev. ed. Washington, D.C.: The Brookings Institution, 1976.

Gunn, Alan. "Is an Interest Deduction for Personal Debt a Tax Expenditure?" *Canadian Taxation* 1/4 (1979): 46–50.

Hickman, Frederic W. "Interest, Depreciation, and Indexing." *Virginia Tax Review* 5 (1986): 773–806.

Hoerner, J. Andrew. "Indexing the Tax System for Inflation: Lessons from the British and Chilean Experiences." *Tax Notes International* 2 (June 1990): 552–56.

Johnson, Calvin H. "Tax Shelter Gain: The Mismatch of Debt and Supply Side Depreciation." *Texas Law Review* 61 (1983): 1013–55.

Johnson, Calvin H. "Is an Interest Deduction Inevitable?" *Virginia Law Review* 6 (1986): 123–82.

Kahn, C. H. *Personal Deductions in the Federal Income Tax*. Princeton, N.J.: Princeton University Press, 1960.

Kayle, Bruce. "Where Has All the Income Gone? The Mysterious Relocation of Interest and Principal in Coupon Stripping and Related Transactions." *Virginia Tax Review* 7 (9187): 303–61.

Klein, William A. "Borrowing to Finance Tax-Favored Investments." *Wisconsin Law Review* (1962): 608–36.

Koppelman, Stanley. "Tax Arbitrage and the Interest Deduction." *Southern California Law Review* 61 (1988): 1143–1217.

Kurtz, Jerome. "Comments on 'Indexing for Inflation and the Interest Deduction.'" *Wayne Law Review* 30 (1984): 969–72.

McIntyre, Michael J. "An Inquiry into the Special Status of Interest Payments." *Duke Law Review* (1981): 765–810. Reproduced in Michael McIntyre, Frank Sander, and David Westfall, *Readings in Federal Taxation*. 2d rev. ed. Mineola, N.Y.: Foundation Press, 1983, pp. 302–46.

McIntyre, Michael J. "Comments on 'Indexing for Inflation and the Interest Deduction.'" *Wayne Law Review* 30 (1984): 973–82.

McIntyre, Michael J. *The International Income Tax Rules of the United States*. 2 vol., looseleaf. Boston: Butterworth Legal Publishers, 1989 with current update.

McIntyre, Michael J. "Contributions Made by the U.S. Tax Reform Act of 1986 to Distributive Justice." In *Flattening the Tax Rate Scale: Alternative Scenarios and Methodologies*, edited by John Head and Richard Krever. Melbourne: Longman Professional, 1990.

McIntyre, Michael J. "Tracing Rules and the Deduction for Interest Payments: A Justification for Tracing and a Critique of Recent U.S. Tracing Rules." *Wayne Law Review* 39 (1992): 67–120.

McMahon, Martin. "Reforming Cost Recovery Allowances for Debt Financed Depreciable Property." *St. Louis University Law Journal* 29 (1985): 1029–132.

Mundstock, George. "Accelerated Depreciation and the Interest Deduction: Can Two Rights Really Make a Wrong?" *Tax Notes* 29 (1985): 1253–60.

Oliver, Philip D. "A Counter-Productive Solution to a Nonexistent Problem." *Tax Law Review* 40 (1985): 351–410.

Shakow, David. "Confronting the Problem of Tax Arbitrage." *Tax Law Review* 43 (1987): 1–50.

Snoe, Joseph A. "My Home, My Debt: Remodeling the Home Mortgage Interest Deduction." *Kentucky Law Journal* 80 (1992): 431–97.

Shoup, Carl S. "Deductions of Homeowners' Mortgage Interest, Interest on Other Consumer Debt, and Property Taxes, under the Individual Income Tax: The Horizontal Equity Issue." *Canadian Tax Journal* 27 (1979): 529–533.

Steuerle, C. Eugene. "Tax Arbitrage, Inflation, and the Taxation of Interest Payments and Receipts." *Wayne Law Review* 30 (1983): 991–1013.

Steuerle, C. Eugene. *Taxes, Loans, and Inflation: How the Nation's Wealth Becomes Misallocated*. Washington, D.C.: The Brookings Institution, 1985.

Steuerle, C. Eugene. *The Tax Decade*. Washington, D.C.: The Urban Institute Press, 1991.

Taggart, John Y. "Denial of the Personal Interest Deduction." *Tax Lawyer* 41 (1988): 195–278.

Vann, Richard J., and Darryl A. Dixon. *Measuring Income under Inflation*. Australian Tax Research Foundation, Research Study No. 12, 1990.

White, Melvin. "Proper Tax Treatment of Deductions for Personal Expense." In House Committee on Ways and Means, 86th Cong., 1st Sess., 1959, *Tax Revision Compendium* 1. Comm. Print, pp. 365–74.

White, Melvin, and Anne White. "Horizontal Equity in the Federal Income Tax Treatment of Homeowners and Tenants." *National Tax Journal* 18 (1965): 225–39.

White, Melvin, and Anne White. "Tax Deductibility of Interest on Consumer Debt." *Public Finance Quarterly* 5 (1977): 3–7.

Whitt, Deborah. "Interest Deductions after the Tax Reform Act of 1986 and the Revenue Act of 1987." *Boston University Journal of Tax Law* 6 (1988): 85–115.

*Cross references:* homeowner preferences, individual income tax; income tax, federal; itemized deductions; original issue and market discount.

# Intergovernmental grants

Mark Schroder
Department of Housing and Urban Development

*Payments generally made from a higher to a lower level of government to subsidize the cost of providing specific public goods or services.*

In a federal system, one level of government may receive funding from another level of government, generally a higher one, either for the provision of a specific public service or for the general conduct of public business. In the United States, the last five decades have witnessed a steady increase in the level of grants from the federal government to state and local governments, whether expressed in constant dollars or as a share of gross domestic product.

The largest single federal grant program ($68 billion in fiscal year 1992) is Medicaid, which pays for the health care of public assistance recipients and certain other groups. The next five largest grant categories are family support (welfare) at $15 billion, highways ($15 billion), housing assistance ($12 billion), compensatory education for disadvantaged students ($6 billion), and child nutrition programs ($6 billion).

## Rationale

It is almost universally believed that some public services are most efficiently delivered by subnational governments. The question is why all such services should not be paid for by the residents of the jurisdiction doing the spending. The scholarly literature employs four different ideas to explain the increasing transfer of resources from higher to lower levels of government:

### Externalities

A particular service provided by a lower-level government may have benefits that spill over to residents of other jurisdictions. Feasible lower-level tax systems (e.g., property or sales) do not capture these external benefits. It is inequitable for residents of the provider jurisdiction to pay for nonresidents'

benefits, and, in the absence of external assistance, the provider jurisdiction would choose an inefficiently low level of service. As spillovers increase, the argument for the higher level of government assuming the function entirely may grow stronger.

### Vertical equity

Higher-level authorities may believe that feasible lower-level tax systems have undesirable distributional consequences. Resources for essential public services that can most efficiently be provided by the lower level of government should be obtained in part from a tax system that has more desirable distributional properties (e.g., income).

### Income elasticity of demand

Demand for public services is highly income-elastic, but lower-level tax systems may not be. As society becomes richer, it demands disproportionately more public services, some of them local, and must use those tax systems most responsive to wealth and income changes to pay for them, regardless of the level of government providing them.

### Fiscal illusion

When the taxing entity is not the same as the spending entity, some level of spending on the particular public service appears to the lower-level authorities as a free good. They will then spend more for that service than their own electorate would be willing to pay for it. The higher-level authority's interest in maintaining the illusion arises from the political influence of groups with special interests in raising expenditures on those services.

Locally provided elementary and secondary education can serve as an illustration for all four arguments. This service cost $216 billion in fiscal year 1991, and states provided more than half the money, in an increasing departure from the tradition of dependence on the local property tax. In an increasingly mobile society, the children educated by one jurisdiction may live and work as adults in other areas, and some of the benefits of their education are lost to the community that paid for it. The property tax base per child is very unevenly distributed across communities, and either legislatures or courts come to believe that providing a minimum standard of education to all children is unfairly burdensome for property-poor communities. The economy demands an increasing proportion of high school graduates, and the traditional property tax base may well not expand as quickly as school enrollments. Finally, the substantial growth in state aid to local schools has been an avowed goal of groups interested in higher aggregate expenditure levels, like teachers' unions.

## Appropriate design of grants programs

The design of grant allocations across jurisdictions does not always reflect the intent of the legislators as well as it could. Grants may be categorical—that is, tied to a particular public service—or untied; they may be awarded competitively or by formula. If they are awarded by formula, they may be awarded with or without a matching requirement; a matching requirement may reflect various efficiency and equity concerns.

### Untied grants

An untied grant (like the former federal revenue-sharing program) invites the lower-level government to choose from a wide menu of spending increases and/or tax reductions.

### Competitive grants

In the federal government, small grant programs are almost necessarily competitive. Competitive processes have both positive and negative features. The higher-level government can use the competition to reward those lower jurisdictions that have made the greatest effort to solve a problem of general concern, or to assist jurisdictions for whom the problem is particularly acute, although the latter approach can give rise to perverse incentives.

It is sometimes argued that competitions stimulate lower-level jurisdictions to give greater consideration to particular problems, even if they fail to receive funding. On the other hand, competitive processes consume scarce resources at both the lower and upper levels of government; much of the time spent in grant writing and proposal evaluation is deadweight loss.

### Categorical grants with no matching requirement

The higher-level authorities may award funds for some public service without requiring the lower-level jurisdiction to devote additional resources to that service. The accepted view of economists is that matching provisions will cause the lower-level government to provide greater amounts of service; the reasons are discussed below.

### Open-ended or limited matching requirements

The higher-level legislators may choose not to continue to match lower-level expenditures above some threshold. An open-ended matching program could easily lead to spending levels in excess of those the legislators are committed to supporting. On the other hand, limited matching programs offer no incentives, and relatively less aid, to those jurisdictions that have high spending propensities for the service in question.

### Efficiency considerations in matching formulas

When creating matching formulas, legislators typically fail to provide adjustments for the extent to which service delivery in one jurisdiction has more or less spillover externalities than in others. The predictable consequence will be inefficient under provision of the service. For example, if differences in the level of welfare benefits motivated migration across state lines, the spillover could lead to inefficiently low levels of benefit in all states. The existence of substantial welfare-motivated migration has never been clearly demonstrated, but if spillover effects became a concern for Congress, the matching formula devised for the allocation of Aid to Families with Dependent Children could be adjusted to compensate states with an excess burden of recipients to taxpayers.

### Effects of categorical grants on spending

A substantial body of scholarly literature, both theoretical and empirical, has analyzed the effects of categorical grant programs on lower-level public service expenditure. Two sorts of findings about price and income effects have arisen from it. First, each public service is presumably a good thing that almost every citizen would like to have a little more of as the price of obtaining it falls. Categorical grants that require matching funds effectively lower the price of the public service. For example, if the federal government pays 80 percent of the cost of an Interstate highway, then each state obtains the benefits of an additional mile of highway at an apparent price of 20 cents on the dollar. Economists have therefore predicted that any given amount of funds delivered in the form of categorical matching grants would stimulate more lower-level spending on the targeted services than the same amount of money provided without matching. The matching requirement lowers the price of additional units of service, while the grant without a matching requirement leaves the price of additional units to the lower-level government unaffected. Most empirical studies confirm this prediction.

Second, money is fungible. Suppose that Dirty City, where the citizens have a total private income of $100 million a year, spends $400,000 a year (0.4%) to control water pollution. Now suppose that Dirty City receives a grant of $200,000 to increase its pollution control activity. Under a variety of economic models of political behavior, the grant is equivalent to some distribution of $200,000 to particular individuals in the community; from this one would anticipate a trivial increase in anti-pollution spending, somewhere around $800 (0.4%) of the grant—a little more if clean water is a luxury good or the mayor is a Sierra Club member), and the remainder would be used for other public purposes and/or reducing community taxes.

The prediction of trivial impact has no empirical support. Instead, it would be more typical to find Dirty City increasing its water pollution control budget from $400,000 to $480,000—less, possibly, than the higher-level authorities wanted, but an increase that is a hundred times larger than what one would expect from the simple fungibility of money. Most empirical studies have found this flypaper effect, so called because grant funding tends to "stick where it hits" (Courant et al. 1979).

The flypaper effect has provoked much controversy and inspired much creativity in the building of new behavioral models, but no consensus has emerged. If citizens are unwilling to spend a large fraction of "their own" tax money on the targeted public service, the question is why they let "their own" government spend a large fraction of grant money on that service rather than on goods and services that they care more about. Tax illusion, special interest pressure, bureaucratic power, institutional restrictions like constitutional caps on property tax rates, and the political interest in stable tax rates (rate cuts based on intergovernmental grants could be destabilizing if future grants were not forthcoming) are among the explanations in the literature.

## Additional readings

Ahmad, Ehtisham. *Financing Decentralized Expenditures: An International Comparison of Grants.* Cheltenham, U.K.: Edward Elgar, 1997.

Bradford, David F., and Wallace E. Oates. "The Analysis of Revenue Sharing in a New Approach to Collective Fiscal Decisions." *Quarterly Journal of Economics* (August 1971): 416–39.

Chubb, John E. "The Political Economy of Federalism." *American Political Science Review* (December 1985): 994–1015.

Courant, Paul N., Edward M. Gramlich, and Daniel L. Rubinfeld. "The Stimulative Effects of Intergovernmental Grants: Or Why Money Sticks Where It Hits." In *Fiscal Federalism and Grants-in-Aid,* edited by Peter Mieszkowski and William H. Oakland. Washington, D.C.: The Urban Institute, 1979.

Fossett, James W. "On Confusing Caution and Greed: A Political Explanation of the Flypaper Effect." *Urban Affairs Quarterly* (September 1990): 95–117.

Gramlich, Edward M. "Intergovernmental Grants: A Review of the Empirical Literature. In *The Political Economy of Fiscal Federalism,* edited by Wallace E. Oates. Lexington, Mass.: Lexington Books, 1975.

Inman, Robert P. "Grants in a Metropolitan Economy—A Framework for Policy. In *Financing the New Federalism: Revenue Sharing, Conditional Grants, and Taxation,* edited by Wallace E. Oates. Baltimore: Johns Hopkins University Press, 1975.

Inman, Robert P. "The Fiscal Performance of Local Government: An Interpretive Review." In *Current Issues in Urban Economics,* edited by Peter Mieszkowski and Mahlon Straszheim. Baltimore: Johns Hopkins University Press, 1979.

Ladd, Helen F., and Fred C. Doolittle. "Which Level of Government Should Assist the Poor?" *National Tax Journal* (September 1982): 323–36.

Logan, Robert R. "Fiscal Illusion and the Grantor Government." *Journal of Political Economy* (December 1986): 1304–18.

Ma, Jun. *Intergovernmental Fiscal Transfers in Nine Countries.* Policy Research Working Paper 1822. Washington, D.C.: World Bank, 1997.

Nathan, Richard P. "State and Local Government under Federal Grants: Toward a Predictive Theory." *Political Science Quarterly* (Spring 1983): 47–57.

Nathan, Richard P., and Fred Doolittle. "Federal Grants: Giving and Taking Away." *Political Science Quarterly* (Spring 1985): 53–74.

Oates, Wallace E. *Fiscal Federalism.* New York: Harcourt Brace Jovanovich, 1972.

Reischauer, Robert D. "General Revenue Sharing—The Program's Incentives." In *Financing the New Federalism: Revenue Sharing, Conditional Grants, and Taxation,* edited by Wallace E. Oates. Baltimore: Johns Hopkins University Press, 1975.

Shah, Anwar. *The Reform of Intergovernmental Fiscal Relations in Developing and Emerging Market Economies.* Policy and Research Series 23. Washington, D.C.: World Bank, 1994.

Shroder, Mark. "Approximately Efficient Federal Matching Grants for Subnational Public Assistance." *National Tax Journal* (June 1992): 155–66.

Singh, Nirvikar, and Ravi Thomas. "Matching Grants versus Block Grants with Imperfect Information." *National Tax Journal* (June 1989): 191–239.

Wilde, J. "Grants in Aid: The Analytics of Design and Responses." *National Tax Journal* (June 1971): 573–84.

*Cross references:* education financing, state and local; fiscal federalism; Tiebout model.

# Inventory accounting

David W. Brazell
Department of the Treasury

*Methods used to match costs incurred in producing, purchasing, transporting, or storing property against revenues received from the sale of that property; different inventory accounting rules apply for financial accounting and income tax purposes.*

## The need for inventory accounting

As used in both financial and income tax accounting, inventory value represents the historic costs of acquiring certain property. The objective of inventory accounting is to allocate the costs incurred in connection with the acquisition, production, and maintenance of inventory to the period when the gross receipts associated with the sale of the merchandise are realized. This allocation is accomplished by capitalizing the costs (which are usually cash outlays, but may also include accrued costs such as depreciation) and by allowing a deduction for them only when the inventory is sold. The cost of goods sold during a given accounting period is determined by adding total inventory costs incurred during that period to the value of the inventory at the beginning of that period, and by deducting the value of the inventory at the end of that period.

## What is inventory?

Generally accepted accounting principles (GAAP) must be followed by publicly traded corporations for financial reporting purposes. These principles define inventory as items of "tangible personal property that (1) are held for sale in the ordinary course of business, (2) are in process of production for such sale, or (3) are to be currently consumed in the production of goods or services to be available for sale" (AICPA 1953). The federal income tax regulations contain a similar definition, but exclude supplies that do not physically become part of merchandise intended for sale. Both definitions exclude property acquired with the intention of earning an investment return (including fixed tangible capital) and all real property. There are two main tax consequences for property being designated as inventory: The character of inventory gains and losses is ordinary, not capital, and inventory may be valued at the "lower of cost or market" (LCM). Exceptions to the second consequence include inventory valued using the "last in, last out" method, which must be valued at cost, and the inventory of security dealers, which must be valued at fair market value.

## Basis of inventory valuation

Statutory authority for requiring inventory tax accounting provides two general restrictions on inventory valuation methods: The method must conform as closely as possible to the best accounting practice in the trade or business of the taxpayer, and it must clearly reflect income. The first requirement usually refers to the degree to which a particular method conforms with GAAP. The second restriction is primarily a requirement that the method be used consistently from year to year.

### Valuation at cost

The basis of valuation most commonly used by businesses that meets the two requirements of the law is (historical) "cost." Manufacturing costs that must be inventoried under GAAP include only those that can be identified specifically with the manufactured product: direct materials costs, direct labor costs, and indirect production costs (also referred to as factory "overhead" or "burden"). Inventory costs for purchased merchandise include direct purchasing costs, among them transportation costs. Before 1987, tax accounting also followed the GAAP definitions of cost. Wholesalers and retailers were required to capitalize direct purchasing costs, while manufacturers were subject to the "full absorption" regulations. These rules specified that indirect costs had to be inventoried only if they were capitalized by the taxpayer in preparing its financial statements. Thus, taxpayers were usually required to keep only one set of inventory records for both tax and financial reporting purposes.

### The uniform capitalization rules

The Tax Reform Act of 1986 added the "uniform capitalization requirements" (UCR) to the Internal Revenue Code. The UCR mandate that taxpayers must allocate to inventory those costs that "directly benefit or are incurred by reason of the performance of production or resale activities" (Reg. §1.263A-1(e)(3)(i)). Consequently, certain administrative overhead—such items as utilities, insurance, data processing, and legal services—must be capitalized into inventory to the extent they are allocated to production or resale activities. Indirect costs that continue to be deductible under the UCR include selling and advertising costs, research and experimentation costs, income taxes, and most interest costs.

UCR regulations authorize a number of simplified accounting techniques that allow firms to first calculate their GAAP inventory values and then identify and allocate their additional UCR costs to inventory. They also contain *de minimus* rules that exempt small resellers and producers from the UCR, and allow taxpayers to elect to use their regular tax inventory values in computing their alternative minimum tax (AMT) income, thereby avoiding an additional tax compliance burden, albeit at the cost of potentially paying additional tax under the AMT.

### Predetermined costs

The use of actual costs in valuing manufacturing inventory can be very complex. Consequently, both GAAP and tax rules authorize methods that utilize predetermined unit costs. If actual costs vary from predetermined costs under these methods, such "variances" need not be allocated to tax inventory if they are not significant, if the taxpayer also deducts them in financial statements, and if both positive and negative variances are treated consistently.

Under GAAP, a manufacturer may use a plant's estimated "practical capacity" production level to estimate fixed overhead unit costs. This allows a lower unit cost to be used to establish inventory cost if actual production falls below the practical capacity level. The method, expressly allowed under full absorption regulations, was disallowed under the UCR regulations. Some taxpayers believe, however, that the Internal Revenue Service did not have the authority to repeal the practical capacity method.

### LCM and subnormal goods

Treasury regulations also authorize the lower-of-cost-or-market (LCM) method of inventory valuation. This method is usually justified by the conservatism principle of GAAP:

> A departure from the cost basis of pricing the inventory is required when the utility of the goods is no longer as great as its cost. Where there is evidence that the utility of goods, in their disposal in the ordinary course of business, will be less than cost, whether due to physical deterioration, obsolescence, changes in price levels, or other causes, the difference should be recognized as a loss of the current period. This is generally accomplished by stating such goods at a lower level commonly designated as *market* (AICPA 1953).

Market is not the full realizable value of a good; it is the replacement cost (by purchase or by reproduction) of the good. GAAP rules limit market on the high side by net realizable value and on the low side by net realizable value reduced by an allowance for an approximately normal profit margin. Income tax regulations define market as "the aggregate of the current bid prices prevailing at the date of the inventory of the basic elements of cost" (Reg. §1.471-4(a)). The tax regulations do not contain the

limits on market specified under GAAP, but they allow net realizable value to be used for normal goods in limited situations. Once an item is valued at market, that value becomes its future "cost."

Regardless of whether a taxpayer uses cost or LCM as its general valuation method, the taxpayer may value "subnormal goods" at net realizable value. These are goods that are unsalable at normal prices or unusable in the normal way because of damage, imperfections, change of style, or other similar reasons.

The availability of write-downs under the LCM method and for subnormal goods has been criticized for providing inappropriate exceptions from income realization accounting principles and as being one-sided by allowing the recognition of losses, but not gains.

## Identification of inventory items

Items in current inventory must be identified in some way and associated with a historical period of acquisition or production. This identification may be accomplished by tracking specific items. More commonly, however, a flow-of-cost assumption is employed. The "first in, first out" (FIFO) method assumes that the remaining items in inventory are those last purchased or last produced. The "last-in-first-out" (LIFO) method is also used. Under LIFO, it is assumed that items in the current inventory were the earliest acquired or manufactured. While a more complicated method, LIFO yields lower inventory values (and lower taxes) in periods of rising costs.

### LIFO requirements

If LIFO is elected for tax purposes, the identified inventory must be evaluated at cost. Other restrictions are also placed on LIFO taxpayers. For example, LIFO may be used only if it is used for all financial reporting purposes. In addition, a corporate taxpayer must include a portion of the change in its LIFO "recapture amount" (the difference in inventory values as computed using the FIFO and LIFO methods) in calculating its AMT income.

### LIFO methods

LIFO inventory is valued under either the "specific-goods" method or, most often, the "dollar-value" method. The standard approach to implementing dollar-value LIFO is the "double-extension" method. Under this method, inventory is placed into one or more "pools." The items in a pool are "extended" (i.e., costed) using both (fixed) base-year unit costs and current-year unit costs to obtain total inventory values at both base-year and current-year costs. The ratio of these two values provides a current-year value of a LIFO cost index. Comparing the ending inventory valued at base-year costs with the base-year value of beginning inventory provides a measure of the year's inventory increment or decrement. If a decrement has occurred, then prior increments (at base-year values) are removed or reduced in reverse chronological order to the extent of the decrement. If an increment has occurred, it is valued at current-year costs using the LIFO cost index and added to the prior increments to obtain ending inventory at historical cost.

Under the double-extension method, a new item entering the inventory must be valued at base-year cost, even if it did not exist in the base year. Such a cost must be constructed or estimated in some acceptable fashion. This method may therefore become impractical because of "technological changes, the extensive variety of items, or extreme fluctuations in the variety of the items" (Reg. §1.472-8(e)(1)). Consequently, other variants of dollar-value LIFO are specifically authorized. The "index" and the "link-chain" methods use a "representative portion" of the inventory pool to estimate the LIFO cost index. Two simplified methods are also authorized, in which cost indexes are developed from price indexes published by the Bureau of Labor Statistics. However, unless a taxpayer is a small business, it can use only 80 percent of the percentage change in the published indexes in constructing its LIFO cost index.

### Components of cost

Items in a LIFO pool are sometimes defined under the "components of cost" (COC) method, which identifies as inventory "items" the three components of cost (direct materials, direct labor, and overhead) that make up the cost of physical products. In implementing the COC method, some taxpayers estimate the base-year quantities of materials, labor, and overhead using current-year technological relationships. With increased efficiency of production over time, this implies a reduction in base-year costs, a smaller inventory increment, and a lower end-of-year inventory value. The COC method has been criticized for not accounting for changes in technology, whereas its defenders claim that the COC method better eliminates inflationary inventory profits and avoids costing problems associated with the introduction of new products.

## Inventory investment in the national income and product accounts

Inventory investment reported in the national income and product accounts (NIPA) differs from accounting change-in-inventory concepts by measuring both beginning and ending inventory values at current-year cost. The NIPA estimators con-

vert historical cost inventory values (as reported under the GAAP rules) into current replacement cost estimates using available price series and estimates of inventory turnover rates. The NIPA also report an inventory valuation adjustment (IVA) that equals the difference between the change in inventory stocks valued at current cost and the change in those stocks valued at historical cost (i.e., the change in book inventory values). The IVA is subtracted from reported profits in calculating NIPA estimates of corporate profits and proprietors' income.

### Additional readings

American Institute of Certified Public Accountants, Inc. (AICPA). *Accounting Research Bulletin* 43, ch. 4 (1953).

Garrett, Richard, James E. Connor, and Annette B. Smith. *Uniform Capitalization Rules: Inventory; Self-Constructed Assets; Real Estate.* Tax Management Portfolio No. 576. Washington, D.C.: Tax Management, Inc., 1996.

Godbout, James C., Diane P. Herndon, Jeremy K. Holt, and Barry A. Tovig. *Inventories: General Principles; LIFO Method.* Tax Management Portfolio No. 578. Washington, D.C.: Tax Management, Inc., 1996.

U.S. Department of Commerce. Bureau of Economic Analysis. *Readings in Concepts and Methods of National Income Statistics.* Washington, D.C.: National Technical Information Service, 1976.

*Cross reference:* uniform capitalization rules.

# Inverse elasticity rule

Harry Watson
George Washington University

*A principle for choosing tax rates to minimize the excess tax burden.*

---

The inverse elasticity rule is one of the few simple rules that derive from the optimal commodity tax literature, a literature that examines how excise taxes should be structured in order to achieve some revenue target while ensuring that the excess burden of taxation is minimized. Because most of the optimal tax rules that have been derived are not very transparent and would require a substantial amount of information were they to be used, some effort has been devoted to finding conditions under which simple rules of thumb might serve as a guide in the choice of optimal tax rates. One such guide is the inverse elasticity rule, the application of which requires that the demands and supplies of all the goods or services that are subject to taxation depend only on their own price.

Supposing that demands of taxed goods or services are sensitive only to their own price, and assuming that production of the taxed goods or services occurs in perfectly competitive industries with constant average costs (so that producer prices are unaffected by taxation) yields the simplest variant of the inverse elasticity rule: The excise tax rates of any pair of taxed goods or services, say $i$ and $j$, should be set so that $\theta_i/\theta_j = \epsilon_j/\epsilon_i$, where $\theta$ is the ad valorem tax rate and $\epsilon$ is the elasticity of demand.

Thus, the tax rates should vary inversely with the responsiveness of consumers to price changes, a relationship that minimizes the excess burden that such taxes can create. Assuming that there are $n$ taxed goods or services and that all their elasticities are known, the problem of selecting optimal excise tax rates is quite simple. By the inverse elasticity rule, it must be that $\theta_2 = (\epsilon_1/\epsilon_2)\theta_1$, $\theta_3 = (\epsilon_1/\epsilon_3)\theta_1$, etc. The values of all these tax rates are simply multiples of $\theta_1$, and the value of $\theta_1$ can be adjusted upward until the revenue target is met.

When producer prices can vary—that is, when the assumption of constant average costs is dropped—and the supplies and demands of taxed goods or services depend only on their own price, the inverse elasticity rule becomes: The ad valorem excise tax rates for any pair of goods or services, say $\theta_i$ and $\theta_j$, should be set so that

$$\frac{\theta_i}{\theta_j} = \frac{1/\epsilon_i + (1 - \theta_i)/\eta_i}{1/\epsilon_j + (1 - \theta_j)/\eta_j}$$

where $\epsilon$ is the consumer's demand elasticity and $\eta$ is the producer's supply elasticity.

As in the previous case, the logic behind this rule is to shift the tax burden to the market in which price changes produce limited responses. If the supplier of good $j$ is not price-sensitive, so $\eta_j$ is small, the tax on good $j$ should be large relative to the taxes on other goods. On the other hand, if the producers of goods $i$ and $j$ are very price-sensitive, so that $\eta_i$ and $\eta_j$ are large, the rule above collapses to the simple variant and tax rates are inversely related to the elasticities of consumers, or $\theta_i/\theta_j = \epsilon_j/\epsilon_i$.

The simplicity of the inverse elasticity rules comes at the cost of assuming that the demands and supplies of taxed goods or services are insensitive to changes in all prices except their own. Generally, one would expect that the impact of a tax on one good would not be limited to the market for that good; the imposition of a tax in one market will lead to supply or demand adjustments in other markets and, concomitantly, changes in the prices of other goods. It is these intermarket effects, which the inverse elasticity rule assumes away, that complicate the search for optimal tax rules.

Thus, the appropriateness of using the inverse elasticity rule hinges on the assumption that these intermarket effects can be ignored. For example, consider levying excise taxes on two different pairs of goods, say gasoline and tobacco versus beer and wine. For most consumers, spending on gasoline is independent of spending on tobacco—one cannot be substituted for the other, nor does one complement the use of the other—so it is likely that the impact of an excise tax on either good on the market for the other good can be ignored. On the other hand, because beer and wine may be substitutes for some consumers, the impact of an excise tax on either good may alter demand for the other, so that intermarket effects cannot be ignored. Ignoring intermarket effects may lead to the inappropriate application of the inverse elasticity rule. Suppose this rule is used to determine whether labor and capital income should face different rates of income taxation. Leaving aside the more complicated features of income taxation, it is possible to interpret a capital income tax as an excise tax that raises the price of future consumption—or reduces the return to saving—and a labor income tax as an excise tax that reduces the wage so that, together, these excise taxes capture the essence of income taxation. Provided the supply of labor was unaffected by the price of future consumption and the demand for future consumption was unaffected by the after-tax wage, it would follow that optimal pattern of labor versus capital income tax rates would be inversely related to the responsiveness of labor supply to the after-tax wage relative to the responsiveness of saving to after-tax rates of return.

This result suggests that whether labor or capital income should face a higher tax rate depends on a simple comparison of elasticity values. However, even if these elasticities could be accurately measured, this outcome cannot be assured unless it is true that labor supply does not respond to after-tax rates of return and saving does not respond to after-tax wage rates. While it is possible that labor supply is not significantly affected by after-tax rates of return, theory and empirical evidence do not support the assumption that saving does not respond to tax-induced changes in labor income, a fact that would preclude the use of the inverse elasticity rule in analyzing income taxation.

Although literal application of the inverse elasticity rule may not be feasible or appropriate in the practical design of tax systems, the spirit behind the rule provides some broad guidance to policymakers—namely, that in setting tax rates one should be mindful of the potential gains that can be had in economic efficiency by imposing heavier tax burdens on goods or activities that are relatively less sensitive to the kinds of changes in market prices that typically result from the imposition of taxes.

*Cross references:* elasticity, demand and supply; excess burden; optimal taxation.

# Investment tax credits

Robert S. Chirinko
Emory University

*Reductions in tax liabilities determined as a percentage of the price of a purchased asset.*

---

Starting with the Revenue Act of 1962, the investment tax credit (ITC) has been set at various rates, suspended, reinstated, repealed, resurrected, increased, and then finally completely eliminated in the Tax Reform Act of 1986. Reinstituting the ITC was part of the Clinton administration's initial economic proposal to Congress, but it was not enacted into law.

Tax credits were initially granted primarily for the purchase of business capital equipment, then extended to other assets and activities (e.g., expenditures on research and development, restoration of historic buildings, and hiring of certain classes of workers). ITCs have constituted a quantitatively important tax expenditure ($21.3 billion in 1985).

This entry is divided into three parts. Part one discusses the history, scope, and types of ITCs. The chief reason for granting these subsidies has been to stimulate economic activity, although which aspect of economic activity was the appropriate target for this stimulus has varied because of changing views about the structure of the economy and the possibilities for constructive public policies. These changes are considered in the second part. Finally, the impact of the ITC on economic activity is reviewed briefly in the third part of this entry.

## History, scope, and types of ITCs

ITCs have been used frequently as an instrument of fiscal policy in the United States. Beginning in 1962, the statutory rate for the ITC was set at 7 percent for spending on business capital equipment with tax lives greater than three years and for special purpose structures replaced contemporaneously with the equipment that they house, support, or serve. The statutory rate was increased to 10 percent in 1975. The Tax Reform Act of 1986 abolished the ITC. Between 1962 and 1986, the ITC was not in force for two periods: suspended from October 1966 to March 1967 and repealed from April 1969 to August 1971. Public utility property (equipment plus structures) has also received a credit, ranging from 3 percent in 1962, to 4 percent in 1971, to 10 percent in 1975. Assets generally become eligible for the tax credit when they are placed in service.

Several complicating factors have driven a wedge between the statutory rates of the investment credit, at time times when it has existed, and its ultimate impact on businesses. Four are discussed here. First, the ITC is not refundable and hence is valuable to a taxpayer only if there is a current tax liability. (Legislation has generally exacerbated this problem by restricting the percentage of the current tax liability that can be reduced by the ITC.) This shortcoming is mitigated by carryback and carryforward provisions, but the delay in realizing the tax credit lowers its value. Problems caused by the absence of a current tax liability were overcome with the safe-harbor leasing provisions in the Economic Recovery Tax Act of 1981 that, in effect, permitted the sale of unused tax credits to firms with current tax liabilities. While such an expansion of markets is generally welcomed by economists, the realization that many large profitable corporations were paying little or no taxes led to a public outcry, and safe-harbor leasing was eliminated at the end of 1983.

Second, the statutory impact of the ITC increases with the tax life of the asset. For example, under the 1962 legislation, eligible property with a tax life of four to six years received one-third of the ITC, and eligible property with a tax life of six to eight years received two-thirds of the ITC. The tax lives determining the percentage of the available credit, as well as the percentages themselves, have been changed periodically. A larger ITC for longer-lived assets can be an important feature in attempting to preserve neutrality of the ITC across assets (Bradford 1980).

Third, the impact of the ITC on investment incentives also depends on whether it reduces the basis used in calculating tax depreciation. The 1962 legislation that introduced the ITC subtracted its value from the basis. This basis reduction (known as the Long Amendment after the chairman of the Senate Finance Committee) was repealed in 1964. Thus, the 7 percent ITC in 1962 was not as large as the 7 percent ITC in 1964. In 1982, the tax depreciation basis was lowered by one-half of the tax credit, thus reducing the value of the ITC.

Fourth, the limited coverage of the ITC creates an incentive to reclassify assets as equipment or special-purpose structures. While the original legislation explicitly excluded any "building and its structural components," this restriction has been circumvented by creative accounting. As a result of this response to incentives, along with a slow expansion of the tax code to broaden the coverage of the ITC, more than 50 percent of the cost of the acquisitions of structures (as defined in the National Income and Product Accounts) was eligible for the ITC in 1975.

The above considerations suggest the difficulty in specifying the impact of the ITC (see Fullerton et al. 1987 for estimates).

For a given effective rate, several different types of ITCs are available to policymakers. The ITC can be targeted to particular classes of capital or be uniform across all capital.

The ITC can be permanent or temporary. An ITC with a credible expiration date will induce firms to accelerate their investment spending to capture the transient tax benefits. It is unclear whether a temporary credit leads to an overall increase in investment spending or just intertemporal substitution with no increase relative to the level of investment that would have prevailed without the tax credit.

The ITC can be unilateral or incremental. A unilateral ITC applies to all investment in a category and has been the type adopted in all previous U.S. legislation for fixed capital. An incremental ITC— proposed by the Kennedy and Clinton administrations—applies to all equipment investment above a threshold, which might be specified as some average of the firm's past investment expenditures or sales, or some industrywide variables. While both types of ITCs provide an incentive to increase investment, the government would expect to lose less revenue for a given amount of investment—that is, would expect a greater "bang-for-the-buck"—with an incremental ITC.

The threshold creates several thorny problems for the incremental ITC. The benefits of an incremental ITC would not be distributed fairly, because firms that have recently undertaken major investment programs would receive relatively less benefit because of their higher threshold. Further difficulties would be faced in the long run, because incentives would exist to "reinvent" the company (in an accounting sense) every few years to lower the threshold. If the incremental ITC is in force for several years, firms would face an intertemporal trade-off that would lower the impact of this fiscal policy. A firm that invests today may raise its threshold (depending on the definition) for calculating tomorrow's tax benefit, thus lowering the overall stimulus afforded by the ITC. These last two concerns suggest that an incremental ITC would be most useful as a temporary policy providing short-term stimulus to the economy.

## Reasons for adopting an ITC

The ITC is one of several fiscal policies that affect firms directly and that are available to policymakers to stimulate economic activity. Other fiscal instruments include the income tax rate, depreciation allowances, and the percentage of asset purchase price eligible for a tax or subsidy. While an ITC, the income tax rate, and depreciation allowances can be adjusted so that they all have the same present value

to an investing firm (see Cost of capital), the ITC carries some additional advantages. Decreases in the income tax rate affect the returns on both existing and new capital and hence are more costly to the government for a given amount of investment incentive. Depreciation allowances are subject to the uncertainty associated with discount rates (perhaps caused by inflation) or repeal. The immediate value imparted by the ITC makes it a more potent fiscal policy instrument than depreciation allowances.

Between 1962 and 1986, the ITC was changed several times. To understand the reasons for tax legislation changes, it is useful to remember that investment plays two pivotal roles in the macroeconomy. The considerable volatility of business investment spending is a prime contributor to short-run fluctuations in the aggregate economy. Additionally, the long-run potential of the economy is directly linked to the amount of capital available to businesses and the efficient allocation of that capital among firms. Because of changing views about the structure of the economy and the possibilities for constructive public policies, the reasons for adopting an ITC have varied between some combination of short-run stabilization and long-run allocation goals.

The Revenue Act of 1962 represented a major innovation in tax policy by introducing the ITC as a fiscal policy instrument. Many economists believe that the ITC was adopted initially to strengthen short-run economic activity in the tradition of Keynesian demand management. However, the first economic report of the Kennedy administration reveals that the 1962 act sought to meet both allocation and stabilization goals (Economic Report of the President 1978: 10; U.S. Treasury, 1979: 365).

Keynesian economics had come to dominate policymaking by the mid-1960s and early 1970s. Consequently, the ITC was viewed solely as a tool for stabilization when suspended in 1966 and reinstated in 1967 (U.S. Treasury 1967: 28–31).

In 1969, the ITC was repealed, and the budget saving was used to remove the income tax surcharge then in effect. Interestingly, despite the ascendancy of Keynesian thought at this time, the repeal was based on the "consideration of the longer-range issues" because "the national priorities of the 1970s did not require or justify this special incentive" (Economic Report of the President 1970: 31).

Stabilization goals reemerged when the ITC was resurrected in 1971 (Economic Report of the President 1972: 69). Concern about a depressed level of aggregate economic activity led to an increase in the ITC in 1975. This increase was to last only two years and was intended to give businesses "an incentive to undertake some investment now that they would otherwise have undertaken only later" (Economic Report of the President 1975: 20). This temporary

ITC was extended on a temporary basis in the Tax Reform Act of 1976.

During the latter part of the 1970s, questions arose as to the usefulness of fiscal policy as a stabilization tool. Lags in recognizing the need for a fiscal stimulus, passing the appropriate legislation, and obtaining the desired spending by firms undermined the usefulness of discretionary fiscal policy. Furthermore, because of deficiencies in both empirical predictions and theoretical foundations, the Keynesian model of the macroeconomy lost favor in the economics profession (see Mankiw 1990). This disenchantment led to a change in emphasis concerning the reasons for adopting the ITC. When the ITC was made permanent (until 1986) in 1979, the goal of growth, not stabilization, was emphasized (Economic Report of the President 1978).

The demise of the stabilization goal was complete by the beginning of the 1980s with the passage of the Economic Recovery Tax Act of 1981 (ERTA). Among other aspects of this fundamental legislation, distortions affecting the intertemporal allocation of resources were emphasized (Economic Report of the President 1982: 7). While ERTA had major effects on raising investment incentives, this legislation affected the ITC only slightly, by increasing the percentage of the credit available to shorter-lived equipment, thus creating a credit uniform across all eligible assets.

The substantial incentives in ERTA, along with ongoing academic and government research, highlighted an additional dimension to efficient resource allocation. Not only must resources be allocated efficiently between consumption and investment, there is an additional issue of allocating a given amount of aggregate investment among capital assets. That taxes not affect the interasset allocation of capital is known as asset neutrality, which was enshrined in the concept of the "level playing field." The uniform ITC in place in the early 1980s posed major problems for creating a level playing field for business capital assets and was eliminated in the Tax Reform Act of 1986 (Fullerton 1994).

Reviewing tax systems in several industrialized countries, Pechman (1987b: 3) echoed the sentiments of many economists at that time in noting a "growing disenchantment almost everywhere with investment incentives. Opinion is widespread that they distort the allocation of resources and generate numerous inequities among industries and firms."

However, the case for asset nonneutrality and an equipment ITC reemerged quickly. As has been the case with the ITC throughout its history, views about investment incentives are affected by economic events and research findings. The impressive growth of several industrializing nations called attention to the strong correlation between growth and investment spending. Influential research by DeLong and Summers (1992), combined with a large body of extant work on developing economies, highlighted the positive externalities that may be associated with equipment investment. These research findings have been disputed, however (Auerbach et al. 1994; DeLong and Summers 1994).

The Clinton administration proposed reinstituting a permanent ITC for equipment investment targeted to small businesses. Moreover, a sluggish economy prompted a call for a temporary incremental ITC. Using the ITC to address both allocation and stabilization goals is similar to the approach taken by the Kennedy administration 30 years before, although the temporary nature of the incremental ITC and the reasons for the permanent ITC differed. However, the Clinton ITCs were not enacted into law.

## The impact of the ITC

The impact of the ITC can be viewed in several different ways. From an accounting perspective, profitability and cash flow are affected initially, although the ultimate effect depends on the general equilibrium response of output prices, input prices, and final sales. Economists tend to focus on the impact of the ITC at the margin; that is, on the final (or additional) dollar of investment spending. From a marginal perspective, the ITC also has several different impacts: the intertemporal allocation of resources between consumption and investment, the interasset allocation of resources among capital assets, the overall level of economic welfare, the marginal cost of funds, and the additional investment per dollar of tax loss. Calculations of the last two effects will be reviewed here.

Assessments of the ITC at the margin cannot be undertaken in isolation; they must consider all taxes impinging on the investment decision. The analytic tool used by economists is the cost of capital, first applied to tax policy analysis by Hall and Jorgenson (1967) and used recently by Jorgenson and Yun (1991) to study tax reforms in the United States. The cost of capital combines in a single measure several taxes affecting the decision to acquire capital (see Cost of capital). Conceptually, the cost of capital is the price of "renting" a unit of capital for one period. The ITC effectively lowers the purchase price of the asset and hence the "rental" that is required from the firm.

In a simulation study representative of those with computational general-equilibrium models, Fullerton and Henderson (1989) calculated the marginal cost of funds—the decrement to total welfare (measured in dollars) from raising an additional dollar of tax revenue—associated with taxes on 38 different types of capital assets. The marginal cost of funds is usually greater than the dollar in new revenue because of distortions introduced by taxes. Given the tax code that existed in 1984, their simulations revealed that reducing the ITC is the most efficient way of raising revenue (with available tax instruments). Because of a reduction of distortions among assets, the marginal cost of funds is only $0.62; hence, by appropriate reductions in the ITC, collecting $1 of revenue leads to a fall in consumer welfare of only $0.62. While several important factors are not represented in this model (e.g., investment externalities and stabilization problems), these calculations suggest that investment decisions are sensitive to the ITC and that its elimination in 1986 was welfare-enhancing.

However, when assessed in terms of econometric investment equations, the ITC appears to have less impact (see Chirinko 1993 for a survey). Estimates of tax policy effects on investment vary widely, and these differences are related to some of the key assumptions and caveats used in specifying the econometric model. For example, Chirinko and Eisner (1982) analyzed the investment equations in six quarterly macroeconometric models. In one partial-equilibrium simulation, a doubling of the ITC for equipment and the institution of a 10 percent credit for structures leads to a "bang for the buck"—the additional investment per dollar of tax loss—of between $0.13 and $1.43 (five years after the ITC increases). The mean value for all six models was $0.84, corresponding to an elasticity (with respect to the cost of capital) of −.052.

A number of these aggregate equations contain overly restrictive assumptions. When the investment equations are reestimated with more general specifications, the mean impact of tax policy is lowered ($0.47 with a corresponding elasticity of −.029) and the range of results across models is narrowed considerably ($0.14 to $0.82).

Thus, simulation studies indicate a more substantial impact of the ITC than do econometric analyses. Reconciling these differences would begin by examining the many assumptions maintained in simulation models that may not accurately describe the economy. Alternatively, econometric estimates of the potency of the ITC may be attenuated by biases arising from aggregation, simultaneity, or measurement error in the cost of capital.

## Additional readings

Auerbach, Alan, Kevin Hasset, and Stephen Oliver. "Reassessing the Social Returns to Investment." *Quarterly Journal of Economics* 109 (August 1994): 789–802.

Ballentine, J. Gregory. "Three Failures in Economic Analysis of Tax Reform." *National Tax Association–Tax Institute of America Proceedings* (1986): 3–6.

Bradford, David F. "Tax Neutrality and the Investment Tax Credit." In *The Economics of Taxation*, edited by Henry J. Aaron and Michael J. Boskin. Washington, D.C.: The Brookings Institution, 1980: 281–98.

Chirinko, Robert S. "Business Fixed Investment Spending: Modeling Strategies, Empirical Results, and Policy Implications." *Journal of Economic Literature* 31 (December 1993): 1875–1911. An extended version of this survey has been published as "Econometric Models and Empirical Findings for Business Investment." A monograph in the Salomon Brothers Center Series *Financial Markets, Institutions & Instruments*. New York: Basil Blackwell, 1993.

Chirinko, Robert S., and Robert Eisner. "The Effect of Tax Parameters in the Investment Equations in Macroeconomic Econometric Models." In *Economic Activity and Finance*, edited by Marshall E. Blume, Jean Crockett, and Paul Taubman. Cambridge, Mass.: Ballinger, 1982, pp. 25–84.

DeLong, J. Bradford, and Lawrence H. Summers. "Macroeconomic Policy and Long-Run Growth." In *Policies for Long-Run Growth*. Kansas City, Mo.: Federal Reserve Bank of Kansas City, 1992, pp. 93–128.

DeLong, J. Bradford, and Lawrence H. Summers. "Equipment Investment and Economic Growth: Reply." *Quarterly Journal of Economics* 109 (August 1994): 803–7.

*Economic Report of the President*. Washington, D.C.: U.S. Government Printing Office, various annual issues.

Fullerton, Don. "Tax Policy." In *American Economic Policy in the 1980s*, edited by Martin S. Feldstein, pp. 165–233. Chicago: University of Chicago Press, 1994.

Fullerton, Don, and Yolanda Kodrzycki Henderson. "The Marginal Excess Burden of Different Capital Tax Instruments." *The Review of Economics and Statistics* 71 (August 1989): 435–42.

Fullerton, Don, Robert Gillette, and James Mackie. "Investment Incentives under the Tax Reform Act of 1986." In *Compendium of Tax Research 1987*, pp. 131–72. Washington, D.C.: Office of Tax Analysis, U.S. Department of the Treasury, 1987.

Hall, Robert E., and Dale W. Jorgenson. "Tax Policy and Investment Behavior." *American Economic Review* 57 (June 1967): 391–414.

Jorgenson, Dale W., and Ralph Landau. *Tax Reform and the Cost of Capital: An International Comparison*. Washington, D.C.: The Brookings Institution, 1993.

Jorgenson, Dale W., and Kun-Young Yun. *Tax Reform and the Cost of Capital*. Oxford: Clarendon Press, 1991.

Mankiw, N. Gregory. "A Quick Refresher Course in Macroeconomics." *Journal of Economic Literature* 28 (December 1990): 1645–60.

Pechman, Joseph A. *Federal Tax Policy*. 5th ed. Washington, D.C.: The Brookings Institution, 1987a.

Pechman, Joseph A., editor. *Comparative Tax Systems: Europe, Canada, and Japan*. Arlington, Va.: Tax Analysts, 1987b.

U.S. Office of Management and Budget. *Budget of the United States Government*. Washington, D.C.: U.S. Government Printing Office, various annual issues. Information on tax developments can be found in the main budget document (under "Budget Receipts: Enacted Legislation" or similar titles) or the supplements entitled "Special Analyses" and "Analytical Perspectives" from 1981 onward.

U.S. Treasury. *The Annual Report of the Secretary of the Treasury on the State of the Finances*. Washington, D.C.: U.S. Government Printing Office, various annual issues from 1962 through 1980 inclusive.

*Cross references:* capital cost recovery; cost of capital; investment tax credits.

# Itemized deductions

## Sally Wallace
Georgia State University

*In computing taxable income (the base on which the federal income tax falls), individuals are permitted to deduct a series of expenditures.*

Itemized deductions from adjusted gross income are allowed for specific activities, catastrophic losses, or other taxes paid under the federal individual income tax system (Internal Revenue Code, Section 63). Taxpayers compute their total itemized deductions, compare this total to the standard deduction allowed for their filing status, and subtract the greater amount from adjusted gross income. While the standard deduction simply provides a threshold for taxation, itemized deductions are targeted at individual circumstances or specific policies (Goode 1976: 147). Itemized deductions have been allowed under the federal income tax law for many years. However, they have been altered over time; some have been disallowed, some have been added, the computations have changed, and so forth.

Taxpayers with income over a threshold amount are subject to a limitation on their total itemized deductions. In 1997, the threshold was $121,200 ($60,600 for married filing separately). For taxpayers with adjusted gross income over the threshold, allowable itemized deductions (other than medical, investment interest, casualty, theft, or wagering losses) are reduced by 3 percent of the excess, to a maximum reduction of 80 percent of total allowable deductions (excluding medical, investment interest, casualty, theft, or wagering losses) (Commerce Clearing House 1996: 281). Taxpayers must use tax form 1040 if they itemize their deductions. In 1993, approximately 28 percent of all federal individual

income tax returns filed used itemized rather than standard deductions.

Of the 43 states and the District of Columbia that have an income tax, 38 allow some itemized deductions in the calculation of taxable income (Advisory Commission on Intergovernmental Relations 1994: 68–69). The majority of these states have adopted most of the same itemized deductions that are allowed by the federal government.

The purpose of itemized deductions is fourfold: to ease the burden of catastrophic expenditures that affect a taxpaying unit's ability to pay tax, to encourage certain types of activities such as home ownership and charitable contributions, to ease the burden of taxes paid to state and local governments, and to allow taxpayers to deduct the cost of legitimate business expenses (Pechman 1987: 92–97). Under current law, there are seven main classes of itemized deductions.

Medical and dental expenses are justified on the grounds that catastrophic medical expenses alter a taxpayer's ability to pay taxes (Pechman 1987: 92). A taxpayer may deduct nonreimbursed medical and dental expenses that exceed 7.5 percent of adjusted gross income. This relatively high floor precludes many taxpayers from taking this deduction; in 1993, only 4.7 percent of total filers used it.

An individual may deduct payment of the following taxes: state and local government income taxes, real estate taxes, personal property taxes, income taxes paid to a foreign country, war profits or excess profits taxes, generation-skipping transfer taxes, and environmental taxes (Commerce Clearing House 1996: 284). Previously, federal excise taxes (e.g., gasoline) and state and local sales taxes were also allowed as deductions, along with some other minor state and local taxes, but these were removed by the mid-1980s. The federal deduction of state and local government taxes effectively reduces the "price" of state and local taxes. If taxpayers itemize and deduct the allowed state and local government taxes, the federal income tax bill is reduced by their deduction times their federal marginal tax rate. Consider the following example: A taxpayer pays $100 in state income and property taxes and faces a federal marginal tax rate of 28 percent. An itemizer would deduct the $100 of state taxes and reduce the federal tax liability bill by $28. In effect, $100 in state taxes cost only $72 ($100 − $28), because of the federal income tax saving received.

There is debate about this deduction. Proponents see it as a means of aiding state and local government budgets by reducing the price of state and local government goods. Opponents argue that it would be more efficient to provide assistance directly with federal aid. Another argument is that the deductibility of taxes serves to level the playing field among higher and lower taxing states. Taxpayers in higher taxing states will receive more federal tax savings through deductibility, thereby reducing their total federal, state, and local tax liability relatively more than for those taxpayers in lower taxing states. Critics ask why the federal government should subsidize higher taxing states, and also point out that because itemizers are higher-income individuals, deductibility will reduce the overall progressivity of the federal-state-local tax system.

Mortgage interest payments and points, and investment interest expenses, are deductible subject to certain limits. Mortgage interest (up to two homes), interest on home equity loans, and interest expenses incurred for investment purposes (up to a limit equal to investment income) are deductible. Before the Tax Reform Act of 1986, consumer interest was also deductible, and the rules for investment interest deductions were generally more lenient. The deduction for investment-related interest expenses is justified as a cost incurred in doing business. Mortgage interest is less easily justified as a deduction. It probably does encourage homeownership, which may help to provide stability in the economy. However, because homeowners do not report income from their owner-occupied homes, the deduction of interest expenses would not seem justified as an expense (Pechman 1987: 94). Additionally, this deduction gives homeowners a great advantage over renters.

Cash and in-kind gifts to charity are another form of itemized deductions. (Between 1982 and 1986, nonitemizers were also allowed to deduct some charitable contributions.) In general, taxpayers can deduct an amount equivalent to up to 50 percent of their adjusted gross income. A limit of 30 percent of adjusted gross income applies to gifts to some types of foundations and organizations. Because charitable contributions are deductible, the federal government in effect pays part of the individual taxpayer's contributions. Whether or not the income tax system should support such contributions has been a matter of limited debate. Some believe that the good done by these charitable organizations is worth the federal government's support (Pechman 1987: 94), while others believe that allowing such deductions is a violation of the separation between church and state (Rosen 1995: 376).

The casualty and theft loss deduction applies only to nonbusiness property. The goal is to protect a taxpayer in the event of catastrophic loss. The deduction is limited to losses in excess of 10 percent of the taxpayer's adjusted gross income.

Job expenses and "miscellaneous itemized expenses" are a separate group of deductions, justified as expenses incurred in the production of income. Job expenses include job-related travel, union dues, job education, uniforms, and subscriptions to professional journals. Miscellaneous deductions include tax preparation fees and expenses incurred in the production or collection of taxable income such as safe deposit box rental, legal and accounting fees, and clerical help. All deductions reported in this group are subject to a 2 percent floor—the taxpayer can deduct only those expenses that exceed 2 percent of adjusted gross income.

Certain other miscellaneous deductions that may be itemized include moving expenses incurred in an earlier period, gambling losses that offset gambling winnings, federal estate tax on income in respect of a decedent (income received but which was also included in the valuation of a decedent's estate for estate tax purposes), and impairment-related work expenses of a disabled person (Commerce Clearing House 1996: 280). These deductions are not subject to any floor.

The data in table 1 summarize the use of itemized deductions for tax year 1993. This information shows that itemized deductions have a significant impact on federal individual income tax revenue. In fact, the tax expenditure estimate of the main itemized deductions for 1996 is well over $100 billion— almost 17 percent of expected federal individual income tax revenue for 1996.

## Additional readings

Advisory Commission on Intergovernmental Relations. *Significant Features of Fiscal Federalism*. Washington, D.C.: Advisory Commission on Intergovernmental Relations, 1994.

Commerce Clearing House. *1996 U.S. Master Tax Guide*. Chicago, 1996.

Goode, Richard. *Individual Income Taxation*. Washington, D.C.: The Brookings Institution, 1976.

Internal Revenue Service, Statistics of Income Division. *SOI Bulletin* (Spring 1995): 21–27.

Pechman, Joseph A. *Federal Tax Policy*. Washington, D.C.: The Brookings Institution, 1987.

Rosen, Harvey S. *Public Finance*. Chicago: Irwin, 1995.

*Cross references:* adjusted gross income; income tax, federal.

**TABLE 1**

**Summary of Itemized Deductions, 1993**

| | Number of Returns | Amount ($ millions) |
|---|---|---|
| Total Itemized Deductions after Limitation | 32,694,192 | $ 480,356 |
| Medical and Dental Expenses Deduction | 5,408,223 | 25,932 |
| Taxes Paid Deduction | 32,155,955 | 167,882 |
| Interest Paid Deduction | 27,359,989 | 194,976 |
| Contributions Deduction | 29,717,271 | 67,166 |
| Moving Expense Deduction | 804,919 | 3,897 |
| Net Miscellaneous Deductions after Limitation | 7,717,250 | 27,877 |
| Other Miscellaneous Deductions | 729,192 | 2,718 |
| Total Returns | 114,626,932 | |
| Total Adjusted Gross Income Reported | | $3,724,124 |

*Source:* Internal Revenue Service (1995).
*Notes:* Total deductions are after limitation.

# J

# Joint Committee on Taxation, U.S. Congress

**Albert Buckberg**
Chief Economist Emeritus
Joint Committee on Taxation

*A well-staffed committee of members made up of the two "fiscal committees" of the Congress (House Committee on Ways and Means and Senate Finance) charged, inter alia, with providing estimates of revenue provisions.*

## Introduction

The Joint Committee on Taxation (JCT) was established in the Revenue Act of 1926. The committee is composed of 10 members, five each from the House Committee on Ways and Means and the Senate Committee on Finance (the five being the chairman and the two senior members from the majority and minority of each committee). The chairmanship rotates annually between the chairmen of the House and Senate committees. The JCT was given two assignments: (1) oversight of the administration of the tax, including income tax refunds above a specified threshold, and (2) technical assistance to the Ways and Means and Finance Committees on tax legislation, which has become the JCT's predominant responsibility.

The chairman and vice chairman appoint the chief of staff. The chief of staff selects the nonpartisan committee staff, which consists of lawyers with experience in tax law, economists holding Ph.D. degrees or completing dissertations, certified public accountants, other accountants, technical assistants, secretaries, and clerks.

## Administrative oversight

Oversight of tax administration is carried out primarily by a small staff, with an office at the Internal Revenue Service (IRS), that reviews income tax refunds and carries out assignments of administrative investigations. The General Accounting Office also performs investigations of selected issues in tax administration at the request of the Joint Committee.

## Legislative assistance

The JCT performs identical roles for the two tax committees during the legislative process. Before public hearings on proposed tax legislation, the JCT staff cooperates with the tax committee's staffs in preparing for public hearings on major legislation. The JCT and congressional tax staffs and the Treasury and IRS tax staffs often meet jointly to explore administrative compliance problems with existing law, implications of proposals for improving compliance, and other tax matters of mutual concern to Congress and the executive branch. The JCT staff prepares documents for the committees that describe present law, analyze its effects on taxpayer activities and private and public administrative problems, describe legislative proposals for changes, and present estimates of the revenue effects of the proposals.

During committee markup sessions, the JCT chief of staff summarizes the materials prepared by the staff and responds to inquiries for clarification and greater detail. As the committees complete their legislative decisions, the JCT staff meets with the legislative counsel of the respective chambers and appropriate committee tax staffs to translate the decisions into statutory language. Members of the tax staffs of the Treasury Department and the IRS also participate in these sessions.

The JCT prepares committee reports on the bills reported by the committees to their respective chambers and statements for the bills' floor managers which describe present law, the reasons for making the changes, and how they will be applied in practice. Tables listing estimates of the effects of the changes on tax revenue are also prepared.

Differences in the provisions of the House and Senate bills are resolved in a conference of the tax committees. Before and during the conference, JCT documentation summarizes the two bills for the conferees and highlights the differences between them. At this time, the JCT chief of staff briefs each committee on the differing bills in detail.

The JCT chief of staff performs a crucial communication role between the two committees. This vital part of his job requires that he develop their confidence in him by having demonstrated to them his mastery of the complex interdependencies of the Internal Revenue Code, but also by having conveyed to them that they can rely on the authenticity of the information. He must relate accurately and coherently the nuances of the political, business, and economic issues considered in each committee when making its decisions. In this role as a trusted and reliable intermediary, the chief of staff smooths the path to a successful conference agreement because the conferees understand the dimensions of the legislative matrix within which both sets of conferees may feel free to negotiate.

After completion of the conference, the JCT prepares the report, which details present law, reasons for changes, the provisions agreed upon, and their expected effects and summarizes the reasons for rejecting other provisions. Revenue estimates are provided for each provision approved by the conference for as many years into the future as budget procedures require.

Throughout the legislative process, the JCT staff prepares revenue estimates that measure the magnitude of each provision's effects. These are the official estimates for congressional tax legislation. Because the net revenue effect of a bill must comply with the limits established in the currently prevailing budget resolution, specific proposed tax changes often need to be offset by changes with the opposite revenue effect. As a result, controversies have arisen among proponents and opponents of proposals. Recently, JCT estimates have been criticized for not adequately measuring revenue and economic growth that would result from major tax structural changes. The JCT convened a public forum on such dynamic forecasting in January 1997 in which results of research into this subject were presented. While sanguine about the potential of dynamic forecasting, the participants indicated that the promise of practical dynamic forecasting lies in the future.

## Additional readings

Bennett, Rob, and R. Eliot Rosen. "An Interview with Former JCT Chief of Staff Ronald Pearlman." *Tax Notes*, January 28, 1991, pp. 328–33.

Rosen, R. Eliot, and Lee A. Sheppard. "Estimating Process Still Evolving on Capital Gains." *Tax Notes*, February 4, 1991, pp. 443–48.

*Cross references:* Finance Committee, U.S. Senate; Office of Tax Policy; Ways and Means Committee.

# L

# Labor supply, taxes and

James P. Ziliak
University of Oregon

*Effects of income and other taxes on the
number of hours worked by taxpayers.*

Many taxes reduce workers' take-home pay. In some cases, the effects of taxation are obvious, as in the case of income and payroll taxes, where workers see the amount of taxes that are withheld from their paychecks. The effects of sales taxes are more subtle and indirect than income and payroll taxes, but broadly similar. Although a sales tax does not directly reduce a worker's pay, it generally raises the prices of goods that people buy, which lowers the purchasing power of labor income. Thus, whether income, payroll, or sales are taxed, an hour of work buys the worker less consumption than it would in the absence of taxation. This issue has been studied most intensively in the context of income taxation.

A question that has long occupied public finance economists is whether taxes reduce the amount that people are willing to work. Economic theory does not offer a definite answer. The reason is that reducing the after-tax wage is likely to pull a person in two different directions. On the one hand, a lower after-tax wage makes a person want to work fewer hours because it is more attractive to spend one's time in leisure pursuits, or in undertaking non-market labor activities (such as home production) that are not taxed. This tendency, known as the substitution effect, tends to reduce a person's work effort. On the other hand, a lower after-tax wage may cause a person to work more hours because each hour of work buys less in the way of goods than if income were not taxed. This tendency, known as the income effect, has the opposite effect. When the substitution effect is stronger than the income effect, taxing income will lower work effort; but when the substitution effect is as strong as the income effect, the net effect of taxing income may be to leave the amount of work effort unchanged.

## Efficiency cost of taxing labor income

Even when taxes do not change the total number of hours worked, they still drive a wedge between the wage the person earns before taxes and the wage received after taxes, which causes a distortion in the person's labor supply that is a potential excess burden, or efficiency cost of taxation. This point is illustrated by the following example. Consider the case of a worker who in the absence of taxation would work 1,000 hours at a before-tax wage of $10 per hour. Now assume that income is taxed at a rate of 20 percent so that the after-tax wage falls from $10 to $8. Suppose further that the substitution effect of the drop in the after-tax wage would, other things being equal, cause the individual to want to reduce hours from 1,000 to 800, but that the fact that the tax lowers the person's income counteracts this tendency so that work effort remains unchanged at 1,000 hours. Although work effort is the same, taxing the person in a way that drives a wedge between the before- and after-tax wage reduces the well-being the person could attain, compared with a tax that did not lower the wage. To see this, assume that the same revenue ($2,000) were raised from the individual by a tax, such as a "head tax" that did not change the person's after-tax wage. Presumably in this case, because the taxpayer could earn $10 per hour instead of $8 as in the case of the income tax, the taxpayer would not want to substitute leisure for work; and indeed, the taxpayer might choose to increase work effort above the original 1,000 hours. Thus, the incentive to substitute leisure for work that results from the tax wedge is masked by the income effect.

The size of this distortion depends on the size of the substitution effect. Thus, if an income tax is imposed on a person who has a "small" substitution effect that is counteracted by a "small" income effect, the tax leaves labor supply unchanged and also has a small efficiency cost. In contrast, a tax imposed on a person who has a "large" substitution effect that is counteracted by a "large" income effect can have a sizable efficiency cost, even though the taxpayer's observed labor supply does not change.

## Policy implications

Because income taxes account for nearly 80 percent of all federal revenues collected, their effects on labor supply figure prominently in debates about tax policy. Assumptions about how people are likely to respond to changes in tax rates were, for example, necessary in order to project the effects on tax revenue of reforms such as the Tax Reform Act of 1986 and the Omnibus Budget Reconciliation Act of 1993.

In the early 1980s, advocates of supply-side tax cuts argued that lower tax rates would expand the tax base by spurring greater work, which would off-set some or all of the effects on taxing income at a lower rate. Echoes of the supply-side debate in the 1990s were heard in an exchange between Martin Feldstein (1993) and the U.S. Treasury. In 1993, the Clinton administration proposed increasing marginal tax rates by more than one-third for the highest-income Americans. In estimating how much revenue the tax increase would produce, it was assumed that hours worked by American taxpayers would not change and that, hence, tax collections would rise by an amount directly proportional to the rate hike. Feldstein countered that the tax increase would lower work effort, both by encouraging primary workers to reduce their hours of work and, especially, by encouraging secondary workers in high-income households to leave the labor force altogether so that tax revenues would rise much less than predicted. Feldstein even constructed a scenario where the response would be so great that tax collections would fall after the tax increase.

The size of the work disincentive of taxes is also relevant to assessing the implications of introducing a single-rate (flat) income tax. For example, if a flat tax is adopted that lowers the marginal tax rate for the typical worker, but the typical worker's labor supply does not respond to the higher after-tax wage, then tax collections will fall. If, instead, a typical worker responds to the higher after-tax wage by supplying more hours to the labor force, then tax collections will not fall as much as the rate cut, and in extreme cases of a large response, revenues may even increase.

### Empirical evidence

Labor economists have spent considerable time and effort trying to determine how sensitive hours worked are to changes in the wage. These estimates are relevant for assessing the magnitude of any work disincentive created by income taxes. Studies of labor supply behavior undertaken in the 1970s, surveyed in Killingsworth (1983) and Pencavel (1986), indicated that labor supply, especially of male heads of households, was fairly unresponsive to changes in the after-tax wage. The basic finding was that persons were found to have a relatively "small" tendency to substitute leisure hours for work when the wage falls, which was offset by a similarly small tendency to work more hours in response to a lower after-tax income. These findings provided the basis for a rough consensus that changes in tax rates were likely to have little or no effect on labor supply. The fact that the estimated size of the substitution effect was small also suggested that any distortion in people's labor supply decisions caused by income taxes was likely to be small, so that cutting tax rates would do little to make people's labor supply decisions more efficient.

This consensus was challenged by a series of studies undertaken in the 1980s, surveyed in Hausman (1985), which found that labor supply was sensitive to changes in the wage rate. These results implied that progressive income taxes had a measurable, and negative, effect on labor supply.

These divergent results stemmed from the divergent methodologies used to estimate the effect of income taxation on labor supply. The earlier studies that found labor supply to be relatively unresponsive to income taxes generally treated the individual's observed marginal tax rate as a "given" and then used standard multivariate regression techniques to estimate the individual's labor supply function. Subsequent research, pioneered by Hausman (1981), attempted to account for the fact that under a progressive income tax, the individual's tax rate is not given, but is determined, in part, by how much labor the person decides to supply, which determines the person's income, income tax bracket, and hence observed marginal tax rate. What the individual faces as a "given" is thus not a single tax rate, but a range of after-tax wages that can be earned that vary with the amount of hours that the person chooses to work.

Taking this fact into account seemed to make a difference. Hausman found significantly larger substitution and income effects than the previous literature. This had two implications. First, Hausman's methodology implied that cutting taxes would lead to some increase in labor supply. Second, his estimates implied that tax rates resulted in a measurable distortion in labor supply decision, which meant that taxing income, especially at progressive rates, imposed an efficiency cost on taxpayers.

Hausman's work was challenged, however, by MaCurdy et al. (1990), who cast doubt on the statistical validity of Hausman's methodology. They argued that Hausman's statistical model rested on too many untenable assumptions. In particular, Hausman's method assumes that the individual worker has complete knowledge of all the marginal tax rates and deductions, and that the pretax wage and nonlabor income are givens and not affected by the amount of labor supplied. The gross wage or pretax wage is not likely to be unaffected by the number of hours worked because the gross wage is typically measured as the ratio of annual earnings over annual hours of work. Most important though, the method used by Hausman has the effect of requiring that a lower wage encourage a person to substitute leisure for work when income is held constant and to work more (fewer) hours when the wage rises (falls). This can have the statistical effect of forcing labor supply to be more responsive to tax changes than what actually happens in the data.

Although MaCurdy et al. recognized the shortcomings of the 1970s vintage literature on labor supply, their research reaches conclusions that are broadly similar to those obtained with improved statistical methods. Thus, if valid, the MaCurdy et al. critique of Hausman's findings calls into question the efficacy of many supply-side arguments in favor of income tax reduction, which have relied on Hausman's estimates.

More recent research on the work-disincentive effects of income taxes has extended the basic model of household labor supply in several ways. One is to do a better job of accounting for factors like people's tastes for and ability to work that are likely to affect how much labor they supply. Another is to recognize the possibility that changes in wages or tax rates can affect the timing of people's labor supply over their life cycle. Lastly, one should also account for the fact that most Western countries tax both wage and interest income, which implies that labor supply decisions made today are based not only on today's wage but also on expected values of the future wage and marginal tax rate (Blomquist 1985).

Ziliak and Kniesner (1998) incorporate these elements into a statistical model of labor supply. Although they use the modeling approach recommended by MaCurdy et al., they find a labor supply response that is larger than that found by MaCurdy et al. but smaller than that found by Hausman (1981). They find, however, that incorporating life-cycle considerations into the model results in an estimated efficiency cost of income taxes that is larger than that found by Hausman.

The general conclusion from much of the research on labor supply that has been done to date is that the labor supply of married men is relatively unresponsive to changes in the tax code. Research on the labor supply of women has produced findings that are more mixed. Several studies of married women have found that their labor supply is fairly sensitive to the wage and, hence, to the tax rate. This finding is of some policy importance to the extent that married women treat their income as being "stacked" on top of the income earned by their spouse and hence subject to high next-dollar marginal tax rates. Other studies, however, do not indicate that income taxation reduces the women's labor supply (Mroz 1987).

Although much of the evidence to date suggests that hours worked by households are not affected a great deal by taxation, this does not imply that the form in which labor compensation is received is similarly unaffected. For example, workers can choose to be paid in the form of cash wages that are taxed or fringe benefits that are not, and there is evidence that the choice of how much labor income to receive in the form of fringe benefits is sensitive to changes in tax rates. In addition, workers can choose to work in activities where it is possible to evade paying some or all taxes. The decision to evade taxes may also depend on the level of tax rates.

## Additional readings

Bound, John, Charles Brown, Greg J. Duncan, and Willard L. Rodgers. "Evidence on the Validity of Cross-Sectional and Longitudinal Labor Market Data." *Journal of Labor Economics* 12 (1994): 345–68.

Blomquist, N. Soren. "Labor Supply in a Two-Period Model: The Effect of a Nonlinear Progressive Income Tax." *Review of Economic Studies* 70 (1985): 515–24.

Feldstein, Martin. "Tax Rates and Human Behavior." The *Wall Street Journal,* May 7, 1993.

Hausman, Jerry. "Labor Supply." In *How Taxes Affect Economic Behavior,* edited by Henry Aaron and Joseph Pechman, pp. 27–72. Washington, D.C.: The Brookings Institution, 1981.

Hausman, Jerry. "Taxes and Labor Supply." In *Handbook of Public Economics 1,* edited by Alan J. Auerbach and Martin Feldstein, pp. 213–63. Amsterdam: North Holland, 1985.

Killingsworth, Mark. *Labor Supply.* Cambridge, U.K.: Cambridge University Press, 1983.

MaCurdy, Thomas, David Green, and Harry Paarsch. "Assessing Empirical Approaches for Analyzing Taxes and Labor Supply." *Journal of Human Resources* 25 (1990): 415–89.

Mroz, Thomas A. "The Sensitivity of an Empirical Model of Married Women's Hours of Work to Economic and Statistical Assumptions." *Econometrica* 55 (1987): 765–99.

Pencavel, John. "Labor Supply of Men." In *Handbook of Labor Economics I,* edited by Orley Ashenfelter and Richard Layard, pp. 3–102. Amsterdam: North Holland, 1986.

Triest, Robert K. "The Effect of Income Taxation on Labor Supply in the United States." *Journal of Human Resources* 25 (1990): 491–516.

Ziliak, James P., and Thomas J. Kniesner. *The Effects of Recent Tax Reforms on Labor Supply.* American Enterprise Institute Studies on Tax Reform, 1998.

*Cross reference:* elasticity, demand and supply.

# Life cycle model

Diane Lim Rogers
U.S. Congressional Budget Office

*A theory of consumer behavior which asserts that a household or individual makes decisions about the timing of consumption and saving so as to maximize lifetime utility subject to a lifetime budget constraint.*

In the purest version of the life cycle model, capital markets are assumed to be "perfect," meaning that consumers can borrow or lend (save) against their own future income at a constant interest rate and to an unlimited extent. Assuming no transfers from parents to children or vice versa, a simplest, two-period version of the pure life cycle model would state that the consumer will choose how much to consume and how much to save in the first period, in a way that maximizes some function of present and future consumption (the "lifetime utility function"). The consumer's budget constraint is that the present value of the stream of consumption must equal (or be less than) the present value of the stream of labor income. Because that stream of income spans the consumer's lifetime, it is often referred to as "lifetime income." Note that no period-by-period budget constraint exists; that is, current-period consumption is not constrained to be equal to or less than current-period income.

An important implication of the pure version of the life cycle model is that consumption in any given period will be dependent only on the consumer's preferences (i.e., the form of the utility function), the rate of interest, and *lifetime* income, but will be independent of current income (controlling for lifetime income). Assuming diminishing marginal utility of consumption, a consumer will maximize utility by "smoothing" consumption between the two periods, no matter how dissimilar present and future incomes are. Thus, if labor income is high during working years but low or zero in retirement, the life cycle model would predict positive amounts saved during the working years (where consumption plus saving would equal labor income) and a drawing down of savings in retirement (where consumption would equal any labor income plus interest-augmented savings from the previous period). The amount of present relative to future consumption will be higher the higher the consumer's rate of time preference (i.e., the more impatient the consumer is) and/or the lower the rate of interest, because the "price" of present consumption relative to future consumption is one plus the rate of interest.

The life cycle model has important implications for the effects of taxation, from both efficiency and distributional standpoints. First, because the model acknowledges that the timing of consumption over the life cycle is subject to consumer choice, it reveals the potential inefficiency caused by taxes that affect the net rate of return on savings. An interest income tax, for example, reduces the net rate of interest and thus the relative price of present to future consumption. Present consumption is thus encouraged by this substitution effect, and (assuming that a no-tax allocation is efficient) this results in a less-than-efficient level of saving in the economy. This inefficiency results even where the total effect of an interest income tax on saving is zero. The income effect of an interest income tax on savers is to save more because real income has fallen, but the sub-stitution effect is to save less, and it is the substitution effect that creates excess burden. The allocative inefficiency caused by interest income taxes will be larger the greater the size of the interest income tax and/or the greater the intertemporal elasticity of substitution (how sensitive consumers are to changes in the interest rate). Empirical evidence on the intertemporal elasticity is quite mixed, although more recent work seems to suggest that the intertemporal elasticity is quite low (Hall 1988).

With respect to distributional concerns, the life cycle model suggests: (1) the desirability of using lifetime (versus annual) incomes as a measure of *current* ability to pay, (2) the superiority of consumption-based (over income-based) taxes, and (3) the lifetime present-value equivalence of consumption and wage-income taxes.

If the pure version of the life cycle model holds, then current consumption should be proportional to lifetime income. Therefore, if current ability to pay taxes is reflected by current consumption, then lifetime income is a better measure of current ability to pay than is annual income. Categorizing households based on annual incomes can give misleading pictures of the incidence of taxes, because households with the same annual income can in reality have very different consumption possibilities and thus very different current abilities to pay taxes. If the life cycle model holds to a more limited extent, however, then current consumption will depend somewhat on both current and lifetime income, and lifetime income will be a less accurate reflection of current ability to pay taxes. [Under such circumstances, lifetime income could still be interpreted as a measure of *lifetime* ability to pay taxes (Fullerton and Rogers 1993).] Recent empirical research suggests that liquidity constraints *do* exist and that they are binding for many households (Zeldes 1989), so that the life cycle model's assumption of unlimited abilities to borrow and lend against future income seems rather unrealistic.

Whether or not liquidity constraints exist, however, the general life cycle theory of consumer behavior implies that consumer well-being ultimately depends on consumption streams, not income streams. It thus suggests that consumption-based taxes are more equitable than income-based taxes. In addition, from a lifetime perspective, interest income taxes appear unfair, because under such taxes lifetime tax liabilities depend on the *timing* of consumption and not just lifetime consumption possibilities. A general consumption tax or a wage-income tax, on the other hand, would impose equal lifetime taxes on two individuals with the same lifetime incomes, independent of how they chose to allocate their consumption over time.

Finally, the lifetime budget constraint in the pure life cycle model suggests that taxes on wage income are equivalent, in lifetime present-value terms, to taxes on consumption. The timing of the two taxes differs, however, because consumption tax burdens will be smoother over the life cycle, while wage-income taxes will be greater when young and smaller following retirement. The pure life cycle model would imply that because capital markets are perfect, the timing of taxes should not affect a consumer's well-being; thus, consumption taxes and wage-income taxes are equivalent for any individual alive when these taxes are fully phased in. During a transition to a new tax, however, the two types of taxes *can* have redistributive effects across generations. For example, switching from a general income tax to a consumption tax will more heavily burden older generations (who have already paid income taxes on their labor income when the switch takes place), compared with a switch to a wage-income tax (Auerbach and Kotlikoff 1987). The present-value equivalence of consumption and wage-income taxes also breaks down in the presence of intergenerational transfers, because with such transfers the present value of consumption need not equal the present value of labor income.

## Additional readings

Auerbach, Alan J., and Laurence J. Kotlikoff. *Dynamic Fiscal Policy*. Cambridge, U.K.: Cambridge University Press, 1987.

Fullerton, Don, and Diane Lim Rogers. *Who Bears the Lifetime Tax Burden?* Washington, D.C.: The Brookings Institution, 1993.

Hall, Robert E. "Intertemporal Substitution in Consumption." *Journal of Political Economy* 96 (April 1988): 339–57.

Zeldes, Stephen P. "Consumption and Liquidity Constraints: An Empirical Investigation." *Journal of Political Economy* 97 (April 1989): 305–46.

*Cross references:* ability to pay; consumption taxation; excess burden; fairness in taxation; generational accounting; incidence of taxes; income tax, federal; saving, taxes and.

# Low-income housing credit

Leonard E. Burman
The Urban Institute

*Designed to encourage the acquisition, construction, and/or rehabilitation of housing for low-income families, this federal tax credit, which is criticized for its inefficiency and complexity, is one of the few mechanisms for low-income housing support.*

This credit, enacted as part of the Tax Reform Act of 1986 and made permanent in 1993, replaced a variety of incentives for investment in low-income housing with a tax subsidy aimed more directly at lower-income households.

## Overview

Under Section 42 of the Internal Revenue Code, qualifying individuals and corporations can claim a tax credit over a 10-year period equal to a percentage of the depreciable costs incurred to provide low-income housing. For new construction and costs of renovation on qualified housing that does not receive additional federal subsidies, the credits may have a present value of up to 70 percent of the depreciable basis in low-income units. A reduced credit with a present value of up to 30 percent is available for housing with other federal subsidies and for the cost of purchasing existing housing that is renovated. The corresponding maximum annual credit percentages were 8.7 percent and 3.7 percent, respectively, in June 1995.

To qualify for the credit, either 20 percent of the units in a housing project must be rented to tenants with incomes below 50 percent of the area's median income, adjusted for family size, or 40 percent of the units must be rented to tenants with incomes below 60 percent of the median income. The rent on a low-income unit is limited to 30 percent of the qualifying income level, assuming a family size equal to 1.5 times the number of bedrooms in the unit.

Past tax credits are recaptured with interest if the project fails to comply with the rent limits and set-aside requirements during the first 15 years. The percentage of credits recaptured phases out in the 11th through 15th years. In addition, project owners must agree to provide low-income units for at least 30 years, although owners may terminate this commitment after 15 years under certain conditions.

State housing authorities authorize credits for housing projects. Credit allocations for each project are supposed to be limited so that investors and project organizers do not reap excessive profits. Each state may allocate up to $1.25 per capita for projects that are not financed with tax-exempt bonds. Total credits allocated for bond-financed projects are limited only by states' authority to issue tax-exempt bonds (for a more detailed description, see Johnson and Schober 1994).

The Joint Committee on Taxation estimates that the tax expenditure on low-income housing credits will total $15 billion from 1995 to 1999. About two-thirds of the credits are claimed by individuals and one-third by corporations. The annual amounts are expected to increase from $2.2 billion in 1995 to $3.7 billion in 1999, because more and more projects qualify for the credits over time. Credits paid in 1999 will go to projects placed in service not just in 1999 but also during the preceding 10 years. Once the credit is fully phased in—around the turn of the century—the tax expenditure should increase at about the rate of growth of the population.

## Analysis

The question "Is the low-income housing credit an efficient way to help poor people meet their housing needs?" can be dissected into two parts. First, how efficient are government subsidies to the supply of housing, compared with demand-based subsidies? Second, if supply subsidies are called for, how efficient is the low-income housing credit, compared with other subsidy mechanisms? The debate on both of these questions has been lively and remains unresolved.

### Efficacy of housing supply programs

If the supply of low-income housing is very elastic in the long run, then production of limited amounts of subsidized housing will simply replace other housing that would otherwise have been provided. Housing supplied or subsidized by the government might increase the average quality of housing available to low-income tenants, but it would have little lasting effect on the quantity or price of housing available to poor people. (See Weicher and Thibodeau 1988 for a discussion of the effects of subsidized housing on the housing market as a whole.) Moreover, because new and substantially rehabilitated housing is expensive to produce, it is likely to be worth far less to tenants than an equal cash supplement, such as housing vouchers. (For a more complete comparison of housing vouchers with low-income housing credits, see Congressional Budget Office 1992.)

Advocates of supply subsidies argue that, in certain housing markets, the supply of housing is inelastic, even in the long run. Apgar (1990) argues that shortages of decent low-rent housing have been getting worse over time. As a result, housing produced or subsidized by the government will permanently increase the stock of housing available. Moreover, because supply is inelastic, supply-based programs can be more efficient than demand subsidies because they generate pecuniary externalities. The augmented supply lowers the price of housing, generating benefits not only for the tenants in the new housing but for others in the market as well (Coate et al. 1994). In contrast, a program like housing vouchers, which expands the demand for housing without affecting the supply, raises the price, harming low-income tenants who do not have vouchers.

Supply is likely to be elastic in markets with high vacancy rates even in the short term, and vacancy rates are relatively high by historical standards. The vacancy rate for rental housing was 7.4 percent in 1994, according to the Commerce Department. By comparison, it was 5.9 percent in 1984 and 5.3 percent in 1970. Since the late 1980s, vacancy rates have been higher than at any time since the 1960s. In the 61 largest metropolitan areas, the average vacancy rate was 7.5 percent in 1993. Only four cities had vacancy rates below 4 percent.

Although vacancy rates are lowest for very low-rent housing (which is the housing most likely to be demolished or abandoned if unoccupied), they are highest at the rent levels qualifying for low-income housing credits. Median family income in 1993 was about $37,000. Based on 60 percent of that income level, monthly rents in credit-eligible housing would average about $550. In 1993, 8.2 percent of housing renting for $500 to $599, and 8.6 percent of housing renting for $450 to $499, was vacant. Overall, two-thirds of the vacant units rented for less than $500. These vacant units—especially the inadequate ones—are likely to leave the stock if better-quality housing is supplied (Weicher 1990).

In the long run, the supply of unsubsidized housing is likely to be very elastic because housing investments have to earn rates of return competitive with other capital. Thus, even in tight markets, subsidized housing starts are likely to displace unsubsidized housing over the long run. However, adjustment to this long-run equilibrium may be slow. Thus, targeted supply subsidies might speed adjustment to equilibrium. For this reason, some analysts advocate supply subsidies as a complement to demand subsidies in tight housing markets (Struyk 1990).

Supply subsidies might also enhance efficiency if they mitigate market failures. The market for low-income housing might fail for several reasons. Lenders might be unwilling to lend to investors in neighborhoods where many poor people live because of class or racial biases (a form of discrimination often referred to as "redlining"). To the extent that discrimination in lending occurs, a capital subsidy might improve the allocation of capital.

In addition, when an area falls into decline, decayed housing creates a negative externality that discourages investment in housing on a small scale. A significant part of property value arises from the characteristics of the neighborhood (indeed, externalities are sometimes referred to as "neighborhood effects" in the economics literature). Thus, if all or most of the housing in a neighborhood were improved, it would be worth more per unit than would one or two improved buildings. As a result, government investment, directly or indirectly, might generate social benefits by improving a neighborhood.

Indirect evidence of such market failures might be the poor quality of housing available for rent to poor families. Harvard University's Joint Center for Housing Studies reports that 22 percent of very poor households (incomes below 25 percent of area median income) lived in structurally inadequate housing in 1991. In rural areas, 31 percent of such households lived in substandard housing. The percentage of households in inadequate housing declines with income, and the income limits for the low-income housing credit are relatively high. Nearly 90 percent of households with incomes between 50 and 80 percent of the median lived in decent housing. In this income range, housing problems were not particular to any region, and cities and rural areas had only slightly more inadequate housing than suburbs. Thus, poor-quality housing is not pervasive. It derives from the inability of a poor household to pay for decent housing. In most housing markets, the primary problem seems not to be market failure, but affordability.

### Advantages and disadvantages of the low-income housing credit

Suppose that policymakers decide that the government should build or subsidize the creation of affordable housing. How does the low-income housing credit compare with other available mechanisms for increasing supply? The credit has obvious political advantages. First, the private sector builds the housing, rather than state or federal governments. Second, the program devolves almost total control over allocation of the credits to state housing agencies, a sterling example of how fiscal federalism (see Fiscal federalism) can be implemented through the tax code. Third, new spending done through the tax code (see Tax expenditures) is viewed as a tax cut, rather than increased government spending.

These advantages come at a high price. The equity capital raised for investment generally comes from syndicates of individual investors or from corporations. Syndicating limited partnerships is technically complex—and expensive. The General Accounting Office has estimated that these costs consume 27 percent of equity invested in low-income housing credit projects. Moreover, because the credit is very complex and risky to investors, who might become ineligible for credits and have to repay past credits with interest if their project fails to comply with the restrictions of the law, investors require high after-tax rates of return. Stegman (1991), using an estimated internal rate of return of 15 percent, estimates that housing produced by syndicates of individuals costs the government nearly twice what a direct capital grant to the project sponsor would cost.

Corporate investors do not have to form syndicates to raise capital, but their lower overhead costs may translate into higher profits rather than smaller subsidies. Lampert (1993), who calls the low-income housing credit "perhaps the last true tax shelter remaining—especially for the widely held corporation," claims that "lofty internal rates of return,

ranging from 15 percent to 25 percent, are possible in today's market."

The costs of the low-income housing credit include the costs of administration by federal and state housing agencies and by the Internal Revenue Service (IRS). Adequate monitoring by state housing agencies and the IRS would be expensive, but, without such monitoring, credits might be allocated to fraudulent claimants, to those who do not comply with the income or rent restrictions of the law, or to investors who earn above-normal rates of return. Public information on the administrative effort of state housing agencies does not exist, but Guttman (1995) reports that the IRS has no internal tracking mechanism to ensure that those who claim the low-income housing credit are eligible for it. As a result, the IRS estimates that $6 billion or more in credits might have been improperly claimed since the tax credit was enacted in 1986. Both the costs of noncompliance and the costs of administration must be added to the total cost of the tax credit approach.

## Additional readings

Apgar, William C., Jr. "Which Housing Policy Is Best." *Housing Policy Debate* 1 (1990): 1–32.

Coate, Stephen, Stephen Johnson, and Richard Zeckhauser. "Pecuniary Redistribution through In-Kind Programs." *Journal of Public Economics* 55 (September 1994): 19–40.

Congressional Budget Office. "The Cost-Effectiveness of the Low-Income Housing Tax Credit Compared with Housing Vouchers." *CBO Staff Memorandum* (April 1992).

Guttman, George. "Despite Assurances to Congress, IRS Slow to Track LIHC Compliance." *Tax Notes* 67 (June 26, 1995): 1715–17.

Johnson, Linda M., and Kathleen F. Schober. "A Practical Guide to the Low-Income Housing Credit." *Taxes* 72 (June 1994): 331–38.

Lampert, Peter M. "Corporate Investment in the Low-Income Housing Credit." *The Journal of Taxation* 79 (December 1993): 344–50.

Stegman, Michael A. "The Excessive Costs of Creative Finance: Growing Inefficiencies in the Production of Low-Income Housing." *Housing Policy Debate* 2 (1991): 357–73.

Struyk, Raymond J. "Comment on William Apgar's 'Which Housing Policy Is Best.'" *Housing Policy Debate* 1 (1990): 41–51.

Weicher, John C. "Comment on William Apgar's 'Which Housing Policy Is Best.'" *Housing Policy Debate* 1 (1990): 33–39.

Weicher, John C., and Thomas G. Thibodeau. "Filtering and Housing Markets: An Empirical Analysis." *Journal of Urban Economics* 23 (January 1988): 21–40.

*Cross reference:* tax-exempt bonds.

# Lump-sum tax

Joseph J. Cordes
George Washington University

*A tax that does not cause those affected by it to change their behavior in response to it.*

In the process of extracting resources from the private sector, taxes generally affect prices faced by consumers and/or producers of the taxed activities. Thus, an income tax causes workers to receive after-tax wages below what their labor is actually worth to their employers, and savers to receive after-tax returns below the before-tax return earned on their savings. Similarly, an excise tax causes buyers to pay a higher price for the taxed good than it costs sellers to produce it. The response of buyers and sellers to these effects of taxation imposes an economic cost, in the form of reduced productivity or consumer well-being, that is referred to as the excess burden of taxation.

A lump-sum tax is levied in such a way that it does not create economic incentives for either buyers or sellers to change their behavior. The classic example of a lump-sum tax is a so-called head tax, in which every taxpayer would simply be assessed some fixed amount of tax, which would not depend in any way on the taxpayer's economic circumstances, as, for example, measured by income or wealth, or on any other characteristics that the taxpayer could change. Because the amount of the tax could not be changed by anything that the taxpayer did, a taxpayer's economic choices would not be affected by the tax, and there would be no excess burden resulting from collecting such a tax.

The role of lump-sum taxes in tax policy is more conceptual than it is practical. Tax economists find it extremely useful to conduct the "thought experiment" of comparing the economic effects of actual taxes, such as income and excise taxes, that raise a given amount of revenue with some hypothetical lump-sum tax that would raise the same amount of money. This allows the analyst to focus on the effects of different ways of raising a given amount of revenue from the private sector.

In practice, it is difficult, if not impossible, to levy lump-sum taxes. One reason is that the distribution of tax burdens that would result under many lump-sum taxes would be widely perceived as unfair. For example, under a head tax, everyone would pay the same amount of tax, without regard to either income or the benefits received from public spending. Such a distribution of the tax burden would be seen as unfair under either the ability-to-pay or benefit principles of taxation. Similarly, it has sometimes been observed that taxes on goods that are "necessities" could be equivalent to lump-sum taxes because consumers need to buy a fixed amount of such goods, without regard to the market price. But taxing necessities is generally seen as unfair because taxpayers will pay a declining share of their income in taxes on necessities as their income rises.

Taxes levied on so-called economic rents may be lump-sum, at least in the short run, and be less likely to be criticized on ability-to-pay grounds. For example, suppose that a profit-maximizing business that holds an exclusive patent on a new technology is able to earn a return of 20 percent when the competitive return to capital is 10 percent in other lines of business. A tax on the excess return of 10 percent would be lump-sum because the owner of the business would have no reason to change behavior. If, for example, the excess profits were taxed at a rate of 50 percent, the best the owner could do would be to earn the maximum total profit of 20 percent, and pay the excess profits tax of 5 percent, leaving an after-tax excess return of 5 percent.

Taxes that are based on past economic behavior would also be examples of lump-sum taxes, provided that the imposition of these taxes was not anticipated by the taxpayer. If the tax is based on decisions made by the taxpayer in the past, there is nothing the taxpayer can do to avoid paying tax in the present. And if the tax was unanticipated at the time the past decision was made, it cannot be said to have affected that decision either.

Yet, even the above examples may not be pure lump-sum taxes to the extent that they affect some margins of choice made by buyers and sellers. Taxing "necessities" at a high enough rate may eventually create economic incentives for buyers and sellers to find substitutes for the taxed goods. Taxes on economic rents will have behavioral effects when the rents represent a reward for risk-taking or entrepreneurship. In such cases, taxing excess profits would change behavior over time, by discouraging risk-taking or reducing the supply of entrepreneurs. Similarly, imposing a tax based on past behavior can change current behavior if taxpayers form expectations about future taxes.

*Cross references:* ability to pay; excess burden; head tax.

# Luxury taxes

Bruce Davie
Department of the Treasury

*Excise taxes on goods or services predominantly consumed by persons with high incomes or wealth.*

Luxury taxes are, for several reasons, as old as taxation itself. By taxing items uniquely or predominantly consumed by the rich, a government attempts to secure revenue from those with an ability to pay while minimizing the number of transactions subject to tax and the number of persons responsible for remitting taxes. Historically, luxuries have often been identified with foreign goods that could easily be taxed upon importation. In modern economies, luxury taxes are insignificant because income taxation and, to a much lesser extent, taxes on estates and wealth are used to satisfy distributional objectives, and broad-based taxes are used to generate most of government revenue. Economists can easily demonstrate the distortional effects of specific excise taxes that lead to deadweight losses of consumer welfare. Luxury taxes also create horizontal inequities among taxpayers in the same income (or consumption) class when taxpayers have different tastes.

Luxury excise taxes are usually imposed on an ad valorem basis at the retail level. In many cases the determination of whether an item meets the definition of a taxable luxury can only be made at the point of sale to a final consumer. Moreover, taxing at the retail level is likely to avoid imposing the tax on an intermediate good—for example, diamonds used as an abrasive in industrial processes. But taxation at retail makes evasion more likely and is more expensive to administer than taxation at the manufacturer level.

In the United States, the federal government has a long, albeit intermittent, history of imposing luxury excise taxes. The first revenue measure enacted under the Constitution, on July 4, 1789, included high-rate tariffs on snuff and carriages, specifically because these items were identified with a luxurious lifestyle. Calling distilled spirits a luxury was one of the arguments made for imposing the first domestic excise tax, in 1791. The tariff on snuff and carriages was supplemented in 1794 with a tax on domestically manufactured snuff (at 8 cents per pound while the tariff rate was 10 cents per pound) and an annual tax on carriages ranging from $2 to $15. The tax on domestic snuff production was soon repealed because administrative costs were high relative to revenues. The annual carriage tax was re-pealed in 1802, along with all other domestic excises (except a tax on salt repealed in 1807), including the tax on distilled spirits. Excise taxes on liquor and carriages were reenacted in 1812, as a wartime measure, along with use taxes on household furniture and watches. All of these domestic excises were repealed in 1817. No luxury taxes, or indeed any other domestic excise taxes, were imposed again until the Civil War.

In addition to incomes, the Civil War Congress taxed legacies and successions; the gross receipts of certain industries; banks; a long list of specified trades, professions, and businesses; alcohol and tobacco products; manufactured goods generally; and certain classes of sales. Stamp taxes were imposed on a wide variety of financial instruments and legal documents. A very minor part of these taxes was specifically directed against luxury consumption. At one time or another during the war, taxes were imposed on the ownership of carriages; yachts; billiard tables; gold and silver plate (with an exemption for silver plate owned by religious societies); pianos, organs, and other musical instruments; and watches. Revenue commissioners routinely recommended their repeal. As one commissioner put it, the amounts collected had paid "but indifferently for the expense of collection." Congress was unwilling to repeal these taxes while the war continued because, as one Ways and Means Committee report put it, "the owners of carriages valued at over $300, and gold watches and silver plate, were among those persons best able to contribute something to the support of the Government under whose protection they have been able to acquire articles indicative of wealth and assured means of support."

Along with explicit luxury taxes, during the Civil War taxes were seemingly aimed at amusements and frivolity. Among the businesses subject to a gross receipts tax (at a 2 percent rate) were operas, theaters, circuses, and museums. Sales of perfume and cosmetics were taxed at a 4 percent rate, photographs and playing cards at 5 percent. Billiard rooms were subject to an annual license tax of $10 per table and bowling alleys of $10 per alley. Circuses, theaters, and museums were required to paid a license tax of $100 in addition to the receipts tax. The license tax for jugglers was $20. Between 1863 and 1871, $16,872.20 was actually collected from jugglers.

By 1871, most Civil War excise taxes had been repealed. Taxes on liquor and tobacco were retained, however, and have been continuously imposed ever since. The tax on perfume and cosmetics was repealed in 1883.

Financing the Spanish American War involved increasing tobacco and fermented liquor (beer) taxes (but not taxes on distilled spirits) and bringing back some luxury taxes. In 1898, special taxes were imposed on proprietors of theaters, bowling alleys, billiard and pool rooms, and other places of amusement. Taxes, administered through the use of stamps, were also imposed on cosmetics and chewing gum. By 1902, all the wartime luxury taxes had been repealed. Alcohol and tobacco taxes, however, remained a major source of revenue.

World War I brought luxury taxes back. Bowling alleys and pool halls were again taxed annually at $10 per alley or table, and a general tax was imposed on admissions. Manufacturers' excise taxes were imposed on automobiles and major home appliances, soft drinks and candy, cameras and film, sporting goods, musical instruments, records, and long-distance telephone messages. An annual use tax was imposed on boats, graduated by size. Retail taxes were imposed on jewelry, furs, cosmetics, and luggage. Wearing apparel was taxed to the extent that its price exceeded relatively high thresholds. These taxes appear to have generated about 5 percent of the government's total revenue by the end of the war. Practically all of the wartime taxes were repealed during the 1920s. At the end of the decade, the only remnant was a tax on theater admissions of more than $3.

As part of the attempt by the Revenue Act of 1932 to bring the federal budget back into balance, manufacturers' excise taxes were reimposed on automobiles, certain consumer durables, jewelry, furs, luggage, cosmetics, and sporting goods. An annual use tax ranging from $10 to $200 was imposed on pleasure boats. The base of the admissions tax was broadened by reducing the threshold level to 40 cents. Some of these taxes were repealed later in the decade.

During World War II, excise tax rates on automobiles and consumer durables were generally increased and additional items subjected to tax. Retail excise taxes were imposed on furs, jewelry, cosmetics, and luggage at a 20 percent rate. The tax rate on admissions was doubled, to 20 percent. Bowling alleys and pool tables were again subject to annual use taxes. The tax on long-distance telephone calls was extended to local telephone service. A few tax rates were reduced after the war, and Congress was considering repeal of all the World War II luxury taxes when the Korean War broke out. Instead, the luxury taxes were retained and the manufacturers' excise tax on automobiles increased from 7 to 10 percent. The World War II/Korean War luxury taxes were not generally repealed until 1965. The manufacturers' tax on automobiles was retained (at a 7 percent rate) until 1971. The tax on telephone services was still in effect (at a 3 percent rate) in 1997, even though its rationale as a wartime luxury tax had disappeared.

Excise taxes explicitly designated as luxury taxes reappeared in the United States with the Omnibus Budget Reconciliation Act of 1990. They were designed to help achieve a specified distribution, by income class, of a whole package of tax increases. Retail excise taxes were imposed at a 10 percent rate on sales of jewelry and furs (to the extent the price exceeded $10,000), automobiles (to the extent the price exceeded $30,000), airplanes (to the extent the price exceeded $250,000), and boats (to the extent the price exceeded $100,000). Complex rules were provided to exempt items used in a trade or business, to deal with leases, to tax additions or modifications made within the first six months of initial purchase, and to exempt used items. For example, limousines used in a limousine service were not taxed, but limousines used by a corporate executive were. In fiscal year 1992, these luxury taxes raised about $300 million, of which 90 percent came from the tax on automobiles.

The luxury taxes enacted in 1990 were widely unpopular, particularly the tax on boats. Boat makers complained that the tax was responsible for the demise of their industry and the unemployment of their workers. With the exception of the tax on automobiles, these taxes were repealed on August 10, 1993. The repeal was retroactive to January 1 of that year, creating the further complication of providing a refund mechanism. The tax on automobiles was modified in 1996 so as to be phased out by 2003.

American states use sales taxes as a major source of revenue but generally have not attempted to impose higher-than-normal rates on luxury goods. The ease with which transactions in luxury goods could move out of state undoubtedly provides the reason. The relatively few instances in which higher-than-normal rates are applied—for example, high rates on hotel and motel room rentals—are almost always explained as attempts to export taxes to nonresidents.

Many countries impose value-added taxes (VATs) at more than one rate. This practice is typically defended on distributional grounds; "necessities" are taxed at a lower rate than "luxuries." With a two-rate system, this practice is more accurately described as taxing a specifically identified list of items at a preferentially low rate and taxing everything else at a higher, regular rate. That is, the "necessities" are specifically defined rather than the "luxuries." Some countries do impose higher-than-normal VAT rates on specifically enumerated luxuries. Other than applying high VAT rates to automobiles, these higher-than-normal rates generally apply to a small portion of total consumption, generate little additional revenue, have little effect on the distribution of aggregate tax burdens, and are difficult to administer. VAT experts view the use of specific excises as a better technique for subjecting luxury goods to high tax rates for sumptuary or distributional purposes.

## Additional readings

Brownlee, W. Elliot. *Federal Taxation in America: A Short History.* New York: Cambridge University Press, 1996.

Davie, Bruce F. "Excise Taxes, Fiscal Year 1992." *Statistics of Income Bulletin* 13 (2) (1993): 36–52.

Dewey, Davis Rich. *Financial History of the United States.* New York: Longmans, Green and Co., 1939.

Due, John F., and John Mikesell, editors. *Sales Taxation: State and Local Structure and Administration.* Washington, D.C.: The Urban Institute Press, 1994.

Pechman, Joseph A. *Federal Tax Policy.* 5th ed. Washington: The Brookings Institution, 1987.

Smith, Harry Edwin. *The United States Federal Internal Tax History from 1861 to 1871.* Boston: Houghton Mifflin, 1914.

Tait, Alan A. *Value Added Tax: International Practice and Problems.* Washington: International Monetary Fund, 1988.

Talley, Louis Alan, Jack Taylor, and Dennis Zimmerman. *History and Economics of U.S. Excise Taxation of Luxury Goods.* Washington, D.C.: The Library of Congress, Congressional Research Service, 91-306 E, April 2, 1991.

The Tax Foundation. *Federal Excise Taxes.* Project Note No. 40. New York, 1956.

U.S. Congress, House, Committee on Ways and Means. *Excise Tax Compendium.* 88th Cong., 2d sess., 1964.

Zimmerman, Dennis. *The Effect of the Luxury Excise Tax on the Sale of Luxury Boats.* The Library of Congress, Congressional Research Service, 92-149 A, February 10, 1992.

*Cross references:* ability to pay; excess burden; excise taxes; fairness in taxation; horizontal equity; vertical equity.

# M

# Marginal effective tax rate

Don Fullerton
University of Texas

*Designed to measure incentives for investment, a calculation that takes into account effects of measurement and timing of income in determining the impact of a tax applied to an additional dollar of capital income.*

The marginal effective tax rate on capital income is the expected pretax rate of return minus the expected after-tax rate of return on a new marginal investment, divided by the pretax rate of return. It typically accounts for an investment tax credit, a statutory tax rate, accelerated depreciation allowances, and historical cost depreciation that falls in real value with inflation. It may include just corporate income taxes, or it may also include personal taxes and local property taxes. It may account for nominal interest deductions, inventory accounting, the alternative minimum tax, and other detailed provisions of the tax law. Several studies have estimated effective marginal tax rates for different assets under different laws (see Jorgenson and Yun 1991 for a time series in the United States and Jorgenson and Landau 1993 for nine different countries).

The marginal effective tax rate is a forward-looking measure that summarizes the incentives to invest in a particular asset as provided by complicated tax laws. It may bear little relation to an industry's "average effective tax rate," defined as the actual tax paid in a particular year divided by the actual capital income in that year, because that measure averages over taxes on income from all past investment (minus credits on that year's new investment).

Any particular estimate of a marginal effective tax rate will depend on particular assumptions about equilibrium in capital markets, the rate of discount, the rate of inflation, expectations of investors, churning, financing, the treatment of risk, and even the choice between the "old view" (where dividend taxes matter) and the "new view" (where they do not). For the simplest example, consider a perfectly competitive firm contemplating a new investment with outlay $q$ that has return $c$ in a world with no uncertainty. Assume that the firm has sufficient tax liability to take associated credits and deduc-

tions and that it does not resell the asset. An investment tax credit at rate $k$ reduces the asset's net cost to $(1-k)q$. The return $c$ grows with inflation at constant rate $\pi$, but the asset depreciates at exponential rate $\delta$. The corporate income tax is levied at statutory rate $u$, and local property tax at rate $w$ is deductible against it. Net returns are discounted at the firm's nominal after-tax discount rate $r$, and the present value of depreciation allowances per dollar of investment is $z$. The particular value for $z$ will reflect the discount rate, the tax lifetime for the asset, the depreciation schedule, and whether allowances are based on historical or replacement cost. In equilibrium, the net outlay must be exactly matched by the present value of new returns:

$$(1-k)q = \int_0^\infty (1-u) \cdot$$
$$(c-wq)e^{(\pi-\delta)t}e^{-rt}dt + uzq \quad (1)$$

This condition can be used to solve for the Hall and Jorgenson (1967) "cost of capital" formula providing $\rho^c$, the real social rate of return in the corporate sector, gross of tax but net of depreciation:

$$\rho^c \equiv \frac{c}{q} - \delta$$
$$= \frac{r-\pi+\delta}{(1-u)}(1-k-uz) + w - \delta \quad (2)$$

In calculations below, common values are used for $r$, $\pi$, and $u$, but each asset has a specific value for $\delta$, $k$, $z$, and $w$. (If $u$ and the corporate discount rate are replaced by the noncorporate entrepreneur's personal marginal tax rate and corresponding discount rate, then equation (2) gives an analogous expression for $\rho^{nc}$, the social rate of return in the noncorporate sector.)

The "marginal effective corporate tax rate" $t$ can be found by setting the property tax $w$ to zero and then taking the gross-of-tax return $(\rho^c)$ minus the net-of-tax return $(r-\pi)$, all divided by the gross-of-tax return. Simple algebra can then be used to demonstrate several important conceptual results. First, this effective rate $t$ is equal to the statutory rate $u$ if the investment tax credit is zero and depreciation allowances are based on replacement cost [because $z$ is then $\delta/(\delta+r-\pi)$]. Second, this effective rate still equals the statutory rate if the investor receives only an immediate deduction equal to the purchase price times the fraction $z = \delta/(\delta+r-\pi)$, the first-year recovery proposal of Auerbach and Jorgenson (1980). Third, the effective tax rate is equal to zero with expensing of new investment (because $z$ is then one). Thus uniform effective taxation of all assets can be achieved either with economic depreciation (all $t = u$) or expensing (all $t = 0$). Fourth, uniform effective tax rates can be achieved at any rate between zero and $u$, if all assets receive an investment tax credit that is proportional to $(1 - z)$. That is, replace $k$ in equation (1) with $k(1 - z)$, where $z$ is based on economic depreciation at replacement cost, and the resulting effective tax rate is $(u - k)$ on all assets.

To account for personal taxes and deductibility of interest, assume that the firm can arbitrage between debt and real capital, as in Bradford and Fullerton (1981). If $i$ is the nominal interest rate, then the corporation can save $i(1 - u)$ by retiring a unit of debt, so any marginal real investment must earn the same rate of return in equilibrium. All nominal net returns are then discounted at the rate $r = i(1 - u)$, whatever the source of finance.

A fraction $c_d$ of corporate investment is financed by debt, and the personal marginal rate of debt holders is $\tau_d$. The net return to debt holders is thus $i(1 - \tau_d)$. A fraction $c_{re}$ of corporate investment is financed by retained earnings, and the return after corporate taxes $i(1 - u)$ results in share appreciation that is taxed at the effective accrued personal capital gains rate $\tau_{re}$. The net return to the shareholder is then $i(1 - u)(1 - \tau_{re})$. The remaining fraction $c_{ns}$ of corporate investment is financed by new shares, subject to personal taxes at rate $\tau_{ns}$, so the net return is $i(1 - u)(1 - \tau_{ns})$. In combination, the real net return in the corporate sector is:

$$s^c = c_d[i(1 - \tau_d)] + c_{re}[i(1 - u)(1 - \tau_{re})]$$
$$+ c_{ns}[i(1 - u)(1 - \tau_{ns})] - \pi \quad (3)$$

The "marginal effective total tax rate" in the corporate sector, including all corporate, personal, and property taxes, is $t = (\rho^c - s^c)/\rho^c$, the tax wedge as a fraction of the pretax return. Similar expressions for the noncorporate sector and owner-occupied housing are detailed in Fullerton (1987).

This inclusion of personal taxes, and more simple algebra, can be used to demonstrate additional important conceptual results. Consider a tax-exempt investor such as a university endowment or a pension fund ($\tau^d = 0$), and suppose that the marginal investment is entirely financed by debt ($c_d = 1$). Then with economic depreciation at replacement cost, the marginal effective total tax rate is now zero. The corporate income tax may collect plenty of revenue on past equity-financed investment, but at the margin the corporate income tax is entirely nondistorting (Stiglitz 1973). The reason is that the normal return to the asset is paid out as interest— which is deductible against the corporate income tax. Thus we get a zero marginal effective tax rate either with expensing *or* with debt finance. As a consequence, we get a negative effective tax rate

with expensing *and* debt finance. Thus, to maintain neutrality, proposals for expensing must also disallow interest deductions.

Under actual laws, the marginal effective tax rate can be large for an asset with no investment tax credit and slow depreciation allowances based on historical cost with high inflation, especially if the weight on debt is low and the weights on equity are high. It can be negative for an asset with an investment tax credit and accelerated depreciation allowances, especially if the weight on debt is high. Differences in effective tax rates among assets can be used to measure the welfare cost of resource misallocations.

Actual estimates of effective tax rates depend on numerical assumptions about parameters. For example, Fullerton (1987) calculates marginal effective total tax rates for 36 assets in 18 industries, using 4 percent inflation, 5 percent real net return, actual depreciation based on historical cost, one-third debt financing, and weighted-average personal tax rates on interest, dividends, and capital gains. Before the Tax Reform Act of 1986, that paper finds corporate-sector effective rates equal to $-0.18$ for equipment, 0.37 for structures, 0.29 for public utility assets, 0.42 for inventories, 0.45 for land, and 0.29 overall. Equipment is subsidized by the combination of investment tax credit, accelerated depreciation, and interest deductions at the high 46 percent statutory corporate tax rate. After the Tax Reform Act of 1986, these rates become 0.37, 0.44, 0.44, 0.41, 0.44, and 0.41, respectively. The overall rate rises from 0.29 to 0.41, suggesting less overall incentive to invest, but the different assets are treated much more uniformly. The subsidy to equipment is eliminated with the repeal of the investment tax credit and with the reduction of the statutory corporate tax rate to 34 percent.

We now turn to a discussion of some caveats. These calculations assume that the asset is held forever, but Gordon et al. (1987) show that investors could sell a building, pay the capital gains tax, increase the basis for the new owner's depreciation, and pay less total tax. Churning can reduce the effective tax rate, narrow the difference between structures and equipment, and thus decrease the efficiency gain from a more level playing field. However, Gravelle (1987) indicates that the net effects on the cost of capital are small and depend on transaction costs. Second, the model assumes that firms can use all credits and deductions. Effects of uncertainty and imperfect loss offsets are discussed in Auerbach (1986). Third, it excludes intangible capital that arises from advertising, research, and development. Summers (1987) suggests that the inclusion of these tax-favored assets would reduce the gain from removing the tax-favored status of equipment, but Fullerton and Lyon (1988) show that the 1986 act still provides efficiency gains by reducing the effective tax rate on other assets such as structures, land, and inventories.

These calculations also assume the same financing for all assets. Gordon et al. (1987) note that structures might use more debt and thus have an effective tax rate that does not exceed equipment, but they provide no evidence on actual financing. Results in Gravelle (1987) support the assumption of equal financing for all assets.

The model includes all major tax provisions as well as considerable disaggregation and detail, such as the half-year convention, the half-basis adjustment, LIFO (last in, first out) inventory accounting, and noncorporate taxes. It ignores some specific provisions, however, such as the minimum tax, passive loss rules, and accounting changes in 1986. Lyon (1990) provides a full discussion of the minimum tax, and Fullerton et al. (1987) show that some of these other provisions have a very small effect on the cost of capital even though they raised noticeable revenue in the five-year budget period.

Results from the Tax Reform Act of 1986 are particularly sensitive to the assumption about the importance of dividend taxes. Calculations reported above correspond to the "new view" because they use observed financing of new investment, where most equity is financed from retained earnings subject to the low capital gains rate, and little equity is financed by new share issues subject to the high personal tax rate on dividends. Thus, the 1986 act's reduction of personal tax rates receives low weight, and the repeal of the investment tax credit helps ensure that the overall effective tax rate rises. In contrast, the "old view" would use observed dividend payout rates of about 50 percent and thus assign a higher 50 percent share to the equity income subjected to high personal taxes on dividends. In this case, the reduction of personal income tax rates is more important, and some estimates find that the Tax Reform Act of 1986 actually lowered overall marginal effective tax rates on income from capital.

### Additional readings

Auerbach, Alan J. "The Dynamic Effects of Tax Law Asymmetries." *Review of Economic Studies* 53 (April 1986): 205–25.

Auerbach, Alan J., and Dale W. Jorgenson. "Inflation-Proof Depreciation of Assets." *Harvard Business Review* 58 (September–October 1980): 113–18.

Bradford, David F., and Don Fullerton. "Pitfalls in the Construction and Use of Effective Tax Rates." In *Depreciation, Inflation and the Taxation of Income from Capital*, edited by Charles R. Hulten. Washington, D.C.: The Urban Institute Press, 1981.

Fullerton, Don. "The Indexation of Interest, Depreciation, and Capital Gains and Tax Reform in the United States." *Journal of Public Economics* 32 (February 1987): 25–51.

Fullerton, Don, and Andrew B. Lyon. "Tax Neutrality and Intangible Capital." In *Tax Policy and the Economy* 2, edited by Laurence H. Summers. Cambridge, Mass.: MIT Press, 1988.

Fullerton, Don, Robert Gillette, and James Mackie. "Investment Incentives under the Tax Reform Act of 1986." In *Compendium of Tax Research 1987*. Washington, D.C.: U.S. Treasury Department, 1987.

Gordon, Roger H., James R. Hines, and Lawrence H. Summers. "Notes on the Tax Treatment of Structures." In *The Effects of Taxation on Capital Accumulation*, edited by Martin Feldstein. Chicago: University of Chicago Press, 1987.

Gravelle, Jane G. "Tax Policy and Rental Housing: An Economic Analysis." Congressional Research Service Report No. 87-536 E. Washington, D.C.: Library of Congress, 1987.

Hall, Robert, and Dale W. Jorgenson. "Tax Policy and Investment Behavior." *American Economic Review* 57 (June 1967): 391–414.

Jorgenson, Dale W., and Ralph Landau, editors. *Tax Reform and the Cost of Capital: An International Comparison*. Washington, D.C.: The Brookings Institution, 1993.

Jorgenson, Dale W., and Kun-Young Yun. *Tax Reform and the Cost of Capital*. Oxford: Clarendon Press, 1991.

Lyon, Andrew B. "Investing Incentives under the Alternative Minimum Tax." *National Tax Journal* 43 (December 1990): 451–65.

Stiglitz, Joseph E. "Taxation, Corporate Financial Policy, and the Cost of Capital." *Journal of Public Economics* 2 (February 1973): 1–34.

Summers, Lawrence H. "Should Tax Reform Level the Playing Field?" *Proceedings of the National Tax Association–Tax Institute of America*, meeting of November 1986 (1987): 119–25.

*Cross references:* average effective tax rate; capital cost recovery; expensing; income tax, corporate.

# Marriage penalty

Leslie A. Whittington
Georgetown University

*An increase in federal individual income tax liability solely as a result of marriage.*

When two individuals marry, their income tax liability may exceed their combined income tax liabilities as singles. This additional tax burden resulting from marriage is referred to as a "marriage penalty" or "marriage tax." Marriage can also reduce the federal tax liability of two people, in which case the reduction in tax is called a "marriage subsidy."

This concept is perhaps best illustrated using a hypothetical couple. Assume that in 1998, two people, each with an annual income of $30,000, decide to marry. Assume also that they have no dependents and that both take the standard deduction rather than itemizing. Subtracting the standard deduction for married couples filing jointly ($6,990) and two personal exemptions ($2,650 each) from total marital income gives the couple a tax liability of $7,879.

If these two individuals remain single, their combined tax liabilities are lower. Each person would have a single tax liability of $3,480, giving them a combined total of $6,960. This hypothetical couple pays $919 more in federal income taxes as a married couple than they would as two single individuals. That difference in tax liability ($919) is the so-called marriage penalty or marriage tax. As demonstrated later, it is also easy to construct examples in which combined taxes fall with marriage.

One common misconception is that married persons have the choice of filing as single or married. This is not true. Married people can elect to each file a separate tax return in lieu of a joint return. However, the tax rate schedule applied to married taxpayers filing separately is not the same as that used for single taxpayers. The total tax liability of a couple rarely differs if they file separately rather than jointly.

## The creation of the marriage penalty

There is no explicit federal policy in the United States with respect to taxing or subsidizing marriage. The marriage penalty results from two features of the federal personal income tax code: the use of the family as the taxable unit and the imposition of progressive taxation. Income tax systems can be marriage-neutral, meaning that it is possible to tax income so that the tax liability of a couple does not change with marriage.

The personal income tax in the United States was largely marriage-neutral before 1948, levying tax on an individual basis. In community property states, however, wives had a claim to the income of their husbands, allowing the husband and wife to each report half of the joint income, resulting in a marriage bonus. This treatment led to geographic inequity, which became more problematic as rates rose, and states whose property laws derived from common law began to follow suit. These events and a variety of other circumstances (see Groves 1963) led, essentially, to the extension of community property treatment to all married couples. In 1948, the practice of income splitting between spouses was adopted. This allowed couples to aggregate their income on a joint tax return, and it doubled the width of each tax bracket for married couples. Each spouse was effectively assessed taxes on half of the joint income regardless of how much of the income that spouse actually earned. This was a major shift in the orientation of the federal income tax because it changed the unit of taxation from the individual to the family.

Originally, family taxation was largely advantageous to married couples because it lowered their average tax rate and thus commonly resulted in a marriage subsidy. However, single taxpayers were relatively disadvantaged. Despite subsequent statutory changes designed to alleviate the burden, income splitting often meant that a single taxpayer's liability could be as much as 40 percent higher than that of a married couple with equal income (Rosen 1977: 424).

The Tax Reform Act of 1969 addressed the disparity between single and married persons' tax liabilities by creating a new tax schedule for single taxpayers, under which the differential between the tax liability of a single person and that of an equal-income married couple could not exceed 20 percent. There was no actual change in the tax burden imposed on married persons, but the introduction of the new single schedule caused their relative position to worsen. This change created the marriage penalty, or marriage tax: in a reversal of the previous situation, the combined tax liability of two single people often increased with marriage. Since the reforms of 1969, numerous modifications have been made to the income tax laws that have altered the magnitude of the marriage penalty, but recent evidence documents that many couples still face a tax penalty because they are married. (For a comprehensive review of the history of the marriage penalty in the United States, see Bittker 1975 or Brozovsky and Cataldo 1994.)

## The magnitude of the marriage penalty

It is relatively straightforward to determine the marriage penalty for a particular couple in the year that they marry. Calculation becomes much more complex when it involves couples who are already married, because it hinges crucially on the assumptions made about the behavior of the people were they to split up. If, for example, a married couple with two children and a home that is mortgaged were not married, what would they pay in taxes? Who would claim the children as dependents and therefore have the right to use the head of household tax schedule? Would both partners purchase homes and take itemized deductions? Would one spouse make alimony payments to the other? Would the spouses change their labor decisions? These issues would all affect the tax burden of the two former partners and thus the marriage penalty. Because the marital split is hypothetical, the value of the marriage penalty cannot be unambiguously determined.

The marriage penalty is often discussed as a very easily measured tax item. However, because of the ambiguity surrounding postmarital tax burdens, there is no one precise algorithm for determining either the average value of the marriage penalty or the precise number of married couples who pay a marriage tax. Several reasonable approaches have been employed to estimate the probable magnitude and coverage of the marriage penalty. The general conclusion is that the tax effects of marriage—both positive and negative—can be quite large.

Recent estimates suggest that the percentage of married couples incurring a marriage tax has risen fairly steadily since the Tax Reform Act of 1969 and that about 57 percent of the married couples in the United States now pay a marriage penalty. Almost 30 percent receive a marriage subsidy, and the remainder experience no change in tax liability as a result of marital status. Estimates of the average marriage penalty in recent years generally range from about $100 to almost $400, but this average masks large variations across the population. For example, among those who paid a marriage penalty in 1994, the average penalty was at least $1,200, and for those incurring a subsidy, the average subsidy was roughly $1,100. Penalties and subsidies can be in excess of $5,000 for some couples.

Dual-income couples are most likely to incur a marriage penalty, especially if their incomes are similar and large. Single-earner couples are likely to gain a tax subsidy through marriage. The large increase in female labor force participation over the past few decades has been one contributing factor to the estimated upward trend in the percentage of families experiencing a marriage penalty and the general increase in the value of that penalty. (For estimates of trends in, and recent values of, the marriage penalty, see Alm and Whittington 1996 and Feenberg and Rosen 1995.)

## Can the marriage penalty be eliminated?

Eliminating the marriage penalty would require a major philosophical shift in the orientation of the federal tax system. An income tax structure cannot be marriage-neutral and progressive and also tax equal-income married couples equally. Contrast the hypothetical couple discussed earlier with an equal-income ($60,000) couple that has a single earner, has no dependent children, and takes the standard deduction. Because the family is the unit of taxation under current law, their marital tax liability is the same as the dual-earner, equal-income married couple.

If the unit of taxation were the individual, the two couples would not pay the same amount of income tax. The single earner in the second couple would now have a tax liability of $11,601, $4,641 more than the dual-earner couple would pay under a system of individual taxation.

Moving toward marriage neutrality necessarily implies moving away from equal tax treatment of equal-income families. It also necessarily implies increasing the tax liability on many married couples who receive a tax subsidy under the current tax system. (See Bittker 1975 and Rosen 1977 for additional discussion.)

## The marriage penalty and human behavior

Defining the taxable unit as the family rather than the individual is controversial. The principal arguments revolve around equity issues (Rosen 1977). However, there are also efficiency issues associated with the tax features. It is well recognized, for example, that the secondary earner in a couple will likely experience an increase in his or her marginal tax rate upon marriage, making market work less attractive.

Recent empirical research also provides support for anecdotal evidence that individuals do consider the tax consequences of marital events in making decisions about marriage. Researchers have found that the marriage penalty negatively influences the probability of marriage and positively affects the probability of divorce. The marriage penalty also influences the timing of marital events. (See Alm and Whittington 1995, 1997; Gelardi 1996; Sjoquist and Walker 1995; Whittington and Alm 1997.)

## Additional readings

Alm, James, and Leslie A. Whittington. "Income Taxes and the Marriage Decision." *Applied Economics* 27 (January 1995): 25–31.

Alm, James, and Leslie A. Whittington. "The Rise and Fall and Rise of the Marriage Tax." *National Tax Journal* 49 (December 1996): 571–89.

Alm, James, and Leslie A. Whittington. "Income Taxes and the Timing of Marital Events." *Journal of Public Economics* 64 (May 1997): 219–40.

Bittker, Boris. "Federal Income Taxation and the Family." *Stanford Law Review* 27 (1975): 1388–1463.

Brozovsky, John, and Anthony J. Cataldo III. "A Historical Analysis of the 'Marriage Penalty Tax.'" *The Accounting Historians Journal* 21 (June 1994): 163–87.

Feenberg, Daniel R., and Harvey S. Rosen. "Recent Developments in the Marriage Tax." *National Tax Journal* 48 (March 1995): 91–101.

Gelardi, Alexander M.G. "The Influence of Tax Law Changes on the Timing of Marriages: A Two-Country Analysis." *National Tax Journal* 49 (March 1996): 17–30.

Groves, Harold M. *Federal Tax Treatment of the Family*. Washington, D.C.: The Brookings Institution, 1963.

Rosen, Harvey S. "Is It Time to Abandon Joint Filing?" *National Tax Journal* 30 (December 1977): 423–28.

Sjoquist, David L., and Mary Beth Walker. "The Marriage Tax and the Rate and Timing of Marriage." *National Tax Journal* 48 (December 1995): 547–58.

Whittington, Leslie A., and James Alm. 1996. "'Til Death or Taxes Do Us Part: The Effect of Income Taxation on Divorce." *Journal of Human Resources* (Spring 1997): 388–412.

*Cross references:* adjusted gross income; family, tax treatment of.

# Median voter theorem

Randall G. Holcombe
Florida State University

*Majority rule decisionmaking will produce the outcome most preferred by the median voter.*

The median voter theorem is a prediction about how demands for public spending are expressed through majority rule voting. According to this hypothesis, the median voter's demand determines the group's demand in the political process. Different models lead to this conclusion, but they all share two fundamental assumptions. First, the alternatives must be capable of being ranked on a single-dimension continuum. Second, when the alternatives are so ranked, each voter has single-peaked preferences—that is, voters prefer outcomes closer to their most preferred alternatives over outcomes that are farther away. A model specifying an institutional structure can then be used with these assumptions about voter preferences to yield the conclusion that majority rule decisionmaking will produce the outcome most preferred by the median voter.

The median voter theorem has been demonstrated using a number of different assumptions about the institutional structure of majority rule voting. Hotelling (1929) suggested the idea in an article on spatial competition, and his framework was developed extensively by Downs (1957) to explain how competition between political parties produces the results most preferred by the median voter. In this model, two political candidates compete for office based on their political platforms, which are located on a single-dimension continuum from political left to political right. Voters always choose the candidates closest to their own position, so both candidates have an incentive to move their platforms toward the center to compete for the median vote. The candidate who gets the median vote also will get all votes to one side of the median and

so will get a majority of the votes and win the election. The process of political competition described by Hotelling and Downs causes both candidates' platforms to converge on the median, producing the outcome most preferred by the median voter.

Bowen (1943) came up with the same conclusion with a model of referendum voting. Bowen's voters are asked to vote on the quantity of a publicly produced good with the understanding that if they vote against that quantity they will be offered an opportunity to vote on a marginally lower quantity. The process continues until voters approve a quantity, and Bowen shows that the quantity approved will be that most preferred by the median voter. The same conclusion is reached by a process in which voters are offered a small amount of the good and if they vote in favor are offered marginal increases as long as they continue to favor them. Again, the quantity produced by majority rule in a referendum setting is the quantity most preferred by the median voter.

Black (1958) describes yet another institutional arrangement in which a committee chooses an outcome by majority rule. Motions are put forward by committee members and compete against each other in pairwise elections. The winning motion remains on the floor and can face a potentially unlimited number of competing motions, but Black shows that the motion most preferred by the median voter can defeat any other motion by majority rule. Black discusses the role of single-peaked preferences in detail and shows how the possibility of cyclical majorities can arise when this assumption is not satisfied.

This overview shows that the median voter theorem can be demonstrated under different institutional arrangements, all pointing to the general conclusion that majority rule decisionmaking produces the outcome most preferred by the median voter. If the median voter theorem is descriptive, it provides researchers with a good model of public-sector demand, which allows theoretical modeling of public-sector resource allocation and provides the basis for empirical models of public-sector supply and demand. Most empirical studies of the median voter theorem tend to support it. For example, Inman (1978) demonstrates that median population characteristics tend to explain public-sector output better than average data, and Holcombe (1980) uses school referendum data to conclude that the median voter theorem describes election outcomes better than other plausible alternatives.

Holcombe (1989) discusses the empirical evidence in more detail and notes that while the evidence is not unanimous, it tends to be consistent with the median voter theorem. This statement is comforting to researchers who want to apply this simple yet powerful theorem to understand how the democratic decisionmaking process allocates economic resources. Furthermore, it provides a useful foundation for empirical models because it suggests that there are equilibrating forces in the political process and that the differences in the characteristics of median voters across jurisdictions can cause differences in the types of public-sector output produced by those jurisdictions.

While the empirical evidence has been generally supportive, a substantial amount of theoretical work has called the median voter theorem into question. This is partly because the theorem rests on simple assumptions that appear not to be met in the real world and partly because the model was used to draw conclusions that were well beyond what it actually implied. The theorem found its strongest acceptance in the early 1970s, and a number of empirical articles in top journals used it to justify the conclusion that the public sector produces what the median voter most prefers. This strong interpretation of the theorem leaves it vulnerable to attack on several grounds. First, some of the assumptions of the theorem may not be satisfied, but more significantly, the theorem deals only with the way majority rule voting aggregates demands, yet this strong interpretation suggests that the theorem describes both the supply and demand sides of the market for public-sector output. If this overly strong interpretation is accepted, any evidence that the public sector does not provide what the median wants can be taken as evidence against the theorem's applicability.

Niskanen's (1971) well-known economic analysis of bureaucracy illustrates this point. Niskanen develops a model of bureaucratic resource allocation that concludes that government bureaucracies produce far more output than the median voter would most prefer, which critics of the theorem took to be evidence against its validity. Yet Niskanen clearly builds his analysis using the median voter theorem to model the demand side of the public sector and then adds a supply side to draw his conclusions. Although Niskanen accepted the median voter theorem as a model public-sector demand aggregation, others took Niskanen's model to imply that the theorem was not applicable to public-sector resource allocation.

More serious questions about the applicability of the median voter theorem arose in the late 1970s, when a group of economists, using sophisticated mathematical models, demonstrated that its conclusion is crucially dependent on the assumption that the political issue space is single-dimension. For example, using a framework similar to Black's, McKelvey (1976) shows that if the issue space is extended even to two dimensions, there is no outcome that can defeat all others by majority rule, even if all voters have single-peaked preferences. This finding suggests that a cyclical majority model would be more descriptive of democratic decision-making than the median voter theorem. A number of economists and political scientists responded by noting that public-sector outcomes in fact tend to be very stable, with programs, institutions, and even elected officials displaying more stability than is observed in the market sector. The evidence seems to weigh against continual voting (or policy) cycles in the public sector.

If one accepts the conclusion that the outcomes from collective choices tend to be stable over time, that still leaves open the question about what produces the stability. It could be that the median voter theorem explains the stability because public-sector demand is a reflection of the preferences of the median voter, whose characteristics do not change much over time. Another possibility is that the institutional structure of the public sector leads democratic decisionmaking to produce stable outcomes. Institutional constraints can have many effects, but two important potential effects deserve mention. First, they can limit the range of options over which groups can make collective choices, which can produce stability but also is a potential source of inefficiency in collective decisionmaking. Second, they can limit the ability of people to participate in the collective decisionmaking process because of high transaction costs. The fact that some people (such as legislators and lobbyists) face lower transaction costs in the political decisionmaking process than others (such as the general public) has given rise to special-interest models of legislation that conclude that representative government tends to favor special interests over the general public interest.

The assumptions behind the median voter model fit U.S. winner-take-all general elections very well, and the implications of the theorem also conform to the American experience. The theorem explains why candidates take similar platforms when running against each other (both are aiming their platforms at the median voter) and why candidates who take extreme positions lose badly (they are too far away from the median voter). The theorem also explains why two is the equilibrium number of political parties in this type of election system. (A third party must compete with a party on one side of the median, making two of the three parties unable to win elections and so not viable in the long run.) Note that although the United States has had only two major parties throughout its history, the Constitution says nothing about political parties, and third parties have continued to spring up, either to disappear (Progressive Party) or to replace one of the two dominant parties (Republican Party). In certain circumstances, the median voter theorem is very descriptive of real-world political processes and lends a great deal of insight into the way majority rule voting aggregates the preferences of voters.

The simple structure of the theorem that allows it to illuminate clearly the demand aggregation characteristics of majority rule voting also limits its applicability. The median voter theorem has nothing to say about the supply side of the public sector, and when its assumptions are violated, voting cycles are possible. Furthermore, the institutional environment can affect election outcomes in ways that are not reflected in the theorem. In this regard, the median voter theorem might be considered similar to the neoclassical model of purely competitive markets. Because of the simplifying assumptions underlying the models, they may be inapplicable to many situations. Still, the models lend powerful insights into the fundamental processes underlying markets and voting. Seen in this way, the median voter theorem provides a good foundation for understanding the way resources are allocated when demands are aggregated through majority rule voting.

## Additional readings

Black, Duncan. *The Theory of Committees and Elections*. Cambridge, U.K.: Cambridge University Press, 1958.

Bowen, Howard R. "The Interpretation of Voting in the Allocation of Economic Resources." *Quarterly Journal of Economics* 58 (November 1943): 27–48.

Downs, Anthony. *An Economic Theory of Democracy*. New York: Harper & Row, 1957.

Holcombe, Randall G. "An Empirical Test of the Median Voter Model." *Economic Inquiry* 18 (April 1980): 260–74.

Holcombe, Randall G. "The Median Voter Model in Public Choice Theory." *Public Choice* 61 (1989): 115–25.

Hotelling, Harold. "Stability in Competition." *Economic Journal* 29 (March 1929): 41–57.

Inman, Robert P. "Testing Political Economy's 'as if' Assumption: Is the Median Income Voter Really Decisive?" *Public Choice* 33 (1978): 45–65.

McKelvey, Richard D. "Intransitivities in Multi-Dimensional Voting Models and Some Implications for Agenda Control." *Journal of Economic Theory* 12 (June 1976): 472–82.

Niskanen, William N. *Bureaucracy and Representative Government*. Chicago: Aldine-Atherton, 1971.

*Cross references:* budget process, federal; budget processes, state; tax illusion; Tiebout model.

# Medicare trust fund

Robert Friedland
National Academy on Aging

*One of the component programs of the Social Security system, an arrangement for federal funding of health care for the elderly and certain disabled persons.*

Medicare was enacted in 1965 under Title XVIII of the Social Security Act to help older persons obtain and pay for medical care. In the early 1960s, before Medicare, only about half of older Americans had any health insurance (compared with 75% of those under 65). Some seeking private coverage were denied on the basis of age or preexisting conditions; others could not afford it. Medicare is divided into two parts—Hospital Insurance (Part A) and Supplementary Medical Insurance (Part B)—which represent two of the four Social Security trust funds (the others address retirement/survivors and disability income). In 1972, the program was extended to certain people under age 65: those with end-stage renal disease (kidney failure) and people receiving Social Security Disability Insurance (DI) benefits for at least two years.

## Who is eligible for Medicare?

In 1996, Medicare covered 38 million people (33 million aged and 5 million disabled), including persons age 65 and over eligible for Social Security benefits (retired workers, spouses of retired or disabled workers, or surviving spouses); persons under age 65 receiving DI for two years (workers and their surviving spouse or adult disabled child); persons of any age with end-stage renal disease (ESRD—workers, spouses, or their children); and persons age 65 or older who are otherwise not eligible but elect to enroll by paying a monthly premium ($311 in 1997).

As a social insurance program, Medicare Part A is an earned benefit for most people and requires no premium upon eligibility. In contrast, participation in Part B is voluntary but is heavily subsidized by taxpayers. Beneficiaries choosing Part B pay a premium based on 25 percent of anticipated Part B program costs ($43.80 per month in 1997). In 1996, more than 97 percent of older and 87 percent of disabled beneficiaries elected Part B.

## Medicare and health care

Medicare is a major payer in the U.S. health care system, accounting for 32 percent of all hospital and 20 percent of all physician payments. It also covers 45 percent of health care spending for the elderly overall, but less for the oldest elderly, who require more nursing home care.

## What does Medicare cover?

Medicare was designed with acute care benefits in mind, such as hospital and physician care. The basic benefit package has changed little since the program's inception; however, many services are now delivered beyond traditional acute care settings.

*Part A*, Hospital Insurance, provides the following coverage:

Inpatient hospital care coverage for the first 60 days less a deductible ($760 in 1997) for each period of acute illness. For days 61 to 90 in a hospital, a beneficiary must pay a daily copayment ($190 in 1997). Beyond 90 days, he or she may elect to draw upon a 60-day lifetime reserve with a daily copayment ($380 in 1997).

Inpatient psychiatric care (190-day lifetime maximum).

Skilled nursing care or rehabilitation associated with recuperation for up to 100 days following a hospitalization. (There is no cost-sharing for the first 20 days; daily copayment for days 21 to 100 was $95 in 1997.)

Home health care, that is, skilled nursing or rehabilitation benefits provided in the home and prescribed by a physician. There are no deductibles, coinsurance, limits on the number of covered days, or required prior hospitalization.

Hospice care (care for the terminally ill, ranging from home health aide services to medical supplies and limited, short-term inpatient care). Coinsurance for some services applies.

*Part B*, Supplementary Insurance, generally pays 80 percent of physician and outpatient services after an annual $100 deductible. Coverage includes physician services; laboratory and other diagnostic tests; X-ray and other radiation therapy; outpatient services at a hospital, rehabilitation facility, or rural health clinic; home dialysis supplies and equipment; ambulance services; physical and speech therapy; mammography screening and screening pap smears; and outpatient mental health services (50% of the approved amount only).

*Not Covered* are such items as outpatient prescription drugs; routine physical examinations; nonsurgical dental services; hearing aids and eyeglasses; and most long-term care in nursing facilities, in the community, or at home.

Beneficiaries face cost-sharing in the form of premiums, deductibles, and coinsurance, as well as the cost of services and products not covered by Medicare. Unlike most private insurance, Medicare does not cap a beneficiary's out-of-pocket costs. In 1994, older persons (excluding those living in nursing homes) on average spent $2,519 on health care, or 21 percent of their average household income. Most elderly beneficiaries (89%) have supplemental coverage, through separately purchased private insurance ("Medigap," 37%), employer retiree coverage (38%), Medicaid (12%), or other sources (2%). Since 1988, state Medicaid programs are required to pay Medicare Part B premiums and cost-sharing for all "Qualified Medicare Beneficiaries," whose incomes are below 100 percent of the federal poverty level and whose assets are below certain levels ($7,890 for individuals, $10,610 for couples in 1997). For those with incomes between 100 and 120 percent of the poverty level, Medicaid pays for their Part B premiums only. Individuals must apply for Medicaid in their state to be eligible.

## Medicare managed care

In 1996, 3.5 million Medicare beneficiaries (9.1%) were enrolled in risk (as opposed to cost-reimbursed) health maintenance organizations (HMOs). These plans must provide all Medicare-covered services and receive a fixed payment that approximates 95 percent of the costs for similar enrollees in fee-for-service, adjusted for average per capita costs. HMOs frequently add coverage (e.g., prescription drugs) and have lower copayments. Government payments to HMOs could be too high, however, if HMOs enroll healthier individuals.

## Medicare expenditures and enrollment

In 1996, Medicare outlays were $200.3 billion. Approximately 9 percent of Medicare spending is for disabled beneficiaries, 5 percent for those with end-stage renal disease, and the rest for the aged. About 5 percent of enrollees account for 50 percent of spending. Beneficiaries with ESRD incur the highest costs per person.

Medicare is projected to grow at an average rate of about 8.5 percent per year, and spending is projected to reach nearly $450 billion in 2005 under current law. Over time, Medicare spending has grown as a percentage of the federal budget and of gross domestic product. Simultaneously, health care costs have outpaced the incomes of older and disabled persons.

What drives these growth figures? In the near term, Medicare projections are based primarily on expected increases in medical prices and the volume and intensity of services and new technologies. These are largely the same factors causing spending growth in the private sector, although Medicare's population is generally in poorer health. Over the long term, powerful forces are projected to push up costs and, thus, expenditures. Technological change is likely to continue being a cost driver. In combination with technology, our demographics are also changing—that is, our society is "aging" as a result of the retirement of the baby boomers and longer life expectancy. Unless dramatic new ways are found to attain efficiency in Medicare, changes will have to occur in enrollment, benefits, or funding.

## Cost containment efforts

Efforts to control Medicare costs have taken many forms, such as fee limits or utilization review to reduce unnecessary services. In the early years, controlling prices to reduce program spending was frequently undermined because the total volume of services rose. In 1983, the Prospective Payment System was created, which set limits on hospital reimbursement for inpatient care by establishing a set amount to be paid for each patient's case, depending on the medical condition or "diagnosis-related group." Hospitals were no longer paid for whatever treatment they provided. Beginning in January 1992, the Medicare Fee Schedule for physician services was implemented. The fee schedule uses a "resource-based relative value scale," which sets a relative value according to the time and complexity of the service performed, rather than paying physicians their usual or customary fees. Despite these changes, Medicare expenditures continued to grow, albeit at a slower rate than might have occurred otherwise. In recent years, skilled nursing facility and home health care have grown much faster than hospital and physician care.

### Medicare financing

Two trust funds are used to finance the Medicare program, the Hospital Insurance (HI) Trust Fund and the Supplementary Medical Insurance (SMI) Trust Fund. Current employees and their employers each pay 1.45 percent of a worker's salary (self-employed workers pay 2.90%) to HI. This tax financed most (89%) of the $124.6 billion in income received by the HI Trust Fund in 1996. Other income sources in 1996 included interest earned on trust fund balances ($10.2 billion or 8.1% of revenues) and revenue from some taxes on Social Security benefits ($4.1 billion or 3% of revenues in 1997). The HI Trust Fund is essentially operating largely on a "pay-as-you-go" basis. There were, however, nearly $131 billion in reserves at the end of 1995. In 1996, expenditures were $5.3 billion more than income, and thus reserves were reduced to about $125 billion by the end of 1996.

Because of these reserves and the taxes on Social Security benefits, workers pay slightly less than the cost of Medicare, but as reserves decline and program costs increase, current worker payroll taxes will no longer be sufficient. In 1996, the program costs as a percentage of taxable income were 3.48 percent. By 2015, this cost rate is projected to reach 5.82 percent; by 2030, it could be 8.63 percent of taxable payroll. The 1997 trustees report projects that the HI Trust Fund will be depleted by 2001, when the cost will be about 4 percent of payroll and the statutory payroll tax will be 2.9 percent of payroll.

In contrast, the SMI Trust Fund, because it is financed on a year-by-year basis, is "adequately financed" in the short run. SMI is financed by premium contributions of enrollees (covering about 25% of costs) and from general federal revenue (covering the remaining 75%). The SMI Trust Fund is not designed to accumulate funds for future benefit payments.

### The future of Medicare and policy debates

Health programs, like retirement programs, are affected by the aging of our society, but unlike retirement programs, they are also affected by the rapid development of medical technology and rising costs of health care. Proposed short-term solutions for the Medicare funding gap include raising payroll taxes, shifting contributions from other trust funds, changing premiums and rates of copayment, expanding managed care, or reexamining cost-sharing to influence the use of certain services. Each of these options has different consequences. More profound restructuring is also likely to be examined, including combining Parts A and B and rethinking the trust fund financing arrangements, increasing beneficiaries' costs, changing the benefits, raising the age of eligibility, and fostering health plan competition to keep health care costs in check.

### Additional readings

Aaron, Henry J. *Serious and Unstable Condition: Financing America's Health Care*. Washington, D.C.: Brookings Institution, 1991.

Moon, Marilyn. *Medicare Now and in the Future*. 2d ed. Washington, D.C.: The Urban Institute, 1993.

*Cross references:* health expenditures, tax treatment; payroll tax, federal; Social Security Trust Fund.

# Mortgage interest deduction
### Richard Green
University of Wisconsin, Madison

*A deduction from adjusted gross income as part of the determination of taxable income, intended to encourage home ownership and encourage spending on owner-occupied housing.*

Before the Tax Reform Act of 1986, consumer interest was generally deductible from gross income. Indeed, the original Income Tax Act of 1913 allowed for the deduction of consumer interest (see Pechman 1987). But since 1986, the only interest expense that consumers have been able to completely deduct from gross income in order to calculate taxable income has been interest paid on specified types of home mortgages.

These mortgages include those on first and second homes with balances totaling less then $1 million. The definition of "home" is quite broad: motor homes and yachts, for example, by virtue of their indoor plumbing and kitchens, qualify as homes for tax purposes. Beyond the $1 million limit, mortgages on which interest is completely deductible may not exceed the maximum of the equity value of the house securing the loan, or, on a refinanced loan, the outstanding balance of the original mortgage plus $100,000.

According to the Treasury Department, in 1997 the value of the mortgage interest deduction to taxpayers was roughly $52 billion.

### Importance of the benefit

In the popular press, the mortgage interest deduction is often characterized as being the principal tax benefit accruing to homeowners. This is certainly not correct. First, fewer than 50 percent of homeowners itemize on their tax returns; the remainder use the standard deduction. This is because the value of itemized deductions for low- to moderate-income homeowners in states with low marginal tax rates will almost certainly be less than the value of the standard deduction, which in 1997 was $6,900 for married couples. Also, according to tabulations from the Survey of Consumer Finances, many households with elderly heads own their homes entirely with equity (i.e., do not have mortgages), and for these households, the mortgage interest deduction has no value.

Second, even for those who do itemize, the mortgage interest deduction does not necessarily produce the largest tax benefit arising from owning. The imputed rent that households earn from their owner-occupied housing (i.e., the rents that households are not required to pay anyone else because they own) goes untaxed. This rent is therefore favored relative to most other types of income, including ordinary income, taxable bond income, dividend income, and capital gains income, which, while favored and deferrable, is still generally taxed. The average loan-to-value ratio in the United States is less than 50 percent. Thus, even if all owners with mortgages itemized on their tax returns, the value of the nontaxation of imputed rent would be larger than that of the mortgage interest deduction.

### Effect of the benefit on choice of financing

One could argue that the effect of the mortgage interest deduction is to put debt on a level playing field with equity as a way to finance housing. This contrasts with the tax treatment of corporate income, where interest is deductible and the opportunity cost of equity capital is not. Many analysts have shown that the U.S. tax system encourages corporations to take on debt. Capozza et al. (1996) have shown how the combination of nontaxation of imputed rent and the absence of a mortgage interest deduction would discourage households from financing housing with debt. In Australia, imputed rent is not taxed and mortgage interest is not deductible, and households there generally pay off their mortgages more quickly than in the United States.

### Mortgage interest deduction and efficiency

For many years, the mortgage interest deduction was viewed as a mechanism that steered investment capital away from plants and equipment and toward the housing market. Laidler (1969) and Rosen (1979), among others, found that the quantity effects of the mortgage interest deduction (and nontaxation of imputed rent) were large, because they assumed that housing was supplied perfectly elastically.

Some more recent work by King (1980) and Poterba (1984) relaxed the assumption of perfect elasticity and still found large quantity effects. But the most recent work (Somerville and Mayer 1997, Skinner 1997, and Capozza et al. 1996) has found housing to be supplied very inelastically, and consequently finds small quantity effects and large price effects (e.g., capitalization effects) arising from the tax preferences for owner-occupied housing. This suggests that the efficiency costs of the mortgage interest deduction are rather small.

An interesting question raised by the mortgage interest deduction is whether it causes market segmentation. Within a housing market, households with the highest marginal tax rates have an incentive to outbid everyone else for owner-occupied housing. Once these households are exhausted, the households with the second highest rates can outbid everyone else, and so on. If this were to happen, tax benefits could be entirely capitalized. If, on the other hand, market values are determined by some average marginal tax rate, households with high tax rates will consume more housing than they would in the absence of the tax preference, and households with low tax rates would consume less (or might even rent).

### The mortgage interest deduction and vertical equity

The mortgage interest deduction generally reduces progressivity in the income tax system, because it gives higher-income taxpayers higher levels of benefits. On the other hand, the extent to which the mortgage interest deduction reduces progressivity depends on the elasticity of housing supply. If housing were inelastically supplied (i.e., could be represented by a vertical supply curve), all tax benefits would be capitalized into prices, and owners would get no net benefits from the mortgage interest deduction. Those benefits that are not capitalized determine the extent to which the mortgage interest deduction hampers progressivity.

## Additional readings

Capozza, Dennis, Richard K. Green, and Patric H. Hendershott. "Taxes, Mortgage Borrowing and Residential Land Prices." In *Economics of Fundamental Tax Reform*, edited by Henry Aaron and William Gale. Washington, D.C.: The Brookings Institution, 1996.

King, M.A. "An Econometric Model of Tenure Choice and the Demand for Housing as a Joint Decision." *Journal of Public Economics* 14(2) (1980): 137–59.

Laidler, David. "Income Tax Incentives for Owner-Occupied Housing." In *The Taxation of Income from Capital*, edited by Arnold Harberger and Martin Bailey. Washington, D.C.: The Brookings Institution, 1969.

Mayer, C., and T. Somerville. "Testing Alternative Paradigms of the Supply of Owner-Occupied Housing." Mimeograph, 1997.

Pechman, Joseph. *Federal Tax Policy.* 5th ed. Washington, D.C.: The Brookings Institution, 1987.

Poterba, James. "Tax Subsidies to Owner-Occupied Housing: An Asset-Market Approach." *Quarterly Journal of Economics* 99 (4) (1984): 729–52.

Rosen, Harvey. "Housing Decisions and the U.S. Income Tax: An Econometric Analysis." *Journal of Public Economics* 11 (1) (1979): 1–23.

*Cross references:* homeowner preferences, individual income tax; implicit taxes; progressivity, measures of; standard deduction, federal.

# Multinational corporations, taxation

Eric Toder
The Urban Institute

*A system of taxation of large U.S. corporations that have foreign operations organized under laws of another country or operate abroad in branch form.*

In the past 20 years, international trade and investment have grown substantially. Much of the growth in international capital flows is attributable to direct foreign investment by multinational corporations.

Multinationals need not own overseas facilities to secure the cost and market access advantages of foreign production; they can (and sometimes do) contract out production to locally owned firms. The usual reason economists advance for direct ownership is that the high transaction costs of negotiating and enforcing rights to the returns from intangible assets (such as patents, production processes, and reputation) make internal ownership of those assets preferable (Markusen 1995).

In the domestic context, a tax on corporate retained earnings protects the income tax base by preventing individual investors from accruing untaxed income within corporations. When the same corporation receives income from production in more than one taxing jurisdiction, however, and when rights to that income accrue to shareholders of different nationalities, both domestic and foreign tax rules determine whether taxation of corporate income is achieving the goal of taxing undistributed income of shareholders at the appropriate rate, without imposing extra tax penalties on international investment flows.

In determining rules for taxing cross-border income flows, two principles of tax neutrality are in conflict. *Locational neutrality* (often called "capital-export" neutrality) means that tax rules should not distort the location of economic activity among countries. This form of neutrality requires that (risk-adjusted) pretax returns be equalized among countries and (with perfect capital markets) would result from profit maximization in the absence of taxes. It could be achieved if all countries taxed the worldwide income (including income accrued within foreign affiliates) on a current basis of all corporations with headquarters within their borders (resident corporations), but allowed a credit for foreign income taxes paid. This would make a corporation's tax rate on profits equal to its home country rate in all locations, without regard for the local country's tax rate. (An alternative concept of locational neutrality, called "national neutrality," would be achieved by any country that taxed the worldwide income of its corporations, but with a deduction instead of a credit for foreign taxes. This rule would encourage corporations to equalize the yield before domestic taxes, but net of foreign taxes, and would therefore equalize the home country's return to investment in all locations.) But unless all countries have the same tax rules, residence-based corporate taxation does not ensure that any one country's multinationals face the same total tax rate on investments in any location as multinationals residing in other countries.

*Producer neutrality* (often called "capital-import" neutrality) requires that the after-tax return to investment in any location be equalized for all corporations, without regard to their country of residence. This could be achieved if all countries taxed income from production within their borders (domestic-source income) at the same rate, regardless of the residence of the investing corporation, and imposed no taxes on foreign-source income of its own resident corporations because it would make the tax rate in any location the same for all corporations. But unless all countries imposed the same tax rate, such a rule would not produce locational neutrality; required pretax returns would be higher in high-tax countries, and world capital stocks would be misallocated.

If all resident corporations in any country are owned exclusively by domestic residents, and domestic saving is inelastic with respect to the after-tax rate of return, the higher tax rates any country may impose on its corporations are likely to be borne by its own savers in the form of lower after-tax yields instead of raising the cost of capital on its resident corporations. For this reason, many international tax experts have favored residence-based taxation on grounds of efficiency (Musgrave 1984). If, however, corporations issue equity on a world market, then higher taxes on profits of any one country's resident multinationals will not be fully shifted backward to shareholders and could, by raising their cost of capital, place resident corporations at a disadvantage relative to corporations with headquarters in other countries. In this sense, residence-based taxation can reduce the "competitiveness" of resident multinationals. (With low elasticities of substitution by investors between foreign and domestic equity, the importance of locational neutrality would outweigh the importance of producer neutrality. See Grubert and Mutti 1995.)

While efficiency considerations arguably favor residence-based taxation, administration and compliance considerations may favor source-based taxation because countries can more easily collect taxes on income accrued within their own borders. Taxing foreign-source income as accrued is especially difficult when a resident corporation or individual has only a minority interest in a foreign entity and cannot compel the entity to report data to domestic tax authorities. The model tax treaties of the Organization for Economic Cooperation and Development (OECD) and the United Nations both give source countries the first rights to tax income accrued by permanent establishments within their borders. The United States and its major trading partners all tax domestic-source income of foreign-owned, as well as domestically owned, corporations.

But determining the allocation of income by country has become more difficult because of the growth of cross-border trade that takes the form of transactions between branches and affiliated companies *within* multinational corporations. When a corporation purchases goods or services from a foreign branch or a wholly owned foreign subsidiary, the price it pays (called a "transfer price") has no effect on the aggregate pretax profits of the corporate group, but does affect the shares of total taxable income reported by the separate entities to different countries. Consequently, multinational corporations have an incentive to set high prices (low prices) for purchases from (sales to) subsidiaries in low-tax countries, in order to raise the amount of income reported to low-tax countries and reduce reported income in high-tax jurisdictions.

Under the "arm's-length" standard, transfer prices between affiliates should be set equal to the prices of sales of comparable goods and services in transactions between unrelated entities. Often, however, appropriate comparable transactions cannot be identified. The most typical case is where a multinational corporation licenses the use of unique intangibles (patents and production processes) it possesses to a foreign subsidiary that uses the intangible assets in production. The royalty charged to the subsidiary cannot be compared to any arm's-length transaction if the corporation does not sell or lease its intangible assets to unrelated parties. To address this problem, the United States has developed detailed transfer pricing regulations that allow alternative methods based on comparable profit rates in cases where suitable comparable transactions do not exist. Such methods, nevertheless, attempt to establish prices or royalties that would be charged at arm's length.

In view of problems in determining appropriate transfer prices, some experts favor replacing the arm's-length system with a system of "formulary apportionment," which ignores intercompany transactions and allocates income for an entire corporate group among jurisdictions in proportion to shares of certain defined variables. Formulary apportionment is used by states within the United States to allocate domestic U.S. profits among states. States typically base their allocation formulas on a weighted average of a company's sales, assets, and payroll among jurisdictions, although some have recently moved toward a sales-only formula.

Opponents of the formulary approach point out that, to be workable, it would require a much greater degree of harmonization among countries' tax systems than exists today or is feasible in the immediate future. In this view, formulary apportionment works (although not without problems and economic distortions) for U.S. states only because states use a common accounting framework with a corporate tax base that is the same, or similar, to the base of the U.S. corporate income tax. Opponents of formulary apportionment note further that, through the efforts of the OECD, the world's major economies have reached a consensus that supports the arm's-length test and rejects formulary apportionment. (A recent Treasury conference examined issues in replacing the current system with a formulary approach. See the papers collected in U.S. Treasury Department [1996].)

In addition to taxing U.S.-source corporate income, the United States taxes the worldwide income of its resident corporations, with a credit for foreign income and withholding taxes paid. But in general, the United States allows corporations to defer tax on most active business income accrued within foreign subsidiaries until that income is repatriated in the form of dividend payments to the parent U.S. multinational. Special rules (the subpart F rules) tax passive income and certain other forms of "easily shiftable" income of foreign subsidiaries on a current basis to limit the erosion of the U.S. tax base that opportunities to accrue income in low-tax jurisdictions would otherwise create.

The United States adjusts for double taxation on that portion of foreign-source income that is taxable (repatriated income and subpart F income) by allowing corporations to claim a credit for foreign taxes paid. (Some other countries exempt foreign-source business income of their resident multinationals but do tax investment income that is generally subject to lower foreign taxes, with a credit or deduction for such taxes. Exemption of some foreign-source income reflects a capital-import neutrality approach.) The U.S. foreign tax credit is limited to the tax liability that would otherwise be payable on the foreign-source income under U.S. tax law. Companies can, however, effectively claim credits in excess of the U.S. tax rate in a high-tax country by earning enough income in low-tax jurisdictions to soak up the excess credits. To limit such "cross-crediting," the U.S. tax law establishes separate "baskets" for different types of income and applies a separate foreign tax credit limit to each "basket."

U.S. multinationals that are unable to use all their foreign tax credits (because of an average foreign tax rate for any basket that is higher than the U.S. tax rate) are said to be in an "excess credit" position. Corporations in an excess credit position have an incentive to characterize more of their income to U.S. authorities as foreign source in order to claim credits against U.S. tax for more of the income taxes they pay to foreign governments. Companies in a long-term excess credit position and companies in an excess limit position also face different effective tax rates on foreign investments. Excess credit companies effectively pay no residual U.S. tax on additional foreign-source income, whereas excess limit companies do pay U.S. tax on additional income from low-tax jurisdictions.

In recent years, numerous studies have estimated how U.S. multinationals respond to the incentives in U.S. international rules (Hines 1996 provides a detailed summary of this work). The research shows that differences in effective tax rates among locations affect both the location of real investment and where firms report income, given the location of real investment, but parameter estimates

vary widely among studies and must be considered imprecise. There is also evidence that deferral and the U.S. foreign tax credit rules affect the decision of multinationals to retain earnings overseas instead of repatriating dividends to U.S. parent companies, although other evidence suggests that the estimated response may only represent changes in timing in response to annual changes in foreign tax credit positions. (See Altshuler et al. 1995. Their evidence is consistent with the argument by Hartman 1985 that repatriation taxes that do not vary over time should not affect the decision to retain earnings abroad.)

The U.S. rules for taxing foreign-source income seek to balance three sometimes contradictory goals—limiting tax preferences for U.S. firms to invest abroad (by limiting disparities in effective tax rates between domestic and foreign investments), protecting the competitiveness of U.S.-resident multinationals (by limiting disparities in effective tax rates on foreign investments of U.S. and foreign multinationals), and protecting the domestic income tax base (by preventing income-shifting to low-tax jurisdictions). Advocates of policy changes differ in the goals they emphasize. Some members of Congress have expressed concern that deferral encourages U.S. corporations to invest abroad instead of at home and have proposed measures to expand subpart F to cover "runaway" plants that produce goods for export to the United States. In contrast, others in Congress and the business community view the U.S. antideferral rules as being too harsh, relative to tax rules imposed on foreign-source income by other capital-exporting countries, and believe they damage U.S.-resident multinationals' competitiveness. Corporations also complain about the complexity of rules designed to limit tax-motivated income shifting.

The communications revolution, including the Internet, raises new challenges for international tax policy and administration. For example, determining the source of income will become more difficult for activities that take place in cyberspace. Furthermore, the ability to transmit money or its equivalent without financial intermediaries, and possibly anonymously, could enhance tax-avoidance opportunities. (For a discussion of tax issues relating to the communication revolution, see U.S. Treasury Department 1996a.)

Some fundamental tax reforms that have been discussed in the United States would have a profound impact on worldwide taxation of multinationals. If, for example, the United States were to replace the income tax with a consumption-based "flat tax" or a national sales tax, multinationals would have a powerful incentive to shift both real and reported income to the United States. (For a more complete discussion, see Grubert and Newlon 1995.) Other countries are likely to respond by taking measures either to protect their domestic tax base (such as taxing U.S.-source income on an accrual basis as "tax haven" income) or to protect their domestic capital stock by reducing corporate income taxes. The prospects for such U.S. reforms have become more remote in the past year but could revive if public dissatisfaction with the U.S. income tax continues to increase.

## Additional readings

Altshuler, Rosanne, T. Scott Newlon, and William C. Randolph. "Do Repatriation Taxes Matter? Evidence from the Tax Returns of U.S. Multinationals." In *Studies in International Taxation*, edited by Martin Feldstein, James R. Hines, and R. Glenn Hubbard. Chicago: University of Chicago Press, 1995.

Grubert, Harry, and John Mutti. "Taxing Multinationals in a World with Portfolio Flows and R&D: Is Capital Export Neutrality Obsolete?" *International Tax and Public Finance* 2 (3) (November 1995): 439–57.

Grubert, Harry, and Scott Newlon. "The International Implications of Consumption Tax Proposals." *National Tax Journal* 48 (4) (December 1995).

Hartman, David G. "Welfare Effects of a Capital Income Tax on Open Economy." National Bureau of Economic Research. Working Paper 1551 (January 1985).

Hines, James R., Jr. "Tax Policy and the Activities of Multinational Corporations." National Bureau of Economic Research. Working Paper 5589 (May 1996).

Markusen, James R. "The Boundaries of Multinational Enterprises and the Theory of International Trade." *Journal of Economic Perspectives* 9 (2) (Spring 1995): 169–89.

Musgrave, Peggy B. "The Taxation of International Capital Income." In *Taxation Issues of the 1980s*, edited by John G. Head. Sydney, Australia: Australian Research Foundation (1984).

U.S. Department of the Treasury, Office of Tax Policy. "Selected Tax Policy Implications of Global Electronic Commerce." November 1996 (1996a).

U.S. Department of the Treasury. Conference on Formula Apportionment, December 12, 1996 (1996b).

*Cross references:* allocation rules, multinational corporations; capital export neutrality; capital import neutrality; foreign tax credit; income tax, federal; national neutrality; taxable income, corporate.

# Multistate Tax Commission

Dan R. Bucks
Multistate Tax Commission

*An organization of member states that serves as an administrative, joint-auditing, and research agency for state governments.*

The Multistate Tax Commission is the governing body and operating agency of the Multistate Tax Compact, an interstate compact with 20 member states, 15 associate member states, and 5 project member states as of mid-1995.

The states created the Multistate Tax Commission (MTC) in 1967 to preserve fiscal federalism and promote fair and effective taxation of interstate and international commerce. The full members of the MTC (i.e., those whose legislatures enacted the compact) are Alabama, Alaska, Arkansas, California, Colorado, District of Columbia, Hawaii, Idaho, Kansas, Michigan, Minnesota, Missouri, Montana, New Mexico, North Dakota, Oregon, South Dakota, Texas, Utah, and Washington. These states govern and pay dues to support the commission and typically participate in a wide range of projects and programs. They are represented on the commission by the directors of their revenue agencies.

The associate members of the MTC are Arizona, Connecticut, Georgia, Louisiana, Maine, Maryland, Massachusetts, New Hampshire, New Jersey, North Carolina, Ohio, Pennsylvania, Tennessee, Wisconsin, and West Virginia. Nonvoting associate members participate in committees and meetings and often join MTC projects or programs. Five project member states also participate in MTC tax-enforcement programs.

The Multistate Tax Compact was written in the mid-1960s, principally by representatives of the Council of State Governments and the National Association of Tax Administrators (predecessor to the Federation of Tax Administrators, the professional association of state revenue agency directors and staff). The compact was drafted as a response to the final report of the Willis Committee, a multiyear congressional investigation of state taxation of interstate commerce. In response to complaints by the American business community that nonuniform state tax methods resulted in substantial compliance burdens and double taxation of income, the Willis Committee proposed federal legislation to preempt significant features of state corporate income taxes and retail sales taxes. The compact and the MTC were developed as mechanisms to help states work voluntarily toward greater uniformity in tax policy and administration, as a substitute for federal preemption of what states perceived to be their sovereign power of taxation. The compact went into effect on August 4, 1967, following its adoption by seven state legislatures. Implementation of the compact and vigorous lobbying by the MTC member states forestalled congressional adoption of the Willis Committee recommendations, which were introduced in a variety of bills throughout the 1970s.

The stated purposes of the Multistate Tax Compact are to: (1) facilitate proper determination of state and local tax liability of multistate taxpayers, including the equitable apportionment of tax bases and settlement of apportionment disputes; (2) promote uniformity or compatibility in significant components of tax systems; (3) facilitate taxpayer convenience and compliance in the filing of tax returns and in other phases of tax administration; and (4) avoid duplicative taxation. Implicit in the history surrounding the development of the compact is a fifth purpose: to prevent federal government preemption of state tax practices that otherwise pass constitutional muster (e.g., that do not impermissibly discriminate against interstate commerce).

The MTC engages in a wide variety of activities and programs in furtherance of these goals. Its standing Uniformity Committee develops model regulations, statutes, and policy guidelines to address areas of taxation of interstate commerce for which nonuniformity has been identified as imposing business compliance burdens and/or as providing an opportunity for business tax avoidance. The MTC has been especially active in developing detailed regulations to implement the Uniform Division of Income for Tax Purposes Act (UDITPA), a model law developed in 1957 that provides the basic set of apportionment rules for the division of the corporate income tax base in nearly all states (Multistate Tax Commission 1995). (UDITPA is embodied in the compact itself as Article IV.) Following a public hearing process, the full commission votes on the formal endorsement of uniform regulations and laws developed by the Uniformity Committee. The MTC then seeks to persuade its member states to adopt these uniformity recommendations as their own policy, which may require action by the state legislature or implementation of formal regulation adoption procedures by the tax agency.

As a legal instrumentality of its member states, the MTC has authority to engage in tax enforcement activities. The MTC's Joint Audit Program has a staff of tax auditors who conduct corporate income tax and retail sales and use tax audits of large multistate companies on behalf of a number of states simultaneously. (The validity of the Multistate Tax Compact and the authority of the MTC to conduct audits were upheld by the U.S. Supreme Court in *U.S. Steel Corp. et al.* v. *Multistate Tax Commission,* 434 US 452 [1978].) Simultaneous multistate auditing achieves economies of scale in this vital tax administration function, and it reduces the burdens and disruption imposed on businesses by the need to respond to information requests from numerous auditors. The MTC National Nexus Program engages in a variety of information-sharing, voluntary taxpayer negotiation, and investigation efforts, all aimed at getting on the states' tax rolls businesses that should be, but are not, paying corporate income and/or retail sales and use taxes.

The commission also functions as a policy and legal development "think tank" for state tax agencies. It conducts research, it sponsors conferences, and its staff members frequently speak and publish to apprise state tax officials of how changes in the structure of the economy and business operations require changes in tax policy and tax law (National Conference of State Legislatures 1993). It has been particularly active in encouraging states to develop and update their tax jurisdiction (or nexus) standards in light of the trend toward conducting interstate business via telecommunications and computer linkages. The MTC frequently files amicus curiae briefs in U.S. Supreme Court cases involving cutting-edge state tax issues.

Finally, the commission is the principal organization of state government officials that seeks to protect state and local taxing prerogatives when these are threatened by proposed federal legislation or executive branch actions. For example, in 1994, the MTC was active in seeking to ensure that the Uruguay Round agreements of the General Agreement on Tariffs and Trade (GATT) did not provide foreign corporations with additional mechanisms with which to challenge otherwise constitutional state and local tax practices. The MTC has also long worked for enactment of federal legislation that would overturn the U.S. Supreme Court's 1967 *National Bellas Hess* decision, which prevents states from imposing on many out-of-state mail-order companies a duty to charge sales/use taxes on sales to their residents. Finally, throughout the 1980s, the MTC successfully lobbied against federal legislation that would have prohibited states from using the combined filing method of "unitary taxation." Combined filing is a variant of state corporate income tax apportionment rules that is followed by most MTC member states with such taxes and that is aimed at preventing state tax avoidance through interstate transfer pricing and related tax planning techniques.

As of mid-1995, the MTC had a staff of about 35 (composed of managers, auditors, attorneys, lobbyists, economists, and administrative support personnel) and an annual budget of approximately $3.5 million. It has headquarters in Washington, D.C., and field audit offices in New York City, Chicago, and Houston.

## Additional readings

Multistate Tax Commission. *Model Regulations, Statutes and Guidelines: Uniformity Recommendations to the States*. Washington, D.C.: Multistate Tax Commission, 1995.

National Conference of State Legislatures and National Governors' Association. *Financing State Government in the 1990s*. Denver: National Conference of State Legislatures, 1993.

*Cross references:* apportionment; fiscal federalism; income tax, corporate, state and local; retail sales tax; tax administration: private and public cooperation; unitary taxation.

# N

## National neutrality

Peggy B. Musgrave
University of California, Santa Cruz

*A tax regime in which the country of residence applies its own tax to all investment income of its resident taxpayers, whether earned at home or abroad, but net of foreign taxes (P. Musgrave 1969: 134, 153–54).*

---

The foreign corporation income tax is treated as a cost of doing business abroad and allowed as a deduction from taxable income. The purpose is to provide equal, and therefore neutral, tax treatment to domestic investment income and that part of foreign investment income which may be said to accrue to the country of residency, that is, what is left over after foreign countries of source have taken their tax share. The economic significance of national neutrality is that it promotes a nationally (as distinct from internationally) efficient allocation of investment, where national efficiency is defined as a condition that promotes maximization of the residency country's national output or income (Feldstein and Hartman 1979).

Under the foreign tax regime of residency taxation with foreign tax credit, investors will find it in their interest to invest abroad until the net after-tax returns are equalized at home and abroad. This meets the goal of international efficiency in resource allocation, but not that of national efficiency. The reason is that the foreign tax part of the return on foreign investment does not accrue to the capital-exporting country but is lost. Foreign investment is therefore carried too far (Musgrave and Musgrave 1973: 571–72): The higher the foreign tax, the larger the national loss. This conflict with national efficiency is further magnified where the foreign tax credit regime encourages the capital-importing country to raise its tax in order to soak up the tax of the crediting country.

For national efficiency to be met and the capital-exporting country's national income to be maximized, foreign investment should be carried to the point at which its return net of foreign tax equals the domestic return before tax. The foreign tax is lost to the national income of the capital-exporting country and is dropped out. This is precisely the rule that the investor will follow in his own interest when granted a deduction (not credit) for foreign tax. The system will then no longer distort investment away from the national interest. Tax treatment is rendered neutral with regard to the treatment of national gain from foreign and domestic investment. As under the criterion of international neutrality, this approach requires the capital-exporting country to tax foreign income as earned, without deferral.

The deduction approach thus ranks ahead of the foreign tax credit with regard to national efficiency. It also has the further advantage of simplifying administration and compliance compared with the complexities presented by the foreign tax credit. At the same time, deductibility does not meet the same standard of international efficiency as does the crediting of foreign tax under a system of capital-export neutrality. A choice has to be made since both goals can only be met simultaneously as the foreign tax approaches zero.

### Additional readings

Feldstein, Martin S., and David Hartman. "The Optimal Taxation of Foreign Source Investment Income." *Quarterly Journal of Economics* 93 (November 1979).

Musgrave, Peggy B. *United States Taxation of Foreign Investment Income: Issues and Arguments*. Cambridge, Mass.: International Tax Program, Harvard Law School, 1969.

Musgrave, Richard, and Peggy B. Musgrave. *Public Finance in Theory and Practice*. 5th ed. New York: McGraw-Hill, 1973.

*Cross references:* capital export neutrality; capital import neutrality; foreign tax credit.

## National Tax Association

Frederick Stocker
Professor Emeritus
Ohio State University

*A continuing forum devoted to fostering study and discussion of contrasting viewpoints on issues in tax theory, practice, and policy.*

---

The National Tax Association (NTA) carries out its purposes through a quarterly publication and by sponsoring conferences, symposia, and study committees. Its scope, while emphasizing taxation, covers all of public finance.

The NTA espouses no particular public finance program, policy, or viewpoint, nor does it promote any legislative agenda. As a nonpolitical, nonpartisan scientific and educational organization (under the terms of Section 501(c)(3) of the Internal Revenue Code), the NTA aims to advance understanding of the theory and practice of taxation at all levels of government.

The association's membership is richly diverse, consisting of tax scholars, administrators, tax policy analysts, taxpayer representatives, tax lawyers, and accountants. Membership is open to all.

Membership in 1998 numbered 1,800, divided (except for some 350 libraries) about equally among three groups—academics, government administrators and policy analysts, and private-sector practitioners and tax executives. The bylaws of the association and its traditions call for balance among these three groups on the association's board of directors and in its elected officers.

## History

The NTA was founded in Columbus, Ohio, in 1907 by a group of the nation's leading professors of public finance, tax administrators, and corporate tax representatives. Their main focus was on reform of the "general" (property) tax, under which states sought, with notable lack of success, to apply a uniform (ad valorem) levy on all classes of assets.

Over the years, the topics addressed by the NTA in its annual conferences have broadened, reflecting evolution of the tax system. Income taxation generated considerable debate before and after adoption of the federal income tax in 1913. Corporate taxation and estate and inheritance taxation also received increasing attention. In the 1930s, state sales tax issues became prominent on the conference agenda.

In 1972, the NTA merged with the Tax Institute of America. Since then, the official (though now seldom used) name has been "National Tax Association–Tax Institute of America" (NTA–TIA).

## Publications

The NTA's quarterly publication, the *National Tax Journal*, a refereed journal founded in 1948, is the premier scholarly journal in the field of taxation and public finance. The *Journal* contains articles on public finance theory, application, and policy. While many of the articles are technical in nature, brief nontechnical summaries make essential analysis and conclusions available to a wide audience of those concerned with taxation.

All members receive the *Journal*. In addition, some 1,800 nonmembers, mainly libraries, subscribe. Annual subscription prices range from $50 to $80.

The association's nontechnical quarterly publication, the *NTA Forum*, contains articles of broad interest to all tax professionals, along with news of association activities.

Every year, the association conducts a survey of research in progress on taxation and public finance and publishes a summary, classified by topic. The 1994 report, for example, entitled *Research in Progress on Taxation and Public Finance Topics*, included 283 projects by 166 different researchers. It is distributed free of charge to all NTA members and can be purchased by nonmembers.

The papers presented at the association's annual conference are published in the *Proceedings of the Annual Conference on Taxation*, a fascinating archive of almost a century of American fiscal thought.

## Awards and recognitions

The association presents an annual award for the outstanding dissertation in public finance, along with two honorable mentions. It also recognizes outstanding lifetime contributions to the field through the Daniel M. Holland medal, awarded to Carl S. Shoup (1993), Richard A. Musgrave (1994), George Break (1996), Richard Goode (1997), and C. Lowell Harris (1998).

## Conferences and symposia

The NTA's principal conference is its Annual Conference on Taxation. Over a period of two and a half days, leading experts on taxation address topics of both current and long-term significance including federal, state, local, and international tax issues. The conference is designed to bring out differing views, reflecting the diversity within the association's membership and the best of contemporary thought.

Since 1970, the NTA has sponsored an annual Spring Symposium having a defined tax policy theme. Papers presented at the symposium are published in the September issue of the *National Tax Journal*.

Since 1971, the association, in cooperation with Wichita State University, has conducted an annual week-long workshop on Valuation of Railroad and Public Utility Property for Tax Purposes. This "Wichita Workshop" offers professional education to corporate and state government officials responsible for valuing these specialized properties. The published workshop papers constitute an authoritative body of literature on valuation matters.

In addition to these three regular annual conferences, the NTA sponsors occasional seminars on special topics in public finance (e.g., Critical Issues in Sales Taxation, Taxation of Business Property, Taxation of Financial Services), sometimes in co-sponsorship with other organizations. Most papers given at these seminars are published commercially.

In keeping with its role for providing a neutral, evenhanded forum for learned examination and policy discussion of "cutting edge" issues in public finance, in 1996 the Association established the Communications and Electronic Commerce Tax Project. Project members represent the broad spectrum of business and government interests concerned with the application of state and local taxes and fees to electronic commerce. Within this context the initial focus has been on issues relating to state and local sales and use taxation of communications and electronic commerce, including gross receipts taxes that are functionally equivalent to sales and use taxes.

The purpose of the project is to develop a broadly available public report that identifies and explores the issues involved in applying state and local taxes and fees to electronic commerce. The report is to include model legislation designed to implement project recommendations.

Membership in the NTA is valuable to all tax professionals, whether their interests are theoretical or applied, or their employment public sector or private. (For information, contact natltaxl @aol.com.)

# Nexus

Paull Mines
Multistate Tax Commission

*In order for a government to levy a tax on an activity or entity, the taxing jurisdiction must demonstrate that the event to be taxed has a presence or connection in the jurisdiction. The question of what constitutes a sufficient connection—or taxable nexus—has created considerable economic, legal, and political controversy. Resolving the nexus question is of increasing importance to the states in an era of sales by catalogue/direct mail and electronic commerce.*

## Concepts and issues

### Federal constitutional nexus

Nexus describes whether a taxpayer, property, or activity has sufficient connection with a state to be subject to that state's taxing jurisdiction. The term today principally refers to federal constitutional limitations on state taxing power that emanate from a state's territorial boundaries and the free flow of interstate commerce. The U.S. Constitution's Due Process Clause (minimum contacts and fairness) and Commerce Clause (contracts that ensure there is not an unreasonable burden on multijurisdictional commerce) define the outermost limit of a state's taxing power.

The most relevant discussion of federal constitutional nexus in these evolutionary times focuses on the Commerce Clause. The most impartial observation one can make is that federal constitutional nexus in 1998 is a controversial concept due to its *cliff* nature (nexus exists or not) and the tax consequences of finding nexus after the fact. Nexus issues in sales and use taxes raise a special problem—the potential imposition of a tax where the seller may have previously forgone any opportunity to be made economically whole from its customer. There are numerous unresolved nexus issues under the U.S. Constitution. These issues remain because of the political unwillingness of Congress to provide a bright-line legislative solution and the judicial restraint of the U.S. Supreme Court, which requires a maturation of each category of issue before providing a judicial resolution. All these aspects of nexus create more than the usual amount of tension associated with taxation in general.

### Other forms of nexus

Nexus also may be used to describe limitations in legislative enactments, including federal legislation enacted under the commerce power of Article I of the U.S. Constitution. Chief among these is PL 86-272, 73 STAT 55 (1959), codified at 15 USC § 381 *et seq.*, which restricts the application of a "net income tax" where the taxpayer's connection to the taxing state is limited to certain specified circumstances. States also define by statute the limits of their own taxing power. State-defined legislative limits may be less than what the U.S. Constitution or federal statutes permit but may never exceed these limits.

Nexus also is suggested in the territorial limitation of formula apportionment of multijurisdictional income that is embodied in the U.S. Supreme Court's unitary business rule. This rule prohibits inclusion of business income in the preapportionment tax base of the taxing state unless the income is derived from a unitary business at least part of which is in the taxing state.

## Analysis of nexus

The following is a possible analytical approach for determining nexus. The approach reflects the Multistate Tax Commission's unfinished uniformity project to develop a guideline on the federal constitutional limits on nexus for sales and use taxes and some special income tax nexus issues.

### Use tax collection nexus

Nexus in the sales and use tax context can arise in the imposition of (1) a sales tax, (2) a use tax, and (3) a use tax collection duty on an out-of-state seller. *National Bellas Hess, Inc.* v. *Department of Revenue*, 386 U.S. 753 (1967), and *Quill Corporation* v. *North Dakota*, 504 U.S. 298 (1992), deal only with the third area, although *Quill* suggests that its nexus principle may apply to sales and use taxes in general. *Quill* also reflects a tension between the Court's technical holding and its descriptive language. The technical holding of *Quill* is an affirmation of the safe harbor of *Bellas Hess*—the Commerce Clause prohibits the imposition of a use tax collection duty if the out-of-state seller's only connection to the customers in the taxing state is through a common carrier or the U.S. mail. The U.S. Supreme Court describes this holding as a "physical presence" rule. Because a connection with the taxing state that exceeds the safe harbor would not necessarily constitute physical presence in all cases, there is an unresolved question of whether the Court uses the physical presence term descriptively or substantively. There is at least one way to resolve the tension: When the taxpayer is outside the safe harbor of *Bellas Hess* but not clearly within the physical presence realm, a use tax collection duty may be imposed, provided it does not unreasonably burden interstate commerce.

### Meaning of physical presence

Assuming physical presence is a substantive term, what does it mean? Many practitioners apply their own textual understanding, suggesting, for example, that intangibles could never give rise to a physical presence. A textual understanding of *Quill's* physical presence term raises conceptual difficulty, however. As Professor Richard Pomp and Michael McIntyre have observed, typically, an out-of-state seller as a judicial person is never physically present in a taxing state ("State Taxation of Mail-Order Sales of Computers after *Quill*: An Evaluation of MTC Bulletin 95-1," *State Tax Notes* 11 (1996): 177, 181). Only the *relationship* of this legal fiction we call a corporation to persons, property, or activities in the taxing state supports a finding of physical presence. Therefore, the determination of physical presence should focus on the out-of-state seller's relationship with employees, independent contractors and agents, property, and activities in the taxing state. The analysis should seek to determine (1) whether the relationship has sufficient substance to conclude that the out-of-state seller is for all practical purposes in the taxing state, and (2) if some of these substantive relationships that exceed the safe harbor of *Bellas Hess* are not physical, whether the imposition of a use tax collection duty would result in an unreasonable burden on interstate commerce.

Among the relationships that support a finding of physical presence under the Commerce Clause is the permanent posting of an employee in the taxing state, regardless of the duties assigned. The temporary presence of an employee is more problematical. If the temporary presence is associated with market enhancement activities, the relationship suggests physical presence; if not, then at least some instances (e.g., an executive giving a speech) probably would not constitute physical presence.

Use of independent contractors and agents raises an issue similar to the temporary presence of employees. If independent contractors and agents are engaged in market enhancement activities, including performing repairs to fulfill the out-of-state seller's warranty, that relationship should be sufficient for physical presence. Some business representatives have argued that independent contractors and agents must actually solicit before physical presence occurs. That kind of reading of the U.S. Supreme Court's holdings seems unreasonably narrow. Additionally, using an independent contractor or agent as a substitute for the permanent presence of an employee (e.g., a leased employee who works full time under the control of the out-of-state seller), even though not involved in market enhancement activities, should be treated the same as the permanent presence of an employee in the taxing state.

*Bellas Hess* limited its safe harbor to contact by common carriers and U.S. mail. Extensive use of contract carriers raises the issue of whether an out-of-state seller using such a carrier has a representative in the taxing state engaged in market enhancement activities. To the extent a contract for delivery can properly be characterized as creating a representational relationship, there seems to be no sound reason not to apply the independent contractor and agent rules.

Some type of minimal presence may not support a finding of nexus. This raises the issue of properly stating a de minimis rule. The U.S. Supreme Court has clearly stated that a "slightest presence" will not support the imposition of a use tax collection duty. Additionally, taking a clue from the Supreme Court's view as to PL 86-272, there is a sense that an inadvertent presence that does not reflect a conscious submission to the jurisdiction of the taxing state should also be protected under de minimis. A possible conclusion is that any presence reflecting a business decision to seek the market of the taxing state through a conscious presence is not de minimis. If this is true, then nexus should flow from a physical presence in the form of a very few sales trips into the taxing state for the purpose of fulfilling the business strategy of the out-of-state seller. The Commerce Clause statement of nexus is "substantial nexus," not "substantial physical presence."

## Sales tax nexus

Nexus to impose a sales tax is different from nexus to impose a use tax collection duty. At a minimum, a sales tax may only be imposed by a state in which the sale occurs. See *Evco* v. *Jones*, 409 U.S. 91 (1972). Additionally, it is difficult to question the simple declarative statement that a state may impose its sales and use tax on any sale or use that occurs within the taxing state. See *Oklahoma Tax Commission* v. *Jefferson Lines, Inc.*, 514 U.S. 175 (1995). Yet some argue that jurisdiction does not attach unless the seller is also physically present through means other than the activity of the sale. This counterargument raises the issue of whether a sale or use can occur in a taxing state without the taxpayer thereby having sufficient connection to the txing state for the transaction to be taxed. It is not clear that the counterargument can rely on the physical presence rule of *Quill* because that case, involving the imposition of a use tax collection duty, assumed the out-of-state seller had not sold or used property in the taxing state.

## Constitutional concept of a sale

If the state where a sale occurs may impose a sales tax, the challenge becomes knowing what constitutes a sale in constitutional terms. The best understanding is that a constitutional sale of tangible goods finally occurs after there has been both (1) transfer of title or possession and (2) passage of risk of loss to the purchaser. See *McGoldrick* v. *Berwind-White Co.*, 309 U.S. 33 (1940); L. Tribe, *American Constitutional Law* 447-48 (2d ed. 1988). Sale of a service or intangible property probably occurs after commencement of delivery. See *Oklahoma*. Regardless of one's reaction to these definitions. it is unlikely that the U.S. Supreme Court would view the bare transfer of title as defining a constitutional sale. See *McGoldrick*.

## Income tax nexus

The income tax nexus issue drawing the most attention is whether *Quill*, a use tax collection duty case, also applies to income taxes. There is significant opposition, especially from the financial institutions industry that does not generally enjoy the benefit of PL 86-272, to recognizing nexus based on something other than physical presence or perhaps something even stricter. The case most often cited in this area is *Geoffrey, Inc.* v. *South Carolina Tax Commission*, 437 S.E. 2d 13 (S.C. 1993), *cert. denied*, 510 U.S. 992 (1993), holding that income tax nexus exists over a company that licensed a trademark in the state and derived income therefrom. The failure to accept that income tax nexus can be based on something less than *Quill* is puzzling to some observers. *Quill* itself may suggest that income tax nexus may well

be a lower threshold: "Although in our cases subsequent to *Bellas Hess* and concerning other types of taxes we have not adopted a similar bright-line, physical-presence requirement, our reasoning in those cases does not compel that we now reject the rule that *Bellas Hess* established in the area of sales and use taxes" (504 U.S. at 317).

For those who argue that a relationship with intangibles cannot establish physical presence, *International Harvester Co.* v. *Wisconsin Department of Taxation*, 322 U.S. 435 (1944), is disquieting. In that case, the Court upheld under a due process challenge a dividends-paid withholding tax against nonresident shareholders. See also *Whitney* v. *Graves*, 299 U.S. 366 (1937). While some argue that due process nexus cases are irrelevant after *Quill*, it is difficult to accept that position when the Court reviewed its earlier due process cases in *Quill* to secure an understanding as to its physical presence concept. In addition, the Court in *Quill* does not suggest that it is adopting anything new. And the administrative burden issue, a strong factor in *Quill*, is quite different for income taxes than for use tax collection. The number of income taxing jurisdictions is exponentially less, and there is more uniformity in income taxes. Further, the taxpayer is paying its own tax and not acting as a collection agent for the state. Therefore, if the taxpayer is wrong in its nexus determination, it pays its own tax and not its customer's tax.

Regardless of whether an income tax nexus standard is ultimately found to be less stringent, arguments that it is more stringent than *Quill* seem misplaced. But in one sense the nexus burden of imposing an income tax is different. The difference takes the form of the unitary business principle described above. There is no unitary business connection requirement for sales and use taxes because a sale or use must occur in the taxing state in order to be taxed. A more accurate description of the nexus requirements of a sales and use tax and an income tax is that they are different, because a sales tax is a transactional tax and the income tax is an operational tax.

# Nonprofit organizations, federal tax treatment

Terry Knoepfle
Karen Froelich
North Dakota State University

*Organizations that engage in charitable and other activities that are deemed to be socially meritorious may be exempt from certain taxes.*

Recent changes to the federal tax laws and related changes in the financial accounting standards applied to tax-exempt organizations will permit greater public scrutiny of the activities of public charities, but also give charities the opportunity to position themselves better in the public eye.

Internal Revenue Code Section 501 exempts dozens of different types of organizations from federal income taxation, including those formed and operated for charitable, religious, scientific, literary, or educational purposes, and those formed to engage in testing for public safety or preventing cruelty to animals or children [IRC §501(c)(3); Treas. Reg. §§ 1.501(a)-(1), 1.501(c)(3)-1(d)(1)]. The criteria for exemption under § 501(c)(3) are that (1) the organization is organized and operated exclusively for exempt purposes as defined by the Internal Revenue Code and regulations; (2) no part of the organization's net earnings inures or will inure to the benefit of any private shareholder or individual; and (3) the organization does not engage in activities a substantial part of which consist of carrying on propaganda or otherwise attempting to influence legislation, or of participating or intervening in any candidate's political campaign for office [IRC § 501(c)(3); Treas. Reg. § 1.501(c)(3)-1].

The Internal Revenue Code authorizes deductions for contributors to an organization that meets the criteria for exemption [IRC §§ 107(c)(2) (income tax), 2522(a)(2) (gift tax), 2055(a)(2) (estate tax)]. Unless expressly excused from making the disclosure, a tax-exempt organization must specifically disclose to contributors what part of their contributions are or are not tax-deductible [IRC §§ 170(c), 6113].

A private foundation may not claim exempt status, and all organizations are presumed to be private foundations until they establish that they are not (IRC § 508). Private foundations, as described in Code Section 509, rely on a narrow group of contributors for revenues and therefore are assumed to serve those contributors' private needs. In contrast, nonprivate foundations, also known as public charities, receive more than one-third of their revenues from public or governmental contributions. An organization meeting Code Section 501(c)(3)'s criteria (plus specific organizations enumerated elsewhere in Section 501) may be variously referred to as a "not-for-profit," "nonprofit," "exempt organization," "public charity," or "nonbusiness" organization.

An organization seeking tax-exempt status must apply for the exemption and submit and establish proof of its exempt character [Treas. Reg. § 1.501(a)-1; Form 1023 (Application for Recognition of Exemption under Section 501(c)(3))]. The application and the documents supporting it are open to public inspection [Internal Revenue Service (IRS) Notice 92-28, 1992-1 C.B515 (June 22, 1992)].

Once an organization has been granted exempt status, it maintains this status unless its circumstances change substantially. Many organizations establish their continuing right to exempt status by filing an annual information return, usually Form 990 [IRC § 6033; Treas. Reg. §§ 1.501(a)-1(d), 1.6033-1]. About 30 percent of exempt organizations must make this annual filing. Only religious organizations, organizations with gross receipts of not more than $25,000 in each tax year, and certain other specified organizations are excused from filing. The filing, as discussed below, must be made available to the public upon request.

If an organization's revenues inure to or benefit private individuals or shareholders, it loses its exempt status [Treas. Reg. § 1.501(c)(3)-1(c)(2)]. To stay tax-exempt, an organization must irrevocably and consistently dedicate its earnings and profits to its exempt purpose.

The private instrument or "excess benefits transaction" rule is applicable when the economic benefit provided by an exempt organization to a key employee or other "disqualified person" exceeds ordinary and necessary expenses as determined by the general fair market value (IRC §§ 162, 4858). Examples of prohibited transactions include compensation to an individual that is unreasonable in relation to the services performed, the payment of most forms of revenue-based incentive compensation, the payment of rentals or interest to such individuals at higher-than-market rates, and the payment of above-market prices for assets purchased from such individuals.

"Disqualified persons" include all persons in a position to exercise substantial influence over the organization's affairs, such as officers, key employees, large donors, their relatives, and entities 35 percent controlled by one of these persons [IRC § 4958(f)]. Sanctions available against these persons were recently increased by the 1996 Taxpayer Bill of Rights 2, in response to recent highly publicized scandals involving the misuse of assets by the United Way and other well-known exempt organizations [IRC § 4958; Taxpayer Bill of Rights 2, PL 104-168 (adopted July 30, 1996, and effective for transactions on and after September 14, 1995)].

Disqualified persons who are found to improperly benefit from an excess benefits transaction with an exempt organization, and managers within the organization who have abetted them, each now must pay a heavy excise tax (25% for the disqualified person; 10% for the abetters) in addition to any income tax owed on the income. The disqualified person must also disgorge the improper benefit: If the excess benefit is not repaid within a specified time, then the disqualified person is subject to an additional excise tax of 200 percent of the benefit received. This two-tiered set of excise taxes is referred to as "intermediate sanctions," because they fall short of the severe penalty of revoking an organization's tax-exempt status.

The 1996 changes allow the Commissioner of Internal Revenue to impose the heavy, two-tier excise taxes and other sanctions on both the private individuals who benefited by an improper transaction and the officers and managers who allowed the organization's assets to be misused, without having to also resort to the harsh sanction of revoking the organization's exempt status. This gives the commissioner the flexibility to correct misuse of an organization's assets by a few individuals, without having to attack the status of an organization that on the whole is properly functioning as an exempt organization.

The 1996 changes also include tighter overall reporting requirements for exempt organizations. An exempt organization that has experienced excess benefits transactions must report, on Form 990, the nature of those transactions, the names of all individuals involved, and the excise taxes. The commissioner may require further disclosures by the disqualified persons (IRC § 4958).

An organization may operate a trade or business that primarily furthers its exempt purposes and still maintain its exempt status [Treas. Reg. § 1.50(c)(3)-1(e)]. It may also own a taxable subsidiary without itself becoming taxable [Priv. Ltr. Rul. 9519057 (February 16, 1995)]. However, an exempt organization may be taxed on income from business enterprises not related to the purpose that supports its tax exemption. This is the "unrelated business income tax," or "UBIT," which applies to gross income, after deductions, derived from (1) the operation of a business enterprise unrelated to the organization's exempt purpose, and (2) rentals of property leased to others if the organization is carrying any indebtedness on the property related to its purchase, acquisition, or improvement. UBIT does not include activities in which the work is performed by volunteers or for the members' convenience, sales of donated merchandise, qualified public entertainment activities, some forms of passive income, or certain other specified activities [IRC §§ 501(b), 511–515]. UBIT activities must be separately reported on Form 990-T.

Similarly, the revenues of a "feeder" organization operated by an exempt organization primarily as a trade or business are taxable even if its profits are payable to the tax-exempt organization [IRC § 502; Treas. Reg. 1.50(a)-1]. On the other hand, a corporation's revenues are tax-exempt if its exclusive purpose is to hold property, collect the income from it, and turn over the entire net after expenses to another exempt organization [IRC §§ 501(c)(2), 503; Treas. Reg. §§ 1.50 (a)-1, 1.50(c)(2)-1].

The Internal Revenue Code tightly restricts lobbying and political contributions by exempt organizations. The code contains several complex definitions of lobbying activities that are subject to different regulatory schemes, making compliance difficult to maintain.

Generally speaking, a Section 501(c)(3) exempt organization will lose its tax-exempt status or be subjected to an excise tax if it participates or intervenes in any individual candidate's political campaign, or if a substantial part of its activities consist of lobbying efforts to influence legislation [IRC § 501(h); Treas. Reg. 1.50(h)-1]. For instance, a bar association that rated judicial candidates lost its tax-exempt status as a charitable and educational organization [*Association of the Bar of the City of New York*, 858 F.2d 876 (2d Cir. 1988), *cert. denied*, 109 S.Ct. 1768 (1989)]. An organization that engages in such activities is considered an "action organization" [IRC § 501(c)(3); Treas. Reg. 1.50(c)(3)-1(c)(3)].

However, a public charity qualifying under § 501(c)(3) may make an election that allows it to make limited and "grass roots" lobbying expenditures [Form 5768 (Election for Lobbying Expenditures)]. The election allows an organization to make expenditures for lobbying within specified dollar limits, with any excess expenditures being subjected to a 25 percent excise tax [IRC §§ 501(h)(4), 491(c); Treas. Reg. § 1.50(h)-1 to -2]. If an organization persistently has excess expenditures from year to year, it loses the protection of this election [Treas. Reg. § 1-501(h)-3].

The federal tax-exempt status enjoyed by exempt organizations has implications beyond exemption from payment of taxes. Form 990, the annual information return, is a major source of financial information about the activities of exempt organizations. Members of the public, press, and regulatory agencies increasingly scrutinize Form 990s, together with an organization's annual reports and financial statements, for purposes of analyzing the organization's use of financial resources. They may look especially hard at the information on Form 990 reporting executive compensation, and at the figures showing the percentage of expenditures used to directly promote exempt purposes of the organization compared with its administrative expenses. Because of this scrutiny, Form 990s are also becoming a tool for organizations to present favorable program-related information to potential donors and other interested persons.

IRS Form 990 is a public document. Recent changes in the tax laws were designed to make Form 990 widely available. In the past, an exempt organization was merely required to keep a copy of its Form 990 available for inspection at its main offices. Now, an exempt organization must proactively make its information returns available to the public [IRC § 6104(e)(1)A; Taxpayer Bill of Rights 2, PL 104-168]. Public access to Form 990 is likely to expand again in the near future as proposed Internet access becomes a reality.

Starting in 1997, an exempt organization must mail its three most recent Form 990s to anyone who requests them. Requests made by mail must be fulfilled within 30 days. The organization may charge reasonable copying fees and postage. Its Form 990 must also be immediately available to anyone who requests it at the organization's main business offices during regular business hours and at every office where the organization has three or more employees. "Availability" includes copying of the return and providing copies of related documents, such as the organization's Form 1023 if requested.

There are penalties for providing incomplete information or failing to provide copies of Form 990 upon request, including a $20 per day fine, up to $10,000 or 5 percent of the organization's gross receipts, with higher rates imposed on organizations with gross receipts in excess of $1 million ($100 per day and $50,000 maximum).

One of the most significant changes in exempt-organization law in 1996 was the revision of Form 990 to reflect changes in financial accounting standards, in particular the changes made by the new Statement of Financial Accounting Standards 116 (Accounting for Contributions Received and Contributions Made) and 117 (Financial Statements of Not-for-Profit Organizations), which resulted in changes to Part IV of Form 990 (balance sheets), and the addition of new Parts IV-A (reconciliation of revenue per audited financial statements with revenue per return) and IV-B (reconciliation of expenses per audited financial statements with expenses per return).

Balance sheets must now be filed with an organization's Form 990 and reconciled with the figures contained therein. Form 990 must include a complete listing of officers, directors, managers, and other highly compensated employees and the compensation paid to each, and report excess benefits transaction information.

The coordination of Form 990 with the financial documents required by the new accounting standards is less than perfect. Form 990 distorts some financial data that may be more accurately presented on the organization's annual financial statements. Reporting under revenue categories such as government funding and program service fees seems particularly prone to distortion. Other areas where discrepancies arise between Form 990 and audited financial statements are total revenues, gross profits from sales, unrealized gains and losses on investments, treatment of donated services and use of facilities, total program expenses, and total salaries and wages. Thus, preparation of Form 990 in light of the new financial accounting standards, so that both present a consistent and accurate picture of financial status, is likely to be an ongoing challenge for exempt organizations.

Another challenge is presented by the increase in IRS audits of exempt organizations. Among the issues being raised in these audits are: lobbying and political contributions by exempt organizations, inurements and private benefits resulting from extraordinary compensation arrangements and excessive executive compensation, the relationships between exempt organizations and related for-profit entities, various unrelated business income tax issues such as failure to report advertising income and the treatment of associate member dues, and the improper structuring of mailing list rentals [recently addressed by the Ninth Circuit in *Sierra Club Inc.* v. *C.I.R.*, 86 F 3d 1526 (9th Cir. 1996)].

## Additional readings

Froelich, Karen A., and Terry W. Knoepfle. "Internal Revenue Service 990 Data: Fact or Fiction?" *Nonprofit and Voluntary Sector Quarterly* (March 1996): 40–52.

Hodgkinson, Virginia A., Murray S. Weitzman, Stephen M. Noga, and Heather A. Gorski. *A Portrait of the Independent Sector: The Activities and Finances of Charitable Organizations*. Washington, D.C.: Independent Sector, 1993.

Monk, Harold J., Brenda Cline, Winford Paschall, Stephen Eason, Marilyn Patterson, and Martha Benson. *Guide to Preparing Nonprofit Financial Statements*. 3rd ed., ch. 1, 4, 5. Fort Worth, Tex.: Practitioners Publishing Company, 1996.

New York University. "Tax Exempt Organizations." *Proceedings of the Fifty-Fourth Institute on Federal Taxation* (1996) § 25.08, 2, 25-144-15-154.

Steinberg, Richard. "Nonprofit Organizations and the Market." In *The Nonprofit Sector: A Research Handbook*, edited by Walter W. Powell. New Haven: Yale University Press, 1987.

*Cross reference:* nonprofit organizations, state tax treatment.

# Nonprofit organizations, state tax treatment

John Mikesell
Indiana University

*Relief from sales and use, property, and corporate income taxes that state and local governments provide for private charitable, religious, and educational nonprofit organizations.*

A number of private charitable, religious, and educational organizations provide services—hospital operation and health-care delivery, assistance for the at-risk young and old, education and training, sponsorship of cultural events, aid to the poor, and so on—that would almost certainly become a state or local responsibility if not provided by a nonprofit organization. Several states also exempt hospitals, regardless of owner. Hence, revenue sacrifice may be justified as a way to encourage service provision without direct government involvement. The non-profit organization may also provide a quality stan-dard against which for-profit providers may be tested.

Nonprofit organizations fall into two groups. The older, philanthropic sector includes entities op-erating on donations, either from endowments (past gifts) or current gifts; sales income contributes a minor part of their finances. Commercial nonprofit organizations, now about two-thirds of all nonprofit organizations, receive virtually all of their income from sales. Despite different financing, these two types of organizations share the basic distinction from proprietary firms: "No one owns the right to share in any profit or surplus of a nonprofit" (Weis-brod 1988: 14).

State and local tax policy toward these organi-zations is inconsistent, partly because governments have not fully adjusted to the commercial nonprofit sector, but partly because of "a larger debate on the appropriate roles for private, nonprofit, and public organizations—a debate about privatization that af-fects many industries all over the world" (Herzlinger and Krasker 1987: 93). Governments often encour-age nongovernmental responses to social problems because they may be less bureaucratic and more sensitive to public wants. At the same time, those governments want to avoid unfair competition be-tween nonprofit and proprietary providers. State and local tax systems have to balance the desire to encourage the nonprofit spirit and to use these or-ganizations to relieve governmental service demands against the concern about unfair competition, es-pecially as higher tax rates increase the advantage from exemption.

## Sales and use taxation

Simple generalizations about how sales and use taxes treat nonprofit organizations, as sellers or as buyers, are impossible, either across states or by type of nonprofit organization. Many nonprofit or-ganizations provide services that are not taxed, re-gardless of seller, but some services are taxed, and nonprofit organizations sell some goods. Sales may be of (1) the core good or service, such as the ser-vices of a nonprofit hospital; (2) a good or service related to the core, such as prints in an art museum shop; or (3) an unrelated good or service sold as a fund-raiser, such as Girl Scout cookies. State policy has been more directed toward the third category,

although the first two are more important for the commercial nonprofit sector.

States traditionally exempt at least some non-profit organizations, especially charitable, religious, and educational institutions, (1) on casual sales; (2) on sales during periodic fund-raising events like fish fries, bean suppers, and similar regional favorites; and (3) on sales of seasonal fund-raising items. (The entity may, however, be taxed on the purchase of supplies for these sales or of merchandise sold, or may need special registration for tax-exempt pur-chase. Some states have experienced political grief when, as they extended sales taxes to include "snack food," they found they had taxed Girl Scout cook-ies.) To provide no sales exemption at all is the ex-ception. Many states extend the normal casual sales exemption with, for instance, a maximum number of days for the sales event, a ceiling on the price of items sold, or limits on total sales. Some states, including Arizona, Nevada, Missouri, and Vermont, exempt all sales by such entities. [*Swaggart Minis-tries* v. *California Board of Equalization* (110 S. Ct. 688) removed the concern that uniform and neutral application of the tax when the seller was a religious organization and the items were religious in nature might be constitutionally prohibited.] A few states make exemption dependent on how proceeds are used—for example, if profits benefit schools or stu-dents—or on whether the organization competes with private business.

Nonprofit organizations purchase many taxable items, and no state provides them a global exemp-tion. However, only California, Hawaii, Louisiana, South Carolina, and Washington provide no exemp-tion for charitable, religious, or educational insti-tutions or hospitals, the entities most often provided preferential treatment, and some specific organiza-tions in even these states have purchase exemptions. About 20 states exempt purchases by virtually all those nonprofit organizations, mostly through ex-emption certificates. The major difference among them is whether the entity determines its own eli-gibility or whether there is a formal application pro-cess. Somewhat more than a dozen states exempt some but not all of the charitable-religious-educational group, either by establishing the gen-eral classification that will be exempt (e.g., youth organizations) or by identifying an extensive list of entities that will be exempt (e.g., the Arkansas Poets Roundtable). There is little uniformity in the extent to which exempt entities may pass their ex-emption to contractors working for them (Healy and Klemm 1990: 336–339).

## Property taxation

All states exempt property held by some nonprofit organizations. Governments often require that these properties be assessed, but few assessment officials attempt a serious valuation, preferring to devote their resources to tax-yielding properties. These exemptions, in common with those for sales and income taxes, are virtually always provided by state action, even though any property tax lost is predominantly from local government, in contrast with the other taxes. That can be a considerable policy problem, because the fiscal impact is not equally distributed across the state (Pfister 1976). Some universities make payments in lieu of taxes, but no uniform systems relieve local fiscal burdens, and voluntary payments are both rare and seldom seen by recipients as fully adequate.

Most states require that property be used primarily for an exempt purpose and that it benefit an indefinite nonexclusive class (Wellford and Gallagher 1988: 123). Some states permit considerable nonexempt use of the property, but most constrain commercial activities on the property. One exception is Kentucky, which exempts property owned by the nonprofit organization without regard to use. The struggle to delimit exempt from taxable use is difficult, and there are few clear standards. Tensions are particularly great in operations of auxiliary enterprises and housing by educational institutions, although exemptions provided fraternal organizations in some states cause similar problems. Most states have specific application procedures before the exemption can be granted; about half also require regular renewal (Balk 1971: 165). Whether fees are associated with use of the exempt property is usually not relevant, although some states do limit fees to the cost of service or require some waiver for those unable to pay. No general standard for nonprofit organization exemption extends across property, sales, and corporate income tax laws, but property tax rules are the most independent of all.

## Income taxation

To receive exemption from corporate income tax, the nonprofit organization may not distribute any profits to those in control of the organization. It is not required to be zero profit, but it must devote any return to its primary exempt purpose. Other conditions are not so simple. A nonprofit organization may earn (1) income from gifts and investment of its resources, (2) income from activities related to its primary exempt purpose, and (3) income from unrelated business activity. Following the federal system, states and their local governments do not tax qualified nonprofit organizations on their income from gifts or investment of endowment, and they do not tax income from the primary exempt purpose, assuming those incomes are used in an appropriate fashion. Income from activities not related to the purpose for which the organization was granted tax-exempt status—that is, not for the charitable or mutual benefit purposes of the or-

ganization—is taxed as "unrelated business income." Many nonprofit organizations use unrelated business activity to provide resources to subsidize their charitable activities. It is the activity, however, not how the profits are used or the status of the operating organization, that determines whether the profits will be taxed. Dividing organization operations between exempt and unrelated has proven administratively difficult.

## Problems

Are the services provided by the nonprofit organization worth the lost tax revenue and does the nonprofit receive an unfair competitive advantage over proprietary firms? Several argue that the property exemption permits uneconomic holdings of real property, especially by religious and educational institutions (Balk 1971; Pfister 1976). The strongest empirical evidence comes from the hospital industry, where government, proprietary, and nonprofit firms all operate, For instance, recent evidence shows the state market share of nonprofit hospitals to be greater where exemption from state corporate income and local property taxes is more valuable—that is, where the tax rates are higher (Gulley and Santerre 1993: 485). This is the clearest direct evidence to date that state and local tax exemptions make a competitive difference. If the commercial nonprofit sector continues its expected growth, state and local governments will find exemption systems established for the charitable nonprofit to be ever more strained by the commercial nonprofit sector.

## Additional readings

Balk, Alfred. *The Free List Property without Taxes*. New York: Russell Sage Foundation, 1971.

Bennett, James, and Gabriel Rudney. "A Commerciality Test to Resolve Commercial Nonprofit Issues." *Tax Notes*, September 1987.

Gulley, O. David, and Rexford E. Santerre. "The Effect of Tax Exemption on the Market Share of Nonprofit Hospitals." *National Tax Journal* 46 (December 1993): 477–86.

Healy, John C., and Kenneth D. Klemm. "Sales and Use Tax Implications for Construction Contractors." *Journal of State Taxation* 8 (4) (1990): 315–40.

Herzlinger, Regina E., and William S. Krasker. "Who Profits from Nonprofit?" *Harvard Business Review* 87 (January–February 1987).

McDermott, Richard E., Gary C. Cornia, and Eugene Beck. "Property Tax Exemption for Nonprofit Hospitals." *Hospital and Health Services Administration* 34 (Winter 1989): 493–506.

Mikesell, John L. "Sales Taxation of Nonprofit Organization Purchases and Sales." In *Sales Taxation, Critical*

*Issues in Policy and Administration*, edited by William F. Fox. Westport, Conn: Praeger, 1992.

Pfister, Richard L. "A Reevaluation of the Justification for the Property Tax Exemption." *Public Finance Quarterly* 4 (October 1976): 431–52.

Steinberg, Richard. "'Unfair' Competition by Nonprofits and Tax Policy." *National Tax Journal* 44 (September 1991): 351–64.

Weisbrod, Burton A. *The Nonprofit Economy*. Cambridge, Mass.: Harvard University Press, 1988.

Wellford, W. Harrison, and Janne G. Gallagher. *Unfair Competition? The Challenge to Charitable Tax Exemption*. Washington, D.C.: National Assembly of National Voluntary Health and Social Welfare Organizations, 1988.

Zimmerman, Dennis. "Nonprofit Organizations, Social Benefits, and Tax Policy." *National Tax Journal* 44 (September 1991): 341–49.

*Cross references:* income tax, corporate, state and local; nonprofit organizations, federal tax treatment; property tax, real property, business; retail sales tax.

# O

# Office of Tax Policy

Lowell Dworin
Department of the Treasury

*Office in the Treasury Department charged
with providing advice and analysis on matters
of tax policy.*

The Treasury Department's Office of Tax Policy
(OTP) provides the Secretary of the Treasury and
other senior administration officials with advice and
analysis on matters of tax policy, including legislative proposals for changes in tax policy, and estimates of the revenue and distributional implications
of the proposed policy changes. The office is also
responsible for estimates of future federal tax receipts and tax expenditures used in the Federal
Budget, for the negotiation of bilateral tax treaties,
and for the promulgation of Treasury regulations
and revenue rulings and procedures (these latter
two responsibilities are shared with the Internal
Revenue Service).

In the early 1960s, the tax policy and research
functions at Treasury were brought together under
an Assistant Secretary for Tax Policy. Stanley Surrey
was the first person to be named to that position.
The economists who had worked in the previously
established Office of Tax Research became members of the Office of Tax Analysis (OTA), reporting
to the Deputy Assistant Secretary for Tax Analysis.
About 10 years later, a second Deputy Assistant
Secretary (for policy analysis) was appointed to supervise the attorneys working in the OTP. Currently,
the OTP contains about 100 economists, attorneys,
and support staff, with the attorneys organized into
offices of the International Tax Counsel (primarily
responsible for international tax issues), the Benefits Tax Counsel (primarily responsible for pension
and similar compensation-related issues), and the
Tax Legislative Counsel (primarily responsible for
all other tax issues).

In recent years, almost all major economic initiatives of both the executive branch and Congress
have included a tax component. In addition, because of their potential impact on tax revenues, the
OTP's work derives not merely from tax initiatives,
but from almost all major policy changes affecting
health care, pensions, welfare, labor, education,
housing, financial institutions, the environment, energy, and other areas of national interest. In the past

few years, the OTP has prepared major studies on
a wide range of topics, including the study that culminated in the historic Tax Reform Act of 1986, and
studies on health and long-term care, insurance,
pensions, financial institutions, partnerships, integration of the corporate and individual tax systems,
and other topics. The OTP also publishes a staff
working paper series, and compilations of staff research in its periodic Compendia of Tax Research.

As senior advisor on tax policy to the Treasury
secretary, the Assistant Secretary for Tax Policy is
often called upon to testify before Congress, and to
respond to communications from the congressional
tax-writing and budget committees, other government agencies, individual members of Congress,
foreign governments, and the public. The OTP has
traditionally sought to represent the interests of the
general public, and in that role it often finds itself
in opposition to proposals that seek to benefit more
narrow interests.

In addition to its legislative responsibilities, the
OTP works closely with the Internal Revenue Service (IRS) to provide taxpayers with regulatory
guidance. Since 1992 it has published a business plan
that typically calls for the completion each year of
more than 100 Treasury regulations and a comparable number of revenue rulings and procedures.
The economists in the OTP are also responsible for
the preparation of hundreds of estimates of the revenue consequences of proposals advanced by both
the administration and the senior members of the
tax-writing committees of Congress, for the official
estimates of federal receipts and tax expenditures
appearing in the president's budget (as well as interim budget revisions), and for determination of
the revenues to be transferred to various trust funds.
The OTP staff also provides monthly receipts forecasts for the Office of the Fiscal Assistant Secretary
for use in forecasting government borrowing needs.

The OTP staff, who are organized into five divisions (Business Tax, Individual Tax, International
Tax, Revenue Estimating, and Economic Modeling
and Computer Applications), assemble statistical
and analytical materials to support policy recommendations. To do this, the staff develop and maintain major simulation models for analyzing the
economic, distributional, and revenue effects of alternative tax proposals and tax systems. Most of the
models use large microdata files from individual and
corporate income tax returns and other databases.
The OTP also oversees the Statistics of Income studies conducted by the IRS to extract data from samples of tax returns for use in the models.

The OTP has been unusually successful in concluding bilateral income tax treaties with other governments. It has also engaged in negotiating multilateral tax and trade agreements and participates in numerous international conferences and meetings. It works with other federal agencies (such as the Pension Benefit Guarantee Corporation) to develop and refine policies that have broad social implications.

*Cross references:* Finance Committee, U.S. Senate; Joint Committee on Taxation, U.S. Congress; Ways and Means Committee.

# Offsetting collections

Pearl Richardson
Congressional Budget Office

*Funds credited against federal budget outlays (expenditures).*

Apart from the proceeds of borrowing, all collections flowing from the public to the federal government are classified in the budget as either offsets against outlays or governmental receipts (also known as "budget receipts" and as "federal revenues"). Offsetting collections include loan repayments, interest, miscellaneous recoveries and refunds, and a wide variety of fees. Governmental receipts generally consist of taxes, customs duties, and miscellaneous collections, including penalties and some fees. The general guidelines for assigning collections to the revenue or spending side of the budget are relatively straightforward (see below), but the terms are confusing and likely to vary with the user.

Offsetting collections show up in the budget as either reimbursements to appropriations or offsetting receipts.

## Reimbursements to appropriations

In some cases, the law specifies that a collection be offset within an expenditure account. Such collections are "reimbursements to appropriations." Reimbursements to appropriations are deposited as credits to the expenditure accounts that they finance and, in many cases, may be spent without further action by Congress. For example, under current law, the Postal Service may use collections from the sale of stamps to finance its operations without a requirement for annual appropriations. Depending on whether the funds originate from within or outside the government, budget documents identify reim-

bursements to appropriations as "offsetting collections from federal sources" (which includes trust and off-budget funds) or as "offsetting collections from nonfederal sources." Reimbursements to appropriations are frequently referred to simply as "offsetting collections," thus creating a confusion of terms.

## Offsetting receipts

If the law does not specify that a collection be assigned to an expenditure account, it will go into a receipt account and be classified as an offset to budget outlays, not as a governmental receipt. Such collections are entitled "offsetting receipts," and if they come from outside the government, they are called "proprietary receipts from the public." Offsetting receipts, including proprietary receipts from the public, appear in the budget as negative outlays.

In brief, where a provision of law authorizes the offset to occur within an expenditure account, the collections are reimbursements to appropriations. All other offsetting collections are called offsetting receipts. Otherwise, there is no real difference between reimbursements to appropriations and offsetting receipts.

## Budget classification guidelines

In 1967, a commission appointed by President Lyndon Johnson recommended guidelines on budget concepts, including the classification for budgetary purposes of funds flowing to the federal government. Among its many other recommendations were several dealing with when to offset collections against expenditures, and when to record them as governmental or budget receipts.

At the time the commission issued its report, the classification of a collection depended entirely upon provisions of law. Over the years, the classification of items had become inconsistent. To remedy the problem, the commission suggested that the nature of a collection should determine its classification. It recommended that collections associated with activities that operated as business-type enterprises or were market-oriented should be included as offsets to related expenditures. But collections from activities that were essentially governmental in character, involving regulation or compulsion, should be reported as receipts.

The commission distinguished between fees imposed for the primary purpose of channeling the private demand for, and use of, valuable resources or materials that happened to be owned by the government and taxes designed to raise revenues for the government or charges associated with the government's regulatory activities. The basis for the distinction was the commission's conviction that budget receipts should reflect the activities in which the government engages by virtue of its powers as a sovereign state.

In examining federal collections, the commission identified the following types as basically governmental in character and recommended that they be treated as budget receipts: income, excise, franchise, and employment taxes; customs receipts; social insurance premiums (the commission recommended classifying those social insurance collections arising from the government's sovereign powers as budget receipts and those arising from noncompulsory insurance activities as offsetting collections); payments of excess earnings of the Federal Reserve system to the Treasury; gifts and contributions; patent and copyright fees; judiciary fees; immigration, passport, and consular fees; and registration and filing fees associated with regulatory activities.

The commission recommended that the following types of collections be treated as offsets to expenditures: repayments of loans and advances; receipts of government enterprises and enterprise funds; charges for permits; hunting and grazing licenses and fees; interest, dividends, rents, and royalties; sales of products; sales of government property; and fees and charges for services and benefits of a voluntary character.

The commission's recommendations were applied administratively (by presidential direction) beginning with the budget for 1969. Thereafter, in principle, all collections except those arising from the sovereign powers of government were offset against outlays.

In practice, the commission's recommendations have generally served as a guide—at least to the extent that business-type fees are offsets against outlays and taxes are always budget receipts. Although the commission's guidelines remain in force today, provisions of law or administrative decisions are increasingly likely to intervene and lead to budget classifications that depart from the guidelines. Provisions of law always take precedence over guidelines.

### Current practice

Since the mid-1980s, the dominant trend in budget classification has been to offset as many collections as possible against outlays, regardless of their nature. Thus, many collections that, based on the recommendations of the President's Commission on Budget Concepts, would be governmental receipts are now offsets against outlays. These collections consist primarily of compulsory fees for regulatory activities (see User charges, federal).

In the 1990s, legislation to reduce the deficit—in particular the Budget Enforcement Act of 1990—and rules within Congress governing the budget process have provided further incentives to levy fees and offset them against outlays. Increases in offsetting receipts or collections count as reductions in spending and thus provide a means for complying with spending limits or meeting budget reconciliation targets. In consequence, user charges have grown, and the practice of levying charges that may be similar to taxes and offsetting them against outlays has become increasingly common. The only measures that are exempt are provisions that actually amend the Internal Revenue Code, levy duties, or assess fines and penalties.

The Office of Management and Budget (OMB) has acknowledged the practice by describing some collections as "offsetting governmental collections" and others as "offsetting governmental receipts." In line with the recommendations of the Commission on Budget Concepts, OMB distinguishes between governmental receipts, which are collections from the public that result from the exercise of the sovereign powers of the government, and offsetting collections, which are derived from business-type transactions.

*Cross reference:* user charges, federal.

# Optimal taxation
## William M. Gentry
Columbia University

*A set of normative prescriptions for tax policy usually based on maximizing social welfare for a given revenue requirement.*

---

Optimal tax theory addresses such questions as: Should the government use income or commodity taxes? Within commodity taxes, how should tax rates vary across commodities? How progressive should the tax system be?

Optimal tax theory encompasses a range of models that focus on particular aspects of the tax system. These different models share three features. First, each model specifies a set of feasible taxes for the government, such as commodity taxes, and the government's revenue needs. The models typically rule out lump-sum taxes, which would cause no economic distortion. Second, each model specifies how individuals and firms respond to taxes. That is, individuals have preferences about goods and leisure; firms have a given technology for producing goods; and individuals and firms interact in a given market structure (often perfect competition). Third, the government has an objective function for evaluating different configurations of taxes. In the simplest models, the government's objective is to minimize the excess burden generated by the tax system while raising a set amount of revenue. The more complicated models balance efficiency considerations with equity concerns. The models that include equity are usually more concerned with vertical equity rather than either horizontal equity or the benefit principle.

One of the oldest strands of the optimal tax literature is the optimal configuration of commodity tax rates. The basic question is whether uniform commodity tax rates—taxing all goods and services at the same rate—are optimal. This problem is commonly referred to as the Ramsey problem after the solution proposed by Frank Ramsey in his 1927 article. The short answer is that, abstracting from the collection costs of administering differentiated tax rates, uniform commodity taxes are rarely optimal.

The simplest version of the Ramsey problem is a static model (i.e., a one-period model without saving) with a representative consumer (alternatively, the model could have many consumers with the same demand functions). The government's objective is to raise a given amount of revenue while minimizing the distortions (excess burden) created by the tax system. This formulation minimizes economic distortion without concern for the fairness of the tax system. The feasible set of taxes includes flat rate taxes on different goods and services but excludes taxes on wage income. Uniform commodity taxes have the appeal of raising all prices by the same magnitude, and thus not distorting the relative prices of different goods. This simple intuition has two problems. First, it ignores the fact that commodity taxes cannot directly tax one especially important good: leisure. Second, it implicitly assumes that supply curves are perfectly elastic so that consumers bear the entire incidence of the taxes.

By maintaining the assumption that supply of all goods is perfectly elastic, Ramsey's solution to this problem yields an elegant rule: The optimal set of commodity taxes leads to an equal percentage reduction in the compensated (Hicksian) demands for all goods. (The compensated demand for a good is derived by fixing utility and calculating how demand changes with a change in price. The compensated demand functions capture the substitution effect of price changes without measuring the income effect.) Thus, rather than having each *price* change by an equal percentage as would be implied by uniform taxation, the optimal tax system has an equal percentage change in the *quantities* of each good. Corlett and Hague (1953) proposed an alternative interpretation of the Ramsey rule. They point out that the optimal tax rates on different goods depend upon the relationship between the demand for the good and leisure. The optimal configuration of commodity taxes has higher tax rates on complements to leisure and lower tax rates on complements to working. The intuition is that, because leisure is the untaxed good, taxing goods that

are complementary to leisure implicitly taxes leisure.

Some of the many extensions to the Ramsey problem provide intuition about possible policy prescriptions. In the special case that demands for different goods are unrelated (i.e., the demand for one good does not depend on the price of other goods), the Ramsey rule simplifies to the "inverse-elasticity rule." The inverse-elasticity rule states that tax rates should be inversely proportional to their elasticity of demand. Goods for which demand is inelastic should have a high tax rate since changing their prices does not create much distortion. Conversely, the government should set lower tax rates on price-elastic goods since small price changes may create large distortions in the quantity demanded.

One criticism of the Ramsey solution, especially the special case of the inverse-elasticity rule, is that the solution may require higher taxes on necessities than on luxury goods since necessities often have relatively inelastic demands. Diamond (1975) extends the Ramsey problem to allow for households with different tastes and incorporates concerns for fairness among the different types of households. In Diamond's model, the government's social welfare function is a weighted average of the utilities of individual consumers. The social welfare weights for the households could depend on the well-being of the household, with higher weights for less-advantaged households. Incorporating fairness into the Ramsey problem modifies the basic result so that the percentage reduction in goods consumed heavily by the households favored by the government (often assumed to be the poorer households) is smaller than the percentage reduction in the goods consumed by households with lower weights in the social welfare function. Thus, equity can be introduced into the optimal commodity tax system by having higher taxes on the goods consumed predominantly by the rich. This result accords with the intuition behind many state governments exempting groceries from their sales tax bases: Because poor people spend a higher fraction of their income on groceries than rich people, the exclusion of groceries from the sales tax base adds fairness to the tax system. This exemption is counter to the basic Ramsey rule because grocery demand is relatively price inelastic.

Another branch of the optimal taxation literature addresses the optimal design of income (direct) taxes. As with optimal commodity taxation, the basic models are static, so they focus primarily on labor income rather than saving decisions or capital income. However, more recent models have added intertemporal saving and investment decisions.

Static models of optimal income taxation are of two types: linear and nonlinear (general) income taxes. Linear income tax systems have two parameters, a demogrant and a marginal tax rate. The demogrant can either be a lump-sum grant of money to each individual, in which case it provides a guaranteed income to each individual, or a lump-sum tax. The marginal tax rate on income distorts the labor supply decision and thus has an efficiency cost. By choosing both parameters, the government can simultaneously raise revenue and redistribute income across income groups. The optimal choice of parameters depends on: (1) how much revenue the government needs to raise; (2) society's preferences for redistribution, as summarized by a social welfare function; (3) how responsive individuals' labor supply decisions are to changes in the after-tax wage; and (4) the distribution of pretax wages in the economy, which determines the inequality of the pretax income distribution. Stern (1976) provides examples suggesting that (1) the optimal linear income tax is quite sensitive to these parameters, and (2) even if society has an extreme aversion to inequality, the marginal income tax rate is less than 100 percent.

General, nonlinear income tax systems allow the marginal tax rate to change continuously with the level of income. As with linear income tax systems, the goal of a nonlinear tax system is to raise revenue (as evidenced by positive average tax rates) in an equitable fashion while minimizing economic distortions created by nonzero marginal tax rates. The problem facing the government is that people have different innate ability levels that the tax authorities cannot observe. If the government could observe these ability levels, then it could levy nondistortionary individual-specific taxes on ability. As a proxy for taxing ability, the government taxes income but must recognize that the income tax gives people incentives to change how hard they work to escape taxation.

The degree of abstraction in models of optimal nonlinear income taxes has limited the policy relevance of their results. One often-cited result is that the marginal tax rate on the highest-income person (who has, presumably, the highest ability) is zero (see Seade 1977). The intuition behind this result is that a nonzero marginal tax rate distorts the labor supply of the highest-ability person. If this tax rate were changed to zero, the highest-ability person might work more, which would make that person better off (having the choice of whether to work more). However, government revenue would not change, because with a positive tax rate, this labor is not provided, and with a zero tax rate, the extra labor supply is not taxed. The logic of this argument applies only at the top of the income distribution, because changes in marginal tax rates below this level affect the taxes paid by people with higher incomes. Unfortunately, this result does not give any information about how high marginal tax rates should be just below the top of the income distribution. Also, from a practical standpoint, it is almost impossible to determine the "top" of the ability or income distribution.

As suggested from these results, the outcomes from optimal tax models depend on the set of possible taxes the government can implement. A long-standing debate surrounds the choice between indirect (e.g., commodity) and direct (e.g., income) taxation. That is, when the government can use both direct and indirect taxes, what is the optimal mix of taxes? Atkinson and Stiglitz (1980, ch. 14) show that commodity taxes are a relatively inefficient way of increasing the equity of a tax system that includes an optimally designed income tax. However, there may be administrative reasons for using indirect taxes.

One major consideration in designing an optimal tax system is how taxes interact with market imperfections. Externalities, such as pollution, are one example of a market imperfection that can affect optimal tax policy. Taxes on activities that create externalities can be one mechanism to reduce the economic inefficiency caused by externalities. For example, a tax on polluting may have the social benefit of reducing the level of pollution. Optimal tax models aimed at correcting externalities suggest that the optimal tax balances the marginal social damage from the externality with the marginal social benefit of the activity that generates the externality. The optimal tax does not necessarily eliminate the activity that generates the externality; for example, even with an optimal tax there may still be some pollution. For more on the corrective role of taxes in the case of externalities, see Baumol and Oates (1988).

While the optimal taxation literature is large and complex, there are several helpful reviews of the material. Rosen (1992, ch. 15) provides a useful introduction to the issues. Auerbach (1985), Stern (1987), and Stiglitz (1987) offer more technical summaries of optimal commodity and income taxation. Slemrod (1990) presents a critical review of the modern optimal tax literature and argues for including issues of administrative costs and compliance to the models.

## Additional readings

Atkinson, Anthony B., and Joseph E. Stiglitz. *Lectures on Public Economics*. New York: McGraw-Hill, 1980.

Auerbach, Alan J. "The Theory of Excess Burden and Optimal Taxation." In *Handbook of Public Economics*, vol. 1, edited by Alan Auerbach and Martin Feldstein, pp. 69–127. Amsterdam: North-Holland, 1985.

Baumol, William J., and Wallace E. Oates. *The Theory of Environmental Policy*. 2d ed. New York: Cambridge University Press, 1988.

Corlett, W.J., and D.C. Hague. "Complementarity and the Excess Burden of Taxation." *Review of Economic Studies* 21 (1953): 21–30.

Diamond, Peter A. "A Many-Person Ramsey Rule." *Journal of Public Economics* 4 (1975): 335–42.

Mirlees, James A. "An Exploration in the Theory of Optimum Income Taxation." *Review of Economic Studies* 38 (1971): 175–208.

Ramsey, Frank P. "A Contribution to the Theory of Taxation." *Economic Journal* 37 (1927): 47–61.

Rosen, Harvey S. *Public Finance.* 3rd ed. Homewood, Ill.: Irwin, 1992.

Seade, Jesus K. "On the Shape of Optimal Tax Schedules." *Journal of Public Economics* 7 (1977): 203–36.

Slemrod, Joel. "Optimal Taxation and Optimal Tax Systems." *Journal of Economic Perspectives* 4 (Winter 1990): 157–78.

Stern, Nicholas H. "On the Specification of Models of Optimum Income Taxation." *Journal of Public Economics* 6 (July–August 1976): 123–62.

Stern, Nicholas H. "The Theory of Optimal Commodity and Income Taxation: An Introduction." In *The Theory of Taxation for Developing Countries*, edited by David Newbery and Nicholas Stern, pp. 22–59. Oxford: Oxford University Press, 1987.

Stiglitz, Joseph E. "Pareto Efficient and Optimal Taxation and the New Welfare Economics." In *Handbook of Public Economics* 2, edited by Alan Auerbach and Martin Feldstein, pp. 991–1042. Amsterdam: North-Holland, 1987.

*Cross references:* labor supply, taxes and; saving, taxes and.

# Original issue and market discount

Ted Sims
George Washington University

*Since interest received is a form of taxable income, special tax issues arise when the nominal interest rate on an obligation differs from that of the market rate.*

Between 1954 and 1984, income taxation of taxable debt underwent a transformation that acknowledged the importance of "discounted" or "present" values to income measurement. (See generally Canellos and Kleinbard 1983, Halperin 1986, and Sims 1992.) As a result, the U.S. income tax more consistently takes interest into account as it accrues. One major stimulus for these changes was the set of issues that arise when the interest rate explicitly provided for in a debt obligation differs from the prevailing market rate, referred to as "original issue discount" and "market" premium or discount. (Closely related problems involve the issuance of debt for property, now dealt with largely by Internal Revenue Code [IRC] § 1274, and the disassembly of debt into its constituent elements in so-called "coupon stripping" transactions, dealt with by IRC § 1286. See Canellos and Kleinbard 1983 and Kayle 1987.)

## Debt

A debt obligation issued for money or property consists of a sequence of discrete (re)payments. *Conventional* debt, most typically a "coupon" bond, is usually issued for a specified "face" (or "stated principal") amount, with a "stated interest rate" and a finite maturity date. If the periodic (coupon) payments before maturity are at the prevailing rate of interest for obligations of comparable risk and maturity, the instrument's value will equal its stated principal amount. But there are other possibilities, of which two extreme versions are of interest. At one extreme, the "consol" (common in the United Kingdom but not the United States) has no maturity date but calls for an infinite stream of periodic payments. At the other, "pure discount" (or "zero-coupon") debt provides for a single repayment at maturity and no periodic payments before then. Between the extremes lies a continuum of types, including instruments whose payments before maturity, while greater than zero, are less than the interest that periodically accrues, and instruments that call for periodic payments in excess of the interest that accrues, with the excess applied to the amortization (reduction) of "principal." Whenever an instrument prescribes periodic payments that are less than accrued interest, the instrument will be valued at a discount to its stated principal amount.

## Income ("accretion") taxation of debt

Theoretically, proper income taxation of all of these variants flows directly from Samuelson (1964), extended to uncertainty by Fane (1987). The value of debt will be invariant to the tax rates of its holder (issuer) if, and only if, in each period the holder includes in gross income (and the issuer deducts in determining taxable income) the accrued change during that period in the instrument's value. The accrued change in value is given by exponential growth. (Samuelson 1964 dealt explicitly with "economic" depreciation, but it is easy to show that allowing economic depreciation is equivalent to taxing exponential accrual of value.) Proper taxation of debt that provides for current payment of interest accrued at a market rate has never been especially controversial. Since the amount *accrued* has also been *paid*, the issuer is simply allowed to deduct under IRC § 163(a) and the holder required to include under IRC § 61(a)(3) the interest "paid or incurred" in each period.

The rate of interest stated on a debt instrument may differ for any of several reasons, from the prevailing market rate, however, and proper taxation then becomes more complex.

### Original issue discount (IRC §§ 1271–1273)

When such a discrepancy exists at the time of issue, it usually takes the form of a stated interest rate that is less than the prevailing market rate, and periodic payments of "stated interest" that are less than what would have been called for by a market rate (the extreme instance being the pure discount bond). Under such circumstances, the instrument's market value at issue will be less than its "stated principal amount." The difference is denoted "original issue discount" (OID) by IRC § 1273(a).

As an economic matter, a discount bond changes value as interest accrues over time. Nevertheless, pre-1954 decisions like *Commissioner v. Caulkins* (1944) suggested that the holder should not be taxed until any accrued gain was technically "realized" under the predecessor of IRC § 1001(a) through either a sale in the market or surrender at maturity; and also that such gain, when realized, might be treated as favorably taxed long-term capital gain under IRC § 1222. (The history is recounted in more detail in several places, including Canellos and Kleinbard 1983, Garlock 1994, Lokken 1986, and Sims 1992). In 1954, Congress provided that realized gain on debt was to be treated as ordinary income to the extent of any original issue discount [IRC § 1271(c)(2)(A)]. [The same treatment was subsequently applied to instruments issued before 1954 by the decision of the Supreme Court in *United States* v. *Midland-Ross Corporation* (1965).] Revisions in 1969 required that OID be periodically accrued and said it could be included in the income of the holder and deducted by the issuer, using a ratable (or linear) methodology to determine how much was to be included each year [IRC § 1272(b); Income Tax Regs. § 1.163-4]. The 1969 revisions thus recognized that interest was accruing over time, but ignored the fact that it was accruing exponentially. In 1982, Congress finally amended the statute to require, as it now does, that OID be taken into account by holders and issuers using a discrete approximation of exponential accrual [IRC §§ 1272(a), 163(e)].

Specifically, for a debt instrument whose "stated redemption price at maturity" exceeds by more than a de minimis amount its actual "issue price," the statute requires a determination of the "yield to maturity," assuming at least annual compounding, that sets the "issue price" equal to the contractually

prescribed subsequent payments. A portion of the aggregate OID is then required to be accrued for tax purposes in each "accrual period," which is typically six months but may be as long as one year, by both the holder and issuer. The portion taken into account is determined for the first period after issue as the product of the instrument's yield-to-maturity and its issue price. The issue price is then adjusted upward by the accrued OID, and the portion of the aggregate OID taken into account in the next accrual period is the product of the yield-to-maturity and the resulting "adjusted" issue price. (In each period, the accrued OID taken into account is reduced by any amount actually payable as interest, which is separately treated under IRC §§ 61 and 163.) This procedure is iterated to the point of surrender [IRC §§ 1273, 1272(a)(3)–(5), 163(e); Garlock 1994; Lokken 1986.] At the close of each accrual period, the holder's basis for determining gain or loss on any subsequent disposition is also adjusted upward by the amount of OID included in gross income during that period [IRC § 1272(d)(2)]. If an instrument subject to the OID rules changes hands in the midst of an accrual period, the OID accrued in that period is prorated on a daily basis between the transferor and transferee [IRC § 1272(a)(1) and (3)]. The procedures prescribed by IRC § 1272, consistently applied, set an instrument's adjusted issue price (and adjusted basis) equal to its stated redemption price by its stipulated maturity date.

While the incorporation of exponential accrual into the taxation of debt seems widely regarded as a salutary, if somewhat complex, development, these provisions have not been free of criticism. In particular, Bankman and Klein (1989) have pointed out that IRC § 1272(a) ignores the impact of the interest rate term structure, although it remains unclear how serious a set of distortions this deficiency produces (see Sims 1992; Strnad 1995).

### Market premium and discount

The market value of a debt instrument may vary from its unrepaid principal balance because of events that occur after issue, including changes in the creditworthiness of the issuer. More commonly, the value of debt will fluctuate with changes in the market rate of interest, declining with rises in the interest rate and rising with declines. Consequently, when debt changes hands in a taxable transfer after issue but before surrender at maturity, it will usually be acquired at "market premium" to or a "market discount" from its unrepaid balance. Such premiums or discounts have the effect of adjusting the instrument's (market) yield-to-maturity so as to set it equal to the prevailing market interest rate. Theoretically, pure accrual taxation would appear to require exponential accrual of the premium or discount to the holder. The statute does not, however, generally so require.

### Premium (IRC § 171)

In particular, the statute allows market premium to be ignored. IRC § 171(d) allows holders of debt acquired in the market at a price that exceeds the amount payable at maturity an election to amortize (deduct) the resulting premium over time [Income Tax Regs. § 1.171-2(a)(1)]. [The election, once made, applies to all bonds then held and subsequently acquired by the electing taxpayer, unless and until revoked with the consent of the authorities, IRC § 171(d)(2).] Until 1986, regulations under IRC § 171 generally provided for ratable amortization of the premium [Income Tax Regs. § 1.171-2(f)(2)(i)]. In 1986, however, in the wake of the general shift to compound interest methodologies legislated in 1982 and 1984, IRC § 171 was amended to require the use of a bond's market yield-to-maturity in the hands of its holder to determine the amount of premium to be amortized each year.

### Discount (IRC §§ 1276–1278)

Even though *original issue* discount was required to be currently included in gross income as early as 1969, and determined using compound interest as of 1982, so-called "market" discount remained essentially untouched. Even though market discount operates to increase the holder's yield, and is therefore essentially "interest," gain from the sale of an instrument acquired in the market at a discount was not taxed until "realized" by sale or other disposition; and, if the instrument qualified under IRC § 1221 as a "capital asset" in the hands of its holder, it was eligible for preferential capital gains taxation.

In 1984, Congress acted to require that, on disposition at a gain of any debt instrument previously acquired in the market at a discount, to the extent it does not exceed the increase in the instrument's value over time resulting from the accrual of market discount, the gain be treated as ordinary income. The holder may, however, elect with respect to any market discount bond to treat the discount as accruing on the basis of the instrument's market yield-to-maturity as of the time it was acquired [IRC § 1276(b)(2)]. In addition, a separate election is available pursuant to which market discount on *all* market discount debt held by the electing taxpayer may be currently included in income using either of the methods prescribed by IRC § 1276(b).

### Borrowing to buy market discount bonds

One way in which the pre-1984 treatment of market discount was exploited was by borrowing to purchase market discount bonds. The interest paid on the borrowing was deducted currently, while the return attributable to the accrual of the discount over time was taxed at a later time, often as long-term capital gain. The recharacterization rule of IRC § 1276(a) forestalled the "conversion" of ordinary income into long-term capital gain using such arrangements, but it would have remained possible, despite IRC § 1276, to achieve deferral through approximately riskless debt-financed investments in market discount bonds. To curtail that remaining possibility, Congress simultaneously enacted IRC § 1277, which defers interest deductions in any year on debt (borrowing the formulation of IRC § 265) "incurred or continued" to "purchase or carry" market discount bonds, to the extent of any untaxed market discount that accrues during that year.

### Interactions between original issue discount and market premium or discount

Instruments acquired at a market premium or discount may obviously include those originally *issued* at a discount. The 1982 and 1984 enactments deal specifically with these possibilities. If, for example, an OID instrument is subsequently acquired in the market at a premium to its "adjusted issue price," the statute, consistent with IRC § 171, permits the resulting "acquisition premium" to be deducted against the accruing OID [IRC § 1272(a)(7)]. Conversely, if such an instrument is subsequently acquired at a discount from the adjusted issue price, the amount of market discount subject to IRC § 1276(a) is limited to the difference between the adjusted issue price (rather than the redemption price at maturity) and the holder's acquisition cost [IRC § 1278(b)(2)(B) and (4)].

### Additional readings

Bankman, Joseph, and William A. Klein. "Accurate Taxation of Long-Term Debt: Taking Into Account the Term Structure of Interest." *Tax Law Review* 44 (1989): 335.

Canellos, Peter C., and Edward D. Kleinbard. "The Miracle of Compound Interest: Interest Deferral and Discount after 1982." *Tax Law Review* 38 (1983): 565.

Fane, George. "Neutral Taxation under Uncertainty." *Journal of Public Economics* 33 (1987): 95–105.

Garlock, David C. *The Federal Income Taxation of Debt Instruments.* Englewood Cliffs, N.J.: Prentice Hall Law and Business, 1994.

Halpering, Daniel I. "Interest in Disguise: Taxing the 'Time Value of Money.'" *Yale Law Journal* 95 (1986): 506.

Kayle, Bruce. "Where Has All the Income Gone? The Mysterious Relocation of Interest and Principal in Coupon Stripping and Related Transactions." *Virginia Tax Review* 7 (1987): 303.

Lokken, Lawrence. "The Time Value of Money Rules." *Tax Law Review* 42 (1986): 1.

Samuelson, Paul. "Tax Deductibility of Economic Depreciation to Insure Invariant Valuations." *Journal of Political Economy* 72 (December 1964): 604–06.

Sims, Theodore S. "Long Term Debt, the Term Structure of Interest and the Case for Accrual Taxation." *Tax Law Review* 47 (1992): 313.

Strnad, Jeff. Taxation of Bonds: The Tax Trading Dimension." *Virginia Law Review* 81 (1995): 47.

*Cross references:* interest deductibility; tax arbitrage; tax shelters.

# Origin principle

George Carlson
Arthur Andersen

*A principle for taxing goods based on where they are produced rather than on where they are sold.*

Under the origin principle of taxation, goods and services are taxed where they are produced or originate, rather than where they are purchased or consumed. Origin-basis treatment can be contrasted with the destination principle, under which goods and services are taxed where they are consumed. The term "origin principle" typically applies to taxes on goods and services, rather than those on income. (A tax on income is normally levied under either the source or residence principle. The term "source principle" refers to the site of the activity generating the income, and "residence principle" to the residence or location of the recipient.)

Consider the case of a sales or value-added tax in Country A. With respect to goods and services that are produced in Jurisdiction A (the origin), but sold in Jurisdiction B (the destination), the origin principle is implemented if Jurisdiction A applies no border tax adjustments to either imports or exports. Specifically, Jurisdiction A should not apply the tax to imports, and should not rebate or "forgive" the tax on exports to Jurisdiction B. The effect of these so-called origin principle border tax adjustments is to ensure that all goods produced in Jurisdiction A (the origin jurisdiction) are taxed, regardless of where they are consumed.

Goods or services sold in Jurisdiction A, but exported and sold elsewhere, are taxed by Jurisdiction A under the origin principle.

International tax and trading rules, established by the General Agreement on Tariffs and Trade (GATT), provide that the origin, but not the destination, principle can be applied to income or social insurance taxes. Thus, a direct tax (income, social insurance, etc.) cannot be applied to imports or rebated on exports. Under the origin principle, direct taxes apply to all domestic production, regardless of where the good or service is sold or consumed. No adjustment is made, under the origin principle, for applying the tax to imports or relieving it on exports. In countries with federal systems of government, such as the United States and Canada, subnational governmental entities may also be able to levy taxes. If so, the movement of goods and services among these subnational units of government requires choosing between the destination and origin principle. In the United States, for example, states tend to follow a destination principle method of taxation. Within a common market or economic union, however, the origin principle could be readily applied, but only if tax rates were roughly similar. Otherwise, the origin principle would serve to discourage activity in the high-tax location or origin of production.

The primary effect of the origin principle is to tax production, rather than consumption. All goods and services produced in the origin jurisdiction are taxed, provided they are not specifically exempted from the tax base. Many jurisdictions, for example, choose to exempt food, medicine, and other "necessities" from taxation for reasons of fairness and equity. But provided a good or service is generally subject to taxation, the origin principle demands that the tax be levied only if the good or service was produced in the origin jurisdiction. Only the origin of the good or service is relevant in determining tax liability. Because the origin of a service (e.g., financial advice) can be less certain than that of a good (e.g., an automobile), it may be more difficult to apply the origin principle to some services than to goods.

A completely general tax applied uniformly to either the consumption or the production of all goods in an economy will not affect the allocation of resources. In an open economy, this implies that the choice of either origin or destination principle border tax adjustments is irrelevant to resource allocation. This result is explained in the Tinbergen Report, which was authorized by the European Coal and Steel Community, the forerunner of the European Economic Community. In particular, assuming a comprehensive tax applying to all products, the choice of either the destination or the origin principle will not affect the distribution of resources or the direction or extent of trade between the countries. There is a monetary difference between the two principles in that a general tax imposed under the origin principle will initially worsen the country's trade balance, causing an offsetting devaluation in its currency, whereas a general tax imposed under the destination principle will have no trade balance repercussions. This is another way of saying that currency depreciation and destination principle border tax adjustments produce the same results. There is, however, a fiscal difference in that taxes are collected by the exporting country under the origin principle.

*Cross references:* border tax adjustments; destination principle.

# P

## Partnerships

George Mundstock
University of Miami School of Law

*Taxation of an unincorporated association (but not a trust or estate) of individuals requiring a set of decision rules for assigning tax obligations of the owner/partner individuals.*

The income tax policy issues presented by the partnership can be traced to the basic decision to respect the character of partnerships under nontax substantive partnership law. Historically, this law treated partnerships as complicated arrangements between partners, and not as legal entities. For example, partnerships could not own real property, because only legal persons could own property, and a partnership was not a legal person. The modern trend in this law, however, has been toward reification. Partnerships now own all property in their own name. U.S. tax law had developed similarly, historically treating partnerships as merely a bundle of relationships (usually referred to as an "aggregate" approach), but increasingly treating partnerships as entities.

Current tax law's provisions for partnerships date back to 1954. At the time, most partnerships were service businesses with a small group of partners. The tax provisions were directed toward this type of partnership. Today, there are capital-intensive partnerships with numerous partners. As articulated below, the current rules work particularly badly with these large partnerships. Even small partnerships present difficult policy issues, however.

A partnership generally determines its taxable income (or loss) and credits as an entity, as if it were an individual. The partnership entity is not a taxpayer, however. The aggregate view results in a partnership's tax items flowing through to the partners as if earned directly by them. In other words, for purposes of determining and taxing most tax items, a partnership is a pass-through entity. This presents two initial concerns. First, because corporations are generally taxed along with their shareholders, pass-through treatment subjects partnerships to only one level of taxation, whereas corporate income is taxed twice. It is difficult to justify this preference for the partnership form. Some argue, however, that the partnership regime, because it does not involve the double taxation of the corporate regime, is the more

attractive of the two (see Integration, corporate tax). Second, pass-through treatment facilitates the use of partnerships as a vehicle for tax shelters (see Tax shelters). Shelter promoters form a partnership and sell partnership interests to the investors seeking shelter. The partnership is particularly attractive for leveraged tax shelters, as a partner is allowed losses attributable to partnership borrowing, even nonrecourse borrowing. This means that a partner can receive losses as a consequence of the partnership investment that are well in excess of the partner's out-of-pocket investment (see Passive activity losses).

The question arises as to what types of business organizations should qualify for this pass-through treatment. Limited partnerships (partnerships with one class of partners that are not liable for partnership debts) are generally taxed as partnerships. Limited partnerships (with active businesses) whose interests are traded in public markets are treated like corporations, however. Some believe that all limited partnerships resemble corporations and should be taxed accordingly. Limited partnerships have been the preferred vehicle for tax shelters. Thus, taxable entity treatment of limited partnerships would restrict tax shelters as well. Recently, states have been enacting new vehicles called "limited liability companies." Limited liability companies resemble partnerships except that all shareholders (not just a limited class, as with limited partnerships) are shielded from liability. These are also generally treated as partnerships for income tax purposes, presenting concerns analogous to those presented by limited partnerships.

A difficult issue associated with pass-through treatment is how tax items are allocated among the partners. These problems build a case against pass-through treatment, because they do not arise if all income or loss is taxed to the partnership. This case is strongest with respect to partnerships with large numbers of partners or with complicated economic arrangements between the partners, because these partnerships present the most involved allocation difficulties.

Allocation problems arise in two situations. First, problems arise with regard to tax items, such as accelerated depreciation and tax credits, for which there is no corresponding identifiable economic item treated separately for nontax purposes. In this case, there is no nontax point of reference from which the tax law can view an item. This makes allocation difficult. For example, assume a 50–50 partnership between two individuals: one providing solely capital and one providing primarily services and some capital. The partnership claims a jobs credit. A 50–50 partnership suggests that the credit should be split evenly between the partners. It might make more sense, however, to allocate the credit in a way that provides the most incentive, perhaps proportionately to the partners' contributions to payment of the underlying wages. This presents its own difficulties, because there is no ready way to determine which partner provided the specific cash used to pay the specific qualified wages.

Second, even when a tax item corresponds to an economic item, allocation problems arise under some of the varied and complex economic arrangements allowed by flexible nontax partnership law. It can be quite difficult to determine the real present economic consequences of a current economic item. This can be seen in an example: Assume that two women form a partnership to acquire an office building and operate it for 15 years. They share revenues 50–50. The first partner puts up the cash used to purchase the building. The second partner agrees to pay all operating expenses (out of her pocket or out of her share of the revenues). How should (economic) depreciation on the building be allocated? At first glance, it would seem that the depreciation should go to the first partner, as she provided the cash for the building. On the other hand, the first partner has more than a building. The first partner has rights against the other partner for 15 years of operating expenses. In effect, the second partner is making a deferred capital contribution. So viewed, the second partner might be allocated some depreciation. In short, allocating even economic items can be quite difficult because the complex relationships involved in many partnerships make it difficult in a given year to measure how much a partner gets richer or poorer as a consequence of the partnership.

One solution to the allocation problem is to allow the partners to allocate tax items (benefits and burdens) as they see fit. Under such a regime, one can expect the partners to allocate items so as to minimize their total tax. For example, the partners would allocate taxable income to low-bracket partners (such as partners with excess net operating losses) and allocate tax-free income, deductions, and credits to high-bracket partners. Such a regime is a form of free transferability of tax benefits. Congress generally rejects transferability, as in safe-harbor leasing and in acquisitions of corporations with net operating losses. This rejection prevents unintended tax benefits. With partnerships, however, tax benefit transfers are possible under current law.

The sale of a partnership interest by a partner presents two policy issues. First, the character (capital or ordinary) of any gain (or loss) must be determined (see Capital gains taxation). An entity view suggests that the gain should be capital. If the

partnership owns property whose sale would result in ordinary income, an aggregate approach concludes that the selling partner is selling his share of the ordinary income asset and should be taxed on his share of the underlying ordinary income. Current law strikes an awkward compromise. Second, the consequences of the sale of a partnership interest on the nonselling partners must be determined. An entity perspective shows no consequences to the other partners, as they are not a party to the sale of the partnership interest. An aggregate view sees the other partners getting a new co-owner of the partnership's assets. This affects how the partnership determines its tax items that are then passed through to the partners. Current law allows the partnership to elect aggregate treatment. However, aggregate treatment is quite unwieldy when applied to a partnership where numerous partnership interests change hands frequently.

The difference between aggregate and entity approaches to the taxation of nonselling partners can be illustrated with an example: A partnership's principal asset at the time that a partnership interest is sold is appreciated land. Later the partnership sells the property. Under an entity approach, the amount of gain to the partnership upon the later sale is the difference between the amount realized by and the cost to the partnership. This gain is allocated among the partners. If the property had been owned directly by the partners (the aggregate view), the total gain would be smaller. Each co-owner (partner) would determine gain by comparing his share of the sale price to his cost. In the case of the new co-owner, her cost would be higher than that of the former owner from whom she bought her interest, because the partnership's property appreciated in value from the time acquired by the partnership to the time the selling partner sold his interest. This results in less gain than if the new co-owner's gain was measured using the old cost. Yet, in the partnership entity regime, the old low cost, not the real high cost of the new co-owner, is used in determining the partnership's gain. In other words, the selling partner paid tax on gain in an amount equal to the difference between his cost and the new cost paid by the new partner. The aggregate approach prevents this gain being taxed again when the underlying property is sold.

Another context in which the tension between the aggregate and entity nature of partnerships has presented difficulties is where, as a consequence of a partnership transaction, a partner's interest in property shifts. The clearest example is a partner transferring property to her partnership. The property might have unrealized gain or loss. Because current law takes an aggregate approach to this transaction (in effect, the partner is transferring the property to herself), this gain or loss is not taxed. To prevent tax avoidance, this gain or loss must be taxed later. Because this gain or loss actually occurred while the property was owned by the contributing partner, these items should be allocated to her (to prevent tax benefit transfers). Current law goes part way toward this result. This problem is particularly troubling when the failure to trace the gain back to the contributing partner results in a partner converting ordinary income to capital gain. Similar problems are presented by a transfer of property from a partnership to a partner, admission of a new partner, retirement of a partner, and non–pro rata cash distributions. Again, entity treatment would avoid most of these concerns.

The hybrid nature of partnerships also causes problems when a service partner receives an interest in the partnership that gives him no right to the assets currently owned by the partnership but entitles him to share in future profits. Practitioners adopt the aggregate approach and conclude that the service partner has received nothing but profits that should only be taxed in the future when earned by the partnership. Others adopt an entity view and note that a present interest in future profits, like coupons on a bond, can have present value and, when this is the case, should be taxed upon receipt.

In conclusion, the evolution of tax policy thinking and the use of partnerships has rendered current law rules inadequate. Wholesale reform is badly needed.

## Additional readings

Auerbach, Alan J. "Should Interest Deductions Be Limited?" In *Uneasy Compromise: Problems of a Hybrid Income/Consumption Tax*, edited by Henry J. Aaron, Harvey Galper, and Joseph A. Pechman. Washington, D.C.: The Brookings Institution, 1988.

McKee, William S., William F. Nelson, and Robert L. Whitmire. *Federal Taxation of Partnerships and Partners*. 2d ed. 2 vols. Boston: Warren, Gorham, & Lamont, 1990.

Willis, Arthur B., John S. Pennell, and Philip F. Postlewaite. *Partnership Taxation*. 2 vols. Colorado Springs: Shepards/McGraw-Hill, Inc., 1989.

*Cross references:* capital gains taxation; passive activity losses; proprietorships; tax shelters.

# Passive activity losses

Bradford L. Ferguson
Sidley and Austin

Frederick W. Hickman
Hopkins and Sutter

*A defined term in Section 469 of the Internal Revenue Code of 1986, introduced by the Tax Reform Act of 1986 for the purpose of limiting "tax shelter" activity and raising revenue.*

The statutory term "passive activity" was intended to encompass investments generally regarded as "tax shelters"—that is, investments in business assets by an investor with little or no personal participation in the business—which are designed to initially generate tax losses or tax credits that can be used to reduce tax liabilities on the investor's income from other sources.

The passive activity loss (PAL) provisions apply to taxpayers other than broadly held corporations. They identify a "basket" consisting of items of income from "passive activities" (excluding portfolio income—i.e., interest, dividends, and other investment income not derived in the ordinary course of a trade or business) and items of deduction and credit deemed to relate to that income. If there is net income in the basket, it is simply added to the taxpayer's other income. But if there is net loss in the basket, it is "disallowed": It may not be used to reduce the taxpayer's other income, except to the extent attributable to final dispositions of property accounted for within the basket. Disallowed PALs may be carried forward to offset any net income in the basket in future years. Tax credits, if any, that relate to income in the basket may be utilized only to offset tax liability deemed attributable to income from the basket.

The loss limitation turns neither on the nature of the activity nor on the loss-creating deductions or credits, but on whether the taxpayer is "passive" with respect to the "activity." If the taxpayer is deemed to be sufficiently engaged in the activity, the net losses or credits from it are unaffected by the limitations, even though they reduce (i.e., "shelter") tax on the taxpayer's income from other sources.

To understand the design of the PAL provisions it is necessary to understand the principal loss-producing deductions and credits involved in tax shelters.

One or more of the deductions for interest, for depreciation, and for the current expensing of costs that relate to future income are likely to be involved in an investment in business assets. Those deductions are likely to produce a net loss for a given investment project in its early years, either because the deductions are skewed toward the front end of the project life, or because the natural pattern of project revenue is skewed toward the back end, or both. The net loss shelters other income from tax, producing positive cash flow in the form of a reduction in the taxes that would otherwise be paid. The benefit is a "timing" benefit: The deducted costs are legitimate, deductible costs, and the "shelter" is a function of the timing of the deduction. While that tax reduction attributable to taking larger deductions in early years is offset by a corresponding increase in tax from taking smaller deductions in later years, the net result is equivalent to a non–interest-bearing loan from the Treasury. It reduces the private financing required and confers an economic benefit that reduces the taxpayer's project cost.

The principal tax credits affected are the credits for rehabilitation of buildings, for low-income housing, and for research and development. (The larger investment tax credit was repealed in 1986.) Because a credit produces a permanent tax reduction, and not just a timing reduction accompanied by a corresponding tax increase later, each dollar of credit produces a larger reduction in project cost than a dollar of tax reduction, which is equivalent to a non–interest-bearing loan.

The tax credits and many of the depreciation and expensing provisions involved were intended by Congress to produce the described tax shelter benefits and thus to be an "incentive" for businesses to invest. The interest deduction is an exception: it does not provide an overall incentive to investment because, unlike the depreciation and expensing deductions, it does not reduce the total amount of income in the tax base, either temporarily or permanently. Every deducted interest payment creates an equal and offsetting item of income for the recipient. But the interest deduction may nonetheless create a net loss from the project for the investing taxpayer in periods in which the gross income from the project is small.

In the 1970s and 1980s, the financing of business assets by means of syndicating tax shelters was widespread. Investors were offered the opportunity to acquire ownership of all or a portion of the asset (directly, or through partnerships), receive income from the business that used it, and become entitled to the interest, depreciation, and expensing deductions and the tax credits that accrue to "owners" of business assets, without participating personally in the operation of the business using the asset. The tax shelter vehicle permitted full use of the deductions and credits attributable to the investment in instances where the business-user, if also the owner, could not have fully used them. Further, so long as the marginal tax rate of the owner-investor was

higher than that of the business-user (before 1982 the top individual rate was 70% and the top corporate rate less than 50%), the arrangement permitted a shift of deductions to a higher-rate bracket without an offsetting shift of income. After the top rate for individuals dropped to 50 percent in 1982, the potential for significant "bracket shifting" disappeared, except in those situations where the business-user has net losses and thus a marginal rate of zero.

There is no persuasive evidence that the tax incentives described produce higher returns on investment, either for user-investors or for tax shelter investors, because the tax reductions represent reductions in investment cost and, like other generally applicable reductions in investment cost, translate into lower output prices. The hoped-for increase in investment and business activity created by tax "incentives," whether or not in tax shelters, occurs to the extent that lower output prices elicit larger demand. Nonetheless, unsophisticated tax shelter investors often believed there was an advantage in taking investment return in the form of reductions in tax on their other income, notwithstanding that investments that reduced taxable income in early years produced commensurately higher taxable income in later years, that many such investments were ultimately unsuccessful, and that virtually all were illiquid. The real advantage to the tax shelter investor—if any—was in the opportunity to make higher-risk, illiquid, business investments that produced commensurately higher returns if successful, and to finance a portion of the investment "automatically" with reductions in tax on other income.

The growth of a market that enables individuals to participate in an expanded variety of business investments and that indirectly makes existing tax incentives more universally available to all operating businesses (rather than only to those businesses that can use them directly and immediately) seems generally desirable. On the other hand, extending investment opportunities heavily laden with tax incentives to less sophisticated investors had some undesirable side effects. There were inevitably abuses that required audit surveillance (as where inflated asset values or essentially nonexistent assets were used to produce inflated depreciation deductions). There were also instances in which the illusory lure of "tax advantage" and the lessened financing requirements permitted promoters to raise financing from unsophisticated tax shelter investors for projects that non–tax shelter owner-investors utilizing the same tax deductions and credits would not find economic.

However, the chief problem with tax shelters—the problem that most concerned Congress and that gave rise to the PAL provisions—was the "appearance" problem. Tax shelter investment packages very visibly produced, in some periods, deductions and credits that individual taxpayers used to reduce their tax on other income. A large segment of the public had been educated to an awareness of that fact and had been exhorted to view it as favoritism to high-income taxpayers. This public perception, justified or not, was seen as corroding public trust in the fairness of the tax system.

The PAL provisions were accordingly tailored to address only taxpayers who visibly used loss deductions and credits from particular investments to shelter "other" income. But if an investment asset is part of a larger activity in which the investor is sufficiently active, the same deductions and credits can continue to shelter not only the investor's income from that activity but any other income.

The aim of the 1986 Tax Reform Act was to broaden the income tax base, to use the revenues generated to reduce tax rates, and to keep the act "revenue neutral." If the PAL provisions had been limited to property involved in tax shelter transactions entered into after 1986, the revenue gain would have been modest. The PAL provisions were accordingly made applicable, with some transitional relief, to preexisting investments, rendering many of them uneconomic, but allowing the official revenue estimates to show a large revenue gain that could be "spent" on tax rate reductions. Investors reacted by restructuring their investments to generate "passive activity income" in the basket sufficient to absorb the disallowed PALs.

Tax shelter transactions did dry up after 1986. The 1982 and 1986 reductions in tax rates, the repeal of the investment tax credit, and the revised limitations on deductions for depreciation, expensing, and interest all lessened the degree of "shelter" provided by such transactions and may have dried them up in any event. However, the PAL rules are widely credited with giving the *coup de grace*.

While the PAL provisions appear simple in basic concept, they are extraordinarily complex in application. Taxpayers plan, primarily, to avoid having PALs, and, secondarily, to the extent that PALs cannot be avoided, to have sufficient passive activity gross income to absorb them. There is no simple test for what is deemed to be "passive." Characterization depends on the nature of the activity and the hours spent by the taxpayer, with different requirements in different contexts. The degree of investor participation is largely irrelevant in a few cases: Virtually all ordinary rental activities are deemed to be passive, and virtually all "working interests" in oil and gas investments are deemed not to be passive.

Elaborate regulations contain numerous exceptions and "recharacterization" rules intended to prevent taxpayers' burying inappropriate nonpassive items in passive activities, or inappropriate passive activity items in nonpassive activities. Perhaps the most critical regulations are those relating to the definition of an "activity," for items may be "passive" if included in one activity but "active" if included in another, or activities may be converted from active to passive, or vice versa, if specific activities or functions are included or excluded. By paring or adding, aggregating or disaggregating specific activities or functions—all in a context in which the potential permutations are legion—passive items can be converted from passive to active or vice versa. While the taxpayer is given much flexibility, detailed planning and analysis is typically required.

The extraordinary complexity of the PAL rules does, ironically, achieve a kind of simplification. The difficulties in planning for investments that will fall under the rules is so great that taxpayers simply avoid them.

The PAL provisions stand as still another example of how the income tax system becomes barnacled with complexity (and is seldom scraped clean) as political goals are compromised, ad hoc, in the legislative process.

*Cross references:* partnerships; tax shelters.

# Payroll tax, federal

Maureen Anne Griffin
Congressional Budget Office

*A group of taxes based on the earnings of employees and self-employed persons.*

As a revenue source, federal payroll tax revenues have grown substantially in the past 60 years. As a share of total receipts, payroll taxes increased from 10 percent in 1937 to 34 percent in 1997. Over the same period, payroll taxes grew from 1 percent to 7 percent of gross domestic product.

## Components of federal payroll taxes

Federal payroll taxes, or social insurance contributions, consist of tax revenues from Social Security, Medicare hospital insurance, unemployment insurance, railroad retirement, and other retirements. Social Security comprises the lion's share of federal payroll taxes—73 percent of the $539 billion collected in 1993. Medicare, the second largest component, comprises 20 percent of payroll tax revenues. The remaining revenue is divided between unemployment insurance (5%), railroad retirement (less than 1%), and other retirements (1%).

### Social Security

Social Security (OASDI, or Old Age, Survivors, and Disability Insurance) began in the late 1930s as a mandatory old-age insurance program for most employees in the private sector. Over time, the program was expanded to include disability insurance and mandatory coverage for almost all workers.

The Social Security Act of 1935 provided monthly benefits to retired workers covered by Social Security. In 1939, benefits were extended to the dependents and survivors of covered workers. The program was further expanded to provide disability insurance to covered workers and their dependents in 1956 and 1958, respectively.

Even in its infancy, coverage under Social Security was broad. All workers in commerce and industry—except railroad workers, who had their own retirement plan—were originally covered under Social Security. Beginning in the 1950s, coverage was expanded to include most workers in the private sector not originally covered. Participation was mandatory for some, such as farm and domestic workers, active military personnel, and self-employed persons, and elective for others, such as nonprofit workers, state and local government workers, and employees of religious bodies. Additional legislation in the mid-1980s expanded coverage to federal workers hired after 1983 and mandated coverage for employees of nonprofit organizations. In 1994, about 95 percent of all jobs in the United States were covered by Social Security. Workers excluded from coverage fall into four major categories: federal civilian employees hired before 1984, railroad workers, certain state and local government workers covered under a retirement system, and workers whose earnings do not meet minimum earnings requirements.

Benefits earned by covered workers are financed primarily by a payroll tax on a worker's wages. (Two other sources of income to finance benefits are income tax revenues from the taxation of some Social Security benefits and interest income earned on the Social Security Trust Fund reserves.) Both the employee and the employer pay taxes based on the worker's earnings up to a maximum amount or taxable maximum earnings base. In 1937, both employee and employer each paid a 1 percent tax, levied on all covered earnings up to $3,000. This captured the full earnings of about 97 percent of all covered workers. Since then, both the tax rate and the maximum taxable earnings base have been increased by myriad legislative measures. The most recent increase in the OASDI tax rate occurred in 1990, when the rate was increased from 6.06 percent to 6.2 percent. The tax rate applicable to self-employed persons has varied over the years; since 1990, self-employed persons have been subject to a tax rate of 12.4 percent, which is equal to the combined employee and employer tax rates. The taxable maximum was increased by a series of ad hoc legislative changes until 1975, when Congress tied the maximum earnings base to changes in the national

average wage. Since then, the taxable maximum earnings base has been automatically indexed each year. In 1996, the taxable maximum earnings base was $62,700, which is expected to capture the full earnings of around 95 percent of the work force.

Social Security tax revenues are allocated between the Old Age and Survivors Insurance (OASI) Trust Fund and the Disability Insurance (DI) Trust Fund. During the 1990s, the DI trust fund was facing exhaustion, so Congress changed the allocation of funds between the OASI and DI trust funds in a series of steps. The final scheduled change in this allocation, 5.3 percent to OASI and 0.9 percent to DI, is scheduled to take effect in 2000.

### Medicare hospital insurance

The Social Security Act was amended in 1965 to include Medicare hospital insurance (HI). This program, which is financed primarily through payroll taxes, provides hospitalization benefits to eligible persons age 65 or older. Generally, eligible persons have paid HI taxes based on their covered earnings.

For many years, the pool of workers paying HI taxes and the taxable maximum earnings base were identical to those under Social Security. In the mid-1980s, however, the HI pool was expanded to include all federal workers and all state and local workers hired after March 31, 1986. In 1991, the HI taxable maximum earnings base was raised from $53,400 to $125,000, and in 1994 it was eliminated entirely, thereby decoupling it from the Social Security base, and making all covered earnings subject to the tax.

The HI tax rate is 1.45 percent on all covered earnings. Both the employee and the employer pay this tax rate, and self-employed persons pay the combined tax rate. While the original tax rate was 0.35 percent in 1966 and has increased steadily over the past three decades, no further increases are currently scheduled.

All revenue generated from the HI payroll tax is deposited in the Hospital Insurance Trust Fund. Revenues in that trust fund are used to finance inpatient hospital, skilled nursing facility, home health, and other institutional services.

### Unemployment insurance

Unemployment insurance (UI) payroll taxes began in the 1930s; the taxes are used to finance unemployment benefits for workers involuntarily unemployed.

Basically, there are two parts to the UI payroll tax: the Federal Unemployment Tax Act (FUTA) tax and the state tax. FUTA taxes finance the administrative expenses of the program, the federal account for state loans, and one-half the expense of extended benefits. State taxes, which are deposited in the U.S. Treasury, finance regular UI benefits and half the expense of extended benefits.

The FUTA program is designed to induce state participation by granting a credit against the federal tax if the state program conforms to federal standards. FUTA generally determines which workers are covered by UI. Originally, coverage was limited to industrial and commercial workers in the private sector. Currently, the vast majority of workers, with the exception of self-employed persons, are eligible for UI benefits. In addition, FUTA mandates a taxable maximum earnings base. Each state determines the amount and duration of benefits, the tax rate, and eligibility requirements.

FUTA currently imposes a 6.2 percent gross tax rate on the first $7,000 paid annually by covered employers to each employee. Employers in states with programs approved by the federal government and with no delinquent federal loans may credit 5.4 percentage points against the 6.2 percent tax rate, making the minimum, net federal tax rate 0.8 percent. Originally, the FUTA tax applied to total annual wages. In 1939, however, a $3,000 taxable wage base was established that exceeded the annual wages of 98 percent of the workers subject to the tax. The taxable wage base was increased three times: to $4,200 in 1972, to $6,000 in 1978, and to $7,000 in 1983.

States must impose a payroll tax on employers for at least the first $7,000 paid annually to each employee to be eligible for the 5.4 percentage point FUTA credit. In 1996, 40 states had taxable wage bases greater than $7,000; Hawaii has the highest base, at $25,800. All state laws have experience ratings that have the effect of varying individual employers' tax rates from the standard rate of 5.4 percent based on their previous unemployment experience. The estimated national average of state tax rates was 2.2 percent in 1995, with rates ranging from 0.6 percent in South Dakota and North Carolina to 4.9 percent in Pennsylvania.

### Railroad retirement

Federal involvement in providing and financing railroad retirement began in the mid-1930s, when declines in the railroad industry imposed tremendous financial hardships on the railroads. The program has been revamped several times; the latest overhaul was in 1974, when the current system was established. The retirement system has two tiers that are financed by federal payroll taxes. (The other components of the retirement system provide supplemental benefits to certain workers. The programs are financed through general fund transfers and a cents-per-hour tax paid by employers.)

Both tiers of the program are financed by a payroll tax on the worker's wages. The tier 1 tax rate is equivalent to the combined Social Security and Medicare HI tax rate. Under tier 1, both employee and employer pay taxes on covered wages up to the applicable maximum taxable earnings base for Social Security ($62,700 in 1996) and all covered wages for HI. Under tier 2, the wage base is equal to what the Social Security tax base would have been without the ad hoc increases in the taxable wage base provided by the Social Security amendments of 1977. In 1996, the tier 2 taxable wage base was $46,500. Unlike tier 1 and Social Security, where both the employer and employee tax rates are 7.65 percent, tier 2 employer's contributions are much greater. The tier 2 employer and employee tax rates are 16.10 percent and 4.90 percent, respectively.

### Other retirements

Basically, revenues classified as "other retirements" in the federal budget are the retirement contributions of federal government workers. [Employer and employee payroll taxes for District of Columbia government employees covered under the Civil Service Retirement System (CSRS) are also included as other retirement revenues in the federal budget.] Federal government workers are covered under one of two programs. For decades, all workers were covered under the CSRS. Under this program, most employees pay a 7 percent tax on all wages. (A higher tax rate is levied on workers in special groups, such as law enforcement officers and congressional staff.) In 1984, a new retirement program for federal workers, the Federal Employees' Retirement System (FERS), was introduced. FERS is mandatory for new workers and elective for CSRS participants. FERS replaced the defined benefit program under CSRS with a program integrated with Social Security. FERS uses Social Security as a base, adds a supplemental benefit financed by a 0.8 percent tax on taxable wages, and then adds a deferred compensation plan. The supplemental tax of 0.8 percent is a payroll tax. (Under both programs, the federal government also makes an employer contribution based on the workers' wages; this, however, is not included in the revenue totals.)

## Incidence of federal payroll taxes

Compared with the other major federal tax source—individual income taxes—payroll taxes have low administration and compliance costs, but this is at the expense of progressivity. Payroll taxes are less progressive than individual income taxes because all payroll taxes tax only earned income, and most include a maximum taxable earnings base. Currently, the effective or average federal payroll taxes are progressive only in the lowest income quintile, virtually flat across the three middle income quintiles, and regressive in the top quintile

(U.S. Congress, Congressional Budget Office 1994). In an effort to increase the progressivity of Social Security, the largest payroll tax, the earned income tax credit (EITC) was introduced in 1975 to lighten the burden on working people below certain incomes. Since then, the EITC has been expanded several times, including the two most recent Omnibus Budget Reconciliation Acts in 1990 and 1993.

## Additional readings

Musgrave, Richard A., and Peggy B. Musgrave. *Public Finance in Theory and Practice*. 4th ed. New York: McGraw-Hill, 1984.

Pechman, Joseph A. *Federal Tax Policy*. 5th ed. Washington, D.C.: The Brookings Institution, 1987.

Rosen, Harvey S. *Public Finance*. Homewood, Ill.: Richard D. Irwin, 1985.

U.S. Congress, Congressional Budget Office. *The Economic and Budget Outlook: Fiscal Years 1995–1999*. 103rd Cong., 2d sess., 1994.

U.S. Congress, House of Representatives, Committee on Ways and Means. *Overview of the Federal Tax System*. 103rd Cong., 1st sess., 1993.

U.S. Congress, House of Representatives, Committee on Ways and Means. *Overview of Entitlement Programs: 1996 Green Book*. 104th Cong., 2d sess., 1996.

*Cross references:* earned income credit; fairness in taxation; Medicare trust fund; Social Security benefits, federal taxation; Social Security Trust Fund.

# Pensions, tax treatment

John A. Turner
International Labor Office

*To encourage (or at least not discourage) saving for retirement, tax policy generally accords favorable treatment toward contributions, investment income, and/or benefits related to income accumulated for retirement.*

---

Private pensions receive favorable tax treatment in the United States and in most other countries. In the United States, an employer's pension contribution is deductible in computing corporate income taxes, and the investment earnings on plan assets are not taxed. The employee is taxed once—personal income tax liability is deferred until the employee receives a distribution from the plan. In comparison, for savings through wage payments, the employee is taxed twice—when wages are received and when investment earnings are received on the subsequent savings.

## Policy aspects of the tax treatment of pension plans

The U.S. tax code requirements to qualify for favorable tax treatment are used to regulate pension plans. To be tax-qualified, a plan must meet minimum standards regarding participation, vesting, and nondiscrimination against lower-paid workers (McGill and Grubbs 1989). For plans not meeting these standards, the employer's contribution must be included in the employee's taxable income if it is to be tax-deductible to the employer.

Favorable tax treatment is justified by the argument that, without a tax subsidy, families would save too little for retirement. A key issue concerning the taxation of pensions is: Do the tax exemptions increase coverage and individual savings or do they simply substitute pensions for other forms of saving? As well as the possible effect on workers' savings, the tax treatment of pensions may affect other microeconomic decisions of workers and employers: (1) wages versus pensions, (2) deferred wages versus pensions, (3) other fringe benefits (such as employer-provided health insurance) versus pensions, (4) Social Security versus pensions, (5) defined benefit versus defined contribution plans, (6) individual plans versus employer-provided plans, (7) self-employment versus corporate employment, (8) lump-sum benefits versus annuities, and (9) pension investments in some types of assets versus others.

## Calculating the tax liability

Private pension plans involve three transactions, which are possible occasions for taxation—contributions, investment income, and benefits payments.

### Contributions

Employer pension contributions and wages are deductible business expenses under the corporate income tax. From a tax perspective, employers are indifferent between paying wages and contributing to pension plans. However, employers are not indifferent between making pension contributions and paying deferred wages. Because there is no way to shelter from the corporate income tax money set aside to pay deferred wages, pensions are preferred by employers to deferred wages when compensation is deferred.

To protect the Treasury against excessive tax deductions, limits are placed on pension contributions. Maximum contributions to a pension plan depend on plan type (e.g., defined benefit, profit-sharing), whether the employee is covered by more than one plan, and whether the plan is top-heavy, which refers to plans (mainly for small firms) where a disproportionate amount of the benefits accrue to the owners of the firm and key employees. Limits are placed on the maximum employee earnings that can be used to determine benefits or contributions. There are also contribution limits based on the extent to which pension assets exceed or fall short of liabilities (Hubbard 1994).

Employer and employee contributions are treated differently by the U.S. tax code. Employer contributions are not taxed as income to the employee, avoiding personal income and Social Security payroll taxation when the contributions are made.

Employee contributions are generally taxable under the personal income tax and the Social Security payroll tax. Employee contributions to salary reduction plans are an exception.

The most common type of salary reduction plan is the 401(k) plan, named after the Internal Revenue Code section that established it. In salary reduction plans, employee contributions are deductible from before-tax earnings, a feature that may explain much of their popularity. While salary reduction plans generally require employee contributions, other pension plans rarely do.

### Investment earnings and assets

Once an employer or employee has contributed to a pension plan, the investment earnings on those funds are not taxed. This aspect of the tax treatment of pension plans is called the "inside buildup." Pension assets maintained in the pension plan are also not taxable. However, when an employer terminates an overfunded defined benefit plan and surplus plan assets revert to the employer, those assets are taxed at the corporate income tax rate plus an excise tax of 20 percent. The excise tax rate is increased to 50 percent unless the employer transfers part of the excess assets to a replacement plan or provides a benefit increase under the terminating plan. This tax treatment discourages firms from terminating overfunded defined benefit plans.

### Distributions of benefits

Pension benefits received at retirement or earlier are taxed under the federal and state personal income tax rates, but are not subject to the Social Security payroll tax. A participant generally recovers tax-free the amounts that have been included previously in his or her taxable income. These tax-free amounts are called "basis," and generally consist of the employee's after-tax contributions. Because of the progressivity of the income tax system, frequently workers have lower marginal income tax rates in retirement than while working. Lump-sum distributions received before retirement are subject

to an excise tax as well as the personal income tax. The excise tax is designed to discourage those distributions, under the theory that pension plan assets should be used exclusively for financing retirement consumption.

### Implications of the tax treatment of pensions

The tax treatment of pensions moves the United States towards a consumption tax system. Earnings saved through a pension are not taxed until received in retirement. A consumption tax avoids the double taxation of savings that occurs under the current income tax system.

The two aspects of the tax advantage of pensions are income-smoothing and the tax-exempt status of pension plan earnings. When income is taxed according to a progressive tax scale, workers can avoid paying high marginal tax rates on pension contributions during their working lives and instead can pay lower inframarginal tax rates when they receive their pension during retirement.

Even if the marginal tax rates the worker paid were the same in retirement as when working, with a progressive tax scale the worker can gain because the first pension dollars are taxed at lower inframarginal rates. The first dollar received in retirement is taxed at the lowest tax rate, and subsequent dollars are taxed at progressively higher marginal rates. Because of the tax advantages of income-smoothing, workers will want larger pensions under a progressive tax system than a flat tax system (Ippolito 1990).

The tax system has reduced the desirability of defined benefit plans relative to defined contribution plans. First, employees can make tax-deductible contributions to defined contribution plans but not to defined benefit plans. Second, the Omnibus Budget Reconciliation Act of 1987 reduced the amount of funding that could be put into a pension plan that was overfunded. This reduced the amount that could accumulate in a defined benefit plan earning the tax-free rate of return, reducing the tax advantage of defined benefit plans relative to defined contribution plans.

### Pension tax expenditures

Tax expenditures for pensions are measured relative to a comprehensive income tax under which the increase in the present value of expected retirement benefits (roughly equal to the employer contribution plus investment earnings) is included in the employee's taxable income. Pension benefits are not taxed. Thus, the Treasury Department's estimate of tax expenditures consists of (1) the revenue loss from exempting employer contributions and investment earnings, offset by (2) the revenue gain from currently taxing private pension benefits. Most of the tax benefits of pensions accrue to middle-income families, those with incomes between $30,000 and $50,000 in the early 1990s. The tax expenditure for pensions is the largest tax expenditure for individuals, representing 18 percent of total tax expenditures for individuals and a revenue loss of $51 billion in 1992 (Dorsey 1992). (This amount includes the tax expenditure for pension plans provided by federal, state, and local governments and other non-business employers.)

The tax expenditure figures indicate the amount of federal income tax revenue lost in a tax year as a result of private pensions. The tax expenditure figures overstate, however, the long-term loss of revenue. A worker's lifetime loss measure would calculate the amount of revenue lost this year as a result of pension accruals for workers and subtract the expected present value of taxes paid on those currently accruing benefits. Unlike health insurance premiums, which are never subject to federal taxation, retirement fund contributions and investment earnings eventually face the individual income tax when paid out to retired workers.

### Additional readings

Dorsey, Stuart. "Taxation of Pensions." In *Trends in Pensions 1992*, edited by John A. Turner and Daniel J. Beller. Washington, D.C.: U.S. Government Printing Office, 1992.

Hubbard, Richard L. "The Tax Treatment of Pensions." In *Pension Funding and Taxation: Implications for Tomorrow*, edited by Dallas L. Salisbury and Nora Super Jones. Employee Benefit Research Institute, 1994.

Ippolito, Richard A. *An Economic Appraisal of Pension Tax Policy in the United States.* Homewood, Ill.: Irwin, 1990.

McGill, Dan M., and Donald S. Grubbs, Jr. *Fundamentals of Private Pensions.* 6th ed. Philadelphia: University of Pennsylvania Press, 1989.

*Cross references:* fringe benefits; individual retirement accounts; saving, taxes and.

# Personal exemption, federal

Joseph J. Cordes
George Washington University

*The amount of money that a taxpayer can deduct from federal adjustable gross income, based on the number of dependents claimed on the tax return.*

In arriving at taxable income, taxpayers are allowed to deduct a certain amount based on the number of dependents claimed on the tax return. People who are claimed as dependents on another taxpayer's tax return cannot claim themselves as dependents on their own tax returns.

In 1997, the amount of the federal personal exemption equaled $2,650 per dependent. Thus, a single taxpayer would be entitled to claim a single personal exemption of $2,650; a married couple could claim two personal exemptions worth $5,300; a married couple with two children would have four personal exemptions worth $10,600; and so on.

For many families, the personal exemption, together with the standard deduction, defines a threshold level of income below which no tax is due. Table 1 shows the levels of this threshold in 1997 for families of different types.

Failing to index the personal exemption for inflation reduces the real value of the threshold level of nontaxable income and raises the average effective tax rate. For example, in 1950, the personal exemption equaled $600. In 1986, the personal exemption was $1,080, even though over the same period the cost of living had risen by more than 350 percent. Thus, over 36 years, the real value of the exemption had fallen by almost half, to $304 in 1950 dollars. Put somewhat differently, had the 1950-level personal exemption been increased for inflation over the same 36-year period, it would have equaled $2,129 in 1986.

The steady erosion in the real value of the personal exemption was halted by the Tax Reform Act of 1986, which raised it to $2,000 by 1989 and which provided that the personal exemption, along with the standard deduction, was to be adjusted annually for inflation beginning in 1990. (Personal exemptions and the standard deduction were also indexed in 1985 and 1986.)

Although the personal exemption is available to most taxpayers, higher-income taxpayers are subject to a phaseout of their personal exemption after their income reaches a certain level. In 1997, the phaseout began at $121,200 for a single taxpayer and at $181,800 for married taxpayers filing jointly. The effect of this provision is to increase the effective marginal tax rate of taxpayers subject to the exemption phaseout.

### Additional reading

Pechman, Joseph. *Federal Tax Policy.* 5th ed. Washington, D.C.: The Brookings Institution, 1987.

*Cross references:* adjusted gross income; inflation indexation of income taxes; marginal effective tax rate; standard deduction, federal.

## TABLE 1

| Family Type | Value of Personal Exemptions | Standard Deduction | Taxable Income Threshold |
|---|---|---|---|
| Single | $2,650 | $4,150 | $6,800 |
| Husband and Wife | $5,300 | $6,900 | $12,400 |
| Single Head of Household and 2 Children | $7,950 | $6,050 | $14,000 |
| Husband, Wife, and 2 Children | $10,600 | $6,900 | $17,500 |

# Portfolio choice

## James Poterba
Massachusetts Institute of Technology

*Differing tax treatments on portfolio income (the name for the group of various types of investments not related to income earned from trade or business) will affect investors' decisions on which investments to buy and sell.*

The personal income tax in the United States levies different tax burdens on different types of capital income. Interest and dividend income in excess of low thresholds is included in taxable income. Capital gains are only taxed upon realization, and then at a preferential rate. Interest paid on state and local government bonds is tax-exempt. As a result of these tax provisions, individual investors in different tax circumstances may choose to hold different portfolios.

This entry begins by summarizing existing theoretical models of individual portfolio choice in the presence of taxation. It then describes the empirical evidence on how asset choice, and in particular the dividend yield on common stock held by different investors, is affected by taxation. The final section describes the rise of targeted retirement saving accounts, such as individual retirement accounts (IRAs) and 401(k) plans, that permit households to defer taxes on capital income.

## Models of portfolio choice with differential taxation

If investors face different marginal tax rates on different assets, if there is heterogeneity in these tax rates in the investor population, and if all assets are riskless, then investors should segregate into asset clienteles. This can be illustrated in a simple model, based on Miller (1977), in which there are only two portfolio assets: corporate debt and corporate equity. Assume that corporate equity is untaxed at the investor level. Investors facing high tax rates should therefore specialize in equity, while investors in

lower tax brackets should hold only corporate debt. Assume further that there are fixed supplies of corporate debt and equity, and that corporate capital earns a fixed pretax rate of return, $f$. Corporate interest payments are deductible from corporate income tax, but corporate profits net of interest are taxed at the corporate income tax rate, $\tau_C$. In this setting, the returns that investors receive from holding bonds and stocks will adjust to clear the stock and bond markets. This requires equality between the return after investor taxes on debt and equity for the lowest-tax-rate investor holding equity. If the pretax rates of return on debt and equity are $r_D$ and $r_E$, respectively, and the tax rate of this marginal investor is $\tau^*$, the after-tax returns received by the marginal investor must satisfy $(1-\tau^*)r_D = r_E$. Normalizing the price of equity to equal unity, $r_E = (1-\tau_C)f$, and $r_D = [(1-\tau_C)/(1-\tau^*)]f$. The value of $\tau^*$ depends on the supply of equity, the distribution of wealth across taxpayers with different marginal tax rates, and the marginal tax rate schedule.

The *pretax* return on debt exceeds that on equity by just enough to compensate the marginal investor for the higher taxes on debt than equity. For an investor with a tax rate ($\tau$) above that of the marginal investor, the incremental after-tax return from holding equity rather than debt is $r_E - (1-\tau)r_D = (1-\tau_C)f - (1-\tau)[(1-\tau_C)/(1-\tau^*)]f = [(\tau-\tau^*)/(1-\tau^*)](1-\tau_C)f$. If the pretax returns on debt and equity were equal, the corresponding incremental return would be $\tau(1-\tau_C)f$. The higher pretax return on debt than equity illustrates the notion of an *implicit tax*: Although equity investors are not taxed on their returns, the relative pretax returns on equity are reduced by the heavier taxation of bonds. This is a pervasive effect of taxes that are specific to particular assets or types of capital income. Scholes and Wolfson (1992) present examples of implicit taxes that arise with respect to both portfolio and real investments.

This simple model illustrates the importance of general equilibrium considerations in analyzing financial markets in the presence of taxes. Asset supplies are not fixed in Miller's (1977) model; they respond to taxes and other market factors. Under the strong assumptions of the model, the tax rate of the marginal investor must equal the corporate tax rate ($\tau=\tau_C$). Any individual firm should therefore

**TABLE 1**

**Probability of Owning Assets in One Class, Conditional on Ownership of Another Asset Category**

| Conditional on Holding | Probability of Holding | | | |
|---|---|---|---|---|
| | Stocks | Bonds | Bills | Tax-Exempt |
| Stocks (17%) | 1.00 | 0.22 | 0.77 | 0.57 |
| Bonds (2%) | 0.89 | 1.00 | 0.98 | 0.78 |
| Bills (30%) | 0.70 | 0.22 | 1.00 | 0.42 |
| Tax-Exempt (11%) | 0.87 | 0.33 | 0.94 | 1.00 |

be indifferent between issuing debt and equity. The model also shows how investors might segment into different clienteles, with different types of investors holding different types of securities.

The Miller (1977) model nevertheless neglects important aspects of actual financial markets. Perhaps most importantly, the returns on most assets are uncertain. In this case, a key determinant of portfolio patterns is whether investors can obtain all possible pretax return streams from assets with their own most-preferred tax treatment. For example, if both debt and equity in the earlier model had risky but identical returns, then the clientele results of the type described above would still be obtained. If investors cannot span the set of pretax returns with tax-preferred assets, however, Auerbach and King (1983) show that simple portfolio clientele results break down. Investors will hold portfolios determined in part by their tax preferences, and in part by their risk preferences. More realistic models generally do not yield stark predictions on clientele formation. Poterba (forthcoming) summarizes this literature in more detail.

## Empirical evidence on taxes and portfolio behavior

Whether taxes affect portfolio decisions can be tested in many ways. At the outset, it is important to investigate whether investors segment into the portfolio clienteles suggested by some models. King and Leape (1984) explored this issue using data from a 1978 survey conducted by SRI International. They found that most investors held incomplete portfolios—that is, they had zero holdings of many broad asset categories such as corporate stock, corporate bonds, and tax-exempt bonds. Leape (1987) tries to model such incompleteness as the optimal response to information and transaction costs; he also surveys much of the previous literature on this issue. Second, King and Leape (1984) found that most investors with relatively tax-favored assets also held more heavily taxed assets, contrary to the prediction of the simple clientele models described above.

Table 1 presents similar evidence based on the 1989 Survey of Consumer Finances (SCF). The en-

tries report the probabilities of holding corporate stock or stock mutual funds (Stocks); corporate bonds or corporate bond mutual funds (Bonds); Treasury bonds, bills, government bond mutual funds, or money-market funds (Bills); and tax-exempt debt or tax-exempt mutual funds (Tax-Exempt), *conditional* on positive holdings of the other asset categories. These tabulations exclude holdings in targeted retirement accounts, such as IRAs and Keoghs.

The data do not suggest the presence of sharp asset-holding clienteles. For example, more than three-quarters of the households holding corporate bonds also hold tax-exempt bonds. While only one-third of those holding tax-exempt bonds also hold corporate bonds, nearly all investors in tax-exempts also have taxable-interest-bearing assets such as government bonds or Treasury bills.

Feldstein (1976) and King and Leape (1984) present more formal tests of the link between investor marginal tax rates and asset purchase decisions. The former study analyzes portfolio data from the 1962 SCF, when the top marginal federal tax rate was 91 percent. Feldstein (1976) finds that a household's income has a substantial effect on the mix of assets it holds, conditional on net worth. He interprets this evidence as showing that marginal tax rates affect portfolio composition, although the perennial problem in cross-sectional analysis of tax effects, separating tax rate effects from income effects, complicates this conclusion.

King and Leape (1984) present similar evidence, although their findings imply a weaker relationship between marginal tax rates and portfolio choice. They find some evidence that tax variables affect the *set* of assets that investors decide to hold, but much weaker evidence on the link between tax rates and the *level* of asset holdings, or the fraction of the portfolio held in different assets.

Poterba and Samwick (1998) analyze both cross-sectional patterns of asset holding in the SCFs conducted between 1983 and 1992, and *changes* in asset holding between the 1983 and 1989 wages of the SCF panel. They introduce a richer set of controls for income-related differences in tax rates than earlier studies, yet they still find substantial effects of marginal tax rates on the set of assets that households hold. The ownership effects are again more pronounced than the effects of taxation on the portfolio shares in different assets. Samwick (1998) presents detailed summary tabulations on portfolio ownership patterns as reported in the SCFs.

The starkest example of an asset that should exhibit a tax-rate-sensitive demand is tax-exempt debt. Feldstein (1976), King and Leape (1984), and Poterba and Samwick (1998) suggest that higher-income households are more likely to hold tax-exempt debt. Only the last of these studies finds an effect for marginal tax rates after controlling for household income.

Feenberg and Poterba (1991) consider the inverse problem, studying the distribution of marginal tax rates among individuals who hold tax-exempt debt. In 1988, a year when the top stated bracket in the federal income tax schedule was 33 percent, less than one-fifth of outstanding tax-exempt debt was held by taxpayers in the 33 percent bracket. Taxpayers with marginal tax rates between 28 and 33 percent held an additional two-thirds of the tax-exempt debt held by individuals. Slightly less than 10 percent of individual holdings of tax-exempt debt were reported by taxpayers with marginal rates of less than 20 percent. The explanation for the nontrivial holdings among low marginal tax rate households may be inertia in portfolio choice, inheritance, or transitory fluctuations in marginal tax rates.

One aspect of taxation and portfolio choice that has been an active subject of empirical research is the relationship between marginal dividend tax rates and the dividend yield on common stock held by different households. Blume et al. (1974), Petit (1977), Lewellen et al. (1978), Chaplinsky and Seyhun (1990), and Scholz (1992) used different methodologies and data sets to test whether individuals who face higher marginal tax rates on dividends relative to capital gains are more likely to invest in low-yield stocks (which are assumed to pay out more of the total return in the form of lightly taxed capital gains).

Most of these studies suggest that taxpayers facing higher dividend tax burdens hold lower-yield stocks, although this effect is substantively small. Blume et al. (1974) studied a unique sample of tax returns from 1971, and found that the ratio of dividends to market value of equity varies by approximately 75 basis points between investors facing the lowest and highest marginal tax rates. Petit (1977) estimates that a 10-point increase in an investor's marginal tax burden on dividend income would reduce his portfolio's dividend yield by approximately 35 basis points. Scholz's (1992) estimates suggest larger tax effects than earlier studies, implying that a 10-percentage-point increase in an investor's marginal dividend tax rate would reduce his portfolio's dividend yield by between 100 and 150 basis points. This estimated effect is larger than simple comparisons of portfolio yields for different groups of investors suggest, and the source of the difference between Scholz's (1992) findings and those in earlier studies is not clear.

Chaplinsky and Seyhun (1990) adopt a somewhat different empirical strategy. They analyze tax return data and show that the ratio of dividends to realized capital gains varies as a function of an investor's tax position. This is not direct evidence of dividend-yield clienteles, because it could also reflect tax effects on decisions to realize capital gains.

The foregoing studies on taxation and equity portfolio choice have focused on the choice of individual equity securities, ignoring open-end mutual funds. These funds are a significant and rapidly growing part of individual portfolios. Because investors do not control the timing of asset sales for the securities owned by mutual funds, as they do for securities held on their own account, mutual funds present individual investors with different tax minimization problems. Dickson and Shoven (1993) discuss the effects of a fund's gain and loss realization strategies on the after-tax return earned by investors. Their results underscore the value of selecting open-end mutual funds that are managed in tax-efficient ways.

## Investing through tax-deferred saving vehicles

The preceding discussion concentrated on investors who hold securities in currently taxable form. Yet during the 1980s, many investors took advantage of new tax provisions that created opportunities for tax-deferred saving. IRAs, described in more detail in Venti and Wise (1992), were a popular saving vehicle from their introduction in 1981 until eligibility restrictions were imposed in the Tax Reform Act of 1986. A second type of tax-deferred saving vehicle, the 401(k) plan, has grown rapidly throughout the 1980s and early 1990s. By 1990, 17.3 million workers participated in 401(k) plans. Poterba et al. (1994a) report that the participation rate of eligible workers exceeds 70 percent, and demonstrate that contributions to IRAs and 401(k) plans represented a substantial fraction of private saving in the United States during the late 1980s.

IRAs as offered in the early 1980s, and 401(k) plans, allow investors the opportunity to defer taxes on current income that is saved through these accounts. Moreover, taxes on the income from assets held in these accounts are deferred until the accounts are drawn down. Withdrawals from these accounts are taxed as ordinary income, and they are subject to an additional 10 percent penalty tax if they are made before age 59½. 401(k) plans frequently offer an additional attraction: Employers may match worker contributions to these plans and often do so at substantial rates.

One of the key questions associated with the increasing importance in household portfolios of assets held in IRAs and 401(k) plans is the degree to which these assets replace those that would otherwise have been held in traditional taxable accounts. Evidence presented in Poterba et al. (1994b) suggests that, with the possible exception of high-income, high-wealth households, households do not view contributions to IRAs and 401(k) plans as substitutes for other types of asset accumulation. Gale and Scholz (1994) present a contrary view and also provide references to many of the earlier studies on this issue.

Both 401(k) plans and IRAs are saving *vehicles* with attractive tax features, not *assets* with attractive tax characteristics. Investors therefore have some discretion in selecting the assets that are held in these accounts. If an investor holds both highly taxed bonds and less-heavily taxed equity in a portfolio, current taxes could be reduced by placing the bonds in the tax-deferred saving vehicle, and the stocks in the taxable account. Whether such a strategy maximizes the investor's long-term, after-tax wealth holdings, however, remains an open question.

## Taxation and portfolio adjustment

This discussion focuses on how taxes affect the composition of household portfolios, neglecting the important related question of how taxation, particularly capital gains taxation, affects decisions to sell assets and make portfolio adjustments. Numerous empirical studies, starting with Feldstein et al. (1980) and surveyed in Poterba (forthcoming), have shown that capital gains realization behavior is affected by the level, and expected change, in capital gains tax rates. The general effect of realization-based capital gains taxation is to encourage investors to defer sale of appreciated assets, but because this applies to all assets that may generate capital gains, the overall effect of such "lock-in" on the mix of assets held in investor portfolios is difficult to assess.

## Additional readings

Auerbach, Alan J., and Mervyn A. King. "Taxation, Portfolio Choice, and Debt-Equity Ratios: A General Equilibrium Model." *Quarterly Journal of Economics* 98 (1983): 587–609.

Blume, Marshall E., Jean Crockett, and Irwin Friend. "Stockholders in the United States: Characteristics and Trends." *Survey of Current Business* 64 (November 1974): 16–40.

Chaplinsky, Susan, and H. Nejat Seyhun. "Dividends and Taxes: Evidence on Tax Reduction Strategies." *Journal of Business* 63 (1990): 239–60.

Dickson, Joel, and John B. Shoven, "Ranking Mutual Funds on an After Tax Basis." Working Paper 4393, National Bureau of Economic Research. Cambridge, Mass., July 1993.

Engen, Eric, William Gale, and J. Karl Scholz. "The Illusory Effects of Savings Incentives on Saving." *Journal of Economic Perspectives* 10 (Fall 1996): 113–38.

Feenberg, Daniel R., and James M. Poterba. "Which Households Own Municipal Bonds? Evidence from Tax Returns." *National Tax Journal* 44 (December 1991): 93–103.

Feldstein, Martin S. "Personal Taxation and Portfolio Composition: An Econometric Analysis." *Econometrica* 44 (July 1976): 631–49.

Feldstein, Martin S., Joel B. Slemrod, and Shlomo Yitzhaki. "The Effects of Taxation on the Selling of Corporate Stock and the Realization of Capital Gains." *Quarterly Journal of Economics* 94 (1980): 777–91.

Gale, William, and John Karl Scholz. "IRAs and Household Saving." *American Economic Review* 84 (December 1994): 1233–60.

King, Mervyn A., and Jonathan I. Leape. "Wealth and Portfolio Composition: Theory and Evidence." Working Paper 1468, National Bureau of Economic Research. Cambridge, Mass., 1984.

Leape, Jonathan I. "Taxes and Transaction Costs in Asset Market Equilibrium." *Journal of Public Economics* 33 (1987): 1–20.

Lewellen, Wilbur G., Kenneth L. Stanley, Ronald C. Lease, and Gary G. Schlarbaum. "Some Direct Evidence on the Dividend Clientele Phenomenon." *Journal of Finance* 33 (December 1978): 1385–99.

Miller, Merton. "Debt and Taxes." *Journal of Finance* 32 (May 1977): 261–75.

Petit, R. Richardson. "Taxes, Transaction Costs, and the Clientele Effect of Dividends." *Journal of Financial Economics* 5 (1977): 419–36.

Poterba, James M. "Taxation, Risk-Taking, and Household Portfolio Behavior." In *Handbook of Public Economics* 3, edited by Alan J. Auerbach and Martin S. Feldstein. Amsterdam: North-Holland, forthcoming.

Poterba, James M., and Andrew Samwick. "Taxation and Household Portfolio Composition: Evidence from Tax Reforms in the 1980s." Mimeograph, Department of Economics, Massachusetts Institute of Technology. Cambridge, Mass., 1998.

Poterba, James M., Steven F. Venti, and David A. Wise. "Do 401(k) Contributions Crowd Out Other Personal Saving?" Working Paper, Massachusetts Institute of Technology. Cambridge, Mass.: 1994a.

Poterba, James M., Steven F. Venti, and David A. Wise. "Targeted Retirement Saving and the Net Worth of Elderly Americans." *American Economic Review* 84 (May 1994b): 180–85.

Poterba, James M., Steven F. Venti, and David A. Wise. "How Retirement Saving Programs Increase Private Saving." *Journal of Economic Perspectives* 10 (Fall 1996): 91–112.

Samwick, Andrew A. "Portfolio Responses to Taxation: Evidence from the End of the Rainbow." In *Does Atlas Shrug? The Economic Consequences of Taxing the Rich*, edited by Joel Slemrod. Cambridge, U.K.: Cambridge University Press, 1998.

Scholes, Myron S., and Mark A. Wolfson. *Taxes and Business Strategy: A Planning Approach.* Englewood Cliffs, N.J.: Prentice Hall, 1992.

Scholz, John Karl. "A Direct Examination of the Dividend Clientele Hypothesis." *Journal of Public Economics* 49 (1992): 261–85.

Venti, Steven F., and David A. Wise. "Government Policy and Personal Retirement Saving." In *Tax Policy and the Economy* 6, edited by James M. Poterba. Cambridge, Mass.: MIT Press, 1992.

*Cross references:* capital gains taxation; dividends, double taxation of; implicit taxes; individual retirement accounts; saving, taxes and; tax-exempt bonds.

# Profit-sharing plans

Dallas Salisbury
Employee Benefit Research Institute

*A type of defined contribution plan in which the employer's only financial obligation is the contribution made.*

Profit-sharing plans are sometimes structured in such a way that employees share in their companies' profits and potentially gain a greater interest in their firms' success.

In 1939, legislation clarified the tax status of deferred plans (defined below). This legislation and the World War II wage freeze resulted in the rapid growth of profit-sharing plans in the 1940s. The Employee Retirement Income Security Act of 1974 (ERISA) furthered this growth by imposing less burdensome regulations on profit-sharing plans than on defined benefit pension plans, thus increasing their attractiveness. The Revenue Act of 1978 created Section 401(k) of the Internal Revenue Code (IRC), which provided for employee pretax contributions to profit-sharing plans.

## Types of plans

There are three basic types of profit-sharing plans.

Under a *cash plan*, at the time profits are determined, contributions are paid directly to employees in the form of cash, checks, or stock. The amount is taxed as ordinary income when distributed.

Under a *deferred plan*, profit-sharing contributions are not paid out currently but rather are deferred to individual accounts set up for each employee. Benefits—and any investment earnings accrued—are distributed at retirement, death, or disability, and sometimes at separation from service or other events, at which point they are taxable.

Under a *combination plan*, the participant has the option of deferring all or part of the profit-

sharing allocation. That portion taken as a deferral is placed into the participant's account, where it and investment earnings accrue tax-free until withdrawal. Any amount taken in cash is taxed currently. For tax purposes, Internal Revenue Service (IRS) qualification of profit-sharing plans is restricted to deferred or combination plans, which may be 401(k) arrangements. According to more recent tabulations of data from the 5500 series of tax forms, 95.7 percent of all 401(k) plans in 1992 were profit-sharing and thrift saving plans.

## Plan qualification rules

Profit-sharing plans, like other retirement plans, must meet a variety of requirements to qualify for preferential tax treatment. These rules, created under ERISA, are designed to protect employee rights and to guarantee that pension benefits will be available for employees at retirement. The rules govern requirements for reporting and disclosure of plan information, fiduciary responsibilities, employee eligibility for plan participation, vesting of benefits, form of benefit payment, and funding. In addition, qualified plans must satisfy a set of IRS nondiscrimination rules [under IRC Sections 401(a)(4), 410(b), and, in some cases, 401(a)(26)] designed to ensure that a plan does not discriminate in favor of highly compensated employees.

## Contributions

### Employer contributions

Plans must define how employer contributions will be allocated to employee accounts. The allocation formula is generally based on compensation. Sometimes the allocation is a flat percentage of pay, or it may be determined by calculating the proportion of each employee's compensation relative to the total compensation of all plan participants. For example, if the employee earns $15,000 annually and total annual compensation for all participants is $300,000, the employee would receive 5 percent of the employer's annual contribution. With the advent of Section 401(k), many employers now offer a matching contribution that is tied to contributions made by the employee.

Some plans base their allocations on compensation and service credits. These plans must be careful to ensure that the wage/service formula meets the regulatory scheme for demonstrating that the formula does not discriminate in favor of highly compensated employees. Allocation formulas may be integrated with Social Security within prescribed limits. Maximum annual contributions (employer and employee, if any) on behalf of each plan participant are limited by the defined contribution limits under Section 415 of the IRC. But the total amount of contributions for all employees that an employer may deduct for federal tax purposes is limited to 15 percent of all covered employees' compensation.

Until recently, an employer's contribution to a profit-sharing plan was limited to the extent of an employer's current or accumulated profits. Currently, an employer does not have to have profits to establish a profit-sharing plan, and total contributions are not restricted to total profits. Plan documents, however, must specify that the plan is a profit-sharing plan.

If an employer's contribution for a particular year is less than the maximum amount for which a deduction is allowed, the unused limit may not be carried forward to subsequent years unless the carryforward exists as of December 31, 1986. These limit carryforwards may be used to increase the general deduction limit to 25 percent until the carryforwards are exhausted.

A deduction carryforward of contributions in excess of the deduction limit for a particular year may be deductible in succeeding taxable years to the extent allowed. Such contributions, however, may be subject to a 10 percent nondeductible excise tax. Excess contributions are defined as the sum of total amounts contributed for the taxable year over the amount allowable as a deduction for that year plus the amount of excess contributions for the preceding year, reduced by amounts returned to the employer during the year, if any, and the portion of the prior excess contribution that is deductible in the current year. In other words, if an excess contribution is made during a taxable year, the excise tax would apply for that year and for each succeeding year until the excess is eliminated. Excess contributions for a year are determined at the close of the employer's taxable year, and the tax is imposed on the employer.

### Employee contributions

Pure profit-sharing plans do not require employee contributions, but some may permit voluntary employee contributions up to certain limits. Employee contributions in the form of a salary reduction are becoming increasingly popular. When pretax salary reduction is allowed, the plan must follow rules for 401(k) arrangements.

## Distributions

### Retirement, disability, and death benefits

The law requires that participants' account balances fully vest at retirement. In addition, plans generally provide for benefits upon death or disability. A plan's vesting provisions determine whether an employee will receive full or partial benefits upon other types of employment termination. However, if the plan is contributory (that is, if employees make con-

tributions), the employee will always receive the benefits that are attributable to "I" or the employee's own contributions.

Profit-sharing plans typically give retiring participants and beneficiaries of deceased participants a choice between a lump-sum payment and installments. Usually, those who terminate employment for reasons other than retirement, death, or disability receive lump-sum distributions, although if the benefit exceeds $3,500, the participant cannot be forced to take an immediate benefit. Distributions from profit-sharing accounts must follow the general distribution rules for all qualified retirement plans. Distributions must begin by the year following the attainment of age 70½ even if the individual has not retired. There are minimum and maximum limits on the amount of annual distribution, both subject to penalty taxes if not followed.

### In-service withdrawals

Some profit-sharing plans provide for partial account withdrawals during active employment. Plans allowing participants to elect account withdrawals impose certain conditions, which vary widely. But generally, the funds must be held in the plan for two years before a withdrawal is allowed. A 10 percent additional income tax applies to most early distributions made before age 59½. The 10 percent additional tax does not apply to distributions that are (1) a result of the participant's death or disability; (2) in the form of an annuity or installments payable over the life or life expectancy of the participant (or joint lives or life expectancies of the participant and the participant's beneficiary); (3) made after the participant has separated from service on or after age 55; (4) used for payment of medical expenses deductible under federal income tax rules; (5) made to or on behalf of an alternate payee pursuant to a qualified domestic relations order; or (6) rolled over to an individual retirement account or other qualified plan within 60 days.

## Conclusion

Profit-sharing offers employees a chance to share in their company's success. The level of company success is directly related to profits, which often define the amount of profit-sharing allocation. So the greater the profits of the company, the larger the potential allocation. However, profit-sharing plans can serve several goals. If the plan is cash only, it is generally viewed as a form of bonus. If profits are good, benefits are paid. Deferred plans are usually intended to supplement other pension plans and thus are generally more appropriate for retirement purposes. With a 401(k) feature, the plan serves as a vehicle for employees to save for their retirement on a pretax basis.

## Additional readings

Allen, Everett T., Jr., Joseph Melone, Jerry Rosenbloom, and Jack L. VanDerhei. *Pension Planning*. 7th ed. Homewood, Ill.: Richard Irwin, 1992.

Employee Benefit Research Institute. *Fundamentals of Employee Benefit Plans*. 5th ed. Washington, D.C., 1996.

U.S. Department of Labor, Bureau of Labor Statistics. *Employee Benefits in Medium and Large Firms, 1993*. Washington, D.C.: U.S. Government Printing Office, 1995.

Watson Wyatt Worldwide. *Top 50: A Survey of Retirement, Thrift and Profit Sharing Plans Covering Salaried Employees at 50 Large U.S. Industrial Companies as of January 1, 1995*. Washington, D.C.: Wyatt Research and Information Center, 1996.

*Cross references:* employee stock ownership plan; fringe benefits; pensions, tax treatment; saving, taxes and.

# Progressivity, measures of

Donald W. Kiefer
Congressional Research Service, Library of Congress

*Although there is wide agreement on the definition of progressivity—the ratio of tax payment to income rises as income rises—there are variants regarding the measurement and valuation or the numerator and denominator.*

A tax is progressive if the ratio of taxes to income rises as income increases, proportional if the ratio is constant for all incomes, and regressive if the ratio falls as income increases. Progressivity measures determine the degree of progressivity (or regressivity) in a tax system and assess whether a tax revision has made a tax more or less progressive.

## Types of progressivity indexes

While the definition of tax progressivity is generally agreed upon, the way to measure it is not. Over the years, a wide variety of indexes of tax progressivity have been suggested and used. These tax progressivity indexes may be categorized in at least two ways: first, by what they measure, and second, by what affects their numerical value.

Some of the progressivity indexes measure the distribution of the tax burden, whereas others measure the effect of the tax system on the distribution of income. There is no universal agreement that the latter type of index should be regarded as a measure of "progressivity," and not all writers who have used

indexes of income redistribution have referred to them as measuring progressivity. Both types of measures will be discussed here.

The numerical value of one group of indexes, which might be called "structural indexes," is a function of the relationship between the amount of income and the amount of tax imposed on that income. The numerical value of the second group of indexes, which might be called "distributional indexes," is a function of the tax structure but also of the distribution of income.

## Structural progressivity indexes

Three commonly used structural progressivity indexes are average-rate progression, liability progression, and residual income progression (see Musgrave and Thin 1948).

Average-rate progression is the ratio of the change in effective tax rate to the change in income over some income interval; the value is positive when the tax is progressive, zero when the tax is proportional, and negative when the tax is regressive. For the U.S. federal income tax, this measure is positive and tends to decline as one moves up the income scale, indicating decreasing progressivity.

Liability progression is the ratio of the percentage change in tax liability to the percentage change in income; this index has a value greater than one when the tax is progressive, equal to one when the tax is proportional, and less than one when the tax is regressive. This measure applied to the federal income tax also indicates decreasing progressivity as one moves up the income scale.

Residual income progression is the ratio of the percentage change in after-tax income to the percentage change in before-tax income. The index is less than one when the tax is progressive, equal to one when the tax is proportional, and greater than one when the tax is regressive. This measure applied to the U.S. federal income tax is less than one and declines as one moves up the income scale, showing increasing progressivity (in contrast to the first two measures).

These measures will differ in what is characterized as a progressivity-neutral tax change. In a progressive tax system, an equal percentage point change in average tax rates will preserve average-rate progression, and proportionate changes in average tax rates will preserve liability progression. A tax change resulting in proportionate changes in after-tax incomes is neutral in terms of residual income progression.

Residual income progression is perhaps the most interesting of these measures from a welfare perspective because it relates to the effects of taxes on the distribution of disposable income.

## Distributional progressivity indexes

The distributional progressivity indexes are grouped here according to the measure of dispersion on which they are based: the concentration index or an index based on the concept of equally distributed equivalent level of income.

### Indexes based on a concentration index

A concentration index is based on a concentration curve. The best known of these measures are the Gini index and the Lorenz curve. With population members ordered from lowest to highest income, the Lorenz curve relates the cumulative share of income (on the vertical axis) to the cumulative share of population (on the horizontal axis). If income is equally distributed, the Lorenz curve lies on a 45° line, because each given fraction of the population has that same fraction of the total income. If income is not equally distributed, a given fraction of the population will have less than the same fraction of the aggregate income, and the Lorenz curve will lie beneath the 45° line, coinciding only at the 100 percent and zero percent points. The Gini index is the ratio of the area between the Lorenz curve and the 45° line to the entire area under the 45° line. The Gini index is 0 when income is equally distributed and rises toward one as income becomes more unequally distributed.

The following distributional progressivity indexes are based on the concentration index:

1. Musgrave and Thin (1948) introduced an index they labeled "Effective Progression," defined as

$$EP = \frac{(1 - G_a)}{(1 - G_b)}$$

where G refers to the Gini index, and the a and b subscripts refer to after-tax and before-tax income, respectively. For $EP > 1$, the tax is progressive; for $EP = 1$, the tax is proportional; for $EP < 1$ the tax is regressive.

2. The progressivity index used by Pechman and Okner (1974) is

$$PO = \frac{G_a - G_b}{G_b}$$

If $PO < 0$, the tax is progressive; if $PO = 0$, the tax is proportional; if $PO > 0$, the tax is regressive.

3. A related index was used by Reynolds and Smolensky (1977):

$$RS = G_a - G_b$$

If $RS < 0$, the tax is progressive; if $RS = 0$, the tax is proportional; if $RS > 0$, the tax is regressive.

4. The index used by Khetan and Poddar (1976) is

$$KP = \frac{(1 - G_b)}{(1 - C_t)}$$

where $C_t$ is the concentration index of taxes; that is, it is calculated like the Gini index with tax liability substituted for income. For $KP > 1$, the tax is progressive; for $KP = 1$, the tax is proportional; for $KP < 1$, the tax is regressive.

5. The index used by Kakwani (1977), which he labeled $P$, is

$$P = C_t - G_b$$

If $P > 0$, the tax is progressive; if $P = 0$, the tax is proportional; if $P < 0$, the tax is regressive.

6. Khetan and Podder (1976) and Suits (1977) developed two closely related indexes. The Suits index, $S$, which is the better known of the two, is the relative concentration index of taxes with respect to income; that is, it is calculated like the Gini index with tax liability substituted for income and income substituted for population. If $S > 0$, the tax is progressive; if $S = 0$, the tax is proportional; if $S < 0$, the tax is regressive. The Khetan-Poddar version is $1/(1 - S)$.

### Indexes based on the concept of equally distributed equivalent level of income

From a social welfare perspective, the Gini index and related concentration indexes suffer from well-known deficiencies. Atkinson (1970) emphasized that underlying any summary statistic of inequality "is some concept of social welfare and it is with this concept that we should be concerned." Atkinson and several other authors—including Dasgupta et al. (1973), Sen (1973), and Blackorby and Donaldson (1978)—examined the social welfare concept underlying the Gini index and found it wanting. For brevity, the specific criticisms of the Gini index will not be detailed here, but an overview is provided in Kiefer (1984).

Kolm (1969), Atkinson (1970), and Sen (1973) developed an alternative inequality index based on the concept of equally distributed equivalent level of income, designated by $Y_{ede}$. Given a social welfare function, $Y_{ede}$ is that level of per capita income which, if equally distributed, would produce the same level of social welfare as the current income distribution. The inequality index, $I$, is equal to one minus the ratio of $Y_{ede}$ to mean income. Blackorby and Donaldson (1983) proposed a tax progressivity index based on this inequality index:

$$BD = \frac{(1 - I_a)}{(1 - I_b)} - 1$$

If $BD > 0$, the tax is progressive; if $BD = 0$, the tax is proportional; if $BD < 0$, the tax is regressive.

Kiefer (1984) proposed an alternative tax progressivity index of the form:

$$K = I_b - I_a$$

If $K > 0$, the tax is progressive; if $K = 0$, the tax is proportional; if $K < 0$, the tax is regressive. This tax progressivity index shows tax changes that make equal improvements in social welfare to be equally progressive regardless of the initial income distribution. The *BD* index does not have this property.

Kiefer (1984) demonstrated that the various distributional tax progressivity indexes may give inconsistent results in comparisons of tax systems and income distributions. Each of the progressivity indexes is, in effect, associated with a unique definition of progressivity. Hence, a conclusion about which of two tax systems is more progressive may be dependent on which distributional tax progressivity measure is used for the evaluation. It is, therefore, incumbent upon the researcher to make a choice among the tax progressivity indexes based on an understanding of their characteristics and implications.

### Additional readings

Atkinson, Anthony B. "On the Measurement of Inequality." *Journal of Economic Theory* 2 (September 1970): 244–63.

Blackorby, Charles, and David Donaldson. "Measures of Relative Equality and Their Meaning in Terms of Social Welfare." *Journal of Economic Theory* 18 (June 1978): 59–80.

Blackorby, Charles, and David Donaldson. "Ethical Social Index Numbers and the Measurement of Effective Tax/Benefit Progressivity." Mimeograph. University of British Columbia, May 1983.

Dasgupta, Partha, Amartya Sen, and David Starrett. "Notes on Measurement of Inequality." *Journal of Economic Theory* 6 (April 1973): 180–87.

Kakwani, Nanak C. "Applications of Lorenz Curves in Economic Analysis." *Econometrica* 45 (April 1977): 719–27.

Khetan, C.P., and S.N. Poddar. "Measurement of Income Tax Progression in a Growing Economy: The Canadian Experience." *Canadian Journal of Economics* 9 (November 1976): 613–29.

Kiefer, Donald W. "Distributional Tax Progressivity Indexes." *National Tax Journal* 37 (December 1984): 497–513.

Kolm, S.C. "The Optimal Production of Social Justice." In *Public Economics,* edited by J. Margolis and H. Guitton, pp. 145–200. London: MacMillan, 1969.

Musgrave, Richard A., and Tun Thin. "Income Tax Progression, 1929–48." *Journal of Political Economy* 56 (December 1948): 498–514.

Pechman, Joseph A., and Benjamin A. Okner. *Who Bears the Tax Burden?* Washington, D.C.: The Brookings Institution, 1974.

Reynolds, Morgan, and Eugene Smolensky. "Post Fisc Distributions of Income in 1950, 1961, and 1970." *Public Finance Quarterly* 5 (October 1977): 419–38.

Sen, Amartya. *On Economic Inequality.* Oxford: Clarendon Press, 1973.

Suits, Daniel B. "Measurement of Tax Progressivity." *American Economic Review* 67 (September 1977): 747–52.

*Cross references:* ability to pay; fairness in taxation.

# Property tax, farm

Donald F. Vitaliano
Rensselaer Polytechnic Institute

*Property that is used in connection with farming frequently receives special treatment under state and local property taxes.*

---

Virtually every state in the Union has some sort of program designed to confer special property tax treatment upon farms. Although such plans were originally conceived as a way to preserve family farming, supporters of preferential treatment of farmland now include environmentalists who see it as way of preserving open spaces from encroaching suburban development. However, the weight of professional judgment and empirical evidence appears not to support such programs, whether judged on their own terms or by the conventional public finance criteria of equity, economic efficiency, and ease of administration.

The impetus to grant relief to farm real estate derives from a (correct) perception by the general public and policymakers that the property tax is regressive in relation to income, rather than a type of wealth tax. This attitude is reinforced by pressure for full-value assessment as communities undergo the transition from rural to suburban, a movement that particularly burdens farm real estate because it is typically assessed at the lowest fraction of market value among the several types of real property. A legitimate case for relief is conceivable if present owners reasonably anticipated continuation of these assessment practices at the time of purchase.

Preservation of family farming may be viewed as a form of income redistribution, whereas open-space preservation has to do with possible market failure. In the absence of market failure, economic efficiency favors full-value taxation because it is neutral in its impact on land-use decisions: The tax burden is unaffected by the use of the land.

Farm property is accorded special treatment in several different ways: preferential assessment at current use value instead of market value; deferred taxation of land kept in farming; credits against state income taxes; purchase of development rights; and land-use zoning. Zoning tends to impose the cost of farm preservation on landowners, and their resistance to it can be expected. But land not subject to significant development pressure may actually increase in value when subjected to strict agricultural zoning resulting from, say, reduced uncertainty and limits on nearby incompatible activities.

Forty-four states rely primarily upon some variant of use-value assessment. The popularity of this type of assessment may be attributed to the fact that it benefits farmers and investors who receive significant amounts of nonfarm income and who would not qualify for much, if any, relief under a tax credit scheme.

The impact of use-value taxation on the rate of conversion of farmland has been found to be negligible by Gloudemans (1974), Gustafson and Wallace (1975), Conklin and Lesher (1977), and Blewett and Lane (1988). Ladd (1980) maintains that use-value assessment has questionable distributional consequences.

The existence of external benefits of open space not reflected in the pecuniary and psychic returns to the farm operator is one type of market failure that may justify a farm tax subsidy. In addition, because automobile drivers do not bear the full social cost of commuting to work, inefficient overexpansion of suburbs may occur. One study suggests that the private supply of open space was 20 percent less than the socially optimal amount in densely populated, higher-income areas of Massachusetts (Lopez et al. 1994). However, the effectiveness of preferential farm property taxation in slowing conversion is likely to be least in just such areas because the value of property tax abatements is usually small relative to potential development profit.

In order to slow the pace of development, preferential taxation must push forward the date at which the landowner chooses to sell out for development. In the simplest case where development income does not grow, the decision to sell merely involves comparison of the present discounted value of net farm income versus the discounted value of the potential net income from the most profitable development option. Thus, development must be able to absorb the opportunity cost of sacrificed farm output plus the capital cost of conversion, such as new structures. This illustrates how shaky is the argument for special property tax treatment of farmland based on running out of land used to grow food and other useful crops. Present and expected future returns from farming clearly incorporate estimates of future food prices. Unless it can be shown that systematic myopia exists, anticipated food scarcity automatically rations land to nonfarming uses by raising the opportunity cost of development.

In the situation where expected development revenues grow through time as land ripens, the timing of the development act is dependent on the gain to the landowner from postponement of development (appropriately discounted to reflect the time value of money) as compared to the forgone development profit during the period of postponement (say, one year). The more rapid the rate of ripening, the sooner the parcel will be developed because of the higher cost of postponement.

Credits against state income tax (often labeled circuit-breaker programs) can, at least in principle, better focus the redistribution of income by explicitly taking into account the overall economic circumstances of the farmer. However, the typical tax credit program omits the increased value of the land as a component of income, a serious deficiency when judged by the widely accepted Haig-Simons definition of income for tax purposes: consumption plus changes in net worth. Wisconsin and Michigan use credits against income tax to grant relief to low-income farmers.

Tax relief, whether via credits or preferential assessment, assumes that the true burden of the property tax is measured by actual tax payments by current landowners. However, if property taxes are capitalized into a decreased market price of the property, as is usually assumed by economists, the current owner bears only that part of the tax that was increased or not anticipated to increase during his ownership tenure. The relief granted may therefore not be justified.

## Empirical evidence

The emphasis of empirical studies relating to farmland taxation has been on the degree of capitalization of the various property tax preferences into the market price of the land. This effort is complicated by the typically weak administration of the property tax. Fractional assessments and lags in updating assessment rolls in many communities mean that farm property is rarely taxed at current market value. This is especially so in rural communities where farming interests effectively control the local government apparatus.

One study used regression analysis to examine 458 sales of arable farmland and pastures, without structures, between 1982 and 1985 in New York state (vineyards and tree croplands were excluded) (Vitaliano and Hill 1994). New York employs use-value assessment of farms voluntarily enrolled in agricultural districts for an eight-year period, which is renewable. No statistically significant effect of the use-value program on the sale price of farmland was detected. The authors suggested that this finding was likely a result of widespread de facto use-value assessment in rural areas, as well as the voluntary nature of the tax abatement program in New York. Another possible reason is that locally financed tax abatement is partly offset by a higher tax rate as the tax base shrinks due to assessment erosion; this effect can be significant in communities where farm property constitutes the bulk of the base and much of it is granted relief, de jure or de facto. Parcels located near strong nonfarm influences (e.g., shopping centers) sold for an average 45 percent more than otherwise similar parcels. Farmers are not likely to forgo these potential gains voluntarily when they are likely to realize many of the tax abatement benefits without participating in the Agricultural District Program.

Michigan's program of credits against state income tax relieved enrolled properties of 80 to 90 percent of annual property taxes, which were capitalized into an average 10 percent higher property value (Anderson and Bunch 1989). These numbers indicate how difficult it is to materially affect the pattern of land use by means of locally financed tax concessions. Few communities could afford to grant widespread abatement of 80 percent or more of farm property taxes. And even in this situation, property values rise by only 10 percent, which is significantly less than the prospective gain from a typical development sale.

Tax relief for farm property, whether justified as income redistribution or correction of market failure, should probably be financed by higher levels of government, either because the sources of these higher-level tax subsidies are more equitable or because the locus of external benefits from open-space preservation is more widespread than the local taxing jurisdiction. Administration of tax concessions to farmland causes problems because use value is not easy to determine. Capitalization of existing net income flows assumes present crops and farm management are optimal. Comparable sales are unhelpful because they will incorporate anticipated development value. Moreover, tax credits require a more comprehensive measure of economic capacity than current definitions.

Overall, the typical use-value farm tax abatement program seems to get low marks in preserving open spaces, either because abatement is not worth as much as development, or because de facto abatement accomplishes the same thing. As a method of income redistribution, the programs are too blunt, granting aid without properly measuring need. An alternative might be a phase-in of full-market assessment or loans at market interest payable upon sale to finance current tax payments. Both of these measures would discourage forced sales, which are often used as a justification of existing abatement programs, even though their extent is largely undocumented. In spite of their shortcomings, current programs appear to be politically popular and are likely to be continued.

## Additional readings

Anderson, John E., and Howard C. Bunch. "Agricultural Property Tax Relief." *Land Economics* 65 (February 1989): 13–22.

Bentick, Brian L., and Thomas F. Pogue. "Development Timing and Property Taxes." *Land Economics* 64 (November 1988): 317–24.

Blewett, Robert A., and Julia I. Lane. "Development Rights and Differential Assessment of Agricultural Land: Fractional Valuation of Farmland Is Ineffective for Preserving Open Space and Subsidizes Speculation." *American Journal of Economics and Sociology* 47 (April 1988): 195–205.

Conklin, Howard E., and William G. Lesher. "Farm Value Assessment as a Means for Reducing Premature and Excessive Agricultural Disinvestment in Urban Fringes." *American Journal of Agricultural Economics* 59 (November 1977): 755–59.

Gloudemans, Robert J. *Use-Value Farmland Assessments: Theory, Practice and Impact.* Chicago: International Association of Assessing Officers, 1974.

Gustafson, Gregory C., and L.T. Wallace. "Differential Assessment as Land Use Policy: The California Case." *Journal of the American Institute of Planners* 41 (September 1975): 379–84.

Henneberry, David M., and Richard I. Barrows. "Capitalization of Agricultural Zoning." *Land Economics* 66 (August 1990): 249–58.

Ladd, Helen F. "The Considerations Underlying Preferential Tax Treatment of Open Space and Agricultural Land." In *Property Tax Preferences for Agricultural Land*, edited by Neal A. Roberts and H. James Brown. New York: Lincoln Institute of Land Policy and Universe Books, Inc., 1980.

Ladd, Helen F. *Local Government Tax and Land Use Policies in the United States.* Northampton, Mass.: Edward Elger, 1998.

Lopez, Rigoberto A., Farhed A. Shah, and Marilyn A. Altobello. "Optimal Allocation of Land." *Land Economics* 70 (February 1994): 53–62.

Vitaliano, Donald F., and Constance Hill. "Agricultural Districts and Farmland Prices." *The Journal of Real Estate Finance and Economics* 8 (May 1994): 213–23.

*Cross reference:* property tax assessment.

# Property tax, real property, business

Marion S. Beaumont
California State University, Long Beach

*Since business is an organizational form of individuals acting collectively, the (usually local) taxation of the business entity is often the most efficient and fair way to assess individuals for public services that accrue to them indirectly; however, the form of the tax may vary depending on policy objectives.*

## Business real property tax

The business real property tax is a component of the property tax base in the United States (all 50 states and the District of Columbia) and in numerous countries worldwide; it is conditioned on the ownership, and measured by the value, of business real property: land and improvements that are permanently attached to the land (structures and other immovables including mines, minerals in place, oil and gas wells). In the United States, the business real property tax is primarily an own-source of tax revenue for local governments. The tax is also a feasible own–local revenue source for new democracies (e.g., in Central Europe) and in developing countries that are hard-pressed to finance their local service requirements (see Smith 1993: 18; World Bank 1988: 161).

## Tax base, valuation, revenue

No single, nationwide business real property tax exists in the United States. Instead, each state's property tax law, often with individual jurisdictional variations, defines the tax base, rates, valuation system, and administration. The Bureau of the Census's quinquennial *Census of Governments*, in which the locally assessed value of taxable real property is listed by use category—residential (single-family, multifamily); commercial; industrial; acreage; and vacant platted lots—is the best source of aggregate business real property tax data. In this taxonomy, *commercial* (retail stores, restaurants, office buildings, hotels) and *industrial* (manufacturing plants, warehouses) parcels of locally assessed real property are the core components of the business real property tax. In 1986, the last year census data are available by use category, commercial and industrial property accounted for only 4 percent of the 108 million locally assessed parcels, but 21 percent of total gross assessed value. In practice, the business real property tax base may also include other locally assessed realty (e.g., multifamily farm acreage) and state-assessed real property. Lack of aggregate-use category data since the 1987 *Census of Governments* is an unfortunate obstacle to understanding the current status and role of the business real property tax in the information age. Devolution of responsibility, from the federal to the state-local sector, for important services and the complexities of deregulation (e.g., telecommunications and electrical industries), environmental concerns (e.g., pollution control; valuation of environmentally sensitive land), public education funding priorities, and economic development pressures all affect the business real property tax and require informed policymaking.

A glimpse of the *potential* business real property tax base in the 1986–95 decade can be noted in the Department of Commerce's estimates of the net stock of fixed reproducible tangible wealth in the United States (Katz and Harman 1997). The total fixed capital stock was $10.2 trillion in 1986 and $15.7 trillion in 1995. In both 1986 and 1995, about one-half of the total net stock of fixed private capital was nonresidential (48.5% in 1986 and 49.3% in 1995); this share declined relative to residential fixed private capital over the decade. By industry, wholesale trade; retail trade; finance, insurance, and real estate; and services showed a relative gain. Structures were 62.5 percent of nonresidential fixed capital in 1986 and 61.6 percent in 1995; equipment's share increased (from 37.5% in 1986 to 38.4% in 1995). Because equipment is more likely to be exempt from property taxes (in 1994, 35 states taxed machinery and equipment and 38 states taxed business fixtures), the wealth estimates suggest a widening gap between the actual gross assessed value (before exemptions) and the potential business real property tax base. In 1995, 36 percent (by very rough estimate) of the potential real property tax base (wealth estimate) was included in the gross assessed value of business real property (census data). In the ratio of gross assessed value of business real property (census data) to the net stock of nonresidential private fixed capital, the numerator (in billions of dollars) is the locally assessed value of the sum of commercial (710.5), industrial (286.9), farm acreage (309.3), multifamily (331.3), and state-assessed (242.9) real property = 1,880.90. The denominator, in billions of dollars, is the total net stock (equipment and structures) of nonresidential private fixed capital = 5,241.5. The ratio of the gross assessed value of real business property in 1986 to the potential real business property tax base is $(1{,}880.90/5{,}241.5) \times 100 = 35.9$ percent.

In most states, firms pay taxes on some personal property. Defined as all property (tangible or intangible) other than real property, personal property (personalty) is movable—not permanently affixed to real estate. Whether a particular item is real or personal property—computer hardware and components, for example—can be controversial and may be specified by statute or litigation. Business inventories are exempt in 38 states, and all commercial/industrial personalty is exempt in 10 states. Intangible personal property (for example, equities, bonds, copyrights, patents, franchises, deposits, and other financial assets) is exempted to some extent in 33 states (Dornfest 1997: 27, 34–35). Litigation, preference of states to tax the income flow from intangibles under a broad-based income tax, and the ease of moving and hiding intangibles to evade taxation are reasons that the trend to exempt intangibles is likely to continue (see Bowman et al. 1990). Numerous other exemptions and exclusions further narrow the business real property tax base (see U.S. Department of Commerce 1988: xix).

Each item in the business real property tax base is appraised to determine its market value, and the assessed (taxable) value is computed as a certain percentage of market value. Market value is usually defined by statute (for example, "full cash value" in California, "fair and reasonable market value" in Alabama), and the assessment procedure is prescribed by law and/or traditional practice. Of the three major approaches to estimating market value—sales comparison, income (or capitalization), and cost—the income and cost approaches, or a combination of value indicators, are preferred to the sales comparison approach alone in commercial/industrial appraisals; comparable sales data are often scarce or nonexistent (see International Association of Assessing Officers 1996). Appraisals are performed by the local assessor, subject to the supervision of a state agency (tax commission, department of revenue, board of equalization). Properties that cross the boundaries of a single local taxing jurisdiction are generally state-assessed. Computer and information management systems facilitate updating assessments and improving property tax administration.

Myriad legal assessment standards (such as Proposition 13's 1975 base or acquisition year methodology in California), differential assessment rules to promote or retain certain uses of property (farm, scenic, and recreational uses; historic preservation; energy conservation; environmental protection), and classified property taxation are among the many legal variations that complicate property valuation. Structural changes and cyclical effects are additional complexities. The assessment ratio (assessment level as a percentage of market value) for commercial/industrial property is generally the same (35 states and the District of Columbia) or higher (15 states) than for residential property. Twenty states and the District of Columbia specify a legal assessment ratio for more than one class of real property (Advisory Commission on Intergovernmental Relations [ACIR] 1992: 140).

Results of an empirical study by Ladd and Yinger (1989) indicated that structural change, from manufacturing to services, does not affect either the revenue-raising capacity of cities (although growth of the property tax base is dampened) or the costs of providing public services. The authors noted that, for most cities, the exemption of business personalty reduced the exportability of property taxes.

Business real property tax revenue is the product of the net (of exemptions) assessed value of business realty and the nominal property tax rate. Increasingly, nominal tax rates are specified by tax rate or expenditure limits rather than by computing the ratio of a jurisdiction's levy to its net assessed value. ACIR estimated business real property tax revenue in 1991 to be $44.1 billion, or approximately 8 percent of state and local government tax revenue (Advisory Commission on Intergovernmental Relations 1993: 7).

## Economic effects

Owners of business realty bear the legal responsibility (statutory incidence), but not necessarily the final burden (economic incidence), of the business real property tax. Property tax incidence, the study of the changes in the distribution of economic welfare resulting from imposition of the tax, has an extensive literature—reviewed by Mieszkowski and Zodrow (1989), Rubinfeld (1987), and Kotlikoff and Summers (1987). Two theories are especially relevant to business real property tax incidence: the "new view" introduced by Mieszkowski (1972) and the "benefit" approach (Hamilton 1975).

According to the "new view," the local general property tax has two (analytic) parts. One is the "average" nationwide effective property tax rate, borne by all owners of capital. The second, the local differential tax rate, has excise tax effects because mobile capital can leave localities with above (the national) average tax rates. In the "new view," if the quantity of capital (property) is fixed in the short run, and if local tax differentials are relatively small, the property tax is a distortionary tax on all capital. Assuming capital ownership rises with income, the property tax burden is distributed progressively.

In biennial empirical studies that conceptualized the "new view," the incidence of the Minnesota business real property tax (the state does not tax personalty) is analyzed in a multistate setting. Minnesota real business tax incidence is analyzed in three steps: (1) impact of initial imposition of the tax; (2) incidence on Minnesota consumers, capital, and labor and on nonresidents; and (3) incidence on Minnesota households by income deciles. Results indicate that the business real property tax incidence on Minnesota residents was distributed to consumers, 34 percent; labor, 2 percent; and capital, 24 percent; and 40 percent was exported to nonresidents (see Minnesota Department of Revenue 1997: 47).

According to the benefit theory, the property tax is a nondistortionary payment for local public services, similar to a user fee. This view is accommodated by extending, through zoning and other land-use restrictions, the all-consumer Tiebout model of efficient provision of local public goods to include commercial/industrial property (see Fischel 1992 and 1985: 305–15). Suggested implementation of the benefit approach is to levy uniform tax rates on value added (see Oakland and Testa 1996).

Among the many implications of the benefit theory are these: Is the present assignment of fiscal instruments and functions in multilevel government efficient (does it minimize deadweight loss) when domestic and global mobility of nonland factors of production is possible? What are the economic effects of federal government subsidization of local public services through permitting income tax deductibility of property tax payments? Are economic development incentives by subnational governments (property tax exemptions and abatements, for example) effective or desirable? Is a winner's curse a likely outcome? The significance of property taxes in business location decisions remains an unsettled issue (see Carroll and Wasylenko 1994; Luce 1994).

Results of an empirical study by Ladd (1975) indicated that the presence of large amounts of business property, particularly commercial property, induced overinvestment in education in Boston SMSA (standard metropolitan statistical area) communities, as local residents perceived a tax price lower than the marginal cost of education services. Proposals to pool the business portion of the property tax base statewide and redistribute the proceeds to local jurisdictions appear to be a less preferred fiscal equalization measure than intergovernmental aid in the United States.

Instead of partitioning the tax base, taxing land at a higher rate than improvements is often suggested. Both theoretical analysis (George 1956) and empirical evidence support, on efficiency grounds, adopting site value taxation, particularly in urban areas. Equity aspects are less convincing (see DiMasi 1987; Beaumont 1992). Open-economy analysis and consideration of longer-term economic effects—for example, lifetime (Fullerton and Rogers 1993) and generational accounting (Auerbach, et al. 1991) models—are interesting newer approaches to understanding the economic effects of the business real property tax.

### Additional readings

Advisory Commission on Intergovernmental Relations. *Significant Features of Fiscal Federalism 1992*. Vol. 2. Report M-180. Washington, D.C., 1992.

Advisory Commission on Intergovernmental Relations. *RTS 1991, State Revenue Capacity and Effort*. Report M-187. Washington, D.C., 1993.

Auerbach, Alan J., Jagadeesh Gokhale, and Laurence J. Kotlikoff. "Generational Accounts: A Meaningful Alternative to Deficit Accounting." In *Tax Policy and the Economy*, edited by David Bradford, pp. 55–110. Cambridge, Mass.: National Bureau of Economic Research, 1991.

Beaumont, Marion S. "Optimal Property Taxation in California: Is Greater Reliance on Land Values Feasible and Desirable?" *Review of Urban and Regional Development Studies* 4 (1992): 162–78.

Bowman, John H., George E. Hoffer, and Michael D. Pratt. "Current Patterns and Trends in State and Local Intangibles Taxation." *National Tax Journal* 43 (1990): 439–50.

Carroll, Robert, and Michael Wasylenko. "Do State Business Climates Still Matter? Evidence of a Structural Change." *National Tax Journal* 47 (1994): 19–33.

Colker, David. "Property Taxation of Telecommunications Companies in California." *Assessment Journal* 4 (May/June 1997): 47–52.

DiMasi, Joseph A. "The Effects of Site Value Taxation in an Urban Area: A General Equilibrium Computational Approach." *National Tax Journal* 40 (1987): 577–90.

Dornfest, Alan S. "State and Provincial Ratio Study Practices: 1997 Survey Results." *Assessment Journal* 4 (November/December 1997): 23–67.

Fischel, William A. *The Economics of Zoning Laws: A Property Rights Approach to American Land Use Controls*. Baltimore, Md.: Johns Hopkins University Press, 1985.

Fischel, William A. "Property Taxation and the Tiebout Model: Evidence for the Benefit View from Zoning and Voting." *Journal of Economic Literature* 30 (1992): 171–77.

Fisher, Ronald C. *State and Local Public Finance*. 2d ed. Chicago: Irwin, 1996: 324–54.

Fullerton, Don, and Diane Lim Rogers. *Who Bears the Lifetime Tax Burden?* Washington, D.C.: The Brookings Institution, 1993.

George, Henry. *Progress and Poverty*. New York: Robert Schalkenbach Foundation, 1956. (First published, 1879.)

Hamilton, Bruce W. "Zoning and Property Taxation in a System of Local Governments." *Urban Studies* 12 (1975): 205–11.

International Association of Assessing Officers. *Property Assessment Valuation*. 2d ed. Chicago: International Association of Assessing Officers, 1996.

Katz, Arnold J., and Shelby W. Harman. "Improved Estimates of Fixed Reproducible Tangible Wealth, 1929–95." *Survey of Current Business* 77 (May 1997): 169–92.

Kotlikoff, Laurence J., and Lawrence H. Summers. "Tax Incidence." In *Handbook of Public Economics* 2, edited by Alan J. Auerbach and Martin S. Feldstein, pp. 1043–92. Amsterdam: North-Holland (Elsevier Science Publishing Company), 1987.

Ladd, Helen F. "Local Education Expenditures, Fiscal Capacity, and the Composition of the Property Tax Base." *National Tax Journal* 28 (1975): 145–58.

Ladd, Helen F., and John Yinger. *America's Ailing Cities: Fiscal Health and the Design of Urban Policy*. Baltimore, Md.: Johns Hopkins University Press, 1989.

Luce, Thomas F., Jr. "Local Taxes, Public Services, and the Intrametropolitan Location of Firms and Households." *Public Finance Quarterly* 22 (April 1994): 139–67.

Mieszkowski, Peter. "The Property Tax: An Excise Tax or a Profits Tax?" *Journal of Public Economics* 1 (1972): 73–96.

Mieszkowski, Peter, and George R. Zodrow. "Taxation and the Tiebout Model: The Differential Effects of Head Taxes, Taxes on Land Rents, and Property Taxes." *Journal of Economic Literature* 27 (1989): 1098–146.

Mikesell, John L. "Selected Business Property Taxation Issues: Personal Property." In *Taxation of Business Property*, edited by John H. Bowman, pp. 161–70. Westport, Conn.: Praeger, 1995.

Minnesota Department of Revenue, Tax Research Division. *1997 Minnesota Tax Incidence Study*. St. Paul, Minn.: Minnesota Department of Revenue, 1997.

Morrison, Donald T. "Tax Valuation of Contaminated Property." In *Taxation of Business Property*, edited by John H. Bowman, pp. 151–60. Westport, Conn.: Praeger, 1995.

Oakland, William, and William A. Testa. "State-Local Business Taxation and the Benefits Principle." Federal Reserve Bank of Chicago *Economic Perspectives* 21 (January/February 1996): 2–19.

Rubinfeld, Daniel L. "The Economics of the Local Public Sector." In *Handbook of Public Economics* 2, edited by Alan J. Auerbach and Martin S. Feldstein, pp. 571–645. Amsterdam: North-Holland (Elsevier Science Publishing Company), 1987.

Smith, Stephen. "The Impact of European Integration on Local Taxation." In *Local Government Taxation: International Report 1993*, edited by Colin Farrington, pp. 17–20. London: The Institute of Revenues, Rating, and Valuation, 1993.

Tiebout, Charles M., "A Pure Theory of Local Expenditures." *Journal of Political Economy* 64 (1956): 416–24.

U.S. Department of Commerce, Bureau of the Census. 1987 *Census of Governments*, vol. 2, *Taxable Property Values*. Washington, D.C.: U.S. Government Printing Office, 1988.

Wasylenko, Michael. "Empirical Evidence on Interregional Business Location Decisions and the Role of Fiscal Incentives in Economic Development." In *Industry Location and Public Policy*, edited by Henry W. Herzog, Jr.,
and Alan M. Schlottmann, pp. 13–30. Knoxville, Tenn.: University of Tennessee Press, 1991.

Wise, David M. "Opening the Closed Circuit: Assessing Electric Utility Property under Deregulation." In *1997 Conference Proceedings, Beyond Borders: Global Solutions for Success*. Chicago: International Association of Assessing Officers, 1997, pp. 405–10.

World Bank. *World Development Report 1988*. New York: Oxford University Press, 1988, pp. 43–185.

*Cross references:* fiscal federalism; incidence of taxes; property tax assessment.

# Property tax, real property, residential

Steven M. Sheffrin
University of California, Davis

*Taxes levied on the value of residential property.*

The residential real property tax is a tax levied on the value of residential structures, both owner-occupied and rented. It is part of the entire system of property taxation that includes taxation on real business property and personal property (see Property tax, real property, business; and Property tax, personal). The residential real property tax accounts for over 56 percent of total real property tax revenues nationwide (Fisher 1988: 126).

Today, the property tax is primarily a local government revenue source, and local governments receive more than 96 percent of property tax revenues. This stands in contrast to the early 1900s, when the property tax provided more than half of state government revenues in the United States. Increased demands placed on state governments led them to seek additional revenue sources and, as a consequence, the share of tax revenue from property taxes declined. The Great Depression of the 1930s accelerated this decline, so that by 1940 the property tax provided less than 8 percent of state tax revenue. The share had fallen to 2 percent by 1980 and remained virtually unchanged throughout the 1980s (Advisory Commission on Intergovernmental Relations 1992, vol. 2, table 65, pp. 126–28).

Although the property tax still dominates local revenue structures, there is a substantial degree of variation in reliance on the property tax by type of local government (counties, cities, school districts, and special districts). Throughout the 1980s, the distribution of the property tax pie remained fairly stable, with school districts receiving the largest piece, 43 percent. Traditionally, the property tax had been the major source of school finance. However, as a result of lawsuits throughout the country attacking inequalities in school finance, state governments are playing an increasing role in financing local education.

The property tax is intended to be a tax on wealth. Initially, the property tax in the United States was an in rem tax—so many dollars per unit—applied to ownership of very specific types of property such as cattle, land, and improvements. However, as new forms of wealth, both tangible and intangible, began to appear in the early 19th century, the structure of the property tax was altered. The base was expanded to include most varieties of property, which necessitated a switch from in rem to ad valorem percentages of value taxation. The last several decades have brought a reversal of this trend toward a more general tax, back to a more specific tax. The emphasis today is clearly on real property, land and improvements.

Unlike several other taxes that are levied against property owners, such as property transfer taxes, real estate and gift taxes, and capital gains taxes, the property tax is a recurrent tax that must be paid on an annual basis. The taxability of a property owner is determined by the product of the tax base—a measure of the property's value—and the tax rate expressed as a percentage of value. The property tax in the United States is far from a uniform tax. There is significant variation in the definition and scope of the tax base and in the magnitude of tax rates across states, and even within states across local taxing jurisdictions.

The base for the residential property tax is typically calculated using an estimate of the market value of the property. The assessed value (taxable value of a property) is often just a fraction (the assessment ratio) of the true market value of the property. The assessment ratio is typically governed by law. For example, in Colorado, residential properties are assessed by law at only 15 percent of market value, whereas all other properties are assessed at 29 percent. If all types of properties were assessed at the same ratio within a jurisdiction, the actual assessment ratio would not really matter; for example, a 50 percent assessment ratio with a 2 percent rate is equivalent to a 100 percent assessment at a 1 percent rate. However, many jurisdictions (such as Colorado) assess different types of properties at different rates. In that case, the assessment ratio is a tool used to distribute the tax burden across different types of properties.

Estimates of market value are provided by the local assessor (see Property tax assessment). The assessor's primary task is to provide estimates of the market value of all taxable properties. For residential property, assessors typically use a method known as the comparable sales approach. This approach involves a comparison of the property being appraised to similar properties that have recently been sold. Statistical analysis of sales prices and property characteristics can identify hedonic prices or implicit values for each characteristic, including locational attributes. These prices can then be applied to the specific characteristics of the property in question. The success of this approach requires data on a substantial number of recent sales of similarly situated properties. For larger rental properties, assessors use the income capitalization method. This approach requires information on income and operating expenses for the property, which may be available from the property owner or can be determined from standardized tables available to assessors. The net income stream generated by the property is discounted (capitalized) at an appropriate rate to determine the property's value.

The rates for the property tax are typically set by local jurisdictions. Local governments have fiscal authority to set or change tax rates in 41 states. Most taxing jurisdictions set rates based on budgetary needs and the available tax base as measured by the assessed valuation in the jurisdiction. In general, the tax rate necessary to support a given budget is the budget divided by assessed valuations.

Because assessment ratios differ across localities, the most informative way to compare the burden of taxation is through effective tax rates, which are defined as the ratio of property taxes to market value. The most comprehensive data on effective tax rates for single-family homes across jurisdictions are from the Advisory Commission on Intergovernmental Relations (1989, vol. 1, table 33, pp. 72–73). Overall, the effective tax rate for the United States as a whole fell from 1.67 percent in 1977 to 1.15 percent in 1987. This decrease occurred in large part because of the tax revolts in the late 1970s and early 1980s, particularly in California and Massachusetts. There is substantial variation in effective tax rates across states. In 1987, New York, Oregon, South Dakota, New Jersey, Nebraska, and Michigan all had effective tax rates exceeding 2 percent. In the same year, seven states had effective tax rates less than 0.75 percent.

The final component of the structure of the property tax is relief provisions. Property tax relief refers to any measure that reduces property taxes below what they otherwise would be. Relief has taken many forms, including homestead exemptions or credits, classification, deferral programs, preferential assessment of farmland, and tax breaks for business, but the most widely employed method for residential property consists of tax credits, or "circuit breakers," to offset property tax liabilities. Used in many states, circuit breakers are typically targeted to low-income and elderly homeowners.

While in the United States residential property taxes are based on the assessed value of property, different systems are used in other parts of the world: Two of these are annual-value and site-value systems.

An annual-value-based system taxes the yearly rental income of properties and hence is more of an income than a wealth tax. Most of such systems in use today are derived from the pre-1989 British property tax system known as "rates." In this system, the tax base is defined to be the annual rent that a property could be expected to earn on the market. Ideally, the annual value base and the capital value base would be essentially equal because capital value is equivalent to the discounted stream of net rental income. However, a number of factors cause the two to differ. Deductions are often allowed to cover the costs of repairs, insurance, taxes, and other expenses. In some cases, the legally allowed deduction is as high as 50 percent of the rent and clearly exceeds actual costs. Moreover, rent controls can cause actual rental payments to differ from market rent.

Site-value taxation is a form of capital value taxation in which improvements are exempt. Site- or land-value systems differ as to whether improvements such as clearing, leveling, drainage, and surrounding infrastructure are included or whether the value of such improvements is ignored. Differences also arise concerning the standard of valuation—highest and best use or current use. This approach has several advantages, among which are lower assessment costs because reassessment is not needed to capture the value of new buildings.

Virtually all jurisdictions that have property taxes have some form of accompanying tax limitations. As of 1991, only six states were free of limitations on property taxes (Advisory Commission on Intergovernmental Relations 1992, vol. 1, table 7, p. 18). Property tax limitations take on a variety of forms. There can be limitations on the growth of the property tax base for individual properties or for a given jurisdiction; there can be limitations on rates; and there can be limitations on the growth of property tax revenues. Overall, limits in assessed value are in place in 10 states; rate limits are in effect in 30 states; and a large number of other states have limits on total property tax revenues.

One of the most dramatic limitations on the property tax base came into effect with the passage of Proposition 13 in California. There, the assessed value of a property can only be increased by a maximum of 2 percent a year until the property is sold, at which point it is assessed at market value. If inflation in housing prices exceeds 2 percent a year, then newly purchased properties will be assessed at substantially higher rates than properties that have not been sold.

Studies have revealed that these limitations on assessed value growth have had dramatic effects on effective tax rates. (See O'Sullivan et al. 1995, ch. 4, for an analysis of effective tax rates.) For example, in Los Angeles County in 1992, 43 percent of homeowners had been in their homes since 1975. On average, the effective tax rate for those homeowners was 0.2 percent, compared with 1 percent for newly purchased homes. In California, the average effective tax rate was 0.55 percent and the statutory rate was 1 percent. These disparities in effective tax rates were challenged in the Supreme Court on grounds that they violated the equal protection clause of the Constitution. However, the Court has generally given wide discretion to states in the design of their fiscal systems, and it upheld Proposition 13 on these grounds. (See O'Sullivan et al. 1995, ch. 1, for an analysis of the legal arguments.)

Who bears the property tax? The economic incidence of the property tax has been the subject of considerable dispute. (A good reference on this topic is Aaron 1975.) According to the traditional or "old view" of property taxation, the land component of property was borne by the landowner, but the part of the tax levied on structures was borne by the inhabitant of the property. The rationale for this view was that land is supplied inelastically while capital, used in structures, was supplied elastically to any jurisdiction. According to the old view, homeowners would therefore bear the full burden of the tax, while renters would bear all the tax except for the part levied on land.

The "new view" of the property tax takes the position that property taxes are levied nationwide. Thus, capital used in structures is taxed throughout the United States, and capital cannot escape the tax. According to this view, owners, not renters, would bear the burden of the tax. Many economists believe that, while the new view may describe the burden of an average national tax, differences from this average should be allocated according to the old view.

## Additional readings

Aaron, Henry J. *Who Pays the Property Tax?* Washington, D.C.: The Brookings Institution, 1975.

Advisory Commission on Intergovernmental Relations. *Significant Features of Fiscal Federalism*. Vol. 1. Washington, D.C.: U.S. Government Printing Office, 1989.

Advisory Commission on Intergovernmental Relations. *Significant Features of Fiscal Federalism*. Vols. 1 and 2. Washington, D.C.: U.S. Government Printing Office, 1992.

Fisher, Ronald C. *State and Local Public Finance*. Glenview, Ill.: Scott, Foresman and Company, 1988.

O'Sullivan, Arthur, Terri A. Sexton, and Steven M. Sheffrin. *Property Taxes and Tax Revolts: 77th Legacy of Proposition 13.* New York: Cambridge University Press, 1995.

*Cross references:* circuit breaker; incidence of taxes; property tax assessment.

# Property tax assessment

Michael E. Bell
MEB Associates, Inc.

*Determining the base of the property tax.*

---

The property tax is unique among state and local revenue sources. It is the largest single source of state and local revenues, it is the only major tax applied in all 50 states, and it is the only major revenue source with a tax base estimated by a government official. Both consumption and income taxes are based on current flows or transactions, the values of which are relatively clear. The property tax, however, is based on a stock of wealth that does not change hands every year. Therefore, the value of property, which is the base of the tax, must be estimated annually. This process of property tax assessment is inherently subjective and requires the talents of highly trained and experienced personnel—generally referred to as assessors, property appraisers, or property valuation administrators. These officials typically work for local governments responsible for determining property values. They are appointed in 10 states and elected in 22 states, and in 14 states the assessing jurisdiction has the option of appointing or electing the assessor.

The definition of the property tax base varies across states. *Locally assessed property* includes both *real property* (land and improvements) and *personal property* (machinery, household goods, automobiles, business inventories, and so forth). Recently, however, the trend in the United States has been to de-emphasize the contribution of personal property to the tax base. Real property is taxed in all 50 states, but motor vehicles are subject to some form of personal property tax in 18 states, household property in 17 states, and business inventories in 18 states; commercial and industrial personal property are taxed in 42 states and agricultural property in 32 states. As a result of these trends, real property accounts for more than 90 percent of total locally assessed taxable property, and personal property accounts for just 9 percent of the taxable base.

In addition to this locally assessed property, the tax base includes *state-assessed property*, which includes large, complex properties whose values are determined at the state level, such as utilities, railroads, oil and gas production properties, and mining properties. In 1991, state-assessed taxable property had an estimated value of $286 million, compared with locally assessed taxable property, which had an assessed value of $6.4 trillion.

Each state, in its constitution or statutes, defines one legal standard for all assessed values. While all standards have a basis in or a relationship to market value, market value and assessed value are not synonymous. Market value is the estimated selling price that a willing buyer would pay to a willing seller in a transaction where neither party is under duress—this is called an arm's-length transaction. Assessed value is the value assigned to each property to determine its property tax liability.

All but five states require every assessing unit to maintain the same assessment level and definition of value—that is, they require uniformity of assessment. With respect to real property, the Bureau of the Census indicates that 20 states and the District of Columbia require assessed values to equal market values (or fair cash value, or true value). An additional 15 states specify a single percentage of market value, or a way of calculating a single percentage annually, to determine assessed value. For 14 states, the single assessment level for real property has disappeared and has been replaced by a "classified property tax," which assesses different types of property (classified by ownership or use characteristics) at different percentages of market value. California is unique because it adjusts the prior year's assessment, but the annual increase is limited to 2 percent, unless the property is sold.

The assessing function—the process of determining assessed values—involves three specific activities: the discovery, listing, and valuation of each parcel of land. Discovery requires the identification of each parcel of real property (or each taxable unit of personal property). This activity is typically manifested in a tax, or cadastral, map that displays parcels of real property, showing for each the boundaries, size, location, parcel identification number, ownership, value, and other spatially oriented details such as easements, rights-of-way, soil types, and flood plains. As a result of this activity, the assessor is custodian of the largest public database on property parcels. The listing activity underlies the preparation of a permanent record of each taxable property. The valuation function is the most important, and complicated, component of the process of determining the assessed value of each parcel.

The ultimate goal of the assessor in the valuation function is to provide the most accurate estimate of what an individual property would sell for on the open market at a given time. Written procedures, establishing the parameters or rules governing subjective judgments that an individual assessor must make, help reduce the variation in estimated market value between different assessors. These standard procedures result in less variation in property assessments, thereby minimizing some of the confusion on the part of both practitioners and the general public.

Whatever the exact provisions of a state's assessment law, assessors employ three common approaches to the valuation of property that are endorsed by the American Institute of Real Estate Appraisers:

1. *Cost approach*—the current cost of reproducing a property minus depreciation from deterioration or functional and economic obsolescence.
2. *Income approach*—the value that the property's potential net earning power will support, based on a capitalization of net income.
3. *Market data approach*—the value indicated by recent sales of comparable properties in the marketplace.

Typically, each of these approaches to valuing property is applied to a specific subset of property uses. For example, market data are more commonly used in valuing single-family residences than in valuing commercial or industrial properties, because the latter are relatively heterogeneous and sell relatively infrequently. However, each approach to value, if accurately carried out, should produce approximately the same estimate of market value—in the absence of serious market disequilibrium. These individual approaches should not be considered mutually exclusive, but rather as alternatives that may be used to verify the results of the "traditional" approach to valuing each property type.

Because the actual market value for an individual parcel is observed only when a sale takes place, local officials and property owners are concerned about how well assessors estimate the value of property that does not sell. To what extent does the assessor's estimated market value—which is the product of the assessment process described above— reflect the "true" market value as indicated by actual sale data? In addition, are properties assessed in a uniform manner? Such uniformity among local property owners *and* between taxing districts is important because property valuations serve as a basis for

—tax levies by overlapping governmental units—for example, counties, school districts, and special districts.
—determinations of net bonded indebtedness, which often is restricted to a percentage of either the local assessed value or market value of property in a jurisdiction.

## TABLE 1

### Assessment/Sales Ratios

| Property | Assessed Value (A) | Sales Price (S) | A/S Ratio | Absolute Deviation |
|---|---|---|---|---|
| 1 | $20,900 | $19,000 | 110.0% | 20 |
| 2 | 28,500 | 30,000 | 95.0 | 5 |
| 3 | 22,950 | 25,500 | 90.0 | 0 |
| 4 | 33,200 | 41,500 | 80.0 | 10 |
| 5 | 31,200 | 52,000 | 60.0 | 30 |
| Total | $136,750 | $168,000 | 81.4% | 65 |

—determinations of authorized levies restricted by tax-rate limits.
—apportionment of state assistance to local governmental units—for example, school aid formula, local government aid formula.

The consequence of nonuniform assessment is an unwarranted shift in the tax burden to the benefit of some property owners, but to the detriment of others. An equitable distribution of the tax burden is achieved only if built upon uniform assessment. With uniform assessment, property owners with properties of equal value pay the same tax—this is *horizontal equity*. Similarly, those with more valuable property pay a higher tax—this is *vertical equity*. Achievement of both types of equity requires uniform assessments.

To evaluate the degree of uniformity across properties and jurisdictions, reasonably accurate and acceptable statistical techniques are used. *Assessment/sales ratio studies* are used in approximately 40 states to measure the degree of assessment inequality in and across jurisdictions. The assessment/sales ratio for an individual parcel is simply the relationship between the assessor's estimated market value and the actual sales price, expressed as a ratio. If perfect assessment uniformity existed in an area, the assessor's estimated market value for a property that sold would be 100 percent of the actual sales price and no ratio would deviate from that level. In practice, however, actual assessment/sales ratios vary substantially.

The uniformity of a group of assessment/sales ratios is initially described by various measures of central tendency. For example, the *mean ratio*, or arithmetic average, of a group of assessment/sales ratios is derived by computing the ratios for individual properties, adding the ratios together, and dividing the total by the number of parcels. For the sample properties in table 1, the mean is 87.0 (435/5). Alternatively, the individual ratios can be arranged from the highest to lowest values and the middle ratio in the series can be selected; this is the *median ratio*. In table 1, the median ratio is 90.0. Another common method of describing the degree of uniformity among a group of assessment/sales ratios is to calculate the *aggregate average*, or the weighted mean. This measure is computed by dividing the assessor's total estimated market value for all properties sold by the total sales prices of those properties. In table 1, the aggregate, or weighted, average ratio is 81.4 ($136,750/$168,000). Thus, the measure of central tendency used to describe a series of individual assessment/sales ratios can influence the perception of how well property is being assessed in an area. The International Association of Assessing Officers (IAAO) has established standards for median assessment/sales ratios of 90 to 110 percent of actual sales price.

A second dimension of the quality of assessment that needs monitoring is the degree to which actual assessment ratios are dispersed around the measure of central tendency. For example, for any particular taxing jurisdiction, the median assessment ratio may equal 1.0, indicating that the estimated value of the median property exactly equaled its actual selling price. However, this provides no information about the variation in the individual ratios in the jurisdiction—that is, how closely clustered around the median those other ratios are.

The *coefficient of dispersion* is the most commonly used measure of the variability of individual assessment/sales ratios—used in 19 states. It measures the deviation of individual parcel ratios from the average ratio as a percentage of the average ratio. The higher the coefficient, the less uniform are the assessments. In Table 1, individual assessment/sales ratios are subtracted from the median ratio, and the difference is recorded in the last column without regard to its sign (absolute deviation from the median). Next, these absolute deviations are summed and divided by the number of homes in the sample (65/5 = 13). This average absolute deviation is expressed as a percentage of the median ratio [(13/90) × 100 = 14.4 percent]. The International Association of Assessing Officers (IAAO) has established a standard for the coefficient of dispersion of under 10 percent for new and/or homogeneous areas and under 15 percent for older or otherwise heterogeneous areas.

Finally, the assessment process has been revolutionized with the advent and application of computers. *Computer-assisted mass appraisal (CAMA)* models analyze extensive real estate market data and/or housing characteristic and sales data to estimate market values of properties not recently sold. CAMA allows frequent reassessment of residential properties. The improved quality of assessments obtained with CAMA models makes it possible to monitor and reassess property on an annual basis to ensure equitable assessment. According to a 1990 Survey of State and Provincial Assessment Administration Practices undertaken by the IAAO and the Lincoln Institute of Land Policy, 16 states monitor computer use by the primary assessing units. State programs are of several kinds: (1) maintaining a centralized computer system that generates values and tax lists or processes locally developed values; (2) providing software, usually with technical assistance and training, to local units; and (3) reviewing and approving contracts for computer-assisted valuation services provided by private firms.

Mapping for assessors is emerging as an integral element of a local *geographic information system (GIS)*. GIS is essentially a multipurpose assemblage of computer capability designed to receive, display, manipulate, or otherwise process digital data with a spatial dimension. All of these new technologies, however, require a commitment of funds on the part of the local jurisdiction for the hardware and software necessary to implement them, in addition to the highly trained (and paid) professional staff necessary to operate them. The cost of these new technologies must be weighed against the improved quality of assessment, and their impact on the coordination of information across governmental functions attained from their use must be measured.

## Additional readings

Bell, Michael, and John Bowman. "Property Tax Law and Administration." In *A Fiscal Agenda for Nevada*, edited by Robert D. Ebel, ch. 10, pp. 276–310. Reno, Nev.: University of Nevada Press, 1990.

Bell, Michael, and John Bowman. "Property Taxes." In *Local Government Finance: Concepts and Practices*, edited by John Petersen and Dennis Strachota. Chicago: Government Finance Officers Association, 1991.

Bureau of the Census, Governments Division. *1992 Census of Governments, Vol. 2—Taxable Property Values, No. 1—Assessed Valuations for Local General Property Taxation*. GC92(2)1, August 1994.

Malme, Jane. "Property Tax Administration in North America." *Property Tax Journal* 9 (4) (December 1990): 235–47.

*Cross references:* property tax, farm; property tax, real property, business; property tax, real property, residential.

# Proprietorships

James E. Long
Auburn University

*Issues arise as to whether taxation will affect an individual's decision to go into business for her/himself (but not in partnership with others).*

Proprietorships are one of the three primary forms of business organization in the United States, the other forms being partnerships and corporations. A proprietorship is a firm owned and operated by a single individual or family. The sole proprietor or self-employed individual has total control over his or her business, receives all of the firm's profits, and is responsible for all its liabilities. About three-fourths of the businesses in the United States are proprietorships, operating primarily in wholesale and retail trade, construction, and agriculture. For example, the hometown hardware store, the local drug store, the family-owned restaurant, and the neighborhood gas station and auto repair shop are likely to be proprietorships. While extremely numerous (more than 15 million) in the economy, proprietorships are usually very small in terms of number of employees and size of sales and profits. In recent years, the average nonfarm proprietorship had annual revenues of about $50,000, compared with $250,000 for the typical partnership and $2.5 million for the average corporation.

The popularity of proprietorships can be traced to several advantages of this type of business organization. The ease of establishing and dissolving a proprietorship is probably its major advantage. After satisfying a few legal formalities (such as obtaining appropriate licenses), the owner-operator commences operations by announcing that goods and services are available for sale to consumers. When the owner decides to end the proprietorship, he or she simply stops doing business with customers. Another advantage is that the owner directly receives all of the proprietorship's profits, which are taxed as self-employment income under the individual income tax, as opposed to being taxed under a separate business income tax such as the corporate income tax. A final advantage of self-employment is that the sole proprietor exerts total control over the business. The opportunity to make business decisions independently of other owners or employers, including the decisions of when to work and how much time to spend working, is surely a major reason why some individuals choose self-employment rather than salaried jobs that may provide higher monetary compensation.

As might be expected, the sole proprietorship also has some disadvantages that limit its effectiveness as a business structure, especially when large, complex, or capital-intensive undertakings are involved. First, the owner-operator personally bears all of the losses of the business and is responsible for all of the firm's liabilities, so the proprietor's personal assets and income are at risk. Second, because of this unlimited financial liability and the absence of a legal life for the business independent of the owner's life, a proprietorship has difficulty attracting the outside capital funds necessary for business expansion.

In terms of their representation in the U.S. labor force, proprietors or self-employed workers steadily declined for roughly a century after the Civil War. In more recent decades, the proportion of civilian employees who are self-employed has fallen, from 22 percent in 1940 to less than 9 percent in 1970. Not surprisingly, this decline in overall self-employment coincides with the shift of the American economy away from agriculture, an industry of historically high proprietorship activity. The long-running decline in self-employment ceased in the early 1970s, however, and the proportion of self-employed workers in nonagricultural sectors has risen over the past two decades. Today, about 10 percent of the entire labor force is self-employed.

The reversal of such a pronounced trend as the decline in self-employment is a significant phenomenon and, understandably, has attracted interest in the determinants of self-employment and proprietorship activity. The possible influence of the tax system on the self-employment choice has received considerable attention in recent years, especially because of relatively large legislated and inflation-driven changes in income tax rates during the 1970s and 1980s. The traditional analysis of how income taxation influences the amount of work effort, by affecting the choice between labor (money income) and leisure, has been expanded to consider the potential impact of taxation on the allocation of working time across different employments.

In a modern economy, individuals can work for business firms or governmental agencies as wage or salaried employees, or they can supply labor to their own enterprise or proprietorship. In theory, the individual income tax is general in the sense that its impact is the same on returns from all types of labor market activity. For example, under a proportional income tax of 30 percent, an additional dollar of salary or business income will yield 70 cents of disposable (after-tax) income for both the corporate accountant and the self-employed one. In this case, the income tax will not influence the choice between self-employment and salaried work.

In practice, however, the income tax is not perfectly general and thus may influence an individual's choice of employment. The returns from self-employment or proprietorship activity are thought to be less heavily taxed than wages or salaries, and this tax advantage might lead individuals to prefer self-employment over salaried jobs. First, wages and salaries are subject to both tax withholding by employers and return filing requirements, whereas taxation of the self-employed depends primarily on voluntary compliance. Studies have found that a larger percentage of proprietorship and self-employment incomes goes unreported to the Internal Revenue Service and other tax authorities, which implies that effective or actual tax burdens are relatively lower for the self-employed than for salaried employees. Second, proprietors can lower their taxable incomes, and hence their tax liabilities, through deductions for expenses incurred in earning income from their business or trade. To the extent that some deductible "business" expenses (e.g., for travel, entertainment, office furnishings) also yield personal (consumption) benefits, the proprietor effectively earns tax-free income. Contributions to individual retirement saving plans represent another tax-deductible expenditure that, as a result of the Tax Reform Act of 1986, has been made more accessible to self-employed persons than to wage or salaried workers. In recent years, Keogh retirement saving plans for proprietors have expanded steadily in terms of both number and annual volume of deposits.

The findings of several empirical studies suggest that rising income tax rates do in fact induce workers to choose self-employment rather than wage or salaried jobs. The individual need not make an all-or-nothing choice, however. These is also some evidence that high-salaried (and high tax bracket) individuals establish proprietorships in addition to their full-time jobs for tax-avoidance purposes. For instance, many high-income employees reporting Schedule F (farm) losses on their individual tax returns are quite possibly "farming the tax code" rather than the soil.

Proprietorship activity may be affected by other fiscal and governmental policies besides the general taxation influences described above. For example, entrepreneurial investment may be influenced by a specific and controversial feature of the income tax structure, its treatment of capital gains income. Advocates of preferential (lower) tax rates on capital gains maintain that full taxation of nominal realized capital gains combined with limited loss offsets deters would-be proprietors from starting new firms. In contrast, self-employment among older Americans has probably been encouraged by the disincentive for full-time salaried employment inherent in the Social Security earnings test. Government regulations and required paperwork are thought to disproportionately burden proprietorships because of their small size relative to partnership and corporate enterprises, which often employ persons specifically to assist in compliance with government mandates. Had governmental information, environmental, safety, and other requirements on firms not increased so sharply over the past two or three decades, the recent reversal of the decline in proprietorship activity in the United States might have been more dramatic.

One potential new government mandate facing American businesses, employer-provided health insurance for all employees, could have an extremely large impact on small business and has attracted much interest in the discussion of health care reform in the United States. Employer-provided health insurance and other fringe benefits are generally paid for by employees through reduced wages. But many small firms and proprietorships pay wages that are already close to the legal minimum and cannot be significantly reduced. Consequently, some analysts believe that mandated insurance coverage is likely to produce labor cost increases large enough to devastate many small businesses.

It is unlikely that proprietorship activity in the United States will ever again reach the scale it once exhibited when the nation was largely rural and agricultural. However, as long as individuals value the flexibility afforded by self-employment, and the desire to be one's own boss exists, proprietorships can be expected to remain a popular form of business organization.

## Additional readings

Blau, David M. "A Time-Series Analysis of Self-Employment in the United States." *Journal of Political Economy* 95 (June 1987): 445–67.

Kahn, C. Harry. *Business and Professional Income under the Personal Income Tax*. Princeton: Princeton University Press (for National Bureau of Economic Research), 1964.

Long, James E. "The Income Tax and Self-Employment." *National Tax Journal* 35 (March 1982): 31–42.

Long, James E. "Income Taxation and the Allocation of Market Labor." *Journal of Labor Research* 3 (Summer 1982): 259–76.

Long, James E. "Farming the Tax Code: The Impact of High Marginal Tax Rates on Agricultural Tax Shelters." *American Journal of Agricultural Economics* (February 1990): 1–12.

Long, James E. "Estimates of Tax-Favored Retirement Saving Behavior of the Self-Employed." *Public Finance Quarterly* 21 (April 1993): 163–77.

Park, Thae S. "Relationship between Personal Income and Adjusted Income: Revised Estimates, 1947–83." *Survey of Current Business* (May 1986): 34–40.

# R

## Rainy day funds

Jed Kee
George Washington University

*A hedge against the unpredictability of the revenue stream and forecasting errors.*

---

Revenue stability—sometimes called rainy day funds, and sometimes known as budget-stabilization funds—is generally defined as the ability of a state-local tax structure to generate a predictable revenue stream that matches expenditures, and that depends upon the elasticity of the tax base. In general, state and local officials prefer a tax base that grows with the economy (income-elastic) because this will allow a corresponding increase in expenditures to meet an expected increased demand for public goods and services. However, an income-elastic structure is less predictable in the budgetary process, where revenue estimates are made 12 months or more in advance of actual tax receipts. Thus, state and local officials face a tradeoff between a stable (inelastic) revenue structure and a responsive (elastic) one. Generally, states tend to have the more elastic base (with a revenue structure consisting primarily of income taxes and sales taxes) and local governments the less elastic base (their revenue structure consisting primarily of property taxes and fees).

Since the early 1980s, state and local governments have been buffeted by a series of outside events (national and regional recessions, federal mandates and a reduction in federal aid, and natural disasters) that have challenged their ability to keep expenditures in line with revenues, thus maintaining a balanced budget. Forty-nine of the 50 states are required, by state constitution or statute, to maintain a balanced operating budget. In response to this dilemma, 45 states have created revenue-stabilization or rainy day funds.

Most state constitutions also require that local governments maintain a balanced budget. Although local governments historically have relied on less elastic revenue sources—the property tax and a variety of user fees and charges—they are more vulnerable to cyclical fluctuations than larger state economies, because of less-diversified economic bases. Even though local governments have reduced their dependence on the stable property tax, it remains the largest source of revenues for most local governments and thus reduces, somewhat, the need for local revenue-stabilization policies.

Rainy day funds are created primarily to make states (with the more income-elastic revenue bases) less vulnerable to business cycles. Thus, states stockpile revenue surpluses during prosperous economic times and draw on those funds during times of economic downturn. Rainy day funds greatly differ among the states, with respect to how they are created and designed, the total amount allowed in the funds, and when the states can draw down on those funds.

Most states authorize rainy day funds in legislation, although seven states do so in their constitution (Delaware, Florida, Louisiana, Oklahoma, South Carolina, Texas, and Virginia). In Alaska, Louisiana, and Texas, deposits to their funds are tied to mineral, oil, and gas revenues, but most states use any surplus general funds. Seven states require legislative action to transfer funds to their rainy day fund. The advantage of this method is that it provides the governor and the legislature with a degree of flexibility on the use of surplus funds; the disadvantage is the political difficulty of comparing the relative priority of the rainy day fund balance to other program priorities. Thirty-one states automatically transfer all or a portion of their unexpended general-fund surplus at the end of their fiscal year; the other states use a variety of formulas (such as growth in personal income). An automatic method of allocation provides the advantage of removing the decision from politics but affords much less flexibility for the governor and the legislature.

While there is no "appropriate" amount that should be accumulated in rainy day funds, a rule of thumb recommended by the National Conference of State Legislatures' Fiscal Affairs and Oversight Committee (and informally used by municipal bond rating agencies) is that the combination of general-fund surpluses and rainy day funds should equal at least 5 percent of total state expenditures. States with highly elastic revenue sources (such as progressive income taxes) might opt for a larger balance because their revenues will fluctuate more during economic swings. For fiscal year 1994–95, state ending balances, in the aggregate, were projected at $8.1 billion and budget stabilization funds at $4.2 billion. The combined reserves equaled approximately 4 percent of the projected expenditures of $343.6 billion. Eight states, however, began the year with a zero balance in their rainy day or budget-stabilization fund.

In order to draw down from the rainy day fund, states have set up procedures designed to ensure that the funds will be used only in emergencies, generally tied to revenue shortfalls (35 of the states), budget deficits (Colorado, Connecticut, and Nebraska), or a decline in the growth of personal income (Arizona, Michigan, and Indiana). Four states (Alabama, Kentucky, Missouri, and North Carolina) allow the governor substantial discretion in the use of the funds.

The major arguments in favor of revenue funds are the following: They allow budget planning without unduly conservative revenue projects; they protect current expenditures during economic downturns, avoiding cyclical reinforcing budget cuts; they provide a permanent improvement in the financial conditions of the state—the fiscal cushion that bond rating agencies examine in determining ratings; and they allow politicians to avoid the unattractive alternative of midyear expenditure cuts or tax increases.

There are several arguments against rainy day funds. Some argue that surplus state revenues should be used to fund needed state projects (generally capital spending) that often are squeezed out of the budget. Others suggest that state surpluses should be returned to the taxpayers in the form of tax relief. Still others suggest alternative methods for maintaining a balanced budget during economic downturns: reducing expenditures, maintaining "contingent" spending (depending upon revenue growth), contingent taxation (triggered by revenue collections below projections), borrowing (either short- or long-term), and maintaining large general-fund balances. All of these methods have their own political and economic costs. Budget cuts and tax increases reinforce rather than counter cyclical downturns. Short-term borrowing, if used with regularity, may adversely affect the state's bond rating. All of these methods carry political risks with the electorate.

Rainy day funds work best when they are used primarily as a hedge against an economic downturn and when there are sufficient balances available to cushion what otherwise might be difficult spending cuts and tax increases. However, they are not useful in dealing with long-term economic problems in a state. The amount of the fund should be sufficient to cover likely revenue shortfalls caused by a state's inability, in its revenue projections, to forecast national economic downturns. Based on the evidence of recent recessions, a 5 to 10 percent state revenue shortfall (below projections) is typical. Because it is politically difficult to accumulate a rainy day fund that equals 10 percent of expenditures, some combination of approaches (including rainy day funds, expenditure reductions, and tax increases) may be necessary to deal with severe economic downturns, especially those that last more than one year.

## Additional readings

Braun, Bradley M., L.E. Johnson, and Robert D. Ley. "State Revenue Shortfalls: Budget Restraints and Policy Alternatives." *The American Journal of Economics and Sociology* 52 (4) (October 1993): 385–97.

Eckl, Corina L. "States Broaden the Scope of Rainy Day Funds." *The Fiscal Letter* (March/April 1995): 1–3 and 8–11. National Conference of State Legislatures.

Gold, Steven D. *Preparing for the Next Recession: Rainy Day Funds and Other Tools for States*. National Conference of State Legislatures. Legislative Finance Paper #41. December 30, 1983.

National Association of State Budget Officers. *Budgeting amid Fiscal Uncertainty: Stabilization Funds and Other Strategies*. Washington, D.C., June 1985.

Vasche, Jon David, and Brad Williams. "Optimal Governmental Budgeting Contingency Reserve Funds." *Public Budgeting and Finance* 7 (1) (Spring 1987): 66–82.

*Cross references:* automatic stabilizers; revenue elasticity (tax elasticity)

# Rehabilitation tax credit

Louis Alan Talley
Congressional Research Service, Library of Congress

*A credit allowed for capital expenditures incurred in rehabilitating either nonresidential real property (commercial property) or qualified residential rental property. No federal tax incentives exist for the rehabilitation of an individual's private residence, but a 10 percent tax credit is allowed for rehabilitation of buildings constructed before 1936 and a 20 percent credit is allowed for certified historic structures.*

## Defining historic structures

Certified historic structures are either individually registered in the National Register of Historic Places or certified by the Secretary of the Interior as having historic significance and being located in a registered historic district. In either case, an application form must be filed with the respective state's historic preservation office, which reviews the certification application and either recommends or denies designation of historic significance. The state office forwards the information and recommendation to the Secretary of the Interior, who certifies that the preservation preserves the historic character of the building or integrates with the historic district.

## Rehabilitation standards

The Secretary of the Interior has 10 standards for rehabilitation of historic structures, to ensure that the historic character of the building is preserved. There are other important provisions such as the substantial rehabilitation test, the types of expenditures qualifying for the credit, provisions for tax-exempt use property, and recapture rules. Projects eligible for the 10 percent credit are also restricted; in particular, at least 75 percent of the external walls must be retained (50 percent as external walls), and 75 percent of the internal structure must be retained.

## Legislative history

The *Tax Reform Act of 1976* first provided for a historic preservation tax incentive, allowing a five-year write-off for rehabilitation expenditures for business and residential rental property. Historic structures were those individually registered in the National Register of Historic Places or certified by the Secretary of the Interior as having historic significance and located in a registered historic district. Structures located in a historic district under state or local statute and certified by the Department of the Interior were also eligible. Penalties imposed for tearing down certified historic structures disallowed the deduction of demolition costs and reduced depreciation for new structures built on sites of previous historic structures.

The *Revenue Act of 1978* extended the 10 percent investment tax credit then in existence to qualified rehabilitation expenditures for nonresidential buildings. Expenditures had to begin at least 20 years after the building was first placed in service and have a useful life of five years or more. If the investment tax credit was claimed, the five-year write-off could not be used. Costs for acquisition, replacement, or enlargement of the building did not qualify, nor was the credit available if more than 25 percent of the exterior walls were replaced. Work on certified historic structures had to be certified by the Secretary of the Interior to qualify for the credit.

The *Economic Recovery Tax Act of 1981* changed the depreciation benefit to a tax credit. This was done partly as a simplification and partly to add counterbalance to new provisions of the 1981 tax law that provided for accelerated cost recovery. The credit was three-tiered: a 15 percent credit for nonresidential buildings at least 30 years old, a 20 percent rate for nonresidential structures at least 40 years old, and a 25 percent credit reserved for certified historic structures. The building's basis for depreciation purposes was reduced by one-half of the credit.

The *Tax Reform Act of 1986* changed the three-tier credit to the current two-tier one and reduced the basis by the full credit, rather than one-half of it. Many of the prior law's provisions were retained, such as the substantial rehabilitation test, the types of expenditures qualifying for the credit, provisions for tax-exempt use property, and recapture rules. The old rules for how much of the structure must be retained to receive the nonhistoric structure credit were replaced by more stringent rules that required retention of at least 75 percent of the external walls, with at least 50 percent remaining as external walls, and of 75 percent of internal structural framework. External wall requirements were deleted from the rules for certified historic structures, because those restorations are supervised by the Secretary of the Interior.

To restrict tax shelter investing, Congress in 1986 prohibited the deduction of losses from a business activity in which the taxpayer does not "materially participate" from any other kind of income (or in this case using tax credits generated in such a business to offset taxes on other income) until the investment is sold. Ownership of a limited partnership interest and rental of property were both defined as passive activities. There were, however, two exceptions for those engaged in rehabilitation activity. First, those investors did not have to "actively participate" in the management of the property to be allowed the credit, so a limited partner could take the credit. Second, taxpayers with higher incomes than those eligible for other "passive losses" were eligible for the credit.

The *Revenue Reconciliation Act of 1989* eliminated the income limitation on taking the credit, and all individuals were permitted a $25,000 deduction equivalent regardless of income. A provision enacted as part of the *Revenue Reconciliation Act of 1993* (PL 103-66) eased restrictions on passive activity losses from rental real estate in general for "eligible" taxpayers.

## Rationale

Rapid depreciation of these investments was adopted as an incentive in response to declining usefulness of older buildings and was designed to promote stability and economic vitality to deteriorating areas through the rehabilitation and preservation of historic structures and neighborhoods. Achievement of this goal was thought to be dependent upon enlistment of private funds in the preservation movement.

Partly as a simplification and partly to counterbalance the new accelerated cost recovery rules, the tax incentives were changed to a tax credit in 1981 and made part of a set of credits for rehabilitating older buildings (varying by type or age). Congress hoped to help revitalize the economic prospects of aging areas and preclude the decay and deterioration of distressed economic localities.

The credit amount was reduced in 1986 because the rate was deemed too high relative to the new lower tax rates, and a reduction from a three- to a two-tiered rehabilitation rate credit was adopted. The credit was retained because Congress was concerned that social and aesthetic values are not necessarily taken into account in project profit projections. A higher credit rate was allowed for preservation of historic structures than for rehabilitations of older qualified buildings first placed in service before 1936. This differential was provided to ensure that the credits would be focused on historic and older buildings.

## Impact and assessment

The credit reduces the taxpayer's cost of preservation projects, which can turn unprofitable rehabilitation into profitable rehabilitation and in some cases make rehabilitation more profitable than new construction. Thus, owners of historic buildings and older commercial structures may be encouraged to renovate them through the use of the tax credit available for substantial rehabilitation expenditures.

It is argued that to the extent that businesses renovate rather than relocate, inner-city jobs can be saved with less relocation of workers and changes in commuter patterns. To the extent commuter patterns are changed, governments may be required to make additional investments in transportation modes (roads, commuter rail, and so forth). Before the tax reform in 1986, historic preservation projects had become a popular tax shelter with rapid growth. The limits on credits under the passive loss restrictions limit the use of this investment as a tax shelter for those taxpayers not engaged in the business of real estate.

Some have questioned why the credit is allowed only for business property. Individual homeowners are precluded from use of the credit but find that many of the reasons stated for the credit would apply equally to the preservation of owner-occupied homes.

Opponents of the credit note that investments are allocated to historic buildings that would not be profitable projects without the credit, resulting in economic inefficiency. Proponents argue that investors fail to consider external benefits (preservation of social and aesthetic values) that are desirable for society at large. Thus, this allocation may be desirable if there are external benefits to society that the investors would not take into account.

It has also been argued that the credit has an adverse effect on administration of the tax law. The Internal Revenue Service finds the present system difficult to administer with approval made by a different department of the government. Elimination of the credit would simplify the tax code.

## Additional readings

Lipton, Richard M. "TRA '93 Eases Rules Affecting Debt-Financed Property and Passive Losses from Realty." *Journal of Taxation* 80 (May 1994): 260–65.

Sage, Judith A., Sonia Elias Gorgy, and Lloyd G. Sage. "The Effect of the Revenue Reconciliation Act of 1993 on Real Estate Owners." *Tax Adviser* 25 (August 1994): 491–97.

U.S. Congress, Joint Committee on Taxation. *General Explanation of the Revenue Act of 1978 (H.R. 13511, 95th Congress; Public Law 95-600).* Washington, D.C.: U.S. Government Printing Office, March 12, 1977, pp. 155–58.

U.S. Congress, Joint Committee on Taxation. *General Explanation of the Economic Recovery Tax Act of 1981 (H.R. 4242, 97th Congress; Public Law 97-34).* Washington, D.C.: U.S. Government Printing Office, December 31, 1981, pp. 111–16.

U.S. Congress, Joint Committee on Taxation. *General Explanation of the Tax Reform Act of 1986 (H.R. 3838, 99th Congress; Public Law 99-514).* Washington, D.C.: U.S. Government Printing Office, May 4, 1987, pp. 148–52.

U.S. Congress, Joint Committee on Taxation. *Description of Selected Federal Tax Provisions That Impact Land Use.* Washington, D.C.: U.S. Government Printing Office, July 11, 1996.

U.S. General Accounting Office. *Historic Preservation Tax Incentives.* Washington, D.C., August 1, 1986.

*Cross references:* business location, taxation and; enterprise zones.

# Research and experimentation tax credit

Joseph J. Cordes
George Washington University

*Tax credit provided to companies based on qualified expenditures on research and development.*

The U.S. tax code provides special treatment of business investments in research and development (R&D) in the form of two provisions: an option to expense R&D expenditures and an incremental tax credit for qualified expenditures on research and experimentation (R&E).

## History of the research and experimentation credit

A tax credit for R&D was first introduced in the Economic Recovery Tax Act of 1981, and with several modifications it has been extended since then. When it was first enacted, businesses could claim a 25 percent tax credit on eligible spending on R&E that exceeded a base amount. The base amount was originally defined to be the average of the three prior years' spending on R&E with an additional limitation that the amount of the base used to determine the credit could not be less than one-half of the taxpayer's qualified expenditures during the taxable year. In effect, this "base period limitation" reduced the effective statutory rate of incremental credit for firms with R&D growing at more than twice the level of base spending from 25 percent to 12.5 percent. Expenses that qualified for the original credit were salaries of R&D personnel, expenses of materials used in R&D, and 65 percent of the cost of R&D services purchased from other providers.

The Tax Reform Act of 1986 reduced the R&E credit from 25 to 20 percent and tightened some of the definitions of the type of R&E spending eligible to receive the credit. These changes in the definition of qualifying R&D were made in response to criticisms that the enactment of the R&E credit in 1981 created incentives for firms to redefine activities as R&D in order to qualify for the credit. A tax credit also was provided for company-funded basic research conducted at universities. Under the original tax credit enacted in 1981, 65 percent of company-funded university research was eligible for the incremental credit. Under the 1986 tax law, company-funded university basic research was given separate treatment. The subsidy provided by the credit was further reduced in 1988 by making half of the credit claimed taxable income by requiring businesses to deduct the tax credit from their expensing deduction.

In 1989, the amount of credit claimed was made 100 percent taxable, and the method of determining the base for calculating the amount of R&E that was eligible for the credit was changed. Instead of using the average of three prior years' R&E spending, the base became the product of a fixed ratio of R&E spending to sales (referred to as the "fixed base percentage") times average gross sales of the business for the preceding four years. As in the earlier version of the credit, the base period limitation was maintained so that the base used to determine the credit could not be less than one-half of the taxpayer's qualified expenditures during the taxable year. So as not to unduly penalize businesses with unusually high R&D-to-sales ratios, the fixed ratio used to determine the base was defined to be the lesser of 0.16 or the actual ratio of R&E to sales for at least three years between 1984 and 1988. Businesses without the requisite number of taxable years

between 1984 and 1988 were assigned a fixed ratio of 0.03. Beginning in 1994, businesses without the requisite number of taxable years were allowed to retain the fixed base percentage for only the first five years, and additional calculations of the fixed base percentage were required in the 6th through 10th years. In 1996, firms were allowed an alternative lower credit rate with a smaller fixed base.

Although initially set to expire, the credit has been extended many times, on occasion on a retroactive basis.

## Policy issues

Since its enactment, the R&E tax credit has provided tax subsidies to industrial spending on R&E in excess of $1 billion per year. The rationale for the subsidy is that investments in industrial R&D often have social returns above the private return captured by the business that makes the investment. The existence of such external benefits from R&D spending means that private investments in R&D may be less than would be socially optimal.

Economists generally agree that certain types of spending on industrial research can generate sizable external benefits and that, for this reason, some form of government subsidy for R&E may be justified. As with other tax expenditures, however, the broad issue of whether the R&E tax credit has subsidized spending on industrial research that otherwise would not have been undertaken has surfaced at several points in the credit's history.

One noteworthy feature of the R&E credit is that from its inception, attempts have been made to avoid providing the credit for R&E spending that businesses would have undertaken in the absence of the credit. Allowing businesses to claim a tax credit only on the amount by which current spending exceeded some predetermined base was intended to make the R&E tax credit an incremental subsidy for spending on R&E that the business would not otherwise have undertaken.

Economists who have studied the credit agree that the initial attempt to define the base was seriously flawed. By defining the base to be the average of the firm's qualified R&D spending in the past three years, an additional $1 of R&D spending in the present allowed a business to claim a tax credit, but at a cost of not being able to claim a comparable tax credit in future years. The reason was that the additional $1 spent in the present reduced the amount of future R&D eligible for the credit by $0.33 in each of the subsequent three years.

This feature of the current credit had two effects. One was that the effective rate of subsidy provided by the credit was significantly reduced from its statutory level of 20 percent to something closer to 3 percent. Another potential effect was that businesses faced incentives to change the timing of their

R&D spending to maximize the amount of credits that could be claimed. Firms with declining R&D spending in a given year faced an incentive to defer R&D spending to subsequent years, while other firms faced incentives to vary or to "cycle" R&D spending over a period of years in order to be able to claim more R&D credits.

This shortcoming was addressed by the change in defining the base that was enacted in 1990. As a result of this change, a firm's base depends on two factors—the fixed base percentage, and the average of three prior years' sales—that are not directly affected by how much the business spends on R&E. Thus, increased spending on R&E today does not automatically make it harder for a business to claim the credit in the future, which had the effect of diluting the effective rate of subsidy provided by the credit.

Even though the base has been defined more satisfactorily, there is still an issue of whether the credit truly encourages a significant amount of R&E spending that otherwise would not have taken place. An important factor is the price sensitivity (elasticity) of spending on R&D. The R&E credit is intended to stimulate spending on R&D by reducing its cost. The amount of additional spending on R&E that is encouraged by the credit thus depends on how sensitive business decisions are to the cost of R&D. If, for example, decisions about spending on R&D depend on considerations other than cost, reducing the after-tax cost of R&D will increase R&D spending by a relatively small amount, and much of the tax subsidy would reward businesses for doing what they would have done in any case. If, however, cost is a consideration, the tax subsidy is more likely to encourage a significant volume of "new" spending on R&D.

Economists who study the behavior of businesses that conduct R&D generally agree that the amount of R&D spending is sensitive to its cost, so that the R&E tax credit has stimulated some additional industrial R&D. There are, however, a range of estimates of how much additional spending has been encouraged per dollar of revenue lost. At the low end, these estimates imply that the R&E credit has stimulated roughly $.30 of extra spending on R&D per dollar of revenue lost, which would mean that it has not been a cost-effective way of encouraging industrial R&E. But other studies estimate that the R&E credit has caused businesses to spend $1.00 or more of additional R&D spending for every dollar of revenue that is forgone, which would make it cost-effective.

### Additional readings

Cordes, Joseph J. "Tax Incentives and R&D Spending: A Review of the Evidence." *Research Policy* 18 (1989): 119–33.

Cordes, Joseph J., Harry S. Watson, and J. Scott Hauger. "The Effects of Tax Reform on High Technology Firms," *National Tax Journal* 40 (3) (1987): 373–91.

Hall, Bronwyn. "R&D Tax Policy during the 1980s: Success or Failure." In *Tax Policy and the Economy*, vol. 7, edited by James Poterba, pp. 1–35. Cambridge, Mass.: MIT Press, 1993.

Moumeneas, T., and M. I. Nadiri. "Public R&D Policies and Cost Behavior of the U.S. Manufacturing Industries." *Journal of Public Economics* 63 (1): 57–83.

Watson, Harry S. "The 1990 Tax Credit: A Uniform Tax on Inputs and Subsidy for R&D." *National Tax Journal* 49 (1): 93–103.

*Cross references:* basis adjustment; expensing; investment tax credits; tax expenditures.

# Residence principle

Joseph J. Cordes
George Washington University

*A basis for assigning tax liabilities to individuals and businesses located in one jurisdiction and earning income in another.*

---

Taxation on the basis of residence, rather than at the source, means that the amount a person pays in taxes depends on where the person lives, rather than on where the income is earned. Consider the case of a resident of the United States who earns interest from a bank account that is located in another country. If the United States and that country agree, typically through a tax treaty, to tax each other's citizens on the basis of residence, the investor would be required to report and pay taxes on the interest income to the United States instead of to the country in which the interest income is earned.

In the United States, individual states often agree to tax citizens of other states on the basis of residence to ease the compliance burden of taxpayers. This can be especially important in border areas where residents of one state may work and earn income in another. For example, in the Washington, D.C., metropolitan area, a resident of the Virginia suburbs who works in Maryland files in, and pays taxes to, Virginia rather than Maryland.

Taxation on the basis of residence means that taxes will be neutral with respect to where taxpayers decide to invest and earn their money. For example, if a U.S. resident faces a choice between investing money in the United States and earning a return of $R_U$, and investing the money abroad and earning a return of $R_F$, the portfolio decision should depend only on which of these two returns is the greatest if the taxpayer is taxed on the basis of residence. If she invests in the United States, she would be taxed on the investment at her U.S. tax rate of $T_{US}$ percent, and after paying taxes would earn an after-tax return of $R_U(1-T_{US})$. If instead she invests abroad, and she is taxed on the basis of residence, she would also be taxed at the U.S. rate, so her after-tax return would be $R_F(1-T_{US})$. If the decision about where to invest is based on the after-tax return, it will depend on which investment pays the highest pretax return, because that investment will result in the highest after-tax return. For this reason, taxation on the basis of residence is seen as facilitating an economically efficient flow of resources among different taxing jurisdictions.

*Cross references:* capital export neutrality; capital import neutrality; national neutrality; source principle.

# Retail sales tax

John F. Due
University of Illinois

*A retail sales tax is a form of sales tax that is levied on the final sale through which a commodity (or service) passes on the path to the final purchaser.*

Technically, a retail sales tax is defined as a tax on sales for use or consumption and not for resale. It is not a tax solely on retailers in the usual distribution sense of that term, but on any firm making final sales as defined. Nor is it a tax confined to sales to final household consumers, because in practice the tax applies to a number of purchases for use in further production, such as machinery and equipment. It is not, therefore, a pure consumption tax related directly to household personal consumption.

## Development

Until the 1930s, retail sales taxation was considered to be beyond the capacity of effective administration, although its use had been suggested on a few occasions—for example, in France during World War I. Use of the tax began in the United States in the early 1930s, as an outgrowth of low-rate business occupation taxes, although it had been used in a minor fashion in the 19th century and again in the 1920s. In 1932, Mississippi, desperate for additional revenue, converted its business occupation levy into a 2 percent tax on retail sales (Wheeless 1966). De-

spite strong protests, the tax proved productive of revenue and capable of adequate administrative effectiveness.

The result of this success led other states to follow—10 in 1933 alone and 29 by 1938 (Due and Mikesell 1994). Introduction then slowed, but it speeded up after the end of World War II. By 1969, only five states did not use the tax—and none has added it since then, despite many proposals, but none has repealed it either. The initial rates, typically 2 percent, have gradually increased, until by 1998 the median rate is 5 percent, ranging from 3 to 7.25 percent. Concurrently, in a number of states, various local governments, primarily cities and counties, levied the tax, with most rates ranging from 2 to 3 percent. Combined state-local rates were typically 7 to 10 percent.

In parallel to the U.S. experience, the tax was introduced in Canada, starting with the city of Montreal in 1935 and the province of Alberta in 1936, although Alberta later repealed the tax (Due 1964). Quebec imposed the tax in 1940, and others followed, until by 1967 all of the provinces employed the tax except Alberta—as is still true.

Elsewhere in the world, while sales taxation spread rapidly, typically other forms were used. The retail tax was used in relatively few countries. These included Zimbabwe, which imposed the tax in 1963 and has continued to use it, although attention has been given recently to its replacement by a value-added tax. This is one of the very few cases in which a retail sales tax has been used successfully by a developing country, but Zimbabwe has a highly commercialized retail sector (Due 1983). South Africa imposed a retail sales tax in the 1970s, but replaced it with a VAT in 1990, and Namibia has what is essentially a retail sales tax.

Other uses can be noted briefly. The tax was imposed in Iceland in 1960, used successfully at high rates—up to 20 percent—and replaced by a VAT in 1989. Norway (1940–1970) and Sweden (1940–1948 and 1960–1969) used retail sales taxes until they replaced them with VATs. Barbados imposed a retail tax in 1975 but repealed it a year later.

The tax had limited use in Latin America, first in Honduras (1964) and then in Costa Rica (1967), Nicaragua (1968), and Paraguay (1968–1992) (Birch and Due 1985). All were ultimately replaced by VATs. The retail tax has been used in several states in India, and the Swiss wholesale sales tax was in fact collected primarily at the retail level; it was replaced by a VAT in 1995.

In the United States and Canada, the sales taxes were introduced primarily to meet the need for additional revenue, not to replace other taxes. They were chosen over income tax increases primarily because of the fear of loss of business investment to other states, the height of federal income taxes, and the greater cyclical stability of revenue relative to income taxes.

The retail sales taxes in the United States have yielded from 30 to 34 percent of state tax revenue in recent years, although they range from less than 20 percent to a high of 58 percent (Florida, 1996), and more than 50 percent in several other states. In Canada, the tax yields an overall 26 percent of provincial tax revenue, ranging from 23 to 45 percent.

The remainder of this entry concentrates on the experience in the United States and Canada, given the tax's current limited use elsewhere.

## Coverage—commodities

The typical retail sales tax applies to all commodities—that is, tangible personal property—other than ones specifically exempted, but only to their final sales; as noted, purchase must be for use or consumption and not for resale. All purchases for resale are therefore free of tax; universally, purchases of materials to be physically incorporated into products are included in the category of sales for resale.

Sales for delivery outside the state are exempt; purchases from out of state are subject to levies called use taxes, imposed at the same rate as the sales tax.

Exemptions of commodities fall into two general classes. First, certain production inputs, particularly those used in manufacturing and agriculture, are specifically exempted (Due and Mikesell 1994; Hellerstein and Hellerstein 1992, ch. 14; Ring 1989). Following the rationale for its use, a retail sales tax should apply only to purchases for household consumption expenditures and thus logically should not apply to any purchases acquired for business use. But in practice, the taxes were not designed in this fashion; use or consumption has been interpreted to mean use by business firms as well as final consumers. This rule, of course, results in multiple applications of the tax to final consumption goods, contrary to the consumption principle. In addition, it may lead to pyramiding—that is, price increases in excess of the tax by application of percentage markups to prices, including tax. It may deter real investment by making investment more costly, and by encouraging firms to reduce the amount of tax by producing goods for use in further production instead of purchasing them.

Accordingly, almost all states and provinces have gradually added various categories of production inputs to the exempt list. About half of the states and several Canadian provinces, for example, exempt machinery and equipment used in manufacturing, and agricultural feed, seed, and fertilizer are universally excluded, as is farm machinery and equipment in a number of states. One result is to complicate somewhat the operation of the taxes and

pave the way for evasion. Determination by the seller of the ultimate use of many goods is difficult.

The second group of exemptions is designed to bring about a distribution of the tax burden that is less regressive and thus more acceptable (Due and Mikesell 1994, ch. 4; Hellerstein and Hellerstein 1992, ch. 3). On this issue, state practice varies substantially. Some states provide virtually no exemptions of this type, others a wide range. Food is the most significant exemption in terms of revenue, granted in 1998 by 25 states and all of the Canadian provinces. It has been a common exemption in other countries as well. Medicines and related items, especially those on prescription, are now exempt in virtually all states and provinces, although the specific coverage differs.

There are other exemptions in various states—books in some, for example, and clothing in a few states. The exemptions, particularly food, have drastic effects on revenue, the food exemption alone reducing the revenue by as much as 20 percent. The exemptions inevitably complicate compliance, audit, and control, because of interpretative problems relating to the coverage of the category and misapplication of the tax by clerks. Food exemption does significantly reduce the regressivity of the tax and the absolute burden on the poor.

There are other exemptions of varying significance, such as sales to government and various charitable and educational institutions, and commodities, such as motor fuel, subject to excises.

This section is concerned with commodities—that is, tangible personal property. Sale of real property is generally never taxed, nor is intangible property, including securities and various credit instruments—basically because purchase is not considered to be consumption.

## Services

The treatment of services varies substantially among the states and has gradually changed over the years (Due and Mikesell 1994, ch. 5; Hellerstein and Hellerstein 1992, ch. 15; Federation of Tax Administrators 1996). The original taxes applied solely to tangible personal property, thus excluding all services, and in a few states—California, for example—the taxes are still primarily of this nature. Only two states, Hawaii and New Mexico, initially followed the opposite taxation pattern: In addition to commodities, virtually all services rendered to customers, but not services of employees, were taxed. South Dakota's treatment later moved relatively close to these. Gradually, other states have added services—some only a few, such as transient accommodations and utilities; others a hundred or so. The result is to increase revenues, but rarely by a high percentage, because the states are reluctant as a matter of principle and politics to include some of the most productive services, from a revenue stand-point, such as medical care and legal services. It is not at all clear that including services brings the pattern of distribution more in line with accepted standards (Fox and Murray 1988; Siegfried and Smith 1991).

One major sector, real property contract work, receives special treatment. Typically, the tax applies to materials purchased for this work, rather than the full contract price including labor.

## Rate structures

Unlike some other forms of sales tax, retail sales taxes typically have uniform rates, in part because of the difficulty for retailers in keeping adequate records of sales at various rates. In the United States, the principal exceptions are the application of lower rates to industrial equipment and machinery, used in lieu of exemption. Rarely is a higher than basic rate applied. Paraguay was an exception, and a few U.S. states tax motel and hotel services, car rental, and alcoholic beverages more heavily than the basic figure; outside the United States, rates have typically been under 10 percent, although Iceland used a 20 percent rate.

For the states, in January 1996, the median state rate was 5 percent. Most of the original taxes had 2 percent rates; by 1959 the median was 3 percent, and rates have slowly but steadily increased since that year. These are state rates only; in the states with municipal sales taxes as well, the overall figure is higher. In Canada, the rates have typically been higher than in the United States, but the exemptions are broader. In 1995, the median rate was 9 percent, with a range from 6.5 percent (Quebec) to 12 percent (Newfoundland).

## Distribution of burden of a retail sales tax

The traditional view of the distributional effects of a retail sales tax is that the tax will be reflected in higher prices to consumers, and thus the burden will be distributed in relation to consumption expenditures. Empirical evidence was provided by Poterba (1996). It is also widely believed that quoting the tax separately from the prices for goods or services, an almost universal practice in the United States and Canada but not in many other countries, facilitates forward shifting by encouraging competing firms to follow the same pricing policies.

It has long been recognized, however, that there are certain to be exceptions. Demand elasticities for various goods will differ, even with a uniform tax rate, and firms may readjust prices so as to push more of the burden onto the goods with inelastic demands. As noted, a portion of the tax rests on goods purchased for use in production; the distribution of this portion of the burden is by no means

clear. Finally, it has long been argued that the over-all higher prices will result in reduced demand for factor units and thus reduce their prices, some of the burden being borne in relation to factor income. But if fiscal policy seeks to maintain the same over-all level of demand for factors, factor prices will not fall.

In summary, while the assumption of exact forward shifting is an oversimplification, it is still generally accepted as the basis for legislative action and analyses of burden distribution.

Many studies have been made of the distribution of burden by income class, on the assumption of forward shifting. In general, these concluded that the tax, without exemptions, will be regressive relative to incomes, and place considerable absolute burden on the lowest income groups. If food is exempt, then regressivity is greatly reduced. Adding services to the coverage does not accomplish much in lessening regressivity.

This general view of regressivity has been criticized on two grounds. First, it is argued that distributional effects should be considered in terms of lifetime income, not annual income; many of the low-income groups are not really poor, but drawing on previously accumulated funds. On a lifetime basis, the recent studies have shown the tax to still be regressive, but much less so (Fullerton and Rogers 1993; Caspersen and Metcalf 1994). The second objection is that many persons in the lowest income groups are receiving incomes (e.g., welfare) that are indexed to the general price level; if the sales tax rises, the transfer payments will also rise (Browning 1985). But many lower-income groups do not benefit from such indexing.

An alternative to food exemption, used by several states, is to provide for credit against state income tax with a refund, or a direct cash payment, to compensate for the tax on the lower-income groups (Case and Ebel, 1989). This is used by nine U.S. states and by the Canadian government on its value-added tax.

The other problem with studies of sales tax incidence is that they basically employ a partial-equilibrium analysis, when a general-equilibrium analysis would be more suitable, because all or most prices are changing. But obtaining adequate data poses serious problems.

## Administration of the taxes

When retail sales taxes have been introduced by national governments, administration has typically been assigned to Customs and Excise along with other indirect taxes. Individual states in the United States have followed various routes. In earlier years, sales tax administration was typically placed as a separate division in the general revenue agency. In recent years, the trend has been toward functional organization, in which each activity involved in sales tax administration has been entrusted to the division performing similar functions for other taxes, including income tax as well, although in practice some specialization of personnel takes place.

In addition to routine registration of firms and handling incoming returns and payments, there are two major aspects of administration. First is control of delinquency—checking on firms not filing returns or paying on time. Second is auditing—inspecting firms' records to ensure that correct amounts are paid (Due and Mikesell 1994, ch. 6). Operations are now highly computerized, so ascertainment of delinquents—those not filing or paying—is relatively easy, with contact then made by letter, phone call, and, if necessary, a visit.

Initial delinquency rates as a percentage of registered firms continues to be relatively high, with a median for all states of about 10 percent, concentrated in smaller firms. But the final action—such as seizure of property—involves no more than 0.1 percent of the firms.

Audits are performed by a relatively well-trained staff, and a variety of techniques are used to establish priorities for audit. But the coverage is very limited—overall, no more than 1.2 percent of registered firms per year in recent years. There are about 7.4 million firms in the United States registered for sales tax purposes (Due and Mikesell 1994: 23).

## Overall effectiveness of the state retail sales taxes

It is very difficult to measure the exact degree of the taxes' operational effectiveness. From all indications, the intrastate operation is relatively effective, with no mass escape of taxable firms and transactions, although some revenue is lost via the underground economy (Due 1974). With interstate transactions, however, there is a substantial loss—as is true with interprovincial sales in Canada as well. A state cannot apply an "export" tax on buyers in other states for constitutional reasons and likely would not wish to do so anyway. Under the use tax sections of the state sales tax legislation, states can tax purchases coming from out of state, and they do reach such purchases from large traditional mail-order houses, as well as the purchases of motor vehicles and other items that must be registered. But they cannot reach many smaller transactions and firms selling into a large number of states with small amounts in each, as well as many of the large mail-order vendors. Such firms could be forced, at considerable cost and nuisance, to conform with the sales-use tax laws of a number of states. These states have sought to lessen the escape, but with only limited effect (Trandel 1992;

Walsh and Jones 1988; Fisher 1980; Fox 1986; Washington Department of Revenue 1990). Federal legislation could greatly enhance the states' power, but this has not been forthcoming. Similar problems arise with the local sales taxes, but typically the purchases are caught by one jurisdiction or another.

The cost of administering state sales taxes ranges at around 1 percent of the revenues; exact figures are difficult to obtain because of joint administration of sales and other taxes in many states.

Estimates of compliance costs for the vendors vary widely; one study suggests an overall figure of about 3 percent—but this figure ranges widely with the type of business (*Tax Administrators News* 1996; Peat et al. 1982).

## The worldwide trend

In general, national governments have moved away from retail sales taxes to VATs, basically for two reasons: to free all purchases used for business from the tax (important for a country's foreign trade position and domestic efficiency in production), and to improve administration because of the superior audit trail. The European community's adoption of the VAT stimulated this shift.

In federal countries, however, the retail sales tax remains supreme at the state level, although in the United States and Canada limited attention has been given to its possible replacement with VATs. The main reason this does not occur is the interstate problem; the interstate sales give rise to serious questions about credit for other states' taxes and engender much greater enforcement problems than does the retail tax. There are serious conflict-of-interest issues among the various states regarding allocation of the share of the total sales (value-added) tax revenue between the states in which the retail sale occurs (with credit for tax paid at pretail sales) and the states of origin. Canada has sought to integrate provincial and federal sales taxes, with only limited success (Hill and Rushton 1993). In the United States, current proposals for a federal retail sales tax would alter the picture drastically.

## Additional readings

Baum, Donald. "Economic Effects of Including Services in the Sales Tax Base: An Applied General Equilibrium Approach." *Public Finance Quarterly* 19 (April 1992): 166–92.

Birch, Melissa H., and John F. Due. "Paraguay: The Retail Sales Tax." *Bulletin for International Fiscal Documentation* 39 (3) (1985): 103–7.

Boucher, Karen J. "Sales Tax on Services: The New Source of State Revenues." *Journal of State Taxation* 7 (3) (Fall 1988): 273–86.

Browning, Edgar K. "Tax Incidence, Indirect Taxes, and Transfers." *National Tax Journal* 38 (December 1985): 525–34.

Case, Bradford, and Robert Ebel. "Using State Consumer Tax Credits for Achieving Equity." *National Tax Journal* 42 (September 1989): 323–38.

Caspersen, Erik, and Gilbert Metcalf. "Is a Value Added Tax Regressive? Annual vs. Lifetime Incidence Measures." *National Tax Journal* 47 (December 1994): 731–46.

Derrick, Frederick W., and Charles E. Scott. "Business and the Incidence of Sales and Use Tax." *Public Finance Quarterly* 21 (April 2, 1993): 210–26.

Due, John F. *Provincial Sales Taxes*. Toronto: Canadian Tax Foundation. rev. ed., 1964.

Due, John F. "Evaluation of the Effectiveness of State Sales Tax Administration." *National Tax Journal* 27 (June 1974): 197–219.

Due, John F. "The Experience of Zimbabwe with a Retail Sales Tax." *Bulletin for International Fiscal Documentation* 37 (February 1983): 51–8.

Due, John F. "The Implications for Australia of the Experience of the United States, Canada, and Other Countries with Retail Sales Tax." In *Changing the Tax Mix*, edited by John G. Head, pp. 225–46. Melbourne: Australian Tax Research Foundation (1986).

Due, John F., and John L. Mikesell. *Sales Taxation*. Washington, D.C.: The Urban Institute, 1994.

Duncombe, William. "Economic Change and the Evolving State Tax Structure: The Case of the Sales Tax." *National Tax Journal* 45 (September 1992): 299–313.

Dye, Richard, and Therese McGuire. "Growth and Variability of State Individual Income and General Sales Taxes." *National Tax Journal* 44 (March 1991): 55–65.

Federation of Tax Administrators. *Sales Taxation of Services: Who Taxes What?* Washington, D.C., 1991.

Federation of Tax Administrators. "Survey on State Taxation of Services." *Tax Administrators News* 60 (December 1996): 109, 112–8.

Fisher, Ronald C. "Local Sales Taxes: Tax Rate Differentials, Sales Loss, and Revenue Estimation." *Public Finance Quarterly* 8 (April 1980): 171–88.

Fox, William F. "Tax Structure and the Location of Economic Activity along State Borders." *National Tax Journal* 39 (December 1986): 387–402.

Fox, William F., ed. *Sales Taxation: Critical Issues in Policy and Administration*. Westport, Conn.: Praeger Publishers, 1992.

Fox, William F., and Charles Campbell. "Stability of the State Sales Tax Income Elasticity." *National Tax Journal* 37 (June 1984): 201–12.

Fox, William F., and Matthew Murray. "Economic Aspects of Taxing Services." *National Tax Journal* 41 (March 1988): 19–36.

Fullerton, Don, and Diane Lim Rogers. *Who Bears the Lifetime Tax Burden?* Washington, D.C.: The Brookings Institution, 1993.

Gold, Steven D. "Simplifying the Sales Tax: Credits or Exemptions?" In *Sales Taxation: Critical Issues in Policy and Administration*, edited by William F. Fox, pp. 157–68. Westport, Conn.: Praeger Publishers, 1992.

Hamilton, Billy, and John L. Mikesell. "Sales Tax Policy during the Next Decade." In *Sales Taxation: Critical Issues in Policy and Administration*, edited by William F. Fox, pp. 27–40. Westport, Conn.: Praeger Publishers, 1992.

Healy, John C., and Kenneth D. Klemm. "Sales and Use Tax Implications for Construction Contractors." *Journal of State Taxation* 8 (1990): 315–40.

Hellerstein, Jerome R., and Walter Hellerstein. *State Taxation*. vol. 2, part S. Boston: Warren, Gorham & Lamont, 1992.

Hellerstein, Walter. "Florida's Sales Tax on Services." *National Tax Journal* 41 (March 1988): 1–18.

Hellerstein, Walter. "Sales Taxation of Services. In *Sales Taxation: Critical Issues in Policy and Administration*, edited by William F. Fox, pp. 41–50. Westport, Conn.: Praeger Publishers, 1992.

Hill, Roderick, and Michael Rushton. "Harmonizing Provincial Sales Taxation with the GST." *Canadian Tax Journal* 41 (April 1993): 101–22.

Mikesell, John L. "Sales Taxation and the Border County Problem." *Quarterly Review of Economics and Business* 11 (Spring 1971): 23–9.

Mikesell, John L. "Fiscal Effects of Differences in Sales Tax Coverage: Revenue Elasticity, Stability, and Reliance." In *Proceedings of the Eighty-fourth Annual Conference on Taxation of the National Tax Association-Tax Institute of America* 84 (1991), pp. 50–7.

Mikesell, John L. "Sales Taxation of Services: Economic Logic versus Fiscal Politics. *State Tax Notes* 5 (August 19, 1993): 361–2.

Mikesell, John L., and Mark Brown. "How Big Is the Local Use Tax Problem for Mail-Order Vendors?" *State Tax Notes* 3 (August 31, 1992): 309–13.

Minnesota Department of Revenue, Tax Research Division. *Minnesota Tax Incidence Study*. St. Paul, Minn., November 1993.

Peat, Marwick, Mitchell & Co. *Report to The American Retail Federation on Costs to Retailers of Sales and Use Tax Compliance*. Washington, D.C., 1982.

Pomp, Richard D., and Oliver Oldman. "A Normative Enquiry into the Base of a Retail Sales Tax: Casual Sales, Used Goods, and Trade-Ins." *National Tax Journal* 43 (December 1990): 427–38.

Poterba, James M. "Retail Price Reactions to Changes in State and Local Sales Taxes." *National Tax Journal* 49 (June 1996): 165–75.

Quick, Perry D., and Michael J. McKee. "Sales Tax on Services: Revenue or Reform?" *National Tax Journal* 41 (September 1988): 395–410.

Ring, Raymond. "The Proportion of Consumers' and Producers' Goods in the General Sales Tax." *National Tax Journal* 42 (June 1989): 167–79.

Rock, Steven M. "The Impact of Deductibility on the Incidence of a General Sales Tax." *National Tax Journal* 37 (March 1984): 105–112.

Siegfried, John J., and Paul A. Smith. "The Distributional Effects of a Sales Tax on Services." *National Tax Journal* 44 (March 1991): 41–53.

*Tax Administrators News* 57 (1) (August 1993). "Vendor Collection of State Sales and Use Tax." P. 88.

Trandel, Gregory A. "Evading the Use Tax on Cross-Border Sales: Pricing and Welfare Effects." *Journal of Public Economics* 49 (December 1992): 313–32.

Walsh, Michael J., and Jonathan D. Jones. "More Evidence on the 'Border Tax' Effect." *National Tax Journal* 41 (June 1988): 261–5.

Washington Department of Revenue. The *Effect of Tax Rate Differences on Retail Trade in Washington Border Counties*. Olympia, 1990.

Wheeless, V.B. *The Sales and Use Tax: Its Origin and Background in Mississippi*. Jackson, Miss.: State Tax Commission, 1966.

*Cross references:* consumption taxation; elasticity, demand and supply; excise taxes; fairness in taxation; incidence of taxes; life cycle model; value-added tax.

# Revenue elasticity (tax elasticity)

Joseph J. Cordes
George Washington University

*Measures the sensitivity of the tax base to changing economic conditions.*

The revenue elasticity of a tax is calculated by dividing the percentage change in revenue by the percentage change in income. For example, if income increased by 100 percent and the revenue raised by a tax on widgets increased by 50 percent, the revenue elasticity of the tax on widgets would equal 0.5 = 50 percent ÷ 100 percent. If, instead, income increased by 100 percent and the revenue raised from taxing widgets increased by 200 percent, the revenue elasticity of the widget tax would be calculated to be 2.0 = 200 percent ÷ 100 percent.

When tax revenues grow (decline) less rapidly than income grows (declines), the calculated revenue elasticity of a tax will be less than one and the tax is said to be inelastic. Conversely, when the tax revenues grow (decline) more rapidly than income grows (declines), the calculated value of the revenue elasticity is greater than one and the tax is said to be elastic. (This definition is similar to that of price elasticity of demand, discussed elsewhere in this volume.)

Two factors come into play in determining a tax's elasticity. One is how responsive or elastic the base of the tax is to income. The other is the structure of the tax rates that are applied to the base.

The role of these factors can be illustrated by considering the revenue elasticity of general sales, income, and property taxes. General sales taxes are typically levied at a single rate, and to a large extent, movements in sales track movements in income very closely, so that, for example, if personal income doubles, spending (which is the base of the sales tax) also doubles. For this reason, the percentage change in sales tax revenues is apt to be virtually the same as the percentage change in income, and the revenue elasticity of a general sales tax is widely taken to be 1.0. In contrast, although specific excise taxes on goods such as motor fuels, tobacco, and alcohol are also generally taxed at a single rate, the change in spending on these goods is less than proportionate to the change in income—that is, when incomes double, we expect spending on such goods to increase less than twofold. Hence, the calculated revenue elasticity of excise taxes is generally less than 1.0. Similarly, property tax revenues are fairly inelastic because assessed property values often increase (decrease) less rapidly than does income.

Income taxes illustrate the role of the tax rate structure in determining revenue elasticity. When income rises, it is taxed at higher rates; hence, income tax revenue grows (declines) more than proportionately relative to income, making the revenue elasticity of a graduated, or progressive, income tax greater than one. By comparison, a flat-rate income tax that taxes the first dollar of income would have a revenue elasticity of one. These examples indicate a close connection between revenue elasticity and the progressivity of a tax. By definition, a progressive tax will have a revenue elasticity greater than one and be an elastic source of revenue, while regressive taxes will have elasticities that are less than one.

Tax elasticity is a two-edged sword. On the one hand, taxes that are elastic act as automatic stabilizers by causing taxes to increase more than income does when times are good and also to fall more than income falls when times are bad. On the other hand, taxes that are elastic are generally less stable sources of public revenue precisely because of their tendency to fluctuate with economic conditions. Taxes that are inelastic provide greater revenue stability but, conversely, do not act as automatic stabilizers.

*Cross references:* automatic stabilizers; elasticity, demand and supply; progressivity, measures of; rainy day funds.

# Revenue estimating, state

Yeang-Eng Braun
Wisconsin Department of Revenue

*As with the federal process, estimating state revenues is, or ought to be, subject to a systematic set of statistical practices and guidelines; however, states differ in the assignment of which agency is responsible for the process and the methodology.*

There are two usages of the term "revenue estimating": (1) the process of forecasting state tax revenue for the current and future fiscal years, also referred to as "state-revenue forecasting," and (2) the process of estimating the impact of a change in the tax law on tax receipts, also referred to as the "fiscal note process."

## State-revenue forecasting

A state generally forecasts its revenue at the start of a budget cycle, with revisions made as warranted by actual tax collections and economic conditions. Most states forecast tax revenues one to two years into the future. The forecast horizon largely depends on whether the budget cycle is an annual or biennial one. States with biennial budgets typically forecast to the end of the current or next biennium, depending on whether they are in the first or second year of their budget.

A state's revenue-estimating process typically involves three steps:

First, a forecast of the national economy is needed in order to determine national economic trends and estimates of economic variables such as gross domestic product, personal income, consumption, employment, interest rates, and inflation. Most states do not produce their own national economic forecast. Instead, they subscribe to national economic forecasting services offered by private firms and universities.

Second, a state-specific economic forecast is developed from the national economic forecast adjusted to reflect the specific economic mix of the state. Some states develop their own state econometric model, and others purchase their state economic forecast from economic forecasting services. The state economic forecast provides information pertaining to the state's economic variables.

Third, the relevant state economic variables are then used to make predictions about each of the sources of revenue. For example, the individual income tax forecast is based on the forecasted level and composition of personal income and the forecasted level of employment, and the sales tax forecast is based on forecasted disposable income and the relative prices of items subject to the sales tax.

Recent tax collection data are also incorporated into the estimation process, but they have to be carefully analyzed and frequently monitored because they can easily be misinterpreted—year-over-year changes in monthly collections are often affected by factors other than underlying economic trends. These factors include law changes, large refunds and audit activity, changes in the timing of employer payroll periods, and differences in the number of workdays for tax processing in each month.

Revenue estimates are never going to be exact, and some errors are inevitable. Some of the common sources of revenue-estimating errors are:

1. Errors in measurement that are reflected in data revisions. Current period estimates of income and employment are often treated as "actual data" even though they may be revised several years later. Thus, if the best estimate of current (and past) income is off, for example, by 1 percent, it is not surprising that forecasts of income, and in turn tax revenues, one or two years from now will be off by 1 or 2 percent.

2. Errors in the economic forecast. The national economic forecast can be wrong because of incorrect assumptions regarding monetary and fiscal policies, consumer and investor confidence, or international events. Of particular importance is the forecast of inflation because state revenue estimates depend on both real and inflationary growth. Even if the national economic forecast is correct, the state forecast may be wrong. This error could be the result of misspecification of the revenue-estimating equations, or the result of unanticipated shocks, such as large layoffs by a major employer. These exogenous shocks tend to be more significant for state forecasts than for national ones.

3. Behavioral changes. A key ingredient to any revenue forecast is time series data. However, the benefit of the historical data is reduced when the tax law is significantly modified. This problem is compounded if tax laws are changed frequently. Under such circumstances, past activity no longer provides a good predictor of future behavior, because new tax systems mean new behavior that can have significant consequences. Forecasters do not have good estimates of the degree of

behavioral response. For example, the 1986 federal tax changes created uncertainties over the impact of those changes on state tax receipts. This was especially the case with capital gains. States were uncertain as to how the higher federal tax on capital gains would influence investors' behavior. The larger the anticipated sale of assets, the larger the state tax windfall. In some states, revenue estimators greatly overestimated the extent to which taxpayers would sell their assets to avoid the larger federal tax payments. These states were caught off guard by their multimillion-dollar shortfalls.

4. Unanticipated events. No matter how sophisticated the estimating models may be, they will not be able to capture all of the events that will affect a state-revenue estimate. Court decisions affecting tax refunds or tax assessments, or the death of a wealthy individual, are cases in point. While such isolated events have an insignificant effect on federal revenues, their impact on state tax collections is noticeable.

Under fortunate circumstances, these errors may offset one another, producing an accurate forecast. Under unfortunate circumstances, these errors may compound each other and produce a very poor forecast. A good revenue estimate is one in which the error is within some reasonable range. While there is no universal measure, an acceptable margin of error (from a statistical point of view) is plus or minus 1 to 3 percent of the estimate.

The organization of the revenue-estimating function varies among states. In some states, that function is performed by the tax collection agency; in others, it is performed by the budget or finance agency. While the forecasting function is primarily the responsibility of the executive branch, some state legislatures have access to a legislative fiscal agency for an independent forecast of revenue.

To keep the revenue forecast from becoming mired in politics, some states rely on "consensus estimating" or "consensus forecasting." Consensus revenue estimating involves representatives from both the executive and legislative branches of government, as well as from the business and academic communities, who have to reach unanimous agreement on the economic assumptions to be used and the revenue estimates.

In a 1991 survey of state-revenue forecasting practices, the Federation of Tax Administrators (1993) found that out of the 45 states that responded, 23 had a single executive agency forecasting state revenue—8 of them the department of taxation or revenue and 15 the finance or budget office. Eighteen states used consensus forecasting. Four states used a hybrid procedure in which the executive and legislative agencies prepare independent forecasts and attempt to reconcile their differences. If an agreement is not reached, the legislature can adopt one as the official forecast, or combine parts of each.

## The fiscal note process

"Revenue estimating" can also refer to the process of estimating the impact of a change in the tax law on tax receipts. This is also referred to as the "fiscal note process" because these estimates are usually reported in a fiscal note accompanying the proposed change in tax laws.

To prepare such an estimate, the projected revenue under current law is compared to the projected revenue under the proposal, and the difference between the two numbers is the fiscal estimate of the proposed law change. In addition, any administrative costs associated with the proposal (e.g., personnel costs, programming costs, or costs for adding lines to a tax form) have to be included in the fiscal estimate of the legislation.

One major issue is whether the fiscal estimate should be "static" (i.e., ignoring the economic impact of the law change), or "dynamic," where economic impacts are taken into account. It is argued that if the economic impacts are taken into account, the net revenue loss associated with tax incentive legislation is reduced or transformed into revenue gains.

Even when the economic impacts are not taken into account in the revenue estimates of a law change, estimators do try to take into account taxpayer behavioral response whenever possible. For example, in estimating the revenue impact of a cigarette tax increase, it is assumed that the increase would be fully passed through to the consumer, resulting in decreased tobacco consumption.

In some cases, a change in a particular section of the tax code may affect other tax provisions as well, and these effects must be added to or subtracted from the fiscal estimate. Consider, for example, a decrease in the standard deduction. This would increase tax revenue, causing some taxpayers to switch from standardized tax forms to itemized returns, and the fiscal effect from switching to itemized deductions would have to be subtracted from the initial fiscal effect.

Of the 45 states responding to the 1991 survey mentioned above (Federation of Tax Administrators 1993), 34 relied on their tax departments for preparing revenue estimates of tax law changes. Of these, only 6 states regularly estimated economic impacts, and another 10 reported that they did so occasionally or on request.

## Additional reading

Federation of Tax Administrators. *State Revenue Forecasting and Estimation Practices*. Research Report No. 139, March 1993. Washington, D.C.

*Cross references:* rainy day funds; revenue estimation, federal; revenue forecasting, federal.

# Revenue estimation, federal

Rosemary D. Marcuss
Department of Commerce

*The (nonpolitical) federal revenue estimation process requires one to consistently, systematically, and rigorously take account of factors ranging from the nation's economic and demographic trends (also estimated) to year-to-year changes in tax laws, rules, and regulations; the methodologies employed by Congress and the executive branch are quite similar, but not the same in all respects.*

In fiscal year 1996, the U.S. federal government collected $1,453 billion in tax receipts, expended $1,560 billion in outlays for goods and services, and borrowed $107 billion in the private credit market. An operation of that scale requires sophisticated financial management. An important component of that management is the estimation of the flow of tax receipts, or revenues. In addition, as part of the process of federal tax policy formulation, summary measures of taxes paid by households and the effects of those taxes on household incomes—so-called distributional estimates—are often requested by policymakers and require estimation. Those estimation processes are related.

The composition of federal revenues, the economic conditions that affect revenues, the data describing those conditions, the models used to estimate those revenues, and the financial reports of the U.S. Department of the Treasury all affect revenue estimation. A closely related subject, the revenue forecasting used in Congress's legislative and budget estimation process, is explained in another entry (see Revenue forecasting, federal). That forecasting process requires estimates of federal revenues for up to 10 future years. Revenue estimation for the current year is described here.

## Composition of federal revenues

About 80 percent of federal revenues come from workers' earnings and other personal income re-

ceipts: about 45 percent from the individual income tax and another 35 percent from payroll taxes, most of which finance the Social Security retirement income system. Roughly 10 percent of revenues come from the corporate income tax. Excise taxes, mostly on transportation-related goods and services and alcohol and tobacco products, make up 4 percent of revenues. Payments from the Federal Reserve System, customs duties, estate and gift taxes, and fees, fines, and penalties account for the remainder.

## How are revenues measured, and who estimates them?

For the most part, tax liabilities are defined in the Internal Revenue Code of 1986. Customs duties, fees, fines, penalties, and Federal Reserve payments are established either in laws other than the Internal Revenue Code or by administrative action. Income and payroll tax liabilities are defined on an annual basis. Most other federal tax liabilities—excise taxes, customs duties, and fees, for the most part—are defined on a per-transaction basis.

The flow of revenue to the U.S. Treasury that proceeds from the liabilities defined in tax law depends on the operating rate of the economy and the schedules established for payment to the U.S. Treasury by individuals and businesses. Given the composition of federal revenues, the economic flows that are most important for determining revenues are wages, salaries, and other types of personal income; corporation income; sales of taxed goods; and the amount of imported goods and services. The process of federal revenue estimation combines numerical tax calculators that reproduce the stipulations of the Internal Revenue Code with approximations of the historical relationships between federal revenue flows and summary measures of their underlying economic determinants, such as the total U.S. sales of goods and services and the aggregate levels of personal and business incomes. Those calculators and approximations of historical relationships constitute statistical models that produce estimates of aggregate tax liabilities by type of tax.

The budget upon which the annual process of presidential budget proposal and congressional consideration is based is a "cash" budget. For example, federal revenues are counted when they are paid into the Treasury, which occurs after the liabilities for the taxes are incurred. Therefore, revenue estimation entails another step after the estimation of liabilities: Payment schedules are applied to the estimates of liabilities to produce estimates of payments to the Treasury. Those cash estimates are used in the annual budget of the president and the Concurrent Budget Resolution—the official congressional budget document. The annual time period upon which those budget calculations are based is a fiscal year that runs from October 1 through September 30.

In contrast, the federal government sector of the National Income and Product Accounts (NIPA), a measure of federal government activity that is not strictly a budget measure, calculates revenues on a mixture of payment and liability bases in order to approximate more closely the effects of taxes on economic activity. The annual time period of the NIPA is the calendar year. The NIPA measure of revenues is used for macroeconomic analysis rather than for budget formulation.

In the annual federal budget process, the responsibility for estimating federal revenues under current tax law for Congress resides with the Congressional Budget Office (CBO). The responsibility for such estimations for the president's budget resides with the Department of the Treasury, which shares budget estimation responsibility with the Office of Management and Budget. The responsibility for estimating the effects on revenue flows of legislated changes in tax law resides with the congressional Joint Committee on Taxation. (For an explanation of the role of legislative estimates, see Federal revenue forecasting.) The CBO, the Joint Committee on Taxation, and the Treasury Department employ similar estimation techniques. The responsibility for estimating the NIPA resides with the Commerce Department's Bureau of Economic Analysis.

## Estimation models for major tax sources

Federal revenue estimation models produce estimates of annual fiscal-year revenues on a cash basis. Revenues from the individual income tax, the most important federal tax in terms of revenue generation, are estimated using a type of statistical estimation technique called "microsimulation." The technique begins with a statistical sample of approximately 100,000 tax returns compiled by the Internal Revenue Service (IRS) from the most recent year for which those data are available (usually two years before the year being analyzed), with "weights" assigned to those sample returns that, combined with the per-return data, reproduce population totals, the number of tax returns, the amount of income subject to tax, deductions, and other tax-payment characteristics for the year of the sample. In order to produce an estimate of total revenue for the current tax year (typically two years later), that tax return data from the sample year is combined with estimates of the number of tax returns, personal income, and other components of tax liability for the current year, along with a calculator that computes the current-year tax liability for each sample return. The liabilities estimated in that process are then "weighted up" to a measure of total tax liability for the estimation year. An estimate of the flow of tax payments to the Treasury,

the final revenue estimate, is then calculated based on the tax payment schedule established by the IRS. Individual income tax revenues totaled $656 billion in fiscal year 1996.

Social insurance payroll taxes consist mostly (more than 90 percent) of contributions to the Social Security system, officially entitled the Old Age, Survivors, Disability, and Hospital Insurance (OASDHI) system. For 1996, each employee contributed 6.2 percent of his or her wage or salary up to a maximum wage or salary of $62,700 to the Old Age, Survivors, and Disability Insurance (OASDI) Trust Fund, which finances payments to the currently retired and disabled. Each employer contributed the same amount. The total combined contribution rate is 12.4 percent. The maximum wage level is adjusted annually, based on the change in average wages economywide. Likewise, each employee and employer contributed another 1.45 percent, but on the employee's total wage or salary without a maximum, to the Hospital Insurance (HI) Trust Fund, which finances Medicare hospital payments for those 65 years and older. The total combined employee and employer rate for HI is 2.9 percent. Self-employed individuals contribute to OASDHI at the combined employee-employer rates.

Another 6 percent of payroll taxes finance the combined federal-state unemployment insurance system. Those unemployment insurance taxes are paid by employers based on wages and salaries up to a maximum per employee that is much lower than that for OASDI, and are levied at a lower, variable rate based on the employment history of that employer and the overall unemployment rate in each state. The remaining 1 percent of payroll tax revenue consists of retirement contributions by certain federal government and railroad system employees.

Like individual income tax revenues, OASDHI revenues are estimated using microsimulation. Rather than being based on a sample of income tax returns from the IRS, OASDHI revenue-estimation microsimulation begins with a sample of wage and salary records for every worker. Those records are maintained by the Social Security Administration, the agency that administers the Social Security system. In order to produce an estimate of total revenue for the current year, the data for the sample year are combined with estimates of current-year wages and salaries, and with a calculator that computes the employer and employee contribution for each worker, based on the worker's earnings, current-year tax rates, and the maximum level of worker income subject to the OASDHI contribution obligation. Rather than provide the earnings sample data to the revenue-estimating agencies, the Social Security Administration estimates OASDHI revenues for both the CBO and the Treasury Department based on earnings and wage index estimates obtained from those agencies. Social insurance payroll tax revenues of all types totaled $508 billion in fiscal year 1996.

Corporation income taxes are estimated statistically, using an equation in which corporate tax liabilities are typically a function of, along with other less important determinants, the top statutory corporation income tax rate, corporate profits and losses, and adjustments for recent changes in tax law. Depreciation deductions taken for tax purposes by corporations that invest in plant and equipment are computed using a calculator based on Internal Revenue Code depreciation rules, combined with estimates of investment. Corporation income tax revenues totaled $172 billion in fiscal year 1996.

The federal excise taxes that generate the bulk of total excise tax revenues are those on motor fuels, alcohol, and tobacco products. Those revenues are also estimated statistically, using equations with statutory tax rates and proxies for tax bases as explanatory variables. For example, an estimation equation for motor fuel excise tax liabilities would typically cast liabilities as a function of variables such as the statutory tax rate, the relative price of gasoline, a measure of overall economic activity such as the gross domestic product, the number of motor vehicles, and average mileage per vehicle. The estimation equation for cigarette excise tax revenues would typically cast liabilities as a function of the statutory tax rate, population, and per capita cigarette consumption. Overall, federal excise tax revenues, including revenues from a large number of other excise taxes levied at lower rates or on smaller bases, totaled $54 billion in fiscal year 1996. Revenues from the remaining, smaller revenue sources are estimated statistically when feasible or by using simple trends extrapolated from historical revenue data.

The revenue estimates on which each annual federal government budget is based are those made available in January of the year in which the budget year begins on the following October 1. The revenue and outlay estimates adopted in that budget are embodied in the congressional Concurrent Budget Resolution for that fiscal year.

## Monitoring revenue collections during the year

The Treasury's Office of Financial Management provides daily and monthly tabulations of federal revenue collections and expenditures. The daily tabulations are made available electronically with a one- to two-day lag. A more detailed tabulation of monthly revenues and outlays is published in the *Monthly Treasury Statement*, which is released about three weeks after the end of the month for which the data are reported. As the fiscal year proceeds, an increasingly clearer picture of the momentum of

tax collections for the year emerges. Typically, by June or so, after a full accounting of the very large final settlements by individuals on their income tax liabilities for the past calendar year that are due by April 15 (payments exceed refunds), extrapolation from monthly payment data surpasses statistical estimation as the more reliable means of revenue estimation for that year.

## Summary measures of taxes paid

The public and congressional tax policy formulation process depends on additional measures of taxes paid by individuals and families, specifically measures of total taxes paid and the resulting effects on the incomes of different types of households, such as those with and without children, elderly households, and households with different amounts of income—so-called "distributional" estimates. One type of distributional measure consists of average effective tax rates (total taxes paid divided by household income) for subgroups of households defined by income ranges. Another type of distributional measure consists of average percentage changes in after-tax income for such subgroups of households. The distributional estimates that allocate all federal taxes to households are based on the generally accepted understanding that, regardless of the entities upon which legal tax liabilities are assessed, individuals ultimately bear the burden of all taxes, as earners, business owners, and consumers.

## Additional readings

Cilke, James M., and Roy A. Wyscarver. "The Individual Income Tax Simulation Model." In *Compendium of Tax Research, 1987*, pp. 43–75. Washington, D.C.: Office of Tax Analysis, U.S. Department of Treasury, 1987.

Sunley, Emil, and Randall D. Weiss. "The Revenue Estimating Process." *Tax Notes* 51 (June 10, 1991): 1299–314.

*Cross references:* revenue elasticity (tax elasticity); revenue estimating, state; revenue forecasting, federal.

# Revenue forecasting, federal

Rosemary D. Marcuss
Department of Commerce

*In the federal jargon, revenue estimating usually refers to the short–medium term, whereas forecasting, which is largely a congressional responsibility, looks several years into the future. As with the estimating process, the methodology involves a systematic, replicable process.*

Forecasts of federal government revenues—and expenditures—for several years into the future are the bedrock of the annual congressional budget formulation process. One type of forecast is that of federal revenues under current tax law. That forecast, combined with a forecast of federal government spending, defines the projected federal budget deficit. Another type of revenue forecast is that of the effect of a legislated change in tax law on the flow of revenues generated under current tax law. This type of forecast, which typically accompanies a congressional committee report on a tax bill, is usually referred to as a legislative revenue estimate. A third type of revenue forecast is a tax-expenditure forecast, or estimate. That is an estimate of the revenues forgone by the U.S. Treasury because of a special preference in the individual income tax. Tax-expenditure estimates are provided for information purposes only: they do not play a role in the congressional budget formulation process. Consequently, they are not described here.

## Revenue forecasts for the annual federal budget process

Each year in late January or early February, the president issues a budget proposal. That budget sets forth a forecast of federal revenues for the budget year, which begins on October 1 of the same year, and for four or five subsequent years. (Of course, every budget consists of both a revenue forecast and an expenditure forecast, but only the revenue forecast is described here.) The revenues in the president's budget are defined as the revenues generated under current tax law amended by any changes in law proposed by the president in that budget, assuming that the economy performs as forecasted by the president. At the same time, the Congressional Budget Office (CBO) presents a budget forecast to Congress based on its assumptions about economic performance. That budget also sets forth a forecast of federal revenues for the budget year and for four or five subsequent years. Those revenues are defined as the revenue generated under current tax law without amendment. That budget forecast is often referred to as a baseline budget forecast. Both the president's and the CBO forecasts include estimates of revenues and outlays for additional years—up to 10 in all—for information purposes.

The congressional federal budget formulation process results in the Concurrent Budget Resolution for the coming fiscal year that stipulates, among other budget goals, a "floor," or minimum level, for federal revenues and the change in revenues from the baseline forecast level necessary to reach that minimum. Nonbinding targets for total revenues and revenue changes for several years beyond the budget year are also included in the Concurrent Budget Resolution. Usually, those revenue targets

are based at least indirectly on the CBO baseline revenue forecast.

## Budget revenue forecasts require macroeconomic forecasts

The federal tax system depends heavily on income and payroll taxes to generate revenues. Excise and other taxes and fees make up less than 10 percent of revenues. Therefore, the flow of revenues to the U.S. Treasury is sensitive to the operating rate of the economy—to the levels of personal and business incomes, to prices, to the amount of business transactions in the private economy, and to other economic flows. The forecasts of revenues generated under current tax law that underpin both the president's budget and the CBO baseline revenue forecast are generated using statistical models that depend on forecasts of such macroeconomic aggregates as explanatory variables. (For an explanation of those forecasting models, see Revenue estimating, federal.) The CBO utilizes its own macroeconomic forecast in its budget forecast. The president's budget usually utilizes the macroeconomic forecast of the "Troika" group whose staff reports to the Secretary of the Treasury, the Chairman of the President's Council of Economic Advisers, and the Director of the Office of Management and Budget.

## Legislative revenue estimates and budget act discipline

Many bills are considered by Congress at each session, some as part of the "omnibus" or comprehensive budget-related legislation resulting from the congressional budget resolution and others separately. The effect of a bill on the federal budget is important to its prospects for enactment. Before bills are considered on the floor of either House, estimates of their effects on federal revenues are provided by the congressional Joint Committee on Taxation. Those legislative estimates—like the estimates for expenditure legislation provided by the CBO—add discipline and consistency to the congressional budget debate. They are usually made available on the spot when bills are brought out of committee for floor debate.

Broadly shared concern about the long-term threat to the economy posed by the large and growing federal budget deficits of the mid-1980s led to enactment of a series of budget procedures that have imposed stringent discipline on legislated tax cuts and expenditure increases. The first such law was the "Gramm-Rudman-Hollings" act of 1985, which established fixed deficit targets for several years that required increasingly drastic expenditure cuts or tax increases to achieve. Those targets were eventually replaced by procedures established by the Budget Enforcement Act of 1990. That act added additional budget constraints to the existing requirements of a minimum revenue level and a maximum expenditure level for the budget year. Those new constraints included the requirement that legislated tax cuts must be offset by some combination of tax increases and entitlement program cuts of the same magnitude. That requirement, which is imposed cumulatively over a two-fiscal-year period rather than on a bill-by-bill basis, is the so-called "pay-as-you-go" budget rule. In an atmosphere in which a desired legislated tax reduction must come at a price, the estimates of revenue effects attributed to each piece of legislation take on central importance in congressional negotiations and debate. That discipline has restrained legislated tax reductions. It has also engendered legislative proposals designed as much to circumvent the budget rules as to improve tax system design.

The Congressional Budget and Impoundment Control Act of 1974, the legislation that put in place the present congressional federal budget process, established the requirement that a bill that affects the budget must be accompanied by an estimate of that effect. In the House of Representatives, the committee report accompanying any bill that affects federal budget revenues or expenditures must include an estimate of the budgetary effect of that bill if an estimate is "timely available." The absence of a report provides grounds under the Budget Act for withholding that bill from consideration on the House floor. In the Senate, a committee issuing a bill for congressional consideration is not required to issue a report, although most bills in fact are accompanied by reports containing estimates of budgetary effects. Jurisdiction over tax legislation resides in the Committee on Ways and Means in the House and the Committee on Finance in the Senate.

Legislative estimates for both tax and spending bills typically include estimates for the budget year and several subsequent years. In the Senate, a bill lacking an estimate of the cumulative effect of the legislation on the budget in years 6 through 10 can be withheld from floor consideration. Recently, the Joint Committee on Taxation has provided legislative revenue estimates for 10 years, as congressional interest in later-year budget effects has increased.

The legislative revenue estimates calculated by the Joint Committee on Taxation are based on the CBO forecast of revenues generated under current tax law, in order to guarantee that the congressional estimates are internally consistent. For example, the estimate for a change in income tax rates would start with the CBO forecast of income tax revenues generated under current law. The estimate for a change in the capital gains tax rate would start with a CBO forecast of capital gains revenues generated under current law. The estimate for a change in the excise tax rate on cigarettes begins the same way.

## Legislative revenue estimates assume a taxpayer reaction

People react to changes in legislated tax rates and tax changes, and those taxpayer reactions are taken into account in revenue estimates. For example, if the excise tax on motor fuels were increased, consumers would cut back on their purchases. The change in revenues brought about by that reduction in purchases would be included as part of the revenue estimate. Likewise, if the tax rate on capital gains were reduced, sales of gains-bearing assets would increase. In other words, more capital gains would be realized. The effect on revenues brought about by that increase in capital gains would be included in the revenue estimate. In the same way, if the top income tax rate facing individuals were increased, those individuals would adjust their portfolio investments and the form and timing of their income, if feasible, in order to reduce the adverse effect of that rate increase. The effect on revenues caused by these adjustments would be included in the revenue estimate. Those taxpayer responses, while sometimes large in terms of their effects on the transactions subject to the tax change, have been assumed, for legislative estimation purposes, to operate within fixed levels of overall, economy-wide taxpayer income. In that sense, the taxpayer reactions assumed for legislative revenue estimates remain consistent with the gross domestic product forecast on which the congressional budget resolution for that year is based.

## "Dynamic" legislative estimates

It is widely agreed that large changes in the federal budget can affect overall prices and economic activity and that important changes in tax rates can affect taxpayers' decisions about working and saving and investors' decisions about the placement of their capital. Few legislative initiatives raise the likelihood of noticeable effects on overall economic output, employment, or prices—most are simply of insufficient scope—but on those occasions when one does, those effects can be included in congressional budget estimates in several ways. Budget estimates that include such effects are often referred to as "dynamic" estimates.

First, the effect on the overall economy (the "dynamic" effect) of legislated budget changes can be factored into the revenue and expenditure forecast on which the congressional budget resolution is based. That is the nature of the so-called "fiscal dividend," or revenue boost and expenditure cut, sometimes built into federal budget forecasts underlying congressional budget resolutions that achieve a balanced budget within the budget forecast period by means of legislated program cuts. The fiscal dividend, which is calculated by the CBO, takes into account the effect of federal budget balance on reducing interest rates, and thereby boosting corporate profits and income tax receipts and reducing federal government interest costs. A budget resolution starting from a budget forecast including such a fiscal dividend indicates the amount of program cuts required to balance the budget after the helpful economic effects that can result from meeting that goal are taken into account.

Alternatively, the economywide or "dynamic" effect of an individual piece of legislation could be included in the estimate of the budget effect of that legislation. Concern has been voiced that tax changes that hypothetically affect the supply of labor or the savings rate—often called "supply-side" effects—cannot receive proper consideration unless the legislative revenue estimate reflects those effects. At present, legislative estimates do not. Inclusion of such effects has been hampered by two impediments: the longer-term nature of those effects juxtaposed against the short-term span (five years) covered by legislative estimates, and the uncertainty surrounding the scale of those effects. At present, when such effects are not precisely measurable, it is generally agreed that the legislative process benefits from a description of those effects. In addition, it is understood that legislation embodying major tax restructuring, such as the replacement of the income tax with a consumption-based tax, would affect the overall economy, and that the effect should be described for Congress if it cannot be numerically estimated.

### Additional readings

Congressional Budget Office. *Budget Estimates: Current Practice and Alternative Approaches.* Washington, D.C., January 1995.

Congressional Budget Office. *The Economic and Budget Outlook, Fiscal Years 1998–2007.* Washington, D.C., January 1997.

Gravelle, Jane. *Dynamic Revenue Estimating.* Washington, D.C.: Congressional Research Service, December 1994.

Joint Committee on Taxation, U.S. Congress. *Methodology and Issues in the Revenue Estimation Process*, JCX-2-95, January 1995, Washington, D.C.

*Cross references:* revenue elasticity (tax elasticity); revenue estimation, federal.

# Ricardian equivalence

Angelo R. Mascaro
Congressional Budget Office

*The proposition, stated by 19th-century British economist David Ricardo, that a given path of government expenditures could, under certain conditions, have the same effects on the economy irrespective of how the expenditures are financed.*

For Ricardo, the proposition of Ricardian equivalence was intended to establish the important principle that the economic cost of government expenditures could not be lessened if, instead of financing the full amount of the expenditure with taxes, government issued debt and levied taxes to finance the payment of interest and the retirement of principal. For modern scholars and policy analysts, the proposition yields a set of conditions for determining how government spending and the method of financing that spending may influence aggregate demand and employment, interest rates, national saving, and capital accumulation.

Ricardo was apparently the first to recognize the theoretical possibility of equivalence if individuals realized that government bonds issued to finance an expenditure could be used to pay taxes levied to retire the debt and that interest income from the bonds could also be used to pay taxes levied to service the debt. By increasing savings to purchase the bonds, and by saving the interest income from the bonds as well, individuals could insulate themselves from all future taxes associated with debt finance. Consequently, if individuals behaved this way, any effects on the economy would arise only from government expenditure itself and not from the method of financing the expenditure.

However, Ricardo doubted individuals would behave in the required way. He believed they would underestimate future tax liabilities and not save to the same extent under debt finance as they would under full and immediate tax finance. Therefore, he gave little weight to the equivalence proposition and regarded debt finance with disfavor because of its likely adverse effects on national saving and investment.

Contemporary analysis of the equivalence proposition, motivated in response to Barro's (1974) analysis of when tax or debt finance would have equivalent effects on interest rates and aggregate demand, has refined the theoretical conditions required for equivalence. In addition to Ricardo's requirement that individuals see through the veil of government debt to the future taxes that must be levied, at least three additional requirements seem necessary for equivalence to hold. (These and other requirements are evaluated in Tobin 1980 and Sweeney 1988.) First, individuals of one generation must be concerned about the welfare of the next. Such concern, or altruism, requires that if the tax liability from debt finance extends into the next generation, enough wealth will have been bequeathed to discharge the future liability and leave the next generation positioned as if the expenditure had been financed entirely by current taxes. Second, institutional imperfections must not exist that would inhibit individuals from sharing their resources between current and future dates through borrowing and lending, or between one generation and the next through gifts and bequests. If imperfections exist, the timing of the taxes could affect aggregate demand, interest rates, savings, and investment and nullify the equivalence proposition. For example, one imperfection emerges when borrowers face liquidity constraints. Such constraints can last when borrowers and lenders do not have identical information, so that capital markets are unable to function efficiently and borrowing is inhibited. Third, the taxes levied under debt finance must not introduce any new distortions relative to the taxes levied under full and immediate tax finance. Lump-sum taxes that do not distort the choice between work and leisure, between current and future consumption, or between consumption and investment provide a case in which equivalence will hold. However, any tax that distorts such choices, as most taxes do, will nullify Ricardian equivalence.

Although most economists agree that the conditions required for exact equivalence do not hold in reality, many disagree strongly as to whether the conditions might hold approximately and, consequently, whether the predictions of Ricardian equivalence might also hold approximately. If approximate equivalence prevails, then the choice of taxes or debt to finance government spending would not matter much, because it would have only small additional effects on aggregate demand, interest rates, saving, and capital accumulation, compared with the effects of the spending itself. If approximate equivalence does not prevail, however, the choice will be important, because the financing method will have additional effects that could be exploited. For example, the potentially adverse effects of increased government spending on private capital accumulation could be offset by increased taxes that reduced private spending on consumption.

The issue of the approximate validity of Ricardian equivalence is an empirical one, and economists have tried to resolve it in two basic ways. Some have tried to determine how closely reality conforms to the theory's assumptions and others have tried to determine how closely reality conforms to the the-

ory's predictions. Because the approximate validity of a theory is often more difficult to test than its exact validity, however, empirical research has yielded ambiguous evidence on approximate equivalence. Some research on the assumptions of Ricardian equivalence has found that bequests from one generation to the next do reflect, in part, the altruistic motive needed for equivalence, but other research finds that bequests reflect unrelated motives as well, including uncertainty about life span, that could nullify equivalence. Analogous ambiguity surrounds the interpretation of evidence of whether liquidity constraints and distortionary taxes support or reject approximate equivalence. Some evidence on the predictions of Ricardian equivalence shows that there is no strong, statistically significant relationship between deficits (or debt) and interest rates, apparently supporting approximate equivalence. Similarly, some evidence on the relationship between taxes and private spending that takes government spending into account finds no strong relationship in the data, also giving apparent support to approximate equivalence. In both cases, however, the interpretation of the evidence has been challenged and confronted with other evidence that apparently rejects approximate equivalence. (The extensive research is surveyed in Bernheim 1988; Seater 1993; Smetters 1995.)

Obviously, the issue of approximate equivalence remains unresolved. Nevertheless, the research on Ricardian equivalence has deepened our understanding of the many channels through which government spending, taxes, deficits, and debt influence the economy.

## Additional readings

Barro, Robert J. "Are Government Bonds Net Wealth?" *Journal of Political Economy* 82 (6) (November/December 1974): 1095–1117.

Bernheim, B. Douglas. "Ricardian Equivalence: An Evaluation of Theory and Evidence." In *NBER Macroeconomics Annual* 1987. Cambridge, Mass.: The MIT Press, 1988.

Ricardo, David. *The Principles of Political Economy and Taxation.* Original work 1817. Reprinted in *The Works and Correspondence of David Ricardo,* vol. 1, edited by Piero Sraffa. Cambridge, U.K.: Cambridge University Press, 1951.

Ricardo, David. "Funding System." Original work 1820. Reprinted in *The Works and Correspondence of David Ricardo,* vol. 4, edited by Piero Sraffa. Cambridge, U.K.: Cambridge University Press, 1951.

Seater, John J. "Ricardian Equivalence." *Journal of Economic Literature* 31 (1) (March 1993): 142, 190.

Smetters, Kent. "Essays on the Intergenerational Transmission of Wealth." Ph.D. Dissertation, Harvard University, 1995.

Sweeney, Richard J. *Wealth Effects and Monetary Theory.* New York: Basil Blackwell, Inc., 1988.

Tobin, James. *Asset Accumulation and Economic Activity.* Chicago: University of Chicago Press, 1980.

# S

# Sales tax relief programs, state

Corina Eckl and Arturo Pérez
National Conference of State Legislatures

*State governments employ a variety of programs to reduce the tax burden (tax regressivity) on low-income families.*

The sales tax is a very important source of revenue for most states. In fiscal year 1996, sales tax revenues accounted for 33 percent of total state own-source revenues and exceeded 50 percent of total state revenues in six states (Federation of Tax Administrators 1998). However, despite its important role in state finances, the sales tax is often criticized because it is regressive: Poor people pay a higher percentage of their income in sales taxes than people with higher incomes. Regressivity increases when necessities, such as food, are included in the taxable base.

This entry reviews state sales tax relief programs. The states have followed two approaches to reduce the regressivity of the sales tax: exemptions of certain purchases—usually food and other necessities—or credits representing a portion of the sales tax paid for these necessities. Because sales tax relief is most often discussed in the context of food purchases, this discussion uses food as the basis for its analysis. The analysis may also apply to purchases of other necessities.

Forty-five states levy a sales tax. In January 1998, 26 of these exempted food purchases from the sales tax and eight provided a sales tax credit or rebate. (Some states also provide relief for other necessities. For example, 43 states provide sales tax exemptions for prescription drugs; eight for nonprescription drugs; 29 for consumer electric and gas utilities; and six for clothing, usually up to a specified dollar limit. In some states, these items remain taxable but at a lower rate.) There are benefits and drawbacks to each form of sales tax relief, making the decision of which form to use—an exemption or a credit—difficult. Policymakers are faced with issues of forgone revenue, targeting, and administrative concerns, just to name a few. The following sections examine the two forms of sales tax relief and identify their advantages and disadvantages using four important tax relief goals: targeting efficiency, certainty of relief, cost containment, and stability of revenue and permanence.

## Targeting efficiency

If the goal of tax relief programs is to target the relief to low-income households, tax credits are better than exemptions. Credits typically target needy recipients because they specify eligibility, usually limiting relief to households below certain income levels. Some states have selected different eligibility requirements and target their programs to senior citizens or disabled persons. Sales tax exemptions are inadequate in their targeting efficiency because they are available to everyone, regardless of their income. In fact, exemptions provide larger amounts of tax relief to middle- and high-income households because these families spend more (in dollar terms) on food than low-income families (who spend a greater proportion of their income on food). Some states have attempted to improve the targeting efficiency of the sales tax exemption by limiting the exemption to certain types of purchases. For example, certain "luxury" foods, such as caviar, or "luxury" clothing, such as formal wear, may be ineligible for the sales tax exemption.

## Certainty of tax relief

Another goal of tax relief programs is to ensure that poor individuals and households actually receive relief. Certainty of sales tax relief is best achieved by a sales tax exemption because relief occurs automatically at the point of purchase. Households are guaranteed relief as long as they are making qualified food purchases. (Depending on a state's definition of food, some purchases—such as food items for immediate consumption—may not qualify for the sales tax exemption.)

Certainty of tax relief also improves if administrative burdens are minimized or eliminated. Because tax exemptions are automatic, no administrative tasks are associated with receiving tax relief. Tax credits, on the other hand, require applications for relief that often must be accompanied by documentation, such as proof of age for programs that are limited to senior citizens or household income for programs that tie the credit to income level. Such requirements may actually undermine the goals of tax relief if they discourage qualified individuals or households from applying for the relief. This has been a serious concern in some states where participation rates have been low. One way to combat low participation rates is through aggressive education and outreach programs.

Although sales tax exemptions relieve the administrative burden for recipients, they impose burdens on sellers of food products who must be careful to apply the exemption to qualified food items yet tax nonqualified food items. The widespread use of Universal Product Code (UPC) scanners has eased this burden considerably, although the burden remains for small or locally owned and operated stores that have not acquired UPC scanner technology.

Another factor related to certainty of tax relief is timing. Timing is improved with an exemption because it occurs immediately—at the time of purchase. As noted above, with a tax credit, relief occurs only after a claim has been made. This imposes a delay between when the tax is paid and when the relief is provided. This delay can be considerable, especially in states where credit programs are tied to personal income tax.

## Cost containment

Exempting food purchases from the sales tax is an expensive way of providing sales tax relief in terms of state revenue collections. According to information provided by state departments of revenue, sales tax exemptions for food cost states anywhere from 6 percent to 29 percent of total sales tax revenues (Pérez 1992). As a result, states with a food exemption lose substantial amounts of revenue, and the bulk of the exemption's benefits go to higher-income families. In order to minimize the revenue loss, some states continue to tax food, but at a lower rate (which can pose an administrative burden for retailers). Others replace the lost revenue by imposing a higher overall sales tax rate on items that remain taxable. In 1994, for example, the statutory sales tax rate in states fully exempting food purchases averaged 5.4 percent. The rate was 4.7 percent in those states fully taxing food (Mikesell 1996).

Because credit programs limit eligibility to certain households, credits are less costly to states than broad exemptions. Costs can increase slightly if states undertake programs to notify eligible households of the tax relief program.

## Stability of revenue

Because the consumption of goods is closely tied to economic conditions, consumer purchases tend to decline when the nation enters a recession. Local or regional fiscal problems can lead to the same effect. This consumption pattern makes the sales tax generally unstable as a source of revenue. This instability increases when food is exempt from the sales tax, for two main reasons: (1) while purchases for some items, such as new cars, furniture, or appliances, may be reduced or eliminated during a recession, food purchases remain fairly constant: and (2) as noted above, the revenue derived from sales taxes

on food can be substantial. If an important goal of a sales tax relief program is to preserve the stability of the sales tax as much as possible, credits are preferable to exemptions.

## Summary of state credit programs

Eight states currently offer a credit program to offset some of the regressivity of the state sales tax on food and other essentials. Hawaii, Idaho, Kansas, New Mexico, Oklahoma, South Dakota, Vermont, and Wyoming each provide some level of tax relief through a credit program aimed at low-income individuals and families, the elderly, the disabled, or taxpayers in general. Of these eight states, only Vermont does not apply its sales tax to food.

Hawaii is the only state that makes the credit program available to all ages. Income restrictions are placed on applicants for the sales tax credit programs in Kansas, New Mexico, Vermont, South Dakota, Wyoming, and Oklahoma. Idaho, Kansas, South Dakota, and Wyoming also use age as an eligibility factor in determining who can receive a tax credit.

Eligible individuals need to file a state income tax return to receive the tax credit in Idaho, New Mexico, Vermont, and Oklahoma. Hawaii offers a flat-rate credit to all residents in addition to offering a graduated credit up to the $30,000 income level, and a tax credit on actual medical expenses. Kansas's credit program is tied to the homestead exemption under the property tax. Because they do not levy a state personal income tax, South Dakota and Wyoming provide direct payments to eligible applicants.

In addition to the tax relief goals discussed above, there may be other broad issues associated with state sales tax relief programs. For instance, state policymakers may want to consider whether and how local governments would be affected by state changes. Another broad issue is the overall regressivity or progressivity of the state's tax system. The sales tax is just one piece of the overall revenue picture, so its regressivity should be examined in the context of the overall tax structure.

There are strong arguments for and against each form of state sales tax relief. It is likely that the states that already exempt food purchases will continue their exemption, barring any disastrous events in state finances. The debate on which form of relief is preferable, therefore, will occur in those states that continue to tax food or those that offer credits but may be rethinking them.

## Additional readings

Due, John F., and John L. Mikesell. *Sales Taxation: State and Local Structure and Administration.* Washington, D.C.: The Urban Institute Press, 1994.

Case, Bradford, and Robert D. Ebel. "Using State Consumer Tax Credits for Achieving Equity." *National Tax Journal* 42 (3) (1989): 323–37.

Federation of Tax Administrators. *1996 State Tax Collections by Source.* FTA Home Page, January 15, 1998.

Gold, Steven D. "Simplifying the Sales Tax: Credits or Exemptions?" In *Sales Taxation: Critical Issues in Policy and Administration.* Washington, D.C.: Praeger Publishers, 1991.

Mikesell, John L. "Should Grocery Food Purchases Bear a Sales Tax Burden?" *State Tax Notes* 11 (11) (September 9, 1996): 753.

Pérez, Arturo. "Food Purchases Add Weight to State Sales Tax Collections." National Conference of State Legislatures. *The Fiscal Letter* 14 (3) (May/June 1992): 4.

*Cross references:* fairness in taxation; progressivity, measures of; retail sales tax; tax equity analysis.

# Saving, taxes and

B. Douglas Bernheim
Stanford University

John Karl Scholz
University of Wisconsin, Madison

*The "right" amount of saving, the decision to allocate income to future rather than current consumption, is important to a nation's economic growth. Tax policy can, and often does, affect the saving decision through a variety of channels.*

The tax treatment of capital income is a potentially important determinant of national saving. It affects private saving by altering the economic benefits associated with thrift, and it affects public saving by altering the balance between government revenues and expenditures. Those who favor tax incentives for saving argue that these incentives would reduce the excess burden associated with the tax system, and that this would stimulate capital accumulation. Policy initiatives to encourage saving include broadbased measures (such as consumption or wage taxation), as well as more narrowly targeted measures (such as individual retirement accounts and other tax-favored vehicles for saving).

## The components of national saving

National saving has two components: private saving and public saving. Private saving takes place in the personal and corporate sectors of the economy. Public saving is the sum of budget surpluses (deficits) for federal, state, and local governments. For the United States, the National Income and Product Accounts (NIPA), published by the Commerce Department, provide extensive data on each of these sectors.

Net national saving fell sharply from 7.2 percent of net national product in 1980 to 3.6 percent in 1994. Net national product is equal to the more familiar concept of gross domestic product (GDP) minus depreciation on existing plant and equipment, while net national saving also measures private and public saving net of depreciation. This decline took place both because the rate of private saving fell during the 1980s, and because the government sector actually was dissaving by running large government budget deficits.

Some economists contend that it is meaningless to decompose national saving into these various pieces. They point out that all economic assets and liabilities ultimately belong to households. Consequently, saving is saving, regardless of where it occurs. If this is correct, then the allocation of national saving among sectors is merely an exercise in accounting and has no behavioral significance (see Ricardian equivalence).

Other economists believe that it is possible to obtain a better understanding of national saving by decomposing it into personal, corporate, and public saving. They argue that, for various reasons, households do not regard an additional dollar of corporate or public saving as equivalent to a dollar of personal saving. This is sometimes referred to as the hypothesis that households do not perfectly pierce either the "corporate veil" or the "government veil."

This issue is of great practical importance. If one accepts the premise that households regard all forms of national saving as equivalent, then it is impossible to influence the level of national saving by adjusting government budget deficits, or by influencing corporate saving, because households simply adjust their behavior to offset these effects. Conversely, if one rejects this premise, then policies that affect government budget deficits and corporate saving will—all else remaining the same—alter national saving.

## How do taxes affect saving?

Tax policy can, in principle, affect saving through a variety of channels. Economists have traditionally emphasized the fact that capital income taxation reduces the after-tax rate of return available on investments, thereby diminishing the rewards associated with thrift. The interest elasticity of saving is a common quantitative measure of the extent to which saving changes in response to movements in the real after-tax rate of return (see the related discussion under Elasticity, demand and supply). The real after-tax rate of return is defined as the difference between the after-tax rate of return and the rate of inflation. If the interest elasticity of saving is positive, then saving rises with the real after-tax rate of return, and falls with the rate of taxation applicable to capital income. When the interest elasticity of saving is larger, saving falls further in response to a given increase in capital income taxation.

Many economists believe that the interest elasticity of saving is positive. They assert that households will save more when saving is more rewarding economically. As a matter of theory, this issue is far from clear. An increase in the real after-tax rate of return effectively reduces the price of future consumption, in the sense that households do not need to sacrifice as much current consumption to achieve a given level of future consumption. Therefore, even if future consumption rises in response to a higher real after-tax rate of return, saving may fall.

A simple calculation illustrates this point. Suppose that a household wishes to accumulate $100,000 over the next 10 years to send a child to college. Suppose also that this household expects to earn 8 percent on its investments, and to pay 25 percent of capital income as taxes. Finally, suppose that the household expects an annual inflation rate of 4 percent. Then the real after-tax rate of return is 2 percent (75% of 8%, minus 4%), and the household can achieve its target by saving roughly $7,160 per year. Now suppose that the government permits this same household to accumulate these resources in a special account, and exempts all associated capital income from taxation. Then the real after-tax rate of return is 4 percent, and the household can achieve its target by saving roughly $6,390 per year.

This example illustrates an important point: If households save for fixed targets, then saving must fall in response to an increase in the real after-tax rate of return, and must rise in response to higher capital income taxation. Of course, asset targets are not usually fixed. With higher real after-tax rates of return, households may set higher targets, particularly for objectives that do not require fixed expenditures, such as retirement. However, even if asset targets rise in response to increases in the real after-tax rate of return, saving may still fall. The interest elasticity of saving will be positive only if saving targets are sufficiently responsive to the real after-tax rate of return.

Much controversy surrounds the empirical measurement of the interest elasticity of saving. Although the evidence is mixed, most of the studies that have relied on macroeconomic data conclude that saving is not very responsive to the after-tax rate of return. These studies are, however, vulnerable to a variety of criticisms that call the reliability of macroeconomic estimates into serious question. Some analysts have also attempted to infer the interest elasticity of saving from simulation models.

Simulation studies have identified some important factors that should make saving more sensitive to the real after-tax rate of return. For example, simulations have shown that an increase in the after-tax rate of return significantly decreases the value of "human wealth" by reducing the present discounted value of all future earnings and pension income. In response to this reduction in wealth, households should consume less and save more. Unfortunately, the simulation methodology cannot reliably establish the interest elasticity of saving. Simulated values of this parameter are highly sensitive to the assumptions on which the simulations are based.

Even if the interest elasticity of saving is small, personal saving may still be sensitive to tax policy. Psychological theories of saving suggest that certain institutional arrangements may increase thrift by promoting self-discipline. For example, an individual might choose to place funds in a tax-favored retirement account, rather than in a more flexible savings vehicle, knowing full well that early withdrawals from the retirement account will be subject to heavy penalties, in part because the existence of these penalties helps to enforce self-discipline. Tax-favored retirement accounts may ultimately stimulate greater total personal saving precisely because households are less likely to invade these accounts prematurely.

Tax policy can also affect corporate saving. The taxation of dividends may discourage cash distributions to shareholders, and encourage the retention of earnings (see Dividends, double taxation of), thereby increasing net saving in the corporate sector. Similarly, high rates of corporate taxation can reduce corporate saving by siphoning off earnings that might otherwise have been reinvested. Of course, these are valid concerns only if households do not perfectly pierce the corporate veil.

Finally, tax policy can affect government saving. Tax reforms that increase revenues without associated increases in spending reduce deficits, or increase surpluses. While this is true of all taxes, the issue deserves special emphasis in the context of capital income taxes. Efforts to stimulate private saving through tax incentives generally require reductions in capital income tax rates, which tend to reduce revenue and increase government deficits. Thus, unless these measures significantly stimulate private saving, they may actually reduce national saving. Of course, effects on government saving are of concern only if households do not perfectly pierce the government veil.

## Possible justifications for favorable tax treatment of capital income

One potential justification for reducing or eliminating capital income taxes is that this might reduce the excess burden associated with taxation (see Excess burden). Capital income taxes distort households' intertemporal choices by, in effect, raising the price of future consumption relative to current consumption. The elimination of capital income taxes would remove this source of excess burden. However, a revenue-neutral reduction in capital income tax revenues would necessitate an increase in other tax rates, which would in turn create other distortions. For example, an increase in the tax burden on labor income would further distort the choice of labor versus leisure. Thus, revenue-neutral cuts in capital income tax will reduce the excess burden associated with taxation only if, on the margin, capital income taxes create more excess burden per dollar of revenue than other taxes (see Optimal taxation and Inverse elasticity rule).

Another potential justification for reducing or eliminating capital income taxes is that this might stimulate domestic capital formation. Capital formation is important because it fuels the growth of employment, wages, and income. Historically, domestic saving has been the most important source of funds for domestic investment, so policies that stimulated saving also promoted investment. In recent years, the progressive integration of international capital markets has permitted saving and investment to diverge. Thus, although domestic investment declined significantly during the 1980s, it did not fall as far as national saving. The impact of lower saving on investment was cushioned to some extent by inflows of foreign capital. Conversely, if the rate of domestic saving were to increase, it is likely that a significant fraction of the incremental funds would be invested abroad, rather than domestically. Nevertheless, many economists believe that domestic saving continues to constrain domestic investment over long time periods.

Finally, many economists believe that an alarming number of Americans have been doing little to prepare themselves financially for economic adversity or retirement. Some analysts argue that this reflects poor planning and limited financial sophistication, rather than deliberate choice. This view leads to a paternalistic justification for encouraging saving by reducing or eliminating capital income taxes.

## Tax provisions and saving

Tax provisions for private and public pensions attempt to increase household and national saving. The tax expenditure for employer-provided pensions is estimated by the Joint Committee on Taxation to have cost $311.1 billion from 1994–1998 (see Tax expenditures; and Pensions, tax treatment). It is justified in part as a way of promoting household saving and ensuring adequate retirement income security for the elderly. Social Security, a publicly pro-

vided pension system, provides income to elderly households (see Social Security benefits, federal taxation).

The effect of private and public pensions on national saving is the sum of their effect on public, business, and household saving. Because Social Security benefits for current retirees are largely funded by the taxes paid by today's workers, only a small fraction of Social Security taxes go toward increasing public saving (see Social Security Trust Fund). In contrast, employer pension obligations are generally fully funded, and hence increase business saving. Thus, private pensions have a larger positive effect on the sum of public and business saving than does Social Security. These programs will have an ambiguous effect on household saving. To the extent that pensions raise lifetime wealth, current consumption would be expected to increase and household saving would decline. If, however, pensions allow people to retire earlier than otherwise, private saving may increase in order to maintain living standards during a longer retirement period.

The crucial empirical issue when thinking about the effects of private and public pensions on saving is, to what extent do people "undo" the effect of pensions by altering private saving? If people reduce private nonpension wealth dollar for dollar in relation to private pension wealth, national saving will fall by roughly the amount of the tax expenditure associated with private pensions. If people respond in a similar way to Social Security wealth, national saving will fall by nearly the full amount of Social Security expenditures. These outcomes would be dramatically different from those that are intended by these programs.

Empirical studies of pensions are hampered by the difficult task of accurately calculating lifetime resources for households. This issue is important, because policies that increase the use of pensions would undoubtedly be accompanied by reductions in other forms of employee compensation. Thus, the effect of increased pension wealth for a household is to reallocate resources toward retirement, holding the present discounted value of lifetime resources constant. Studies that have most carefully addressed the effect of private pensions and Social Security on household saving find that for every dollar of pension and Social security wealth, private wealth falls by 10 to 50 cents, depending on the study. These estimates suggest that Social Security may have an important depressing effect on national saving. In contrast, private pensions, because they are fully funded, increase national saving. The empirical literature on this topic is far from definitive, however.

Given the low rates of household saving in the United States and the concern that Social Security depresses national saving, the country has experimented, particularly since 1981, with narrowly targeted personal saving incentives. These voluntary accounts—individual retirement accounts (IRAs), 401(k) plans, and Keogh accounts—feature preferential tax treatment of contributions and investment earnings, annual contribution limits, and penalties for early withdrawals (see Individual retirement accounts). Since 1986, contributions to these saving incentives have amounted to about one-third of personal saving as measured by the NIPA.

There are sound conceptual reasons to doubt the effectiveness of voluntary saving incentives. First, contributions are capped. A single taxpayer, for example, can make no more than $2,000 in tax-deductible IRA contributions each year. For any taxpayer who would have saved more than $2,000 in the absence of IRAs, the availability of an IRA does not affect the costs or benefits to be had from an additional dollar of saving, and therefore provides no incentive on the margin for the taxpayer to increase saving. Yet the IRA will reduce federal tax receipts. In addition, the IRA may actually induce the taxpayer to consume more, because it increases his or her total after-tax resources. For both of these reasons, the IRA would contribute to a lower rate of national saving. 401(k) and Keogh plans have higher contribution limits (the 401(k) limit was $9,240 in 1994) and hence are more likely than IRAs to provide marginal incentives.

Second, even if a taxpayer would not (in the absence of a saving incentive) have saved more than the contribution limit in a given year, he or she could take full advantage of the saving incentive deduction either by drawing down previously accumulated assets or by borrowing. Contributions funded either by shifting existing assets or by borrowing do not increase household saving. Instead, they depress national saving by reducing federal tax receipts, thereby adding to the federal budget deficit.

Determining the effectiveness of these narrowly targeted saving incentives is difficult, given currently existing data. First, saving at the household level is very difficult to measure. Second, households with similar characteristics may save vastly different amounts, which complicates estimations using empirical models. Third, households may have different motives for saving. Some may save primarily for retirement, others may save to meet unexpected expenses, and others may follow simple rules of thumb or not save at all. If underlying motives to save are not well understood, it is difficult to predict the effects of policies that alter the incentives to save. These pitfalls contribute to widely different estimates of the effects of IRAs and 401(k) plans in the empirical literature.

Because it is difficult to design narrowly targeted saving incentives that do not reward taxpayers for borrowing, reshuffling existing assets, or redirecting saving from conventional instruments into tax-favored accounts, many economists believe a consumption-based tax system would be much more successful in promoting household saving (see Consumption taxation). Under the income tax, a dollar of income saved and consumed 10 years from now yields a considerably smaller amount of after-tax consumption in constant dollars than it would if it were consumed immediately. This is because income is taxed as it is earned, and again as it is saved. With an interest rate of 5 percent and a marginal tax rate of 28 percent, for example, the tax system imposes a greater than 12 percent penalty on saving after 10 years. Because of the bias toward current consumption in the tax system, many proposals to stimulate saving are designed to make the tax system more neutral toward intertemporal consumption decisions.

The present tax system could be changed to an expenditure-based system by, among other changes, eliminating contribution limits and early withdrawal penalties on IRA-type saving plans and phasing out taxation of capital income. By removing saving from the tax base, an expenditure tax eliminates distortions in intertemporal consumption decisions. Many economists believe a switch from a progressive income tax to a progressive expenditure tax would significantly increase economic efficiency. Expenditure tax advocates also argue that the tax system would be administratively simpler. Expenditure tax critics, however, argue that income is a more appropriate basis for taxation, and that the difficulties that arise with implementing an expenditure tax are large enough to make it an impractical policy alternative.

## Additional readings

Bernheim, B. Douglas. "The Economic Effects of Social Security: Towards a Reconciliation of Theory and Measurement." *Journal of Public Economics* 33 (1987): 273–304.

Bernheim, B. Douglas. *The Vanishing Nestegg: Reflections on Saving in America.* New York: Priority Press Publications, 1991.

Bradford, David F. *Untangling the Income Tax.* Cambridge, Mass.: Harvard University Press, 1986.

Campbell, John and N. Gregory Mankiw. "Consumption, Income, and Interest Rates: Reinterpreting the Time Series Evidence." *NBER Macroeconomics Annual,* 1989.

Dicks-Mireaux, Louis and Mervyn King. "Pension Wealth and Household Savings: Tests of Robustness." *Journal of Public Economics* 23 (1984): 115–39.

Engen, Eric M., William G. Gale, and John Karl Scholz. "Do Saving Incentives Work?" *Brookings Papers on Economic Activity* 1 (1994): 85–180.

Feldstein, Martin. "The Welfare Cost of Capital Income Taxation." *Journal of Political Economy* (1978).

Gale, William G., and John Karl Scholz. "IRAs and Household Saving." *American Economic Review* 84 (5) (December 1994): 1233–41.

Graetz, Michael J. "Expenditure Tax Design." In *What Should Be Taxed—Income or Expenditure?* edited by Joseph A. Pechman, pp. 161–276. Washington, D.C.: The Brookings Institution, 1980.

Kotlikoff, Laurence J. "Taxation and Savings: A Neoclassical Perspective," *Journal of Economic Literature* 22 (December 1984): 1576–1629.

Poterba, James M., Steven F. Venti, and David A. Wise. "Do 401(k) Contributions Crowd Out Other Personal Saving?" *Journal of Public Economics* 58 (September 1995): 1–32.

Shefrin, Hersh and Richard Thaler. "The Behavioral Life-Cycle Hypothesis. "*Economic Inquiry* 26 (1988): 609–43.

Summers, Lawrence H. "Capital Taxation and Accumulation in a Life Cycle Growth Model." *American Economic Review* 71 (4) (September 1981): 533–44.

Venti, Steven, and David Wise. "Have IRAs Increased U.S. Saving? Evidence from Consumer Expenditure Surveys." *Quarterly Journal of Economics* 105 (1990): 661–98.

*Cross references:* consumption taxation; individual retirement accounts; pensions, tax treatment; Ricardian equivalence.

# Seigniorage

Gail E. Makinen
Congressional Research Service

*A source of government revenue that comes from money creation.*

Given that money is socially useful and, hence, that a demand for it exists, it is possible for the supplier of money to derive some revenue or profit from providing it. Seigniorage (and brassage, a related term) was originally applied to mean a charge imposed by a mint when bullion was converted into coins (money). As such, it represented the difference between the face and the bullion value of the coin. Seigniorage later became synonymous with the real revenue or profit government derives from the creation of money. Although this is often omitted from discussions of seigniorage, the word applies to the net revenue or net profit from supplying money because the maintenance of the existing money stock is not costless (even when full-bodied coins are used).

As monetary systems evolved, their ability to produce seigniorage changed, the nature of seigniorage became less obvious, and the initial collector of this revenue also changed.

When paper money supplied by government came to be substituted for full-bodied coins, the potential for seigniorage rose dramatically, because the same amount of money could be supplied at a much lower resource cost to the government. Seigniorage continued to be measured as the difference between the face value of the notes and the cost to produce and maintain them in circulation.

The introduction of commercial banking and deposit money not only made the form of seigniorage less obvious, but potentially reduced the amount that could be extracted from the monetary system. To see this, suppose that only deposit money is used and that its supply is controlled by an asset called reserves (or high-powered money) which is supplied by the central bank (it could also be supplied by the treasury). Further, assume that the relationship between reserves and deposit money is one to five. If the central bank wants the commercial banks to supply more deposit money, it can do so by supplying more reserves. One way to supply these reserves is through buying government securities in the market. The acquisition of additional securities by the central bank will reduce the government's net payment of interest, because central bank profits are remitted to the treasury. This interest "saving" is then a measure of gross seigniorage. However, because the interest is saved year after year, the present value of these "savings" is the appropriate measure of gross seigniorage. On an annual basis, this present value is equal to the amount of reserves or high-powered money created in any year.

The ability of a deposit-only money system to reduce seigniorage can be seen when it is compared to an all-currency system. Given that the same amount of money is used in both systems, in the deposit-only system, seigniorage is earned only on the system's reserves or high-powered money. And these reserves are equal in value, in the example above, to only one-fifth of the currency that would exist in an all-currency system.

A major way of earning additional seigniorage in the deposit-only system is to raise the reserve requirement. When it is raised to 100 percent, the two systems will yield the same gross seigniorage (given that the central bank will supply the reserves necessary for the money stock to remain the same in both systems). However, because 100 percent reserve banking is not common, actual seigniorage will be less in a deposit-only system or in a mixed deposit–currency system relative to a currency-only system.

When central banks replace treasuries as suppliers of paper money, the major change is in the institution that initially collects the seigniorage. In the United States, the Federal Reserve supplies currency largely through buying federal government securities in the market. Because the net earnings or profits of the Federal Reserve are remitted to the Treasury, the Fed holdings of government securities are, in effect, an interest-free loan to the government. The present value of the reduced-interest bill of the federal government, then, measures the amount of gross seigniorage. Not all of the Fed's holdings of government securities, however, are acquired through supplying paper money. Some are acquired through supplying reserves to depository institutions. Thus, on a present value basis, it is the change in the sum of currency in circulation and the reserves of depository institutions, called high-powered money, that represents the gross seigniorage earned per year. When the expenses of the Federal Reserve are subtracted from this total, a measure of net seigniorage results. (The Federal Reserve has additional sources of revenue, such as interest earned on its holding of nongovernment securities and discounts, and other costs such as capital gains or losses on its holdings of foreign exchange and on the sale of government securities, that can alter the total amount of net seigniorage.)

Because the federal budget is prepared on a cash-flow basis, the amount listed per year in the budget document as seigniorage is different from the seigniorage computed on a present value basis. Most of seigniorage in the budget represents the sum paid per year by the Federal Reserve to the Treasury, representing the net earnings from its entire portfolio of assets. In the budget document, this measure of net seigniorage is recorded as a part of "Other Revenue" subtitled "Miscellaneous Receipts." During the 1950s, '60s, '70s, and '80s, it averaged, as a percent of total federal receipts, 0.6, 1.2, 1.8, and 2.2 percent, respectively. In addition, the Treasury itself earns a small amount of seigniorage on coinage, representing the difference between the face value of the coins and the operating costs of the U.S. Mint.

*Cross reference:* inflation tax.

# Severance tax, state

James A. Richardson
Louisiana State University

*State governments employ special taxes on the severing of nonrenewable resources from the land.*

Thirty-nine states raise revenues or regulate behavior by taxing the severing of renewable and nonre-newable resources from land or water within the taxing jurisdiction of the state. The severance tax is levied on a variety of resources, with 11 states taxing timber products, 27 states taxing oil and gas, 16 states taxing coal, 2 states taxing fish, and 27 states taxing a variety of minerals ranging from iron ore and phosphates to sand and gravel.

Revenues from the severance tax to all states amounted to $4.4 billion, or 1.1 percent of total state tax collections in 1996. Ten states, having significant endowments of oil and gas or coal, collected 82 percent of total severance tax collections. These states—with their percent of the U.S. oil, gas, and coal production; their severance tax rates on oil, gas, and coal; and the significance of severance taxes—are shown in table 1. Texas and Alaska dominate oil production; Texas and Louisiana dominate natural gas production, although some of this gas is produced in the federal outercontinental shelf and is not subject to state severance taxes. Wyoming, West Virginia, and Kentucky dominate coal production in the United States.

Oil and gas states receive the overwhelming majority of the severance tax. Texas, Alaska, Louisiana, Oklahoma, and New Mexico claimed 63 percent of all severance taxes collected, and Wyoming, West Virginia, and Kentucky received just over 12 percent. Alaska and Wyoming are the states most dependent on severance tax collections.

Oil severance tax rates vary across the states, from 0.4 percent in Wyoming to 15.0 percent in Alaska. The tax base is typically the value of the oil at the wellhead. The natural gas severance tax is levied either on the value of natural gas at the wellhead or on a thousand cubic feet (MCF) basis. The complication of administering the oil and gas severance tax is that, while the tax is levied at the wellhead, typically no market transaction occurs at that point; the value of oil and natural gas at the wellhead is, therefore, a computation based on the price the oil or gas is sold for at the first market transaction less any transportation and processing expenses incurred between the wellhead and the first market transaction. This complication does not occur if the severance tax is levied on a per volume basis.

Coal is taxed on a cents per ton basis or as a percent of market value. The three prime coal-producing states use percent of value as the tax base, although the rates vary from 4.5 percent in Kentucky to 9.5 percent for surface-mined coal in Wyoming. The coal in the western states of Wyoming and Montana has less sulfur content than the coal in Kentucky and West Virginia, creating an environmental advantage for the western coal.

State severance taxes had national implications in the 1970s because of rising energy prices, federal controls on domestic oil and natural gas prices, and several severance tax increases. Nonproducing

## TABLE 1

### Resource Production, Severance Tax Rates, and Significance of Severance Tax Collections for Selected States

| States | Severance Tax Rate | | | Percent of U.S. Production | | | Tax as a % of Total Tax Collection |
|---|---|---|---|---|---|---|---|
| | Oil | Gas | Coal | Oil | Gas | Coal | |
| Alaska | 15.0%[1] | 10.0%[1] | — | 23.7% | 2.4% | — | 63.0% |
| Kentucky | 4.5%[1] | 4.5%[1] | 4.5%[1] | 0.2% | 0.4% | 16.0% | 2.9% |
| Louisiana | 12.5%[1] | 10.1¢/mcf[2] | 10¢/ton | 16.0% | 27.2%[4] | — | 7.4% |
| Montana | | | | | | 3.8% | 7.0% |
| Surface-mined | | | 10%–15% | 0.7% | 0.2% | | |
| Underground-mined | | | 3%–4%[3] | | | | |
| New Mexico | 7.08%[1] | 7.08% | $1.13–$1.17/ton[3] | 2.6% | 5.6% | — | 10.1% |
| N. Dakota | 11.5%[1] | 4.7¢/mcf | 77¢/ton | 1.3% | | | 11.7% |
| Oklahoma | 7.085%[1] | 7.085%[1] | — | 4.0% | 11.6% | — | 6.9% |
| Texas | 4.6%[1] | 7.5%[1] | — | 25.6% | 34.2% | — | 3.9% |
| West Virginia | 5.0%[1] | 5.0%[1] | 5.0%[1] | — | 0.1% | 16.8% | 5.7% |
| Wyoming | 0.4%[1] | 0.4%[1] | | 3.7% | 4.2% | 19.4% | 30.2% |
| Surface-mined | | | 9.5%[1] | | | | |
| Underground-mined | | | 7.25%[1] | | | | |

[1]Of value.
[2]mcf = thousand cubic feet. Indexed to price of natural gas.
[3]Depends on BTU per lb.
[4]Includes federal offshore.

states feared that producing states were shifting their tax burden to consumers in nonproducing states. However, the fears of tax exportation failed to materialize. First, only three states increased their severance taxes after January 1974, the time of the initial Arab oil embargo. Alaska increased the tax rate on oil from 12.5 to 15.0 percent, and Montana and Wyoming increased their severance taxes on coal. Louisiana had increased its severance tax on oil from 26 cents per barrel to 12.5 percent of value in 1973. Second, the ability to export any severance tax through price increases was facilitated more by federal price controls than by states having a disproportionate share of these energy resources. Third, in a free market, increases in severance taxes are more likely to be exported, if at all, through effects on wages, royalties, lease payments, and other input payments than via consumer prices. The elimination of the federal price controls and the general availability of energy resources in the 1980s and 1990s have substantially reduced the tax-exporting opportunities of producing states.

State policies relating to severance taxes focus on the choice of the tax base, the predictability and stability of the revenue stream, the long-term depletion of the resource, and the impact at the margin on resource development and production. As illustrated in table 1, states have chosen value over volume as the appropriate tax base for energy resources. The only major gas producer with a volume tax is Louisiana, but this 10.1 cents per MCF is indexed to increases or decreases in the price of natural gas. The severance tax base for other minerals, timber products, and fish varies from gross proceeds, to tons, to cords.

Severance tax revenues are related to long-term production prospects and price conditions. Oil and gas production has been declining in the United States since 1970. The fiscal advantage of having oil and gas resources is not permanent, but states have ample time to plan for the replacement of this tax base because the production declines are gradual and predictable. The long-term depletion of the energy reserves can be accommodated for current and future citizens by a permanent trust fund that converts the depletable oil and gas or coal resource into a nondepletable financial asset. A permanent trust fund preserves the use of the natural wealth of a state for future generations.

Price variation is another matter. In 1981, oil prices had moved close to $40 per barrel, but by early 1987, they were closer to $10 per barrel. Severance tax collections, or the lack thereof, forced the major oil- and gas-producing states to raise other taxes or to curtail state programs. These states faced budgetary turmoil throughout the 1980s and even into the 1990s. Price variation is not predictable and is created by short-run disturbances, not long-run trends. Hence, states that use severance taxes to fund key state programs have to be aware of the "boom and bust" cycle associated with such revenues. Price variation in energy resources can be accommodated by "rainy day funds" that grow when energy prices are high and then are used when energy prices fall.

Energy-producing states became accustomed to the industrial development that accompanied the discovery of oil, natural gas, or coal, just as they became accustomed to the severance taxes as a means of financing public programs. Any impedi-

**TABLE 2**

**Resource Development/Resource Consumption Process**

| Owners of mineral rights | Resource Development |
|---|---|
| Exploration/development | |
| Drilling activity | ↑ |
| Production | Tax Levied |
| Transportation | |
| Refiner/processor | ↓ |
| Industrial users | |
| Retailer | |
| Final consumer | Resource Consumption |

ment to the exploration, development, or production of the energy resources has an adverse impact on employment and economic activity within the energy-producing states. High severance taxes could be one such impediment.

Severance taxes postpone the depletion of energy reserves. The degree of economic distortion caused by the severance tax depends on who in the production line actually pays the taxes. The ultimate incidence of the severance tax becomes the critical issue. Participants in the development/consumption process are listed in table 2. The severance tax is imposed on those severing the resource.

Contractual relationships link the suppliers of energy resources. The principal features of the contract with the owners of the mineral rights are royalty rates, bonus payments, and rental fees. The explorer/developer/producer shares the risk with the landowner by paying upon production, as opposed to a strictly upfront purchase of the resource rights. The royalty rate is the percentage of production value that accrues to the landowner. Higher severance taxes may lead to lower royalty rates as the tax is shifted back to the landowner. Bonuses represent cash payments made at the initiation of the contract. Higher severance tax rates reduce bonus payments if royalty rates are not reduced. Rental payments are penalty payments for not drilling within a specified amount of time and are usually related to bonus payments. Rental payments may be reduced by higher severance taxes. Transactions between the person who originally owned the mineral rights and the person who eventually drills can become even more complicated. For example, a person purchasing the right to drill can farm out the drilling to another operator in exchange for a share of the production.

In the long run, severance taxes can be shifted back to the owners of the mineral rights. In the short run, however, contractual obligations between mineral owners and producers will prevent an increase in the severance tax from being shifted immediately back to the landowner. Higher severance tax rates raise the operating costs leading to earlier abandonment of existing fields for a given price projection.

Higher severance tax rates can also neutralize new technology. In particular, enhanced recovery methods will not be as profitable if severance tax rates are raised. Secondary recovery methods, including water flooding and internal combustion, are commonly used in mature producing states. Tertiary recovery methods, such as chemically induced pressurization, are much more expensive and sensitive to higher severance tax rates. Energy states are concerned with employment policies in the 1990s. Higher severance taxes are weighed against any possible employment loss, and severance tax reductions are weighed against possible employment gains.

## Additional readings

Burness, Stuart. "On the Taxation of Nonreplenishable Natural Resources." *Journal of Environmental Economics and Management* 3 (4) (March 1976): 289–311.

Cuciti, Peggy, Harvey Galper, and Robert Lucke. "State Energy Revenues." In *Fiscal Federalism and the Taxation of Natural Resources*, edited by Charles McClure, Jr., and Peter Mieszkowski, pp. 11–60. Lexington, Mass.: D.C. Heath, 1983.

Deacon, Robert J. "Taxation, Depletion, and Welfare: A Simulation Study of the U.S. Petroleum Resource." *Journal of Environmental Economics and Management* 24 (March 1993): 159–87.

English, Jeffrey E., and Mark S. Klan. "Optimal Taxation: Timber and Externalities." *Journal of Environmental Economics and Management* 18 (May 1990): 263–75.

Friedman, Julia Mason. "Taxation of Timber." In *Final Report of the Minnesota Tax Study Commission*, edited by Robert D. Ebel and Therese J. McGuire, pp. 399–410. Boston: Butterworths, 1986.

Olson, Kent W., and James W. Kleckley. "Severance Tax Stability." *National Tax Journal* 42 (March 1989): 69–78.

Richardson, James A., and Loren C. Scott. "Resource Location Patterns and State Severance Taxes: Some Empirical Evidence." *Natural Resources Journal* (Winter 1983): 352–64.

Richardson, James A. "Severance Tax Reform." In *Reforming State Tax Systems*, edited by Steven D. Gold. National Conference of State Legislatures, December 1986.

Ward, Frank A., and Joe Kerkvliet. "Quantifying Exhaustible Resource Theory: An Application to Mineral Taxation Policy." *Resources and Energy Economics* 15 (June 1993): 203–41.

*Cross references:* energy taxes; environmental taxes, state; site value taxation; tax exportation.

# Site value taxation; single tax

Joan M. Youngman
Lincoln Institute of Land Policy

Site value taxes—*Taxes on the value of land in its original, unimproved state.*

Single tax—*A site value tax proposed to replace all other taxes as the sole source of government revenue.*

---

The unusual economic characteristics of land, particularly its nearly inelastic supply and its growth in value with community development, have long supported special approaches to its taxation. Because real property taxes generally combine land and building values in a single tax base, those interested in distinct taxes on land itself have focused on various alternatives: graded property taxes at higher rates on land than buildings; land value taxes limited to land value rather than land and buildings; site value taxes, reaching land in its original state before private capital improvements; and the single tax, a site value tax serving as the sole source of government tax revenue. Graded taxes have been used in several U.S. states and Canadian provinces, and land value taxes have been imposed in Jamaica and individual cities in Australia and New Zealand.

"Site value" denotes that portion of land wealth not attributable to private investment: land alone, without consideration of privately financed improvements to its original state. The "single tax" that would replace all other forms of taxation with a site value tax was brought to greatest popular attention by Henry George (1839–1897), a 19th-century social reformer and author of the 1879 work *Progress and Poverty*. This product of George's long self-education, even typeset by the author himself, garnered enormous attention. It drew the support of admirers as diverse as Tolstoy, George Bernard Shaw, and Sun Yat-sen, and it inspired reform efforts ranging from land tax legislation to the formation of utopian communities. *Progress and Poverty* deals with many issues, but the single tax is its central prescription for redress of the inequities it passionately assails. It constitutes a compelling work of literature, as well as a political and economic tract.

The case for site value taxation is based on both efficiency and equity. The existence of a tax base in nearly inelastic supply offers the possibility of collecting revenue without distorting prices and economic incentives. Similarly, taxation of a form of wealth not due to individual human effort does not claim the product of the taxpayer's own labor. By excluding value resulting from private investments, such as grading and planting, site value taxation is designed to reach only the "unearned increment," the value resulting from community development and thus properly claimed by the community itself. While a tax on site value could be set at any rate, Henry George advocated a confiscatory tax equal to the full annual rental value of the unimproved land. He wrote:

> What I, therefore, propose, as the simple yet sovereign remedy, which will raise wages, increase the earnings of capital, extirpate pauperism, abolish poverty, give remunerative employment to whoever wishes it, afford free scope to human powers, lessen crime, elevate morals, and taste, and intelligence, purify government and carry civilization to yet nobler heights, is— *to appropriate rent by taxation* (George 1979 ed.: 405–6).

The greatest difficulties facing such a policy concern treatment of land claims established under a previously settled regime of property rights. A confiscatory tax would not reach only future unearned increments; it would also abolish property values held by investors who recently purchased land in reliance on past tax practices. William Vickery included as a "basic desiderata in a land tax base" the principle of legitimacy: "Expectations legitimately developed in the past must be sufficiently honored to create confidence in the expectations intended to be generated by the new tax regime" (Holland 1970: 26). Henry George considered such claims spurious when land title could be undermined by legal technicalities, pointing out that "if Quirk, Gammon & Snap can mouse out a technical flaw in your parchments or hunt up some forgotten heir who never dreamed of his rights, not merely the land, but all your improvements, may be taken away from you" (George 1979 ed.: 366–67). George had little use for compromise, such as John Stuart Mill's proposal that legislation provide for confiscating value increments realized after its implementation. George replied, "Because I was robbed yesterday, and the day before, and the day before that, is it any reason that I should suffer myself to be robbed today and tomorrow?" (George 1979 ed.: 365). The political problems raised by such an approach have generally left land value taxes well below the level of full annual rental value. Conversely, special opportunities exist for introducing land taxes in economies in transition from state ownership to private rights in property, because equitable issues concerning settled expectations are obviated if new owners take title with full understanding of their future tax liabilities.

Many important issues in site value taxation, as in land value taxation generally, concern assessment, administration, and implementation. For example, market value is often equated with value at "highest and best use," the most profitable use that is legal and feasible, and a heavy or even confiscatory tax on land value would be intended in part as an incentive to development. Yet no consensus exists today that development uniformly constitutes the "highest and best use" of land in a social sense. In all 50 U.S. states and in many other nations, property tax benefits for farmland, forests, and open space explicitly seek to counteract the economic incentive for conversion of such land to other uses. George considered taxation at highest and best use to be a central advantage of his proposal: "The monopolist of agricultural land would be taxed as much as though his land were covered with houses and barns, with crops and with stock. The owner of a vacant city lot would have to pay as much for the privilege of keeping other people off of it until he wanted to use it, as his neighbor who has a fine house upon his lot" (George 1979 ed.: 437–38). The burden of any annual wealth tax on cash-poor property owners generates intense political pressure for relief. This is dramatized by the reluctance of elderly homeowners to take advantage of mitigation provisions, such as tax deferral and reverse-annuity programs, that would encumber their property, seeking a reduction in the tax itself instead.

Much research on land taxation and site value taxation has focused on their effects on land prices and development decisions. The nondistortionary aspects of a tax on a commodity in inelastic supply contrast with the development incentive exerted by a tax based not on current rental income but on potential sale value. That incentive varies with the tax rate. Under a confiscatory tax equal to the rental value of the unimproved site, development to full economic potential would be imperative. At the tax rates commonly found in contemporary property tax systems, the role of the property tax in development decisions is less clear. The difficulty of taxing land at its highest and best use, even at the generally low rates currently prevailing, indicates the problems that would confront a tax patterned on George's model.

Studies on the influence of land taxes on development use differing assumptions as to whether the tax would reach the full potential land value or only value at current use (e.g., Mills 1981; Tideman 1982). As noted earlier, general reliance on highest and best use valuation means that, in the absence of special statutory exceptions, land value for tax purposes should reflect the most profitable use that is feasible and legal (although the value of buildings and other improvements not suited to that use may be reduced to reflect this obsolescence or depreciation). The fact that such explicit valuation provisions coexist with genuine uncertainty as to actual assessment practices illustrates the need for further study of the administration of the tax in order to gauge its effects.

Problems of this type already arise under the land tax component of current real property taxes. A tax on the value of the original and unimproved site would raise many additional valuation and assessment challenges. For example, in suggesting use of a legally defined "standard state" as the basis for assessment, Vickery wrote: "[T]o value land in an original substandard state requires an even greater feat of the imagination than the valuation of the land in a standard state: how, for example, would one value the site of the World Trade Center on the assumption that it was still a part of the bed of the North River? What is substandard for one purpose might be superior for another. The fill that is an advantage for the construction of a four-story walk-up may simply have to be removed for the skyscraper; it might be much easier to dredge mud and pump water" (Holland 1970 ed.: 28). Site value taxation could also require legal innovations, such as an appeals process protecting taxpayers' rights to contest their individual assessments while preserving the integrity of a mapping system under which taxable values of neighboring parcels stand in predictable relationship to one another.

## Additional readings

Bentick, Brian L. "The Impact of Taxation and Valuation Practices on the Timing and Efficiency of Land Use." *Journal of Political Economy* 87 (1979): 859–68.

Bentick, Brian L. "A Tax on Land Value May Not Be Neutral." *National Tax Journal* 35 (1982): 113.

Brueckner, Jan K. "A Modern Analysis of the Effects of Site Value Taxation." *National Tax Journal* 39 (1986): 49–58.

Calvo, Guillermo A., Laurence J. Kotlikoff, and Carlos Alfredo Rodriguez. "The Incidence of a Tax on Pure Rent: A New (?) Reason for an Old Answer." *Journal of Political Economy* 87 (1979): 869–74.

George, Henry. *Progress and Poverty.* New York: Robert Schalkenback Foundation, centenary ed. of original 1879 work, 1979.

Holland, Daniel M., editor. *The Assessment of Land Value.* Madison: The University of Wisconsin Press, for the Committee on Taxation, Resources, and Economic Development, 1970.

Ladd, Helen F., and Katharine L. Bradbury. "City Taxes and Property Tax Bases." *National Tax Journal* 41 (1988): 503–23.

Lindholm, Richard W., and Arthur D. Lynn, Jr. *Land Value Taxation: The Progress and Poverty Centenary.* Madison: The University of Wisconsin Press, for the Committee on Taxation, Resources, and Economic Development, 1982.

Mills, David E. "The Non-Neutrality of Land Value Taxation." *National Tax Journal* 34 (1981): 125–29.

Mills, David E. "Reply to Tideman." *National Tax Journal* 35 (1982): 115.

Tideman, T. Nicolaus. "A Tax on Land Value Is Neutral." *National Tax Journal* 35 (1982): 109–11.

*Cross reference:* lump-sum tax.

# Social Security benefits, federal taxation

David Weiner
Congressional Budget Office

*A portion of Social Security benefits counted as taxable income for taxpayers with incomes above specified thresholds.*

**TABLE 1**

**Number of Returns Reporting Taxable Benefits and Revenues Collected**

| Tax Year | Number of Tax Returns Including Benefits in AGI (millions) | Revenues Credited to the Social Security and Disability Insurance Trust Fund from Benefit Taxation (billions of dollars) |
|---|---|---|
| 1984 | 2.6 | 3.0 |
| 1985 | 2.9 | 3.4 |
| 1986 | 3.2 | 3.7 |
| 1987 | 3.6 | 3.2 |
| 1988 | 4.0 | 3.4 |
| 1989 | 4.7 | 2.5 |
| 1990 | 5.1 | 5.0 |
| 1991 | 5.3 | 6.1 |
| 1992 | 5.5 | 6.1 |
| 1993 | 5.7 | 5.6 |
| 1994 | 5.9 | 5.3 |
| 1995 | 6.6 | 5.8 |
| 1996 | 7.4 | 6.8 |

*Sources:* Department of the Treasury, Internal Revenue Service, *Statistics of Income Bulletin*, Spring 1998 and Fall 1998; Social Security Administration, *Annual Supplement to the Social Security Bulletin*, 1997.

In the years following the original enactment of the Social Security system, administrative rulings by the Treasury Department, in 1938 and 1941, excluded Social Security benefits from the income tax base. At that time, incomes were low enough that even if benefits had been included there would have been little effect on taxes collected. From that time until 1983, several proposals were made to subject benefits to taxation, but nothing was implemented until the Social Security Amendments of 1983.

The Social Security Amendments of 1983 required that taxpayers with incomes above specified levels include up to 50 percent of their Social Security benefits in their adjusted gross income (AGI).The amendments, which followed the recommendations of the National Commission on Social Security Reform, credited the additional revenue raised from benefit taxation to the Social Security Trust Fund (see table 1). The Social Security Amendments of 1983 were in response to a projected shortfall in the Social Security Trust Funds and included other provisions to strengthen the long-term actuarial balance of the funds such as phased-in increases in the payroll tax rate and the retirement age.

Not all taxpayers must include a portion of benefits as income when calculating income taxes. The 1983 amendments set a threshold below which benefits were totally excluded from income. Individuals with incomes below $25,000 and couples with incomes below $32,000 included no benefits when calculating their taxable income. A special definition of income was used to test whether an individual was below the threshold. It included:

1. AGI (without regard to Social Security benefits)
2. Half of Social Security benefits

3. Tax-exempt interest income

The threshold was designed to alleviate the impact of benefit taxation on lower-income families. Although tax-exempt interest is excluded from AGI, it was included in this special income definition so that a family with high total income would not be excluded from benefit taxation if a large fraction of its income was in the form of tax-exempt interest. The 1983 amendments did not index the thresholds for inflation, so as incomes increase over time, a greater fraction of the beneficiaries are over the threshold and must include a portion of their benefits in income for tax purposes. This feature of the amendments was deliberate and was designed to gradually extend the inclusion of benefits in AGI to all beneficiaries. (Not all beneficiaries would pay tax on their benefits, even if they all included benefits in the calculation of AGI, because other aspects of the tax system—the personal exemption and standard deduction, for example—would reduce the taxable income of many beneficiaries to zero.)

The 1983 amendments phased in the taxation of benefits. A family whose income increased from the threshold to one dollar over the threshold did not have to include half of its benefits in AGI. For each dollar a family's income was over the threshold, it was required to include 50 cents of benefits in AGI, up to a maximum of half of its benefits. This phase-in avoided problems of a "notch," but it did increase implicit marginal tax rates for those in the phase-in range. These higher implicit marginal rates reduced the incentives to work and save.

The formula for taxing benefits was changed as part of the Omnibus Budget Reconciliation Act of 1993 (OBRA93). As a result of this act, taxpayers with incomes over a second set of thresholds, $34,000 for individuals and $44,000 for couples, must include up to 85 percent of their benefits. The act had no impact on taxpayers with incomes below these thresholds. Under the 1993 act, taxpayers first calculate the taxable portion of benefits according to the formula established in the 1983 amendments, and then they do a second calculation if their incomes are above the 1993 act's higher thresholds. Like the 1983 amendments, the additional taxation of benefits is phased in. The phase-in rate is 85 percent (as opposed to the 50 percent phase-in under the 1983 amendments) and raises implicit marginal tax rates for those in the new phase-in range.

The 1993 changes in benefit taxation were part of a general effort to reduce the deficit. The increase in the inclusion percentage was justified in part as making the taxable portion of Social Security benefits parallel to private contributory pension plans. The additional revenue from this change was not to be transferred to the Old-Age and Survivors Insurance Trust Fund from which the benefits were paid. Instead, it was dedicated to the Hospital Insurance Trust Fund.

The proper tax treatment of Social Security depends in part on whether Social Security is viewed as a pension program or a tax-transfer program. If benefit payments are unrelated to payroll taxes, then full taxation of benefits would be justified. If, on the other hand, benefit payments are directly related to payroll taxes in the same way that pension benefits are related to pension contributions, then only a portion of the benefits should be subject to tax.

The Social Security program has elements of both a tax-transfer program and a pension program. Benefits are related to payroll taxes, but the benefit formula has a redistributive element. Lower-wage earners get a higher fraction of their wages in benefits than do those with higher wages. This suggests that only a fraction of benefits should be subject to taxation, but the exact percentage would differ among beneficiaries because the benefit formula is not uniform.

The 85 percent inclusion percentage enacted in OBRA93 is based on a hypothetical individual earning at the maximum earnings level over the course of his or her lifetime, retiring around 1993, and earning benefits over an average expected lifetime. For that individual, total payroll taxes paid divided by total benefits paid is approximately 15 percent. Because income taxes were already paid on that 15 percent, only 85 percent of the benefits should be subject to tax.

While the 85 percent inclusion formula approximates the proper tax treatment for a hypothetical case, the current law (as of 1994) rules still under-

state the fraction of benefits that might be included. Most beneficiaries earn below the maximum earnings level and receive benefits that are more than 85/15 of their payroll taxes. (This discussion assumes that the proper tax treatment of Social Security parallels that of private contributory pension plans. However, most private plans are noncontributory or do not tax pension plan contributions—a significant tax preference. If Social Security benefits were treated in the same way, a smaller percentage of benefits would be subject to tax.) Also, the current taxation rules exclude many beneficiaries from taxation at 85 percent since the 85 percent inclusion rate is phased in.

### Additional readings

National Commission on Social Security Reform. *Report of the National Commission on Social Security Reform.* 1983.

Pattison, David. "Taxation of Social Security Benefits under the New Income Tax Provisions: Distributional Estimates for 1994." *Social Security Bulletin* (Summer 1994): 44–50.

Sammartino, Frank J., and Richard Kasten. "The Distributional Consequences of Taxing Social Security Benefits: Current Law and Alternative Schemes." *Journal of Post Keynesian Economics* (Fall 1985): 28–46.

U.S. Congress, House. *Social Security Amendments of 1983: Conference Report.* 98th Cong., 2d sess., 1983.

*Cross references:* payroll tax, federal; Social Security Trust Fund.

# Social Security Trust Fund

Robert Friedland
National Academy on Aging

*Social security is a broad term for a variety of programs intended to soften the financial impact of change in employment status, health, and family status.*

---

Social Security is a national, federally administered program that covers almost all workers. It does not cover about 20 percent of state and local employees and some federal employees hired before 1984. For all others, the program is compulsory, requiring that workers contribute based on earnings and entitling them to a benefit when they retire. While benefits are a statutory right, the provisions of the program—such as payroll contributions or amount of benefits—can be modified, and indeed have been several times in the past six decades.

Social Security's financial structure is based on the principle of employees making contributions and earning, through employment, the right to protection for themselves and their families against the risk of reduced income and economic uncertainty from retirement or the death of a breadwinner. (The other trust funds protect workers and their spouses and children against risks related to disability and costs of health care.) This underlying principle led to the use of payroll taxes as the primary source of financing.

Social Security consists of four trust funds: (1) Old-Age and Survivors Insurance (OASI), (2) Disability Insurance (DI), (3) Hospital Insurance (HI, or Medicare Part A), and (4) Supplementary Medical Insurance (SMI or Medicare Part B). The biggest trust fund, in terms of revenues received, benefits paid, and the number of beneficiaries, is the Old-Age and Survivors Insurance Fund, followed by the Hospital Insurance Trust Fund, the Supplementary Medical Insurance Fund, and the Disability Insurance Fund.

Each of these trust funds and the programs they reflect is quite different. What they share, however, is the political logic for establishing a trust fund. The Social Security Act was passed in 1935. President Roosevelt was adamant that Social Security be financed by workers and that their "contributions" go into a trust fund. This was to underscore the notion of an earned right to benefits and to give workers the sense that their "contributions" were safe. Because contributions paid into the fund were intended to pay current beneficiaries, the political message was not consistent with the financing that would actually take place. However, Roosevelt's political instinct was to ensure that the program would be popular and hence politically secure. In 1965, Medicare was added to the Social Security Act. The political success of OASI was the basis for proposing a similar mechanism for what is now known as Part A of Medicare. The fact that Medicare has two distinct trust funds with very different financing is, in part, a reflection of the nature of the legislative process that combined three distinct proposals into what is now Medicare. Because each Social Security trust fund is so different, this entry focuses primarily on just the federal OASI Trust Fund.

Under the Federal Insurance Contributions Act (FICA), each Social Security-covered worker pays a payroll tax of 5.35 percent of earnings for OASI (retirement and survivor's coverage) and 0.85 percent for DI (disability coverage), up to a maximum. The maximum taxable earnings are indexed for wage growth each year. In 1997, OASI and DI taxable earnings were $65,400. (Employees also pay 1.45 percent for HI—Medicare Part A—with no cap on earnings.) Employers are responsible for paying the same percentage of an employee's payroll as the employee pays. Self-employed workers pay the full 15.3 percent of their payroll for OASI, DI, and HI.

The OASI Trust Fund also receives part of the income taxes paid by higher-income Social Security beneficiaries. Although most benefits are free from income taxes, single individuals with a combined income over $25,000 ($32,000 if married) pay income taxes on up to half of their benefits, and single individuals with combined income over $34,000 ($44,000 if married) pay tax on up to 85 percent of the benefits. Another source of trust fund earnings is interest income. Surplus Social Security funds are invested in special U.S. Treasury securities, which earn interest. Most of the financing is from payroll taxes (89%), followed by interest earnings (9.5%) and taxes on higher-income beneficiaries (1.6%). In 1996, total contributions to OASI were $356.8 billion—$317.2 billion from payroll taxes, $5.8 billion from taxes on benefits, and $34 billion from interest.

## Who receives benefits from OASI?

Social Security benefits are earned by working in covered employment. They are not related to an individual's other income or assets. Beneficiaries must have worked at least 10 years in covered employment to qualify. For persons attaining age 62 in 1991 or after, benefits are calculated based on a worker's highest average indexed earnings over 35 years. Like contributions, credited earnings are subject to a maximum. When calculating benefits, earnings are adjusted for wage growth. Benefit amounts are also adjusted annually based on increases in the Consumer Price Index.

Social Security (OASI) pays benefits when the worker retires (or to survivors when the worker dies). Full benefits are calculated based on retirement at age 65 (increasing to age 67 for workers born after 1959). Retirees can claim benefits at age 62, but those benefits are permanently reduced to reflect the actuarial equivalent of retiring at age 65 (increasing to age 67 by 2027).

In December 1996, approximately 37.8 million retired workers and survivors received OASI benefits (26.9 million retired workers, 2.3 million children, and 8.6 million other adults). Total benefit payments were $308 billion. The average monthly benefit at the end of 1995 was $720 for a retired worker and $700 for all OASI beneficiaries. The benefit structure is designed to pay higher benefits to higher earners; however, the *proportion* of earnings replaced after retirement is higher for lower-paid workers. For example, if a worker always had earnings equal to the U.S. average, he could expect to receive a benefit of about 43 percent of pay. If he always had the maximum amount of taxable earnings, he could expect a benefit of about 24 percent of that maximum. These benefit calculations are complicated by Social Security's auxiliary family benefits—for example, spousal retirement and survivor benefits—which are offered at no additional cost to the worker.

## Social Security's achievements

Social Security is a major source of income for the elderly, providing 36 percent of total incomes and raising the elderly to an income standard roughly equivalent to the rest of the population. Nonetheless, it was never intended to be the only source of income in retirement. Because the program is not means-tested, workers and employers can plan private pension and personal savings strategies around Social Security benefits. The popularity of Social Security (supported by more than 80% of the population for more than 50 years) stems from the underlying concept of an earned right to benefits, as well as its record of enhancing dignity and stabilizing families. Social Security allows the elderly to live independently for more time.

## Adequacy versus individual equity

Social Security attempts to balance two goals: adequacy and individual equity. Adequacy means making sure benefits are sufficient to meet the basic needs of the people the program is designed to protect. This goal is balanced against individual equity—that is, making sure that the amount people pay into the system is directly related to what they receive in return.

The Social Security benefit structure is a compromise between these two goals. It attempts to achieve adequacy by having inflation adjustments and a weighted formula that provides proportionately larger benefits to workers with lower incomes and workers with families, and by paying auxiliary benefits (such as spousal benefits) to certain family members. It attempts to achieve individual equity by having benefits that are related to earnings, where higher wages, and therefore higher payroll tax contributions, lead to higher benefits. While there is a minimum adequate benefit for lower earners, everyone in the system is protected against economic risks, and everyone pays for that protection.

## How OASI differs from private pensions

Both Social Security retirement and private pensions operate on the principle of pooled risk—that is, workers collectively provide for subsequent benefits. However, Social Security has several unique features not found in most pension plans:

—Social Security participation is compulsory, covering almost all workers. (Private and other public pensions cover 56% of the civilian, nonagricultural work force.)
—Social Security benefits have a cost-of-living adjustment.
—Survivor benefits are paid to each child.
—Social Security does not require long-term employment in one place and allows workers to move from job to job.
—Social Security benefits are taxed somewhat less than other pension benefits.

Although most Americans can expect to retire, many do not save adequately. Therefore, Social Security attempts to protect the larger group from decisions made by those who inadequately prepare for retirement and who would have to rely on other public resources when they are no longer able to work.

## Trust fund outlook

Since the changes of 1983, Social Security has operated on a "partially prefunded" basis, meaning future benefits are anticipated and partially funded in advance. Alternatively, Social Security could be funded on a "pay-as-you-go" basis, where taxes and benefits are adjusted so that there is no reserve accumulation. (Only a contingency reserve would be needed to maintain liquidity.) This was essentially the structure from the mid-1950s to the mid-1970s.

Contributions now flowing into the trust fund exceed benefits paid out and are projected to continue to do so until about 2012. Trust fund assets are then projected to decline, and to be depleted by 2031. The trust fund's ability to meet payment obligations is referred to as the trust fund ratio. The trust fund ratio reflects the percentage of a particular year's outgo that the fund is capable of paying with assets available at that year's beginning. This is displayed in figure 1, which contains three ratio projections—low cost, high cost, and intermediate cost—where high cost reflects the most pessimistic economic and demographic assumptions.

Table 1 displays a 90-year overview of OASI's historical and projected income, outgo, beneficiaries, and outgo as a percent of gross domestic product. In 1995, 141 million people worked in Social Security–covered employment.

## Retirement of the baby boomers

Changes in demographics resulting from the retirement of the "baby boom" generation have received a lot of attention. What does the retirement of the baby boomers mean for Social Security? When the baby boomers retire (from about 2010 to 2030), their Social Security benefits will be supported by a relatively smaller taxpaying work force. By having a prefunded surplus, the Social Security system shifts

## FIGURE 1

### Estimated Trust Fund Ratios for OASI

*(Assets as a % of annual expenditures)*

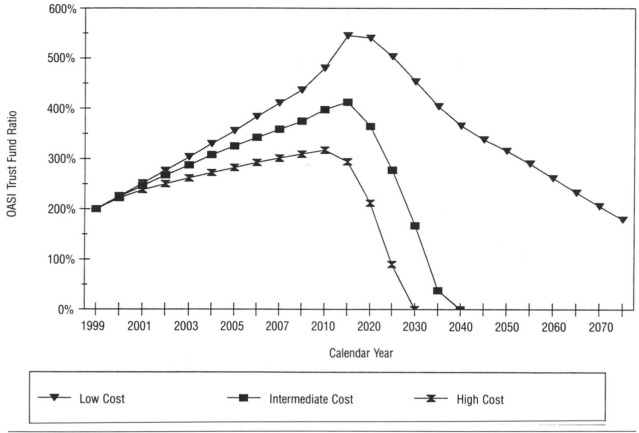

*Source: 1999 Annual Report of the Board of Trustees of the Federal Old-Age and Survivors Insurance and Disability Insurance Trust Funds*, table II.F20.

## TABLE 1

### OASI Operations, 1960–2050

| Calendar Year | Income ($ billions)* | Beneficiaries (in thousands) | Outgo ($ billions) | Outgo as a Percent of GDP |
|---|---|---|---|---|
| 1960 | 9.8 | 13,740 | 11.1 | 2.16 |
| 1970 | 29.9 | 22,618 | 27.3 | 2.70 |
| 1980 | 98.2 | 30,385 | 103.2 | 3.81 |
| 1990 | 264.5 | 35,266 | 223.5 | 4.02 |
| 2000** | 397.2 | 38,984 | 372.2 | 4.00 |
| 2010** | 664.1 | 45,237 | 629.4 | 4.04 |
| 2020** | 1,067.2 | 58,603 | 1,235.6 | 4.92 |
| 2030** | 1,684.7 | 70,531 | 2,256.7 | 5.76 |
| 2040** | 2,673.1 | 74,529 | 3,641.2 | 5.74 |
| 2050** | 4,193.1 | 76,745 | 5,697.8 | 5.59 |

*Income consists of tax revenues only; it does not include interest.
**Projected, intermediate estimate based on data in 1997 Trustees Report.

some of the retirement burden from future workers to the baby boom group itself. Analysts have shown that baby boomers as a group will pay in taxes about what they receive back in benefits, adjusted for inflation, plus a real rate of return of 2 percent. (Lower-wage workers and workers with families will get back more, higher-paid workers and single workers less.) When today's younger workers retire, Social Security will have a lower rate of return than for previous retirees. However, overall, it will have a positive return.

Building up Social Security surpluses has the potential to add to national saving and a buildup in capital stock. This could increase worker productivity and allow the economy to support a growing number of retirees; however, other government borrowing—resulting from large budget deficits *outside* of Social Security—undermines this goal.

The outlook for the retirement of the baby boomers and future workers in general (not just for Social Security) depends on several factors. If the economy grows, this larger "economic pie" can support increased retirees' consumption and a higher standard of living for future workers. How can this growth be achieved? Economic growth depends on increased productive capacity—that is, growth in capital stock through increased saving, investment in plant and equipment, new technology, and infrastructure, and growth in labor through increased productivity and a growing labor force (the latter, for example, through later retirement, longer work hours, or increased immigration).

*Cross references:* Medicare trust fund; payroll tax, federal.

# Source principle

Joseph J. Cordes
George Washington University

*A basis for assigning tax liabilities to individuals and businesses who are located in one jurisdiction, while earning income in another.*

Taxation at the source, rather than on the basis of residence, means that the amount that a taxpayer pays in taxes depends on where the income is earned rather than on where the taxpayer resides. Consider the case of a multinational company with headquarters in the United States that earns income from an affiliate located in another country. Income taxation at the source means that the company would be required to report and pay taxes on the income to

the foreign country. Typically, in order to prevent the income from being taxed twice, the company would then be allowed to claim a credit, based on taxes paid to the foreign government, against taxes owed to the United States on the foreign-source income.

There is broad agreement among tax scholars that jurisdictions have the right to tax income and production that occurs within their boundaries. But, in order to avoid double-taxation of individuals and businesses who are located in one jurisdiction and earn income in another, the taxpayer's home jurisdiction needs to forgo taxing the income of residents that is earned elsewhere. Administratively, this is usually accomplished, as in the example above, by allowing residents who are taxed at the source to take a credit for taxes paid to other jurisdictions against taxes they would otherwise owe to their home jurisdiction.

In the United States, the issue of whether to tax income at the source or on the basis of residence comes up in many metropolitan areas because people live in the suburbs but work in the city.

Commuter taxes are an example of attempts to tax people living in urban areas at the source.

*Cross references:* commuter taxes; multinational corporations, taxation; residence principle.

# Standard deduction, federal

Joseph J. Cordes
George Washington University

*The fixed amount of money that taxpayers who do not itemize deductions can deduct from federal adjustable gross income, based on the taxpayer's filing status.*

In arriving at taxable income, taxpayers who do not itemize deductions are allowed to subtract a fixed sum, which varies with their filing status, from adjusted gross income. In 1997, the standard deduction for non-aged, nonblind taxpayers equaled $4,150 for single filers, $6,900 for a married couple filing jointly, and $6,050 for a head of household. Taxpayers who are 65 or older and/or blind were allowed to take larger standard deductions, ranging from $5,150 for a single filer who is either blind or aged to $10,100 for a married couple who file jointly and who are both aged and blind. Along with personal exemptions, the standard deduction has been indexed for inflation, beginning first in 1985–86, and then starting again in 1990. Together with the personal exemption, the standard deduction defines a threshold level of income below which no tax is due (see Personal exemption, federal). In addition, the more generous the amount of the standard deduction, the fewer the number of taxpayers who will itemize deductions. Historically, between six and seven out of 10 taxpayers have claimed the standard deduction instead of itemizing deductions on their federal tax returns.

*Cross references:* adjusted gross income; income tax, federal; inflation indexation of income taxes; personal exemption, federal.

# Subchapter S corporation

George A. Plesko
Northeastern University

*An incorporated business that, having met certain eligibility requirements and made an effective federal tax election, is generally not subject to the federal corporate-level income tax.*

The income (and losses) of a Subchapter S corporation flow through to shareholders as they are realized by the entity, much like a partnership rather than a corporation. As a general principle, actual distributions of dividends to shareholders are received free of tax up to the basis of each shareholder in his or her shares. These corporations continue to share all other attributes of incorporated entities (e.g., separate legal entity, limited liability, unlimited life).

For tax purposes there are four forms of business organizations: C corporations (all other than S), S corporations, partnerships, and proprietorships. The choice may have important tax consequences.

Subchapter S of the Internal Revenue Code (§ 1361 through § 1379), for and by which these corporations are named and governed, was enacted in 1958 and substantially revised in 1982 and 1996. The basic eligibility requirements to be met by a Subchapter S corporation are: (1) that it be a U.S. corporation with no more than 75 shareholders, with married couples counting as a single shareholder, (2) that only individuals may be shareholders, with the exception of some estates and trusts, (3) that it may not have a nonresident alien as a shareholder, (4) that it may have only one class of stock, and (5) that it may not be a bank, an insurance company, or a member of an affiliated group, or any of certain other types of corporations. Individual states set their own rules for the state income

tax treatment of S corporations, which range from full conformability to federal rules to the nonrecognition of S corporations, which subjects all of the entity's income to the state corporate income tax.

An S election requires the unanimous consent of shareholders. Unlike C corporations, S corporations must generally use a calendar year tax year, but may choose either the cash or the accrual method of accounting. Unlike C corporation shareholders, an S corporation employee who owns more than 2 percent of the corporation's stock will face partnership treatment of fringe benefits.

Additional taxes may apply to C corporations converting to S corporations. A C corporation that used the last in, first out (LIFO) in its inventory accounting will have to pay a recapture tax. If the corporation has carryovers of net operating losses or tax credits, they cannot be used by the S corporation. An S corporation that formerly was a C corporation may also be taxed on its passive income (e.g., interest, dividends, rents, and royalties) if it has Subchapter C earnings and profits at the time of conversion. A final issue in the conversion decision is the "built-in gains" tax of IRC § 1374, enacted in 1986. This provision requires an S corporation to pay a corporate-level tax on any pre-conversion Subchapter C "built-in" gains if they are realized within 10 years of the conversion. (Conversions that took place before 1987 remain subject to an earlier form of the rule that contained a three-year recognition period.)

While an S corporation can voluntarily revoke its status at any time, care must be exercised to ensure that S treatment is not involuntarily terminated. Involuntary termination can take place if the corporation fails to continuously meet the eligibility requirements listed above. A voluntary revocation during the first two and one-half months of a tax year is effective for that year; otherwise it will take effect at the beginning of the next taxable year. A termination becomes effective on the date the firm violates any of the eligibility requirements. A firm that either revokes or terminates its S status cannot elect to become an S corporation again for five years (although relief can be granted for accidental termination). This prohibits firms from making frequent changes to take advantage of the differing tax treatments accorded S and C corporations.

Subchapter S is an attractive option for startup firms that are able to meet the eligibility requirements. In the early years of operation, when firms are likely to have negative income, the losses would flow through to shareholders and be deducted against their individual income. Losses passed through to shareholders are deductible up to each individual's basis in the corporation's stock and debt. Losses in excess of basis can be carried forward to offset future Subchapter S income. The S corporation's income is taxable to the individual shareholder as it is received or accrued, regardless of whether the income is distributed (as in a partnership). The amount of income recognized by each shareholder increases his or her basis in the corporation. This basis affects the amount of distributions receivable tax-free. Unlike a partnership, all gains and losses must be allocated pro rata to each share.

For closely held corporations, S and C status can be used as part of a tax-minimizing strategy. In the case of loss corporations, S is preferred because the losses can be immediately deducted at the individual level. For profitable corporations, election of S status would eliminate the corporate-level tax. However, in some cases (particularly before the Tax Reform Act of 1986), an S election may subject the income to an individual tax rate that is higher than the corporate rate. In 1986, the maximum tax rates were 46 percent for corporations and 50 percent for individuals (as recently as 1981 individual tax rates were 70%). When shareholder rates are higher than the corporate rate, a strategy of paying the corporate tax as a C corporation and not distributing income to shareholders may result in less tax being paid in the current year, and a deferral of the individual tax. If capital gains are more favorably taxed than ordinary income, the deferral of income also benefits from lower tax rates if it is ultimately recognized through a sale of the stock in the corporation. There are various strategies to remove income from the taxable corporate sector without paying two levels of tax. Because these are closely held corporations, managers and employees of the firm may also be shareholders. Thus, payments of wages and salaries, deductible at the corporate level, will be taxed only once when received by individuals (and not at all in the case of some benefits). In addition, subject to some constraints, the corporation could reduce its exposure to the corporate tax by borrowing from its shareholders because interest payments (and rents and royalties) are deductible at the corporate level (Plesko 1994).

After the Tax Reform Act of 1986, the maximum individual and corporate marginal tax rates were reduced, with the maximum corporate rate (34%) being higher than that for individuals (28%). This had the effect of making C corporations less attractive as a means of minimizing taxes. Since 1986, the use of S corporations has expanded dramatically, even though in 1993 the maximum individual federal income tax rates were raised above the maximum corporate rate. An S election eliminates one of the two taxes, amounting to integration of the corporate and shareholder taxes by election.

S corporations grew from 6.2 percent of corporate returns in 1960 to 20.1 percent in 1980 to 24.1 percent in 1986. The number of S corporations increased to 1,575,092 of the 3,716,650 corporate returns filed in 1990 (42.4%). Accompanying the growth in the number of S corporations is their share of corporate economic activity. Before 1986, S corporations were responsible for less than 6 percent of business receipts, increasing to 10.1 percent in 1987. In 1990, S corporations were responsible for 14.2 percent of total receipts. Despite these increases in returns, S corporations remain a small proportion of corporate assets: In 1990, 4.1 percent of corporate assets were in S corporations. Petska and Wilson (1994) provide information on trends in business organizations during the 1980s.

While 35 was, until the 1996 legislation, the maximum number of shareholders allowed under federal law, the constraint seemed to affect only a small percentage of firms; the typical firm had fewer than three shareholders and more than 90 percent of firms had 10 or fewer (Nelson 1992; Plesko 1994). In 1990, the average S corporation had $472,550 in assets, compared to an average of approximately $8.1 million for non-S corporations. Thirty-two percent of S corporations are in services, 26.7 percent in trade. The smallest number of S corporations are in mining (1 percent of the total), agriculture (3.5 percent), and transportation and utilities (4.1 percent) (Internal Revenue Service 1993). Nelson (1993) and Plesko (1995) provide data on the characteristics of business corporations after the Tax Reform Act of 1986.

Limited liability corporations (LLCs) and limited liability partnerships (LLPs) have become popular alternatives to S corporations. Recognized in nearly all 50 states, these entities offer the same benefits of limited liability and pass-through tax treatment as S corporations, but have fewer operational restrictions. For example, LLCs have no limits on the number of shareholders of classes of stocks.

## Additional readings

Internal Revenue Service. *Corporation Income Tax Returns*, Publication 16. Washington, D.C.: U.S. Government Printing Office, various years.

McNulty, J.K. *Federal Income Taxation of S Corporations.* Westbury, N.Y.: Foundation Press, 1992.

Nelson, Susan C. "S Corporations since the Tax Reform Act of 1986." *Proceedings of the Eighty-Fourth Annual Conference, Williamsburg, 1991.* Columbus, Ohio: NTA-TIA, 1992, pp. 18–24.

Nelson, Susan C. "S Corporations: The Record of Growth after Tax Reform." *Journal of S Corporation Taxation* 5 (Fall 1993): 138-61.

Petska, T.B., and R.A. Wilson. "Trends in Business Structure and Activity, 1980–1990." *SOI Bulletin* 13 (Spring 1994): 27–72.

Plesko, George A. "Corporate Taxation and the Financial Characteristics of Firms." *Public Finance Quarterly* (July 1994): 311–34.

Plesko, George A. "Gimme Shelter? Closely Held Corporations since Tax Reform." *National Tax Journal* 48 (September 1995): 409–16.

*Cross references:* dividends, double taxation of; income tax, corporate, federal; income tax, federal; partnerships.

# Sumptuary taxes

Bruce F. Davie
Department of the Treasury

*Excise taxes intended to discourage the consumption of specific commodities or services.*

The term sumptuary taxation has gone out of fashion. An earlier generation of writers used the term to categorize taxes imposed for moral or religious reasons. Contemporary economists would describe a tax intended to discourage consumption of a specific commodity as adjusting for a negative externality. Politicians and journalists might use the term "sin taxes."

Excise taxes have been and are widely used by governments to discourage consumption of specific commodities; taxes on alcoholic beverages and tobacco products are the obvious examples. Using the old-fashioned term "sumptuary tax" helps to clarify thinking about excise taxes of this sort. The need for clarity is illustrated by the literature regarding cigarette taxes and smoking. Those who view tobacco taxes as instruments for adjusting for externalities are interested in measuring the negative externalities and reaching a conclusion with respect to whether the tax, as a policy instrument for increasing the price by an amount that corresponds to the measured externalities, is too high, too low, or about right. Those who view cigarette taxes from a sumptuary stance argue for taxes above the externality-adjusting level because they regard protection of every individual's health a public policy obligation. In this view, it is a moral imperative to reduce consumption below what would occur when consumers are fully aware of the risks of smoking and cigarette prices include measured externalities.

Both advocates of externality-adjusting excise taxes and advocates of sumptuary taxes would agree that the revenue generated by the tax is not a primary objective. Similarly, they would agree that the distribution of either tax among taxpayers classified by income or consumption levels is largely irrelevant. For both, the object of the tax is to get the gross-of-tax price "right."

Sumptuary taxes set at "too high" a level verge upon prohibition through the tax system rather than by regulation. Because the social costs of prohibition can be significant—for example, the costs of controlling smuggling and illicit domestic production and distribution—a sumptuary tax rate that is in some sense optimal is not a rate that minimizes consumption. Clearly, sumptuary taxation involves issues that go well beyond traditional tax analysis.

The United States has a long history of sumptuary taxation of alcoholic beverages and tobacco products mixed with revenue-raising objectives. The first domestic tax enacted by the United States, in 1791, was on distilled spirits at rates ranging from 7 to 18 cents per gallon, depending on the alcohol content, or proof, of the liquor, and imposed on the distiller. The first secretary of the treasury, Alexander Hamilton, sought a revenue source not dependent on foreign trade. Sumptuary motives were also involved. As Hamilton put it, "The consumption of ardent spirits particularly, no doubt very much on account of their cheapness, is carried on to an extreme, which is truely to be regretted, as well in regard to the health and morals, as to the economy of the community (quoted in Forsythe 1977: 40). The tax was resisted in western Pennsylvania and other areas where whiskey was used as a medium of exchange. In 1794, troops had to be called out to put down the "Whiskey Rebellion." The military operation was successful in establishing the power of the new government to collect taxes, but the tax continued to be unpopular. Soon after the Jeffersonians took power, the whiskey tax was repealed. It was reenacted briefly during the War of 1812 and then not again until the Civil War, primarily as a revenue-raising measure. At the time, only a few members of Congress argued for the tax on sumptuary grounds. During the 1860s taxes were also imposed on beer, tobacco products, and wine, but again, sumptuary objectives were secondary to revenue. Taxes on alcoholic beverages and tobacco products have been part of the federal taxes ever since the Civil War. The sumptuary character of these taxes, and of similar state and local taxes, seems to form a substantial part of their continuing public acceptance.

The 10 percent tax on wagers on sporting events, elections, and contests enacted in 1951 might be regarded as a sumptuary tax. Its intent was to aid law enforcement efforts aimed at illegal bookmaking. The rate was reduced to 2 percent in 1974 and, in the case of legal wagers such as sports betting in Nevada, to 0.25 percent in 1982. Exemptions are provided for state lotteries, and state-sanctioned horse races and similar events. Given the low rate on legal wagers and the broad exemptions, the tax on wagers seems to have a role only in enforcement of laws against illegal bookmaking and thus is not truly sumptuary in nature.

Sumptuary taxes present special administrative problems because they are typically high relative to the value of the product, increasing the payoff to successful tax evasion. The enforcement problem is further complicated by the typical rules allowing the product to be exported or used for a purpose other than human consumption on a tax-free basis. For these reasons, sumptuary taxes involve systems of inspection and control not typical of other excise taxes.

Structuring a tax to accomplish a sumptuary objective also presents difficulties. Instead of an *ad valorem* tax, taxes on liquor and tobacco are usually *in rem* taxes based on volume and weight, respectively. For example, the U.S. tax on distilled spirits applicable in 1997 was $13.50 per proof gallon; wine was taxed at rates ranging from $1.07 to $3.15 per gallon, depending on alcohol content, with wines having an alcohol content of more than 24 percent taxed like distilled spirits; and beer was taxed at a rate of $18 per 31-gallon barrel. In terms of alcohol content, the distilled spirits tax results in a tax of about 21 cents per ounce, the beer tax about 10 cents per ounce, and the wine tax about 8 cents per ounce. These differences seem to reflect political judgments about the relative degree to which sumptuary taxes should be imposed on different classes of alcoholic beverages. Because these taxes are not structured solely on alcohol content, definitional problems continually emerge as new products come on the market. Inflation has the effect of eroding the real value of *in rem* taxes. Despite ad hoc increases in tax rates on alcohol and tobacco, in real terms U.S. rates were generally lower in 1997 than in 1951.

## Additional readings

Congressional Budget Office. *Federal Taxation of Tobacco, Alcoholic Beverages, and Motor Fuels*. Washington, D.C., June 1990.

Cook, Phillip J., and Michael Moore. "This Tax's for You: The Case for Higher Beer Taxes." *National Tax Journal* 47 (3) (September 1994): 559–74.

Forsythe, Dall W. *Taxation and Political Change in the Young Nation, 1781–1833*. New York: Columbia University Press, 1977.

Gravelle, Jane, and Dennis Zimmerman. "Cigarette Taxes to Fund Health Care Reform." *National Tax Journal* 47 (3) (September 1994): 575–90.

Smith, Harry Edwin. *The United States Federal Internal Tax History from 1861 to 1871*. Boston: Houghton Mifflin, 1914.

Viscusi, W. Kip. *Smoking: Making the Risky Decision*. New York: Oxford University Press, 1992.

*Cross references:* excess burden; luxury taxes; retail sales tax; severance tax, state; tobacco taxes.

# T

# Tax abatement programs

Dick Netzer
Urban Research Center

*Most states and many local governments offer some type of business tax reduction to selectively promote an economic activity. These incentives come in various forms, such as income tax credits, sales tax exemptions or rate reductions, and, most commonly, full or partial forgiveness of the local property tax for some period of years on real estate that is being rehabilitated or developed. The efficiency benefits of such abatements are the topic of considerable debate and empirical examination.*

Tax incentives to foster the types of economic behavior preferred by legislative bodies take on a variety of forms and names—exemptions, deductions, credits, and abatements. The last ordinarily refer to time-limited reductions, possibly to zero, in the *increase* in tax liability that would otherwise be triggered by the economic action that is to be encouraged. However, state and local government policymakers are not rigid in their nomenclature, and the term "abatement" is frequently used to describe tax incentive programs that are called by other names in most places. Moreover, time-limited reductions in tax liability may be made permanent by changes in the law, or by repeated extensions of the original time period.

The great majority of the states have programs for the abatement of some state or local taxes. Usually, but not invariably, it is local government—rather than state government—taxes that are abated, and for the most part, the programs concern local property taxes. The typical form of the abatement—say, to encourage new office building construction in an older central business district—is the following: The assessed value of the land underlying the new building is frozen at its level at the time the abatement is requested (the almost universal undervaluation of sites by American local assessors ensures that this value will be a low one) for a specified number of years, and the taxes on the new building are abated at a declining rate over that period. At the end of the period, the property becomes fully taxpaying.

Some programs are highly automatic, or "as-of-right." Once an official agency determines that the action of the taxpayer (construction of a new building or purchase of equipment ordinarily subject to the state sales tax, for example) qualifies, both the amount of the tax reductions and their timing are set, with no administrative discretion. Other programs involve considerable negotiation about the specific expenditures that are eligible, the size of the tax reduction, and even the schedule. In some cases, a state government agency must approve local government actions. "As-of-right" provisions tend to be more common for programs designed to encourage housing investment than for those concerned with business investment decisions, and more common for investments located in specific places, such as old industrial sections of large cities, that are the objects of local economic development policy (see Enterprise zones).

Informal tax abatement by local assessors—by simply neglecting to list new buildings on the tax rolls for a year or two, or more—is as old as the American property tax. Indeed, that, along with systematic undervaluation, was the predominant instrument of economic development policy in smaller cities and towns for many decades. The first major formal tax abatement programs appear to have developed in New York state in the 1920s, to encourage the construction of new housing. One program, confined to New York City, provided for an abatement schedule that began at 100 percent for new owner-occupied housing; another was the first in a long series of tax abatement programs for new construction and major rehabilitation of multifamily housing.

More than 30 states authorize property tax abatements for new business investment, in most cases focusing on the manufacturing industry (National Association of State Development Agencies 1991). Smaller numbers authorize abatements for investment in specified types of housing—in either residential or nonresidential urban renewal areas—and in the preservation of historic properties. A few abate sales tax on purchases of specific types of business equipment or other intermediate business purchases. Also, there are numerous abatements specific to a single industry, like shipbuilding or railroads (in New York State, the abatement is termed an "exemption," but the size of the exemption is inversely related to the railroad's net operating income, and it changes each year).

In most places, the revenue losses associated with tax abatements are quite small relative to total tax revenue (the costs are usually estimated on the assumption that economic behavior is unaffected by the tax incentive, which, of course, is not the intent of the program (see Tax expenditures). For example, revenue losses in the state of Washington from time-limited economic development property tax abatements in the 1991–1993 biennium were estimated at less than 0.05 percent of total property tax levies (Washington State Department of Revenue, January 1992, and March 1992). At the other extreme, time-limited property tax abatements in New York City were valued at roughly 7.1 percent of the total tax levy; three-fourths of the abatements were for housing and the rest for commercial and industrial property (New York City Department of Finance 1993). Economists generally have been skeptical about the efficacy of tax abatement programs in achieving policy goals. For housing tax abatements, the goal is the expansion in the supply of housing services, that being a final, rather than intermediate, product. For tax abatements designed to promote local economic development, the intermediate product is an increase in business investment in a community and the final product an increase in local employment, income, and—ultimately—tax revenue. The key empirical questions are: (1) the extent to which the tax abatements are captured by investments and other economic actions that are truly induced by the program, rather than actions that would have occurred in its absence; (2) whether, in the case of economic development incentives, there really are those final products in the form of increased income; and (3) whether the tax-favored investments impose large external costs, such as new infrastructure requirements, within the local jurisdiction.

The most important question is the first one; the answer largely determines both the benefits and costs of a tax abatement program. Most of the program costs are likely to consist of the taxes forgone on the investment that would have occurred in any case; the taxes forgone on the induced investment are not costs in any economic sense.

The empirical evidence is sketchy (Wolkoff 1985; Netzer 1991; Wassmer 1992; Coffman 1993). This is not surprising, in view of the difficulty of specifying the independent policy variable for use in multivariate analysis across taxing jurisdictions and finding enough observations. It is hard enough to estimate the locational effects of differentials and changes in the level and nature of general state–local taxes (see Business location, taxation and), but a typical state tax policy regression study will use straightforward tax policy variables like effective rates of the major taxes, top marginal rates, and measures of the total tax burden and can rely on the fact that the major taxes apply more or less uniformly to a vast number of firms. In contrast, with regard to economic development tax abatements, there is considerable interstate variation in the spe-

cific provisions of similar-sounding measures, and rates of participation in similar programs differ greatly over time and place, with resulting variation in the composition of those firms that do participate.

In rare instances, such as projects that are in the form of real estate developments, separately incorporated with sale of the equity interest fairly soon after the physical investment has been put in place, rates of return with and without the tax abatement subsidy can be calculated, yielding reliable conclusions about the causal role of the subsidy (White 1983).

Another approach has been used in some studies: calculating the break-even point—that is, the proportion of the increase in investment or employment experienced (or promised) by the firms receiving the subsidy that must be induced by the subsidy if the benefits are to equal the costs of the subsidy. If the break-even point is very low, then it really is not important to worry about the other causes for the new investment; if the break-even point is very high, then the assumption must be that the program will not be cost effective.

One consideration in measuring cost-effectiveness of tax abatement policy is the level of government from whose perspective the analysis is performed. In one study, the break-even point for the local government was an encouraging 8.8 percent, but that included substantial increases in state school aid to offset the local tax losses. When that possibility was excluded, the break-even point rose to a very discouraging 41.7 percent (Morse and Farmer 1986).

In general, the empirical analyses of tax abatement programs for economic development purposes show negative results: most of the tax abatements do accrue to investments that would have been made in the absence of the tax incentives. The empirical evidence on housing tax abatements is more ambiguous, and there do seem to be strong effects on the timing of housing investments for those programs that are expected to be temporary.

There is, nonetheless, an economic logic to property tax abatements for new investment: Local property taxes at a given rate will have a far stronger negative effect on new investment than on old investment. This is a point of special importance for those jurisdictions that habitually impose differentially high effective tax rates on investment in new commercial and multifamily residential structures, a practice that continues to exist in a number of states.

## Additional readings

Coffman, Richard B. "Tax Abatements and Rent-Seeking." *Urban Studies* 30 (April 1993): 593–98.

Durchslag, Melvyn R. "Property Tax Abatement for Low-Income Housing: An Idea Whose Time May Never

Arrive." *Harvard Journal on Legislation* 30 (Summer 1993): 367–82.

McDonald, J. F. "An Economic Analysis of Local Inducements for Business." *Journal of Urban Economics* 13 (November 1983): 322–33.

Menezes, Marco, and Lawrence W. Morgan. "P.A. 198: Michigan's Industrial Property Tax Abatement Law: Fortuity or Futility?" *Cooley Law Review* 7 (1990): 139–77.

Morgan, W.E., and M.M. Hackbart. "An Analysis of State and Local Industrial Tax Exemption Programs." *Southern Economic Journal* 41 (October 1974): 200–05.

Morse, G.W., and M.C. Farmer. "Location and Investment Effects of a Tax Abatement Program." *National Tax Journal* 39 (June 1986): 229–36.

National Association of State Development Agencies. *Directory of Incentives for Business Investment and Development in the United States.* 3rd ed. Washington, D.C.: The Urban Institute Press, 1991.

Netzer, Dick. "An Evaluation of Interjurisdictional Competition through Economic Development Incentives." In *Competition among States and Local Governments,* edited by Daphne A. Kenyon and John Kincaid. Washington, D.C.: The Urban Institute Press, 1991.

New York City Department of Finance. *Annual Report on Tax Expenditures, Fiscal Year 1993.* November 1993.

Reese, Laura A. "Municipal Fiscal Health and Tax Abatement Policy." *Economic Development Quarterly* 5 (February 1991): 23–32.

Washington State Department of Revenue. *Tax Exemptions—1992.* Olympia, January 1992.

Washington State Department of Revenue. *Tax Statistics 1991.* Olympia, March 1992.

Wassmer, Robert W. "Property Tax Abatement and the Simultaneous Determination of Local Fiscal Variables in a Metropolitan Area." *Land Economics* 68 (August 1992): 263–82.

White, Michelle J. "J51: Incentive, Subsidy, or Windfall?" *New York Affairs* 7 (4) (Winter/Spring 1983): 112–25.

Wolkoff, Michael J. "Chasing a Dream: The Use of Tax Abatements to Spur Urban Economic Development." *Urban Studies* 22 (August 1985): 305–15.

Zoeckler, Robert L. "The Tax Abatement Program for Historic Properties in Georgia." *Georgia State Bar Journal* 28 (February 1992): 129–33.

*Cross references:* business location, taxation and; enterprise zones.

# Taxable income, corporate
Michael McDonald
Ernst & Young

*The computed base of gross income less allowable deductions on which the federal (and state, for states that "conform" to federal statute) income tax rates are applied.*

---

Corporations have been subject to income tax since 1913. Although the tax code has changed extensively in the past 80 years, the "classical" system of separate, and substantially unintegrated, individual and corporate income taxes has remained unchanged. This entry describes the tax-based measure of corporate profits, corporate taxable income. It defines the base of the corporate income tax, identifies its components, compares this profits measure to similar measures in financial accounting and national income accounts, and discusses recent historical trends.

Since 1987, corporations have calculated two separate measures of taxable income—"regular" taxable income, and taxable income under the corporate alternative minimum tax (AMT). This entry describes regular taxable income.

## Determining taxable income

To determine taxable income, corporations use Form 1120, the Corporation Income Tax Return. Income and deduction items are reported separately, and many items require supporting forms and schedules. A description of the components of taxable income follows the tax form.

### Income

The corporate tax classifies income into two broad categories: ordinary income and capital gains. Ordinary income includes gross sales less cost of goods sold, dividends, interest (except interest on certain municipal bonds), rents, and royalties. Most corporations must use accrual accounting for tax purposes, and therefore recognize income when it is earned. To calculate cost of goods sold, corporations have some flexibility to choose the valuation of end-of-year inventory (at historical cost, market value, or the lower of cost or market value), and the assumed flow of cost—last in, first out (LIFO), first in, first out (FIFO), or specific identification—to minimize tax liability.

Corporate capital gains are taxed when they are realized, not as they accrue. This is similar to the treatment of capital gains under the individual tax. Also similar to individual tax treatment, capital gains may be netted against capital losses. Unlike the individual tax, however, capital losses cannot offset ordinary income. Finally, and unlike the individual tax, corporate capital gains do not enjoy a preferential tax rate. (Before 1987, corporate capital gains were taxed at a lower rate than ordinary income. For example, in 1986, capital gains faced a maximum rate of 28%, considerably lower than the 46% top rate on ordinary income.)

### Deductions

Corporations are allowed deductions for the ordinary and necessary costs of doing business. The major components of these costs are salaries and wages, pension contributions and other employee benefit costs, interest expenses, state and local taxes, rents, charitable contributions, bad debt losses, advertising expenses, tangible capital asset depreciation, and intangible asset amortization. For all but the last two deductions, corporations generally deduct these costs in the year the liability is incurred, as required under accrual accounting. When corporations purchase tangible capital assets (i.e., investment in plants, equipment, or structures), they are not allowed to deduct the full cost in the year of acquisition. Instead, they use a permitted depreciation method (usually more accelerated than straight-line) over each asset's determined cost-recovery period to calculate the deduction. Corporations may generally amortize intangible assets, including goodwill, over 15 years.

### Total income less total deductions

If total deductions exceed total income, then a corporation has *negative net income*, or a loss. This has two implications. First, the corporation has no taxable income for the year. Second, the corporation may carry back the loss to offset any net income earned over the previous three years, and receive a refund. If the corporation is unable to offset the entire loss by this carryback, it may carry the remaining loss forward for up to 15 years to offset future net income. Corporations offset this future income with the "net operating loss deduction."

If total income exceeds total deductions, then a corporation has *positive net income* and may take two additional deductions, called the special statutory deductions, to derive its taxable income. The first deduction is the intercorporate dividends-received deduction (DRD). The DRD is 70 percent for "portfolio stock" (stock for which the corporation owns less than 20%), 100 percent for wholly owned subsidiaries, and 80 percent for most other stock. The DRD is designed to limit the tax burden on corporate income. If corporations pay tax on income received from other corporations, that income would be taxed more than once at the corporate level. A 100 percent intercorporate DRD helps ensure that income is taxed only once at the corporate level.

The second deduction is the net operating loss deduction. Corporations may offset income with unused (i.e., carried forward) losses from previous years. The income remaining after a corporation takes this deduction is its taxable income.

## Corporate taxable income versus other profit measures

Corporate taxable income described above is a measure of profits consistent with corporate tax law. There are two other popular measures of corporate profits that are in certain ways conceptually different from taxable income. These are "pre-tax book income," used in financial statements, and "corporate profits," used in the National Income and Product Accounts (NIPA). Each of these concepts seeks to measure "economic" income (from the standpoint of accounting and national production, respectively).

### Pre-tax book income

Corporations that file financial statements to shareholders use generally accepted accounting principle (GAAP) rules to measure profits. Although pre-tax book income is similar to taxable income, they differ in some important ways. Unlike taxable income, pre-tax book income (1) includes certain unrealized capital gains and losses in income, (2) excludes the DRD, (3) uses straight-line, rather than accelerated, depreciation for tangible assets, (4) includes certain tax-exempt income, such as interest from municipal bonds, (5) amortizes goodwill over 40 years, rather than 15 years, and (6) allows for a reserve of bad debts, rather than a specific charge off. In addition, GAAP's rules for consolidating affiliated corporations are different from tax law.

### NIPA corporate profits

The NIPA seek to measure the value of national output, called gross domestic product (GDP). One way GDP is calculated is by summing all the income earned and the costs incurred in producing the output. NIPA corporate profits (technically "NIPA corporate profits with IVA [inventory valuation adjustment] and CCA [capital consumptions allowance]") is one of the income components.

Although NIPA corporate profits relate to, and can be reconciled with, corporate taxable income, the two measures are not identical. Unlike taxable income, NIPA corporate profits (1) values all depreciation and inventory at replacement cost, which prevents inflationary gains from being counted as income, (2) excludes capital gains income, (3) excludes *all* intercorporate dividends, (4) includes income earned by certain federal agencies, primarily the Federal Reserve, which is not part of the tax base, (5) includes income earned by pass-through corporations, primarily Subchapter S corporations and regulated investment corporations, which are not subject to the corporate tax, and (6) includes state and local taxes, which corporations deduct to determine taxable income. (Besides these six, there are about a dozen other comparatively minor differences between taxable income and NIPA corporate profits).

### Recent historical trends

Corporate taxable income increased from $147 billion in 1975 to $494 billion in 1992. On average, corporate taxable income has grown by 7.0 percent per year, but this overall growth has been quite uneven, with alternating periods of growth and decline. For example, taxable income declined from 1979 to 1982 and from 1988 to 1991. The historical series reflects the business cycle. However, unlike NIPA pretax profits, which has a relatively consistent meaning year after year, corporate taxable income changes definition according to changes in tax law. It is important to view the historical trend in light of some major tax changes enacted during the period that changed the definition of taxable income.

The Economic Recovery Tax Act of 1981 (ERTA) generally provided tax relief to corporations. It allowed corporations to substantially accelerate depreciation deductions (which by definition would be offset by lower deductions in subsequent years). The ERTA made taxable income lower than it otherwise would have been in the years immediately following the act.

The Tax Equity and Fiscal Responsibility Act of 1982 (TEFRA) and the Deficit Reduction Act of 1984 (DEFRA) began the process of undoing the effects of the ERTA. They scaled back some depreciation benefits, introduced compliance measures, and reduced perceived tax shelters, expanding the corporate tax base.

The Tax Reform Act of 1986 (TRA86) continued the base-broadening trend. It established a new depreciation system that was less generous than under the ERTA, capitalized certain inventory costs that were formerly deducted, disallowed or limited some deductions, and brought more business activities into the taxable realm.

TRA86 increased both the level and the share of taxes paid by corporations. Higher corporate taxes increased the incentive for firms to avoid the corporate tax. This is demonstrated by the substantial growth in S corporation income since 1986. S corporations pass income directly to shareholders, and so have no taxable income. S corporation income increased from $24 billion in 1986 to $73 billion in 1992, and as a share of total corporate income

it more than doubled over this period. This has contributed to the relative decline of corporate taxable income to gross domestic product since 1988.

### Additional readings

Steurle, C. Eugene. *The Tax Decade*. Washington, D.C.: The Urban Institute Press, 1992.

U.S. Department of Commerce, Bureau of Economic Analysis. *Corporate Profits: Profits before Tax, Profit Tax Liability, and Dividends*. May 1985.

U.S. Department of the Treasury, Internal Revenue Service. *Source Book: Corporation Income Tax Returns*. Publication 1053. Various years.

*Cross references:* alternative minimum tax, corporate; capital cost recovery; dividends, double taxation of; income tax, federal; inventory accounting; subchapter S corporation.

# Tax administration, federal

Edward J. Nannenhorn
General Accounting Office

*A general overview of the Internal Revenue Service, the federal agency that has primary responsibility for tax administration.*

The federal government levies individual and corporate income taxes, social insurance taxes, excise taxes, estate and gift taxes, customs duties, and other miscellaneous taxes and fees. Both the government and taxpayers have roles in calculating and documenting the amount of tax owed, remitting the tax, and ensuring compliance. Individual and business taxpayers are responsible for learning about and understanding their responsibilities, calculating taxes owed, preparing tax returns and other documents, and sending appropriate documents and payments to the government. The Internal Revenue Service (IRS) is the federal agency with primary responsibility for tax administration. The IRS receives and processes tax returns and other documents, processes payments, enforces compliance through audits and other programs, collects delinquent taxes, and provides a number of services to help taxpayers understand their responsibilities. In 1996, the IRS collected $1,376.1 billion, the largest single component of which was the individual income tax (table 1).

## TABLE 1

### Summary: Internal Revenue Net Collections (1996)

| Source | Amount ($ billions) |
| --- | --- |
| Individual Income Tax | $656.0 |
| Withheld | 533.1 |
| Other | 212.2 |
| Refunds | (89.3) |
| Corporate Income | 171.4 |
| Employment Taxes | 491.3 |
| Estate and Gift Taxes | 17.2 |
| Excise Taxes | 40.2 |
| Total | 1,376.1 |

*Source:* IRS 1996 Data Book.

## IRS organization

In fiscal year 1996, the IRS had a budget of about $7.2 billion and employed about 106,000 people. A largely decentralized agency, the IRS employs people at its national office in Washington, D.C., and in 4 regional offices, 33 district offices, 10 service centers, and other offices across the country. The national office sets nationwide policies under the direction of the commissioner of Internal Revenue. IRS regional offices largely coordinate the activities of the various IRS offices within each region. The 33 district offices and 30 subdistrict offices perform examination, collection, criminal investigation, and some types of taxpayer service functions for specific geographical regions. At IRS service centers, tax returns and payments are processed, taxpayer services are provided, and certain types of compliance checks are performed. The IRS also operates 3 computing centers and about 400 walk-in taxpayer service sites.

Table 2 shows how IRS staff and budget funds were allocated in 1996.

## Tax return and payment processing

The administration of the current federal tax system relies on large numbers of tax returns, information returns, and payment documents, all of which need to be processed by the IRS. In 1996, the IRS processed about 208 million tax returns. The individual income tax, a tax levied on individuals rather than businesses alone, generates the majority of returns. While some low-income individuals do not have to file, the individual income tax (including individual estimated tax) accounted for about 75 percent of all tax returns. Table 3 shows the number and type of tax returns processed by the IRS in 1996.

In order to verify income received by individuals and help collect individual income tax, businesses are required to withhold income tax on wages and salaries and provide information returns to the IRS, documenting the payment of a number of forms of income to individuals. More than a billion information returns were sent to the IRS in 1995; about 200 million reporting wages and salaries paid, and about 360 million showing the payment of dividend or interest income (table 4).

In addition to filing employment tax returns each quarter, businesses remit employment taxes and withheld income taxes through the Federal Tax Deposit (FTD) System. The majority of federal revenue is remitted through this system, rather than through payments made by individuals to the IRS when filing their returns. Depending on the amount of tax owed, businesses are required to deposit payments along with associated deposit coupons with Federal Reserve and private-sector banks on a monthly or semiweekly basis. These banks send the coupons to the IRS for processing and transfer funds to Treasury accounts. In 1996, the IRS processed more than 100 million federal tax deposits.

Processing tax returns is a labor-intensive, error-prone process for the large number of returns filed on paper. The IRS now receives most information returns on magnetic tape, and can scan FTD coupons and the relatively simple 1040EZ individual income tax return. However, information from other returns must still be keyed into IRS databases, a process that leads to errors. While the IRS has had some recent success in encouraging 1040EZ filers to file by telephone, efforts to encourage other taxpayers to file electronically through paid preparers or through personal computers have had limited success to date.

## Enforcement activity and compliance

The IRS can identify noncompliance with the individual income tax through audits and by matching amounts reported on tax returns with the amounts reported on information returns (document matching). Essentially all returns filed are checked for misreporting income subject to information reporting. Document matching is also used to identify individuals who may have been required to file a tax return but did not.

The IRS checks individual taxpayer compliance through three types of audits. During a *field audit*, IRS agents will visit a taxpayer's residence or business. During an *office audit*, a taxpayer will be asked to visit an IRS district office or service center and talk to a tax auditor. In addition to these traditional types of audits, the IRS recently began to classify as audits all contacts between service center tax examiners who discover possible discrepancies between returns and information returns and other third-party information (table 4).

Individual income tax returns are selected for audit largely on the basis of the amount of additional taxes likely to result. The IRS has used a discriminant function (DIF) methodology to rank returns by their likelihood of resulting in additional taxes.

## TABLE 2

### IRS Budget Overview: Major Categories and Subcategories (1996 Actual)

| Budget Activity | Staff (full-time equivalents) | Amounts ($ thousands) |
|---|---|---|
| Processing, Assistance, Management | 31,431 | 1,723,572 |
| Submission Processing | 20,460 | 780,512 |
| Inspection | 1,292 | 100,092 |
| Management Services | 1,531 | 119,967 |
| Taxpayer Services | 8,031 | 492,436 |
| Resource Management | 117 | 230,565 |
| Tax Law Enforcement | 66,740 | 4,170,191 |
| Examination | 27,327 | 1,555,387 |
| Collection | 17,916 | 855,058 |
| Chief Counsel | 4,995 | 361,674 |
| Tax Fraud and Financial Investigation | 4,805 | 377,135 |
| Document Matching | 2,086 | 72,756 |
| Resource Management (Compliance) | 5,981 | 725,020 |
| Employee Plans and Exempt Organizations | 2,191 | 128,207 |
| Statistics of Income/Compliance Research | 900 | 57,746 |
| International | 535 | 37,208 |
| Information Systems | 8,471 | 1,346,458 |
| Services and Compliance | 5,296 | 623,615 |
| TSM (Tax System Modernization) Modernized Development | 2,016 | 585,056 |
| Support Systems | 688 | 92,294 |
| Modernized Operational | 471 | 45,493 |
| Total | 106,642 | 7,240,221 |

*Source:* IRS Budget Estimates, Fiscal Year 1998 President's Budget.
*Note:* Totals may include rounding error.

## TABLE 3

### Number of Returns by Principal Type (1996)

| Type of return | Number of returns (millions) |
|---|---|
| Individual Income Tax | 118.8 |
| 1040 | 66.2 |
| 1040A | 23.3 |
| 1040EZ | 21.4 |
| 1040 other | 7.9 |
| Estimated Individual Tax | 36.0 |
| Fiduciary (including estimated tax) | 3.9 |
| Partnership | 1.6 |
| Corporation Income Tax | 4.9 |
| Employment Taxes | 28.6 |
| Estate and Gift Taxes | .3 |
| Excise Taxes | .8 |
| Employee Plans/Exempt Organizations | 1.4 |
| Supplemental Documents | 12.6 |
| Total | 208.9 |

*Source:* 1996 IRS Data Book.

DIF scoring has been based on findings from the IRS Taxpayer Compliance Measurement Program (TCMP), which has conducted extensive line-by-line audits of randomly selected taxpayers in order to find patterns of noncompliance. However, because the last TCMP study of individual taxpayers was conducted in 1988, DIF formulas may have become less useful in identifying returns for audit that are most likely to result in additional taxes. Other returns selected for audit are those that fall under special IRS compliance efforts. For example, the IRS audited many tax shelter returns in the 1980s and has put special emphasis on earned income credit returns in the past few years.

The IRS examined about 2 percent of all returns filed by corporations in 1995. IRS audit rates for corporations vary significantly according to the size of the business. For corporations with less than $250,000 in assets, the audit rate was about 1 percent. In contrast, about 50 percent of large corporations (assets more than $250 million) were examined.

After reviewing a taxpayer's support for a return, IRS agents or auditors decide whether to recommend changes to tax liability. If a change is recommended, the taxpayer can agree with the recommended change or appeal through the IRS Office of Appeals or the Tax Court. For individual income tax returns, about 85 percent of field or office audits result in additional recommended taxes, and about 65 percent of service center contacts result in a tax change. For corporations, about 76 percent of audits by revenue agents and about 53 percent of service center contacts result in a change in tax liability. It should be noted, however, that in cases in which businesses have no current-year tax liability, audit

TABLE 4

**Returns Filed, Examination Coverage (1996 examinations, numbers in thousands)**

| Category | 1995 Returns | Total Audits | Revenue Agent or Auditor Contact | Service Center Contact | Percentage Coverage (Total Audits) | Percentage Coverage (Agent or Auditor Contact) |
|---|---|---|---|---|---|---|
| All individuals | 116,060 | 1,942 | 762 | 1,180 | 1.67 | 0.66 |
| Income < $100,000 | 103,494 | 1,534 | 507 | 1,027 | 1.48 | 0.49 |
| Income > $100,000 | 4,541 | 129 | 76 | 53 | 2.84 | 1.67 |
| Schedule C | 7,256 | 262 | 171 | 90 | 3.61 | 2.36 |
| Schedule F | 769 | 18 | 9 | 8 | 2.30 | 1.17 |

*Source:* 1996 IRS Data Book.

TABLE 5

**Income Tax Gap Estimates, 1992**

| Source of Tax Gap | Tax Gap Amount (billions) | Percent of Total |
|---|---|---|
| Individual Tax Gap | 94.0 | 73.9 |
| Corporate Tax Gap | 33.1 | 26.1 |
|   Small Corporations | 7.0 | 5.5 |
|   Large Corporations | 23.7 | 18.7 |
|   Other | .4 | 0.3 |
|   Corporate Remittance Gap | 2.0 | 1.6 |
| Total Tax Gap | 127.1 | 100 |

*Source:* IRS.

findings that increase income may increase future tax liability by reducing net operating loss deductions.

Evidence on the degree of compliance with the current tax system comes primarily from IRS tax gap studies. For the individual and corporate income taxes, these studies have used TCMP data as their primary source of information on compliance. In the aggregate, the IRS finds that taxpayers voluntarily pay about 83 percent of income taxes owed; after IRS enforcement and collection efforts, they ultimately pay about 87 percent of taxes owed. It should be noted that the tax gap estimates for large corporations use taxes recommended by revenue agents as a measure of true liability. For large corporations, it is not uncommon for additional recommended taxes to be reduced significantly during the appeals process. Table 5 shows the most recent IRS tax gap estimates.

Table 6 shows the components of the individual income tax gap. Nonfiling, underpayment by individuals who did file returns, and underreporting of income are all important sources of noncompliance, and underreporting of income is the most important in dollar terms. The table also shows that compliance, in percentage terms, is much higher for the types of income subject to information reporting— such as wages, interest, and dividends—than for other types of income, such as income of sole proprietorships. The IRS estimates that compliance for wage income, which is subject to withholding, is about 99 percent.

Analysts have also used TCMP data to investigate how compliance is related to income levels and marginal tax rates. Christian (1994) presents evidence that the frequency of underreporting some amount of income increases with income and with marginal tax rates, but voluntary compliance levels increase slightly with income. Feinstein (1991), using data from the 1982 and 1985 TCMP studies, found a significantly negative relationship between tax rates and evasion.

In 1993, the IRS estimated the employment tax gap for years 1984–1997. (This gap results from taxpayers underreporting and misreporting tax liability and not remitting tax that is reported as due.) Overall, the IRS estimated that the gross (before enforcement action) employment tax gap for 1997 would be about $45 billion and that the noncompliance rate would be about 9 percent. About 60 percent of the total employment tax gap was estimated to be the result of underreporting of self-employment tax liability.

## Taxpayer services

The IRS has received heavy criticism in the area of taxpayer services in the past few years. It provides a number of services to taxpayers, including tax forms and publications, educational programs, walk-in assistance, and toll-free telephone assistance. While some taxpayer services seem to work well, taxpayers have had significant problems trying to reach the IRS by phone.

Although it has recognized the need to upgrade its information systems since it began the Tax System Modernization program in 1986, the IRS has not succeeded in implementing new processes or technology to significantly improve its ability to answer taxpayer questions or resolve problems. Many IRS problems in this area can be traced to antiquated information systems that are not linked. As a result, IRS personnel often cannot gain access to the data needed to answer taxpayer questions or resolve account-related problems quickly.

## TABLE 6

**Individual Income Tax Gap Components, 1992**

| Component | Amount ($ Net billions) | | Net Misreporting Percentage | |
|---|---|---|---|---|
| | Low | High | Low | High |
| Nonfiling gap | 13.5 | 13.8 | N/A | N/A |
| Underpayment gap | 8.4 | 8.4 | N/A | N/A |
| Underreporting gap | 71.3 | 73.1 | N/A | N/A |
| wage income | 3.1 | 3.2 | 0.9 | 0.9 |
| interest income | 0.9 | 0.9 | 2.2 | 2.3 |
| dividends | 1.3 | 1.3 | 7.6 | 7.8 |
| pensions and annuities | 1.7 | 1.8 | 3.9 | 4.0 |
| capital gains | 2.4 | 2.5 | 6.9 | 7.2 |
| sales of business assets | 0.7 | 0.7 | 27.1 | 28.0 |
| nonfarm proprietor income | 16.4 | 16.9 | 31.3 | 32.3 |
| informal supplier income | 12.3 | 12.3 | 81.4 | 81.4 |
| rents and royalties | 3.6 | 3.7 | 16.6 | 17.2 |
| adjustments | 0.2 | 0.2 | 1.9 | 2.0 |
| deductions | 5.0 | 5.1 | 4.3 | 4.4 |
| exemptions | 2.8 | 2.9 | 4.4 | 4.5 |
| tax credits | 6.0 | 6.2 | 38.9 | 40.2 |

*Source:* IRS.

In response to the IRS's problems in providing services and modernizing its information systems, the National Commission on Restructuring the IRS recommended that the overall governance of the agency be turned over to an oversight board. As envisioned by the commission, an oversight board would bring private-sector expertise to the agency, especially in the areas of customer service and technology. Legislation to implement these recommendations is currently before Congress.

## Additional readings

Andreoni, James, Brian Erard, and Jonathon Feinstein. "Tax Compliance." Social Systems Research Institute working paper 9610. University of Wisconsin–Madison, April 1996.

Christian, Charles W. "Voluntary Compliance with the Individual Income Tax: Results from the 1988 TCMP Study." *The IRS Research Bulletin, 1993/1994.* Publication 1500 (rev. 9–94).

Feinstein, Jonathon S. "An Econometric Analysis of Income Tax Evasion and Its Detection." *RAND Journal of Economics* 22 (1) (1991): 14–35.

Internal Revenue Service. *1996 Data Book* (publication 55B). U.S. Government Printing Office, 1996.

Internal Revenue Service. *Federal Tax Compliance Research: Individual Income Tax Gap Estimates for 1985, 1988, and 1992.* Publication 1415 (rev. 4-96). Washington, D.C., 1996.

Internal Revenue Service Research Division. "Federal Tax Compliance Research: Gross and Net Employment Tax Gap Estimates for 1984–1997." Publication 1415-E (rev. 10-93). Washington, D.C., 1993.

Slemrod, Joel, editor. *Why People Pay Taxes: Tax Compliance and Enforcement.* Ann Arbor: University of Michigan Press, 1992.

Slemrod, Joel, and Jon Bakija. *Taxing Ourselves: A Citizen's Guide to the Great Debate over Tax Reform.* Cambridge, Mass.: The MIT Press, 1996.

Steuerle, C. Eugene. *Who Should Pay for Collecting Taxes?* Washington, D.C.: American Enterprise Institute for Public Policy Research, 1986.

U.S. General Accounting Office. "Tax Administration: Audit Trends and Results for Individual Taxpayers." GAO/GGD-96-91, April 26, 1996.

U.S. General Accounting Office. "Managing IRS: IRS Needs to Continue Improving Operations and Services." Statement of Lynda D. Willis, director of Tax Policy and Administration Issues. GAO/T-GGD/AIMD-96-170, July 29, 1996.

U.S. General Accounting Office. "Taxpayer Compliance: Analyzing the Nature of the Income Tax Gap." Statement of Lynda D. Willis, director of Tax Policy and Administration Issues. GAO/T-GGD-97-35, January 9, 1997.

*Cross references:* adjusted gross income; income tax, federal.

# Tax administration mechanisms for intergovernmental cooperation

Harley T. Duncan
Federation of Tax Administrators

Charles E. McLure, Jr.
Hoover Institution, Stanford University

*Several cooperative agreements that exist between state tax administrators and the Internal Revenue Service are designed to improve tax compliance and enforcement.*

Despite the highly independent system of tax administration resulting from the sovereignty accorded the states by the U.S. Constitution, there are a number of cooperative arrangements between state and federal tax authorities and among various groups of states. These arrangements are aimed primarily at improving tax compliance and enforcement; relatively few address the administrative and compliance burdens faced by multistate taxpayers— a lacuna that has been the focus of recent criticism.

Each state has its own tax administration agency (commonly known as the department of revenue) that is responsible for the collection of taxes imposed by that state. State tax agencies are generally headed by individuals who are appointed by the governor, the elected chief executive of the state. In three states, the head of the tax agency is a statewide elected official, and several state revenue agencies are governed by a multimember commission appointed by the state's governor.

State tax agencies are usually organized around the core functions of tax administration rather than being organized by type of tax. A revenue department has major organizational subunits devoted to identification and registration of taxpayers, processing of returns and remittances, taxpayer accounting, audit and enforcement, and taxpayer education and assistance, as well as various organizational support functions such as legal services, personnel, facilities, and information systems. For taxpayers desiring to adjudicate actions of the tax authority, there is at least one level of administrative appeal within the revenue agency, with rights of subsequent appeal to other administrative tribunals and the state judicial system.

## Federal-state exchanges of information

The cornerstone of cooperative tax administration in the United States is an active exchange of information between federal and state tax authorities to support enforcement of the personal and corpora-tion income tax. Federal law authorizes the U.S. Internal Revenue Service (IRS) to provide federal tax return information to state tax agencies, provided it is used solely for tax administration purposes and is properly safeguarded against unauthorized disclosure or release. (State tax statutes likewise authorize the exchange of return information with other states and with the federal government under appropriate safeguards.) All states have entered into an exchange-of-information agreement with the IRS, through which they receive an abundance of tax information. Information exchanged includes copies of all federal audits or other adjustments to a taxpayer's return, identification of taxpayers filing a federal income tax return with an address in the receiving state, extracts of items of income and expense reported on the federal tax return, and information reports filed by third-party payers (e.g., banks, brokerage firms, and employers) with respect to taxpayers in a particular state.

Given the basic level of conformity between state and federal income tax bases, the information is often used to assess additional state tax directly. For example, one of the most effective information exchanges is an IRS program that matches third-party reports of income to entries on taxpayer returns. The IRS assesses additional federal tax where income has been omitted and provides information on the adjustment to the state tax authority in which the taxpayer resides. The state customarily issues an automated assessment of additional state tax unless the income is exempted by the state. States also compare the exchanged data with state files to ensure consistency in amounts reported to federal and state tax authorities and to identify nonfiling taxpayers. With the massive amounts of information involved, nearly all information is exchanged on computer-readable or electronic media instead of paper.

Federal data and federal audit reports are the only, or at least the predominant, means of independently auditing state individual income tax returns in many states. The rates of state individual income taxes (generally 5–8% of taxable income) are such that it is not cost-effective (particularly compared with the yield on audits of state corporation income taxes and retail sales taxes) to maintain a substantial cadre of state revenue agents to conduct on-site audits of individual income tax returns.

States also use the results of federal corporation tax audits for enforcement. Because the computation of state tax generally begins with federal taxable income, states rely extensively on federal examination activities for verification of the tax base and the proper treatment of various transactions, particularly those involving international operations. State agencies devote their audit activities primarily to verifying the apportionment of income across states, examining the taxpayer's treatment of certain types of transactions, and determining the membership of the unitary group if the state employs combined reporting.

In addition, states have recently gained access to data from other federal agencies to aid in tax enforcement activities. They receive regular reports from the U.S. Customs Service on imported goods that they use to identify goods to which the retail sales and use tax may apply or to identify potential taxpayers who may not be registered.

Historically, information flowed mostly from the federal government to the states. In recent years, however, states have begun providing more information to federal tax administrators. In particular, federal administrators use state lists of registered sales-tax payers to identify nonfilers of federal employment and corporation taxes and to cross-check reported receipts. They also use files maintained by other state agencies that license individuals engaged in various trades and professions as a source of leads (e.g., on nonfilers). Finally, state driver's license files provide a good source of address information and potential assets in seizure situations. Here again, the data are exchanged under legal agreements regarding the use and safeguarding of the data, and most information is exchanged in computer-usable form.

There are relatively few instances in which the states and federal government conduct joint audits of individual taxpayers, except in the motor fuel excise tax area if earlier investigative work by either the federal or state tax authority has revealed evidence of criminal tax evasion.

Cooperative efforts between state and federal agencies in the administration of excise taxes on alcoholic beverages or tobacco products are few, except for occasional working arrangements between individual agencies and local governments. Federal law, however, does require that manufacturers of tobacco products and alcoholic beverages provide reports to state tax authorities on all products shipped to wholesalers in the state. This practice helps ensure that tax is paid on all products entering the distribution chain in a particular state.

Likewise, little cooperation exists in the collection of delinquent tax obligations, even though a delinquent taxpayer may owe money to both state and federal authorities. This situation is often a source of friction between tax authorities, with one level attempting to assert priority over the other where resources are not sufficient to satisfy both obligations.

## Cooperative taxpayer assistance

Beyond the audit and enforcement efforts, state and federal tax authorities have undertaken a wide range of cooperative taxpayer service and education activities. Of particular note are cooperative or joint programs for providing training and education to tax practitioners and preparers as well as providing cooperative registration and filing assistance to new businesses. State and federal authorities often offer on-site taxpayer assistance at a single site.

The most ambitious effort builds on a computerized or electronic filing program begun by the IRS several years ago. States were, at the same time, beginning to enter the electronic filing arena. To avoid duplicative efforts and simplify matters for taxpayers, most states decided to enter into a cooperative filing effort with the IRS rather than develop their own individual filing program. At present, 31 states are participating in the joint Fed State electronic filing program. Under the program, the federal and state individual income tax returns for persons using a participating tax preparer can be filed in a single electronic transmission with the IRS, which in turn provides the state return to the appropriate state tax authority.

## Collaborative training efforts

A final area of collaboration between state and federal tax authorities is in training personnel. This cooperation takes three forms:

—State tax agency personnel can take part in all IRS-sponsored training sessions if space is available. Personnel have access to a wide range of courses from short-term, specialized courses to more basic courses lasting several weeks (e.g., basic criminal investigation). This cooperation enables states to leverage the resources of the IRS to meet certain training needs for which it would be impractical to develop their own offerings.

—State and federal tax authorities have on occasion jointly developed specialized training programs. Most recently, they cooperated in developing basic and advanced courses in motor fuel audit and investigation; more than 1,200 state and federal agents have attended the course over the past three years.

—IRS personnel regularly participate, both as instructors and students, in training sessions conducted by state agencies or their representatives. For example, the Federation of Tax Administrators (FTA) sponsors training workshops and conferences on current topics and techniques in tax administration for state agency personnel.

## Procedures for cooperation

The process by which these cooperative tax administration activities are initiated, developed, and implemented is diverse and somewhat dependent on the nature of the initiative. Outside the information and data exchange area, the cooperative efforts are generated largely by individual state tax authorities and their counterpart IRS district office. Representatives from the IRS and state tax agency regularly meet to examine ways to cooperate, and out of such liaisons many individual initiatives grow. Once developed and tested, they are likely to be replicated in other states. But the implementation of many efforts may not occur in all areas of the country.

A similar coordinate mechanism exists at the national level for efforts affecting all states. The FTA holds regular liaison sessions with the executive leadership of the IRS to discuss and coordinate cooperative activities. The IRS maintains a small national office staff (about 15 persons) dedicated to assisting states in working with the IRS and in providing information on the types of cooperative activities being conducted across the country. Numerous IRS staff throughout the country and in various functions devote at least part of their time to working with states. Leadership and staff of the IRS and FTA play a lead role in designing and implementing nationwide efforts such as the joint electronic filing program and the information exchange program. They are also active in facilitating the adoption of state–district-level initiatives by other regions of the country.

This essay is an abridged version of Duncan, Harley T., and Charles E. McLure, Jr. "Tax Administration in the United States of America: A Decentralized System." *Bulletin of the International Bureau of Fiscal Documentation* 51 (February 1997): 74–85.

*Cross references:* budget processes, state; budget process, federal.

# Tax administration: private and public cooperation in state tax administration and promoting best practices

Harley T. Duncan
Federation of Tax Administrators

Charles E. McLure, Jr.
Hoover Institution, Stanford University

*Several organizations, public and private, cooperate both informally and by law in the administration of state and local taxes.*

Several multistate organizations, private and public, contribute to coordination and collaboration for the purpose of (a) improving state tax compliance through information sharing; (b) improving the uniformity of state tax laws and practices to increase compliance and reduce complexity for taxpayers; (c) conducting administrative operations on a combined basis to reduce administrative costs and the complexity of operating in multiple states; and (d) educating the public and their clientele on recent developments in taxation, tax policy, and best practices.

The private organizations include the Committee on State Taxation (COST), an adjunct of the Council of State Chambers of Commerce, which consists of roughly 400 multistate companies. The primary purpose of COST is to advocate for multistate taxpayers before state and federal legislative and judicial bodies and to provide training to member companies. Similarly, the Tax Executives Institute (TEI) is an organization of tax professionals from major multistate and international corporations domiciled in the United States and Canada. Its mission includes professional development and advocacy before state and federal policymakers. The Institute of Property Taxation (IPT) consists of tax professionals and representatives in the property, sales, and use tax areas. Its mission is limited to professional development for its members and working with appropriate state and local tax authorities on matters of mutual interest.

There are five key public vehicles for cooperation. The two most prominent—the Federation of Tax Administrators (FTA) and the Multistate Tax Commission (MTC)—are discussed in separate entries in this volume. The three other cooperative arrangements are discussed below.

## Regional cooperative agreements

In several areas of the country, state tax agencies have joined together to adopt regional agreements to encourage information sharing among the states as a means of improving tax compliance on interstate sales. These regional agreements provide that information gathered on transactions meeting specified criteria will be shared among the states. In practice, however, these regional information exchanges fall far short of providing information on all interstate sales owing to the following two political realities that force tax administrators to be particularly attentive to the political interests in their state to avoid losing the support of elected officials: (1) providing information to other states may lead to increased taxation of companies (or their products) operating in the state providing the information, and (2) substantial portions of their economy may benefit from compliance difficulties currently faced by other states.

Certain of the agreements (primarily in the Great Lakes, Midwest, and Southeast regions) call for active encouragement of retailers to register in all states into which they ship goods. New York, New Jersey, and Connecticut have extended this type of agreement to include a mechanism under which a retailer can file a single return with one state to satisfy its sales tax obligations in each of the three states. The Southeast also includes procedures for routinely sharing certain corporation income tax information.

## Bilateral exchanges

Each state has entered into agreements to exchange tax return information with nearly all other states. This exchange may be accomplished either through the Uniform Exchange of Information Agreement developed by the FTA and executed by about 45 states or through separate bilateral exchange agreements. Under these bilateral arrangements, states routinely share compliance information with other states on a taxpayer-by-taxpayer and a state-by-state basis. The exchanges may be more comprehensive. Thus, New York, New Jersey, and Connecticut routinely exchange information on individual taxpayers in the New York City metropolitan area who work in one state, but reside in another, to ensure consistent sourcing of the income and proper computation of credits for taxes paid in another state.

## International Fuel Tax Agreement

In the past several years, states have been required by federal law to join the International Fuel Tax Agreement (IFTA) as a means of reducing the administrative burden on taxpayers through participation in a joint tax administration project. All states (and some Canadian provinces) are now members of IFTA, which provides a mechanism for apportioning the motor fuel excise tax liability of an interstate or multijurisdictional motor carrier among the states in which it operates.

In the United States, a carrier pays tax at the time fuel is purchased or "at the pump" but is then responsible for apportioning the tax paid on its entire fleet on the basis of miles traveled in each jurisdiction. Before the adoption of IFTA, a carrier was responsible for filing quarterly returns in each jurisdiction in which it operated, detailing its mileage, purchases, consumption, and any tax or refund owed.

Under the agreement, the carrier files only a single tax return with the state in which it is domiciled or based, together with information on its operations (purchases, mileage, etc.) in all jurisdictions for the reporting period. The "base state" provides information to other jurisdictions, reconciling the tax owed by the carrier in all jurisdictions and otherwise providing for the administration of the other jurisdictions' taxes on behalf of the carrier. The base state also audits carriers on behalf of all other jurisdictions. In short, the interstate carrier deals only with the tax authority in its base state, which is responsible for all contacts on behalf of the carrier with other jurisdictions.

New York State has taken the joint administration of IFTA one step further. It has developed a data processing facility that provides tax return and remittance processing services for IFTA jurisdictions, including two Canadian provinces. The processing center captures all data from returns filed with it and handles all financial transactions among the states involved and other IFTA jurisdictions. The states are individually responsible for registering and auditing carriers and dealing with delinquent carriers. IFTA began as a voluntary cooperative effort among a relatively small number of states—three at the outset. However, because of the perceived benefits, the interstate trucking industry pushed hard for further participation and eventually secured enactment of a federal law requiring states to participate in IFTA if they wished to continue imposing the apportioned fuel use tax beyond September 30, 1996. Although some states initially resisted enactment of the requirement, all complied with its provisions by the deadline.

## Additional readings

This essay is an abridged version of Duncan, Harley T., and Charles E. McLure, Jr. "Tax Administration in the United States of America: A Decentralized System." *Bulletin of the International Bureau of Fiscal Documentation* 51 (February 1997): 74–85.

Duncan, Harley T. "Interstate Cooperative Efforts to Enforce State Sales and Use Taxes." *Proceedings of the 81st Annual Conference on Taxation.* Columbus, Ohio: National Tax Association–Tax Institute of America, 1989.

Special Committee on State Taxation of Interstate Commerce, Committee on the Judiciary, U.S. House of Representatives, pursuant to Public Law 86-272. The special committee operated from 1962 to 1966. These hearings were generally known as the "Willis Committee" hearings, named after the committee chairman, Rep. Edwin E. Willis of Louisiana.

*Cross reference:* Multistate Tax Commission.

# Tax amnesty

Ronald C. Fisher
Michigan State University

*A program offering reduced financial and/or legal penalties to taxpayers who voluntarily agree to pay outstanding past tax liabilities.*

---

Programs that might be called "formal tax amnesties" are unique, one-time opportunities that typically apply for a very limited period and usually occur just before an increase in tax enforcement and penalties. These formal amnesties should be distinguished from the more common practice by many tax authorities of negotiating payments and penalties if taxpayers offer to settle past disputes or liabilities, which might be called "informal amnesties."

## Amnesty practice and experience

Thirty-four state governments in the United States held formal tax amnesties in the years 1982 to 1992, with the first really substantial amnesties occurring in 1984 in Illinois and Massachusetts. Because these state amnesties differed widely in their coverage and characteristics, collections varied from as little as $100,000 (from Illinois's first amnesty) and $200,000 (North Dakota in 1983) to highs of more than $360 million (New York, 1986) and $450 million (California, 1985). Even the largest programs were relatively small, however, as no amnesty collections were more than $20 per capita or 2 percent of annual state revenue. Tax amnesties also have been used by many local governments in the United States and by other nations, although the focus of research has been on these state programs.

Amnesties can be distinguished by the number of eligible taxes, whether they apply to both underreporting and nonfiling, whether taxpayers with previously identified liabilities (accounts receivable) are eligible, the nature and magnitude of the reduced penalties, and whether they preceded enhanced enforcement and stricter penalties. Three-quarters of state amnesty programs applied to all taxes (or all administered by the state revenue department); except for a few specialized amnesties limited to minor taxes, most included the general sales and personal income taxes. Participants included both individuals and firms—taxes collected from business, including corporate income taxes, have been part of many amnesties.

Most tax amnesties applied to both underreporting of transactions or tax base and failure to file, although the statute of limitations typically is shorter for underreporting. Of more importance is whether delinquent taxpayers who have been identified by tax authorities or who have had outstanding liabilities assessed before the amnesty are allowed to participate. Fewer than half of state amnesties included these taxpayers (often identified as accounts receivable), but they were included in nearly all of the state amnesties that generated substantial revenue. Thus, in those cases, amnesty can be thought of as a convenient, low-cost method of collecting known, outstanding debts.

All amnesties waived any potential criminal penalties, and most eliminated or substantially reduced the financial penalties that applied to underpayment. In most states, amnesty participants did have to pay interest on the outstanding liabilities, although about a third of state amnesties also reduced or eliminated interest charges. Perhaps surprisingly, Alm and Beck (1991) reported evidence that reducing interest charges tended to increase the revenue generated by the amnesty (increased revenue from more participation offsetting the loss of interest payments).

Finally, many states used amnesties to smooth the transition to a regime of stricter enforcement (about 60 percent of amnesties) and higher penalties (75 percent). Typical amnesty advertising focused on such slogans as "Don't Say We Didn't Warn You" (Colorado) and "Get To Us Before We Get To You" (Michigan). Amnesties and enhanced enforcement seem complementary in two ways—the new enforcement and penalties in the future create an incentive for taxpayers to participate in an amnesty, and the amnesty may make the change to a new tax collection regime seem fairer by providing taxpayers an opportunity to avoid what might be perceived as an arbitrary or unannounced change in policy. As expected, amnesties that were to be followed by enhanced enforcement did seem to have more participation and generate larger amounts of collections (Alm and Beck, 1991).

## Success of tax amnesty

Tax amnesties have three main objectives. The first is to generate revenue in the short run. As noted, states that offered the broadest programs with the greatest incentives to participate were most successful in achieving this objective. Second, governments want to increase revenue in the long run by changing the behavior of some taxpayers, inducing taxpayers who had been evaders to comply fully in the future. Third, governments hope to generate information both about amnesty participants, which could be used to enforce compliance by those individuals in the future, and about tax compliance and evasion in general, which could be used to improve tax collection and enforcement programs.

It is evident, however, that the long-run implications of amnesties are ambiguous. The potential gain from identification of past evaders and improved compliance by them in the long run must be weighed against three factors that might reduce compliance of others in the long run. First, some complying taxpayers might decide not to pay taxes fully in the future and to wait for an amnesty. To mitigate against this potential problem, all states holding amnesties emphasize the unique, one-time aspect of the opportunity, promising not to hold another amnesty (for the same tax) soon. Second, there is concern that some compliers might become disillusioned by the perceived unfairness of offering relief to past noncompliers, leading to less compliance overall. And third, some worry that the amnesty experience and attention might provide information about the ease of and opportunities for evasion.

In fact, state amnesties attracted a variety of taxpayers but not necessarily the most serious evaders (Fisher et al. 1989; Joulfaian 1989). Among the large multitax amnesties, the individual income tax accounted for the majority of tax cases resolved but a smaller share of collections, because many of these participants used the amnesty to pay very small amounts (in many instances less than $100). In addition, not having filed (rather than having filed incorrectly) was the most common form of evasion among participants, and most of these nonfilers used amnesty to file for one or two years. In many cases, participating nonfilers had paid most tax due through withholding or quarterly payments but had not filed a return to settle their accounts. In Michigan, for instance, 60 percent of the taxpayers using amnesty to file individual income tax returns had already paid at least 80 percent of the total tax owed (Fisher et al. 1989: 23). Some had even filed federal returns.

Businesses participated in amnesties mostly to resolve corporate income and sales tax matters (Fisher and Goddeeris 1989). Corporate income tax cases were particularly important, accounting for a larger share of amnesty collections than did sales tax cases. Many of the income tax cases, as with individuals, involved small amounts, with a few firms in each case paying large amounts that represented a substantial percentage of amnesty collections. In those states that allowed taxpayers with known outstanding liabilities or audits in progress to participate, collections from accounts receivable often represented at least half of amnesty collections for corporate income and sales taxes. In at least one state, however, many business participants used amnesty to file for several years, including a large number who had never filed returns.

It seems, then, that relatively few individual taxpayers who participated in amnesties were "hardcore evaders," having evaded large amounts of taxes over long periods of time, and that a relatively larger number of chronic business tax evaders may have been detected by amnesties. Certainly some individual and business taxpayers who had a serious past history of evasion or who were completely outside the tax system were uncovered. Still, most participants might be called "marginal tax evaders"—taxpayers who received only a small gain or who found themselves in the situation reluctantly or by accident. Not surprisingly, therefore, examination of tax enforcement had no long-run effect on revenue collections (Alm and Beck 1993). Possibly, any long-run gains from returning or adding taxpayers to the rolls were offset by new evasions.

## Future for tax amnesties

Tax amnesties seem to have been most successful in generating immediate revenue, part of which represented known liabilities that were collected sooner or at lower cost than from enhanced enforcement alone. Amnesties also have provided states useful information about taxpayers, tax compliance problems, and tax collection and enforcement policies. But it seems that amnesties generally did not succeed in generating long-term additions to revenue as a result of additional taxpayers and improved compliance. Neither, however, did amnesties seem to hurt revenue collection.

As two-thirds of U.S. states, including most of the larger states, recently have held amnesties, and it is counterproductive to repeat them often, additional major state amnesties should not be expected. However, New York held a second amnesty (November 1996 through January 1997) just 10 years after its first one. Arkansas recently conducted its first state tax amnesty (September through November 1997). A federal tax amnesty for the United States has been discussed, but the state results coupled with the substantially different nature of federal tax evasion have generated little momentum for a federal tax amnesty. Tax amnesties for local governments and other nations are likely to continue.

## Additional readings

Alm, James, and William Beck. "Tax Amnesties and Tax Revenues." *Public Finance Quarterly* 18 (October 1990): 433–53.

Alm, James, and William Beck. "Wiping the Slate Clean: Individual Response to State Amnesties." *Southern Economic Journal* 57 (April 1991): 1043–53.

Alm, James, and William Beck. "Tax Amnesties and Compliance in the Long Run: A Time Series Analysis." *National Tax Journal* 46 (March 1993): 53–60.

Alm, James, Michael McKee, and William Beck. "Amazing Grace: Tax Amnesties and Compliance." *National Tax Journal* 43 (March 1990): 23–37.

Andreoni, James. "The Desirability of a Permanent Tax Amnesty." *Journal of Public Economics* 45 (July 1991): 1435–59.

Crane, Steven E., and Farrokh Nourzad. "Amnesty for State Tax Evaders: Lessons from the California Experience." In *Proceedings of the 81st Annual Conference, 1988.* Columbus, Ohio: National Tax Association–Tax Institute of America, 1989.

Crane, Steven E., and Farrokh Nourzad. "Tax Rates and Tax Evasion: Evidence from California Amnesty Data." *National Tax Journal* 43 (June 1990): 189–99.

Fisher, Ronald C., and John H. Goddeeris. "Participation in Tax Amnesties: The Case of Business Taxes." In *Proceedings of the 81st Annual Conference, 1988.* Columbus,

Ohio: National Tax Association–Tax Institute of America, 1989.

Fisher, Ronald C., John H. Goddeeris, and James C. Young. "Participation in Tax Amnesties: The Individual Income Tax." *National Tax Journal* 42 (March 1989): 15–27.

Goddeeris, John H., Susan W. Martin, and James C. Young. "Tax Amnesty in Michigan: Characteristics of Individual Income Tax Participants." *Journal of State Taxation* 7 (Winter 1989): 373–95.

Joulfaian, David. "Participation in Tax Amnesties: Evidence from a State." In *Proceedings of the 81st Annual Conference, 1988.* Columbus, Ohio: National Tax Association–Tax Institute of America, 1989.

Leonard, Herman B., and Richard J. Zeckhauser. "Amnesty, Enforcement, and Tax Policy." In *Tax Policy and the Economy*, edited by Lawrence Summers. Cambridge, Mass.: MIT Press, 1986.

Lerman, Allen. "Issues in Amnesty from the Federal Viewpoint." *National Tax Journal* 39 (September 1986): 325–32.

Malik, Arun, and Robert Schwab. "The Economics of Tax Amnesty." *Journal of Public Economics* 46 (October 1991): 29–49.

Mikesell, John L. "Amnesties for State Tax Evaders: The Nature of and Response to Recent Programs." *National Tax Journal* 39 (December 1986): 507–25.

Parle, William M., and Mike W. Hirlinger. "Evaluating the Use of Tax Amnesty by State Governments." *Public Administration Review* (May/June 1986): 246–55.

Spencer, Linda. "More States Conduct Tax Amnesty Programs." *Journal of State Taxation* 7 (Winter 1989): 361–71.

*Cross reference:* tax evasion.

# Tax and revenue capacity

Daphne A. Kenyon
Simmons College

*A measure that compares the relative potential tax and revenue bases ("representative capacity") of similar jurisdictions, such as the U.S. states. Tax and revenue capacity show how much revenue would be raised in each state if all states (and their local governments) applied uniform rates to a uniform set of bases.*

Tax and revenue capacity describes a government's ability to generate receipts from its own sources (i.e., exclusive intergovernmental transfers) in order to fund public services. Tax capacity refers to the potential ability (the capacity) of a government to generate receipts from taxes—compulsory payments to governments for which there is no direct quid pro quo consequent to the payment. The government essentially considers its flow of receipts independent from expenditures for any specific service. Revenue capacity measures, in addition to taxes, potential "nontax" governmental receipts to be derived from sources such as user charges and fees, interest earnings, net lottery receipts, special assessments, and sales of property. It is important to note that tax and revenue capacity are not synonymous with fiscal capacity or adequacy, which incorporate an expenditure dimension into the measurement. In this essay, the term *tax capacity* will be used to refer to both tax and revenue capacity, except where explicit distinctions are drawn.

Tax capacity is an idea that derives from applied public finance rather than economic theory. One controversy in the capacity literature involves the extent to which various measures of capacity have sound theoretical foundations (Fastrup 1986; Barro 1986). To the extent that tax capacity links to a theoretical construct, it can be thought of as being determined by the budget constraints facing a government or group of governments in a particular geographic area.

Several measures of capacity exist, all in the form of index numbers that compare the tax capacity of one state to a national or regional average or one local government to other local governments in the same state. Tax capacity measures are used to compare and monitor trends in the fiscal health of states and local governments, target grants to those governments with lesser abilities to raise revenue, or evaluate the distribution of intergovernmental grants.

Four commonly referenced indices of the capacity of state and local governments to mobilize revenues, by state, are per capita personal income (PCI), the representative tax system (RTS), the representative revenue system (RRS), and total taxable resources (TTR). Measures and rankings for 1994 are shown in table 1. The 1994 data are presented because this is the latest year for which all four measures have been estimated.

PCI, which is readily available by state from the Department of Commerce, includes labor compensation; proprietors' income; net rent, interest, and dividends; and transfer payments. PCI is the most commonly used measure of capacity in federal grant formulas; indeed, it was the only capacity measure used until 1987. (For example, the federal matching rate for Medicaid funding is inversely related to state PCI.) Despite its widespread use, PCI has been roundly criticized as a measure of governmental receipts-generating capacity. The two major criticisms are that it does not measure income sufficiently comprehensively (e.g., it omits corpo-

## TABLE 1

**Indices of 1994 State Tax and Revenue Capacity
(100 = U.S. Average)**

| State | PCI Index | PCI Rank | TTR Index | TTR Rank | RTS Index | RTS Rank | RRS Index | RRS Rank |
|---|---|---|---|---|---|---|---|---|
| Alabama | 85 | 41 | 81 | 44 | 83 | 48 | 84 | 47 |
| Alaska | 110 | 8 | 125 | 5 | 131 | 3 | 157 | 1 |
| Arizona | 89 | 38 | 88 | 36 | 93 | 35 | 92 | 35 |
| Arkansas | 79 | 49 | 78 | 48 | 81 | 50 | 80 | 49 |
| California | 103 | 13 | 105 | 13 | 105 | 14 | 105 | 15 |
| Colorado | 101 | 20 | 104 | 14 | 110 | 11 | 108 | 13 |
| Connecticut | 129 | 2 | 133 | 2 | 136 | 2 | 136 | 2 |
| Delaware | 103 | 15 | 128 | 3 | 116 | 8 | 115 | 8 |
| District of Columbia | 137 | 1 | 232 | 1 | 124 | 7 | 129 | 4 |
| Florida | 101 | 19 | 93 | 28 | 100 | 20 | 100 | 20 |
| Georgia | 93 | 33 | 96 | 21 | 95 | 28 | 94 | 28 |
| Hawaii | 109 | 10 | 114 | 8 | 125 | 6 | 122 | 6 |
| Idaho | 87 | 40 | 82 | 42 | 90 | 40 | 88 | 43 |
| Illinois | 108 | 11 | 109 | 10 | 107 | 12 | 108 | 12 |
| Indiana | 94 | 30 | 93 | 29 | 97 | 23 | 95 | 27 |
| Iowa | 93 | 31 | 91 | 34 | 93 | 34 | 92 | 36 |
| Kansas | 96 | 25 | 93 | 30 | 97 | 26 | 96 | 25 |
| Kentucky | 82 | 47 | 84 | 39 | 85 | 46 | 84 | 46 |
| Louisiana | 83 | 43 | 86 | 38 | 92 | 37 | 93 | 34 |
| Maine | 92 | 34 | 84 | 40 | 89 | 43 | 88 | 42 |
| Maryland | 112 | 6 | 108 | 11 | 107 | 13 | 109 | 11 |
| Massachusetts | 115 | 5 | 119 | 6 | 112 | 10 | 114 | 9 |
| Michigan | 102 | 17 | 99 | 19 | 101 | 19 | 101 | 19 |
| Minnesota | 100 | 21 | 104 | 15 | 104 | 15 | 103 | 17 |
| Mississippi | 76 | 51 | 72 | 51 | 71 | 51 | 71 | 51 |
| Missouri | 96 | 26 | 93 | 31 | 94 | 33 | 93 | 33 |
| Montana | 83 | 44 | 77 | 49 | 96 | 27 | 93 | 32 |
| Nebraska | 98 | 22 | 95 | 23 | 95 | 30 | 94 | 29 |
| Nevada | 110 | 9 | 110 | 9 | 141 | 1 | 133 | 3 |
| New Hampshire | 111 | 7 | 104 | 16 | 113 | 9 | 112 | 10 |
| New Jersey | 125 | 3 | 126 | 4 | 128 | 5 | 128 | 5 |
| New Mexico | 81 | 48 | 82 | 43 | 90 | 42 | 92 | 37 |
| New York | 115 | 4 | 119 | 7 | 101 | 18 | 105 | 14 |
| North Carolina | 90 | 37 | 94 | 27 | 91 | 38 | 91 | 38 |
| North Dakota | 89 | 39 | 81 | 45 | 93 | 36 | 91 | 39 |
| Ohio | 97 | 24 | 95 | 24 | 97 | 25 | 96 | 22 |
| Oklahoma | 82 | 45 | 79 | 47 | 87 | 44 | 85 | 45 |
| Oregon | 92 | 35 | 92 | 32 | 98 | 21 | 96 | 24 |
| Pennsylvania | 103 | 16 | 97 | 20 | 97 | 24 | 97 | 21 |
| Rhode Island | 102 | 18 | 96 | 22 | 94 | 32 | 95 | 26 |
| South Carolina | 83 | 42 | 83 | 41 | 86 | 45 | 85 | 44 |
| South Dakota | 94 | 29 | 88 | 37 | 91 | 39 | 89 | 41 |
| Tennessee | 92 | 36 | 92 | 33 | 90 | 41 | 90 | 40 |
| Texas | 93 | 32 | 95 | 25 | 95 | 31 | 94 | 30 |
| Utah | 79 | 50 | 81 | 46 | 85 | 47 | 84 | 48 |
| Vermont | 94 | 28 | 89 | 35 | 95 | 29 | 94 | 31 |
| Virginia | 103 | 14 | 104 | 17 | 104 | 16 | 104 | 16 |
| Washington | 106 | 12 | 103 | 18 | 103 | 17 | 103 | 18 |
| West Virginia | 82 | 46 | 75 | 50 | 81 | 49 | 80 | 50 |
| Wisconsin | 95 | 27 | 95 | 26 | 97 | 22 | 96 | 23 |
| Wyoming | 97 | 23 | 108 | 12 | 128 | 4 | 122 | 7 |

*Sources:* Compson and Navratil (1997), Tannenwald (1997), 1996 U.S. Statistical Abstract, and calculations by author.

rate income other than dividends) and that it does not take into account a government's potential to expand its capacities by exporting taxes.

The RTS was developed for the U.S. Advisory Commission on Intergovernmental Relations (ACIR) in 1962 by Selma Mushkin and Alice Rivlin and has been refined since then, with new state estimates published every few years. The RTS index is constructed by estimating the national average effective tax rates that apply to a large number of different tax bases (e.g., personal income, corporation income, severance); applying those representative rates to each state's actual tax bases; and computing the relative per capita revenue each state would raise if it levied those tax rates. The RTS has never been used to help determine the distribution of federal grants in the United States, but Canada has used an RTS method for distributing grants under its federal-provincial equalization program since 1967. Many European countries also employ some form of RTS in their intergovernmental transfer arrangements (Bird and Wallich 1995).

The RTS has an advantage over PCI in that the RTS implicitly takes some tax-exporting opportunities into account by including severance taxes and selective sales taxes related to tourist activity among its tax bases. The primary criticism of the RTS is that it cannot be derived from the theory of government budget constraint. For example, the RTS adds sales tax capacity to income tax capacity in computing total tax capacity. The theorist would argue that tax capacity depends primarily on resident income and that there is no independent sales tax capacity. Another criticism of the RTS is that it does not take into account tax exporting through federal deductibility of state and local taxes.

The RRS, which is very similar to the RTS, was developed by the ACIR in 1986. The ACIR RRS includes the tax bases used in the RTS plus the revenue bases of rents and royalties, lotteries, and user charges. As shown in table 1, most states have nearly identical rankings under the RTS and the RRS.

TTR is defined as the unduplicated sum of income produced within a state and income received by its residents that a state can potentially tax. As the concept is currently implemented, TTR is calculated by assigning a share of the nation's gross domestic product (GDP) to each state. A state's share is equal to the state's average share of the nation's personal income and GDP. TTR is currently used as a measure of receipts-generating capacity for the Community Mental Health Services and Substance Abuse Prevention and Treatment block grants (Compson and Navratil 1997). TTR is more comprehensive than PCI and may be considered more theoretically consistent than either the RTS or the RRS, but TTR does not account for tax exporting through federal tax deductibility.

Table 1 shows how the measure of tax or revenue capacity used would affect the states (although the relative values of the indices are likely to change over time). The RTS and the RRS give very similar results, but these two indices sometimes differ considerably from the other capacity measures. For 11 states (Alaska, Delaware, District of Columbia, Hawaii, Louisiana, Montana, Nevada, New Mexico, New York, North Dakota, and Wyoming), there is at least a 10-point difference in index numbers among the four alternative measures of tax or revenue capacity.

Measures of tax or revenue capacity can also be generated for local governments within states or for cities across the United States, but such research is at a more preliminary stage than that for the state capacity measures described here (Ferguson and Ladd 1986; Texas Advisory Commission on Intergovernmental Relations 1986). Current efforts to advise less-developed countries or transition economies use capacity measures as guides for grant programs (Bahl 1994; Ma 1997).

## Additional readings

Advisory Commission on Intergovernmental Relations. *RTS 1991: State Revenue Capacity and Effort*. Washington, D.C.: U.S. Government Printing Office, 1993.

Bahl, Roy. "Revenues and Revenue Assignment: Intergovernmental Fiscal Relations in the Russian Federation." In *Russia and the Challenge of Fiscal Federalism*, edited by Christine I. Wallich. Washington, D.C.: The World Bank, 1994.

Barro, Stephen M. "State Fiscal Capacity Measures: A Theoretical Critique." In *Measuring Fiscal Capacity*, edited by H. Clyde Reeves. Boston, Mass.: Oelgeschlager, Gunn & Hain, 1986.

Bird, Richard, and Christine Wallich. "Financing Local Government in Hungary." In *Decentralization of the Socialist State*, edited by Richard Bird, Robert Ebel, and Christine Wallich. Washington, D.C.: The World Bank, 1995.

Cohen, Carol, Robert Lucke, and John Shannon. "The ACIR Representative Tax System for Estimating the Fiscal Capacity of the Fifty State-Local Systems." In *Measuring Fiscal Capacity*, edited by H. Clyde Reeves. Boston, Mass.: Oelgeschlager, Gunn & Hain, 1986.

Compson, Michael, and John Navratil. "An Improved Method for Estimating the Total Taxable Resources of the States." Research Paper No. 9702, Office of the Assistant Secretary for Economic Policy, U.S. Department of the Treasury. Washington, D.C.: U.S. Government Printing Office, 1997.

Fastrup, Jerry C. "Fiscal Capacity, Fiscal Equalization, and Federal Grant Formulas." In *Federal-State-Local Fiscal Relations: Technical Papers, Vol. I*, Office of State and

Local Finance, U.S. Department of the Treasury. Washington, D.C.: U.S. Government Printing Office, 1986.

Ferguson, Ronald F., and Helen F. Ladd. "Measuring the Fiscal Capacity of U.S. Cities." In *Measuring Fiscal Capacity*, edited by H. Clyde Reeves. Boston, Mass.: Oelgeschlager, Gunn & Hain, 1986.

Ma, Jun. "Intergovernmental Fiscal Transfers in Nine Countries: Lessons for Developing Countries." Policy Research Working Paper 1822. Washington, D.C.: The World Bank, 1997.

Rafuse, Robert. *Representative Expenditures: Addressing the Neglected Dimension of Fiscal Capacity*. Washington, D.C.: Advisory Commission on Intergovernmental Relations, 1990.

Sawicky, Max B. "The 'Total Taxable Resources' Definition of State Revenue-Raising Ability." In *Federal-State-Local Fiscal Relations: Technical Papers, Vol. 1*, Office of State and Local Finance, U.S. Department of the Treasury. Washington, D.C.: U.S. Government Printing Office, 1985.

Tannenwald, Robert. "Come the Devolution: Will the States Be Able to Respond?" A paper presented to the National Tax Association/Boston Federal Reserve Bank Colloquium on Devolution. Boston, Mass., September 12, 1997.

Texas Advisory Commission on Intergovernmental Relations. "Local Government Fiscal Capacity Measures: A Profile of State Studies." In *Federal-State-Local Fiscal Relations: Technical Papers, Vol. I*, Office of State and Local Finance, U.S. Department of the Treasury. Washington, D.C.: U.S. Government Printing Office, 1986.

*Cross references:* tax and revenue effort; tax competition; tax exportation.

# Tax and revenue effort

Daphne A. Kenyon
Simmons College

*Tax and revenue effort refers to the extent to which a government uses the potential receipts-generating capacity (tax or revenue bases) available to it.*

Tax and revenue effort is measured as a ratio of revenues collected to capacity, so there are potentially as many effort indices as there are indices of capacity.

As with the term *capacity*, tax or revenue effort refers to comparisons among governments and not to the fiscal well-being of taxpayers (individuals or businesses). This distinction between a government's fiscal status and that of its taxpayers may be significant if some governments are able to generate large amounts of revenues from nonresidents through tax exporting. Thus, a government may have a high tax or revenue effort that places a low burden on its taxpayers if it can take advantage of opportunities for tax exporting.

Effort measures can be used to monitor the fiscal health of state or local governments. Effort can be an indicator of fiscal stress, because attempts to collect more revenues on a given base or shrinkage of the revenue base can be considered fiscally stressful events (Benson et al. 1988). Measures of effort have also been used in grant formulas to reward those governments raising a higher level of revenues. For example, the General Revenue Sharing program (1972–86) allocated greater funds to those states with higher tax effort, measured as the ratio of state and local tax revenue to aggregate state personal income.

Since 1962, the U.S. Advisory Commission on Intergovernmental Relations (ACIR) has published periodic estimates of state and local tax or revenue effort together with its state capacity estimates. The most recent estimates of capacity and effort using the representative tax system (RTS) and the representative revenue system (RRS), developed by Tannenwald (1997), are shown in table 1. The RTS and the RRS measure effort as the ratio of actual revenues collected to estimated revenue capacity.

Those states whose collections exceed their estimated capacity have an effort index greater than 100. States that rank in the top five for both tax and revenue effort are the District of Columbia, Wisconsin, and New York. States that rank in the bottom five for both tax and revenue effort are Nevada, New Hampshire, and Tennessee.

Because the RTS methodology includes separate capacity and effort index measures for each of the many different tax bases, additional uses can be made of the effort measurements. Any state can use disaggregated tax effort measures to determine potential revenue-raising opportunities or overuse of particular tax bases relative to the U.S. average. For example, New Hampshire was assigned these disaggregated tax effort indices in 1994: general sales and gross receipts, 0; total selective sales taxes, 80; personal income taxes, 5; corporate net income and net worth taxes, 113; and total property taxes, 199 (Tannenwald 1997). These figures indicate unused capacity with respect to general sales and gross receipts, selective sales, and personal income taxes; and utilization of capacity in excess of the U.S. average for corporate net income and property taxes.

An individual tax effort index under the RTS methodology can be interpreted as a measure of relative effective tax rate, thanks to the uniform methodology used to estimate the size of each of the many potential tax bases for each state. Effec-

## TABLE 1

### Indices of 1994 State Tax and Revenue Capacity and Effort
(100 = U.S. Average)

| State | RTS Capacity | RTS Effort | RRS Capacity | RRS Effort |
|---|---|---|---|---|
| Alabama | 83 | 80 | 84 | 94 |
| Alaska | 131 | 103 | 157 | 110 |
| Arizona | 93 | 97 | 92 | 94 |
| Arkansas | 81 | 86 | 80 | 88 |
| California | 105 | 96 | 105 | 98 |
| Colorado | 110 | 85 | 108 | 89 |
| Connecticut | 136 | 106 | 136 | 94 |
| Delaware | 116 | 89 | 115 | 97 |
| District of Columbia | 124 | 149 | 129 | 127 |
| Florida | 100 | 91 | 100 | 96 |
| Georgia | 95 | 93 | 94 | 99 |
| Hawaii | 125 | 107 | 122 | 107 |
| Idaho | 90 | 90 | 88 | 96 |
| Illinois | 107 | 96 | 108 | 90 |
| Indiana | 97 | 91 | 95 | 97 |
| Iowa | 93 | 103 | 92 | 108 |
| Kansas | 97 | 99 | 96 | 100 |
| Kentucky | 85 | 95 | 84 | 95 |
| Louisiana | 92 | 78 | 93 | 91 |
| Maine | 89 | 110 | 88 | 104 |
| Maryland | 107 | 103 | 109 | 97 |
| Massachusetts | 112 | 105 | 114 | 100 |
| Michigan | 101 | 105 | 101 | 105 |
| Minnesota | 104 | 109 | 103 | 112 |
| Mississippi | 71 | 97 | 71 | 106 |
| Missouri | 94 | 83 | 93 | 82 |
| Montana | 96 | 85 | 93 | 87 |
| Nebraska | 95 | 100 | 94 | 103 |
| Nevada | 141 | 69 | 133 | 75 |
| New Hampshire | 113 | 81 | 112 | 78 |
| New Jersey | 128 | 104 | 128 | 98 |
| New Mexico | 90 | 96 | 92 | 101 |
| New York | 101 | 159 | 105 | 144 |
| North Carolina | 91 | 96 | 91 | 97 |
| North Dakota | 93 | 90 | 91 | 99 |
| Ohio | 97 | 95 | 96 | 95 |
| Oklahoma | 87 | 89 | 85 | 95 |
| Oregon | 98 | 96 | 96 | 103 |
| Pennsylvania | 97 | 101 | 97 | 97 |
| Rhode Island | 94 | 111 | 95 | 100 |
| South Carolina | 86 | 88 | 85 | 103 |
| South Dakota | 91 | 83 | 89 | 86 |
| Tennessee | 90 | 81 | 90 | 87 |
| Texas | 95 | 89 | 94 | 90 |
| Utah | 85 | 93 | 84 | 101 |
| Vermont | 95 | 109 | 94 | 102 |
| Virginia | 104 | 86 | 104 | 89 |
| Washington | 103 | 105 | 103 | 107 |
| West Virginia | 81 | 95 | 80 | 99 |
| Wisconsin | 97 | 116 | 96 | 113 |
| Wyoming | 128 | 82 | 122 | 93 |

*Source:* Tannenwald (1997).

tive and nominal tax rates can differ greatly when some states employ a broad tax base and others a narrow one.

Analysts can also use the tax effort measures to evaluate the extent to which an individual state's tax mix differs from that of the average state. The New Hampshire figures cited above indicate that the state relies much more on property taxes than the average state, somewhat more on corporate income taxes, less on selective sales taxes, and much less on general sales and personal income taxes.

A number of states have computed receipts-generating effort indices for their local governments. For example, Maryland computes capacity and effort for its counties and the city of Baltimore, and Virginia computes revenue capacity and effort for all of its cities and counties (Advisory Commission on Intergovernmental Relations 1993: 5). In addition, several states use some measure of revenue effort as a factor in allocating grant funds to local governments (Texas Advisory Commission on Intergovernmental Relations 1986: 276).

There are important limits in the information that can be gleaned from fiscal effort measures, however. High fiscal effort may be an indication of many different phenomena: above-average expenditure needs, voter tastes for above-average government spending, waste in government spending, successful efforts of interest groups pressing for more government spending, or below-average tax or revenue capacity. Further, because effort is a ratio of revenues to capacity, effort indices will rise either when revenues are raised or when capacity falls. Both changes would lead to fiscal stress, but each has very different policy implications for relieving that stress.

## Additional readings

Advisory Commission on Intergovernmental Relations. *RTS 1991: State Revenue Capacity and Effort.* Washington, D.C.: U.S. Government Printing Office, 1993.

Benson, Earl D., Barry R. Marks, and K.K. Raman. "Tax Effort as an Indicator of Fiscal Stress." *Public Finance Quarterly* 16 (April 1988): 203–217.

Gold, Steven D. "Measuring Fiscal Effort and Fiscal Capacity: Sorting Out Some of the Controversies." In *Measuring Fiscal Capacity*, edited by H. Clyde Reeves. Boston, Mass.: Oelgeschlager, Gunn & Hain, 1986.

Tannenwald, Robert. "Come the Devolution: Will the States Be Able to Respond?" A paper presented to the National Tax Association/Boston Federal Reserve Bank Colloquium on Devolution. Boston, Mass., September 12, 1997.

Texas Advisory Commission on Intergovernmental Relations. "Local Government Fiscal Capacity Measures: A Profile of State Studies." In *Federal-State-Local Fiscal Relations: Technical Papers, Vol. I*, Office of State and

Local Finance, U.S. Department of the Treasury. Washington, D.C.: U.S. Government Printing Office, 1986.

*Cross reference:* tax and revenue capacity.

# Tax arbitrage

Andrew A. Samwick
Dartmouth College

*Profit opportunities created by differential taxation of gains and losses.*

An arbitrage is the opportunity to buy and sell the same asset in two different markets in order to profit from a price differential. By purchasing the asset in the market where it is cheaper and selling it in the market where it is more expensive, the investor can earn the difference in prices without incurring any risk. In a tax arbitrage, the price differential is the result of a feature of the tax code that treats gains and losses generated by an asset asymmetrically.

The assets that form the basis of tax arbitrages are typically financial rather than real. Consequently, buying and selling an asset at different prices is equivalent to lending and borrowing the same cash flows at different after-tax interest rates. Under a pure income tax system, interest paid on borrowed funds is deductible from taxable income, and interest received on loaned funds is included in taxable income. Tax arbitrage occurs whenever it is possible to use borrowed funds whose interest expenses are fully deductible to lend in the same market at an interest rate that is not fully taxed. The size of the deductions will exceed that of the receipts, and the investor's tax burden on income from other sources will be reduced.

Under the current tax code, the primary source of deductible interest payments for households is home mortgages or other home equity loans. A household can engage in a "debt" tax arbitrage by taking out a home equity loan and investing the proceeds in municipal bonds, the interest on which is untaxed. Alternatively, the household could use the loan to buy taxable bonds and hold them in an individual retirement account (IRA) or make larger contributions to a pension plan that invests in taxable bonds. Investment income on assets in these retirement accounts is tax-deferred until retirement. An additional tax advantage may exist if the household's marginal tax rate is lower in retirement than during its working years. (A similar tax arbitrage is also available to a corporation that sponsors a pension plan in which a fund is established to provide for promised future benefits. No income tax is paid

on contributions to the pension fund or the income earned on the fund until the fund is distributed to pensioners. The corporation could simultaneously issue a bond, on which interest is fully deductible, make a larger contribution to its pension fund, and invest the contribution in a taxable bond of similar duration and risk to the one it issued.)

Households can also engage in "equity" tax arbitrages. The asymmetry in the tax treatment of equities is that capital gains and losses are taxed only when they are realized, not when they are accrued. Because the household determines when to buy or sell its stock, losses can be taken immediately while gains are postponed. A tax arbitrage can therefore be constructed simply by simultaneously buying and short-selling two highly correlated portfolios of stocks. At the end of a year, one of the positions will have increased in value and the other will have decreased. The latter can be liquidated to generate a loss for tax purposes. The investor can then maintain the tax arbitrage by taking an offsetting position in a new portfolio of stocks that is highly correlated with the position that has increased in value. The effective tax rate on the gains when all positions are liquidated is further reduced by either a preferential statutory tax rate of 28 percent on capital gains (for high-income investors) or the step-up of basis of the value of capital gains at death. (This example is based on Stiglitz (1985), who shows how strategies of this sort can be used to eliminate an investor's tax liability on all capital income and, in some cases, on all ordinary income as well.)

Provisions in the tax code and other capital market imperfections prevent households from fully exploiting either of these tax arbitrages. In the debt tax arbitrage, the government allows interest deductions primarily in conjunction with real estate holdings. The size of the debt that can be issued to finance the purchase of tax-preferred assets is therefore limited by the size of the real estate. There are also fairly low limits on the amounts that can be contributed to IRAs and other tax-preferred accounts. It is also important to note that neither the mortgage borrowing, nor the real estate on which it is based, nor the tax-preferred assets that are purchased are riskless. Banks will charge a premium over the risk-free rate for the mortgage that may exceed the tax advantages to the municipal bond or retirement account.

These obstacles are even more pronounced for the equity arbitrage. Transaction costs associated with trading stocks are not negligible, particularly when short-sales are involved. There are also fairly low limits on how much of a net capital loss can be used to offset noncapital income in a given year rather than being carried forward. Households without substantial other capital income will find the tax arbitrage strategy less profitable. More important, the equity tax arbitrage cannot be constructed simply by buying and selling two different shares of the same security. The investor must find two different portfolios that are highly correlated. Because this correlation will in practice be less than perfect, the investor will be exposed to risk. (Standard portfolio theory has strong conclusions regarding the optimality of holding well-diversified portfolios of risky assets. Asset pricing models typically imply that idiosyncratic risk that could have been diversified away is not reflected in the price of securities. Tax arbitrage using different portfolios implies an exposure to some idiosyncratic risk.) An investor's willingness to exploit a potential tax arbitrage may be limited by aversion to this risk.

A corporate tax arbitrage that has been of interest to policymakers is that of accelerated depreciation. The reduction in the present value of an asset over time is called its economic depreciation. Under an income tax, this depreciation should be deducted from the firm's taxable income each year. Historically, the federal tax code has allowed firms to claim depreciation expenses in a fashion that is accelerated relative to the asset's economic depreciation. In the period before the Tax Reform Act of 1986 (TRA86), two common forms of accelerated depreciation were the accelerated cost recovery system (ACRS) and the investment tax credit (ITC). When the asset is sold, the gain is taken with respect to the depreciated basis, but the gain may be treated preferentially. A corporation that borrows to purchase an asset that is eligible for accelerated depreciation is engaging in a tax arbitrage similar to the debt tax arbitrage described above. (See Warren (1985) for a thorough discussion of depreciation and tax arbitrage.) As in the debt tax arbitrage, an investor's risk aversion will limit the extent to which this arbitrage is exploited. Additionally, because the asset involved is real rather than financial, diminishing marginal returns to investment may limit the amount of funds that can be arbitraged in this way.

In the years before TRA86, there was a thriving tax shelter industry that was based on extending this corporate tax arbitrage to individual investors. Tax shelters were typically packaged as limited partnerships, which combined the advantages of limited liability found in corporations with the pass-through of profits and losses to the taxable incomes of the partners. Before TRA86, the top marginal tax rate for individual investors exceeded that of corporations, so the ability to deduct interest payments suggested that noncorporate entities should borrow to purchase depreciable assets and then lease them to corporations. (An obvious tax arbitrage would be for a corporation to sell its asset to a limited partnership and then agree to lease it back in perpetuity. Such sale-leaseback arrangements are prohibited by law.) TRA86 contained a number of provisions that were targeted at tax shelters, including the repeal of the ITC, the lengthening of depreciation schedules, the lowering of top marginal tax rates, and the passive activity loss limitations (PALLs). The PALLs limited the extent to which losses from activities in which the investor did not materially participate (i.e., limited partnerships) could offset gains from other sources. (Cordes and Galper (1985) discuss tax shelters before TRA86. Samwick (1996) analyzes the impact of TRA86's several anti-tax shelter provisions on their subsequent decline.)

Tax arbitrages can be understood as unintended consequences of government tax policy. Because home ownership, retirement security, investment, and the like are viewed as desirable social objectives, the federal government has attempted to promote them through the tax code. But the government cannot, for example, require that households use their IRAs only for retirement. Each special provision permits the possibility that it will be used only to lower households' tax liabilities and not to further the government's objective. Tax policy has been modified to strike a balance between promoting the objective and limiting abuse. In the case of IRAs and pensions, there are ceilings on contributions for both individuals and corporations. The size of the tax preference on particular assets may be tied to the investor's willingness to bear risk, such as the limited offset of capital losses against contemporaneous noncapital income and the PALLs. The most obvious abuses are simply prohibited directly by law, such as the buying and selling of the same security in the equity tax arbitrage or sale-leaseback arrangements between corporate and noncorporate entities.

These restrictions also play a role in establishing equilibrium asset prices. Asset markets cannot be in equilibrium if there are exploitable arbitrage opportunities. The price of each asset must be such that no investor has an opportunity to profit by tax arbitrage. This implies that the risk-adjusted after-tax return on all investments must be equal at the margin or that the marginal investment is prohibited by a legal or institutional constraint. Tax policy will therefore have an impact on the rates of return of all assets and the distribution of asset holdings in the population, but in equilibrium, no investor will be able to profit by engaging in another tax arbitrage. Cordes and Galper (1985) discuss tax shelters before TRA86. Samwick (1996) analyzes the impact of TRA86's several anti-tax shelter provisions on their subsequent decline.

### Additional readings

Cordes, Joseph J., and Harvey Galper. "Tax Shelter Activity: Lessons from Twenty Years of Experience." *National Tax Journal* 38 (September 1985): 305–24.

Miller, Merton H. "Debt and Taxes." *Journal of Finance* 32 (May 1977): 261–76.

Ross, Stephen A. "Arbitrage and Martingales with Taxation." *Journal of Political Economy* 95 (April 1987): 371–93.

Samwick, Andrew A. "Tax Shelters and Passive Losses after the Tax Reform Act of 1986." In *Empirical Foundations of Household Taxation,* edited by Martin Feldstein and James M. Poterba. Chicago: University of Chicago Press, 1996.

Stiglitz, Joseph E. "The General Theory of Tax Avoidance." *National Tax Journal* 38 (September 1985): 325–37.

Warren, Jr., Alvin C. "Accelerated Capital Recovery, Debt, and Tax Arbitrage." *Tax Lawyer* 38 (3) (1985): 549–74.

*Cross references:* capital cost recovery; capital gains taxation; depreciation recapture; expensing; individual retirement accounts; interest deductibility; investment tax credits; partnerships; passive activity losses; tax shelters.

# Tax competition

## Robert Tannenwald
Federal Reserve Bank of Boston

*The design of tax policy to attract and to retain geographically mobile capital, labor, and consumption.*

Always a contentious issue, tax competition is more salient and more controversial today than ever before. Over the past 15 years, profound technological and political changes have enhanced the geographic mobility of capital, extended firms' geographic range, and therefore heightened economic competition in the United States and throughout the world. These developments have stimulated interest in tax competition at all levels of government, from the municipal to the supranational.

## Forms of tax competition

Tax competition can be *explicit* or *implicit* (Kenyon 1991). Governments engage in explicit tax competition when they enact tax laws and regulations *expressly* designed to enhance the attractiveness of their jurisdiction to businesses, residents, employees, or consumers. The purest form of such competition is "smokestack chasing," offers of tax benefits to a specific company on condition that it locate facilities within a particular jurisdiction. For example, in 1993 the city of Tuscaloosa and the state of Alabama offered Daimler-Benz, Inc., an estimated $150 million in tax incentives to build a new Mercedes-Benz plant in Tuscaloosa.

Governments engage in implicit tax competition when they modify their pursuit of other tax policy goals—such as equity, neutrality, simplicity, revenue adequacy, or tax exporting—in order to mitigate anticompetitive consequences. An example was Florida's decision in December 1987 to abandon its attempt to tax services under its sales tax. Earlier that year, Florida had incorporated a wide array of services into its sales tax base in order to enhance the tax's lucrativeness, equity, and neutrality. After several interest groups, especially those representing advertisers and the media, claimed that taxing them would drive businesses out of the state, the state reversed itself.

## Effectiveness of tax-competitive strategies

Hundreds of empirical studies have investigated the extent to which a jurisdiction's tax characteristics influence its attractiveness to businesses, employees, residents, and consumers (literature surveys can be found in Bartik 1991, Wasylenko 1991, and Tannenwald 1993). Most studies conclude that (1) taxes are a less powerful determinant of business location and expansion than centrality of location, wage rates, regulatory burden, and the availability of appropriately skilled labor; and (2) because sites within a metropolitan area tend to be similar with respect to these prime locational determinants, taxes are a more effective instrument of intrametropolitan competition than of intermetropolitan or interstate competition.

Evidence concerning the effectiveness of tax policy as an instrument of interstate and intermetropolitan economic competition is inconclusive, however. Until about 15 years ago, most academic studies found very little connection between interstate tax differences and interstate differences in economic performance. Since about 1980, empirical studies have produced mixed results. While many studies still conclude that taxes "don't matter," several others have found that differences among states in tax characteristics do affect economic growth and site selection by firms. Moreover, there is still little agreement among academic studies about which interstate tax differences are the most significant locational determinants. Recent studies indicate that tax characteristics exerting a significant effect in the 1960s and 1970s exerted no such effect during the 1980s (see, e.g., McGuire and Wasylenko 1987 and Wasylenko and Carroll 1994). (See Business location, taxes.)

## The difficulty of evaluating a jurisdiction's tax competitiveness

No statistics are widely recognized as superior indicators of tax competitiveness. This is not surprising, given the absence of conclusive empirical evidence on which tax characteristics, if any, most heavily influence location.

Neoclassical economic theory, however, provides some insight into the characteristics of a good indicator of tax competitiveness. The prototypical neoclassical firm should be most concerned about how taxes imposed at a given site affect the long-run rate of return on its investments. Consequently, it should be most sensitive to interjurisdictional differences in the burden of those taxes that most directly affect its profitability, such as taxes on corporate profits, industrial and commercial property, and the purchase of intermediate goods.

The neoclassical firm should also be concerned about the burden of state and local taxes paid by individuals, such as the personal income tax, the residential property tax, and the retail sales tax. Such taxes can indirectly affect a firm's bottom line by inducing workers to demand higher pretax compensation. Highly compensated managers and professionals are more likely than other workers to make their wage demands stick because they are well-informed and possess scarce, valuable skills. Consequently, a jurisdiction's tax competitiveness theoretically should be affected by how heavily it taxes its high-income households.

Estimating how the burden of business taxes and taxes on high-income households varies across subnational jurisdictions is hindered by (1) the absence of subnational data on business profits, (2) the tendency of state and municipal governments not to report the division of their property tax and sales receipts between residential and nonresidential taxpayers, and (3) differences across jurisdictions in the ability of firms to export the burden of their taxes to taxpayers in other jurisdictions (see Incidence of taxes and Tax exportation).

Despite these empirical difficulties, many states and municipalities closely monitor their tax competitiveness with whatever imperfect statistics are available. Four of the most widely monitored and publicized indicators of state tax competitiveness are (1) total receipts from taxes levied by all state and municipal jurisdictions within the state's boundaries divided by the total personal income of its residents, (2) total state and municipal taxes per capita, (3) total receipts from all own-source revenues (fees and charges as well as taxes) as a percentage of statewide personal income, and (4) total receipts from all own-source revenues per capita. None of these indicators focuses on those taxes that theoretically should concern businesses the most.

As table 1 shows, the ranking of many states varies dramatically from measure to measure.

Perhaps the most misleading, widely cited indicator of a state's tax competitiveness is "business's share": the percentage of all state and local taxes imposed within a state for which businesses, as opposed to households, are liable. In constructing this measure, analysts classify each state and local tax according to whether it is paid by businesses or households. For each state, taxes paid by both types of taxpayers, such as the property tax and sales tax, are decomposed into their business and household components. The statistic was first constructed by the U.S. Advisory Commission on Intergovernmental Relations (1981). The tax system of a state collecting a relatively large share of its taxes from businesses, as opposed to households, is sometimes criticized as "uncompetitive" and "unfair" to business. Estimates of business's share in fiscal year 1990 for the 50 states and the District of Columbia are displayed in the fifth column of table 1.

Unlike the indicators shown in first four columns of the table, business's share focuses on those state and local taxes that should concern businesses the most. Nevertheless, the share of a state's taxes collected from businesses has little to do with how heavily or fairly its businesses are taxed. Business's share is influenced primarily by two characteristics of a state's economy: its capital intensity and the importance of extractive industries in its industrial mix (Tannenwald 1994). In states with capital-intensive economies, the bases of major business taxes, such as profits (the return to capital) and nonresidential property, are large relative to the bases of major household taxes, such as personal income. Business taxes *as a percentage of* profits, however, are not necessarily high. States rich in extractable resources, such as Alaska, Wyoming, and Montana, generate a large fraction of their revenues from severance taxes and property taxes on natural resources. The burden of these taxes is borne by energy consumers throughout the world, companies engaged in mineral extraction, or owners of mineral rights, not by business as a whole. In these states, business's share bears little relationship to how heavily the typical business is taxed.

In recent years, economists have experimented with *the representative firm approach* to evaluating a jurisdiction's tax competitiveness. Businesses representative of selected industries are assumed to invest in a new facility at various sites. All nontax costs are assumed to be constant across sites. Each firm's liability for taxes levied by all levels of government is computed at each site before and after the investment is undertaken. The more taxes levied at a given site depress the rate of return on the new facility, the less competitive is the site (see Papke and Papke 1981 and Tannenwald 1993). A similar approach has been tried with representative

**TABLE 1**

## Selected Frequently Cited Indicators of State Tax Competitiveness

| | 1995 State and Local Taxes as a Percentage of Personal Income | Rank | 1995 State and Local Taxes Per Capita ($) | Rank | 1995 State and Local General Own-Source Revenue as a Percentage of Personal Income | Rank | 1995 State and Local General Own-Source Revenue Per Capita ($) | Rank | 1990 Business Share of State and Local Taxes (percent) | Rank |
|---|---|---|---|---|---|---|---|---|---|---|
| Alabama | 9.6 | 2 | 1,713.0 | 51 | 15.8 | 39 | 2,806.0 | 47 | 33.8 | 11 |
| Alaska | 19.0 | 51 | 4,460.0 | 1 | 54.8 | 1 | 12,872.1 | 1 | 78.8 | 1 |
| Arizona | 12.4 | 42 | 2,291.6 | 29 | 16.7 | 26 | 3,092.0 | 39 | 31.8 | 19 |
| Arkansas | 0.6 | 9 | 1,764.6 | 50 | 15.3 | 43 | 2,538.9 | 51 | 24.4 | 41 |
| California | 11.6 | 27 | 2,570.1 | 15 | 16.8 | 25 | 3,736.4 | 13 | 30.1 | 24 |
| Colorado | 10.7 | 11 | 2,332.9 | 26 | 16.2 | 32 | 3,528.7 | 19 | 28.4 | 33 |
| Connecticut | 12.7 | 44 | 3,687.4 | 4 | 15.4 | 42 | 4,480.7 | 4 | 32.2 | 15 |
| Delaware | 11.9 | 35 | 2,703.9 | 12 | 19.7 | 6 | 4,462.7 | 5 | — | — |
| District of Columbia | 14.0 | 49 | 4,401.1 | 2 | 17.1 | 19 | 5,390.1 | 2 | 45.7 | 4 |
| Florida | 10.6 | 8 | 2,252.3 | 31 | 16.1 | 34 | 3,433.0 | 24 | 34.5 | 10 |
| Georgia | 11.2 | 19 | 2,214.5 | 32 | 16.6 | 28 | 3,278.3 | 33 | 25.5 | 38 |
| Hawaii | 12.8 | 45 | 3,057.8 | 6 | 18.0 | 10 | 4,299.9 | 9 | 24.1 | 43 |
| Idaho | 11.5 | 26 | 2,062.2 | 40 | 17.5 | 15 | 3,136.6 | 37 | 24.1 | 44 |
| Illinois | 11.2 | 16 | 2,618.8 | 14 | 14.9 | 45 | 3,496.1 | 21 | 29.3 | 27 |
| Indiana | 11.0 | 13 | 2,201.0 | 34 | 16.4 | 29 | 3,292.4 | 32 | 26.2 | 37 |
| Iowa | 12.3 | 39 | 2,465.5 | 20 | 17.9 | 11 | 3,598.0 | 16 | 19.3 | 50 |
| Kansas | 11.5 | 22 | 2,369.3 | 24 | 16.6 | 27 | 3,426.8 | 25 | 36.6 | 9 |
| Kentucky | 11.9 | 36 | 2,100.8 | 38 | 17.0 | 21 | 2,986.5 | 43 | 31.9 | 18 |
| Louisiana | 10.5 | 6 | 1,838.5 | 47 | 17.2 | 18 | 3,010.3 | 41 | 44.1 | 5 |
| Maine | 12.7 | 43 | 2,466.3 | 19 | 16.9 | 23 | 3,298.6 | 30 | 23.2 | 46 |
| Maryland | 11.2 | 18 | 2,757.9 | 10 | 14.8 | 46 | 3,660.3 | 14 | 25.5 | 39 |
| Massachusetts | 11.7 | 32 | 2,980.1 | 8 | 15.8 | 40 | 4,018.9 | 10 | 20.7 | 48 |
| Michigan | 11.1 | 15 | 2,453.7 | 21 | 16.0 | 35 | 3,536.8 | 18 | 28.7 | 29 |
| Minnesota | 13.6 | 47 | 2,996.2 | 7 | 19.8 | 5 | 4,357.8 | 7 | 24.2 | 42 |
| Mississippi | 11.4 | 21 | 1,776.3 | 49 | 17.5 | 16 | 2,733.8 | 49 | 32.2 | 16 |
| Missouri | 10.5 | 7 | 2,147.8 | 36 | 14.4 | 48 | 2,938.8 | 44 | 29.4 | 26 |
| Montana | 11.6 | 30 | 2,037.6 | 42 | 17.6 | 14 | 3,094.0 | 38 | 51.5 | 3 |
| Nebraska | 11.6 | 29 | 2,397.6 | 23 | 16.9 | 24 | 3,480.8 | 22 | 21.0 | 47 |
| Nevada | 11.3 | 2 | 2,567.1 | 16 | 16.0 | 36 | 3,636.7 | 15 | 31.2 | 20 |
| New Hampshire | 9.7 | 3 | 2,267.1 | 30 | 13.7 | 51 | 3,216.9 | 34 | 37.3 | 8 |
| New Jersey | 11.9 | 34 | 3,284.7 | 5 | 16.2 | 33 | 4,462.5 | 6 | 29.5 | 25 |
| New Mexico | 12.9 | 46 | 2,147.0 | 37 | 20.7 | 3 | 3,464.2 | 23 | 33.0 | 12 |
| New York | 15.3 | 50 | 3,932.5 | 3 | 20.1 | 4 | 5,174.8 | 3 | 28.5 | 31 |
| North Carolina | 11.5 | 25 | 2,209.7 | 33 | 16.4 | 30 | 3,146.6 | 35 | 26.6 | 36 |
| North Dakota | 11.8 | 33 | 2,183.4 | 35 | 18.2 | 9 | 3,378.1 | 27 | 32.4 | 13 |
| Ohio | 11.6 | 28 | 2,405.3 | 22 | 15.9 | 38 | 3,305.0 | 29 | 28.4 | 32 |
| Oklahoma | 11.1 | 14 | 1,935.1 | 44 | 16.3 | 31 | 2,843.6 | 46 | 32.0 | 17 |
| Oregon | 11.5 | 24 | 2,309.2 | 27 | 17.8 | 12 | 3,581.9 | 17 | 28.7 | 30 |
| Pennsylvania | 11.2 | 17 | 2,476.6 | 17 | 15.1 | 44 | 3,355.3 | 28 | 31.0 | 22 |
| Rhode Island | 12.0 | 37 | 2,660.5 | 13 | 15.9 | 37 | 3,517.7 | 20 | 23.7 | 45 |
| South Carolina | 10.9 | 12 | 1,922.0 | 45 | 17.3 | 17 | 3,050.3 | 40 | 30.5 | 23 |
| South Dakota | 9.9 | 4 | 1,914.2 | 46 | 14.4 | 49 | 2,795.8 | 48 | 25.4 | 40 |
| Tennessee | 9.4 | 1 | 1,790.4 | 48 | 14.0 | 50 | 2,672.4 | 50 | 32.4 | 14 |
| Texas | 10.7 | 10 | 2,066.3 | 39 | 15.5 | 41 | 2,998.1 | 42 | 42.8 | 6 |
| Utah | 12.3 | 38 | 2,058.8 | 41 | 18.7 | 7 | 3,137.3 | 36 | 28.2 | 34 |
| Vermont | 10.4 | 5 | 2,307.3 | 28 | 14.8 | 47 | 3,294.9 | 31 | 29.1 | 28 |
| Virginia | 12.4 | 41 | 2,468.6 | 18 | 17.1 | 20 | 3,412.9 | 26 | 26.8 | 35 |
| Washington | 12.3 | 40 | 2,727.9 | 11 | 17.7 | 13 | 3,933.6 | 11 | 31.0 | 21 |
| West Virginia | 13.7 | 48 | 2,831.4 | 9 | 18.4 | 8 | 3,819.7 | 12 | 20.4 | 49 |
| Wisconsin | 11.5 | 23 | 1,954.9 | 43 | 17.0 | 22 | 2,890.6 | 45 | 42.6 | 7 |
| Wyoming | 11.7 | 31 | 2,358.1 | 25 | 21.5 | 2 | 4,336.2 | 8 | 68.3 | 2 |

*Sources:* U.S. Bureau of the Census and Robert Tannenwald, "Massachusetts's Tax Competitiveness," *New England Economic Review* (January/February 1994), page 39.

households (see, for example, Government of the District of Columbia 1993 and Tannenwald 1994).

## Costs and benefits of interjurisdictional tax competition

Critics of interjurisdictional tax competition contend that (1) state and local tax incentives generally produce little "bang for the buck," rewarding firms for behavior that they would have exhibited anyway; (2) tax competition ultimately lowers the revenues of all competing jurisdictions without enhancing the competitive standing of any, thereby resulting in insufficient spending for needed state and local public services; (3) tax incentives confer windfalls according to a capricious pattern, favoring firms in some industries but not others, and therefore distort the nation's interindustry allocation of resources; and (4) tax competition discourages subnational governments from progressive taxation (see Ability to pay). They fear that highly skilled managers and professional workers, who tend to earn high incomes, will respond to heavy tax burdens by migrating to other jurisdictions.

Proponents of interjurisdictional competition make four arguments in its favor. One is that it curbs governments' inherent tendency to maximize revenues and exploit taxpayers (the "Leviathan principle"). A second is that such competition encourages states and municipalities to tax their constituents according to the "benefit principle"—that is, in proportion to the benefits they receive from state and municipal services. Departure from this principle will cause some of those paying taxes in excess of benefits received to move to another jurisdiction. Distributing tax burdens in proportion to benefits received is a second normative principle of tax fairness that complements the principle of ability to pay (see Benefit principle). Their third argument is that, much as free-market pricing leads to efficient resource allocation in the private sector, so benefit taxation maximizes allocative efficiency within the public sector and promotes an optimal public/private mix of goods and services (see Tiebout model). Fourth, they argue that while interjurisdictional competition encourages regressive taxation, progressive taxation at the federal level can offset the resulting inequities without the attendant distortions in location.

Proponents of interjurisdictional tax competition generally acknowledge that its benefits can be fully realized only when fiscal disparities across competing jurisdictions are small (see Fiscal disparities.) Otherwise, jurisdictions with low fiscal capacity (see Fiscal capacity) and/or high fiscal need will be at an inherent competitive disadvantage no matter what competitive tactics they pursue. Fiscally comfortable jurisdictions will be able to provide a given level of services at a lower average tax burden than their more fiscally stressed competitors. For this reason, tax competition is most beneficial when pursued within a federal context, in which higher levels of government redistribute resources across jurisdictions to maintain a level interjurisdictional "playing field."

## Alternatives to explicit tax competition in economic development policy

The high costs of explicit interjurisdictional tax competition, as well as persistent doubts about its effectiveness, have spurred states and municipalities to pursue economic development strategies designed to foster business *creation and expansion* rather than *to attract* and *to retain* existing firms. For example, the National Governors' Association argued in a formal policy statement adopted in 1993 that "state competition [for business investments] should not be characterized by how much direct assistance a state can provide to individual companies . . . [but] on how each state attempts to provide a business climate in which existing businesses can operate profitably and expand and new businesses can be established and survive" (Kayne and Shonka 1994: 25).

Some groups and individuals have urged the federal government to regulate the use of tax incentives at the subnational level and to renew revenue sharing arrangements in order to curb incentives for explicit tax competition (see, e.g., Rivlin 1991).

## Additional readings

Bartik, Timothy J. *Who Benefits from State and Local Economic Development Policies?* Kalamazoo, Mich.: W.E. Upjohn Institute for Employment Research, 1991.

Government of the District of Columbia. *Tax Rates and Tax Burdens in the District of Columbia: A Nationwide Comparison.* Washington, D.C., 1993.

Kayne, Jay, and Molly Shonka. *Rethinking State Development Policies and Programs.* Washington, D.C.: National Governors' Association, 1994.

Kenyon, Daphne A. *Interjurisdictional Tax and Policy Competition: Good or Bad for the Federal System?* Washington, D.C.: U.S. Advisory Commission on Intergovernmental Relations, 1991.

McGuire, Therese, and Michael Wasylenko. *Employment Growth and State Government Fiscal Behavior: A Report on Economic Development for States from 1973 to 1984.* Trenton, N.J.: New Jersey State and Local Expenditure and Revenue Policy Commission, 1987.

Papke, James A., and Leslie E. Papke. "Microanalytic Simulation for Analyses of Intersite Business Tax Differentials." In *Proceedings of the Seventy-Fourth Annual*

*Conference.* Columbus: National Tax Association–Tax Institute of America, 1981.

Rivlin, Alice M. "Distinguished Lecture on Economics in Government: Strengthening the Economy by Rethinking the Role of Federal and State Governments." *Journal of Economic Perspectives* 5 (Spring 1991): 3–14.

Tannenwald, Robert. *Massachusetts Tax Competitiveness.* Boston: Massachusetts Special Commission on Business Tax Policy, 1993.

Tannenwald, Robert. "Massachusetts Tax Competitiveness." *New England Economic Review* (January/February 1994): 31–49.

U.S. Advisory Commission on Business Tax Policy. *Regional Growth: Interstate Tax Competition.* Washington, D.C.: U.S. Government Printing Office, 1981.

U.S. Department of Commerce, Bureau of the Census. *Governmental Finances 1990–91.* Washington, D.C.: U.S. Government Printing Office, 1993.

Wasylenko, Michael. "Empirical Evidence on Interregional Business Location Decisions and the Role of Fiscal Incentives in Economic Development." In *Industry Location and Public Policy*, edited by Henry W. Herzog, Jr., and Alan M. Schlottmann. Knoxville: University of Tennessee Press, 1991.

Wasylenko, Michael, and Robert Carroll. "Do State Business Climates Still Matter? Evidence of a Structural Change." *National Tax Journal* 47 (March 1994): 19–38.

*Cross references:* benefit principle; business location, taxation and; enterprise zones; tax abatement programs; tax and revenue capacity.

# Tax equity analysis

Donald Phares
University of Missouri—St. Louis

*A review of the concept and process for understanding the distribution of the tax burden among people (individuals, families, households).*

A tax system is a complex set of instruments employed to accomplish public purposes. Tax evaluation could use many criteria such as adequacy, efficiency, or responsiveness, but a factor that often receives both taxpayer and legislative attention is "equity." Who pays and how much? What impact does taxation have on taxpayers with different economic status? Is it "fair"?

Why is equity of concern? A broad response is "fairness." But the core answers are more complex. How is the cost of public programs apportioned? Who bears the burden and how much is it? What are the impacts of changes in a tax system and how should they be apportioned? How do equity concerns weigh against other evaluation criteria? How focal should equity be as a determinant of tax policy? The real answers are far more involved than "to be fair."

Looking back at the seeds of Proposition 13 in California, Proposition 2-1/2 in Massachusetts, or their progeny, many public fiscal limitations over the past few decades had equity, de facto, as a focal issue. Taxpayers felt that they were paying too much and that the cost was not fairly distributed. Such concern continues.

## Key issues

In considering equity, several points are pivotal. First, a revenue system's overall impact should be considered, not just the marginal effect of one component. During legislative deliberations, attention necessarily might be on a specific item, but the marginal change should be factored into overall impact.

Second, nontax sources, such as fees and charges, play an increasingly more important role in public finances; their impact, often ignored, needs to be considered also. Third, equity is traditionally evaluated in the context of ability to pay. This is complicated by varying interpretations of what defines ability to pay, who should pay, and how much. Fourth, revenue systems are economically open. Taxes are not contained by jurisdictional boundaries. A relatively large percentage of tax burdens may be "exported." Taxes may also be "imported" from other jurisdictions. To the extent that exporting and importing occur, burden and equity for a revenue system are affected.

## Gauging the equity of tax systems

Equity for a tax system cannot be established a priori. Determination is a function of rather complex theoretical and empirical analysis. The following will sketch this out.

### What is equity?

Equity (vertical) analysis most commonly examines the pattern of tax burdens moving across an income spectrum from low to high. It reflects how effective tax rates vary with income.

Estimating tax burdens and then equity is an exercise in applied economic analysis. It involves the use of economic theory and various quantitative techniques. The lexicon of equity analysis tends to become "application-specific" and needs to be set out clearly in order for discussion to be interpreted properly. The most commonly encountered terms are:

*Burden*: The claim on economic status, usually income, resulting from the imposition of a tax.

*Effective rate*: A measure of tax burden that relates taxes paid to ability-to-pay.

*Nominal rate*: The statutory rate.

*Equity*: The pattern of the tax burdens' effective rate, across the income spectrum. Equity patterns are usually classified as: *regressive*—burden declines as income rises; *proportional*—burden is invariant with income; *progressive*—burden increases as income increases.

*Impact*: The impact on those legally required to pay.

*Incidence*: Contrasted with impact, the actual economic impact on those who must ultimately bear the burden.

*Shifting*: The movement (shifting) of the burden from its point of legal impact to its final economic resting place (incidence).

*Exporting*: The geographical movement of taxes from where legally imposed to residents of other jurisdiction(s) or, with state/local taxes, also to the federal tax system.

*Importing*: The movement of taxes into one jurisdiction from another.

### How is equity determined?

Determination of equity involves blending economic theory on shifting/incidence, the interjurisdictional movement of revenues, and the application of quantitative techniques to summarize the resultant information. Stated in its simplest terms, divide the income spectrum into groupings that are appropriate to policy, and then determine the taxes that are paid by each group as a percentage of income. This gives an effective rate. Then examine the pattern of effective rates across the income spectrum. This pattern reflects the equity of specific taxes or sets of taxes.

Several steps are entailed. First, determine payments for each income group by applying shifting/incidence theory. A tax on business provides a good illustration. Businesses do not bear the burden of tax payments. Rather, they are shifted to consumers as higher prices, workers as lower compensation, owners as reduced returns, or some combination. Applying shifting/incidence theory permits estimation of actual tax burdens.

Second, revenues are not constrained by boundaries. They move because of the openness of our economic system. Tax imposed in one area can exert its economic incidence on residents elsewhere. Estimation of effective rates, and therefore the pattern of burden, must account for such tax movement to accurately reflect the actual burden and equity

within the area of concern. Also, part of the state/local tax burden may be shifted to the federal revenue structure through IRS deductibility provisions.

A final consideration is measurement of ability to pay, the denominator of an effective rate. Measures vary from very narrow ones such as adjusted gross income (AGI) to much more sophisticated ones such as "permanent income," a lifetime income flow. A key issue for tax policy is current burden and the current income to pay it. This focuses more on the immediacy of tax policy to fund public programs. While AGI is generally considered too narrow a definition of ability to pay, a broader measure such as money income is closer to measuring ability to pay in an immediate policy-relevant context—that is, to pay current taxes out of current income.

With payments of taxes measured for the numerator and ability to pay for the denominator of an effective rate, burden across income groups can be estimated. Determination of equity then entails an examination of the *pattern* of these burdens across the income spectrum. The following summarizes the components that comprise effective rates:

$$ER_{ij} = \frac{T_{ij}}{Y_{ij}}$$

ER = effective rate (burden)
Y = ability-to-pay
T = (C-E-F+I);
*i* = income group
*j* = specific tax or set of taxes

where
C = revenue
E = exported taxes
F = exporting due to IRS provisions (state/local only)
I = imported taxes

### Measures of equity

The final task in equity analysis is to examine the *pattern* of effective rates as it varies with income. The expression above defines effective rates for income classes but does not portray the pattern of burden. Equity is concerned with this pattern. To reflect this, an index is needed to depict the magnitude of variation and allow a general classification (regressive, proportional, progressive). Such an index greatly facilitates comparisons for policy options.

One widely used equity measure employs regression analysis using data on the effective rate and income by income class. The index becomes the coefficient from the regression equation and reflects the change in burden as income changes; it is usually estimated in percentage terms. If this index is negative (burden falls as income rises), equity is regressive; if it is positive (burden increases with income), it is progressive; if there is no statistical association between burden and income, equity is proportional. Quantitative comparisons can be made by examining the magnitude of the indexes.

A second equity index, the Suits index, has been used quite widely of late. It examines the concentration of tax payments by income class. It ranges in value from +1.0 where all payment is made by the highest class (extreme progressivity), through 0.0 where the burden is evenly spread across classes (proportionality), to −1.0 where the lowest class makes all payment (extreme regressivity).

The clear advantage of such indices is the ability to make comparisons. Is one tax more equitable than another? How regressive/progressive is a tax system? What impact do policy changes have? How do jurisdictions compare? What change has occurred over time?

## Limitations of equity analysis

Equity analysis does have limitations. One relates to applying theoretical information on shifting/incidence to make quantitative estimates of effective rates. Economic theory is used to reflect how a tax shifts from point of legal impact to economic incidence. This relates to shifting not only among economic groups but also geographically. Sales taxes may be shifted to consumers; a residential property tax may be shifted to renters; business taxes may affect owners. Each, in turn, may be exported geographically. The primary objective is to determine who pays, how much they pay, and where they reside. A difficulty is that there is not universal agreement about shifting/incidence. As an example, debate continues over who pays the corporation income tax and, more recently, who pays the property tax. Both instances focus on burden being shifted to consumers or being borne by owners. Needless to say, equity is sensitive to the assumptions.

Frequently this is resolved by relying on professional judgment, selecting assumptions that are reasonable, and defining them as "benchmarks." Sensitivity analysis is then used with alternative assumptions to determine a range.

A second limitation is that equity tends to focus on taxes. Clearly taxes affect private economic status. However, expenditures also affect economic status. An above-average burden may be offset by above-average spending on public programs; the revenue burden is accompanied by an expenditure benefit. An apparently regressive tax system may be mitigated by increased spending benefits for lower-income households.

It should also be noted that the type of equity study discussed here does not examine what the situation is *within* any given income group, which also may be of interest for certain policy issues.

Finally, a tax's equity must be weighted against the magnitude of the burden the tax imposes. A highly regressive tax on a necessity, such as food, is very different from a highly regressive tax on an item of choice, such as tobacco.

## Policy relevance of equity analysis

What is the relevance of equity for revenue policy? Consider the following questions: Who bears the burden of public programs—who pays? How redistributive is a tax system; what is its impact on different economic groups? How do taxes vary in equity? How does tax policy affect burden/equity for different economic groups? What changes have occurred over time? Are they consistent with policy intent? How do specific changes affect a revenue system? How do jurisdictions compare? How does equity, as one goal, relate to other goals such as revenue efficiency, responsiveness, and adequacy or public acceptance?

Although this entry focuses on tax equity, it should be noted that equity analysis can also deal with public expenditures, other revenue sources such as fees and charges, and the total budgetary impact of the government budget on private well-being. Also, the level of analysis can vary from a very specific change in policy (i.e., a tax credit or exemption) to the broad impact of any "collection" of public revenues or expenditures to entire government sectors (federal, state, local).

## Additional readings

Musgrave, Richard A., and Peggy B. Musgrave. *Public Finance in Theory and Practice*. New York: any edition.

Phares, Donald. *State-Local Tax Equity: An Empirical Analysis of the Fifty States*. Lexington, Mass.: Lexington Books, 1973.

Phares, Donald. *Who Pays State and Local Taxes?* Cambridge, Mass.: Oelgeschlager, Gunn & Hain Publishers, 1980.

Phares, Donald. "The Role of Tax Burden Studies in State Tax Policy." *Reforming State Tax Systems*, edited by Steven D. Gold. Denver: National Conference of State Legislatures, 1987.

Slemrod, Joel B., editor. *Tax Progressivity and Income Inequality*. New York: Cambridge University Press, 1994.

*Cross references:* ability to pay; benefit principle; fairness in taxation; horizontal equity; incidence of taxes; progressivity, measures of; revenue elasticity (tax elasticity); tax exportation; vertical equity.

# Tax evasion

James Alm

University of Colorado at Boulder

*Illegal and intentional actions taken by individuals or firms to reduce their tax payments.*

---

Tax evasion is one of the most common economic crimes. Noncompliance has been present since the introduction of taxes: People do not like paying taxes, and they pursue many avenues to reduce their payments. Legal methods known as tax avoidance take full advantage of the tax code. Tax evaders fail to pay legally due obligations. Individuals and firms evade taxes by underreporting incomes, overstating deductions and exemptions, or failing to file returns.

Tax evasion is important for many reasons. It reduces tax collections, thereby affecting taxes that compliant taxpayers face and public services that citizens receive. Evasion creates resource use misallocations when individuals alter their behavior to cheat on their taxes. It alters the distribution of income in unpredictable ways. Evasion may contribute to feelings of unfair treatment and disrespect for the law. It affects the accuracy of macroeconomic statistics. More broadly, without recognizing the existence of evasion it is not possible to understand the true impact of taxation.

Tax evasion raises many issues. How extensive is it? What leads individuals to cheat on their taxes? What is the evidence on individual behavioral responses? What are appropriate government policies toward evasion? Each issue is considered. (For comprehensive surveys on tax evasion, see Tanzi (1982), Roth et al. (1989), Cowell (1990), Elffers (1991), and Slemrod (1992).)

## Measurement of tax evasion

A major difficulty in analyzing evasion is in its measurement. After all, individuals have incentives to conceal their cheating. Several methods have been developed to measure evasion, all subject to imprecision and controversy.

One method relies on information generated by the tax authority as part of its audit process. The Internal Revenue Service (IRS) conducts line-by-line audits of individual tax returns for its Taxpayer Compliance Measurement Program (TCMP). These audits yield an estimate of the taxpayer's "true" income, allowing measures of individual and aggregate tax evasion to be calculated. However, TCMP data have some serious deficiencies: The audits do not detect all underreported income, nonfi-

lers are not often captured, honest errors are not identified, and final audit adjustments are not included.

Another direct method involves surveys. These surveys are typically designed to elicit taxpayers' attitudes about their reporting, but such surveys can also be used to estimate noncompliance. However, the accuracy of surveys is uncertain. Individuals may not remember their reporting decisions, they may not respond truthfully or at all, and the respondents may not be representative.

Indirect methods attempt to infer the magnitude of unreported income from its traces in other, observable areas. One approach looks at discrepancies between income and expenditures in budget surveys or in national income accounts. Another looks at discrepancies between "official" labor force participation rates and estimates of "true" participation rates. A third approach looks for traces of unreported income in monetary aggregates. All of these methods are subject to serious criticisms. They may simply compound measurement errors, they attribute all discrepancies to unreported income, and often they are able only to estimate the change in unreported income over some period, not its absolute level.

Despite these measurement difficulties, it appears that tax evasion is a widespread and growing problem in the United States. The most reliable estimates project the amount of unpaid federal income taxes at $127 billion for 1992 and suggest an annual growth rate of roughly 10 percent since 1973 (Internal Revenue Service 1996). State and local governments also report problems with noncompliance and evasion. Evidence from other countries suggests that the American experience is not an isolated one.

## Theories of tax evasion behavior

The basic theory used in nearly all compliance research builds on the economics-of-crime model, in which an individual maximizes the expected utility of the tax evasion gamble, balancing the benefits of successful cheating against the risky prospect of detection and punishment. This approach concludes that compliance depends upon audit and fine rates. Indeed, its central conclusion is that an individual pays taxes only for fear of detection and punishment, and will pay more taxes with an increase in the fine or the audit rate. Surprisingly, an increase in the tax rate generally has an ambiguous effect on reported income; under plausible assumptions, compliance actually rises with higher tax rates.

However, it is clear to many observers that compliance cannot be explained entirely by the level of enforcement. The levels of audit and penalty rates are set at such low levels that most individuals would evade if they are rational because it is unlikely that cheaters will be caught and penalized.

This observation suggests that the compliance decision must be affected by factors not mentioned in the basic model, or must be affected in ways not captured appropriately by the theory. Many attempts have been made to expand the basic model to include other factors, such as

—Government services,
—Uncertainty and complexity,
—Endogenous audit rules,
—Use of paid preparers,
—Labor supply and occupational choice,
—Tax avoidance,
—Structure of taxation,
—Overweighting of low probabilities,
—Honesty, morality, and social norms,
—Tax amnesties (see Tax amnesty).

Other factors may well be relevant. No single theory has been able to incorporate more than a few of these factors in a meaningful way.

## Evidence on tax evasion behavior

There is a growing body of empirical literature on the responses of individuals in their tax evasion behavior. As emphasized above, availability of data is a major difficulty, and the empirical work draws creatively on many sources. The most extensively used source is TCMP data. Others include taxpayer returns, survey data, national income accounts, and laboratory experiments.

In its entirety, this work suggests the following conclusions:

—A higher audit rate leads to more compliance, at least to a point, with an estimated reported income-audit rate elasticity ranging from 0.1 to 0.2.
—A higher fine rate leads to marginally more compliance, with an estimated reported income-fine rate elasticity less than 0.1.
—A higher tax rate leads to less compliance, with an estimated reported income-tax rate elasticity of $-0.5$ to $-3.0$.
—There is strong evidence that audit rates are endogenous and that this endogeneity increases the efficiency of the tax agency.
—An increase in tax complexity leads to greater use of a tax practitioner, and the average level of noncompliance is higher for returns prepared with paid assistance.
—The audit selection criteria of state and federal enforcement agencies are somewhat different, which suggests that sharing information could increase agency revenues.
—Rewards can provide a significant positive inducement for greater compliance.

—Many individuals substantially overweight the probability of an audit.
—Individuals pay more in taxes when faced with a public program that they have selected, that they value, and that they know enjoys widespread support.
—The social norm of compliance can be affected by the institutions that face individuals and by individual participation in the selection of those institutions.
—Demographic variables are important determinants of behavior.

Given the underlying data problems, this empirical work needs to be treated cautiously. Still, these results indicate that the enforcement agency can increase compliance by changing its enforcement strategy, but that there are limits to strategies based only on greater enforcement.

## Government policies

Governments everywhere wish to increase tax compliance. The standard policy prescription has long been an increase in penalty and audit rates. Both theoretical and empirical work indicate that greater enforcement can increase compliance; indeed, sufficient—and draconian—increases in penalties and audit rates could substantially eliminate evasion.

However, it is unlikely that such extreme measures will be implemented. There is a widespread belief that "the punishment should fit the crime." Moreover, higher penalty and audit rates entail costs, both to the government that must use real resources in its efforts and to the individuals who suffer a loss in utility from greater enforcement. Finally, it may be inappropriate to increase the IRS budget, even if a dollar spent on enforcement increases collections by more than one dollar. The additional budget allocation represents a real resource cost, while the additional revenues are simply a transfer from the private to the public sector. Instead, the optimal amount of government enforcement must equate its marginal costs and benefits, where the benefits should include added revenues but also should reflect the impacts of government-induced honesty and the loss in individual expected utility.

It may well be that the best government policy is a pragmatic one that recognizes that evasion cannot—and should not—be completely eliminated. Such a policy should include greater enforcement, but should also emphasize the use of source withholding, a reliance on computers, social obligations of compliance, positive rewards, the wise use of taxpayer dollars, and individual participation in the decision process. Until more is known about evasion, this strategy may well be the best.

There is much that we do not know about tax evasion. We are constantly struggling to measure its extent, to discover its motivations, to estimate individual responses, and to implement appropriate policies. As long as there are taxes, this struggle will continue.

## Additional readings

Cowell, Frank A. *Cheating the Government: The Economics of Tax Evasion*. Cambridge, Mass.: The MIT Press, 1990.

Elffers, Henk. *Income Tax Evasion: Theory and Measurement*. Deventer: Kluwer, 1991.

Internal Revenue Service. *Federal Tax Compliance Research: Individual Income Tax Gap Estimates for 1985, 1988, and 1992*. Publication 7285. Washington, D.C.: U.S. Department of the Treasury, 1996.

Roth, Jeffrey A., John T. Scholz, and Ann Dryden Witte, eds. *Taxpayer Compliance. Vol. 1, An Agenda for Research* and *Vol. 2, Social Science Perspectives*. Philadelphia: University of Pennsylvania Press, 1989.

Slemrod, Joel, ed. *Why People Pay Taxes*. Ann Arbor: The University of Michigan Press, 1992.

Tanzi, Vito, ed. *The Underground Economy in the United States and Abroad*. Lexington, Mass.: D.C. Heath and Company, 1982.

*Cross reference:* tax administration, federal.

# Tax-exempt bonds

Dennis Zimmerman
Congressional Research Service, Library of Congress

*A bond, issued by a state or local government, the interest on which is exempt from taxation.*

State and local governments issue debt ($267 billion in 1997) in exchange for the use of the savings of individuals and corporations. This debt obligates state and local governments to make interest payments for the use of these savings and to repay, some time in the future, the amount borrowed (the bond proceeds).

The first income tax law in the United States, in 1913, excluded from taxable income the interest income earned by holders of the debt obligations of states and their political subdivisions. In 1988 the U.S. Supreme Court in *South Carolina* v. *Baker* (485 U.S. 505 [1988]) rejected the assertion that any federal taxation of interest income derived from this debt is unconstitutional because the exemption is protected by the Tenth Amendment and the doctrine of intergovernmental tax immunity. The Court denied the claim of constitutional protection and found tax exemption to be dependent upon statute and regulation. In short, Congress has the right to tax this interest income if it chooses—which it has not done.

Because the interest income on state and local debt is excluded from federal income taxation, the interest rate on this "tax-exempt" debt is lower than the interest rate on taxable debt. For this reason, tax-exempt debt has its own "market" and is an important factor in several economic policy issues.

## Characteristics of tax-exempt bonds

### Maturity

State and local governments must borrow money for long periods of time and for short periods of time. Long-term debt instruments are usually referred to as bonds and carry maturities in excess of one year ($221 billion in 1997). Because public capital facilities provide services over a long period of time, it makes sense to pay for these facilities over a long period of time. Thus, long-term bonds are an effort to match the timing of the payments for the capital facilities (taxes raised to fund interest and principal payments) to the flow of services from the capital facilities. An attempt to pay for capital facilities "up front" is likely to result in a less-than-optimal rate of public capital formation, as current taxpayers vote against paying taxes now for benefits provided to future citizens.

Short-term debt instruments are usually referred to as notes and carry maturities of 12 months or less ($46 billion in 1997). Notes usually are paid from specific taxes due in the near future or from anticipated intergovernmental revenue and are often referred to as tax and revenue anticipation notes (TRANS). These short-term notes are issued because governments are faced with the necessity of planning a budget for the year (or in some cases for two years). This requires a balancing of revenue forecasts (see Revenue forecasting, federal) against forecasts of the demand for services and spending. Not infrequently, the inevitable unforeseen circumstances that undermine any forecast cause a revenue shortfall that must be financed with short-term borrowing. In addition, even when the forecasts are met, the timing of expenditures may precede the arrival of revenues, creating the necessity to borrow within an otherwise balanced fiscal year. Finally, temporarily high interest rates that prevail at the time bonds are issued to finance a capital project may induce short-term borrowing in anticipation of a drop in rates.

## Security

General obligation debt, which is the sum of short-plus long-term bonds, pledges the "full faith and credit" of the issuing government, an unconditional pledge of its powers of taxation to guarantee its liability for interest and principal repayment ($106 billion in 1997). Revenue bonds, or nonguaranteed debt ($161 billion in 1997), pledge only the earnings from revenue-producing activities, most often the earnings from the facilities being built with the revenue bond proceeds. Should these earnings prove to be inadequate to repay interest and principal, the issuing government is under no obligation to utilize its taxing powers to finance the shortfall.

## New issue versus refunding

New-issue bonds ($140 billion in 1997) finance new capital facilities. Refunding-issue bonds ($60 billion in 1997) replace outstanding bond issues with bonds that carry more favorable terms, such as lower interest rates. The refunding issue usually does not add to the stock of outstanding bonds or the stock of capital facilities; its proceeds are used to pay off (retire) the remaining principal of the original bond issue. Advance refunding bonds are issued before the date on which the original bonds are refunded and add to the outstanding stock of bonds without adding to the stock of capital facilities.

## Arbitrage

State and local governments do not pay federal income tax, and absent federal constraint they have unlimited capacity to issue debt at low interest rates and reinvest the bond proceeds in higher-yielding taxable debt instruments, thereby earning arbitrage profits (see Tax arbitrage). Unchecked, state and local governments could substitute arbitrage earnings for a substantial portion of their own citizens' tax effort.

Such activity lies outside the purpose of tax exemption, and the federal tax law requires that tax-exempt bond proceeds be used as quickly as possible to pay contractors for the construction of capital facilities. Because it is impossible for bonds to be issued on the day every contractor must be paid for expenses incurred in building public capital facilities, a two-year period is granted to spend an increasing share of the bond proceeds. Bond issues that have unspent proceeds in excess of the allowed amounts during this two-year spend-down schedule must rebate any arbitrage earnings to the U.S. Treasury. Bond issues are considered to be taxable arbitrage bonds if a governmental unit, in violation of the arbitrage restriction in the tax code, purposely invests a substantial portion of the proceeds in assets that earn interest rates that exceed the tax-exempt interest rate by more than one-eighth of a percentage point.

## Public purpose versus private purpose

Before the late 1960s, nothing in the tax law prevented state and local officials from issuing bonds and using the proceeds to finance investments for private individuals and businesses. This "conduit" financing became an increasingly larger share of the total volume of bonds, rising from 21 percent of total bond volume in 1975 to 73 percent of total bond volume in 1984. Unfortunately, these bonds generated no public capital facilities (the reason for having tax-exempt bonds).

Most of the legislation pertaining to tax-exempt bonds over the 30 years from 1968 to 1998 represents an effort to reduce this "conduit" financing. The legislation restricted tax exemption to bonds issued for activities that satisfy some broadly defined "public" purpose, that is, for which federal taxpayers are likely to receive substantial benefits. Bonds are considered to satisfy a public purpose if they meet either of two criteria: No more than 10 percent of the proceeds is used directly or indirectly by a nongovernmental entity; and no more than 10 percent of the proceeds is secured directly or indirectly by property used in a trade or business. Bonds that satisfy either of these tests are termed "governmental" bonds and can be issued without limit. Bonds that fail both of these tests are considered to primarily benefit private individuals or businesses, are termed "private-activity" bonds, and are ineligible for tax-exempt financing.

Some activities that fail the two tests are considered to provide some public benefits in addition to private benefits. These activities, termed qualified private activities, can be financed with tax-exempt bonds. The annual volume of bonds issued within a state for all qualified private activities is restricted to the greater of $50 per state resident or $150 million. The majority of bonds issued for these qualified private activities finance mortgages for owner-occupied housing, student loans for postsecondary education, and loans for private manufacturing facilities. By 1990, legislative changes had succeeded in reducing private-activity bonds to 20 percent of total bond volume.

## Tax-exempt bonds and economic issues

The lower interest rate of tax-exempt bonds relative to taxable bonds makes these bonds an important factor in four economic policy issues.

## Intergovernmental fiscal relations

In the context of the U.S. system of fiscal federalism (see Fiscal federalism), federal taxpayers have decided that it makes economic sense to subsidize (reduce the cost of) state and local services. The lower interest rate of tax-exempt bonds is one form of subsidy; two others are grants-in-aid (which increase the income of the governmental unit) and the deduction of state and local income and property taxes from federal taxable income (which reduces the tax price (see Tax price) of state and local government services). During the 1980s, the real value of intergovernmental aid provided via tax-exempt bonds grew dramatically, while the real value of grants-in-aid and tax deductibility declined. Providing aid via tax-exempt bonds rather than grants-in-aid allows state and local governments to determine the total cost to the federal government (bond issuance is unconstrained except for private-activity bonds); costs more than a dollar to provide a dollar of aid; allows state and local taxpayers to decide which goods and services should be subsidized; and keeps administrative costs relatively low.

### Federal budget deficit

The desire to control the deficit was an important factor in legislative efforts in the 1980s to restrict state and local use of private-activity bonds. The exclusion of interest income from federal income taxation imposes a revenue loss on the federal government and contributes to the federal deficit; in fact, this revenue loss is among the largest of all preferential tax provisions listed in the federal government's tax expenditure budget. The revenue loss is calculated as the taxes that would have been collected if tax-exempt bond purchasers had instead purchased taxable debt and received taxable interest income. The revenue loss from the outstanding stock of tax-exempt debt in 1997 is estimated to be $24.9 billion.

### Resource allocation

The exclusion of interest income lowers the cost of capital for facilities that can be financed with tax-exempt bonds, thereby raising their after-tax rate of return and reallocating resources (savings) away from noneligible facilities. This absence of neutral taxation occurs in three areas. First, because almost all public investment is eligible for tax-exempt financing and most private investment is not eligible, it increases public investment relative to private investment. Second, it increases private investment in the subset of private activities that are eligible for tax-exempt financing and decreases investment in nonqualifying private activities. And third, it changes state and local production processes toward more use of capital, which is subsidized, and away from labor, which is not subsidized.

All of these changes impose losses of national income on society, because the pretax rate of return on most of these subsidized investments is lower than the pretax rate of return on the unsubsidized investments that are displaced. The welfare of federal taxpayers is enhanced only if taxpayers value the social benefits produced by the subsidized investments more than the lost national income.

### Tax equity

Tax-exempt bonds present an opportunity for individuals and corporations to shelter their income from federal income taxation. Because the bonds are most valuable to taxpayers with relatively high marginal tax rates, the reduced tax liability tends to reduce the progressivity of the distribution of the tax burden by income class and raises concerns about high-income taxpayers' use of tax-exempt bonds to escape their social duty as taxpayers.

If one ignores or dismisses as of little value the social objectives of the interest income exclusion that is used to justify resource reallocation, one is left with the conclusion that tax-exempt bonds are, from the federal perspective, little more than a vehicle for investors to shelter a portion of their income from federal taxation. This is not, however, a balanced view. It is true that one can use tax-exempt bonds to reduce one's marginal tax rate to zero, but this is accompanied by an implicit tax in the form of a lower pretax rate of return that generates a positive marginal effective tax rate. Furthermore, society's vertical equity objectives are not expressed by the statutory rate structure, but by the effective rate structure that results from each income class's access to the numerous exemptions, deductions, exclusions, credits, deferrals, and so forth. This suggests that any effort to alter tax-exempt bonds on equity grounds is likely to be countered by adjustments in other tax preferences that leave the overall pattern of marginal effective tax rates by income class relatively unchanged.

## Additional readings

Fortune, Peter. "The Municipal Bond Market, Part I: Politics, Taxes and Yields." *New England Economic Review* (September/October 1991): 13–36.

Fortune, Peter. "The Municipal Bond Market, Part II: Problems and Policies." *New England Economic Review* (May/June 1992): 47–64.

Hilhouse, Albert M. *Municipal Bonds: A Century of Experience.* New York: Prentice Hall, 1936.

Ott, David J., and Allan H. Meltzer. *Federal Tax Treatment of State and Local Securities.* Washington, D.C.: The Brookings Institution, 1963.

Petersen, John E., and Ronald Forbes. *Innovative Capital Financing.* Chicago: American Planning Association, 1985.

Public Securities Association. *Fundamentals of Municipal Bonds.* New York, 1989.

Zimmerman, Dennis. *The Private Use of Tax-Exempt Bonds: Controlling Public Subsidy of Private Activity*. Washington, D.C.: The Urban Institute Press, 1991.

*Cross references:* cost of capital; fairness in taxation; implicit taxes; marginal effective tax rate; progressivity, measures of; tax arbitrage; tax expenditures; vertical equity.

# Tax expenditures

Jane G. Gravelle
Congressional Research Service, Library of Congress

*Revenue losses resulting from federal tax provisions that grant special tax relief designed to encourage certain kinds of behavior by taxpayers or to aid taxpayers in special circumstances.*

Tax expenditures may, in effect, be viewed as spending programs channeled through the tax system. They are classified in the same functional categories as the federal budget.

Section 3(3) of the Congressional Budget and Impoundment Control Act of 1974 specifically defines tax expenditures as:

> . . . those revenue losses attributable to provisions of the Federal tax laws which allow a special exclusion, exemption, or deduction from gross income or which provide a special credit, a preferential rate of tax, or a deferral of tax liability; . . . .

In the legislative history of the Congressional Budget Act, provisions classified as tax expenditures are contrasted with those provisions that are part of the "normal structure" of the individual and corporate income tax necessary to collect government revenues. Tax expenditures, therefore, do not cover all departures from the economist's concept of income. In particular, they do not include imputed and unrealized income (such as capital gains accruals and imputed rent on owner-occupied housing). Nor do they measure tax penalties (such as the failure to index for inflation).

The measurement of tax expenditures is sometimes arbitrary. For example, the single largest business tax expenditure, for depreciation, is based simply on differences between regular tax depreciation and depreciation used in the alternative minimum tax. Tax expenditures represent cash flow measures of benefits, as would be the case in a budget document, rather than the economic value of a subsidy. Thus, the depreciation tax expenditure reflects the difference in current depreciation deductions and not the timing value of accelerated depreciation.

## Tax expenditure budget

The listing of tax expenditures, taken in conjunction with the listing of direct spending programs, is intended to allow Congress to scrutinize all federal programs relating to the same goals—both nontax and tax—when developing its annual budget. Only when tax expenditures are considered will congressional budget decisions take into account the full spectrum of federal programs. The tax expenditure budget also identifies provisions that could be considered in any base-broadening tax reform program.

Because any qualified taxpayer may reduce tax liability through use of a tax expenditure, such provisions are comparable to entitlement programs under which benefits are paid to all eligible persons. Because tax expenditures are generally enacted as permanent legislation, they are not renewed each year and thus are not subject to automatic review. Indeed, the original rationale for some tax expenditures may no longer be relevant.

Tax expenditure budgets that list the estimated annual revenue losses associated with each tax expenditure have to be published in the administration's budget (since 1975) and by the Budget Committees (since 1976). The congressional Joint Committee on Taxation has also published estimates. The tax expenditure concept is still being refined; therefore, the classification of certain provisions as tax expenditures continues to be discussed.

As defined in the 1974 act, the concept of tax expenditure refers to corporation and individual income taxes. Other parts of the Internal Revenue Code—excise taxes, employment taxes, estate and gift taxes—also have exceptions, exclusions, refunds and credits (such as a gasoline tax exemption for nonhighway uses) that are not included in the formal tax expenditure budget.

## Major forms of tax expenditures

Tax expenditures may take any of the following forms:
1. Exclusions, exemptions, and deductions, which reduce taxable income;
2. Preferential tax rates, which apply lower rates to part or all of a taxpayer's income;
3. Credits, which are subtracted from taxes as ordinarily computed;
4. Deferrals of tax, which result from delayed recognition of income or from allowing in the current year deductions that are properly attributable to a future year.

The amount of tax relief per dollar of each exclusion, exemption, and deduction increases with the taxpayer's tax rate. A tax credit is subtracted directly from the tax liability that would otherwise be due; thus, the amount of tax reduction is the amount of the credit—which does not depend on the marginal tax rate.

## Order of presentation

The tax expenditures are presented in an order that generally parallels the budget functional categories used in the congressional budget; tax expenditures related to "national defense" are listed first, those related to "international affairs" are listed next, and so on. This parallel format is consistent with the requirement of section 301(d)(6) of the act, which requires that the Budget Committees present the estimated levels of tax expenditures "by major functional categories" in the tax expenditure budgets that they publish in their April 15 reports.

Although it is not strictly correct to add tax expenditure items, a sum of tax expenditures provides some information on their size and importance. Data from the Joint Committee on Taxation show $510 billion in tax expenditures in fiscal year 1997—$445 billion in the individual income tax and $65 billion in the corporate tax. In both cases, the largest major budget function was commerce and housing, reflecting, in the individual tax case, tax benefits for owner-occupied housing and capital income, and, in the corporate tax case, depreciation and industry-specific tax provisions. The second-largest category for individuals was in income security, with pension benefits the largest single tax expenditure in that area.

If tax expenditures are viewed in terms familiar to tax practitioners rather than budget analysts, the largest category of benefits for individuals was in itemized deductions ($108 billion), followed by investment income subsidies ($103 billion), with about half resulting from capital gains and the remainder largely from life insurance, tax-exempt bonds, and individual retirement accounts (IRAs). Employer fringe benefits were also large ($71 billion for pensions and $77 billion for other fringe benefits). Retirement income exclusions and other benefits for the elderly were also substantial at $47 billion. Business-related provisions for individuals were relatively small ($12 billion). For corporate tax expenditures, depreciation accounted for $27 billion, industry-specific provisions $11 billion, tax-exempt bonds $6 billion, and small business benefits $5 billion.

## Distributional issues

Tax expenditures tend to benefit higher-income individuals compared with many other spending programs, which has caused some observers to refer to them as "upside-down" subsidies. Not only are higher-income individuals likely to be subject to higher tax rates, but they are also more likely to itemize deductions, to have significant capital investments, and to own their homes—all characteristics that are associated with tax expenditures. Of course, if we were to adopt a broader-based tax system, we might also adopt flatter tax rates, so that eliminating tax expenditures need not necessarily lead to a more progressive tax system.

## Additional readings

Brannon, Gerard M. "Tax Expenditures and Income Distribution: A Theoretical Analysis of the Upside-Down Subsidy Argument." In *The Economics of Taxation*, edited by Henry J. Aaron and Michael J. Boskin, pp. 87–98. Washington, D.C.: The Brookings Institution, 1980.

Ladd, Helen. *The Tax Expenditure Concept after 25 Years*. Presidential Address to the National Tax Association. Proceedings of the National Tax Association, 1994.

Surrey, Stanley S., and Paul R. McDaniel. "The Tax Expenditure Concept and the Legislative Process." In *The Economics of Taxation*, edited by Henry J. Aaron and Michael J. Boskin, pp. 123–144. Washington, D.C.: The Brookings Institution, 1980.

U.S. Congress, Joint Committee on Taxation. *Estimates of Federal Tax Expenditures for Fiscal Years 1997–2001*. Prepared for the Committee on Ways and Means and the Committee on Finance. Committee Print, 104th Cong., 2nd sess. Washington, D.C.: U.S. Government Printing Office, November 26, 1996.

U.S. Congress, Senate Committee on the Budget. 104th Cong., 2nd sess. *Tax Expenditures: Compendium of Background Material on Individual Provisions*. Washington, D.C.: U.S. Government Printing Office, December 1996.

U.S. General Accounting Office. *Tax Expenditures: A Primer*. PAD 80-26. Washington, D.C.: U.S. Government Printing Office, 1979.

U.S. Office of Management and Budget. "Tax Expenditures." *Budget of the United States Government Fiscal Year 1998, Analytical Perspectives*. Washington, D.C.: U.S. Government Printing Office, 1997.

*Cross references:* capital gains taxation; fringe benefits; individual retirement accounts; mortgage interest deduction; tax-exempt bonds.

# Tax exportation

Donald Phares
University of Missouri—St. Louis

*The process by which a tax levied by one jurisdiction is shifted ("exported") to a taxpayer of another jurisdiction.*

Having "someone else" help pay the bills is obviously less painful for governments as well as for households. States have grown more sensitive to the opportunities for exporting tax burdens to nonresidents. While a great deal of attention has focused on tourism- or energy-rich states and their ability to export their taxes, the issue is broader. Other states, because of fiscal and economic circumstance, can also shift some of their tax burden onto nonresidents. Exporting is not an isolated phenomenon affecting only states such as Alaska, Florida, Nevada, or Texas. It influences the fiscal environment in every state.

## How are taxes exported?

Taxes can be exported in two general ways. The first derives from Internal Revenue Service (IRS) provisions that allow itemization of state and local taxes on income and property. In 1970, all property, income, general sales, and gasoline taxes were allowed; in 1980, gasoline taxes were eliminated; and by 1995 so were general sales taxes.

The second mechanism relates to the open movement of goods and services, capital, and people across state borders. This economic flow, combined with ownership, migration, and journey-to-work patterns, means that taxes flow out of (and then into) each state. This entry discusses each general type of exporting. Tax importing, the flip side of the issue, has received far less scrutiny.

### Federal offset exporting

For those who itemize for federal tax purposes, each dollar deducted shifts part of the tax burden onto the federal revenue structure. Its impact then is in accordance with the incidence characteristics of this system and into the future through deficit financing. Because two major state and local taxes (income and property) can still be itemized, the impact is, de facto, a subsidy through the federal tax system. The more a state uses deductible taxes, the larger the potential exporting and subsidy. The subsidy amount is not dollar for dollar, however. It is a function of the extent to which the taxpayer uses deductible taxes, the income level of the taxpayer, and the taxpayer's federal marginal tax rate. For example, $1,000 itemized in the 36 percent tax bracket reduces federal taxes by $360.

It needs to be emphasized that these tax burdens do not disappear; they are shifted from state and local to federal taxpayers, and then their impact is through the federal tax system. The net effect state by state, however, does vary considerably.

Although recent studies exist of the importance of the tax offset for individual states, no examination of its aggregate importance has been made since 1980 (Phares).

Almost $21 billion in state/local taxes was shifted to the federal revenue structure as a result of IRS provisions in 1980, up from $8.8 billion in 1970. The figure for 1995 would be even greater. The largest contributor is the individual income tax, for two reasons. First, most states use this tax and rely on it heavily as a revenue source. Second, this state tax liability rises with an individual's income, and thus this deduction is worth more (although less now than in 1970 or 1980) on the federal return. The next largest contributor is real property taxes, followed by general sales and personal property taxes. Past estimates showed that just shy of 50 percent of total exporting derived from IRS provisions.

### Price/migration exporting

The second type of exporting results from the openness of state economies and the ease with which economic activity flows among states; while boundaries represent legal or political definitions, they do not constrain taxes. Taxes move freely with goods and services, people, and capital flows. The more "open" a state's economy, the greater the possibility for shifting part of its tax burden.

Price/migration exporting is similar in focus to the concerns of tax shifting and incidence—that is, to trace the movement (shifting) of a tax from its point of legal impact to its final economic resting place (incidence). A tax on tobacco, for example, is legally imposed on the seller but is shifted to the final consumer. Price/migration exporting uses this input but must go one step further. Not only must the "interpersonal" movement of a tax be traced, from tobacco *seller* to tobacco *consumer*, but the spatial location of the burden also must be determined. For example, casinos in Nevada pay gaming taxes. This burden, however, does not fall on the casino but on gamblers. The task is to determine in what state a gambler resides. While the tax has been legally imposed by Nevada, most of the burden falls on nonresidents who have visited for recreation. Thus, the tax is shifted in two distinct senses—first, from a business, the casino, to a consumer, the gambler; and second, geographically from Nevada to residents elsewhere.

Table 1 shows some states that exemplify this type of spatial tax movement. While these are blatant cases, all states export to some extent.

As is obvious from this brief discussion, the full theoretical and empirical model estimating this exporting is too complex to present here (see McLure 1966, 1967, or Phares 1980). Again, recent data on the price-migration effect are not available but, as with the federal offset, the amount is quite large ($22 billion in 1980).

The dominant category is income taxes. Some income tax is derived from individuals, but most is corporate-related. Corporate ownership is not confined to state of location, and price/migration exporting reflects movement of the burden to the owner's state of residence. The second-largest category is severance taxes, which grew dramatically during the 1970s as a result of the rising price of oil and gas, and the yield from taxing resource extraction. Most of this tax burden falls on residents outside the levying state. Overall, price/migration exporting rose 125 percent during the 1970s and 1980s, slightly less than the 135 percent for federal offset exporting.

## Policy implications

Tax exporting is a significant factor affecting the fiscal environment among states. The amounts involved are substantial and probably account for nearly one-fifth of all state and local taxes for 1980.

Contained within aggregate numbers, however, is detail on each state. It is in this context that relative fiscal and economic behavior is influenced and policies altered. While the U.S. average for exported taxes is 18 percent, there is considerable variance around this mean. Although Tennessee exported only 11 percent of its taxes, Delaware was able to shift one-third of its burden onto out-of-state residents or onto the federal tax system. Such differentials might influence policy in several areas.

### Interstate competition

To the extent its taxes can be shifted to nonresidents or the federal revenue system, a state enjoys, de facto, a lower tax status. To the extent that low taxes favorably influence business and residential locational decisions, a comparative advantage exists. Considering taxation in the context of all other factors affecting locational decisions, high-export states such as Texas, Nevada, or Delaware might gain an advantage.

### Fiscal capacity

Formulas have been an important and integral part of allocating revenues to public programs. The oldest and most complex are undoubtedly the state school aid formulas. General revenue-sharing, housing and community development, and the Comprehensive Employment and Training Act (CETA) were three more notable examples of formula-driven aid programs. Elements of many distribution schemes have included tax effort and capacity. Both can be affected by tax exportation.

### Implicit federal aid

The implicit subsidy (tax expenditure) to state and local taxpayers, through IRS provisions for the deduction of state and local taxes, amounted to more than $40 billion in 1997. This form of aid, albeit implicit, has become a major component in the overall system of intergovernmental transfers and has grown. With current trends in aid programs and proposed cutbacks, it may soon dominate. The federal tax system has been used to subsidize a vast array of activities and to encourage certain types of "socially beneficial" behavior. This tax break for state and local operations has grown to become large but is also less visible.

### Federal tax reform proposals

Recent proposals from Washington have focused on eliminating (limiting) deductibility for state and local taxes. No doubt the sheer cost to the U.S. Treasury weighs heavily. Elimination of these provisions, however, could have dramatic implications for the fiscal operations of states and localities. An additional tax burden would be shifted *onto* state and local taxpayers and *off of* the federal revenue system. This would undoubtedly affect the array of public goods and services provided. It would raise

## TABLE 1

### High Tax Export States

| State | Type of Exported Tax | Reason |
| --- | --- | --- |
| Nevada | Selective sales | Gambling activity |
| Delaware | Corporation taxes | Corporate headquarters |
| Alaska, Texas | Severance taxes | Natural resources |
| Hawaii | General excise tax | Tourism |
| Florida | Specific tourism taxes | Tourism |

the real cost of these public operations, it could increase taxpayer resistance to new or increased taxes, and it conceivably might even lead to a new round of "taxpayer revolt" activity.

### Tax-adjusted price of state-local goods

Individual economic decisions respond to the price of factors, goods, and services. State and local public goods are similar in terms of taxpayer (qua consumer) response. When part of the cost of these public operations is shifted to residents of other states or the federal tax structure, the net cost of public goods is lowered. A state such as Delaware that exports perhaps one-third of its taxes can, de facto, provide public goods for a lower tax cost to its residents. Examined in a relative context across states, this can lead to differential responses to the provision of public goods, depending upon exportability.

## Conclusion

This entry has outlined the manner by which taxes levied at the state and local levels can be rearranged within the federal system, with about half related to IRS provisions and the rest to the flow of economic activity among states. This rearrangement has a potential impact on fiscal decisionmaking in the American federal system. While the impact is somewhat hidden, it certainly should not escape attention.

## Additional readings

McLure, Charles. "An Analysis of Regional Tax Incidence, with Estimation of Interstate Incidence of State and Local Taxes." Department of Economics, Princeton University, Ph.D. dissertation, 1966.

McLure, Charles. "Tax Exporting in the United States: Estimates for 1962." *National Tax Journal* 20 (March 1967): 49–77.

Metcalf, Gilbert E. "Tax Exporting, Federal Deductibility, and State Tax Structure." *Journal of Policy Analysis and Management* 12 (1993): 109–26.

Phares, Donald. *Who Pays State and Local Taxes?* Cambridge, Mass.: Oelgeschlager, Gunn & Hain Publishers, 1980.

Phares, Donald. "Missourians and the Taxes They Pay." St. Louis: University of Missouri—St. Louis, Public Policy Research Centers, March 1996.

*Cross references:* fairness in taxation; incidence of taxes; itemized deductions; severance tax, state; tax and revenue capacity; tax equity analysis.

# Tax illusion

## Michael L. Marlow
California Polytechnic State University

*Even the rational fiscal voter who looks at the benefits and costs of public programs may lack adequate information (perhaps because of the complexity of the tax code itself), thereby underestimating the true costs of public activities.*

Voters base their demand for public programs on expected costs and benefits. A long-standing issue in public finance concerns the ability of demanders to understand the true nature of costs and benefits of programs because, without perfect information, demands must be based on perceived, as opposed to actual, costs and benefits. The tax illusion hypothesis proposes that voters base their demands on an illusion that the costs of public programs are lower than true costs. An important implication of the tax illusion hypothesis is that, because the net benefit for any public program is measured as the difference between benefits and costs, net benefits are overestimated whenever costs are underestimated. This hypothesis therefore predicts that the public sector overexpands whenever net benefits are overestimated by misinformed voters.

One possible reason why voters may underestimate costs of public programs is complexity of the tax system. Consider, for example, that until 1942 the Internal Revenue Service collected income tax after the year was over and that now these taxes are withheld from each paycheck received. Taxes are also collected at grocery stores, gasoline stations, bars, sporting events, and department stores, and they are attached to utility bills and interest income earned on savings. There is little question that tax sources are plentiful. Moreover, if voters feel they have little recourse about changing their tax burdens, they may be even less inclined to calculate the true costs than if they perceive that knowing the true costs might allow them to lower their tax burdens.

A related hypothesis is that voters underestimate costs of public programs when governments operate budget deficits (Buchanan and Wagner 1977). This implies, for example, that voters perceive that $100 billion of public spending costs less when financed through public debt than through taxation. This would represent just another form of tax illusion, or what might be referred to as deficit illusion because budget deficits reflect taxes that are deferred to the future. Underestimation occurs when voters believe that taxes paid today cost more than the present value of taxes paid tomorrow that are required to pay off today's deficit.

The implication of the deficit illusion hypothesis is the same as before: When voters underestimate future tax burdens associated with deficit finance, public programs appear cheaper than they really are. Consequently, these voters overestimate the net benefits of public programs, which results in higher demands for programs than if current spending were financed entirely by current taxes. An important implication of the deficit illusion hypothesis is that some portion of federal spending expansion since 1969 reflects overspending. This implication follows from the prediction that deficit illusion causes voters to approve more spending than if expansion of public debt had not caused them to underestimate the full costs of public programs.

Two possible remedies for removing tax and deficit illusions are simplification of tax policies and constitutional limitations on budget deficits. While most states have some constitutional or legislative limitations on taxes and deficits, the federal government does not operate under any such rule (see Tax limitations). Proponents of adopting these rules at the federal level predict that these changes would allow voters to approve public spending on the basis of true costs and, possibly, to lower funding of public programs as well.

Critics of the deficit illusion hypothesis argue that voters are not likely to systematically underestimate financing burdens and that therefore overexpansion of the public sector is unlikely (Barro 1978). This view is consistent with the Ricardian equivalence proposition, which hypothesizes that voters recognize, for given levels of public spending, the equivalence between taxes and public debt. Voters therefore do not operate under an illusion that public debt offers a cheaper alternative to taxation. Unlike the tax and benefit illusion hypotheses, this hypothesis predicts that the public sector neither overexpands nor underexpands.

There is also a longstanding counterhypothesis that, while voter illusion exists, it arises over the benefits, not the costs, of public programs (Downs 1960). This hypothesis proposes that, because voters underestimate the benefits of programs, underexpansion of public programs occurs from the resulting underestimation of net benefits. Other than policies that attempt to inform voters about the true nature of benefits, it is not clear what remedies would dispel benefit illusion and promote government programs more in line with their true costs and benefits.

There is mixed empirical support for the hypothesis that voters underestimate the tax bills of public programs (e.g., for support see Wagner 1976, and for rejection see Greene and Munley 1979). However, a survey of the empirical evidence finds little overall support for the hypothesis (Oates 1988). While the deficit illusion hypothesis is especially interesting in light of the record of federal deficits for 1970–1997, little empirical research has been conducted on its influence on public-sector expansion, and therefore testing of this hypothesis is likely to be the subject of expanded interest in the near future.

## Additional readings

Barro, Robert J. "Comments from an Unreconstructed Ricardian." *Journal of Monetary Economics* (August 1978): 569–81.

Buchanan, James M., and Richard E. Wagner. *Democracy in Deficit. The Political Legacy of Lord Keynes.* New York: Academic Press, 1977.

Downs, Anthony. "Why the Government Budget Is Too Small in a Democracy." *World Politics* (July 1960): 541–63.

Greene, Kevin V., and Vincent G. Munley. "Generating Growth in Public Expenditures: The Role of Employee and Constituent Demand." *Public Finance Quarterly* (January 1979): 82–109.

Oates, Wallace E. "On the Nature and Measurement of Fiscal Illusion: A Survey." In *Taxation and Fiscal Federalism: Essays in Honour of Russell Mathews,* edited by Geoffrey Brennan, Bhajan S. Grewel, and Peter D. Groenewegen, pp. 65–82. Canberra: Australian National University Press, 1988.

Wagner, Richard E. "Revenue Structure, Fiscal Illusion, and Budgetary Choice." *Public Choice* (1976): 45–61.

*Cross references:* budget process, federal and state; Ricardian equivalence; Tiebout model.

# Tax limitations

Perry Shapiro
University of California, Santa Barbara

*Using a combination of constitutional and/or statutory approaches, some state and local governments place an overall cap on tax proceeds. Often accomplished by initiative, the "tax revolt" was primarily a late 1970s–1980s phenomenon.*

All 50 states in the country limit taxes and expenditures in some way. The most prevalent limitation is the requirement of a balanced state budget; in fact, all states but Vermont have one. Other common restrictions include supermajority vote requirements for passage of tax increases, line-item gubernatorial vetoes, bond limitations, and indexation of income taxes. Tax limitations, however, generally refer instead to legislation that constrains specific sources and uses of tax revenue. The 1970s and 1980s witnessed an explosion of tax limitations in the United States, highlighted by such well-known political struggles as California's Proposition 13.

The tax rebellion of the 1970s and 1980s was billed by advocates as a popular revolt against governments that were unresponsive to popular will. They cast government as a Leviathan, the monopoly supplier of public services with an unbridled ability to finance its supply through taxation and inflation. Tax and expenditure limitations were advocated as a means for taming the public sector.

This interpretation poses an interesting question, however. Why, in a stable democracy, should fiscal policy diverge so far from the collective will? Economists have long theorized that the mix of goods and services provided by the government in any jurisdiction is the mix and quantity that is demanded by the median voter. While there are always voters who desire more than the amount provided and voters who desire less, the voter with the median preference in a majority-rule society should be satisfied. Tax limitation bills cannot capture a majority vote in such a world, so the median voter model cannot adequately explain the recent popularity of the tax limitation movement.

New Jersey passed the first limitation of state fiscal authority in 1976 and was followed, in one form or another, by 20 states over the next 10 years. While these state laws differ widely, several regularities can be observed. A vast majority of states with active legislation restrict expenditures rather than tax revenues. Only 17 states have active tax and expenditure limitations; New Jersey allowed its legislation to expire, Nevada and Rhode Island have nonbinding limits (only the governor's budget proposal is restricted), and Utah has not passed the necessary enabling legislation. Most of these states tie spending growth directly to the growth in state personal income; several adjust in addition for inflation. Almost all states retain the option to override the terms of the limitation with a simple two-thirds majority vote of the legislature during emergencies, although several require voter or governor approval. Only Oklahoma has no provisions for a waiver. In addition, five state governments are mandated to rebate surplus revenues to taxpayers either through revision of future tax rates or through refunds or credits in proportion to tax liability, four have no explicit provision for treatment of surpluses, and the rest transfer surplus funds to reserve accounts for future use. A more detailed description of state-by-state tax and expenditure limitation legislation can be found in Advisory Commission on Intergovernmental Relations (ACIR) 1989b.

The tax revolt was a citizen effort. Not surprisingly, tax and expenditure limitation measures are more common in states that have citizen initiative laws. Of the 26 states that have those laws, nearly one-half have passed tax and expenditure limitation bills. Only one state in four that lacked popular access to state government passed a tax and expenditure limitation bill. It must be noted, however, that in only five states was passage of a limitation measure accomplished by citizen initiative. Thus, it is unclear whether the differential is because states with citizen initiative laws have an a priori greater proclivity to bind government or whether the presence of the initiative induces elected officials to comply with popular will.

While legislation that constrains state fiscal authority is a relatively recent phenomenon, local government has a long history with tax limitations. The first property tax limitation was enacted by Rhode Island in 1870 (ACIR 1977: 11). However, the number of states with limitations on municipal taxation and spending almost doubled from 14 to 26 between 1976 and 1987 (Preston and Ichniowski 1991). Among the statutes passed in the 1970s and 1980s, California's Proposition 13 and Massachusetts's Proposition 2½ were unique. Both directly reduced taxes. Other limitations laws merely constrained the rate of future tax growth.

Because local governments derive most of their revenues from property taxes, the traditional form of tax limitation has been control of property tax rates. A recent shift toward limiting the growth of property tax levies has occurred, however. In 1987, 19 states limited the total property tax burden that could be levied on property owners, compared with 9 in 1976. Levy limits frequently stipulate a maximum permissible rate of growth in property tax collections, although most allow for population growth and inflation. Between 1976 and 1987, allowable growth rates ranged from 0 percent in Kansas to 10 percent in Mississippi. Arizona, California, and Idaho have coupled tax rate limitations with limits on assessment increases, which, in effect, indirectly constrains the growth in property tax levies (Preston and Ichniowski 1991). A smaller number of states restrict own-source municipal expenditures or revenues directly, although few rely exclusively on this mechanism.

The presence of popular referenda is equally important as a determinant of local-level tax limitations. In fact, more than three-quarters of states with citizen initiative laws had local tax limitations during the peak reform years, 1976 to 1987, whereas only 42 percent of the states without such provisions had limitations during the same period. As with state-level limitations, however, a causal chain between referenda and tax limitation cannot be inferred.

Economists have proposed numerous explanations of the tax limitation movement and potential failure of the median voter model. Many postulate the existence of a Leviathan government, unresponsive to popular will. For example, one compelling version theorizes that government has grown too large because of imperfections in the agenda formation process that favor high demanders of public goods and services. An alternative theory suggests that limitation measures might reflect discontent with the method of finance rather than the level of service, particularly at the local level. In this view, limitations might reflect the desire to shift the burden from local property taxes to more progressive state income taxes. Yet another idea suggests that voters might be expecting something for nothing.

Denzau et al. (1979) motivate Leviathan by suggesting that ballot initiatives are a public good, available to all irrespective of whether one contributes. Because participation in the political process is costly and because tax burden is generally more widely dispersed than are benefits, Denzau et al. model a government that becomes effectively controlled by a dominant coalition of high demanders. It is conceivable, however, that low demanders could form such a special interest group also. As a result, the outcome of democratic voting reflects only voter demand along a narrow array of predetermined alternatives, and a constitutional spending limit provides one means of widening the array.

Table 1 presents the historical trend of the public sector. There was clear growth in the relative size of government, for the nation as a whole, from 1927 to 1987. Federal, state, and local government own-source revenues constituted 12.7, 30.9, and 37.1 percent and direct expenditures 11.7, 31.6, and 38.6 percent of gross national product (GNP) in 1927, 1967, and 1987 respectively. However, the majority of the increase took place well before the beginning of the tax revolt in the mid-1970s. In fact, the greatest period of relative government growth occurred directly after WWII; the 1970s witnessed stability in the relative size of government. If government growth precipitated the tax revolution, then rebellion should have occurred sooner. Also disconcerting is the fact that reform efforts were concentrated at the state and local government levels even though growth in state and local revenues and expenditures was modest in contrast to growth in the federal budget. Furthermore, local government grew in relative size the least, yet it was arguably the biggest target of reform efforts.

Analysis at the national level may conceal important state and local patterns. For instance, excessive public welfare is a common focal point for pro-limitation argument. State and local public welfare expenditures increased steadily from 0.78 percent of GNP in 1955 to 1.76 percent of GNP in 1975, the eve of the rebellion. However, state and local

public welfare did not decline after passage of so many limitation measures (ACIR 1989b: 31). Additionally, local government is heavily reliant on property taxes, though property taxes as a percentage of local revenues decreased steadily from 92.4 percent in 1942 to 73.7 percent in 1987 (ACIR 1989b: 79). This trend, however, disguises an increasing burden on property owners in the years prior to the tax revolt. Local property taxes increased from 2.4 percent of GNP in 1948 to 3.7 percent of GNP in 1972, the eve of the tax rebellion, before returning to 2.5 percent of GNP in the 1980s (ACIR 1989b: 35).

Many explanations center on state-specific events. Take California; its fiscal history has been well documented. Oakland found that state and local taxes as a percentage of personal income were higher and increased faster than the national average over the 20 years preceding Proposition 13. By 1977, they were almost 4 percentage points higher than the national average. California's budget may have gotten out of line, and Proposition 13 may have been the voters' way of reasserting control. Shapiro and Sonstelie (1982) used the passage of Proposition 13 as a natural experiment to test whether California's municipal governments were behaving according to the median voter or the Leviathan model. They found evidence for the latter.

Proposition 13 primarily affected property taxes, however. Shapiro proposed another explanation based on a public opinion survey, conducted just before the election, which suggested that expenditure levels for most public services, except for administrative costs and welfare, were not perceived as too high. Because the share of property taxes paid by citizens had risen from 45 to 53 percent between 1973 and 1978, and because the state had a $7 billion surplus, Shapiro suggests that Proposition 13 might have reflected a desire to shift financial responsibility from local to state government. The desirability of state financing, however, was inversely related to income because California income taxes were progressive; low-income groups were the primary beneficiaries. Shapiro found no support for the hypothesis empirically, though, because, in the survey, support for Proposition 13 did not differ systematically across incomes. He did, however, find support for Leviathan because estimated demand for school and county expenditures was between 7 and 8 percent too high. Oakland was critical of the methodology employed and unwilling to dismiss the hypothesis.

Fischel (1989) has advanced the role played by the California Supreme Court in precipitating Proposition 13. Tiebout argued that the free rider problem could be overcome for local public goods because communities could offer different mixes and levels of local services and like-minded individuals would choose to settle together. In this way,

**TABLE 1**

Government Own-Source Revenues and Direct Expenditures, Relative to GNP

| | Revenues as a Percent of GNP | | | | Expenditures as a Percent of GNP | | | |
|---|---|---|---|---|---|---|---|---|
| Year | Federal | State and Local | State | Local | Federal | State and Local | State | Local |
| 1927 | 4.64 | 8.02 | 2.07 | 5.95 | 3.54 | 8.11 | 1.51 | 6.60 |
| 1940 | 6.97 | 10.76 | 4.99 | 5.77 | 9.14 | 11.20 | 3.54 | 7.65 |
| 1952 | 20.42 | 8.09 | 4.08 | 4.02 | 19.62 | 8.78 | 3.07 | 5.71 |
| 1957 | 19.31 | 9.33 | 4.60 | 4.74 | 19.19 | 11.72 | 4.14 | 7.58 |
| 1962 | 18.52 | 10.72 | 5.24 | 5.48 | 18.39 | 12.28 | 4.44 | 7.84 |
| 1967 | 19.76 | 11.17 | 5.73 | 5.44 | 18.60 | 12.98 | 4.86 | 8.12 |
| 1972 | 18.42 | 13.15 | 6.96 | 6.19 | 17.20 | 15.71 | 5.98 | 9.73 |
| 1973 | 18.66 | 13.12 | 7.14 | 5.98 | 17.03 | 15.12 | 5.74 | 9.38 |
| 1974 | 19.58 | 13.31 | 7.31 | 6.00 | 17.15 | 15.32 | 5.85 | 9.47 |
| 1975 | 18.99 | 13.57 | 7.46 | 6.12 | 18.26 | 16.78 | 6.69 | 10.09 |
| 1976 | 18.22 | 13.89 | 7.80 | 6.09 | 18.06 | 17.00 | 6.90 | 10.10 |
| 1977 | 19.27 | 13.84 | 7.83 | 6.01 | 18.05 | 16.24 | 6.47 | 9.77 |
| 1978 | 19.17 | 13.42 | 7.63 | 5.80 | 17.79 | 15.35 | 6.07 | 9.28 |
| 1979 | 19.97 | 13.15 | 7.57 | 5.58 | 18.02 | 15.17 | 5.93 | 9.24 |
| 1980 | 20.70 | 13.49 | 7.78 | 5.71 | 19.27 | 15.82 | 6.34 | 9.48 |
| 1981 | 21.65 | 13.64 | 7.86 | 5.78 | 20.46 | 15.30 | 6.50 | 8.81 |
| 1982 | 21.72 | 14.54 | 8.27 | 6.28 | 22.44 | 16.52 | 6.68 | 9.84 |
| 1983 | 19.96 | 14.79 | 8.37 | 6.42 | 23.07 | 16.58 | 6.83 | 9.75 |
| 1984 | 19.99 | 14.71 | 8.37 | 6.35 | 21.98 | 15.35 | 6.44 | 8.90 |
| 1985 | 20.10 | 15.28 | 8.69 | 6.59 | 23.04 | 16.34 | 6.71 | 9.64 |
| 1986 | 20.03 | 15.84 | 9.04 | 6.79 | 23.18 | 16.93 | 6.91 | 10.02 |
| 1987 | 21.06 | 16.08 | 9.16 | 6.92 | 22.92 | 15.71 | 6.95 | 8.76 |

*Sources:* The data are drawn from tables 1, 12, and 13 of ACIR 1989b; U.S. Bureau of the Census, p. 139; and *Economic Report of the President*, p. 294. Note that a typographical error in table 12 of ACIR has been corrected.

property taxes behaved like user costs. In attempting to equalize educational opportunity statewide, the court ruled in the second *Serrano* v. *Priest* decision (1976) that all California school districts must equate, within $100, expenditures per student. This restriction meant that public school expenditures could no longer signal community demand for education, and thus most property taxes were a deadweight loss. The block of voters in communities with greater than average demand for education, who generally reside in affluent areas, and who ordinarily would have opposed the proposition, were silent.

A final argument is more cynical. Citrin (1979: 13) recognizes that "the public's readiness to demand and consume government programs is understandably greater than its willingness to pay for them." It is unclear whether support for tax limitation measures reflects a belief about the proper size of government or antagonism toward particular programs, welfare in particular. Considering California, Citrin concluded that, while Proposition 13 certainly expressed a collective preference for lower taxes, maintaining the status quo was a prominent, and in some areas a majority, view.

Tax limitations are an important component of state and local fiscal policy in the United States. The tax limitation movement reached its peak during the frenzied 1970s and 1980s with the adoption, in one form or another, of legislation in a majority of

states. The legislation remains active in most of these states. The causes appear to be numerous, although it is clear that state and local government did grow faster than the willingness of the electorate to finance it. Furthermore, citizen access to referenda is strongly correlated with the passage of tax limitation legislation.

## Additional readings

Advisory Commission on Intergovernmental Relations. *State Limitations on Local Taxes and Expenditures.* Washington, D.C.: U.S. Government Printing Office, February 1977.

Advisory Commission on Intergovernmental Relations. *Significant Features of Fiscal Federalism 1989. Vol. 1.* Washington, D.C.: U.S. Government Printing Office, January 1989 (1989a).

Advisory Commission on Intergovernmental Relations. *Significant Features of Fiscal Federalism 1989. Vol. 2.* Washington, D.C.: U.S. Government Printing Office, August 1989 (1989b).

Bails, Dale G. "The Effectiveness of Tax-Expenditure Limitations: A Re-evaluation." *American Journal of Economics and Sociology* 49 (April 1990): 223–38.

Citrin, Jack. "Do People Want Something for Nothing: Public Opinion on Taxes and Government Spending." *National Tax Journal* 32 (June 1979): 113–30.

Courant, Paul N., Edward M. Gramlich, and Daniel L. Rubinfeld. "Why Voters Support Tax Limitation Amendments: The Michigan Case." *Tax and Expenditure Limitations*, COUPE Papers on Public Economics. Washington, D.C.: The Urban Institute Press, 1981.

Denzau, Arthur, Robert MacKay, and Carolyn Weaver. "Spending Limitations, Agenda Control, and Voters' Expectations." *National Tax Journal* 32 (June 1979): 189–200.

*Economic Report of the President*. Washington, D.C.: U.S. Government Printing Office, February 1990.

Elder, Harold W. "Exploring the Tax Revolt: An Analysis of the Effects of State Tax and Expenditure Limitations Laws." *Public Finance Quarterly* 20 (January 1992): 47–63.

Fischel, William A. "Did Serrano Cause Proposition 13?" *National Tax Journal* 42 (December 1989): 465–73.

Ladd, Helen F., and Julie Boatright Wilson. "Why Voters Support Tax Limitations: Evidence from Massachusetts' Proposition 2-1/2." *National Tax Journal* 35 (June 1982): 121–47.

Magleby, David B. *Direct Legislation: Voting on Ballot Propositions in the United States*. Baltimore: The Johns Hopkins University Press, 1984.

Oakland, William H. "Discussion of Perry Shapiro, 'Popular Response to Public Spending Disequilibrium: An Analysis of the 1978 California Property Tax Limitation Initiative.'" *Tax and Expenditure Limitations*, COUPE Papers on Public Economics. Washington, D.C.: The Urban Institute Press, 1981.

Preston, Anne E., and Casey Ichniowski. "A National Perspective on the Nature and Effects of the Local Property Tax Revolt, 1976–1986." *National Tax Journal* 44 (June 1991): 123–45.

Shapiro, Perry. "Popular Response to Public Spending Disequilibrium: An Analysis of the 1978 California Property Tax Limitation Initiative." *Tax and Expenditure Limitations*, COUPE Papers on Public Economics. Washington, D.C.: The Urban Institute Press, 1981; also see Oakland.

Shapiro, Perry, and Jon Sonstelie. "Did Proposition 13 Slay Leviathan?" *The American Economic Review* 72 (May 1982): 184–90.

Shapiro, Perry, David Puryear, and John Ross. "Tax and Expenditure Limitation in Retrospect and in Prospect." *National Tax Journal* 32 (June 1979): 1–10.

Tiebout, Charles. "A Pure Theory of Local Expenditures." *Journal of Political Economy* 64 (October 1956): 416–24.

U.S. Bureau of the Census. *Historical Statistics of the United States: Colonial Times to 1957*. Washington, D.C., 1960, Library of Congress Card No. A 60-9150.

*Cross references:* education financing, state and local; tax price; Tiebout model.

# Taxpayer compliance measurement program (TCMP)

William Lefbom
Internal Revenue Service (Emeritus)

*An IRS program designed to assess the degree of noncompliance with law and regulation.*

The taxpayer compliance measurement program (TCMP) was designed by the Internal Revenue Service (IRS) in the early 1960s to measure the extent to which taxpayers voluntarily comply with tax laws. TCMP is designed to measure the degree to which taxpayers file an accurate return and pay on a timely basis before any direct enforcement actions. The purpose was to define the extent and characteristics of noncompliance so that optimal solutions could be initiated to improve compliance. These solutions have included recommendations for changing the laws, improved IRS workload (audit) selection systems, changed emphasis in enforcement programs, tax form design, and educational efforts.

To achieve the desired compliance measurement objectives, the IRS randomly selects a sample of accounts, potential nonfilers, or returns; conducts a thorough investigation or audit; and captures the results on a database. The term "investigation" is used in this entry to describe the techniques used by the IRS collection function to determine if a potential nonfiler has already filed, is not required to file, or has not filed a required tax return. The IRS uses the term "examination" instead of "audit." The term "audit" is used in this entry because it is the more commonly understood word used to describe an IRS examination of books, records, financial transactions, and so forth to determine the accuracy of the tax return submitted by the taxpayer.

## Scope of TCMP surveys

The IRS developed terms to define the many different surveys conducted since 1963. The term "phase" is used to designate what compliance aspect is being measured, and the IRS uses roman numerals to designate a phase. A "cycle" is used to designate the specific period the survey measures. Eleven phases and 35 cycles were completed from 1963 through 1996. Surveys designated Phase I are designed to measure timely payment, Phase II and IX surveys measure compliance in filing of returns, and Phase III, IV, V, VI, VII, VIII, X, and XI surveys measure the accuracy of a filed return. The following surveys have been completed: Phase I (Surveys of Delinquent Accounts)—7 cycles, last survey 1984; Phase

II (Delinquent Returns Non-Farm Business Surveys)—3 cycles, last survey 1969; Phase III (Surveys to Measure Accuracy of Individual Income Tax Returns)—10 cycles, last survey 1988; Phase IV (Surveys to Measure Accuracy of Corporation Income Tax Returns)—5 cycles, last survey 1988; Phase V (Survey to Measure Accuracy of Estate Tax Returns)—1 cycle, only survey 1971; Phase VI (Surveys to Measure Accuracy of Exempt Organization Returns)—3 cycles, last survey 1988; Phase VII (Survey to Measure Accuracy of Fiduciary Income Returns)—1 cycle, only survey 1975; Phase VIII (Survey to Measure Accuracy of Employee Plans Returns)—1 cycle, only survey 1980; Phase IX (Delinquent Returns Individual Income Tax)—2 cycles, last survey 1988; Phase X (Survey to Measure Accuracy of Partnership Returns)—1 cycle, only survey 1982; Phase XI (Survey to Measure Accuracy of S Corporation Returns)—1 cycle, only survey 1985.

## TCMP process

The TCMP process from initial planning to the beginning of the analysis of results takes five years, and the IRS has generally followed these steps:

### Preliminary planning

This step determines the overall scope and objectives of the survey—for example, what type of return, the period of sample selection, whether results are to be used for workload selection formulas, preliminary sample design, approval to commit resources, development of a detailed action plan. A memorandum on the "scope and objectives" of a specific survey summarizes these tasks.

### Sample design and computer selection programming

All TCMP surveys are based on audits or investigations of a random *stratified* sample. Income levels (individual income taxes), asset size (corporations), and availability of information returns (delinquent return surveys) are some of the criteria that determine the strata. The selection of potential nonfilers or returns within a sample stratum is entirely random, but the sample rate varies greatly by stratum. The size of the sample, within a stratum, is determined by the survey scope and objectives, which are normally the measurement of compliance and the development of workload selection formulas. One of the means the IRS has used for identifying which returns to audit is a mathematical technique known as discriminant function (DIF). DIF formulas are developed for each audit class, based on TCMP. Samples are normally designed to be large enough to measure compliance and develop DIF formulas *for each audit class*. DIF requirements greatly increase the sample size that would be required if

compliance measurement were the only objective. Data from tax returns and information returns submitted by taxpayers or third parties are transcribed (or electronically transmitted to the IRS) and retained on a master file. The master file is programmed to identify selected returns when they post to the system based on the strata criteria and sample selection rate. For delinquent return surveys, the master file is programmed to stratify potential nonfilers, for a specific year, based primarily on information returns and prior tax year return information. (The most recent TCMP survey of potential nonfilers also sampled individuals who are not on the master file system and for whom no information return data were available to the IRS.)

### Selection of returns or potential nonfilers

The sampling of filed returns normally takes place weekly for an entire year—for example, sampling of tax year 1988 individual income tax returns would start in January 1989 and continue through the end of December 1989. The sampling of potential nonfilers, however, occurs at one time, after information returns have been received, processed and correlated. The sampling of potential nonfilers of tax year 1988 individual income tax returns took place in April 1990, for instance. The sampled returns or investigations of potential nonfilers are controlled so that every sampled case is included in the survey unless there is a legitimate reason for excluding one from the sample—for example, if a taxpayer died after filing and there is no executor that can provide any type of information for use in an audit.

### Development of a questionnaire

An instrument is used to collect the data necessary to meet the scope and objectives of the survey. (The IRS uses the term "check sheet" to describe this instrument.) The IRS tries to obtain only data that can be obtained by a thorough audit or investigation. The only information *sought from the taxpayer* during the audit or investigation is what is necessary to determine the accuracy of the return, or determine if the taxpayer meets tax return filing requirements in case of delinquent return surveys. Generally, a check sheet designed to measure the accuracy of a return will contain most of the line items on the tax return as reported by the taxpayer and determined by the examiner to be the correct amount—for example, interest income reported and the amount the examiner determines is correct, which may be the same, higher, or lower.

### Training and audits or investigations

The employees assigned to conduct TCMP audits or investigations are not trained in survey methodology or research, but they do understand tax law, so their training emphasizes the importance of an in-depth audit or investigation and the accurate completion of the check sheet. The taxpayer selected for the audit or investigation is entitled to all the normal appeals processes. The taxpayer may receive a "no change" report, receive a refund, be required to pay additional taxes, or even be the subject of a criminal referral if fraud is uncovered. IRS examiners are required to review all potential issues to determine if the return is correct as filed. The IRS relies on the professional judgment of its employees to ensure that all potential issues that would affect the reported tax liability are explored. All TCMP audits or investigations are subject to a separate technical review. Particular emphasis is placed on use of proper auditing techniques to detect unreported income. Normally, at least 18 months are allowed for the audit portion of a TCMP survey. The most complex returns, which take the longest time to audit, are normally the last to be filed and, therefore, sampled. The taxpayer may not agree with the examiner's recommendations and may request an appeal. The results of the audit are normally set forth on the check sheet before any appeals organization or tax court decisions that could increase or decrease the tax changes recommended by the examiner or investigator.

### Datafile creation

The check sheets are designed so that numerous validity or consistency tests can be applied to ensure data integrity. In earlier surveys, the check sheets were sent to a central processing center where they were key entered and subject to testing. In more recent surveys, the check sheets are entered in field offices, to move the timing and placement of error correction closer to the source. The datafile would include all items from the check sheet and other items from the IRS master file.

### Output tables and preliminary analysis

Diagnostic tables, which provide frequency counts and values for check sheet line items, serve as another check to ensure data integrity. The TCMP database is then available for analysis of compliance and the development of DIF formulas for workload selection. A public use file like that developed by the statistics of income program is not developed for TCMP because availability of a micro-level file could enable someone to determine tax return line item variables and relative weights associated with high tax change returns—the same general means the IRS uses to develop scoring formulas (DIF) for workload (audit) selection. The IRS believes the formulas might be approximated and individuals might improperly manipulate their tax returns to avoid the possibility of being audited.

An example of a tabulation is "Table 10," frequently used within the IRS. This table contains, for each line item on the tax return, the amount reported, the amount increased, decreased, not reported but established (by the examination), and reported and changed to zero. This table is aggregated by audit class. While the IRS produces the table for internal use, it has occasionally provided the table to academics and others having an interest in overall tax compliance and the components of compliance such as proper reporting of income, deductions, and credits.

### Voluntary compliance level

An aggregate measure that has been used since the first TCMP cycles is the voluntary compliance level (VCL). The IRS wanted one simple measure that depicted overall compliance for a year and for each audit class. The VCL is calculated by dividing the tax reported on the return by the tax reported plus the tax increase determined by the examiner. The result is multiplied by 100. The IRS also develops "tax gap" estimates—the amount of "true" tax liability for a particular tax year that is not paid voluntarily and timely—primarily from TCMP data. Tax gap estimates include compliance percentages, in addition to amounts. The tax gap compliance percentages (or the inverse noncompliance percentages) are much broader than the VCL measures, and the two measures are not comparable. (There have been media articles that compared the VCL to tax gap percentages and incorrectly implied a major decline in voluntary compliance.)

### Published results from TCMP surveys

The primary focus of TCMP is to improve tax administration. Measurements of voluntary compliance that result from TCMP are provided to congressional tax-writing committees and the General Accounting Office. These results may only reflect a specific aspect of tax compliance, which may be the subject of a hearing. The IRS makes publicly available two documents that may contain summary measures from completed TCMP surveys.

*The IRS Research Bulletin, Publication 1500*, formerly known as the *Trend Analysis and Related Statistics*, is generally published once a year. The 1993/1994 *Bulletin* includes articles and tables on the accuracy of the latest survey to measure accuracy of filed 1988 individual income tax returns and to compare them with secured delinquent returns. Earlier issues include articles on compliance levels from the most recently completed TCMP survey and compliance trends from prior surveys.

*The Statistics of Income (SOI) Bulletin, Publication 1136*, published quarterly, occasionally includes compliance measures from TCMP surveys.

The Summer 1993 and Fall 1994 issues contain articles and tables on tax year 1988 individual income tax return filing compliance.

## Additional readings

Internal Revenue Service. *The IRS Research Bulletin.* Washington, D.C.: U.S. Government Printing Office, various years.

Internal Revenue Service. *Statistics of Income (SOI) Bulletin.* Pittsburgh: Government Printing Office, various years. Superintendent of Documents, P.O. Box 371954, Pittsburgh PA 15250-7954.

*Cross references:* income tax, federal; tax administration, federal; tax administration: public and private cooperation.

# Tax price

Walter Hettich
California State University

*A concept developed in analogy to price as observed in private markets.*

The tax price is usually defined as the payment required of a consumer for an extra unit of a public good (Stiglitz 1988). The term may also be used more broadly to indicate the marginal or average unit cost of public services to a particular taxpayer or group of taxpayers.

Tax price differs from *tax rate* by making an explicit connection between tax payments and the consumption of public services. While it is related to the term *user fees*, its meaning is more general, because an implicit tax price exists in all cases regardless of whether consumers are being charged for the good or service.

Tax price is most often used in theoretical discussions of how to equate the demand and supply of public services. In the private economy, market prices play an important function in establishing such equality by serving as crucial signals to buyers and sellers. Under competitive conditions, adjustment of prices in response to shortages or surpluses leads to market equilibrium and to an efficient use of resources in production and consumption. Economists have asked whether there are charges or payments that can serve a similar role in the public sector.

The main conceptual difficulty arises from the special nature of public goods. It is often pointed out that public services such as defense do not diminish in availability when one more consumer is added; those already living in the community continue to enjoy the same level of protection as before. Furthermore, it is not feasible to exclude anyone residing in the country from benefiting from expenditures on national defense. These characteristics make it impossible to use private market institutions and market prices to match demand and supply in the case of public goods and to allocate such goods among consumers in an efficient manner.

Theorists have proposed various mechanisms to determine tax prices that would provide appropriate signals to the consumers of public goods. The most famous contribution was made in 1919 by Lindahl (1958), who suggested a mechanism to let consumers react to individually differentiated tax prices. Price ratios for public and private goods were to be adjusted separately for each consumer until everyone demanded the same amount of the public good, an equilibrium situation having efficiency properties similar to a private market solution. Lindahl's work implies that consumers pay differing unit prices for the same amount of public good in equilibrium, reflecting variations in their demand for the good. This outcome is necessary because quantity cannot be adjusted separately by each individual, as is possible for goods sold in private markets.

While Lindahl's work provides a conceptual solution for determining equilibrium tax prices, it has a theoretical shortcoming. Participants in the scheme who understand its functioning can reduce their payments by misrepresenting their true demand in response to announced price ratios, leading to free riding on their part. If such actions are prevalent, the mechanism no longer yields efficient tax prices. Economists have attempted to devise other approaches that would force participants to reveal their true demands (Clarke 1971, Feldman 1980), but as yet no mechanism with broad applicability in practice has been discovered.

Lindahl's model is a simplified and highly stylized representation of public goods provision. While it clears up important theoretical issues, it is not descriptive of how decisions are made. In democratic societies, taxpayers express their demands for public goods and services primarily by voting. This has led to analyses of voting mechanisms and their role in the determination of public-sector output.

An approach frequently used in research on the public sector is the *median voter model*. Under the conditions specified in this framework, the voter with the median demand for a public good determines the equilibrium level of output. In making choices, this voter relates his or her tax price to the benefit from additional units of public output until tax price equals the value of the last unit of the good provided. Researchers who use this model attempt to determine tax prices faced by the median voter in particular political decision contexts, such as referenda on bond issues, in order to test the model against actual data.

Outcomes in a median voter framework generally differ from those in Lindahl equilibrium. Depending on the conditions facing the median or decisive voter, budgets may be higher or lower than with efficient pricing. This is not surprising because results hinge on the tax price of a particular voter and do not represent the marginal responses of all participants. While tax price remains important, it no longer simulates the role played by prices in efficient private markets. The necessity of using a collective choice process exacts a cost if market efficiency is taken as a standard of comparison.

While the median voter model links budgetary choices to voting, it is based on rather strict assumptions concerning the nature of preferences and the number of dimensions in which decisions are made. In situations where choices are complex, with several issues being decided simultaneously, the model no longer yields predictable, stable outcomes. In alternative frameworks more suited for analyzing complex tax and expenditure situations, such as expected vote maximization, the links between tax prices for particular public goods and budget size are less direct, even though voters still relate the overall benefits from increased public output to the cost of paying additional taxes.

As mentioned, the difficulties for appropriate pricing arise primarily from the nature of public goods. However, not all goods or services provided by governments are "public" in the full sense of the term, because they are subject to not being diminishable in consumption and to not being excludable. Some are closer in nature to private goods, although they may have a public aspect or component. An example is provided by higher education, where students capture a large proportion of benefits from the activity privately in the form of increased earnings after completion of studies, and where exclusion by price can readily be practiced. In such a context, user fees (i.e., tuition) can be applied. If their level were to be determined by considerations of economic efficiency alone, such fees would represent prices similar to those observed in private markets, although they would contain an element of subsidy to reflect any public component or externality attached to the good. In practice, determination of such charges or fees represents additional factors reflecting the political mechanism through which decisions are made and distributional considerations that may be important in public policy.

Because of the size and complexity of the modern public sector, it is hard for the average voter to link changes in his or her tax burden directly to changes in specific public benefits. The individual pays a multitude of taxes, each of which may be subject to special provisions, such as exemptions, deductions, and credits, making it difficult to cal-

culate marginal tax payments. One should also note that some taxes can be shifted, giving rise to complex questions of *incidence*. As a result, it may be next to impossible to know how an individual's tax liability will be affected by a small increase in public expenditures and thus to estimate an appropriate marginal tax price. Similar problems will also arise if we attempt to determine actual average tax prices.

Although economists are aware of the difficulties of implementation, they continue to employ the concept in theoretical discussions. Analysis based on tax price clarifies important issues about the similarities and differences of the public and private sectors and yields conclusions of a general nature that are useful in policy-making. It strongly suggests that efficiency in public resource use will be improved by mechanisms establishing a closer link between the consumption of publicly provided goods and the cost to those who benefit from these goods.

## Additional readings

Clarke, E.H. "Multipart Pricing of Public Goods." *Public Choice* (Fall 1971): 17–33.

Feldman, Alan M. *Welfare Economics and Social Choice Theory.* Boston: Kluwer Nijhoff Publishing, 1980.

Lindahl, E. "Just Taxation—A Positive Solution" (translated) in *Classics in the Theory of Public Finance*, edited by R.A. Musgrave and A.T. Peacock. New York: St. Martin's Press, 1958.

Stiglitz, Joseph. *Economics of the Public Sector.* 2d ed. New York: Norton, 1988.

*Cross references:* benefit principle; median voter theorem; tax illusion; user charges, federal.

# Tax reform, federal

C. Eugene Steuerle
The Urban Institute

*A review of the federal government experience in reviewing and adjusting its revenue system to adjust to changes in the national economy, demography, and its institutional and political arrangements. The term usually refers to broad rather than piecemeal change in law.*

Changes to the tax laws are almost always labeled reforms, but reform as improvement, not merely amendment, generally is based upon bringing the law into closer adherence to certain principles or goals. The public finance principles of efficiency, growth, equal treatment of those in equal situations (horizontal equity or fairness), progressivity, and simplicity provide a useful listing around which tax changes can be analyzed.

Taxes generally are not good in and of themselves. They provide the means by which government is financed, and hence their benefits relate to the expenditure side of the budget. By themselves, taxes nearly always distort behavior, add complications to the lives of at least some taxpayers, and, in practice, create problems of equity between some who pay and some who are equally capable of paying, but from whom payment is more difficult to extract. Much of tax reform, therefore, is aimed at minimizing the costs of taxation—reducing the inefficiencies of taxation—more than at maximizing some efficiencies it somehow adds to society.

## Historical context

At the end of the 19th century and the beginning of the 20th, many federal reform efforts were aimed at displacing or replacing old taxes with new taxes. During the 19th century, government was financed primarily through tariffs. Today large tariffs are generally viewed as both unfair and inefficient, but in the earlier period they could be assessed conveniently at the time that goods were transferred from sellers to buyers, and an accounting was engaged at the port or dock. With the rise of the corporation and the large organization, however, more elaborate accounting schemes allowed better assessment of returns to factors of production such as labor and capital. It was this development, more than any other, that allowed replacement of tariffs by income and wage taxes as the primary sources of revenues to the federal government.

As income taxes grew in size and importance, more and more attention was paid to their design, rather than their adoption, expansion, or contraction, as a major reform option. Many fights, of course, also ensued over the size of the tax system, but the revenue goal here was closely related to how large government expenditures should be, an issue that extends far beyond tax reform. But the issues were often combined and confused. In some periods, such as wartime, consensus on the need for expenditures left as a remaining debate only the issue of who should pay. In other periods, many policymakers argued for higher or lower taxes primarily on the basis of what expenditures could be financed. In these cases, the tax debate often could not be separated from the issue of size of government.

Another confusion in the tax reform debate often arose in considerations of the design of the tax base and its interaction with the progressivity of the system itself. While tax progressivity generally can be determined by the setting of tax rates, even under widely varying tax bases, reform often began with statutory rates themselves considered as fixed.

Hence, when the base changed, the reform often had distributional consequences across income classes even if the initial goals of reform were unrelated to redistribution. For instance, barring offsetting changes in the tax rate structure, cutting back on a particular tax preference might be favored or opposed primarily on the grounds of what it did to the relative tax burdens of the rich or poor.

Still another source of confusion arose over use of the tax system for growth or macroeconomic purposes versus other improvements in well-being, such as might be achieved through more standard improvements in efficiency. In the United States, these issues arose particularly in tax reform debates in the post–World War II era. In tax reform options put forward in the early 1960s, for instance, President Kennedy made a strong pitch that tax reductions would help spur the economy and produce economic growth by expanding demand. At the same time, he proposed a number of changes to the tax base to make it more inclusive of different sources of income. The macroeconomic goal at the time was associated closely with Keynesian economics, and the argument put forward was that the additional money circulating in the economy would spur demand. In 1981, President Reagan put forward a tax reform proposal that also used macroeconomic arguments. Indeed, its primary features were very similar to those adopted during the Kennedy round of tax reform in the early 1960s: rate reduction and expansion of incentives for investment in physical capital, particularly equipment. In the 1981 round, however, the justification put forward was that lower tax rates would spur suppliers of labor and capital to work harder and save more; the term "supply side" was applied to this macroeconomic argument. Thus, a similarly designed tax change was justified in both cases by an appeal to macroeconomics, yet the theory or apologetics used were very different (Steuerle 1992).

When the macroeconomic justification was used, as it was for several tax reductions between the early 1960s and 1981, it often tended to dominate not only the debate, but the outcome. In many of these years, tax reduction was thought to bring about an expansion of the economy, a higher rate of growth, or a quicker turn out of recession. Many of the gains were argued to be immediate in their effect. Defining the base properly, on the other hand, was a long-term objective that could always be put off until another day. Thus, in the 1960s round the question of definition was essentially abandoned and the macroeconomic goal given preference, while in 1981 almost no base broadening was proposed, and later congressional expansions tended to erode the base further.

For many tax reformers, the issues of defining the tax base in a way that would promote efficiency, fairness, and simplicity often were given far too little weight because of the greater attention given to size of revenues, progressivity of the system, and macroeconomic incentives to spur either supply or demand. To the reformers, the issues could be separated. Given a tax base, the level of revenues and degree of progressivity could be determined by adjusting the tax rate schedule, including allowances for low-income individuals. Hence, the issue of what would be included in the base for the most part was a separable issue. If a given deduction was eliminated, for instance, any revenue raised could be offset by a reduction in rates, and any effect on progressivity could be offset by a change in the rate schedule itself.

Base broadening to include more items of income, better compliance with respect to items that were reported poorly, and reductions in preferences began to receive much more attention after 1981. At that time, the issue was again driven by a concern that went beyond tax reform: large levels of government deficit. Several base-broadening reforms in the 1980s were enacted as part of deficit reduction bills. President Reagan's strong antipathy to raising tax rates, coupled with Congress's reluctance or inability to deal with entitlement types of spending, left base broadening not so much a popular option as one of the least unpopular of choices for reducing the deficit.

In 1984 to 1986, the nation engaged in an extensive debate over a tax reform that would center almost entirely on the tax base itself and the lower rates that might be possible if that base were appropriately expanded. The effort for the most part attempted to put aside the issues of total revenues, progressivity, and short-term macroeconomic incentives for growth. Thus, the reform was designed approximately to be "revenue neutral" and "distributionally neutral." A large number of deductions, exclusions, credits, and other preferences were either pared or eliminated. Rates were reduced significantly, but unlike either the Kennedy round of rate reductions or the Reagan 1981 round, they were paid for through other tax changes. Like all reforms, the 1986 Tax Reform Act was made possible by a combination of opportunities: a president who especially disliked high tax rates, the rapid expansion of tax shelters, the increased income taxation of the poor, and growing concerns over taxation of the family.

By the time the act was signed into law, it involved the most comprehensive reform of this type ever achieved for the income tax. According to Witte (1991), "Of the 72 provisions which tightened tax expenditures, 14 tax expenditures were eventually repealed, a figure approximately equal to the total that had been repealed from 1913 to 1985." Treasury had advocated repeal of 38 tax expenditures. Another detailed analysis, by Neubig and Joulfaian (1988), indicated that under some simpli-

fying assumptions, tax reforms produced the equivalent of $193 billion in tax expenditure reduction for the year 1988. Base broadening was directly responsible for $77 billion of this total, and the rate reduction it made possible indirectly reduced the value of tax expenditures by $1.6 billion.

## Further reform options

Debate over federal tax reform will continue as long as there is a tax system. Many discussions in the modern era combine different reform options into a single package. Among the principal reforms suggested are the following:

### Conversion of income tax to a consumption tax

Should the tax base be reduced to exclude all purchases of capital equipment and net saving? Many current proposals would begin, as a base, with a subtraction method value-added tax applied to business—that is, by taking current income and subtracting net purchases of assets (Bradford 1986). To this system would be added an individual tax—either on wages at the individual level, or a complementary consumption tax at the individual level—which essentially would attempt to allow subtraction of savings from income. Some versions of these more elaborate reforms would maintain or expand an estate tax (Aaron and Galper 1985), and thus could be considered more as extending the accounting period for the income tax from a year to a lifetime, rather than excluding from taxation any income that was not consumed by the person who earned it.

### Value-added taxes

More narrow reforms would simply add a value-added tax (VAT) to the existing tax system. In many cases, the VAT would follow more traditional types of consumption taxes adopted in other countries. The motives are diverse—increasing revenues to support some expenditure like health care, increasing the share of government burden paid by the elderly, who now receive a substantial share of government expenditures, financing the reduction in taxes on labor or on capital, and adopting a tax with a border tax adjustment (rebate of taxes) for exports.

### Flat rate taxes

Still other reforms would convert the tax system into one with a single rate of tax applying to most of the tax base. Strictly speaking, most of these proposals allow some income to be taxed at a zero rate, so they are not flat. Most current proposals also are consumption tax proposals in that they allow the cost of capital equipment to be written off (expensed) right away rather than depreciated over time (Hall and Rabushka 1985). If carried out throughout the tax structure, flat taxes have the advantage of dramatically reducing the requirements for individual filing. That is, if the same rate applies to all income, it is not necessary to know to whom the income accrues. A payer—employer, bank, corporation—could simply pay over a flat rate tax on the tax base, and the amount paid over or withheld on behalf of eventual recipients would be exactly equal to the final tax owed. No filing or reconciliation would be required. This goal might also be achieved in part through essentially flat taxes on particular items of income—a schedular approach more popular in many other industrialized countries. Generally speaking, a flat rate tax would also reduce taxes for those with the highest incomes and increase the share of the tax burden borne by those with incomes in the middle range.

### Income tax reform

Many reforms would expand the efforts of the 1980s to define the tax base in a manner considered appropriate. Often these involve eliminating social preferences, cutting back on the value of various exclusions or deductions, and eliminating the taxation of items that would not legitimately be included in a system that more purely taxed income once and only once. There might be a reduction in the special preferences applied to health insurance purchased by employers, for example. Or integration of corporate and personal income taxes would eliminate the double taxation of capital income earned and paid out to equity owners of corporations.

### Integration of tax and transfer systems

In recent years, there has been increased realization not only that expenditures are hidden in the tax system, but that taxes are hidden in the expenditure system. Most transfers from the government involve some sort of implicit tax. The Social Security benefit formula, for instance, provides for lower returns on taxes of higher-income individuals. Welfare systems typically phase out benefits as income rises. Means testing may be applied to a variety of health benefits. Each of these tax systems tends to develop independently, leading to a combined tax system that is little understood or appreciated. Some reforms would aim themselves more directly at determining an integrated rate structure for the systems as a whole. Here, of course, tax and expenditure reform become inseparable.

### Tax simplification

Seldom, if ever, has tax reform focused primarily upon simplification. Although it was one of the goals of the 1986 reform, it was achieved only in part for moderate-income taxpayers, while filing became

more complex for many businesses or individuals with significant capital income. Simplification might be sought through one of the broader reforms listed above, or it could be pursued step by step within the existing income tax framework.

### Additional readings

Aaron, Henry A., and Harvey Galper. *Assessing Tax Reform*. Washington, D.C.: The Brookings Institution, 1985.

Bradford, David F. *Untangling the Income Tax*. Cambridge, Mass.: Harvard University Press, 1986.

Hall, Robert E., and Alvin Rabushka. *The Flat Tax*. Stanford, Calif.: Hoover Institution Press, 1985.

Neubig, Thomas, and David Joulfaian. "The Tax Expenditure Budget before and after the Tax Reform Act of 1986." Office of Tax Analysis Paper 60. Washington, D.C.: U.S. Department of the Treasury, 1988.

Steuerle, C. Eugene. *The Tax Decade*. Washington, D.C.: The Urban Institute Press, 1992.

Witte, John F. "The 1986 Tax Reform: A New Era in Politics?" *American Politics Quarterly* (October 1991).

*Cross references:* consumption taxation; excess burden; fairness in taxation; flat tax; integration, corporate tax; payroll tax, federal; pensions, tax treatment; tax administration, federal; tax equity analysis; value-added tax, national.

# Tax reform, state

Steven D. Gold
National Conference of State Legislatures (1978–1996)

*A review of the 20th century for periods in which there have been broad changes made in the way state tax systems work.*

State tax reform changes the structure of state and local taxes so that revenue is obtained with greater equity and fewer economic distortions and in sufficient quantity to allow governments to provide the services that citizens want and are willing to pay for.

### History

State tax reform has gone through five major phases in the 20th century:

#### 1911–1929

During this period, states gradually began to develop their modern tax systems:

—Wisconsin established the first broad-based personal income tax in 1911, and 13 other states had adopted one by 1929.

—Sixteen states imposed corporate income taxes, again following Wisconsin's precedent.

—Every state enacted a gasoline tax between 1919 and 1929.

—After Iowa created the first state cigarette tax in 1921, seven states followed suit later in that decade.

### Depression-era reform

The Great Depression provided a tremendous impetus to state tax reform, particularly because the property tax, which had been the bulwark of state-local fiscal systems, became extremely onerous in a period of widespread unemployment, low income, and declining property values. Many states relieved some of the pressure on the property tax by adopting new broad-based taxes. Mississippi pioneered the general sales tax in 1930, and by 1939 half of the 48 states had adopted one. In addition, 16 states enacted broad-based personal income taxes, and 15 states established taxes on corporate income. The first taxes on distilled spirits were also imposed, with 29 states passing one between 1933 and 1939, and 19 more states began to tax cigarettes.

### Baby boom reform

State tax reform resumed after World War II. One driving force was demographic—the tremendous costs of educating the baby boom generation. More than half of state-local spending was for elementary-secondary education in many states in the early 1960s. In addition, state government began a transformation in the 1960s, modernizing its institutions and greatly expanding systems of higher education, health, and social services.

From 1947 to 1960, 11 more states adopted sales taxes, and 3 added corporate income taxes, but no new personal income taxes were established. Reform accelerated between 1961 and 1971, with 9 new broad-based personal income taxes, 9 corporate income taxes, and 10 sales taxes. State-local tax revenue soared from 9.2 percent of personal income in 1960 to 12.3 percent in 1973.

The foundation for many of the reforms during this period was laid by tax studies conducted by economists. These studies drew upon the academic community to provide comprehensive analyses of state tax systems and options for improving them. The seminal studies of this kind were directed by Harvey Brazer in Michigan and Minnesota. James Papke also directed five of these studies.

### 1973–1981

Demographic pressures abated after 1973 as public school enrollment decreased. The nature of reform changed in this period, focusing more on relieving and limiting taxes than on raising them. New Jersey's personal income tax, adopted in 1976, was the only new broad-based levy.

Important developments focused especially on the property tax, the personal income tax, and formal tax limitations:

—Property tax relief was a high priority. The property tax fell from 4.6 percent of personal income in 1973 to 3.3 percent in 1982. The most important factor was increased state aid, especially for schools, but many states also relieved localities of responsibility for functions like welfare and Medicaid. There was also increased reliance on local sales and income taxes and user charges, expanded credits and exemptions for homeowners and other property owners, and new state-imposed limitations on property taxes or local spending.

—Circuit breakers—state-financed tax credits whose value depends on both household income and property tax liability—spread rapidly, with their number growing from 5 in 1970 to 29 in 1979.

—Personal income tax revenue continued to grow faster than personal income, but its increase was slowed by two developments—the adoption of indexation by numerous states, and tax rate reductions, especially in states where tax rates were above average.

—Limitations on the growth of state taxes or spending proliferated. New Jersey adopted the first one in 1976, restricting the growth of state appropriations to the rate of increase of personal income. By 1982, 19 states had similar measures, in some cases tying growth to the inflation rate and population increases.

—Limitations also spread on property taxes or local spending. The most well known were Proposition 13 in California (1978), which limits the effective property tax rate to 1 percent of market value and also restricts assessment increases, and Proposition 2½ in Massachusetts (1980), which permits property tax revenue to grow only 2.5 percent per year and places a 2.5 percent ceiling on the effective tax rate. Many other states imposed limitations on annual revenue increases in 1971 and later years.

—The proliferation of tax and spending limitations was one aspect of the so-called tax revolt that was signaled by Proposition 13. Other results were wider use of indexation, permanent tax reductions and one-time rebates, and a temporary reluctance to raise taxes.

These changes had two important results: first, to slow the rise in the share of personal income going to state and local taxes, and second, to centralize taxes at the state level. In the 1950s and 1960s, state and local taxes had risen much faster than personal income, but they did not in the 1970s. At the same time, the share of revenue collected by states rose from 55.3 percent in 1970 to 61.3 percent in 1980.

### Since 1982

The back-to-back recessions of the early 1980s resulted in widespread state fiscal distress, and most states responded with substantial tax increases in 1982 and 1983. Although tax reform was not a prominent feature of these tax increases, many governors and legislators recognized that serious problems existed in their tax policies. They responded by establishing tax studies to analyze the deficiencies of their state tax systems. More than half of the states conducted such studies in the 1980s.

These studies helped prepare states to respond to federal tax reform. The Tax Reform Act of 1986 offered most states substantial potential windfalls because it broadened the federal definition of income subject to taxation and curtailed numerous itemized deductions; these provisions are normally used (with minor modifications) in determining state taxable income. Unless they lowered tax rates or took other actions, states would have received substantial increases in tax revenue.

In fact, most states responded to federal tax reform by mimicking it—cutting and flattening tax rates, raising standard deductions and personal exemptions, and targeting relief to low-income households. States generally conformed to the federal base-broadening changes (except for taxation of Social Security benefits) and in fact repealed many of their own provisions that did not conform to the federal tax code. The majority of states avoided most if not all of the potential revenue windfall.

The early 1990s witnessed a considerable amount of state tax reform. The most important accomplishments were the following:

—Connecticut enacted a new personal income tax.
—Thirteen states restructured income tax rates, in nearly all cases increasing progressivity (although four of these changes were temporary).
—Twelve states broadened the personal income tax base by reducing deductions.
—Twenty-eight states broadened the sales tax base (although two of these expansions were subsequently repealed entirely).

—Twenty-two states expanded tax relief for the poor or other households with relatively low incomes.
—Most states that enacted large tax increases made their tax systems more balanced in the sense that they increased reliance on a major tax that was previously underutilized. (This generalization excludes states that do not impose either the sales or the income tax.)

Although this list is impressive, much of the base broadening and tax relief for the poor was relatively modest in scope. Only Connecticut and New Jersey instituted sweeping reforms, and many of the reforms in New Jersey were subsequently repealed.

When state fiscal conditions improved in 1994 and 1995, reform focused primarily on income tax relief, increasing personal exemptions or credits and reducing tax rates.

Two other important areas of reform in the first half of the 1990s involved school property taxes and tax limitations. Seven states raised state taxes to substantially increase the state share of school costs, and five states enacted stringent new tax limitations or required extraordinary legislative majorities or popular votes to increase state taxes.

### The unfinished agenda

A report published in 1993 by the major groups representing elected state officials argued that an impending crisis will engulf state governments unless they reform their tax systems. They based this conclusion on the view that many states have structural deficits, with revenue growth falling persistently short of the spending required to maintain existing levels of services. The report maintained that state tax systems are outmoded because they do not reflect major changes in the economy. It referred to the growth of the service sector, which is much more lightly taxed than the goods-producing part of the economy; technological and regulatory changes in industries such as telecommunications and financial services; the increasingly multinational nature of corporations; and the growth of retirement income, which is usually granted more favorable treatment by states than by the federal income tax.

The tax reform agenda varies among states, depending on the nature of their existing tax system and their economic situation. While most states rely substantially on each of the three major taxes (personal income, general sales, and corporate income), some do not. While some state sales taxes have broad coverage of services, most do not. While many personal income taxes have relatively broad bases and rate structures that have been reformed within the past decade, many others have not changed their rates in more than 25 years or still have costly deductions or exclusions that have been abandoned by most other states.

Nine states (as of 1997) do not impose a broad-based personal income tax (Alaska, Florida, Nevada, New Hampshire, South Dakota, Tennessee, Texas, Washington, and Wyoming), and five states have no general sales tax (Alaska, Delaware, Montana, New Hampshire, and Oregon). Most of these states have high tax rates on the property tax and/or whichever general tax they do not employ (unless they have vast oil production [Alaska] or a large gaming industry [Nevada], in which case they utilize these special tax bases).

In this era of "fend-for-yourself federalism" (a phrase coined by John Shannon), most state tax systems have been decentralizing, and local tax revenue has risen faster than state tax revenue every year since 1985. As this trend builds pressure on property taxes, states must pay increasing attention to local tax reform. Often the result is that states grant local governments greater authority to levy sales taxes, and sometimes it leads to reform of property tax administration.

Tax relief for the poor advanced substantially in the late 1980s; nearly half of the states now exempt poor families from the state income tax. But the regressive tax systems of many states still impose high burdens on low-income households.

## Conclusion

The two greatest periods of state tax reform came during the fiscal crises caused by the Great Depression and the cost of educating the baby boom generation. Reform has occurred more slowly in the past quarter century. One important reason is that a severe fiscal crisis makes it more feasible politically to overcome reform obstacles, and recent fiscal crises have not been as severe and long-lasting as those in the 1930s and the 1960s. Another factor is that now reform usually requires more subtlety than it did when the solution was adoption of a new broad-based tax, either the income or the sales tax. With most states already imposing both of those taxes, what is needed is broadening of tax bases, changes of tax rates, and carefully designed tax credits or exemptions that target relief rather than spread it widely.

## Additional readings

Bahl, Roy, editor. *Taxation and Economic Development: Blueprint for Ohio Tax Reform.* Columbus: Battelle Press, 1996.

Ebel, Robert, editor. *A Fiscal Agenda for Nevada.* Reno: University of Nevada Press, 1990.

Ebel, Robert, and Therese McGuire, editors. *Final Report of the Minnesota Tax Study Commission.* Boston: Butterworth, 1986.

Fox, William F., editor. *Sales Taxation: Critical Issues in Policy and Administration.* Westport, Conn.: Praeger, 1992.

Gold, Steven D., editor. *Reforming State Tax Systems.* Denver: National Conference of State Legislatures, 1986.

Gold, Steven D., editor. *The Unfinished Agenda for State Tax Reform.* Denver: National Conference of State Legislatures, 1988.

Gold, Steven D., editor. *The State Fiscal Agenda for the 1990s.* Denver: National Conference of State Legislatures, 1990.

Gold, Steven D., and Jennifer McConnick. "State Tax Reform in the Early 1990s." *State Tax Notes* (May 2, 1994): 1146–61.

Snell, Ronald K., editor. *Financing State Government in the 1990s.* Washington, D.C.: National Governors' Association and National Conference of State Legislatures.

*Cross references:* circuit breaker; fairness in taxation; income tax, corporate, state and local; property tax, real property, business; property tax, real property, residential; retail sales tax; tax limitations; tax reform, federal.

# Tax shelters

Jack Taylor
Congressional Research Service, Library of Congress

*Popularly, investments that take such advantage of preferential tax provisions that they reduce taxes on other activities; more generally, any arrangements undertaken to minimize taxes.*

The opportunity to "shelter" income from taxation arises because different sources of income are taxed at different rates. Moving income from higher-tax sources to lower-tax sources reduces the total tax bill and "shelters" income from tax, whether the move involves investing in tax-favored activities such as oil and gas exploration or contracting with one's employer to receive some of one's compensation in the form of tax-free health insurance rather than taxable wages. Both of these would be, in the broad meaning of the term, "tax shelters."

However, the term is more often heard in a narrower meaning. Popular usage pictures an investment or enterprise designed to take extraordinary advantage of provisions that reduce taxes, so that the investment or enterprise not only bears no current tax, but also generates losses or credits that can be used to reduce taxes on other income. In this usage, the investment shelters both its own income and income from other sources.

It is this popular definition that has had the important impact on tax policy, and public perceptions of the rich "sheltering" their income from tax have littered the Internal Revenue Code with restrictions on tax shelters and penalties for "abusive" ones. This perception of tax shelters has even been credited with helping to bring about the Tax Reform Act of 1986 (Steuerle 1992; Shaviro 1993). There are at least three explicit definitions of a "tax shelter" in the code, and several more by implication, and all relate more closely to the popular definition than to the more general definition.

The popular definition might also be thought of as the "commercial" definition. In the 1970s and early 1980s, tax shelter investments were aggressively marketed on the promise that they would generate no current tax themselves and would also reduce taxes on other income.

Many of the restrictions currently placed on tax shelter investing are aimed at these promotions of tax shelters rather than the investments themselves. This reflects another aspect of the tax shelter phenomenon: The tax differentials introduced to encourage activities that are deemed socially desirable or to assist groups deemed socially worthy are the differentials that make tax shelters possible. Any restrictions placed on tax shelters necessarily also restrict the incentives for the desirable activity. Reform of tax shelter provisions has been constantly inhibited by this dilemma.

## Tax shelters, past

Classic tax shelters ended (for the moment) with the Tax Reform Act of 1986 (TRA86), which not only restricted them directly but also reduced both overall tax rates (so sheltering was no longer as lucrative) and differences in tax rates (so finding worthwhile shelters was harder). Before TRA86, however, high marginal tax rates and large differences in rates for different income sources created an ideal climate for tax shelters.

The classic tax shelter consisted of combining several tax code provisions that allowed reduced or deferred taxes. Deductions greater than economic costs, such as percentage depletion of minerals or accelerated depreciation of buildings, were an essential element; the tax shelter investor did not want real economic losses. This element alone provided a tax shelter; excess deductions taken against otherwise taxable income at least postponed taxes until the property was sold.

But the reduced tax rate on capital gains gave an added benefit. The deductions could be taken against income otherwise taxed at rates of up to 70 percent (the maximum rate on ordinary income at

one time), and the deferred tax, when finally paid upon the sale of the investment, could be calculated at the capital gains rate, which was 50 or 60 percent less. (This did not work for equipment, because all gain due to depreciation was taxed at ordinary rates at sale.)

A third important element could also be added: leverage. If the investment generated enough income to pay actual economic expenses and interest, as was common in real estate investments, for example, it could be largely financed by borrowed funds and the investor's return on his own invested capital greatly enhanced.

Because transaction costs and risk in such investments tend to be high, they were originally restricted mostly to the rich. In the 1960s and 1970s, however, there was a growing trend toward packaging and marketing tax shelters for the middle class. Limited partnerships were a particularly favored vehicle; they allowed participation of many smaller investors, allocation of losses and credits to the limited partners, and strict limits on risk.

Aggressively marketed tax shelters became notorious. "Rent-a-cow" shelters advertised in *The Wall Street Journal*: Cattle breeders sold their herds to investors and leased them back, giving the investors the deductions for raising calves, and also capital gains tax rates when the herd was sold. Motion picture film syndicates made films for the sole purpose of generating large artificial losses; the films might never even be shown. The investors often risked no money, because nonrecourse financing was part of the deal.

The elements of these classic tax shelters can be summarized as: (1) deferral or elimination of tax through deductions in excess of current economic costs; (2) conversion of income taxed at ordinary rates into income taxed at reduced rates; and (3) leverage. To market tax shelter investments to smaller investors, syndication or some other form of packaging was required. The tax reform efforts from 1969 to 1986 attacked each of these elements on a multitude of fronts.

## Tax shelters, present

The tax code in the late 1990s honors tax shelters mostly by the effort it makes to prevent them (although it still allows quite a few).

Many of the basic rules that created tax shelter opportunities, particularly excessive depreciation deductions, investment credits, and large rate differentials for capital gains, no longer exist. In addition, however, there are a number of explicit provisions undermining tax shelters. It is no longer possible to take deductions larger than one's investment (at-risk rules, Internal Revenue Code Section 465), to deduct investment interest in excess of investment income (Section 163(d)), or to deduct losses and credits from a business in which one is not an active participant from other sources of income (the "passive activity" rules, Section 469). Finally, if one slips through these and several other restrictive provisions, a second tax computation, required of anyone with extraordinary tax preference items, may result in the payment of an "alternative minimum tax" (Section 55–59).

Certain defined tax shelters are required to be registered (Section 6111) and to provide IRS with a list of their investors (Section 6112). For these purposes, tax shelters are defined as investments that offer an investor deductions and credits greater than twice his investment and are either registered syndications, or that involve five or more investors or total investment of $250,000 or more. There are penalties for "abusive" tax shelters, defined as partnerships or other entities offering fraudulent deductions or credits (Section 6700). There are special rules (and yet more definitions) for economic performance (Section 461(i)(3)) and for substantial understatement of tax (Section 6662(d)(2)(C)). Special hedging transaction rules are provided for "syndicates," defined as partnerships or similar entities allocating more than 35 percent of their losses to limited partners (Section 1256(e)(3)(B)).

Tax reform did not eliminate all tax shelters from the code. One can still borrow money to place in an individual retirement account, reduce taxable income by an equivalent amount, defer taxes until retirement, and possibly pay at a lower tax rate. Oil and gas syndications, small rental real estate investments, and rentals by real estate "professionals" are among the many tax shelters explicitly allowed under the passive activity loss rules.

These remaining shelters, however, are rather anemic compared with the robust ones of the past. In fact, TRA86 virtually ended the tax shelter industry.

## Tax shelters, future

As the underlying philosophy of TRA86 has become blurred, the basic changes that made tax shelters uneconomic have begun to erode. The rate differential between ordinary income and capital gains for the top income tax bracket has gone from zero to 11.6 percentage points. The passive activity loss exemption for real estate professionals and a number of other retreats from TRA86 were made in the Omnibus Budget Reconciliation Act of 1993.

Perennially popular tax proposals contain the elements of classic tax shelters. Incentives to encourage investment and capital gains rate differentials are the two most important elements in tax shelters, and they are prominent elements in many recent tax proposals. The more "incentives" there are, the more "tax shelters" there will be.

Even a consumption-based tax might not end tax shelters; consumption taxes always have rate differentials between consumption items and investment items. If consumption is taxed directly, converting consumption spending into investment spending would shelter consumption. If consumed income is taxed, one would want to convert consumed income into saved income. Either of these could be accomplished by turning personal spending into business spending. One could even imagine ways in which such shelters could be marketed. In any tax, if rate differentials exist, tax shelters are possible.

## Additional readings

Cordes, Joseph J., and Harvey Galper. "Tax Shelter Activity: Lessons from Twenty Years of Evidence." *National Tax Journal* 38 (September 1985): 305–24.

Nelson, Susan. "Taxes Paid by High-Income Taxpayers and the Growth of Partnerships." *SOI Bulletin* 5 (Fall 1985): 55–60.

Shaviro, Daniel N. "Rethinking Anti-Tax Shelter Rules: Protecting the Earned Income Base." *Taxes* 71 (December 1993): 859–81.

Steuerle, C. Eugene. *The Tax Decade.* Washington, D.C.: The Urban Institute Press, 1992, pp. 90–92.

Stiglitz, Joseph E. "The General Theory of Tax Avoidance." *National Tax Journal* 38 (September 1985): 325–37.

U.S. Congress, Joint Committee on Internal Revenue Taxation. *Tax Shelter Investments.* JCS-8-76, April 14, 1976. Washington, D.C.: U.S. Government Printing Office, 1976.

U.S. Congress, Joint Committee on Taxation. *Tax Reform Proposals: Tax Shelters and Minimum Tax.* JCS-34-85, August 7, 1985. Washington, D.C.: U.S. Government Printing Office, 1985.

U.S. Congress, Joint Committee on Taxation. *General Explanation of the Tax Reform Act of 1986.* JCS-10-87, May 4, 1987. Washington, D.C.: U.S. Government Printing Office, 1987, pp. 209–61.

*Cross references:* alternative minimum tax, corporate; alternative minimum tax, personal; capital cost recovery; deferral of tax; depreciation recapture; partnerships; passive activity losses; tax arbitrage; tax expenditures; tax reform, federal.

# Telecommunications and electronic commerce, state taxation

Matthew N. Murray
University of Tennessee

*The trend toward deregulation of the telecommunications industry, coupled with the rapid development of new technologies and the emergence of new competitors, is leading to a rethinking of how states should and can tax telecommunications (a medium of delivery) and electronic commerce (transactions of goods and services). These issues are often complicated by the unique ways in which some communications activities have been treated historically for tax purposes.*

The telecommunications industry, including both providers and consumers, has been exposed to a unique structure of taxation by the states since the inception of telegraphy services in the 1800s. Providers of electronic commerce (other than traditional telecommunications firms) have been taxed largely as ordinary business entities that provide intangible services; consumers of electronic commerce may confront general or specific transactions taxes depending on the location and nature of their purchases.

## Industry definitions

Telecommunications is defined here as an electronic mode of transmitting data, information, and audio/video signals. This includes both one-way and two-way signals using traditional land-line phones, cellular phones, paging devices, satellites, microwave systems, and so on. Telecommunications is best viewed as a medium or mode of delivery, not the actual content of the information transmitted over the medium. By analogy, it is similar to a common carrier delivery truck that provides transportation or a natural gas pipeline that provides transmission services. The common carrier analogy is useful because telecommunications firms have little or no control over the content provided over the medium by others.

The intent here is to provide an economic distinction between transactions, rather than to develop a definition tied to specific technologies or industry practices. This approach is not, however, free of problems, because services and content are often bundled, and it is not always possible to observe explicit prices for transmission and other components of the bundle.

Some would expand the definition of telecommunications to include, in addition to basic services such as local and long-distance calling, enhanced services such as call forwarding and voice mail. A common feature of enhanced services is that there is additional value added beyond simply transmission. But including enhanced services, or going the next step to include content, can lead to administrative and compliance problems. Generally, this clouds the distinction between transmission, often used as a distinct productive input by business establishments, and services or content, which often reflect final consumption by individuals and households. This in turn makes it difficult to discern exempt from taxable sales, leads to multiple taxation, and complicates efforts to assign tax collection and remittance responsibilities under transaction taxes.

Electronic commerce includes services and content provided using telecommunications media. Examples include voice mail, on-line banking, the acquisition of computer software, and the purchase of tangible property through a site on the World Wide Web. Two important categories of electronic service are Internet service providers, firms that provide access to the Internet, and on-line service providers, firms that provide access to proprietary subscriber networks or independent services. The services and content available directly via electronic commerce are inherently intangible. Accordingly, tax policy toward electronic commerce will hinge largely on the way in which states treat service providers as opposed to providers of tangible products.

## Tax treatment of telecommunications

The historical roots of the taxation of telecommunications begin with the telegraph companies that were granted the privilege of conducting business and stringing wires on public rights-of-way by states and their constituent local governments in the 1800s. The initial privilege (franchise) taxes were generally flat-rate levies applied to miles of wire, numbers of poles, or receipts. These taxes were productive revenue sources with low administration and compliance costs. By the mid-1930s, telecommunications firms had fallen under the regulatory auspices of both federal and state governments. This regulated environment allowed firms to shift taxes forward to consumers so that taxes were not burdensome to the telecommunications providers.

The traditional telecommunications firm of today confronts many different taxes at the state and local levels, depending on where business is conducted. Most states impose a corporate income tax on the activities of telecommunications firms. This corporate tax structure often entails unique formulary apportionment of multijurisdictional earnings, as opposed to the use of the traditional three-factor formula that includes sales, property, and payroll. The situs of the sales component of the corporate apportionment formula is typically determined on an origin basis—that is, where the activity is produced rather than where it is consumed. This is different from the treatment of sales of tangible goods, where sales are allocated on a destination basis. The state-level corporate franchise tax also would generally apply to telecommunications firms, unless specifically exempted.

Sales (or specific transactions) taxes may fall on transmission activities, services, content, or some combination thereof, depending on the jurisdiction. Most states tax transmission—interstate or intrastate calls—under the general sales tax. (Following *Goldberg* v. *Sweet*, 488 U.S. 252, 1989, states can tax interstate calls if they are billed in the state, and if the call either originates in the state or has an in-state destination. No apportionment is required of these taxes.) Additional telecommunications service or transaction taxes may apply to specifically enumerated services (beyond simply transmission). Sales tax is paid on most input purchases, although central office switching equipment is often exempt. A particularly thorny problem is whether transmission companies should be responsible for tax collection on the sales made by providers of services and content. There are some cases (900 calls) where the collection responsibility does fall on the transmission companies. Some states have taken this course (using the concept of *attributional nexus*) because they cannot impose collection obligations on service and content providers directly for lack of nexus.

A minority of states apply gross receipts taxation to telecommunications firms. Local gross receipts (or explicit privilege/franchise) taxes also are common, and the ability of local governments to impose such taxes was sustained by the Telecommunications Reform Act of 1996. (The same act preempted local sales taxation of direct broadcast satellite services.) The lack of uniformity in tax structure across jurisdictions raises compliance costs substantially. In addition, a wedge can be created between firms traditionally obligated to pay such taxes (including telecommunications firms and cable operators) and their modern competitors (such as the Internet) that escape gross receipts taxation.

Finally, telecommunication firms are exposed to a unique system of property taxation. This includes the unit (as opposed to summation) method of assessment, relatively higher assessment ratios, assessments applied to both real and personal property, and often central state (versus local) assessment.

The trend toward deregulation, especially the breakup of AT&T in 1982 and the Telecommunications Reform Act of 1996, coupled with the rapid development of new technologies and new competitors, is unraveling some of the peculiarities of this historical system of taxation. Competition, in lieu of the old monopoly structure, means that firms confront a more level playing field in the market. But if tax structure differs for functionally equivalent media (services), which is often the case, tax-induced advantages and disadvantages will surface for different firms. For example, an Internet service provider that offered long-distance calling might escape gross receipts and transaction taxation, giving it a tax advantage over the traditional telecommunications provider.

## Taxation of electronic commerce

The tax structure confronting providers of electronic services and content (which may include traditional telecommunications providers) is similar to the structure that would confront any firm selling intangibles and services. Under most state corporate income tax systems, the three-factor apportionment formula will allocate sales to where they are produced rather than to where services are sold. In general, nexus is not as easily established for sellers of intangible property relative to sellers of tangible products. One consequence is that a firm could penetrate the markets of many states through electronic contacts, but pay corporate income tax solely in the domiciled jurisdiction. A small number of states (*market states*) assign the sale of intangibles on a destination basis. This approach can reduce the incentives to relocate the firm to a state with a low corporate income tax rate. Throwback provisions for unallocated income are less common for firms selling intangibles and services. Incorporated electronic marketers will generally confront the same state-level franchise taxes that other corporations confront.

Gross receipts taxes on electronic commerce are uncommon. The reason is that such taxes often have their roots in the privilege/franchise tax. And because electronic marketers are not franchise monopolies and generally do not use public rights-of-way, they typically are not exposed to such taxes. Exceptions can exist for public utilities (e.g., telecommunications companies) and monopoly franchises (e.g., cable operators) that provide services in addition to transmission.

Most tax issues regarding electronic commerce center on transaction taxes. Special transaction or excise taxes for specific services (e.g., 900 calls) may apply at the state and local levels. Inconsistency in structure is a burden to compliance, and it is inequitable and distortionary. At best, industry views these taxes as a nuisance.

Under the general sales tax, states tax services primarily on an enumerative basis, meaning that each component or category of the base must be identified explicitly through statutory language or administrative rulings. An extensive array of services and intangibles escape taxation, although it is common state practice to apply tax if the service is bundled with a tangible product. (An example is repair services and parts.) This means that absent statutory intent or administrative interpretation, most electronic commerce will escape sales taxation as well. There are numerous efforts to place certain forms of electronic commerce (such as Internet access charges) under the category of telecommunications services, which are taxed to varying degrees by most states. This leads to considerable uncertainty about the taxable status of transactions and to significant differences in tax structure across jurisdictions. Moreover, the general enumerative approach will not keep up with rapid changes in technology, and continual revisions to the sales tax structure will impart significant burdens on taxpayers and tax administrators alike.

Balance is needed as the sales tax is applied to electronic commerce to ensure a level playing field. Currently, one can purchase computer software from electronic vendors in many states without paying tax on it, but the same purchase would be taxable if delivered on disk. In other cases, states may seek to impose tax on information services such as electronic newspapers that would be exempt if sold in traditional tangible form. While the issue is balance, balance can be achieved in two ways. The first entails leveling up, or imposing sales tax on electronic services that would have been taxed if delivered in nonelectronic form. The second is leveling down, or removing tax from currently sales-taxable activities so that they are on a par with electronically provided services.

Collection of the sales tax on electronic commerce is complicated by the electronic nature of transactions and constitutional nexus constraints. Because tax administrators have little or no hope of directly observing electronic transactions, they must turn to buyers or sellers, as happens with sales of tangible property. But the buyer generally is not known to tax authorities, and voluntary compliance with use tax requirements on electronic commerce will be incomplete at best. Sellers with nexus would argue that they do not know the situs of delivery (consumption) and therefore they cannot charge and remit tax. This is a serious problem that will likely be resolved through development of practical, workable rules for determining situs.

More problematic is the firm without nexus. Electronic commerce severs the direct link between buyer and seller, analogous to the situation for catalog sales, tangible commodities, and common carriers. But the *substantial nexus* requirements of the Commerce Clause for electronic commerce are more difficult to establish than for marketers of tangible goods. Hence, it is more difficult to assign tax

collection obligations to marketers of electronic services and content. As states attempt to redefine nexus to bring electronic commerce into the sales tax net, they are being met by court challenges throughout the United States. Perhaps the best remedy from a tax policy perspective is congressional action that would define nexus based on economic contacts with a state.

Finally, sales tax will apply to most tangible inputs and specifically enumerated and taxed services that go into the production of electronically provided services and content. While industry would like broader resale exemptions, these are uncommon outside the manufacturing sector (where final sales are generally subject to sales tax). The disparate taxation of inputs, coupled with uncertainty regarding tax status, raises compliance costs, is inefficient, and results in double taxation.

*Cross references:* income tax, corporate, state and local; National Tax Association; retail sales tax.

# Tiebout model

## Wallace E. Oates
University of Maryland and University Fellow, Resources for the Future

## Robert M. Schwab
University of Maryland

*A classic statement of why people may move across jurisdictional boundaries—"vote with their feet"—as a way to live in a jurisdiction that best fits their (tax and spending) preferences.*

In the field of public finance, the Tiebout model has come to serve as the cornerstone or organizing principle for the theory of local finance. The model provides a market-like conception of the working of the local public sector that generates outcomes with efficiency properties much like those of competitive markets. In the Tiebout model, mobile households choose a community of residence from a broad menu of alternatives on the basis of the levels of public services offered and the associated tax liability. Local tax bills function much like prices in a market, so that individuals make location choices that reflect their preferences for public services and the cost of services they consume.

The origins and intent of the model are instructive, if somewhat curious. Charles Tiebout, in a terse and informal paper of only 8½ pages in the *Journal of Political Economy* in 1956, outlined his conception of the local public sector not so much to set forth a theory of local finance as to contest a central proposition in public expenditure theory. As explicated by Paul Samuelson, Richard Musgrave, and others, this proposition maintains that public goods cannot be provided by a decentralized pricing system. It was Tiebout's intent to show that this contention is not universally true—that a class of public goods ("local public goods") exists for which there is, in principle at least, such a decentralized pricing mechanism.

The original paper envisions a world in which a large number of local governments offer a wide variety of levels of local services for which they charge a "tax-price" equal to the marginal cost of servicing an additional household. In this setting, Tiebout notes, "Spatial mobility provides the local public-goods counterpart to the private market's shopping trip. . . . Just as the consumer may be visualized as walking to a private market place to buy his goods, the prices of which are set, we place him in the position of walking to a community where the prices (taxes) of communities are set" (page 422). This is a world in which consumer-voters, instead of voting for public outputs at the ballot box, vote "with their feet." In so doing, they both reveal their preferences for local public goods and consume efficient levels of these goods. The model produces an equilibrium in which we have perfectly homogeneous communities in terms of individual household demands for local public goods; people who have high levels of demand join with others who have similarly high levels of demand, and the converse is also true.

On first glance, the stark simplicity of the model involving a set of seemingly unrealistic assumptions raises serious questions about its application to understandng the real worlds of local finance. In particular, Tiebout assumed a world of footloose consumers who move costlessly among local jurisdictions *solely* in response to fiscal considerations; the Tiebout household is unconstrained by travel costs to a location of employment or by any other nonfiscal ties to a particular locality. Moreover, Tiebout's original paper is disturbingly silent on a number of key issues. There is little explicit discussion of where the "supply" of communities comes from or how each determines its fiscal package. There is virtually no treatment of the form of local taxes; the reader is left with the vague sense that each community somehow charges its residents some kind of price for the public services they consume, but the form this "tax" takes is unspecified. The article thus leaves us with the tantalizing and perplexing question of the potential of the Tiebout model for understanding, predicting, and prescribing fiscal behavior in the local public sector.

Much of the later work on both the theory and empirical study of local finance has been devoted to answering these questions. For example, in the United States (and a number of other countries), local governments rely primarily on property taxation. Such taxes on the value of local residences (land and structures) seem to bear little resemblance to a Tiebout "price" for local services. But, as Hamilton (1975) showed, if communities use local zoning ordinances that effectively set lower limits on consumption of housing (an ordinance that specifies a minimum lot size may be a reasonable approximation), the property tax becomes a perfect benefit tax; it is transformed into a price for the consumption of local public services, just as envisioned in the Tiebout model.

Moreover, a large body of empirical work confirms the pervasiveness of certain kinds of Tiebout behavior. It comes as no surprise, for example, to find that people are willing to pay more to live in communities that have superior schools and are relatively safe from crime. In an early paper, Oates (1969) found that after controlling for other factors, the value of local houses is positively correlated with measures of outputs of local public services. He found, in addition, that higher rates of local property taxation resulted, other things equal, in lower house values. There is now a large body of empirical literature that finds fiscal differentials across communities in the form of both variations in outputs of local services and differences in local tax burdens largely capitalized into local property values. This evidence is consistent with the view that people do, in fact, "shop" among communities in their selection of a locality in which to live; in so doing, they bid up the prices of houses in fiscally favored jurisdictions. This literature, interestingly, has provided an empirical handle on the important issues of people's valuation of local services. By measuring the differences in the selling prices of houses in different jurisdictions, we can obtain estimates of what people are willing to pay for higher levels of local services, including things like better schools, lower crime rates, and higher levels of environmental quality. In addition, Fischel (1975) and others have shown how the model can be extended to encompass mobile business property within local jurisdictions.

The Tiebout model, in its extended form, has thus gained considerable currency as a useful way to characterize the operation of the local public sector. Notably, in large metropolitan areas, households and business firms have a large number of jurisdictions from which to choose. For example, an individual who works in the central city typically has a diverse menu of suburban communities as potential places to reside (Fischel 1981). And the evidence suggests that local public services and taxes play an important role in determining the choice of a community of residence.

The Tiebout vision of local finance has some important implications for fiscal outcomes. From a perspective solely of economic efficiency, a Tiebout equilibrium has the same attractive properties as a competitive market. Individuals survey alternative levels of local public policy outputs and, facing tax prices equal to marginal cost, they select their desired level of consumption of these services in much the same way that they choose their preferred levels of consumption of private goods. The result is an efficient allocation of resources of the local public sector.

Such an outcome, however, is less satisfying on equity grounds. Because people's demands for local public services (as measured by what they are willing to pay) are highly correlated with income, a Tiebout model can be expected to exhibit a high degree of segregation by income. We would expect, in a Tiebout world, to find communities composed of high-income households that consume high levels of public services in sharp contrast with communities of lower-income households with inferior levels of public services. This, of course, is simply a manifestation of the high demand for goods (private or public) that accompanies higher levels of income. This prediction of the Tiebout model concerning economic segregation, incidentally, also finds considerable empirical support: There is typically much less inequality in the distribution of income within a local municipality in a metropolitan area than across the metropolitan area as a whole (Hamilton et al. 1975).

The nature of many local public goods is likely to reinforce this pattern of segregation by income. For many goods, the level of public services depends not only on expenditures by local governments but also on the characteristics of the population. Consider education, for example. A student's achievement depends in part on the textbooks and teachers the school provides. But it also depends on the characteristics of the student's family and classmates. The empirical evidence suggests that peer group effects are significant and often quite large (see, for example, Henderson et al. 1978; Summers and Wolfe 1997).

Suppose low-income children reduce the academic performance of children from high-income families. As argued by Schwab and Oates (1991), high-income families would then be willing to live in mixed-income communities only if low-income families compensated them for this negative externality by paying higher taxes. Such "super-regressive taxes" are implausible and, on equity grounds, very unattractive. Thus, the mixing of families with different incomes may be even less likely than the original version of the Tiebout model would suggest.

The wide variation in the quality of local public services, especially public schools, that results from such residential segregation by income has caused much concern. Through the 1960s, local governments provided the majority of funds for primary and secondary public education in the United

States. Because property taxes traditionally have been the primary source of local tax revenue, the resources devoted to education were to a large extent a function of the local property tax base. Critics argued that this system of finance was inherently unfair and, beginning with *Serrano* v. *Priest* (1971) in California, they challenged the constitutionality of local education funding.

By 1996, the supreme courts in 43 states had heard cases on the constitutionality of school finance systems. The courts have overturned systems in 16 states and upheld them in 20; seven cases are pending. In addition, further litigation has been filed in a number of states where the state supreme court had ruled. In California, for example, there have been three separate decisions in the *Serrano* case; New Jersey has six versions of *Robinson* v. *Cahill*, and there are indications that its current active challenge, *Abbott* v. *Burke*, may surpass the *Robinson* record of repeated litigation.

Most states where the courts have overturned school financing plans have responded either by shifting the financing of public schools explicitly to the state level or by introducing equalizing state grants that redistribute funds to poorer districts. And, as Murray et al. (1997) show, these new measures significantly reduced the inequality in school spending. It is noteworthy that the real culprit here is not local property taxation per se; the reliance on practically any local tax base is bound to involve large differentials in tax bases across local jurisdictions that give rise to substantial variations in levels of spending on local public services.

In spite of its extreme simplification, the Tiebout model thus provides a number of important insights into the workings of the local public sector. We see, in particular, the role that locational choice plays in the local fiscal system and the kinds of constraints that the mobility of households imposes on local fiscal decisions. From an efficiency perspective, a Tiebout world has much appeal. A large number of small competing local communities provides powerful incentives for the efficient provision of local public services while offering consumer households a wide variety of fiscal packages from which to choose. The local public sector, in short, provides a close analogue in its operation to the functioning of a competitive market. But such a world, in which communities are characterized by a high degree of segregation by income, implies very limited scope for redistributive activities within communities and large potential differentials in levels of local public services across these communities. This situation places the major responsibility for socially desired income redistributions for the support of low-income households and poorer local jurisdictions with higher levels of government. However we may feel about this tension between efficiency and our various equity objectives, the Tiebout model focuses our attention on some powerful economic and social forces that must be addressed in the design of public policy (see Hamilton 1987 for a more technical treatment of the Tiebout model).

There are some interesting parallels between Tiebout's paper and Coase's classic 1960 paper on externalities. Both were written four decades ago. Research in economics has a notoriously short half-life, yet both remain seminal contributions to public economics literature today. As one small indicator, Tiebout's paper was cited in economics journals roughly 300 times over the past four years. Both papers are deceptively simple, and neither is filled with the pages and pages of equations we now expect to find in journal articles. Both offered new, fundamental insights that set the field off in important new directions. Perhaps the most important lesson we can learn from Tiebout and Coase is that mathematical elegance is rarely a substitute for important ideas.

### Additional readings

Coase, Ronald. "The Problem of Social Cost." *Journal of Law and Economics* 3 (October 1960): 1–44.

Fischel, William A. "Fiscal and Environmental Considerations in the Location of Firms in Suburban Communities." In *Fiscal Zoning and Land Use Controls*, edited by Edwin S. Mills and Wallace E. Oates, pp. 119–73. Lexington, Mass.: D.C. Heath, 1975.

Fischel, William A. "Is Local Government Structure in Large Urbanized Areas Monopolistic or Competitive?" *National Tax Journal* 34 (March 1981): 95–104.

Hamilton, Bruce W. "Zoning and Property Taxation in a System of Local Governments." *Urban Studies* 12 (June 1975): 205–11.

Hamilton, Bruce W. "Tiebout Hypothesis." In *The New Palgrave: A Dictionary of Economics* 4, edited by John Eatwell, Murray Milgate, and Peter Newman, pp. 640–2. London: Macmillan & Co., 1987.

Hamilton, Bruce W., Edwin S. Mills, and David Puryear. "The Tiebout Hypothesis and Residential Income Segregation," in Mills and Oates, eds., pp. 101–18.

Henderson, Vernon, Peter Mieszkowski, and Yvon Sauvageau. "Peer Group Effects and Educational Production Functions." *Journal of Public Economics* 10 (August 1978): 97–106.

Murray, Sheila E., William N. Evans, and Robert M. Schwab. "Education Finance Reform and the Distribution of Education Resources," working paper. College Park: University of Maryland, January 1997.

Oates, Wallace E. "The Effects of Property Taxes and Local Public Spending on Property Values: An Empirical Test of Tax Capitalization and the Tiebout Hypothesis." *Journal of Political Economy* 77 (November/December 1969): 344–58.

Schwab, Robert M., and Wallace E. Oates. "Community Composition and the Provision of Local Public Goods: A Normative Analysis." *Journal of Public Economics* 44 (March 1991): 217–37.

Summers, Anita A., and Barbara L. Wolfe. "Do Schools Make a Difference?" *American Economic Review* 67 (September 1977): 639–52.

Tiebout, Charles M. "A Pure Theory of Local Expenditures." *Journal of Political Economy* 64 (October 1956): 416–24.

*Cross references:* education financing, state and local; tax competition; tax price; zoning, property taxes, and exactions.

# Tobacco taxes

W. Kip Viscusi
Harvard University

*Tobacco products are subject to a variety of special federal, state, and local taxes.*

Tobacco products such as cigarettes, like other consumer products, are subject to sales taxes. However, they are also subject to excise taxes at the federal, state, and local levels. These taxes have been of substantial economic interest both because of the economic functions the taxes serve and because of the moneys raised through these taxes.

### Economic rationales for tobacco taxes

In addition to raising money, cigarette taxes may serve other economic functions. Cigarette taxes and alcohol taxes are the two most prominent "sin" taxes now imposed on consumer goods. (See Alcoholic beverage taxes, federal.) The rationale for tobacco taxes, though, stems not necessarily from religious or ethical beliefs but rather from economic aspects of smoking behavior, including the social costs. Excise taxes will raise the price of smoking to consumers, thus potentially discouraging smoking. Deterring smoking in this manner may be viewed as socially desirable if cigarette smokers are making mistaken consumption decisions. For example, if cigarette smokers underestimate the risks associated with smoking or do not fully internalize the costs imposed on society, there would be a rationale for discouraging this behavior through a tax.

Much of the recent impetus for cigarette taxes has stemmed from a concern with the social costs associated with smoking. If smoking cigarettes and other tobacco consumption activities generate social costs, such as higher medical care expenditures, then cigarette taxes can serve as a mechanism for recouping this social cost. In effect, cigarette smokers will pay with each purchase for the cost inflicted by their smoking activity. A variety of proposals relating to the first Clinton administration's health insurance plans sought to finance these efforts in part through tobacco taxes because of a belief that the social costs were substantial.

Evidence regarding the rationality of smoking decisions for the smoker remains much debated. Several decades of government warnings and annual reports by the Surgeon General have publicized the risks associated with smoking. Survey evidence suggests that smokers are now not only aware of the risk, but may in fact overestimate the hazards. Evidence regarding habituation or addiction problems associated with smoking remains controversial as well. Quitting smoking is clearly difficult, but some economists have hypothesized that addictions of this type may be the result of rational individual choices.

The potential role for government intervention is greater with respect to societal costs if net damages are inflicted. There are, however, many conflicting aspects of net damages. Smoking shortens life, which reduces retirement benefit costs, but it leads to ill health, which increases medical care costs. The overall effect on society hinges on the net influence of these and other competing factors.

## Profile of tobacco taxes

Tobacco taxes are among the most prominent excise taxes levied on consumer products. Estimates by Fullerton and Rodgers (1993) suggest that as a percentage of the purchase price, the implied tax rate on tobacco products is higher than it is for alcoholic beverages, gasoline, automobiles, or utilities.

The federal government and the states tax cigarettes roughly equally. For fiscal year 1996, federal cigarette taxes were $0.24 per pack and state taxes averaged $0.317 per pack. These values ranged from a low tax of $0.25 per pack from the tobacco-producing state of Virginia to a high of $0.815 per pack in Washington state. Municipalities in eight states have imposed taxes as well, ranging from $0.01 to $0.35 per pack. (The federal tax was increased in 1997 to $0.34 per pack in 2000–01 and $0.39 per pack thereafter.)

The dollar magnitude of these tobacco taxes is substantial. In fiscal year 1996, federal tobacco tax revenues were $5.7 billion and state tax revenues were $7.3 billion. The total value of all excise taxes on cigarettes was $13.5 billion.

Tobacco taxes are generally set at tax rates per package, which are revised periodically through legislation. Until the most recent changes enacted in 1997, federal cigarette taxes have had only five levels over the past half century, rising from $0.07 per pack in 1942 to $0.24 per pack in 1993. The incidence of

tobacco taxes is highly regressive. Smoking rates increase as the income level of the group declines, so that the poor segment of the population tends to be hit particularly hard by cigarette taxes. The population group whose annual earnings are below $10,000 pay cigarette taxes of 1.5 percent more per person than the group with incomes of $50,000 or more. The average taxes paid per person in 1990 were $81 for this poorest group and $49 for the most affluent group. Thus, cigarette taxes are regressive in absolute terms and even more regressive as a percentage of income.

## Cigarette taxes and smoking behavior

Like raising the price of any good, raising cigarette taxes reduces consumer demand for the product. What this effect on demand will be depends on the estimated elasticity of demand with respect to the total price of cigarettes.

Dozens of studies have estimated cigarette demand functions. Most of the demand elasticities are clustered in the range from $-0.4$ to $-1.0$, meaning that for every cigarette tax that raises the price of smoking by 10 percent there should be a 4 to 10 percent decrease in the consumption of cigarettes.

This price responsiveness will not be uniform for all population segments. Some estimates suggest that teenagers are particularly price-sensitive, with a demand elasticity that is perhaps as high as $-1.4$. If so, a 10 percent increase in the purchase price would consequently reduce teenage smoking by 14 percent.

Cigarette taxes also reduce cigarette consumption in much the same way that heightened perceptions of the risk would. Estimates presented in Viscusi (1992) indicate that the average national excise tax for cigarettes has the same effect in discouraging smoking behavior as would a belief that there was a 27 percent chance that smoking would cause lung cancer, assuming a price elasticity of demand of $-0.7$.

## Estimates of the social costs of smoking

Most of the economic analyses of tobacco taxes have been concerned with how these taxes relate to the financial costs associated with smoking. The justification for such taxes hinges, however, on the presence of net positive social costs.

The empirical evidence suggests that the net effects may be surprising. The study by Shoven et al. (1989) found that smoking leads to a reduction in Social Security costs through the premature mortality of smokers. This analysis was extended by Manning et al. (1991) to consider not only pension effects but also the effects on medical insurance, nursing home expenditures, and related financial costs. Their study found that at low discount rates of about 3 percent or less, cigarette smoking generated net financial savings, even excluding the role of excise taxes, and that at very high discount rates, there would be a net social cost of smoking. Gravelle and Zimmerman (1994) extended this analysis both to update it and to include a sensitivity analysis with respect to the role of environmental tobacco smoke (ETS), or "second-hand smoke." The basic conclusions regarding the self-financing aspect of cigarette smoking remained unchanged.

The most recent extension is that by Viscusi (1995), who updated the earlier results and also recognized the influence of the changing riskiness of cigarettes. This analysis, using a 3 percent discount rate, suggested that cigarette smoking imposed a medical care cost per pack of $0.50, a sick leave cost per pack of $0.01, a group life insurance cost per pack of $0.13, and a cost per pack of fires of $0.02. The offsetting savings were nursing home care cost savings of −$0.22 and retirement pension savings of −$1.10. On balance, then, cigarette smoking saves society −$0.32 per pack, even excluding the role of excise taxes.

These cost figures, however, exclude the potential societal costs associated with ETS. Depending on the risk assumptions that are employed and the lag time between smoking and the health effects, these much-debated ETS risks can potentially alter the desirability of an offsetting excise tax. For all but the most extreme risk assumptions, however, the current level of excise tax is sufficient to offset the total value of the health risks to society, where these calculations assume an implicit value of life of $5 million. The extent to which excise taxes are needed to offset the financial costs on society will hinge in large part on how the assessment of ETS risks is resolved.

### Additional readings

Fullerton, Don, and Diane Lim Rodgers. *Who Bears the Lifetime Tax Burden?* Washington, D.C.: The Brookings Institution, 1993.

Gravelle, Jane, and Dennis Zimmerman. "Cigarette Taxes to Fund Health Care Reform: An Economic Analysis." Washington, D.C.: Congressional Research Service, 1994.

Manning, Willard G., Emmet B. Keeler, Joseph P. Newhouse, Elizabeth M. Sloss, and Jeffrey Wasserman. *The Costs of Poor Health Habits.* Cambridge, Mass.: Harvard University Press, 1991.

Shoven, John B., Jeffrey O. Sundberg, and John P. Bunker. "The Social Security Costs of Smoking." In *The Economics of Aging*, edited by David A. Wise, pp. 231–351. Chicago: University of Chicago Press, 1989.

Tobacco Institute. *The Tax Burden on Tobacco: Historical Compilation 1996*, vol. 30. Washington, D.C., 1997.

Viscusi, W. Kip. *Smoking: Making the Risky Decision.* New York: Oxford University Press, 1992.

Viscusi, W. Kip. "Cigarette Taxation and the Social Consequences of Smoking." In *Tax Policy and the Economy*, vol. 9, edited by James Poterba, pp. 51–101. National Review of Economic Research, 1995.

*Cross references:* alcoholic beverage taxes, federal; retail sales tax; sumptuary taxes.

# Transfer pricing, federal

T. Scott Newlon
Department of the Treasury

*Taxes are often measured by the price attached to the transfer of goods, foods, services, and/or funds across national borders; however, when multinationals make transfers "within company," prices must be estimated.*

Transfer prices are the prices established for transfers of goods or intangibles, the lending of money, or the provision of services from one company to a related company or from one part of a company to another part located in a different tax jurisdiction. Transfer prices are used by the U.S. government and by most other countries in determining the income, for tax purposes, of companies engaging in such transfers.

## Role of transfer prices in the firm

Transfer pricing is most relevant in the context of the transfer within a multinational firm of goods, intangibles, services, or funds across national borders. Such transactions may occur between a parent company and a foreign subsidiary, between two subsidiary companies that have a common parent, or between a branch office of a company and another part of the company. The prices established for such transactions are important for tax purposes because they affect the amount of taxable income reported in each of the countries in which the multinational firm operates. For example, a higher price on a sale of goods from a parent company to a foreign subsidiary generally means that more revenue is reported in the tax jurisdiction of the parent and greater deductions are reported in the tax jurisdiction of the subsidiary. Where tax rates differ across countries, an incentive exists for multinational firms to set their transfer prices to shift income from high-tax jurisdictions to low-tax jurisdictions.

An incentive to use transfer prices to shift income between related companies can exist even when both companies are located in the same tax jurisdiction. If the companies do not consolidate for tax purposes, and one of the companies is reporting income while the other is reporting losses, then the overall tax liability of the two companies can be reduced by shifting income from the income-reporting to the loss-reporting company.

Transfer prices can also serve a role in promoting the efficient operation of a firm. Where management is decentralized, transfer prices may serve as shadow prices on which the firm's managers may base their decisions. This role may place some limitations on the flexibility of the firm to optimize the setting of transfer prices for tax purposes, particularly in jurisdictions where it is illegal to keep two sets of books.

## The separate entity approach and the arm's-length standard

Transfer prices are relevant for the determination of the taxable income of a multinational firm in each of the countries in which it operates because most countries adopt the *separate entity approach* to the taxation of multinational firms. Under this approach, a multinational firm's operations in a country are treated as if they were an entity distinct from the multinational firm's operations in other countries, so that only the income accruing from the activities and transactions of the operations in that country is taxable there.

Countries that impose substantial taxes on company income and adopt the separate entity approach need to set and enforce some standard for setting transfer prices in order to limit tax base erosion brought about by the manipulation of transfer prices on cross-border transactions. The standard generally adopted is the *arm's-length standard*, which dictates that transfer prices should be set at the level that would have prevailed had the transactions taken place between unrelated parties under the same circumstances.

The arm's-length standard is the international norm for determining transfer prices for tax purposes. In the United States, the Income Tax Regulations under Section 482 of the Internal Revenue Code require the use of the arm's-length standard in determining transfer prices for federal tax purposes. The arm's-length standard is also enshrined in nearly all of the bilateral tax treaties the United States has entered into, as well as the model income tax treaties of the Organization for Economic Cooperation and Development (OECD) and the United Nations. The arm's-length standard was also affirmed as the international norm for transfer pricing in the OECD's 1979 report *Transfer Pricing and Multinational Enterprises* and the OECD's 1995 revision of that report entitled *Transfer Pricing Guidelines for Multinational Enterprises and Tax Administrations*.

Two features of the arm's-length standard may account for its broad international acceptance. First, the arm's-length standard treats vertically or horizontally integrated firms the same for tax purposes as firms that are not integrated. In principle, the same tax liability should accrue from a given business, whether that business is carried out by a company acquiring inputs and selling its outputs to unrelated parties or by a company that has integrated across borders and acquires inputs or sells its outputs to related parties within a multinational firm (unless the total amount of income is different in the two cases as a result of integration economies). Second, the arm's-length standard provides a clear principle for determining transfer prices that all countries can understand and accept, thereby providing a basis for agreement among countries about the appropriate division of a multinational firm's income among them. Such an agreement avoids subjecting the income of multinational firms to taxation by multiple jurisdictions, a result that would inhibit and distort cross-border investment.

The U.S. states generally use *formulary apportionment* rather than the separate entity approach and the arm's-length standard to determine how the income from a business operating in more than one state should be allocated among those states. Under formulary apportionment, each state typically allocates to itself a portion of the total U.S. income of such a business, using a formula based on some measure of the size of the business's activities in the state relative to the size of the total business. Typical formulas use one or more of property, payroll, and sales as the apportionment factors. The Canadian provinces and Swiss cantons follow a similar approach.

## Application of the arm's-length standard

The arm's-length standard is generally applied by comparing the results of a transaction between related parties (called a *controlled transaction* to denote that it is between parties under a certain degree of common control) to the actual results, or the results that would be anticipated, from transactions between unrelated parties (called *uncontrolled transactions*). Various transfer pricing methods are used in practice. The methods differ in the type of transaction results they compare: prices, gross profit margins, net profit measures, or profit splits.

The most important factor affecting the reliability of the results of a transfer pricing method is generally considered to be the *comparability* of the controlled transaction being evaluated to the transactions and activities of unrelated parties that are being used as a basis for comparison. Comparability is determined based on those factors in the open market that could be expected to affect the particular result (price or profit measure) being compared. For example, the price or profit margin for a sale of goods might be affected by the characteristics of the product, the contractual terms of the transaction, and the market conditions. The importance of specific comparability criteria may vary depending upon the result that is being compared. For example, the characteristics of a product conveyed in a transaction would be expected to have a greater impact on the price in the transaction than on the profit margin realized from the transaction, while the vintage of plant and equipment used in producing a product might affect a measure of the profit margin on sales of the product, but would be unlikely to affect the sales price for the product.

Six principal transfer pricing methods are provided in the Section 482 regulations and in the OECD's *1995 Transfer Pricing Guidelines*:

### Comparable uncontrolled price method

The appropriate transfer price is determined based on the price established in uncontrolled transactions involving similar goods or services conveyed under similar terms and conditions. In the Section 482 regulations, this method is labeled the *comparable uncontrolled transaction method* when it is applied to transfers of intangibles. This method is considered to be the most accurate way to determine transfer prices when closely similar transactions between unrelated parties can be found, because it is based directly on a market price.

### Cost-plus method

This method is often applied in situations in which the buyer receives a product manufactured by the seller or services provided by the seller. The appropriate transfer price is determined by applying a markup to the production cost of the good or service. The markup is derived from the gross profit margin that is realized by sellers in similar sales to unrelated parties under similar circumstances.

### Resale price method

This method is frequently applied in situations in which a product is purchased from a related party and resold to an unrelated party. The appropriate transfer price is determined by deducting an appropriate markup from the resale price. The markup is derived from the gross profit margin obtained by resellers in similar purchases and resales of goods involving unrelated parties. This method is also sometimes referred to as the *resale minus method*.

### Comparable profits method or transactional net margin method

The appropriate transfer price is determined based on some measure of the profit rate or profit margin derived by one of the parties to the controlled transactions from its business activities associated with those transactions. The appropriate transfer price is the price that results in that party earning the same profit rate or profit margin as is earned by independent parties engaged in similar activities under similar circumstances. The profit rate measure is generally based on *operating profit*—that is, revenue after deduction for all nonfinancial costs.

### Profit-split method

This method explicitly measures and divides the joint profit from controlled transactions. Most profit-split applications divide the joint profit based on the relative value of the factors of production each party contributes to the earning of the joint profit.

### Conceptual and practical problems

Several problems that arise in applying the arm's-length standard can lead to opportunities for income shifting by multinational firms, disputes between taxpayers and tax authorities, substantial compliance burdens and uncertainty for taxpayers, and substantial enforcement burdens for tax authorities.

One of the most important problems is that it is often difficult to identify uncontrolled transactions that can be used in establishing appropriate transfer prices for controlled transactions. A principal reason for a firm to become multinational is that it possesses valuable intangible assets such as unique skills, know-how, and technology, and there is an economic advantage to the firm in exploiting those assets itself in other markets rather than attempting to transfer them to an independent company over which it has limited control. Where such valuable intangible assets are present, the transactions and activities of the multinational firm may be unique in important respects.

Even if closely comparable transactions exist, it may be impossible for taxpayers or tax authorities to identify them, because that information may not be public. Tax authorities are often at a particular disadvantage in this regard because they may have much less information about the taxpayer's business and industry than does the taxpayer.

When potentially comparable uncontrolled transactions are identified, it can be difficult to make adjustments to reflect differences from the controlled transaction in question. Transactions frequently have a complex set of attributes in terms of the characteristics of the property conveyed, the contractual terms, and the market conditions.

The large number of related-party transactions within multinational firms also represents a problem. It can place a significant compliance burden on firms wishing to ensure that all their controlled transactions satisfy the arm's-length standard. Tax authorities can incur significant enforcement costs in attempting to identify and evaluate such transactions.

Fundamental differences in relationships between related and unrelated parties can also complicate application of transfer pricing methods. For example, if integration economies are present, then related parties dealing with each other have lower costs, and therefore higher profits, than unrelated parties would have under similar circumstances. Determining how such cost savings should be reflected in transfer prices (that is, how integration benefits should be divided between the parties) is problematic.

*Cross references:* allocation rules, multinational corporations; foreign tax credit; multinational corporations, taxation.

# Transfer taxes, real estate

John O. Behrens

*State and local government–imposed taxes at the time of transfer or recording of real estate transactions.*

---

The real estate transfer tax (one of the so-called documentary taxes) is imposed at the time of transfer or recordation and is nonrecurring. It is a levy on the transfer of real property, usually measured by the sales price or the price exclusive of mortgages or other liens. Transfer taxes usually make up a minor share of state or local revenue. The exact annual yield nationwide is difficult to identify because in some states the total constitutes part of revenue from all documentary taxes (such as transfer of stocks, bonds, debentures, and certificates of indebtedness). Documentary taxes as a group constituted less than 1 percent of all state tax revenue in 1997 (1 percent for the 30 states reporting such revenue).

Virginia imposed the first transfer tax in 1922, followed by South Carolina in 1923 and Florida in 1931. By 1940, Alabama, Maryland, Tennessee, and Washington also had transfer taxes. Now, they exist in 35 states and the District of Columbia. Arizona also has a flat fee of $2 per real estate transfer.

From 1932 until it was repealed in 1968, states were covered by the federal Stamp Tax on Convey-

ance of Realty Sold. The documentary stamps affixed to the deed of conveyance on payment were perceived to be indicative of the sale price, data essential for professional assessors. The federal government urged the states to adopt transfer taxes when the federal levy was repealed.

Three recent court cases, taken together, test but in the end leave intact the conventional wisdom that market value, or a reasonable proxy, remains the most accepted basis for transfer tax liability, even though adjustments may be necessary in particular legal or economic situations—*A. Bradley Askin* v. *District of Columbia* (DC Superior Court, Tax Division, N. 5572-93, April 1991, 1995); *Gottfried, Inc.* v. *Wisconsin Department of Revenue* (429 NW 2d 508, 1988); and *Wisconsin Department of Revenue* v. *Mark* (483 NW 2d 168, 1992).

## Rate patterns and varieties

Rates (percentage of taxable consideration) range from 0.01 percent in Colorado to 2.2 percent in the District of Columbia. In 11 states the taxable consideration is the amount remaining after deduction of mortgages and other liens. In all other states, the taxable consideration is the sales price or its equivalent. Transfers under $100 are exempt in 13 states, and Colorado, Iowa, and New York exempt transfers under $500. Each state has several other exemptions, including transfers in which a federal, state, or local government is a party; any tax deed; deeds without consideration between husband and wife; and instruments intended only to secure a debt.

## Transfer tax procedures for property tax benefits

There is a connection between real estate transfer tax administrators and local property tax assessors and recording officials. In many areas, county registrars of deeds or treasurers (town clerks in Connecticut and Vermont) collect the taxes for the states. Stamps are used as evidence of payment in 25 states, 14 of them among the 28 that have documentation requirements comprehensive enough to be of value to local tax assessors. (These are "declarations" in 14 states and "affidavits" in 14 others plus the District of Columbia that require the address and legal description, use of the property, and conditions of the sale or other transfer.)

Arizona, Colorado, Connecticut, Georgia, Illinois, Iowa, Kansas, Minnesota, New Hampshire, New York, Ohio, South Carolina, Vermont, Wisconsin, and the District of Columbia require considerable detail about location and property use, sale price, and conditions of sale. In Georgia, Iowa, and New York, the declaration or affidavit is a prerequisite for recording the transfer, and Arizona, New York, and Vermont require inclusion of the assessor's parcel identifier. In Iowa, either party may sign the declaration. Since 1995 in New Hampshire, the purchaser or other transferee must file a completed questionnaire with the Department of Revenue Administration.

## Local real estate transfer taxes

Local real estate transfer taxes may be levied in the following states: *California*—counties (0.11%) and cities at one-half the county rate; *Delaware*—counties (no more than 1% of property value, first-time homeowners exempt); *Florida*—counties (surtax not to exceed 0.45%, except single-family residences), collected by the state; *Illinois*—Chicago (6% on leases of personal property, and 0.75% transfer stamp tax) and Cook County (0.05% transfer); *Maryland*—home-rule counties (0.5% unless exempt from the state tax); *Nevada*—counties with 100,000 to 400,000 population (up to 0.1%, subject to voter approval); *New York*—New York City (1% on one- to three-family homes and condominiums up to $500,000, then 1.425%; for other property, 1.425% up to $500,000, then 2.625%; half the applicable rate on real estate investment trusts [REITs]; 1.75% of secured debt on all other property) and Erie County (0.5% above $500, excluding the value of liens and encumbrances under $500,000); *Pennsylvania*—Philadelphia (3% of property value) and Pittsburgh (1.5% of property value plus 0.5% for the school district); *Ohio*—counties (not to exceed 0.30%); *South Carolina*—counties, mandated (0.11% of value over $100); *Virginia*—cities and counties (one-third of state recordation tax).

## Selected other levies

Five states levy other taxes that are sometimes included within the realty transfer category: *Alabama*—leasehold interest in nonproducing oil, gas, and other minerals, in lieu of all ad valorem taxes (5 cents per acre up to 10 years, 10 cents per acre for 10 to 20 years, 15 cents per acre for more than 20 years, minimum $1); *Connecticut*—(1) farm and forest land conveyance tax applicable to sales of designated "open space" if conveyed or changed in classification within 10 years (10% of sale price or market value in the first year, down 1% each year to 1% for the 10th year), and (2) controlling interest in an entity having an interest in Connecticut realty over $2,000 value (1.11% except in an enterprise zone); *Mississippi*—leasehold interest in nonproducing oil, gas, or other minerals (3 cents per mineral or royalty acre up to 10 years, 6 cents for 10 to 20 years, and 8 cents for more than 20 years; minimum $1); *New York*—(1) transfer gains tax (10% on $1 million or more on use for business purposes and $1 million or more aggregate on condominium or co-

operative property) and (2) REITs (0.2% based on trust contract dates); *Vermont*—gains from land sale or exchange of land (amount realized minus the basis as determined by the Internal Revenue Code—from 80% for less than four months to 5% for more than five but less than six years).

## Transfer taxes and the information age

Despite their relatively modest revenue potential, transfer taxes are helpful as documentation and as information sources for property tax assessors. These, among other aspects of property taxes, are being transformed by computer-assisted mass appraisal and geographic information systems. Central to that achievement is mastery of the three approaches to value—depreciated cost, capitalized income, and comparable sales.

Two developments rate attention:

1. Since passage of the Tax Reform Act of 1986, the Internal Revenue Service (IRS) has required (IRC § 6045e) that the party responsible for closing a sale report the selling price on Form 1099-S, by which the IRS could accumulate a database of an estimated 10 million sales prices annually. The Taxpayer Relief Act of 1997 excluded sales of personal residences after May 1997 if the gain on the sale is $500,000 or less for married sellers and $250,000 or less for single sellers.

2. The 1988 American Bar Association (ABA) Model Law on Real Property Transfer Information (developed by the ABA's sections on Taxation, and Real Property, Probate, and Trust Law) provides that, at the time of recordation, at least one transferor and transferee, or their attorneys or agents, file a joint declaration containing the address and assessor's parcel number, date of conveyance document or actual date of transfer, names and addresses of the transacting parties, and price paid. The declaration would be a public record. No state has adopted the Model Law provision specifically, but such legislation has support in several states, and support can be expected to increase with technology developments.

## Additional readings

Advisory Commission on Intergovernmental Relations. *Intergovernmental Aspects of Documentary Taxes*. Washington, D.C., September 1964.

Advisory Commission on Intergovernmental Relations. *State and Local Taxes*. ACIR Legislative Program, vol. 3. Washington, D.C., November 1975.

International Association of Assessing Officers. *Standard on Ratio Studies*. Chicago, July 1990.

Rifkin, Bernard. "Transfer Taxes: A National Survey." *Real Property, Probate and Trust Journal* 19 (Winter 1984): 1035–97.

*State Tax Reporter*. Chicago: Commerce Clearing House, various dates.

U.S. Department of Commerce, Bureau of the Census. *State Government Tax Collections*. Washington, D.C., selected annual issues.

U.S. Department of Commerce, Bureau of the Census. *State and Local Ratio Studies, Property Tax Assessment, and Transfer Taxes*. State and Local Government Special Studies, no. 99. Washington, D.C., October 1980.

U.S. Department of Commerce, Bureau of the Census. *Taxable Property Values and Assessment–Sales Price Ratios*. 1982 Census of Governments, vol. 2 (Washington, D.C., February 1984). (*Taxable Property Values*, 1987 Census of Governments, vol. 2; and *Assessed Values for Local General Property Taxation*, 1992 Census of Governments, vol. 2, no. 1, *do not* contain any de facto levels of assessment [ratios of assessed value to sales price] because no ratio studies were completed for those years.)

# Tribal taxation, state

Judy Zelio
National Conference of State Legislatures

*Because of Indian tribes' special status, determined by federal-Indian agreements, the states must enter cooperative agreements with Indian tribes to levy and collect taxes within the state whose boundaries surround the tribal government boundaries.*

Because of historical treaty and trust responsibilities, the federal government provides funds to Indian tribal governments. But under growing pressure to cut spending, the federal government has appeared increasingly eager for tribal governments to assume a greater share of the costs of reservation services as well as administrative responsibilities. Tribal governments traditionally have been reluctant to levy taxes on their members because of general hostility to taxation and the extensive poverty that exists on many Indian reservations. But some tribes are assuming heavier burdens of social and educational services. They also are making greater efforts to raise revenues through operation of various tribal businesses and through tax collection. This entry discusses state-tribal cooperation on tax issues.

Tribes are governmental entities and retain limited sovereignty under federal law, including the right to make their own laws and be governed by them. Outside the boundaries of a reservation, Indian people are subject to the same state tax laws that apply to everyone else, unless a federal law or treaty confers a special immunity, or unless a state grants exemptions. States have some powers to tax on reservations, but these powers are limited by congressional authority over Indian matters, and particularly so when Indian economic interests are affected.

Beyond those guidelines, there are three sets of conditions under which states generally may and may not impose taxes on tribal members or on tribal lands.

One is *state income taxes*. States may tax the income of tribal members who live and work off the reservation, but they may not tax the income of tribal members who live and work on their tribe's reservation. In addition, states may impose taxes on income and nontrust property of Indian individuals who are not members of the tribe on whose reservation they work and reside. States also may tax non-Indians' income earned on a reservation.

A second set is *property taxes*. State and local governments have the power to levy taxes on most real property owned by non-Indians within reservation boundaries. Similarly, land owned by individual Indian people may be subject to property taxation. Most land owned by tribes and land held in trust by the federal government is not taxable.

The third set is *state sales and use taxes*. Indian people are liable for state sales taxes on transactions conducted off reservation lands, unless a state chooses to exempt tribal members from this obligation. States may not tax sales to and by tribal members when the transactions occur on tribal or trust lands. However, states may tax sales to and by non-Indians on tribal lands. Non-Indians are liable for state taxes on purchases they make on Indian lands, and tribes are obligated to help collect validly imposed state taxes on such sales.

Even though states may have the right to impose taxes on Indian lands under certain conditions, the collection of those taxes may be problematic. Retail outlets located on Indian lands and operated by tribes (or in some cases Indian individuals) sometimes offer products—especially gasoline and cigarettes, whose price elsewhere includes state excise taxes—at lower prices than non-Indian businesses can set, creating a competitive advantage for Indian retailers. Sales of this nature can mean tax revenue losses for states. Although in most states non-Indian buyers are obligated to pay state taxes on these retail purchases, they often do not do so unless the Indian retailers agree to cooperate with state officials. Some states and tribes have agreements in place to work on these issues. States and tribes that together examine tax issues as an economic question rather than a purely legal one sometimes find their overall interests served by a tax-sharing arrangement reached through a negotiated agreement.

A state-tribal tax agreement is an arrangement between two governments that addresses specific jurisdictional issues in taxation. State-tribal agreements require government-to-government discussion between tribal and state officials. Such discussions allow tribal and state leaders to talk directly and specifically about revenue needs, economic development objectives, and the practical, political, and economic concerns that arise from tax conflicts. This approach—unlike litigation—enables the tribe and the state, not a court, to decide whether results are satisfactory.

States must negotiate a separate agreement with each tribal government. If a tax conflict is to be resolved, both the tribe and the state must assent to the terms of any agreements. Agreements may not be possible with all tribes within a state's borders. Each state also must consider whether it is necessary to enact an enabling statute before creating such agreements.

Several states have addressed state-tribal tax issues through legislation and regulations: Florida (1977), Mississippi (1986), Montana (1993), Nevada (1991), New Mexico (1992), Oklahoma (1992), Washington (1985), and Wisconsin (1987). Minnesota has tax agreements with 10 different tribes. These agreements, which use formulas to determine refunds to tribes from sales and motor vehicle excise taxes, cigarette taxes, alcoholic beverage taxes, and petroleum taxes, attempt to preserve the tribes' and tribal members' immunity while collecting the state tax legally owed by nonmembers of the tribe.

Other states and tribes also have reached agreements that illustrate a variety of approaches: Louisiana and the Chitimacha Tribe (1990); Nevada and the Reno Sparks Tribe (1991); Montana and the Fort Peck and Assiniboine Sioux Tribes (1992); Oklahoma and the Cherokee Nation and four other tribes (1992); Oregon and the Warm Springs Confederated Tribes (1979); South Dakota and the Standing Rock Sioux, Rosebud Sioux, Cheyenne River Sioux, and Oglala Sioux Tribes (beginning in 1971); and Wisconsin and seven different tribes (agreements were updated in 1996). New Mexico and some pueblos have explored the development of a unified tax collection system that would allow shared revenues. New York has explored such agreements in the past and may continue to do so because of a 1994 U.S.

Supreme Court decision (*New York* v. *Milhelm Attea and Bros., Inc.*) that upheld a state law imposing certain restrictions on wholesalers' cigarette sales on reservations.

Tax revenues are essential to the operation of government, the delivery of services, and the development of infrastructure. Rather than compete for revenue from the same sources—either non-Indian businesses operating on a reservation or transactions between tribal businesses and non-Indians—a number of states and tribes are choosing to negotiate tax-sharing agreements and forgo expensive and time-consuming litigation. In the negotiation process, both sides can discuss, in a nonadversarial environment, revenue needs and economic concerns.

## Additional readings

Cohen, Felix S. *Handbook of Federal Indian Law, with Reference Tables and Index*. Washington, D.C.: U.S. Government Printing Office, 1942. Reprinted, Albuquerque: University of New Mexico Press, 1972.

Canby, William C., Jr. *American Indian Law in a Nutshell*. 2d ed. St. Paul: West Publishing Co., 1988.

Duncan, Harley. "Issues in State-Tribal Taxation." Bulletin B-232. Washington, D.C.: Federation of Tax Administrators, Nov. 21, 1991.

Endreson, Douglas B.L. *Resolving Tribal-State Tax Conflicts*. Washington, D.C.: National Indian Policy Center, June 1991.

Getches, David H. and Charles F. Wilkinson. *Federal Indian Law: Cases and Materials*. 2d ed. St. Paul: West Publishing Co., 1986.

Michael, Joel. "Taxation in Indian Country." In *Indians, Indian Tribes and State Government*. Research Department, Minnesota House of Representatives, February 1993.

Montana Committee on Indian Affairs (Eddye McClure, Connie Erickson, Stephen Maly, and Susan Byorth Fox, staff). *The Tribal Nations of Montana: A Handbook for Legislators*. Helena: Montana Legislative Council, March 1995.

Pevar, Stephen L. *The Rights of Indians and Tribes: The Basic ACLU Guide to Indian and Tribal Rights*. 2d ed. Carbondale: Southern Illinois University Press, 1992.

Reed, James A., and Judy A. Zelio. *States and Tribes: Building New Traditions*. Denver: National Conference of State Legislatures, 1995.

*Cross reference:* gaming taxation, state.

# U

## Uniform capitalization rules

Gerard M. Brannon
Consultant

*When the law requires that an expenditure be treated as a capital rather than a current expense, special rules are promulgated for how this transaction is valued for income tax purposes.*

When to expense or capitalize business costs is an aspect of a serious problem in a Haig-Simons income tax—namely, that the requirement for taking account of changes in wealth calls for annual valuations of assets, which in many cases are not provided by our market institutions.

Income tax laws in all countries contain compromises with the theoretical demands of annual valuations. For investment assets, appreciation is ignored until realization. Fixed business assets not sold are presumed only to decline in value according to an arbitrary depreciation schedule. In addition, there are many rules, such as those relating to the cost of goods sold and the basis of inventory, distinguishing *deductible* current expenses, which presumably create no increased value (beyond cash receipts) and *capitalizable* outlays, which are presumed to create increased unrealized value equal to the expenditure thereon and which therefore are not to be deducted.

If a business cost is incurred to increase future income, the assumption of business rationality suggests that the future income should exceed the current cost by the normal rate of return compounded. The time value of money suggests that a current deduction for the cost and deferral of the related income is equivalent to making the return on the cost tax-free (Johnson 1994; Mundstock 1990).

The policy issue in many of these compromises involves balancing accuracy against complexity in income measurement. Moreover, in some situations better income measurement is sacrificed for an expected incentive effect, which is the case with accelerated depreciation and research and development outlays.

That partial deductibility of capital expenditures in the U.S. tax law has been characterized as an "Uneasy Compromise" (Aaron et al. 1988). Some commentators see the unsatisfactory state of these compromises as the strongest case for a consumption, or cash flow, tax. Such a tax is equivalent to allowing a deduction for all capital expenditures or allowing an exemption for investment income (Bradford 1986).

Much of the tax reform effort in the United States in the past decade has been a move toward purifying the income concept by eliminating several accounting compromises that allowed expensing of capital investments. These accounting changes were attractive to Congress, in part because they provided politically acceptable revenue increases. They generally involved short-run "transitional" revenues that appeared larger in the five-year revenue window used in congressional committee reports than their actual steady-state effect. The general form of these changes was a reduction of currently deductible business costs, leaving higher year-end capital accounts. These changes ranged from tightening of depreciation rules, to statutory changes in long-term contract accounting, to formulaic deferral of long-term insurance acquisition costs.

One such change was the enactment in 1986 of Section 263A of the Internal Revenue Code, which authorized the Treasury to issue detailed regulations to require that certain current outlays be capitalized—that is, included in the basis of property held for sale or use. These rules are commonly referred to as the uniform capitalization or Unicap rules.

Historically, for business taxpayers in wholesale and retail trade, direct costs—the costs of raw materials and wages of workers in production—were not deducted but instead were allocated as cost of goods. To the extent that these goods were sold, the allowable business deduction was for cost of goods *sold*. Costs allocated to goods not (yet) sold became the basis of inventory. Indirect costs such as taxes and interest were simply deductible.

Manufactured inventories were, by regulation, subject to rules requiring that some indirect costs be capitalized by adding them to the cost of goods sold, the "full absorption" rules. Congress applied similar rules to accounting for long-term contracts in 1982. The Treasury tax reform proposals in 1985 recommended unifying the rules for including indirect costs in costs of goods produced. Congress carried the proposal further by applying it to costs of goods purchased for resale as well as costs of goods produced for either sale or use.

Section 263A broadly requires that nearly all indirect costs be allocated to the cost of goods and thus be deductible only to the extent that the goods were sold. Broadly, the indirect costs covered included the allocable portion of the costs that benefit assets produced or acquired for resale, among them general, administrative, and overhead costs; depreciation; fringe benefits; and interest allocable to the goods involved. The regulations allow various simplifications. In certain circumstances, for instance, the taxpayer may establish a historical ratio of indirect to direct inventory costs and use that ratio to comply with the new rules. (Details of this legislation as elaborated by regulations are provided in Garrett and Connor 1992.)

The transition rule provided that the basis of inventories on hand be immediately written up (and be available for deduction again), but the write-up is treated as a change in accounting and thus has to be added to income over a four-year period. Effectively, any extra deductions the taxpayer obtained from the old rule, to the extent that the related goods were still on hand, were returned to income over a four-year period. Enactment of the Unicap rules was credited with a revenue gain of $35 billion over five years. About 70 percent of this was a result of the transition effect.

Despite the high-sounding name of "uniform" rules, the new section comes with exceptions. Separate rules provided under the code continue generous deductibility for research and development expenses, for intangible expenses of oil and gas wells, for certain mineral development costs, and for the developmental outlays of tree growers, and these expenses are not allocated to the costs of goods. Some small businesses that are required to do inventory accounting are still exempt from the Section 263A refinements. Farmers who generally are excused from the rigors of accrual accounting will continue to be exempt from the need to do any inventory accounting. In addition, many costs in a business, such as advertising aimed at name recognition, are still deductible, which increases the business's year-end value. The effect of these outlays is commonly recognized in the sale of a business as "goodwill." (For a discussion of the implication of deducting expenses that give rise to goodwill, see Gravelle and Taylor 1992 and the entry on Expensing.)

Legislative activity in requiring more capitalization continued after 1986. The Omnibus Budget Reconciliation Act of 1990 (OBRA90) provided that the acquisition costs for long-term insurance policies should be capitalized and deducted over an arbitrary period. Similarly, three years later OBRA93 conformed accounting required for dealers in securities more closely to the Haig-Simons concept by requiring that inventories be "marked-to-market"—that is, that unrealized appreciation in inventory securities be included in income.

The Internal Revenue Service has indicated an intention to require capitalization of a number of environmental costs that increase the value of property (Technical Advice Memorandum 920004).

The courts have also been concerned with issues of deductibility versus capitalization. The Supreme Court in *INDOPCO* v. *Commissioner* (112 Sup. Ct. 1039 (1992)) held that professional fees incurred in a tax-free acquisition produced significant future benefits and were thus capitalizable, not deductible, even though the fees produced no separate and distinct asset. This decision is seen by some as presaging other situations where historically deductible costs might come under a capitalization rule (Johnson 1994). The IRS has itself indicated that it is reconsidering the deductibility of loan origination costs by a bank (IRS Announcement 93-60, March 30, 1993).

## Additional readings

Aaron, Henry, Joseph Pechman, and Harvey Galper, editors. *Uneasy Compromise: Problems of a Hybrid Income-Consumption Tax*. Washington, D.C.: The Brookings Institution, 1988.

Bradford, David. *Untangling the Income Tax*. Cambridge, Mass.: Harvard University Press, 1986.

Garrett, Richard, and James Connor. *Unified Capitalization Rules*. Washington, D.C.: Tax Management Portfolio Series, Tax Management Inc., 1992.

Gravelle, Jane, and Jack Taylor. "Tax Neutrality and the Tax Treatment of Purchased Intangibles." *National Tax Journal* 45 (March 1992): 77.

Johnson, Calvin. "Capitalization after the Government's Big Win in *INDOPCO*: The Saga Continues." *Tax Notes* 63 (June 6, 1994): 1323.

Mundstock, George. "Franchises, Intangible Capital and Assets." *National Tax Journal* 43 (September 1990): 299.

U.S. Congress, Joint Committee on Taxation. *General Explanation of the Tax Reform Act of 1986*. Washington, D.C.: Government Printing Office, 1986.

*Cross references:* adjusted gross income; inventory accounting.

# Unitary taxation

Walter Hellerstein
University of Georgia

*Use of the unit rule to determine a multijurisdictional taxpayer's tax base.*

Unitary taxation is a methodology for determining a multijurisdictional taxpayer's tax base. It is commonly associated with the taxing methodology employed by the U.S. states for determining the portion of a multijurisdictional corporation's income that may be attributed to and taxed by the state. The underlying principle, however, has its roots in property taxation.

The unitary business principle derives from the "unit rule" developed in the late 19th century for apportioning property values of railroad, telegraph, and express companies to state or local taxing jurisdictions. To ascertain the value of a company's property that was properly attributable to the taxing jurisdiction, states and localities would determine the value of the entire operating system and then assign to the state or locality a proportion of the system value based on the ratio of the amount of some identifiable factor within the state to the amount of such factor in the entire system. For example, a railroad's property would typically be apportioned to the state by reference to the ratio of the miles of track within the state to the total miles of track in the system.

When taxpayers complained that taxing jurisdictions were exceeding their power by taking account of extraterritorial values for purposes of determining the proper value of the taxpayer's property attributable to the taxing state or locality, the U.S. Supreme Court responded that a railroad must be regarded for most purposes "as a unit"; that the "track of the road is but one track from one end of it to the other and, except in its use as one track, is of little value"; that each taxing jurisdiction through which the railroad passes has "an interest much more important than it has in the limited part of it lying within its boundary"; and that it doubted there was any better mode of determining the value of that portion of the track within the taxing jurisdiction than to ascertain the value of the whole road and apportion the value within the jurisdiction by its relative length to the whole (*Tate Railroad Tax Cases*, 92 U.S. 575, 608 (1875)).

The U.S. Supreme Court subsequently expanded the concept of the "unit rule" beyond cases in which there was a contiguous physical unity to cases in which there was operational—but no physical—unity. Thus it sustained the power of a state to consider the value of all of an express company's horses, wagons, and furniture in determining the value of such property that ought to be attributed to the state, even though there was no physical link, such as a railroad track or telephone line, between the taxpayer's in-state and out-of-state property.

When the U.S. Supreme Court began to confront constitutional challenges to apportioned corporate net income taxes in the 1920s, it applied the same "unit rule" or unitary taxation principles it had developed in adjudicating the constitutionality of apportioned property taxes. The Court recognized that when corporate income was "largely earned by a series of transactions beginning with manufacture in [one state] and ending with sales in other states," apportionment was a reasonable method for assigning the taxpayer's income to each of the various states in light of the "impossibility of allocating the profits earned by the processes conducted within its borders" (*Underwood Typewriter Co.* v. *Chamberlain*, 254 U.S. 113, 120–21 (1920)).

The existence of a unitary business thus became the critical factor in determining whether a state could consider income earned outside its borders in ascertaining by an apportionment formula the portion of the taxpayer's income that the state could tax. Under the unitary business principle, if the taxpayer was carrying on a single unitary business within and without the state, the state had the requisite connection to the out-of-state activities of the business to justify inclusion in the taxpayer's apportionable tax base of all of the income generated by the combined effect of the out-of-state and in-state activities. By the same token, if the taxpayer's income-producing activities carried on within the state were not unitary with its income-producing activities carried on elsewhere, the state was constitutionally constrained from including the income arising from those out-of-state activities in the taxpayer's apportionable tax base. In short, as the U.S. Supreme Court declared, "the linchpin of apportionability in the field of state income taxation is the unitary business principle" (*Mobil Oil Corp.* v. *Commissioner of Taxes*, 445 U.S. 425, 439 (1980)).

In delineating the contours of a unitary business, the U.S. Supreme Court focused on the underlying factors that created an organic connection between the corporation's activities within and without the state and that warranted the state's consideration of the corporation's out-of-state activities in determining the income derived from its in-state activities. Thus the Court observed that it was "unity of use and management of a business" (*Butler Bros.* v. *McColgan*, 315 U.S. 501, 508 (1942)) that justified the state's inclusion of income generated by out-of-state activities in the apportionable tax base. The Court described a unitary business as one characterized by "functional integration, centralization of management, and economies of scale" (*Mobil Oil Corp.* v. *Commissioner of Taxes*, 445 U.S. 425, 438 (1980)). It emphasized the fundamental notion that, for a business to be unitary, "the out-of-state activities of the purported 'unitary business' must be related in some concrete way to the in-state activities" (*Container Corp. of America* v. *Franchise Tax Bd.*, 463 U.S. 159, 166 (1983)), and there must be "some sharing or exchange of value not capable of precise identification—beyond the mere flow of funds arising out of a passive investment or a distinct business operation."

The Court also made clear that everything a taxpayer happened to own did not necessarily constitute part of its unitary business. For example, when North Dakota sought to include the value of interstate railroads' stocks and bonds in its apportionable property tax base, the Court observed that "[t]he only reason for allowing a state to look beyond its borders when it taxes the property of foreign corporations is that it may get the true value of the things within it, when they are part of an organic system of wide extent, that gives them a value above what they would otherwise possess" (*Wallace* v. *Hines*, 253 U.S. 66, 69 (1920)). The purpose is not, the Court continued, "to expose the heel of the system to a mortal dart—not, in other words, to open to taxation what is not within the State." Consequently, the bonds secured by mortgage of lands in other states and other property that "adds to the riches of the corporation but does not affect the North Dakota part of the road" could not be included in the apportionable tax base.

The Court applied the same principle when dealing with the question whether items of income could be included in the taxpayer's apportionable tax base. It concluded that a state in which a taxpayer was not domiciled could not require the taxpayer to include income from investments that did not serve an "operational function" in the taxpayer's business (*Allied-Signal, Inc.* v. *Director, Division of Taxation*, 504 U.S. 768 (1992)). Consequently, the state could not tax an apportioned share of the gain that the taxpayer derived from its investment in another corporation, when the investment did not serve as working capital for the taxpayer and when the other corporation's activities were unrelated to those carried on by the taxpayer in the taxing state.

In recent years, the most controversial aspect of the unitary business principle has been in its application to multicorporate enterprises. Once formulary apportionment is accepted as a method of dividing the income of a single corporation that conducts a unitary business in more than one state, there is no justification, in principle at least, for failing to apply formulary apportionment to the income of a group of controlled corporations that compose a unitary business. The only difference between the two cases lies in the form of business organization—that is, the organization of a business enterprise through subsidiaries, as distinguished from branches, a factor that should not affect a state's power to determine the portion of the income of a unitary business that is fairly attributable to the state.

The pioneer case extending the unitary business principle to the income of a multicorporate enterprise involved a Delaware corporation that owned a chain of retail stores selling shoes and accessories. Each store was organized as a separate subsidiary corporation in the state in which it did business. The parent corporation manufactured no goods, but conducted its central management, purchasing, distributing, advertising, and administrative activities in St. Louis. The California subsidiary, which carried on a purely intrastate business, paid for the goods and services it received from the parent at the parent company's cost, plus overhead charges.

The taxpayer sought to have its California net income tax determined solely on the basis of that separate corporation's activities in California. The tax commissioner rejected this approach and instead applied an apportionment formula to the income of the entire chain of stores in order to determine the net income of the taxpayer that was apportionable to California. The taxpayer contended that the statute did not authorize the extension of the apportionment formula to the income and factors of out-of-state corporations that were not taxable in the state. The court rejected the contention, observing that "[n]o difference in principle is discernible" whether the business is carried on by a single corporation or a group of related corporations. The income of the individual corporate taxpayer could be determined by reference to the combined income of the group of related corporations so long as the individual corporate taxpayer's business "is an integral part of a larger and unitary system" (*Edison California Stores, Inc.* v. *McColgan*, 176 P.2d 697 (Cal. 1947), on rehearing, 183 P.2d 16, 21 (Cal. 1947)).

The furthest extension of the unitary business principle has occurred in the context of *multinational* multicorporate enterprises. The U.S. Supreme Court first addressed the constitutionality of the application of the unitary business principle to a multinational multicorporate enterprise in 1983, when California sought to determine the income of a corporation doing business in California by reference to worldwide combined income of all of the affiliated corporations that were conducting a unitary business. The Court sustained California's application of the unitary business principle on a worldwide basis to a group of affiliated corporations with a U.S. parent, despite the taxpayer's contention that the application of the unitary method led to international multiple taxation and prevented the U.S. government from speaking with one voice in foreign policy.

In 1994, the U.S. Supreme Court reaffirmed the constitutionality of the application of the unitary business principle as a basis for taxing the income of a corporation on a worldwide unitary basis when it sustained the application of the method to a multinational multicorporate group with a foreign parent (*Barclays Bank PLC* v. *Franchise Tax Board*, 512 U.S. 298 (1994)). The Court reiterated the position it had taken a decade earlier, and it found no significant distinction between the application of the unitary method to a foreign-based, as distinguished from a United States-based, multinational multicorporate group.

The executive branch of the U.S. government, foreign governments, and the international business community have expressed their strong opposition to the states' application of the unitary method in the context of international commerce because it is contrary to the accepted international norm for taxation of related corporations. The international norm strictly respects the separate corporate entity and makes adjustments to the income separately reported by such entities only when transfers between the related corporations do not reflect arm's-length pricing. Even though opponents of worldwide unitary taxation have been unsuccessful in challenging it in court, the states have responded to this opposition legislatively. With a few narrow exceptions, states limit the application of the unitary business principle to U.S. "water's edge" income.

## Additional readings

Hellerstein, Jerome R., and Walter Hellerstein. *State Taxation*. 2 vols. 2d ed. Boston: Warren, Gorham, Lamont, 1993.

Hellerstein, Jerome R., and Walter Hellerstein. *State and Local Taxation*. 6th ed. St. Paul: West Publishing Company, 1997.

Hellerstein, Walter. "State Taxation of Corporate Income from Intangibles: *Allied-Signal* and Beyond." *Tax Law Review* 48 (Fall 1993): 739–878.

*Cross references:* apportionment; income tax, corporate, state and local.

# User charges, federal

Pearl Richardson
Congressional Budget Office

*Charges representing an attempt to match those who pay for federal services with those who receive them.*

Although seemingly straightforward, the terms "user charge" and "user fee" have no set meaning. Federal agencies have defined user fees broadly, as prices that the government charges identifiable individuals or entities for a service or good that it controls, and, more narrowly, as prices the government charges to recover its costs of providing special benefits to an identifiable recipient beyond those that accrue to the general public. The narrower definition rests on a distinction between special benefits to individuals and businesses and general benefits to the public—a distinction that is often clearer in theory than in practice. The leasing of government-owned land to private firms, for example, clearly confers a special benefit; providing for

the national defense is obviously a general benefit. But between these extremes lie a wide variety of services that may provide both special benefits to particular individuals or businesses and general benefits to the public.

User charges may take the form of fees or dedicated excise taxes and may include not only payments for benefits but also assessments to lessen a burden that individuals or businesses impose (or might impose) on third parties. Liability-based charges are the mirror image of beneficiary-based charges and are an attempt to match those who pay for corrective actions with those who might cause the conditions requiring them.

There are four distinct types of federal user charges: user fees, regulatory fees, benefit-based taxes, and liability-based taxes.

*User fees* are payments made by individuals or businesses for goods or services provided by the government, consumed voluntarily, and not generally shared by other members of society. User fees are levied for goods and services that are beneficiary-based. Apart from being charged by the government, user fees are similar in kind, although not necessarily in amount, to payments made in ordinary business transactions in the private sector and often may be for the kinds of goods and services that the private sector also provides.

User fees include royalties on natural resources; canal, bridge, and highway tolls; insurance premiums; and lease and rental payments. They also include charges for the use of federal land, such as grazing livestock; the use of federal facilities, such as campsites in national parks; services, such as mail delivery, waste disposal, and enrichment of uranium; permits and licenses not associated with regulatory programs; and recurring sales of products, such as power, or resources, such as water, minerals, and timber.

*Regulatory fees* are charges based on the government's power to regulate particular businesses or activities. These charges include fees for regulatory and judicial services; immigration, passport, and consular fees; Customs Service user fees; fees for testing, inspection, and grading services; patent, trademark, and copyright fees; and registration, filing, permit, and license fees associated with regulatory programs. In general, these charges, which may be beneficiary-based or liability-based, or both, are for functions that traditionally are performed by government, and only rarely by the private sector.

Regulatory fees stem from the powers that the government exercises as a sovereign state, such as the powers to levy taxes and duties and to regulate commerce. Regulatory fees include charges for licenses, which the government may require as a condition for permitting a commercial activity, and charges for such services as inspections, which may benefit the fee payer, lessen the fee payer's imposition of costs or risks on others or on society as a whole, or both. Frequently, such charges are for activities undertaken to ensure that a firm has followed prescribed measures to avert environmental or other damage to public health and safety.

The government often sets safety standards for certain types of industrial activity and charges firms for the cost of inspecting their plants to ensure compliance. From the standpoint of the regulated party, such services seem to benefit the payer little, and thus the charges seem to be more like taxes than fees for service. From the standpoint of the federal government, however, such charges compensate for—and the final prices of goods and services should reflect—the costs that a business imposes or might impose on society when it pollutes or otherwise damages a public resource. Regulatory services thus may be either for direct benefits (such as passports or patents) to identifiable private individuals or for measures that safeguard public health and safety. Although all regulatory fees stem from the sovereign power of government, the issue of who benefits from certain types of regulatory activity has been controversial at times.

*Beneficiary-based taxes* are charges levied on bases correlated in varying degrees with the use of a publicly provided good or service. Benefit taxes may be proxies for user fees and are usually dedicated to trust or special funds.

Most benefit taxes are related to transportation and nature conservation. More frequently than not, they are excises. Excise and other taxes are user charges when the law creates a relationship between the collection of a tax on a product and the provision of a good or service. Generally, the relationship involves dedicating the tax to a trust or special fund for a purpose that directly or indirectly benefits the payer. For example, taxes on air passenger tickets, air cargo, noncommercial jet fuel, and aviation gasoline, and a head tax on international departures and arrivals, are dedicated to the Airport and Airways Trust Fund, which finances airport construction and improvements, development of the airway system, and a portion of Federal Aviation Administration operations.

Similarly, taxes on gasoline, diesel fuel, gasohol, tires and innertubes, truck and trailer sales, and highway vehicles weighing more than 55,000 pounds are dedicated to the Highway Trust Fund, which finances the maintenance and improvement of roads and bridges and supports highway safety and traffic control projects within the federal highway system. The taxes on trucks and trailers, highway vehicles, and tires for heavy vehicles are intended to approximate charges for highway wear and tear. (A more exact relationship between charges and use of the highways would also take distance into account.)

Beneficiary-based taxes differ from fees, not only in the structure of the charge but also in the degree of connection between the payers of the charge and the benefits or services that are financed with the proceeds. Taxes are more likely than fees to be levied at uniform rates with less regard for differences in cost for facilities within a system or for differences in the use of the system. For example, nearly all purchasers of gasoline pay the motor fuels excise tax, even though individuals vary widely in their use of Interstate highways. The charge is thus more loosely related to the benefit it provides than is, say, a highway toll. But it is more closely related to a benefit than, for example, the income tax.

Benefit taxes frequently involve some amount of cross-subsidy, which occurs when one group pays fees that reflect more than its share of costs, while another group pays fees that reflect less than its share. In these cases, the higher-paying group is subsidizing the lower-paying group. Although typically less with fees, cross-subsidies may occur with either fees or benefit taxes.

*Liability-based taxes* are excises levied for the purpose of abating hazards or compensating for injuries. Where possible, the government collects damages from responsible parties. But at times, taxes on products that might have some connection with the cause of damages serve as a proxy for recovering damages from responsible parties. Thus, for example, certain taxes on gasoline, diesel and other motor fuels, methanol and ethanol fuels, aviation fuels, and fuels used by vessels in inland waterways are dedicated to the Leaking Underground Storage Tank (LUST) Trust Fund, which covers cleanup costs when damage has occurred and the party responsible is insolvent or fails to deal with the problem. Taxes on domestically mined coal finance the Black Lung Disability Trust Fund, which was set up to compensate miners disabled by pneumoconiosis (black lung disease) or to recompense their survivors. Taxes on vaccines are dedicated to the Vaccine Injury Compensation Trust Fund, which provides funds to compensate people for injuries resulting from prescribed diphtheria, pertussis, tetanus, measles, mumps, rubella, and polio vaccines administered after October 1, 1988.

These charges illustrate a trend toward using dedicated taxes to pay for environmental and other damage imposed on third parties. Liability-based taxes are likely to be reflected in consumer prices and may be said to represent an attempt—however imprecise—to include within the final prices of certain goods the costs imposed on society of producing or consuming them. In this respect, they are analogous to certain liability-based regulatory fees, just as benefit-based taxes are analogous to user fees.

Taxes levied on the source of an environmental danger may reduce the activity that causes the danger. Taxes levied on the sources of health or environmental hazards also may substitute for insurance programs. How much they do depends on the strength of the relationships between the taxes and the potential liabilities that they finance. The more direct the relationship, the more effective the tax will be in averting or compensating for actual damage.

The strength of the relationships between current excise taxes and the liabilities they finance varies. For example, the excise taxes dedicated to the Leaking Underground Storage Tank Trust Fund finance control and cleanup once damage has occurred but do nothing directly to reduce or prevent it. These taxes also fall short of functioning as insurance charges because they finance cleanup of damages that occurred before the taxes were enacted. The taxes levied for the Vaccine Injury Compensation Fund, in contrast, cover prospective damages, and thus more closely approximate insurance payments.

## Additional readings

Hopkins, Thomas D., editor. *Federal User Fees, Proceedings of a Symposium*. Administrative Conference of the United States, 1987.

U.S. Congress, Congressional Budget Office. *The Growth of Federal User Charges*. Washington, D.C., August 1993.

"User Charges." U.S. Government, Executive Office of the President, Office of Management and Budget, Circular A-25, *Federal Register*, vol. 52, no. 126, July 1, 1987, pp. 24890–92.

*Cross references:* Airport and Airway Trust Fund; benefit principle; environmental taxes, federal; environmental taxes, state; fuel taxes, federal; tax price.

# V

## Value-added tax, national

Alan Tait
International Monetary Fund

*Broad-based tax on business designed to measure net dollar value generated in a country.*

The usual value-added tax (VAT) is a general sales tax on all goods and services. It is levied at each stage of production and accumulates so that it is equivalent to a tax on all final household consumption. It has become the most popular sales tax in the world. It started in France in 1948, was adopted by the European Community (EC) in 1968, and has since spread to more than 100 countries. The only major economies that do not use some form of the VAT are Australia and the United States.

The VAT is designed to raise large amounts of revenue (typically 5 to 10% of gross domestic product) without creating economic distortions. In practice, many countries, because of political pressures to use the tax system to correct social inequities and because of their inability to tax certain sectors, use exemptions and multiple rates that erode the neutrality of the VAT. Such complications make the VAT more complex and expensive to administer and increase the opportunities for evasion.

Value added is the difference between the amount received for a good or service (output) and the cost to a trader of buying the materials and services from other traders (input). This difference, output minus input, usually consists of wages and salaries, profits, rents, and interest paid and constitutes the value added of the business. Clearly, value added can be measured either by subtracting inputs from outputs (the subtractive base) or by adding together the constituents. A tax on the additive base could be viewed as a tax on profits, rents, wages, and salaries and as a tax additional to conventional income taxes. For this reason, and because it would have to be on an annual base, levied at a single rate, it is not used. Instead, nearly all countries use the subtractive type of VAT pioneered in France. This variant does not actually require the trader to calculate value added by subtracting inputs from outputs, but taxes every sale and purchase and nets out the difference in tax liabilities for each trader.

In this way, a trader registered for the VAT charges a proportional tax rate on all sales. Likewise, he pays a VAT charged on his purchases by his suppliers. Each taxable period (usually a month), the trader credits the tax paid on his purchases against the tax liability on his sales, and the difference is his net VAT liability to be paid to the authorities. Actual value added is never calculated; it is only the difference between two tax liabilities, on outputs and inputs, that is computed. The emphasis placed on each transaction means that the evidence for each sale or purchase, the invoice, becomes a crucial document to monitor and administer the VAT. For this reason, this EC type of VAT is often called the "credit-invoice VAT."

An alternative subtractive method is to use company accounts to deduct purchases from sales and apply the tax rate to the value added derived from these accounts. This is used in Japan (the accounts method) and is administered by the income tax administration. The revenue should be the same as that when the credit-invoice method is used, but only a single VAT rate can be levied (5% in Japan). Companies make provisional tax payments through the year, and a reconciliation is performed when the accounts are closed at the end of the year.

The sum of all value added at each stage of production is equal to the final retail price. So a VAT is equivalent to a retail sales tax (RST) and should have similar effects. However, an RST is applied only at the final sale to a consumer, and it is frequently the easiest transaction to misrepresent and the most difficult for the tax administrators to check. As the VAT is levied at each stage and cumulates, the invoices for each transaction provide a better audit trail than the single retail sale. An RST at higher rates invites increasing evasion, and for this reason a VAT has been preferred as a sales tax when levied at high rates. In addition, under an RST it is often difficult to ensure that tax is not levied again on sales where inputs have already been taxed (cascading); under a truly general VAT, cascading is eliminated.

The EC adopted the VAT because it was a sales tax that could be identified precisely on exports and imports; it could be rebated entirely on exports by using a zero rate (the credit for taxes on purchases against a zero tax liability on the export sale ensures the exporter is compensated for all VAT levied on earlier stages of production). Likewise, the VAT could be levied on imports, regardless of the stage of production, at a rate identical to that used for domestic production. The assumption is that the VAT is passed forward fully in prices. The destination principle states that the VAT paid should be that levied in the country where the final consumption (sale) is made so the consumer's choice is not influenced by different countries' tax rates.

Another advantage of the VAT over the RST is that capital goods can be exempted entirely from the tax. Purchase of capital goods involves paying the VAT, but credit should be claimed at once against the next tax period's VAT liability on sales. When capital purchases are large—for instance, involving extensive plant and machinery or a new building—the credit in a single tax period can far outweigh the tax liability; this net credit should be repaid at once by the government, although some administrations allow it to be set only against future VAT liabilities.

The VAT base should include all goods and services. To the extent that it does not, double taxation and cascading occurs and the neutrality of the VAT is eroded. Some sectors are difficult to tax. Small traders should not have to register; the time and trouble taken to monitor their liabilities is not compensated by the revenues. Thresholds for registration vary greatly; Denmark taxes all traders with an annual turnover above US$1,500, whereas Japan applies the full VAT to traders with a turnover above US$3.5 million (those between US$200,000 and US$3.5 million use a simplified scheme). Generous minimum thresholds simplify administration, and most difficult-to-tax categories drop out (small farmers, street traders, one-man suppliers of business services).

Second-hand goods are usually taxed only on their markup; because there is no VAT on the purchase, no credit is available if a VAT is applied to the value of the final sale. Of course, the largest category of second-hand goods is the existing stock of residential houses. The usual treatment is to tax the real estate agents' margins on sales of old houses but to tax new houses fully, including the profit element of the builder.

Financial services are exempt from the VAT (except in Israel and partially in New Zealand—see discussion in Tait 1991: 12). The charge for financial services is often a spread that may be only a few base points in the final charge to the consumer. Only part of this charge is for the service of financial intermediation, and it is impossible to unbundle it from the fees. This exemption from the VAT means that banks and insurance companies pay a VAT on their purchases (which can be substantial—e.g., computers, buildings) and cannot claim any credit for their payment. Presumably their VAT liability is passed forward to their customers, who then charge a VAT again on that price including the VAT; hence, distortions and cascading are introduced.

Frequently, governments argue that items that feature prominently in low-income household budgets, such as food, should not be taxed. Whether all food (e.g., in the United Kingdom) or only "essential" food is zero-rated, this favored treatment erodes revenue, creates problems of definition, and involves valuable administrative time in settling "border" disputes. Moreover, it uses the VAT to try to attain distributional ends for which the tax is ill-suited. The VAT is levied primarily for revenue; progressive income and wealth taxes, and carefully judged government expenditures to help at-risk groups, can be better designed to meet the distributional responsibilities of the budget.

The same argument applies to the claims made to use multiple rates of VAT to tax essentials at lower rates and luxury goods at higher rates. It is undoubtedly correct that a single-rate VAT is regressive, but it is easier to administer and less open to evasion. The EC is moving to use only two rates: equal to or lower than 5 percent for food, water, pharmaceuticals, passenger transport, books, agricultural materials, and cultural events, and 15 percent or higher for everything else. Typically, much higher rates on "luxury" goods generate little revenue, are difficult to administer, and generate evasion. Equity should be the responsibility of other parts of the fiscal system (see Vertical equity).

It has also been claimed that the introduction of the VAT is inflationary. Undoubtedly, because it is an additional tax on household consumption reflected in higher prices, adopting a VAT will lead to a once-and-for-all jump in the price level. Whether this would lead, in turn, to an accelerated rise in prices depends on the wage-price nexus and whether the money supply is expanded to accommodate the rising prices. The evidence is that in most countries the introduction of a VAT led to a once-and-for-all shift in the price level but not to a change in the rate of inflation.

The VAT is not a cheap tax to administer. The revenue raised should be equivalent to an RST at an identical tax rate, but more taxpayers must be registered and more tax returns made. Much money is collected only to be returned. Much fraud is possible through suppression of sales figures, barter transactions, understated debtors, false invoices, misdescriptions, multiple claims, customs fraud, and fictitious businesses. The costs of VAT administration vary widely depending on the exemptions, thresholds, zero-rating, number of tax rates, frequency of audit, and role played by other collection agencies (e.g., customs). In the EC, the ratio of staff to taxpayers varies from 1:123 in Belgium to 1:726 in Italy. A 1993 U.S. study reckoned that with a registration threshold of US$25,000, an annual audit rate of 10.6 percent, and an average audit length of 12 hours (more or less the norms for the United Kingdom and New Zealand), 18,850 staff years would be needed for 12 million taxpayers (1:637). If the threshold is set at US$100,000, the ratio drops to 1:529.

The United States has debated the possibility of adopting a VAT on numerous occasions. It has been seen as a way to reduce the budget deficit, finance Social Security, replace the corporate and personal income tax, and finance a health scheme or defense. In the United States, a 5 percent VAT, if education, financial services, and all medical care are zero-rated, would yield about US$98 billion in 1998 (about 6.3% of revenues) (Congressional Budget Office 1995: 393). This yield is much lower than is common in Europe, and it suggests that to make the administrative costs worthwhile (US$1 billion for government and US$6–10 billion compliance costs for business) the rate might have to move toward the typical worldwide rates of VAT (10 to 20%). However, it must be remembered that such a federally administered VAT would be supplemental to existing state sales taxes typically levied at 4 to 8 percent.

## Additional readings

Department of the Treasury. *Tax Reform for Fairness, Simplicity and Growth. Vol. 3. Value-Added Tax.* Washington, D.C., November 1984.

Tait, Alan A. *Value-Added Tax: International Practice and Problems.* Washington, D.C.: International Monetary Fund, 1988.

Tait, Alan A., editor. *Value-Added Tax: Administrative and Policy Issues.* Washington, D.C.: International Monetary Fund, 1991.

U.S. Congress, Congressional Budget Office. *Reducing the Deficit: Spending and Revenue Options.* Washington, D.C., February 1995.

U.S. General Accounting Office: Report to the Joint Committee on Taxation, U.S. Congress. *Tax Policy: Value-Added Tax: Administrative Costs.* Washington, D.C., May 1993.

*Cross references:* consumption taxation; retail sales tax; tax reform, federal; value-added tax, state.

# Value-added tax, state

Robert D. Ebel
National Tax Association

*A broad-based tax on the business enterprise that is designed to measure the net dollar value contributed to the output and income generated in a state.*

---

State tax receipts are derived primarily from taxes on individual income and consumption, while the contribution of general business taxes has declined (Advisory Commission on Intergovernmental Relations 1994: table 59). The merits of a continued shift away from taxes on production and toward the receipt and disposition of income are questionable. Not only is there evidence that a state's economic competitiveness can be reduced by an overreliance on personal income taxes (Gold 1991), but considerations of law as well as economic efficiency also suggest that a strategy of broadening the general sales tax base does not have the attractiveness often promised. (Not only has *Quill* v. *North Dakota* made inaccessible a large and growing portion of the state retail sales tax base—that of interstate mail order sales—but the presumed merits of the equity and revenue productivity arguments for broadening the general sales tax base to services also have been undermined by research showing tax pyramiding is a much more serious problem than many have thought. See Ebel and Zimmerman 1991: 20–33.)

Such problems, combined with the likelihood that Congress will increasingly continue to shift domestic spending responsibilities from the federal government to the states, has led several state tax study groups to recommend that states consider adopting a broad tax based on the "value added" of business enterprise, as a means of creating a more stable and efficient tax system.

The bulk of attention and analysis regarding the value-added tax (VAT) has been national (it is now employed in some form in more than 100 countries) rather than subnational. The only major economies that do not use a VAT in some form are Australia and the United States.

The idea of a state VAT is not new. The earliest recommendations were advanced by the Brookings Institution in separate studies for Iowa (1930) and Alabama (1932). Hawaii became the first governmental unit operating within the United States to employ the value-added concept (the business excise tax, 1932–35). However, it was not until 1953 (with the strong support of the business community) that a state VAT was adopted; Michigan used it as a replacement for its corporate net income tax. After having its tax base eroded with numerous special provisions, in 1968 Michigan dropped its VAT in favor of a conventional corporate profits tax (Ebel 1972). By 1975, legislators determined that its business tax system had become unstable and overly complex, and again replaced the corporate profits tax (plus several "nuisance" taxes) with its current VAT, the Single Business Tax. In 1993, New Hampshire became the second state to enact the tax (the "Business Enterprise Tax"). As of this writing (1999), a state VAT is being actively considered in Tennessee, West Virginia, and the District of Columbia.

## Definition

A value-added tax is levied on corporate and noncorporate entities (sole proprietorships, partnerships) alike, and at all stages of the production and distribution process. The taxpayer calculates value added either by subtracting from its gross receipts all of its purchases from other firms (*subtraction approach*), or by summing up its payments to the factors of production of labor, land, capital, and entrepreneurship—that is, the sum of payrolls, rent, interest, and profits (*addition approach*). Either way, tax base size is the same. The choice is largely one of administrative convenience and ease of taxpayer compliance.

If a business operates in several states, it would allocate its share of total value added to the taxing state using the same type of apportionment method the states now require for corporate income tax purposes. The firm then applies the tax rate to the value added attributable to the state to determine tax due.

## Treatment of capital

In addition to choosing between adding or subtracting, the policymaker must choose between one of two variants of the tax base: income or consumption. (A third option, the "gross product variant," is rarely given serious consideration because it disallows any deduction for capital.) Here, the issue is how to structure the taxpayer's deduction for the capital equipment purchased from other firms. The choice focuses on the period over which the deduction will be allowed.

The *income variant* (IVA) adopts the familiar process of establishing a depreciation schedule over some period of years. This is the same procedure that applies to net income (profits) taxes. Under the *consumption variant* (CVA), which Michigan has adopted, the full amount of the capital purchase is deducted in the same year it is purchased. From the perspective of both the size of the total tax base and industry-by-industry impacts, the choice is not significant. However, for any one year, or for any single firm, the choice could be important.

## A retail sales tax in disguise?

The IVA-CVA distinction can lead to the question of whether the VAT is, in effect, a retail sales tax. The answer depends on whether the tax is being applied nationally or by a state. If one were to levy a consumption VAT nationally, for example, the tax would be equivalent to a national sales tax. The income tax, however, would look more like a proportional tax on business income.

For state policy purposes, however, even the sales tax (CVA) or national income (IVA) equivalence is misleading, for at least two reasons. First, because a state operates in an economy that is characterized by a free flow of factors and products across its borders (states cannot levy tariffs, impose quotas, restrict migration), there may be little systematic relationship between the size of the retail base and the amount of income and product generated in a state.

Second, in computing a VAT for state tax purposes, the taxpayer will apply a formula for apportioning its total tax base between the taxing state and other states in which it has affiliates (if any). Thus, structurally similar national and state tax policies have very different economic characteristics (except in a sales-only apportionment approach). That the state VAT more closely resembles a levy on production (income as it originates) than sales (income at its point of disposition) leads to an important policy implication: For a state, the VAT is a complement to, not a substitute for, a retail sales tax.

## Evaluation

In comparison to its alternative, the corporate net income tax (or, in Washington state, a tax on business gross receipts), the VAT gets high marks when judged against the conventional criteria of revenue productivity and stability, efficiency (neutrality) with respect to private-sector decisions, and simplicity. In each case, this is a result of the broad-based nature of the tax base. Its revenue advantages are largely that, unlike a profits tax, the VAT base includes payroll, making the VAT stable and predictable compared with the net income alternative (Kleine 1978) but also allowing the state to automatically capture the total income originating in the relatively low-profit-margin but high-growth service and trade sectors.

The VAT is also superior on efficiency grounds. Unlike a profits levy, which is a tax on the return to capital, the VAT is levied on all factor returns. Moreover, because the VAT is levied regardless of type of legal organization and includes payrolls in its base, it will require a tax payment regardless of its level of profitability.

In calculating tax liability, a firm can take the entries for the tax form directly off its financial statements or its federal income tax returns. In fact, under the subtraction method, the state VAT form is nearly the same line-for-line as the state corporate income tax form. This does not make it a model of simplicity, however. Many of the same problems of a net income tax will exist with the VAT, most notably those related to rules for apportioning that tax base for multistate business activities.

But embedded in its merits are the elements of its political unacceptability. Primary among these is the argument that because the VAT taxes all firms that receive government benefits, a firm with zero, or even negative, profits has a tax obligation. While this makes economic sense (even the zero-profit firm benefits from government services), the "no profit– no tax" argument has political impact). Also politically problematic is that what levels the competitive playing field for all the factors of production, most notably capital, is viewed quite properly as a loss of an indirect hidden subsidy to another factor—labor.

## Additional readings

Advisory Commission on Intergovernmental Relations. *Significant Features of Fiscal Federalism.* 1994 ed., vol. 2. Washington, D.C., 1994, Table 59.

Berghaus, V. Hummell IV, and William F.J. Ardinger. "The Policy and Structure of the Business Enterprise Tax." *New Hampshire Bar Journal* 34 (December 1993): 5–18 and 128–29.

Cordes, Joseph J., and Harry S. Watson. "Business Franchise and Insurance Taxes in the D.C. Tax System." A Paper Prepared for the District of Columbia Tax Revision Commission, 1998. Available at www.dctrc.org.

District of Columbia Tax Revision Commission. *Taxing Simply, Taxing Fairly, The Final Report of the District of Columbia Tax Revision Commission.* Washington, D.C.: 1998, pp. 41–59. Available at www.dctrc.org.

Ebel, Robert D. *Michigan Business Activities Tax.* East Lansing: Michigan State University, 1972.

Ebel, Robert D., and Christopher Zimmerman. "Sales Tax Trends and Issues." In *Sales Taxation,* edited by William F. Fox, pp. 20–33. Westport, Conn.: Praeger Publishers, 1991.

Gold, Steven D. "Interstate Competition and Personal Income Tax Policy in the 1980s." In Daphne A. Kenyon and John Kincaid, *Competition among States and Local Governments,* pp. 205–17. Washington, D.C.: The Urban Institute, 1991.

Kenyon, Daphne A. "A New State VAT?" *National Tax Journal* 49 (September 1996): 381–409.

Kleine, Robert J. *The Michigan Single Business Tax.* Washington, D.C.: U.S. Advisory Commission on Intergovernmental Relations, 1978.

*Cross references:* apportionment; consumption taxation; destination principle; origin principle; value-added tax, national.

# Vertical equity

Joseph J. Cordes
George Washington University

*A principle used to judge the fairness of taxes, which holds that taxpayers with different incomes should pay different amounts of tax.*

Along with horizontal equity, vertical equity is a basic yardstick that is used to gauge whether tax burdens are fairly distributed. The application of the concept of vertical equity differs depending on whether taxes are judged according to the benefit principle or the ability-to-pay principle.

If judgments about tax fairness are based on the benefit principle, and one assumes that the benefits that taxpayers receive from government spending vary with their income, taxation according to the benefit principle would require that taxpayers with different incomes pay different amounts of tax. Depending on how benefits varied with income, however, vertical equity could require that benefit tax burdens be distributed regressively, proportionately, or progressively, depending on whether benefits from public goods and services rose less than proportionately, proportionately, or more than proportionately as income increased.

In contrast to the benefit principle, regressive taxes would not be seen as vertically equitable under the principle of ability to pay. But whether vertical equity under the ability-to-pay standard requires that taxes be proportional or progressive depends on one's views about the distribution of income. Those who believe that the after-tax distribution of income should be the same as the pretax distribution would favor proportional taxes; those who believe that taxes should help to equalize the distribution of income favor progressive taxes, which narrow the dispersion in the distribution of after-tax incomes. In policy debates about the distribution of the tax burden, there has traditionally been a general, though not universal, presumption that vertical equity requires that tax burdens be distributed at least somewhat progressively.

## Vertical equity and consumption vs. income taxation

As in the case of horizontal equity, one issue that arises in applying the concept of vertical equity has to do with the measure of income that is used to group taxpayers into different income groups. The most commonly used yardstick is annual income, comprehensively measured. Many economists, however, believe that a taxpayer's lifetime income is a better measure. One's judgment about whether taxing consumption is inconsistent with vertical equity depends on which definition of income one uses. If the pure version of the life cycle model holds, taxes on consumption will be proportional with respect to lifetime income because current consumption is proportional to lifetime income. The same taxes, however, will generally be regressive with respect to annual income. The reason is that over the taxpayer's lifetime, consumption tends to be a larger share of income in years when the taxpayer's annual income is low, and a smaller share in years when income is high.

## Application to tax policy

The concept of vertical equity plays an important role in ongoing evaluation of tax policy. Distributional tables, which describe how the benefits of tax cuts or the burdens of tax increases are distributed by income, play an important role in debates about changes in tax law at both the federal and the state levels.

## Additional readings

Kaplow, Louis. "Horizontal Equity: Measures in Search of a Principle." *National Tax Journal* 42 (2) (1989): 139–55.

Kiefer, Donald. "Distributional Tax Progressivity Indexes." *National Tax Journal* 37 (December 1984): 494–513.

Musgrave, Richard. "Horizontal Equity Once More." *National Tax Journal* 43 (2) (1990): 113–23.

*Cross references:* ability to pay; benefit principle; consumption taxation; fairness in taxation; horizontal equity; life cycle model; progressivity, measures of; tax reform, federal and state; value-added tax, national.

# Ways and Means Committee

Albert Buckberg
Chief Economist Emeritus
Joint Committee on Taxation

*The committee in the House of Representatives that originates tax and other revenue legislation.*

---

The Committee on Ways and Means of the House of Representatives originates legislation to raise the revenues that are deposited in the Treasury to the general fund or to dedicated trust funds, all of which finance the federal government's expenditures.

Its purview includes the individual and corporation income taxes, payroll taxes, and excise taxes that finance spending from the general fund and the trust funds, as well as other taxes—estate and gift taxes, tariffs, and miscellaneous receipts—that are credited to the general fund. Matters relating to the issue of debt to finance budget deficits also fall within the jurisdiction of the committee. Ways and Means also authorizes all spending for several social programs and from certain trust funds.

## Financing government

Ways and Means initiates legislation to provide revenues for the federal budget that are grouped under the general fund and the various trust funds. Spending from the general fund is financed by general revenues, which include the individual and corporation income taxes, some excise taxes, estate and gift taxes, tariffs, and miscellaneous receipts. Trust fund outlays are financed directly from revenues dedicated specifically to each trust fund—primarily payroll taxes on wages and salaries and excise taxes. Pubic debt is issued for two purposes: to finance budget deficits, and as an investment medium for surplus reserves of trust funds.

Individual and corporation income taxes in 1996 accounted for 57 percent of budget receipts, with individual income taxes providing 79 percent of that revenue. Social insurance payroll taxes and contributions—equal amounts contributed by employee and employer—constituted 35 percent of budget receipts. The remaining 8 percent consisted primarily of excise taxes—mostly dedicated to trust funds, estate and gift taxes, tariffs, and miscellaneous receipts.

Ways and Means has initiated all major legislation relating to income taxes since the 16th amendment to the Constitution authorized such taxation, including major revisions in 1942, 1948, 1962, 1969, 1971, 1978, 1981, and 1986. Social insurance tax rates have been changed as needed to finance current trust fund outlays and to maintain adequate trust fund reserves. Other trust fund financing has been adjusted for the same purposes, usually in response to revised spending authorizations.

The committee retains jurisdiction over the limit on outstanding federal debt and generally the terms and conditions of the several types and maturities of debt issue. It is conceivable that the debt limit would be increased solely to provide the investment medium for trust fund reserves when the general fund is in balance.

The committee's spending responsibilities vary between setting criteria for distributing benefits from federally administered social programs to establishing guidelines for state administration of some federal social programs. These programs relate to (1) loss of earnings because of retirement, disability, survivorship (widows and orphans), and cyclical unemployment, and trade assistance encompassing unemployment compensation and retraining benefits, (2) protection of retirement pension benefits by regulation of private pension funds, (3) supplemental benefits for needy and disabled elderly, (4) hospital and medical care insurance, primarily for senior citizens, and some medical care for the needy, (5) child welfare and child care, and (6) assorted social service and social welfare programs. The committee originates tax provisions to supplement and facilitate realization of these social objectives.

## Committee history

The Committee was established as the Select Committee on Ways and Means on July 24, 1789. It was discharged less than two months later as Alexander Hamilton asserted the suzerainty of the Treasury Department over the fiscal affairs of the new republic. The committee was reestablished as a select committee after Hamilton left office and has operated continuously since the first session of the Fourth Congress. It was designated formally as a standing committee on January 7, 1802.

Until 1865, the committee's jurisdiction included (1) raising revenues, (2) appropriations, and (3) banking. After the Civil War, separate committees were created to deal with appropriations and banking, and until the 1930s the jurisdiction of Ways and Means was limited to (1) revenue measures generally and related to insular possessions, (2) tariffs, (3) reciprocal trade agreements, (4) the bonded debt of the United States, (5) tax-exempt foundations and charitable trusts, and (6) national social security, except health care supported from general revenues. Social programs were added to its jurisdiction beginning with the Social Security Act of 1935, and the scope of such programs has expanded since then.

The committee has 36 members and a sizable professional, technical, and clerical staff. For additional staff resources, the committee relies on the staff of the Joint Committee on Taxation and may request added technical assistance from the Congressional Budget Office, the Congressional Research Service in the Library of Congress, and the General Accounting Office.

*Cross references:* Finance Committee, U.S. Senate; Joint Committee on Taxation, U.S. Congress.

# Wealth taxation

Gregg A. Esenwein
Congressional Research Service, Library of Congress

*Taxation of the wealth or net worth (assets less liabilities) of an individual.*

Although the idea of a national wealth tax is not in vogue, it was once seriously considered by the Treasury Department as a means of retiring the national debt incurred during World War I. On the other hand, several European nations currently use and have a long history of using national wealth taxes as a source of revenue. The three main arguments usually advanced in support of wealth taxation are that public services increase the value of property and, hence, should be paid for by property owners; that wealth is the best barometer of ability to pay; and that wealth taxes can be used to help prevent the concentration of wealth among a few individuals or families (Musgrave and Musgrave 1976).

From a theoretical perspective, a tax on lifetime wealth (net worth) is identical to a tax on lifetime net capital income. However, if these taxes are levied on an annual basis, their equivalence erodes and they have different incidence and efficiency effects.

## The tax base

In theory, a tax on net worth or wealth would be based on a valuation of all of the assets owned by a taxpayer less all of his liabilities on a given date. In other words, an inventory of all assets would be taken and a market value established for each asset. The taxpayer's debts would be subtracted from this aggregation of gross wealth, leaving the taxpayer's net worth as the tax base.

Wealth can take a variety of forms. It can consist of financial assets, land, housing, consumer durables, jewelry, and future earning potential. It is important to note that, in theory, a full accounting of a taxpayer's assets would require the inclusion of the capitalized value of a taxpayer's future earning potential. For example, at a given point the value of an animal, say a horse, represents the capitalized value of its potential future services. Because the value of the horse would be included in a wealth tax, so too should the capitalized value of the potential future services of the taxpayer himself (Rolph and Break 1961).

As a practical matter, however, it would be virtually impossible to measure accurately the value of an individual's potential future services. As a result, in practice, a wealth tax would be assessed only on physical capital.

At any given point, this stock of assets represents a taxpayer's claim to resources in the economy. These assets also yield a return that can take various forms—of money income, capital appreciation, enjoyment, or satisfaction (Organization for Economic Cooperation and Development 1988). This relationship between wealth and the return to wealth offers a convenient way to understand the linkage between wealth and income taxation.

Wealth represents a stock, whereas income represents a flow from that stock. Wealth is measured at a point in time, while income is measured over a period of time. Hence, when measured correctly over the lifetime of the taxpayer, taxing wealth is equivalent to taxing net capital income. For example, consider the situation where the average asset yield (the return to wealth including both money and nonmoney yields) is 5 percent. In this situation, a 1 percent tax on wealth would be equivalent to a 20 percent tax on income. The tax owed for every $100 of wealth would be $1, which is the same as taxing the $5 flow (income) from the stock (wealth) at 20 percent.

## Equity

It has been argued that wealth would make a more equitable tax base than income. One reason is that wealth gives the holder advantages that can exceed the income derived from it—independence, security, power, and prestige to its owner, for instance. Furthermore, the consumption of wealth requires no sacrifice of current leisure. These advantages mean that the owner of wealth has extra taxpaying capacity that is not fully reflected in the flow of income (OECD 1988). Hence, it is argued that wealth provides a superior measure of ability to pay and as such is better suited than income as a means of distributing the tax burden across the income spectrum.

It has also been argued that wealth is superior to income as a tax base from the perspective of horizontal equity. This line of reasoning suggests that, over a given period, taxpayers with identical incomes do not necessarily have identical command over resources. However, at a given point in time, taxpayers with identical net worth do have the same command over resources. As a result, horizontal equity is best satisfied by assessing the tax on the basis of wealth, not income (Rolph and Break 1961).

These arguments, however, are predicated on the assumption that a wealth tax would be assessed on individuals based on their global holdings of wealth. In practical terms, given the international legal and administrative difficulties of such a procedure, it is highly doubtful that such an assessment could be made. In a second-best world, the validity of the arguments that wealth is a more equitable tax base than income is not as clear.

### Efficiency

Some have speculated that because wealth taxation is related to past rather than present or future activities, it might prove to be an efficient tax. It would introduce fewer distortions in labor/leisure choices and savings/consumption choices than would an income- or consumption-based tax. This argument, however, is valid only if the wealth tax is assessed once, and then on the basis of lifetime wealth. An annual wealth tax, on the other hand, would probably have much the same effects on economic efficiency as would an annual income tax.

From a practical perspective, some circumstance is conceivable in which an annual wealth tax that was used as a partial substitute for an income tax might result in some efficiency gains relative to the situation under the annual income tax. These would occur if the wealth tax encouraged investment to move from low-yield to high-yield assets. For example, idle land might be brought into production because under a wealth tax an assessment would be made on the value of the land whether or not it was producing income.

At the same time, however, a wealth tax with high tax rates might increase the distortion in saving-consumption choices. Indeed, at high enough rates, a wealth tax could even produce dissaving (consumption of capital) in the economy.

Many of the efficiency gains that are commonly attributed to a wealth tax could possibly be achieved by broadening the base of the income tax through inclusion of imputed and noncash income.

### Simplicity/administration

For developing nations, a wealth tax may have some simplicity and administrative advantages over other forms of taxes. These derive primarily from the visibility of the tax base when the majority of assets consists of immovable property. In these situations, it is much easier to value assets such as cattle rather than the income they produce (Musgrave and Musgrave 1976).

In developed nations, however, wealth taxes tend to be rather complex and difficult to administer. This stems from the fact that many assets can be hidden—for instance, jewelry and collectibles—and others are difficult to value. In addition, because net worth is the tax base, liabilities also have to be valued, a task that can be difficult in a sophisticated and mature economy. It does appear that in developed nations with a wealth tax, the wealth tax provides some administrative advantages by serving as a cross-check for income tax returns.

### Additional readings

Dugger, William M. "The Wealth Tax: A Policy Proposal." *Journal of Economic Issues* 24 (March 1990): 133–44.

Musgrave, Richard A., and Peggy B. Musgrave. *Public Finance in Theory and Practice.* Boston: McGraw-Hill, 1976, pp. 342–66.

Organization for Economic Cooperation and Development. *Taxation of Net Wealth, Capital Transfers and Capital Gains of Individuals.* Paris: OECD, 1988.

Rolph, Earl R., and George F. Break. *Public Finance.* New York: Ronald Press Company, 1961, pp. 194–209.

Shoup, Carl S. *Public Finance.* Chicago: Aldine Publishing Company, 1969, pp. 357–81.

Thurow, Lester C. "Net Worth Taxes." *National Tax Journal* 25 (September 1972): 417–23.

*Cross references:* fairness in taxation; property tax, real property, business; property tax, real property, residential.

# Withholding of taxes

Allen H. Lerman
Department of the Treasury

*Deduction of taxes by a payor of wages or other income for direct payment to the taxing authority.*

Withholding is a method of tax collection under which a payor of wages or other income deducts (i.e., withholds) the tax from the gross payment due to a worker or other payee. The payor submits the deducted tax to the taxing authority for credit to the account of the payee. Amounts "withheld" may constitute full payment of the tax obligation, or may be credited toward the payment of a tax liability that is determined separately, often after the end of the calendar year. Withholding is an important method of collecting various wage and income taxes from employees. It may also be used to collect taxes on other payments, such as pensions, interest, and dividends, as well as income taxes on payments made to recipients who reside outside the jurisdiction of the taxing authority. Typically, the payor who withholds the tax is treated as an agent of the taxing authority, and the payee receives credit for the tax payment based on the withholding, whether or not the amount withheld is paid to the taxing authority.

Major portions of the federal individual income tax and of the Social Security and Medicare taxes imposed on employees are paid through withholding. Withheld taxes represent more than 45 percent of total federal tax receipts. Most states and localities use withholding as the main means of collecting income and wage taxes.

Periodically, employers and other withholding agents pay the aggregate amount of withheld taxes to the taxing authority. Withheld federal income, Social Security, and Medicare taxes (together with the employers' matching Social Security and Medicare taxes) are paid to the Internal Revenue Service (IRS), generally through deposits at local banking institutions. The frequency of required deposits ranges from quarterly to daily, and depends on the amounts withheld but undeposited, or the amounts withheld during previous periods. At the end of each calendar year, employers report each worker's earnings and the amounts withheld from each worker's pay to the IRS. The amounts so reported are reconciled to the aggregate amounts of withheld taxes previously paid by each employer.

## Social Security and Medicare taxes

Employees pay a Social Security tax for old age, survivors, and disability insurance (OASDI) of 6.2 percent of earnings up to an annual ceiling ($72,600 for 1999 and indexed annually). Employees are also taxed 1.45 percent of wages, with no annual limit, for the hospital insurance portion (Part A) of Medicare. These taxes are collected via withholding from wage payments. Social Security taxes have been imposed since 1937 and Medicare taxes since 1966, although wage bases and rates have varied.

Because the Social Security and Medicare taxes are imposed at a uniform percentage of covered wages and the amount of wages is known by the employer, the amount of tax withheld generally matches the employee's tax liability. However, be-

cause each employer must withhold OASDI on wages up to the annual ceiling, workers who have two or more employers during a year and whose total annual wages exceed the ceiling may have too much OASDI withheld. Workers may treat such excesses as withheld federal individual income tax and may claim credit for the excess on their individual income tax returns.

In fiscal year 1998, about $220 billion was withheld from employee wages for Social Security and Medicare taxes. That represented more than 45 percent of total Social Security and Medicare taxes; another 45 percent came from the employers' matching shares, and the remainder from taxes on self-employment income.

## Federal individual income taxes

Federal income tax withholding is required for wages and salaries, which represent more than 75 percent of all income reported on income tax returns. There is mandatory or optional withholding on certain other types of payments, including pensions and lump sum distributions from Individual Retirement Accounts (IRAs), and certain payments to persons living outside the United States. "Backup withholding" may be required for such items as interest, dividends, and proceeds from the sale of certain securities, if the payee does not provide a valid taxpayer identification number to the payor. Unless withholding (or a taxpayer's quarterly payments of estimated taxes) covers either 90 percent of the current year's tax liability as shown on the tax return or 100 percent of the prior year's tax liability, the taxpayer is generally subject to penalties, which are calculated as if they were interest on the underpayment. (To avoid penalties, taxpayers with incomes over $150,000 must have paid, depending on the year, 105 percent to 112 percent of the prior year's tax liability. There are no penalties if the unpaid balance is less than $1,000 [$500 for years prior to 1998].)

Withholding was introduced in 1943, when personal exemptions were reduced and typical wage earners, rather than just a small portion of the population, began to have federal income tax liability. Withholding assured that taxpayers would be able to pay their newly imposed tax liabilities even if they became unemployed, incurred other financial crises, or failed to set aside some of their wages for taxes.

For 1996, $407 billion of withheld income tax was shown on 104 million of the 120 million federal income tax returns filed. Withholding represented 75 percent of the gross income tax payments, and the other major forms of payments were estimated tax payments and payments made with tax returns. Refunds were due on 72 percent of all tax returns, but on nearly 80 percent of returns where withholding was the only form of payment. A total of $129 billion was either refunded to taxpayers or credited to their estimated tax payments for 1997. For returns with overpayments, average overpayment was $1,490.

Since the 1970s, about three-fourths of each year's income tax returns have been overpaid, with aggregate overpayments averaging 15 to 20 percent of tax liability. Taxpayers tend to have reasonably similar refunds from year to year. Part-year employment and head of household filing status may lead to overwithholding; workers having two jobs concurrently and two-earner married couples tend to be underwithheld. In the aggregate, the withholding provisions do not have a significant bias toward either over- or underwithholding. (In 1992, in an attempt to provide economic stimulus by reducing the aggregate amount of overwithholding, a slight bias toward underwithholding for most workers was incorporated into the withholding rate schedules. In 1995, the underwithholding bias began to be phased out.) Thus, the reasons for persistent aggregate overpayments are not clear. Anecdotal evidence suggests three possibilities, but the relative importance of each is not known: (1) Overwithholding may be an intentional form of forced savings; (2) taxpayers may be unable or unwilling to use the withholding system's provisions to match their withholding to their tax liability; or (3) taxpayers may tolerate overwithholding to avoid having unexpected balances due.

## Structure of wage and salary withholding

The withholding system for wages and salaries is a simplified analogue of the income tax system. Withholding under graduated rate schedules, which mirror the income tax rate schedules, applies to gross wages less exclusions, which reflect personal exemptions, standard deductions, and, optionally, itemized deductions and other common provisions that affect tax liability.

The assumptions underlying the system are that each worker is employed at only one job at a time, works for the entire year at a constant salary, has no nonwage income, and does not itemize deductions or have any tax credits. When these assumptions hold, withholding for workers who use the "single" or "married filing jointly" filing statuses closely approximates actual tax liability. Workers may have their withholding adjusted to reflect itemized deductions, certain "statutory adjustments to income," tax credits, income not subject to tax, and potential underwithholding from two-job or two-earner situations. Although withholding is designed to cover only the tax liability attributable to wages and salaries, many workers cover their liability on nonwage income via withholding instead of making quarterly estimated tax payments directly to the IRS.

An Employee's Withholding Allowance Certificate (IRS Form W-4) is used by a worker to provide information to the employer for use in determining the amount of income tax to be withheld from the worker's wages. Every employer is supposed to provide each new employee with a Form W-4, and workers may also complete Forms W-4 at other times to change their withholding. The worker uses the Form W-4's instructions and worksheets along with information about the number of the worker's dependents, other income, tax credits, itemized deductions, and other jobs to determine the number of "withholding allowances" that generally will result in withholding closely approximating tax liability. If the number of allowances calculated is negative, the employee is instructed to claim zero allowances, and further instructions help the employee to determine the additional dollar amount of withholding required to minimize or prevent underwithholding. On Form W-4, the worker also indicates whether withholding is to be at the tax rates for single taxpayers or for married taxpayers filing joint tax returns.

Originally, withholding allowances were equivalent to personal exemptions, and the size of a withholding allowance remains the same as the size of an exemption. Currently, all withholding adjustments for a worker are translated into withholding allowances on the Form W-4 worksheets. This method reduces the amount of information the employer needs to handle and permits workers to adjust their withholding without giving employers confidential personal and financial information. (Unless an employee claims an unusually large number of allowances, Form W-4 is not sent to the Internal Revenue Service, and the federal government never knows the number of withholding allowances claimed by specific workers.)

The withholding system includes a little-understood and widely ignored provision, called the special withholding allowance (SWA), which ensures that workers receive the proper amount of the standard deduction for withholding regardless of whether the worker or the married couple have one job or two jobs concurrently. One-job workers and one-earner families who fail to claim the SWA will tend to be overwithheld. Failure to understand and claim the SWA may account for a significant portion of aggregate overwithholding. An optional adjustment for the potential underwithholding also may occur in a progressive tax system when income is earned from two or more jobs.

All of a worker's allowances may be claimed on one job of the employee (or the employee and spouse), or the allowances may be divided among several jobs. Workers risk being underwithheld and incurring penalties for underwithholding if the total number of allowances claimed on all jobs exceeds the number resulting from the worksheet computations. Employees may claim fewer than the suggested number of allowances, and it appears that many do. The aggregate levels of overwithholding since the mid-1980s and the size of the average tax overpayments might be explained by workers claiming approximately two fewer withholding allowances than suggested by the Form W-4 worksheets.

For each wage payment, the employer uses the information on Form W-4 together with the amount of earnings to determine the amount of income tax to be withheld. Net wages are calculated as gross wages less the value of the withholding allowances claimed by the worker. Withholding is determined from the net wages and the withholding rate schedules, but is increased by any extra dollar amount of withholding requested by the worker. The resulting amount is deducted or "withheld" from the worker's gross wage.

## Additional readings

Lerman, Allen H. "Measuring the Accuracy of Federal Income Tax Withholding." Presentation at the 1988 Annual Meeting of the National Association of Tax Administrators. Mimeograph.

Pechman, Joseph A. *Federal Tax Policy.* 5th ed. Washington, D.C.: The Brookings Institution, 1987.

U.S. Internal Revenue Service. *Statistics of Income, Individual Income Tax Returns, 1992.* Washington, D.C.: U.S. Government Printing Office, 1995.

*Cross reference:* tax administration, federal.

# Z

## Zero rating

Joseph J. Cordes
George Washington University

*A means of exempting goods from taxation under a value-added tax.*

---

One way of making a consumption-based value-added tax (VAT) less regressive is to tax certain goods, often regarded as necessities, at lower rates at one or more stages of the distribution process. Zero rating is the most common form of reduced rating. The way zero rating would work under the credit invoice method of collecting a value-added tax is illustrated in table 1.

The example assumes that the VAT rate that applies to non-zero-rated sales is 5 percent. As may be seen, a tax is initially remitted on value added at the manufacturing stage, but is then effectively forgiven in subsequent stages of production. Wholesalers receive a credit for the VAT that they pay on purchases from manufacturers, but they are not themselves required to pay a VAT on their sales to retailers because the good is zero-rated.

Zero rating of goods under a credit invoice VAT needs to be distinguished from exempting businesses from taxation under a VAT. VAT exemptions are granted, usually to small businesses, as a matter of administrative convenience. When transactions are exempt from a VAT, the business does not remit any VAT on sales, but it also is not allowed to claim a credit for VAT paid on purchases from other producers. Thus, exempting transactions breaks the chain of VAT credits and does not reduce the rate at which goods are taxed.

Zero rating of goods, such as necessities, is often seen as a way of reducing the regressivity of a VAT. But studies have found that zero rating is a fairly ineffective means of reducing the burden of a VAT on low-income consumers. A main reason is that when some goods are zero-rated, the tax rate must be increased on other goods to raise a given amount of revenue.

### Additional reading

Congressional Budget Office. *Effects of Adopting a Value-Added Tax*. Washington, D.C., 1992.

*Cross references:* progressivity, measures of; value-added tax, national; value-added tax, state; vertical equity.

## Zoning, property taxes, and exactions

William A. Fischel
Dartmouth College

*The division of a municipality into areas in which some land uses are allowed and others are not is often accompanied by fees and taxes that recognize the fiscal impact (costs and benefits) of development and changes in land use.*

---

### The fiscal powers of zoning

Zoning is the division of a municipality into contiguous areas (zones) in which some land uses are allowed and others are forbidden. Zoning exists in almost all American urban and suburban areas and, increasingly, in many rural areas. The only large city not to have zoning is Houston, Texas, whose citizens persistently vote against its adoption. Only Hawaii has statewide zoning, but a few states, such as Ver-

**TABLE 1**

### Zero Rating under the Credit Invoice Method

|  | Manufacturing | Wholesale | Retail | Total Tax |
|---|---|---|---|---|
| Sales | 1,000 | 2,000 | 2,500 | |
| Purchases (excluding VAT) | 0 | 1,000 | 2,000 | |
| Tax on non-zero-rated sales | 50 | NA | NA | |
| Tax on zero-rated sales | NA | 0 | 0 | |
| VAT credit on purchases | 0 | 50 | 0 | |
| VAT owed | 50 | 0 | 0 | 0 |

mont, Oregon, and Florida, supervise and coordinate local decisions more closely than others. Even in active states, however, it is rare for a statewide body to tell a local government that it must accept a proposed land use that it does not want.

The 1928 "Standard State Zoning Enabling Act" was one of the most successful model acts to have been promulgated by the federal government. Its influence is still evident. The words of the original model offer a useful summary of the enormous grant of authority to the municipality over the private use of land:

> Section 1: Grant of Power.—For the purpose of promoting health, safety, morals, or general welfare of the community, the legislative body of cities and incorporated villages is hereby empowered to regulate and restrict the height, number of stories, and size of buildings and other structures, the percentage of a lot that may be occupied, the size of yards, courts, and other open spaces, the density of population, and the location and use of buildings, structures, and land for trade, industry, or other purpose.

This grant of power allows communities to regulate in great detail the capital-to-land ratio. It is not merely use and lot size that are regulated; the height and bulk of buildings and their placement on the lot are clearly subject to the collective will.

> Section 2: Districts.—For any or all of said purposes the local legislative body may divide the municipality into districts of such number, shape, and area as may be deemed best suited to carry out the purposes of this act; and within such districts it may regulate and restrict the erection, construction, reconstruction, alteration, repair, or use of buildings, structures, or land. All such regulations shall be uniform for each class or kind of buildings throughout each district, but the regulations in one district may differ from those in other districts.

The police power, of which zoning is an example, does not require the community to compensate owners of private property for adverse effects of regulations. The uniformity of regulations within zones mentioned above is scant protection for landowners because the community can determine the borders of the zones. These borders and permissible uses within each zone may be changed by the vote of municipal authorities. Modern ordinances also often make many of the uses subject to discretionary review by a zoning board or planning commission whose members are elected or appointed by elected officials.

> Section 3: Purposes in View.—Such regulations shall be made in accordance with a comprehensive plan and designed to lessen congestion in the streets; to secure safety from fire, panic, and other dangers; to promote health and the general welfare; to provide adequate light and air; to prevent overcrowding of land; to avoid undue concentration of population; to facilitate adequate provision of transportation, water, sewerage, schools, parks, and other public requirements. Such regulations shall be made with reasonable consideration, among other things, to the character of the district and its peculiar suitability for particular uses, and with a view to conserving the value of buildings and encouraging the most appropriate use of land throughout such municipality.

The comprehensive plan mentioned above is seldom a binding document, but it sometimes has been invoked by courts as a reason to overturn ad hoc rezonings. Like zoning rules and boundaries, however, comprehensive plans can be changed when the community desires. They are not a major constraint on a municipality's ability to determine what it will become.

Section 3 also clearly indicates the fiscal basis for zoning. The possibility of substitution of regulation (which does not require much public expenditure) for taxation and spending is evident in zoning's earliest documents. A community that limits the number of new houses so as to avoid school costs is not doing something that is prohibited by most zoning enabling acts.

Economists sometimes regard "fiscal zoning" as different from "externality zoning," but the law makes no such distinction. Many state statutes and state courts nowadays are hostile to the more blatant forms of fiscal zoning. As a result, modern planning documents hide such intentions in more acceptable language (Bogart 1993). Expressions of the need to preserve farmland, wetlands, open space, and historic sites in areas that might otherwise be developed are usually all that are necessary to preserve the ordinance from attack as fiscally motivated "exclusionary" zoning.

A commonplace in zoning is that no landowner has a vested right to any particular zoning law. Changes that are adverse to a landowner's prospective use of the land occur often. Established uses and buildings, however, are seldom required to be discontinued or reconfigured when zoning laws are changed. Existing homeowners, who are most influential in suburban zoning politics, can thus impose higher standards for development for prospective residents without cost to themselves. Either their own homes are in an already developed zone separate from developable space in the rest of the community, or their homes are grandfathered under the newly restrictive law.

Recently, a few development-minded landowners have persuaded courts to order government agencies to pay for the consequences of downzonings (that is, more restrictive regulations) under the constitutional rubric of "regulatory takings." This doctrine poses some financial threat to local government discretion, but it is typically successful only when the landowner can claim that there is no economically viable use under the new law, a condition easily avoided by most governments.

## Fiscal zoning and property taxes

Zoning permits municipalities to shape their property tax bases without having to compensate disappointed landowners. The newer (less developed) the town, the more power it typically has, but even older communities can govern their tax base extensively through controls on redevelopment. The controls are typically negative; communities cannot force landowners to build things they do not want. But given the comprehensiveness of zoning regulation, private developers must be willing to accommodate community concerns before that can proceed.

The community's fiscal concerns have several dimensions. The simplest to describe is that communities want new development to "pay its own way" in property taxes. If it is assumed that an additional residence will cause, on average, the expenditure of $5,000 per year in municipal services (schools, roads, police), and that local property taxes average 2.5 percent of value per year, the community will "break even" if the new residence is assessed for tax purposes at $200,000.

Zoning cannot declare what the minimum housing value must be. However, as the foregoing list of powers indicated, quality constraints that accomplish the same outcome (a $200,000 house) are within both the authority and the ability of the local government. Even unsophisticated governments can hire consultants who have access to published rules of thumb for what each type of development costs the town.

Hamilton (1975) showed that if there is a large number of communities free to tailor the level of services to the tastes of households (and there are scores in most large metropolitan areas), the property tax will have no deadweight loss under fiscal zoning. People will shop around—vote with their feet—for the community that best fits their demands in the manner proposed by Tiebout (1956).

Hamilton showed that in these circumstances residents will get exactly what they pay for in local taxes. The property tax becomes a fee for local services, and there is no misallocation in those local government services that are limited to the borders of the community. Shirking payment is impossible because zoning makes it impossible to build a house that confers a fiscal benefit on the occupant. The property tax has no deadweight loss in this system because it is not really a tax at all.

The Tiebout-Hamilton system is criticized often as being unrealistic. But that is only because it is an elegant model. In reality, local officials do not simply aim for a single minimum-value house. They are able to discriminate among land uses and put them in a limited zone even if they cannot ban them altogether. Thus, condominiums and apartments, which may seem to be a fiscal burden to a community, may be allowed, but only in such a small area that their prices will be quite high, reflecting the fiscal benefit of owning or renting them (Hamilton 1975). In other cases, community authorities may require that developers of housing also come up with projects whose fiscal payoffs cover the burdens of more schoolchildren. More subtle applications of zoning regulation can control the population of the community (Ellickson 1977; Oates 1977), although explicit racial zoning was banned long ago.

## Exaction, property taxes, and municipal corporations

Zoning allows community authorities to demand that developers pay monetary exactions to offset their fiscal or environmental costs. Exactions are essentially payments in exchange for discretionary zoning permits or rezonings. Exactions were traditionally used to pay for public infrastructure that was added to accommodate new development. Even this limited range of exactions suggests that the property tax "subsidy" to suburban sprawl or new development is a dubious claim. To look only at the average property taxes paid by a new development overlooks the exactions and payments in kind (developer-built sidewalks and sewers) that were very likely required as a condition of zoning approval and that offset the higher costs.

Since 1970, exactions have become so expansive that the developer can be required to pay for community services that have only the most tangential relationship to the project (Altshuler and Gómez-Ibáñez 1993). Courts that are protective of property rights have attempted to limit the extent of exactions, but economists should not be fooled into believing that this makes much difference. The reason exactions are paid at all is that the community's regulatory powers are so great. Developers who do not respond to community concerns simply do not get permits.

A more general theory, one that goes beyond the Tiebout-Hamilton model, sees zoning as the means by which municipal corporations establish and protect their collective property rights (Nelson 1977; Fischel 1985). These corporations are run for the benefit of those who control the political power in the community. In the suburbs, where politics is reasonably transparent, the median voter gets his or her way, and the median voter is a homeowner. Social scientists would profitably view suburban zoning and, for that matter, all municipal activity, as being managed to maximize the net worth of homeowners (Sonstelie and Portney 1978).

The homeowner, not being irrational, does not want to "minimize taxes," because minimization could be achieved by providing no local services, which would reduce the value of the home. The homeowner does not want to maximize the nonresidential tax base because the hazardous waste processor that is willing to pay 90 percent of the local taxes may nonetheless reduce home values. Nor does the homeowner want to exclude all commercial activity in order to maximize the local quality of the environment. That would mean forgoing other good things like convenience to commercial activities and, in more rural places, nearness to jobs.

The model that both fits the facts and is consistent with economic theory is that the homeowner is interested in maximizing net worth (Brueckner 1983). That usually (although not always) means maximizing the value of the homeowner's major asset, the home. (The exception occurs when a homeowner can be bought out by a developer with a lump sum payment that offsets the reduction in the home's value.) The approach nevertheless recognizes that transaction costs and agency problems may forestall value-enhancing deals among homeowners, land developers, and political authorities.

In bigger cities, such problems may sometimes result in zoning that serves interests other than those of the voters. But this is no different in principle from the agency problems that affect private corporations, in which managers sometimes govern in ways that are not in the best interest of stockholders. Zoning is a critical part of a municipality's corporate charter, and public finance would be richer if it recognized this fact.

## Additional readings

Altshuler, Alan A., and Jose A. Gómez-Ibáñez, with Arnold M. Howitt. *Regulation for Revenue: The Political Economy of Land Use Exactions*. Cambridge, Mass.: Lincoln Institute of Land Policy, 1993.

Bogart, William T. "'What Big Teeth You Have!' Identifying the Motivations for Exclusionary Zoning." *Urban Studies* (December 1993): 1669–81.

Brueckner, Jan K. "Property Value Maximization and Public Sector Efficiency." *Journal of Urban Economics* 14 (July 1983): 1–15.

Ellickson, Robert C. "Suburban Growth Controls: An Economic and Legal Analysis." *Yale Law Journal* 86 (January 1977): 385–511.

Fischel, William A. *The Economics of Zoning Laws: A Property Rights Approach to American Land Use Controls*. Baltimore: Johns Hopkins University Press, 1985.

Hamilton, Bruce W. "Capitalization of Intrajurisdictional Differences in Local Tax Process." *American Economic Review* 66 (December 1966): 743–53.

Hamilton, Bruce W. "Zoning and Property Taxation in a System of Local Governments." *Urban Studies* 12 (June 1975): 205–211.

Ladd, Helen F. *Local Government Tax and Land Use Policies in the United States*. Northampton, Mass.: Edward Elger, 1998, chapter 2.

Nelson, Robert H. *Zoning and Property Rights*. Cambridge, Mass.: MIT Press, 1977.

Oates, Wallace E. "The Use of Local Zoning Ordinances to Regulate Population Flows and the Quality of Local Services." In *Essays in Labor Market Analysis*, edited by Orley Ashenfelter and Wallace Oates. New York: John Wiley, 1977.

Sonstelie, Jon C., and Paul R. Portney. "Profit Maximizing Communities and the Theory of Local Public Expenditures." *Journal of Urban Economics* 5 (April 1978): 263–77.

Tiebout, Charles M. "A Pure Theory of Local Expenditures." *Journal of Political Economy* 64 (October 1956): 416–24.

*Cross references:* infrastructure financing; property taxes, real property, business; property taxes, real property, residential; Tiebout model.

# Index

Italicized page numbers indicate main reference.

# About the Editors

**Joseph J. Cordes**, a visiting fellow at the Urban Institute, served as associate dean for faculty affairs and programs in the Columbian College of Arts and Sciences at George Washington University from 1986 to 1989 and was chair of the department of economics from 1991 to 1997. He was a Brookings economic policy fellow in the U.S. Treasury Department's Office of the Assistant Secretary for Tax Policy from 1980 to 1981. From 1989 to 1991 he was deputy assistant director for tax analysis at the Congressional Budget Office. He is coeditor (with Milton M. Carrow and Robert Paul Churchill) of *Democracy, Social Values and Public Policy* (Greenwood-Praeger, 1998) and has published over 50 articles on tax policy, government regulation, government spending, and nonprofit organizations.

**Robert D. Ebel** is principal economist at the World Bank Institute for Intergovernmental Relations and Local Financial Management and executive director of the National Tax Association. Prior to joining the World Bank, he was director of government finance research for the U.S. Advisory Commission on Intergovernmental Relations (ACIR), and the director of state tax studies in Hawaii, Minnesota, and, while he worked at the Urban Institute, Nevada. He is also the recent past chairman of the District of Columbia Tax Revision Commission and manager of the World Bank's Fiscal Decentralization Initiative in Central and Eastern Europe. He is the author of several studies on taxation and fiscal decentralization. His most recent book, coedited with Richard Bird and Christine Wallich, is *Decentralization of the Socialist State: Intergovernmental Finance in Transition Economies* (World Bank, 1996).

**Jane G. Gravelle** is a senior specialist in economic policy at the Library of Congress's Congressional Research Service, where she specializes in taxation, particularly the effects of tax policies on economic growth and resource allocation. She has served at the Labor Department and the Treasury Department's Office of Tax Analysis and has taught at Boston University. Recent papers have addressed consumption taxes, dynamic revenue estimating, investment subsidies, capital gains taxes, individual retirement accounts, enterprise zones, and corporate tax revisions. She is the editor of the *Tax Expenditure Compendium* and the author of *The Economic Effects of Taxing Capital Income* (MIT Press, 1994). She serves on the editorial board of the *National Tax Journal*. She won the National Tax Association's 1981 award for outstanding doctoral dissertation in public finance.